Health, United States, 2005

With Chartbook on Trends in the Health of Americans

U.S. DEPARTMENT OF HEALTH AND HUMAN SERVICES
Centers for Disease Control and Prevention
National Center for Health Statistics

November 2005
DHHS Publication No. 2005-1232

U.S. Department of Health and Human Services

Michael O. Leavitt
Secretary

Centers for Disease Control and Prevention

Julie Louise Gerberding, M.D., M.P.H.
Director

National Center for Health Statistics

Edward J. Sondik, Ph.D.
Director

For sale by the Superintendent of Documents, U.S. Government Printing Office
Internet: bookstore.gpo.gov Phone: toll free (866) 512-1800; DC area (202) 512-1800
Fax: (202) 512-2250 Mail: Stop SSOP, Washington, DC 20402-0001

ISBN 0-16-072854-1

Preface

Health, United States, 2005 is the 29th report on the health status of the Nation and is submitted by the Secretary of the Department of Health and Human Services to the President and Congress of the United States in compliance with Section 308 of the Public Health Service Act. This report was compiled by the National Center for Health Statistics (NCHS), Centers for Disease Control and Prevention (CDC). The National Committee on Vital and Health Statistics served in a review capacity.

The *Health, United States* series presents national trends in health statistics. Each report includes an executive summary, highlights, a chartbook, trend tables, extensive appendixes, and an index.

Chartbook

The fourth *Chartbook on Trends in the Health of Americans* updates and expands information from previous chartbooks and introduces this year's special feature on adults 55–64 years of age, a rapidly growing segment of the adult population. The economic and health status of this age group is of interest as the majority of its members are poised to enter retirement and to become eligible for Medicare. The chartbook assesses the Nation's health by presenting trends and current information on selected determinants and measures of health status and utilization of health care. Determinants of health considered in the chartbook include demographic factors, poverty, health insurance coverage, and health behaviors and risk factors, including obesity, cigarette smoking, and physical activity. Additional risk factors this year include teen seat belt use, drinking and driving, and multiple cardiovascular risk factors for adults. Measures of health status include prevalence of asthma attacks in children, headache and lower back pain in adults, limitation of activity due to chronic health conditions, and several measures of mortality. A new section on health care utilization includes use of mammography and Pap tests, visits to physician offices and outpatient departments, injury-related visits by children to emergency departments, and insertion of cardiac stents—an increasingly common hospital procedure for treatment of coronary artery disease, particularly for older persons. Many measures are shown separately for persons of different ages because of the strong effect of age on health. Selected figures also highlight differences in determinants and measures of health status and utilization of health care by such characteristics as sex, race, Hispanic origin, education, and poverty status.

Trend Tables

The chartbook section is followed by 156 trend tables organized around four major subject areas: health status and determinants, health care utilization, health care resources, and health care expenditures. A major criterion used in selecting the trend tables is availability of comparable national data over a period of several years. The tables present data for selected years to highlight major trends in health statistics. Earlier editions of *Health, United States* may present data for additional years that are not included in the current printed report. Where possible, these additional years of data are available in Excel spreadsheet files on the *Health, United States* Web site. Tables with additional data years are listed in Appendix III.

Racial and Ethnic Data

Many tables in *Health, United States* present data according to race and Hispanic origin consistent with Department-wide emphasis on expanding racial and ethnic detail when presenting health data. Trend data on race and ethnicity are presented in the greatest detail possible after taking into account the quality of data, the amount of missing data, and the number of observations. New standards for Federal data on race and ethnicity are described in Appendix II under *Race*.

Education and Income Data

Many tables in *Health, United States* present data according to socioeconomic status, using education and poverty level as proxy measures. Poverty level is based on family income data and number of persons in the household. Data are presented in the greatest detail possible after taking into account the quality of data, the amount of missing data, and the number of observations. Due to the complexity and sensitivity of collecting education and income information, only a few national data systems obtain data on education and income, including the National Health Interview Survey (NHIS), the National Health and Nutrition Examination Survey, and the National Survey of Family Growth. Education and income are obtained directly from survey respondents, and nonresponse rates, especially for income data, are particularly high. NCHS imputes missing family income data for the NHIS starting with data year 1990, and tables with NHIS data shown in *Health, United States* utilize the imputed poverty data. Education and income information are not generally available from records-based data collection systems including the National Health Care Surveys (see Appendix I). State vital statistics systems currently report mother's education on the birth certificate and, based on information from an informant, decedent's education on the death certificate. See Appendix II, *Education; Family income; Poverty level.*

Changes in This Edition

Each volume of *Health, United States* is prepared to maximize its usefulness as a standard reference source while maintaining its continuing relevance. Comparability is fostered by including similar trend tables in each volume. Timeliness is maintained by (1) adding new tables each year to reflect emerging topics in public health and (2) improving the content of ongoing tables. *Health, United States, 2005* includes eight new trend tables on multiple births (table 5) based on birth certificate data; prevalence of respiratory conditions (table 56), headache and low back pain (table 57), hearing and vision limitations (table 59), leisure-time physical activity (table 72), and adult vaccinations (table 76), all based on National Health Interview Survey data; the nutritional status of the U.S. population based on National Health and Nutrition Examination Survey data (table 71); and factors that affect growth in personal health care expenditures (table 121) based on data from the Centers for Medicare & Medicaid Services.

Appendixes

Appendix I describes each data source used in the report and provides references for further information about the sources. Data sources are listed alphabetically within two broad categories: (1) Government Sources and (2) Private and Global Sources.

Appendix II is an alphabetical listing of terms used in the report. It also presents standard populations used for age adjustment (tables I, II, and III); ICD codes for causes of death shown in *Health, United States* from the Sixth through Tenth Revisions and the years when the Revisions were in effect (tables IV and V); comparability ratios between ICD–9 and ICD–10 for selected causes (table VI); ICD–9–CM codes for external cause-of-injury, diagnostic, and procedure categories (tables VII, IX, and X); industry codes according to the 2002 North American Industry Classification System (table VIII); National Drug Code (NDC) Therapeutic Class recodes of generic analgesic drugs (table XI); and sample tabulations of NHIS data comparing the 1977 and 1997 Standards for Federal data on race and Hispanic origin (tables XII and XIII).

Appendix III lists tables for which additional years of trend data are available electronically in Excel spreadsheet files on the *Health, United States* Web site and CD-ROM, described below under Electronic Access.

Index

The Index to Trend Tables and Chartbook Figures is a useful tool for locating data by topic. Tables are cross-referenced by such topics as Child and adolescent health; Elderly population age 65 years and over; Women's health; Men's health; State data; American Indian, Asian, Black, and Hispanic origin populations; Education; Poverty status; Disability; and Metropolitan and nonmetropolitan data.

Electronic Access

Health, United States may be accessed in its entirety on the World Wide Web at www.cdc.gov/nchs/hus.htm. From the *Health, United States* Web site, one may also register for the *Health, United States* electronic mailing list to receive announcements about release dates and notices of updates to tables.

Health, United States, 2005, the chartbook, and each of the trend tables are available as Acrobat .pdf files on the Web. Chartbook figures are available as downloadable PowerPoint® slides. Trend tables and chartbook data tables are available as downloadable Excel spreadsheet files. Trend tables listed in Appendix III include additional years of data not shown in the printed report or .pdf files. Both .pdf and spreadsheet files for selected tables will be updated on the Web if more current data become available near the time when the printed report is released. Readers who register with the electronic mailing list will be notified of these table updates. Previous editions of *Health, United States* and chartbooks, starting with the 1993 edition, also may be accessed from the *Health, United States* Web site.

Health, United States is also available on CD-ROM, where it can be viewed, searched, printed, and saved using Adobe Acrobat software on the CD-ROM.

Copies of the Report

Copies of *Health, United States, 2005,* and the CD-ROM can be purchased from the Government Printing Office (GPO) through links to GPO on the National Center for Health Statistics Web site, Publications and Information Products page.

Questions?

For answers to questions about this report, contact:

Office of Information Services
Information Dissemination Staff
National Center for Health Statistics
Centers for Disease Control and Prevention
3311 Toledo Road, Fifth Floor
Hyattsville, MD 20782
Phone: 301-458-INFO or toll free 866-441-NCHS
E-mail: nchsquery@cdc.gov
Internet: www.cdc.gov/nchs

Acknowledgments

Overall responsibility for planning and coordinating the content of this volume rested with the Office of Analysis and Epidemiology, National Center for Health Statistics (NCHS), under the direction of Amy B. Bernstein and Diane M. Makuc.

Production of ***Health, United States, 2005,*** highlights, trend tables, and appendixes was managed by Kate Prager. Trend tables were prepared by Amy B. Bernstein, Alan J. Cohen, Margaret A. Cooke, La-Tonya D. Curl, Catherine R. Duran, Sheila Franco, Virginia M. Freid, Ji-Eun Lee, Andrea P. MacKay, Mitchell B. Pierre, Jr., Rebecca A. Placek, Kate Prager, Laura A. Pratt, and Henry Xia, with assistance from Stephanie N. Gray. Appendix II tables and the index were assembled by Anita L. Powell. Production planning and coordination of trend tables were managed by Rebecca A. Placek. Administrative and word processing assistance were provided by Carole J. Hunt, Lillie C. Featherstone, and Brenda L. Wolfrey.

Production of the ***Chartbook on Trends in the Health of Americans*** was managed by Virginia M. Freid. Production of the Special Feature on Adults 55-–64 Years of Age was managed by Amy B. Bernstein. Data and analysis for specific charts were provided by Amy B. Bernstein, Margaret A. Cooke, Sheila Franco, Virginia M. Freid, Deborah D. Ingram, Ellen A. Kramarow, Ji-Eun Lee, Andrea P. MacKay, Patricia N. Pastor, and Kate Prager. Graphs were drafted by La-Tonya D. Curl and data tables were prepared by Rebecca A. Placek. Technical assistance and programming were provided by Lara Akinbami, Alan J. Cohen, Catherine R. Duran, Lois Fingerhut, Richard F. Gillum, Mitchell B. Pierre, Jr., Henry Xia, and Marc W. Zodet.

Publications management and editorial review were provided by Demarius V. Miller. Oversight review for publications and electronic products was provided by Linda L. Bean. The designer was Sarah Hinkle. Production was done by Jacqueline M. Davis and Zung T. Le. Printing was managed by Patricia L. Wilson and Joan D. Burton.

Electronic access through the NCHS Internet site and CD-ROM were provided by Christine J. Brown, Jacqueline M. Davis, Dorothy Day, Zung T. Le, Demarius V. Miller, Sharon L. Ramirez, and Patricia L. Wilson.

Data and technical assistance were provided by staff of the following NCHS organizations: *Division of Health Care Statistics*: Irma E. Arispe, Catharine W. Burt, Donald K. Cherry, Carol J. DeFrances, Marni J. Hall, Esther Hing, Lola Jean Kozak, Karen L. Lipkind, Linda F. McCaig, Robert Pokras, Susan M. Schappert, Jane E. Sisk, and Genevieve W. Strahan; *Division of Health Examination Statistics*: Lisa Broitman, Margaret D. Carroll, Bruce Dye, and Clifford L. Johnson; *Division of Health Interview Statistics*: Patricia F. Adams, Veronica E. Benson, Barbara Bloom, Viona I. Brown, Margaret L. Cejku, Pei-Lu Chiu, Robin A. Cohen, Richard H. Coles, Marcie Cynamon, Achintya Dey, Cathy C. Hao, Kristina Kotulak-Hays, Susan S. Jack, Jane B. Page, Eve Powell-Griner, Jeannine Schiller, Charlotte A. Schoenborn, Mira L. Shanks, Anne K. Stratton, and Luong Tonthat; *Division of Vital Statistics*: Robert N. Anderson, Elizabeth Arias, Anjani Chandra, Thomas D. Dunn, Brady E. Hamilton, Donna L. Hoyert, Kenneth D. Kochanek, Marian F. MacDorman, Joyce A. Martin, Gladys M. Martinez, T.J. Mathews, Arialdi M. Minino, William D. Mosher, Sherry L. Murphy, Gail A. Parr, Manju Sharma, Stephanie J. Ventura, and Jim Weed; *Office of Analysis and Epidemiology*: Mark S. Eberhardt, Lois Fingerhut, Deborah D. Ingram, Richard J. Klein, and Patricia A. Knapp; and *Office of International Statistics*: Juan Rafael Albertorio-Diaz and Francis C. Notzon.

Additional data and technical assistance were also provided by the following organizations of the Centers for Disease Control and Prevention: *Epidemiology Program Office*: Samuel L. Groseclose and Patsy A. Hall; *National Center for Chronic Disease Prevention and Health Promotion*: Joy Herndon, Sherry Everett Jones, Laura K. Kann, Steve Kinchen, Shari L. Shanklin, and Lilo T. Strauss; *National Center for HIV, STD, and TB Prevention*: Melinda Flock and Luetta Schneider; *National Immunization Program*: Natalie J. Darling and Meena Khare; by the following organizations within the Department of Health and Human Services: *Agency for Healthcare Research and Quality*: David Kashihara and Steven Machlin; *Centers for Medicare & Medicaid Services*: Cathy A. Cowan, Cherron A. Cox, Frank Eppig, Denise F. Franz, David A. Gibson, Deborah W. Kidd, Helen C. Lazenby, Katharine R. Levit, Anna Long, Joanne S. Mack, Anne B. Martin, and Carter S. Warfield; *National Institutes of Health*: Jessica Campbell, Catherine C. Cowie, and Lynn A. G. Ries; *Office of the Secretary, DHHS*: Mitchell Goldstein; *Substance Abuse and Mental Health Services Administration*: Daniel Foley, Joseph C. Gfroerer, and Ronald Manderscheid; and by the following governmental and nongovernmental organizations: *U.S. Bureau of the Census Bureau*: Joseph Dalaker and Bernadette D. Proctor; *Bureau of Labor Statistics*: Alan Blostin, Stella Cromartie, Kay Ford, Daniel Ginsburg,

Elizabeth Rogers, John Stinson, and Peggy Suarez; *Department of Veterans Affairs*: Michael F. Grindstaff; *Alan Guttmacher Institute*: Rebecca Wind; *American Association of Colleges of Pharmacy*: Jennifer M. Patton; *American Association of Colleges of Podiatric Medicine*: Carol E. Gill; *American Dental Education Association*: Richard Weaver; *Association of Schools of Public Health*: Mah-Sere K. Sow; *Cowles Research Group*: C. McKeen Cowles; and *InterStudy*: Richard Hamer.

All those associated with *Health, United States* would like to give their special thanks to

Dr. Kate Prager

who is retiring this year. In her capacity as Special Assistant for *Health, United States* for the past 13 years, Dr. Prager's painstaking review of everything from the validity of the content to the formatting of footnotes has ensured that all aspects of the book are accurate and accessible. She has performed the work of analyst, technical editor, manager, government liaison, and every other possible role involved in producing a book of this scope and has done so with skill, dedication, and patience. We would like to express our gratitude for all she has contributed to the publication over the years and wish her well in her post-*Health, United States* life. She will be greatly missed.

Contents

Contents

Executive Summary and Highlights

Chartbook on Trends in the Health of Americans

Trend Tables

Appendixes

List of Chartbook Figures

Population

Health Insurance and Expenditures

Health Risk Factors

Morbidity and Limitation of Activity

Health Care Utilization

Mortality

Special Feature: Adults 55–64 Years of Age

List of Trend Tables

Health Status and Determinants

Population

Fertility and Natality

Mortality

Determinants and Measures of Health

Utilization of Health Resources

Ambulatory Care

Inpatient Care

Health Care Resources

Personnel

Facilities

Health Care Expenditures and Payors

National Health Expenditures

Health Care Coverage and Major Federal Programs

State Health Expenditures and Health Insurance

Executive Summary and Highlights

Executive Summary

Health, United States, 2005, is the 29th annual report on the health status of the Nation prepared by the Secretary of the Department of Health and Human Services for the President and Congress. In a chartbook and 156 detailed tables, it provides an annual picture of health for the entire Nation. Trends are presented in health status and health care utilization, resources, and expenditures.

For those entrusted with safeguarding the Nation's health, monitoring the health of the American people is an essential step in making sound health policy and setting priorities for research and programs. Measures of the population's health provide essential information for assessing how the Nation's resources should be directed to improve the health of the population. Examination of emerging trends identifies diseases, conditions, and risk factors that warrant study and intervention. *Health, United States* presents trends and current information on measures and determinants of the Nation's health. It also identifies differences in health and health care among people of differing races and ethnicities, genders, education and income levels, and geographic locations, and it shows whether these differences are narrowing or increasing. Given the increasing diversity of the Nation and the continuing changes in the health care infrastructure, this is a challenging task, but it is a critically important undertaking.

Overall Health of the Nation

The health of the Nation continues to improve overall, in part because of the significant resources devoted to public health programs, research, health care, and health education. Over the past century many diseases have been controlled or their morbidity and mortality substantially reduced. Notable achievements in public health have included the control of infectious diseases such as typhoid and cholera through decontamination of water; implementation of widespread vaccination programs to eradicate or contain polio, diphtheria, pertussis, and measles; fluoridation of water to drastically reduce the prevalence of dental caries; and improvements in motor vehicle safety through vehicle redesign and efforts to increase use of seatbelts and motorcycle helmets (1). A sharp decline in deaths from cardiovascular disease is a major public health achievement that resulted in large part from public education campaigns emphasizing a healthy lifestyle and increased use of cholesterol and hypertension-lowering medications (2). Yet even as progress is made in improving both the quantity and quality of life, increased longevity is accompanied by increased prevalence of chronic conditions and their associated pain and disability. In recent years, progress in some arenas—declines in infant and cause-specific mortality, morbidity from chronic conditions, reduction in prevalence of risk factors including smoking and lack of exercise—has not been as rapid as in earlier years or trends have been moving in the wrong direction. It is equally important to keep in mind that these improvements have not been equally distributed by income, race, ethnicity, education, and geography.

Health Status and Its Determinants

Life expectancy in the United States continues to show a long-term upward trend, although the most dramatic increases were in the early part of the 20th century. In 2003 American men could expect to live 3 years longer, and women more than 1 year longer, than they did in 1990. Infant mortality and mortality from heart disease, stroke, and cancer continued to decline in recent years (figures 26, 27, 29, and tables 22, 27, and 29). In 2002 the infant mortality rate in the United States increased for the first time since 1958; preliminary data indicate a small, but not statistically significant, decline in 2003 (3,4).

Childhood infectious diseases such as mumps and measles have all but disappeared (table 51), but the prevalence of many chronic diseases is increasing in part associated with increased longevity and aging of the population (figure 1 and table 1). In 1999–2002, more than 9 percent of persons 20 years of age and over and about one-fifth of adults 60 years and over had diabetes, including those with diabetes previously diagnosed by a physician and those with undiagnosed diabetes determined by results of a fasting blood sugar test (table 55). A substantial proportion of the population also experiences discomfort from conditions such as arthritis, headache, and back pain, which can affect quality of life. In 2003, 15 percent of adults suffered with severe headache or migraine during the past 3 months (figure 17 and table 57). Nearly twice as many adults reported low back pain (figure 17 and table 57).

Of particular concern in recent years has been the increase in overweight and obesity, which are risk factors for many chronic diseases and disabilities including heart disease, hypertension, and back pain. The rising number of children and adolescents who are overweight, and the high percentage of Americans who are not physically active (figures 13–15 and tables 72–74) raise additional concerns about Americans' future health (5).

Decreased cigarette smoking among adults is a prime example of a trend that has contributed to overall declines in mortality. However, the rapid drop in cigarette smoking in the two decades following the first Surgeon General's Report in 1964 has slowed in recent years. About 24 percent of men and 19 percent of women were current smokers in 2003 (figure 10 and table 63).

Prevalence of risky behaviors has also improved over time, including the percent of high school students in grades 9–12 who rode with a driver who had been drinking alcohol. This statistic decreased from 40 percent to 30 percent between 1991 and 2003, yet further reductions are certainly necessary (figure 12) (6).

Health Care Utilization and Resources

People use health care services for many reasons: to treat illnesses, injuries, and health conditions; to prevent or delay future health care problems; to reduce pain and increase quality of life; and to obtain information about their health status and prognoses. The study of trends in health care utilization provides important information on these phenomena and spotlights areas that warrant further study. Utilization trends may also be used to project future health care needs and expenditures, as well as training and supply needs.

Admissions to hospitals and length of stay declined substantially in the 1980s and 1990s, but these declines appear to be leveling off (tables 97–99). The diagnoses recorded on inpatient hospital stays are changing, as are the procedures performed on inpatients (table 100). Hospitalizations for procedures that can be performed on an outpatient basis, such as lens extractions and knee arthroscopies, have all but disappeared from inpatient settings. Instead, inpatient care is becoming more intensive and complex, with more procedures such as insertions of cardiac stents and hip replacements being performed, particularly on older persons (figure 25 and table 100). In addition to changes in the location of services, the types of services being provided have changed. In particular, the number of drugs prescribed or administered during visits to physicians and hospital outpatient departments is increasing (table 92).

Americans are increasingly using many types of preventive or early-detection health services. Since the late 1980s the percentages of older adults who had received pneumococcal and influenza vaccine have increased sharply but remain below desired levels (table 76). The percentage of children 19–35 months of age vaccinated for many childhood infectious diseases is at a high level (81 percent), and the percentage of children receiving varicella (chickenpox) vaccine has increased sharply since it was first recommended in 1996 (table 77). Rates of Pap smears and mammograms have increased since 1987 when national data first became regularly available (figures 21, 22, and tables 86 and 87).

As the nature of health care changes, so do the supply of health providers and the sites where services are provided. Services that historically were provided in inpatient settings are increasingly offered in outpatient settings, and the number of physical therapy providers, comprehensive outpatient rehabilitation facilities, and ambulatory surgical centers certified by the Centers for Medicare & Medicaid Services has increased since the 1980s (table 117). As a result of this shifting in the sites of care, the supply of some other providers or service sites has declined, such as the number of inpatient mental health organizations and the associated number of beds (table 113).

Expenditures and Health Insurance

The United States spends more on health per capita than any other country, and health spending continues to increase rapidly. Much of this spending is for care that controls or reduces the impact of chronic diseases and conditions affecting an aging population. Prescription drugs and cardiac operations are two notable examples. In 2003 national health care expenditures in the United States totaled $1.7 trillion, a 7.7 percent increase from 2002 (table 119). Since 1995 the average annual rate of increase for prescription drug expenditures was higher than for any other type of health expenditure (table 122), indicating the growing importance of prescription drugs. The source of payment for personal health care varies according to the type of care provided. In 2003, government sources were the primary payers of hospital and nursing home care, paying for about three-fifths of these types of services, while private health insurance paid for almost one-half of physician services and prescription drugs (table 123).

Access to health care is determined by many factors, including the supply of providers and the ability to use and pay for available care. The percent of the population under 65 years of age with no health insurance coverage fluctuated about 16–18 percent between 1994 and 2003 (figure 6 and table 134). The percent of the population with private health insurance decreased between 1999 and 2003 (figure 6 and table 132). This decrease was offset by an increase in Medicaid coverage (table 133), resulting in little change in the percentage uninsured. Employer-sponsored health insurance in particular has been declining in recent years. Between 2001 and 2003 the proportion of the population under 65 years of age with health insurance obtained through the workplace (a current or former employer or union) declined from 67 to 63 percent (table 132).

Disparities in Risk Factors, Access, and Utilization

Efforts to improve Americans' health in the 21st century will be shaped by important changes in demographics. Ours is a Nation that is growing older and becoming more racially and ethnically diverse. In 2004 nearly one-third of adults and about two-fifths of children were identified as black, Hispanic, Asian, or American Indian or Alaska Native. Fourteen percent of Americans in 2004 identified themselves as Hispanic, 12 percent as black, and 4 percent as Asian (figure 3).

Health, United States, 2005, identifies major disparities in health and health care that exist by socioeconomic status, race, ethnicity, and insurance status. Persons living in poverty are considerably more likely to be in fair or poor health and to have disabling conditions, and less likely to have used many types of health care. In 2003 adults living in poverty were almost twice as likely to report having trouble seeing—even with eyeglasses or contact lenses—as higher income persons (table 59), and were also almost twice as likely to report having had an asthma attack in the past year (table 56). Non-Hispanic black children 3–10 years of age had higher asthma attack prevalence rates than non-Hispanic white or Hispanic children, and this disparity has been increasing in recent years (figure 16).

Large disparities in infant mortality rates remain among racial and ethnic groups (figure 28 and table 19). The gap in life expectancy between the black and white populations has narrowed, but persists (table 27). Disparities in risk factors, access to health care, and morbidity also remain. Hispanic and American Indian persons under 65 years are more likely to be uninsured than those in other racial and ethnic groups (table 134). Obesity, a major risk factor for many chronic diseases, varies by race and ethnicity (tables 73 and 74). In 2003 the rate of recent mammogram screening for white and black women was similar but rates for Asian and Hispanic women remained at a lower level (figure 21 and table 86).

Many aspects of the health of the Nation have improved, but the health of some racial and ethnic groups has improved less than others. The large differences in health status by race and Hispanic origin documented in this report may be explained by factors including socioeconomic status, health practices, psychosocial stress and resources, environmental exposures, discrimination, and access to health care (7). Socioeconomic and cultural differences among racial and ethnic groups in the United States will likely continue to influence future patterns of disease, disability, and health care use.

Special Feature: Adults 55–64 Years of Age

The population group age 55–64 years is projected to be the fastest growing segment of the adult population over the next decade. In 2004 there were about 29 million persons in this age group. The 55–64 age group is projected to increase by 11 million persons over the 2004–2014 period (figure 30), to 40 million persons by 2014. "Baby boomers" are those born during the post-World War II period, between 1946 and 1964. In 2004 the oldest baby boomers were 55–58 years of age, and just beginning to enter the 55–64 year age group. Many more boomers will age into the group in the next 10 years. In future decades the population age 65 years and over will increase dramatically—yet the population age 55–64 years will not decline because more boomers will replace the ones that age into older age groups. Focusing on this age group may provide insight into program and policy interventions that could improve access and quality of care for Americans age 55–64 years as well as highlight implications for the Medicare program as this large group ages into Medicare and Social Security. This year's *Chartbook on Trends in the Health of Americans* includes a Special Feature focusing on health care use and expenditures for adults age 55–64 years of age, and determinants of care including employment status, income, health insurance, and risk factors.

People age 55–64 years often have more frequent and more severe health problems than younger people. The prevalence of diabetes, hypertension, heart disease, and other chronic diseases increases with age (tables 55 and 69). There is also evidence that prevalence of some risk factors associated with heart disease—hypertension and obesity—has been increasing among this group while the prevalence of elevated cholesterol has declined (figure 34). Between 1988–94 and 1999–2002, the percent with at least one of these heart disease risk factors increased for men age 55–64 years from 64 to 72 percent and remained steady for women at 73–75 percent. Utilization of prescription drugs for these conditions has increased substantially. Between 1995–96 and 2002–03 the rate of cholesterol-lowering drugs prescribed during physician and hospital outpatient department visits among men 55–64 years of age almost tripled and among women increased more than three-fold (figure 36). Increasing drug utilization overall also has economic implications. The average annual expenses for all prescription drugs and out-of-pocket expenses for drugs increased substantially between 1997 and 2002 for this group (2002 dollars; figure 37).

Americans age 55–64 years are more likely to have health insurance coverage than younger adults age 18–54 (table 134). However as they grow older and begin to develop health problems, they do not have the guarantee of health insurance coverage that Medicare offers to almost all older adults age 65 years and over. Those still employed may delay retirement plans and continue to work in order to maintain health insurance coverage for themselves or their spouses until they reach age 65. In 2002–03 more than one-half of adults 55–64 years of age were employed with 17 percent retired and 12 percent unemployed due to disability (data table for figure 31).

Uninsured 55–64 year-olds may be at risk for high out-of-pocket expenditures, or of delaying or not receiving needed nonurgent care. Persons 55–64 years of age without health insurance were considerably less likely to have health care visits in the past year than persons with private insurance. About one-half of the uninsured 55–64 year-olds saw a general physician (family medicine practitioner, internist, or general practitioner) at least once in the past year compared with 80 percent of those with private insurance (figure 35). When the uninsured 55–64 year-olds do become eligible for Medicare, they may use more health care resources as a result of health care that was delayed at earlier ages (8).

Many Americans age 55–64 years are relatively well off; however certain subgroups including unmarried persons, women, and minorities are at a greater risk of living in poverty, lacking health insurance, and being disabled (data tables for figures 31–33). Among both men and women 55–64 years of age, non-Hispanic black and Hispanic adults were about twice as likely to be living in poverty as non-Hispanic white adults in 2003. Levels of disability reported as a reason for unemployment were also higher among non-Hispanic black men and particularly among non-Hispanic black women age 55–64 years than among other racial and ethnic groups (figure 31). Those without health insurance or adequate income are particularly vulnerable to the financial and physical burdens of disease and disability.

To improve the health of all Americans and to enable policymakers to chart future trends, target resources most effectively, and set program and policy priorities, it is critical that the Nation keep collecting and disseminating reliable and accurate information about all components of health, including current health status, the determinants of health, resources, and outcomes. The following highlights from *Health, United States, 2005 With Chartbook on Trends in the Health of Americans* summarize the latest findings gathered from across the public and private health care sectors to help the Department of Health and Human Services, the President, and Congress in carrying out this essential mission.

References

1. Ten great public health achievements—United States, 1900–1999. MMWR 48(12):241–3. 1999. Available at www.cdc.gov/mmwr/preview/mmwrhtml/00056796.htm accessed on February 18, 2005.
2. Achievements in Public Health, 1900–1999: Decline in deaths from heart disease and stroke—United States, 1900–1999. MMWR 48(30):649–56. 1999. Available at www.cdc.gov/mmwr/preview/mmwrhtml/mm4830a1.htm accessed on June 1, 2005.
3. MacDorman MF, Martin JA, Mathews TJ, Hoyert DL, Ventura SJ. Explaining the 2001–2002 infant mortality increase: Data from the linked birth/infant death data set. National vital statistics reports; vol 53 no 12. Hyattsville, Maryland: National Center for Health Statistics. 2005. Available at www.cdc.gov/nchs/data/nvsr/nvsr53/nvsr53_12.pdf accessed on March 3, 2005.

4. Hoyert DL, Kung H, Smith BL. Deaths: Preliminary data for 2003. National vital statistics reports; vol 53 no 15. Hyattsville, Maryland. National Center for Health Statistics. 2005. Available at www.cdc.gov/nchs/data/nvsr/nvsr53/nvsr53_15.pdf accessed on March 3, 2005.

5. Flegal KM, Carroll MD, Ogden CL et al. Prevalence and trends in obesity among U.S. adults, 1999–2000. JAMA 288(14):1723–7. 2002.

6. Centers for Disease Control and Prevention, Surveillance summaries. Youth risk behavior surveillance—United States, 2003. MMWR 53(SS02):1–96. 2004. Available at www.cdc.gov/mmwr/preview/mmwrhtml/ss5302a1.htm accessed on March 3, 2005.

7. Williams DR, Rucker TD. Understanding and addressing racial disparities in health care. Health Care Financing Review 21(4):75–90. 2000.

8. McWilliams JM, Zaslavsky AM, Meara E, Ayanian JZ. Impact of Medicare coverage on basic clinical services for previously uninsured adults. JAMA 290(6):757–64. 2003.

Highlights

Health, United States, 2005, is the 29th report on the health status of the Nation. In a chartbook and 156 trend tables, it presents current and historic information on the health of the U.S. population. The trend tables are organized around four major subject areas: health status and determinants, health care utilization, health care resources, and health care expenditures and payors. The 2005 Chartbook on Trends in the Health of Americans focuses on selected determinants and measures of health and includes a special feature on adults 55–64 years of age, a rapidly growing segment of the adult population. The economic and health status of this age group is of interest as it is poised to enter retirement and to become eligible for Medicare. Highlights of the featured topic, adults age 55–64 years, follow other major findings from the report.

Health Status and Determinants

Population characteristics

Demographic changes in the U.S. population will shape future efforts to improve health and health care. Two major changes are the increasing racial and ethnic diversity of the Nation and the growth of the older population.

From 1950 to 2004 the proportion of the **population age 75 years and over** rose from 3 to 6 percent. It is projected that by 2050, 12 percent, or about one in eight Americans, will be 75 years of age or over (figure 2).

The **racial and ethnic composition** of the Nation has changed over time. The Hispanic population and the Asian population have grown more rapidly than other racial and ethnic groups in recent decades. In 2004, 14 percent of the U.S. population identified themselves as Hispanic and 4 percent as Asian (figure 3).

In 2003, 12.5 percent of Americans were living in **poverty,** up from 12.1 percent in 2002 and 11.7 percent in 2001. In 2003 more than 60 percent of black and Hispanic children under 18 years of age and more than one-half of the black and Hispanic population age 65 years and over were poor or near poor (figures 4 and 5 and table 2).

Fertility

Birth rates for teens continued their steady decline while birth rates for women 25–44 years of age increased in 2003.

The **birth rate for teenagers** declined for the 12th consecutive year in 2003, to 41.6 births per 1,000 women age 15–19 years, the lowest rate in more than six decades. The birth rate for 15–17 year olds in 2003 was 42 percent lower than the recent peak in 1991, and the birth rate for older teens 18–19 years of age was 25 percent lower than in 1991 (table 3).

In 2003 the **fertility rate** for Hispanic women (96.9 births per 1,000 Hispanic women 15–44 years) was 66 percent higher than for non-Hispanic white women (58.5 per 1,000) (table 3).

In 2003 the **birth rate for unmarried women** increased to almost 45 births per 1,000 unmarried women age 15–44 years. The birth rate for unmarried black women was essentially unchanged at 66.3 per 1,000 in 2003, and the birth rate for unmarried Hispanic women increased for the fifth year in a row to 92.2 per 1,000 (table 10).

The rate of **triplet and higher order births** at 187.4 per 100,000 live births in 2003 has been relatively stable since 1998, but was over 400 percent higher than the rate in 1980. The increase in multiple births was most marked among women 30 years of age and over (table 5).

Health Behaviors and Risk Factors

Health behaviors and risk factors have a significant effect on health outcomes. Cigarette smoking increases the risk of lung cancer, heart disease, emphysema, and other respiratory diseases. Overweight and obesity increase the risk of death and disease as well as the severity of disease. Regular physical activity lessens the risk of disease and enhances mental and physical functioning. Heavy and chronic use of alcohol and use of illicit drugs increase the risk of disease and injuries.

The percent of **adults who smoke cigarettes** continues to decline. Between 1990 and 2003, the percent of men who smoked declined from 28 to 24 percent and the percent of women who smoked declined from 23 to 19 percent (figure 10).

Between 1997 and 2003 the percent of **high school students who reported smoking cigarettes** in the past month declined from 36 percent to 22 percent, reversing an upward trend that began in the early 1990s. Despite these declines, 26 percent of high school seniors were current smokers in 2003 and 13 percent smoked cigarettes on 20 or more days in the past month (figures 10 and 11).

Cigarette smoking during pregnancy is a risk factor for poor birth outcomes such as low birthweight and infant death. In 2003 the proportion of mothers who smoked cigarettes during pregnancy declined to less than 11 percent, down from 20 percent in 1989. The smoking rate during pregnancy for mothers age 18–19 years (17 percent) remained higher than that for older mothers (figure 10 and table 12).

Low birthweight is associated with elevated risk of death and disability in infants. In 2003 the low birthweight rate (less than 2,500 grams, or 5.5 pounds, at birth) increased to 7.9 percent, up from 7.0 percent in 1990 (table 13).

In 2003, 22 percent of male high school students rarely or never **used a seat belt** compared with 15 percent of female high school students. The percent of high school students in grades 9–12 who **rode with a driver who had been drinking alcohol** decreased from 40 percent to 30 percent between 1991 and 2003 (figure 12).

In 2003, 67 percent of **high school students** reported **regular physical activity**. Seventy-three percent of male high school students and 60 percent of female high school students reported regular physical activity. Only 50 percent of non-Hispanic black female students were physically active on a regular basis (figure 13).

In 2003, one-third of **adults** 18 years of age and over engaged in **regular leisure-time physical activity**. Nonpoor adults were more likely to engage in regular leisure-time physical activity (37 percent) than near poor or poor persons (23–25 percent). About one-half of poor and near poor adults were inactive compared with less than one-third of nonpoor adults (percents are age adjusted) (figure 14 and table 72).

Between 1971–74 and 1999–2000, the average energy intake in **kilocalories** (Kcals) increased 7 percent among men 20–74 years of age and almost 22 percent among women 20–74 years. For both men and women, the percent of Kcals from fat decreased while the percent of Kcals from carbohydrates increased (table 71).

The prevalence of **overweight and obesity among adults** 20–74 years of age increased from 47 percent in 1976–80 to 65 percent in 1999–2002. During this period the prevalence of obesity among adults 20–74 years of age doubled from 15 to 31 percent (percents are age adjusted) (figure 15 and table 73).

Between 1976–80 and 1999–2002 the prevalence of **overweight among children** 6–11 years of age more than doubled from 7 to 16 percent and the prevalence of overweight among **adolescents** 12–19 years of age more than tripled from 5 to 16 percent (figure 15 and table 74).

In 2003 among current drinkers age 18 years and over, 40 percent of men and 20 percent of women reported drinking **five or more alcoholic drinks** on at least 1 day in the past year (age adjusted). This level of alcohol consumption was most common among young adults 18–24 years of age. Nearly 60 percent of young men and 42 percent of young women consumed five or more alcoholic drinks in a day (table 68).

In 2003 the prevalence of **illicit drug use** within the past month among youths 12–17 years of age was 11 percent. The percent of youths and young adults reporting illicit drug use increased with age, from 4 percent among 12–13 year olds to 19 percent among those age 16–17 years and 20 percent among those 18–25 years (table 66).

Morbidity

Summary measures of morbidity presented in this report include limitation of activity due to chronic health conditions, limitations in activities of daily living, and self-assessed (or family member-assessed) health status. Additional measures of morbidity include the incidence and prevalence of specific diseases, vision and hearing trouble, injury-related emergency department use, and suicide attempts.

In 2003 the percent of persons reporting their **health status** as fair or poor was more than three times as high for persons living below the poverty level as for those with family income more than twice the poverty level (20 percent and 6 percent, age adjusted). Levels of fair or poor health were nearly twice as high among Hispanic persons and non-Hispanic black persons as among non-Hispanic white persons (table 60).

In 2003 **limitation of activity** due to chronic health conditions was reported for 7 percent of **children** under the age of 18 years. Among preschool children (under 5 years) the conditions most often mentioned were speech problems, asthma, and mental retardation or other developmental problems. Among school-age children (5–17 years), learning disabilities and Attention Deficit Hyperactivity Disorder (ADHD) were frequently mentioned (figure 18 and table 58).

Arthritis and other musculoskeletal conditions were the leading cause of **activity limitation** among **working-age adults** 18–64 years of age in 2002–03. Mental illness was the second most frequently mentioned condition causing activity limitation among adults 18–44 years of age and the third most frequently mentioned among adults 45–54 years (figure 19).

Among **persons age 65 years and over**, arthritis, and heart disease and other circulatory conditions were the two most frequently reported causes of **activity limitation** in 2002–03. The next most commonly reported cause of activity limitation was diabetes for those 65–84 years and vision problems and senility for those 85 years and over (figure 20).

In 2003, 9 percent of the adult population reported trouble seeing even with contact lenses or glasses and 3 percent were deaf or reported a lot of trouble hearing. **Vision and hearing trouble** increase with age. Twenty-one percent of persons age 75 years and over had trouble seeing and 15 percent were deaf or had a lot of trouble hearing (table 59).

In 2003, 15 percent of adults age 18 years and over reported **severe headache or migraine** during the past 3-month period. Severe headaches and migraines were more common among women than men (21 percent compared with 9 percent, age adjusted) and declined with age from 25 percent among women age 18–44 years to 7 percent among women age 75 years and over (figure 17 and table 57).

In 2003, 28 percent of adults age 18 years and over reported **low back pain** lasting a day or more in the last 3-month period. Women had higher prevalence of low back pain than men (figure 17 and table 57).

In 2003 **tuberculosis** incidence declined for the 11th consecutive year to 5.2 cases per 100,000 population, down from 10.3 in 1990 and 12.3 in 1980 (table 51).

New **pediatric AIDS cases** have declined steadily since 1994 when U.S. Public Health Service guidelines recommended testing and treatment of pregnant women and neonates to reduce perinatal HIV transmission. The vast majority of pediatric AIDS cases occur through perinatal exposure. In 2003, an estimated 59 new AIDS cases occurred among children under the age of 13 years, compared with an estimated 187 cases in 1999 (table 52).

Incidence rates for **all cancers combined** declined in the 1990s for males but not for females. Between 1990 and 2001 age-adjusted cancer incidence rates declined on average nearly 1 percent or more per year for black males, non-Hispanic white males, American Indian or Alaska Native males, and Asian or Pacific Islander males. Among non-Hispanic white females cancer incidence increased on average 0.4 percent per year between 1990 and 2001, a significant increase (table 53).

The most frequently diagnosed **cancer sites in males** are prostate, followed by lung and bronchus, and colon and rectum. Cancer incidence at these sites is higher for black males than for males of other racial and ethnic groups. In 2001 age-adjusted cancer incidence rates for black males exceeded those for white males by 50 percent for prostate, 49 percent for lung and bronchus, and 16 percent for colon and rectum (table 53).

Breast cancer is the most frequently diagnosed cancer among females. Breast cancer incidence is higher for non-Hispanic white females than for females in other racial and ethnic groups. In 2001 age-adjusted breast cancer incidence rates for non-Hispanic white females exceeded those for black females by 33 percent, for Asian or Pacific Islander females by 52 percent, and for Hispanic females by 74 percent (table 53).

In 1999–2002, 9.3 percent of adults 20 years of age and over had **diabetes**. Thirty percent of adults with diabetes were undiagnosed in 1999–2002, similar to the percent in 1988–94 (table 55).

In 2003, about 3 percent of **adults** age 18 years and over and 6 percent of **children** age 3–17 years had an **asthma attack** during the past 12-month period (figure 16 and table 56).

In 2003 among **adults** age 18 years and over, 14 percent reported being diagnosed with **sinusitis** and 9 percent with **hay fever**. Women were more likely than men to report these diagnoses (table 56).

Between 1993 and 2003 the percent of high school students who reported attempting suicide (8–9 percent) and whose **suicide attempts** required medical attention (just under 3 percent) remained fairly constant. Girls were more likely than boys to consider or attempt suicide. However, in 2002 adolescent boys (15–19 years of age) were five times as likely to die from suicide as were adolescent girls, in part reflecting their choice of more lethal methods, such as firearms (tables 46 and 62).

The prevalence of **serious psychological distress** was 3 percent in 2002–03 among civilian noninstitutionalized adults 18 years of age and over. Four percent of persons age 45–54 years had serious psychological distress, more than younger and older age groups. Persons living below the poverty line were more than four times as likely as those above 200 percent of poverty to have serious psychological distress (9 percent compared with 2 percent, age adjusted) (table 61).

Poor children are more likely to have **untreated dental caries** than children in families with incomes above the poverty level. In 1999–2002, 33 percent of poor children 6–17 years of age had untreated dental caries compared with 13 percent of children in families with incomes at least twice the poverty level (table 85).

Between 1988–94 and 1999–2002, approximately one-quarter (24–28 percent) of adults 18–64 years of age had **untreated dental caries**, down from nearly one-half (48 percent) of adults in 1971–74 (table 85).

Mortality Trends

Life expectancy and infant mortality rates are often used to gauge the overall health of a population. Life expectancy shows a long-term upward trend and infant mortality shows a long-term downward trend.

In 2003 **life expectancy** at birth for the total population reached a record high of 77.6 years (preliminary data), up from 75.4 years in 1990 (table 27).

In 2003 the preliminary **infant mortality** rate was 6.9 infant deaths per 1,000 live births, similar to the rate in 2002 (7.0 per 1,000). In 2002 the infant mortality rate increased for the first time in more than 40 years. The rise in infant mortality in 2002 was concentrated among neonatal deaths occurring in the first week of life, due largely to an increase in the number of infants born weighing less than 750 grams (1 pound 10 1/2 ounces) (figure 27 and table 22).

Between 1950 and 2003 the age-adjusted **death rate for the total population** declined 43 percent to 831 deaths per 100,000 population (preliminary data). This reduction was driven largely by declines in mortality from heart disease, stroke, and unintentional injury (figure 29 and table 29).

Mortality from **heart disease**, the leading cause of death, declined almost 4 percent in 2003 (preliminary data), continuing a long-term downward trend. The 2003 age-adjusted death rate for heart disease was 60 percent lower than the rate in 1950 (figure 29 and tables 29 and 31).

Mortality from **cancer**, the second leading cause of death, decreased more than 2 percent in 2003 (preliminary data), continuing the decline that began in 1990. Overall cancer age-adjusted death rates rose from 1960 to 1990 and then reversed direction (figure 29 and tables 29 and 31).

Mortality from **stroke**, the third leading cause of death, declined almost 5 percent in 2003 (preliminary data). Between 1950 and 2003, the age-adjusted death rate for stroke declined 70 percent (figure 29 and tables 29 and 31).

In 2003 mortality from **chronic lower respiratory diseases** (CLRD), the fourth leading cause of death, decreased almost 5 percent from its peak in 1999 (preliminary data). Age-adjusted death rates for CLRD generally rose between 1980 and 1999, mainly as a result of steadily increasing death rates for females, most noticeably for females age 55 years and over (figure 29 and tables 29, 31, and 41).

Mortality from **unintentional injuries**, the fifth leading cause of death, decreased more than 2 percent in 2003 (preliminary data). Age-adjusted death rates for unintentional injuries generally declined from 1950 until 1992 and then increased slightly (figure 29 and tables 29 and 31).

Disparities in Mortality

As overall death rates have declined, racial and ethnic disparities in mortality persist, but the gap in life expectancy between the black and white populations has narrowed. Disparities in mortality also persist among persons of different education levels.

Large disparities in **infant mortality** rates among **racial and ethnic groups** continue. In 2002 infant mortality rates were highest for infants of non-Hispanic black mothers (13.9 deaths per 1,000 live births), Hawaiian mothers (9.6 per 1,000), American Indian mothers (8.6 per 1,000), and Puerto Rican mothers (8.2 per 1,000); and lowest for infants of mothers of Chinese origin (3.0 per 1,000 live births) and Cuban mothers (3.7 per 1,000) (table 19).

Infant mortality increases as **mother's level of education** decreases among infants of mothers 20 years of age and over. In 2002 the mortality rate for infants of mothers with less than 12 years of education was 58 percent higher than for infants of mothers with 13 or more years of education. This disparity was more marked among non-Hispanic white infants, for whom mortality among infants of mothers with less than a high school education was more than twice that for infants of mothers with more than a high school education (table 20).

Between 1990 and 2003 **life expectancy at birth** increased 3.0 years for **males** and 1.3 years for **females** (preliminary data). The gap in life expectancy between males and females narrowed from 7.0 years in 1990 to 5.3 years in 2003 (figure 26 and table 27).

Between 1990 and 2003 **mortality from lung cancer** declined for **men** and increased for **women.** Although these trends reduced the sex differential for this cause of death, the age-adjusted death rate for lung cancer was still 74 percent higher for men than for women in 2003 (preliminary data) (table 39).

Since 1990 mortality from **chronic lower respiratory diseases** remained relatively stable for **men** while it increased for **women**. These trends reduced the gap between the sexes for this cause of death. In 1990 the age-adjusted death rate for males was more than 100 percent higher than for females. In 2003 (preliminary data) the difference between the rates had been reduced to 38 percent (table 41).

Between 1990 and 2003 **life expectancy at birth** increased more for the **black** than for the **white population**, thereby narrowing the gap in life expectancy between these two racial groups. In 1990 life expectancy at birth for the white population was 7.0 years longer than for the black population. By 2003 the difference had narrowed to 5.2 years, based on preliminary data (table 27).

Overall mortality was 30 percent higher for **black Americans** than for white Americans in 2003 (preliminary data) compared with 37 percent higher in 1990. In 2003 age-adjusted death rates for the black population exceeded those for the white population by 43 percent for **stroke**, 31 percent for **heart disease**, 23 percent for **cancer**, and almost 750 percent for **HIV disease** (table 29).

The **5-year survival rate** for black females diagnosed in 1992–2000 with breast cancer was 14 percentage points lower than the 5-year survival rate for white females (74 percent compared with 88 percent) (table 54).

In 2003 **breast cancer mortality** for black females was 37 percent higher than for white females (preliminary data), compared with less than 15 percent higher in 1990 (based on age-adjusted death rates) (table 40).

Homicide rates among young black males 15–24 years of age and **young Hispanic males** were about 50 percent lower in 2002 than in 1992 and 1993 when homicide rates peaked for these groups. Despite these downward trends, homicide was still the leading cause of death for young black males and the second leading cause for young Hispanic males in 2002, and their homicide rates remained substantially higher than for young non-Hispanic white males (table 45).

HIV disease mortality peaked in 1995 and then fell sharply with the advent of new drug therapies. However, the decline in HIV disease mortality has slowed in recent years. Between 1999 and 2003 (preliminary data), age-adjusted death rates for HIV disease declined about 4 percent per year on average for males and were unchanged for females (table 42).

In 2002 the death rate for **motor vehicle-related injury for young American Indian males** 15–24 years of age was almost 40 percent higher and the suicide rate was almost 60 percent higher than the rates for those causes for young white males. Death rates for the American Indian population are known to be underestimated (tables 44 and 46).

In 2002 death rates for **stroke for Asian males** 45–54 and 55–64 years of age were about 15 percent higher than for white males of those ages. Since 1990, stroke mortality for Asian males and females 45–74 years of age has generally exceeded that for white males and females of those ages. Death rates for the Asian population are known to be underestimated (table 37).

Death rates vary by **educational attainment**. In 2002 the age-adjusted death rate for persons 25–64 years of age with fewer than 12 years of education was 2.7 times the rate for persons with at least one year of college (table 34).

Occupational Health

Improvements in workplace safety constitute a major public health achievement in the twentieth century. Despite important improvements in workplace safety practices, preventable injuries and deaths continue to occur.

In 2003 approximately 2.3 million **workplace injuries and illnesses** in the private sector involved days away from work, job transfer, or restricted duties at work for a rate of 2.6 cases per 100 full-time workers. Transportation and warehousing reported the highest injury and illness rate, 5.4 cases per 100. The next highest rates were reported by the manufacturing (3.8 per 100) and construction industries (3.6 per 100) (table 50).

In 2003, 5,043 **occupational injury deaths** occurred in the private sector or 4.7 fatal occupational injuries per 100,000 employed private sector workers. Natural resources and mining had the highest fatality rate (55.7 per 100,000). Natural resources industries include agriculture, forestry, fishing, and hunting. The next highest fatality rates were for the construction (14.3 per 100,000) and trade, transportation, and utilities industries (5.6 per 100,000) (table 49).

A total of 2,715 **pneumoconiosis deaths**, for which pneumoconiosis was either the underlying or nonunderlying cause of death, occurred in 2002, compared with 4,151 deaths in 1980. Pneumoconiosis is primarily associated with workplace exposures to dusts, including asbestos and dust in coal mines (table 48).

Health Care Utilization and Health Care Resources

Major changes continue to occur in the delivery of health care in the United States, driven in part by changes in payment policies intended to rein in rising costs and by advances in technology that have allowed more complex treatments to be performed on an outpatient basis. Use of hospital inpatient services overall has decreased, yet inpatient care is becoming more complex with more cardiac procedures performed, especially on older persons. New types of health care providers including ambulatory surgery centers and end-stage renal disease facilities have emerged that provide services previously available only in hospitals.

In 2000–2003 the most common **external causes of injury for visits to hospital emergency departments** for children and adolescents were falls, being struck by or against a person or object, and motor vehicle traffic-related injuries (figure 23).

In 2002–03 the percent of **hospital emergency department injury visits** due to falls for adults increased with age from 10–13 percent of visits for persons 18–44 years to 19 percent for persons 45–64 years and 41 percent for persons 65 years of age and over (table 89).

In 2002–03 visit rates to **physician offices and hospital outpatient departments** among persons 18–44 years of age were twice as high for women as for men, largely due to medical care associated with female reproduction. This gender difference narrowed among middle-age adults and disappeared among persons 65 years of age and over (figure 24).

In 2003 the **hospital emergency department** visit rate for black persons was almost twice the rate for white persons (71 visits compared with 38 visits per 100 persons, age adjusted). Adults 75 years and over had a higher rate of visits to the hospital emergency department than other age groups (64 visits per 100 persons) (table 88).

In 2003, 63 percent of all **surgical operations** in community hospitals were performed on outpatients, up from 51 percent in 1990 and 16 percent in 1980 (table 101).

The long-term decline in **hospital discharge rates** and **average length of stay** appears to be over. In 2003 the hospital discharge rate was 120 discharges per 1,000 population, 5 percent higher than in 2000. In 2003 average length of stay was 4.8 days, compared with 4.9 days in 2000–2002 (data are age adjusted) (table 97).

Between 1992–93 and 2002–03 **hospital stays with at least one operation on vessels of the heart** performed on persons 75 years of age and over increased from 79 to 128 hospital stays per 10,000 persons (table 100).

Between 1996–97 and 2002–03 the rate of coronary stent insertion for adults age 45 years and over more than doubled from 22 to 49 per 10,000 population. Among adults age 75 years and over, hospitalizations that included this procedure more than tripled from 23 to 73 per 10,000 population (figure 25).

Between 1992–93 and 2002–03 **hospital stays with at least one diagnostic radiology procedure** performed on persons 18 years of age and over decreased substantially from 78 to 35 hospital stays per 10,000 persons (rates are age adjusted) (table 100).

Between 1995 and 2003 the number of **allopathic medicine graduates** was nearly 16,000 per year, and osteopathic medicine graduates increased from 1,800 to 2,600 per year (table 109).

Between 1990 and 2003 the number of **community hospital beds** declined from about 927,000 to 813,000. In 2003 community hospital occupancy increased to 66 percent from a low of 63 percent in 1995 (table 112).

Between 1990 and 2002, the overall number of **inpatient mental health beds** in the United States declined by 22 percent. In VA medical centers the number of mental health beds declined by 55 percent, in State and county mental hospitals and private psychiatric hospitals the decline was more than 40 percent, and in psychiatric units of non-Federal general hospitals the decline was 25 percent (table 113).

In 2003 there were 6,900 Medicare-certified **home health agencies**, down from 10,800 in 1997. During this period, the number of Medicare-certified **hospices** remained stable at about 2,300 (table 117).

In 2003 there were nearly 1.8 million **nursing home beds** in facilities certified for use by Medicare and Medicaid beneficiaries. Between 1995 and 2003 nursing home bed occupancy in those facilities was relatively stable, estimated at 83 percent in 2003 (table 116).

Preventive Health Care

Preventive health services help reduce morbidity and mortality from disease. Use of several different types of preventive services has been increasing, but disparities persist in use of preventive health care by race, ethnicity, and family income.

The percent of mothers receiving **prenatal care** in the first trimester of pregnancy has continued to edge upward from 76 percent in 1990 to 84 percent in 2003. Although increases occurred for all racial and ethnic groups, in 2003 the percent of mothers with early prenatal care still varied substantially, from 71 percent for American Indian mothers to 92 percent for mothers of Cuban origin (table 7).

In 2003, 81 percent of children 19–35 months of age received the **combined vaccination** series of four doses of DTaP (diphtheria-tetanus-acellular pertussis) vaccine, three doses of polio vaccine, one dose of MMR (measles-mumps-rubella vaccine), and three doses of Hib (Haemophilus influenzae type b) vaccine. Children living below the poverty threshold were less likely to have received the combined vaccination series than were children living at or above poverty (76 percent compared with 83 percent) (table 77).

In 2003, 66 percent of noninstitutionalized adults 65 years of age and over reported an **influenza vaccination** within the past year, approximately the same percent since 1999 and more than double the percent in 1989. In 2002 and 2003 the percent of older adults ever having received a **pneumococcal vaccine** was 56 percent, up sharply from 14 percent in 1989 (table 76).

In 2003, 70 percent of women age 40 years and over had a **mammogram** within the past 2 years. Poor women living below the poverty threshold were less likely to have a recent mammogram (55 percent) than were women in families with incomes at least twice the poverty threshold (74 percent) (figure 21 and table 86).

In 2003, 79 percent of women age 18 years and over reported a **Pap smear** within the past 3 years. Among women 25–44 years of age, Pap smear use was lowest for women with less than a high school education (72 percent) and highest for women with at least some college education (91 percent) (figure 22 and table 87).

Access to Care

People need ready access to care both for preventive care and for prompt treatment of illness and injuries. Health insurance coverage is a major determinant of access to care. Other indicators of access include having a usual source of health care and having a recent contact with a provider of health care.

Between 1994 and 2003, the percent of the **population under 65 years of age with no health insurance coverage** (public or private) ranged between 16.1 and 17.5 percent. Among the under 65 population, the poor and near poor (those with family incomes less than 200 percent of poverty) were much more likely than the nonpoor to be uninsured (figures 6 and 7).

The likelihood of being uninsured varies substantially among the **States**. In 2001–03 the average percent of the population with **no health insurance coverage** ranged from 8 percent in Minnesota to 25 percent in Texas (table 156).

In 2003, 10 percent of **children** under 18 years of age had **no health insurance coverage**. Between 2000 and 2003 among children in families with income just above the poverty level (1–1.5 times poverty), the percent uninsured dropped from 25 to 16 percent. However, children in low-income families remain substantially more likely than children in higher-income families to lack coverage (table 134).

Persons of **Hispanic origin and American Indians** under 65 years of age are more likely to have **no health insurance coverage** than are those in other racial and ethnic groups. In 2003 among the Hispanic-origin population, persons of Mexican origin were the most likely to lack health insurance coverage (38 percent). Non-Hispanic white persons were the least likely to lack coverage (12 percent) (figure 7 and table 134).

In 2003 **uninsured persons** under 65 years of age were about 3 times as likely as insured persons to have had **no health care visits** within the past 12 months (38 percent compared with 13 percent, age adjusted) (table 75).

In 2002–03, 12 percent of **children** under 18 years of age had **no health care visit** to a doctor or clinic within the past 12 months. Uninsured children were more than 3 times as likely as insured children to lack a recent visit (32 percent compared with 10 percent) (table 79).

Six percent of **children** under 18 years of age had **no usual source of health care** in 2002–03. Uninsured children were nearly 10 times as likely as insured children to lack a usual source of care (29 percent compared with 3 percent) (table 80).

Twenty-seven percent of young **children** under 6 years of age had an **emergency department (ED) visit** within the past 12 months in 2003. Young children living below the poverty level were more likely than those in families with income more than twice poverty to have had an ED visit within the past 12 months (34 percent compared with 24 percent) (table 81).

Seventeen percent of **working-age adults** 18–64 years of age had **no usual source of health care** in 2002–03. Working-age males were nearly twice as likely as working-age females to lack a usual source of care (22 percent compared with 12 percent, age adjusted) (table 82).

In 2003, 75 percent of **children** 2–17 years of age had a **dental visit** in the past year. Children living below or near the poverty level were less likely than children living in families with income more than twice poverty to have had a recent dental visit (66–67 percent compared with 81 percent) (table 84).

Use of hospital inpatient care is greater among the poor than among the nonpoor whose family income is at least twice the poverty level. In 2003 among persons under 65 years of age, the hospital discharge rate for the poor was nearly twice the rate for nonpoor (150 and 82 per 1,000 population, age adjusted) (table 96).

Health Care Expenditures and Payors

After double-digit annual growth in national health expenditures in the 1980s, the rate of growth slowed during the 1990s. In the current decade the rate of growth edged up again and continued to accelerate until 2002. The rate of growth was slower in 2003 than in the previous year. The United States continues to spend more on health than any other industrialized country. Major payors for health care include public programs such as Medicare and Medicaid, and private health insurers such as health maintenance organizations and other managed care entities.

In 2003 **national health care expenditures** in the United States totaled $1.7 trillion, a 7.7 percent increase compared with about 9 percent per year increases in 2001 and 2002. In the mid-1990s annual growth had slowed somewhat, following an average annual growth rate of 11 percent during the 1980s (table 119).

The United States spends a larger **share of the gross domestic product (GDP) on health** than does any other major industrialized country. In 2002 the United States devoted 15 percent of the GDP to health compared with 11 percent each in Switzerland and Germany and nearly 10 percent in Iceland, France, Canada, Norway, and Greece, countries with the next highest shares (table 118).

In 2003 national health expenditures grew 7.7 percent, compared with 4.9 percent growth in the gross domestic product (GDP). **Health expenditures as a percent of the GDP** increased to 15.3 percent in 2003, up from 14.9 percent in 2002 (figure 8 and table 119).

In 2004, the increase in the medical care component of the **Consumer Price Index** (CPI) was 4.4 percent, continuing to outpace overall inflation (2.7 percent). The CPI for hospital services showed the greatest price increase (6.0 percent) compared with other components of medical care (table 120).

Expenditures by Type of Care and Source of Funds

In recent years expenditures for prescription drugs have grown at a faster rate than any other type of health expenditure. Hospital care, however, continues to account for the largest share of health care spending.

Expenditures for hospital care accounted for 31 percent of all national health expenditures in 2003. Physician services accounted for 22 percent of the total in 2003, prescription drugs for 11 percent, and nursing home care for 7 percent (table 122).

Between 2000 and 2003 **community hospital expenses** increased at an average annual rate of 8 percent compared with a 5-percent increase between 1995 and 2000 (table 129).

Between 1995 and 2003 the average annual rate of increase for **prescription drug expenditures** was 14 percent, higher than for any other health expenditure (table 122).

Prescription drug expenditures increased 11 percent in 2003 and 15–16 percent in 2001 and 2002. Prescription drugs posted a 3-percent increase in the Consumer Price Index in 2003 and 2004 and a 5-percent price increase in 2001 and 2002 (tables 120 and 122).

In 2003, 46 percent of **prescription drug expenditures** were paid by private health insurance (up from 24 percent in 1990), 30 percent by out-of-pocket payments (down from 59 percent in 1990), and 19 percent by Medicaid. Although Medicare is the Federal program that funds health care for persons age 65 years and over, and older Americans are the highest per capita consumers of prescription drugs, Medicare paid less than 2 percent of prescription drug expenses in 2003 (table 123).

In 2002, 91 percent of persons age 65 years and over in the civilian noninstitutionalized population had a **prescribed medicine expense** compared with 61 percent of younger people. Women 65 years of age and over averaged $920 out-of-pocket for prescribed medicine compared with $674 for men in 2002. Among those under 65 years of age, out-of-pocket expenses averaged $265 for women and $212 for men in 2002 (table 124).

In 2002, 96 percent of **persons age 65 years and over** in the civilian noninstitutionalized population reported **medical expenses** that averaged about $7,800 per person with expense. Seventeen percent of expenses were paid out-of-pocket, 14 percent by private insurance, and 66 percent by public programs (mainly Medicare and Medicaid) (tables 124 and 125).

The burden of **out-of-pocket expenses** for health care varies considerably by age. In 2002 about two-fifths of those 65 years of age and over with health care expenses paid $1,000 or more out-of-pocket, compared with one-quarter of those 45–64 years of age, and less than one-ninth of adults 18–44 years of age (table 126).

In 2003, 33 percent of **personal health care expenditures** were paid by the Federal Government and 11 percent by State and local government; private health insurance paid 36 percent and consumers paid 16 percent out-of-pocket (figure 9 and table 123).

In 2003 the major **sources of funds for hospital care** were Medicare (30 percent) and private health insurance (34 percent). **Physician services** were also primarily funded by private health insurance (one-half) and Medicare (one-fifth). In contrast, **nursing home care** was financed primarily by Medicaid (almost one-half) and out-of-pocket payments (more than one-quarter). The Medicare share of nursing home expenditures has risen from 3 percent in 1990 to 12 percent in 2003 (table 123).

Publicly Funded Health Programs

The two major publicly funded health programs are Medicare and Medicaid. Medicare is funded through the Federal Government and covers the health care of persons 65 years of age and over and disabled persons. Medicaid is jointly funded by the Federal and State Governments to provide health care for certain groups of low-income persons. In recent years, Medicaid has expanded to cover a greater proportion of the low-income adult population—and the State Children's Health Insurance Program (SCHIP) now covers many low-income children. Medicaid benefits and eligibility vary by State.

In 2004 the **Medicare** program had 42 million enrollees and expenditures of $309 billion (table 139).

In 2004 **hospital insurance** (HI) accounted for 55 percent of **Medicare** expenditures. Expenditures for home health agency care continued to hover around 3 percent of HI expenditures, down from 14 percent in 1995. Expenditures for hospice care nearly doubled from 2 to 4 percent of HI expenditures between 2000 and 2004 (table 139).

In 2004 **supplementary medical insurance** (SMI) or Part B of Medicare accounted for 45 percent of **Medicare** expenditures. It typically covers outpatient health expenses including physician fees. Fourteen percent of SMI expenditures in 2004 were payments to managed care organizations, down from 20–22 percent in 1999–2000. Nearly 40 percent of the $138 billion SMI expenditures in 2004 went to physicians under the physician fee schedule (table 139).

Of the 35 million **Medicare enrollees in the fee-for-service program** in 2002, 11 percent were 85 years of age and over and 16 percent were disability beneficiaries under 65 years of age. Among fee-for-service Medicare enrollees age 65 years and over, payments ranged from an average of $4,600 per year for enrollees age 65–74 years to $9,000 for those 85 years and over (table 140).

In 2001, 80 percent of Medicare beneficiaries were non-Hispanic white, 9 percent were non-Hispanic black, and 7 percent were Hispanic. One-fifth of Hispanic beneficiaries and one-quarter of non-Hispanic black beneficiaries were persons under 65 years of age entitled to **Medicare through disability**, compared with 12 percent of non-Hispanic white beneficiaries (table 141).

In 2002 **Medicare payments per fee-for-service enrollee** varied by State from less than $4,500 in Hawaii and South Dakota to $7,200 or more in New Jersey, the District of Columbia, Louisiana, Maryland, and New York (table 153).

In 2001 **Medicaid** paid vendors $186 billion on behalf of 46 million recipients (table 142).

In 2003 **Medicaid enrollment** increased to 12.3 percent of the noninstitutionalized population under 65 years of age, up from 9.5 percent in 2000. In 2003 among children under 18 years of age, 26 percent were covered by Medicaid or the State Children's Health Insurance Program, a 6 percentage point increase since 2000 (table 133).

In 2001 children under the age of 21 years accounted for 46 percent of **Medicaid recipients** but only 16 percent of expenditures. Aged, blind, and disabled persons accounted for nearly one-quarter of recipients and nearly 70 percent of expenditures (table 142).

In 2001, 20 percent of **Medicaid payments** went to nursing facilities, 14 percent to inpatient general hospitals, 16 percent to capitated payment services, and 13 percent to prescribed drugs (table 143).

In 2001 **Medicaid payments per recipient varied by State** from less than $3,000 in California, Tennessee, Georgia, and Washington to more than $7,000 in New York and New Hampshire. On average, payments were lower in the Southeast, Southwest, and Far West States than in the New England and Mideast States (table 154).

Private Health Insurance

Almost 70 percent of the population under 65 years of age has private health insurance, most of which is obtained through the workplace. In private industry, about 7 percent of employees' total compensation is devoted to health insurance. This share has increased in recent years. Most health insurance is now provided through some form of managed care organization, including health maintenance organizations (HMOs), preferred provider organizations (PPOs), and point-of-service plans (POSs). Less than one-quarter of all persons in the United States were enrolled in HMOs in 2004. HMO enrollment peaked in 1999 and has declined slowly since then.

In 2002 and 2003 the proportion of the population under 65 years of age with **private health insurance** was 69 percent. Between 1995 and 2001 the proportion had fluctuated between 71 and 73 percent after declining from 77 percent in 1984 (figure 6 and table 132).

Between 2001 and 2003 the proportion of the population under 65 years of age with **health insurance obtained through the workplace** (a current or former employer or union) declined from 67 to 63 percent. This decline disproportionately affected the poor and near poor and Hispanic persons (table 132).

In 2005 **private employers** paid an estimated 6.8 percent of total compensation for health insurance, or $1.64 for each employee-hour worked. The corresponding estimates for State and local governments were 10.2 percent and $3.63, based on March 2005 reporting (table 128).

Enrollment in HMOs totaled 69 million persons or 23 percent of the U.S. population in 2004. HMO enrollment varied from 16–19 percent in the South and Midwest to 30–34 percent in the Northeast and West. HMO enrollment increased steadily through the 1990s but has declined since then. Between 1998 and 2004 the number of HMO plans decreased from 651 to 412 plans (table 137).

Special Feature: Adults 55–64 Years of Age

The population 55–64 years of age is a rapidly growing segment of the adult population. As persons in this group age and begin to develop health problems, they do not have the guarantee of health insurance coverage that Medicare now offers to almost all older adults age 65 and over, and employer-sponsored post-retirement health insurance offers have been declining. While many Americans age 55–64 years are relatively well off both physically and financially, other Americans in this age group face a burden from chronic and debilitating diseases, poverty, lack of health insurance, and reduced access to health care.

The **population 55–64 years of age** is a rapidly growing segment of the adult population. In 2004 this age group numbered about 29 million persons. Over the next 10-year period, the 55–64 age group will increase by 11 million persons to an estimated 40 million persons (figure 30).

In 2002–03 more than one-half of adults 55–64 years of age were **employed**. Non-Hispanic white men and Hispanic men were more likely to be working (about 65 percent) than non-Hispanic black men (57 percent). Among women, a little over one-half of non-Hispanic white women were working compared with 46 percent of non-Hispanic black women and 41 percent of Hispanic women (figure 31).

Non-Hispanic black adults age 55–64 years were more likely than other racial and ethnic groups to report being **unemployed because of disability**. In 2002–03, 22 percent of non-Hispanic black adults age 55–64 years were unemployed due to disability compared with 15 percent of Hispanic and 10 percent of non-Hispanic white adults in this age group (figure 31).

In 2003, more than one-fifth of adults 55–64 years of age had income below 200 percent of **poverty** compared with almost two-fifths of older persons (figures 5 and 32).

In 2002–03, 83 percent of **married** adults 55–64 years of age were covered by **private health insurance** compared with about 60 percent of widowed, separated, divorced, and single adults (figure 33).

Between 1988–94 and 1999–2002, the percent of men age 55–64 years who had one or more of the **cardiovascular risk factors** of obesity, high cholesterol, and hypertension increased from 64 to 72 percent (figure 34).

In 2002–03, persons age 55–64 years with private health insurance were about twice as likely to report **medical care visits** in the past 12 months to specialist physicians, eye doctors, and physical or occupational therapists compared with those without insurance. Those with private insurance were almost 50 percent more likely than the uninsured to report a recent visit to a general physician (family medicine practitioner, internist, or general practitioner) (figure 35).

Between 1995–96 and 2002–03 the rate of **cholesterol-lowering drugs** prescribed during physician and hospital outpatient department visits among men 55–64 years of age almost tripled from 20 to 57 drugs per 100 population and among women more than tripled from 15 to 49 drugs per 100 population (figure 36).

In 2002 the out-of-pocket **prescribed medicine expense** among adults 55–64 years of age was $425 compared with $286 in 1997 (2002 dollars). Women age 55–64 years had an average out-of-pocket prescribed medicine expense of $495 in 2002 compared with $351 for men in this age group (figure 37).

Chartbook on Trends in the Health of Americans

Figure 1. Total population and older population: United States, 1950-2050

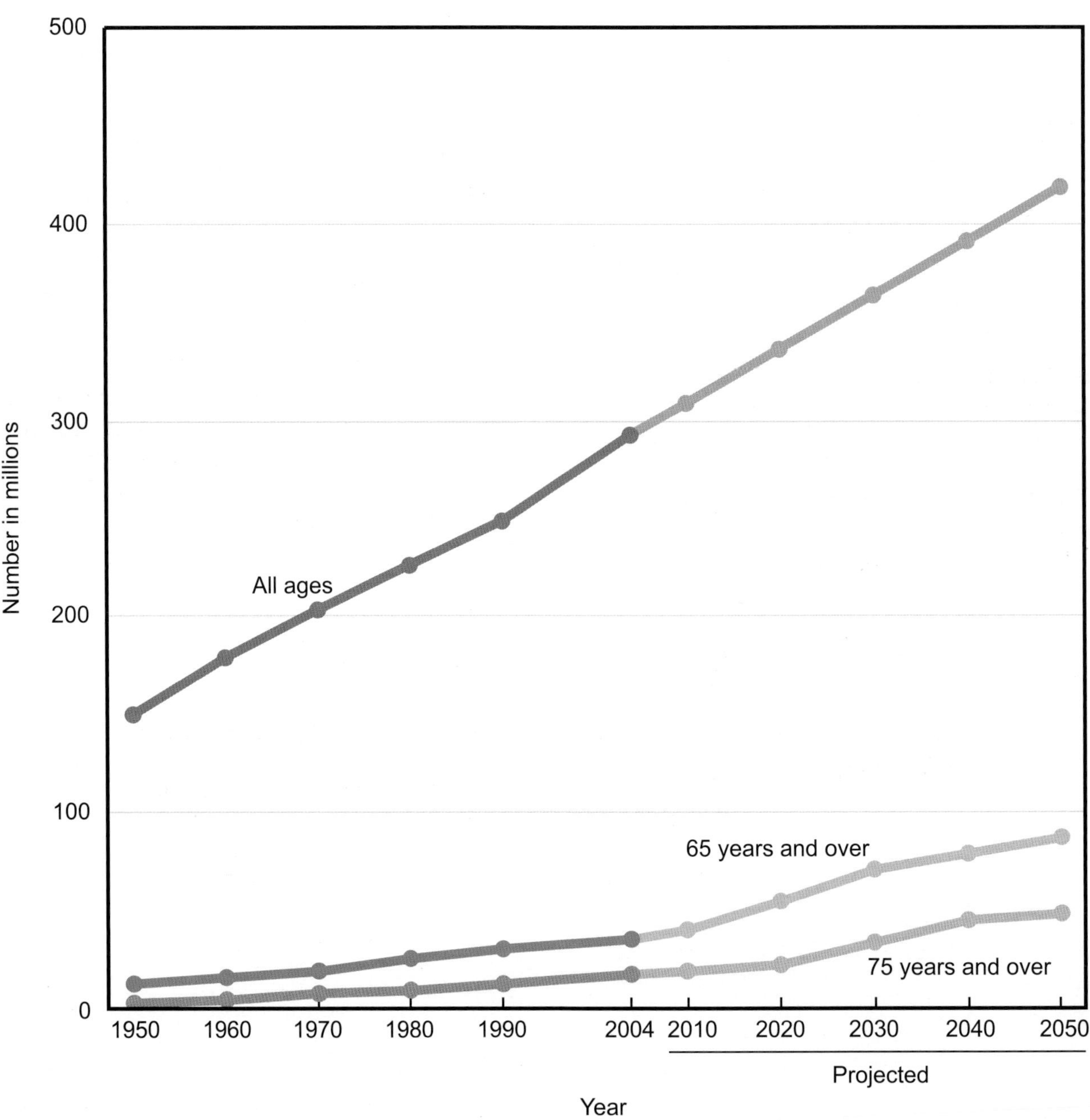

NOTE: See Data Table for data points graphed and additional notes.

SOURCE: U.S. Census Bureau.

Age

From 1950 to 2004 the total resident population of the United States increased from 150 million to 294 million, representing an average annual growth rate of 1 percent (figure 1). During the same period, the population 65 years of age and over grew twice as rapidly and increased from 12 to 36 million persons. The population 75 years of age and over grew 2.9 times as quickly as the total population, increasing from 4 to 18 million persons. Projections indicate that the rate of population growth from now to 2050 will be slower for all age groups, and older age groups will continue to grow more than twice as rapidly as the total population.

Between 1950 and 2004, the U.S. population grew older (figure 2). From 1950 to 2004 the population under 18 years of age fell from 31 to 25 percent of the total population, while persons 55–64 years increased from 9 to 10 percent of total persons, persons 65–74 years remained at about 6 percent, and persons 75 years and over increased from 3 to 6 percent of the total.

From 2004 to 2050 it is anticipated that the percent of the population 55 years and over will increase substantially. The population age 55–64 years of age, featured in this chartbook, is projected to be the fastest growing segment of the adult population during the next 10 years (figure 30). In future decades both the population age 55–64 and the population age 65 years and over will increase dramatically as the baby boomers, born in the post-World War II period of 1946 through 1964, age. By 2029, all of the baby boomers will be age 65 and over. Between 2004 and 2050 the population 65–74 years of age will increase from 6 to 9 percent of the total and the population 75 years and over will increase from 6 to 12 percent. By 2040 the population 75 years and over will exceed the population 65–74 years of age.

The aging of the population has important consequences for the health care system (1,2). As the older fraction of the population increases, more services will be required for the treatment and management of chronic and acute health conditions. Providing health care services needed by Americans of all ages will be a major challenge in the 21st century.

Figure 2. Percent of population in five age groups: United States, 1950, 2004, and 2050

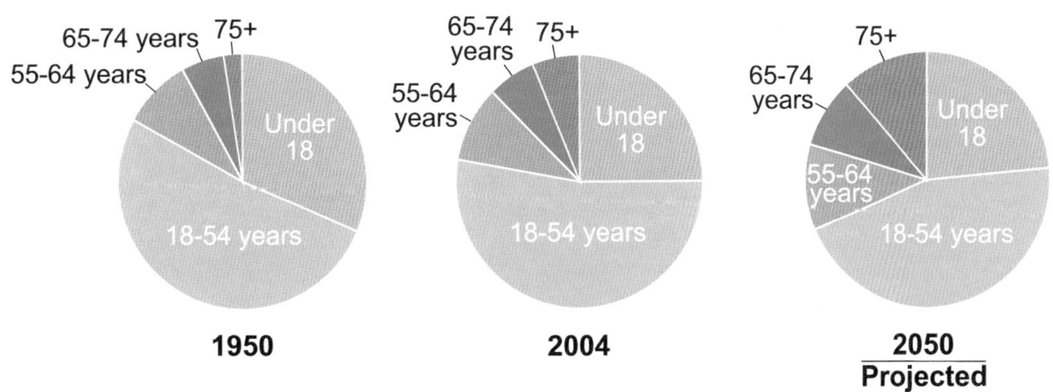

NOTE: See Data Table for data points graphed and additional notes.

SOURCE: U.S. Census Bureau.

Race and Ethnicity

Changes in the racial and ethnic composition of the population have important consequences for the Nation's health because many measures of disease and disability differ significantly by race and ethnicity (*Health, United States, 2005,* trend tables). One of the overarching goals of U.S. public health policy is elimination of racial and ethnic disparities in health.

Diversity has long been a characteristic of the U.S. population, but the racial and ethnic composition of the Nation has changed over time. In recent decades the percent of the population that is of Hispanic origin or Asian has more than doubled (figure 3). In 2004 nearly 30 percent of adults and almost 40 percent of children identified themselves as Hispanic, black, Asian, American Indian or Alaska Native, or Native Hawaiian or Other Pacific Islander.

In the 1980 and 1990 decennial censuses, Americans could choose only one racial category to describe their race (1). Beginning with the 2000 census the question on race was modified to allow the choice of more than one racial category. Although overall a small percent of persons of non-Hispanic origin selected two or more races in 2000, the percent of children described as being of more than one race was more than twice as high as the percent of adults. The number of American adults identifying themselves or their children as multiracial is expected to increase in the future (2).

The percent of persons reporting two or more races varies considerably among racial groups. For example, the percent of persons reporting a specified race in combination with one or more additional racial groups was 1.4 percent for white persons and 37 percent for American Indians or Alaska Natives in 2000 (3).

Figure 3. Percent of population in selected race and Hispanic origin groups by age: United States, 1980-2004

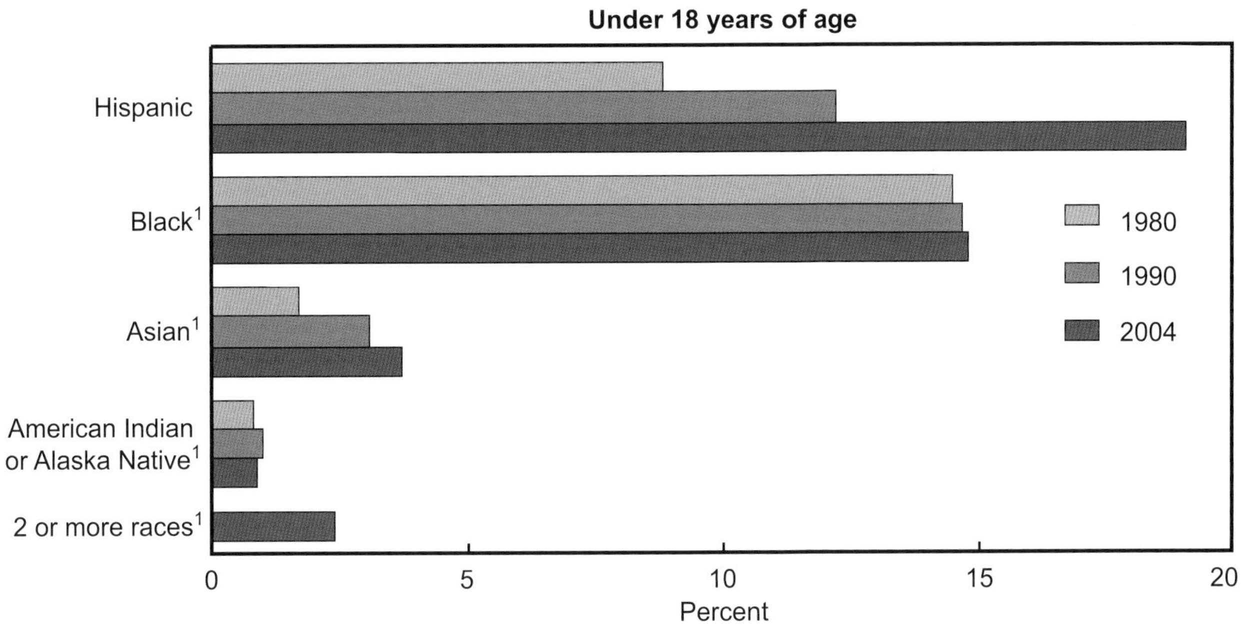

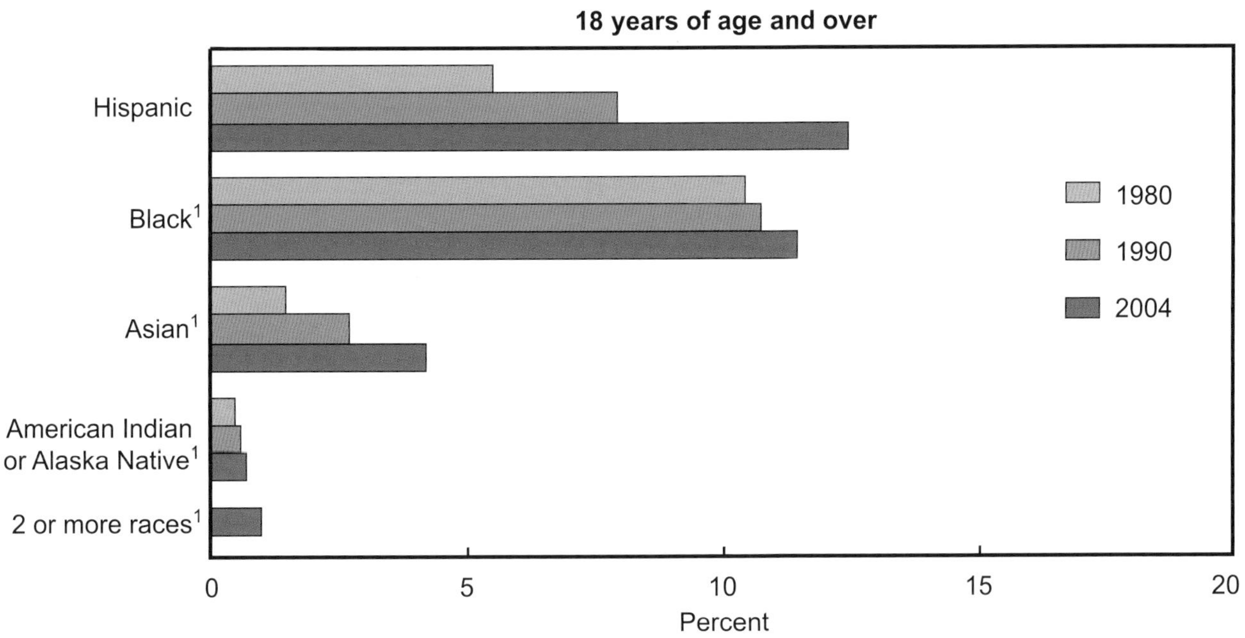

[1] Not Hispanic

NOTES: Persons of Hispanic origin may be of any race. Race data for 2004 are not directly comparable with data for 1980 and 1990. Individuals could report only one race in 1980 and 1990, and more than one race in 2004. Persons who selected only one race in 2004 are included in single-race categories; persons who selected more than one race in 2004 are shown as having 2 or more races and are not included in single-race categories. In 1980 and 1990 the category "Asian" includes Asian and Native Hawaiian or Other Pacific Islander; in 2004 this category includes only Asian. See Data Table for data points graphed and data for Native Hawaiian or Other Pacific Islander.

SOURCE: U.S. Census Bureau.

Poverty

Children and adults in families with incomes below or near the Federal poverty level have poorer health outcomes than those with higher incomes (see Appendix II, Poverty level for a definition of the Federal poverty level). Although, in some cases, illness can lead to poverty, more often poverty causes poor health by its connection with inadequate nutrition, substandard housing, exposure to environmental hazards, unhealthy lifestyles, and decreased access to and use of health care services (1).

In 2003 the overall percent of Americans living in poverty increased to 12.5 percent, up from 12.1 percent in 2002, 11.7 percent in 2001, and 11.3 percent in 2000. The increases in the poverty rate in 2001–03 were the first since 1993. Most of the increase in the poverty rate from 2000 to 2001 was accounted for by working-age adults who are less likely to receive income from government programs than are children and persons 65 years of age and over. In 2002 the poverty rate increased for all ages. Although the poverty rate increased overall in 2003, there was little effect on adults. A slight increase among working age adults was counterbalanced by a slight decrease among those age 65 and over.

Children under 18 years of age bore the brunt of the 2003 increase, which was added to an already high poverty rate for children (2). Starting in 1974 children became more likely than either working-age adults or older Americans to be living in poverty (figure 4). In 1974 poverty among children started increasing and remained at 20 percent or above from 1981 to 1997. Since then, the children's poverty rate gradually declined to 16.2 percent in 2000 but had increased to 17.6 percent by 2003. In 2003, 12.9 million children lived in poverty (data table for figure 5).

Prior to 1974 persons 65 years of age and over were more likely to live in poverty than people of other ages. With the availability of inflation-adjusted government social insurance programs, such as Social Security and Supplemental Security Income, the poverty rate of older Americans declined rapidly until 1974 and continued to decline gradually until the end of the 1990s to 9.7 percent in 1999 (3). From 2000 to 2002 the poverty rate among persons 65 years of age and over increased to 10.4, but in 2003 it decreased to 10.2 percent.

Figure 4. Poverty by age: United States, 1966-2003

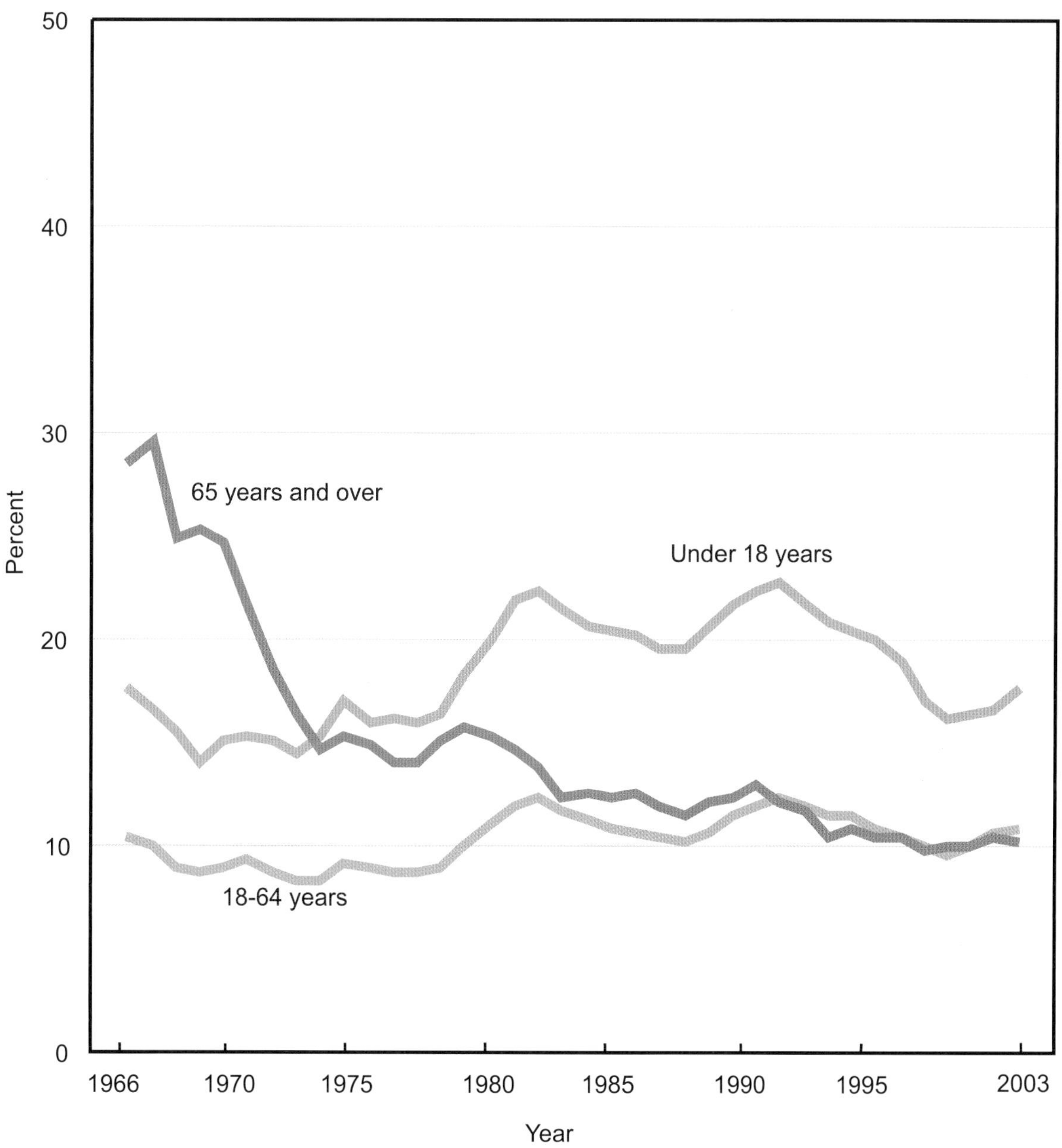

NOTES: Data shown are the percent of persons with family income below the poverty level. See Data Table for data points graphed and additional notes.

SOURCE: U.S. Census Bureau, Current Population Survey.

Poverty *(Continued)*

In 2003 the percent of persons living in poverty also continued to differ significantly by race and ethnicity (figure 5). At all ages, a higher percent of Hispanic and black persons than non-Hispanic white persons were poor. In 2003, 30–34 percent of Hispanic and black children were poor compared with 10–13 percent of Asian and non-Hispanic white children. The 2003 increase in the poverty rate among children from 16.7 to 17.6 percent had a larger impact on black and Hispanic children than on non-Hispanic white children. Similarly, among persons 65 years of age or over one-fifth of Hispanic and nearly one-quarter of black persons were poor, compared with eight percent of non-Hispanic white persons and 14 percent of Asians. In 2001–03, more than one in five American Indian and Alaska Native persons lived in poverty. Poverty estimates for American Indian and Alaska Native persons are based on 3 years of data combined for all age groups in order to produce an estimate (2).

In the first years of this century the burden of poverty appears to be increasing for those who are least able to bear it, namely those with already very high poverty rates (children, and black and Hispanic persons). The record pace of immigration combined with higher poverty levels among immigrants and the present upward trend in the poverty rate may lead to even higher poverty rates over the next few years (4).

Figure 5. Low income by age, race and Hispanic origin: United States, 2003

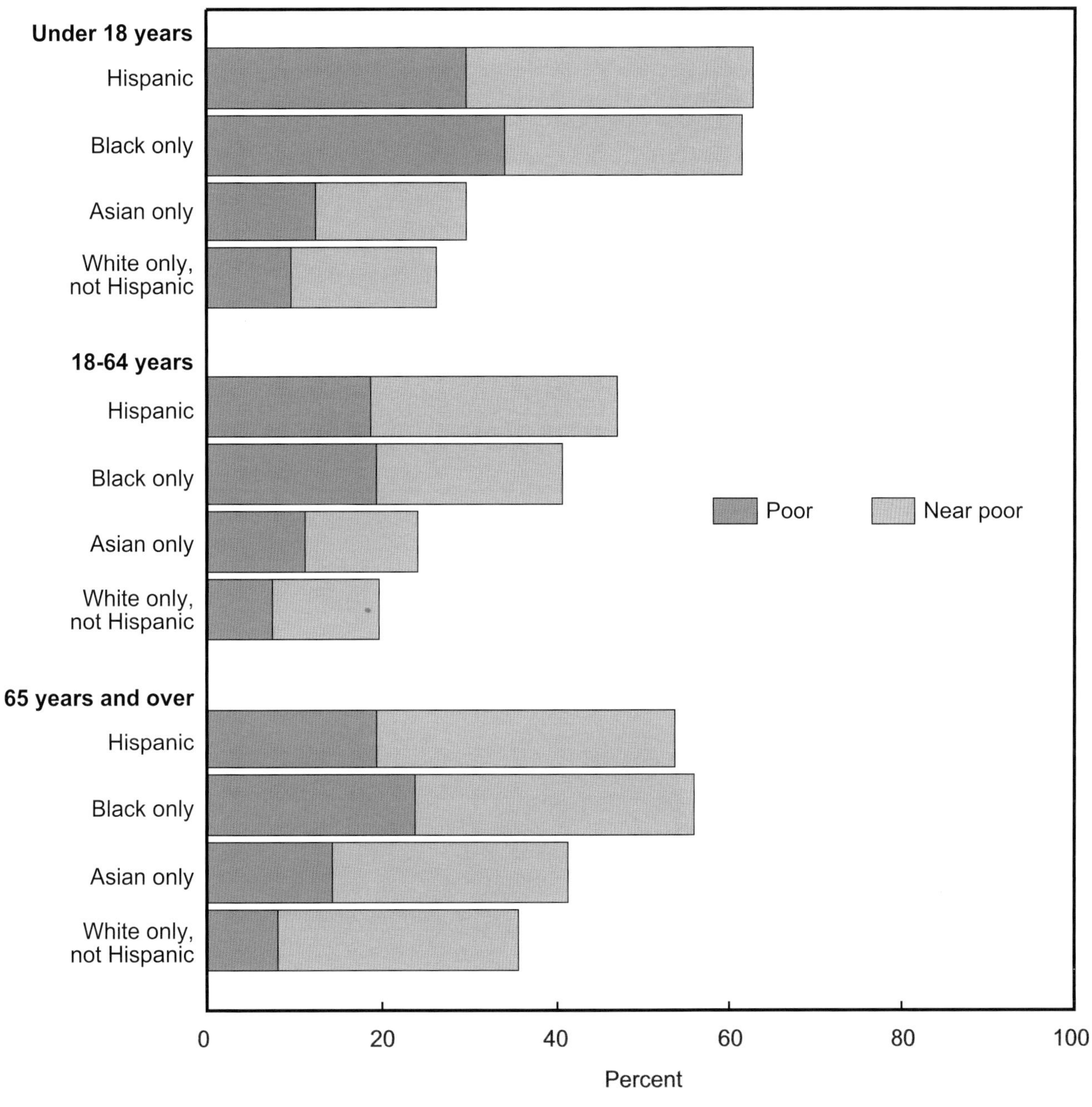

NOTES: Poor is defined as family income less than 100 percent of the poverty level and near poor as 100-199 percent of the poverty level. Persons of Hispanic origin may be of any race. Black and Asian races include persons of Hispanic and non-Hispanic origin. See Data Table for data points graphed and additional notes.

SOURCE: U.S. Census Bureau, Current Population Survey.

Health Insurance

Health insurance coverage is an important determinant of access to health care (1). Uninsured children and adults under 65 years of age are substantially less likely to have a usual source of health care or a recent health care visit than their insured counterparts (*Health, United States, 2005,* tables 75, 79, 80, and 82). Uninsured persons are more likely to forego needed health care due to cost concerns (1,2). The major source of coverage for persons under 65 years of age is private employer-sponsored group health insurance. Private health insurance may also be purchased on an individual basis, but is generally more costly and provides less adequate coverage than group insurance. Public programs such as Medicaid and the State Children's Health Insurance Program provide coverage for many low-income children and adults.

Between 1984 and 1994 private coverage declined among persons under 65 years of age while Medicaid coverage and uninsurance increased. Since 1998 the percent of the nonelderly population with no health insurance coverage has been between 16–17 percent, Medicaid between 9–12 percent, and private coverage between 69–73 percent (figure 6). In 2002 and 2003 the percent with private health insurance decreased. This decrease was offset by an increase in the percent with Medicaid, resulting in little change in the percent uninsured.

In 2003, 17 percent of Americans under 65 years of age reported having no health insurance coverage. The percent of adults under 65 years of age without health insurance coverage decreases with age. In 2003 adults 18–24 years of age were most likely to lack coverage and those 55–64 years of age were least likely (figure 7). Persons with incomes below or near the poverty level were at least three times as likely to have no health insurance coverage as those with incomes twice the poverty level or higher. Hispanic persons and non-Hispanic black persons were more likely to lack health insurance than non-Hispanic white persons. Persons of Mexican origin were more likely to be uninsured than non-Hispanic black persons or other Hispanics. Access to health insurance coverage through employment is lowest for Hispanic persons (*Health, United States, 2005,* table 132). The growing number of Hispanic immigrants of which Mexicans are the largest group (31 percent of all United States immigrants in 2004 were from Mexico) may be expected to further reduce the percent of the population with health insurance through employment and increase the percent with no coverage (3).

Figure 6. Health insurance coverage among persons under 65 years of age: United States, 1984-2003

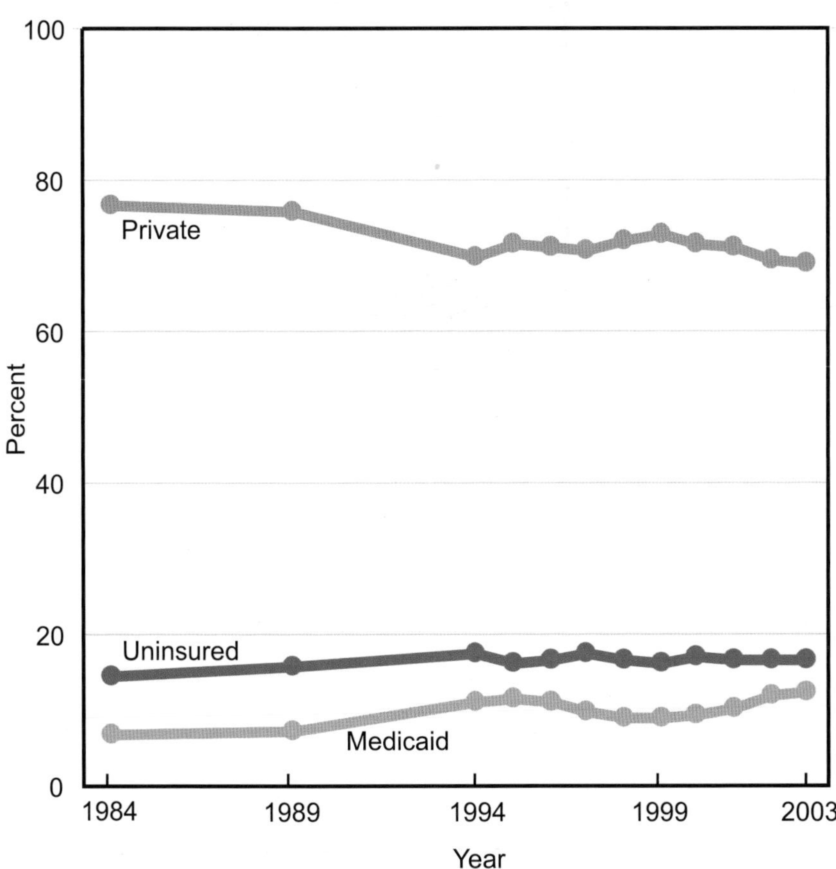

NOTE: See Data Table for data points graphed, standard errors, and additional notes.

SOURCE: Centers for Disease Control and Prevention, National Center for Health Statistics, National Health Interview Survey.

Figure 7. No health insurance coverage among persons under 65 years of age by selected characteristics: United States, 2003

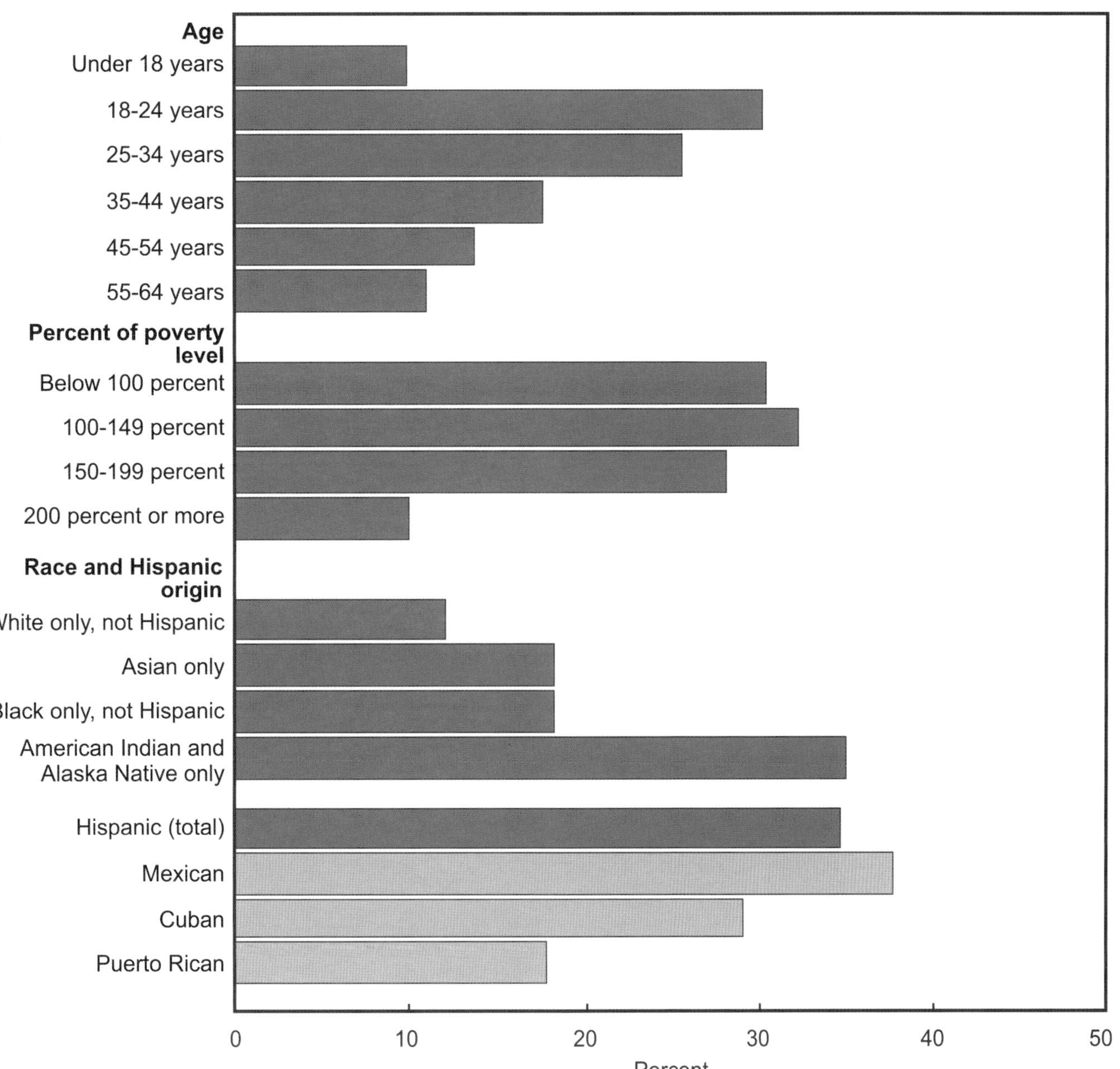

NOTES: Persons of Hispanic origin may be of any race. Asian and American Indian and Alaska Native races include persons of Hispanic and non-Hispanic origin. See Data Table for data points graphed, standard errors, and additional notes.

SOURCE: Centers for Disease Control and Prevention, National Center for Health Statistics, National Health Interview Survey.

Health Care Expenditures

In 2003 the United States spent 15 percent of its Gross Domestic Product (GDP) on health care, a greater share than any other developed country for which data are collected by the Office of Economic Cooperation and Development (figure 8, *Health, United States, 2005*, table 118). After almost a decade of stability from 1992 to 2000, a period of robust economic growth, the share of GDP devoted to health increased sharply from 2000 to 2003, although the 7.7 percent rate of spending increased more slowly in 2003 than in 2002.

In 2003 the United States spent $1.7 trillion on health, an average of $5,671 per person (*Health, United States, 2005*, table 119). Personal health care expenditures include spending for therapeutic goods or services to treat or prevent a specific disease or condition in an individual and comprised 86 percent of national health expenditures in 2003. The remaining 14 percent was spent on administration, government public health activities, research, and construction (*Health, United States, 2005*, table 123) (1).

Overall, private health insurance paid for 36 percent of total personal health expenditures in 2003, the Federal Government 33 percent, State and local government 11 percent, and out-of-pocket payments paid for 16 percent (figure 9). Since 1980 the share of total expenditures paid out-of-pocket declined by 11 percentage points (*Health, United States, 2005*, table 123). This decline resulted from an expansion of benefits in both private health insurance plans and in government programs.

In 2003, more than one-third of personal health care expenditures were for hospital care, one-quarter for physician care, one-eighth for prescription drugs, 8 percent for nursing home care, and the remaining one-fifth for "other" personal health care including visits to non-physician medical providers, medical supplies, and other health services (figure 9). Since 1980 the share of total personal health care expenditures devoted to hospital care has decreased from 47 percent to 36 percent and the prescription drug expenditure share has doubled, reflecting the shift in health care from inpatient to ambulatory care settings and the increasing contribution of prescription drugs to health care (*Health, United States, 2005*, table 123).

Figure 8. National health expenditures as a percent of Gross Domestic Product: United States, 1960-2003

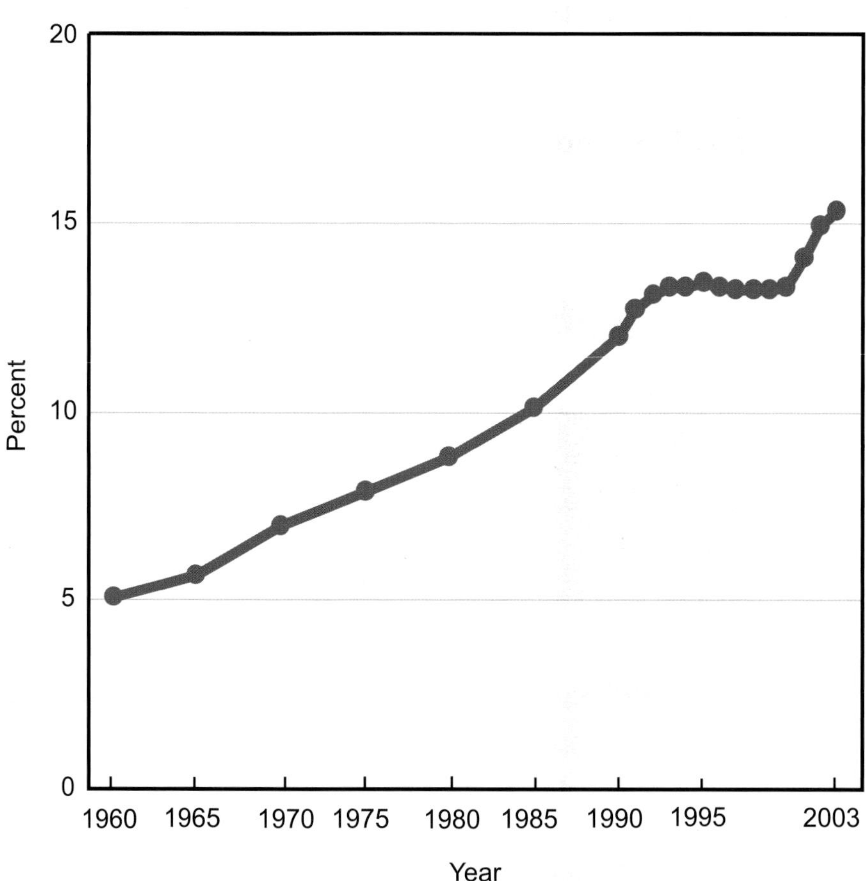

NOTE: See Data Table for data points graphed and additional notes.

SOURCE: Centers for Medicare & Medicaid Services, Office of the Actuary, National Health Statistics Group.

Health Care Expenditures
(Continued)

The source of payment for personal health care varies according to type of care provided. In 2003, government sources were the primary payers of hospital and nursing home care, paying for about three-fifths of these types of services (data table for figure 9). Thirty percent of hospital expenditures were paid by Medicare (the Federal health program for persons 65 years of age and over and the disabled) and 17 percent by Medicaid (the joint Federal and State program for the poor). Nearly one-half of nursing home care was paid by Medicaid, while Medicare paid for only a small part (12 percent in 2003) of nursing home care, primarily short-stays and rehabilitative services. Private health insurance paid for almost one-half of physician services and prescription drugs.

In 2003, 30 percent of expenditures for prescription drugs were paid by recipients out-of-pocket compared with more than twice that percent in 1980 (69 percent) (*Health, United States, 2005,* table 123). Out-of-pocket expenditures for physician services declined to 10 percent in 2003, from 30 percent in 1980. Declines in out-of-pocket expenditures for nursing home services since 1980 have been accompanied by a concurrent increase in government (primarily Medicaid) and private health insurance expenditures through 2003. However, the inflation in health care costs over recent years means that consumers may still have significant out-of-pocket expenditures for their health care. This is the case especially for older persons with worse health and higher total expenditures and persons with large prescription drug expenses, since drug expenses are less likely to be covered by health insurance than hospital and physician expenses. In 2002, more than 40 percent of noninstitutionalized adults 65 years of age and over with medical expenses spent at least $1,000 out-of-pocket (*Health, United States, 2005,* table 126).

Figure 9. Personal health care expenditures according to source of funds and type of expenditures: United States, 2003

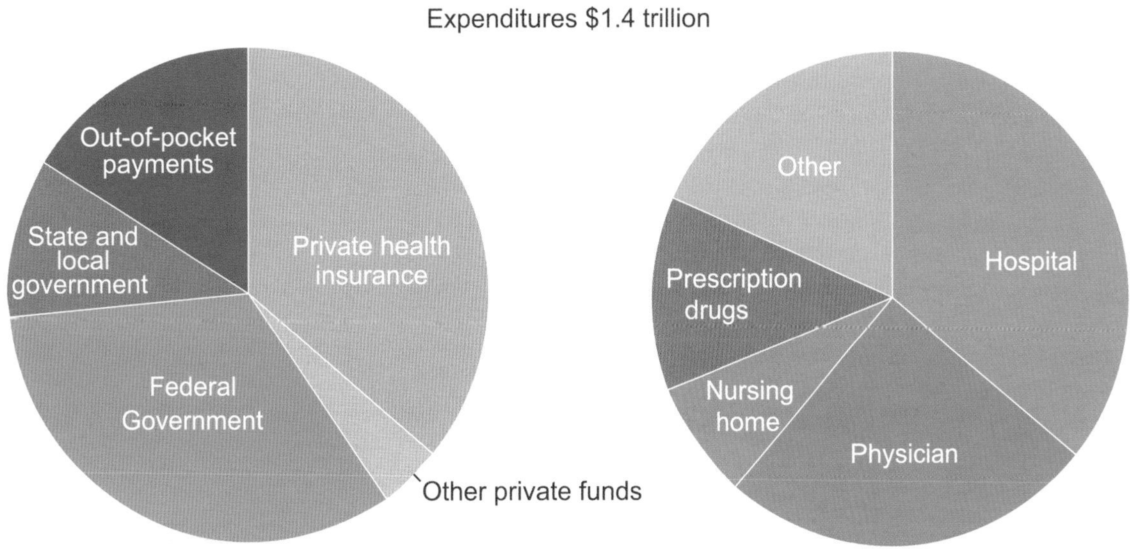

NOTE: See Data Table for data points graphed and additional notes.

SOURCE: Centers for Medicare & Medicaid Services, Office of the Actuary, National Health Accounts.

Tobacco Use

Smoking is associated with a significantly increased risk of heart disease, stroke, lung and other types of cancer, and chronic lung diseases (1). Decreasing cigarette smoking among adolescents and adults is a major public health objective for the Nation. Preventing smoking among teenagers and young adults is critical because smoking usually begins in adolescence (2). Smoking during pregnancy contributes to elevated risk of miscarriage, premature delivery, and having a low birthweight infant (3).

Cigarette smoking among adult men and women declined substantially following the first Surgeon General's Report on smoking in 1964 (figure 10). Since 1990 the percent of adults who smoke has continued to decline but at a slower rate than previously. During the 1990s declines in the percent of adults 18 years and over who smoke were the result of increasing rates of never smoking. In contrast, the percent of former smokers remained relatively stable during that time (4). By 2003, 24 percent of men and 19 percent of women were smokers, down from one-half of men and one-third of women in 1965. Cigarette smoking by adults continues to be strongly associated with educational attainment. Adults with less than a high school education were almost three times as likely to smoke as those with a bachelor's degree or more education (*Health, United States, 2005*, table 64).

Among mothers with a live birth, the percent reporting smoking cigarettes during pregnancy declined between 1989 and 2002 (3,5). Eleven percent of mothers with a live birth in 2002 reported smoking cigarettes during pregnancy. Maternal smoking has declined for all racial and ethnic groups, but differences among these groups persist (*Health, United States, 2005*, table 12 includes 2003 data for 47 States and the District of Columbia). In 2002 the percent of mothers reporting tobacco use during pregnancy was highest for American Indian or Alaska Native mothers (20 percent), non-Hispanic white mothers (15 percent), and Hawaiian mothers (14 percent).

Figure 10. Cigarette smoking among men, women, high school students, and mothers during pregnancy: United States, 1965-2003

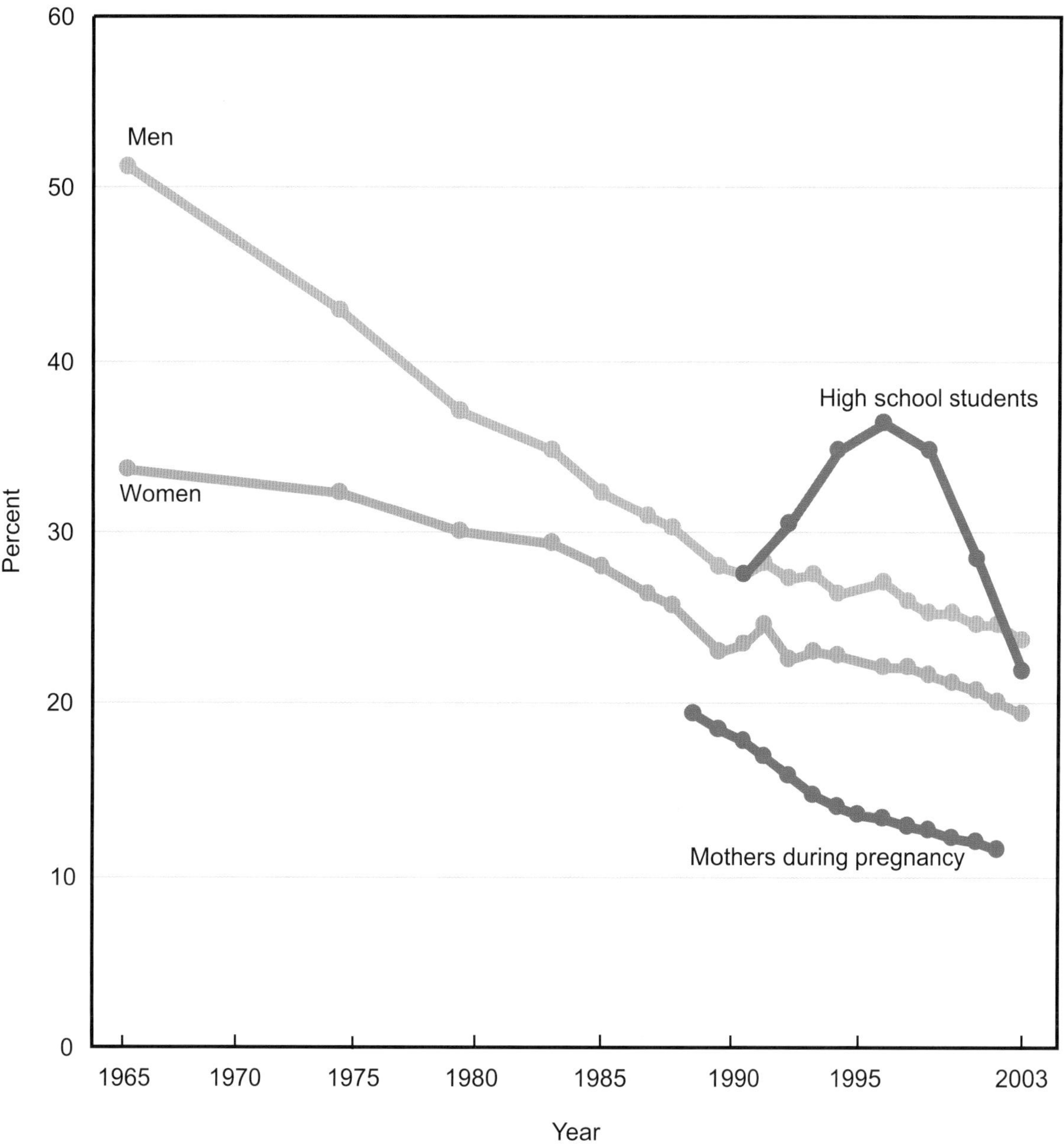

NOTES: Percents for men and women are age adjusted. See Data Table for data points graphed, standard errors, and additional notes. Cigarette smoking is defined as: (for men and women 18 years of age and over) at least 100 cigarettes in lifetime and now smoke every day or some days; (for students in grades 9-12) 1 or more cigarettes in the 30 days preceding the survey; and (for mothers with a live birth) during pregnancy.

SOURCES: Centers for Disease Control and Prevention, National Center for Health Statistics, National Health Interview Survey (data for men and women); National Vital Statistics System (data for mothers during pregnancy); National Center for Chronic Disease Prevention and Health Promotion, Youth Risk Behavior Survey (data for high school students).

Tobacco use *(Continued)*

Antismoking efforts have entailed a two-prong approach; encouraging young persons not to begin smoking and helping current smokers to quit smoking. Cigarette smoking among high school students in grades 9–12 decreased between 1997 and 2003 after increasing in the early 1990s (figure 10). In 2003, 22 percent of high school students reported smoking cigarettes on one or more days of the 30 days preceding the survey and 10 percent reported smoking frequently that is, on 20 days or more in the 30 days preceding the survey (data table for figure 11). Cigarette smoking and frequent cigarette smoking for high school girls were more prevalent among non-Hispanic white girls than among Hispanic or non-Hispanic black girls (figure 11). Among high school boys, current and frequent cigarette smoking were generally similar by race and ethnicity. Cigarette smoking—and especially frequent cigarette smoking—was more common in upper grades than lower grades. By grade 12, 29 percent of boys and 23 percent of girls were current smokers with about one-half of them smoking on a frequent basis. Many high school students who were frequent smokers have already become nicotine dependent (6). In 2003 almost 7 percent of students had used smokeless tobacco (e.g., chewing tobacco, snuff, or dip), and 15 percent of students had smoked cigars on one or more days of the 30 days preceding the survey (7).

Figure 11. Current and frequent cigarette smoking among high school students by sex, race and Hispanic origin, and grade level: United States, 2003

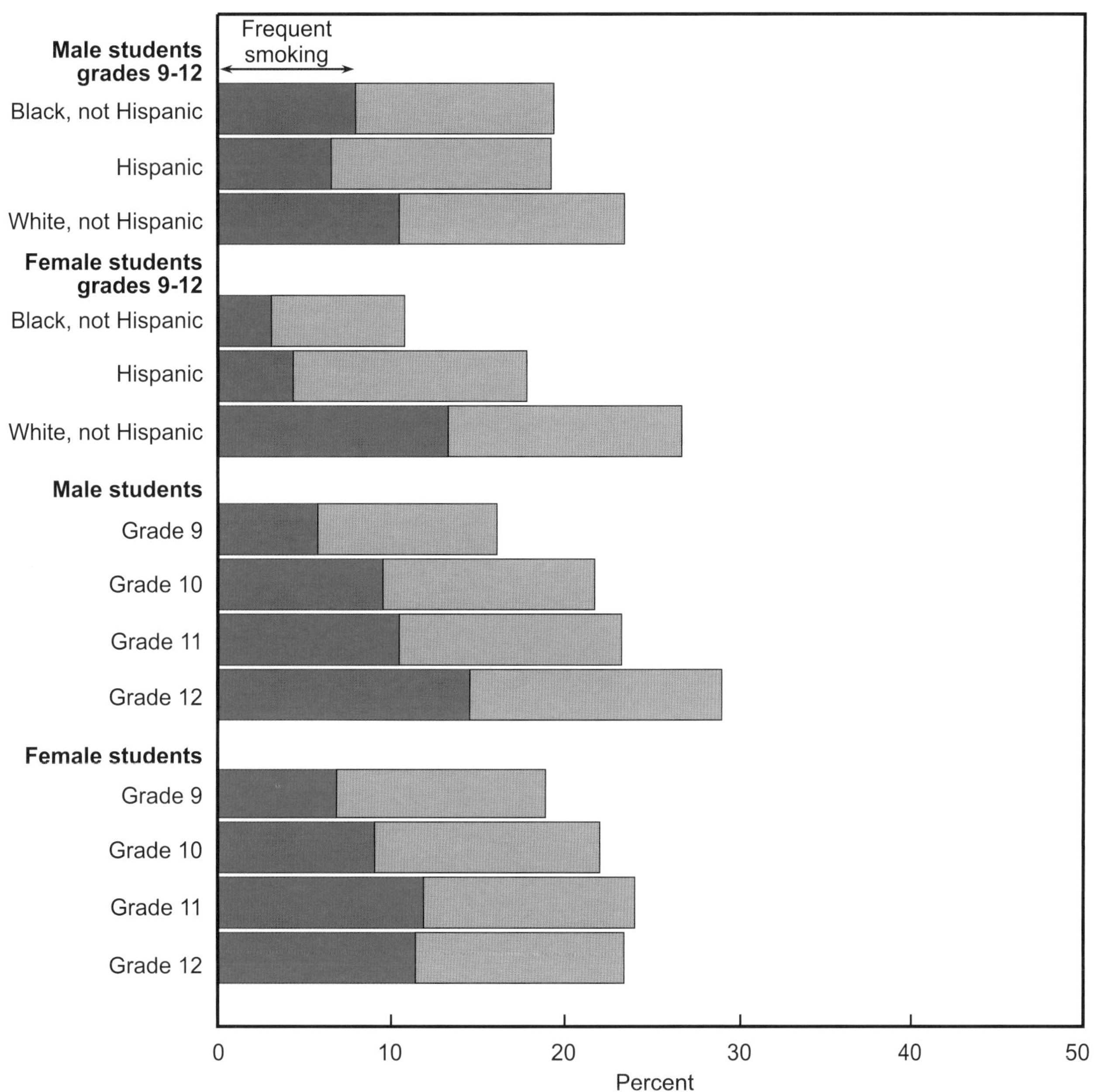

NOTES: Current cigarette smoking is defined as having smoked cigarettes on 1 or more days of the 30 days preceding the survey; frequent cigarette smoking is defined as having smoked cigarettes on 20 or more of the 30 days preceding the survey. See Data Table for data points graphed and standard errors.

SOURCE: Centers for Disease Control and Prevention, National Center for Chronic Disease Prevention and Health Promotion, Youth Risk Behavior Survey.

Teenagers and Cars

Between 1970 and 2002 death rates for motor vehicle-related injuries for teenagers and young adults 15–24 years of age decreased by 40 percent. Yet, teenagers and young adults have among the highest death rates for motor vehicle-related injuries of any age group; one-third of deaths for 15–24 year-olds were the result of motor vehicle-related injuries in 2002 (*Health, United States, 2005,* table 44 and (1)). Research has shown that seatbelts, when properly used reduce the risk of fatal injury to front-seat passenger car occupants by 45 percent and the risk of moderate to critical injury by 50 percent (2). In States with strong seatbelt laws teenage seatbelt use is consistently higher (3). Alcohol use and cars are a deadly combination. In 2003 one-fifth of young drivers 16–20 years of age involved in fatal motor vehicle traffic-related crashes were intoxicated (4). In 2002 three-quarters of young drivers who had been drinking and were killed in a crash were not wearing seatbelts (5).

Between 1991 and 2003 the percent of high school students in grades 9–12 who never or rarely wore seatbelts while riding in a car driven by someone else decreased from 26 percent to 18 percent (data table for figure 12). Although the percent not wearing a seatbelt declined for both male and female students, 22 percent of male high school students compared with 15 percent of female high school students rarely or never used a seatbelt in 2003 (figure 12).

Among high school students, riding with a driver who had been drinking was more common than lack of seatbelt use or drinking and driving. The percent of high school students in grades 9–12 who rode with a driver who had been drinking alcohol decreased from 40 percent to 30 percent between 1991 and 2003. In 2003 male and female high school students were equally as likely to ride with a driver who had been drinking.

The percent of 11–12th grade high school students who drove after drinking alcohol declined from almost 25 percent to 18 percent between 1991 and 2003. Although the percent drinking and driving declined for both males and females, in 2003 male students in grades 11–12 were nearly twice as likely as female students to drink and drive (22 percent compared with 12 percent).

Figure 12. Seatbelt use and drinking and driving among high school students by sex: United States, 1991-2003

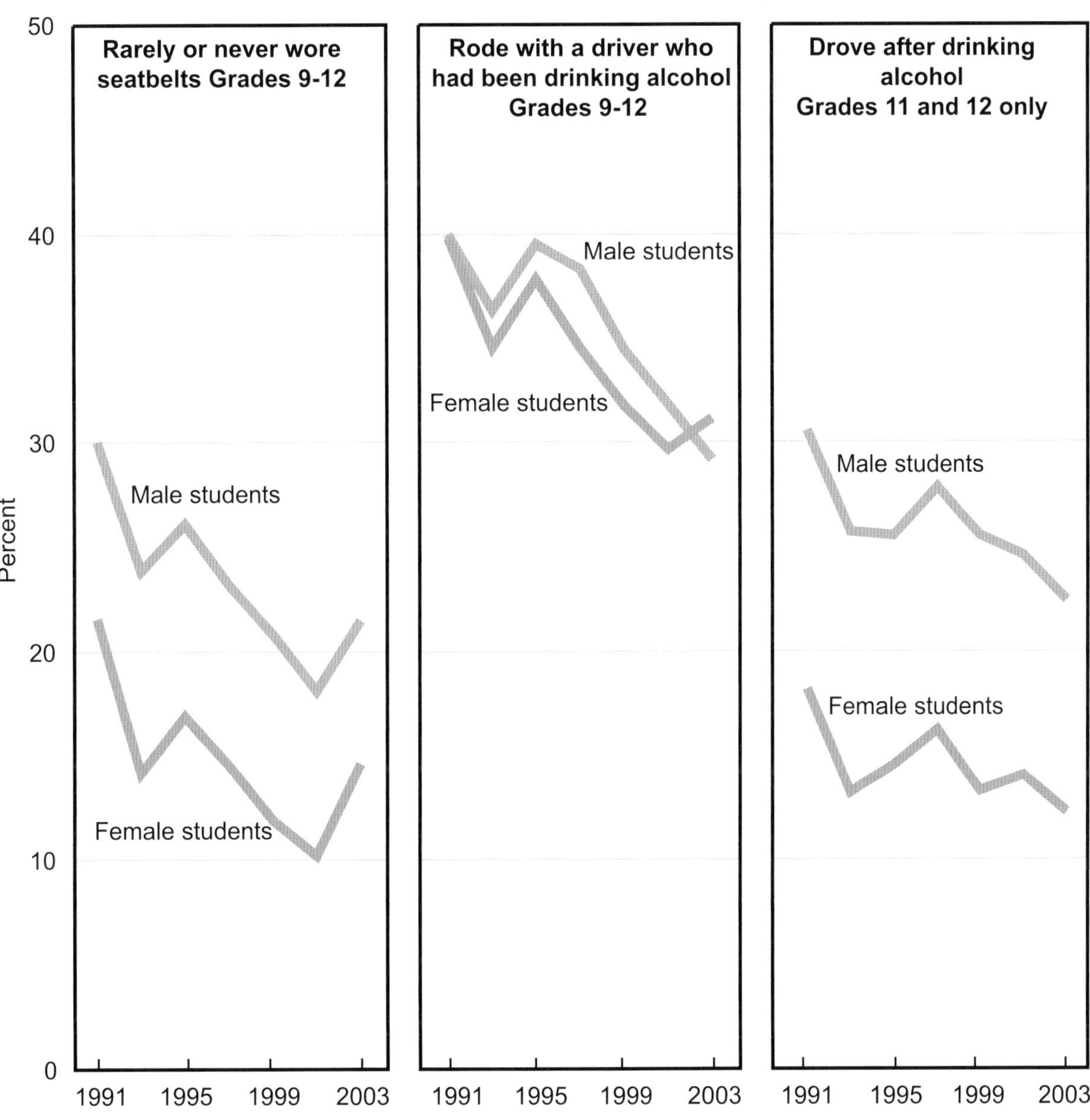

NOTE: See Data Table for data points graphed, standard errors, and additional notes.

SOURCE: Centers for Disease Control and Prevention, National Center for Chronic Disease Prevention and Health Promotion, Youth Risk Behavior Survey.

Physical Activity

Most diseases result from a complex interaction between inherited risk factors and environmental risk factors such as diet, lifestyle, and social factors (1). Adopting a healthy lifestyle, which includes being physically active, eating nutritiously, and avoiding tobacco, can prevent or help to control many diseases. Benefits of regular physical activity include a reduced risk of premature mortality and reduced risks of coronary heart disease, diabetes, colon cancer, hypertension, and osteoporosis. Regular physical activity also improves symptoms associated with musculoskeletal conditions and mental health conditions such as depression and anxiety. In addition physical activity can enhance physical functioning and aid in weight control (2). Physical activity, along with a healthy diet, plays an important role in the prevention of overweight and obesity. Monitoring levels of regular physical activity is of particular concern due to the increasing prevalence of overweight and obesity in the United States.

Although vigorous physical activity produces the greatest cardiovascular benefits, moderate amounts of physical activity are also associated with lower levels of mortality. Among older persons, even small amounts of physical activity may improve cardiovascular functioning (3). National recommendations for physical activity encourage all Americans to engage in regular physical activity and reduce sedentary activities to promote health, psychological well-being, and a healthy body weight. Current 2005 recommendations are for adolescents to engage in at least 60 minutes of physical activity and for adults to engage in at least 30 minutes of moderate physical activity on most days of the week. Additional recommendations target older age groups and weight loss or weight maintenance goals (4).

Physical activity for high school students includes physical education classes, sports teams, and other forms of activity. Between 1999 and 2003 the percent of high school students nationwide who participated in regular physical activity declined slightly from 70 percent to 67 percent (see figure 13 data table for definition of regular physical activity). Male students are more likely than female students to be physically active. In 2003, 73 percent of male high school students and 60 percent of female high school students reported regular physical activity. Among female non-Hispanic black students, only 50 percent were active (figure 13). The percent participating in regular physical activity declines with advancing grade in school. In 2003, 72 percent of 9th graders compared with 60 percent of 12th graders engaged in regular physical activity. The decline in regular physical activity with advancing age is explained in part by patterns of enrollment in high school physical education (PE) classes. In 2003, 71 percent of 9th graders were enrolled in PE classes compared with 40 percent of 12th graders (5). Nationwide, only 28 percent of high school students attended daily PE classes in 2003 while 38 percent of high school students watched at least 3 hours of television on an average school day.

School is one place where teenagers can participate in organized exercise and sports activities and learn the benefits of physical activity to health. Childhood and adolescence may be pivotal times for developing the habit of regular physical activity and preventing sedentary behavior among adults. Positive experiences with physical activity at a young age help lay the basis for being regularly active throughout life (2).

Figure 13. High school students engaging in regular physical activity by sex, race and Hispanic origin, and grade: United States, 2003

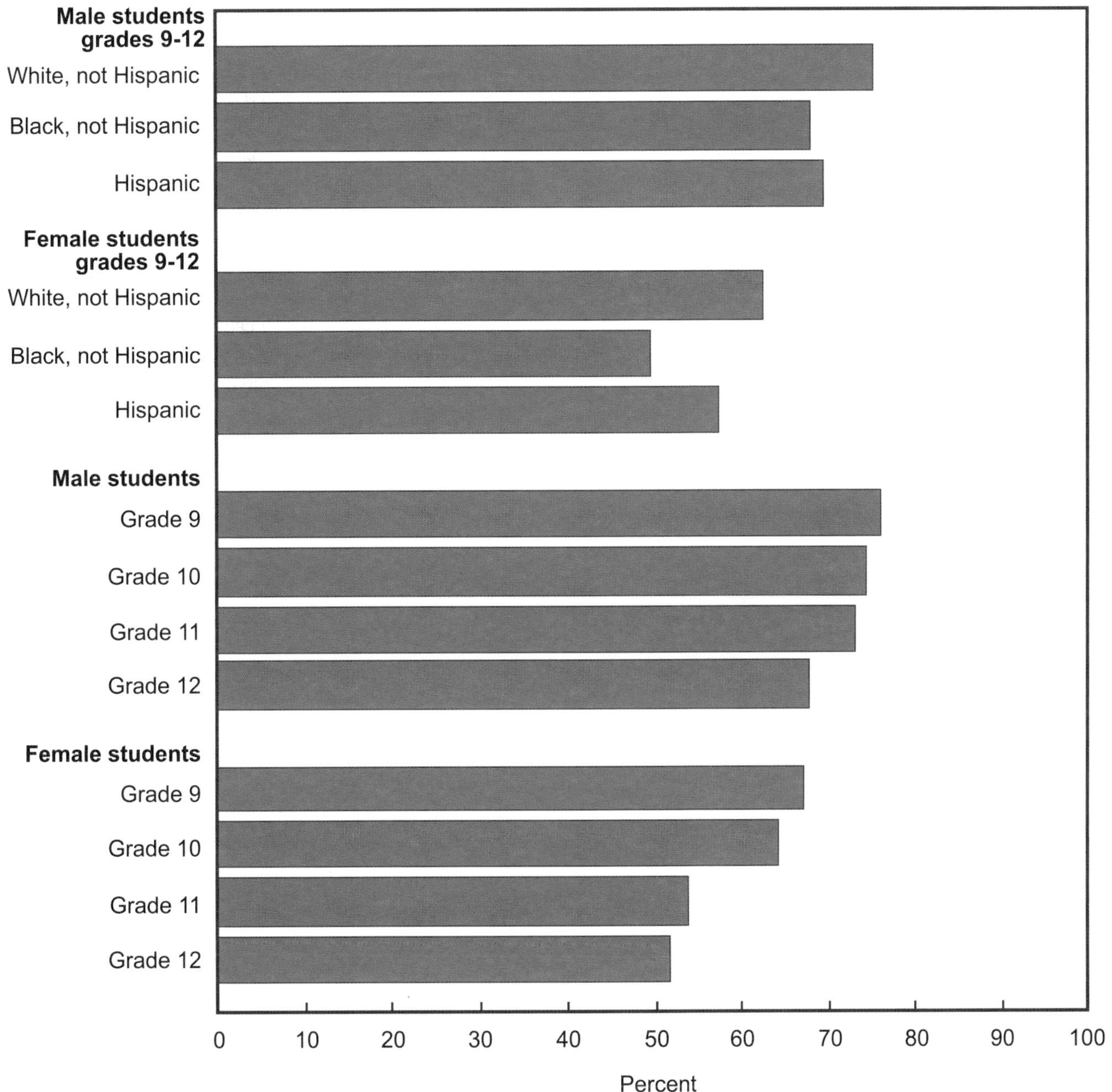

NOTES: Regular physical activity is at least 20 minutes of vigorous activity on 3 or more days or 30 minutes of moderate activity on 5 or more days during the past 7 days. See Data Table for data points graphed, standard errors, and additional notes.

SOURCE: Centers for Disease Control and Prevention, National Center for Chronic Disease Prevention and Health Promotion, Youth Risk Behavior Survey.

Physical Activity *(Continued)*

The trend in leisure-time physical activity among adult men and women has remained stable in recent years (*Health, United States, 2005,* table 72). In 2003, 3 in 10 adults engaged in regular leisure-time activity (see figure 14 data table for definition of leisure-time activity continuum), 3 in 10 had some leisure-time activity, and nearly 4 in 10 adults were inactive in their leisure time. Men were more likely than women to have regular leisure-time activity. While regular leisure-time activity decreases substantially with age from its peak of 42 percent among young adults 18–24 years of age, significant portions of older adults maintain an active lifestyle. More than one-quarter of noninstitutionalized adults 65–74 years of age and nearly one-fifth of adults 75 years of age and over reported regular leisure-time physical activity.

Leisure-time physical activity patterns also vary by poverty status, with adults living below or near poverty less likely to have regular leisure-time physical activity and more likely to be inactive (figure 14). In 2003 about one-half of adults who were poor or near poor were inactive in leisure time compared with about one-third of adults living in families with income more than twice poverty. Conversely, about one-quarter of adults living in or near poverty had regular leisure-time physical activity compared with more than one-third of adults living in families with higher incomes (percents are age adjusted).

Leisure time presents one opportunity for engaging in sufficient physical activity to maintain good health. Other opportunities include physical activity associated with occupation or transportation (for example, walking or biking to work and school). Adults who are inactive in leisure time may compensate for it by being physically active at work. However, an analysis of type of work among adults who are inactive in leisure time showed that only a small proportion—about 1 in 5 adults—reported a category of employment that involved physical activity (6).

Figure 14. Leisure-time physical activity among adults 18 years of age and over by poverty status: United States, 2003

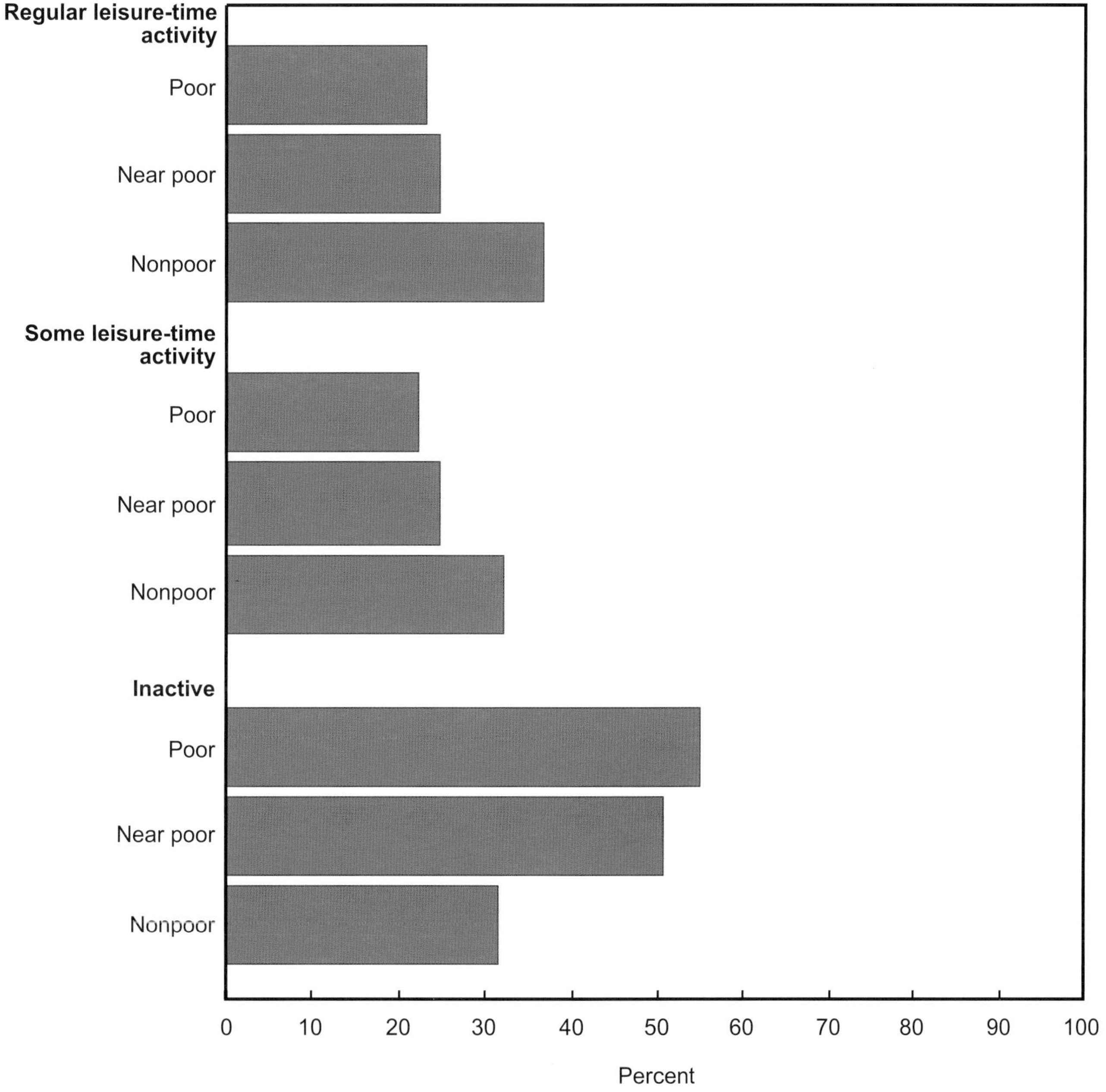

NOTES: Data are for the civilian noninstitutionalized population and are age adjusted. Inactive adults reported no sessions of light/moderate or vigorous leisure-time physical activity of at least 10 minutes duration. Adults with some leisure-time physical activity were not inactive but did not meet the requirements for regular activity. Adults with regular leisure-time activity reported at least 20 minutes of vigorous activity 3 times per week or 30 minutes of light/moderate activity 5 times per week. See Data Table for data points graphed, standard errors, and additional notes.

SOURCE: Centers for Disease Control and Prevention, National Center for Health Statistics, National Health Interview Survey.

Overweight and Obesity

Epidemiologic and actuarial studies have shown that surplus body weight is associated with excess morbidity and mortality (1). Among adults, overweight and obesity elevate the risk of heart disease, diabetes, and some types of cancer. Overweight and obesity are also factors that increase the severity of disease associated with hypertension, arthritis, and other musculoskeletal problems (2). Obesity also has serious health consequences among younger persons. Among children and adolescents, obesity increases the risk of high cholesterol, hypertension, and diabetes (3). Diet, physical activity, genetic factors, environment, and health conditions all contribute to overweight in children and adults. The potential health benefits from reduction in the prevalence of overweight and obesity are of significant public health importance.

National Health and Nutrition Examination Surveys (NHANES) collect data from physical exams in a mobile examination center. Results from a series of NHANES indicate that the prevalence of overweight and obesity changed little between the early 1960s and 1976–80 (figure 15). Findings from the 1988–94 and 1999–2002 surveys, however, showed substantial increases in overweight and obesity among adults. The upward trend in overweight since 1980 reflects primarily an increase in the percent of adults 20–74 years of age who are obese. In 1999–2002, 65 percent of adults were overweight with 31 percent obese.

The percent of children (6–11 years of age) and adolescents (12–19 years of age) who are overweight has also risen. Among children and adolescents, the percent overweight has increased since 1976–80. In 1999–2002 about 16 percent of children and adolescents were overweight. The prevalence of overweight among adolescents varies by race and ethnicity. In 1999–2002, 14 percent of non-Hispanic white adolescents, 21 percent of non-Hispanic black adolescents, and 23 percent of Mexican-origin adolescents were overweight (4).

The prevalence of obesity varies among adults by sex, race, and ethnicity (*Health, United States, 2005,* table 73). In 1999–2002, 28 percent of men and 34 percent of women 20–74 years of age were obese. The prevalence of obesity among women differed significantly by racial and ethnic group. In 1999–2002 one-half of non-Hispanic black women were obese compared with nearly one-third of non-Hispanic white women. In contrast, the prevalence of obesity among men differed little by race and ethnicity (28–29 percent).

The rise in overweight and obesity is reflected in the average weight of adult men and women in the United States (5). Adult men and women are roughly an inch taller than they were in 1960–62, but are nearly 25 pounds heavier on average. The average weight of men age 20–74 years increased from 166 pounds in 1960–62 to 191 pounds in 1999–2002 and the average weight of women increased from 140 pounds to 164 pounds during the same period.

Figure 15. Overweight and obesity by age: United States, 1960-2002

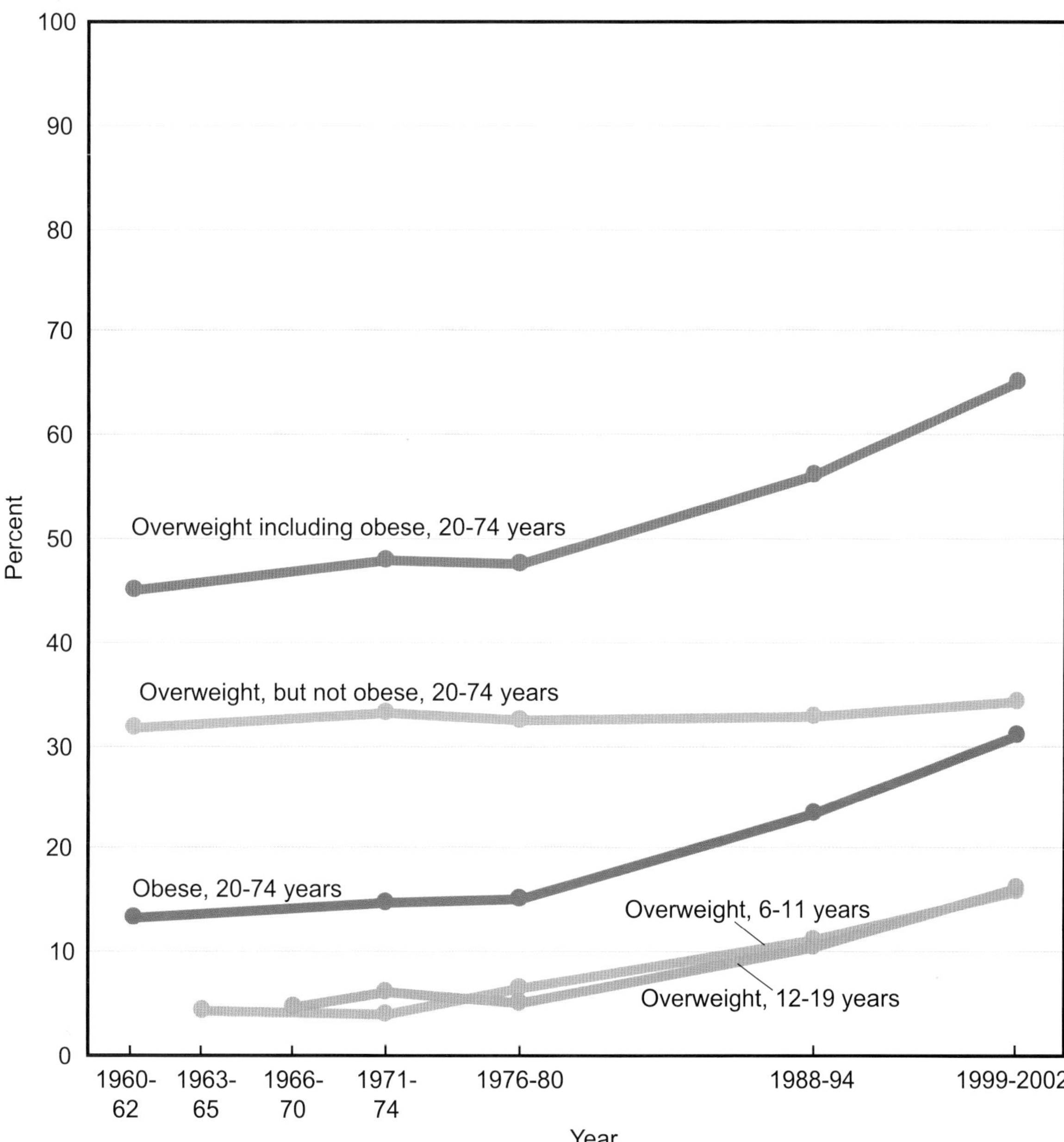

NOTES: Percents for adults are age adjusted. For adults: overweight including obese is defined as a body mass index (BMI) greater than or equal to 25, overweight but not obese as a BMI greater than or equal to 25 but less than 30, and obese as a BMI greater than or equal to 30. For children: overweight is defined as a BMI at or above the sex- and age-specific 95th percentile BMI cut points from the 2000 CDC Growth Charts: United States. Obese is not defined for children. See Data Table for data points graphed, standard errors, and additional notes.

SOURCES: Centers for Disease Control and Prevention, National Center for Health Statistics, National Health Examination Survey and National Health and Nutrition Examination Survey.

Asthma in Children Age 3–17

Asthma is a chronic lung disease that affects breathing. It is characterized by episodes of inflammation and narrowing of small airways in response to "triggers," which include allergens, infections, exercise, or exposure to respiratory irritants, such as tobacco smoke and pollutants. These attacks or episodes may involve shortness of breath, cough, wheezing, chest pain or tightness, mucus production, or a combination of these symptoms (1,2).

Asthma is a leading cause of childhood illness and disability although childhood deaths from asthma are rare (1,3). Attacks can cause considerable discomfort and anxiety in both children and their families, and may limit athletic and other activities. Children under the age of 3 years may experience wheezing, which can later develop into asthma, but in the majority of cases the wheezing is associated with diminished airway function at birth or other respiratory diseases (4). Therefore, a definitive diagnosis of asthma is difficult to make in children less than 3 years of age.

In 2002–03, about 6 percent of children 3–17 years of age, more than 3.6 million children, had an asthma attack within the past year (5). Racial and ethnic disparities in prevalence of and health care utilization for the disease have been documented and have persisted over time (6). Non-Hispanic black children 3–10 years of age have higher asthma attack prevalence rates than either non-Hispanic white or Hispanic children, and this disparity has been increasing in recent years (figure 16). In 2002–03 attack prevalence rates among children age 3–10 years were 9 percent for non-Hispanic black children, compared with about 5 percent for Hispanic and non-Hispanic white children. Additional years of data will be required to see if this gap continues to increase over time. In 2002–03 the race and ethnic differentials in asthma attack prevalence were smaller in older children age 11–17 years.

In 2003 there were approximately 132,000 hospital discharges for children age 3–17 years with a first-listed diagnosis of asthma, 475,000 emergency department visits, and 4.6 million visits to office-based physicians and hospital outpatient clinics with a first-listed diagnosis of asthma (7,8,9). Nearly 70 percent of asthma hospitalizations among children age 3–17 years were for young children 3–10 years of age, although this age group comprised about one-half of all children age 3–17 years (7,10).

Despite an increased number of asthma medications that help prevent the onset of attacks, new clinical practice guidelines, and intervention programs designed to improve asthma management among children, asthma attack prevalence rates among young black children are rising. Poor black children are at the highest risk of asthma-associated morbidity (6). Poor outcomes associated with asthma attacks can generally be prevented if families and children are properly educated and have access to quality health care (3). Disparities by race and poverty status in attack rates may be due to social, cultural, or environmental differences between races that disproportionally affect poor families' ability to effectively identify and manage children's asthma (6).

Figure 16. Asthma attack among children by age, race and Hispanic origin: United States, 1998-2003

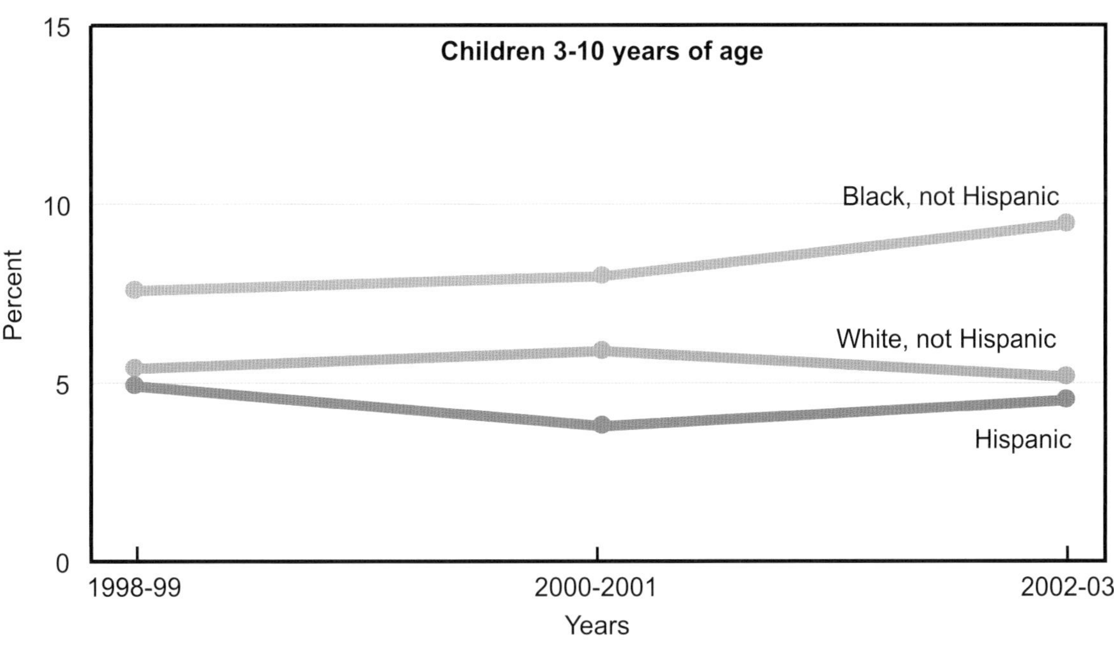

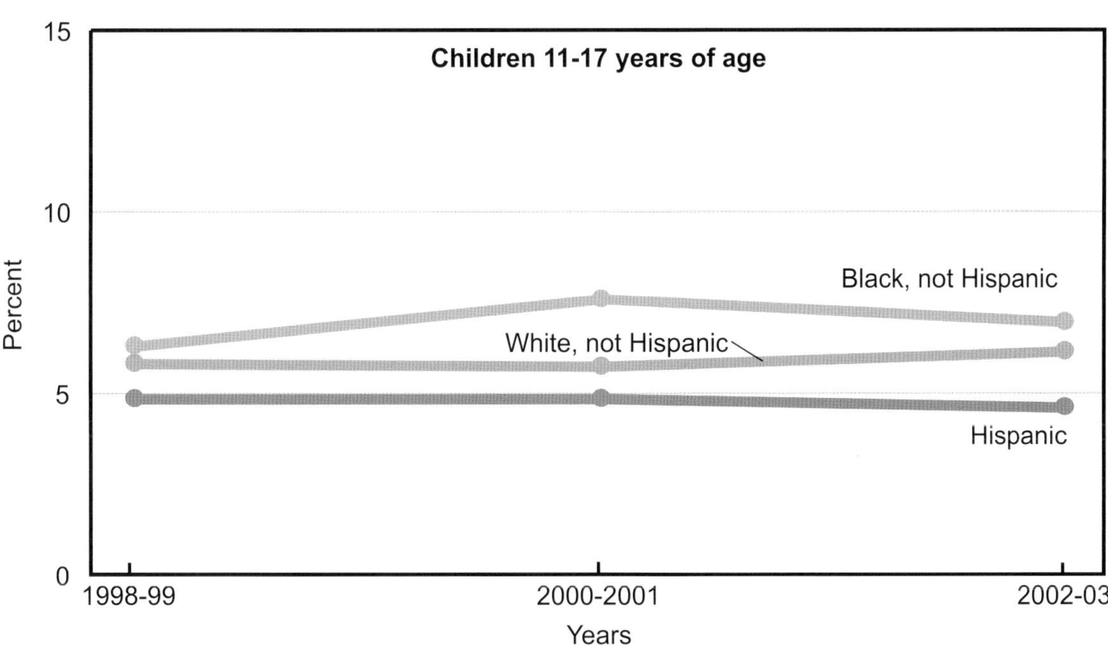

NOTES: Asthma attack in past 12 months. See Data Table for data points graphed, standard errors, and additional notes.

SOURCE: Centers for Disease Control and Prevention, National Center for Health Statistics, National Health Interview Survey.

Headache and Low Back Pain

Headache and low back pain are two common sources of pain and constitute a significant public health concern. They interfere with an individual's ability to work, enjoy social activities, and negatively affect quality of life (1). These conditions have considerable medical and economic consequences for society by placing a large burden on the health care system in terms of diagnosis, treatment, and medication management. In addition there are substantial indirect costs associated with reduced productivity. Americans spend at least $50 billion a year on low back pain, the most common cause of job-related disability and a leading contributor to missed work (2). The cost to American employers due to missed work and reduced productivity associated with migraine headaches is estimated at $13 billion per year (3).

Headache can be classified into three major types: tension, migraine, and cluster (3,4). Tension headache, the most common form of headache, is of mild to moderate intensity and occurs on both sides of the head. Migraine is described as an intense pulsing or throbbing pain in one area of the head often accompanied by extreme sensitivity to light and sound, nausea, and vomiting. Cluster, so named because of the characteristic grouping or clustering of headache, is one of the least common types of headache. With typical cluster headache, the pain is almost always one-sided and usually localized in the eye region.

Low back pain is the second most common neurological ailment in the United States—only headache (when all types and severity levels are considered) is more common (2). Low back pain may reflect nerve or muscle irritation or bone lesions. Most low back pain follows injury or trauma to the back, but pain may also be caused by degenerative conditions such as arthritis or disc disease, osteoporosis, or other causes. Obesity, smoking, weight gain during pregnancy, stress, poor physical condition, posture inappropriate for the activity being performed, and poor sleeping position can also contribute to low back pain.

In the National Health Interview Survey, the presence of pain is measured by asking adult respondents 18 years of age and over about "severe headache or migraine," "low back pain," and other selected types of pain during the past 3 months. Respondents are instructed to report pain that lasted a whole day or more and not to include minor aches or pains. Respondents who reported both severe headache or migraine and low back pain were counted separately for each condition. Comparable national data on pain have been available since 1997 (see Appendix I, National Health Interview Survey). Between 1997 and 2003 the percent of adults 18 years of age and over reporting severe headache or migraine and low back pain remained relatively stable (*Health, United States, 2005*, table 57).

In 2003, 15 percent of adults suffered with severe headache or migraine during the past 3 months (figure 17 and data table for figure 17). Severe headache or migraine was more than twice as common among women as men (21 percent compared with 9 percent). The presence of severe headache or migraine diminished with age; rates among men and women 65 years of age and over were less than one-half the level reported among younger men and women.

In 2003, 27 percent of adults reported low back pain—nearly double the level of adults with severe headache or migraine (figure 17 and data table for figure 17). Low back pain was slightly more common among women than men (30 percent compared with 25 percent). In contrast to the pattern for severe headache or migraine, which diminished with age for men and women, the prevalence of low back pain increased with age. Among men low back pain peaked in the 45–64 year age group and then decreased at older ages while for women the prevalence of low back pain was similar for middle-aged and older women.

Diagnosis, treatment, and medication management of headache and low back pain have considerable impact on the ambulatory health care system (5,6). In 2003 adults 18 years of age and over made 3.5 million visits to physician offices and hospital outpatient departments with a patient's stated reason for visit (up to three reasons were recorded) of headache or migraine, and 3.6 million visits with a reason for visit of back pain (which includes low back pain) (7). Visit rates were higher for women than for men; more than twice as high for headache or migraine and for back pain. Ambulatory care visits for headache or migraine and back pain reflect only a portion of total health care costs for these conditions as they include care only for persons who access the health care system. Additional medical costs are born by persons who self-treat these conditions with over-the-counter drugs or utilize complementary and alternative medicine (CAM) therapies (8).

Figure 17. Adults 18 years of age and over with severe headache or migraine or low back pain in the past 3 months by age and sex: United States, 2003

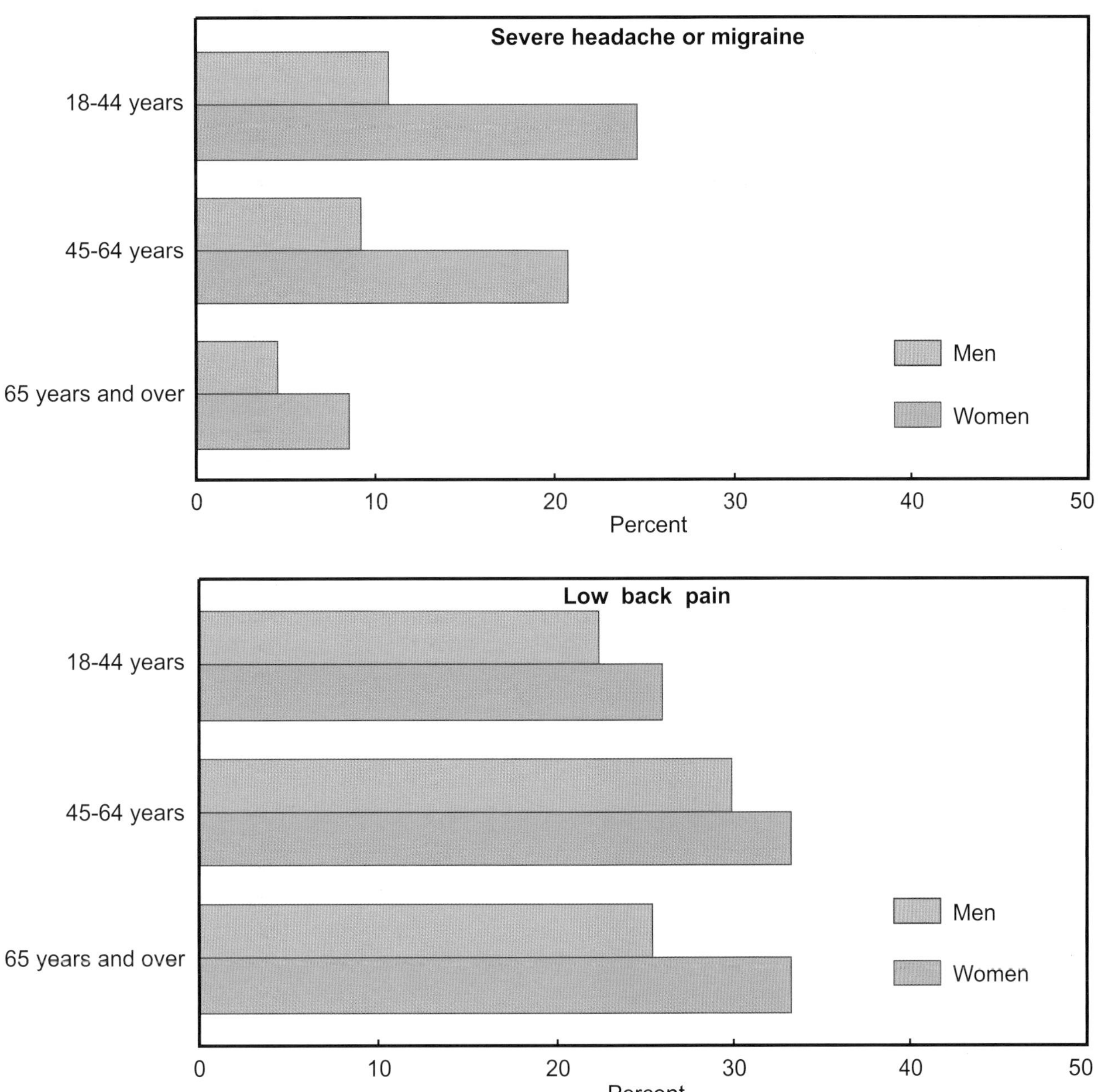

NOTE: See Data Table for data points graphed, standard errors, and additional notes.

SOURCE: Centers for Disease Control and Prevention, National Center for Health Statistics, National Health Interview Survey.

Children

Limitation of activity due to chronic physical, mental, or emotional conditions is a broad measure of health and functioning that gauges a child's ability to undertake major age-appropriate activities. Play is the primary activity for preschool children, whereas schoolwork is the primary activity for children 5 years of age and over.

The National Health Interview Survey identifies children with activity limitation through questions about specific limitations in play, self-care, walking, memory, and other activities and through a question about current use of special education or early intervention services. A child is classified as having an activity limitation due to a chronic condition if at least one of the conditions causing limitations is a chronic physical, mental, or emotional problem. Estimates of the number of children with an activity limitation may differ depending on the type of disabilities included and the methods used to identify them (1).

Comparable national data on activity limitation have been available since 1997 (see Appendix I, National Health Interview Survey). Between 1997 and 2003, 6–7 percent of children were reported to have limitation of activity (*Health, United States, 2005*, table 58). The percent of children with limitation of activity varies by age and sex. In 2002–03 the percent of children with activity limitation was significantly higher among school-age children than among preschoolers, primarily due to the number of school-age children identified solely by participation in special education. About three-quarters of school-age children with an activity limitation were identified as having a limitation solely by participation in special education. Limitation of activity occurred more often among boys than among girls (2). Physiological, maturational, behavioral, and social differences between boys and girls have been suggested as explanations for the higher prevalence of activity limitation in boys (3).

In 2002–03 the leading chronic health conditions causing activity limitation in children differed by age (figure 18). Among preschool children, the chronic conditions most often mentioned were speech problems, asthma, and mental retardation or other developmental problems. Among school-age children, learning disability and Attention Deficit Hyperactivity Disorder (ADHD) were among the most frequently mentioned causes of activity limitation.

Approximately 20 percent of school-age children with an activity limitation had more than one condition causing activity limitation. Among school-age children, the most common combinations of causal conditions were learning disability and ADHD; learning disability and speech problems; and ADHD and other mental, emotional, or behavioral problems (2).

Figure 18. Selected chronic health conditions causing limitation of activity among children by age: United States, 2002-03

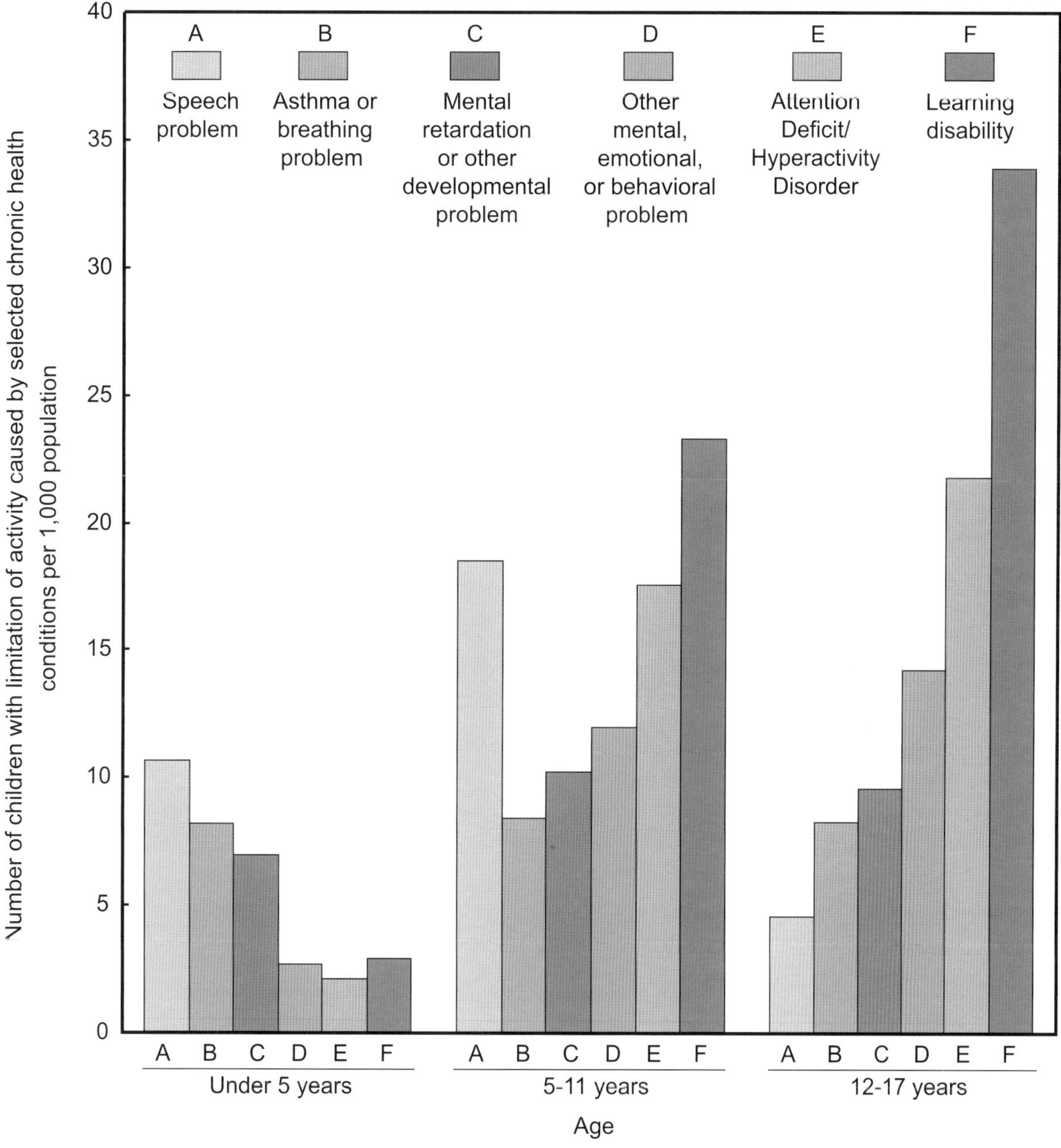

NOTES: Children with more than one chronic health condition causing activity limitation are counted in each category. See Data Table for data points graphed, standard errors, and additional notes.

SOURCE: Centers for Disease Control and Prevention, National Center for Health Statistics, National Health Interview Survey.

Working-Age and Older Adults

Chronic physical, mental, or emotional conditions can cause limitations in one's ability to function and carry out normal activities, such as working, keeping house, raising children, or even functioning independently. Limitation of activity increases with age and the impact of activity limitations may vary by age (1). For working-age adults 18–64 years, the most significant effect of limitations may be on their ability to work or keep house. For older adults 65 years of age and over, the impact of activity limitations on quality of life and independence may be the chief concerns. Limitations in activity are more common among older persons due to their greater likelihood of having disabling chronic conditions. However, examination of trends in conditions causing limitation of activity in younger populations provides important information on their current and projected health care needs and associated costs (2).

In the National Health Interview Survey, limitation of activity in adults is defined as limitations in handling personal care needs (activities of daily living), routine needs (instrumental activities of daily living), having a job outside the home, walking, remembering, and other activities. Comparable national data on activity limitation have been available since 1997 (see Appendix I, National Health Interview Survey). Between 1997 and 2003 the percent of noninstitutionalized working-age adults reporting any activity limitation caused by a chronic health condition remained relatively stable (*Health, United States, 2005*, table 58). In 2003, 6 percent of younger adults 18–44 years of age reported activity limitation, in contrast to 21 percent of adults 55–64 years of age.

Health surveys that measure limitation of activity have typically asked about chronic conditions causing these restrictions. Health conditions usually refer to broad categories of disease and impairment rather than medical diagnoses and reflect the understanding the general public has of factors causing disability or limitation of activity (3). In figure 19, persons who reported more than one chronic health condition as the cause of their activity limitation were counted in each category. Among working-age adults, arthritis and other musculoskeletal conditions were the most frequently mentioned chronic conditions causing limitation of activity in 2002–03. Among persons 45–64 years of age, heart and other circulatory conditions were the second most common cause of activity limitation. Other common conditions causing activity limitation included mental illness and diabetes.

For younger working adults 18–44 years of age, mental illness was the second leading cause of activity limitation and fractures and joint injury were the third most common causes of activity limitation.

Figure 19. Selected chronic health conditions causing limitation of activity among working-age adults by age: United States, 2002-03

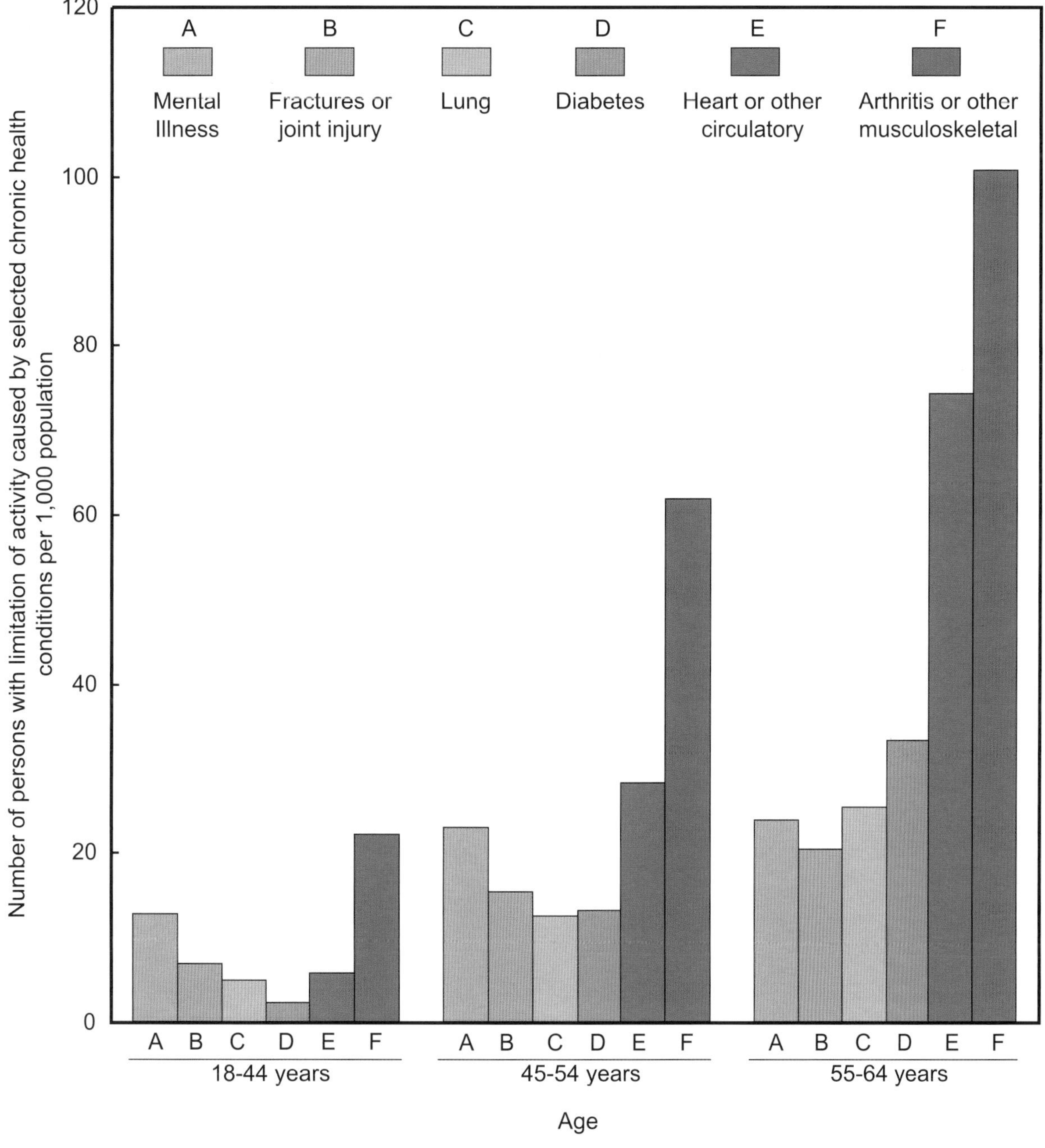

NOTES: Data are for the civilian noninstitutionalized population. Persons may report more than one chronic health condition as the cause of their activity limitation. See Data Table for data points graphed, standard errors, and additional notes.

SOURCE: Centers for Disease Control and Prevention, National Center for Health Statistics, National Health Interview Survey.

Working-Age and Older Adults
(Continued)

In 2003 more than one-third of noninstitutionalized adults 65 years of age and over living in the community reported limitation of activity (*Health, United States, 2005*, table 58). The percent with limitation of activity was more than twice as high among the oldest adults 85 years of age and over compared with adults 65–74 years of age (64 percent compared with 26 percent) (4).

For both older and working-age adults, the most common chronic conditions causing activity limitation were similar, though the rates were higher among older adults. Arthritis and other musculoskeletal conditions were the most frequently mentioned chronic conditions causing any limitation of activity among noninstitutionalized older persons in 2002–03 (figure 20). Heart disease and other circulatory conditions, including stroke, were the second most commonly reported conditions. For the oldest age group, adults 85 years and over, senility (which likely encompasses Alzheimer's disease and other types of dementia), vision, and hearing were commonly reported causes of limitation in activity.

Needing help with personal care needs such as eating, bathing, dressing, or getting around inside the home, known as activities of daily living or ADLs, is a more severe type of limitation (see related *Health, United States, 2005*, table 58). The percent of adults 65 years of age and over who reported needing help with ADLs increased with age from 3 percent of persons 65–74 years to 10 percent of persons 75 years and over. Among older adults, the percent reporting ADL limitations was higher among Hispanic and non-Hispanic black than non-Hispanic white elders. ADL limitations were more common among those living in institutions. Over 90 percent of institutionalized Medicare beneficiaries were limited in ADLs (5).

Twelve percent of noninstitutionalized older persons reported limitations in instrumental activities of daily living (IADLs) in 2003. IADLs are activities related to independent living and include preparing meals, managing money, shopping for groceries, performing housework, and using a telephone. Like other types of activity limitation, limitations in IADLs increase with age. Seven percent of those age 65–74 reported IADL limitations, compared with 18 percent of those 75 years and over (*Health, United States, 2005*, table 58). Among those 65 years of age and over, IADL limitation was higher for women than men, higher for the poor than the nonpoor, and higher for non-Hispanic black than non-Hispanic white adults.

Figure 20. Selected chronic health conditions causing limitation of activity among older adults by age: United States, 2002-03

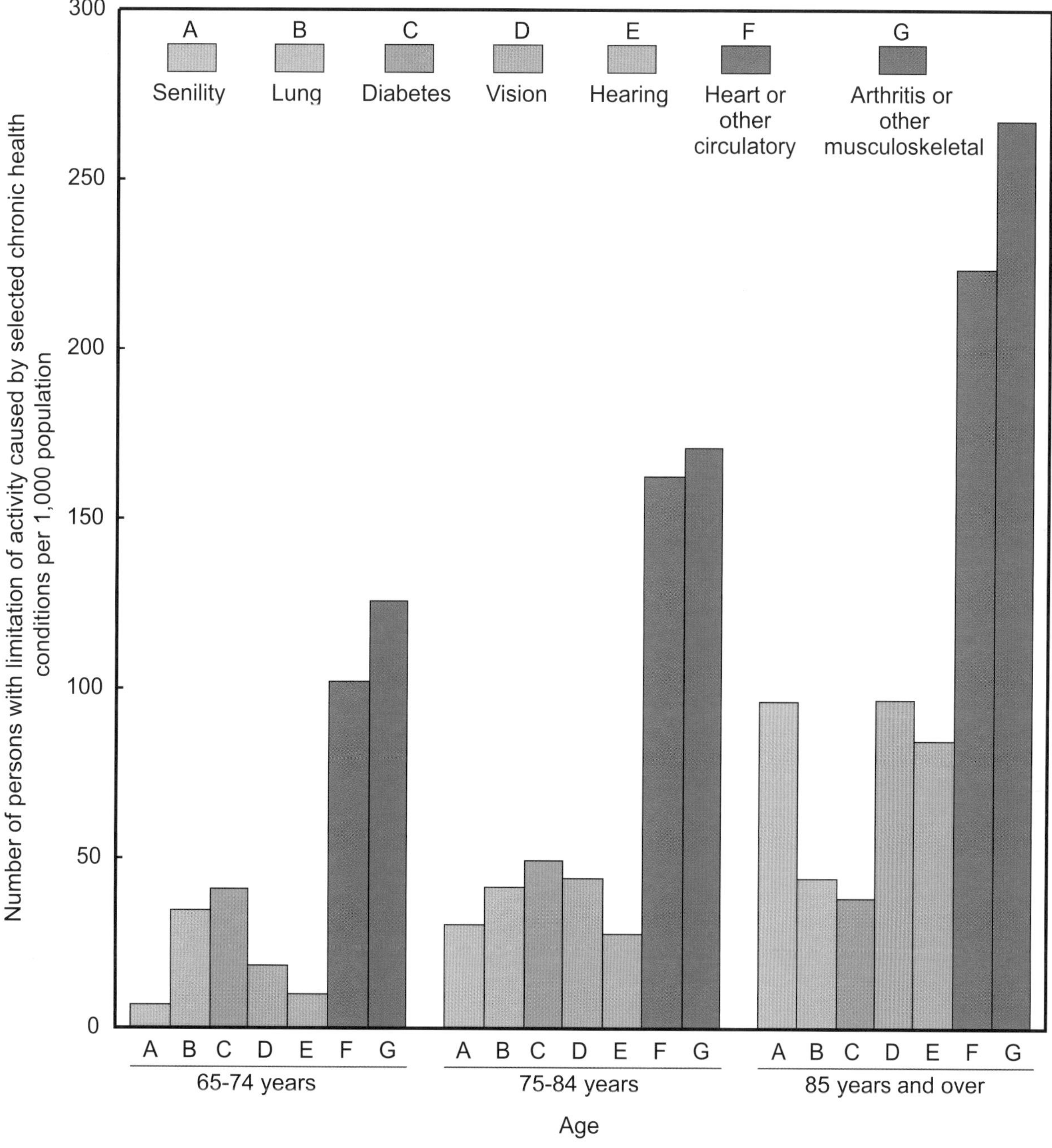

NOTES: Data are for the civilian noninstitutionalized population. Persons may report more than one chronic health condition as the cause of their activity limitation. See Data Table for data points graphed, standard errors, and additional notes.

SOURCE: Centers for Disease Control and Prevention, National Center for Health Statistics, National Health Interview Survey.

Mammography

Breast cancer is the most common type of newly diagnosed cancer among women and the second leading cause of cancer deaths for women. In 2002 approximately 204,000 women in the United States were diagnosed with breast cancer and nearly 42,000 women died from the disease (1,2). Rates of newly diagnosed breast cancer, breast cancer survival rates, and death rates vary among race and ethnic groups (*Health, United States, 2005*, tables 40, 53, 54). Breast cancer incidence and death rates are higher among white and black women than among Asian and Hispanic women. Although breast cancer survival rates have been improving, race differentials in survival persist. Between 1974–79 and 1992–2000, the 5-year relative survival rate for white women increased from 75 to 88 percent and for black women, from 63 to 74 percent. Death rates from breast cancer have been declining since the early 1990s but the percentage decrease in mortality has been substantially greater among white women than among black women.

Regular mammography screening has been shown to be effective in reducing breast cancer mortality. In 2002 the U.S. Department of Health and Human Services released its updated recommendation from the U.S. Preventive Services Task Force (USPSTF) that called for screening mammography, with or without clinical breast examination, every 1 to 2 years for women age 40 years and over. The USPSTF, with concurrence from the National Cancer Institute, lowered the recommended age for initiating routine screening from 50 to 40 years of age, but found that the strongest evidence of the mortality benefit for women undergoing mammography screening was among women age 50–69 years (3).

Between 1999 and 2003, 70 percent of women age 40 years and over had a recent mammogram within the past 2 years, more than double the percent in 1987 (age-adjusted, *Health, United States, 2005*, table 86). During the period 1987–99, the percent of women with a recent mammogram increased substantially for most race and ethnic groups, except for Asian women, for whom mammography rates have been relatively stable since 1993 (figure 21). In the early 1990s, compared with other racial and ethnic groups, non-Hispanic white women had the highest recent mammography rates. Starting in 1993, recent mammography rates for non-Hispanic black and white women have been similar and generally higher than for other race and ethnic groups. In 2003 mammography rates for non-Hispanic white and black women (71 percent) were higher than rates for Asian and Hispanic women (58 and 65 percent).

Barriers to mammography for Asian and Hispanic women may include language and acculturation, cultural beliefs, and health system barriers such as lack of insurance and no usual source of regular medical care. Several studies report lower rates of screening mammography among Spanish-speaking Hispanic patients compared with English-proficient Hispanics and non-Hispanics (4,5). With the growing number of recent immigrants in the United States, including large numbers of Asian and Hispanic immigrants, identification of potential barriers to mammography screening is critical to improving screening rates in these populations.

Disparities in mammography screening among underserved women with low income or less education also continue to exist. In 2003 poor women remained less likely than women with higher incomes to have a recent mammogram (55 percent compared with 74 percent, data table for figure 21). Women age 40 years and over with no high school diploma or GED also remained much less likely than women with at least some college education to have a recent mammogram (58 percent compared with 75 percent).

Reducing death rates from breast cancer is contingent on increasing mammography screening rates to detect the disease at an early stage and providing access to followup treatment for women who are diagnosed with breast cancer (6). Many public and private initiatives, including the National Breast and Cervical Cancer Early Detection Program (NBCCEDP) help low income, uninsured, and underserved women obtain access to both screening and followup care (7). The Breast Cancer Treatment and Prevention Act, passed in 2000, also helps to make treatment more available to women screened by the NBCCEDP and allowed States the option of providing Medicaid coverage to low-income women enrolled in NBCCEDP who have a diagnosis of breast cancer, cervical cancer, or a related precancerous condition. Other efforts to increase mammogram usage include mammography coverage for Medicaid and Medicare enrollees, endorsement of screening by professional associations and health plan guidelines, and inclusion as a quality of care measure.

Figure 21. Use of mammography within the past 2 years for women 40 years of age and over by race and Hispanic origin: United States, 1987-2003

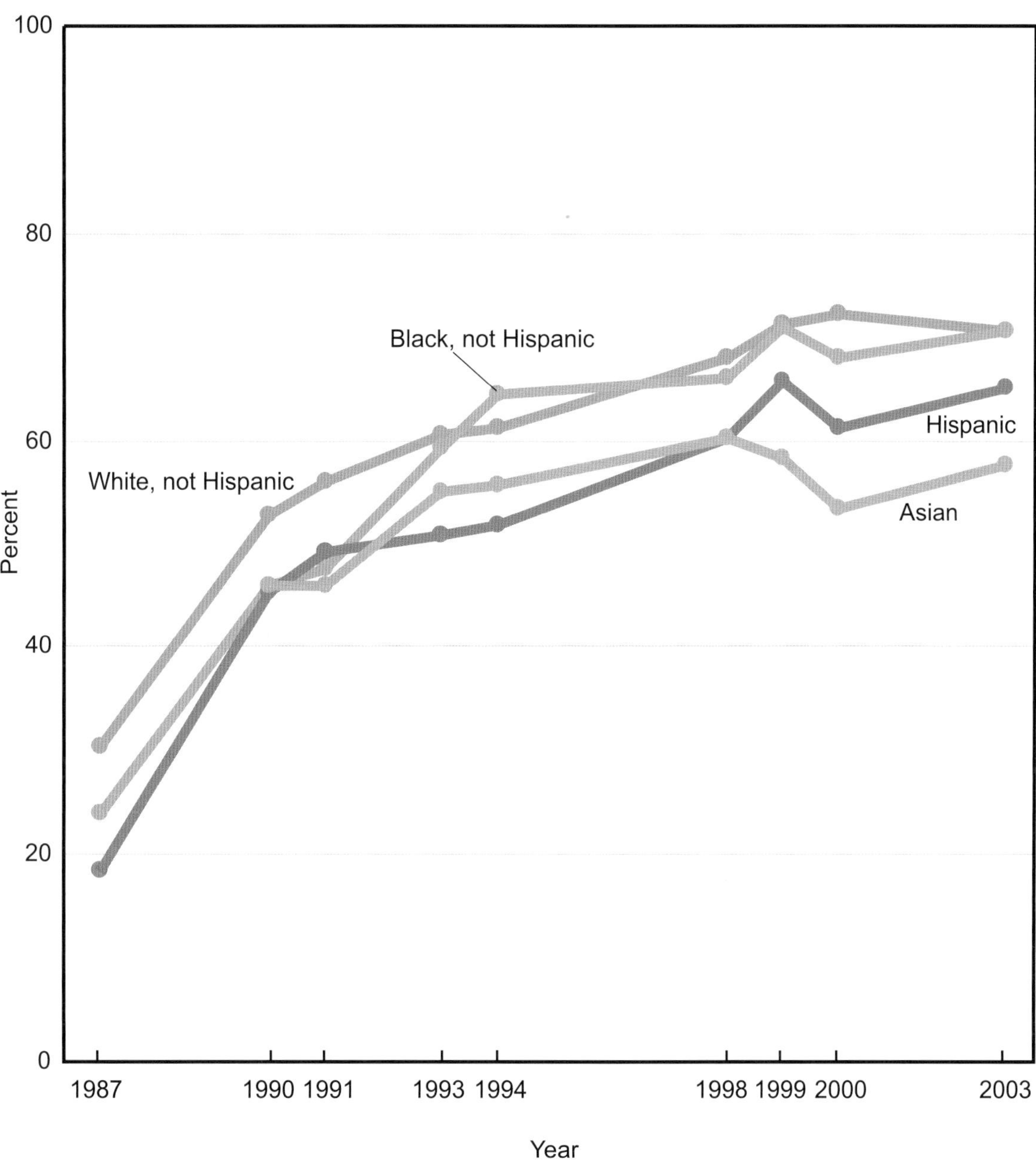

NOTES: Persons of Hispanic origin may be of any race. Asian race includes persons of both Hispanic and non-Hispanic origin. See Data Table for data points graphed, standard errors, and additional notes.

SOURCE: Centers for Disease Control and Prevention, National Center for Health Statistics, National Health Interview Survey.

Pap Smear

A Pap smear is a microscopic examination of cells scraped from the cervix that is used to detect cancerous or precancerous conditions of the cervix and other medical conditions. If detected, precancerous conditions can be treated before they become malignant. Between 1975 and 2001 use of the Pap smear is credited with cutting the age adjusted cervical cancer incidence in half, from 14.8 to 7.9 cases per 100,000 women; and with reducing the age adjusted cervical cancer death rate from 5.6 to 2.7 deaths per 100,000 women (1). In 2002 cervical cancer was the reported cause of death for 4,000 women in the United States (2). The U.S. Preventive Services Task Force, the American Cancer Society, and the American College of Obstetricians and Gynecologists all recommend regular Pap smear screening for cervical cancer, although recommendations vary as to the frequency, timing, risk factors, and age of women to be screened (3–5).

Between 1987 and 2003 the percent of women 18 years of age and over with a Pap smear within the past 3 years increased from 74 percent to 79 percent, with increases occurring among women of all race and ethnic groups (figure 22). However, Pap smear screening rates vary considerably by race and ethnicity. In 2003 non-Hispanic black women had the highest rate of screening, 84 percent. Both non-Hispanic black and non-Hispanic white women were considerably more likely to report having a recent Pap smear than Asian and Hispanic women in 2003. Screening rates for both Asian and Hispanic women increased between 1987 and 1993, but have remained fairly stable through 2003. Pap smear screening rates remained lower for Asian and Hispanic women than for non-Hispanic black and non-Hispanic white women.

Several studies have examined barriers to cervical cancer screening for Hispanic and Asian women. Demographic and socioeconomic variables were found to be important predictors of Pap smear screening for Hispanic and Asian women, as they are for the general U.S. population (6). In addition, language and acculturation has been shown to predict Pap smear utilization among Hispanic and Asian women, with more recent immigrants and those with English language barriers, fatalistic views on cancer, and culturally-based embarrassment reporting less frequent receipt of Pap smear (7–9).

Incidence rates of cervical cancer were highest for Hispanic women and rates for black women were also higher than the average for all women (10). Despite their high Pap smear screening rates, black women had the highest death rates from cervical cancer in 1997–2001, 5.6 deaths per 100,000 women. Hispanic women also had cervical cancer death rates higher than that of non-Hispanic white and Asian women. In contrast, both the incidence rate of cervical cancer and the death rate for Asian women—who had the lowest screening level—were in line with the average rates for women of all races and ethnicities combined. The reasons for the higher death rates among black women despite their high screening rates are not fully understood. This higher mortality among black women may be in part due to diagnosis at more advanced cancer stages and lower socioeconomic status (11).

For women in whom precancerous lesions have been detected through Pap smears, the likelihood of survival is nearly 100 percent with appropriate evaluation, treatment, and followup (12). The National Breast and Cervical Cancer Early Detection Program (NBCCEDP) and other initiatives help low income, uninsured, and underserved women to obtain access to both screening and followup care for cervical cancer.

Figure 22. Use of Pap smear within the past 3 years for women 18 years of age and over by race and Hispanic origin: United States, 1987-2003

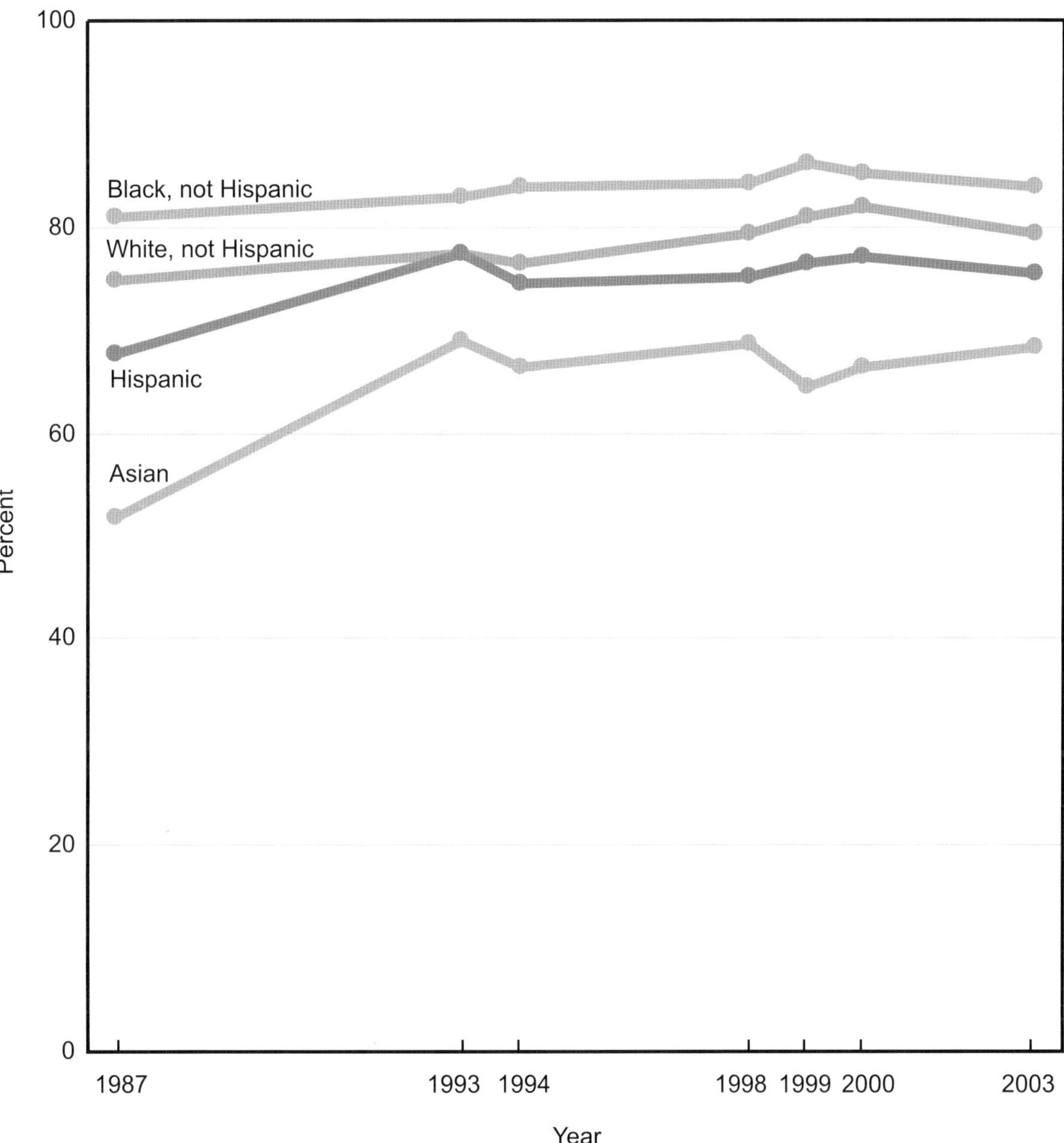

NOTES: Persons of Hispanic origin may be of any race. Asian race includes persons of both Hispanic and non-Hispanic origin. See Data Table for data points graphed, standard errors, and additional notes.

SOURCE: Centers for Disease Control and Prevention, National Center for Health Statistics, National Health Interview Survey.

Injury-Related Emergency Department Visits Among Children and Adolescents

Injuries are a substantial and preventable public health concern. Injury-attributable medical expenditures cost as much as $117 billion in 2000 (1). Whereas the most severe injuries can result in death, nonfatal injuries cause substantial pain and disability. Injuries account for a significant proportion of deaths among young persons. In 2002 injuries accounted for about 45 percent of deaths for children 1–9 years, 50 percent at 10–14 years, and 78 percent of deaths for persons age 15–19 years (2,3). In 2003 there were nearly 20 million visits with a first-listed diagnosis of injury to hospital emergency departments (EDs), hospital outpatient departments (OPDs), and physician offices for children and young adults less than 20 years of age (4). Forty-six percent of visits to these three sites for injury care were made in physicians' offices, an additional 46 percent in EDs, and 8 percent to OPDs.

EDs are often the initial site of care for serious injuries. Many injury-related visits to physician offices and OPDs are for care and observation following treatment of an initial injury. Over 60 percent of ED injury visits by persons of all ages resulted in a referral to another physician or hospital outpatient clinic (5). A larger proportion of ED visits by children and adolescents are for injuries than ED visits by middle-age and older adults. In 2003 almost 30 percent of ED visits by children and adolescents under 20 years of age were for injury diagnoses compared with 19 percent of ED visits for persons 45 years and over (4).

The National Hospital Ambulatory Medical Care Survey collects information on injury-related visits from medical records of hospital EDs. For injury-related visits two important pieces of information are coded from the medical record—the medical diagnosis and the external cause of injury. The external cause of injury, which is defined as the classification of environmental events, circumstances, and conditions that were the cause of injury, provides important public health information in terms of injury prevention. For example, an injury diagnosis might be contusions or fracture, and the external cause of injury might be cut or a fall.

In 2000–2003 the most common external causes of injury for visits to EDs for children and adolescents under 20 years of age were falls, being struck by or against a person or object, motor vehicle traffic-related injuries, and cuts. The likelihood of ED visits for these four external causes of injury varied considerably by age (figure 23 and data table for figure 23). Young children under 10 years of age were more likely to have ED visits from falls than from other causes (figure 23). Falls were the most common cause of ED injury visits among infants under 1 year of age with visit rates peaking in the toddler years. Children 10 years of age and over were more likely to have ED injury visits due to being struck by or against an object or person, often occurring during sports activities. Sports and recreation are the most common activities associated with pediatric injury-related ED visits in the United States (6). Visit rates for motor vehicle traffic-related injuries rise rapidly as teenagers begin to reach driving age, with motor vehicle traffic-related injury visit rates peaking at age 18. Most injury visits in the ED are classified as unintentional rather than intentional. However, it is noteworthy that with increasing age among teenagers, the proportion of visits coded to intentional 'struck by or against' increases from 23 percent at age 15 years to 30 percent at age 19 years (4).

Figure 23. Injury-related visits to hospital emergency departments among children under 20 years of age by first-listed external cause and age: United States, average annual 2000-2003

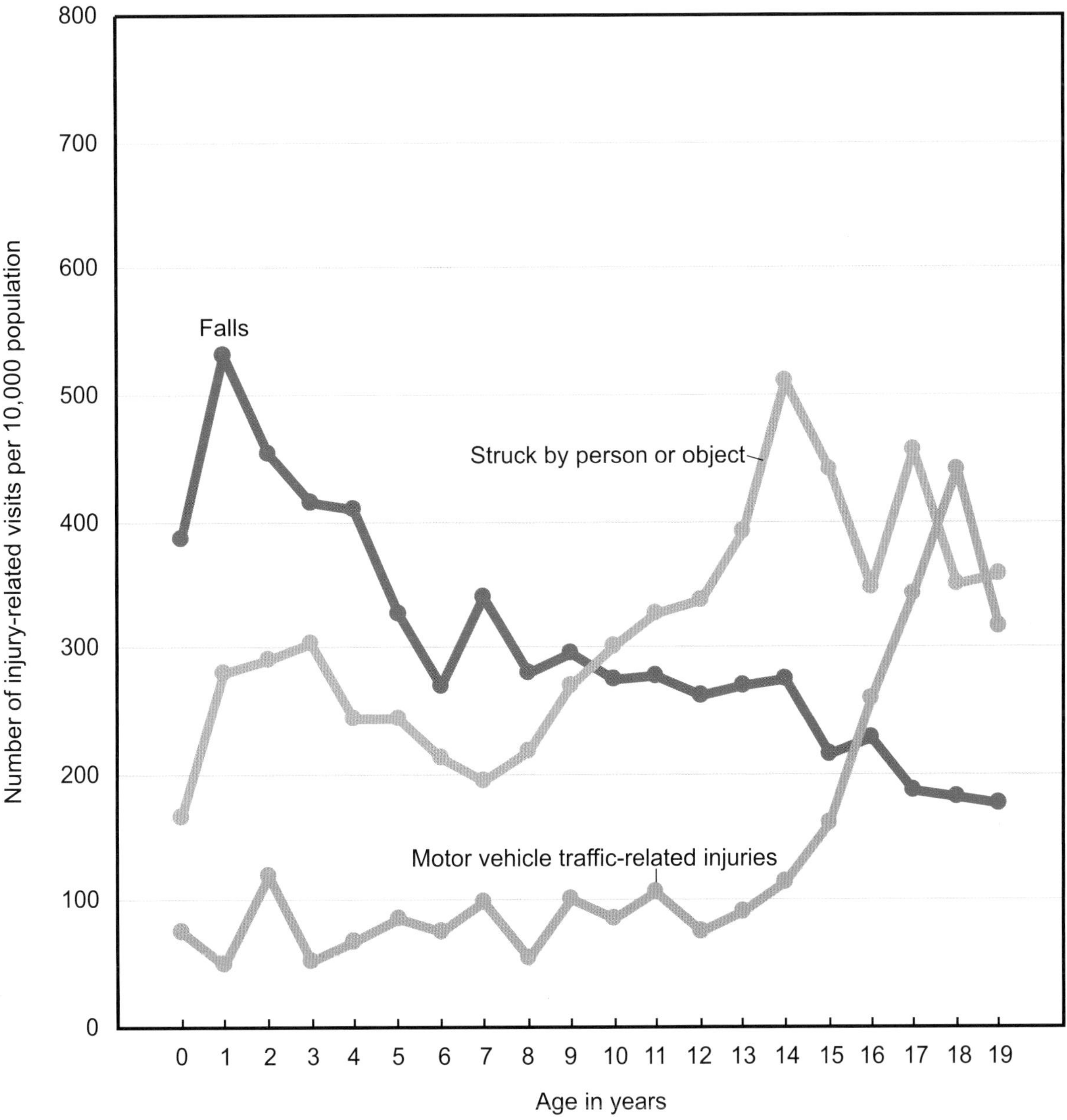

NOTES: External cause of injury is the classification of environmental events, circumstances, and conditions that were the cause of injury. See Data Table for data points graphed, standard errors, and additional notes.

SOURCE: Centers for Disease Control and Prevention, National Center for Health Statistics, National Hospital Ambulatory Medical Care Survey.

Visits to Physician Offices and Hospital Outpatient Departments

Americans of all ages visit physician offices and hospital outpatient departments (OPDs) to receive preventive and screening services, diagnosis and treatment of health conditions, medical counseling, and other types of ambulatory health care. In 2002–03 there were, on average, 1 billion visits per year to physician offices and OPDs (data table for figure 24). Many OPD clinics provide preventive services and primary care very similar to the services received in private physicians' offices. About 8 percent of these visits were made in OPDs overall, but OPDs were more frequently used sites of care for certain population groups. Visit rates to OPDs were nearly twice as high for black persons as for white persons (*Health, United States, 2005*, table 88). Physician expenditures are a major component of all personal health care expenditures and their price tag continues to increase (*Health, United States, 2005*, table 119).

Data from the National Ambulatory Medical Care Survey and the National Hospital Ambulatory Medical Care Survey, which are abstracted from medical records, provide a snapshot of care from office-based physicians and hospital outpatient departments. Visit rates to physician offices and hospital OPDs have increased since the mid-1990s. Between 1996–97 and 2002–03 the average number of ambulatory care visits for persons of all ages rose from 3.1 to 3.6 visits per person (data table for figure 24). This increase was driven by rising visit rates among men 65 years of age and over and women 45 years of age and over (figure 24).

Gender differences in visits to physician offices and hospital OPDs vary by age. The largest gender difference in visit rates occurs among adults 18–44 years of age. In this age group visit rates for women were twice as high as for men, largely due to care associated with female reproduction. This gender difference continues to narrow among middle-age adults and disappears among the oldest age group. In 2002–03 among adults 45–54 years of age visit rates for women were 45 percent higher than for men, 35 percent higher among adults 55–64 years, 10 percent higher among adults 65–74 years, and visit rates were similar among men and women 75 years of age and over.

Clinical advances; new medications and increased use of existing medications; rising burden of risk factors such as overweight and obesity; and increasing prevalence of chronic diseases such as asthma, diabetes, and hypertension contribute to rising visit rates (1–5). Medical advances such as identifying the benefits of lower cholesterol, blood pressure, and blood sugar levels lead to more visits for screening and treatment including drug monitoring. Contributing to the rise in visit rates is the increased use of both prescription and over-the-counter drugs. Drugs are becoming a more frequently utilized therapy for reducing morbidity and mortality and improving the quality of life of Americans. Almost two-thirds (62 percent) of visits to physician offices and hospital OPDs in 2001–02 had at least one drug associated with the visit; among adults 65 years of age and over nearly 20 percent of visits had 5 or more drugs associated with the visit (6). The prevalence of many chronic conditions and diseases increases with age, and as the baby boom generation continues to age its impact on the ambulatory care system will be felt more strongly (*Health, United States, 2005*, figures 30–37).

Figure 24. Visits to physician offices and hospital outpatient departments by sex and age: United States, 1996-2003

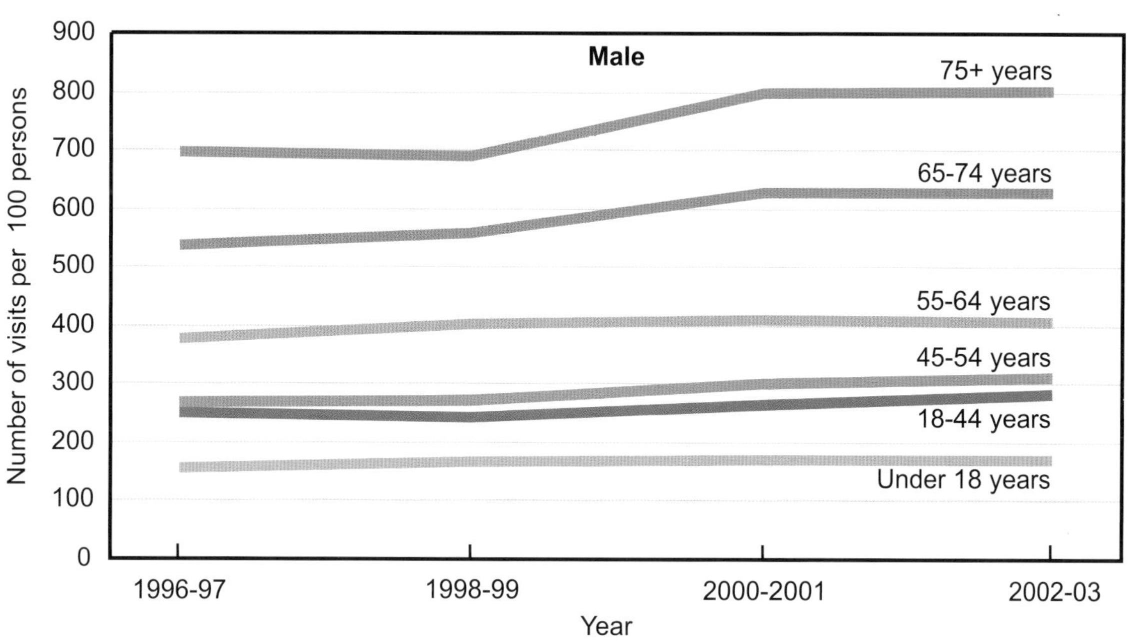

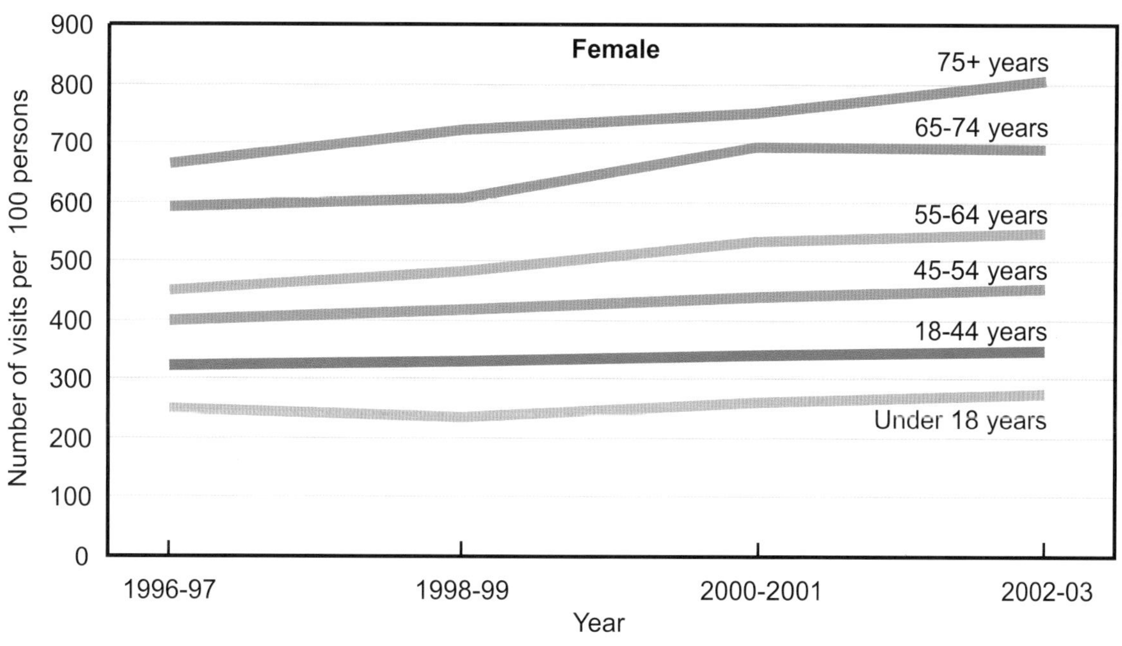

NOTE: See Data Table for data points graphed, standard errors, and additional notes.

SOURCES: Centers for Disease Control and Prevention, National Center for Health Statistics, National Ambulatory Medical Care Survey and National Hospital Ambulatory Medical Care Survey.

Hospital Procedures: Cardiac Stents

Heart disease is the leading cause of morbidity and mortality in the United States. Blockages to the coronary arteries (coronary artery disease) are a major cause of heart disease and heart attacks and their associated disability and mortality. Technological advances in treatment of blocked arteries include the introduction of coronary artery bypass graft (CABG) surgery (also called cardiac revascularization) in the late 1960s, percutaneous transluminal coronary angioplasty (PTCA, also called balloon angioplasty), introduced in the late 1970s and now often called percutaneous coronary intervention (PCI). Both procedures are preceded by cardiac catheterization, which measures the location and extent of coronary artery blockage. Whether CABG, PTCA, or some other alternative procedure is used depends on various factors such as where the blockage is, how many blockages there are, and the extent of the blockage (1,2).

The code for coronary artery stenting was introduced in 1996. Stenting is performed in combination with the PTCA procedure. A stent is a wire mesh tube used to prop open an artery that has recently been cleared using angioplasty. Since the mid-1990s angioplasty has increasingly been used with the insertion of stents because of lower rates of renarrowing of opened arteries (restenosis) (2). According to the American Heart Association, 70–90 percent of percutaneous transluminal coronary angioplasty (PTCA) procedures involve the placement of a stent (3).

Among adults 45 years of age and over, there were more than half a million hospital discharges with at least one coronary stent insertion procedure performed in 2002–03 (data table for figure 25). Between 1996–97 and 2002–03 the rate of coronary stent insertion procedure for adults age 45 years and over more than doubled from 22 to 49 per 10,000 population (data table for figure 25). Among adults age 75 years and over, the rate of hospitalizations that included this procedure more than tripled from 23 per 10,000 population in 1996–97 to 73 in 2002–03 (figure 25). For persons 45–64 years the rate of stent procedures per population stabilized after 1999, but for persons 65 years and over the rate continued to rise, in part because PTCA and stenting are considerably less invasive than CABG and can be performed on older persons who are likely to have other medical conditions that preclude more extensive open-heart CABG surgery (4,5). In contrast to rising rates of stent insertions, rates for CABG procedures declined among adults 45–64 years of age and remained stable for adults 75 years and over (*Health, United States, 2005*, table 100).

Together, medical innovations such as CABG, PTCA, the intracoronary stent, and other procedures developed during the last 30 years have contributed to improved survival for heart attack patients. It is estimated that around 70 percent of survival improvement in heart attack mortality is a result of these technological changes (2). New drug-eluting stents show promise of reducing restenosis and subsequent heart attacks still further (6).

Figure 25. Hospital inpatient procedures for insertion of coronary artery stent(s) among adults 45 years of age and over by age: United States, 1996-2003

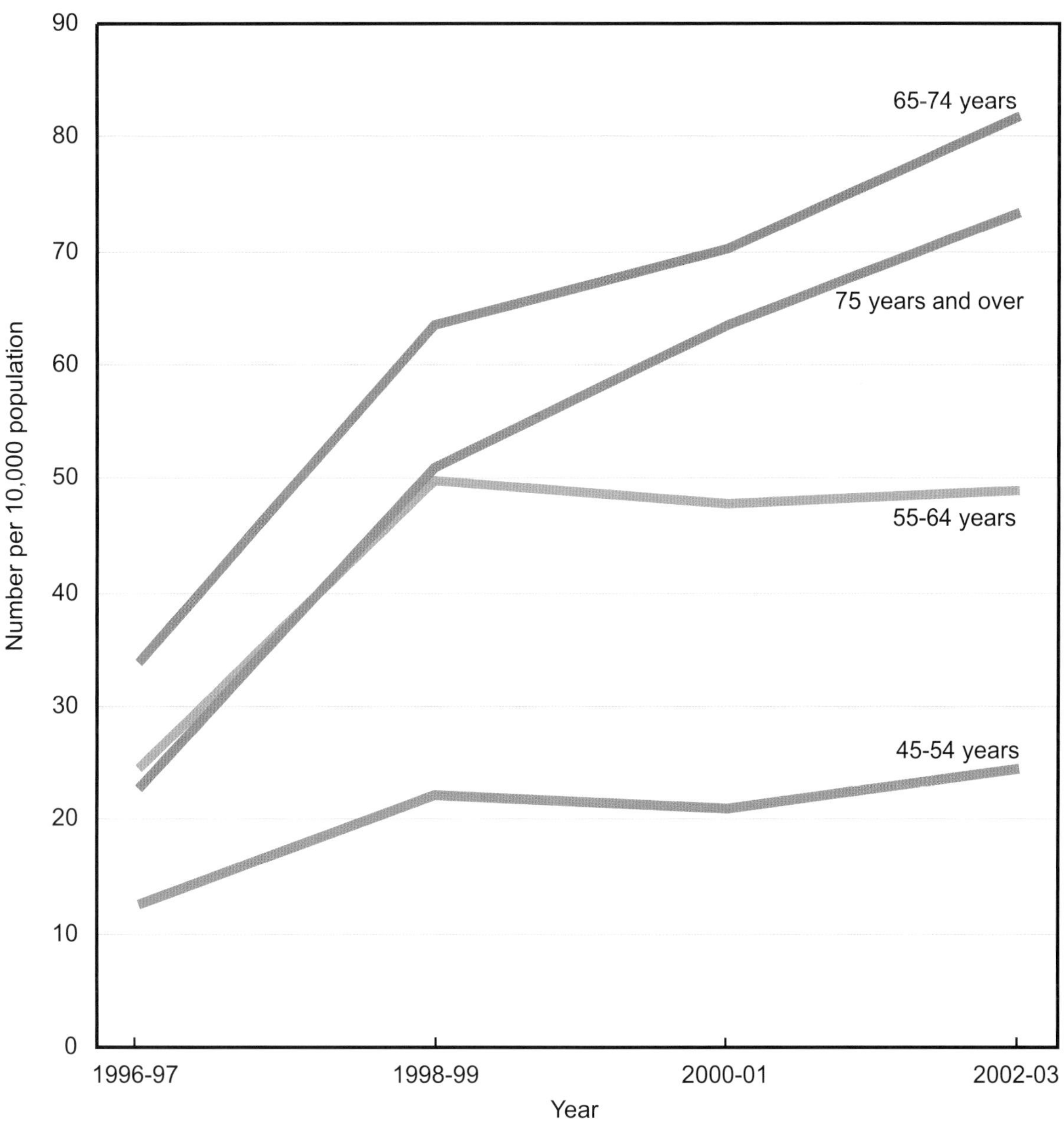

NOTES: Up to four procedures were coded for each hospital stay. Stent procedures were "any-listed" procedures. See Data Table for data points graphed, standard errors, and additional notes.

SOURCE: Centers for Disease Control and Prevention, National Center for Health Statistics, National Hospital Discharge Survey.

Life Expectancy

Life expectancy is a measure often used to gauge the overall health of a population. As a summary measure of mortality, life expectancy represents the average number of years of life that could be expected if current death rates were to remain constant. Shifts in life expectancy are often used to describe trends in mortality. Life expectancy at birth is strongly influenced by infant and child mortality. Life expectancy later in life reflects death rates at or above a given age and is independent of the effect of mortality at younger ages (1).

From the turn of the 20th century through 2002, life expectancy at birth increased from 48 to 75 years for men and from 51 to 80 years for women (figure 26). Improvements in nutrition, housing, hygiene, and medical care contributed to decreases in death rates throughout the lifespan. Prevention and control of infectious diseases had a profound impact on life expectancy in the first half of the 20th century (2).

Life expectancy at age 65 has also increased since the beginning of the 20th century. Among men, life expectancy at age 65 rose from 12 to 17 years and among women from 12 to 20 years. In contrast to life expectancy at birth, which increased sharply early in the century, life expectancy at age 65 improved primarily after 1950. Improved access to health care, advances in medicine, healthier lifestyles, and better health before age 65 are factors underlying decreased death rates among older Americans (3).

While the overall trend in life expectancy for the United States was upward throughout the 20th century, the gain in years of life expectancy for women generally exceeded that for men until the 1970s, widening the gap in life expectancy between men and women. The increasing gap during those years is attributed to increases in male mortality due to ischemic heart disease and lung cancer, both of which rose largely as the result of men's early and widespread adoption of cigarette smoking (4). After the 1970s the gain in life expectancy for men exceeded that for women, and the gender gap in life expectancy began to narrow. Between 1990 and 2002 the total gain in life expectancy for women was 1.1 year compared with 2.7 years for men, reflecting proportionately greater decreases in heart disease and cancer mortality for men than for women and proportionately larger increases in chronic lower respiratory disease mortality among women (4).

Longer life expectancies at birth in many other developed countries suggest the possibility of improving longevity in the United States (*Health, United States, 2005*, table 26). Decreasing death rates of less advantaged groups could raise life expectancy in the United States (*Health, United States, 2005*, table 27).

Figure 26. Life expectancy at birth and at 65 years of age by sex: United States, 1901-2002

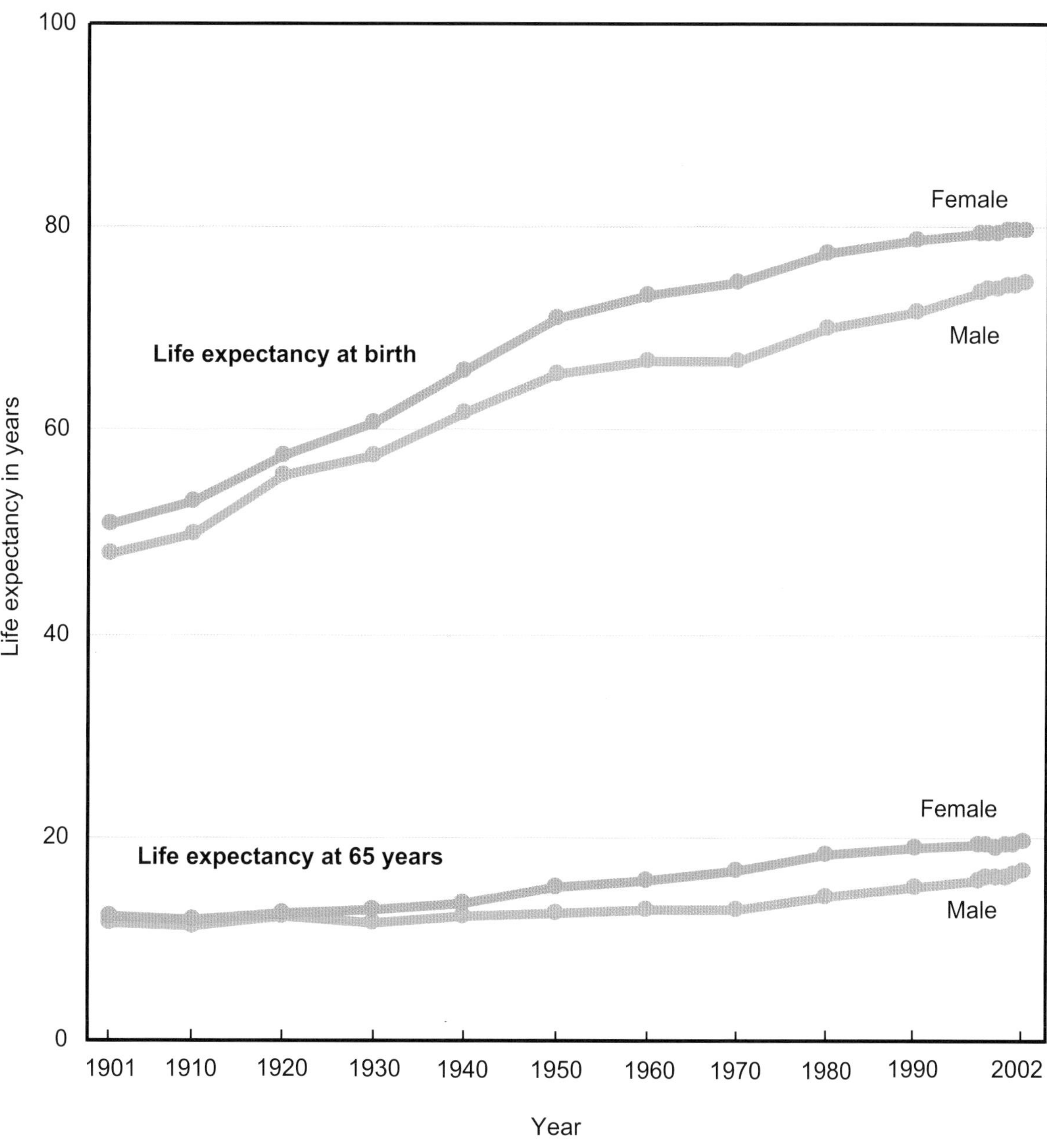

NOTE: See Data Table for data points graphed and additional notes.

SOURCE: Centers for Disease Control and Prevention, National Center for Health Statistics, National Vital Statistics System.

Infant Mortality

Infant mortality, the risk of death during the first year of life, is related to the underlying health of the mother, public health practices, socioeconomic conditions, and availability and use of appropriate health care for infants and pregnant women. Disorders related to short gestation and low birthweight and congenital malformations are the leading causes of death during the neonatal period (less than 28 days of life). Sudden Infant Death Syndrome (SIDS) and congenital malformations rank as the leading causes of infant deaths during the postneonatal period (28 days through 11 months of life) (1).

Between 1950 and 2001 the infant mortality rate declined by almost 77 percent (figure 27 and *Health, United States, 2005*, table 22). In 2002 the infant mortality rate increased to 7.0 infant deaths per 1,000 live births up from 6.8 in 2001 (2,3). This was the first year since 1958 that the rate had not declined or remained unchanged. The rise in infant mortality in 2002 was concentrated among neonatal deaths occurring in the first week of life. A special analysis of the 2002 linked birth/infant death data set found that the increase in infant mortality was due to an increase in the number of infants born weighing less than 750 grams (1 lb 10 1/2 oz), the majority of whom die during the first year of life (4).

Preliminary 2003 data indicated a small, but nonsignificant, decline in the infant mortality rate (5). More information on infant mortality patterns in 2003 will be available when the final mortality data and the linked birth/infant death data set for 2003 are available.

Declines in infant mortality over the past five decades have been linked to improved access to health care, advances in neonatal medicine, and public health education campaigns such as the "Back to Sleep" campaign to curb fatalities caused by SIDS (6).

Infant mortality rates have declined for all racial and ethnic groups, but large disparities remain (*Health, United States, 2005*, table 19). During 2000–2002 the infant mortality rate was highest for infants of non-Hispanic black mothers (figure 28). Infant mortality rates were also high among infants of American Indian or Alaska Native mothers, Puerto Rican mothers, and Hawaiian mothers. Infants of mothers of Chinese origin had the lowest infant mortality rates.

Figure 27. Infant, neonatal, and postneonatal mortality rates: United States, 1950-2002

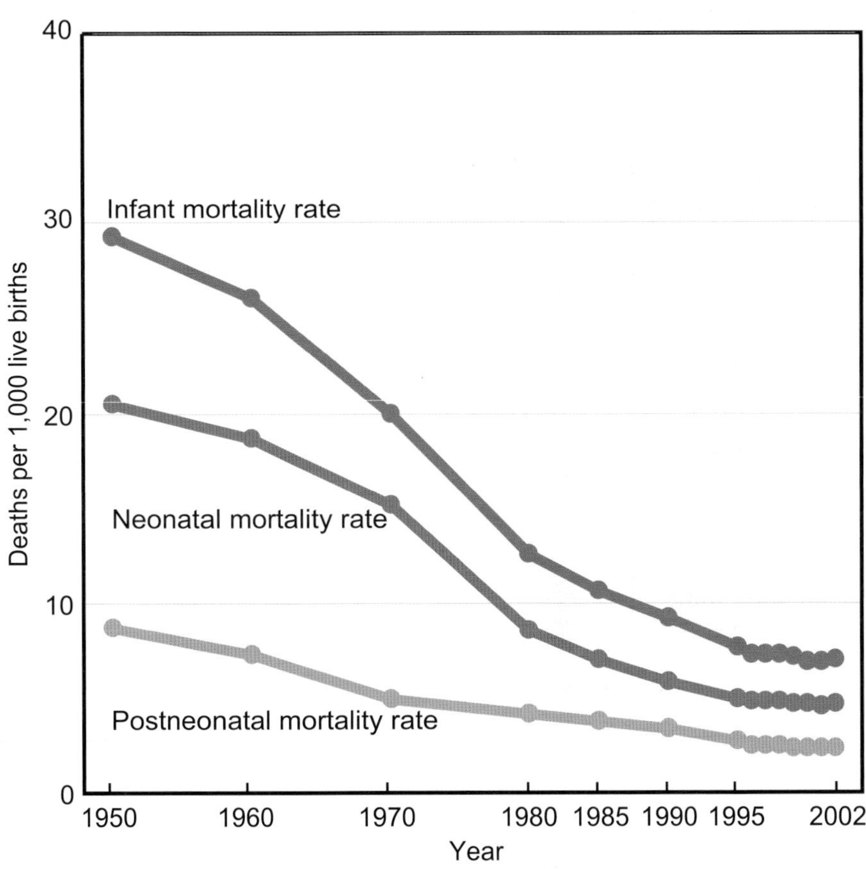

NOTES: Infant is defined as under 1 year of age, neonatal as under 28 days of age, and postneonatal as between 28 days and 1 year of age. See Data Table for data points graphed and additional notes.

SOURCE: Centers for Disease Control and Prevention, National Center for Health Statistics, National Vital Statistics System.

Figure 28. Infant mortality rates by detailed race and Hispanic origin of mother: United States, 2000-2002

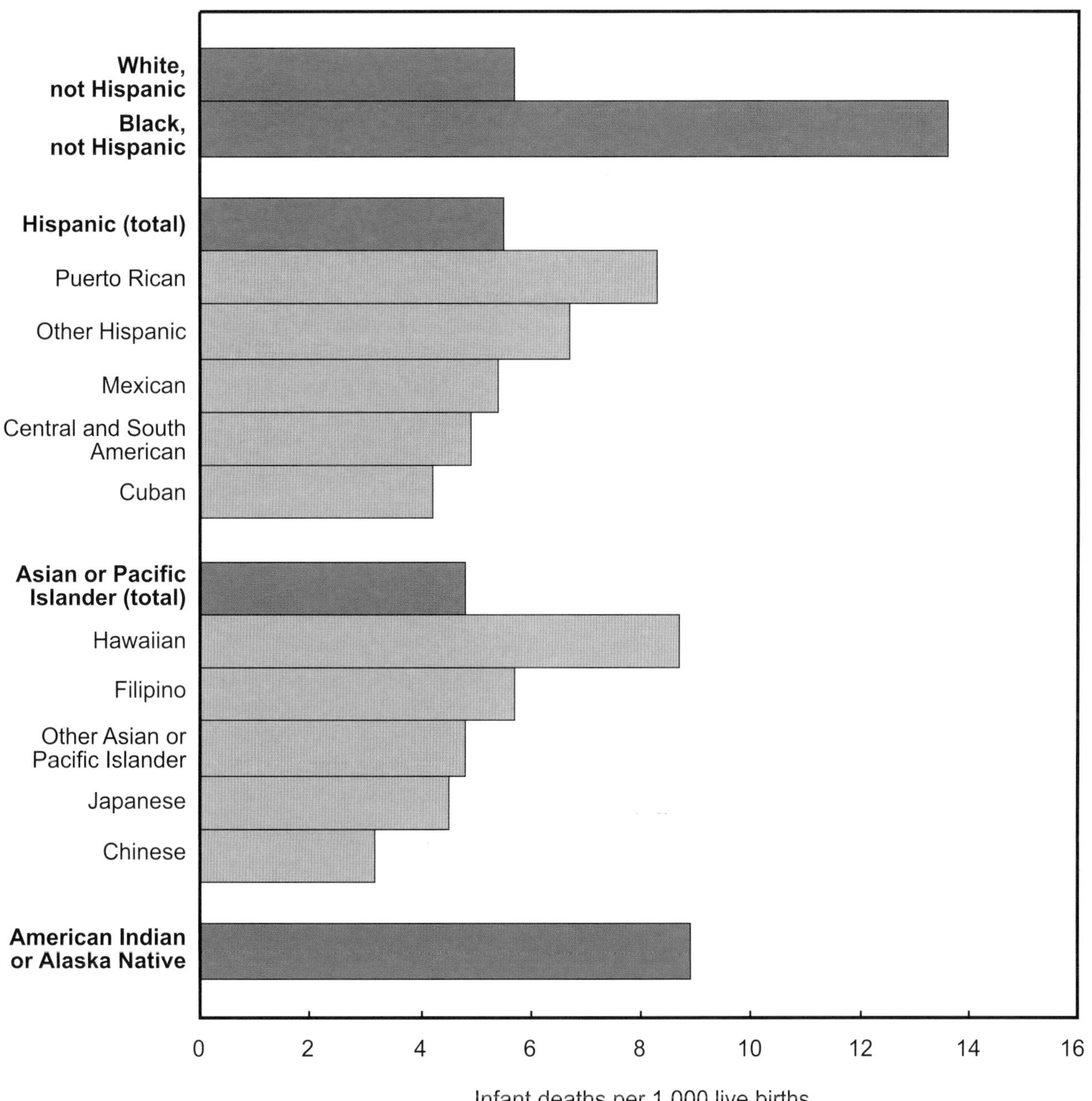

NOTES: Infant is defined as under 1 year of age. Persons of Hispanic origin may be of any race. Asian or Pacific Islander and American Indian or Alaska Native races include persons of Hispanic and non-Hispanic origin. See Data Table for data points graphed and additional notes.

SOURCE: Centers for Disease Control and Prevention, National Center for Health Statistics, National Linked Birth/Infant Death Data Sets.

Leading Causes of Death for All Ages

In 2002 a total of 2.4 million deaths were reported in the United States (*Health, United States, 2005*, table 31). The overall age-adjusted death rate was 42 percent lower in 2002 than it was in 1950. The reduction in overall mortality during the last half of the twentieth century was driven mostly by declines in mortality for such leading causes of death as heart disease, stroke, and unintentional injuries (figure 29).

Throughout the second half of the twentieth century, heart disease was the leading cause of death and stroke was the third leading cause. In 2002 the age-adjusted death rate for heart disease was 59 percent lower than the rate in 1950. The age-adjusted death rate for stroke declined 69 percent since 1950 (*Health, United States, 2005*, tables 36 and 37). Heart disease and stroke mortality are associated with risk factors such as high blood cholesterol, high blood pressure, smoking, and dietary factors. Other important factors include socioeconomic status, obesity, and physical inactivity. Factors contributing to the decline in heart disease and stroke mortality include better control of risk factors, improved access to early detection, and better treatment and care, including new drugs and expanded uses for existing drugs (1).

Cancer was the second leading cause of death throughout the period. Overall age-adjusted death rates for cancer rose between 1960 and 1990 and then reversed direction. Between 1990 and 2002 overall death rates for cancer declined more than 10 percent. In the 1980s cancer death rates for females increased faster and in the 1990s declined more slowly than rates for males, reducing the disparity in cancer death rates. Rates for males were 63 percent higher than rates for females in 1980 and 46 percent higher in 2002. The trend in the overall cancer death rate reflects the trend in the death rate for lung cancer (*Health, United States, 2005*, tables 38 and 39). Since 1970 the death rate for lung cancer for the total population has been higher than the death rate for any other cancer site. Lung cancer is strongly associated with smoking.

Chronic lower respiratory diseases (CLRD) was the fourth leading cause of death in 2002. The age-adjusted death rate for CLRD in 2002 was 54 percent higher than the rate in 1980. The upward trajectory for CLRD death rates is a result of steadily increasing death rates for females, which increased 150 percent between 1980 and 2002, whereas death rates for males increased only 7 percent. The increasing trend for females is most noticeable for females age 55 years and over (*Health, United States, 2005*, table 41). CLRD is strongly associated with smoking.

The fifth leading cause of death in 2002 was unintentional injuries. Age-adjusted death rates for unintentional injuries declined during the period 1950–92 (*Health, United States, 2005*, table 29). Since 1992, however, unintentional injury mortality has gradually increased. Despite recent increases, the death rate for unintentional injuries in 2002 was still 53 percent lower than the rate in 1950. The risk of death due to unintentional injuries is greater for males than females and the risk varies with age. For males age 15–64 years in 2002, the risk of death due to unintentional injuries was 2–3 times the risk for females of those ages. For ages under 15 years and ages 65 years and over, the gender disparity was smaller. The risk of death due to unintentional injuries increased steeply after age 64 years for both males and females (2).

Although overall unintentional injury mortality has increased slightly since the early 1990s, the trend in motor vehicle-related injury mortality, which accounts for approximately one-half of all unintentional injury mortality, has been generally downward since the 1970s (*Health, United States, 2005*, table 44). The decline in death rates for motor vehicle-related injuries is a result of safer vehicles and highways; behavioral changes such as increased use of safety belts, child safety seats, and motorcycle helmets; and decreased drinking and driving (3).

Death rates generally increase with age for chronic diseases such as heart disease, cancer, stroke, and CLRD, as well as for unintentional injuries. Age-adjusted death rates for black persons exceed those for white persons of the same gender for heart disease, stroke, and cancer. Socioeconomic factors are strongly associated with risk of death. Adult males and females with a high school education or less had death rates more than twice as high as the rates for those with more than a high school education in 2002 (*Health, United States, 2005*, table 34).

Figure 29. Death rates for leading causes of death for all ages: United States, 1950-2002

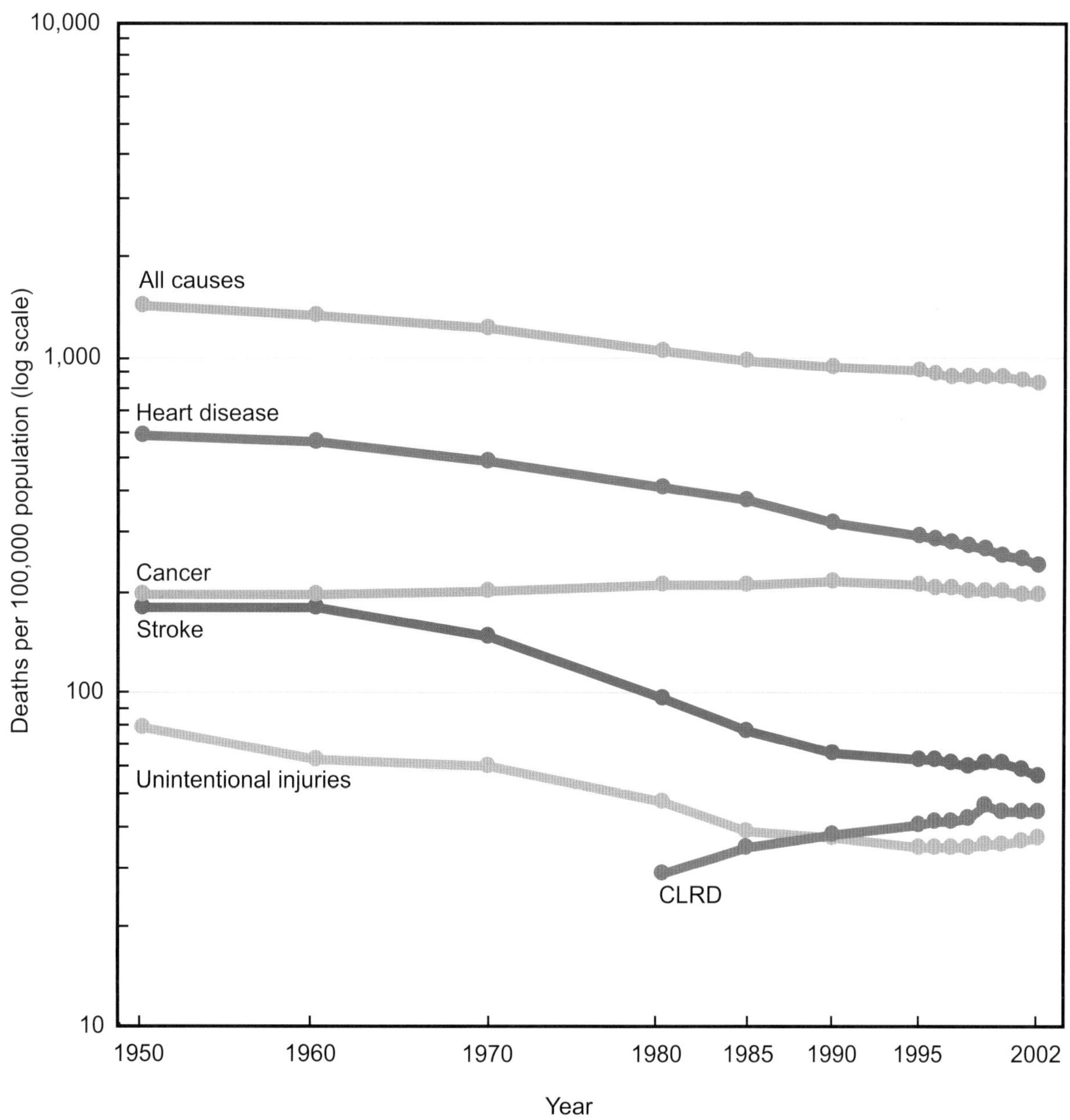

NOTES: Rates are age adjusted. Causes of death shown are the five leading causes of death for all ages in 2002. CLRD is chronic lower respiratory diseases. Starting in 1999 data were coded according to ICD-10. See Data Table for data points graphed and additional notes.

SOURCE: Centers for Disease Control and Prevention, National Center for Health Statistics, National Vital Statistics System.

Introduction

As they approach age 65, many Americans eagerly anticipate the day when they can have more leisure time. This "preretirement age" population, defined in this Special Feature as all adults 55–64 years of age, is projected to be the fastest growing segment of the adult population during the next 10 year period. In 2004 there were about 29 million persons in this age group. The 55–64 age group is projected to increase by 11 million persons over the 2004–14 period, to 40 million persons by 2014 (figure 30). Persons born during the explosive rise in population following World War II, between 1946 and 1964, are referred to as "baby boomers." In 2004 the oldest baby boomers were 55–58 years of age and are just beginning to enter the preretirement age group, with many more boomers aging into the 55–64 age group in the next 10 year period. In future decades the population age 65 years and over will increase dramatically—yet the population age 55–64 will not decline for the next few decades—because more boomers will replace the ones that age into older age groups. By 2029, the youngest of the baby boomers will have reached age 65.

Adults age 55–64 have more frequent and more severe health problems than younger people. The prevalence of diabetes, hypertension, heart disease, and other chronic diseases increase with age (*Health, United States, 2005*, tables 55, 69, 70). In addition, hypertension and obesity have been increasing over time for this age group. Between 1988–94 and 1999–2002 hypertension prevalence rose from 42 to 50 percent and obesity increased from 31 to 39 percent among adults 55–64 years (1).

Between 1997 and 2003 the percent of adults 55–64 years of age who had at least one health care visit in the past year rose from 85 to 89 percent and the percent with 4 or more visits rose from 43 to 50 percent (*Health, United States, 2005*, table 75). Strengthened efforts to identify and modify risk factors for chronic diseases may contribute to this greater use of health care services. This increased vigilance in screening and modifying risk factors is intended to reduce morbidity and improve quality of life. All Americans, including those age 55–64 years, are targeted for identification and intervention of heart disease risk factors (e.g., high serum cholesterol, high blood sugar, overweight, and high blood pressure) and cancer screening (2–5). Clinical guidelines have also increased the number of candidates for hypertension-lowering therapy and blood sugar control. Rates of office visits with prescribed cholesterol-lowering and blood glucose regulating drugs have increased dramatically in recent years (figure 36).

Figure 30. Aging of the population 45 years of age and over: United States, 2004, 2014, and 2024

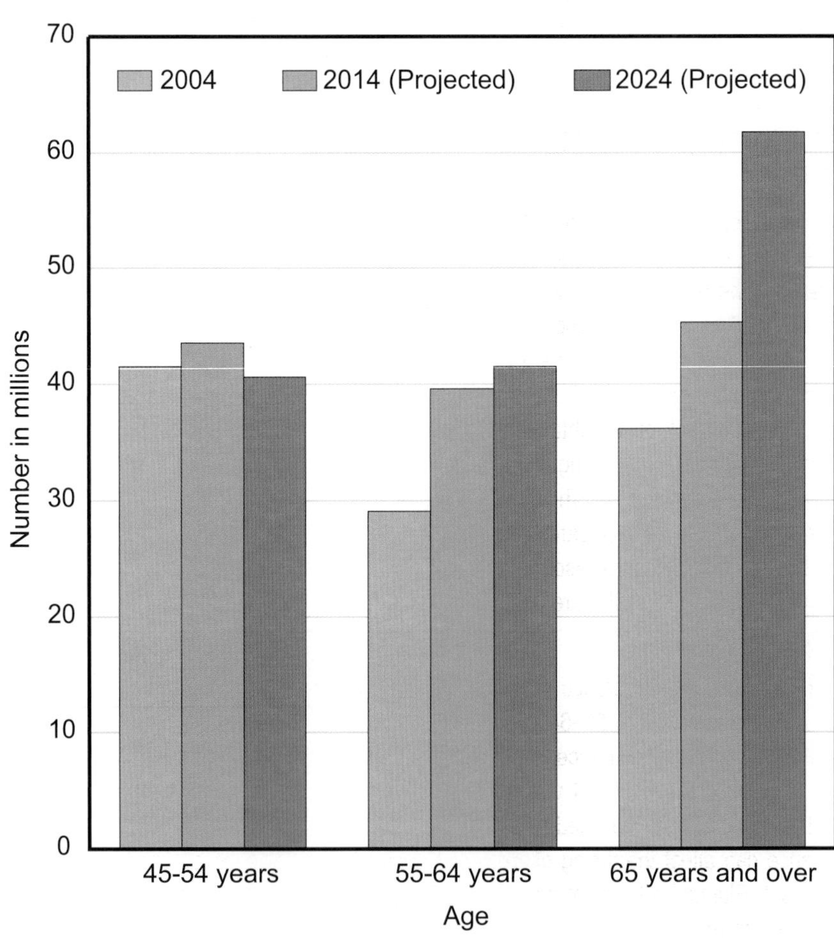

NOTE: See Data Table for data points graphed and additional notes.

SOURCE: U.S. Census Bureau.

Health insurance coverage is an important determinant of access to health services and is of particular importance for people with chronic conditions that require ongoing care. Whereas Americans age 55–64 years are more likely to be insured than other working-age adults under age 65, preretirement age adults do not have the guarantee of health insurance coverage that Medicare offers to almost all older adults age 65 and over (*Health, United States, 2005*, table 134). The 11 percent of 55–64 year olds who have no health insurance may find it difficult to buy insurance in the private market (data table for figure 33). Private nongroup health insurance is generally considerably more expensive than employer-sponsored health insurance, and preexisting health conditions often increase premiums in the nongroup market (6).

Uninsured persons may postpone or not receive care that could have prevented or delayed the progression of various diseases and conditions. Those uninsured due to disability or the inability to work because of a health condition are at particular risk of not obtaining needed services or of incurring high out-of-pocket expenditures. When they do become eligible for Medicare they may use more health care resources as a result of deferring health care that was needed at earlier ages (7).

The changing health insurance market is also affecting people age 55–64 who currently have health insurance. Among employed persons age 55–64 years with health care coverage, the need for health insurance can affect the timing of their retirement. Planned retirement may be postponed to maintain individual or dependent health insurance coverage. Many employers that continue to offer retirees health benefits have reduced benefits, particularly prescription drug coverage, and many have shifted costs they previously paid to their retirees through expenditure caps and various increases in cost-sharing provisions such as increased premiums, copayments and deductibles (8,9). Future cuts in retiree health insurance benefits have implications both for currently employed 55–64 year olds, as well as for the growing number of aging baby boomers entering that age group.

While many Americans age 55–64 are in good health and relatively well off financially, minorities, primarily African Americans, American Indians, and persons of Hispanic origin, are more likely than non-Hispanic white Americans to have chronic health problems, live in poverty, lack insurance coverage, and be unable to work because of a disability (figures 31–33) (10,11). The percent of the population that is black or Hispanic is increasing. If current racial and ethnic disparities do not narrow, this trend could indicate even higher prevalence of obesity, diabetes, hypertension, and other diseases more common in minorities and a corresponding higher burden on the health care system.

This special feature focuses on the health care use and its determinants for the population age 55–64 years including their employment status, income, health insurance, heart disease risk factors, and health care utilization and expenses. Focusing on this age group may provide insight into program and policy interventions that could both improve access and quality of care for Americans age 55–64 years as well as to highlight implications for the Medicare system as this large age group looms at its doorstep.

Employment Status

In 2002–03, 58 percent of adults 55–64 years of age were employed (data table for figure 31) compared with nearly 80 percent of younger adults 35–54 years of age (1). Adults 55–64 years of age who were not working were either retired, unemployed due to disability, keeping house, looking for work, or not working for some other reason. Employment, or past employment, is a determinant of access to health care both in terms of supplying income to pay for care and also because employer-sponsored health insurance is frequently offered to employees. Persons who are not working because of a disability often have considerable medical expenditures and thus have a greater need for health insurance than less disabled persons.

Men 55–64 years of age were more likely to be working at a job or business for pay than women (figure 31). Data from the National Health Interview Survey show that about two-thirds of men 55–64 years of age were working for pay in 2002–03 compared with about one-half of women in that age group (data table for figure 31). Although men were more likely than women to be working, the percent of women 55–64 years in the labor force has increased substantially over the past 20 years. Between 1982 and 2002 the percent of women 55–64 years who were employed increased 32 percent, whereas the percent of men 55–64 years who were employed decreased slightly (2). In 2002–03 there was no difference between men and women in the percent who were retired (17 percent) or who said they were unemployed due to disability (12 percent) when asked the reason they had not been working for pay at a job or business the previous week. Women were more likely to be taking care of house or family than were men.

In 2002–03 employment status differed by race and ethnicity. Non-Hispanic white men and Hispanic men were more likely to be working (about 65 percent) than non-Hispanic black men (57 percent). Among women, a little over one-half of non-Hispanic white women were working compared with 46 percent of non-Hispanic black women and 41 percent of Hispanic women. Hispanic women in this age group were more likely to be taking care of home or family than non-Hispanic women. Hispanic men and women were less likely to be retired than non-Hispanic adults 55–64 years.

Unemployment due to disability was higher for non-Hispanic black men and women age 55–64 years than for other racial and ethnic groups. In 2002–03, about one-fifth of non-Hispanic black men and one-quarter of non-Hispanic black women were unemployed due to a disability compared with 15 percent of Hispanic adults and 10 percent of non-Hispanic white adults. This self-reported higher prevalence of unemployment because of disability among black adults is confirmed by data on Medicare enrollment for the disabled, which includes those with end-stage renal disease. In 2001, 16 percent of the disabled Medicare enrollees age 45–64 years were black adults, higher than would be expected given that they represent 11 percent of the population in this age group (*Health, United States, 2005*, tables 1 and 141). African Americans have higher rates of enrollment in the Medicare End-Stage Renal Disease Program, which is in part explained by their higher prevalence of diabetes and hypertension, risk factors for kidney disease (3,4). Hispanic adults accounted for 11 percent of disabled Medicare beneficiaries age 45–64 years, though they represented only 8 percent of the population in this age group in 2001. Higher rates of unemployment due to disability for black and Hispanic adults may be explained in part by higher prevalence of heart, kidney, and other diseases (5). In addition, health problems are more often disabling for Hispanic and black workers because their jobs are more likely to be physically demanding than the jobs of white workers and less likely to be able to accommodate a disabled or partially disabled worker (6).

Figure 31. Employment status among adults 55-64 years of age by sex, race and Hispanic origin: United States, 2002-03

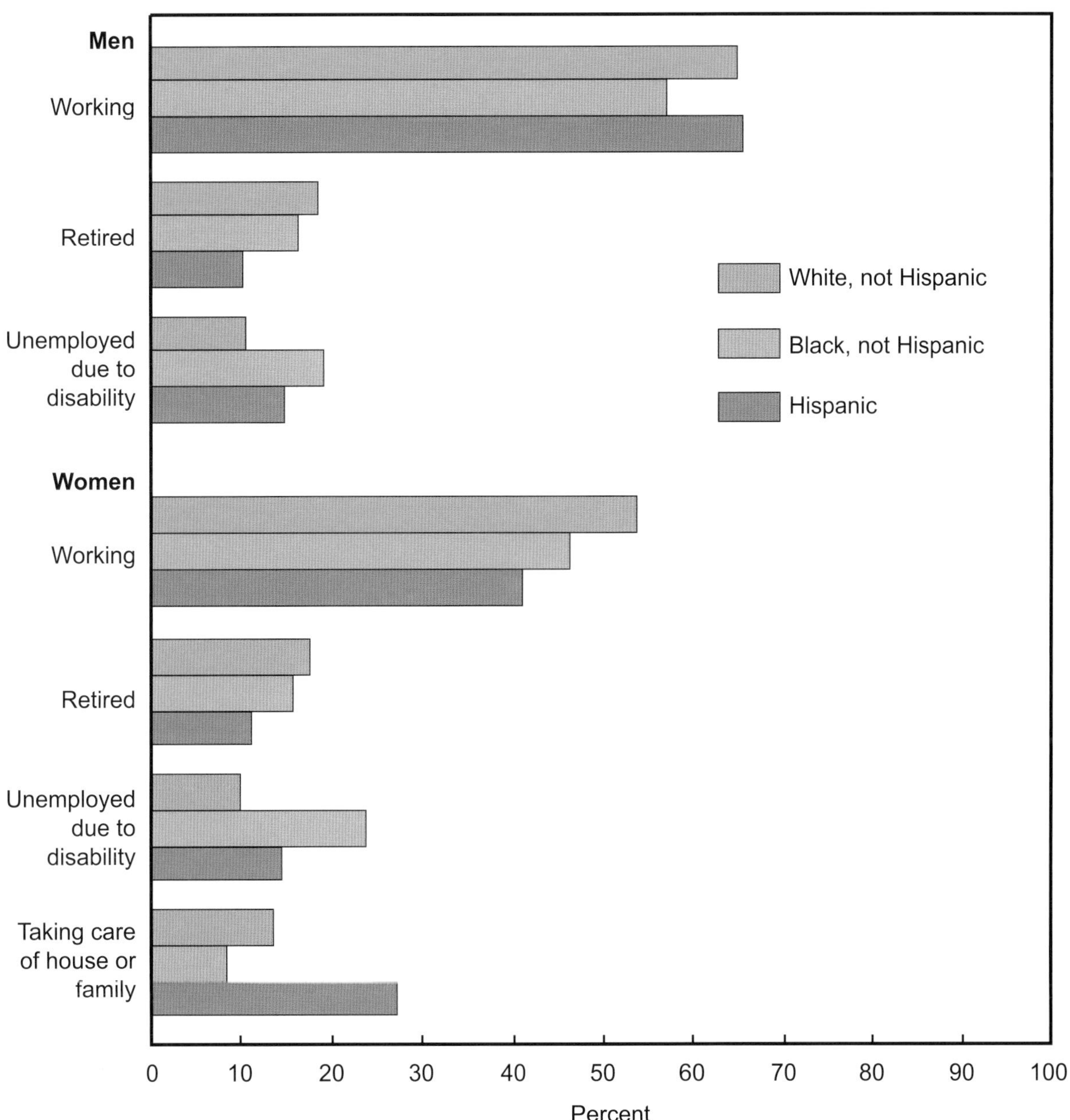

NOTES: Data are for the civilian noninstitutionalized population. Persons of Hispanic origin may be of any race. See Data Table for data points graphed, standard errors, and additional notes.

SOURCE: Centers for Disease Control and Prevention, National Center for Health Statistics, National Health Interview Survey.

Low Income

People with low income are more likely to be in poor health and have a higher prevalence of many serious chronic diseases than those with higher incomes (*Health, United States, 2005*, tables 56, 57, 60, 61, 85). Their worse health is a result of many factors including a higher prevalence of health risk factors, poor nutrition and housing, occupational and environmental hazards, and other social ills (1). Poor health may also contribute to poverty by reducing the ability to earn income. People living below or near the poverty level are also more likely to lack health insurance, which, combined with their low incomes reduces their access to health care (*Health, United States, 2005*, tables 75, 134, figure 7).

In general the preretirement age population 55–64 years has higher incomes than older persons age 65 and over. In 2003 more than one-fifth of the population age 55–64 had incomes below 200 percent of poverty, compared with almost two-fifths of older persons age 65 years and over. More older adults than preretirement age adults had incomes in the 100–199 percent of poverty range. The percent living below 100 percent of poverty, however, was similar for the two groups (about 10 percent) (2).

There is large variation in the poverty distribution by gender and race and Hispanic origin for the preretirement age population (figure 32). In 2003 women 55–64 years of age were more likely than men to be living in poverty (10 percent compared with 8 percent). Both non-Hispanic black and Hispanic men and women were about twice as likely to be living in or near poverty as non-Hispanic white adults. In addition, non-Hispanic black and Hispanic women were more likely to be poor than their male counterparts.

It is unclear how the poverty distribution for this age group will change in the future. The baby boom generation is better educated and wealthier than previous generations and it is likely that as they age they will maintain their economic advantage compared with current retirees (3,4). However, beginning in 2001 the poverty rate for the total population has been rising. In addition, because poverty rates differ by population subgroup, differential population growth and immigration rates may affect future disparities in income (5).

Income for persons age 55–64 is not likely to increase and will probably decrease upon retirement. Persons 55–64 currently living in poverty most often cannot expect future increases in their employment-based incomes (3,6). Employment prospects at this age for poor and near poor persons diminish and are most often limited to low income jobs with few fringe benefits (6).

Figure 32. Low income among adults 55-64 years of age by sex, race and Hispanic origin: United States, 2003

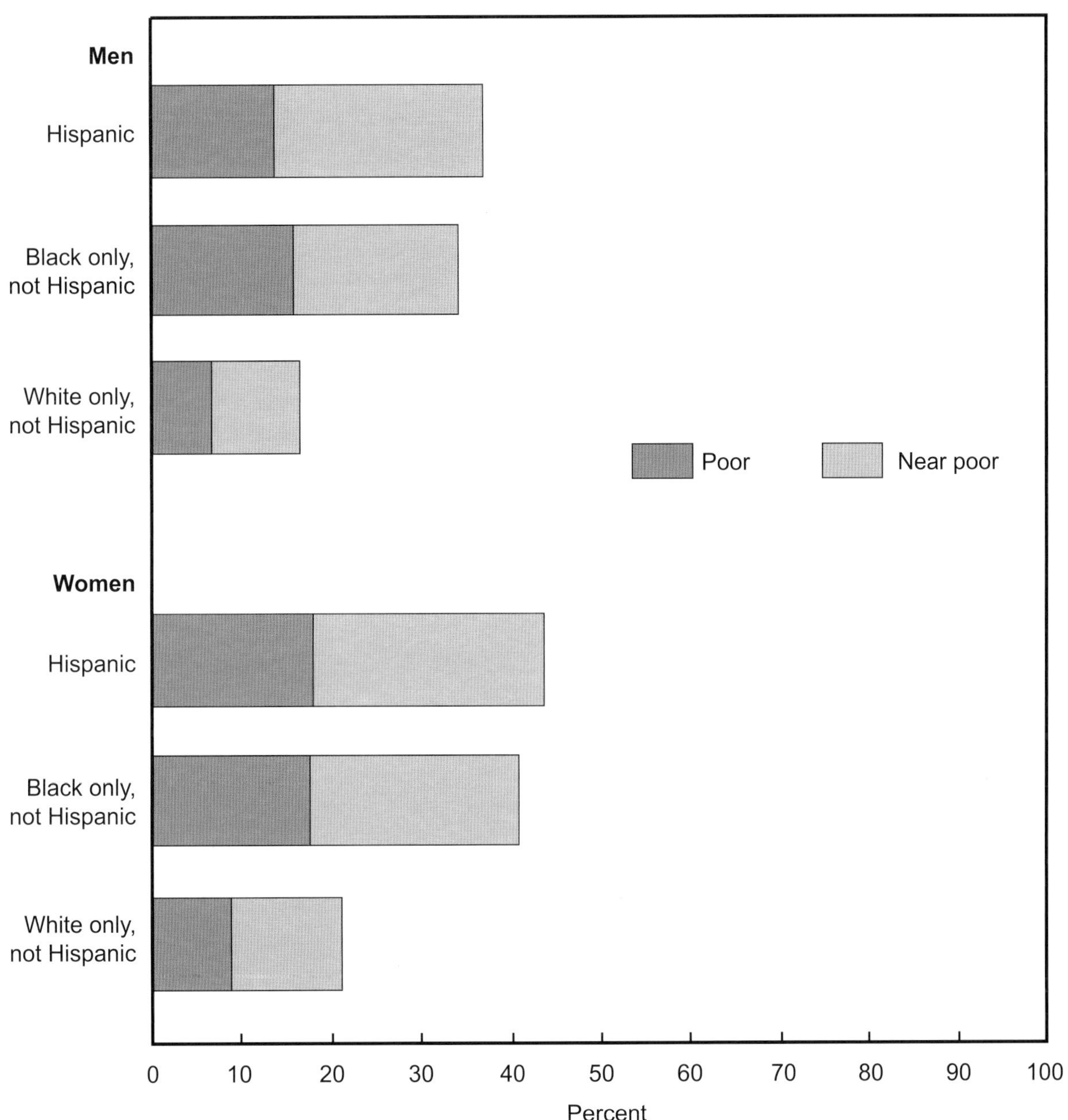

NOTES: Poor is defined as family income less than 100 percent of the poverty level and near poor as 100-199 percent of the poverty level. See Data Table for data points graphed and additional notes.

SOURCE: U.S. Census Bureau, Current Population Survey.

Health Insurance Coverage

Adults 55–64 years of age are reaching a time of life when health problems are likely to become more frequent and more serious. Consequently, persons of this age group are likely to have greater health care needs, on average, than younger persons. Unless adults 55–64 years are disabled or suffer from certain serious chronic conditions, they are not eligible for Medicare, the Federal health program for the disabled and those 65 years of age and over. Some people in this group may have incomes low enough to qualify for Medicaid, the joint Federal and State program serving the poor, or may qualify for other coverage such as from the Department of Veterans Affairs, which is available for persons who have served in the military. However, most adults 55–64 years of age do not qualify for public health insurance coverage and are heavily reliant on private health insurance to finance their health care needs.

Employer-sponsored private health insurance is usually preferable to individually-purchased private health insurance both in terms of more generous benefits and the lower costs resulting from group plan underwriting rates and the financial contributions by employers to the health plan (1–3). Post-retirement health insurance offers by large private-sector firms have been declining (4). Among employers that are continuing to offer retirees health benefits, most have made changes to their benefit packages, including dropping retiree coverage for new employees and shifting costs onto others. Sixty-four percent of firms reported that they are very likely to increase retiree contributions to premiums, and 54 percent are very likely to increase cost sharing (5). This trend is likely to affect both currently employed 55–64 year olds as well as those who will enter the 55–64 year old age group in the future.

In 2002–03 among persons 55–64 years there was a strong relationship between marital status and health insurance regardless of gender. Married persons often have two opportunities to obtain health insurance—through their own employment or their spouse's. Among married preretirement age adults 83 percent were covered by private health insurance compared with about 60 percent of widowed, separated or divorced, and single adults (figure 33). Levels of public coverage were over 2 times as high for unmarried adults as married adults. Among those who were widowed, separated or divorced, or single the percent with no health insurance ranged from 16–18 percent compared with 9 percent for married adults.

Although there was little difference between men and women in the relationship between health insurance coverage and marital status, there were significant differences in marital status for men and women. In 2002–03 preretirement age men were more likely to be married than women (79 percent compared with 66 percent). Women were more than 3 times as likely to be widowed as men (11 percent compared with 3 percent), reflecting both the greater longevity of women and the tendency for women to be a few years younger than their husbands. Women were also more likely to be separated or divorced than men (19 percent compared with 14 percent). These differences were even more pronounced by sex and race and Hispanic origin. Forty-one percent of non-Hispanic black women were currently married compared with 80 percent of non-Hispanic white men (6). Because being married is associated with higher rates of health insurance, minority women, in particular, are more at risk for being uninsured than other groups, as well as more likely to live in poverty (figure 32).

Figure 33. Health insurance coverage among adults 55-64 years of age by marital status: United States, 2002-03

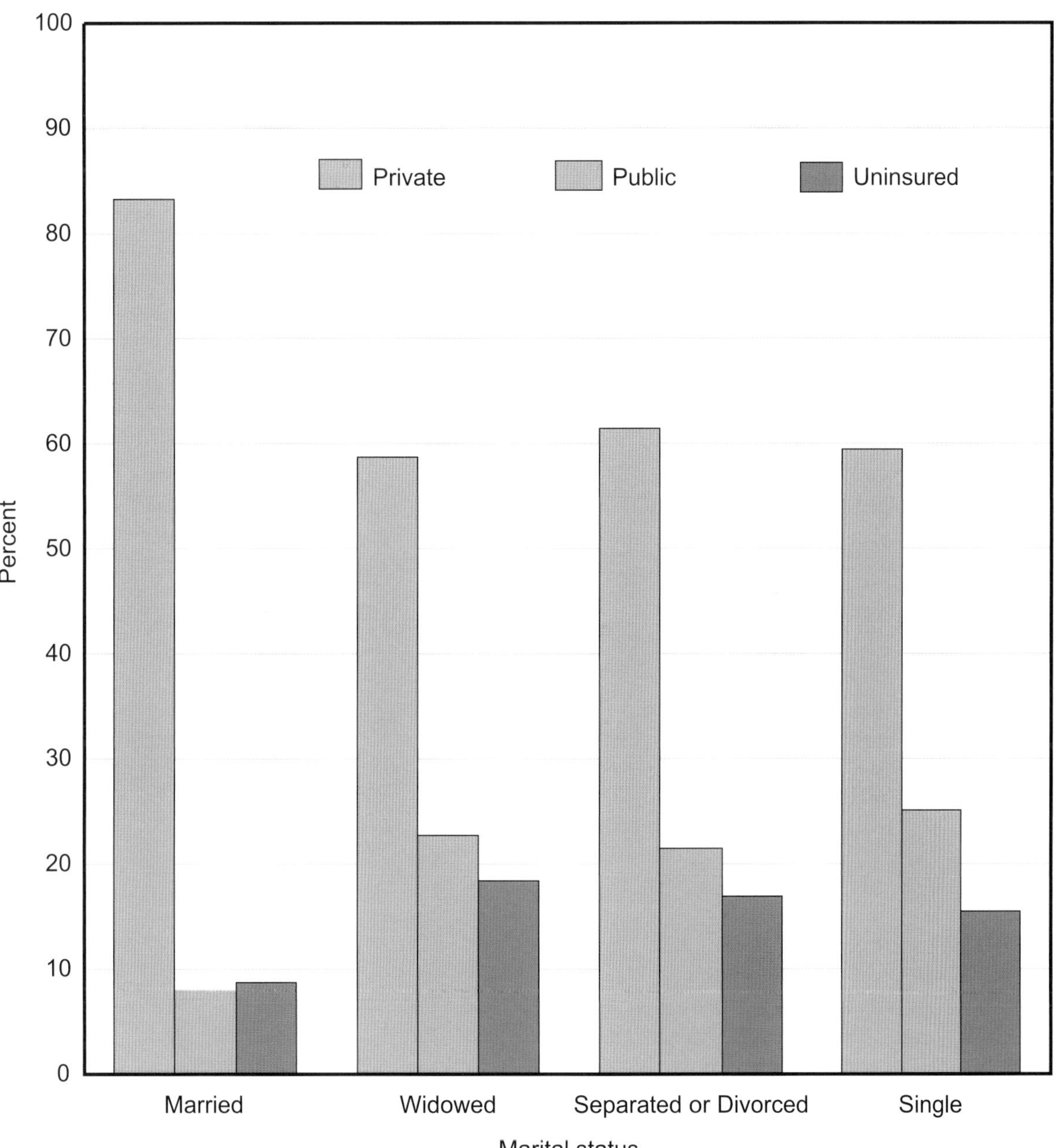

NOTES: Public includes Medicare, Medicaid, SCHIP, Military, and other State and government sponsored health plans. Uninsured adults are not covered by private or public coverage. See Data Table for data points graphed, standard errors, and additional notes.

SOURCE: Centers for Disease Control and Prevention, National Center for Health Statistics, National Health Interview Survey.

Cardiovascular Risk Factors

Hypertension, obesity, and high cholesterol are all independent risk factors for the leading causes of death in the United States—heart disease and stroke (1,2). Hypertension is also a major risk factor for congestive heart failure and kidney failure. Being obese is associated with increased risk of morbidity and mortality (3). High cholesterol increases the likelihood of developing heart disease and raises the risk of heart attacks among those with heart disease (4).

Previous research has found that the prevalence rates for obesity, hypertension, and cholesterol abnormalities are higher at older ages and that having each of these three risk factors substantially increases the risk for cardiovascular morbidity (2,5). People with multiple risk factors are at higher jeopardy for coronary heart disease and stroke than those with a single risk factor and the likelihood of heart disease and stroke increases as the number of risk factors increases.

The National Health and Nutrition Examination Survey (NHANES) collects information on hypertension, high cholesterol, and obesity through in-person household interviews, and physical exams and blood work conducted in a mobile examination center. Hypertension is defined as having either elevated blood pressure (systolic pressure of at least 140 mmHg or diastolic pressure of at least 90 mmHg) or taking antihypertensive medication. High serum cholesterol is defined as having total serum cholesterol greater than or equal to 240 mg/dL. Obesity is defined as having a body mass index greater than or equal to 30 (see Appendix II, Body mass index).

The percent of adults 55–64 years of age who have hypertension increased from 42 to 50 percent between 1988–94 and 1999–2002 (data table for figure 34). During the same time period, obesity increased from 31 to 39 percent of adults in this age group. In contrast, the percent of Americans age 55–64 with elevated cholesterol decreased between 1988–94 and 1999–2002, in part due to growing awareness about the risks of high cholesterol and the increased use of cholesterol-lowering medications.

Between 1988–94 and 1999–2002 the percent of adults 55–64 years of age with one or more of the three cardiovascular risk factors examined remained level at about 70 percent (data table for figure 34). However, the pattern differed for men and women (figure 34). In 1988–94 women 55–64 years of age were more likely than men to have one or more risk factor for cardiovascular disease (73 percent compared with 64 percent). By 1999–2002 the percent of men with one or more risk factors had risen to the level for women.

In 1999–2002 women in this age group were more likely than men to have elevated cholesterol and hypertension and the more serious condition of combinations of two or three cardiovascular risk factors. In 1999–2002, 39 percent of women and 24 percent of men age 55–64 years had two or three of these risk factors (data table for figure 34). Almost one-half of non-Hispanic black adults had two or three of the risk factors, compared with just under one-third of non-Hispanic white and Mexican adults (6).

Figure 34. Cardiovascular risk factors (hypertension, obesity, and high cholesterol) among adults 55-64 years of age by sex: United States, 1988-94 and 1999-2002

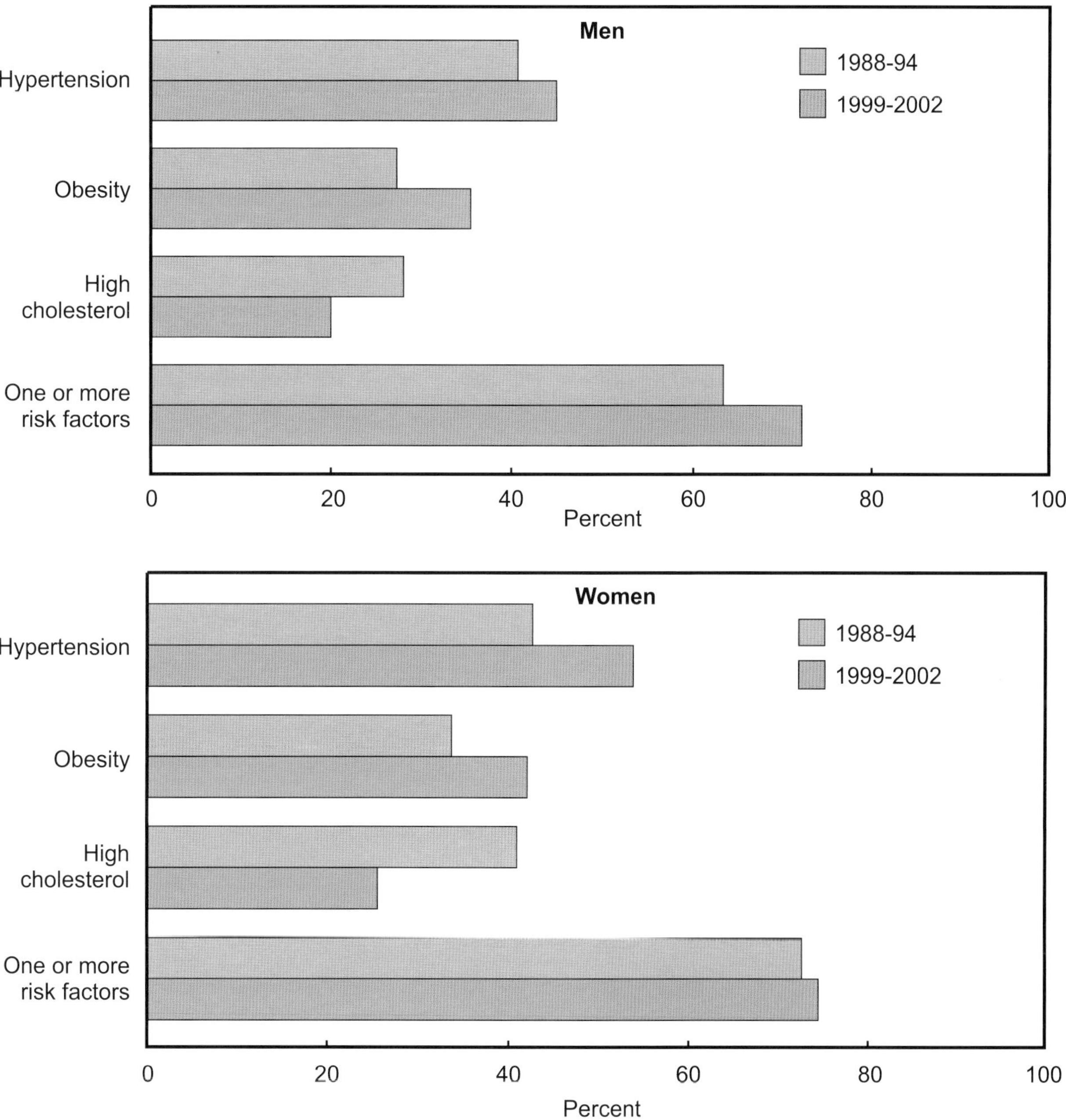

NOTES: Hypertension is defined as either having elevated blood pressure (systolic pressure of at least 140 mmHg or diastolic pressure of at least 90 mmHg) or taking antihypertensive medication. Obesity is defined as a body mass index (BMI) greater than or equal to 30. High serum cholesterol is defined as having measured total serum cholesterol greater than or equal to 240 mg/dL (6.20 mmol/L).

See Data Table for data points graphed, standard errors, and additional notes.

SOURCE: Centers for Disease Control and Prevention, National Center for Health Statistics, National Health and Nutrition Examination Survey.

Use of Health Care Services

People seek care from health professionals to receive preventive and screening services, diagnosis and treatment, counseling, and other health care services. Visits run the continuum from emergency and critical care to services designed to maintain quality of life and functioning. Visits to health professionals are influenced by factors in addition to medical need. Health insurance coverage, ability to pay for services not covered by health insurance, capability to travel to the services, availability of services, and compliance with health care professionals' recommendations to obtain tests or treatment all influence visit patterns (1). These factors vary by race and Hispanic origin, sex, and marital status (figures 31–33). In 2002–03, nearly 90 percent of the population 55–64 years of age had at least one visit to a health care provider such as a primary care physician, specialist physician, therapist, eye doctor, or mental health professional in the past 12-month period (2).

Persons age 55–64 years who have Medicare coverage are eligible primarily through being permanently disabled or having end-stage renal disease. Persons in this age group who have Medicaid coverage also qualify primarily through medical need as well as poverty status (see Appendix II, Medicare and Medicaid). Because of these eligibility criteria, persons age 55–64 years with public coverage have worse health status than the general population age 55–64. A greater percent of persons 55–64 years of age with public coverage reported at least one visit to a general physician, specialist physician, physical or other therapist, or mental health professional than those with private coverage or the uninsured, in part reflecting the higher disease burden in this group (figure 35).

Uninsured persons 55–64 years of age were considerably less likely to have ambulatory health care visits from many types of health care providers in the past year than persons with private insurance. About one-half of the uninsured saw a general physician compared with more than three-quarters of those with private insurance. The percent with a visit to an eye doctor was similar for those with public and private insurance coverage but lower for those without insurance. The uninsured were about one-half as likely to report visits to specialist physicians, eye doctors, and physical or other therapists compared with those with private insurance.

Uninsured persons age 55–64 were about as likely as those with private coverage to report being told by a health care professional that they have one of several common chronic conditions, including arthritis, hypertension, diabetes, heart disease, and serious psychological distress (2). Because the uninsured are less likely to obtain medical care, prevalence rates of diagnosed conditions may be underestimated for many conditions such as hypertension and diabetes that are difficult to diagnose without medical tests.

There is evidence that lack of health insurance among midlife adults discourages routine care that may delay or reduce the future impact of chronic conditions (3,4). Previously uninsured persons may increase their use of clinical services once they reach age 65 and became eligible for Medicare (5). "Catch-up" use of Medicare services by newly-eligible participants has implications for future Medicare expenditures.

Figure 35. Visits to health professionals in the past 12 months among adults 55-64 years of age by health insurance status: United States, 2002-03

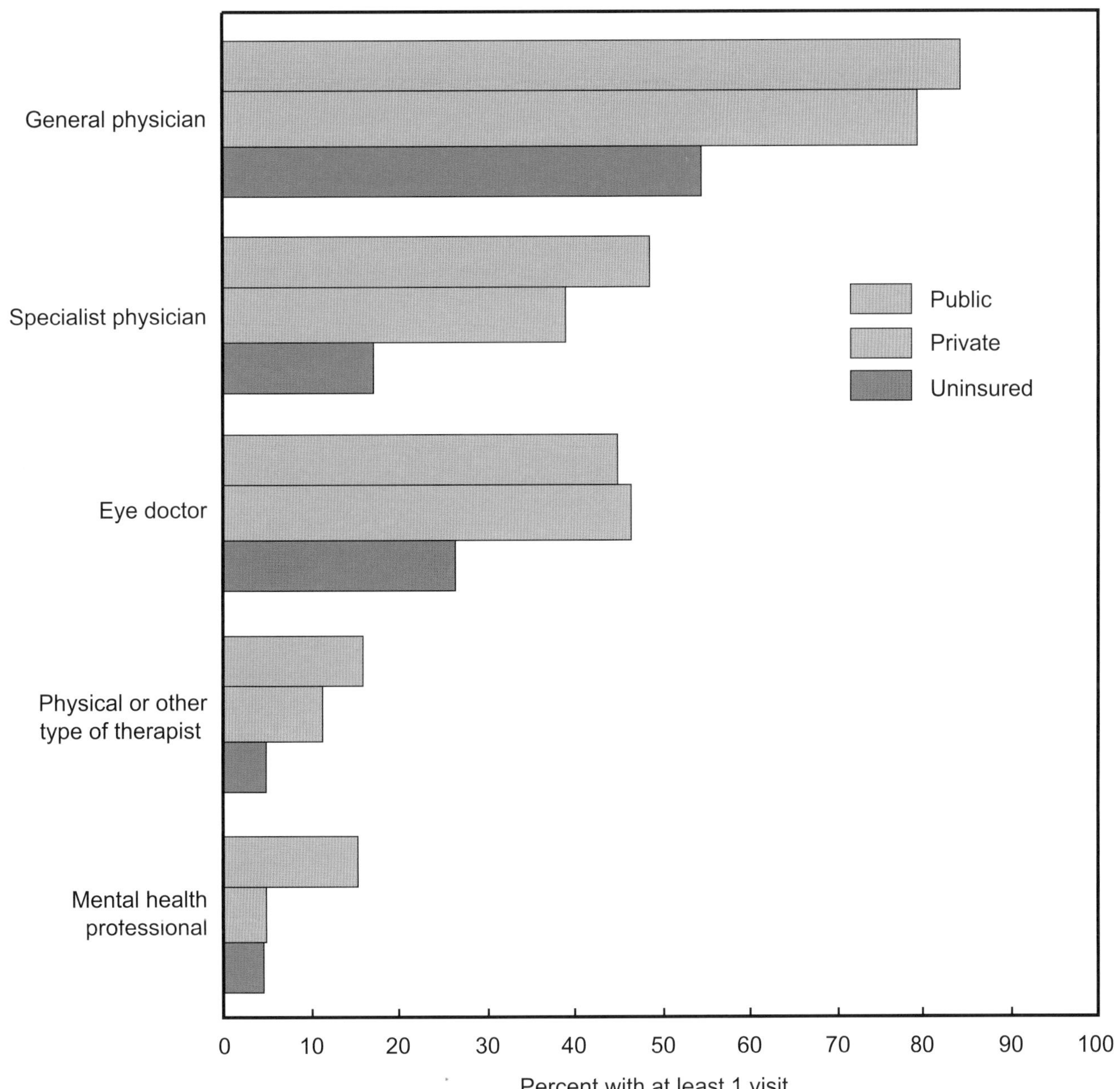

NOTES: Respondents were asked if they had seen or talked to selected types of health professionals within the past 12 months. Physical or other type of therapist includes visits to an audiologist or physical, speech, respiratory, or occupational therapist. See Data Table for data points graphed, standard errors, and additional notes.

SOURCE: Centers for Disease Control and Prevention, National Center for Health Statistics, National Health Interview Survey.

Blood Glucose Regulators and Cholesterol-Lowering Drugs Prescribed During Medical Visits

Drugs—both prescription and over the counter—are becoming a more frequently utilized therapy for reducing morbidity and mortality and improving the quality of life of Americans (1). Prevalence of many chronic conditions and diseases increases with age, with concurrent use of medications designed to help control or prevent complications associated with those conditions. In 1999–2002, 73 percent of adults 55–64 years of age reported taking at least one prescription drug during the past month compared with 62 percent in 1988–94 (2).

Factors contributing to the increase in utilization of medications include the growth of third-party insurance coverage for drugs; the availability of effective new drugs; marketing to physicians and increasingly directly to consumers; and more aggressive clinical guidelines recommending increased use of medications for conditions such as high cholesterol, high blood pressure, chronic asthma, and diabetes (3,4). A greater emphasis on screening for common conditions and beginning medication therapy before permanent damage to body systems occurs has also contributed to greater use of drug therapy.

Data on drugs associated with medical visits are available from the National Ambulatory Medical Care Survey (NAMCS) and National Hospital Ambulatory Medical Care Survey (NHAMCS Outpatient Department Component). These surveys abstract information from medical records of physician office and hospital outpatient department visits, including information on the number and type of prescription and over-the-counter drugs, immunizations, allergy injections, and anesthetics that were prescribed during the in-person visit. Until 2002, up to six medications could be recorded on the visit record. Beginning in 2003, up to eight medications may be recorded. A visit with drugs is defined as a visit where at least one drug was prescribed, ordered, supplied, administered, or continued. Drug rates are presented as drugs per 100 population, which is calculated as the number of drugs recorded during visits for the 2-year period divided by the sum of the population estimates for both years, times 100. If more than one drug in a selected drug class was recorded on the visit record, then that drug class was counted multiple times. Data from NAMCS and NHAMCS provide information on overall medication prescribing patterns in addition to documenting the burden and complexity that medication management presents to the health care system and to consumers.

The prevalence of diagnosed diabetes among adults 55–64 years of age has been increasing (5). Diabetes is associated with numerous serious health complications, including amputations, heart disease, eye disease and blindness, and kidney disease (6,7). Improved glucose control decreases the risk of complications. Diabetes treatment may include dietary management, increased physical activity, oral medications, and insulin. New and better types of oral diabetes medications have been introduced over the past two decades. The rate of blood glucose regulators prescribed during physician and hospital outpatient department visits increased between 1995–96 and 2002–03, for both men and women (figure 36). In 2002–03 the rates of these drugs prescribed were similar for men and women age 55–64 at 45–48 drugs per 100 persons.

High cholesterol is a known risk factor for heart disease. Updated national guidelines and growing awareness about the risks of high cholesterol have contributed to greater diagnosis and treatment of elevated serum cholesterol (8). Cholesterol levels can be reduced by lifestyle modifications, including losing excess weight and increasing physical activity. If such modifications do not reduce cholesterol to target levels, then drug therapy may be warranted. Between 1995–96 and 2002–03 the rate of cholesterol-lowering drugs prescribed during medical visits among those 55–64 years of age more than doubled (data table for figure 36). By 2002–03 the rate of cholesterol-lowering drugs prescribed among men age 55–64 years had increased to 57 drugs per 100 men. Over the same time period, the rate of cholesterol-lowering drugs prescribed for women increased from 15 to 49 drugs per 100 women (figure 36).

Figure 36. Blood glucose regulators and cholesterol-lowering drugs prescribed during medical visits among adults 55-64 years of age by sex: United States, 1995-96 and 2002-03

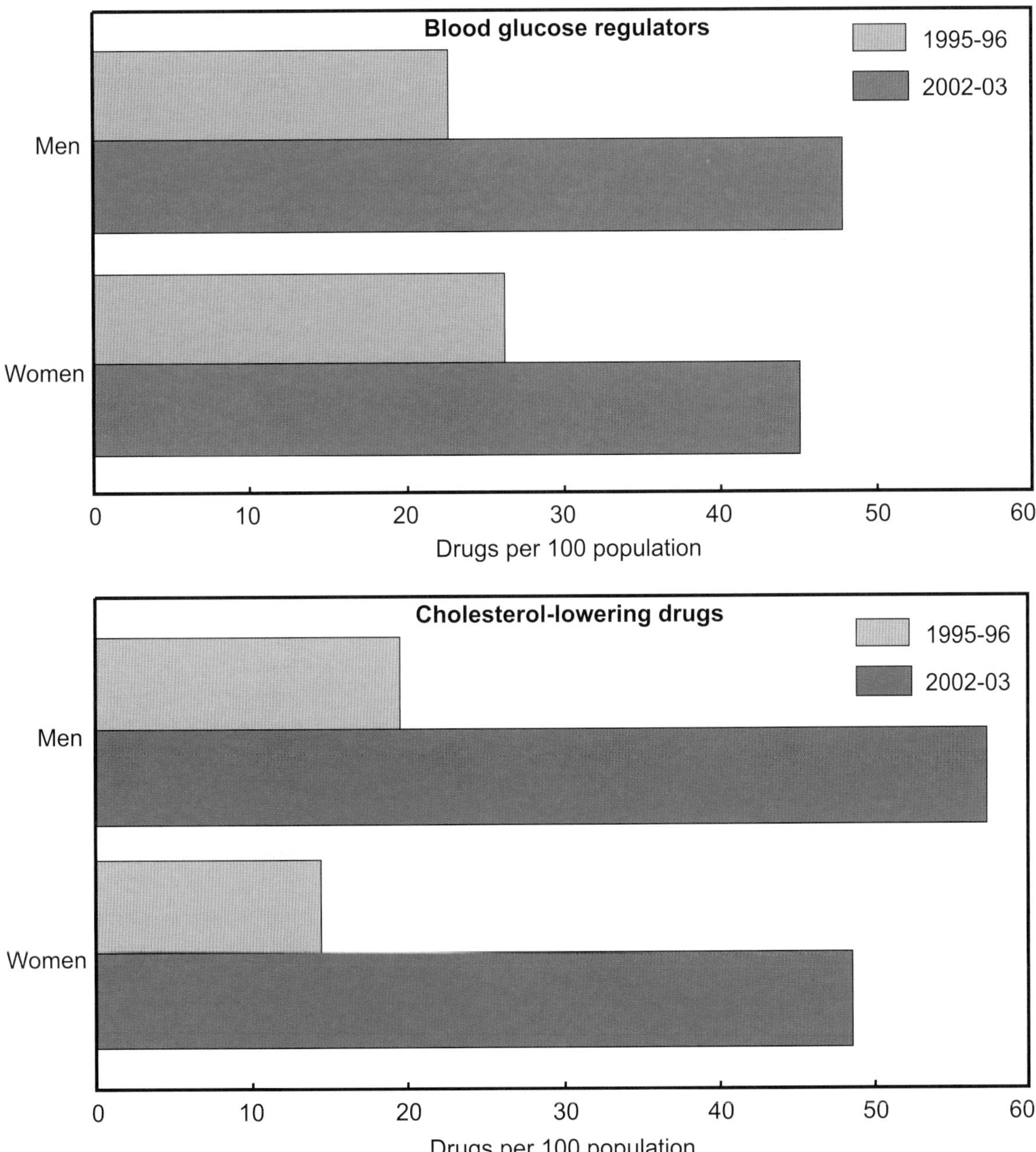

NOTES: Medical visits with drugs prescribed are in-person visits to physician office and hospital outpatient departments with at least one drug prescribed, ordered, supplied, administered, or continued during the visit. Drugs per 100 population are calculated as the number of drugs recorded during visits for the 2-year period divided by the sum of the population estimates for both years, times 100.

See Data Table for data points graphed, specific drugs included, standard errors, and additional notes.

SOURCE: Centers for Disease Control and Prevention, National Center for Health Statistics, National Ambulatory Medical Care Survey and National Hospital Ambulatory Medical Care Survey.

Total Health Care Expense and Prescribed Medicine Expense

As people age their health care needs increase, resulting in higher health care expenses for adults 55–64 years of age than for younger adults. These higher expenses are financed by third party payers (private health insurers, publicly-financed health programs and other miscellaneous sources), as well as by individuals through out-of-pocket payments. Between 1997 and 2002 the out-of-pocket portion of health care expenses in real (2002) dollars increased from 17 percent to 20 percent and rose on average from $753 to $971 per person per year (data table for figure 37). By contrast, the amount of health expenses per person paid by all other sources remained stable during the period. Increased average out-of-pocket payments for all health services may particularly burden poorer, sicker (especially chronically ill), and uninsured adults 55–64 years of age and may result in their foregoing needed services (1).

Drugs—both prescription and over the counter—are becoming a more frequently utilized therapy for reducing morbidity and mortality among adults 55–64 years of age (figure 36). Between 1997 and 2002 prescription drug expenses as a percent of total health care expenses increased from 14 to 23 percent (data table for figure 37). In 2002 average expenses for prescription drugs were about $1,100 per person, a 75-percent increase over 1997 (figure 37). Women had higher average prescribed medicine expenses per person per year than men in both time periods.

The percent of prescription drug expenses paid out-of-pocket declined from 1997 to 2002 (45 percent compared with 38 percent) indicating increased coverage of drug expenses by private health insurance and publicly-funded health programs. Despite expanded coverage of prescription drugs by third party payers, the use of more drugs and the use of more expensive drugs resulted in average out-of-pocket expenses for prescription drugs that were about 50 percent higher in 2002 than in 1997 (figure 37). In some cases high out-of-pocket costs may deter people from obtaining needed prescription drugs, which may result in deteriorating health status (1,2).

Figure 37. Total prescribed medicine expense per person per year among adults 55-64 years of age by source of payment and sex: United States, 1997 and 2002

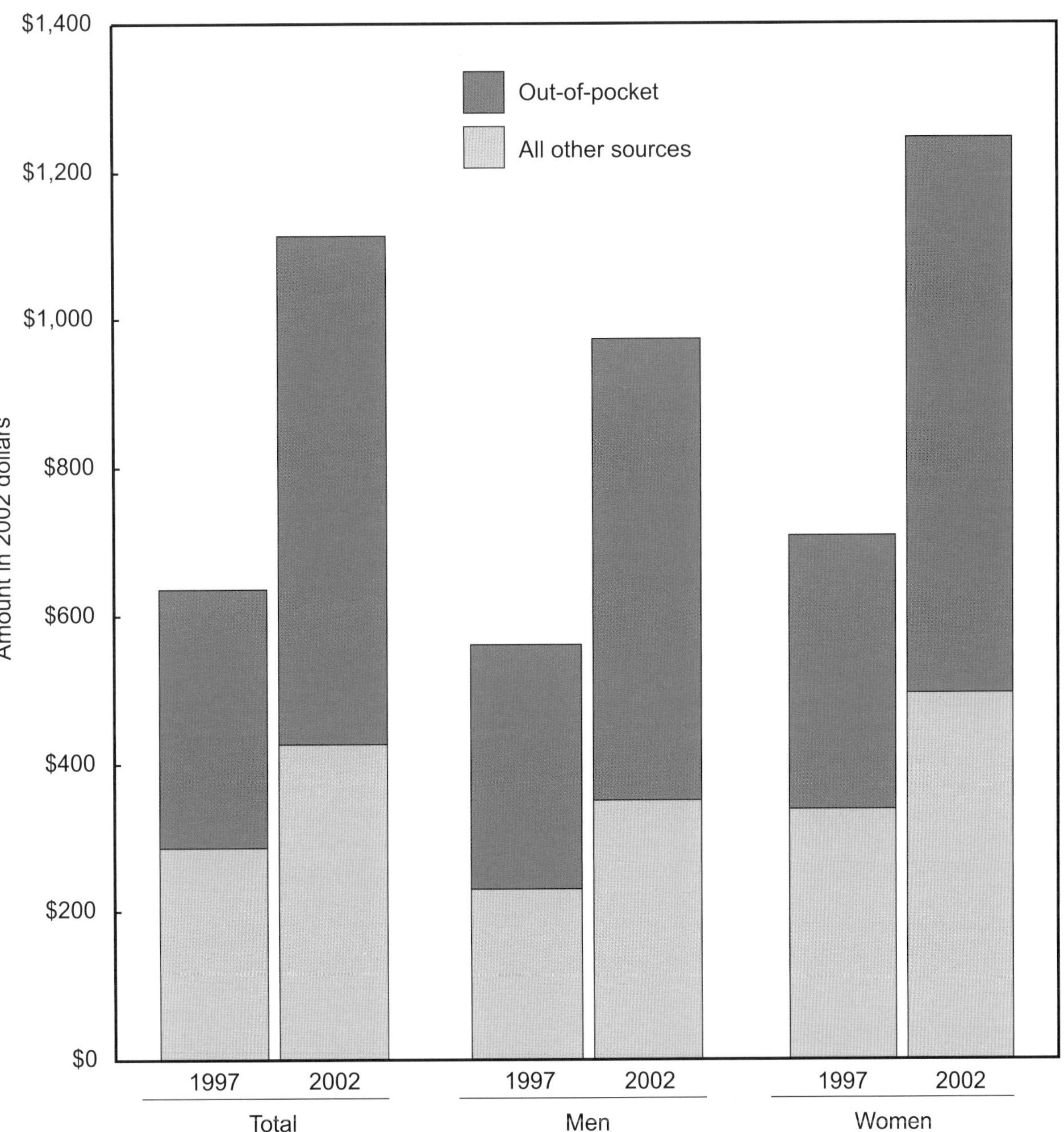

NOTE: See Data Table for data points graphed, standard errors, and additional notes.

SOURCE: Agency for Healthcare Research and Quality, Center for Financing, Access and Cost Trends, Medical Expenditures Panel Survey.

References

Figures 1 and 2: Age

1. Wolf DA. Population change: Friend or foe of the chronic care system? Health Aff 20(6):28–42. 2001. Available at content.healthaffairs.org/cgi/content/abstract/20/6/28 accessed on February 17, 2005.
2. Goulding MR, Rogers ME, Smith SM. Public health and aging: Trends in aging—United States and worldwide. MMWR 52(06):101–6. 2003. Available at www.cdc.gov/mmwr/preview/mmwrhtml/mm5206a2.htm accessed on February 17, 2005.

Figure 3: Race and Ethnicity

1. Grieco EM, Cassidy RC. Overview of race and Hispanic origin. Census 2000 Brief. United States Census 2000. March 2001.
2. Waters MC. Immigration, intermarriage, and the challenges of measuring racial/ethnic identities. Am J Public Health 90(11):1735–7. 2000.
3. U.S. Census Bureau: Census 2000 Modified Race Data Summary File: 2000 Census of Population and Housing, September 2002.

Figures 4 and 5: Poverty

1. Pamuk E, Makuc D, Heck K, Reuben C, Lochner K. Socioeconomic Status and Health Chartbook. Health, United States, 1998. Hyattsville, MD: National Center for Health Statistics. 1998.
2. DeNavas-Walt C, Proctor B, Mills R. Income, poverty, and health insurance coverage in the United States: 2003. Current population reports, series P-60 no 226. Washington: U.S. Government Printing Office. 2004. Available at www.census.gov/prod/2004pubs/p60–226.pdf accessed on February 23, 2005.
3. Hungerford T, Rassette M, Iams H, Koenig M. Trends in the economic status of the elderly. Soc Sec Bull vol 64 no 3. 2001–02.
4. Camarota SA. Economy slowed, but immigration didn't: The foreign-born population 2000–2004. Center for Immigration Studies, November 2004. Available at www.cis.org/articles/2004/back1204.html accessed on January 7, 2005.

Figures 6 and 7: Health Insurance

1. Institute of Medicine. Committee on the Consequences of Uninsurance. Series of reports: Coverage matters: insurance and health care; Care without coverage; Health insurance is a family matter; A shared destiny: community effects of uninsurance; Hidden costs, value lost: uninsurance in America. Washington: National Academy Press. 2001–2003.
2. Ayanian JZ, Weissman JS, Schneider EC, et al. Unmet health needs of uninsured adults in the United States. JAMA 285(4):2061–9. 2000.
3. Camarota, SA. Economy slowed, but immigration didn't: The foreign-born population 2000–2004. Center for Immigration Studies, November 2004. Available at www.cis.org/articles/2004/back1204.pdf accessed on January 7, 2005.

Figures 8 and 9: Health Care Expenditures

1. Smith C, Cowan C, Sensenig A, et al. Trends: Health spending growth slows in 2003. Health Affairs. 24(1): 185–94. 2005. Available at content.healthaffairs.org/cgi/reprint/hlthaff.24.1.185v1 accessed on January 26, 2005.

Figures 10 and 11: Tobacco Use

1. U.S. Department of Health and Human Services. The health consequences of smoking: A report of the Surgeon General. 2004. Atlanta, GA: Centers for Disease Control and Prevention. 2004. Available at www.cdc.gov/tobacco/sgr/sgr_2004/index.htm accessed on May 2, 2005.
2. U.S. Department of Health and Human Services. Preventing tobacco use among young people: A report of the Surgeon General. Atlanta, GA: Centers for Disease Control and Prevention. 1994. Available at www.cdc.gov/tobacco/sgr/sgr_1994/ accessed on March 17, 2005.
3. Mathews TJ. Smoking during pregnancy in the 1990s. National vital statistics reports; vol 49 no 7. Hyattsville, MD: National Center for Health Statistics. 2001. Available at www.cdc.gov/nchs/data/nvsr/nvsr49/nvsr49_07.pdf accessed on February 17, 2005.
4. Centers for Disease Control and Prevention, National Center for Health Statistics, National Health Interview Survey, unpublished analysis.
5. Martin JA, Hamilton BE, Sutton PD, et al. Births: Final data for 2002. National vital statistics reports; vol 52 no 10. Hyattsville, MD: National Center for Health Statistics. 2003. Available at www.cdc.gov/nchs/data/nvsr/nvsr52/nvsr52_10.pdf accessed on February 17, 2005.
6. Centers for Disease Control and Prevention. Trends in cigarette smoking among high school students—United States, 1991–2001. MMWR 51(19):409–12. 2002. Available at www.cdc.gov/mmwr/preview/mmwrhtml/mm5119a1.htm accessed on March 17, 2005.
7. Centers for Disease Control and Prevention. Youth Risk Behavior Surveillance—United States, 2003. MMWR 53(SS02):1–96. 2004. Available at www.cdc.gov/tobacco/research_data/youth/YRBS_ss5302a1.htm accessed on March 17, 2005.

Figure 12: Teenagers and Cars

1. Kochanek KD, Murphy SL, Anderson RN, Scott C. Deaths: Final data for 2002. National vital statistics reports; vol 53 no 5. Hyattsville, MD: National Center for Health Statistics. 2004. Available at www.cdc.gov/nchs/data/nvsr/nvsr53/nvsr53_05.pdf accessed on March 18, 2005.
2. National Highway Traffic Safety Administration. Motor Vehicle Traffic Crash Fatality and Injury Estimates for 2000; U.S. Department of Transportation, Washington: 2001.
3. McCartt AT, Shabanova VI. Teenage Seat belt Use: White Paper. The National Safety Council's Air Bag & Seat Belt Safety Campaign. 2002. Available at www.nsc.org/public/teen0702.pdf accessed on March 28, 2005.
4. Subramanian R. Alcohol Involvement in Fatal Motor Vehicle Traffic Crashes, 2003. National Highway Traffic Safety Administration, U.S. Department of Transportation, Washington: DOT HS 809 822, March 2005. Available at www.nrd.nhtsa.dot.gov/pdf/nrd-30/NCSA/Rpts/2005/809822.pdf accessed on March 28, 2005.
5. National Highway Traffic Safety Administration. Motor Vehicle Occupant Protection FACTS. Available at www.nhtsa.dot.gov/people/injury/airbags/OccupantProtectionFacts/young_adults.htm accessed on March 28, 2005.

Figures 13 and 14: Physical Activity

1. Centers for Disease Control and Prevention, Office of Genomics and Disease Prevention. Genomics and Population Health: United States, 2003. Atlanta, GA. 2004. Available at www.cdc.gov/genomics accessed on August 12, 2004.
2. U.S. Department of Health and Human Services. Physical activity and health: A report of the Surgeon General. Atlanta, GA: Centers for Disease Control and Prevention. 1996. Available at www.cdc.gov/nccdphp/sgr/sgr.htm accessed on January 10, 2005.
3. Mensink GB, Ziese T, Kok FJ. Benefits of leisure-time physical activity on the cardiovascular risk profile at older age. Int J Epidemiol 28(4):659–66. 1999.
4. U.S. Department of Health and Human Services and U.S. Department of Agriculture. Dietary Guidelines for Americans, 2005. Available at www.healthierus.gov/dietaryguidelines/ accessed on March 3, 2005.
5. Grunbaum JA, Kann L, Kinchen S, et al. Youth Risk Behavior Surveillance—United States, 2003. In: CDC Surveillance Summaries. MMWR 53(SS-2). 2004. Available at www.cdc.gov/mmwr accessed on January 10, 2005.
6. Centers for Disease Control and Prevention, National Center for Health Statistics, National Health Interview Survey, unpublished analysis.

Figure 15: Overweight and Obesity

1. National Institutes of Health. Clinical guidelines on the identification, evaluation, and treatment of overweight and obesity in adults: The evidence report. NIH pub no 98–4083. 1998. Available at www.nhlbi.nih.gov/guidelines/obesity/ob_gdlns.htm accessed on March 18, 2005.
2. U.S. Department of Health and Human Services. The Surgeon General's call to action to prevent and decrease overweight and obesity. Rockville, MD. 2001. Available at www.surgeongeneral.gov/topics/obesity/ accessed on March 18, 2005.
3. Dietz WH. Health consequences of obesity in youth: Childhood predictors of adult disease. Pediatrics 101(3 Pt 2):518–25. 1998.
4. Centers for Disease Control and Prevention, National Center for Health Statistics, National Health and Nutrition Examination Survey, unpublished analysis.
5. Ogden CL, Fryar CD, Carroll MD, Flegal KM. Mean body weight, height, and body mass index, United States 1960–2002. Advance data no 347. Hyattsville, MD: National Center for Health Statistics. 2004. Available at www.cdc.gov/nchs/data/ad/ad347.pdf accessed on March 18, 2005.

Figure 16: Asthma in Children Age 3–17

1. National Center for Health Statistics. Asthma prevalence, health care use and mortality, 2002. Available at www.cdc.gov/nchs/products/pubs/pubd/hestats/asthma/asthma.htm accessed on February 3, 2005.
2. National Asthma Education and Prevention Program. Guidelines for the diagnosis and management of asthma: Update on selected topics 2002. NIH pub no 02–5074. Bethesda, MD: National Heart, Lung, and Blood Institute. 2003. Available at www.nhlbi.nih.gov/guidelines/asthma/asthupdt.htm accessed on March 17, 2005.
3. Akinbami LJ, Schoendorf KC. Trends in childhood asthma: Prevalence, health care utilization, and mortality. Pediatrics 110(2):315–22. 2002.
4. Martinez FD, Wright AL, Taussig LM, et al. Asthma and wheezing in the first six years of life. N Engl J Med 332(3):133–8. 1995.
5. Centers for Disease Control and Prevention, National Center for Health Statistics, National Health Interview Survey, unpublished analysis.
6. Akinbami LJ, LaFleur BJ, Schoendorf KC. Racial and income disparities in childhood asthma in the United States. Ambulatory Pediatrics 2:382–7. 2002.
7. Centers for Disease Control and Prevention, National Center for Health Statistics, National Hospital Discharge Survey, unpublished analysis.

8. Centers for Disease Control and Prevention, National Center for Health Statistics, National Hospital Ambulatory Medical Care Survey, unpublished analysis.
9. Centers for Disease Control and Prevention, National Center for Health Statistics, National Ambulatory Medical Care Survey, unpublished analysis.
10. U.S. Census Bureau. Monthly postcensal resident populations by single year of age, sex, race, and Hispanic origin [file for July 1, 2003]. Available at www.census.gov/popest/national/asrh/2003_nat_res.html accessed on May 13, 2005.

Figure 17: Headache and Low Back Pain

1. Bingefors K, Isacson D. Epidemiology, co-morbidity, and impact on health-related quality of life of self-reported headache and musculoskeletal pain—a gender perspective. Eur J Pain 8(5):435–50. 2004.
2. National Institute of Neurological Disorders and Stroke. Low Back Pain Fact Sheet. Available at www.ninds.nih.gov/health_and_medical/pubs/back_pain.htm accessed on October 18, 2004.
3. National Institute of Neurological Disorders and Stroke, in Cooperation with the American Academy of Neurology, American Headache Society and National Headache Foundation. 21st century prevention and management of migraine headaches. Clinical Courier 19(8), 2001. Available at www.ninds.nih.gov/doctors/OP129D_Clinical_Courier_fa.pdf accessed on October 25, 2004.
4. National Headache Foundation. Headache fact sheet. Available at www.headaches.org/consumer/presskit/NHAW04/Categories%20of%20Headache.pdf accessed on October 28, 2004.
5. American Academy of Neurology. Practice Parameter: Evidence-based guidelines for migraine headache (an evidence-based review). Available at www.neurology.org/cgi/reprint/55/6/754.pdf accessed on November 1, 2004.
6. American Academy of Orthopaedic Surgeons (AAOS). AAOS clinical guideline on low back pain/sciatica (acute) (phases I and II). Rosemont, IL: American Academy of Orthopaedic Surgeons (AAOS); 2002. Available at www.guideline.gov/summary/summary.aspx?ss=15&doc_id=5369&nbr=3672 accessed on January 11, 2005.
7. Centers for Disease Control and Prevention, National Center for Health Statistics. National Ambulatory Medical Care Survey and National Hospital Ambulatory Medical Care Survey (OPD), unpublished analysis.
8. Barnes PM, Powell-Griner E, McFann K, Nahin RL. Complementary and alternative medicine use among adults: United States, 2002. Advance data; no 343. Hyattsville, MD: National Center for Health Statistics. 2004. Available at www.cdc.gov/nchs/data/ad/ad343.pdf accessed on November 1, 2004.

Figure 18: Morbidity and Limitation of Activity: Children

1. Newacheck PW, Strickland B, Shonkoff JP, et al. An epidemiologic profile of children with special health care needs. Pediatrics 102(1):117–23. 1998.
2. Centers for Disease Control and Prevention, National Center for Health Statistics, National Health Interview Survey, unpublished analysis.
3. Gissler M, Jarvelin M-R, Louhiala P, Hemminki E. Boys have more health problems in childhood than girls: follow-up of the 1987 Finnish birth cohort. Acta Paediatr 88:310–4. 1999.

Figures 19 and 20: Morbidity and Limitation of Activity: Working-age and Older Adults

1. Guralnik JM, Fried LP, Salive ME. Disability as a public health outcome in the aging population. Annu Rev Public Health 17:25–46. 1996.
2. Bhattacharya J, Cutler DM, Goldman DP, et al. Disability forecasts and future Medicare costs. Chapter 3 in Frontiers in health policy research, volume 7. Cutler DM and Garber AM, editors. Boston: the MIT Press, 2004.
3. Fujiura GT, Rutkowski-Kmitta V. Counting disability. In: Albrecht GL, Seelman KD, Bury M, eds. Handbook of disability studies. Thousand Oaks, California: Sage Publications, 69–96. 2001.
4. Centers for Disease Control and Prevention, National Center for Health Statistics, National Health Interview Survey, unpublished analysis.
5. Federal Interagency Forum on Aging-Related Statistics. Older Americans 2004: Key indicators of well-being. Washington. 2004.

Figure 21: Mammography

1. American Cancer Society. Cancer Facts and Figures 2002. Available at www.cancer.org/downloads/STT/CancerFacts&Figures2002TM.pdf accessed on May 17, 2005.
2. Kochanek KD, Murphy SL, Anderson RN, Scott C. Deaths: Final data for 2002. National vital statistics reports: vol 53 no 5. Hyattsville, MD: National Center for Health Statistics. 2004. Available at www.cdc.gov/nchs/data/nvsr/nvsr53/nvsr53_05.pdf accessed on February 18, 2005.
3. U.S. Preventive Services Task Force. Screening for breast cancer: Recommendations and rationale. February 2002. Agency for Healthcare Research and Quality, Rockville, MD. Available at www.ahrq.gov/clinic/3rduspstf/breastcancer/brcanrr.htm accessed on September 29, 2004.
4. Fiscella K, Franks P, Doescher MP, et al. Disparities in health care by race, ethnicity, and language among the insured: findings from a national sample. Med Care 40:52–59. 2002.

5. Goel MS, Wee CC, McCarthy EP, et al. Racial and ethnic disparities in cancer screening: The importance of foreign birth as a barrier to care. J Gen Intern Med 18:1028–35. 2003.

6. Lawson HW, Henson R, Bobo JK, Kaeser MK. Implementing recommendations for the early detection of breast and cervical cancer among low-income women. MMWR Recomm Rep. 49(RR-2):37–55. 2000. Available at www.cdc.gov/mmwr/PDF/RR/RR4902.pdf accessed on January 26, 2005.

7. National Center for Chronic Disease Prevention and Health Promotion. Centers for Disease Control and Prevention. The national breast and cervical cancer early detection program: saving lives through screening, 2004/2005 fact sheet. Available at cdc.gov/cancer/nbccedp/about2004.htm accessed on January 21, 2005.

Figure 22: Pap Smear

1. Ries LAG, Eisner MP, Kosary CL, et al. (eds). SEER Cancer Statistics Review, 1975–2001. Table V-3. National Cancer Institute. Bethesda, MD. 2004. Available at seer.cancer.gov/csr/1975_2001/ accessed on January 5, 2005.

2. Kochanek KD, Murphy SL, Anderson RN, Scott C. Deaths: Final data for 2002. National vital statistics reports; vol 53 no 5. Hyattsville, MD: National Center for Health Statistics. 2004. Available at www.cdc.gov/nchs/data/nvsr/nvsr53/nvsr53_05.pdf accessed on February 18, 2005.

3. U.S. Preventive Services Task Force. Screening for cervical cancer: Recommendations and rationale. AHRQ pub no 03–515A. January 2003. Agency for Healthcare Research and Quality. Rockville, MD. Available at www.ahrq.gov/clinic/3rduspstf/cervicalcan/cervcanrr.htm accessed on January 3, 2005.

4. Saslow D, Runowicz CD, Solomon D, et al. American Cancer Society guideline for the early detection of cervical neoplasia and cancer. CA Cancer J Clin 52(6):342–62. 2002.

5. The American College of Obstetricians and Gynecologists. ACOG News Release: Revised cervical cancer screening guidelines require reeducation of women and physicians. Available at www.acog.org/from_home/publications/press_releases/nr05–04-04–1.cfm accessed on January 5, 2005.

6. Swan J, Breen N, Coates RJ, et al. Progress in cancer screening practices in the United States: Results from the 2000 National Health Interview Survey. Cancer 97(6):1528–40. 2003.

7. Chaudhry S, Fink A, Gelberg L, Brook R. Utilization of Papanicolaou smears by South Asian women living in the United States. J Gen Intern Med 18:377–84. 2003.

8. Alba D, Sweningson JM, Chandy C, Hubbell FA. Impact of English language proficiency on receipt of Pap smears among Hispanics. J Gen Intern Med 19(9):967–70. 2004.

9. Austin LT, Ahmad F, McNally MJ, Stewart DE. Breast and cervical cancer screening in Hispanic women: A literature review using the health belief model. Women's Health Issues 12(3):122–8. 2002.

10. Ries LAG, Eisner MP, Kosary CL, et al. (eds). SEER Cancer Statistics Review, 1975–2001. Table V-7. National Cancer Institute. Bethesda, MD. 2004. Available at seer.cancer.gov/csr/1975_2001/results_merged/topic_race_ethnicity.pdf accessed on January 6, 2005.

11. Schwartz KL, Crossley-May H, Vigneau, FD, et al. Race, socioeconomic status and stage at diagnosis for five common malignancies. Cancer Causes Control 14:761–6. 2003.

12. Lawson HW, Henson R, recommendations for the early detection of breast and cervical cancer among low-income women. MMWR Recomm Rep. 49(RR-2):37–55. 2000. Available at www.cdc.gov/mmwr/PDF/RR/RR4902.pdf accessed on January 26, 2005.

Figure 23: Injury-related Emergency Department Visits Among Children and Adolescents

1. Centers for Disease Control and Prevention. Medical expenditures attributable to injuries—United States, 2000. MMWR Jan 16;53(1):1–4. 2004. Available at www.cdc.gov/mmwr/preview/mmwrhtml/mm5301a1.htm accessed on February 18, 2005.

2. Anderson RN, Minino AM, Fingerhut LA, et al. Deaths: Injuries, 2002. National vital statistics reports, forthcoming.

3. Kochanek KD, Murphy SL, Anderson RN, et al. Deaths: Final data for 2002. National vital statistics reports; vol 53 no 5. Hyattsville, MD: National Center for Health Statistics. 2004. Available at www.cdc.gov/nchs/data/nvsr/nvsr53/nvsr53_05.pdf accessed on February 18, 2005.

4. Centers for Disease Control and Prevention, National Center for Health Statistics, National Ambulatory Medical Care Survey and National Hospital Ambulatory Medical Care Survey, unpublished analysis.

5. Burt CW, Fingerhut LA. Injury visits to hospital emergency departments: United States, 1992–95. National Center for Health Statistics. Vital Health Stat 13(131). 1998. Available at www.cdc.gov/nchs/data/series/sr_13/sr13_131.pdf accessed on February 18, 2005.

6. Simon TD, Bublitz C, Hambidge SJ. External causes of pediatric injury-related emergency department visits in the United States. Acad Emer Med 11:1042–8. 2004.

Figure 24: Visits to Physician Offices and Hospital Outpatient Departments

1. NAEPP Expert Panel Report. Guidelines for the diagnosis and management of asthma—Update on selected topics 2002. Update 2002: Expert panel report. Available at www.nhlbi.nih.gov/guidelines/asthma/index.htm accessed on January 10, 2005.
2. National Cholesterol Education Program. Executive summary of the third report of the National Cholesterol Education Program (NCEP) expert panel on detection, evaluation, and treatment of high blood cholesterol in adults (adult treatment panel III). JAMA. Vol 285 (19):2486–97. 2001.
3. National Institutes of Health. Clinical guidelines on the identification, evaluation, and treatment of overweight and obesity in adults: The evidence report. NIH pub no 98–4083. September 1998. Available at www.nhlbi.nih.gov/guidelines/obesity/ob_gdlns.htm accessed on February 18, 2005.
4. U.S. Department of Health and Human Services. The Surgeon General's call to action to prevent and decrease overweight and obesity. Rockville, MD. 2001. Available at www.surgeongeneral.gov/topics/obesity/ accessed on February 18, 2005.
5. National Institutes of Health. The seventh report of the joint national committee on prevention, detection, evaluation, and treatment of high blood pressure. NIH pub no 04–5230. August 2004. Available at www.nhlbi.nih.gov/guidelines/hypertension/ accessed on February 18, 2005.
6. National Center for Health Statistics. Health, United States, 2004 with Chartbook on Trends in the Health of Americans. Hyattsville, MD: National Center for Health Statistics. 2004.

Figure 25: Hospital Procedures: Cardiac Stents

1. Holubkov R, Detre KM, Sopko G, et al. Trends in coronary revascularization 1989 to 1997: The bypass angioplasty revascularization investigation (BARI) survey of procedures. Am J of Cardiol 84:157–61. 1999.
2. Cutler DM, McClellan MM. Is technological change in medicine worth it? Health Affairs 20(5):11–29. 2001.
3. Heart and Stroke Encyclopedia, American Heart Association online encyclopedia. Available at www.americanheart.org/downloadable/heart/1056719919740HSFacts2003text.pdf accessed on November 30, 2004.
4. Cohen HA, Williams DO, Holmes DR, et al. Impact of age on procedural and 1-year outcome in percutaneous transluminal coronary angioplasty: A report from the NHLBI Dynamic Registry. American Heart Journal. September 2003.
5. MacGillivray TE, Vlahakes GJ. Perspective: Angioplasty versus minimally invasive bypass surgery. N Engl J Med 347(8):5551–2. 2002.
6. Michaels AD, Chatterjee K. Angioplasty versus bypass surgery for coronary artery disease. Circulation 106:e187–e190. 2002.

Figure 26: Life Expectancy

1. Arriaga EE. Measuring and explaining the change in life expectancies. Demography 21(1):83–96. 1984.
2. Centers for Disease Control and Prevention. Achievements in public health, 1900–1999: Control of infectious diseases. MMWR 48(29):621–9. 1999. Available at www.cdc.gov/mmwr/preview/mmwrhtml/mm4829a1.htm accessed on February 18, 2005.
3. Fried LP. Epidemiology of aging. Epidemiol Rev 22(1):95–106. 2000.
4. Arias E. United States life tables, 2002. National vital statistics reports; vol 53 no 6. Hyattsville, MD: National Center for Health Statistics. 2004. Available at www.cdc.gov/nchs/data/nvsr/nvsr53/nvsr53_06.pdf accessed on February 18, 2005.

Figures 27 and 28: Infant Mortality

1. Anderson RN, Smith BL. Deaths: Leading causes for 2002. National vital statistics reports; vol 53 no 17. Hyattsville, MD: National Center for Health Statistics. 2005. Available at www.cdc.gov/nchs/data/nvsr/nvsr53/nvsr53_17.pdf accessed on April 1, 2005.
2. Kochanek KD, Murphy SL, Anderson RN, Scott C. Deaths: Final data for 2002. National vital statistics reports; vol 53 no 5. Hyattsville, MD: National Center for Health Statistics. 2004. Available at www.cdc.gov/nchs/data/nvsr/nvsr53/nvsr53_05.pdf accessed on April 1, 2005.
3. Mathews TJ, Menacker F, MacDorman MF. Infant mortality statistics from the 2002 period linked birth/infant death data set. National vital statistics reports; vol 53 no 10. Hyattsville, MD: National Center for Health Statistics. 2004. Available at www.cdc.gov/nchs/data/nvsr/nvsr53/nvsr53_10.pdf accessed on April 1, 2005.
4. MacDorman MF, Martin JA, Mathews TJ, Hoyert DL, Ventura SJ. Explaining the 2001–02 infant mortality increase: Data from the linked birth/infant death data set. National vital statistics reports; vol 53 no 12. Hyattsville, MD: National Center for Health Statistics. 2005. Available at www.cdc.gov/nchs/data/nvsr/nvsr53/nvsr53_12.pdf accessed on April 1, 2005.
5. Hoyert DL, Kung H, Smith BL. Deaths: Preliminary data for 2003. National vital statistics reports; vol 53 no 15. Hyattsville, MD. National Center for Health Statistics. 2005. Available at www.cdc.gov/nchs/data/nvsr/nvsr53/nvsr53_15.pdf accessed on April 1, 2005.
6. American Academy of Pediatrics Task Force on Infant Positioning and SIDS. Positioning and sudden infant death syndrome (SIDS): update. Pediatrics 98(6 Pt 1):1216–8. 1996.

Figure 29: Leading Causes of Death for All Ages

1. Centers for Disease Control and Prevention. Decline in deaths from heart disease and stroke—United States, 1900–1999. MMWR 48(30):649–56. 1999. Available at www.cdc.gov/mmwr/preview/mmwrhtml/mm4830a1.htm accessed on February 18, 2005.
2. Centers for Disease Control and Prevention, National Center for Health Statistics, National Vital Statistics System, table 250R. Available at www.cdc.gov/nchs/data/dvs/mortfinal2002_work250r.pdf accessed on May 16, 2005.
3. Centers for Disease Control and Prevention. Motor-vehicle safety: A 20th century public health achievement. MMWR 48(18):369–74. 1999. Available at www.cdc.gov/mmwr/preview/mmwrhtml/mm4818a1.htm accessed on February 18, 2005.

Figure 30: Adults 55–64 Years of Age: Introduction

1. Centers for Disease Control and Prevention, National Center for Health Statistics, National Health and Nutrition Examination Survey, unpublished analysis.
2. National Cholesterol Education Program. Executive summary of the third report of the national cholesterol education program (NCEP) expert panel on detection, evaluation, and treatment of high blood cholesterol in adults (adult treatment panel III). JAMA 285(19):2486–97. 2001.
3. Screening for type 2 diabetes mellitus in adults: recommendations and rationale. United States Preventive Services Task Force—Independent Expert Panel. 1996 (revised 2003 Feb). Available at www.guideline.gov/summary/summary.aspx?doc_id=3523 accessed on February 18, 2005.
4. Screening for hypertension in adults. Available at www.guideline.gov/summary/summary.aspx?ss=15&doc_id=3226&nbr=2452 accessed on January 10, 2005.
5. U.S. Preventive Services Task Force. Guidelines for screening for colorectal cancer. Available at www.ahrq.gov/clinic/3rduspstf/colorectal/ accessed on January 10, 2005.
6. U.S. Government Accountability Office. Private health insurance: Millions relying on individual market face cost and coverage trade-offs. GAO/HEHS-97–8. Washington: U.S. General Accounting Office. 1996.
7. McWilliams JM, Zaslavsky AM, Meara E, Ayanian JZ. Impact of Medicare coverage on basic clinical services for previously uninsured adults. JAMA 290(6):757–64. 2003.
8. Stuart B, Singhal PK, Fahlman CF, Doshi J, Briesacher B. Employer-Sponsored Health Insurance and Prescription Drug Coverage for New Retirees: Dramatic Declines in Five Years. Health Aff (web exclusive) July 23:W3–334-W3–341. 2003. Available at content.healthaffairs.org/cgi/content/full/hlthaff.w3.334v1/DC1 accessed on February 18, 2005.
9. Claxton G, Gil I, Finder B, et al. Employer Health Benefits, 2004 Annual Survey. Report by the Henry J. Kaiser Family Foundation and the Health Research & Educational Trust (HRET). 2004. Available at www.kff.org/insurance/7148/index.cfm accessed on January 10, 2005.
10. Zsembik BA, Peek MK, Peek CW. Race and ethnic variation in the disablement process. J Aging Health 12(2):229–49. 2000.
11. Liao Y, Tucker P, Giles WH. Health status of American Indians compared with other racial/ethnic minority populations—Selected states, 2001–02. MMWR 52(47):1148–52. Available at www.cdc.gov/mmwr/preview/mmwrhtml/mm5247a3.htm accessed on March 14, 2005.

Figure 31: Adults 55–64 Years of Age: Employment Status

1. Centers for Disease Control and Prevention, National Center for Health Statistics, National Health Interview Survey, unpublished analysis.
2. Toossi M. Labor force projections to 2012: the graying of the U.S. workforce. Mon Labor Rev (February):37–57:2004.
3. Medicare and Medicaid Statistical Supplement, 2001. Health Care Financ Rev. Available at www.cms.hhs.gov/review/supp/2001/table6a.pdf accessed on November 24, 2004.
4. Sowers JR, Ferdinand KC, Bakris GL, Douglas JG. Hypertension-related disease in African Americans: Factors underlying disparities in illness and its outcome. Postgrad Med 112(4):24–48. 2002.
5. Choi NG, Schlichting-Ray L. Predictors of transitions in disease and disability in pre- and early-retirement populations. J Aging Health 13(3):379–409. 2001.
6. Flippen C, Tienda M. Pathways to retirement: patterns of labor force participation and labor market exit among the pre-retirement population by race, Hispanic origin, and sex. J Geront: Social Sciences 55B(1):S14–S27. 2000.

Figure 32: Adults 55–64 Years of Age: Low Income

1. Pamuk E, Makuc D, Heck K, Reuben C, Lochner K. Socioeconomic status and health chartbook. Health, United States, 1998. Hyattsville, MD. 1998.
2. DeNavas-Walt C, Proctor BD, Mills RJ. Income, poverty, and health insurance coverage in the United States: 2003. Current population reports, series P-60 no 226. Washington: U.S. Government Printing Office. 2004.
3. Butrica BA, Iams HM, Smith KE. It's all relative: understanding the retirement prospects of baby-boomers. Center for Retirement Research at Boston College, CRRWP 2003–21. November 2003.
4. U.S. Government Accountability Office. Older Workers: Demographic Trends Pose Challenges for Employers and Workers. GAO-02–85, November 2001.

5. Camarota SA. Economy slowed, but immigration didn't: the foreign-born population 2000–2004. Center for Immigration Studies, November 2004. Available at www.cis.org/articles/2004/back1204.html accessed on June 6, 2005.
6. Rubin RM, White-Means SI. Income Distribution of older Americans. Mon Labor Rev. November 2000, 123:19–30. 2000.

Figure 33: Adults 55–64 Years of Age: Health Insurance Coverage

1. Holahan J. Health insurance coverage of the near elderly. The Henry J. Kaiser Family Foundation, Kaiser Commission on Medicaid and the Uninsured, pub no 7114, July 2004. Available at www.kff.org/uninsured/7114.cfm accessed on January 10, 2005.
2. Monheit AC, Vistnes JP, Eisenberg JM. Moving to Medicare: Trends in the health insurance status of near-elderly workers, 1987–1996. Health Aff 20(2):204–13. 2001.
3. Jensen GA. Health insurance of the near elderly: A growing concern. Med Care 36(2):107–9. 1998.
4. Claxton G, Gil I, Finder B, et al. Employer health benefits, 2004 annual survey. Kaiser Family Foundation and Health Research and Educational Trust (HRET). 2004. Available at www.kff.org/insurance/7148/index.cfm accessed on January 10, 2005.
5. Fronstin P, Salisbury D. Retiree health benefits: Savings needed to fund health care in retirement. EBRI Issue Brief No 254, February 2003.
6. Centers for Disease Control and Prevention, National Center for Health Statistics, National Health Interview Survey, unpublished analysis.

Figure 34: Adults 55–64 Years of Age: Cardiovascular Risk Factors

1. National Cholesterol Education Program. Executive summary of the third report of the national cholesterol education program (NCEP) expert panel on detection, evaluation, and treatment of high blood cholesterol in adults (adult treatment panel III). JAMA 285(19):2486–97. 2001.
2. Yusuf HR, Giles WH, Croft JB, et al. Impact of multiple risk factor profiles on determining cardiovascular disease risk. Prev Med 27(1):1–9. 1998.
3. National Institutes of Health. Clinical guidelines on the identification, evaluation, and treatment of overweight and obesity in adults: The evidence report. NIH pub no 98–4083. September 1998. Available at www.nhlbi.nih.gov/guidelines/obesity/ob_gdlns.htm accessed on February 18, 2005.
4. National Cholesterol Education Program. Detection, Evaluation, and Treatment of High Blood Cholesterol in Adults (Adult Treatment Panel III). Final Report. NIH pub no 02–5215. 2002. Available at www.nhlbi.nih.gov/guidelines/cholesterol/atp3full.pdf accessed on May 13, 2005.
5. Brown CD, Higgins M, Donato KA, et al. Body mass index and the prevalence of hypertension and dyslipidemia. Obes Res 8(9):605–19. 2000.
6. Centers for Disease Control and Prevention, National Center for Health Statistics, National Health and Nutrition Examination Survey, unpublished analysis.

Figure 35: Adults 55–64 Years of Age: Use of Health Care Services

1. Baker DW, Shapiro MF, Schur CL. Health insurance and access to care for symptomatic conditions. Arch Intern Med 160(9):1269–74. 2000.
2. Centers for Disease Control and Prevention, National Center for Health Statistics, National Health Interview Survey, unpublished analysis.
3. Johnson RW, Crystal S. Uninsured status and out-of-pocket costs at midlife. Health Serv Res 35(5):911–32. 2000.
4. Sudano Jr JJ, Baker DW. Intermittent lack of health insurance coverage and use of preventive services. Am J Public Health 93(1):130–7. 2003.
5. McWilliams JM, Zaslavsky AM, Meara E, Ayanian JZ. Impact of Medicare coverage on basic clinical services for previously uninsured adults. JAMA 290(6);757–64. 2003.

Figure 36: Adults 55–64 Years of Age: Blood Glucose Regulators and Cholesterol-lowering Drugs Prescribed During Medical Visits

1. National Center for Health Statistics. Health, United States, 2004 with Chartbook on trends in the health of Americans. Hyattsville, MD. 2004.
2. Centers for Disease Control and Prevention, National Center for Health Statistics, National Health and Nutrition Examination Survey, unpublished analysis.
3. Berndt ER. The U.S. pharmaceutical industry: Why major growth in times of cost containment? Health Aff 20(2):100–14. 2001.
4. Chockley N. The emerging impact of direct-to-consumer prescription drug advertising. Testimony before the Subcommittee on Consumer Affairs, Foreign Commerce and Tourism of the Senate Committee on Commerce, Science and Transportation, July 24, 2001. Available at commerce.senate.gov/hearings/072401Chockley.pdf accessed on February 18, 2005.
5. National Center for Health Statistics. Health, United States, 2003 with Chartbook on trends in the health of Americans. Hyattsville, MD. 2003.

6. National Diabetes Data Group. Diabetes in America, 2nd Edition. Bethesda, MD: National Institutes of Health, 1995. (NIH pub no 95–1468).

7. Ross SA. Controlling diabetes: the need for intensive therapy and barriers in clinical management. Diabetes Res Clin Pract 65S(1):S29–S34. 2004.

8. National Cholesterol Education Program. Detection, Evaluation, and Treatment of High Blood Cholesterol in Adults (Adult Treatment Panel III). Final Report. NIH pub no 02–5215. 2002. Available at www.nhlbi.nih.gov/guidelines/cholesterol/atp3full.pdf.

Figure 37: Adults 55–64 Years of Age: Total Health Expense and Prescribed Medicine Expense

1. Piette JD, Heisler M, Wagner TH. Cost-related medication underuse among chronically ill adults: the treatments people forgo, how often, and who is at risk. Am J Public Health e94 (10):1782–87. 2004.

2. Heisler M, Langa KM, Eby EL, et al. The health effects of restricting prescription medication use because of cost. Med Care 42(7):626–34. 2004.

Technical Notes

Data Sources and Comparability

Data for *The Chartbook on Trends in the Health of Americans* come from numerous surveys and data systems and cover a broad range of years. Detailed descriptions of data sources are contained in Appendix I. Interpretation of trend data is affected by major changes such as periodic survey redesign, changes in data collection methodology, changes in wording and order of questions, interruptions or changes in timing of data collection, and changes in data coding systems. Comparability issues are discussed in the notes that accompany each figure and data table, and in the survey description in Appendix I. For example, the National Health Interview Survey was redesigned in 1997 to improve its efficiency and flexibility. The survey redesign affects comparisons before and after 1997 for many measures.

Data Presentation

Many measures in *The Chartbook on Trends in the Health of Americans* are shown for persons of different age groups because of the strong effect age has on most health outcomes. Selected figures in the chartbook highlight current differences in health and health determinants by variables such as sex, race and Hispanic origin, and poverty. Some estimates are age adjusted using the age distribution of the 2000 standard population, and this is noted in the data tables that accompany each chart (see Appendix II, Age adjustment). For some charts data years are combined to increase sample size and reliability of the estimates. Time trends for some measures are not presented because of the relatively short amount of time that comparable national estimates are available.

Graphic Presentation

Line charts for which only selected years of data are displayed have dot markers on the data years. Line charts for which data are displayed for every year in the trend are shown without the use of dot markers. Most trends are shown on a linear scale to emphasize absolute differences over time. The linear scale is the scale most frequently used and recognized, and it emphasizes the absolute changes between data points over time (1). The time trend for overall mortality measures is shown on a logarithmic (or log) scale to emphasize the rate of change and to enable measures with large differences in magnitude to be shown on the same chart. Log scales emphasize the relative or percentage change between data points. Readers are cautioned that one potential disadvantage to log scale is that the absolute magnitude of changes may appear less dramatic (2). When interpreting data on a log scale, the following points should be kept in mind:

1. A sloping straight line indicates a constant rate (not amount) of increase or decrease in the values,
2. A horizontal line indicates no change,
3. The slope of the line indicates the rate of increase or decrease, and
4. Parallel lines, regardless of their magnitude, depict similar rates of change (1).

Tabular Presentation

Following the technical notes are data tables that present the data points graphed in each chart. Some data tables contain additional data that were not graphed because of space considerations. Standard errors for data points are provided for many measures. Additional information clarifying and qualifying the data are included in table notes and Appendix I and II references.

References

1. Page RM, Cole GE, Timmreck TC. Basic epidemiological methods and biostatistics: a practical guidebook. Sudbury, Massachusetts: Jones and Bartlett Publishers, 1995.
2. Jekel JF, Elmore JG, Katz DL. Epidemiology biostatistics and preventive medicine. Philadelphia, Pennsylvania: W.B. Saunders Company, 1996.

Data table for figure 1. Total population and older population: United States, 1950–2050

Year	*All ages*	*65 years and over*	*75 years and over*
		Number	
1950	150,216,110	12,256,850	3,852,395
1960	179,325,657	16,207,237	5,359,338
1970	203,211,926	20,065,502	7,630,046
1980	226,545,805	25,549,427	9,968,822
1990	248,709,873	31,078,895	13,033,400
2000	281,421,906	34,991,753	16,600,767
2004	293,622,764	36,221,951	17,777,261
2010	308,935,581	40,243,713	18,974,204
2020	335,804,546	54,631,891	22,852,732
2030	363,584,435	71,453,471	33,505,538
2040	391,945,658	80,049,634	44,579,726
2050	419,853,587	86,705,637	48,763,200

NOTES: Data are for the resident population. Data for 1950 exclude Alaska and Hawaii. Data for 2010–2050 are projected. See Appendix II, Population.

SOURCES: U.S. Census Bureau, 1980 Census of Population, General Population Characteristics, United States Summary (PC80–1-B1) [data for 1950–80]; 1990 Census of Population, General Population Characteristics, United States Summary (CP-1–1) [data for 1990]; Table 1. Annual estimates of the population by sex and five-year age groups for the United States: April 1, 2000 to July 1, 2003 (NC-EST2003–01) available at www.census.gov/popest/national/asrh/NC-EST2003/NC-EST2003–01.xls accessed on November 21, 2004 [data for Census 2000]; U.S. Census Bureau: Monthly Postcensal Resident Populations, from April 1, 2000 to July 1, 2004 by age, sex, race, and Hispanic origin available at www.census.gov/popest/national/asrh/2003_nat_res.html, July 1, 2004 file, accessed on December 21, 2004 [data for 2004]; U.S. Interim Projections by Age, Sex, Race, and Hispanic Origin Detail File available at www.census.gov/ipc/www/usinterimproj accessed on December 21, 2004 [data for projections].

Data table for figure 2. Percent of population in five age groups: United States, 1950, 2000, 2004, and 2050

Year	*All ages*	*Under 18 years*	*18–54 years*	*55–64 years*	*65–74 years*	*75 years and over*
				Percent		
1950	100.0	31.3	51.8	8.8	5.6	2.6
2000	100.0	25.7	53.3	8.6	6.5	5.9
2004	100.0	24.9	52.8	9.9	6.3	6.1
2050	100.0	23.5	45.0	10.9	9.0	11.6

NOTES: Data are for the resident population. Data for 1950 exclude Alaska and Hawaii. Data for 2050 are projected. See Appendix II, Population.

SOURCES: U.S. Census Bureau, 1980 Census of Population, General Population Characteristics, United States Summary (PC80 1 B1) [data for 1950]; Table 1. Annual estimates of the population by sex and five-year age groups for the United States: April 1, 2000 to July 1, 2003 (NC-EST2003–01) available at www.census.gov/popest/national/asrh/NC-EST2003/NC-EST2003–01.xls accessed on November 21, 2004 [data for Census 2000]; U.S. Census Bureau: Monthly Postcensal Resident Populations, from April 1, 2000 to July 1, 2004 by age, sex, race, and Hispanic origin available at www.census.gov/popest/national/asrh/2003_nat_res.html, July 1, 2004 file, accessed on December 21, 2004 [data for 2004]; U.S. Interim Projections by Age, Sex, Race, and Hispanic Origin Detail File available at www.census.gov/ipc/www/usinterimproj accessed on December 21, 2004 [data for projections].

Data table for figure 3. Percent of population in selected race and Hispanic origin groups by age: United States, 1980–2004

Race and Hispanic origin	All ages				Under 18 years				18 years and over			
	1980	1990	2000	2004	1980	1990	2000	2004	1980	1990	2000	2004
Total	100.0	100.0	100.0	100.0	100.0	100.0	100.0	100.0	100.0	100.0	100.0	100.0
Hispanic or Latino	6.4	9.0	12.5	14.1	8.8	12.2	17.1	19.1	5.5	7.9	11.0	12.4
Not Hispanic or Latino												
White	79.9	75.7	69.5	67.4	74.2	68.9	61.3	58.9	82.1	78.1	72.3	70.2
Black or African American	11.5	11.8	12.2	12.3	14.5	14.7	14.9	14.8	10.4	10.7	11.3	11.4
Asian	1.6	2.8	3.7	4.1	1.7	3.1	3.5	3.7	1.5	2.7	3.8	4.2
American Indian or Alaska Native	0.6	0.7	0.7	0.8	0.8	1.0	1.0	0.9	0.5	0.6	0.7	0.7
Native Hawaiian or Other Pacific Islander	. . .	. . .	0.1	0.1	. . .	. . .	0.2	0.2	. . .	. . .	0.1	0.1
2 or more races	. . .	. . .	1.2	1.3	. . .	. . .	2.2	2.4	. . .	. . .	0.9	1.0

. . . Category not applicable.

NOTES: Data are for the resident population. Persons of Hispanic origin may be of any race. Race data for 2000 and beyond are not directly comparable with data for 1980 and 1990. Individuals could report only one race in 1980 and 1990, and more than one race beginning in 2000. Persons who selected only one race in 2000 and beyond are shown in single-race categories; persons who selected more than one race in 2000 and beyond are shown as having 2 or more races and are not included in the single-race categories. In 1980 and 1990, the category "Asian" includes Asian and Native Hawaiian or Other Pacific Islander; in 2000 and beyond this category includes only Asian. See Appendix II, Hispanic origin; Race.

SOURCES: U.S. Census Bureau: U.S. population estimates, by age, sex, race, and Hispanic origin: 1980 to 1991. Current population reports, series P-25, no 1095. Washington. U.S. Government Printing Office, February 1993 [data for 1980, 1990]; U.S. Census Bureau: Monthly Postcensal Resident Populations, from July 1, 2000 to July 1, 2004 by age, sex, race, and Hispanic origin, www.census.gov/popest/national/asrh/2003_nat_res.html [data for April 1, 2000 and July 1, 2004] accessed on December 21, 2004.

Data table for figure 4. Poverty by age: United States, 1966–2003

Year	*All ages*	*Under 18 years*	*18–64 years*	*65 years and over*
	Percent of persons with family income below the poverty level			
1966	14.7	17.6	10.5	28.5
1967	14.2	16.6	10.0	29.5
1968	12.8	15.6	9.0	25.0
1969	12.1	14.0	8.7	25.3
1970	12.6	15.1	9.0	24.6
1971	12.5	15.3	9.3	21.6
1972	11.9	15.1	8.8	18.6
1973	11.1	14.4	8.3	16.3
1974	11.2	15.4	8.3	14.6
1975	12.3	17.1	9.2	15.3
1976	11.8	16.0	9.0	15.0
1977	11.6	16.2	8.8	14.1
1978	11.4	15.9	8.7	14.0
1979	11.7	16.4	8.9	15.2
1980	13.0	18.3	10.1	15.7
1981	14.0	20.0	11.1	15.3
1982	15.0	21.9	12.0	14.6
1983	15.2	22.3	12.4	13.8
1984	14.4	21.5	11.7	12.4
1985	14.0	20.7	11.3	12.6
1986	13.6	20.5	10.8	12.4
1987	13.4	20.3	10.6	12.5
1988	13.0	19.5	10.5	12.0
1989	12.8	19.6	10.2	11.4
1990	13.5	20.6	10.7	12.2
1991	14.2	21.8	11.4	12.4
1992	14.8	22.3	11.9	12.9
1993	15.1	22.7	12.4	12.2
1994	14.5	21.8	11.9	11.7
1995	13.8	20.8	11.4	10.5
1996	13.7	20.5	11.4	10.8
1997	13.3	19.9	10.9	10.5
1998	12.7	18.9	10.5	10.5
1999	11.9	17.1	10.1	9.7
2000	11.3	16.2	9.6	9.9
2001	11.7	16.3	10.1	10.1
2002	12.1	16.7	10.6	10.4
2003	12.5	17.6	10.8	10.2

NOTES: Data are for the civilian noninstitutionalized population. Starting in 1999 estimates of poverty have been calculated using Census 2000-based population weights. Starting in 2000 estimates are based on an expanded household sample. Implementation of these changes had no effect on the all ages poverty rate for 2000 and a 0.1–0.3 percent difference in the age-specific poverty rates for 2000. See Appendix II, Poverty level. See related *Health, United States, 2005,* table 2.

SOURCES: U.S. Census Bureau, Current population survey, March 1967–2004. U.S. Bureau of the Census. DeNavas-Walt C, Proctor B, and Mills R. Income, Poverty, and Health Insurance Coverage in the United States: 2003. Current population reports, series P-60, no 226. Washington: U.S. Government Printing Office. 2004.

Data table for figure 5. Low income by age, race and Hispanic origin: United States, 2003

Age, race and Hispanic origin	*Poor*	*Near poor*	*Poor*	*Near poor*
	Percent		Number in millions	
All ages				
All races and origins	12.5	18.6	35.9	53.5
Hispanic or Latino	22.5	30.1	9.1	12.2
Black or African American only	24.4	24.0	8.8	8.6
Asian only	11.8	15.2	1.4	1.8
White only, not Hispanic or Latino	8.2	15.4	15.9	30.0
Under 18 years				
All races and origins	17.6	21.5	12.9	15.7
Hispanic or Latino	29.7	32.9	4.1	4.5
Black or African American only	34.1	27.2	3.9	3.1
Asian only	12.5	17.2	0.3	0.5
White only, not Hispanic or Latino	9.8	16.6	4.2	7.2
18–64 years				
All races and origins	10.8	15.5	19.4	27.9
Hispanic or Latino	18.7	28.2	4.6	6.9
Black or African American only	19.4	21.2	4.2	4.6
Asian only	11.3	12.8	0.9	1.0
White only, not Hispanic or Latino	7.6	12.2	9.4	14.9
65 years and over				
All races and origins	10.2	28.5	3.6	9.9
Hispanic or Latino	19.5	34.0	0.4	0.7
Black or African American only	23.7	32.2	0.7	0.9
Asian only	14.3	27.2	0.2	0.3
White only, not Hispanic or Latino	8.0	27.8	2.3	7.9

NOTES: Data are for the civilian noninstitutionalized population. Poor is defined as family income less than 100 percent of the poverty level and near poor as 100–199 percent of the poverty level. Persons of Hispanic origin may be of any race. Black and Asian races include persons of both Hispanic and non-Hispanic origin. See related *Health, United States, 2005,* table 2. See Appendix II, Hispanic origin; Poverty; Race.

SOURCES: DeNavas-Walt C, Proctor B, and Mills R. Income, Poverty, and Health Insurance Coverage in the United States: 2003. Current population reports, series P-60 no 226. Washington: U.S. Government Printing Office. 2004; Age and sex of all people, family members, and unrelated individuals iterated by income-to-poverty ratio and race: 2003, available at ferret.bls.census.gov/macro/032004/pov/new01_000.htm accessed on October 29, 2004.

Data table for figure 6. Health insurance coverage among persons under 65 years of age: United States, 1984–2003

	Health insurance coverage					
	Private		*Medicaid*		*Uninsured*	
Year	*Percent*	*SE*	*Percent*	*SE*	*Percent*	*SE*
1984	76.8	0.6	6.8	0.3	14.5	0.4
1989	75.9	0.4	7.2	0.2	15.6	0.3
1994	69.9	0.4	11.2	0.3	17.5	0.3
1995	71.3	0.4	11.5	0.2	16.1	0.2
1996	71.2	0.5	11.1	0.3	16.6	0.3
1997	70.7	0.4	9.7	0.2	17.5	0.2
1998	72.1	0.4	8.9	0.2	16.6	0.2
1999	72.8	0.3	9.1	0.2	16.1	0.2
2000	71.5	0.4	9.5	0.2	17.0	0.3
2001	71.2	0.4	10.4	0.2	16.4	0.3
2002	69.4	0.4	11.8	0.2	16.8	0.2
2003	68.9	0.4	12.3	0.2	16.5	0.3

SE Standard error.

NOTES: Data are for the civilian noninstitutionalized population. Medicaid includes other public assistance through 1996; includes State-sponsored health plans starting in 1997; and includes State Children's Health Insurance Program (SCHIP) starting in 1999. Uninsured persons are not covered by private insurance, Medicaid, SCHIP, public assistance (through 1996), State-sponsored or other government-sponsored health plans (starting in 1997), Medicare, or military plans. Persons with Indian Health Service only are considered uninsured. Percents do not add to 100 because the percent of persons with Medicare, military plans, and other government-sponsored plans is not shown and because persons with both private insurance and Medicaid appear in both categories. Starting with *Health, United States, 2005,* estimates for 2000 and later years use weights derived from the 2000 census. Estimates for 2000–2002 were recalculated using 2000-based weights and may differ from previous editions of *Health, United States.* See Appendix II, Health insurance coverage. See related *Health, United States, 2005,* tables 132–134.

SOURCE: Centers for Disease Control and Prevention, National Center for Health Statistics, National Health Interview Survey.

Data table for figure 7. No health insurance coverage among persons under 65 years of age by selected characteristics: United States, 2003

Characteristic	*Percent*	*SE*
Age		
Under 65 years	16.5	0.3
Under 18 years	9.8	0.3
18–24 years	30.1	0.7
25–34 years	25.4	0.5
35–44 years	17.5	0.4
45–54 years	13.6	0.4
55–64 years	10.9	0.4
Percent of poverty level		
Below 100 percent	31.1	0.8
100–149 percent	31.9	1.0
150–199 percent	27.6	1.0
200 percent or more	10.0	0.2
Race and Hispanic origin		
White only, not Hispanic or Latino	11.9	0.3
Asian only	18.2	1.3
Black or African American only, not Hispanic or Latino	18.1	0.6
American Indian and Alaska Native only	35.0	3.3
Hispanic or Latino (total)	34.7	0.7
Mexican	37.8	0.8
Cuban	29.1	2.7
Puerto Rican	17.7	1.5

SE Standard error.

NOTES: Data are for the civilian noninstitutionalized population. Persons of Hispanic origin may be of any race. Total for Hispanic includes groups not shown separately. Asian only and American Indian and Alaska Native only races include persons of Hispanic and non-Hispanic origin. Uninsured persons are not covered by private insurance, Medicaid, State Children's Health Insurance Program (SCHIP), State-sponsored or other government-sponsored health plans, Medicare, or military plans. Persons with Indian Health Service only are considered uninsured. Missing family income data were imputed for 33 percent of persons under 65 years of age in 2003. Starting with *Health, United States, 2005,* estimates for 2000 and later years use weights derived from the 2000 census. See Appendix II, Family income; Health insurance coverage; Hispanic origin; Poverty; Race. See related *Health, United States, 2005,* table 134.

SOURCE: Centers for Disease Control and Prevention, National Center for Health Statistics, National Health Interview Survey.

Data table for figure 8. National health expenditures as a percent of Gross Domestic Product: United States, 1960–2003

Year	*Percent*
1960	5.1
1965	5.7
1970	7.0
1975	7.9
1980	8.8
1985	10.1
1990	12.0
1991	12.7
1992	13.1
1993	13.3
1994	13.3
1995	13.4
1996	13.3
1997	13.2
1998	13.2
1999	13.2
2000	13.3
2001	14.1
2002	14.9
2003	15.3

NOTES: See related *Health, United States, 2005,* table 119. See Appendix I, National Health Accounts.

SOURCE: Centers for Medicare & Medicaid Services, Office of the Actuary, National Health Statistics Group, National Health Accounts.

Data table for figure 9. Personal health care expenditures according to source of funds and type of expenditures: United States, 2003

Personal health care expenditures and source of funds	*Total*	*Type of expenditures*				
		Hospital care	*Physician services*	*Nursing home*	*Prescription drugs*	*Other*
			Amount in billions			
All personal health care expenditures	$1,440.8	$515.9	$369.7	$110.8	$179.2	$265.1
			Percent distribution			
All personal health care expenditures	100.0	35.8	25.7	7.7	12.4	18.4
Source of funds			Percent distribution			
All sources of funds	100.0	100.0	100.0	100.0	100.0	100.0
Out-of-pocket payments	16.0	3.2	10.2	27.9	29.7	34.9
Private health insurance	36.0	34.4	49.7	7.6	46.3	25.0
Other private funds	4.2	4.1	6.9	3.8	0.0	3.4
Government	43.8	58.3	33.3	60.7	24.1	36.7
Medicaid	17.2	16.9	7.1	46.1	18.8	19.1
Medicare	19.1	30.3	19.9	12.4	1.6	10.6
Other government	7.5	11.1	6.3	2.2	3.7	7.0
Federal	33.3	46.9	27.4	41.1	14.1	24.8
State and local	10.5	11.4	5.9	19.7	10.0	11.9

NOTES: Other expenditures include dental services, other professional services, home health care, nonprescription drugs and other medical nondurables, vision products and other medical durables, and other personal health care, not shown separately. See related *Health, United States, 2005,* tables 122–123. See Appendix I, National Health Accounts.

SOURCE: Centers for Medicare and Medicaid Services, Office of the Actuary, National Health Accounts.

Data table for figure 10. Cigarette smoking among men, women, high school students, and mothers during pregnancy: United States, 1965–2003

Year	*Men*		*Women*		*High school students*		*Mothers during pregnancy*
	Percent	*SE*	*Percent*	*SE*	*Percent*	*SE*	*Percent*
1965	51.2	0.3	33.7	0.3	- - -	- - -	- - -
1974	42.8	0.5	32.2	0.4	- - -	- - -	- - -
1979	37.0	0.5	30.1	0.5	- - -	- - -	- - -
1983	34.8	0.6	29.4	0.4	- - -	- - -	- - -
1985	32.2	0.5	27.9	0.4	- - -	- - -	- - -
1987	30.9	0.4	26.5	0.4	- - -	- - -	- - -
1988	30.3	0.4	25.7	0.3	- - -	- - -	- - -
1989	- - -	- - -	- - -	- - -	- - -	- - -	19.5
1990	28.0	0.4	22.9	0.3	- - -	- - -	18.4
1991	27.6	0.4	23.5	0.3	27.5	1.4	17.8
1992	28.1	0.5	24.6	0.5	- - -	- - -	16.9
1993	27.3	0.6	22.6	0.4	30.5	1.0	15.8
1994	27.6	0.5	23.1	0.5	- - -	- - -	14.6
1995	26.5	0.6	22.7	0.5	34.8	1.2	13.9
1996	- - -	- - -	- - -	- - -	- - -	- - -	13.6
1997	27.1	0.4	22.2	0.4	36.4	1.1	13.2
1998	25.9	0.4	22.1	0.4	- - -	- - -	12.9
1999	25.2	0.5	21.6	0.4	34.8	1.3	12.6
2000	25.2	0.4	21.1	0.4	- - -	- - -	12.2
2001	24.6	0.4	20.7	0.4	28.5	1.0	12.0
2002	24.6	0.4	20.0	0.4	- - -	- - -	11.4
2003	23.7	0.4	19.4	0.4	21.9	1.1	- - -

SE Standard error.
- - - Data not available.

NOTES: Data for men and women are for the civilian noninstitutionalized population. Percents for men and women are age adjusted to the 2000 standard population using five age groups: 18–24 years, 25–34 years, 35–44 years, 45–64 years, and 65 years and over. Age-adjusted estimates in this table may differ from other age-adjusted estimates based on the same data and presented elsewhere if different age groups are used in the adjustment procedure. Cigarette smoking is defined as follows: among men and women 18 years and over, those who ever smoked 100 cigarettes in their lifetime and now smoke every day or some days; among high school students in grades 9–12, those who smoked cigarettes on 1 or more of the 30 days preceding the survey; and among mothers with a live birth, those who smoked during pregnancy. Data from States that did not require the reporting of mother's tobacco use during pregnancy on the birth certificate are not included. Starting with *Health, United States, 2005*, estimates from the National Health Interview Survey for 2000 and later years use weights derived from the 2000 census. Estimates for 2000–2002 from the National Health Interview Survey were recalculated using 2000-based weights and may differ from previous editions of *Health, United States*. See Appendix II, Age adjustment; Tobacco use. See related *Health, United States, 2005*, tables 12 and 63–65.

SOURCES: Centers for Disease Control and Prevention, National Center for Health Statistics, National Health Interview Survey (data for men and women); National Vital Statistics System (data for mothers during pregnancy); National Center for Chronic Disease Prevention and Health Promotion, Youth Risk Behavior Survey (data for high school students).

Data table for figure 11. Current and frequent cigarette smoking among high school students by sex, race and Hispanic origin, and grade level: United States, 2003

	All students				*Male students*				*Female students*			
	Current smoker		*Frequent smoker*		*Current smoker*		*Frequent smoker*		*Current smoker*		*Frequent smoker*	
Characteristic	*Percent*	*SE*	*Percent*	*SE*	*Percent*	*SE*	*Percent*	*SE*	*Percent*	*SE*	*Percent*	*SE*
Race and Hispanic origin												
All students, grades 9–12	21.9	1.1	9.7	0.7	21.8	1.1	9.6	0.8	21.9	1.4	9.7	0.9
Hispanic or Latino	18.4	1.2	5.5	0.7	19.1	1.8	6.6	1.2	17.7	1.1	4.4	0.7
Not Hispanic or Latino:												
White	24.9	1.2	11.8	0.8	23.3	1.3	10.4	0.9	26.6	1.9	13.2	1.2
Black or African American	15.1	1.4	5.5	0.8	19.3	1.9	7.9	1.3	10.8	1.5	3.1	0.7
Grade												
Grade 9	17.4	1.2	6.3	0.8	16.0	1.2	5.7	1.0	18.9	1.9	6.9	1.3
Grade 10	21.8	1.5	9.2	1.0	21.7	1.7	9.5	1.2	21.9	1.9	9.0	1.3
Grade 11	23.6	1.6	11.2	1.3	23.2	1.8	10.5	1.3	24.0	2.0	11.8	1.9
Grade 12	26.2	1.4	13.1	1.2	29.0	2.0	14.5	1.5	23.3	1.6	11.4	1.2

SE standard error.

NOTES: Current cigarette smoking is defined as having smoked cigarettes on 1 or more days of the 30 days preceding the survey; frequent cigarette smoking is defined as having smoked cigarettes on 20 or more of the 30 days preceding the survey. See Appendix II, Hispanic origin; Race.

SOURCE: Centers for Disease Control and Prevention, National Center for Chronic Disease Prevention and Health Promotion, Youth Risk Behavior Survey.

Data table for figure 12. Seatbelt use and drinking and driving among high school students by sex: United States, 1991–2003

	All students		*Male students*		*Female students*	
Year	*Percent*	*SE*	*Percent*	*SE*	*Percent*	*SE*
			Rarely or never wore a seatbelt (Grades 9–12)			
1991	25.9	2.7	30.0	3.0	21.6	2.6
1993	19.1	1.3	23.8	1.7	14.2	1.1
1995	21.7	1.7	26.1	2.1	16.9	1.8
1997	19.3	1.8	23.2	2.1	14.5	1.5
1999	16.4	1.4	20.8	1.5	11.9	1.5
2001	14.1	0.8	18.1	1.1	10.2	0.8
2003	18.2	2.1	21.5	2.2	14.6	2.2
			Rode with a driver who had been drinking alcohol (Grades 9–12)			
1991	39.9	1.1	40.0	1.2	39.8	1.2
1993	35.3	1.3	36.3	1.5	34.5	1.6
1995	38.8	1.9	39.5	2.2	37.8	2.2
1997	36.6	1.1	38.3	1.3	34.5	1.1
1999	33.1	1.1	34.4	1.3	31.7	1.4
2001	30.7	1.0	31.8	1.2	29.6	1.1
2003	30.2	1.1	29.2	1.3	31.1	1.0
			Drove after drinking alcohol (Grades 11 and 12 only)			
1991	24.6	1.5	30.6	2.2	18.2	1.0
1993	19.6	1.4	25.7	1.6	13.2	1.6
1995	20.1	1.8	25.5	2.3	14.5	1.9
1997	22.7	2.4	27.9	2.8	16.2	2.2
1999	19.5	1.3	25.5	1.4	13.3	1.7
2001	19.3	1.2	24.6	1.5	14.1	1.1
2003	17.5	1.0	22.4	1.5	12.3	1.0

SE Standard error.

NOTES: Students who rarely or never wore a seatbelt when riding in a car driven by someone else; students who during the past 30 days rode one or more times in a car or other vehicle driven by someone who had been drinking alcohol; and students who during the past 30 days drove a car or other vehicle one or more times when they had been drinking alcohol. See Appendix II, Hispanic origin; Race.

SOURCE: Centers for Disease Control and Prevention, National Center for Chronic Disease Prevention and Health Promotion, Youth Risk Behavior Survey.

Data table for figure 13. High school students engaging in regular physical activity by sex, race and Hispanic origin, and grade: United States, 1999, 2001, and 2003

Sex, race and Hispanic origin, and grade	1999		2001		2003	
	Percent	*SE*	*Percent*	*SE*	*Percent*	*SE*
All students, grades 9–12	69.5	0.9	68.8	0.7	66.6	1.1
White, not Hispanic	71.8	1.1	70.7	0.8	69.0	1.5
Black, not Hispanic	60.0	2.4	63.6	2.0	58.8	1.9
Hispanic	64.8	2.2	64.6	1.4	63.5	1.4
Male students, grades 9–12	76.3	1.4	75.8	0.8	73.1	1.1
White, not Hispanic	78.1	1.9	77.1	0.9	75.2	1.3
Black, not Hispanic	68.0	4.2	74.6	1.4	68.2	2.0
Hispanic	75.6	2.4	72.3	1.6	69.7	2.0
Female students, grades 9–12	62.7	1.2	62.1	1.2	59.9	1.5
White, not Hispanic	65.2	1.3	64.7	1.4	62.5	2.0
Black, not Hispanic	52.5	1.7	53.3	2.9	49.6	2.4
Hispanic	54.2	2.6	57.0	2.2	57.4	2.3
All students:						
Grade 9	77.2	2.1	75.7	1.4	71.9	1.5
Grade 10	68.9	2.4	70.4	0.9	69.2	1.6
Grade 11	62.5	1.3	65.6	1.2	63.5	1.4
Grade 12	67.6	1.9	61.1	1.4	59.8	1.4
Male students:						
Grade 9	81.6	2.2	79.9	1.6	76.2	1.5
Grade 10	76.3	1.9	76.4	1.1	74.4	1.8
Grade 11	70.4	2.2	75.6	1.3	73.0	1.4
Grade 12	75.5	1.9	70.5	2.2	67.9	1.7
Female students:						
Grade 9	72.8	3.0	71.9	1.9	67.3	2.1
Grade 10	61.5	3.7	64.4	1.7	64.1	1.9
Grade 11	54.4	2.0	55.8	1.6	53.8	1.9
Grade 12	59.7	2.6	52.1	1.2	51.6	1.8

SE Standard error.

NOTES: Regular physical activity is defined as engaging in recommended amounts of moderate activity (does not cause sweating or hard breathing) for at least 30 minutes on 5 or more of the past 7 days; or vigorous activity (causes sweating and hard breathing) for at least 20 minutes on 3 or more of the past 7 days. The recommended amounts of physical activity for high school students are based on the Healthy People 2010 objectives 22–6 and 22–7 (U.S. Department of Health and Human Services. Healthy People 2010. 2nd ed. 2 vols. Washington: U.S. Government Printing Office, November 2000. Available at www.health.gov/healthypeople). See Appendix II, Hispanic origin; Race.

SOURCE: Centers for Disease Control and Prevention, National Center for Chronic Disease Prevention and Health Promotion, Youth Risk Behavior Survey.

Data table for figure 14. Leisure-time physical activity among adults 18 years of age and over by poverty status: United States, 2003

Poverty level	Leisure-time physical activity level					
	Inactive		Some leisure-time activity		Regular leisure-time activity	
	Percent	SE	Percent	SE	Percent	SE
18 years and over, age adjusted	37.6	0.5	29.5	0.4	32.8	0.4
18 years and over, crude	37.6	0.5	29.6	0.4	32.8	0.4
18 years and over, age adjusted						
Poor	55.1	1.2	22.0	0.8	22.9	1.0
Near poor	50.5	0.9	24.8	0.7	24.7	0.7
Nonpoor	31.4	0.5	32.0	0.4	36.7	0.5

SE Standard error.

NOTES: Data are for the civilian noninstitutionalized population. Data are age adjusted to the 2000 standard population using five age groups: 18–44 years, 45–54 years, 55–64 years, 65–74 years, and 75 years and over. Adults were asked about the frequency and duration of vigorous and light/moderate physical activity during leisure time. Adults classified as inactive reported no sessions of light/moderate or vigorous leisure-time physical activity of at least 10 minutes duration; adults classified with some leisure-time physical activity reported at least one session of light/moderate or vigorous physical activity of at least 10 minutes duration but did not meet the definition of regular leisure-time activity; adults classified with regular leisure-time physical activity reported three or more sessions per week of vigorous activity of at least 20 minutes duration or five or more sessions per week of light/moderate activity lasting at least 30 minutes in duration. Poor persons are defined as below the poverty threshold. Near poor persons have incomes of 100 percent to less than 200 percent of the poverty threshold. Nonpoor persons have incomes of 200 percent or greater than the poverty threshold. Missing family income data were imputed for 36 percent of adults in 2003. Starting with *Health, United States, 2005,* estimates for 2000 and later years use weights derived from the 2000 census. See Appendix II, Age adjustment; Family income; Physical activity, leisure-time; Poverty. See related *Health, United States, 2005,* table 72.

SOURCE: Centers for Disease Control and Prevention, National Center for Health Statistics, National Health Interview Survey.

Data table for figure 15. Overweight and obesity by age: United States, 1960–2002

Year	Children 6–11 years		Adolescents 12–19 years		Adults 20–74 years					
	Overweight				Overweight including obese		Overweight but not obese		Obese	
	Percent	SE	Percent	SE	Percent	SE	Percent	SE	Percent	SE
1960–62	---	---	---	---	44.8	1.0	31.5	0.5	13.3	0.6
1963–65	4.2	0.4	---	---	---	---	---	---	---	---
1966–70	---	---	4.6	0.3	---	---	---	---	---	---
1971–74	4.0	0.5	6.1	0.6	47.7	0.7	33.1	0.6	14.6	0.5
1976–80	6.5	0.6	5.0	0.5	47.4	0.8	32.3	0.6	15.1	0.5
1988–94	11.3	1.0	10.5	0.9	56.0	0.9	32.7	0.6	23.3	0.7
1999–2002	15.8	1.1	16.1	0.8	65.2	0.8	34.1	0.8	31.1	1.0

SE Standard error.
--- Data not available.

NOTES: Data are for the civilian noninstitutionalized population. Percents for adults are age adjusted to the 2000 standard population using five age groups: 20–34 years, 35–44 years, 45–54 years, 55–64 years, and 65–74 years. Age-adjusted estimates in this table may differ from other age-adjusted estimates based on the same data and presented elsewhere if different age groups are used in the adjustment procedure. For children: Overweight is defined as a body mass index (BMI) at or above the sex- and age-specific 95th percentile BMI cut points from the 2000 CDC Growth Charts: United States (See: www.cdc.gov/growthcharts/); obese is not defined for children. For adults: Overweight including obese is defined as a BMI greater than or equal to 25; overweight but not obese as a BMI greater than or equal to 25 but less than 30; and obese as a BMI greater than or equal to 30. Data for 1966–70 are for adolescents 12–17 years, not 12–19 years. Pregnant adolescents were excluded beginning in 1971–74. Pregnant women 20 years of age and over were excluded in all years. See Appendix II, Age adjustment; Body mass index (BMI). See related *Health, United States, 2005,* tables 73 and 74.

SOURCES: Centers for Disease Control and Prevention, National Center for Health Statistics, National Health Examination Survey and National Health and Nutrition Examination Survey.

Data table for figure 16. Asthma attack among children by age, race and Hispanic origin: United States, 1998–2003

Race	1998–99		2000–2001		2002–03	
	Percent	*SE*	*Percent*	*SE*	*Percent*	*SE*
			Children 3–17 years			
Total	5.6	0.2	5.9	0.2	5.9	0.2
Race and Hispanic origin						
Hispanic or Latino	4.9	0.4	4.2	0.3	4.5	0.4
Not Hispanic or Latino:						
White only	5.6	0.3	5.8	0.3	5.7	0.3
Black or African American only	7.0	0.5	7.8	0.5	8.2	0.6
			Children 3–10 years			
Total	5.6	0.3	5.9	0.3	5.8	0.3
Race and Hispanic origin						
Hispanic or Latino	4.9	0.5	3.8	0.4	4.5	0.5
Not Hispanic or Latino:						
White only	5.4	0.3	5.9	0.4	5.2	0.3
Black or African American only	7.6	0.8	8.0	0.7	9.4	0.9
			Children 11–17 years			
Total	5.7	0.3	5.9	0.3	6.1	0.3
Race and Hispanic origin						
Hispanic or Latino	4.8	0.6	4.8	0.5	4.6	0.5
Not Hispanic or Latino:						
White only	5.8	0.4	5.7	0.4	6.1	0.4
Black or African American only	6.3	0.7	7.6	0.8	6.9	0.7

SE Standard error.

NOTES: Respondents (generally the parent) were asked if they had ever been told by a doctor or other health professional that the child had asthma. For those who answered "yes," respondents were asked about episodes of asthma or asthma attacks in the past 12 months. Data are for the civilian noninstitutionalized population. Starting with *Health, United States, 2005,* estimates for 2000 and later years use weights derived from the 2000 census. Total includes children of all races not shown separately. See Appendix II, Hispanic origin; Race.

SOURCE: Centers for Disease Control and Prevention, National Center for Health Statistics, National Health Interview Survey.

Data table for figure 17. Adults 18 years of age and over with severe headache or migraine or low back pain in the past 3 months by age and sex: United States, 2003

	Severe headache or migraine						Low back pain					
	Both sexes		Men		Women		Both sexes		Men		Women	
	Percent	*SE*	*Percent*	*SE*	*Percent*	*SE*	*Percent*	*SE*	*Percent*	*SE*	*Percent*	*SE*
18 years and over, crude	15.2	0.3	9.4	0.3	20.5	0.4	27.5	0.3	25.2	0.5	29.6	0.4
18–44 years	17.8	0.4	10.8	0.4	24.6	0.6	24.2	0.4	22.4	0.6	26.0	0.6
45–64 years	15.1	0.4	9.2	0.5	20.7	0.6	31.5	0.6	29.8	0.8	33.2	0.8
65 years and over	6.9	0.4	4.6	0.5	8.5	0.5	29.9	0.7	25.4	1.0	33.2	1.0

SE Standard error.

NOTES: Data are for the civilian noninstitutionalized population. Respondents were asked: "During the past 3 months, did you have a severe headache or migraine?" and "During the past 3 months, did you have low back pain?" Respondents were instructed to report pain that lasted a whole day or more and to not report fleeting or minor aches or pains. Starting with *Health, United States, 2005,* estimates for 2000 and later years use weights derived from the 2000 census. See related *Health, United States, 2005,* table 57.

SOURCE: Centers for Disease Control and Prevention, National Center for Health Statistics, National Health Interview Survey.

Data table for figure 18. Selected chronic health conditions causing limitation of activity among children by age: United States, 2002–03

Type of chronic health condition	Under 5 years		5–11 years		12–17 years	
	Rate	*SE*	*Rate*	*SE*	*Rate*	*SE*
	Number of children with limitation of activity caused by selected chronic health conditions per 1,000 population					
Speech problem	10.7	1.0	18.5	1.1	4.6	0.5
Asthma or breathing problem	8.2	0.9	8.4	0.7	8.3	0.8
Mental retardation or other developmental problem	7.0	0.8	10.2	0.8	9.6	0.8
Other mental, emotional, or behavioral problem	2.7	0.5	12.0	1.0	14.2	1.1
Attention Deficit/Hyperactivity Disorder	2.1	0.4	17.6	1.2	21.8	1.3
Learning disability	2.9	0.5	23.3	1.2	33.9	1.7

SE Standard error.

NOTES: Data are for noninstitutionalized children. Children with limitation of activity caused by chronic health conditions may be identified by enrollment in special programs (special education or early intervention services) or by reporting a limitation in their ability to perform activities usual for their age group because of a physical, mental, or emotional problem. Conditions refer to response categories in the National Health Interview Survey. The selected health conditions, regardless of duration, are classified as chronic in this analysis. Children who were reported to have more than one chronic health condition as the cause of their activity limitation were counted in each reported category. Starting in 2001 the condition list for children was expanded to include categories for Attention Deficit/Hyperactivity Disorder (ADD or ADHD) and learning disability. Thus, comparable data for this figure are not available prior to 2001. Starting with *Health, United States, 2005,* estimates for 2000 and later years use weights derived from the 2000 census. See Appendix II, Condition; Limitation of activity. See related *Health, United States, 2005,* table 58.

SOURCE: Centers for Disease Control and Prevention, National Center for Health Statistics, National Health Interview Survey.

Data table for figure 19. Selected chronic health conditions causing limitation of activity among working-age adults by age: United States, 2002–03

Type of chronic health condition	*18–44 years*		*45–54 years*		*55–64 years*	
	Rate	*SE*	*Rate*	*SE*	*Rate*	*SE*
	Number of persons with limitation of activity caused by selected chronic health conditions per 1,000 population					
Mental illness	12.9	0.5	23.1	1.1	24.1	1.4
Fractures or joint injury	7.0	0.4	15.5	0.9	20.6	1.2
Lung	5.0	0.3	12.6	0.8	25.6	1.3
Diabetes	2.5	0.2	13.4	0.8	33.4	1.5
Heart or other circulatory	5.9	0.3	28.4	1.2	74.3	2.4
Arthritis or other musculoskeletal	22.2	0.7	61.9	1.8	100.7	2.6

SE Standard error.

NOTES: Data are for the civilian noninstitutionalized population. Conditions refer to response categories in the National Health Interview Survey; some conditions include several response categories. "Mental illness" includes depression, anxiety or emotional problem, and other mental conditions. "Heart or other circulatory" includes heart problem, stroke problem, hypertension or high blood pressure, and other circulatory system conditions. "Arthritis or other musculoskeletal" includes arthritis or rheumatism, back or neck problem, and other musculoskeletal system conditions. Persons may report more than one chronic health condition as the cause of their activity limitation. Starting with *Health, United States, 2005,* estimates for 2000 and later years use weights derived from the 2000 census. See related *Health, United States, 2005,* table 58. See Appendix II, Condition; Limitation of activity.

SOURCE: Centers for Disease Control and Prevention, National Center for Health Statistics, National Health Interview Survey.

Data table for figure 20. Selected chronic health conditions causing limitation of activity among older adults by age: United States, 2002–03

Type of chronic health condition	*65–74 years*		*75–84 years*		*85 years and over*	
	Rate	*SE*	*Rate*	*SE*	*Rate*	*SE*
	Number of persons with limitation of activity caused by selected chronic health conditions per 1,000 population					
Senility	6.8	0.8	30.5	2.0	96.1	6.5
Lung	34.7	2.0	41.4	2.5	44.4	5.6
Diabetes	41.1	1.9	49.4	2.7	38.4	4.6
Vision	18.2	1.5	44.3	2.6	96.6	7.3
Hearing	10.0	1.1	27.8	2.0	84.9	6.8
Heart or other circulatory	101.9	3.3	162.6	5.1	223.5	10.2
Arthritis or other musculoskeletal	125.8	3.6	171.0	4.7	267.6	10.6

SE Standard error.

NOTES: Data are for the civilian noninstitutionalized population. Conditions refer to response categories in the National Health Interview Survey; some conditions include several response categories. "Vision" includes vision conditions or problems seeing and "hearing" includes hearing problems. "Heart or other circulatory" includes heart problem, stroke problem, hypertension or high blood pressure, and other circulatory system conditions. "Arthritis or other musculoskeletal" includes arthritis or rheumatism, back or neck problem, and other musculoskeletal system conditions. "Senility" is the term offered to respondents on a flashcard, but this category may include Alzheimer's disease or other types of dementia reported by the respondent. Persons may report more than one chronic health condition as the cause of their activity limitation. Starting with *Health, United States, 2005,* estimates for 2000 and later years use weights derived from the 2000 census. See related *Health, United States, 2005,* table 58. See Appendix II, Condition; Limitation of activity.

SOURCE: Centers for Disease Control and Prevention, National Center for Health Statistics, National Health Interview Survey.

Data table for figure 21. Use of mammography within the past 2 years for women 40 years of age and over by selected characteristics: United States, selected years 1987–2003

Characteristic	*Year*								
	1987	*1990*	*1991*	*1993*	*1994*	*1998*	*1999*	*2000*	*2003*
	Percent of woman having a mammogram within the past 2 years								
All women 40 years and over, crude	28.7	51.4	54.6	59.7	60.9	66.9	70.3	70.4	69.7
Race and Hispanic origin									
40 years and over, crude:									
Hispanic or Latino	18.3	45.2	49.2	50.9	51.9	60.2	65.7	61.2	65.0
Asian only	*	46.0	45.9	55.1	55.8	60.2	58.3	53.5	57.6
Not Hispanic or Latino:									
White only	30.3	52.7	56.0	60.6	61.3	68.0	71.1	72.2	70.5
Black or African American only	23.8	46.0	47.7	59.2	64.4	66.0	71.0	67.9	70.5
Poverty status									
40 years and over, crude:									
Poor	14.6	30.8	35.2	41.1	44.2	50.1	57.4	54.8	55.4
Near poor	20.9	39.1	44.4	47.5	48.6	56.1	59.5	58.1	60.8
Nonpoor	35.2	59.2	62.2	67.3	68.5	72.6	75.0	75.9	74.3
Education									
40 years and over, crude:									
No high school diploma or GED	17.8	36.4	40.0	46.4	48.2	54.5	56.7	57.7	58.1
High school diploma or GED	31.3	52.7	55.8	59.0	61.0	66.7	69.2	69.7	67.8
Some college or more	37.7	62.8	65.2	69.5	69.7	72.8	77.3	76.2	75.1
	Standard error								
All women 40 years and over, crude	0.7	0.6	0.5	0.7	0.7	0.5	0.5	0.6	0.5
Race and Hispanic origin									
40 years and over, crude:									
Hispanic or Latino	2.3	2.4	2.4	3.2	3.4	1.7	1.8	1.7	1.6
Asian only	*	4.5	4.1	5.6	5.5	4.0	4.3	4.3	3.6
Not Hispanic or Latino:									
White only	0.7	0.7	0.6	0.8	0.8	0.6	0.6	0.6	0.6
Black or African American only	2.0	1.5	1.5	2.1	1.9	1.6	1.5	1.5	1.5
Poverty status									
40 years and over, crude:									
Poor	1.3	1.1	1.3	1.8	2.0	1.6	1.9	1.7	1.6
Near poor	1.1	1.1	1.0	1.4	1.4	1.3	1.4	1.3	1.3
Nonpoor	1.0	0.7	0.7	0.8	0.9	0.6	0.6	0.6	0.6
Education									
40 years and over, crude:									
No high school diploma or GED	0.9	1.1	0.9	1.4	1.6	1.2	1.2	1.2	1.3
High school diploma or GED	1.1	0.8	0.8	1.2	1.2	0.9	1.0	0.9	1.0
Some college or more	1.2	0.9	0.8	1.0	1.0	0.8	0.7	0.7	0.7

* Estimates are considered unreliable. Data not shown have a relative standard error greater than 30 percent.

NOTES: Data are for the civilian noninstitutionalized population. Persons of Hispanic origin may be of any race. Asian only race includes persons of both Hispanic and non-Hispanic origin. Poor persons are defined as below the poverty threshold. Near poor persons have incomes of 100 percent to less than 200 percent of the poverty threshold. Nonpoor persons have incomes of 200 percent or greater than the poverty threshold. Poverty status was unknown for 11 percent of women 40 years of age and over in 1987. Missing family income data were imputed for 19–23 percent of women 40 years of age and over in 1990–94 and 35–39 percent in 1998–2003. Education categories shown are for 1998 and subsequent years. In 1994 and earlier years the following categories based on number of years of school completed were used: less than 12 years, 12 years, and 13 years or more. Starting with *Health, United States 2005,* estimates for 2000 and later years use weights derived from the 2000 census. Estimates for 2000 were recalculated using 2000-based weights and may differ from previous editions of *Health, United States.* See related *Health, United States 2005,* table 86. See Appendix II, Education; Family income; Hispanic origin; Mammography; Poverty level; Race.

SOURCE: Centers for Disease Control and Prevention, National Center for Health Statistics, National Health Interview Survey.

Data table for figure 22. Use of Pap smears within the past 3 years for women 18 years of age and over by selected characteristics: United States, 1987–2003

Characteristic	Year						
	1987	*1993*	*1994*	*1998*	*1999*	*2000*	*2003*
	Percent of woman having a Pap smear within the past 3 years						
All women age 18 years and over, crude	74.4	77.7	76.8	79.1	80.8	81.2	79.0
Race and Hispanic origin							
18 years and over, crude:							
Hispanic or Latino	67.6	77.2	74.4	75.2	76.3	77.0	75.4
Asian only	51.9	68.8	66.4	68.5	64.4	66.4	68.3
Not Hispanic or Latino:							
White only	74.7	77.3	76.5	79.3	81.0	81.8	79.3
Black or African American only	80.9	82.7	83.8	84.2	86.0	85.1	83.8
Poverty status							
18 years and over, crude:							
Poor	64.3	70.3	68.8	69.8	73.6	72.0	70.5
Near poor	68.2	71.2	68.8	70.6	72.5	73.4	71.4
Nonpoor	80.0	82.1	81.9	83.5	84.3	85.0	83.0
Education							
25 years and over, crude:							
No high school diploma or GED	57.1	61.9	60.9	65.0	66.1	69.9	64.9
High school diploma or GED	76.4	78.2	76.0	77.4	79.3	79.8	75.9
Some college or more	84.0	84.4	85.2	86.9	87.8	88.0	86.2
	Standard error						
All women age 18 years and over, crude	0.5	0.5	0.5	0.4	0.4	0.4	0.4
Race and Hispanic origin							
18 years and over, crude:							
Hispanic or Latino	2.0	1.9	1.8	1.0	1.0	1.1	1.1
Asian only	5.0	4.0	3.5	2.8	3.0	2.8	2.6
Not Hispanic or Latino:							
White only	0.5	0.5	0.6	0.4	0.5	0.4	0.5
Black or African American only	1.2	1.3	1.2	0.9	0.9	0.8	1.0
Poverty status							
18 years and over, crude:							
Poor	1.4	1.4	1.3	1.1	1.1	1.1	1.1
Near poor	1.0	1.0	1.1	0.9	0.9	0.9	0.9
Nonpoor	0.6	0.5	0.6	0.4	0.4	0.4	0.4
Education							
25 years and over, crude:							
No high school diploma or GED	1.1	1.3	1.2	0.9	1.0	1.0	1.0
High school diploma or GED	0.8	0.7	0.8	0.7	0.7	0.7	0.8
Some college or more	0.7	0.6	0.6	0.5	0.4	0.4	0.5

NOTES: Data are for the civilian noninstitutionalized population. Persons of Hispanic origin may be of any race. Asian only race includes persons of both Hispanic and non-Hispanic origin. Poor persons are defined as below the poverty threshold. Near poor persons have incomes of 100 percent to less than 200 percent of the poverty threshold. Nonpoor persons have incomes of 200 percent or greater than the poverty threshold. Poverty status was unknown for 9 percent of women 18 years of age and over in 1987. Missing family income data were imputed for 17–20 percent of women 18 years of age and over in 1990–94 and 31–36 percent in 1998–2003. Education categories shown are for 1998 and subsequent years. In years prior to 1998 the following categories based on number of years of school completed were used: less than 12 years, 12 years, and 13 years or more. Starting with *Health, United States 2005,* estimates for 2000 and later years use weights derived from the 2000 census. Estimates for 2000 were recalculated using 2000-based weights and may differ from previous editions of Health, United States. See related *Health, United States 2005,* table 87. See Appendix II, Education; Family income; Hispanic origin; Pap smear; Poverty level; Race.

SOURCE: Centers for Disease Control and Prevention, National Center for Health Statistics, National Health Interview Survey.

Data table for figure 23. Injury-related visits to hospital emergency departments among children under 20 years of age by first-listed external cause and age: United States, average annual 2000–2003

	All injury-related visits	*All causes*	*Falls*	*Struck by*	*Motor vehicle traffic-related injuries*	*Cut*
Both sexes	Injury-related visits per 10,000 population					
Under 1 year	1,376.5	1,032.4	386.0	166.3	76.0	*
1 year old	1,868.0	1,493.4	531.9	279.8	49.7	51.2
2 years old	1,816.7	1,541.6	452.7	290.6	118.3	87.8
3 years old	1,614.6	1,354.7	414.8	302.9	50.9	85.3
4 years old	1,354.6	1,178.6	408.3	242.7	67.3	88.3
5 years old	1,359.1	1,112.0	325.2	244.6	86.6	92.1
6 years old	1,161.0	972.0	269.7	212.5	74.1	76.7
7 years old	1,160.8	996.1	339.0	193.9	97.4	53.1
8 years old	1,102.6	929.5	280.9	217.3	53.1	81.9
9 years old	1,276.3	1,072.2	295.4	270.3	99.7	75.2
10 years old	1,291.9	1,105.7	274.0	300.7	86.1	67.6
11 years old	1,355.6	1,177.0	276.1	326.2	106.4	87.6
12 years old	1,324.0	1,141.7	260.6	336.9	76.3	87.5
13 years old	1,397.3	1,204.6	268.1	391.9	91.5	64.6
14 years old	1,724.2	1,485.8	273.8	510.2	113.3	120.3
15 years old	1,567.5	1,376.4	215.8	441.3	159.4	96.4
16 years old	1,672.7	1,408.5	227.8	346.1	259.1	136.0
17 years old	1,931.9	1,593.9	186.0	455.4	341.2	149.5
18 years old	2,044.3	1,665.0	182.4	348.3	439.2	233.0
19 years old	1,947.2	1,542.6	176.5	357.5	315.1	170.4
Both sexes	Standard error					
Under 1 year	105.7	96.0	56.9	31.3	13.9	10.5
1 year old	109.6	97.9	52.9	35.6	11.9	13.4
2 years old	94.5	81.7	42.3	32.6	21.3	16.8
3 years old	92.7	75.9	37.7	35.2	11.1	17.5
4 years old	85.1	79.6	41.7	32.2	15.2	20.4
5 years old	84.3	74.2	35.1	27.8	23.2	18.3
6 years old	80.0	71.2	29.1	30.3	15.6	15.7
7 years old	71.2	64.3	38.5	23.7	18.9	11.8
8 years old	66.8	60.5	30.9	27.0	11.9	20.3
9 years old	79.4	74.1	38.0	38.5	21.2	15.4
10 years old	76.2	73.6	29.8	33.9	19.5	13.8
11 years old	74.5	68.5	30.3	33.4	18.1	16.6
12 years old	84.2	77.9	24.8	33.9	16.4	15.6
13 years old	74.2	67.4	35.3	34.2	16.1	11.7
14 years old	101.9	94.1	34.7	51.0	24.7	18.9
15 years old	83.8	77.5	23.6	44.7	21.6	18.2
16 years old	77.4	71.8	30.6	36.1	27.7	22.8
17 years old	91.5	86.3	25.8	47.1	35.4	23.3
18 years old	104.2	90.3	28.2	34.9	42.4	29.3
19 years old	91.4	78.0	24.5	34.5	32.4	23.1

* Relative standard error greater than 30 percent.

NOTES: Rates are for the civilian noninstitutionalized population. An emergency department visit was considered injury related if the checkbox for injury was indicated, the physician's diagnosis was injury related (*International Classification of Diseases, Ninth Revision, Clinical Modification* (ICD–9–CM) 800–999), an external cause of injury code was present (ICD–9–CM E800–E999), or the patient's reason for visit was injury related. External cause of injury is the classification of environmental events, circumstances, and conditions that were the cause of injury. Falls include E880–E886, E888, E957, E968.1, and E987 from the ICD–9–CM; struck by includes E916–E917, E960.0, E968.2, E973, and E975; motor vehicle traffic-related injury includes E810–E819, E958.5, E968.5, and E988.5; cut includes E920, E956, E966, E974, and E986. See Appendix II, External cause of injury; Injury visit.

SOURCE: Centers for Disease Control and Prevention, National Center for Health Statistics, National Hospital Ambulatory Medical Care Survey.

Data table for figure 24. Visits to physician offices and hospital outpatient departments by sex and age: United States, 1996–2003

	1996–97	*1998–99*	*2000–2001*	*2002–03*
Both sexes	Visits in thousands			
Total	833,022	873,025	970,880	1,024,122
Under 18 years	178,143	172,228	189,609	202,841
18–44 years	260,687	271,465	282,616	288,063
45–54 years	109,646	121,157	142,323	154,672
55–64 years	88,141	100,882	117,109	129,913
65–74 years	103,035	104,393	120,115	119,510
75 years and over	93,369	102,899	119,108	129,122
Male				
Total	336,321	351,822	393,207	414,317
Under 18 years	91,607	88,935	97,771	105,322
18–44 years	83,091	88,853	92,451	93,258
45–54 years	42,877	46,526	56,115	61,388
55–64 years	38,121	43,542	48,330	52,830
65–74 years	43,711	45,039	51,408	51,657
75 years and over	36,915	38,926	47,133	49,863
Female				
Total	496,700	521,203	577,673	609,804
Under 18 years	86,536	83,293	91,838	97,520
18–44 years	177,597	182,612	190,165	194,805
45–54 years	66,769	74,630	86,208	93,284
55–64 years	50,020	57,340	68,779	77,084
65–74 years	59,325	59,354	68,708	67,853
75 years and over	56,454	63,973	71,975	79,259

See footnotes at end of table.

Data table for figure 24. Visits to physician offices and hospital outpatient departments by sex and age: United States, 1996–2003—Continued

	1996–97		*1998–99*		*2000–2001*		*2002–03*	
	Rate	*SE*	*Rate*	*SE*	*Rate*	*SE*	*Rate*	*SE*
Both sexes	Number of visits per 100 persons							
Total	313.7	8.5	322.7	9.7	348.6	10.4	360.2	9.4
Under 18 years	250.1	10.2	239.3	10.4	262.2	10.7	278.6	12.3
18–44 years	240.6	7.7	250.2	9.1	257.9	10.4	261.5	8.3
45–54 years	334.1	11.3	346.2	11.5	371.5	12.9	385.6	13.8
55–64 years	414.7	13.6	444.6	15.3	473.8	17.0	479.5	15.7
65–74 years	567.7	19.4	583.8	21.8	663.5	25.3	661.7	23.1
75 years and over	676.4	25.1	708.4	31.3	770.1	31.5	804.1	28.5
Male								
Total	259.4	7.7	266.8	8.5	289.8	8.8	298.6	8.7
Under 18 years	251.2	11.3	241.5	11.2	264.2	11.3	282.9	13.4
18–44 years	155.1	6.0	166.3	6.7	171.0	8.0	171.0	6.6
45–54 years	267.6	9.8	272.7	11.1	300.2	12.1	313.5	13.2
55–64 years	376.4	14.2	402.3	16.8	408.4	17.2	406.4	15.3
65–74 years	537.4	20.1	558.5	23.4	627.7	25.1	629.0	24.1
75 years and over	698.2	29.2	689.4	34.1	798.4	32.2	803.7	32.6
Female								
Total	365.3	9.8	375.8	11.8	404.6	12.7	419.0	11.1
Under 18 years	248.9	9.7	236.9	10.7	260.1	11.1	274.1	12.1
18–44 years	324.4	10.7	331.7	13.7	342.6	14.4	350.2	12.3
45–54 years	397.6	14.9	416.3	14.3	439.5	16.3	454.4	17.1
55–64 years	449.6	16.4	483.1	17.2	533.9	20.8	547.0	19.8
65–74 years	592.2	22.6	604.6	25.0	693.0	30.9	688.9	27.1
75 years and over	662.9	25.5	720.4	32.7	752.6	34.9	804.3	30.2

SE Standard error.

NOTES: For 1996–99 data, population estimates are 1990-based postcensal estimates as of July 1 and are adjusted for net underenumeration using the 1990 National Population Adjustment Matrix from the U.S. Census Bureau. For data years 2000 and beyond population estimates are based on the 2000 census. See Appendix I, Population Census and Population Estimates. See related *Health, United States, 2005,* table 88. Starting with *Health, United States, 2005,* data from 2001 and onwards use a revised weighting scheme. See Appendix I, National Ambulatory Medical Care Survey.

SOURCE: Centers for Disease Control and Prevention, National Center for Health Statistics, National Ambulatory Medical Care Survey and National Hospital Ambulatory Medical Care Survey.

Data table for figure 25. Hospital inpatient procedures for insertion of coronary artery stent(s) among adults 45 years of age and over by age and sex: United States 1996–2003

Sex and year	45 years and over: Hospital discharges with any listed stent procedure, average annual	45 years and over, crude		45–54 years		55–64 years		65–74 years		75 years and over	
		Rate	SE	Rate	SE	Rate	SE	Rate	SE	Rate	SE
	Number in thousands	Number per 10,000 population									
All persons											
1996–97	191	21.7	1.7	12.5	1.1	24.7	2.2	33.7	3.2	22.8	2.6
1998–99	388	42.1	3.5	22.2	2.2	49.8	4.9	63.4	5.3	50.9	4.8
2000–2001	436	44.2	3.2	21.1	1.6	47.7	3.5	70.3	5.6	63.4	6.2
2002–03	510	49.3	3.8	24.5	2.2	49.0	3.8	81.8	7.0	73.3	6.7
Men											
1996–97	131	32.5	2.5	19.9	1.7	39.9	4.0	48.5	5.0	32.1	3.6
1998–99	249	58.8	4.7	34.8	3.4	73.1	7.8	85.5	7.1	65.0	5.6
2000–2001	279	61.4	4.5	32.4	2.8	69.9	5.4	95.2	7.9	88.3	8.7
2002–03	336	70.3	5.3	39.2	3.7	71.3	5.3	113.9	10.2	106.7	11.3
Women											
1996–97	60	12.5	1.2	5.5	0.8	10.7	1.4	21.6	2.5	17.4	2.3
1998–99	140	28.0	2.6	10.0	1.5	28.5	3.0	45.2	4.6	42.4	5.1
2000–2001	157	29.5	2.3	10.3	1.1	27.2	2.2	49.8	4.3	48.8	5.3
2002–03	174	31.3	2.8	10.3	1.3	28.4	3.2	55.0	5.8	53.3	5.0

SE Standard error.

NOTES: Up to four procedures were coded for each non-Federal hospital stay. Data in this table are for any listed procedures, that is, if more than one stenting procedure is performed during the same hospital stay, it is counted only once. Effective with the 2003 National Hospital Discharge Survey, a new procedure code for the insertion of drug-eluting coronary artery stents is available. Procedure groupings and code numbers are based on the *International Classification of Diseases, 9th Revision, Clinical Modification* (ICD–9–CM). See Appendix II, table X.

SOURCE: Centers for Disease Control and Prevention, National Center for Health Statistics, National Hospital Discharge Survey.

Data table for figure 26. Life expectancy at birth and at 65 years of age by sex: United States, 1900–1902 through 2002

Year	At birth		At 65 years	
	Male	*Female*	*Male*	*Female*
	Life expectancy in years			
1900–1902	47.9	50.7	11.5	12.2
1909–11	49.9	53.2	11.2	12.0
1919–21	55.5	57.4	12.2	12.7
1929–31	57.7	60.9	11.7	12.8
1939–41	61.6	65.9	12.1	13.6
1949–51	65.5	71.0	12.7	15.0
1959–61	66.8	73.2	13.0	15.8
1969–71	67.0	74.6	13.0	16.8
1979–81	70.1	77.6	14.2	18.4
1989–91	71.8	78.8	15.1	19.0
1997	73.6	79.4	15.9	19.2
1998	73.8	79.5	16.0	19.2
1999	73.9	79.4	16.1	19.1
2000	74.3	79.7	16.2	19.3
2001	74.4	79.8	16.4	19.4
2002	74.5	79.9	16.6	19.5

NOTES: Death rates used to calculate life expectancies for 1997–1999 are based on postcensal 1990-based population estimates; life expectancies for 2000 and beyond are calculated with death rates based on census 2000. See Appendix I, Population Census and Population Estimates. Life expectancies prior to 1997 are from decennial life tables based on census data and deaths for a 3-year period around the census year. The middle year in each 3-year period is plotted in figure 26. Beginning in 1997, the annual life tables are complete life tables based on a methodology similar to that used for decennial life tables. Alaska and Hawaii were included beginning in 1959. For decennial periods prior to 1929–31, data are limited to death registration States: 1900–1902 and 1909–11, 10 States and the District of Columbia; 1919–21, 34 States and the District of Columbia. Deaths to nonresidents were excluded beginning in 1970. See Appendix II, Life expectancy. See related *Health, United States, 2005,* table 27.

SOURCE: Arias, E. United States life tables, 2002. National vital statistics reports; vol 53 no 6. Hyattsville, MD: National Center for Health Statistics. 2004.

Data table for figure 27. Infant, neonatal, and postneonatal mortality rates: United States, 1950–2002

Year	*Infant*	*Neonatal*	*Postneonatal*
		Deaths per 1,000 live births	
1950	29.2	20.5	8.7
1960	26.0	18.7	7.3
1970	20.0	15.1	4.9
1980	12.6	8.5	4.1
1985	10.6	7.0	3.7
1990	9.2	5.8	3.4
1995	7.6	4.9	2.7
1996	7.3	4.8	2.5
1997	7.2	4.8	2.5
1998	7.2	4.8	2.4
1999	7.1	4.7	2.3
2000	6.9	4.6	2.3
2001	6.8	4.5	2.3
2002	7.0	4.7	2.3

NOTES: Infant is defined as under 1 year of age, neonatal as under 28 days of age, and postneonatal as between 28 days and 1 year of age. See related *Health, United States, 2005,* table 22.

SOURCE: Centers for Disease Control and Prevention, National Center for Health Statistics, National Vital Statistics System.

Data table for figure 28. Infant mortality rates by detailed race and Hispanic origin of mother: United States, 2000–2002

Race and Hispanic origin of mother	*Infant deaths per 1,000 live birth*
White, not Hispanic or Latino	5.7
Black or African American, not Hispanic or Latino	13.6
Hispanic or Latino	5.5
Puerto Rican	8.3
Other and unknown Hispanic or Latino	6.7
Mexican	5.4
Central and South American	4.9
Cuban	4.2
Asian or Pacific Islander	4.8
Hawaiian	8.7
Filipino	5.7
Other Asian or Pacific Islander	4.8
Japanese	4.5
Chinese	3.2
American Indian or Alaska Native	8.9

NOTES: Infant is defined as under 1 year of age. Persons of Hispanic origin may be of any race. Asian or Pacific Islander and American Indian or Alaska Native races include persons of Hispanic and non-Hispanic origin. See Appendix II, Hispanic origin; Race. See related *Health, United States, 2005,* table 19.

SOURCE: Centers for Disease Control and Prevention, National Center for Health Statistics, National Vital Statistics System, National Linked Birth/Infant Death Data Sets.

Data table for figure 29. Death rates for leading causes of death for all ages: United States, 1950–2002

Year	*All causes*	*Heart disease*	*Cancer*	*Stroke*	*Chronic lower respiratory diseases*	*Unintentional injuries*
	Deaths per 100,000 population					
1950	1,446.0	586.8	193.9	180.7	- - -	78.0
1960	1,339.2	559.0	193.9	177.9	- - -	62.3
1970	1,222.6	492.7	198.6	147.7	- - -	60.1
1980	1,039.1	412.1	207.9	96.2	28.3	46.4
1985	988.1	375.0	211.3	76.4	34.5	38.5
1990	938.7	321.8	216.0	65.3	37.2	36.3
1995	909.8	293.4	209.9	63.1	40.1	34.4
1996	894.1	285.7	206.7	62.5	40.6	34.5
1997	878.1	277.7	203.4	61.1	41.1	34.2
1998	870.6	271.3	200.7	59.3	41.8	34.5
1998 (Comparability-modified)	870.6	267.3	202.6	62.3	43.5	35.4
1999	875.6	266.5	200.8	61.6	45.4	35.3
2000	869.0	257.6	199.6	60.9	44.2	34.9
2001	854.5	247.8	196.0	57.9	43.7	35.7
2002	845.3	240.8	193.5	56.2	43.5	36.9

- - - Data not available.

NOTES: Death rates are age adjusted to the year 2000 standard population using 10-year age groups from under 1 year, 1–4 years, 5–14 through 75–84 years, and 85 years and over. Causes of death shown are the five leading causes of death for all persons in 2002. The 1950 death rates are based on the 6th revision of the *International Classification of Disease* (ICD-6), 1960 death rates on the ICD-7, 1970 death rates on the ICDA-8, and 1980–98 death rates on the ICD-9. The 1998 (Comparability-modified) death rates use comparability ratios to adjust the rate to be comparable to records classified according to ICD-10. Starting in 1999 death rates are based on ICD-10. Comparability ratios across revisions for selected causes are available at www.cdc.gov/nchs/data/statab/comp2.pdf, and final comparability ratios for ICD-9 to ICD-10 are available at ftp://ftp.cdc.gov/pub/Health_Statistics/NCHS/Datasets/Comparability/icd9_icd10/. Death rates for chronic lower respiratory diseases are available from 1980 when a category that included bronchitis, emphysema, asthma, and other chronic lung diseases was introduced in ICD-9. Cancer refers to malignant neoplasms; stroke to cerebrovascular diseases; and unintentional injuries is preferred to accidents in the public health community. Rates for 1991–99 were computed using intercensal population estimates based on the 2000 census. Rates for 2000 were computed using 2000 census counts. Rates for 2001–02 were computed using postcensal estimates based on the 2000 census. See Appendix I, Population Census and Population Estimates. See Appendix II, Age adjustment; Cause of death; Comparability ratio. See related *Health, United States, 2005,* tables 29, 31, 35, 36, 37, 38, and 41.

SOURCE: Centers for Disease Control and Prevention, National Center for Health Statistics, National Vital Statistics System.

Data table for figure 30. Aging of the population 45 years of age and over: United States, 2004, 2014, and 2024

Age	*2004*	*2014*	*2024*	*2004–2014*	*2004–2024*
	Number in millions			Percent change	
Total population	293.6	319.7	346.7	8.9	18.1
0–19 years	81.5	84.6	91.4	3.9	12.2
20–44 years	105.2	106.5	111.3	1.3	5.8
45–54 years	41.6	43.6	40.7	4.7	–2.3
55–64 years	29.1	39.6	41.6	35.9	42.9
65 years and over	36.2	45.3	61.7	25.2	70.2

NOTE: Data for 2014 and 2024 are projections.

SOURCE: U.S. Census Bureau: Monthly Postcensal Resident Populations, from April 1, 2000 to July 1, 2004 by age, sex, race, and Hispanic origin available at www.census.gov/popest/national/asrh/2003_nat_res.html, July 1, 2004 file, accessed on January 24, 2005 [data for 2004]; U.S. Interim Projections detail file by age, sex, race, and Hispanic origin available at www.census.gov/ipc/www/usinterimproj accessed on January 21, 2005 [data for projections].

Data table for figure 31. Employment status among adults 55–64 years of age by sex, race and Hispanic origin: United States, 2002–03

			Race and Hispanic origin					
					Not Hispanic or Latino			
	All		*Hispanic or Latino*		*White only*		*Black or African American only*	
Sex and employment status	*Percent*	*SE*	*Percent*	*SE*	*Percent*	*SE*	*Percent*	*SE*
Both sexes								
Working	57.8	0.5	52.6	1.2	59.1	0.6	51.1	1.3
Retired	17.1	0.4	10.7	0.8	18.0	0.5	16.0	0.9
Unemployed due to disability	11.6	0.3	14.5	0.8	10.2	0.3	21.7	1.1
Taking care of house or family	7.6	0.2	14.8	0.8	7.2	0.2	5.2	0.6
Looking for work	2.0	0.1	2.7	0.4	1.9	0.1	2.4	0.4
Other	3.9	0.2	4.7	0.5	3.7	0.2	3.6	0.4
Men								
Working	64.4	0.6	65.5	1.7	64.9	0.7	57.2	1.8
Retired	17.4	0.5	10.3	1.1	18.4	0.6	16.3	1.4
Unemployed due to disability	11.5	0.4	14.7	1.2	10.4	0.5	19.2	1.6
Taking care of house or family	0.5	0.1	*	*	*0.4	0.1	*1.2	0.4
Looking for work	2.4	0.2	3.3	0.6	2.2	0.2	*3.2	0.7
Other	3.7	0.2	5.2	0.8	3.5	0.3	*2.9	0.6
Women								
Working	51.7	0.6	41.2	1.6	53.6	0.7	46.3	1.6
Retired	16.8	0.5	11.0	1.0	17.6	0.5	15.7	1.1
Unemployed due to disability	11.7	0.4	14.4	1.1	9.9	0.4	23.8	1.4
Taking care of house or family	14.2	0.4	27.1	1.5	13.5	0.5	8.3	0.9
Looking for work	1.6	0.1	2.1	0.4	1.5	0.2	*1.8	0.4
Other	4.0	0.2	4.3	0.6	3.9	0.3	4.2	0.6

SE Standard error.

* Estimates are considered unreliable. Data preceded by an asterisk have a relative standard error (RSE) of 20–30 percent. Data not shown have an RSE of greater than 30 percent.

NOTES: Data are for the civilian noninstitutionalized population. Persons of Hispanic origin may be of any race. Employment status is determined using the answers to two questions on the National Health Interview Survey: "Which of the following were you doing last week?" The category working includes working for pay at a job or business and with a job or business but not at work. Sample persons who were not working were asked: "What is the main reason you did not work or have a job or business last week?" Persons who said they were on a planned vacation from work or on family or maternity leave were included in the working category. The remaining categories responded retired, disabled, taking care of house or family, or looking to the follow up question. Other includes going to school, temporarily unable to work for health reasons (but not working and not looking for work), on layoff, have job contract (off season), and other not specified. Starting with *Health, United States, 2005,* estimates for 2000 and later years use weights derived from the 2000 census. See Appendix II, Hispanic origin; Race.

SOURCE: Centers for Disease Control and Prevention, National Center for Health Statistics, National Health Interview Survey.

Data table for figure 32. Low income among adults 55–64 years of age by sex, race and Hispanic origin: United States, 2003

Sex and poverty status	Total	Race and Hispanic origin: Hispanic	Not Hispanic or Latino: White only	Not Hispanic or Latino: Black only
		Percent		
Both sexes				
Poor	9.4	15.9	7.8	16.8
Near poor	13.1	24.6	11.1	21.2
Nonpoor	77.5	59.5	81.1	62.0
Men				
Poor	8.2	13.9	6.8	15.8
Near poor	11.4	23.2	9.6	18.5
Nonpoor	80.3	62.9	83.6	65.7
Women				
Poor	10.4	17.8	8.8	17.6
Near poor	14.7	25.8	12.5	23.3
Nonpoor	74.9	56.4	78.7	59.1

NOTES: Data are for the civilian noninstitutionalized population. Total includes all other races not shown separately. Persons of Hispanic origin may be of any race. Poor is defined as family income less than 100 percent of the poverty level, near poor as 100–199 percent of the poverty level, and nonpoor as 200 percent or above the poverty level. See Appendix II, Family income; Hispanic origin; Poverty level; Race.

SOURCE: DeNavas-Walt C, Proctor B, and Mills R. Income, Poverty, and Health Insurance Coverage in the United States: 2003. Current population reports, series P-60 no 226. Washington: U.S. Government Printing Office. 2004; Age and sex of all people, family members, and unrelated individuals iterated by income-to-poverty ratio and race: 2003, available at ferret.bls.census.gov/macro/032004/pov/new01_000.htm accessed on October 29, 2004.

Data table for figure 33. Health insurance coverage among adults 55–64 years of age by marital status: United States, 2002–03

Characteristic	Total private		Private Employer-sponsored		Other private		Public		Uninsured	
	Percent	SE	Percent	SE	Percent	SE	Percent	SE	Percent	SE
Race and Hispanic origin										
Total	76.7	0.4	68.5	0.5	8.2	0.3	12.1	0.3	11.2	0.3
Hispanic or Latino	52.2	1.4	47.1	1.3	5.1	0.6	19.1	1.0	28.7	1.2
Not Hispanic or Latino:										
White only	81.4	0.5	72.7	0.6	8.7	0.3	10.0	0.4	8.7	0.3
Black or African American only	61.8	1.3	56.0	1.5	5.9	0.7	22.7	1.1	15.5	0.9
Marital status										
Married	83.3	0.5	75.4	0.6	7.9	0.3	8.0	0.3	8.7	0.3
Widowed	58.8	1.5	49.8	1.5	8.9	0.8	22.8	1.3	18.4	1.2
Separated or divorced	61.5	1.0	52.8	1.0	8.8	0.6	21.4	0.9	17.0	0.8
Single	59.4	1.8	50.2	1.9	9.2	1.1	25.1	1.6	15.5	1.3

(Health insurance coverage)

SE Standard error.

NOTES: Data are for the civilian noninstitutionalized population. Persons of Hispanic origin may be of any race. Public insurance includes Medicare, Medicaid, SCHIP, Military, and other State and government sponsored health plans. Health insurance categories are mutually exclusive. Persons who reported both public and private coverage are classified as having private coverage. Uninsured persons are not covered by private insurance or public insurance. Persons with Indian Health Service only are considered uninsured. Starting with *Health, United States, 2005,* estimates for 2000 and later years use weights derived from the 2000 Census. See Appendix II, Health insurance coverage; Hispanic origin; Race.

SOURCE: Centers for Disease Control and Prevention, National Center for Health Statistics, National Health Interview Survey.

Data table for figure 34. Cardiovascular risk factors (hypertension, obesity, and high cholesterol) among adults 55–64 years of age by sex: United States, 1988–94 and 1999–2002

Sex and selected cardiovascular risk factors	*1988–94*		*1999–2002*	
	Percent	*SE*	*Percent*	*SE*
Both sexes				
Individual selected cardiovascular risk factors:				
Hypertension	41.7	1.5	49.5	1.6
Obesity	30.7	1.5	38.9	2.0
High cholesterol	34.9	1.4	22.8	1.3
Number of selected cardiovascular risk factors:				
None	31.5	1.6	26.6	2.0
One or more	68.5	1.6	73.4	2.0
One	37.1	1.6	42.0	1.8
Two or three	31.4	1.4	31.4	1.5
Men				
Individual selected cardiovascular risk factors:				
Hypertension	40.6	2.3	45.0	1.8
Obesity	27.2	2.2	35.5	2.4
High cholesterol	28.0	2.1	19.9	1.9
Number of selected cardiovascular risk factors:				
None	36.5	2.2	27.8	2.6
One or more	63.5	2.2	72.2	2.6
One	35.9	2.1	48.7	2.8
Two or Three	27.6	2.1	23.5	1.6
Women				
Individual selected cardiovascular risk factors:				
Hypertension	42.6	2.3	53.9	2.2
Obesity	33.7	1.8	42.1	3.0
High cholesterol	40.9	1.9	25.6	1.5
Number of selected cardiovascular risk factors:				
None	27.3	2.3	25.5	2.7
One or more	72.7	2.3	74.5	2.7
One	38.0	1.9	35.4	2.2
Two or Three	34.7	1.8	39.1	2.4

NOTES: In this analysis cardiovascular disease risk factors are: hypertension, obesity, and high cholesterol. Hypertension is defined as either having elevated blood pressure (systolic pressure of at least 140 mmHg or diastolic pressure of at least 90 mmHg) or taking antihypertensive medication. Hypertension is based on the average of blood pressure measurements taken. Obesity is defined as a body mass index (BMI) greater than or equal to 30. See Appendix II, Body mass index. High serum cholesterol is defined as having measured total serum cholesterol greater than or equal to 240 mg/dL (6.20 mmol/L). Data are for the civilian noninstitutionalized population. Starting with *Health, United States, 2005,* estimates for 2000 and later years use weights derived from the 2000 census.

SOURCE: Centers for Disease Control and Prevention, National Center for Health Statistics, National Health and Nutrition Examination Survey.

Data table for figure 35. Visits to health professionals in the past 12 months among adults 55–64 years of age by health insurance status: United States, 2002–03

	Total		*Public*		*Private*		*Uninsured*	
Type of health professional	*Percent*	*SE*	*Percent*	*SE*	*Percent*	*SE*	*Percent*	*SE*
General physician	77.4	0.5	84.2	1.2	79.5	0.6	54.4	1.8
Specialist physician	38.0	0.6	48.5	1.7	39.2	0.8	17.2	1.5
Eye doctor	44.2	0.7	45.0	1.7	46.5	0.8	26.4	1.6
Physical or other type of therapist	11.3	0.4	16.1	1.3	11.4	0.5	4.9	0.8
Mental health professional	6.3	0.3	15.5	1.2	5.0	0.3	4.6	0.8

SE Standard error.

NOTES: Data are for the civilian noninstitutionalized population. Respondents were asked if they had seen or talked to selected types of health professionals within the past 12 months. Percents are respondents who reported at least one visit. General physician includes visits to a doctor in general practice, family medicine, or internal medicine. Specialist physician includes visits to a doctor who specializes in a particular medical disease or problem (other than obstetrician or gynecologist, psychiatrist, or ophthalmologist). Eye doctor includes visits to an optometrist, ophthalmologist, or eye doctor (someone who prescribes eyeglasses). Physical or other type of therapist includes visits to an audiologist or physical, speech, respiratory, or occupational therapist. Mental health professional includes visits to a psychiatrist, psychologist, psychiatric nurse, or clinical social worker. Total includes about 1 percent of adults with unknown health insurance coverage. Public coverage includes Medicare, Medicaid, SCHIP, Military, and other State and government sponsored health plans. Uninsured persons are not covered by private insurance or public insurance. Persons with Indian Health Service only are considered uninsured. See Appendix II, Health insurance coverage.

SOURCE: Centers for Disease Control and Prevention, National Center for Health Statistics, National Health Interview Survey.

Data table for figure 36. Blood glucose regulators and cholesterol-lowering drugs prescribed during medical visits among adults 55–64 years of age by sex: United States, 1995–96 and 2002–03

	1995–96		*2002–03*	
Selected drug classes and sex	*Drugs per 100 population*	*SE*	*Drugs per 100 population*	*SE*
Blood glucose regulators				
Both sexes	24.5	2.2	46.4	3.9
Men	22.7	2.6	47.8	5.5
Women	26.2	2.5	45.0	4.8
Cholesterol-lowering drugs				
Both sexes	16.9	1.4	52.8	3.9
Men	19.6	2.1	57.3	5.2
Women	14.5	1.7	48.6	4.4

SE Standard error.

NOTES: Medical visits with drugs prescribed are in-person visits to physician office and hospital outpatient departments with at least one drug prescribed, ordered, supplied, administered, or continued during the visit. Drugs per 100 population are calculated as the number of drugs recorded during visits for the 2-year period divided by the sum of the population estimates for both years, times 100. If more than one drug in the selected drug class was recorded on the visit record, then that drug class was counted multiple times. Until 2002, up to six prescription and nonprescription medications were recorded on the visit record. Beginning with the 2003 data, up to eight prescription and nonprescription medications are recorded on the visit record. If only up to six drugs are included for the 2003 data, the 2002–03 rate of blood glucose regulators is 5 percent lower than including up to eight drugs. The 2002–03 rate of cholesterol-lowering drugs, including only up to six drugs for 2003, is 4 percent lower. Drugs were classified according to the National Drug Code therapeutic classes. See Appendix II, Drugs; National Drug Code (NDC) Directory therapeutic classes. See related *Health, United States, 2005,* tables 91 and 92.

SOURCE: Centers for Disease Control and Prevention, National Center for Health Statistics, National Ambulatory Medical Care Survey and National Hospital Ambulatory Medical Care Survey.

Data table for figure 37. Total health care expense and prescribed medicine expense per person per year among adults 55–64 years of age by source of payment and sex: United States, 1997 and 2002

	Source of payment											
	Expense per person				*Out-of-pocket expense per person*				*"All other sources" expense per person*			
	1997	*SE*	*2002*	*SE*	*1997*	*SE*	*2002*	*SE*	*1997*	*SE*	*2002*	*SE*
Total health expense	$4,510	$433	$4,848	$202	$753	$35	$971	$34	$3,757	$418	$3,877	$195
Men	4,640	668	4,615	274	674	50	818	41	3,966	660	3,797	268
Women	4,392	519	5,070	285	824	50	1,116	48	3,569	497	3,954	278
Prescribed medicine expense	$637	$25	$1,114	$39	$286	$15	$425	$18	$351	$15	$689	$30
Men	560	32	974	44	230	16	351	21	331	22	623	33
Women	706	37	1,247	56	338	24	495	25	369	20	752	44

SE Standard error.

NOTES: Data are for the civilian noninstitutionalized population. 1997 estimates have been adjusted to 2002 dollars using the Consumer Price Index (All Urban Consumers; U.S. City Average; All items). Table includes persons with no expense. "All other sources" includes private health insurance, public coverage and other miscellaneous sources. Total health expense include expenses for inpatient hospital and physician services, ambulatory physician and nonphysician services, prescribed medicines, home health services, dental services, and other medical equipment, supplies, and services that were purchased or rented during the year. Excludes expenses for over-the-counter medications, preventive care services, phone contacts with health providers, and premiums for health insurance. Prescribed medicine expense include expenses for all prescribed medications that were purchased or refilled during the survey year. See related *Health, United States, 2005,* tables 124 and 126.

SOURCE: Agency for Healthcare Research and Quality, Center for Cost and Financing Studies. 1997 and 2002 Medical Expenditure Panel Surveys.

Trend Tables

Table 1 (page 1 of 3). Resident population, according to age, sex, race, and Hispanic origin: United States, selected years 1950–2003

[Data are based on decennial census updated by data from multiple sources]

Sex, race, Hispanic origin, and year	Total resident population	Under 1 year	1–4 years	5–14 years	15–24 years	25–34 years	35–44 years	45–54 years	55–64 years	65–74 years	75–84 years	85 years and over
All persons						Number in thousands						
1950	150,697	3,147	13,017	24,319	22,098	23,759	21,450	17,343	13,370	8,340	3,278	577
1960	179,323	4,112	16,209	35,465	24,020	22,818	24,081	20,485	15,572	10,997	4,633	929
1970	203,212	3,485	13,669	40,746	35,441	24,907	23,088	23,220	18,590	12,435	6,119	1,511
1980	226,546	3,534	12,815	34,942	42,487	37,082	25,635	22,800	21,703	15,581	7,729	2,240
1990	248,710	3,946	14,812	35,095	37,013	43,161	37,435	25,057	21,113	18,045	10,012	3,021
2000	281,422	3,806	15,370	41,078	39,184	39,892	45,149	37,678	24,275	18,391	12,361	4,240
2001	284,797	4,034	15,336	41,065	39,948	39,607	45,019	39,188	25,309	18,313	12,574	4,404
2002	288,369	4,034	15,575	41,037	40,590	39,928	44,917	40,084	26,602	18,274	12,735	4,593
2003	290,811	4,004	15,766	40,969	41,206	39,873	44,371	40,805	27,900	18,337	12,869	4,713
Male												
1950	74,833	1,602	6,634	12,375	10,918	11,597	10,588	8,655	6,697	4,024	1,507	237
1960	88,331	2,090	8,240	18,029	11,906	11,179	11,755	10,093	7,537	5,116	2,025	362
1970	98,912	1,778	6,968	20,759	17,551	12,217	11,231	11,199	8,793	5,437	2,436	542
1980	110,053	1,806	6,556	17,855	21,419	18,382	12,570	11,009	10,152	6,757	2,867	682
1990	121,239	2,018	7,581	17,971	18,915	21,564	18,510	12,232	9,955	7,907	3,745	841
2000	138,054	1,949	7,862	21,043	20,079	20,121	22,448	18,497	11,645	8,303	4,879	1,227
2001	139,813	2,064	7,841	21,033	20,485	20,014	22,403	19,236	12,154	8,297	4,987	1,299
2002	141,661	2,064	7,962	21,013	20,821	20,203	22,367	19,676	12,784	8,301	5,081	1,390
2003	143,037	2,046	8,060	20,977	21,183	20,222	22,134	20,044	13,424	8,349	5,154	1,445
Female												
1950	75,864	1,545	6,383	11,944	11,181	12,162	10,863	8,688	6,672	4,316	1,771	340
1960	90,992	2,022	7,969	17,437	12,114	11,639	12,326	10,393	8,036	5,881	2,609	567
1970	104,300	1,707	6,701	19,986	17,890	12,690	11,857	12,021	9,797	6,998	3,683	969
1980	116,493	1,727	6,259	17,087	21,068	18,700	13,065	11,791	11,551	8,824	4,862	1,559
1990	127,471	1,928	7,231	17,124	18,098	21,596	18,925	12,824	11,158	10,139	6,267	2,180
2000	143,368	1,857	7,508	20,034	19,105	19,771	22,701	19,181	12,629	10,088	7,482	3,013
2001	144,984	1,969	7,495	20,033	19,463	19,594	22,616	19,952	13,155	10,016	7,587	3,105
2002	146,708	1,970	7,614	20,025	19,769	19,726	22,550	20,408	13,817	9,973	7,654	3,203
2003	147,773	1,958	7,706	19,992	20,024	19,650	22,237	20,761	14,475	9,988	7,714	3,269
White male												
1950	67,129	1,400	5,845	10,860	9,689	10,430	9,529	7,836	6,180	3,736	1,406	218
1960	78,367	1,784	7,065	15,659	10,483	9,940	10,564	9,114	6,850	4,702	1,875	331
1970	86,721	1,501	5,873	17,667	15,232	10,775	9,979	10,090	7,958	4,916	2,243	487
1980	94,976	1,487	5,402	14,773	18,123	15,940	11,010	9,774	9,151	6,096	2,600	621
1990	102,143	1,604	6,071	14,467	15,389	18,071	15,819	10,624	8,813	7,127	3,397	760
2000	113,445	1,524	6,143	16,428	15,942	16,232	18,568	15,670	10,067	7,343	4,419	1,109
2001	114,659	1,609	6,124	16,398	16,235	16,103	18,461	16,240	10,497	7,311	4,504	1,176
2002	115,966	1,603	6,212	16,363	16,482	16,214	18,368	16,553	11,045	7,288	4,580	1,257
2003	116,875	1,594	6,296	16,322	16,726	16,159	18,129	16,807	11,590	7,308	4,638	1,307
White female												
1950	67,813	1,341	5,599	10,431	9,821	10,851	9,719	7,868	6,168	4,031	1,669	314
1960	80,465	1,714	6,795	15,068	10,596	10,204	11,000	9,364	7,327	5,428	2,441	527
1970	91,028	1,434	5,615	16,912	15,420	11,004	10,349	10,756	8,853	6,366	3,429	890
1980	99,835	1,412	5,127	14,057	17,653	15,896	11,232	10,285	10,325	7,951	4,457	1,440
1990	106,561	1,524	5,762	13,706	14,599	17,757	15,834	10,946	9,698	9,048	5,687	2,001
2000	116,641	1,447	5,839	15,576	14,966	15,574	18,386	15,921	10,731	8,757	6,715	2,729
2001	117,693	1,536	5,826	15,554	15,238	15,385	18,245	16,493	11,162	8,659	6,784	2,809
2002	118,780	1,528	5,915	15,519	15,471	15,412	18,115	16,794	11,716	8,590	6,825	2,895
2003	119,474	1,525	5,999	15,488	15,658	15,310	17,813	17,034	12,263	8,576	6,859	2,950

See notes at end of table.

Table 1 (page 2 of 3). Resident population, according to age, sex, race, and Hispanic origin: United States, selected years 1950–2003

[Data are based on decennial census updated by data from multiple sources]

Sex, race, Hispanic origin, and year	Total resident population	Under 1 year	1–4 years	5–14 years	15–24 years	25–34 years	35–44 years	45–54 years	55–64 years	65–74 years	75–84 years	85 years and over
	Number in thousands											
Black or African American male												
1950	7,300	- - -	[1]944	1,442	1,162	1,105	1,003	772	459	299	[2]113	- - -
1960	9,114	281	1,082	2,185	1,305	1,120	1,086	891	617	382	137	29
1970	10,748	245	975	2,784	2,041	1,226	1,084	979	739	461	169	46
1980	12,585	269	967	2,614	2,807	1,967	1,235	1,024	854	567	228	53
1990	14,420	322	1,164	2,700	2,669	2,592	1,962	1,175	878	614	277	66
2000	17,407	313	1,271	3,454	2,932	2,586	2,705	1,957	1,090	683	330	87
2001	17,710	334	1,263	3,462	3,033	2,574	2,727	2,067	1,131	691	340	88
2002	17,979	344	1,290	3,454	3,107	2,589	2,726	2,149	1,177	701	349	93
2003	18,190	336	1,301	3,444	3,180	2,613	2,705	2,218	1,232	711	355	96
Black or African American female												
1950	7,745	- - -	[1]941	1,446	1,300	1,260	1,112	796	443	322	[2]125	- - -
1960	9,758	283	1,085	2,191	1,404	1,300	1,229	974	663	430	160	38
1970	11,832	243	970	2,773	2,196	1,456	1,309	1,134	868	582	230	71
1980	14,046	266	951	2,578	2,937	2,267	1,488	1,258	1,059	776	360	106
1990	16,063	316	1,137	2,641	2,700	2,905	2,279	1,416	1,135	884	495	156
2000	19,187	302	1,228	3,348	2,971	2,866	3,055	2,274	1,353	971	587	233
2001	19,486	317	1,221	3,356	3,040	2,846	3,076	2,405	1,404	979	605	238
2002	19,769	330	1,249	3,351	3,091	2,855	3,079	2,503	1,464	987	616	243
2003	19,958	323	1,260	3,337	3,140	2,862	3,052	2,579	1,531	999	627	247
American Indian or Alaska Native male												
1980	702	17	59	153	161	114	75	53	37	22	9	2
1990	1,024	24	88	206	192	183	140	86	55	32	13	3
2000	1,488	28	109	301	271	229	229	165	88	45	18	5
2001	1,524	29	109	298	280	232	232	175	95	49	21	5
2002	1,535	21	101	295	287	237	233	181	101	51	22	6
2003	1,553	21	96	293	294	240	232	187	107	53	24	6
American Indian or Alaska Native female												
1980	718	16	57	149	158	118	79	57	41	27	12	4
1990	1,041	24	85	200	178	186	148	92	61	41	21	6
2000	1,496	26	106	293	254	219	236	174	95	54	28	10
2001	1,530	28	105	290	263	220	238	185	102	58	30	11
2002	1,541	20	98	287	271	223	238	192	109	60	32	12
2003	1,558	21	93	286	278	224	235	198	115	62	33	13
Asian or Pacific Islander male												
1980	1,814	35	130	321	334	366	252	159	110	72	30	6
1990	3,652	68	258	598	665	718	588	347	208	133	57	12
2000	5,713	84	339	861	934	1,073	947	705	399	231	112	27
2001	5,919	92	344	875	937	1,104	983	754	431	247	122	30
2002	6,180	95	358	900	946	1,163	1,040	793	461	261	130	33
2003	6,419	94	367	917	983	1,211	1,068	832	496	277	138	36
Asian or Pacific Islander female												
1980	1,915	34	127	307	325	423	269	192	126	71	33	9
1990	3,805	65	247	578	621	749	664	371	264	166	65	17
2000	6,044	81	336	817	914	1,112	1,024	812	451	305	152	41
2001	6,275	88	342	833	922	1,143	1,057	869	486	321	167	47
2002	6,618	91	352	868	936	1,235	1,118	919	529	337	181	53
2003	6,783	89	354	882	947	1,254	1,137	950	565	351	196	59
Hispanic or Latino male												
1980	7,280	187	661	1,530	1,646	1,256	761	570	364	200	86	19
1990	11,388	279	980	2,128	2,376	2,310	1,471	818	551	312	131	32
2000	18,162	395	1,506	3,469	3,564	3,494	2,653	1,551	804	474	203	50
2001	19,018	417	1,533	3,606	3,606	3,699	2,828	1,684	869	501	224	53
2002	19,991	426	1,598	3,721	3,656	3,978	3,027	1,823	935	523	244	60
2003	20,599	442	1,682	3,832	3,759	4,016	3,101	1,910	991	542	261	65
Hispanic or Latino female												
1980	7,329	181	634	1,482	1,546	1,249	805	615	411	257	117	30
1990	10,966	268	939	2,039	2,028	2,073	1,448	868	632	403	209	59
2000	17,144	376	1,441	3,318	3,017	3,016	2,476	1,585	907	603	303	101
2001	17,955	401	1,467	3,450	3,085	3,163	2,624	1,714	978	635	331	107
2002	18,770	408	1,530	3,545	3,147	3,354	2,782	1,832	1,040	658	356	121
2003	19,300	424	1,611	3,659	3,235	3,363	2,815	1,908	1,097	680	380	128

See notes at end of table.

Table 1 (page 3 of 3). Resident population, according to age, sex, race, and Hispanic origin: United States, selected years 1950–2003

[Data are based on decennial census updated by data from multiple sources]

Sex, race, Hispanic origin, and year	Total resident population	Under 1 year	1–4 years	5–14 years	15–24 years	25–34 years	35–44 years	45–54 years	55–64 years	65–74 years	75–84 years	85 years and over
White, not Hispanic or Latino male	Number in thousands											
1980	88,035	1,308	4,772	13,317	16,554	14,739	10,284	9,229	8,803	5,906	2,519	603
1990	91,743	1,351	5,181	12,525	13,219	15,967	14,481	9,875	8,303	6,837	3,275	729
2000	96,551	1,163	4,761	13,238	12,628	12,958	16,088	14,223	9,312	6,894	4,225	1,062
2001	96,966	1,228	4,719	13,082	12,885	12,634	15,816	14,669	9,680	6,836	4,291	1,126
2002	97,329	1,198	4,729	12,941	13,086	12,480	15,534	14,851	10,168	6,793	4,348	1,201
2003	97,660	1,173	4,718	12,797	13,237	12,393	15,225	15,025	10,660	6,796	4,390	1,245
White, not Hispanic or Latino female												
1980	92,872	1,240	4,522	12,647	16,185	14,711	10,468	9,700	9,935	7,707	4,345	1,411
1990	96,557	1,280	4,909	11,846	12,749	15,872	14,520	10,153	9,116	8,674	5,491	1,945
2000	100,774	1,102	4,517	12,529	12,183	12,778	16,089	14,446	9,879	8,188	6,429	2,633
2001	101,070	1,169	4,482	12,385	12,393	12,449	15,810	14,900	10,244	8,059	6,471	2,707
2002	101,363	1,140	4,496	12,263	12,567	12,296	15,531	15,091	10,740	7,970	6,489	2,780
2003	101,555	1,121	4,488	12,125	12,673	12,188	15,201	15,261	11,236	7,935	6,499	2,829

- - - Data not available.
[1]Population for age group under 5 years.
[2]Population for age group 75 years and over.

NOTES: The race groups, white, black, American Indian or Alaska Native, and Asian or Pacific Islander, include persons of Hispanic and non-Hispanic origin. Persons of Hispanic origin may be of any race. Starting with *Health, United States, 2003*, intercensal population estimates for the 1990s and 2000 are based on census 2000. Population estimates for 2001 and later years are 2000-based postcensal estimates. Population figures are census counts as of April 1 for 1950, 1960, 1970, 1980, 1990, and 2000; estimates as of July 1 for other years. See Appendix I, Population Census and Population Estimates. Populations for age groups may not sum to the total due to rounding. Although population figures are shown rounded to the nearest 1,000, calculations of birth rates and death rates shown in this volume are based on unrounded population figures for decennial years and for all years starting with 1991. See Appendix II, Rate. Unrounded population figures are available in the spreadsheet version of this table. See www.cdc.gov/nchs/hus.htm. Data for additional years are available. See Appendix III.

SOURCES: U.S. Bureau of the Census: 1950 Nonwhite Population by Race. Special Report P-E, No. 3B. Washington. U.S. Government Printing Office, 1951; U.S. Census of Population: 1960, Number of Inhabitants, PC(1)-A1, United States Summary, 1964; 1970, Number of Inhabitants, Final Report PC(1)-A1, United States Summary, 1971; U.S. population estimates, by age, sex, race, and Hispanic origin: 1980 to 1991. Current population reports, series P–25, no 1095. Washington. U.S. Government Printing Office, Feb. 1993; National Center for Health Statistics. Estimates of the July 1, 1991-July 1, 1999, April 1, 2000, and July 1, 2001-July 1, 2003 United States resident population by age, sex, race, and Hispanic origin, prepared under a collaborative arrangement with the U.S. Census Bureau, Population Estimates Program. Available at www.cdc.gov/nchs/about/major/dvs/popbridge/popbridge.htm. 2004.

Table 2 (page 1 of 2). Persons and families below poverty level, according to selected characteristics, race, and Hispanic origin: United States, selected years 1973–2003

[Data are based on household interviews of the civilian noninstitutionalized population]

Selected characteristics, race, and Hispanic origin[1]	*1973*	*1980*	*1985*	*1990*	*1995*	*2000*[2]	*2001*	*2002*	*2003*
All persons				Percent below poverty					
All races	11.1	13.0	14.0	13.5	13.8	11.3	11.7	12.1	12.5
White only	8.4	10.2	11.4	10.7	11.2	9.5	9.9	10.2	10.5
Black or African American only	31.4	32.5	31.3	31.9	29.3	22.5	22.7	24.1	24.4
Asian only	- - -	- - -	- - -	12.2	14.6	9.9	10.2	10.1	11.8
Hispanic or Latino	21.9	25.7	29.0	28.1	30.3	21.5	21.4	21.8	22.5
Mexican	- - -	- - -	28.8	28.1	31.2	22.9	22.8	- - -	- - -
Puerto Rican	- - -	- - -	43.3	40.6	38.1	25.6	26.1	- - -	- - -
White only, not Hispanic or Latino	7.5	9.1	9.7	8.8	8.5	7.4	7.8	8.0	8.2
Related children under 18 years of age in families									
All races	14.2	17.9	20.1	19.9	20.2	15.6	15.8	16.3	17.2
White only	9.7	13.4	15.6	15.1	15.5	12.4	12.8	13.1	13.9
Black or African American only	40.6	42.1	43.1	44.2	41.5	30.9	30.0	32.1	33.6
Asian only	- - -	- - -	- - -	17.0	18.6	12.5	11.1	11.4	12.1
Hispanic or Latino	27.8	33.0	39.6	37.7	39.3	27.6	27.4	28.2	29.5
Mexican	- - -	- - -	37.4	35.5	39.3	29.5	28.8	- - -	- - -
Puerto Rican	- - -	- - -	58.6	56.7	53.2	32.1	33.0	- - -	- - -
White only, not Hispanic or Latino	- - -	11.3	12.3	11.6	10.6	8.5	8.9	8.9	9.3
Related children under 18 years of age in families with female householder and no spouse present									
All races	- - -	50.8	53.6	53.4	50.3	40.1	39.3	39.6	41.8
White only	- - -	41.6	45.2	45.9	42.5	33.9	34.7	34.7	37.0
Black or African American only	- - -	64.8	66.9	64.7	61.6	49.3	46.6	47.5	49.8
Asian only	- - -	- - -	- - -	32.2	42.4	38.0	26.7	29.8	37.4
Hispanic or Latino	- - -	65.0	72.4	68.4	65.7	49.8	49.3	47.9	50.6
Mexican	- - -	- - -	64.4	62.4	65.9	51.4	50.9	- - -	- - -
Puerto Rican	- - -	- - -	85.4	82.7	79.6	55.3	52.9	- - -	- - -
White only, not Hispanic or Latino	- - -	- - -	- - -	39.6	33.5	28.0	29.0	29.2	30.7
All persons				Number below poverty in thousands					
All races	22,973	29,272	33,064	33,585	36,425	31,581	32,907	34,570	35,861
White only	15,142	19,699	22,860	22,326	24,423	21,645	22,739	23,466	24,272
Black or African American only	7,388	8,579	8,926	9,837	9,872	7,982	8,136	8,602	8,781
Asian only	- - -	- - -	- - -	858	1,411	1,258	1,275	1,161	1,401
Hispanic or Latino	2,366	3,491	5,236	6,006	8,574	7,747	7,997	8,555	9,051
Mexican	- - -	- - -	3,220	3,764	5,608	5,460	5,698	- - -	- - -
Puerto Rican	- - -	- - -	1,011	966	1,183	814	839	- - -	- - -
White only, not Hispanic or Latino	12,864	16,365	17,839	16,622	16,267	14,366	15,271	15,567	15,902
Related children under 18 years of age in families									
All races	9,453	11,114	12,483	12,715	13,999	11,005	11,175	11,646	12,340
White only	5,462	6,817	7,838	7,696	8,474	6,834	7,086	7,203	7,624
Black or African American only	3,822	3,906	4,057	4,412	4,644	3,495	3,423	3,570	3,750
Asian only	- - -	- - -	- - -	356	532	407	353	302	331
Hispanic or Latino	1,364	1,718	2,512	2,750	3,938	3,342	3,433	3,653	3,982
Mexican	- - -	- - -	1,589	1,733	2,655	2,537	2,613	- - -	- - -
Puerto Rican	- - -	- - -	535	490	610	329	319	- - -	- - -
White only, not Hispanic or Latino	- - -	5,174	5,421	5,106	4,745	3,715	3,887	3,848	3,957

See footnotes at end of table.

Table 2 (page 2 of 2). Persons and families below poverty level, according to selected characteristics, race, and Hispanic origin: United States, selected years 1973–2003

[Data are based on household interviews of the civilian noninstitutionalized population]

Selected characteristics, race, and Hispanic origin[1]	*1973*	*1980*	*1985*	*1990*	*1995*	*2000*[2]	*2001*	*2002*	*2003*
Related children under 18 years of age in families with female householder and no spouse present				Number below poverty in thousands					
All races	---	5,866	6,716	7,363	8,364	6,300	6,341	6,564	7,085
White only	---	2,813	3,372	3,597	4,051	3,090	3,291	3,271	3,580
Black or African American only	---	2,944	3,181	3,543	3,954	2,908	2,741	2,855	3,026
Asian only	---	---	---	80	145	162	105	85	119
Hispanic or Latino	---	809	1,247	1,314	1,872	1,407	1,508	1,501	1,727
Mexican	---	---	553	615	1,056	938	1,001	---	---
Puerto Rican	---	---	449	382	459	242	236	---	---
White only, not Hispanic or Latino	---	---	---	2,411	2,299	1,832	1,953	1,949	2,033

- - - Data not available.

[1]The race groups, white, black, and Asian, include persons of Hispanic and non-Hispanic origin. Persons of Hispanic origin may be of any race. Starting with data year 2002 race-specific estimates are tabulated according to 1997 Standards for Federal Data on Race and Ethnicity and are not strictly comparable with estimates for earlier years. The three single race categories shown in the table conform to 1997 Standards. For 2002 and later years, race-specific estimates are for persons who reported only one racial group. Prior to data year 2002, data were tabulated according to 1977 Standards in which the category "Asian only" included Native Hawaiian and Other Pacific Islander. Estimates for single race categories prior to 2002 are based on answers to the Current Population Survey questionnaire which asked respondents to choose only a single race. See Appendix II, Race.

[2]Estimates are consistent with 2001 data through implementation of Census 2000-based population controls and a 28,000 household sample expansion.

NOTES: Estimates of poverty for 1991–98 are based on 1990 postcensal population estimates. Estimates for 1999 and later years are based on 2000 census population controls. Poverty status is based on family income and family size using Bureau of the Census poverty thresholds. See Appendix II, Poverty status. The Current Population Survey is not large enough to produce reliable annual estimates for American Indian or Alaska Native persons, or for Native Hawaiians. The 2001–03 average poverty rate for American Indian or Alaskan Native only or in combination was 20.0 percent, representing 883,000 persons; for American Indian or Alaska Native only was 23.2 percent, representing 612,000 persons. Data for additional years are available. See Appendix III.

SOURCES: U.S. Census Bureau, Current Population Survey 2000–2004 Annual Social and Economic Supplements; DeNavas-Walt C, Proctor BD, Mills RJ. Income, Poverty and Health Insurance Coverage in the United States: 2003. Current population reports, series P–60, no 226. Washington: U.S. Government Printing Office. 2004.

Table 3 (page 1 of 2). Crude birth rates, fertility rates, and birth rates by age of mother, according to race and Hispanic origin: United States, selected years 1950–2003

[Data are based on birth certificates]

Race, Hispanic origin, and year	Crude birth rate[1]	Fertility rate[2]	Age of mother									
				15–19 years								
			10–14 years	Total	15–17 years	18–19 years	20–24 years	25–29 years	30–34 years	35–39 years	40–44 years	45–54 years[3]
All races			Live births per 1,000 women									
1950	24.1	106.2	1.0	81.6	40.7	132.7	196.6	166.1	103.7	52.9	15.1	1.2
1960	23.7	118.0	0.8	89.1	43.9	166.7	258.1	197.4	112.7	56.2	15.5	0.9
1970	18.4	87.9	1.2	68.3	38.8	114.7	167.8	145.1	73.3	31.7	8.1	0.5
1980	15.9	68.4	1.1	53.0	32.5	82.1	115.1	112.9	61.9	19.8	3.9	0.2
1985	15.8	66.3	1.2	51.0	31.0	79.6	108.3	111.0	69.1	24.0	4.0	0.2
1990	16.7	70.9	1.4	59.9	37.5	88.6	116.5	120.2	80.8	31.7	5.5	0.2
1995	14.6	64.6	1.3	56.0	35.5	87.7	107.5	108.8	81.1	34.0	6.6	0.3
1999	14.2	64.4	0.9	48.8	28.2	79.0	107.9	111.2	87.1	37.8	7.4	0.4
2000	14.4	65.9	0.9	47.7	26.9	78.1	109.7	113.5	91.2	39.7	8.0	0.5
2001	14.1	65.3	0.8	45.3	24.7	76.1	106.2	113.4	91.9	40.6	8.1	0.5
2002	13.9	64.8	0.7	43.0	23.2	72.8	103.6	113.6	91.5	41.4	8.3	0.5
2003	14.1	66.1	0.6	41.6	22.4	70.7	102.6	115.6	95.1	43.8	8.7	0.5
Race of child:[4] White												
1950	23.0	102.3	0.4	70.0	31.3	120.5	190.4	165.1	102.6	51.4	14.5	1.0
1960	22.7	113.2	0.4	79.4	35.5	154.6	252.8	194.9	109.6	54.0	14.7	0.8
1970	17.4	84.1	0.5	57.4	29.2	101.5	163.4	145.9	71.9	30.0	7.5	0.4
1980	14.9	64.7	0.6	44.7	25.2	72.1	109.5	112.4	60.4	18.5	3.4	0.2
Race of mother:[5] White												
1980	15.1	65.6	0.6	45.4	25.5	73.2	111.1	113.8	61.2	18.8	3.5	0.2
1985	15.0	64.1	0.6	43.3	24.4	70.4	104.1	112.3	69.9	23.3	3.7	0.2
1990	15.8	68.3	0.7	50.8	29.5	78.0	109.8	120.7	81.7	31.5	5.2	0.2
1995	14.1	63.6	0.8	49.5	29.6	80.2	104.7	111.7	83.3	34.2	6.4	0.3
1999	13.7	64.0	0.6	44.0	24.4	73.0	105.0	114.9	90.7	38.5	7.4	0.4
2000	13.9	65.3	0.6	43.2	23.3	72.3	106.6	116.7	94.6	40.2	7.9	0.4
2001	13.7	65.0	0.5	41.2	21.4	70.8	103.7	117.0	95.8	41.3	8.0	0.5
2002	13.5	64.8	0.5	39.4	20.5	68.0	101.6	117.4	95.5	42.4	8.2	0.5
2003	13.6	66.1	0.5	38.3	19.8	66.2	100.6	119.5	99.3	44.8	8.7	0.5
Race of child:[4] Black or African American												
1960	31.9	153.5	4.3	156.1	- - -	- - -	295.4	218.6	137.1	73.9	21.9	1.1
1970	25.3	115.4	5.2	140.7	101.4	204.9	202.7	136.3	79.6	41.9	12.5	1.0
1980	22.1	88.1	4.3	100.0	73.6	138.8	146.3	109.1	62.9	24.5	5.8	0.3
Race of mother:[5] Black or African American												
1980	21.3	84.9	4.3	97.8	72.5	135.1	140.0	103.9	59.9	23.5	5.6	0.3
1985	20.4	78.8	4.5	95.4	69.3	132.4	135.0	100.2	57.9	23.9	4.6	0.3
1990	22.4	86.8	4.9	112.8	82.3	152.9	160.2	115.5	68.7	28.1	5.5	0.3
1995	17.8	71.0	4.1	94.4	68.5	135.0	133.7	95.6	63.0	28.4	6.0	0.3
1999	16.8	68.5	2.5	79.1	50.5	120.6	137.9	97.3	62.7	30.2	6.5	0.3
2000	17.0	70.0	2.3	77.4	49.0	118.8	141.3	100.3	65.4	31.5	7.2	0.4
2001	16.3	67.6	2.0	71.8	43.9	114.0	133.2	99.2	64.8	31.6	7.2	0.4
2002	15.7	65.8	1.8	66.6	40.0	107.6	127.1	99.0	64.4	31.5	7.4	0.4
2003	15.7	66.3	1.6	63.8	38.2	103.7	126.1	100.4	66.5	33.2	7.7	0.5
American Indian or Alaska Native mothers[5]												
1980	20.7	82.7	1.9	82.2	51.5	129.5	143.7	106.6	61.8	28.1	8.2	*
1985	19.8	78.6	1.7	79.2	47.7	124.1	139.1	109.6	62.6	27.4	6.0	*
1990	18.9	76.2	1.6	81.1	48.5	129.3	148.7	110.3	61.5	27.5	5.9	*
1995	15.3	63.0	1.6	72.9	44.6	122.2	123.1	91.6	56.5	24.3	5.5	*
1999	14.2	59.0	1.4	59.9	36.5	98.0	120.7	90.6	53.8	24.3	5.7	0.3
2000	14.0	58.7	1.1	58.3	34.1	97.1	117.2	91.8	55.5	24.6	5.7	0.3
2001	13.7	58.1	1.0	56.3	31.4	94.8	115.0	90.4	55.9	24.7	5.7	0.3
2002	13.8	58.0	0.9	53.8	30.7	89.2	112.6	91.8	56.4	25.4	5.8	0.3
2003	13.8	58.4	1.0	53.1	30.6	87.3	110.0	93.5	57.4	25.4	5.5	0.4

See footnotes at end of table.

Table 3 (page 2 of 2). Crude birth rates, fertility rates, and birth rates by age of mother, according to race and Hispanic origin: United States, selected years 1950–2003

[Data are based on birth certificates]

Race, Hispanic origin, and year	Crude birth rate[1]	Fertility rate[2]	Age of mother: 10–14 years	15–19 years: Total	15–19 years: 15–17 years	15–19 years: 18–19 years	20–24 years	25–29 years	30–34 years	35–39 years	40–44 years	45–54 years[3]
			Live births per 1,000 women									
Asian or Pacific Islander mothers[5]												
1980	19.9	73.2	0.3	26.2	12.0	46.2	93.3	127.4	96.0	38.3	8.5	0.7
1985	18.7	68.4	0.4	23.8	12.5	40.8	83.6	123.0	93.6	42.7	8.7	1.2
1990	19.0	69.6	0.7	26.4	16.0	40.2	79.2	126.3	106.5	49.6	10.7	1.1
1995	16.7	62.6	0.7	25.5	15.6	40.1	64.2	103.7	102.3	50.1	11.8	0.8
1999	15.9	60.9	0.4	21.4	12.4	33.9	58.9	100.8	104.3	52.9	11.3	0.9
2000	17.1	65.8	0.3	20.5	11.6	32.6	60.3	108.4	116.5	59.0	12.6	0.8
2001	16.4	64.2	0.2	19.8	10.3	32.8	59.1	106.4	112.6	56.7	12.3	0.9
2002	16.5	64.1	0.3	18.3	9.0	31.5	60.4	105.4	109.6	56.5	12.5	0.9
2003	16.8	66.3	0.2	17.4	8.8	29.8	59.6	108.5	114.6	59.9	13.5	0.9
Hispanic or Latino mothers[5,6,7]												
1980	23.5	95.4	1.7	82.2	52.1	126.9	156.4	132.1	83.2	39.9	10.6	0.7
1990	26.7	107.7	2.4	100.3	65.9	147.7	181.0	153.0	98.3	45.3	10.9	0.7
1995	24.1	98.8	2.6	99.3	68.3	145.4	171.9	140.4	90.5	43.7	10.7	0.6
1999	22.5	93.0	1.9	86.8	56.9	129.5	157.3	135.8	92.3	44.5	10.6	0.6
2000	23.1	95.9	1.7	87.3	55.5	132.6	161.3	139.9	97.1	46.6	11.5	0.6
2001	23.0	96.0	1.6	86.4	52.8	135.5	163.5	140.4	97.6	47.9	11.6	0.7
2002	22.6	94.4	1.4	83.4	50.7	133.0	164.3	139.4	95.1	47.8	11.5	0.7
2003	22.9	96.9	1.3	82.3	49.7	132.0	163.4	144.4	102.0	50.8	12.2	0.7
White, not Hispanic or Latino mothers[5,6,7]												
1980	14.2	62.4	0.4	41.2	22.4	67.7	105.5	110.6	59.9	17.7	3.0	0.1
1990	14.4	62.8	0.5	42.5	23.2	66.6	97.5	115.3	79.4	30.0	4.7	0.2
1995	12.5	57.5	0.4	39.3	22.0	66.2	90.2	105.1	81.5	32.8	5.9	0.3
1999	12.1	57.7	0.3	34.1	17.1	59.4	90.6	108.6	89.5	37.3	6.9	0.4
2000	12.2	58.5	0.3	32.6	15.8	57.5	91.2	109.4	93.2	38.8	7.3	0.4
2001	11.8	57.7	0.3	30.3	14.0	54.8	87.1	108.9	94.3	39.8	7.5	0.4
2002	11.7	57.4	0.2	28.5	13.1	51.9	84.3	109.3	94.4	40.9	7.6	0.5
2003	11.8	58.5	0.2	27.4	12.4	50.0	83.5	110.8	97.6	43.2	8.1	0.5
Black or African American, not Hispanic or Latino mothers[5,6,7]												
1980	22.9	90.7	4.6	105.1	77.2	146.5	152.2	111.7	65.2	25.8	5.8	0.3
1990	23.0	89.0	5.0	116.2	84.9	157.5	165.1	118.4	70.2	28.7	5.6	0.3
1995	18.2	72.8	4.2	97.2	70.4	139.2	137.8	98.5	64.4	28.8	6.1	0.3
1999	17.1	69.9	2.6	81.0	51.7	123.9	142.1	99.8	63.9	30.6	6.5	0.3
2000	17.3	71.4	2.4	79.2	50.1	121.9	145.4	102.8	66.5	31.8	7.2	0.4
2001	16.6	69.1	2.1	73.5	44.9	116.7	137.2	102.1	66.2	32.1	7.3	0.4
2002	16.1	67.4	1.9	68.3	41.0	110.3	131.0	102.1	66.1	32.1	7.5	0.4
2003	15.9	67.1	1.6	64.7	38.7	105.3	128.1	102.1	67.4	33.4	7.7	0.5

- - - Data not available.

* Rates based on fewer than 20 births are considered unreliable and are not shown.

[1]Live births per 1,000 population.

[2]Total number of live births regardless of age of mother per 1,000 women 15–44 years of age.

[3]Prior to 1997 data are for live births to mothers 45–49 years of age per 1,000 women 45–49 years of age. Starting in 1997 data are for live births to mothers 45–54 years of age per 1,000 women 45–49 years of age. See Appendix II, Age.

[4]Live births are tabulated by race of child. See Appendix II, Race, Birth File.

[5]Live births are tabulated by race and/or Hispanic origin of mother. See Appendix II, Race, Birth File.

[6]Prior to 1993, data from States lacking an Hispanic-origin item on the birth certificate were excluded. See Appendix II, Hispanic origin.

[7]Rates in 1985 were not calculated because estimates for the Hispanic and non-Hispanic populations were not available.

NOTES: Data are based on births adjusted for underregistration for 1950 and on registered births for all other years. Beginning in 1970, births to persons who were not residents of the 50 States and the District of Columbia are excluded. Starting with *Health, United States, 2003,* rates for 1991–99 were revised using intercensal population estimates based on Census 2000. Rates for 2000 were computed using Census 2000 counts and starting in 2001 rates were computed using 2000-based postcensal estimates. See Appendix I, Population Census and Population Estimates. The race groups, white, black, American Indian or Alaska Native, and Asian or Pacific Islander, include persons of Hispanic and non-Hispanic origin. Persons of Hispanic origin may be of any race. Interpretation of trend data should take into consideration expansion of reporting areas and immigration. Data for additional years are available. See Appendix III.

SOURCES: Centers for Disease Control and Prevention, National Center for Health Statistics, National Vital Statistics System, Birth File. Martin JA, Hamilton BE, Sutton PD, Ventura SJ, Menacker F, Munson ML. Births: Final Data for 2003. National vital statistics reports; vol 54, no 2. Hyattsville, Maryland: National Center for Health Statistics, 2005; Hamilton BE, Sutton PD, Ventura SJ. Revised birth and fertility rates for the 1990s and new rates for Hispanic populations, 2000 and 2001: United States. National vital statistics reports; vol 51, no 12. Hyattsville, Maryland: National Center for Health Statistics, 2003; Ventura SJ. Births of Hispanic parentage, 1980 and 1985. Monthly vital statistics report; vol 32, no 6 and vol 36, no 11, suppl. Public Health Service. Hyattsville, Maryland. 1983 and 1988; Internet release of *Vital statistics of the United States, 2000, vol 1, natality,* tables 1–1 and 1–7 at www.cdc.gov/nchs/datawh/statab/unpubd/natality/natab2000.htm.

Table 4 (page 1 of 2). Live births, according to plurality, and detailed race and Hispanic origin of mother: United States, selected years 1970–2003

[Data are based on birth certificates]

Plurality of birth and race and Hispanic origin of mother	*1970*	*1971*	*1975*	*1980*	*1985*	*1990*	*1995*	*2000*	*2002*	*2003*
All births					Number of live births					
All races	3,731,386	3,555,970	3,144,198	3,612,258	3,760,561	4,158,212	3,899,589	4,058,814	4,021,726	4,089,950
White	3,109,956	2,939,568	2,576,818	2,936,351	3,037,913	3,290,273	3,098,885	3,194,005	3,174,760	3,225,848
Black or African American	561,992	553,750	496,829	568,080	581,824	684,336	603,139	622,598	593,691	599,847
American Indian or Alaska Native	22,264	23,254	22,690	29,389	34,037	39,051	37,278	41,668	42,368	43,052
Asian or Pacific Islander[1]	---	27,004	28,884	74,355	104,606	141,635	160,287	200,543	210,907	221,203
Chinese	7,044	7,222	7,778	11,671	16,405	22,737	27,380	34,271	33,673	---
Japanese	7,744	7,846	6,725	7,482	8,035	8,674	8,901	8,969	9,264	---
Filipino	8,066	7,946	10,359	13,968	20,058	25,770	30,551	32,107	33,016	---
Hawaiian	---	3,718	3,711	4,669	4,938	6,099	5,787	6,608	6,772	---
Other Asian or Pacific Islander	---	272	311	36,565	55,170	78,355	87,668	118,588	128,182	---
Hispanic or Latino[2]	---	---	---	307,163	372,814	595,073	679,768	815,868	876,642	912,329
Mexican	---	---	---	215,439	242,976	385,640	469,615	581,915	627,505	654,504
Puerto Rican	---	---	---	33,671	35,147	58,807	54,824	58,124	57,465	58,400
Cuban	---	---	---	7,163	10,024	11,311	12,473	13,429	14,232	14,867
Central and South American	---	---	---	21,268	40,985	83,008	94,996	113,344	125,981	135,586
Other and unknown Hispanic or Latino	---	---	---	29,622	43,682	56,307	47,860	49,056	51,459	48,972
Not Hispanic or Latino:[2]										
White	---	---	---	1,256,777	1,407,460	2,626,500	2,382,638	2,362,968	2,298,156	2,321,904
Black or African American	---	---	---	300,480	337,448	661,701	587,781	604,346	578,335	576,033
Twin births										
All races	---	63,298	59,192	68,339	77,102	93,865	96,736	118,916	125,134	128,665
White	---	49,972	46,715	53,104	60,351	72,617	76,196	93,235	98,304	101,297
Black or African American	---	12,452	11,375	13,638	14,646	18,164	17,000	20,626	20,423	20,633
American Indian or Alaska Native	---	362	348	491	537	699	769	900	982	1,047
Asian or Pacific Islander[1]	---	320	505	1,045	1,536	2,320	2,771	4,155	5,425	5,688
Chinese	---	80	120	135	232	368	507	748	929	---
Japanese	---	98	115	103	131	161	217	218	317	---
Filipino	---	92	176	173	247	388	542	612	757	---
Hawaiian	---	46	92	69	74	101	98	109	157	---
Other Asian or Pacific Islander	---	4	2	565	852	1,302	1,407	2,468	3,265	---
Hispanic or Latino[2]	---	---	---	5,154	6,550	10,713	12,685	16,470	18,128	19,472
Mexican	---	---	---	3,599	4,292	6,701	8,341	11,130	12,052	12,954
Puerto Rican	---	---	---	631	705	1,226	1,248	1,461	1,654	1,666
Cuban	---	---	---	102	201	228	312	371	409	465
Central and South American	---	---	---	371	665	1,463	1,769	2,361	2,787	3,141
Other and unknown Hispanic or Latino	---	---	---	451	687	1,095	1,015	1,147	1,226	1,246
Not Hispanic or Latino:[2]										
White	---	---	---	23,004	28,402	60,210	62,370	76,018	79,949	81,691
Black or African American	---	---	---	7,278	8,400	17,646	16,622	20,173	20,064	20,010
Triplet and higher order multiple births										
All races	---	1,034	1,066	1,337	1,925	3,028	4,973	7,325	7,401	7,663
White	---	834	909	1,104	1,648	2,639	4,505	6,551	6,541	6,733
Black or African American	---	196	151	211	240	321	352	521	609	650
American Indian or Alaska Native	---	0	2	9	13	4	20	18	23	33
Asian or Pacific Islander[1]	---	0	4	9	23	61	96	235	228	247
Chinese	---	0	0	3	2	13	21	29	30	---
Japanese	---	0	4	6	0	0	3	8	17	---
Filipino	---	0	0	0	4	15	15	57	47	---
Hawaiian	---	0	0	0	0	3	3	6	12	---
Other Asian or Pacific Islander	---	0	0	0	17	30	54	135	122	---
Hispanic or Latino[2]	---	---	---	78	106	235	355	659	737	784
Mexican	---	---	---	43	82	121	202	391	435	480
Puerto Rican	---	---	---	12	14	28	35	73	106	88
Cuban	---	---	---	0	3	9	24	15	28	28
Central and South American	---	---	---	8	4	59	59	122	123	140
Other and unknown Hispanic or Latino	---	---	---	15	3	18	35	58	45	48
Not Hispanic or Latino:[2]										
White	---	---	---	490	779	2,358	4,050	5,821	5,754	5,922
Black or African American	---	---	---	128	132	306	340	506	591	631

See footnotes at end of table.

Table 4 (page 2 of 2). Live births, according to plurality, and detailed race and Hispanic origin of mother: United States, selected years 1970–2003

[Data are based on birth certificates]

- - - Data not available.

[1]For 2003, data are not shown for Asian or Pacific Islander subgroups during the transition from single race to multiple race reporting. See Appendix II, Race, Birth File.

[2]Prior to 1993, data from States lacking an Hispanic-origin item on the birth certificate were excluded. See Appendix II, Hispanic origin.

NOTES: The race groups, white, black, American Indian or Alaska Native, and Asian or Pacific Islander, include persons of Hispanic and non-Hispanic origin. Persons of Hispanic origin may be of any race. Interpretation of trend data should take into consideration expansion of reporting areas and immigration. Data for non-Hispanic white and non-Hispanic black, 1980–88, have been revised and differ from previous editions of *Health, United States*.
Data for additional years are available. See Appendix III.

SOURCES: Centers for Disease Control and Prevention, National Center for Health Statistics, National Vital Statistics System, Birth File. Martin JA, Hamilton BE, Sutton PD, Ventura SJ, Menacker F, Munson ML. Births: Final Data for 2003. National vital statistics reports; vol 54, no 2. Hyattsville, Maryland: National Center for Health Statistics, 2005; Births: Final data for each data year 1997–2002. National vital statistics reports. Hyattsville, Maryland; Final natality statistics for each data year 1970–96. Monthly vital statistics report. Hyattsville, Maryland.

Table 5. Twin and higher order multiple births, according to race, Hispanic origin, and age of mother: United States, selected years 1971–2003

[Data are based on birth certificates]

Plurality of birth and race, Hispanic origin, and age of mother	*1971*	*1975*	*1980*	*1985*	*1990*	*1995*	*1997*	*1999*	*2000*	*2001*	*2002*	*2003*
Twin births						Number per 1,000 live births						
All races	17.8	18.8	18.9	20.5	22.6	24.8	26.8	28.9	29.3	30.1	31.1	31.5
White	17.0	18.1	18.1	19.9	22.1	24.6	26.7	28.8	29.2	30.0	31.0	31.4
Black or African American	22.5	22.9	24.0	25.2	26.5	28.2	30.0	32.0	33.1	33.7	34.4	34.4
American Indian or Alaska Native	15.6	15.3	16.7	15.8	17.9	20.6	20.6	21.7	21.6	22.3	23.2	24.3
Asian or Pacific Islander[1]	11.9	17.5	14.1	14.7	16.4	17.3	19.2	21.4	20.7	22.9	25.7	25.7
Chinese	11.1	15.4	11.6	14.1	16.2	18.5	19.8	24.1	21.8	24.5	27.6	- - -
Japanese	12.5	17.1	13.8	16.3	18.6	24.4	22.7	25.0	24.3	24.2	34.2	- - -
Filipino	11.6	17.0	12.4	12.3	15.1	17.7	17.5	18.8	19.1	23.3	22.9	- - -
Hawaiian	*12.4	24.8	14.8	15.0	16.6	16.9	16.7	23.6	16.5	26.8	23.2	- - -
Other Asian or Pacific Islander	*	*	15.5	15.4	16.6	16.0	19.4	21.0	20.8	22.1	25.5	- - -
Hispanic or Latino[2]	- - -	- - -	16.8	17.6	18.0	18.7	19.5	20.1	20.2	20.3	20.7	21.3
Mexican	- - -	- - -	16.7	17.7	17.4	17.8	18.5	18.9	19.1	19.0	19.2	19.8
Puerto Rican	- - -	- - -	18.7	20.1	20.8	22.8	23.0	25.4	25.1	26.8	28.8	28.5
Cuban	- - -	- - -	14.2	20.1	20.2	25.0	28.6	32.7	27.6	27.1	28.7	31.3
Central and South American	- - -	- - -	17.4	16.2	17.6	18.6	20.6	22.0	20.8	21.6	22.1	23.2
Other and unknown Hispanic or Latino	- - -	- - -	15.2	15.7	19.4	21.2	21.1	20.6	23.4	22.4	23.8	25.4
Not Hispanic or Latino:[2]												
White	- - -	- - -	18.3	20.2	22.9	26.2	28.8	31.5	32.2	33.5	34.8	35.2
Black or African American	- - -	- - -	24.2	24.9	26.7	28.3	30.0	32.1	33.4	33.9	34.7	34.7
Age of mother:												
Under 20 years	11.6	12.7	12.8	13.0	14.3	14.2	15.0	15.2	15.8	15.3	15.8	15.3
20–24 years	16.2	17.6	17.4	18.3	19.2	19.9	20.4	22.0	22.0	22.3	22.4	22.4
25–29 years	19.8	20.9	20.5	21.6	23.5	24.8	26.3	28.3	28.2	28.7	29.0	29.6
30–34 years	23.7	24.5	23.5	25.5	27.6	30.6	33.7	35.8	36.5	37.7	38.9	39.2
35–39 years	27.3	25.8	25.3	26.3	30.2	35.7	39.3	42.6	43.5	44.9	47.7	47.8
40–44 years	22.3	23.3	23.0	20.5	24.7	32.3	38.6	44.5	45.2	48.1	52.5	51.3
45–49 years	*18.1	*	*	*18.9	*23.8	101.9	133.2	155.7	153.1	170.1	189.7	189.2
50–54 years	- - -	- - -	- - -	- - -	- - -	- - -	347.2	344.8	313.7	368.2	384.0	374.6
Triplet and higher order multiple births						Number per 100,000 live births						
All races	29.1	33.9	37.0	51.2	72.8	127.5	173.6	184.9	180.5	185.6	184.0	187.4
White	28.4	35.3	37.6	54.2	80.2	145.4	195.9	209.2	205.1	208.6	206.0	208.7
Black or African American	35.4	30.4	37.1	41.2	46.9	58.4	88.3	93.9	83.7	91.2	102.6	108.4
American Indian or Alaska Native	*	*	*	*	*	*53.7	*	*	*	*76.4	*54.3	*76.7
Asian or Pacific Islander	*	*	*	*22.0	43.1	59.9	103.1	101.8	117.2	128.8	108.1	111.7
Hispanic or Latino[2]	- - -	- - -	25.4	28.4	39.5	52.2	72.7	76.3	80.8	83.3	84.1	85.9
Not Hispanic or Latino:[2]												
White	- - -	- - -	39.0	55.3	89.8	170.0	230.8	251.8	246.3	253.3	250.4	255
Black or African American	- - -	- - -	42.6	39.1	46.2	57.8	90.0	95.2	83.7	90.0	102.2	109.5
Age of mother:												
Under 20 years	9.1	10.9	14.8	13.8	15.9	17.6	20.7	13.6	23.2	22.0	21.5	12.8
20–24 years	25.4	28.1	31.4	35.0	32.4	35.3	46.8	41.9	44.2	56.1	50.0	48.4
25–29 years	43.7	45.4	42.8	66.3	73.9	118.3	151.0	153.3	163.3	152.9	153.5	158.9
30–34 years	36.4	53.5	58.3	71.2	126.3	217.2	293.6	327.9	307.3	317.4	297.7	309.1
35–39 years	35.7	45.1	47.6	70.0	156.8	285.3	403.2	417.5	368.5	387.0	406.0	409.5
40–44 years	*	*	*	*	*57.6	273.6	315.4	428.5	415.5	354.5	393.6	330.7
45–49 years	*	*	*	*	*	*1,466.8	2,100.2	2,108.3	1,586.6	2,043.8	2,010.0	1,919.6
50–54 years	- - -	- - -	- - -	- - -	- - -	- - -	*	*	*9,019.6	*	*	*

- - - Data not available.

* Rates preceded by an asterisk are based on fewer than 50 births. Rates based on fewer than 20 births are considered unreliable and are not shown.

[1]For 2003, data are not shown for Asian or Pacific Islander subgroups during the transition from single race to multiple race reporting. See Appendix II, Race, Birth File.

[2]Prior to 1993, data from States lacking an Hispanic-origin item on the birth certificate were excluded. See Appendix II, Hispanic origin. Data for non-Hispanic white and non-Hispanic black women for years prior to 1989 are not nationally representative and are provided for comparison with Hispanic data.

NOTES: The race groups, white, black, American Indian or Alaska Native, and Asian or Pacific Islander, include persons of Hispanic and non-Hispanic origin. Persons of Hispanic origin may be of any race. Interpretation of trend data should take into consideration expansion of reporting areas and immigration. Data for additional years are available. See Appendix III.

SOURCES: Centers for Disease Control and Prevention, National Center for Health Statistics, National Vital Statistics System, Birth File; Martin JA, Park MM. Trends in Twin and Triplet Births: 1980–97. National vital statistics reports; vol 47, no 24. Hyattsville, Maryland: National Center for Health Statistics, 1999.

Table 6. Women 15–44 years of age who have not had at least 1 live birth, by age: United States, selected years 1960–2002

[Data are based on birth certificates]

Year[1]	15–19 years	20–24 years	25–29 years	30–34 years	35–39 years	40–44 years
			Percent of women			
1960	91.4	47.5	20.0	14.2	12.0	15.1
1965	92.7	51.4	19.7	11.7	11.4	11.0
1970	93.0	57.0	24.4	11.8	9.4	10.6
1975	92.6	62.5	31.1	15.2	9.6	8.8
1980	93.4	66.2	38.9	19.7	12.5	9.0
1985	93.7	67.7	41.5	24.6	15.4	11.7
1986	93.8	68.0	42.0	25.1	16.1	12.2
1987	93.8	68.2	42.5	25.5	16.9	12.6
1988	93.8	68.4	43.0	25.7	17.7	13.0
1989	93.7	68.4	43.3	25.9	18.2	13.5
1990	93.3	68.3	43.5	25.9	18.5	13.9
1991	93.0	67.9	43.6	26.0	18.7	14.5
1992	92.7	67.3	43.7	26.0	18.8	15.2
1993	92.6	66.7	43.8	26.1	18.8	15.8
1994	92.6	66.1	43.9	26.2	18.7	16.2
1995	92.5	65.5	44.0	26.2	18.6	16.5
1996	92.5	65.0	43.8	26.2	18.5	16.6
1997	92.8	64.9	43.5	26.2	18.4	16.6
1998	93.1	65.1	43.0	26.1	18.2	16.5
1999	93.4	65.5	42.5	26.1	18.1	16.4
2000	93.7	66.0	42.1	25.9	17.9	16.2
2001	94.0	66.6	41.7	25.5	17.6	16.0
2002	94.4	66.8	41.5	24.9	17.3	15.8

[1] As of January 1.

NOTES: Data are based on cohort fertility. See Appendix II, Cohort fertility. Percents are derived from the cumulative childbearing experience of cohorts of women, up to the ages specified. Data on births are adjusted for underregistration and population estimates are corrected for underregistration and misstatement of age. Beginning in 1970 births to persons who were not residents of the 50 States and the District of Columbia are excluded. Some data for 2001–02 were revised and differ from previous editions of *Health, United States*.

SOURCES: Centers for Disease Control and Prevention, National Center for Health Statistics, National Vital Statistics System, Birth File. Table 1–32 at www.cdc.gov/nchs/datawh/statab/unpubd/natality/natab99.htm; *Vital statistics of the United States, 2001, vol 1, natality.* In preparation, forthcoming on CD-ROM.

Table 7. Prenatal care for live births, according to detailed race and Hispanic origin of mother: United States, selected years 1970–2003

[Data are based on birth certificates]

Prenatal care, race, and Hispanic origin of mother	*1970*	*1975*	*1980*	*1985*	*1990*	*1995*	*1997*	*1999*	*2000*	*2001*	*2002*	*2003*
Prenatal care began during 1st trimester						Percent of live births[1]						
All races	68.0	72.4	76.3	76.2	75.8	81.3	82.5	83.2	83.2	83.4	83.7	84.1
White	72.3	75.8	79.2	79.3	79.2	83.6	84.7	85.1	85.0	85.2	85.4	85.7
Black or African American	44.2	55.5	62.4	61.5	60.6	70.4	72.3	74.1	74.3	74.5	75.2	75.9
American Indian or Alaska Native	38.2	45.4	55.8	57.5	57.9	66.7	68.1	69.5	69.3	69.3	69.8	70.8
Asian or Pacific Islander[2]	---	---	73.7	74.1	75.1	79.9	82.1	83.7	84.0	84.0	84.8	85.4
Chinese	71.8	76.7	82.6	82.0	81.3	85.7	87.4	88.5	87.6	87.0	87.2	---
Japanese	78.1	82.7	86.1	84.7	87.0	89.7	89.3	90.7	91.0	90.1	90.5	---
Filipino	60.6	70.6	77.3	76.5	77.1	80.9	83.3	84.2	84.9	85.0	85.4	---
Hawaiian	---	---	68.8	67.7	65.8	75.9	78.0	79.6	79.9	79.1	78.1	---
Other Asian or Pacific Islander	---	---	67.4	69.9	71.9	77.0	79.7	81.8	82.5	82.7	83.9	---
Hispanic or Latino[3]	---	---	60.2	61.2	60.2	70.8	73.7	74.4	74.4	75.7	76.7	77.5
Mexican	---	---	59.6	60.0	57.8	69.1	72.1	73.1	72.9	74.6	75.7	76.5
Puerto Rican	---	---	55.1	58.3	63.5	74.0	76.5	77.7	78.5	79.1	79.9	81.2
Cuban	---	---	82.7	82.5	84.8	89.2	90.4	91.4	91.7	91.8	92.0	92.1
Central and South American	---	---	58.8	60.6	61.5	73.2	76.9	77.6	77.6	77.4	78.7	79.2
Other and unknown Hispanic or Latino	---	---	66.4	65.8	66.4	74.3	76.0	74.8	75.8	77.3	76.7	77.0
Not Hispanic or Latino:[3]												
White	---	---	81.2	81.4	83.3	87.1	87.9	88.4	88.5	88.5	88.6	89.0
Black or African American	---	---	60.8	60.2	60.7	70.4	72.3	74.1	74.3	74.5	75.2	75.9
Prenatal care began during 3d trimester or no prenatal care												
All races	7.9	6.0	5.1	5.7	6.1	4.2	3.9	3.8	3.9	3.7	3.6	3.5
White	6.3	5.0	4.3	4.8	4.9	3.5	3.2	3.2	3.3	3.2	3.1	3.0
Black or African American	16.6	10.5	8.9	10.2	11.3	7.6	7.3	6.6	6.7	6.5	6.2	6.0
American Indian or Alaska Native	28.9	22.4	15.2	12.9	12.9	9.5	8.6	8.2	8.6	8.2	8.0	7.6
Asian or Pacific Islander[2]	---	---	6.5	6.5	5.8	4.3	3.8	3.5	3.3	3.4	3.1	3.1
Chinese	6.5	4.4	3.7	4.4	3.4	3.0	2.4	2.0	2.2	2.4	2.1	---
Japanese	4.1	2.7	2.1	3.1	2.9	2.3	2.7	2.1	1.8	2.0	2.1	---
Filipino	7.2	4.1	4.0	4.8	4.5	4.1	3.3	2.8	3.0	3.0	2.8	---
Hawaiian	---	---	6.7	7.4	8.7	5.1	5.4	4.0	4.2	4.8	4.7	---
Other Asian or Pacific Islander	---	---	9.3	8.2	7.1	5.0	4.4	4.1	3.8	3.8	3.5	---
Hispanic or Latino[3]	---	---	12.0	12.4	12.0	7.4	6.2	6.3	6.3	5.9	5.5	5.3
Mexican	---	---	11.8	12.9	13.2	8.1	6.7	6.7	6.9	6.2	5.8	5.6
Puerto Rican	---	---	16.2	15.5	10.6	5.5	5.4	5.0	4.5	4.6	4.1	3.7
Cuban	---	---	3.9	3.7	2.8	2.1	1.5	1.4	1.4	1.3	1.3	1.3
Central and South American	---	---	13.1	12.5	10.9	6.1	5.0	5.2	5.4	5.7	4.9	4.7
Other and unknown Hispanic or Latino	---	---	9.2	9.4	8.5	6.0	5.3	6.3	5.9	5.4	5.3	5.4
Not Hispanic or Latino:[3]												
White	---	---	3.5	4.0	3.4	2.5	2.4	2.3	2.3	2.2	2.2	2.1
Black or African American	---	---	9.7	10.9	11.2	7.6	7.3	6.6	6.7	6.5	6.2	6.0

--- Data not available.

[1]Excludes live births for whom trimester when prenatal care began is unknown.

[2]For 2003, data are not shown for Asian or Pacific Islander subgroups during the transition from single race to multiple race reporting. See Appendix II, Race, Birth File.

[3]Prior to 1993, data from States lacking an Hispanic-origin item on the birth certificate were excluded. See Appendix II, Hispanic origin. Data for non-Hispanic white and non-Hispanic black women for years prior to 1989 are not nationally representative and are provided for comparison with Hispanic data.

NOTES: Data for 2003 exclude Pennsylvania and Washington that implemented the 2003 Revision to the U.S. Standard Certificate of Live Birth. Prenatal care data based on the 2003 Revision are not comparable with data based on the 1989 Revision to the U.S. Standard Certificate of Live Birth. See Appendix II, Prenatal Care. Data for 1970 and 1975 exclude births that occurred in States not reporting prenatal care. The race groups, white, black, American Indian or Alaska Native, and Asian or Pacific Islander, include persons of Hispanic and non-Hispanic origin. Persons of Hispanic origin may be of any race. Interpretation of trend data should take into consideration expansion of reporting areas and immigration. Data for additional years are available. See Appendix III. Some data for 1980–88 were revised and differ from previous editions of *Health, United States.*

SOURCES: Centers for Disease Control and Prevention, National Center for Health Statistics, National Vital Statistics System, Birth File. Martin JA, Hamilton BE, Sutton PD, Ventura SJ, Menacker F, Munson ML. Births: Final Data for 2003. National vital statistics reports; vol 54, no 2. Hyattsville, Maryland: National Center for Health Statistics, 2005; Births: Final data for each data year 1997–2002. National vital statistics reports. Hyattsville, Maryland; Final natality statistics for each data year 1970–96. Monthly vital statistics report. Hyattsville, Maryland.

Table 8 (page 1 of 2). Early prenatal care according to race and Hispanic origin of mother, geographic division, and State: United States, average annual 1995–97, 1998–2000, and 2001–2003

[Data are based on birth certificates]

Geographic division and State	All races			Not Hispanic or Latino: White			Not Hispanic or Latino: Black or African American		
	1995–97	1998–2000	2001–2003	1995–97	1998–2000	2001–2003	1995–97	1998–2000	2001–2003
	Percent of live births with early prenatal care (beginning in the 1st trimester)								
United States [1]	81.9	83.1	83.7	87.4	88.3	88.8	71.4	73.9	75.2
New England	88.1	89.4	89.6	90.7	91.8	92.0	77.0	80.5	80.5
Connecticut	88.4	88.9	88.5	92.1	92.5	92.4	78.5	81.2	81.9
Maine	89.3	88.9	87.8	89.8	89.3	88.2	82.0	81.3	76.1
Massachusetts	87.3	89.4	89.8	90.4	92.3	92.6	75.6	79.7	79.3
New Hampshire	89.6	90.5	91.6	90.0	91.1	92.4	78.3	75.5	81.3
Rhode Island	89.6	90.6	90.6	92.1	92.9	93.2	79.3	83.3	82.1
Vermont	87.6	87.9	89.6	87.8	88.1	89.9	74.6	75.6	73.3
Middle Atlantic [1]	81.2	82.2	81.0	87.9	88.5	88.5	67.3	69.7	69.3
New Jersey	82.0	81.2	80.1	89.7	89.5	89.0	65.3	64.4	63.5
New York	79.2	81.0	81.5	87.2	88.2	88.2	68.3	71.2	71.6
Pennsylvania [1]	83.8	85.1	- - -	87.6	88.4	- - -	66.8	71.7	- - -
East North Central	83.1	83.7	85.0	87.3	87.9	88.8	69.3	71.0	73.6
Illinois	81.6	82.5	84.8	88.9	89.7	90.7	68.5	70.4	73.7
Indiana	80.4	80.4	81.2	82.8	83.2	84.3	65.9	67.0	69.3
Michigan	84.0	84.1	85.4	88.1	88.6	89.4	70.5	70.3	71.0
Ohio	85.1	86.2	87.6	87.7	88.5	89.7	71.4	75.0	78.3
Wisconsin	84.0	84.2	84.4	87.9	87.9	88.1	66.8	68.8	71.5
West North Central	85.0	85.8	86.4	87.8	88.7	89.4	71.6	74.5	76.8
Iowa	87.2	87.7	88.7	88.5	89.2	90.3	73.4	75.6	78.0
Kansas	85.6	86.2	87.1	89.0	89.6	90.3	75.7	77.4	79.8
Minnesota	83.7	84.6	85.5	87.0	88.2	89.8	63.6	66.8	69.7
Missouri	85.6	87.0	88.0	88.2	89.3	90.0	72.5	76.6	79.8
Nebraska	84.2	83.8	83.3	87.0	87.0	87.0	71.9	70.9	70.5
North Dakota	84.5	86.1	86.4	86.3	88.5	89.2	76.0	76.5	81.9
South Dakota	81.9	81.6	78.1	85.6	85.7	82.8	69.4	73.3	62.2
South Atlantic	83.8	84.7	84.3	89.2	89.9	89.8	73.1	75.8	76.4
Delaware	83.8	84.1	86.2	88.8	88.8	90.5	73.1	75.8	81.1
District of Columbia	63.4	73.1	75.7	87.4	90.8	90.4	58.3	68.0	70.1
Florida	83.3	83.8	85.1	88.3	88.9	89.7	72.1	73.3	76.6
Georgia	85.1	86.9	85.0	90.5	91.7	90.8	77.3	80.4	79.5
Maryland	88.3	87.0	83.8	93.2	92.3	90.5	78.8	78.7	76.1
North Carolina	83.6	84.7	84.4	89.7	90.8	90.9	72.1	75.7	76.0
South Carolina	79.5	80.5	78.3	86.8	87.0	84.8	67.4	70.9	70.1
Virginia	84.5	85.2	85.2	89.7	90.2	90.5	72.4	75.0	76.8
West Virginia	82.0	84.9	86.0	82.6	85.6	86.5	66.0	70.4	75.2
East South Central	82.4	83.7	84.1	87.4	88.4	88.7	69.8	72.5	74.7
Alabama	81.9	82.8	83.2	88.4	89.5	89.8	69.5	71.2	73.6
Kentucky	84.9	86.6	86.8	86.3	87.7	88.1	73.6	78.3	80.3
Mississippi	78.6	81.1	83.8	88.2	89.4	90.5	67.9	71.8	76.3
Tennessee	83.3	83.8	83.0	87.2	87.9	87.8	71.5	73.1	72.5
West South Central	78.3	79.6	80.6	85.5	86.6	87.0	71.2	74.1	75.1
Arkansas	75.7	78.8	80.3	80.6	83.0	84.1	61.9	68.7	71.3
Louisiana	81.0	82.8	83.7	88.7	90.0	90.5	70.5	73.0	74.5
Oklahoma	78.5	79.4	77.3	81.8	82.8	81.4	66.9	71.2	69.5
Texas	78.0	79.1	80.6	86.4	87.3	88.1	74.1	76.3	76.9
Mountain	77.9	77.7	77.8	84.6	84.9	85.3	70.5	71.8	72.4
Arizona	73.7	75.9	76.6	83.3	86.0	87.5	69.8	74.0	77.6
Colorado	81.6	81.5	79.4	86.8	88.0	86.5	75.4	75.6	71.3
Idaho	79.1	80.0	81.8	81.9	82.7	84.0	75.6	71.7	83.3
Montana	82.2	83.1	83.6	84.5	85.8	86.5	79.3	82.7	81.5
Nevada	76.5	74.7	75.8	83.3	83.3	85.3	66.7	67.2	69.6
New Mexico	69.8	67.7	68.9	79.0	75.2	76.8	62.7	62.4	67.9
Utah	83.9	80.6	79.7	86.9	84.2	83.7	68.5	60.5	60.6
Wyoming	82.5	82.3	84.8	84.3	84.0	86.2	71.3	73.1	86.3
Pacific [1]	80.7	83.2	85.8	86.1	87.6	89.3	77.9	80.5	83.1
Alaska	81.5	80.3	80.2	84.2	83.4	83.6	82.9	82.9	83.0
California	80.3	83.5	86.4	86.7	89.1	90.4	77.9	80.8	83.2
Hawaii	83.8	85.5	83.5	89.7	90.8	88.0	89.6	91.1	92.0
Oregon	79.9	80.8	81.5	82.6	83.6	84.5	76.2	77.3	76.8
Washington [1]	83.1	82.8	- - -	86.0	85.9	- - -	76.6	75.9	- - -

See footnotes at end of table.

Table 8 (page 2 of 2). Early prenatal care according to race and Hispanic origin of mother, geographic division, and State: United States, average annual 1995–97, 1998–2000, and 2001–2003

[Data are based on birth certificates]

Geographic division and State	Hispanic or Latino[2]			American Indian or Alaska Native[3]			Asian or Pacific Islander[3]		
	1995–97	1998–2000	2001–2003	1995–97	1998–2000	2001–2003	1995–97	1998–2000	2001–2003
	Percent of live births with early prenatal care (beginning in the 1st trimester)								
United States[1]	72.2	74.4	76.7	67.5	69.2	69.8	81.1	83.6	84.8
New England	76.9	79.8	81.5	75.2	79.0	84.6	81.7	85.0	86.0
Connecticut	77.1	78.8	77.9	74.9	79.0	85.0	85.6	87.2	88.3
Maine	79.3	81.0	80.4	74.4	73.8	79.3	79.6	84.6	82.8
Massachusetts	75.7	79.3	82.8	71.9	78.3	89.4	80.7	84.3	85.4
New Hampshire	78.8	79.4	83.5	78.9	84.2	86.9	84.3	86.9	87.6
Rhode Island	82.8	85.2	86.8	79.2	82.3	81.3	80.0	82.6	83.5
Vermont	82.6	83.3	81.5	*	*83.0	*87.5	75.0	83.0	87.6
Middle Atlantic[1]	69.0	71.7	72.7	73.4	76.7	75.6	76.7	78.8	79.8
New Jersey	70.9	69.8	68.3	75.3	74.1	68.7	82.9	83.5	84.3
New York	67.9	72.3	74.8	71.9	75.0	77.3	73.7	76.0	77.5
Pennsylvania[1]	70.6	73.3	---	75.2	81.1	---	77.9	80.8	---
East North Central	71.5	72.1	76.0	71.8	74.5	75.8	80.4	83.1	85.1
Illinois	71.4	72.9	78.4	73.7	75.2	81.1	83.2	85.5	86.9
Indiana	66.6	63.5	64.8	69.7	71.8	72.4	80.8	82.0	81.6
Michigan	72.8	72.1	75.4	73.9	75.0	79.5	85.1	86.0	88.2
Ohio	76.2	76.7	78.1	78.7	81.1	80.8	86.2	87.8	90.1
Wisconsin	70.6	70.3	70.0	67.5	72.2	71.4	59.6	64.7	68.5
West North Central	67.1	69.5	72.4	66.4	66.7	66.0	72.1	76.9	80.4
Iowa	71.0	72.6	74.8	70.0	74.8	75.5	81.9	82.9	86.6
Kansas	64.7	68.3	73.6	79.9	77.0	82.0	81.3	85.5	85.6
Minnesota	60.8	63.6	67.3	60.5	62.2	63.5	59.3	66.8	73.4
Missouri	76.8	78.1	79.1	77.1	77.0	80.2	83.6	87.3	88.0
Nebraska	66.7	68.3	69.2	66.7	68.9	67.6	81.4	82.0	81.9
North Dakota	76.4	75.8	80.4	69.9	68.8	66.2	77.4	85.5	87.2
South Dakota	73.2	71.1	65.0	63.5	62.9	59.3	74.3	78.9	75.6
South Atlantic	77.5	77.9	76.8	74.3	73.5	76.0	84.5	86.8	86.2
Delaware	68.6	71.3	73.4	*80.4	76.4	82.4	84.5	86.7	91.6
District of Columbia	60.6	70.3	71.3	*	*	*	67.1	76.8	82.2
Florida	80.7	81.4	83.2	71.8	65.2	68.1	86.6	87.8	88.7
Georgia	74.4	78.6	72.8	83.2	83.7	80.7	85.7	89.6	89.3
Maryland	81.3	80.8	71.0	85.4	81.8	81.5	89.3	89.9	83.7
North Carolina	68.4	68.5	69.9	72.2	74.4	79.5	80.9	83.2	84.6
South Carolina	66.2	61.4	60.2	73.1	79.1	75.3	76.6	79.2	76.3
Virginia	71.3	72.9	70.4	81.0	80.8	81.5	82.5	85.3	85.4
West Virginia	74.3	74.9	69.2	*78.0	*77.4	*66.7	81.4	80.7	83.6
East South Central	67.3	63.3	61.2	75.0	78.4	76.8	82.2	84.9	84.4
Alabama	63.0	59.3	52.7	79.7	76.5	83.3	82.2	86.4	87.6
Kentucky	74.7	70.7	71.6	77.9	83.7	84.7	84.0	87.4	84.7
Mississippi	78.1	74.6	74.7	72.1	78.0	70.9	78.8	82.0	85.3
Tennessee	64.9	60.9	60.1	73.1	77.9	75.1	82.7	84.0	82.8
West South Central	70.2	72.0	74.6	69.7	71.3	71.5	84.8	87.0	87.5
Arkansas	59.0	64.3	69.2	68.7	73.1	75.1	73.2	77.7	80.6
Louisiana	82.4	85.4	83.5	80.1	80.0	82.4	81.6	85.3	87.3
Oklahoma	68.6	67.9	64.8	68.5	70.0	69.5	81.1	81.7	79.4
Texas	70.2	72.0	75.0	72.8	74.8	77.7	85.8	87.9	88.5
Mountain	64.8	64.9	66.0	60.0	63.1	64.6	77.4	78.7	79.0
Arizona	62.8	65.0	66.7	59.5	64.8	66.9	80.7	84.7	84.3
Colorado	67.6	66.5	66.0	70.4	71.6	65.3	78.9	82.1	80.6
Idaho	61.3	64.2	69.3	60.5	62.7	69.5	80.0	78.5	82.8
Montana	75.7	78.9	79.9	67.2	65.2	65.9	75.2	81.6	82.8
Nevada	64.0	61.5	63.4	69.4	66.2	70.5	78.9	78.9	80.3
New Mexico	66.6	65.0	66.3	54.9	58.1	59.5	73.4	75.6	75.6
Utah	64.9	62.6	62.8	58.4	56.7	56.8	70.1	65.6	65.3
Wyoming	71.6	73.0	77.2	65.6	69.5	72.7	84.3	82.5	84.3
Pacific[1]	75.0	79.0	83.5	72.0	72.6	73.1	82.4	85.0	86.7
Alaska	78.8	80.5	79.4	75.7	72.9	70.7	77.1	76.3	76.5
California	75.3	79.5	83.9	70.0	73.4	75.4	83.0	85.8	87.9
Hawaii	82.0	83.8	82.1	83.1	83.2	81.5	81.5	83.8	81.9
Oregon	65.4	68.3	70.4	66.2	67.5	70.5	78.8	81.5	81.9
Washington[1]	70.1	71.0	---	71.9	71.9	---	79.4	81.1	---

* Percents preceded by an asterisk are based on fewer than 50 births. Percents not shown are based on fewer than 20 births.
[1]Data for 2003 exclude Pennsylvania and Washington that implemented the 2003 Revision to the U.S. Standard Certificate of Live Birth. Prenatal care data based on the 2003 Revision are not comparable with data based on the 1989 Revision to the U.S. Standard Certificate of Live Birth. See Appendix II, Prenatal Care.
[2]Persons of Hispanic origin may be of any race.
[3]Includes persons of Hispanic and non-Hispanic origin.

SOURCE: Centers for Disease Control and Prevention, National Center for Health Statistics, National Vital Statistics System, Birth File.

Table 9. Teenage childbearing, according to detailed race and Hispanic origin of mother: United States, selected years 1970–2003

[Data are based on birth certificates]

Maternal age, race, and Hispanic origin of mother	*1970*	*1975*	*1980*	*1985*	*1990*	*1995*	*1998*	*1999*	*2000*	*2001*	*2002*	*2003*
Age of mother under 18 years						Percent of live births						
All races	6.3	7.6	5.8	4.7	4.7	5.3	4.6	4.4	4.1	3.8	3.6	3.4
White	4.8	6.0	4.5	3.7	3.6	4.3	3.9	3.7	3.5	3.3	3.1	3.0
Black or African American	14.8	16.3	12.5	10.6	10.1	10.8	8.9	8.2	7.8	7.3	6.9	6.6
American Indian or Alaska Native	7.5	11.2	9.4	7.6	7.2	8.7	8.4	7.9	7.3	6.8	6.6	6.6
Asian or Pacific Islander[1]	---	---	1.5	1.6	2.1	2.2	2.0	1.8	1.5	1.3	1.1	1.1
Chinese	1.1	0.4	0.3	0.3	0.4	0.3	0.3	0.2	0.2	0.2	0.2	---
Japanese	2.0	1.7	1.0	0.9	0.8	0.8	0.8	0.7	0.6	0.5	0.6	---
Filipino	3.7	2.4	1.6	1.6	2.0	2.2	2.1	1.8	1.6	1.5	1.2	---
Hawaiian	---	---	6.6	5.7	6.5	7.6	7.8	6.2	5.7	4.9	4.5	---
Other Asian or Pacific Islander	---	---	1.2	1.8	2.4	2.5	2.3	2.0	1.7	1.5	1.3	---
Hispanic or Latino[2]	---	---	7.4	6.4	6.6	7.6	6.9	6.7	6.3	5.8	5.6	5.4
Mexican	---	---	7.7	6.9	6.9	8.0	7.2	7.0	6.6	6.2	6.0	5.8
Puerto Rican	---	---	10.0	8.5	9.1	10.8	9.2	8.5	7.8	7.4	6.9	6.9
Cuban	---	---	3.8	2.2	2.7	2.8	2.9	2.9	3.1	2.7	2.7	2.4
Central and South American	---	---	2.4	2.4	3.2	4.1	3.6	3.5	3.3	3.1	2.8	2.8
Other and unknown Hispanic or Latino	---	---	6.5	7.0	8.0	9.0	8.8	8.1	7.6	6.8	6.5	6.3
Not Hispanic or Latino:[2]												
White	---	---	4.0	3.2	3.0	3.4	3.0	2.8	2.6	2.3	2.2	2.1
Black or African American	---	---	12.7	10.7	10.2	10.8	9.0	8.3	7.8	7.3	6.9	6.6
Age of mother 18–19 years												
All races	11.3	11.3	9.8	8.0	8.1	7.9	7.9	7.9	7.7	7.5	7.1	6.9
White	10.4	10.3	9.0	7.1	7.3	7.2	7.2	7.2	7.1	6.9	6.6	6.4
Black or African American	16.6	16.9	14.5	12.9	13.0	12.4	12.6	12.4	11.9	11.5	11.1	10.7
American Indian or Alaska Native	12.8	15.2	14.6	12.4	12.3	12.7	12.5	12.3	12.4	12.5	11.9	11.6
Asian or Pacific Islander[1]	---	---	3.9	3.4	3.7	3.5	3.3	3.3	3.0	3.0	2.7	2.4
Chinese	3.9	1.7	1.0	0.6	0.8	0.6	0.6	0.7	0.7	0.8	0.7	---
Japanese	4.1	3.3	2.3	1.9	2.0	1.7	1.6	1.4	1.4	1.2	1.1	---
Filipino	7.1	5.0	4.0	3.7	4.1	4.1	4.1	4.0	3.7	3.6	3.3	---
Hawaiian	---	---	13.3	12.3	11.9	11.5	11.0	11.9	11.7	11.3	10.2	---
Other Asian or Pacific Islander	---	---	3.8	3.5	3.9	3.8	3.5	3.5	3.2	3.1	2.8	---
Hispanic or Latino[2]	---	---	11.6	10.1	10.2	10.3	10.0	10.0	9.9	9.7	9.3	8.9
Mexican	---	---	12.0	10.6	10.7	10.8	10.3	10.4	10.4	10.3	9.8	9.5
Puerto Rican	---	---	13.3	12.4	12.6	12.7	12.7	12.6	12.2	11.8	10.9	11.0
Cuban	---	---	9.2	4.9	5.0	4.9	4.0	4.8	4.4	4.8	5.5	5.5
Central and South American	---	---	6.0	5.8	5.9	6.5	6.6	6.5	6.5	6.3	5.7	5.6
Other and unknown Hispanic or Latino	---	---	10.8	10.5	11.1	11.1	11.4	11.4	11.3	10.5	10.2	9.6
Not Hispanic or Latino:[2]												
White	---	---	8.5	6.5	6.6	6.4	6.4	6.4	6.1	5.9	5.6	5.4
Black or African American	---	---	14.7	12.9	13.0	12.4	12.7	12.5	12.0	11.6	11.1	10.8

- - - Data not available.
[1]For 2003, data are not shown for Asian or Pacific Islander subgroups during the transition from single race to multiple race reporting. See Appendix II, Race, Birth File.
[2]Prior to 1993, data from States lacking an Hispanic-origin item on the birth certificate were excluded. See Appendix II, Hispanic origin. Data for non-Hispanic white and non-Hispanic black women for years prior to 1989 are not nationally representative and are provided for comparison with Hispanic data.

NOTES: The race groups, white, black, American Indian or Alaska Native, and Asian or Pacific Islander, include persons of Hispanic and non-Hispanic origin. Persons of Hispanic origin may be of any race. Interpretation of trend data should take into consideration expansion of reporting areas and immigration. Data for additional years are available. See Appendix III. Some data for 1980–88 were revised and differ from previous editions of *Health, United States*.

SOURCES: Centers for Disease Control and Prevention, National Center for Health Statistics, National Vital Statistics System, Birth File.

Table 10. Nonmarital childbearing according to detailed race and Hispanic origin of mother, and maternal age: United States, selected years 1970–2003

[Data are based on birth certificates]

Race, Hispanic origin of mother, and maternal age	*1970*	*1975*	*1980*	*1985*	*1990*	*1995*	*1998*	*1999*	*2000*	*2001*	*2002*	*2003*
	Live births per 1,000 unmarried women 15–44 years of age[1]											
All races and origins	26.4	24.5	29.4	32.8	43.8	44.3	43.3	43.3	44.0	43.8	43.7	44.9
White[2]	13.9	12.4	18.1	22.5	32.9	37.0	36.9	37.4	38.2	38.5	38.9	40.4
Black or African American[2]	95.5	84.2	81.1	77.0	90.5	74.5	71.6	69.7	70.5	68.2	66.2	66.3
Asian or Pacific Islander	---	---	---	---	---	---	---	---	20.9	21.2	21.3	22.2
Hispanic or Latino[3]	---	---	---	---	89.6	88.7	82.8	84.9	87.2	87.8	87.9	92.2
White, not Hispanic or Latino	---	---	---	---	24.4	28.1	27.9	27.9	28.0	27.8	27.8	28.6
	Percent of live births to unmarried mothers											
All races and origins	10.7	14.3	18.4	22.0	28.0	32.2	32.8	33.0	33.2	33.5	34.0	34.6
White	5.5	7.1	11.2	14.7	20.4	25.3	26.3	26.8	27.1	27.7	28.5	29.4
Black or African American	37.5	49.5	56.1	61.2	66.5	69.9	69.1	68.9	68.5	68.4	68.2	68.2
American Indian or Alaska Native	22.4	32.7	39.2	46.8	53.6	57.2	59.3	58.9	58.4	59.7	59.7	61.3
Asian or Pacific Islander[4]	---	---	7.3	9.5	13.2	16.3	15.6	15.4	14.8	14.9	14.9	15.0
Chinese	3.0	1.6	2.7	3.0	5.0	7.9	6.4	6.9	7.6	8.4	9.0	---
Japanese	4.6	4.6	5.2	7.9	9.6	10.8	9.7	9.9	9.5	9.2	10.3	---
Filipino	9.1	6.9	8.6	11.4	15.9	19.5	19.7	21.1	20.3	20.4	20.0	---
Hawaiian	---	---	32.9	37.3	45.0	49.0	51.1	50.4	50.0	50.6	50.4	---
Other Asian or Pacific Islander	---	---	5.4	8.5	12.6	16.2	15.2	14.5	13.8	13.7	13.5	---
Hispanic or Latino[3]	---	---	23.6	29.5	36.7	40.8	41.6	42.2	42.7	42.5	43.5	45.0
Mexican	---	---	20.3	25.7	33.3	38.1	39.6	40.1	40.7	40.8	42.1	43.7
Puerto Rican	---	---	46.3	51.1	55.9	60.0	59.5	59.6	59.6	58.9	59.1	59.8
Cuban	---	---	10.0	16.1	18.2	23.8	24.8	26.4	27.3	27.2	29.8	31.4
Central and South American	---	---	27.1	34.9	41.2	44.1	42.0	43.7	44.7	44.3	44.8	46.0
Other and unknown Hispanic or Latino	---	---	22.4	31.1	37.2	44.0	45.3	45.8	46.2	44.2	44.4	46.7
Not Hispanic or Latino:[3]												
White	---	---	9.5	12.4	16.9	21.2	21.9	22.1	22.1	22.5	23.0	23.6
Black or African American	---	---	57.2	62.0	66.7	70.0	69.3	69.1	68.7	68.6	68.4	68.5
	Number of live births, in thousands											
Live births to unmarried mothers	399	448	666	828	1,165	1,254	1,294	1,309	1,347	1,349	1,366	1,416
Maternal age	Percent distribution of live births to unmarried mothers											
Under 20 years	50.1	52.1	40.8	33.8	30.9	30.9	30.1	29.3	28.0	26.6	25.4	24.3
20–24 years	31.8	29.9	35.6	36.3	34.7	34.5	35.6	36.4	37.4	38.2	38.6	38.8
25 years and over	18.1	18.0	23.5	29.9	34.4	34.7	34.3	34.3	34.6	35.2	35.9	36.9

- - - Data not available.

[1]Rates computed by relating births to unmarried mothers, regardless of age of mother, to unmarried women 15–44 years of age. Population data for unmarried American Indian or Alaska Native women are not available for rate calculations. Prior to 2000, population data for unmarried Asian or Pacific Islander women were not available for rate calculations.

[2]For 1970 and 1975, birth rates are by race of child.

[3]Prior to 1993, data from States lacking an Hispanic-origin item on the birth certificate were excluded. See Appendix II, Hispanic origin. Data for non-Hispanic white and non-Hispanic black women for years prior to 1989 are not nationally representative and are provided for comparison with Hispanic data.

[4]For 2003, data are not shown for Asian or Pacific Islander subgroups during the transition from single race to multiple race reporting. See Appendix II, Race, Birth File.

NOTES: National estimates for 1970 and 1975 for unmarried mothers are based on births occurring in States reporting marital status of mother. Changes in reporting procedures for marital status occurred in some States during the 1990s. Interpretation of trend data should also take into consideration expansion of reporting areas and immigration. See Appendix II, Marital status. The race groups, white, black, American Indian or Alaska Native, and Asian or Pacific Islander, include persons of Hispanic and non-Hispanic origin. Persons of Hispanic origin may be of any race. Starting with *Health, United States, 2003*, rates for 1991–99 were revised using intercensal population estimates based on Census 2000. Rates for 2000 were computed using Census 2000 counts and starting with 2001, rates were computed using 2000-based postcensal estimates. Data for additional years are available. See Appendix III. Some data for 1980–88 were revised and differ from previous editions of *Health, United States*.

SOURCES: Centers for Disease Control and Prevention, National Center for Health Statistics, National Vital Statistics System, Birth File. Martin JA, Hamilton BE, Sutton PD, Ventura SJ, Menacker F, Munson ML. Births: Final Data for 2003. National vital statistics reports; vol 54, no 2. Hyattsville, Maryland: National Center for Health Statistics, 2005; Hamilton BE, Sutton PD, Ventura SJ. Revised birth and fertility rates for the 1990s and new rates for Hispanic populations, 2000 and 2001: United States. National vital statistics reports; vol 51, no 12. Hyattsville, Maryland: National Center for Health Statistics, 2003; Births: Final data for each data year 1997–2002. National vital statistics reports. Hyattsville, Maryland; Final natality statistics for each data year 1993–96. Monthly vital statistics report. Hyattsville, Maryland; Ventura SJ. Births to unmarried mothers: United States, 1980–92. Vital Health Stat 21(53). 1995.

Table 11. Maternal education for live births, according to detailed race and Hispanic origin of mother: United States, selected years 1970–2003

[Data are based on birth certificates]

Education, race, and Hispanic origin of mother	*1970*	*1975*	*1980*	*1985*	*1990*	*1995*	*1998*	*1999*	*2000*	*2001*	*2002*	*2003*
Less than 12 years of education					Percent of live births [1]							
All races	30.8	28.6	23.7	20.6	23.8	22.6	21.9	21.7	21.7	21.7	21.5	21.6
White	27.1	25.1	20.8	17.8	22.4	21.6	21.2	21.3	21.4	21.7	21.6	21.8
Black or African American	51.2	45.3	36.4	32.6	30.2	28.7	26.9	26.0	25.5	24.9	24.4	24.0
American Indian or Alaska Native	60.5	52.7	44.2	39.0	36.4	33.0	32.7	32.2	31.6	31.0	30.8	30.5
Asian or Pacific Islander [2]	- - -	- - -	21.0	19.4	20.0	16.1	12.9	12.4	11.6	10.8	10.3	9.9
Chinese	23.0	16.5	15.2	15.5	15.8	12.9	11.4	12.0	11.7	11.9	11.3	- - -
Japanese	11.8	9.1	5.0	4.8	3.5	2.6	2.4	2.0	2.1	1.8	2.2	- - -
Filipino	26.4	22.3	16.4	13.9	10.3	8.0	6.9	6.3	6.2	6.0	5.3	- - -
Hawaiian	- - -	- - -	20.7	18.7	19.3	17.6	18.5	16.8	16.7	15.4	14.3	- - -
Other Asian or Pacific Islander	- - -	- - -	27.6	24.3	26.8	21.2	15.9	14.8	13.5	12.2	11.6	- - -
Hispanic or Latino [3]	- - -	- - -	51.1	44.5	53.9	52.1	49.3	49.1	48.9	48.8	48.1	47.5
Mexican	- - -	- - -	62.8	59.0	61.4	58.6	55.2	55.2	55.0	55.0	54.2	53.6
Puerto Rican	- - -	- - -	55.3	46.6	42.7	38.6	35.9	34.4	33.4	32.3	31.5	29.9
Cuban	- - -	- - -	24.1	21.1	17.8	14.4	13.0	12.3	11.9	11.8	11.8	11.5
Central and South American	- - -	- - -	41.2	37.0	44.2	41.7	38.5	37.9	37.2	36.5	35.8	35.3
Other and unknown Hispanic or Latino	- - -	- - -	40.1	36.5	33.3	33.8	33.6	32.5	31.4	30.4	31.7	30.1
Not Hispanic or Latino: [3]												
White	- - -	- - -	18.1	15.7	15.2	13.3	12.8	12.6	12.2	12.0	11.7	11.5
Black or African American	- - -	- - -	37.3	33.4	30.0	28.6	26.7	25.9	25.3	24.8	24.3	23.8
16 years or more of education												
All races	8.6	11.4	14.0	16.7	17.5	21.4	23.4	24.1	24.7	25.2	25.9	26.6
White	9.6	12.7	15.5	18.6	19.3	23.1	25.1	25.7	26.3	26.7	27.3	27.9
Black or African American	2.8	4.3	6.2	7.0	7.2	9.5	11.0	11.4	11.7	12.1	12.7	13.4
American Indian or Alaska Native	2.7	2.2	3.5	3.7	4.4	6.2	6.8	7.2	7.8	8.2	8.7	8.5
Asian or Pacific Islander [2]	- - -	- - -	30.8	30.3	31.0	35.0	39.7	40.9	42.8	44.0	45.7	47.1
Chinese	34.0	37.8	41.5	35.2	40.3	49.0	53.8	54.3	55.6	55.9	57.3	- - -
Japanese	20.7	30.6	36.8	38.1	44.1	46.2	49.1	49.5	51.1	52.0	53.5	- - -
Filipino	28.1	36.6	37.1	35.2	34.5	36.7	39.2	39.6	40.5	41.8	43.3	- - -
Hawaiian	- - -	- - -	7.9	6.5	6.8	9.7	11.0	12.7	13.5	13.2	14.6	- - -
Other Asian or Pacific Islander	- - -	- - -	29.2	30.2	27.3	30.5	36.7	38.5	40.7	42.6	44.4	- - -
Hispanic or Latino [3]	- - -	- - -	4.2	6.0	5.1	6.1	7.0	7.4	7.6	7.9	8.3	8.7
Mexican	- - -	- - -	2.2	3.0	3.3	4.0	4.7	5.0	5.1	5.3	5.5	5.9
Puerto Rican	- - -	- - -	3.0	4.6	6.5	8.7	9.5	10.3	10.4	11.1	11.8	12.9
Cuban	- - -	- - -	11.6	15.0	20.4	26.5	28.6	29.9	31.0	30.8	30.5	31.3
Central and South American	- - -	- - -	6.1	8.1	8.6	10.3	12.5	13.2	14.1	14.8	15.5	16.0
Other and unknown Hispanic or Latino	- - -	- - -	5.5	7.2	8.5	10.5	11.5	12.0	12.5	13.2	13.2	14.4
Not Hispanic or Latino: [3]												
White	- - -	- - -	16.6	19.4	22.6	27.7	30.4	31.4	32.5	33.3	34.3	35.5
Black or African American	- - -	- - -	5.8	6.7	7.3	9.5	11.0	11.4	11.7	12.2	12.7	13.4

- - - Data not available.

[1] Excludes live births for whom education of mother is unknown.

[2] For 2003, data are not shown for Asian or Pacific Islander subgroups during the transition from single race to multiple race reporting. See Appendix II, Race, Birth File.

[3] Prior to 1993, data shown only for States with an Hispanic-origin item and education of mother item on the birth certificate. See Appendix II, Education; Hispanic origin. Data for non-Hispanic white and non-Hispanic black women for years prior to 1989 are not nationally representative and are provided for comparison with Hispanic data.

NOTES: Data for 2003 exclude Pennsylvania and Washington that implemented the 2003 Revision to the U.S. Standard Certificate of Live Birth. Education data based on the 2003 Revision are not comparable with data based on the 1989 Revision to the U.S. Standard Certificate of Live Birth. In 1992–2002, education of mother was reported on the birth certificate by all 50 States and the District of Columbia. Prior to 1992, data from States lacking an education of mother item were excluded. See Appendix II, Education. The race groups, white, black, American Indian or Alaska Native, and Asian or Pacific Islander, include persons of Hispanic and non-Hispanic origin. Persons of Hispanic origin may be of any race. Maternal education groups shown in this table generally represent the group at highest risk for unfavorable birth outcomes (less than 12 years of education) and the group at lowest risk (16 years or more of education). Interpretation of trend data should take into consideration expansion of reporting areas and immigration. Data for additional years are available. See Appendix III. Some data for 1980–88 were revised and differ from previous editions of *Health, United States.*

SOURCE: Centers for Disease Control and Prevention, National Center for Health Statistics, National Vital Statistics System, Birth File.

Table 12. Mothers who smoked cigarettes during pregnancy, according to mother's detailed race, Hispanic origin, age, and education: United States, selected years, 1989–2003

[Data are based on birth certificates]

Characteristic of mother	1989	1990	1995	1998	1999	2000	2001	2002	2003
Race of mother	Percent of mothers who smoked[1,2]								
All races	19.5	18.4	13.9	12.9	12.6	12.2	12.0	11.4	10.7
White	20.4	19.4	15.0	14.0	13.6	13.2	13.0	12.3	11.6
Black or African American	17.1	15.9	10.6	9.5	9.3	9.1	9.0	8.7	8.1
American Indian or Alaska Native	23.0	22.4	20.9	20.2	20.2	20.0	19.9	19.7	18.1
Asian or Pacific Islander[3]	5.7	5.5	3.4	3.1	2.9	2.8	2.8	2.5	2.2
Chinese	2.7	2.0	0.8	0.8	0.5	0.6	0.7	0.5	- - -
Japanese	8.2	8.0	5.2	4.8	4.5	4.2	3.8	4.0	- - -
Filipino	5.1	5.3	3.4	3.3	3.3	3.2	3.2	2.9	- - -
Hawaiian	19.3	21.0	15.9	16.8	14.7	14.4	14.8	13.7	- - -
Other Asian or Pacific Islander	4.2	3.8	2.7	2.4	2.3	2.3	2.3	2.1	- - -
Hispanic origin and race of mother[4]									
Hispanic or Latino	8.0	6.7	4.3	4.0	3.7	3.5	3.2	3.0	2.7
Mexican	6.3	5.3	3.1	2.8	2.6	2.4	2.4	2.2	2.0
Puerto Rican	14.5	13.6	10.4	10.7	10.5	10.3	9.7	9.0	7.9
Cuban	6.9	6.4	4.1	3.7	3.3	3.3	3.0	2.8	2.4
Central and South American	3.6	3.0	1.8	1.5	1.4	1.5	1.3	1.3	1.1
Other and unknown Hispanic or Latino	12.1	10.8	8.2	8.0	7.7	7.4	6.8	6.5	6.6
Not Hispanic or Latino:									
White	21.7	21.0	17.1	16.2	15.9	15.6	15.5	15.0	14.3
Black or African American	17.2	15.9	10.6	9.6	9.4	9.2	9.1	8.8	8.3
Age of mother[1]									
Under 15 years	7.7	7.5	7.3	7.7	7.8	7.1	6.0	5.8	5.3
15–19 years	22.2	20.8	16.8	17.8	18.1	17.8	17.5	16.7	15.4
15–17 years	19.0	17.6	14.6	15.5	15.5	15.0	14.4	13.4	11.9
18–19 years	23.9	22.5	18.1	19.2	19.5	19.2	19.0	18.2	17.1
20–24 years	23.5	22.1	17.1	16.5	16.7	16.8	17.0	16.7	16.1
25–29 years	19.0	18.0	12.8	11.4	11.0	10.5	10.3	9.9	9.4
30–34 years	15.7	15.3	11.4	9.3	8.6	8.0	7.6	7.1	6.5
35–39 years	13.6	13.3	12.0	10.6	9.9	9.1	8.6	7.8	6.8
40–54 years[5]	13.2	12.3	10.1	10.0	9.5	9.5	9.3	8.4	8.0
Education of mother[6]	Percent of mothers 20 years of age and over who smoked[2]								
0–8 years	18.9	17.5	11.0	9.5	8.9	7.9	7.2	6.8	6.2
9–11 years	42.2	40.5	32.0	29.3	29.0	28.2	27.6	26.8	25.5
12 years	22.8	21.9	18.3	17.1	16.9	16.6	16.5	16.0	15.2
13–15 years	13.7	12.8	10.6	9.6	9.4	9.1	9.2	8.8	8.5
16 years or more	5.0	4.5	2.7	2.2	2.1	2.0	1.9	1.7	1.6

[1]Data from States that did not require the reporting of mother's tobacco use during pregnancy on the birth certificate are not included. Reporting area for tobacco use increased from 43 States and the District of Columbia (DC) in 1989 to 49 States and DC in 2000–02, and decreased to 47 States and DC in 2003. See Appendix II, Cigarette smoking.

[2]Excludes live births for whom smoking status of mother is unknown.

[3]Maternal tobacco use during pregnancy was not reported on the birth certificates of California, which in 2003 accounted for 30 percent of the births to Asian or Pacific Islander mothers. For 2003, data are not shown for Asian or Pacific Islander subgroups during the transition from single race to multiple race reporting. See Appendix II, Race, Birth File.

[4]Data from States that did not require the reporting of either Hispanic origin of mother or tobacco use during pregnancy on the birth certificate are not included. Reporting area for tobacco use and Hispanic origin of mother increased from 42 States and DC in 1989 to 49 States and DC in 2000–02. In 2003 California did not require reporting of tobacco use during pregnancy. Data for 2003 also exclude Pennsylvania and Washington that implemented the 2003 Revision to the U.S. Standard Certificate of Live Birth. Tobacco use data based on the 2003 Revision are not comparable with data based on the 1989 Revision to the U.S. Standard Certificate of Live Birth. See Appendix II, Hispanic origin; Cigarette smoking.

[5]Prior to 1997 data are for live births to mothers 45–49 years of age.

[6]Data from States that did not require the reporting of either mother's education or tobacco use during pregnancy on the birth certificate are not included. Reporting area for tobacco use and education of mother increased from 42 States and DC in 1989 to 49 States and DC in 2000–02. In 2003 California did not require reporting of tobacco use during pregnancy. Data for 2003 also exclude Pennsylvania and Washington that implemented the 2003 Revision to the U.S. Standard Certificate of Live Birth. Tobacco use and education data based on the 2003 Revision are not comparable with data based on the 1989 Revision to the U.S. Standard Certificate of Live Birth. See Appendix II, Education; Cigarette smoking.

NOTES: The race groups, white, black, American Indian or Alaska Native, and Asian or Pacific Islander, include persons of Hispanic and non-Hispanic origin. Persons of Hispanic origin may be of any race. Interpretation of trend data should take into consideration expansion of reporting areas and immigration. Data for additional years are available. See Appendix III.

SOURCES: Centers for Disease Control and Prevention, National Center for Health Statistics, National Vital Statistics System, Birth File. Martin JA, Hamilton BE, Sutton PD, Ventura SJ, Menacker F, Munson ML. Births: Final Data for 2003. National vital statistics reports; vol 54, no 2. Hyattsville, Maryland: National Center for Health Statistics, 2005; Births: Final data for each data year 1997–2002. National vital statistics reports. Hyattsville, Maryland; Final natality statistics for each data year 1989–96. Monthly vital statistics report. Hyattsville, Maryland.

Table 13. Low-birthweight live births, according to mother's detailed race, Hispanic origin, and smoking status: United States, selected years 1970–2003

[Data are based on birth certificates]

Birthweight, race, Hispanic origin of mother, and smoking status of mother	*1970*	*1975*	*1980*	*1985*	*1990*	*1995*	*1998*	*1999*	*2000*	*2001*	*2002*	*2003*
Low birthweight (less than 2,500 grams)					Percent of live births[1]							
All races	7.93	7.38	6.84	6.75	6.97	7.32	7.57	7.62	7.57	7.68	7.82	7.93
White	6.85	6.27	5.72	5.65	5.70	6.22	6.52	6.57	6.55	6.68	6.80	6.94
Black or African American	13.90	13.19	12.69	12.65	13.25	13.13	13.05	13.11	12.99	12.95	13.29	13.37
American Indian or Alaska Native	7.97	6.41	6.44	5.86	6.11	6.61	6.81	7.15	6.76	7.33	7.23	7.37
Asian or Pacific Islander[2]	---	---	6.68	6.16	6.45	6.90	7.42	7.45	7.31	7.51	7.78	7.78
Chinese	6.67	5.29	5.21	4.98	4.69	5.29	5.34	5.19	5.10	5.33	5.52	---
Japanese	9.03	7.47	6.60	6.21	6.16	7.26	7.50	7.95	7.14	7.28	7.57	---
Filipino	10.02	8.08	7.40	6.95	7.30	7.83	8.23	8.30	8.46	8.66	8.61	---
Hawaiian	---	---	7.23	6.49	7.24	6.84	7.15	7.69	6.76	7.91	8.14	---
Other Asian or Pacific Islander	---	---	6.83	6.19	6.65	7.05	7.76	7.76	7.67	7.76	8.16	---
Hispanic or Latino[3]	---	---	6.12	6.16	6.06	6.29	6.44	6.38	6.41	6.47	6.55	6.69
Mexican	---	---	5.62	5.77	5.55	5.81	5.97	5.94	6.01	6.08	6.16	6.28
Puerto Rican	---	---	8.95	8.69	8.99	9.41	9.68	9.30	9.30	9.34	9.68	10.01
Cuban	---	---	5.62	6.02	5.67	6.50	6.50	6.80	6.49	6.49	6.50	7.04
Central and South American	---	---	5.76	5.68	5.84	6.20	6.47	6.38	6.34	6.49	6.53	6.70
Other and unknown Hispanic or Latino	---	---	6.96	6.83	6.87	7.55	7.59	7.63	7.84	7.96	7.87	8.01
Not Hispanic or Latino:[3]												
White	---	---	5.69	5.61	5.61	6.20	6.55	6.64	6.60	6.76	6.91	7.04
Black or African American	---	---	12.71	12.62	13.32	13.21	13.17	13.23	13.13	13.07	13.39	13.55
Cigarette smoker[4]	---	---	---	---	11.25	12.18	12.01	12.06	11.88	11.90	12.15	12.40
Nonsmoker[4]	---	---	---	---	6.14	6.79	7.18	7.21	7.19	7.32	7.48	7.66
Very low birthweight (less than 1,500 grams)												
All races	1.17	1.16	1.15	1.21	1.27	1.35	1.45	1.45	1.43	1.44	1.46	1.45
White	0.95	0.92	0.90	0.94	0.95	1.06	1.15	1.15	1.14	1.16	1.17	1.17
Black or African American	2.40	2.40	2.48	2.71	2.92	2.97	3.08	3.14	3.07	3.04	3.13	3.07
American Indian or Alaska Native	0.98	0.95	0.92	1.01	1.01	1.10	1.24	1.26	1.16	1.26	1.28	1.30
Asian or Pacific Islander[2]	---	---	0.92	0.85	0.87	0.91	1.10	1.08	1.05	1.03	1.12	1.09
Chinese	0.80	0.52	0.66	0.57	0.51	0.67	0.75	0.68	0.77	0.69	0.74	---
Japanese	1.48	0.89	0.94	0.84	0.73	0.87	0.84	0.86	0.75	0.71	0.97	---
Filipino	1.08	0.93	0.99	0.86	1.05	1.13	1.35	1.41	1.38	1.23	1.31	---
Hawaiian	---	---	1.05	1.03	0.97	0.94	1.53	1.41	1.39	1.50	1.55	---
Other Asian or Pacific Islander	---	---	0.96	0.91	0.92	0.91	1.12	1.09	1.04	1.06	1.17	---
Hispanic or Latino[3]	---	---	0.98	1.01	1.03	1.11	1.15	1.14	1.14	1.14	1.17	1.16
Mexican	---	---	0.92	0.97	0.92	1.01	1.02	1.04	1.03	1.05	1.06	1.06
Puerto Rican	---	---	1.29	1.30	1.62	1.79	1.86	1.86	1.93	1.85	1.96	2.01
Cuban	---	---	1.02	1.18	1.20	1.19	1.33	1.49	1.21	1.27	1.15	1.37
Central and South American	---	---	0.99	1.01	1.05	1.13	1.23	1.15	1.20	1.19	1.20	1.17
Other and unknown Hispanic or Latino	---	---	1.01	0.96	1.09	1.28	1.38	1.32	1.42	1.27	1.44	1.28
Not Hispanic or Latino:[3]												
White	---	---	0.87	0.91	0.93	1.04	1.15	1.15	1.14	1.17	1.17	1.18
Black or African American	---	---	2.47	2.67	2.93	2.98	3.11	3.18	3.10	3.08	3.15	3.12
Cigarette smoker[4]	---	---	---	---	1.73	1.85	1.87	1.91	1.91	1.88	1.88	1.92
Nonsmoker[4]	---	---	---	---	1.18	1.31	1.44	1.43	1.40	1.42	1.45	1.44

--- Data not available.

[1]Excludes live births with unknown birthweight. Percent based on live births with known birthweight.

[2]For 2003, data are not shown for Asian or Pacific Islander subgroups during the transition from single race to multiple race reporting. See Appendix II, Race, Birth File.

[3]Prior to 1993, data from States lacking an Hispanic-origin item on the birth certificate were excluded. See Appendix II, Hispanic origin. Data for non-Hispanic white and non-Hispanic black women for years prior to 1989 are not nationally representative and are provided for comparison with Hispanic data.

[4]Percent based on live births with known smoking status of mother and known birthweight. Data from States that did not require the reporting of mother's tobacco use during pregnancy on the birth certificate are not included. Reporting area for tobacco use increased from 43 States and the District of Columbia (DC) in 1989 to 49 States and DC in 2000–02. In 2003 California did not require reporting of tobacco use during pregnancy. Data for 2003 also exclude Pennsylvania and Washington that implemented the 2003 Revision to the U.S. Standard Certificate of Live Birth. Tobacco use data based on the 2003 Revision are not comparable with data based on the 1989 Revision to the U.S. Standard Certificate of Live Birth. See Appendix II, Cigarette smoking.

NOTES: The race groups, white, black, American Indian or Alaska Native, and Asian or Pacific Islander, include persons of Hispanic and non-Hispanic origin. Persons of Hispanic origin may be of any race. Interpretation of trend data should take into consideration expansion of reporting areas and immigration. Data for additional years are available. See Appendix III. Some data for 1980–88 were revised and differ from previous editions of *Health, United States*.

SOURCES: Centers for Disease Control and Prevention, National Center for Health Statistics, National Vital Statistics System, Birth File. Martin JA, Hamilton BE, Sutton PD, Ventura SJ, Menacker F, Munson ML. Births: Final Data for 2003. National vital statistics reports; vol 54, no 2. Hyattsville, Maryland: National Center for Health Statistics, 2005; Births: Final data for each data year 1997–2002. National vital statistics reports. Hyattsville, Maryland; Final natality statistics for each data year 1970–96. Monthly vital statistics report. Hyattsville, Maryland.

Table 14. Low-birthweight live births among mothers 20 years of age and over, by mother's detailed race, Hispanic origin, and education: United States, selected years 1989–2003

[Data are based on birth certificates]

Education, race, and Hispanic origin of mother	*1989*	*1990*	*1995*	*1998*	*1999*	*2000*	*2001*	*2002*	*2003*
Less than 12 years of education	Percent of live births weighing less than 2,500 grams[1]								
All races	9.0	8.6	8.4	8.4	8.3	8.2	8.2	8.2	8.4
White	7.3	7.0	7.1	7.2	7.2	7.1	7.1	7.1	7.3
Black or African American	17.0	16.5	16.0	15.0	15.0	14.8	14.6	15.0	15.2
American Indian or Alaska Native	7.3	7.4	8.0	8.0	8.1	7.2	8.3	8.4	8.0
Asian or Pacific Islander[2]	6.6	6.4	6.7	7.4	7.1	7.2	7.5	7.4	7.5
Chinese	5.4	5.2	5.3	5.9	5.2	5.3	4.9	4.4	- - -
Japanese	4.0	10.6	11.0	5.0	11.0	6.8	8.4	4.7	- - -
Filipino	6.9	7.2	7.5	7.9	8.4	8.6	8.5	9.0	- - -
Hawaiian	11.0	10.7	9.8	8.5	7.2	9.4	8.9	7.8	- - -
Other Asian or Pacific Islander	6.8	6.4	6.7	7.8	7.5	7.5	8.1	8.1	- - -
Hispanic or Latino[3]	6.0	5.7	5.8	5.9	5.9	6.0	6.0	6.0	6.2
Mexican	5.3	5.2	5.4	5.6	5.5	5.6	5.7	5.7	5.9
Puerto Rican	11.3	10.3	10.5	10.7	10.5	10.9	10.4	10.4	11.2
Cuban	9.4	7.9	9.2	7.4	6.7	8.4	6.7	7.5	7.9
Central and South American	5.8	5.8	6.2	6.2	6.0	6.2	6.4	6.2	6.4
Other and unknown Hispanic or Latino	8.2	8.0	7.7	7.7	8.0	8.6	8.2	7.8	8.1
Not Hispanic or Latino:[3]									
White	8.4	8.3	8.9	9.1	9.2	9.0	9.1	9.3	9.5
Black or African American	17.6	16.7	16.2	15.3	15.2	15.2	14.9	15.3	15.7
12 years of education									
All races	7.1	7.1	7.6	7.9	8.0	7.9	8.1	8.2	8.4
White	5.7	5.8	6.4	6.7	6.8	6.8	7.0	7.0	7.2
Black or African American	13.4	13.1	13.3	13.1	13.3	13.0	13.1	13.4	13.5
American Indian or Alaska Native	5.6	6.1	6.5	6.9	6.9	6.7	7.2	7.1	7.2
Asian or Pacific Islander[2]	6.4	6.5	7.0	7.2	7.4	7.4	7.5	7.9	7.8
Chinese	5.1	4.9	5.7	4.7	5.8	5.6	5.4	5.2	- - -
Japanese	7.4	6.2	7.4	8.0	8.9	7.2	8.6	7.1	- - -
Filipino	6.8	7.6	7.7	8.0	8.0	8.1	9.2	8.7	- - -
Hawaiian	7.0	6.7	6.6	6.7	8.7	6.8	7.5	8.3	- - -
Other Asian or Pacific Islander	6.5	6.7	7.1	7.6	7.3	7.7	7.4	8.2	- - -
Hispanic or Latino[3]	5.9	6.0	6.1	6.4	6.2	6.2	6.4	6.5	6.5
Mexican	5.2	5.5	5.6	6.0	5.8	5.8	6.0	6.1	6.1
Puerto Rican	8.8	8.3	8.7	9.4	8.6	8.8	9.3	9.3	9.8
Cuban	5.3	5.2	6.7	6.0	6.5	6.5	5.8	6.0	6.4
Central and South American	5.7	5.8	5.9	6.2	6.2	6.0	6.3	6.4	6.6
Other and unknown Hispanic or Latino	6.1	6.6	7.1	7.3	7.1	7.3	7.7	7.7	7.4
Not Hispanic or Latino:[3]									
White	5.7	5.7	6.5	6.8	7.0	6.9	7.2	7.3	7.5
Black or African American	13.6	13.2	13.4	13.3	13.4	13.1	13.3	13.5	13.7
13 years or more of education									
All races	5.5	5.4	6.0	6.5	6.6	6.6	6.7	7.0	7.1
White	4.6	4.6	5.3	5.8	5.8	5.8	6.0	6.2	6.4
Black or African American	11.2	11.1	11.4	11.5	11.6	11.6	11.6	12.0	12.0
American Indian or Alaska Native	5.6	4.7	5.7	5.9	6.1	6.5	6.7	7.0	7.3
Asian or Pacific Islander[2]	6.1	6.0	6.6	7.2	7.2	7.0	7.3	7.6	7.6
Chinese	4.5	4.4	5.1	5.3	4.9	4.8	5.3	5.7	- - -
Japanese	6.6	6.0	7.1	7.4	7.6	7.0	6.9	7.7	- - -
Filipino	7.2	7.0	7.6	8.0	8.0	8.3	8.3	8.4	- - -
Hawaiian	6.3	4.7	5.0	6.6	6.3	4.5	7.7	7.2	- - -
Other Asian or Pacific Islander	6.1	6.2	6.7	7.5	7.6	7.4	7.6	7.9	- - -
Hispanic or Latino[3]	5.5	5.5	5.9	6.3	6.2	6.2	6.4	6.6	6.8
Mexican	5.1	5.2	5.6	5.8	5.6	5.8	6.0	6.2	6.3
Puerto Rican	7.4	7.4	7.9	8.2	8.2	7.9	8.0	8.9	9.1
Cuban	4.9	5.0	5.6	6.3	6.9	5.9	6.7	6.4	6.9
Central and South American	5.2	5.6	5.8	6.5	6.3	6.3	6.3	6.5	6.8
Other and unknown Hispanic or Latino	5.4	5.2	6.1	6.8	6.4	6.6	7.0	7.0	7.6
Not Hispanic or Latino:[3]									
White	4.6	4.5	5.2	5.7	5.8	5.8	6.0	6.2	6.4
Black or African American	11.2	11.1	11.5	11.6	11.7	11.7	11.7	12.1	12.1

[1]Excludes live births with unknown birthweight. Percent based on live births with known birthweight.
[2]For 2003, data are not shown for Asian or Pacific Islander subgroups during the transition from single race to multiple race reporting. See Appendix II, Race, Birth File.
[3]Prior to 1993, data shown only for States with an Hispanic-origin item and education of mother item on the birth certificate. See Appendix II, Education; Hispanic origin.

NOTES: Data for 2003 exclude Pennsylvania and Washington that implemented the 2003 Revision to the U.S. Standard Certificate of Live Birth. Education data based on the 2003 Revision are not comparable with data based on the 1989 Revision to the U.S. Standard Certificate of Live Birth. In 1992–2002, education of mother was reported on the birth certificate by all 50 States and the District of Columbia. Prior to 1992, data from States lacking an education of mother item were excluded. See Appendix II, Education. The race groups, white, black, American Indian or Alaska Native, and Asian or Pacific Islander, include persons of Hispanic and non-Hispanic origin. Persons of Hispanic origin may be of any race. Interpretation of trend data should take into consideration expansion of reporting areas and immigration. Data for additional years are available. See Appendix III.

SOURCE: Centers for Disease Control and Prevention, National Center for Health Statistics, National Vital Statistics System, Birth File.

Table 15 (page 1 of 2). Low-birthweight live births, according to race and Hispanic origin of mother, geographic division, and State: United States, average annual 1995–97, 1998–2000, and 2001–2003

[Data are based on birth certificates]

Geographic division and State	All races			Not Hispanic or Latino: White			Not Hispanic or Latino: Black or African American		
	1995–97	1998–2000	2001–2003	1995–97	1998–2000	2001–2003	1995–97	1998–2000	2001–2003
	Percent of live births weighing less than 2,500 grams[1]								
United States	7.41	7.59	7.81	6.34	6.60	6.90	13.15	13.18	13.33
New England	6.59	7.00	7.28	5.86	6.28	6.61	11.78	12.08	11.86
Connecticut	7.21	7.61	7.55	5.92	6.40	6.47	12.67	12.83	12.46
Maine	5.97	5.96	6.29	6.01	5.99	6.31	*13.55	*10.45	*8.47
Massachusetts	6.57	7.04	7.42	5.89	6.36	6.74	11.22	11.53	11.56
New Hampshire	5.38	6.08	6.37	5.26	5.85	6.26	*8.24	*9.26	11.70
Rhode Island	7.03	7.35	7.94	6.22	6.63	7.23	11.06	12.55	11.80
Vermont	5.94	6.09	6.47	5.86	6.02	6.53	*	*	*
Middle Atlantic	7.64	7.82	7.93	6.10	6.49	6.72	13.08	12.90	12.75
New Jersey	7.69	7.96	8.02	6.08	6.46	6.86	13.71	13.69	13.22
New York	7.70	7.80	7.81	5.98	6.44	6.52	12.40	12.19	12.06
Pennsylvania	7.49	7.74	8.05	6.24	6.56	6.88	14.09	13.81	13.93
East North Central	7.57	7.74	7.91	6.38	6.57	6.88	13.82	13.86	13.85
Illinois	7.92	7.98	8.14	6.34	6.51	6.94	14.34	14.16	14.16
Indiana	7.61	7.71	7.71	6.93	7.13	7.11	13.50	13.01	13.11
Michigan	7.69	7.89	8.05	6.32	6.31	6.76	13.55	14.38	14.08
Ohio	7.62	7.84	8.21	6.57	6.85	7.22	13.57	13.30	13.63
Wisconsin	6.23	6.57	6.67	5.40	5.75	5.93	13.25	13.45	13.35
West North Central	6.60	6.76	6.98	6.09	6.24	6.48	12.90	12.88	12.38
Iowa	6.23	6.23	6.54	5.95	5.98	6.31	12.01	12.36	12.38
Kansas	6.76	7.00	7.11	6.28	6.64	6.81	12.88	12.58	12.52
Minnesota	5.85	6.01	6.27	5.58	5.69	5.81	11.84	11.05	10.29
Missouri	7.61	7.71	7.88	6.56	6.67	6.99	13.47	13.68	13.32
Nebraska	6.54	6.69	6.91	6.25	6.30	6.64	11.47	12.78	12.56
North Dakota	5.73	6.38	6.32	5.66	6.39	6.14	*11.54	*10.25	*8.50
South Dakota	5.65	5.96	6.73	5.62	5.85	6.53	*9.40	*13.14	*8.54
South Atlantic	8.40	8.52	8.75	6.65	6.89	7.26	13.13	13.08	13.31
Delaware	8.55	8.54	9.55	6.82	6.68	7.99	13.74	14.05	14.39
District of Columbia	13.70	12.68	11.54	5.89	6.40	6.16	16.29	15.35	14.52
Florida	7.86	8.06	8.36	6.60	6.88	7.18	12.27	12.34	12.85
Georgia	8.70	8.63	8.91	6.58	6.71	7.15	12.94	12.77	13.07
Maryland	8.63	8.77	9.02	6.33	6.52	7.00	13.54	13.15	13.07
North Carolina	8.75	8.83	8.97	6.98	7.24	7.60	13.77	13.76	14.03
South Carolina	9.22	9.67	9.88	6.87	7.22	7.58	13.47	14.31	14.58
Virginia	7.69	7.87	7.99	6.18	6.48	6.66	12.59	12.44	12.71
West Virginia	8.05	8.14	8.70	7.86	7.94	8.54	14.02	13.78	12.61
East South Central	8.86	9.23	9.56	7.29	7.65	8.03	13.33	13.90	14.44
Alabama	9.18	9.45	9.82	7.24	7.50	7.88	13.24	13.64	14.27
Kentucky	7.77	8.20	8.55	7.31	7.66	8.06	12.49	13.72	13.85
Mississippi	9.93	10.37	11.09	7.23	7.55	8.19	13.10	13.84	14.91
Tennessee	8.77	9.16	9.25	7.33	7.79	8.05	13.95	14.35	14.30
West South Central	7.65	7.84	8.15	6.59	6.85	7.28	13.13	13.37	13.76
Arkansas	8.35	8.69	8.74	7.07	7.47	7.62	13.12	13.56	14.08
Louisiana	9.91	10.13	10.53	6.89	7.11	7.67	14.29	14.48	14.64
Oklahoma	7.20	7.34	7.85	6.71	6.97	7.50	12.68	12.52	13.72
Texas	7.19	7.39	7.72	6.39	6.63	7.06	12.37	12.66	13.14
Mountain	7.26	7.34	7.46	6.96	7.11	7.19	14.04	13.20	13.77
Arizona	6.78	6.91	6.93	6.65	6.69	6.75	13.11	12.61	12.90
Colorado	8.70	8.45	8.80	8.22	8.08	8.51	15.44	14.13	14.82
Idaho	5.98	6.30	6.34	5.80	6.17	6.28	*10.19	*	*9.25
Montana	6.18	6.67	6.85	5.90	6.62	6.72	*	*	*
Nevada	7.52	7.45	7.73	7.13	7.31	7.40	13.89	12.94	13.55
New Mexico	7.61	7.76	8.14	7.52	7.95	7.93	13.10	12.59	14.63
Utah	6.50	6.71	6.47	6.29	6.54	6.29	13.52	14.01	14.04
Wyoming	8.27	8.51	8.58	8.14	8.49	8.37	*11.43	*16.95	*11.83
Pacific	6.02	6.10	6.36	5.42	5.53	5.86	11.89	11.57	11.73
Alaska	5.56	5.80	5.83	5.10	5.22	4.96	12.64	10.65	10.13
California	6.11	6.18	6.43	5.55	5.67	5.99	12.02	11.73	11.90
Hawaii	7.18	7.54	8.34	4.97	5.47	6.67	9.87	10.60	11.93
Oregon	5.43	5.46	5.82	5.21	5.24	5.70	10.92	10.59	10.50
Washington	5.56	5.71	5.90	5.21	5.31	5.57	10.70	10.26	10.46

See footnotes at end of table.

Table 15 (page 2 of 2). Low-birthweight live births, according to race and Hispanic origin of mother, geographic division, and State: United States, average annual 1995–97, 1998–2000, and 2001–2003

[Data are based on birth certificates]

Geographic division and State	*Hispanic or Latino*[2]			*American Indian or Alaska Native*[3]			*Asian or Pacific Islander*[3]		
	1995–97	*1998–2000*	*2001–2003*	*1995–97*	*1998–2000*	*2001–2003*	*1995–97*	*1998–2000*	*2001–2003*
	Percent of live births weighing less than 2,500 grams[1]								
United States	6.33	6.41	6.57	6.62	6.90	7.31	7.07	7.39	7.70
New England	8.10	8.30	8.18	9.16	7.39	8.39	7.09	7.44	7.83
Connecticut	8.64	9.12	8.29	*12.87	*	10.31	8.38	7.29	7.91
Maine	*5.75	*6.42	*5.53	*	*	*	*6.05	*5.50	*5.91
Massachusetts	7.91	8.13	8.34	*7.53	*6.46	*6.78	6.70	7.47	7.81
New Hampshire	*7.34	5.48	5.26	*	*	*	*6.16	7.14	6.29
Rhode Island	7.46	7.11	8.03	*10.40	11.36	11.63	7.70	8.72	10.42
Vermont	*	*	*	*	*	*	*	*	*
Middle Atlantic	7.70	7.61	7.52	8.39	9.27	8.40	7.09	7.39	7.70
New Jersey	7.33	7.32	7.15	11.21	11.03	10.63	7.29	7.73	7.75
New York	7.64	7.52	7.45	7.15	8.58	7.01	6.99	7.26	7.62
Pennsylvania	9.23	9.14	8.95	8.40	9.68	10.00	7.20	7.21	7.97
East North Central	6.22	6.38	6.39	6.25	6.83	7.65	7.37	7.93	7.99
Illinois	6.01	6.28	6.37	7.61	8.56	9.81	8.01	8.30	8.36
Indiana	6.79	6.11	6.27	*8.74	*8.52	*9.13	6.51	7.30	7.75
Michigan	6.46	6.52	6.36	6.10	6.80	6.73	7.03	7.69	7.72
Ohio	7.26	7.51	7.17	8.56	7.57	10.68	6.87	7.89	7.93
Wisconsin	6.45	6.41	6.01	4.95	5.92	6.59	6.67	7.35	7.27
West North Central	6.22	6.04	6.06	6.26	6.29	7.08	6.89	7.22	7.68
Iowa	6.40	5.76	6.21	*7.28	8.74	8.54	8.30	7.22	7.38
Kansas	5.87	5.99	6.02	8.87	5.11	7.14	6.35	7.67	7.55
Minnesota	6.46	5.82	5.78	6.73	6.54	7.00	6.54	7.17	7.69
Missouri	6.36	6.19	6.10	7.29	7.78	7.83	7.27	6.74	7.36
Nebraska	6.10	6.64	6.15	6.12	5.99	7.05	7.24	8.00	8.22
North Dakota	*7.49	*5.69	*6.58	5.52	5.82	7.07	*	*	*6.67
South Dakota	*7.20	*5.05	8.42	5.49	6.10	6.78	*	*7.72	13.04
South Atlantic	6.35	6.32	6.47	9.15	8.92	9.71	7.39	7.64	7.96
Delaware	7.55	6.99	7.22	*	*	*	8.74	7.83	9.49
District of Columbia	7.10	6.85	7.79	*	*	*	*7.60	*9.15	*6.76
Florida	6.50	6.50	6.74	8.31	6.68	7.72	7.78	8.52	8.24
Georgia	5.54	5.57	5.81	*6.09	9.06	8.91	7.66	7.05	8.29
Maryland	6.08	6.55	6.94	*8.16	8.35	11.74	7.05	7.44	7.53
North Carolina	6.05	6.23	6.14	9.98	10.33	10.81	7.54	7.68	7.98
South Carolina	6.43	6.39	6.59	*10.79	*8.72	*9.73	7.56	7.06	8.83
Virginia	6.50	6.21	6.09	*7.71	*7.38	*10.87	6.94	7.32	7.53
West Virginia	*	*	*7.75	*	*	*	*5.83	*7.54	*9.31
East South Central	6.58	6.53	6.59	7.57	7.71	8.03	7.35	7.84	7.84
Alabama	6.38	6.38	6.97	*6.53	*6.82	11.20	7.48	8.03	7.65
Kentucky	7.05	6.85	7.24	*9.39	*9.33	*8.85	6.55	7.16	7.50
Mississippi	6.18	6.09	6.52	*7.23	7.22	6.36	6.69	7.48	7.00
Tennessee	6.59	6.60	6.13	*7.90	*8.53	*7.16	7.88	8.20	8.31
West South Central	6.54	6.68	6.93	6.15	6.41	6.78	7.49	7.72	7.92
Arkansas	5.97	6.09	5.92	*6.58	*6.80	7.77	8.44	8.54	6.79
Louisiana	5.97	6.92	6.83	7.40	7.41	10.54	8.12	8.21	8.04
Oklahoma	6.20	6.06	6.32	6.01	6.22	6.51	6.85	6.58	7.63
Texas	6.55	6.70	6.97	6.36	7.03	6.41	7.44	7.74	7.98
Mountain	7.24	7.16	7.31	6.54	7.01	7.17	8.41	8.38	8.60
Arizona	6.51	6.66	6.63	6.41	6.87	6.89	7.19	7.60	8.28
Colorado	8.67	8.21	8.40	8.47	8.76	9.86	9.48	10.04	10.21
Idaho	6.82	6.77	6.63	7.68	7.43	5.88	*6.77	7.48	6.38
Montana	7.82	6.81	7.91	6.60	7.17	7.38	*9.74	*	*8.09
Nevada	6.24	6.19	6.63	6.84	8.00	6.36	9.16	8.21	8.62
New Mexico	7.81	7.77	8.30	6.05	6.54	7.16	9.27	8.54	7.17
Utah	7.66	7.26	6.97	6.94	7.47	6.42	7.55	7.41	7.30
Wyoming	8.39	7.32	8.83	8.26	7.70	11.10	*	*15.48	*
Pacific	5.51	5.58	5.80	6.00	6.21	6.65	6.78	7.06	7.40
Alaska	6.28	6.12	5.91	5.35	5.91	5.94	5.71	7.39	6.67
California	5.50	5.57	5.81	6.24	6.00	6.66	6.67	6.92	7.26
Hawaii	6.89	7.66	8.36	*8.00	*6.77	*	7.82	8.06	8.81
Oregon	5.77	5.59	5.40	5.77	6.09	7.59	6.07	6.23	6.59
Washington	5.31	5.45	5.39	6.30	6.96	7.32	5.93	6.71	6.58

* Percents preceded by an asterisk are based on fewer than 50 births. Percents not shown are based on fewer than 20 births.
[1]Excludes live births with unknown birthweight.
[2]Persons of Hispanic origin may be of any race.
[3]Includes persons of Hispanic and non-Hispanic origin.

NOTES: For information on very low birthweight live births, see table 47 in Martin JA, Hamilton BE, Sutton PD, Ventura SJ, Menacker F, Munson ML. Births: Final Data for 2003. National vital statistics reports; vol 54, no 2. Hyattsville, Maryland: National Center for Health Statistics, 2005.

SOURCE: Centers for Disease Control and Prevention, National Center for Health Statistics, National Vital Statistics System, Birth File.

Table 16. Legal abortions and legal abortion ratios, according to selected patient characteristics: United States, selected years 1973–2001

[Data are based on reporting by State health departments and by hospitals and other medical facilities]

Characteristic	*1973*	*1975*	*1980*	*1985*	*1990*	*1995*	*1997*	*1998*[1]	*1999*[1]	*2000*[2]	*2001*[2]
					Number of legal abortions reported in thousands						
Centers for Disease Control and Prevention	616	855	1,298	1,329	1,429	1,211	1,186	884	862	857	853
Alan Guttmacher Institute[3]	745	1,034	1,554	1,589	1,609	1,359	1,335	1,319	1,315	1,313	1,303
					Abortions per 100 live births[4]						
Total	19.6	27.2	35.9	35.4	34.4	31.1	30.6	26.4	25.6	24.5	24.6
Age											
Under 15 years	123.7	119.3	139.7	137.6	81.8	66.4	72.9	75.0	70.9	70.8	74.4
15–19 years	53.9	54.2	71.4	68.8	51.1	39.9	40.7	39.1	37.5	36.1	36.6
20–24 years	29.4	28.9	39.5	38.6	37.8	34.8	34.5	32.9	31.6	30.0	30.4
25–29 years	20.7	19.2	23.7	21.7	21.8	22.0	22.4	21.6	20.8	19.8	20.0
30–34 years	28.0	25.0	23.7	19.9	19.0	16.4	16.1	15.7	15.2	14.5	14.7
35–39 years	45.1	42.2	41.0	33.6	27.3	22.3	20.9	20.0	19.3	18.1	18.0
40 years and over	68.4	66.8	80.7	62.3	50.6	38.5	35.2	33.8	32.9	30.1	30.4
Race											
White[5]	32.6	27.7	33.2	27.7	25.8	20.3	19.4	18.9	17.7	16.7	16.5
Black or African American[6]	42.0	47.6	54.3	47.2	53.7	53.1	54.3	51.2	52.9	50.3	49.1
Hispanic origin[7]											
Hispanic or Latino	- - -	- - -	- - -	- - -	- - -	27.1	26.8	27.3	26.1	22.5	23.0
Not Hispanic or Latino	- - -	- - -	- - -	- - -	- - -	27.9	27.2	27.1	25.2	23.3	23.2
Marital status											
Married	7.6	9.6	10.5	8.0	8.7	7.6	7.4	7.1	7.0	6.5	6.5
Unmarried	139.8	161.0	147.6	117.4	86.3	64.5	65.9	62.7	60.4	57.0	57.2
Previous live births[8]											
0	43.7	38.4	45.7	45.1	36.0	28.6	26.4	25.5	24.3	22.6	26.4
1	23.5	22.0	20.2	21.6	22.7	22.0	22.3	21.4	20.6	19.4	18.0
2	36.8	36.8	29.5	29.9	31.5	30.6	31.0	30.0	29.0	27.4	25.5
3	46.9	47.7	29.8	18.2	30.1	30.7	31.1	30.5	29.8	28.5	26.4
4 or more[9]	44.7	43.5	24.3	21.5	26.6	23.7	24.5	24.3	24.2	23.7	21.9
					Percent distribution[10]						
Total	100.0	100.0	100.0	100.0	100.0	100.0	100.0	100.0	100.0	100.0	100.0
Period of gestation											
Under 9 weeks	36.1	44.6	51.7	50.3	51.6	54.0	55.4	55.7	57.6	58.1	59.1
9–10 weeks	29.4	28.4	26.2	26.6	25.3	23.1	22.0	21.5	20.2	19.8	19.0
11–12 weeks	17.9	14.9	12.2	12.5	11.7	10.9	10.7	10.9	10.2	10.2	10.0
13–15 weeks	6.9	5.0	5.1	5.9	6.4	6.3	6.2	6.4	6.2	6.2	6.2
16–20 weeks	8.0	6.1	3.9	3.9	4.0	4.3	4.3	4.1	4.3	4.3	4.3
21 weeks and over	1.7	1.0	0.9	0.8	1.0	1.4	1.4	1.4	1.5	1.4	1.4
Previous induced abortions											
0	- - -	81.9	67.6	60.1	57.1	55.1	53.4	53.8	53.7	54.7	55.5
1	- - -	14.9	23.5	25.7	26.9	26.9	27.5	27.0	27.1	26.4	25.8
2	- - -	2.5	6.6	9.8	10.1	10.9	11.5	11.4	11.5	11.3	11.0
3 or more	- - -	0.7	2.3	4.4	5.9	7.1	7.6	7.8	7.7	7.6	7.7

- - - Data not available.

[1]In 1998 and 1999 Alaska, California, New Hampshire, and Oklahoma did not report abortion data to CDC. For comparison, in 1997 the 48 corresponding reporting areas reported about 900,000 legal abortions. [2]In 2000 and 2001 Alaska, California, and New Hampshire did not report abortion data to CDC.

[3]No surveys were conducted in 1983, 1986, 1989, 1990, 1993, 1994, 1997, 1998, or 2001. Data for these years were estimated by interpolation.

[4]For calculation of ratios by each characteristic, abortions with characteristic unknown were distributed in proportion to abortions with characteristic known.

[5]For 1989 and later years, white race includes women of Hispanic ethnicity. [6]Before 1989 black race includes races other than white.

[7]Reporting area increased from 20–22 States, the District of Columbia (DC), and New York City (NYC) in 1991–95 to 31 States and NYC in 2001. California, Florida, Illinois, and Arizona, States with large Hispanic populations, do not report Hispanic ethnicity.

[8]For 1973–75 data indicate number of living children.

[9]For 1975 data refer to four previous live births, not four or more. For five or more previous live births, the ratio is 47.3.

[10]For calculation of percent distribution by each characteristic, abortions with characteristic unknown were excluded.

NOTES: See Appendix I, Abortion Surveillance and Alan Guttmacher Institute Abortion Provider Survey, for methodological differences between these two data sources. The number of areas reporting adequate data (less than or equal to 15 percent missing) for each characteristic varies from year to year. See Appendix I, Abortion Surveillance. Some data for 2000 have been revised and differ from the previous edition of *Health, United States*. Data for additional years are available. See Appendix III.

SOURCES: Centers for Disease Control and Prevention, National Center for Chronic Disease Prevention and Health Promotion: Abortion Surveillance, 1973, 1975, 1979–80. Public Health Service, Atlanta, Ga., 1975, 1977, 1983; CDC MMWR Surveillance Summaries. Abortion Surveillance, United States, 1984 and 1985, Vol. 38, No. SS-2, 1989; 1990, Vol. 42, No. SS-6, 1993; 1995, Vol. 47, No. SS-2, 1998; 1997, Vol. 49, No. SS-11, 2000; 1998, Vol. 51, No. SS-3, 2002; 1999, Vol. 51, No. SS-9, 2002; 2000, Vol. 52, No. SS-12, 2003; 2001, Vol. 53, No. SS-9, 2004. Alan Guttmacher Institute Abortion Provider Survey. Finer LB and Henshaw SK: Abortion incidence and services in the United States in 2000. Perspectives on Sexual and Reproductive Health. 35(1), 2003; and Finer LB, Henshaw SK. Estimates of U.S. abortion incidence in 2001 and 2002. The Alan Guttmacher Institute. May 2005 at www.guttmacher.org/pubs/2005/05/18/ab_incidence.pdf.

Table 17 (page 1 of 4). Contraceptive use among women 15–44 years of age, according to age, race, Hispanic origin, and method of contraception: United States, 1982, 1988, 1995, and 2002

[Data are based on household interviews of samples of women in the childbearing ages]

Race, Hispanic origin, and year[1]	Age in years				
	15–44	15–19	20–24	25–34	35–44
	Number of women in population in thousands				
All women:[2]					
1982	54,099	9,521	10,629	19,644	14,305
1988	57,900	9,179	9,413	21,726	17,582
1995	60,201	8,961	9,041	20,758	21,440
2002	61,561	9,834	9,840	19,522	22,365
Not Hispanic or Latino:					
White only:					
1982	41,279	7,010	8,081	14,945	11,243
1988	42,575	6,531	6,630	15,929	13,486
1995	42,154	5,865	6,020	14,471	15,798
2002	39,498	6,069	5,938	12,073	15,418
Black or African American only:					
1982	6,825	1,383	1,456	2,392	1,593
1988	7,408	1,362	1,322	2,760	1,965
1995	8,060	1,334	1,305	2,780	2,641
2002	8,250	1,409	1,396	2,587	2,857
Hispanic or Latino:					
1982	4,393	886	811	1,677	1,018
1988	5,557	999	1,003	2,104	1,451
1995	6,702	1,150	1,163	2,450	1,940
2002	9,107	1,521	1,632	3,249	2,705
	Percent of women in population using contraception				
All women:[2]					
1982	55.7	24.2	55.8	66.7	61.6
1988	60.3	32.1	59.0	66.3	68.3
1995	64.2	29.8	63.5	71.1	72.3
2002	61.9	31.5	60.7	68.6	69.9
Not Hispanic or Latino:					
White only:					
1982	57.3	23.6	58.7	67.8	63.5
1988	63.0	34.0	62.6	67.7	71.5
1995	66.2	30.5	65.4	72.9	73.6
2002	64.6	35.0	66.3	69.9	71.4
Black or African American only:					
1982	51.6	29.8	52.3	63.5	52.0
1988	56.8	35.7	61.8	63.5	58.7
1995	62.3	36.1	67.6	66.8	68.3
2002	57.6	32.9	50.8	67.9	63.8
Hispanic or Latino:					
1982	50.6	*	*36.8	67.2	59.0
1988	50.4	*18.3	40.8	67.4	54.3
1995	59.0	26.1	50.6	69.2	70.8
2002	59.0	20.4	57.4	66.2	72.9

See footnotes at end of table.

Table 17 (page 2 of 4). Contraceptive use among women 15–44 years of age, according to age, race, Hispanic origin, and method of contraception: United States, 1982, 1988, 1995, and 2002

[Data are based on household interviews of samples of women in the childbearing ages]

Method of contraception and year	Age in years				
	15–44	*15–19*	*20–24*	*25–34*	*35–44*
	Percent of contracepting women				
Female sterilization					
1982	23.2	–	*4.5	22.1	43.5
1988	27.6	*	*4.6	25.0	47.6
1995	27.8	*	4.0	23.8	45.0
2002	27.0	–	3.6	21.7	45.8
Male sterilization					
1982	10.9	*	*3.6	10.1	19.9
1988	11.7	*	*	10.2	20.8
1995	10.9	–	*	7.8	19.5
2002	10.2	–	*	7.2	18.2
Implant[3]					
1982	. . .	. . .	. . .	. . .	. . .
1988	. . .	. . .	. . .	. . .	. . .
1995	1.3	*	3.7	*1.3	*
2002	1.2	*	*	*1.9	*
Injectable[3]					
1982	. . .	. . .	. . .	. . .	. . .
1988	. . .	. . .	. . .	. . .	. . .
1995	3.0	9.7	6.1	2.9	*0.8
2002	5.4	13.9	10.2	5.3	*1.8
Birth control pill					
1982	28.0	63.9	55.1	25.7	*3.7
1988	30.8	58.8	68.2	32.6	4.3
1995	27.0	43.8	52.1	33.4	8.7
2002	31.0	53.8	52.5	34.8	15.0
Intrauterine device					
1982	7.1	*	*4.2	9.7	6.9
1988	2.0	–	*	2.1	3.1
1995	0.8	–	*	*0.8	1.1
2002	2.2	*	1.8	3.7	*
Diaphragm					
1982	8.1	*6.0	10.2	10.3	4.0
1988	5.7	*	*3.7	7.3	6.0
1995	1.9	*	*	1.7	2.8
2002	0.6	–	*	*	*
Condom					
1982	12.0	20.8	10.7	11.4	11.3
1988	14.6	32.8	14.5	13.7	11.2
1995	23.4	45.8	33.7	23.7	15.3
2002	23.8	44.6	36.0	23.1	15.6
Periodic abstinence-calendar rhythm					
1982	3.3	2.0	3.1	3.3	3.7
1988	1.7	*	1.1	1.8	2.0
1995	3.3	*	*1.5	3.7	3.9
2002	2.0	*	*2.3	*1.7	*2.4
Periodic abstinence-natural family planning					
1982	0.6	–	*	0.9	*
1988	0.6	–	*	0.7	0.7
1995	*0.5	–	*	*0.7	*
2002	*0.4	–	–	*	*
Withdrawal					
1982	2.0	2.9	3.0	1.8	1.3
1988	2.2	3.0	3.4	2.8	0.8
1995	6.1	13.2	7.1	6.0	4.5
2002	8.8	15.0	11.9	10.7	4.7
Other methods[4]					
1982	4.9	2.6	5.4	4.8	5.3
1988	3.2	*	1.8	3.8	3.5
1995	3.2	*	3.2	3.1	3.4
2002	1.7	*	*	*1.5	*1.8

See footnotes at end of table.

Table 17 (page 3 of 4). Contraceptive use among women 15–44 years of age, according to age, race, Hispanic origin, and method of contraception: United States, 1982, 1988, 1995, and 2002

[Data are based on household interviews of samples of women in the childbearing ages]

Method of contraception and year	*Not Hispanic or Latino*[1] *White only*	*Not Hispanic or Latino*[1] *Black or African American only*	*Hispanic or Latino*[1]
	Percent of contracepting women		
Female sterilization			
1982	22.0	30.0	23.0
1988	25.6	37.8	31.7
1995	24.5	39.9	36.6
2002	23.9	39.2	33.8
Male sterilization			
1982	13.0	*1.5	*
1988	14.3	*0.9	*
1995	13.7	*1.8	*4.0
2002	12.9	*	4.7
Implant[3]			
1982	. . .	. . .	. . .
1988	. . .	. . .	. . .
1995	*1.0	*2.4	*2.0
2002	*0.8	*	*1.3
Injectable[3]			
1982	. . .	. . .	. . .
1988	. . .	. . .	. . .
1995	2.4	5.4	4.7
2002	4.2	9.4	7.3
Birth control pill			
1982	26.4	37.9	30.2
1988	29.5	38.2	33.4
1995	28.7	23.7	23.0
2002	34.9	23.1	22.1
Intrauterine device			
1982	5.8	9.3	19.2
1988	1.5	3.2	*5.0
1995	0.7	*	*
2002	1.7	*	5.3
Diaphragm			
1982	9.2	*3.2	*
1988	6.6	*2.0	*
1995	2.3	*	*
2002	*	*	–
Condom			
1982	13.1	6.3	*6.9
1988	15.2	10.1	13.7
1995	22.5	24.9	21.2
2002	21.7	29.6	24.1
Periodic abstinence-calendar rhythm			
1982	3.2	2.9	3.9
1988	1.6	1.9	*
1995	3.3	*1.7	3.2
2002	2.3	*	*
Periodic abstinence-natural family planning			
1982	0.7	0.3	–
1988	0.7	*	*
1995	0.7	*	*
2002	*	*	*
Withdrawal			
1982	2.1	1.3	2.6
1988	2.0	1.4	4.5
1995	6.4	3.3	5.7
2002	9.5	4.9	6.3
Other methods[4]			
1982	4.6	7.3	5.0
1988	3.0	4.4	2.6
1995	3.3	3.8	*2.2
2002	*1.7	*1.9	*1.2

See footnotes at end of table.

Table 17 (page 4 of 4). Contraceptive use among women 15–44 years of age, according to age, race, Hispanic origin, and method of contraception: United States, 1982, 1988, 1995, and 2002

[Data are based on household interviews of samples of women in the childbearing ages]

– Quantity zero.
- - - Data not available.
* Estimates are considered unreliable. Data preceded by an asterisk have a relative standard error of 20–30 percent.
. . . Data not applicable.
[1]Persons of Hispanic origin may be of any race. Starting with data year 1995, race-specific estimates are tabulated according to 1997 Standards for Federal data on Race and Ethnicity and are not strictly comparable with estimates for earlier years. Starting with data year 1995, race-specific estimates are for persons who reported only one racial group. Prior to data year 1995, data were tabulated according to 1977 Standards. Estimates for single race categories prior to 1995 included persons who reported one race or, if they reported more than one race, identified one race as best representing their race. See Appendix II, Race.
[2]Includes women of other or unknown race not shown separately.
[3]Data collected starting with the 1995 survey.
[4]In 2002, includes female condom, foam, cervical cap, Today Sponge®, suppository or insert, jelly or cream, and other methods. See Appendix II, Contraception, for the list of other methods in previous surveys.

NOTES: Data show up to four methods of contraception used in the month of interview. Percents may not add to the total because more than one method could have been used in the month of interview. These data replace estimates of most effective method used and may differ from previous editions of *Health, United States*. Standard errors for selected years are available in the spreadsheet version of this table. See www.cdc.gov/nchs/hus.htm.

SOURCE: Centers for Disease Control and Prevention, National Center for Health Statistics, National Survey of Family Growth.

Table 18. Breastfeeding by mothers 15–44 years of age by year of baby's birth, according to selected characteristics of mother: United States, average annual 1986–88 to 1999–2001

[Data are based on household interviews of samples of women in the childbearing ages]

Selected characteristics of mother	*1986–88*	*1989–91*	*1992–94*	*1995–98*	*1999–2001*
			Percent of babies breastfed		
Total	54.1	53.3	57.6	64.4	66.5
Age at baby's birth					
Under 20 years	28.4	34.7	41.0	49.5	47.3
20–24 years	48.2	44.3	50.0	55.9	59.3
25–29 years	58.2	56.4	57.4	68.1	63.5
30–44 years	68.6	66.0	70.2	72.8	80.0
Race and Hispanic origin [1]					
Not Hispanic or Latino:					
White	59.1	58.4	61.7	66.5	68.7
Black or African American	22.3	22.4	26.1	47.9	45.3
Hispanic or Latino	55.6	57.0	63.8	71.2	76.0
Education [2]					
No high school diploma or GED	31.8	36.5	44.6	50.6	46.6
High school diploma or GED	47.4	45.5	51.1	55.9	61.6
Some college, no bachelor's degree	62.2	61.4	64.3	70.1	75.6
Bachelor's degree or higher	78.4	80.6	82.5	82.0	81.3
Geographic region					
Northeast	51.3	53.5	56.5	61.6	66.9
Midwest	52.3	49.6	51.7	61.7	61.9
South	44.6	43.6	48.6	58.1	60.9
West	71.4	69.5	77.3	78.1	78.9
			Percent of babies who were breastfed 3 months or more		
Total	34.6	31.8	33.6	45.8	48.4
Age at baby's birth					
Under 20 years	18.5	*10.5	*11.7	30.0	30.0
20–24 years	26.1	24.1	25.1	36.6	41.8
25–29 years	36.9	32.3	35.6	46.3	43.7
30–44 years	50.1	46.8	46.7	57.5	62.4
Race and Hispanic origin [1]					
Not Hispanic or Latino:					
White	37.7	35.2	36.6	47.8	49.7
Black or African American	11.6	11.5	13.3	29.6	33.7
Hispanic or Latino	38.2	33.9	35.0	49.7	54.3
Education [2]					
No high school diploma or GED	21.8	17.6	25.2	33.9	37.0
High school diploma or GED	28.2	28.0	27.4	36.9	43.1
Some college, no bachelor's degree	38.7	33.1	38.7	49.6	52.8
Bachelor's degree or higher	55.0	56.1	59.3	64.5	64.1
Geographic region					
Northeast	29.9	37.2	36.4	48.2	48.8
Midwest	30.3	31.5	30.1	42.0	42.8
South	27.7	20.1	26.2	38.9	44.4
West	52.4	42.9	45.3	58.2	59.2

* Estimates are considered unreliable. Data preceded by an asterisk have a relative standard error of 20–30 percent.

[1]Persons of Hispanic origin may be of any race. All race-specific estimates are tabulated according to 1997 Standards for Federal data on Race and Ethnicity and are for persons who reported only one racial group. See Appendix II, Race.

[2]Educational attainment is presented only for women 22–44 years of age. Education is as of year of interview. GED stands for General Educational Development high school equivalency diploma. See Appendix II, Education.

NOTES: Data are based on single births to mothers 15–44 years of age at interview, including those births that occurred when the mothers were younger than 15 years of age. Data on breastfeeding during 1986–94 are based on responses to questions in the National Survey of Family Growth (NSFG) Cycle 5, conducted in 1995. Data for 1995–2001 are based on the NSFG Cycle 6 conducted in 2002. Standard errors are available in the spreadsheet version of this table. See www.cdc.gov/nchs/hus.htm. Data have been revised to reflect the duration of breastfeeding among all babies, and replace duration of breastfeeding data only among breastfed babies reported in previous editions of *Health, United States.*

SOURCE: Centers for Disease Control and Prevention, National Center for Health Statistics, National Survey of Family Growth, Cycle 5 1995, Cycle 6 2002.

Table 19 (page 1 of 2). Infant, neonatal, and postneonatal mortality rates, according to detailed race and Hispanic origin of mother: United States, selected years 1983–2002

[Data are based on linked birth and death certificates for infants]

Race and Hispanic origin of mother	*1983*[1]	*1985*[1]	*1990*[1]	*1995*[2]	*1998*[2]	*1999*[2]	*2000*[2]	*2001*[2]	*2002*[2]
	Infant[3] deaths per 1,000 live births								
All mothers	10.9	10.4	8.9	7.6	7.2	7.0	6.9	6.8	7.0
White	9.3	8.9	7.3	6.3	6.0	5.8	5.7	5.7	5.8
Black or African American	19.2	18.6	16.9	14.6	13.8	14.0	13.5	13.3	13.8
American Indian or Alaska Native	15.2	13.1	13.1	9.0	9.3	9.3	8.3	9.7	8.6
Asian or Pacific Islander	8.3	7.8	6.6	5.3	5.5	4.8	4.9	4.7	4.8
Chinese	9.5	5.8	4.3	3.8	4.0	2.9	3.5	3.2	3.0
Japanese	*5.6	*6.0	*5.5	*5.3	*3.4	*3.5	*4.5	*4.0	*4.9
Filipino	8.4	7.7	6.0	5.6	6.2	5.8	5.7	5.5	5.7
Hawaiian	11.2	*9.9	*8.0	*6.5	9.9	*7.0	9.0	*7.3	9.6
Other Asian or Pacific Islander	8.1	8.5	7.4	5.5	5.7	5.1	4.8	4.8	4.7
Hispanic or Latino[4,5]	9.5	8.8	7.5	6.3	5.8	5.7	5.6	5.4	5.6
Mexican	9.1	8.5	7.2	6.0	5.6	5.5	5.4	5.2	5.4
Puerto Rican	12.9	11.2	9.9	8.9	7.8	8.3	8.2	8.5	8.2
Cuban	7.5	8.5	7.2	5.3	*3.7	4.6	4.6	4.2	3.7
Central and South American	8.5	8.0	6.8	5.5	5.3	4.7	4.6	5.0	5.1
Other and unknown Hispanic or Latino	10.6	9.5	8.0	7.4	6.5	7.2	6.9	6.0	7.1
Not Hispanic or Latino:									
White[5]	9.2	8.6	7.2	6.3	6.0	5.8	5.7	5.7	5.8
Black or African American[5]	19.1	18.3	16.9	14.7	13.9	14.1	13.6	13.5	13.9
	Neonatal[3] deaths per 1,000 live births								
All mothers	7.1	6.8	5.7	4.9	4.8	4.7	4.6	4.5	4.7
White	6.1	5.8	4.6	4.1	4.0	3.9	3.8	3.8	3.9
Black or African American	12.5	12.3	11.1	9.6	9.4	9.5	9.1	8.9	9.3
American Indian or Alaska Native	7.5	6.1	6.1	4.0	5.0	5.0	4.4	4.2	4.6
Asian or Pacific Islander	5.2	4.8	3.9	3.4	3.9	3.2	3.4	3.1	3.4
Chinese	5.5	3.3	2.3	2.3	2.7	1.8	2.5	1.9	2.4
Japanese	*3.7	*3.1	*3.5	*3.3	*2.5	*2.8	*2.6	*2.5	*3.7
Filipino	5.6	5.1	3.5	3.4	4.6	3.9	4.1	4.0	4.1
Hawaiian	*7.0	*5.7	*4.3	*4.0	*7.2	*4.9	*6.2	*3.6	*5.6
Other Asian or Pacific Islander	5.0	5.4	4.4	3.7	3.9	3.3	3.4	3.2	3.3
Hispanic or Latino[4,5]	6.2	5.7	4.8	4.1	3.9	3.9	3.8	3.6	3.8
Mexican	5.9	5.4	4.5	3.9	3.7	3.7	3.6	3.5	3.6
Puerto Rican	8.7	7.6	6.9	6.1	5.2	5.9	5.8	6.0	5.8
Cuban	*5.0	6.2	5.3	*3.6	*2.7	*3.5	*3.2	*2.5	*3.2
Central and South American	5.8	5.6	4.4	3.7	3.6	3.3	3.3	3.4	3.5
Other and unknown Hispanic or Latino	6.4	5.6	5.0	4.8	4.5	4.8	4.6	3.9	5.1
Not Hispanic or Latino:									
White[5]	5.9	5.6	4.5	4.0	3.9	3.8	3.8	3.8	3.9
Black or African American[5]	12.0	11.9	11.0	9.6	9.4	9.6	9.2	9.0	9.3
	Postneonatal[3] deaths per 1,000 live births								
All mothers	3.8	3.6	3.2	2.6	2.4	2.3	2.3	2.3	2.3
White	3.2	3.1	2.7	2.2	2.0	1.9	1.9	1.9	1.9
Black or African American	6.7	6.3	5.9	5.0	4.4	4.5	4.3	4.4	4.5
American Indian or Alaska Native	7.7	7.0	7.0	5.1	4.4	4.3	3.9	5.4	4.0
Asian or Pacific Islander	3.1	2.9	2.7	1.9	1.7	1.7	1.4	1.6	1.4
Chinese	4.0	*2.5	*2.0	*1.5	*1.3	*1.2	*1.0	*1.3	*0.7
Japanese	*	*2.9	*	*	*	*	*	*	*
Filipino	*2.8	2.7	2.5	2.2	1.6	1.9	1.6	*1.5	1.7
Hawaiian	*4.2	*4.3	*3.8	*	*	*	*	*3.7	*4.0
Other Asian or Pacific Islander	3.0	3.0	3.0	1.9	1.8	1.8	1.4	1.6	1.4
Hispanic or Latino[4,5]	3.3	3.2	2.7	2.1	1.9	1.8	1.8	1.8	1.8
Mexican	3.2	3.2	2.7	2.1	1.9	1.8	1.8	1.7	1.8
Puerto Rican	4.2	3.5	3.0	2.8	2.6	2.4	2.4	2.5	2.4
Cuban	*2.5	*2.3	*1.9	*1.7	*	*	*	*1.7	*
Central and South American	2.6	2.4	2.4	1.9	1.7	1.4	1.4	1.6	1.6
Other and unknown Hispanic or Latino	4.2	3.9	3.0	2.6	2.0	2.5	2.3	2.1	2.0
Not Hispanic or Latino:									
White[5]	3.2	3.0	2.7	2.2	2.0	1.9	1.9	1.9	1.9
Black or African American[5]	7.0	6.4	5.9	5.0	4.5	4.6	4.4	4.5	4.6

See footnotes at end of table.

This table will be updated on the Web. Go to www.cdc.gov/nchs/hus.htm.

Table 19 (page 2 of 2). Infant, neonatal, and postneonatal mortality rates, according to detailed race and Hispanic origin of mother: United States, selected years 1983–2002

[Data are based on linked birth and death certificates for infants]

Race and Hispanic origin of mother	1983–85[1,6]	1986–88[1,6]	1989–91[1,6]	1996–98[2,6]	1997–99[2,6]	2000–2002[2,6]
	Infant[3] deaths per 1,000 live births					
All mothers	10.6	9.8	9.0	7.2	7.1	6.9
White	9.0	8.2	7.4	6.0	5.9	5.7
Black or African American	18.7	17.9	17.1	13.9	13.8	13.5
American Indian or Alaska Native	13.9	13.2	12.6	9.3	9.1	8.9
Asian or Pacific Islander	8.3	7.3	6.6	5.2	5.1	4.8
Chinese	7.4	5.8	5.1	3.4	3.3	3.2
Japanese	6.0	6.9	5.3	4.3	4.1	4.5
Filipino	8.2	6.9	6.4	5.9	6.0	5.7
Hawaiian	11.3	11.1	9.0	8.2	8.6	8.7
Other Asian or Pacific Islander	8.6	7.6	7.0	5.5	5.2	4.8
Hispanic or Latino[4,5]	9.2	8.3	7.5	5.9	5.8	5.5
Mexican	8.8	7.9	7.2	5.8	5.6	5.4
Puerto Rican	12.3	11.1	10.4	8.1	8.0	8.3
Cuban	8.0	7.3	6.2	4.7	4.6	4.2
Central and South American	8.2	7.5	6.6	5.2	5.1	4.9
Other and unknown Hispanic or Latino	9.8	9.0	8.2	6.8	6.7	6.7
Not Hispanic or Latino:						
White[5]	8.8	8.1	7.3	6.0	5.9	5.7
Black or African American[5]	18.5	17.9	17.2	13.9	13.9	13.6
	Neonatal[3] deaths per 1,000 live births					
All mothers	6.9	6.3	5.7	4.8	4.8	4.6
White	5.9	5.2	4.7	4.0	3.9	3.8
Black or African American	12.2	11.7	11.1	9.3	9.4	9.1
American Indian or Alaska Native	6.7	5.9	5.9	4.7	4.8	4.4
Asian or Pacific Islander	5.2	4.5	3.9	3.5	3.4	3.3
Chinese	4.3	3.3	2.7	2.3	2.2	2.3
Japanese	3.4	4.4	3.0	2.6	2.8	2.9
Filipino	5.3	4.5	4.0	4.1	4.0	4.1
Hawaiian	7.4	7.1	4.8	5.6	6.1	5.2
Other Asian or Pacific Islander	5.5	4.7	4.2	3.6	3.5	3.3
Hispanic or Latino[4,5]	6.0	5.3	4.8	3.9	3.9	3.8
Mexican	5.7	5.0	4.5	3.8	3.8	3.6
Puerto Rican	8.3	7.2	7.0	5.4	5.5	5.9
Cuban	5.9	5.3	4.6	3.5	3.4	3.0
Central and South American	5.7	4.9	4.4	3.6	3.6	3.4
Other and unknown Hispanic or Latino	6.1	5.8	5.2	4.5	4.3	4.5
Not Hispanic or Latino:						
White[5]	5.7	5.1	4.6	3.9	3.9	3.8
Black or African American[5]	11.8	11.4	11.1	9.3	9.4	9.2
	Postneonatal[3] deaths per 1,000 live births					
All mothers	3.7	3.5	3.3	2.5	2.4	2.3
White	3.1	3.0	2.7	2.1	2.0	1.9
Black or African American	6.4	6.2	6.0	4.6	4.5	4.4
American Indian or Alaska Native	7.2	7.3	6.7	4.6	4.3	4.5
Asian or Pacific Islander	3.1	2.8	2.6	1.8	1.7	1.5
Chinese	3.1	2.5	2.4	1.2	1.1	1.0
Japanese	2.6	2.5	2.2	*1.7	*1.3	*1.6
Filipino	2.9	2.4	2.3	1.9	1.9	1.6
Hawaiian	3.9	4.0	4.1	*2.6	*2.5	3.5
Other Asian or Pacific Islander	3.1	2.9	2.8	1.8	1.8	1.5
Hispanic or Latino[4,5]	3.2	3.0	2.7	2.0	1.9	1.8
Mexican	3.2	2.9	2.7	2.0	1.9	1.8
Puerto Rican	4.0	3.9	3.4	2.7	2.5	2.4
Cuban	2.2	2.0	1.6	*1.3	*1.2	*1.2
Central and South American	2.5	2.6	2.2	1.6	1.5	1.5
Other and unknown Hispanic or Latino	3.7	3.2	3.0	2.3	2.3	2.1
Not Hispanic or Latino:						
White[5]	3.1	3.0	2.7	2.1	2.0	1.9
Black or African American[5]	6.7	6.5	6.1	4.6	4.5	4.5

* Estimates are considered unreliable. Rates preceded by an asterisk are based on fewer than 50 deaths in the numerator. Rates not shown are based on fewer than 20 deaths in the numerator.

[1]Rates based on unweighted birth cohort data.

[2]Rates based on a period file using weighted data. See Appendix I, National Vital Statistics System, Linked Birth/Infant Death Data Set.

[3]Infant (under 1 year of age), neonatal (under 28 days), and postneonatal (28 days–11 months).

[4]Persons of Hispanic origin may be of any race. [5]Prior to 1995, data shown only for States with an Hispanic-origin item on their birth certificates. See Appendix II, Hispanic origin. [6]Average annual mortality rate.

NOTES: The race groups white, black, American Indian or Alaska Native, and Asian or Pacific Islander include persons of Hispanic and non-Hispanic origin. National linked files do not exist for 1992–94. Data for additional years are available. See Appendix III.

SOURCE: Centers for Disease Control and Prevention, National Center for Health Statistics, National Vital Statistics System, Linked Birth/Infant Death Data Set.

This table will be updated on the Web. Go to www.cdc.gov/nchs/hus.htm.

Table 20. Infant mortality rates for mothers 20 years of age and over, according to mother's education, detailed race, and Hispanic origin: United States, selected years 1983–2002

[Data are based on linked birth and death certificates for infants]

Education, race, and Hispanic origin of mother	1983[1]	1990[1]	1995[2]	2001[2]	2002[2]	1983–85[1,3]	1986–88[1,3]	1989–91[1,3]	1997–99[2,3]	2000–2002[2,3]
Less than 12 years of education	Infant deaths per 1,000 live births									
All mothers	15.0	10.8	8.9	7.6	7.9	14.6	13.8	11.1	8.2	7.8
White	12.5	9.0	7.6	6.5	6.7	12.4	11.4	9.2	7.1	6.7
Black or African American	23.4	19.5	17.0	14.0	15.6	21.8	21.1	20.3	14.7	14.8
American Indian or Alaska Native	14.5	14.3	12.7	12.9	8.6	15.2	16.8	13.8	10.2	10.5
Asian or Pacific Islander[4]	9.7	6.6	5.7	5.5	4.5	9.5	8.2	6.9	5.5	5.3
Hispanic or Latino[5,6]	10.9	7.3	6.0	5.1	5.3	10.6	9.9	7.5	5.6	5.2
Mexican	8.7	7.0	5.8	4.9	5.0	9.5	8.3	7.1	5.5	5.0
Puerto Rican	15.3	10.1	10.6	7.8	10.1	14.1	12.8	11.7	8.7	9.2
Cuban	*14.5	*	*	*	*	*10.5	*9.4	*8.2	*6.4	*
Central and South American	9.8	7.0	5.1	5.0	5.7	8.6	9.2	6.8	5.4	5.2
Other and unknown Hispanic or Latino	9.2	9.9	7.3	5.8	6.0	10.1	10.6	10.0	6.8	6.4
Not Hispanic or Latino:										
White[6]	12.8	10.9	9.9	9.0	9.4	12.6	11.8	11.0	9.2	9.2
Black or African American[6]	24.7	19.7	17.3	14.3	15.9	22.6	21.6	20.6	15.0	15.1
12 years of education										
All mothers	10.2	8.8	7.8	7.3	7.6	10.0	9.6	8.9	7.5	7.4
White	8.7	7.1	6.4	6.0	6.3	8.5	8.0	7.2	6.1	6.1
Black or African American	17.8	16.0	14.7	12.9	13.6	17.7	17.1	16.4	14.0	13.3
American Indian or Alaska Native	15.5	13.4	7.9	9.6	8.8	13.4	11.6	12.3	8.8	8.7
Asian or Pacific Islander[4]	10.0	7.5	5.5	5.9	5.3	9.3	7.9	7.5	5.7	5.4
Hispanic or Latino[5,6]	8.4	7.0	5.9	5.1	5.4	9.1	8.3	6.8	5.5	5.2
Mexican	6.9	6.8	5.7	4.7	5.2	7.8	8.2	6.5	5.2	4.9
Puerto Rican	9.5	8.5	6.5	9.2	8.1	10.8	10.1	8.6	7.9	8.1
Cuban	*6.9	*8.0	*	*	*	8.6	6.6	7.6	4.5	*3.6
Central and South American	8.7	6.5	6.1	4.8	4.6	8.7	7.4	6.3	5.1	4.5
Other and unknown Hispanic or Latino	8.8	7.4	6.5	5.6	7.2	8.8	7.7	7.0	6.1	6.2
Not Hispanic or Latino:										
White[6]	8.7	7.1	6.5	6.2	6.7	8.3	7.9	7.3	6.3	6.4
Black or African American[6]	17.8	16.1	14.8	13.1	13.7	17.9	17.4	16.5	14.1	13.4
13 years or more of education										
All mothers	8.1	6.4	5.4	5.1	5.0	7.8	7.2	6.4	5.2	5.0
White	7.2	5.4	4.7	4.3	4.2	6.9	6.2	5.5	4.4	4.2
Black or African American	15.3	13.7	11.9	11.7	11.1	15.3	14.9	13.7	11.3	11.4
American Indian or Alaska Native	12.5	6.8	5.9	6.7	7.3	10.4	8.4	8.1	7.0	6.9
Asian or Pacific Islander[4]	6.6	5.1	4.4	3.7	4.0	6.7	5.9	5.1	4.2	3.9
Hispanic or Latino[5,6]	9.0	5.7	5.0	4.6	4.5	7.4	7.0	5.8	4.8	4.6
Mexican	*8.3	5.5	5.2	4.7	4.7	7.6	6.4	5.7	4.9	4.6
Puerto Rican	10.9	7.3	6.3	5.9	5.4	8.1	6.9	7.8	6.0	5.9
Cuban	*	*5.3	*5.3	*4.0	*3.0	5.5	5.9	4.2	3.9	3.9
Central and South American	*7.1	5.6	3.7	4.1	4.2	7.2	7.6	5.4	4.1	4.0
Other and unknown Hispanic or Latino	11.6	5.4	5.2	3.8	3.9	7.9	7.5	5.6	4.3	4.0
Not Hispanic or Latino:										
White[6]	7.0	5.4	4.6	4.3	4.2	6.8	6.1	5.4	4.4	4.2
Black or African American[6]	14.8	13.7	12.0	11.8	11.2	14.7	14.9	13.8	11.4	11.5

* Estimates are considered unreliable. Rates preceded by an asterisk are based on fewer than 50 deaths. Rates not shown are based on fewer than 20 deaths.

[1]Rates based on unweighted birth cohort data.

[2]Rates based on a period file using weighted data. See Appendix I, National Vital Statistics System, Linked Birth/Infant Death Data Set.

[3]Average annual mortality rate.

[4]The States not reporting maternal education on the birth certificate accounted for 49–51 percent of the Asian or Pacific Islander births in the United States in 1983–87, 59 percent in 1988, and 12 percent in 1989–91. Starting in 1992 maternal education was reported by all 50 States and the District of Columbia.

[5]Persons of Hispanic origin may be of any race.

[6]Prior to 1995, data shown only for States with an Hispanic-origin item and education of mother on their birth certificates. See Appendix II, Education; Hispanic origin. The Hispanic-reporting States that did not report maternal education on the birth certificate during 1983–88 together accounted for 28–85 percent of the births in each Hispanic subgroup (except Cuban, 11–16 percent, and Puerto Rican, 6–7 percent in 1983–87); and in 1989–91 accounted for 27–39 percent of Central and South American and Puerto Rican births and 2–9 percent of births in other Hispanic subgroups.

NOTES: Prior to 1995, data for all mothers and by race are shown only for States reporting education of mother on their birth certificates. See Appendix II, Education. The race groups white, black, American Indian or Alaska Native, and Asian or Pacific Islander include persons of Hispanic and non-Hispanic origin. Persons of Hispanic origin may be of any race. National linked files do not exist for 1992–94. Data for additional years are available. See Appendix III.

SOURCE: Centers for Disease Control and Prevention, National Center for Health Statistics, National Vital Statistics System, Linked Birth/Infant Death Data Set.

This table will be updated on the Web. Go to www.cdc.gov/nchs/hus.htm.

Table 21. Infant mortality rates according to birthweight: United States, selected years 1983–2002

[Data are based on linked birth and death certificates for infants]

Birthweight	1983[1]	1985[1]	1990[1]	1995[2]	1998[2]	1999[2]	2000[2]	2001[2]	2002[2]
	Infant deaths per 1,000 live births[3]								
All birthweights	10.9	10.4	8.9	7.6	7.2	7.0	6.9	6.8	7.0
Less than 2,500 grams	95.9	93.9	78.1	65.3	62.3	61.3	60.2	59.4	60.3
Less than 1,500 grams	400.6	387.7	317.6	270.7	252.4	249.5	246.9	246.9	253.2
Less than 500 grams	890.3	895.9	898.2	904.9	869.6	857.7	847.9	856.8	863.6
500–999 grams	584.2	559.2	440.1	351.0	319.4	318.6	313.8	313.0	321.5
1,000–1,499 grams	162.3	145.4	97.9	69.6	60.6	59.2	60.9	59.4	57.7
1,500–1,999 grams	58.4	54.0	43.8	33.5	29.0	29.1	28.7	27.6	26.9
2,000–2,499 grams	22.5	20.9	17.8	13.7	12.7	12.0	11.9	11.4	11.7
2,500 grams or more	4.7	4.3	3.7	3.0	2.7	2.6	2.5	2.5	2.4
2,500–2,999 grams	8.8	7.9	6.7	5.5	4.9	4.7	4.6	4.5	4.5
3,000–3,499 grams	4.4	4.3	3.7	2.9	2.6	2.5	2.4	2.3	2.3
3,500–3,999 grams	3.2	3.0	2.6	2.0	1.8	1.7	1.7	1.7	1.6
4,000 grams or more	3.3	3.2	2.4	2.0	1.7	1.8	1.6	1.6	1.5
4,000–4,499 grams	2.9	2.9	2.2	1.8	1.7	1.6	1.5	1.5	1.4
4,500–4,999 grams	3.9	3.8	2.5	2.2	2.0	1.9	2.1	2.0	2.0
5,000 grams or more[4]	14.4	14.7	9.8	8.5	*4.3	*7.9	*6.1	*6.5	*5.1

* Estimates are considered unreliable. Rates preceded by an asterisk are based on fewer than 50 deaths in the numerator.
[1]Rates based on unweighted birth cohort data.
[2]Rates based on a period file using weighted data; unknown birthweight imputed when period of gestation is known and proportionately distributed when period of gestation is unknown. See Appendix I, National Vital Statistics System, Linked Birth/Infant Death Data Set.
[3]For calculation of birthweight-specific infant mortality rates, unknown birthweight has been distributed in proportion to known birthweight separately for live births (denominator) and infant deaths (numerator).
[4]In 1989 a birthweight-gestational age consistency check instituted for the natality file resulted in a decrease in the number of deaths to infants coded with birthweights of 5,000 grams or more and a discontinuity in the mortality trend for infants weighing 5,000 grams or more at birth. Starting with 1989 the rates are believed to be more accurate.

NOTES: National linked files do not exist for 1992–94. Data for additional years are available. See Appendix III.

SOURCE: Centers for Disease Control and Prevention, National Center for Health Statistics, National Vital Statistics System, Linked Birth/Infant Death Data Set.

This table will be updated on the Web. Go to www.cdc.gov/nchs/hus.htm.

Table 22. Infant mortality rates, fetal mortality rates, and perinatal mortality rates, according to race: United States, selected years 1950–2002

[Data are based on death certificates, fetal death records, and birth certificates]

Race and year	Infant[1]	Neonatal[1] Under 28 days	Neonatal[1] Under 7 days	Postneonatal[1]	Fetal mortality rate[2]	Late fetal mortality rate[3]	Perinatal mortality rate[4]
All races	Deaths per 1,000 live births						
1950[5]	29.2	20.5	17.8	8.7	18.4	14.9	32.5
1960[5]	26.0	18.7	16.7	7.3	15.8	12.1	28.6
1970	20.0	15.1	13.6	4.9	14.0	9.5	23.0
1980	12.6	8.5	7.1	4.1	9.1	6.2	13.2
1985	10.6	7.0	5.8	3.7	7.8	4.9	10.7
1990	9.2	5.8	4.8	3.4	7.5	4.3	9.1
1995	7.6	4.9	4.0	2.7	7.0	3.6	7.6
1996	7.3	4.8	3.8	2.5	6.9	3.6	7.4
1997	7.2	4.8	3.8	2.5	6.8	3.5	7.3
1998	7.2	4.8	3.8	2.4	6.7	3.4	7.2
1999	7.1	4.7	3.8	2.3	6.7	3.4	7.1
2000	6.9	4.6	3.7	2.3	6.6	3.3	7.0
2001	6.8	4.5	3.6	2.3	6.5	3.3	6.9
2002	7.0	4.7	3.7	2.3	---	---	---
Race of child:[6] White							
1950[5]	26.8	19.4	17.1	7.4	16.6	13.3	30.1
1960[5]	22.9	17.2	15.6	5.7	13.9	10.8	26.2
1970	17.8	13.8	12.5	4.0	12.3	8.6	21.0
1980	11.0	7.5	6.2	3.5	8.1	5.7	11.9
Race of mother:[7] White							
1980	10.9	7.4	6.1	3.5	8.1	5.7	11.8
1985	9.2	6.0	5.0	3.2	6.9	4.5	9.5
1990	7.6	4.8	3.9	2.8	6.4	3.8	7.7
1995	6.3	4.1	3.3	2.2	5.9	3.3	6.5
1996	6.1	4.0	3.2	2.1	5.9	3.3	6.4
1997	6.0	4.0	3.2	2.0	5.8	3.2	6.3
1998	6.0	4.0	3.1	2.0	5.7	3.1	6.2
1999	5.8	3.9	3.1	1.9	5.7	3.0	6.1
2000	5.7	3.8	3.0	1.9	5.6	2.9	5.9
2001	5.7	3.8	3.0	1.9	5.5	2.9	5.9
2002	5.8	3.9	3.1	1.9	---	---	---
Race of child:[6] Black or African American							
1950[5]	43.9	27.8	23.0	16.1	32.1	---	---
1960[5]	44.3	27.8	23.7	16.5	---	---	---
1970	32.6	22.8	20.3	9.9	23.2	---	34.5
1980	21.4	14.1	11.9	7.3	14.4	8.9	20.7
Race of mother:[7] Black or African American							
1980	22.2	14.6	12.3	7.6	14.7	9.1	21.3
1985	19.0	12.6	10.8	6.4	12.8	7.2	17.9
1990	18.0	11.6	9.7	6.4	13.3	6.7	16.4
1995	15.1	9.8	8.2	5.3	12.7	5.7	13.8
1996	14.7	9.6	7.8	5.1	12.5	5.5	13.3
1997	14.2	9.4	7.8	4.8	12.5	5.5	13.2
1998	14.3	9.5	7.8	4.8	12.3	5.3	13.1
1999	14.6	9.8	7.9	4.8	12.6	5.4	13.2
2000	14.1	9.4	7.6	4.7	12.4	5.4	13.0
2001	14.0	9.2	7.6	4.8	12.1	5.3	12.8
2002	14.4	9.5	7.8	4.8	---	---	---

--- Data not available.
[1]Infant (under 1 year of age), neonatal (under 28 days), early neonatal (under 7 days), and postneonatal (28 days–11 months).
[2]Number of fetal deaths of 20 weeks or more gestation per 1,000 live births plus fetal deaths.
[3]Number of fetal deaths of 28 weeks or more gestation per 1,000 live births plus late fetal deaths.
[4]Number of late fetal deaths plus infant deaths within 7 days of birth per 1,000 live births plus late fetal deaths.
[5]Includes births and deaths of persons who were not residents of the 50 States and the District of Columbia.
[6]Infant deaths are tabulated by race of decedent; live births and fetal deaths are tabulated by race of child. See Appendix II, Race.
[7]Infant deaths are tabulated by race of decedent; fetal deaths and live births are tabulated by race of mother. See Appendix II, Race.

NOTES: Infant mortality rates in this table are based on infant deaths from the mortality file (numerator) and live births from the natality file (denominator). Inconsistencies in reporting race for the same infant between the birth and death certificate can result in underestimated infant mortality rates for races other than white or black. Infant mortality rates for minority population groups are available from the Linked Birth/Infant Death Data Set and are presented in tables 19–20 and 23–24. Data for additional years are available. See Appendix III.

SOURCE: Centers for Disease Control and Prevention, National Center for Health Statistics, National Vital Statistics System: Kochanek KD, Murphy SL, Anderson RN, Scott C. Deaths: Final data for 2002. National vital statistics reports. vol 53 no 5. Hyattsville, Maryland: National Center for Health Statistics. 2004; and unpublished numbers.

This table will be updated on the Web. Go to www.cdc.gov/nchs/hus.htm.

Table 23 (page 1 of 2). Infant mortality rates, according to race, Hispanic origin, geographic division, and State: United States, average annual 1989–91, 1997–99, and 2000–2002

[Data are based on linked birth and death certificates for infants]

Geographic division and State	All races			Not Hispanic or Latino: White			Not Hispanic or Latino: Black or African American		
	1989–91[1]	1997–99[2]	2000–2002[2]	1989–91[1]	1997–99[2]	2000–2002[2]	1989–91[1]	1997–99[2]	2000–2002[2]
	Infant[3] deaths per 1,000 live births								
United States	9.0	7.1	6.9	7.3	5.9	5.7	17.2	13.9	13.6
New England[4]	7.3	5.7	5.4	6.2	4.7	4.5	15.1	11.8	12.1
Connecticut	7.9	6.7	6.4	5.9	4.8	4.9	17.0	13.4	14.3
Maine	6.6	5.5	5.1	6.2	5.6	5.0	*	*	*
Massachusetts	7.0	5.2	4.8	5.9	4.4	4.0	14.2	10.8	10.5
New Hampshire[4]	7.1	4.8	4.9	7.2	4.4	4.5	*	*	*
Rhode Island	8.7	6.7	6.7	7.5	4.8	5.3	*13.6	*12.4	*12.6
Vermont	6.6	6.2	5.5	6.3	6.0	5.5	*	*	*
Middle Atlantic	9.2	6.7	6.4	6.6	5.0	5.0	18.5	13.3	12.5
New Jersey	8.4	6.5	6.1	6.1	4.3	4.0	17.8	13.9	13.6
New York	9.5	6.4	6.1	6.3	4.6	4.8	18.4	11.9	11.2
Pennsylvania	9.2	7.4	7.3	7.2	5.8	5.9	19.1	16.0	14.4
East North Central	9.8	8.0	7.7	7.7	6.4	6.2	19.1	16.0	15.9
Illinois	10.7	8.5	7.8	7.6	6.2	5.9	20.5	17.1	15.8
Indiana	9.4	7.9	7.7	8.4	7.0	7.0	17.3	15.2	13.9
Michigan	10.5	8.1	8.1	7.7	6.1	6.0	20.7	16.1	16.9
Ohio	9.0	8.0	7.7	7.7	6.8	6.3	16.2	14.5	15.3
Wisconsin	8.4	6.8	6.9	7.4	5.6	5.6	17.0	15.7	17.9
West North Central	8.5	6.9	6.6	7.4	6.1	5.8	17.5	15.2	14.1
Iowa	8.2	6.1	5.8	7.8	5.7	5.5	15.8	17.2	*11.4
Kansas	8.5	7.3	7.0	7.8	7.1	6.4	15.4	12.0	14.7
Minnesota	7.3	6.0	5.5	6.4	5.4	4.7	18.5	12.5	10.8
Missouri	9.7	7.6	7.7	8.0	6.1	6.3	18.0	16.4	15.6
Nebraska	8.1	7.2	7.0	7.2	6.3	6.2	18.3	17.0	15.0
North Dakota	8.0	7.3	7.8	7.3	6.7	6.8	*	*	*
South Dakota	9.5	8.5	6.4	7.5	7.1	5.4	*	*	*
South Atlantic	10.4	8.3	8.0	7.6	6.2	6.0	17.2	14.1	13.7
Delaware	11.2	8.3	9.6	8.2	6.0	7.9	20.1	16.1	14.9
District of Columbia	20.3	14.1	11.4	*8.2	*	*	23.9	17.4	15.3
Florida	9.4	7.2	7.2	7.2	6.0	5.7	16.2	12.5	13.0
Georgia	11.9	8.4	8.7	8.4	6.0	6.3	17.9	13.3	13.4
Maryland	9.1	8.6	7.7	6.3	5.5	5.3	15.0	14.8	12.7
North Carolina	10.7	9.2	8.4	8.0	6.9	6.4	16.9	15.9	15.1
South Carolina	11.8	9.8	9.0	8.4	6.5	6.0	17.2	15.8	14.9
Virginia	9.9	7.5	7.2	7.4	5.8	5.5	18.0	13.3	13.6
West Virginia	9.1	8.3	7.9	8.8	8.2	7.7	*15.7	*12.7	*11.7
East South Central	10.4	8.8	8.8	8.1	6.8	6.8	16.5	14.6	15.0
Alabama	11.4	9.8	9.3	8.6	7.3	6.8	16.8	14.8	14.7
Kentucky	8.7	7.4	6.7	8.1	6.9	6.4	14.4	12.2	10.8
Mississippi	11.5	10.3	10.5	7.9	6.7	7.0	15.2	14.5	14.7
Tennessee	10.2	8.2	9.0	7.8	6.2	7.0	18.2	15.0	17.0
West South Central[4]	8.4	7.0	6.8	7.2	6.4	6.2	14.2	12.3	12.3
Arkansas	9.8	8.5	8.3	8.1	7.5	7.5	15.2	12.8	12.8
Louisiana[4]	10.2	9.3	9.8	7.5	6.4	6.9	14.3	13.7	13.7
Oklahoma[4]	8.0	8.2	8.0	7.3	7.9	7.4	12.7	13.4	14.5
Texas	7.9	6.3	5.9	6.9	5.8	5.5	14.1	11.1	11.1
Mountain	8.4	6.7	6.2	7.9	6.2	5.7	16.9	12.7	13.5
Arizona	8.8	7.1	6.7	8.2	6.5	6.5	17.3	13.7	14.4
Colorado	8.7	6.8	6.0	8.0	6.3	5.2	16.7	13.7	13.7
Idaho	8.9	6.8	6.6	8.9	6.6	6.2	*	*	*
Montana	9.0	7.0	6.9	8.0	6.2	6.4	*	*	*
Nevada	8.6	6.8	6.0	7.8	6.8	5.1	16.9	11.8	13.7
New Mexico	8.4	6.7	6.4	8.1	6.7	6.0	*17.2	*	*15.8
Utah	7.0	5.4	5.3	6.8	5.3	5.0	*	*	*
Wyoming	8.4	6.7	6.5	8.0	6.3	6.3	*	*	*
Pacific	7.7	5.7	5.5	7.0	5.1	4.9	15.4	12.0	11.2
Alaska	9.2	6.5	6.8	7.2	5.5	5.1	*	*	*
California	7.6	5.7	5.4	6.9	5.0	4.7	15.4	12.2	11.4
Hawaii	7.0	6.9	7.2	5.5	5.8	6.3	*13.6	*	*
Oregon	8.0	5.6	5.5	7.4	5.4	5.6	21.3	*8.8	*10.4
Washington	8.0	5.4	5.5	7.4	4.9	5.2	15.1	11.4	9.5

See footnotes at end of table.

This table will be updated on the Web. Go to www.cdc.gov/nchs/hus.htm.

Table 23 (page 2 of 2). Infant mortality rates, according to race, Hispanic origin, geographic division, and State: United States, average annual 1989–91, 1997–99, and 2000–2002

[Data are based on linked birth and death certificates for infants]

Geographic division and State	Hispanic or Latino[5]			American Indian or Alaska Native[6]			Asian or Pacific Islander[6]		
	1989–91[1]	1997–99[2]	2000–2002[2]	1989–91[1]	1997–99[2]	2000–2002[2]	1989–91[1]	1997–99[2]	2000–2002[2]
	Infant[3] deaths per 1,000 live births								
United States	7.5	5.8	5.5	12.6	9.1	8.9	6.6	5.1	4.8
New England[7]	8.1	7.6	6.5	*	*	*	5.8	3.8	3.9
Connecticut	7.9	8.9	7.1	*	*	*	*	*	*3.7
Maine	*	*	*	*	*	*	*	*	*
Massachusetts	8.3	6.3	6.0	*	*	*	5.7	*3.5	3.7
New Hampshire[7]	- - -	*	*	*	*	*	*	*	*
Rhode Island	*7.2	*8.3	8.0	*	*	*	*	*	*
Vermont	*	*	*	*	*	*	*	*	*
Middle Atlantic	9.1	6.3	6.0	*11.6	*	*7.9	6.4	4.2	3.4
New Jersey	7.5	6.4	6.3	*	*	*	5.6	4.4	3.3
New York	9.4	5.9	5.5	*15.2	*	*	6.4	4.0	3.4
Pennsylvania	10.9	8.2	8.6	*	*	*	7.8	*4.7	*4.0
East North Central	8.7	7.2	6.5	11.6	8.4	9.7	6.1	6.0	5.6
Illinois	9.2	6.9	6.4	*	*	*	6.0	6.3	6.5
Indiana	*7.2	7.4	6.4	*	*	*	*	*6.4	*
Michigan	7.9	7.0	6.7	*10.7	*	*	*6.1	6.0	4.9
Ohio	8.0	8.8	7.6	*	*	*	*4.8	*4.9	*4.8
Wisconsin	*7.3	9.2	6.2	*11.9	*9.2	*11.5	*6.7	*5.7	*5.2
West North Central	9.3	6.5	7.0	17.1	12.3	10.9	7.4	6.6	5.6
Iowa	*11.9	*5.6	*6.7	*	*	*	*	*	*
Kansas	8.7	5.8	7.1	*	*	*	*	*	*
Minnesota	*8.4	7.0	6.5	17.3	*10.9	*10.3	*5.1	7.0	6.1
Missouri	*9.1	*5.6	7.2	*	*	*	*9.1	*5.7	*4.5
Nebraska	*8.8	8.7	7.2	*18.2	*	*15.8	*	*	*
North Dakota	*	*	*	*13.8	*13.8	*13.4	*	*	*
South Dakota	*	*	*	19.9	15.2	11.6	*	*	*
South Atlantic	7.4	5.1	5.4	12.7	10.7	8.5	6.8	5.2	5.3
Delaware	*	*	*7.9	*	*	*	*	*	*
District of Columbia	*8.8	*	*7.5	*	*	*	*	*	*
Florida	7.1	4.7	5.2	*	*8.5	*5.8	*6.2	4.5	5.1
Georgia	9.0	4.9	6.0	*	*	*	*8.2	*5.0	6.8
Maryland	7.2	5.4	5.7	*	*	*	7.5	*5.2	*4.5
North Carolina	*7.5	6.7	5.6	12.2	13.7	10.6	*6.3	*5.8	5.9
South Carolina	*	*7.5	*4.6	*	*	*	*	*	*
Virginia	7.6	5.0	4.8	*	*	*	6.0	5.2	4.6
West Virginia	*	*	*	*	*	*	*	*	*
East South Central	*5.9	6.7	6.2	*	*	*10.1	*7.7	*6.2	*5.4
Alabama	*	*7.5	*7.0	*	*	*	*	*	*
Kentucky	*	*	*4.8	*	*	*	*	*	*
Mississippi	*	*	*	*	*	*	*	*	*
Tennessee	*	*7.0	6.2	*	*	*	*	*	*
West South Central[7]	7.0	5.5	5.1	8.4	7.9	7.5	6.7	4.4	4.4
Arkansas	*	*6.2	*4.5	*	*	*	*	*	*
Louisiana[7]	- - -	*	*6.0	*	*	*	*	*	*8.1
Oklahoma[7]	- - -	5.1	5.7	7.8	8.0	7.6	*	*	*
Texas	7.0	5.5	5.1	*	*8.6	*	6.8	4.4	4.0
Mountain	7.9	6.7	6.2	11.6	8.8	8.6	8.1	5.7	5.9
Arizona	8.0	7.1	6.0	11.4	8.6	9.4	*8.5	*6.1	*5.3
Colorado	8.5	7.0	6.2	*16.5	*	*11.8	*7.8	*5.9	*6.2
Idaho	*7.2	7.0	8.8	*	*	*	*	*	*
Montana	*	*	*	16.7	*12.0	*9.9	*	*	*
Nevada	7.0	5.6	5.1	*	*	*	*	*4.7	*4.7
New Mexico	7.8	6.5	6.3	9.8	7.7	6.8	*	*	*
Utah	*7.0	5.9	6.5	*10.0	*	*	*10.7	*6.5	*8.4
Wyoming	*	*	*	*	*	*	*	*	*
Pacific	7.1	5.3	5.1	14.6	8.9	9.3	6.5	5.3	4.9
Alaska	*	*	*	15.7	9.1	11.2	*	*	*
California	7.0	5.3	5.1	11.0	8.9	7.6	6.4	4.9	4.5
Hawaii	10.7	*7.0	*6.0	*	*	*	7.1	7.4	7.3
Oregon	8.5	6.2	5.1	*15.7	*	*	*8.4	*5.2	*3.7
Washington	7.6	5.0	5.1	19.6	9.6	10.6	6.2	4.9	4.8

* Estimates are considered unreliable. Rates preceded by an asterisk are based on fewer than 50 deaths. Rates not shown are based on fewer than 20 deaths.
- - - Data not available. [1]Rates based on unweighted birth cohort data.
[2]Rates based on period file using weighted data. See Appendix I, National Vital Statistics System, Linked Birth/Infant Death Data Set. [3]Under 1 year of age.
[4]Rates for white and black are substituted for non-Hispanic white and non-Hispanic black for Louisiana 1989, Oklahoma 1989–90, and New Hampshire 1989–91.
[5]Persons of Hispanic origin may be of any race. [6]Includes persons of Hispanic origin.
[7]Rates for Hispanic origin exclude data from States not reporting Hispanic origin on the birth certificate for 1 or more years in a 3-year period.

NOTE: National linked files do not exist for 1992–94.

SOURCE: Centers for Disease Control and Prevention, National Center for Health Statistics, National Vital Statistics System, Linked Birth/Infant Death Data Set.

This table will be updated on the Web. Go to www.cdc.gov/nchs/hus.htm.

Table 24 (page 1 of 2). Neonatal mortality rates, according to race, Hispanic origin, geographic division, and State: United States, average annual 1989–91, 1997–99, and 2000–2002

[Data are based on linked birth and death certificates for infants]

Geographic division and State	All races			Not Hispanic or Latino: White			Not Hispanic or Latino: Black or African American		
	1989–91[1]	1997–99[2]	2000–2002[2]	1989–91[1]	1997–99[2]	2000–2002[2]	1989–91[1]	1997–99[2]	2000–2002[2]
	Neonatal[3] deaths per 1,000 live births								
United States	5.7	4.8	4.6	4.6	3.9	3.8	11.1	9.4	9.2
New England[4]	5.1	4.4	4.0	4.2	3.6	3.3	11.0	8.8	9.0
Connecticut	5.7	5.1	4.8	4.2	3.7	3.8	12.5	10.0	10.1
Maine	4.5	3.9	3.8	4.2	3.9	3.7	*	*	*
Massachusetts	4.9	4.0	3.7	4.1	3.4	3.0	10.4	8.3	8.0
New Hampshire[4]	4.3	3.6	3.4	4.4	3.4	3.1	*	*	*
Rhode Island	6.4	5.0	5.1	5.3	3.9	3.8	*9.8	*	*10.2
Vermont	4.1	4.4	3.5	3.9	4.4	3.6	*	*	*
Middle Atlantic	6.3	4.7	4.5	4.6	3.5	3.6	12.3	9.2	8.6
New Jersey	5.8	4.6	4.3	4.5	3.2	2.9	11.4	9.6	9.3
New York	6.5	4.5	4.3	4.3	3.2	3.4	12.6	8.2	7.8
Pennsylvania	6.2	5.1	5.2	4.9	4.0	4.3	12.5	11.1	9.6
East North Central	6.3	5.4	5.3	4.9	4.3	4.2	12.1	10.6	10.4
Illinois	7.0	5.7	5.3	5.1	4.3	4.2	12.7	11.1	10.0
Indiana	6.0	5.2	5.1	5.2	4.6	4.6	11.5	10.3	8.6
Michigan	6.9	5.5	5.6	4.9	4.0	4.2	14.0	11.0	11.4
Ohio	5.5	5.3	5.3	4.8	4.6	4.2	9.8	9.4	10.4
Wisconsin	5.1	4.6	4.6	4.6	3.7	3.9	9.1	10.5	11.3
West North Central	5.0	4.5	4.3	4.5	4.0	3.7	10.2	10.0	9.6
Iowa	4.8	4.0	3.7	4.5	3.7	3.5	*10.5	*11.3	*8.4
Kansas	4.9	4.8	4.6	4.6	4.7	4.0	8.3	8.1	10.3
Minnesota	4.3	3.9	3.6	3.9	3.6	3.2	10.7	8.1	6.4
Missouri	6.0	4.9	5.1	5.0	3.9	4.1	10.6	10.8	10.7
Nebraska	4.5	4.9	4.8	4.2	4.3	4.3	*9.8	*11.6	*10.9
North Dakota	5.0	4.4	5.1	4.7	4.5	4.5	*	*	*
South Dakota	5.1	4.6	3.4	4.5	4.2	3.0	*	*	*
South Atlantic	6.9	5.7	5.5	4.9	4.1	4.0	11.7	10.0	9.6
Delaware	7.5	5.9	7.0	5.8	3.8	5.8	12.4	12.8	11.1
District of Columbia	14.1	9.8	8.3	*5.2	*	*	16.7	12.4	10.9
Florida	6.2	4.8	4.8	4.7	3.9	3.6	10.5	8.3	8.7
Georgia	7.9	5.8	5.8	5.5	4.0	4.1	12.0	9.4	9.2
Maryland	5.9	6.2	5.6	3.9	3.8	3.8	10.2	10.8	9.2
North Carolina	7.3	6.5	5.9	5.3	4.8	4.4	11.9	11.5	11.0
South Carolina	7.7	6.9	6.2	5.4	4.3	3.9	11.3	11.6	10.6
Virginia	6.8	5.3	4.9	4.8	3.9	3.6	13.0	9.8	9.6
West Virginia	5.8	5.3	5.1	5.6	5.2	5.0	*9.7	*8.1	*9.8
East South Central	6.6	5.6	5.6	5.0	4.2	4.2	10.6	9.5	9.8
Alabama	7.5	6.3	5.9	5.7	4.6	4.2	11.1	9.9	9.4
Kentucky	5.0	4.7	4.2	4.6	4.4	4.0	8.9	7.6	6.3
Mississippi	7.1	6.2	6.6	4.9	3.9	4.2	9.5	9.0	9.5
Tennessee	6.5	5.2	5.8	4.9	3.9	4.3	11.8	9.9	11.4
West South Central[4]	5.0	4.4	4.2	4.2	3.9	3.7	8.4	7.6	7.7
Arkansas	5.4	5.1	4.9	4.5	4.4	4.2	8.5	7.5	8.1
Louisiana[4]	6.3	6.0	6.3	4.8	4.1	4.3	8.5	8.9	8.9
Oklahoma[4]	4.4	5.0	4.8	4.1	4.9	4.6	6.3	8.1	8.5
Texas	4.7	3.9	3.6	4.1	3.5	3.3	8.5	6.7	6.7
Mountain	4.8	4.2	4.1	4.4	3.9	3.7	10.1	8.2	8.9
Arizona	5.3	4.6	4.3	4.9	4.3	4.2	11.0	9.0	9.6
Colorado	5.0	4.5	4.2	4.7	4.0	3.5	10.9	9.8	10.5
Idaho	5.3	4.4	4.5	5.2	4.3	4.1	*	*	*
Montana	4.6	3.7	4.5	4.2	3.2	4.3	*	*	*
Nevada	4.3	3.8	3.6	3.8	3.5	2.9	*8.3	*	7.4
New Mexico	5.0	3.9	4.0	4.8	4.3	3.5	*	*	*
Utah	3.7	3.5	3.5	3.6	3.3	3.4	*	*	*
Wyoming	3.9	3.8	4.3	3.8	3.5	4.3	*	*	*
Pacific	4.6	3.7	3.6	4.0	3.3	3.2	9.2	7.5	7.2
Alaska	4.1	3.1	3.1	3.7	2.9	*2.9	*	*	*
California	4.6	3.8	3.6	4.1	3.3	3.1	9.2	7.7	7.5
Hawaii	4.3	4.7	5.0	3.5	*3.9	5.3	*	*	*
Oregon	4.4	3.6	3.6	4.0	3.4	3.6	*11.6	*	*
Washington	4.3	3.4	3.5	3.8	3.0	3.3	9.7	7.1	6.0

See footnotes at end of table.

This table will be updated on the Web. Go to www.cdc.gov/nchs/hus.htm.

Table 24 (page 2 of 2). Neonatal mortality rates, according to race, Hispanic origin, geographic division, and State: United States, average annual 1989–91, 1997–99, and 2000–2002

[Data are based on linked birth and death certificates for infants]

Geographic division and State	Hispanic or Latino[5]			American Indian or Alaska Native[6]			Asian or Pacific Islander[6]		
	1989–91[1]	1997–99[2]	2000–2002[2]	1989–91[1]	1997–99[2]	2000–2002[2]	1989–91[1]	1997–99[2]	2000–2002[2]
	Neonatal[3] deaths per 1,000 live births								
United States	4.8	3.9	3.8	5.9	4.8	4.4	3.9	3.4	3.3
New England[7]	5.5	5.7	4.9	*	*	*	4.4	*2.6	3.1
Connecticut	5.3	6.5	5.3	*	*	*	*	*	*
Maine	*	*	*	*	*	*	*	*	*
Massachusetts	5.8	5.1	4.6	*	*	*	*3.9	*2.5	*2.7
New Hampshire[7]	- - -	*	*	*	*	*	*	*	*
Rhode Island	*4.9	*5.4	*6.0	*	*	*	*	*	*
Vermont	*	*	*	*	*	*	*	*	*
Middle Atlantic	6.2	4.5	4.2	*	*	*	4.1	3.0	2.3
New Jersey	5.1	4.6	4.3	*	*	*	*3.4	3.1	2.2
New York	6.4	4.2	3.9	*	*	*	4.1	2.9	2.3
Pennsylvania	7.3	5.5	5.8	*	*	*	*5.2	*3.4	*2.7
East North Central	5.9	5.1	4.5	*6.2	*5.3	*5.0	3.6	4.1	4.3
Illinois	6.4	4.8	4.4	*	*	*	3.9	4.4	4.8
Indiana	*4.7	5.2	4.8	*	*	*	*	*	*
Michigan	5.2	4.8	4.7	*	*	*	*	*3.9	*3.8
Ohio	*5.4	6.7	5.3	*	*	*	*	*3.0	*4.0
Wisconsin	*3.9	7.3	4.4	*	*	*	*	*4.2	*3.8
West North Central	5.3	4.5	4.9	6.1	5.3	5.3	4.6	4.5	3.9
Iowa	*	*3.9	*4.9	*	*	*	*	*	*
Kansas	*5.4	*3.7	4.9	*	*	*	*	*	*
Minnesota	*	*4.7	4.6	*4.9	*	*	*3.2	*4.5	*4.2
Missouri	*	*4.6	*5.2	*	*	*	*	*	*
Nebraska	*	*6.5	*4.6	*	*	*	*	*	*
North Dakota	*	*	*	*	*	*	*	*	*
South Dakota	*	*	*	*8.2	*6.1	*4.7	*	*	*
South Atlantic	5.2	3.6	3.7	7.4	8.0	5.8	4.6	3.5	4.0
Delaware	*	*	*	*	*	*	*	*	*
District of Columbia	*	*	*	*	*	*	*	*	*
Florida	5.1	3.2	3.6	*	*	*	*4.4	*2.9	3.8
Georgia	*5.7	3.3	4.0	*	*	*	*5.3	*3.2	5.4
Maryland	*4.7	*4.4	4.2	*	*	*	*4.5	*4.0	*3.6
North Carolina	*5.5	4.8	3.8	*7.7	11.2	*8.1	*	*3.6	*4.4
South Carolina	*	*5.5	*3.6	*	*	*	*	*	*
Virginia	*4.8	3.8	3.5	*	*	*	*4.1	4.0	3.2
West Virginia	*	*	*	*	*	*	*	*	*
East South Central	*	4.3	3.9	*	*	*	*	*4.7	*3.6
Alabama	*	*	*4.6	*	*	*	*	*	*
Kentucky	*	*	*	*	*	*	*	*	*
Mississippi	*	*	*	*	*	*	*	*	*
Tennessee	*	*4.9	*3.8	*	*	*	*	*	*
West South Central[7]	4.2	3.5	3.2	4.3	4.4	3.7	4.1	2.7	2.9
Arkansas	*	*4.1	*3.1	*	*	*	*	*	*
Louisiana[7]	- - -	*	*	*	*	*	*	*	*7.1
Oklahoma[7]	- - -	*3.1	*3.3	*3.7	4.5	3.9	*	*	*
Texas	4.2	3.5	3.2	*	*	*	4.0	2.8	2.5
Mountain	4.7	4.3	4.2	5.8	4.4	4.3	4.6	3.6	3.7
Arizona	5.0	4.6	4.1	5.4	4.4	4.4	*	*	*
Colorado	4.4	4.8	4.6	*	*	*	*	*	*4.7
Idaho	*	*4.3	6.8	*	*	*	*	*	*
Montana	*	*	*	*7.6	*5.3	*5.9	*	*	*
Nevada	*4.1	3.4	3.3	*	*	*	*	*	*
New Mexico	4.9	3.6	4.3	4.9	*3.6	*3.5	*	*	*
Utah	*3.6	4.0	4.1	*	*	*	*	*	*5.0
Wyoming	*	*	*	*	*	*	*	*	*
Pacific	4.5	3.6	3.5	6.5	4.3	4.1	3.7	3.4	3.3
Alaska	*	*	*	*5.7	*3.3	*3.9	*	*	*
California	4.4	3.6	3.5	6.3	*4.6	*4.0	3.6	3.1	3.0
Hawaii	*6.6	*4.3	*3.8	*	*	*	4.2	5.0	4.9
Oregon	6.5	4.7	3.6	*	*	*	*5.3	*3.8	*
Washington	4.9	3.4	3.2	*8.5	*5.6	*4.1	*2.7	3.1	3.2

* Estimates are considered unreliable. Rates preceded by an asterisk are based on fewer than 50 deaths. Rates not shown are based on fewer than 20 deaths.
- - - Data not available. [1]Rates based on unweighted birth cohort data.
[2]Rates based on period file using weighted data. See Appendix I, National Vital Statistics System, Linked Birth/Infant Death Data Set.
[3]Infants under 28 days of age.
[4]Rates for white and black are substituted for non-Hispanic white and non-Hispanic black for Louisiana 1989, Oklahoma 1989–90, and New Hampshire 1989–91.
[5]Persons of Hispanic origin may be of any race. [6]Includes persons of Hispanic origin.
[7]Rates for Hispanic origin exclude data from States not reporting Hispanic origin on the birth certificate for 1 or more years in a 3-year period.

NOTE: National linked files do not exist for 1992–94.

SOURCE: Centers for Disease Control and Prevention, National Center for Health Statistics, National Vital Statistics System, Linked Birth/Infant Death Data Set.
This table will be updated on the Web. Go to www.cdc.gov/nchs/hus.htm.

Table 25. Infant mortality rates and international rankings: Selected countries, selected years 1960–2002

[Data are based on reporting by countries]

Country[2]	1960	1970	1980	1990	2000	2001	2002	International rankings[1] 1960	International rankings[1] 2002
	Infant[3] deaths per 1,000 live births								
Australia	20.2	17.9	10.7	8.2	5.2	5.3	5.0	5	17
Austria	37.5	25.9	14.3	7.8	4.8	4.8	4.1	24	8
Belgium	31.2	21.1	12.1	8.0	4.8	4.5	4.9	20	16
Bulgaria	45.1	27.3	20.2	14.8	13.3	14.4	13.3	30	36
Canada	27.3	18.8	10.4	6.8	5.3	5.2	5.4	14	23
Chile	120.3	82.2	33.0	16.0	11.7	8.3	7.8	36	32
Costa Rica	67.8	65.4	20.3	15.3	10.2	10.8	11.2	33	34
Cuba	37.3	38.7	19.6	10.7	7.2	6.2	6.5	23	27
Czech Republic	20.0	20.2	16.9	10.8	4.1	4.0	4.2	4	10
Denmark	21.5	14.2	8.4	7.5	5.3	4.9	4.4	8	12
England and Wales	22.4	18.5	12.1	7.9	5.6	5.5	5.2	9	21
Finland	21.0	13.2	7.6	5.6	3.8	3.2	3.0	6	4
France	27.5	18.2	10.0	7.3	4.6	4.5	4.1	15	8
Germany[4]	35.0	22.5	12.4	7.0	4.4	4.3	4.3	22	11
Greece	40.1	29.6	17.9	9.7	6.1	5.1	5.9	25	25
Hong Kong	41.5	19.2	11.2	6.2	3.0	2.6	2.3	26	1
Hungary	47.6	35.9	23.2	14.8	9.2	8.1	7.2	31	29
Ireland	29.3	19.5	11.1	8.2	6.2	5.7	5.1	17	20
Israel[5]	31.0	18.9	15.6	9.9	5.4	5.1	5.4	19	23
Italy	43.9	29.6	14.6	8.2	4.5	4.7	4.7	29	14
Japan	30.7	13.1	7.5	4.6	3.2	3.1	3.0	18	4
Netherlands	17.9	12.7	8.6	7.1	5.1	5.4	5.0	2	17
New Zealand	22.6	16.7	13.0	8.4	6.3	5.6	6.2	10	26
Northern Ireland	27.2	22.9	13.4	7.5	5.1	6.1	4.7	13	14
Norway	18.9	12.7	8.1	7.0	3.8	3.9	3.5	3	7
Poland	54.8	36.7	25.5	19.3	8.1	7.7	7.5	32	30
Portugal	77.5	55.5	24.3	11.0	5.5	5.0	5.0	35	17
Puerto Rico	43.3	27.9	18.5	13.4	9.9	9.2	9.8	27	33
Romania	75.7	49.4	29.3	26.9	18.6	18.4	17.3	34	37
Russian Federation[6]	---	---	22.0	17.6	15.2	14.6	13.2	---	35
Scotland	26.4	19.6	12.1	7.7	5.7	5.5	5.3	12	22
Singapore	34.8	21.4	11.7	6.7	2.5	2.2	2.9	21	3
Slovakia	28.6	25.7	20.9	12.0	8.6	6.2	7.6	16	31
Spain	43.7	28.1	12.3	7.6	3.9	3.5	3.4	28	6
Sweden	16.6	11.0	6.9	6.0	3.4	3.7	2.8	1	2
Switzerland	21.1	15.1	9.1	6.8	4.9	5.0	4.5	7	13
United States	26.0	20.0	12.6	9.2	6.9	6.8	7.0	11	28

- - - Data not available.

[1]Rankings are from lowest to highest infant mortality rates (IMR). Countries with the same IMR receive the same rank. The country with the next highest IMR is assigned the rank it would have received had the lower-ranked countries not been tied, i.e., skip a rank. Some of the variation in IMRs is due to differences among countries in distinguishing between fetal and infant deaths.

[2]Refers to countries, territories, cities, or geographic areas with at least 1 million population and with "complete" counts of live births and infant deaths as indicated in the United Nations Demographic Yearbook.

[3]Under 1 year of age.

[4]Rates for 1990 and earlier years were calculated by combining information from the Federal Republic of Germany and the German Democratic Republic.

[5]Includes data for East Jerusalem and Israeli residents in certain other territories under occupation by Israeli military forces since June 1967.

[6]Excludes infants born alive after less than 28 weeks' gestation, of less than 1,000 grams in weight and 35 centimeters in length, who die within 7 days of birth.

NOTE: Some rates for selected countries and selected years were revised and differ from the previous edition of *Health, United States.*

SOURCES: Organization for Economic Cooperation and Development (OECD): OECD Health Data 2004 3rd edition, A Comparative Analysis of 30 Countries, www.oecd.org/els/health/; United Nations: 2000 Demographic Yearbook, United Nations Publication, Sales No. E/F.02.XIII.1, New York, 2002; World Health Organization Statistical Information System (WHOSIS), www3.who.int/whosis/; United States and Puerto Rico: Centers for Disease Control and Prevention, National Center for Health Statistics. Vital Statistics of the United States, vol. II, mortality part A (selected years). Public Health Service. Washington; Sweden: Statistics Sweden; Costa Rica: Dirección General de Estadísticas y Censos. Elaboración y estimación, Centro Centroamericano de Población, Universidad de Costa Rica, populi.eest.ucr.ac.cr/observa/index1.htm; Russian Federation: Goskomstat, www.gks.ru/eng/. Israel: Central Bureau Statistics of Israel, www.cbs.gov.il/engindex.htm.

Table 26 (page 1 of 2). Life expectancy at birth and at 65 years of age, according to sex: Selected countries, selected years 1980–2001

[Data are based on reporting by countries]

Country	Male 1980	Male 1990	Male 1995	Male 1999	Male 2000	Male 2001	Male 2001	Female 1980	Female 1990	Female 1995	Female 1999	Female 2000	Female 2001	Female 2001
At birth	Life expectancy in years						Rank	Life expectancy in years						Rank
Australia	71.0	73.9	75.0	76.2	76.6	77.0	7	78.1	80.1	80.8	81.8	82.0	82.4	7
Austria	69.0	72.2	73.3	74.8	75.1	75.6	14	76.1	78.8	79.9	80.8	81.1	81.5	11
Belgium	70.0	72.7	73.4	74.4	74.6	74.9	21	76.8	79.4	80.2	80.8	80.8	81.1	15
Bulgaria	68.5	68.3	67.4	68.4	68.5	68.6	34	73.9	75.0	74.9	75.1	75.1	75.4	35
Canada	71.7	74.4	75.1	76.3	76.7	77.1	5	78.9	80.8	81.1	81.7	82.0	82.2	8
Chile	- - -	71.1	71.8	72.4	72.6	72.7	29	- - -	76.9	77.8	78.4	78.6	78.7	30
Costa Rica	71.9	74.7	74.0	75.0	75.4	75.6	14	77.0	79.1	78.6	79.8	80.2	79.9	24
Cuba	72.2	74.6	75.4	73.3	74.7	74.7	22	- - -	76.9	77.7	77.5	79.0	79.2	28
Czech Republic[1]	66.8	67.6	69.7	71.4	71.7	72.1	30	73.9	75.4	76.6	78.2	78.4	78.5	31
Denmark	71.2	72.0	72.7	74.2	74.5	74.7	22	77.3	77.7	77.8	79.0	79.3	79.3	27
England and Wales	70.8	73.1	74.3	75.3	75.6	76.0	11	76.8	78.6	79.5	80.1	80.3	80.6	20
Finland	69.2	70.9	72.8	73.8	74.2	74.6	25	77.6	78.9	80.2	81.0	81.0	81.5	11
France	70.2	72.8	73.9	75.0	75.2	75.5	18	78.4	80.9	81.8	82.5	82.7	82.9	4
Germany[2]	69.6	72.0	73.3	74.7	75.0	75.6	14	76.1	78.4	79.7	80.7	81.0	81.3	14
Greece	72.2	74.6	75.0	75.5	75.5	75.4	19	76.8	79.5	80.3	80.6	80.6	80.7	18
Hong Kong	71.6	74.6	76.0	77.7	78.0	78.4	1	77.9	80.3	81.5	83.2	83.9	84.6	2
Hungary	65.5	65.1	65.3	66.4	67.4	68.1	35	72.7	73.7	74.5	75.2	75.9	76.4	34
Ireland	70.1	72.1	72.9	73.9	73.9	74.7	22	75.6	77.6	78.4	78.8	79.1	79.7	26
Israel	72.2	75.1	75.5	76.6	76.7	77.1	5	75.8	78.5	79.5	80.7	81.1	81.6	10
Italy	70.6	73.6	74.9	76.1	76.6	76.7	8	77.4	80.1	81.3	82.2	82.5	82.8	6
Japan	73.4	75.9	76.4	77.1	77.7	78.1	2	78.8	81.9	82.9	84.0	84.6	84.9	1
Netherlands	72.5	73.8	74.6	75.3	75.5	75.8	13	79.2	80.9	80.4	80.5	80.5	80.7	18
New Zealand	70.0	72.4	74.2	76.0	76.0	76.0	11	76.3	78.3	79.5	80.9	80.9	80.9	17
Northern Ireland	68.3	72.1	73.5	74.5	74.8	75.2	20	75.0	78.0	78.9	79.6	79.8	80.1	22
Norway	72.3	73.4	74.8	75.6	76.0	76.2	10	79.2	79.8	80.8	81.1	81.4	81.5	11
Poland	66.0	66.7	67.6	68.2	69.7	70.2	32	74.4	76.3	76.4	77.2	77.9	78.3	32
Portugal	67.7	70.4	71.6	72.6	73.2	73.5	27	75.2	77.4	78.7	79.5	80.0	80.3	21
Puerto Rico	70.8	69.1	69.6	70.7	70.8	71.0	31	76.9	77.2	78.9	79.8	79.9	80.0	23
Romania	66.6	66.6	65.5	67.2	67.8	67.7	36	71.9	73.1	73.5	74.2	74.8	75.0	36
Russian Federation	61.4	63.8	58.3	60.0	59.2	59.1	37	73.0	74.4	71.7	72.5	72.4	72.3	37
Scotland	69.0	71.1	72.1	72.8	73.1	73.3	28	75.2	76.7	77.7	78.4	78.6	78.8	29
Singapore	69.8	73.1	74.2	75.6	76.1	76.5	9	74.7	77.6	78.6	79.7	80.8	81.1	15
Slovakia[1]	66.8	66.6	68.4	69.0	69.2	69.6	33	74.3	75.4	76.3	77.2	77.4	77.7	33
Spain	72.5	73.3	74.3	75.1	75.7	75.6	14	78.6	80.3	81.5	82.1	82.5	82.9	4
Sweden	72.8	74.8	76.2	77.1	77.4	77.6	3	78.8	80.4	81.4	81.9	82.0	82.1	9
Switzerland	72.8	74.0	75.3	76.8	76.9	77.4	4	79.6	80.7	81.7	82.5	82.6	83.0	3
United States	70.0	71.8	72.5	73.9	74.1	74.4	26	77.4	78.8	78.9	79.4	79.5	79.8	25

See footnotes at end of table.

Table 26 (page 2 of 2). Life expectancy at birth and at 65 years of age, according to sex: Selected countries, selected years 1980–2001

[Data are based on reporting by countries]

Country	Male							Female						
	1980	*1990*	*1995*	*1999*	*2000*	*2001*	*2001*	*1980*	*1990*	*1995*	*1999*	*2000*	*2001*	*2001*
At 65 years	Life expectancy in years						Rank	Life expectancy in years						Rank
Australia	13.7	15.2	15.7	16.6	16.9	17.2	3	17.9	19.0	19.5	20.2	20.4	20.7	5
Austria	12.9	14.3	14.9	15.6	16.0	16.3	13	16.3	17.8	18.6	19.2	19.4	19.8	8
Belgium	13.0	14.3	14.8	15.4	15.5	15.8	18	16.9	18.5	19.1	19.4	19.5	19.7	12
Bulgaria	12.7	12.9	12.8	13.0	12.8	13.1	30	14.7	15.4	15.4	15.4	15.4	15.8	32
Canada	14.5	15.7	16.0	16.5	16.4	17.1	6	18.9	19.9	20.0	20.3	20.5	20.6	6
Chile	- - -	14.6	14.9	15.2	15.3	15.4	23	- - -	17.6	18.1	18.5	18.6	18.7	22
Costa Rica	16.1	17.1	16.7	17.1	17.2	17.1	6	18.1	19.3	18.6	19.3	19.6	19.4	15
Cuba	- - -	- - -	- - -	15.6	16.7	16.8	10	- - -	- - -	- - -	17.5	19.0	19.3	17
Czech Republic[1]	11.2	11.6	12.7	13.6	13.7	14.0	27	14.3	15.2	16.0	16.9	17.1	17.2	28
Denmark	13.6	14.0	14.1	14.9	15.2	15.2	24	17.6	17.8	17.5	18.1	18.3	18.4	24
England and Wales	12.9	14.1	14.8	15.5	15.8	16.1	14	16.9	17.9	18.3	18.8	19.0	19.2	19
Finland	12.5	13.7	14.5	15.1	15.5	15.7	19	16.5	17.7	18.6	19.2	19.3	19.6	13
France	13.6	15.5	16.1	16.5	16.7	16.9	8	18.2	19.8	20.6	20.9	21.2	21.3	3
Germany[2]	13.0	14.0	14.7	15.5	15.7	16.0	16	16.7	17.6	18.5	19.2	19.4	19.6	13
Greece	14.6	15.7	16.1	16.3	- - -	- - -	- - -	16.8	18.0	18.4	18.7	- - -	- - -	- - -
Hong Kong	13.9	15.3	16.2	17.2	17.3	17.7	2	13.9	18.8	19.5	21.0	21.5	22.1	2
Hungary	11.6	12.0	12.1	12.2	12.7	13.0	31	14.6	15.3	15.8	15.9	16.4	16.7	30
Ireland	12.6	13.3	13.6	14.1	14.6	15.0	25	15.7	16.9	17.3	17.5	17.8	18.3	25
Israel	14.4	15.9	16.0	16.6	16.9	17.2	3	15.8	17.8	18.0	19.0	19.3	19.8	8
Italy	13.3	15.1	15.8	16.2	16.6	- - -	- - -	17.1	18.8	19.6	20.1	20.4	- - -	- - -
Japan	14.6	16.2	16.5	17.0	17.5	17.8	1	17.7	20.0	20.9	21.9	22.4	22.7	1
Netherlands	13.7	14.4	14.7	15.1	15.3	15.5	22	18.0	18.9	19.0	19.1	19.2	19.3	17
New Zealand	13.2	14.7	15.4	16.5	16.5	16.5	11	17.0	18.3	19.0	19.8	19.8	19.8	8
Northern Ireland	11.9	13.7	14.4	15.0	15.3	15.7	19	15.8	17.5	18.0	18.4	18.5	18.7	22
Norway	14.3	14.6	15.1	15.6	16.0	16.1	14	18.0	18.5	19.1	19.5	19.7	19.8	8
Poland	12.0	12.7	12.9	13.2	13.6	13.9	28	15.5	16.9	16.6	17.0	17.3	17.6	27
Portugal	12.9	13.9	14.6	14.9	15.3	15.6	21	16.5	17.0	17.8	18.3	18.7	18.9	21
Puerto Rico	- - -	- - -	- - -	- - -	- - -	- - -	- - -	- - -	- - -	- - -	- - -	- - -	- - -	- - -
Romania	12.6	13.3	12.9	13.0	13.5	13.5	29	14.2	15.3	15.4	15.5	15.9	16.1	31
Russian Federation	11.6	12.1	10.9	11.2	11.1	11.1	33	15.6	15.9	15.1	15.2	15.2	15.3	33
Scotland	12.3	13.1	13.8	14.4	14.7	14.9	26	16.2	16.7	17.3	17.6	17.8	18.0	26
Singapore	12.6	14.5	14.6	15.4	15.8	16.0	16	15.4	16.9	17.3	17.9	19.0	19.2	19
Slovakia[1]	12.3	12.2	12.7	13.0	12.9	13.0	31	15.4	15.7	16.1	16.6	16.5	16.8	29
Spain	14.8	15.4	16.0	16.1	16.5	- - -	- - -	17.9	19.0	19.8	20.1	20.4	- - -	- - -
Sweden	14.3	15.3	16.0	16.4	16.7	16.9	8	17.9	19.0	19.6	19.9	20.0	20.1	7
Switzerland	14.4	15.3	16.1	16.8	16.9	17.2	3	17.9	19.4	20.2	20.6	20.7	21.0	4
United States	14.1	15.1	15.6	16.1	16.3	16.4	12	18.3	18.9	18.9	19.1	19.2	19.4	15

- - - Data not available.

[1]In 1993 Czechoslovakia was divided into two Nations, the Czech Republic and Slovakia. Data for years prior to 1993 are from the Czech and Slovak regions of Czechoslovakia.

[2]Until 1990 estimates refer to the Federal Republic of Germany; from 1995 onwards data refer to Germany after reunification.

NOTES: Rankings are from highest to lowest life expectancy (LE) for the most recent year available. Since calculation of LE estimates varies among countries, comparisons among them and their interpretation should be made with caution. See Appendix II, Life expectancy. Countries with the same LE receive the same rank. The country with the next lower LE is assigned the rank it would have received had the higher-ranked countries not been tied, i.e., skip a rank. Some estimates for selected countries and selected years were revised and differ from the previous edition of *Health, United States*.

SOURCES: Organization for Economic Cooperation and Development (OECD) Health Data 2004 3rd edition, A Comparative Analysis of 30 Countries, www.oecd.org/els/health/; European health for all database, World Health Organization Regional Office for Europe, www.who.dk/hfadb; Centers for Disease Control and Prevention, National Center for Health Statistics. Vital statistics of the United States (selected years). Public Health Service. Washington, DC. www.cdc.gov/nchs/fastats/lifexpec.htm; Puerto Rico: Commonwealth of Puerto Rico, Department of Health, Auxiliary Secretariat for Planning, Evaluation, Statistics, and Information Systems: Unpublished data; Singapore: Singapore Department of Statistics, Population Statistics Section, www.singstat.gov.sg/stats/singstat/internet.html; England and Wales, Northern Ireland, and Scotland: Government Actuary's Department, London www.gad.gov.uk; Hong Kong: Government of Hong Kong, Special Administrative Region, Department of Health, http://info.gov.hk/dh/index.htm; Costa Rica: Instituto Nacional de Estadística y Censos (INEC) y Centro Centroamericano de Población (CCP) http://ccp.ucr.ac.cr/observa/series/serie3.htm; Chile: Instituto Nacional de Estadísticas, Departamento de Demografía. Gobierno de Chile. Ministerio de Salud Departamento de Estadísticas e Información de Salud; Puerto Rico (1999–2001): Pan American Health Organization, Special Program for Health Analysis. Regional Initiative for Health Basic Data, Technical Information Health System, Washington, DC 2001. Cuba and Singapore (2000–2001): WHO Statistical Information System (WHOSIS) www3.who.int/whosis/core/core_select.cfm

Table 27. Life expectancy at birth, at 65 years of age, and at 75 years of age, according to race and sex: United States, selected years 1900–2002

[Data are based on death certificates]

Specified age and year	All races			White			Black or African American[1]		
	Both sexes	Male	Female	Both sexes	Male	Female	Both sexes	Male	Female
At birth				Remaining life expectancy in years					
1900[2,3]	47.3	46.3	48.3	47.6	46.6	48.7	33.0	32.5	33.5
1950[3]	68.2	65.6	71.1	69.1	66.5	72.2	60.8	59.1	62.9
1960[3]	69.7	66.6	73.1	70.6	67.4	74.1	63.6	61.1	66.3
1970	70.8	67.1	74.7	71.7	68.0	75.6	64.1	60.0	68.3
1980	73.7	70.0	77.4	74.4	70.7	78.1	68.1	63.8	72.5
1985	74.7	71.1	78.2	75.3	71.8	78.7	69.3	65.0	73.4
1990	75.4	71.8	78.8	76.1	72.7	79.4	69.1	64.5	73.6
1991	75.5	72.0	78.9	76.3	72.9	79.6	69.3	64.6	73.8
1992	75.8	72.3	79.1	76.5	73.2	79.8	69.6	65.0	73.9
1993	75.5	72.2	78.8	76.3	73.1	79.5	69.2	64.6	73.7
1994	75.7	72.4	79.0	76.5	73.3	79.6	69.5	64.9	73.9
1995	75.8	72.5	78.9	76.5	73.4	79.6	69.6	65.2	73.9
1996	76.1	73.1	79.1	76.8	73.9	79.7	70.2	66.1	74.2
1997	76.5	73.6	79.4	77.1	74.3	79.9	71.1	67.2	74.7
1998	76.7	73.8	79.5	77.3	74.5	80.0	71.3	67.6	74.8
1999	76.7	73.9	79.4	77.3	74.6	79.9	71.4	67.8	74.7
2000[4]	77.0	74.3	79.7	77.6	74.9	80.1	71.9	68.3	75.2
2001	77.2	74.4	79.8	77.7	75.0	80.2	72.2	68.6	75.5
2002	77.3	74.5	79.9	77.7	75.1	80.3	72.3	68.8	75.6
At 65 years									
1950[3]	13.9	12.8	15.0	- - -	12.8	15.1	13.9	12.9	14.9
1960[3]	14.3	12.8	15.8	14.4	12.9	15.9	13.9	12.7	15.1
1970	15.2	13.1	17.0	15.2	13.1	17.1	14.2	12.5	15.7
1980	16.4	14.1	18.3	16.5	14.2	18.4	15.1	13.0	16.8
1985	16.7	14.5	18.5	16.8	14.5	18.7	15.2	13.0	16.9
1990	17.2	15.1	18.9	17.3	15.2	19.1	15.4	13.2	17.2
1991	17.4	15.3	19.1	17.5	15.4	19.2	15.5	13.4	17.2
1992	17.5	15.4	19.2	17.6	15.5	19.3	15.7	13.5	17.4
1993	17.3	15.3	18.9	17.4	15.4	19.0	15.5	13.4	17.1
1994	17.4	15.5	19.0	17.5	15.6	19.1	15.7	13.6	17.2
1995	17.4	15.6	18.9	17.6	15.7	19.1	15.6	13.6	17.1
1996	17.5	15.7	19.0	17.6	15.8	19.1	15.8	13.9	17.2
1997	17.7	15.9	19.2	17.8	16.0	19.3	16.1	14.2	17.6
1998	17.8	16.0	19.2	17.8	16.1	19.3	16.1	14.3	17.4
1999	17.7	16.1	19.1	17.8	16.1	19.2	16.0	14.3	17.3
2000[4]	18.0	16.2	19.3	18.0	16.3	19.4	16.2	14.2	17.7
2001	18.1	16.4	19.4	18.2	16.5	19.5	16.4	14.4	17.9
2002	18.2	16.6	19.5	18.2	16.6	19.5	16.6	14.6	18.0
At 75 years									
1980	10.4	8.8	11.5	10.4	8.8	11.5	9.7	8.3	10.7
1985	10.6	9.0	11.7	10.6	9.0	11.7	10.1	8.7	11.1
1990	10.9	9.4	12.0	11.0	9.4	12.0	10.2	8.6	11.2
1991	11.1	9.5	12.1	11.1	9.5	12.1	10.2	8.7	11.2
1992	11.2	9.6	12.2	11.2	9.6	12.2	10.4	8.9	11.4
1993	10.9	9.5	11.9	11.0	9.5	12.0	10.2	8.7	11.1
1994	11.0	9.6	12.0	11.1	9.6	12.0	10.3	8.9	11.2
1995	11.0	9.7	11.9	11.1	9.7	12.0	10.2	8.8	11.1
1996	11.1	9.8	12.0	11.1	9.8	12.0	10.3	9.0	11.2
1997	11.2	9.9	12.1	11.2	9.9	12.1	10.7	9.3	11.5
1998	11.3	10.0	12.2	11.3	10.0	12.2	10.5	9.2	11.3
1999	11.2	10.0	12.1	11.2	10.0	12.1	10.4	9.2	11.1
2000[4]	11.4	10.1	12.3	11.4	10.1	12.3	10.7	9.2	11.6
2001	11.5	10.2	12.4	11.5	10.2	12.3	10.8	9.3	11.7
2002	11.5	10.3	12.4	11.5	10.3	12.3	10.9	9.5	11.7

- - - Data not available. [1]Data shown for 1900–60 are for the nonwhite population. [2]Death registration area only. The death registration area increased from 10 States and the District of Columbia in 1900 to the coterminous United States in 1933. See Appendix II, Registration area.

[3]Includes deaths of persons who were not residents of the 50 States and the District of Columbia.

[4]Life expectancies (LEs) for 2000 were revised and may differ from those shown previously. LEs for 2000 were computed using population counts from census 2000 and replace LEs for 2000 using 1990-based postcensal estimates.

NOTES: Populations for computing life expectancy for 1991–99 are 1990-based postcensal estimates of U.S. resident population. See Appendix I, Population Census and Population Estimates. In 1997 life table methodology was revised to construct complete life tables by single years of age that extend to age 100 (Anderson RN. Method for Constructing Complete Annual U.S. Life Tables. National Center for Health Statistics. Vital Health Stat 2(129). 1999). Previously abridged life tables were constructed for 5-year age groups ending with 85 years and over. Life table values for 2000 and later years were computed using a slight modification of the new life table method due to a change in the age detail of populations received from the U.S. Census Bureau. Data for additional years are available. See Appendix III.

SOURCES: Centers for Disease Control and Prevention, National Center for Health Statistics, National Vital Statistics System; Grove RD, Hetzel AM. Vital statistics rates in the United States, 1940–1960. Washington: U.S. Government Printing Office, 1968; life expectancy trend data available at www.cdc.gov/nchs/about/major/dvs/mortdata.htm; Kochanek KD, Murphy SL, Anderson RN, Scott C. Deaths: Final data for 2002. National vital statistics reports. Vol 53 no 5. Hyattsville, Maryland: National Center for Health Statistics. 2004.

This table will be updated on the Web. Go to www.cdc.gov/nchs/hus.htm.

Table 28 (page 1 of 2). Age-adjusted death rates, according to race, Hispanic origin, geographic division, and State: United States, average annual 1979–81, 1989–91, and 2000–2002

[Data are based on death certificates]

Geographic division and State	All persons			White	Black or African American	American Indian or Alaska Native	Asian or Pacific Islander	Hispanic or Latino[1]	White, not Hispanic or Latino
	1979–81	1989–91	2000–02	2000–02	2000–02	2000–02	2000–02	2000–02	2000–02
	Age-adjusted death rate per 100,000 population[2]								
United States	1,022.8	942.2	853.3	835.7	1,097.7	687.0	486.0	642.7	843.1
New England	979.9	882.4	798.8	798.8	895.1	*	374.6	555.7	795.3
Connecticut	961.5	857.5	773.0	764.1	918.5	*	321.0	580.4	756.5
Maine	1,002.9	918.7	847.9	847.3	773.1	*	494.8	*	845.3
Massachusetts	982.6	884.8	801.8	805.3	878.1	*	379.6	582.0	804.0
New Hampshire	982.3	891.7	796.2	798.4	796.2	*	373.3	392.7	785.8
Rhode Island	990.8	889.6	811.7	811.0	926.3	*	456.6	460.8	810.0
Vermont	990.2	908.6	800.5	803.3	*	*	*	*	805.2
Middle Atlantic	1,059.1	967.8	829.6	819.6	977.7	*	393.8	606.7	819.0
New Jersey	1,047.5	956.0	829.4	810.7	1,077.0	*	372.5	567.6	819.8
New York	1,051.8	973.7	797.2	797.9	870.5	*	401.7	608.0	791.0
Pennsylvania	1,076.4	963.4	873.3	851.2	1,157.9	*	393.9	734.0	850.0
East North Central	1,048.0	957.9	880.0	853.9	1,154.7	*	408.1	552.5	855.2
Illinois	1,063.7	973.8	863.9	829.3	1,163.1	*	413.1	535.2	835.7
Indiana	1,048.3	962.0	910.8	896.6	1,152.1	*	305.7	591.7	899.9
Michigan	1,050.2	966.0	884.0	847.6	1,161.8	*	397.5	658.5	841.5
Ohio	1,070.6	967.4	910.9	889.9	1,143.2	*	404.6	587.5	888.9
Wisconsin	956.4	879.1	807.6	795.3	1,098.9	*	478.7	350.3	798.9
West North Central	951.6	876.6	821.8	807.3	1,138.4	*	455.5	613.3	803.5
Iowa	919.9	848.2	781.4	779.1	1,085.6	*	477.1	631.2	779.2
Kansas	940.1	867.2	843.6	832.4	1,178.3	*	307.5	595.8	825.6
Minnesota	892.9	825.2	749.2	742.2	969.0	1,205.4	532.4	579.0	734.5
Missouri	1,033.7	952.4	914.2	892.5	1,167.9	*	421.3	735.4	892.7
Nebraska	930.6	867.9	799.9	789.7	1,112.3	1,199.8	439.7	554.0	787.3
North Dakota	922.4	818.4	761.8	745.3	*	1,438.4	*	*	724.4
South Dakota	941.9	846.4	786.0	749.9	*	1,471.0	*	*	751.6
South Atlantic	1,033.1	951.3	870.0	829.1	1,106.3	*	388.4	588.2	842.3
Delaware	1,069.7	1,001.9	872.2	843.8	1,061.5	*	388.1	707.1	843.7
District of Columbia	1,243.1	1,255.3	1,035.5	658.4	1,258.3	*	520.4	176.9	697.4
Florida	960.8	870.9	796.4	774.1	1,046.1	*	323.5	623.6	796.1
Georgia	1,094.3	1,037.4	958.9	913.4	1,136.7	*	410.2	366.5	919.9
Maryland	1,063.3	985.2	881.8	828.2	1,094.5	*	402.4	280.2	838.6
North Carolina	1,050.4	986.0	920.2	875.0	1,133.5	946.5	367.5	295.7	879.4
South Carolina	1,104.6	1,030.0	952.5	895.7	1,136.8	*	407.0	332.8	899.2
Virginia	1,054.0	963.1	867.0	833.7	1,085.6	*	441.2	490.4	836.4
West Virginia	1,100.3	1,031.5	998.8	999.6	1,119.6	*	*	342.7	1,002.2
East South Central	1,079.3	1,031.6	996.5	963.2	1,191.2	*	423.0	409.0	965.8
Alabama	1,091.2	1,037.9	996.7	956.8	1,161.5	*	332.0	315.2	961.0
Kentucky	1,088.9	1,024.5	991.7	984.4	1,176.0	*	427.8	843.7	984.1
Mississippi	1,108.7	1,071.4	1,035.2	972.1	1,194.8	*	499.1	221.9	975.3
Tennessee	1,045.5	1,011.8	982.0	948.9	1,236.8	*	443.5	331.7	952.2
West South Central	1,036.8	974.9	915.3	891.2	1,166.6	*	432.7	736.1	912.6
Arkansas	1,017.0	996.3	961.8	935.7	1,191.2	*	609.0	244.2	943.5
Louisiana	1,132.6	1,074.6	1,002.7	933.6	1,205.9	*	492.2	539.0	940.0
Oklahoma	1,025.6	961.4	970.8	969.2	1,165.7	*	455.9	731.0	972.9
Texas	1,014.9	947.6	877.4	861.0	1,140.2	*	418.3	744.5	884.4
Mountain	961.8	878.2	810.1	805.0	990.8	928.6	529.0	745.4	805.3
Arizona	951.5	873.5	795.3	786.0	974.8	979.9	462.7	758.3	782.5
Colorado	941.1	856.1	787.0	787.0	957.8	520.2	499.3	763.7	782.9
Idaho	936.7	856.6	797.8	796.1	1,163.2	960.8	579.1	607.6	797.8
Montana	1,013.6	890.2	842.8	825.0	1,091.9	1,271.6	*	725.7	821.9
Nevada	1,077.4	1,017.4	915.9	920.3	1,082.4	706.0	560.8	532.5	952.3
New Mexico	967.1	891.9	815.0	808.5	881.7	894.7	537.3	795.7	799.8
Utah	924.9	823.2	780.2	779.3	1,020.8	804.8	673.4	642.5	781.8
Wyoming	1,016.1	897.4	854.9	849.1	822.6	1,266.5	*	800.8	848.8

See footnotes at end of table.

This table will be updated on the Web. Go to www.cdc.gov/nchs/hus.htm.

Table 28 (page 2 of 2). Age-adjusted death rates, according to race, Hispanic origin, geographic division, and State: United States, average annual 1979–81, 1989–91, and 2000–2002

[Data are based on death certificates]

Geographic division and State	All persons			White	Black or African American	American Indian or Alaska Native	Asian or Pacific Islander	Hispanic or Latino[1]	White, not Hispanic or Latino
	1979–81	1989–91	2000–02	2000–02	2000–02	2000–02	2000–02	2000–02	2000–02
	Age-adjusted death rate per 100,000 population[2]								
Pacific	966.5	900.1	776.1	791.6	1,042.5	*	536.4	612.1	813.1
Alaska	1,087.4	944.6	825.4	780.1	841.8	1,143.8	551.6	702.8	781.2
California	975.5	911.0	770.9	786.5	1,053.6	*	506.1	611.8	815.1
Hawaii	801.2	752.2	660.1	686.6	427.7	*	652.4	1,107.2	674.0
Oregon	953.9	893.0	828.8	831.7	1,038.2	*	504.3	496.0	837.8
Washington	947.7	869.4	792.3	796.4	982.5	943.4	534.1	535.4	799.9

* Data for States with population under 10,000 in the middle year of a 3-year period or fewer than 50 deaths for the 3-year period are considered unreliable and are not shown. Data for American Indian or Alaska Native in States with more than 10 percent misclassification of American Indian or Alaska Native deaths on death certificates or without information on misclassification are also not shown. (Support Services International, Inc. Methodology for adjusting IHS mortality data for miscoding race-ethnicity of American Indians and Alaska Natives on State death certificates. Report submitted to Indian Health Service. 1996.) Division death rates for American Indian or Alaska Native are not shown when any State within the division does not meet reliability criteria.

[1]Caution should be used when comparing death rates by Hispanic origin and race among States. Estimates of death rates may be affected by several factors including possible misreporting of race and Hispanic origin on the death certificate, migration patterns between United States and country of origin for persons who were born outside the United States, and possible biases in population estimates. See Appendix I, National Vital Statistics System, Mortality File and Appendix II, Hispanic origin; Race.

[2]Average annual death rates, age-adjusted using the year 2000 standard population. See Appendix II, Age adjustment. Denominators for rates are resident population estimates for the middle year of each 3-year period, multiplied by 3. The 2001 populations used to compute rates for 2000–02 are based on census 2000. See Appendix I, Population Census and Population Estimates.

NOTES: The race groups, white, black, American Indian or Alaska Native, and Asian or Pacific Islander, include persons of Hispanic and non-Hispanic origin. Persons of Hispanic origin may be of any race. Death rates for the American Indian or Alaska Native and Asian or Pacific Islander populations are known to be underestimated. See Appendix II, Race, for a discussion of sources of bias in death rates by race and Hispanic origin.

SOURCES: Centers for Disease Control and Prevention, National Center for Health Statistics, National Vital Statistics System; numerator data from annual mortality files; denominator data from State population estimates prepared by the U.S. Bureau of the Census: 1980 from April 1, 1980 MARS Census File; 1990 from April 1, 1990 MARS Census File; 2001 from National Center for Health Statistics. Estimates of the July 1, 2001, resident populations of the United States by State and county, race, age, sex, and Hispanic origin, prepared under a collaborative arrangement with the U.S. Census Bureau. Available at: www.cdc.gov/nchs/about/major/dvs/popbridge/popbridge.htm. 2003.

This table will be updated on the Web. Go to www.cdc.gov/nchs/hus.htm.

Table 29 (page 1 of 4). Age-adjusted death rates for selected causes of death, according to sex, race, and Hispanic origin: United States, selected years 1950–2002

[Data are based on death certificates]

Sex, race, Hispanic origin, and cause of death[1]	1950[2]	1960[2]	1970	1980	1990	1995	2000[3]	2001	2002
All persons	Age-adjusted death rate per 100,000 population[4]								
All causes	1,446.0	1,339.2	1,222.6	1,039.1	938.7	909.8	869.0	854.5	845.3
Diseases of heart	586.8	559.0	492.7	412.1	321.8	293.4	257.6	247.8	240.8
Ischemic heart disease	---	---	---	345.2	249.6	219.7	186.8	177.8	170.8
Cerebrovascular diseases	180.7	177.9	147.7	96.2	65.3	63.1	60.9	57.9	56.2
Malignant neoplasms	193.9	193.9	198.6	207.9	216.0	209.9	199.6	196.0	193.5
Trachea, bronchus, and lung	15.0	24.1	37.1	49.9	59.3	58.4	56.1	55.3	54.9
Colon, rectum, and anus	---	30.3	28.9	27.4	24.5	22.5	20.8	20.1	19.7
Prostate[5]	28.6	28.7	28.8	32.8	38.4	37.0	30.4	29.1	27.9
Breast[6]	31.9	31.7	32.1	31.9	33.3	30.5	26.8	26.0	25.6
Chronic lower respiratory diseases	---	---	---	28.3	37.2	40.1	44.2	43.7	43.5
Influenza and pneumonia	48.1	53.7	41.7	31.4	36.8	33.4	23.7	22.0	22.6
Chronic liver disease and cirrhosis	11.3	13.3	17.8	15.1	11.1	9.9	9.5	9.5	9.4
Diabetes mellitus	23.1	22.5	24.3	18.1	20.7	23.2	25.0	25.3	25.4
Human immunodeficiency virus (HIV) disease	---	---	---	---	10.2	16.2	5.2	5.0	4.9
Unintentional injuries	78.0	62.3	60.1	46.4	36.3	34.4	34.9	35.7	36.9
Motor vehicle-related injuries	24.6	23.1	27.6	22.3	18.5	16.3	15.4	15.3	15.7
Suicide[7]	13.2	12.5	13.1	12.2	12.5	11.8	10.4	10.7	10.9
Homicide[7]	5.1	5.0	8.8	10.4	9.4	8.3	5.9	7.1	6.1
Male									
All causes	1,674.2	1,609.0	1,542.1	1,348.1	1,202.8	1,143.9	1,053.8	1,029.1	1,013.7
Diseases of heart	697.0	687.6	634.0	538.9	412.4	371.0	320.0	305.4	297.4
Ischemic heart disease	---	---	---	459.7	328.2	286.5	241.4	228.5	220.4
Cerebrovascular diseases	186.4	186.1	157.4	102.2	68.5	65.9	62.4	59.0	56.5
Malignant neoplasms	208.1	225.1	247.6	271.2	280.4	267.5	248.9	243.7	238.9
Trachea, bronchus, and lung	24.6	43.6	67.5	85.2	91.1	84.2	76.7	75.2	73.2
Colon, rectum, and anus	---	31.8	32.3	32.8	30.4	27.4	25.1	24.2	23.7
Prostate	28.6	28.7	28.8	32.8	38.4	37.0	30.4	29.1	27.9
Chronic lower respiratory diseases	---	---	---	49.9	55.4	54.8	55.8	54.0	53.5
Influenza and pneumonia	55.0	65.8	54.0	42.1	47.8	42.8	28.9	26.6	27.0
Chronic liver disease and cirrhosis	15.0	18.5	24.8	21.3	15.9	14.2	13.4	13.2	12.9
Diabetes mellitus	18.8	19.9	23.0	18.1	21.7	25.0	27.8	28.1	28.6
Human immunodeficiency virus (HIV) disease	---	---	---	---	18.5	27.3	7.9	7.5	7.4
Unintentional injuries	101.8	85.5	87.4	69.0	52.9	49.6	49.3	50.2	51.5
Motor vehicle-related injuries	38.5	35.4	41.5	33.6	26.5	22.8	21.7	21.8	22.1
Suicide[7]	21.2	20.0	19.8	19.9	21.5	20.3	17.7	18.2	18.4
Homicide[7]	7.9	7.5	14.3	16.6	14.8	12.8	9.0	10.8	9.4
Female									
All causes	1,236.0	1,105.3	971.4	817.9	750.9	739.4	731.4	721.8	715.2
Diseases of heart	484.7	447.0	381.6	320.8	257.0	236.6	210.9	203.9	197.2
Ischemic heart disease	---	---	---	263.1	193.9	171.3	146.5	139.9	133.6
Cerebrovascular diseases	175.8	170.7	140.0	91.7	62.6	60.5	59.1	56.4	55.2
Malignant neoplasms	182.3	168.7	163.2	166.7	175.7	173.6	167.6	164.7	163.1
Trachea, bronchus, and lung	5.8	7.5	13.1	24.4	37.1	40.4	41.3	41.0	41.6
Colon, rectum, and anus	---	29.1	26.5	23.8	20.6	19.1	17.7	17.2	16.7
Breast	31.9	31.7	32.1	31.9	33.3	30.5	26.8	26.0	25.6
Chronic lower respiratory diseases	---	---	---	14.9	26.6	31.8	37.4	37.6	37.4
Influenza and pneumonia	41.9	43.8	32.7	25.1	30.5	28.1	20.7	19.2	19.9
Chronic liver disease and cirrhosis	7.8	8.7	11.9	9.9	7.1	6.2	6.2	6.2	6.3
Diabetes mellitus	27.0	24.7	25.1	18.0	19.9	21.8	23.0	23.1	23.0
Human immunodeficiency virus (HIV) disease	---	---	---	---	2.2	5.3	2.5	2.5	2.5
Unintentional injuries	54.0	40.0	35.1	26.1	21.5	21.0	22.0	22.5	23.5
Motor vehicle-related injuries	11.5	11.7	14.9	11.8	11.0	10.3	9.5	9.3	9.6
Suicide[7]	5.6	5.6	7.4	5.7	4.8	4.3	4.0	4.0	4.2
Homicide[7]	2.4	2.6	3.7	4.4	4.0	3.7	2.8	3.3	2.8

See footnotes at end of table.

This table will be updated on the Web. Go to www.cdc.gov/nchs/hus.htm.

Table 29 (page 2 of 4). Age-adjusted death rates for selected causes of death, according to sex, race, and Hispanic origin: United States, selected years 1950–2002

[Data are based on death certificates]

Sex, race, Hispanic origin, and cause of death[1]	1950[2]	1960[2]	1970	1980	1990	1995	2000[3]	2001	2002
White[8]	Age-adjusted death rate per 100,000 population[4]								
All causes	1,410.8	1,311.3	1,193.3	1,012.7	909.8	882.3	849.8	836.5	829.0
Diseases of heart	584.8	559.0	492.2	409.4	317.0	288.6	253.4	243.5	236.7
Ischemic heart disease	- - -	- - -	- - -	347.6	249.7	219.1	185.6	176.5	169.8
Cerebrovascular diseases	175.5	172.7	143.5	93.2	62.8	60.7	58.8	55.8	54.2
Malignant neoplasms	194.6	193.1	196.7	204.2	211.6	206.2	197.2	193.9	191.7
Trachea, bronchus, and lung	15.2	24.0	36.7	49.2	58.6	58.1	56.2	55.6	55.3
Colon, rectum, and anus	- - -	30.9	29.2	27.4	24.1	22.0	20.3	19.6	19.2
Prostate[5]	28.4	27.7	27.4	30.5	35.5	34.2	27.8	26.6	25.7
Breast[6]	32.4	32.0	32.5	32.1	33.2	30.1	26.3	25.5	25.0
Chronic lower respiratory diseases	- - -	- - -	- - -	29.3	38.3	41.5	46.0	45.6	45.4
Influenza and pneumonia	44.8	50.4	39.8	30.9	36.4	33.0	23.5	21.7	22.6
Chronic liver disease and cirrhosis	11.5	13.2	16.6	13.9	10.5	9.7	9.6	9.6	9.6
Diabetes mellitus	22.9	21.7	22.9	16.7	18.8	20.9	22.8	23.0	23.1
Human immunodeficiency virus (HIV) disease	- - -	- - -	- - -	- - -	8.3	11.4	2.8	2.6	2.6
Unintentional injuries	77.0	60.4	57.8	45.3	35.5	33.9	35.1	36.0	37.5
Motor vehicle-related injuries	24.4	22.9	27.1	22.6	18.5	16.3	15.6	15.6	16.0
Suicide[7]	13.9	13.1	13.8	13.0	13.4	12.6	11.3	11.7	12.0
Homicide[7]	2.6	2.7	4.7	6.7	5.5	5.0	3.6	4.9	3.7
Black or African American[8]									
All causes	1,722.1	1,577.5	1,518.1	1,314.8	1,250.3	1,213.9	1,121.4	1,101.2	1,083.3
Diseases of heart	586.7	548.3	512.0	455.3	391.5	363.8	324.8	316.9	308.4
Ischemic heart disease	- - -	- - -	- - -	334.5	267.0	244.9	218.3	211.6	203.0
Cerebrovascular diseases	233.6	235.2	197.1	129.1	91.6	86.9	81.9	78.8	76.3
Malignant neoplasms	176.4	199.1	225.3	256.4	279.5	267.7	248.5	243.1	238.8
Trachea, bronchus, and lung	11.1	23.7	41.3	59.7	72.4	69.0	64.0	62.5	61.9
Colon, rectum, and anus	- - -	22.8	26.1	28.3	30.6	29.3	28.2	27.6	26.8
Prostate[5]	30.9	41.2	48.5	61.1	77.0	76.6	68.1	66.1	62.0
Breast[6]	25.3	27.9	28.9	31.7	38.1	38.0	34.5	34.4	34.0
Chronic lower respiratory diseases	- - -	- - -	- - -	19.2	28.1	30.1	31.6	30.9	31.2
Influenza and pneumonia	76.7	81.1	57.2	34.4	39.4	36.4	25.6	24.1	24.0
Chronic liver disease and cirrhosis	9.0	13.6	28.1	25.0	16.5	12.0	9.4	9.3	8.5
Diabetes mellitus	23.5	30.9	38.8	32.7	40.5	46.7	49.5	49.2	49.5
Human immunodeficiency virus (HIV) disease	- - -	- - -	- - -	- - -	26.7	54.2	23.3	22.8	22.5
Unintentional injuries	79.9	74.0	78.3	57.6	43.8	41.0	37.7	37.6	36.9
Motor vehicle-related injuries	26.0	24.2	31.1	20.2	18.8	16.7	15.7	15.4	15.0
Suicide[7]	4.5	5.0	6.2	6.5	7.1	6.8	5.5	5.5	5.3
Homicide[7]	28.3	26.0	44.0	39.0	36.3	29.7	20.5	21.2	21.0
American Indian or Alaska Native[8]									
All causes	- - -	- - -	- - -	867.0	716.3	771.2	709.3	686.7	677.4
Diseases of heart	- - -	- - -	- - -	240.6	200.6	204.6	178.2	159.6	157.4
Ischemic heart disease	- - -	- - -	- - -	173.6	139.1	141.4	129.1	114.0	114.0
Cerebrovascular diseases	- - -	- - -	- - -	57.8	40.7	48.6	45.0	41.3	37.5
Malignant neoplasms	- - -	- - -	- - -	113.7	121.8	138.2	127.8	131.0	125.4
Trachea, bronchus, and lung	- - -	- - -	- - -	20.7	30.9	37.4	32.3	34.2	33.1
Colon, rectum, and anus	- - -	- - -	- - -	9.5	12.0	14.9	13.4	12.0	14.2
Prostate[5]	- - -	- - -	- - -	20.7	17.8	21.7	19.6	19.0	15.2
Breast[6]	- - -	- - -	- - -	10.8	13.7	15.0	13.6	11.8	13.8
Chronic lower respiratory diseases	- - -	- - -	- - -	14.2	25.4	27.6	32.8	30.0	30.1
Influenza and pneumonia	- - -	- - -	- - -	44.4	36.1	36.1	22.3	22.5	20.4
Chronic liver disease and cirrhosis	- - -	- - -	- - -	45.3	24.1	27.4	24.3	22.6	22.8
Diabetes mellitus	- - -	- - -	- - -	29.6	34.1	45.9	41.5	40.4	43.2
Human immunodeficiency virus (HIV) disease	- - -	- - -	- - -	- - -	1.8	6.5	2.2	2.7	2.2
Unintentional injuries	- - -	- - -	- - -	99.0	62.6	55.3	51.3	51.3	53.8
Motor vehicle-related injuries	- - -	- - -	- - -	54.5	32.5	29.1	27.3	25.9	28.8
Suicide[7]	- - -	- - -	- - -	11.9	11.7	10.6	9.8	10.5	10.2
Homicide[7]	- - -	- - -	- - -	15.5	10.4	9.9	6.8	6.8	8.4

See footnotes at end of table.

This table will be updated on the Web. Go to www.cdc.gov/nchs/hus.htm.

Table 29 (page 3 of 4). Age-adjusted death rates for selected causes of death, according to sex, race, and Hispanic origin: United States, selected years 1950–2002

[Data are based on death certificates]

Sex, race, Hispanic origin, and cause of death[1]	1950[2]	1960[2]	1970	1980	1990	1995	2000[3]	2001	2002
Asian or Pacific Islander[8]			Age-adjusted death rate per 100,000 population[4]						
All causes	---	---	---	589.9	582.0	554.8	506.4	492.1	474.4
Diseases of heart	---	---	---	202.1	181.7	171.3	146.0	137.6	134.6
Ischemic heart disease	---	---	---	168.2	139.6	128.0	109.6	103.0	98.6
Cerebrovascular diseases	---	---	---	66.1	56.9	55.2	52.9	51.2	47.7
Malignant neoplasms	---	---	---	126.1	134.2	131.8	121.9	119.5	113.6
Trachea, bronchus, and lung	---	---	---	28.4	30.2	29.9	28.1	28.2	25.6
Colon, rectum, and anus	---	---	---	16.4	14.4	14.0	12.7	13.2	12.5
Prostate[5]	---	---	---	10.2	16.8	18.0	12.5	11.6	10.2
Breast[6]	---	---	---	11.9	13.7	13.9	12.3	12.9	12.8
Chronic lower respiratory diseases	---	---	---	12.9	19.4	19.3	18.6	17.7	15.8
Influenza and pneumonia	---	---	---	24.0	31.4	29.1	19.7	19.0	17.5
Chronic liver disease and cirrhosis	---	---	---	6.1	5.2	3.9	3.5	3.5	3.2
Diabetes mellitus	---	---	---	12.6	14.6	16.8	16.4	16.9	17.4
Human immunodeficiency virus (HIV) disease	---	---	---	---	2.2	3.2	0.6	0.7	0.8
Unintentional injuries	---	---	---	27.0	23.9	20.2	17.9	17.4	17.9
Motor vehicle-related injuries	---	---	---	13.9	14.0	11.4	8.6	8.1	8.4
Suicide[7]	---	---	---	7.8	6.7	6.7	5.5	5.4	5.4
Homicide[7]	---	---	---	5.9	5.0	4.7	3.0	4.2	2.9
Hispanic or Latino[8,9]									
All causes	---	---	---	---	692.0	700.2	665.7	658.7	629.3
Diseases of heart	---	---	---	---	217.1	211.0	196.0	192.2	180.5
Ischemic heart disease	---	---	---	---	173.3	166.4	153.2	149.9	138.3
Cerebrovascular diseases	---	---	---	---	45.2	46.3	46.4	44.9	41.3
Malignant neoplasms	---	---	---	---	136.8	138.5	134.9	132.3	128.4
Trachea, bronchus, and lung	---	---	---	---	26.5	25.9	24.8	23.8	23.7
Colon, rectum, and anus	---	---	---	---	14.7	14.1	14.1	14.1	13.7
Prostate[5]	---	---	---	---	23.3	27.4	21.6	23.5	21.6
Breast[6]	---	---	---	---	19.5	18.7	16.9	16.3	15.5
Chronic lower respiratory diseases	---	---	---	---	19.3	22.6	21.1	20.7	20.6
Influenza and pneumonia	---	---	---	---	29.7	26.2	20.6	20.5	19.2
Chronic liver disease and cirrhosis	---	---	---	---	18.3	17.4	16.5	15.8	15.4
Diabetes mellitus	---	---	---	---	28.2	35.7	36.9	36.7	35.6
Human immunodeficiency virus (HIV) disease	---	---	---	---	16.3	24.9	6.7	6.2	5.8
Unintentional injuries	---	---	---	---	34.6	32.2	30.1	30.7	30.7
Motor vehicle-related injuries	---	---	---	---	19.5	16.4	14.7	15.0	15.2
Suicide[7]	---	---	---	---	7.8	7.2	5.9	5.7	5.7
Homicide[7]	---	---	---	---	16.2	12.5	7.5	8.3	7.3

See footnotes at end of table.

This table will be updated on the Web. Go to www.cdc.gov/nchs/hus.htm.

Table 29 (page 4 of 4). Age-adjusted death rates for selected causes of death, according to sex, race, and Hispanic origin: United States, selected years 1950–2002

[Data are based on death certificates]

Sex, race, Hispanic origin, and cause of death[1]	*1950*[2]	*1960*[2]	*1970*	*1980*	*1990*	*1995*	*2000*[3]	*2001*	*2002*
White, not Hispanic or Latino[9]				Age-adjusted death rate per 100,000 population[4]					
All causes	---	---	---	---	914.5	882.3	855.5	842.9	837.5
Diseases of heart	---	---	---	---	319.7	289.9	255.5	245.6	239.2
Ischemic heart disease	---	---	---	---	251.9	219.9	186.6	177.5	171.0
Cerebrovascular diseases	---	---	---	---	63.5	60.8	59.0	56.0	54.6
Malignant neoplasms	---	---	---	---	215.4	208.9	200.6	197.4	195.6
Trachea, bronchus, and lung	---	---	---	---	60.3	59.6	58.2	57.7	57.5
Colon, rectum, and anus	---	---	---	---	24.6	22.3	20.5	19.9	19.5
Prostate[5]	---	---	---	---	36.1	34.4	28.0	26.7	25.8
Breast[6]	---	---	---	---	33.9	30.6	26.8	26.0	25.6
Chronic lower respiratory diseases	---	---	---	---	39.2	42.1	47.2	47.0	46.9
Influenza and pneumonia	---	---	---	---	36.5	33.0	23.5	21.7	22.6
Chronic liver disease and cirrhosis	---	---	---	---	9.9	9.0	9.0	9.0	9.0
Diabetes mellitus	---	---	---	---	18.3	20.1	21.8	22.1	22.2
Human immunodeficiency virus (HIV) disease	---	---	---	---	7.4	9.8	2.2	2.1	2.1
Unintentional injuries	---	---	---	---	35.0	33.4	35.3	36.2	38.0
Motor vehicle-related injuries	---	---	---	---	18.2	16.1	15.6	15.5	16.0
Suicide[7]	---	---	---	---	13.8	13.1	12.0	12.5	12.9
Homicide[7]	---	---	---	---	4.0	3.6	2.8	4.0	2.8

--- Data not available.
[1]Underlying cause of death code numbers are based on the applicable revision of the *International Classification of Diseases* (ICD) for data years shown. For the period 1980–98, causes were coded using ICD–9 codes that are most nearly comparable with the 113 cause list for ICD–10. See Appendix II, tables IV and V.
[2]Includes deaths of persons who were not residents of the 50 States and the District of Columbia.
[3]Starting with 1999 data, cause of death is coded according to ICD–10. See Appendix II, Comparability ratio and tables V and VI.
[4]Age-adjusted rates are calculated using the year 2000 standard population. See Appendix II, Age adjustment.
[5]Rate for male population only.
[6]Rate for female population only.
[7]Figures for 2001 include September 11-related deaths for which death certificates were filed as of October 24, 2002. See Appendix II, table V for terrorism-related ICD–10 codes.
[8]The race groups, white, black, Asian or Pacific Islander, and American Indian or Alaska Native, include persons of Hispanic and non-Hispanic origin. Persons of Hispanic origin may be of any race. Death rates for the American Indian or Alaska Native and Asian or Pacific Islander populations are known to be underestimated. See Appendix II, Race, for a discussion of sources of bias in death rates by race and Hispanic origin.
[9]Prior to 1997, excludes data from States lacking an Hispanic-origin item on the death certificate. See Appendix II, Hispanic origin.

NOTES: Starting with *Health, United States, 2003*, rates for 1991–99 were revised using intercensal population estimates based on census 2000. Rates for 2000 were revised based on census 2000 counts. Rates for 2001 and 2002 were computed using 2000-based postcensal estimates. See Appendix I, Population Census and Population Estimates. Data for additional years are available. See Appendix III.

SOURCES: Centers for Disease Control and Prevention, National Center for Health Statistics, National Vital Statistics System; Grove RD, Hetzel AM. Vital statistics rates in the United States, 1940–1960. Washington: U.S. Government Printing Office. 1968; numerator data from National Vital Statistics System, annual mortality files; denominator data from national population estimates for race groups from table 1 and unpublished Hispanic population estimates for 1985–96 prepared by the Housing and Household Economic Statistics Division, U.S. Bureau of the Census; additional mortality tables available at www.cdc.gov/nchs/datawh/statab/unpubd/mortabs.htm; Kochanek KD, Murphy SL, Anderson RN, Scott C. Deaths: Final data for 2002. National vital statistics reports. Vol 53 no 5. Hyattsville, Maryland: National Center for Health Statistics. 2004.

This table will be updated on the Web. Go to www.cdc.gov/nchs/hus.htm.

Table 30 (page 1 of 4). Years of potential life lost before age 75 for selected causes of death, according to sex, race, and Hispanic origin: United States, selected years 1980–2002

[Data are based on death certificates]

Sex, race, Hispanic origin, and cause of death[2]	Crude	Age adjusted[1]					
	2002	1980	1990	1995	2000[3]	2001	2002
All persons	Years lost before age 75 per 100,000 population under 75 years of age						
All causes	7,563.2	10,448.4	9,085.5	8,626.2	7,578.1	7,531.2	7,499.6
Diseases of heart	1,226.7	2,238.7	1,617.7	1,475.4	1,253.0	1,221.1	1,212.7
Ischemic heart disease	802.5	1,729.3	1,153.6	1,013.2	841.8	809.7	792.0
Cerebrovascular diseases	209.8	357.5	259.6	246.5	223.3	211.9	208.1
Malignant neoplasms	1,644.7	2,108.8	2,003.8	1,841.6	1,674.1	1,651.7	1,622.7
Trachea, bronchus, and lung	430.4	548.5	561.4	497.3	443.1	431.2	423.4
Colorectal	143.0	190.0	164.7	152.0	141.9	142.4	141.0
Prostate[4]	56.9	84.9	96.8	83.5	63.6	61.8	60.1
Breast[5]	328.4	463.2	451.6	398.6	332.6	328.1	316.8
Chronic lower respiratory diseases	185.9	169.1	187.4	190.4	188.1	185.8	184.5
Influenza and pneumonia	83.2	160.2	141.5	126.9	87.1	82.3	82.7
Chronic liver disease and cirrhosis	162.3	300.3	196.9	173.7	164.1	164.7	160.5
Diabetes mellitus	186.5	134.4	155.9	174.7	178.4	180.5	184.3
Human immunodeficiency virus (HIV) disease	160.8	- - -	383.8	595.3	174.6	167.8	161.8
Unintentional injuries	1,082.2	1,543.5	1,162.1	1,057.2	1,026.5	1,036.8	1,079.2
Motor vehicle-related injuries	588.9	912.9	716.4	616.3	574.3	572.5	585.8
Suicide[6]	348.2	392.0	393.1	384.7	334.5	342.6	346.7
Homicide[6]	276.1	425.5	417.4	378.6	266.5	311.0	274.4
Male							
All causes	9,429.3	13,777.2	11,973.5	11,289.2	9,572.2	9,507.1	9,470.0
Diseases of heart	1,675.5	3,352.1	2,356.0	2,117.4	1,766.0	1,708.3	1,706.9
Ischemic heart disease	1,154.6	2,715.1	1,766.3	1,531.5	1,255.4	1,201.8	1,179.6
Cerebrovascular diseases	222.2	396.7	286.6	276.9	244.6	233.5	227.6
Malignant neoplasms	1,720.0	2,360.8	2,214.6	2,008.5	1,810.8	1,782.4	1,754.2
Trachea, bronchus, and lung	507.3	821.1	764.8	645.6	554.9	535.9	520.5
Colorectal	164.8	214.9	194.3	179.4	167.3	166.6	168.2
Prostate	56.9	84.9	96.8	83.5	63.6	61.8	60.1
Chronic lower respiratory diseases	193.3	235.1	224.8	213.1	206.0	200.7	200.7
Influenza and pneumonia	95.7	202.5	180.0	155.7	102.8	96.9	97.3
Chronic liver disease and cirrhosis	224.8	415.0	283.9	254.8	236.9	233.6	226.6
Diabetes mellitus	213.3	140.4	170.4	194.6	203.8	209.6	217.2
Human immunodeficiency virus (HIV) disease	234.4	- - -	686.2	991.2	258.9	247.7	237.0
Unintentional injuries	1,561.1	2,342.7	1,715.1	1,531.6	1,475.6	1,490.1	1,542.2
Motor vehicle-related injuries	832.3	1,359.7	1,018.4	851.1	796.4	803.5	817.2
Suicide[6]	560.6	605.6	634.8	628.4	539.1	552.3	555.7
Homicide[6]	434.8	675.0	658.0	589.6	410.5	480.5	425.0
Female							
All causes	5,706.1	7,350.3	6,333.1	6,057.5	5,644.6	5,609.2	5,580.0
Diseases of heart	780.1	1,246.0	948.5	883.9	774.6	765.4	748.8
Ischemic heart disease	452.0	852.1	600.3	537.8	457.6	444.3	430.2
Cerebrovascular diseases	197.4	324.0	235.9	218.7	203.9	192.1	190.3
Malignant neoplasms	1,569.7	1,896.8	1,826.6	1,698.9	1,555.3	1,538.4	1,507.7
Trachea, bronchus, and lung	353.9	310.4	382.2	365.2	342.1	336.6	335.4
Colorectal	121.3	168.7	138.7	127.5	118.7	120.4	115.9
Breast	328.4	463.2	451.6	398.6	332.6	328.1	316.8
Chronic lower respiratory diseases	178.6	114.0	155.9	171.0	172.3	172.8	170.0
Influenza and pneumonia	70.7	122.0	106.2	100.2	72.3	68.7	69.1
Chronic liver disease and cirrhosis	100.1	194.5	115.1	96.6	94.5	98.8	97.4
Diabetes mellitus	159.8	128.5	142.3	155.9	154.4	153.0	153.1
Human immunodeficiency virus (HIV) disease	87.5	- - -	87.8	205.7	92.0	89.4	88.1
Unintentional injuries	605.7	755.3	607.4	580.1	573.2	578.3	610.3
Motor vehicle-related injuries	346.6	470.4	411.6	378.4	348.5	337.2	349.8
Suicide[6]	136.7	184.2	153.3	140.8	129.1	131.9	136.6
Homicide[6]	118.1	181.3	174.3	163.2	118.9	137.4	119.6

See footnotes at end of table.

This table will be updated on the Web. Go to www.cdc.gov/nchs/hus.htm.

Table 30 (page 2 of 4). Years of potential life lost before age 75 for selected causes of death, according to sex, race, and Hispanic origin: United States, selected years 1980–2002

[Data are based on death certificates]

Sex, race, Hispanic origin, and cause of death[2]	Crude	Age adjusted[1]					
	2002	1980	1990	1995	2000[3]	2001	2002
	Years lost before age 75 per 100,000 population under 75 years of age						
White[7]							
All causes	7,117.6	9,554.1	8,159.5	7,744.9	6,949.5	6,941.6	6,936.6
Diseases of heart	1,168.3	2,100.8	1,490.3	1,353.0	1,149.4	1,115.0	1,111.8
Ischemic heart disease	803.1	1,682.7	1,113.4	975.2	805.3	773.0	759.5
Cerebrovascular diseases	181.4	300.7	213.1	205.2	187.1	175.6	173.5
Malignant neoplasms	1,665.9	2,035.9	1,929.3	1,780.5	1,627.8	1,610.2	1,582.8
Trachea, bronchus, and lung	446.3	529.9	544.2	487.1	436.3	427.5	418.5
Colorectal	141.6	186.8	157.8	145.0	134.1	135.0	134.0
Prostate[4]	51.6	74.8	86.6	73.0	54.3	53.1	51.3
Breast[5]	318.8	460.2	441.7	381.5	315.6	309.6	297.5
Chronic lower respiratory diseases	194.2	165.4	182.3	185.7	185.3	184.7	183.5
Influenza and pneumonia	77.4	130.8	116.9	108.3	77.7	72.7	75.1
Chronic liver disease and cirrhosis	169.4	257.3	175.8	164.6	162.7	164.4	162.9
Diabetes mellitus	168.3	115.7	133.7	149.4	155.6	156.2	160.3
Human immunodeficiency virus (HIV) disease	84.8	---	309.0	422.6	94.7	88.4	84.7
Unintentional injuries	1,095.5	1,520.4	1,139.7	1,040.9	1,031.8	1,049.0	1,101.6
Motor vehicle-related injuries	599.7	939.9	726.7	623.6	586.1	585.1	604.0
Suicide[6]	381.2	414.5	417.7	411.6	362.0	373.5	380.1
Homicide[6]	158.0	271.7	234.9	220.2	156.6	204.0	159.7
Black or African American[7]							
All causes	11,640.8	17,873.4	16,593.0	15,809.7	12,897.1	12,579.7	12,401.0
Diseases of heart	1,869.2	3,619.9	2,891.8	2,681.8	2,275.2	2,248.9	2,212.8
Ischemic heart disease	992.5	2,305.1	1,676.1	1,510.2	1,300.1	1,260.6	1,218.7
Cerebrovascular diseases	399.3	883.2	656.4	583.6	507.0	491.3	474.1
Malignant neoplasms	1,834.1	2,946.1	2,894.8	2,597.1	2,294.7	2,228.4	2,196.6
Trachea, bronchus, and lung	451.8	776.0	811.3	683.0	593.0	557.5	561.9
Colorectal	175.4	232.3	241.8	226.9	222.4	219.6	213.7
Prostate[4]	107.3	200.3	223.5	210.0	171.0	164.1	160.3
Breast[5]	446.8	524.2	592.9	577.4	500.0	501.7	495.9
Chronic lower respiratory diseases	193.1	203.7	240.6	244.0	232.7	220.5	222.8
Influenza and pneumonia	134.4	384.9	330.8	269.8	161.2	152.1	146.7
Chronic liver disease and cirrhosis	139.8	644.0	371.8	250.3	185.6	181.5	161.3
Diabetes mellitus	330.8	305.3	361.5	400.8	383.4	392.6	396.7
Human immunodeficiency virus (HIV) disease	670.9	---	1,014.7	1,945.4	763.3	743.5	720.6
Unintentional injuries	1,157.8	1,751.5	1,392.7	1,272.1	1,152.8	1,133.4	1,129.3
Motor vehicle-related injuries	581.1	750.2	699.5	621.8	580.8	571.7	558.5
Suicide[6]	199.6	238.0	261.4	254.2	208.7	201.5	196.5
Homicide[6]	1,023.9	1,580.8	1,612.9	1,352.8	941.6	963.6	962.2
American Indian or Alaska Native[7]							
All causes	7,532.8	13,390.9	9,506.2	9,332.5	7,758.2	7,991.8	8,278.0
Diseases of heart	766.9	1,819.9	1,391.0	1,296.3	1,030.1	1,027.7	959.9
Ischemic heart disease	495.2	1,208.2	901.8	877.3	709.3	695.2	648.4
Cerebrovascular diseases	160.9	269.3	223.3	255.3	198.1	193.5	201.7
Malignant neoplasms	850.9	1,101.3	1,141.1	1,099.5	995.7	1,099.5	1,066.0
Trachea, bronchus, and lung	161.9	181.1	268.1	267.7	227.8	238.7	226.3
Colorectal	88.5	78.8	82.4	103.5	93.8	87.9	115.7
Prostate[4]	23.0	66.7	42.0	51.1	44.5	35.2	36.3
Breast[5]	159.6	205.5	213.4	195.9	174.1	175.2	187.1
Chronic lower respiratory diseases	99.9	89.3	129.0	145.3	151.8	139.3	137.0
Influenza and pneumonia	87.4	307.9	206.3	199.7	124.0	141.3	100.9
Chronic liver disease and cirrhosis	430.1	1,190.3	535.1	604.8	519.4	506.0	495.8
Diabetes mellitus	262.5	305.5	292.3	360.6	305.6	297.3	344.7
Human immunodeficiency virus (HIV) disease	74.9	---	70.1	246.9	68.4	88.1	79.9
Unintentional injuries	1,833.0	3,541.0	2,183.9	1,980.9	1,700.1	1,632.0	1,764.6
Motor vehicle-related injuries	1,164.5	2,102.4	1,301.5	1,210.3	1,032.2	989.4	1,089.3
Suicide[6]	451.2	515.0	495.9	445.2	403.1	420.6	420.8
Homicide[6]	393.1	628.9	434.2	432.7	278.5	287.0	366.5

See footnotes at end of table.

This table will be updated on the Web. Go to www.cdc.gov/nchs/hus.htm.

Table 30 (page 3 of 4). Years of potential life lost before age 75 for selected causes of death, according to sex, race, and Hispanic origin: United States, selected years 1980–2002

[Data are based on death certificates]

Sex, race, Hispanic origin, and cause of death[2]	Crude	Age adjusted[1]					
	2002	1980	1990	1995	2000[3]	2001	2002
Asian or Pacific Islander[7]		Years lost before age 75 per 100,000 population under 75 years of age					
All causes	3,461.5	5,378.4	4,705.2	4,333.2	3,811.1	3,798.7	3,635.5
Diseases of heart	483.0	952.8	702.2	664.9	567.9	547.1	539.4
Ischemic heart disease	306.6	697.7	486.6	440.6	381.1	369.4	352.0
Cerebrovascular diseases	165.5	266.9	233.5	220.0	199.4	198.8	186.5
Malignant neoplasms	904.7	1,218.6	1,166.4	1,122.1	1,033.8	1,029.6	990.3
Trachea, bronchus, and lung	151.6	238.2	204.7	197.0	185.8	180.8	173.8
Colorectal	83.9	115.9	105.1	99.5	91.6	97.2	92.8
Prostate[4]	15.8	17.0	32.4	25.3	18.8	13.3	20.8
Breast[5]	182.1	222.2	216.5	237.8	200.8	205.0	188.4
Chronic lower respiratory diseases	38.5	56.4	72.8	65.8	56.5	52.1	44.8
Influenza and pneumonia	34.6	79.3	74.0	64.3	48.6	45.4	38.0
Chronic liver disease and cirrhosis	37.0	85.6	72.4	48.4	44.8	44.5	40.0
Diabetes mellitus	64.9	83.1	74.0	83.5	77.0	83.8	76.4
Human immunodeficiency virus (HIV) disease	25.6	- - -	77.0	110.4	19.9	21.6	24.8
Unintentional injuries	443.2	742.7	636.6	525.7	425.7	431.4	431.1
Motor vehicle-related injuries	280.9	472.6	445.5	351.9	263.4	275.9	269.7
Suicide[6]	175.5	217.1	200.6	211.1	168.6	166.4	162.7
Homicide[6]	135.5	201.1	205.8	202.3	113.1	165.1	127.5
Hispanic or Latino[7,8]							
All causes	5,256.3	- - -	7,963.3	7,426.7	6,037.6	5,982.2	5,865.9
Diseases of heart	524.0	- - -	1,082.0	962.0	821.3	791.6	796.9
Ischemic heart disease	324.0	- - -	756.6	665.8	564.6	539.1	540.1
Cerebrovascular diseases	133.0	- - -	238.0	232.0	207.8	201.4	193.4
Malignant neoplasms	734.1	- - -	1,232.2	1,172.0	1,098.2	1,099.1	1,052.9
Trachea, bronchus, and lung	88.7	- - -	193.7	173.9	152.1	154.9	150.5
Colorectal	61.2	- - -	100.2	97.9	101.4	95.8	96.7
Prostate[4]	20.7	- - -	47.7	60.8	42.9	49.4	44.1
Breast[5]	150.4	- - -	299.3	257.7	230.7	233.6	205.1
Chronic lower respiratory diseases	46.0	- - -	78.8	82.1	68.5	67.6	69.0
Influenza and pneumonia	52.6	- - -	130.1	108.5	76.0	66.1	65.5
Chronic liver disease and cirrhosis	165.7	- - -	329.1	281.4	252.1	247.7	237.9
Diabetes mellitus	127.7	- - -	177.8	228.8	215.6	212.1	207.1
Human immunodeficiency virus (HIV) disease	154.1	- - -	600.1	865.0	209.4	190.3	179.1
Unintentional injuries	1,030.4	- - -	1,190.6	1,017.9	920.1	945.8	958.1
Motor vehicle-related injuries	633.4	- - -	740.8	593.0	540.2	554.0	569.6
Suicide[6]	193.6	- - -	256.2	245.1	188.5	185.1	185.6
Homicide[6]	381.3	- - -	720.8	575.4	335.1	365.2	330.2

See footnotes at end of table.

This table will be updated on the Web. Go to www.cdc.gov/nchs/hus.htm.

Table 30 (page 4 of 4). Years of potential life lost before age 75 for selected causes of death, according to sex, race, and Hispanic origin: United States, selected years 1980–2002

[Data are based on death certificates]

Sex, race, Hispanic origin, and cause of death[2]	Crude	Age adjusted[1]					
	2002	1980	1990	1995	2000[3]	2001	2002
White, not Hispanic or Latino[8]	Years lost before age 75 per 100,000 population under 75 years of age						
All causes	7,394.1	- - -	8,022.5	7,607.5	6,960.5	6,970.9	6,997.9
Diseases of heart	1,282.4	- - -	1,504.0	1,368.2	1,175.1	1,144.4	1,143.8
Ischemic heart disease	888.4	- - -	1,127.2	988.7	824.7	794.7	781.3
Cerebrovascular diseases	188.9	- - -	210.1	199.6	183.0	170.6	169.4
Malignant neoplasms	1,832.4	- - -	1,974.1	1,814.2	1,668.4	1,652.3	1,629.7
Trachea, bronchus, and lung	513.0	- - -	566.8	507.0	460.3	451.9	443.7
Colorectal	156.1	- - -	162.1	147.8	136.2	138.5	137.6
Prostate[4]	57.5	- - -	89.2	73.6	54.9	53.2	51.7
Breast[5]	347.5	- - -	451.5	389.3	322.3	315.9	305.9
Chronic lower respiratory diseases	221.7	- - -	188.1	190.6	193.8	194.3	193.3
Influenza and pneumonia	81.3	- - -	112.3	105.8	76.4	72.9	75.8
Chronic liver disease and cirrhosis	167.4	- - -	162.4	151.4	150.9	153.0	152.1
Diabetes mellitus	174.0	- - -	131.2	142.8	150.2	151.0	155.8
Human immunodeficiency virus (HIV) disease	69.1	- - -	271.2	362.1	76.0	71.0	67.8
Unintentional injuries	1,093.1	- - -	1,114.7	1,026.1	1,041.4	1,057.2	1,117.4
Motor vehicle-related injuries	585.2	- - -	715.7	618.0	588.8	584.1	603.3
Suicide[6]	413.5	- - -	433.0	427.7	389.2	405.3	413.9
Homicide[6]	110.9	- - -	162.0	148.6	113.2	160.1	114.8

- - - Data not available.
* Rate based on fewer than 20 deaths is considered unreliable and is not shown.
[1]Age-adjusted rates are calculated using the year 2000 standard population. See Appendix II, Age adjustment.
[2]Underlying cause of death code numbers are based on the applicable revision of the *International Classification of Diseases* (ICD) for data years shown. For the period 1980–98, causes were coded using ICD–9 codes that are most nearly comparable with the 113 cause list for ICD–10. See Appendix II, tables IV and V.
[3]Starting with 1999 data, cause of death is coded according to ICD–10. To estimate change between 1998 and 1999, compare the 1999 rate with the comparability-modified rate for 1998. See Appendix II, Comparability ratio and tables V and VI.
[4]Rate for male population only.
[5]Rate for female population only.
[6]Figures for 2001 include September 11 related deaths for which death certificates were filed as of October 24, 2002. See Appendix II, table V for terrorism-related ICD–10 codes.
[7]The race groups, white, black, Asian or Pacific Islander, and American Indian or Alaska Native, include persons of Hispanic and non-Hispanic origin. Persons of Hispanic origin may be of any race. Death rates for the American Indian or Alaska Native and Asian or Pacific Islander populations are known to be underestimated. See Appendix II, Race, for a discussion of sources of bias in death rates by race and Hispanic origin.
[8]Prior to 1997, excludes data from States lacking an Hispanic-origin item on the death certificate. See Appendix II, Hispanic origin.

NOTES: Starting with *Health, United States, 2003*, rates for 1991–99 were revised using intercensal population estimates based on Census 2000. Rates for 2000 were revised based on Census 2000 counts. Rates for 2001 and 2002 were computed using 2000-based postcensal estimates. See Appendix I, Population Census and Population Estimates. See Appendix II for definition of years of potential life lost (YPLL) and method of calculation. Data for additional years are available. See Appendix III.

SOURCES: Centers for Disease Control and Prevention, National Center for Health Statistics, National vital statistics system; numerator data from annual mortality files; denominator data from national population estimates for race groups from table 1 and unpublished Hispanic population estimates for 1990–96 prepared by the Housing and Household Economic Statistics Division, U.S. Bureau of the Census.

This table will be updated on the Web. Go to www.cdc.gov/nchs/hus.htm.

Table 31 (page 1 of 4). Leading causes of death and numbers of deaths, according to sex, race, and Hispanic origin: United States, 1980 and 2002

[Data are based on death certificates]

Sex, race, Hispanic origin, and rank order	1980 Cause of death	1980 Deaths	2002 Cause of death	2002 Deaths
All persons				
. . .	All causes	1,989,841	All causes	2,443,387
1	Diseases of heart	761,085	Diseases of heart	696,947
2	Malignant neoplasms	416,509	Malignant neoplasms	557,271
3	Cerebrovascular diseases	170,225	Cerebrovascular diseases	162,672
4	Unintentional injuries	105,718	Chronic lower respiratory diseases	124,816
5	Chronic obstructive pulmonary diseases	56,050	Unintentional injuries	106,742
6	Pneumonia and influenza	54,619	Diabetes mellitus	73,249
7	Diabetes mellitus	34,851	Influenza and pneumonia	65,681
8	Chronic liver disease and cirrhosis	30,583	Alzheimer's disease	58,866
9	Atherosclerosis	29,449	Nephritis, nephrotic syndrome and nephrosis	40,974
10	Suicide	26,869	Septicemia	33,865
Male				
. . .	All causes	1,075,078	All causes	1,199,264
1	Diseases of heart	405,661	Diseases of heart	340,933
2	Malignant neoplasms	225,948	Malignant neoplasms	288,768
3	Unintentional injuries	74,180	Unintentional injuries	69,257
4	Cerebrovascular diseases	69,973	Cerebrovascular diseases	62,622
5	Chronic obstructive pulmonary diseases	38,625	Chronic lower respiratory diseases	60,713
6	Pneumonia and influenza	27,574	Diabetes mellitus	34,301
7	Suicide	20,505	Influenza and pneumonia	28,918
8	Chronic liver disease and cirrhosis	19,768	Suicide	25,409
9	Homicide	18,779	Nephritis, nephrotic syndrome and nephrosis	19,695
10	Diabetes mellitus	14,325	Chronic liver disease and cirrhosis	17,401
Female				
. . .	All causes	914,763	All causes	1,244,123
1	Diseases of heart	355,424	Diseases of heart	356,014
2	Malignant neoplasms	190,561	Malignant neoplasms	268,503
3	Cerebrovascular diseases	100,252	Cerebrovascular diseases	100,050
4	Unintentional injuries	31,538	Chronic lower respiratory diseases	64,103
5	Pneumonia and influenza	27,045	Alzheimer's disease	41,877
6	Diabetes mellitus	20,526	Diabetes mellitus	38,948
7	Atherosclerosis	17,848	Unintentional injuries	37,485
8	Chronic obstructive pulmonary diseases	17,425	Influenza and pneumonia	36,763
9	Chronic liver disease and cirrhosis	10,815	Nephritis, nephrotic syndrome and nephrosis	21,279
10	Certain conditions originating in the perinatal period	9,815	Septicemia	18,918
White				
. . .	All causes	1,738,607	All causes	2,102,589
1	Diseases of heart	683,347	Diseases of heart	606,876
2	Malignant neoplasms	368,162	Malignant neoplasms	482,481
3	Cerebrovascular diseases	148,734	Cerebrovascular diseases	139,719
4	Unintentional injuries	90,122	Chronic lower respiratory diseases	115,395
5	Chronic obstructive pulmonary diseases	52,375	Unintentional injuries	90,866
6	Pneumonia and influenza	48,369	Diabetes mellitus	58,459
7	Diabetes mellitus	28,868	Influenza and pneumonia	58,346
8	Atherosclerosis	27,069	Alzheimer's disease	55,058
9	Chronic liver disease and cirrhosis	25,240	Nephritis, nephrotic syndrome and nephrosis	32,615
10	Suicide	24,829	Suicide	28,731
Black or African American				
. . .	All causes	233,135	All causes	290,051
1	Diseases of heart	72,956	Diseases of heart	77,621
2	Malignant neoplasms	45,037	Malignant neoplasms	62,617
3	Cerebrovascular diseases	20,135	Cerebrovascular diseases	18,856
4	Unintentional injuries	13,480	Diabetes mellitus	12,687
5	Homicide	10,172	Unintentional injuries	12,513
6	Certain conditions originating in the perinatal period	6,961	Homicide	8,287
7	Pneumonia and influenza	5,648	Human immunodeficiency virus (HIV) disease	7,835
8	Diabetes mellitus	5,544	Chronic lower respiratory diseases	7,831
9	Chronic liver disease and cirrhosis	4,790	Nephritis, nephrotic syndrome and nephrosis	7,488
10	Nephritis, nephrotic syndrome, and nephrosis	3,416	Septicemia	6,137

See footnotes at end of table.

This table will be updated on the Web. Go to www.cdc.gov/nchs/hus.htm.

Table 31 (page 2 of 4). Leading causes of death and numbers of deaths, according to sex, race, and Hispanic origin: United States, 1980 and 2002

[Data are based on death certificates]

Sex, race, Hispanic origin, and rank order	1980		2002	
	Cause of death	Deaths	Cause of death	Deaths
American Indian or Alaska Native				
...	All causes	6,923	All causes	12,415
1	Diseases of heart	1,494	Diseases of heart	2,467
2	Unintentional injuries	1,290	Malignant neoplasms	2,175
3	Malignant neoplasms	770	Unintentional injuries	1,488
4	Chronic liver disease and cirrhosis	410	Diabetes mellitus	744
5	Cerebrovascular diseases	322	Cerebrovascular diseases	567
6	Pneumonia and influenza	257	Chronic liver disease and cirrhosis	547
7	Homicide	217	Chronic lower respiratory diseases	452
8	Diabetes mellitus	210	Suicide	324
9	Certain conditions originating in the perinatal period	199	Influenza and pneumonia	293
10	Suicide	181	Homicide	267
Asian or Pacific Islander				
...	All causes	11,071	All causes	38,332
1	Diseases of heart	3,265	Malignant neoplasms	9,998
2	Malignant neoplasms	2,522	Diseases of heart	9,983
3	Cerebrovascular diseases	1,028	Cerebrovascular diseases	3,530
4	Unintentional injuries	810	Unintentional injuries	1,875
5	Pneumonia and influenza	342	Diabetes mellitus	1,359
6	Suicide	249	Influenza and pneumonia	1,171
7	Certain conditions originating in the perinatal period	246	Chronic lower respiratory diseases	1,138
8	Diabetes mellitus	227	Suicide	661
9	Homicide	211	Nephritis, nephrotic syndrome and nephrosis	649
10	Chronic obstructive pulmonary diseases	207	Septicemia	423
Hispanic or Latino				
...	---	---	All causes	117,135
1	---	---	Diseases of heart	27,887
2	---	---	Malignant neoplasms	23,141
3	---	---	Unintentional injuries	10,106
4	---	---	Cerebrovascular diseases	6,451
5	---	---	Diabetes mellitus	5,912
6	---	---	Chronic liver disease and cirrhosis	3,409
7	---	---	Homicide	3,129
8	---	---	Chronic lower respiratory diseases	3,058
9	---	---	Influenza and pneumonia	2,824
10	---	---	Certain conditions originating in the perinatal period	2,402
White male				
...	All causes	933,878	All causes	1,025,196
1	Diseases of heart	364,679	Diseases of heart	296,904
2	Malignant neoplasms	198,188	Malignant neoplasms	249,867
3	Unintentional injuries	62,963	Unintentional injuries	58,467
4	Cerebrovascular diseases	60,095	Chronic lower respiratory diseases	55,409
5	Chronic obstructive pulmonary diseases	35,977	Cerebrovascular diseases	52,959
6	Pneumonia and influenza	23,810	Diabetes mellitus	28,110
7	Suicide	18,901	Influenza and pneumonia	25,381
8	Chronic liver disease and cirrhosis	16,407	Suicide	23,049
9	Diabetes mellitus	12,125	Alzheimer's disease	15,874
10	Atherosclerosis	10,543	Nephritis, nephrotic syndrome and nephrosis	15,850
Black or African American male				
...	All causes	130,138	All causes	146,835
1	Diseases of heart	37,877	Diseases of heart	37,094
2	Malignant neoplasms	25,861	Malignant neoplasms	32,627
3	Unintentional injuries	9,701	Unintentional injuries	8,612
4	Cerebrovascular diseases	9,194	Cerebrovascular diseases	7,828
5	Homicide	8,274	Homicide	6,896
6	Certain conditions originating in the perinatal period	3,869	Human immunodeficiency virus (HIV) disease	5,301
7	Pneumonia and influenza	3,386	Diabetes mellitus	5,207
8	Chronic liver disease and cirrhosis	3,020	Chronic lower respiratory diseases	4,341
9	Chronic obstructive pulmonary diseases	2,429	Nephritis, nephrotic syndrome and nephrosis	3,427
10	Diabetes mellitus	2,010	Influenza and pneumonia	2,768

See footnotes at end of table.

This table will be updated on the Web. Go to www.cdc.gov/nchs/hus.htm.

Table 31 (page 3 of 4). Leading causes of death and numbers of deaths, according to sex, race, and Hispanic origin: United States, 1980 and 2002

[Data are based on death certificates]

Sex, race, Hispanic origin, and rank order	1980 Cause of death	1980 Deaths	2002 Cause of death	2002 Deaths
American Indian or Alaska Native male				
...	All causes	4,193	All causes	6,750
1	Unintentional injuries	946	Diseases of heart	1,412
2	Diseases of heart	917	Malignant neoplasms	1,081
3	Malignant neoplasms	408	Unintentional injuries	1,003
4	Chronic liver disease and cirrhosis	239	Diabetes mellitus	336
5	Cerebrovascular diseases	163	Chronic liver disease and cirrhosis	319
6	Homicide	162	Suicide	258
7	Pneumonia and influenza	148	Cerebrovascular diseases	236
8	Suicide	147	Chronic lower respiratory diseases	220
9	Certain conditions originating in the perinatal period	107	Homicide	185
10	Diabetes mellitus	86	Influenza and pneumonia	133
Asian or Pacific Islander male				
...	All causes	6,809	All causes	20,483
1	Diseases of heart	2,174	Diseases of heart	5,523
2	Malignant neoplasms	1,485	Malignant neoplasms	5,193
3	Unintentional injuries	556	Cerebrovascular diseases	1,599
4	Cerebrovascular diseases	521	Unintentional injuries	1,175
5	Pneumonia and influenza	227	Chronic lower respiratory diseases	743
6	Suicide	159	Diabetes mellitus	648
7	Chronic obstructive pulmonary diseases	158	Influenza and pneumonia	636
8	Homicide	151	Suicide	469
9	Certain conditions originating in the perinatal period	128	Nephritis, nephrotic syndrome and nephrosis	320
10	Diabetes mellitus	103	Homicide	277
Hispanic or Latino male				
...	---	---	All causes	65,703
1	---	---	Diseases of heart	14,798
2	---	---	Malignant neoplasms	12,235
3	---	---	Unintentional injuries	7,698
4	---	---	Cerebrovascular diseases	3,003
5	---	---	Diabetes mellitus	2,779
6	---	---	Homicide	2,635
7	---	---	Chronic liver disease and cirrhosis	2,437
8	---	---	Suicide	1,651
9	---	---	Chronic lower respiratory diseases	1,625
10	---	---	Human immunodeficiency virus (HIV) disease	1,440
White female				
...	All causes	804,729	All causes	1,077,393
1	Diseases of heart	318,668	Diseases of heart	309,972
2	Malignant neoplasms	169,974	Malignant neoplasms	232,614
3	Cerebrovascular diseases	88,639	Cerebrovascular diseases	86,760
4	Unintentional injuries	27,159	Chronic lower respiratory diseases	59,986
5	Pneumonia and influenza	24,559	Alzheimer's disease	39,184
6	Diabetes mellitus	16,743	Influenza and pneumonia	32,965
7	Atherosclerosis	16,526	Unintentional injuries	32,399
8	Chronic obstructive pulmonary diseases	16,398	Diabetes mellitus	30,349
9	Chronic liver disease and cirrhosis	8,833	Nephritis, nephrotic syndrome and nephrosis	16,765
10	Certain conditions originating in the perinatal period	6,512	Septicemia	15,191
Black or African American female				
...	All causes	102,997	All causes	143,216
1	Diseases of heart	35,079	Diseases of heart	40,527
2	Malignant neoplasms	19,176	Malignant neoplasms	29,990
3	Cerebrovascular diseases	10,941	Cerebrovascular diseases	11,028
4	Unintentional injuries	3,779	Diabetes mellitus	7,480
5	Diabetes mellitus	3,534	Nephritis, nephrotic syndrome and nephrosis	4,061
6	Certain conditions originating in the perinatal period	3,092	Unintentional injuries	3,901
7	Pneumonia and influenza	2,262	Chronic lower respiratory diseases	3,490
8	Homicide	1,898	Septicemia	3,434
9	Chronic liver disease and cirrhosis	1,770	Influenza and pneumonia	3,103
10	Nephritis, nephrotic syndrome, and nephrosis	1,722	Human immunodeficiency virus (HIV) disease	2,534

See footnotes at end of table.

This table will be updated on the Web. Go to www.cdc.gov/nchs/hus.htm.

Table 31 (page 4 of 4). Leading causes of death and numbers of deaths, according to sex, race, and Hispanic origin: United States, 1980 and 2002

[Data are based on death certificates]

Sex, race, Hispanic origin, and rank order	1980 Cause of death	1980 Deaths	2002 Cause of death	2002 Deaths
American Indian or Alaska Native female				
. . .	All causes	2,730	All causes	5,665
1	Diseases of heart	577	Malignant neoplasms	1,094
2	Malignant neoplasms	362	Diseases of heart	1,055
3	Unintentional injuries	344	Unintentional injuries	485
4	Chronic liver disease and cirrhosis	171	Diabetes mellitus	408
5	Cerebrovascular diseases	159	Cerebrovascular diseases	331
6	Diabetes mellitus	124	Chronic lower respiratory diseases	232
7	Pneumonia and influenza	109	Chronic liver disease and cirrhosis	228
8	Certain conditions originating in the perinatal period	92	Influenza and pneumonia	160
9	Nephritis, nephrotic syndrome, and nephrosis	56	Nephritis, nephrotic syndrome and nephrosis	124
10	Homicide	55	Septicemia	100
Asian or Pacific Islander female				
. . .	All causes	4,262	All causes	17,849
1	Diseases of heart	1,091	Malignant neoplasms	4,805
2	Malignant neoplasms	1,037	Diseases of heart	4,460
3	Cerebrovascular diseases	507	Cerebrovascular diseases	1,931
4	Unintentional injuries	254	Diabetes mellitus	711
5	Diabetes mellitus	124	Unintentional injuries	700
6	Certain conditions originating in the perinatal period	118	Influenza and pneumonia	535
7	Pneumonia and influenza	115	Chronic lower respiratory diseases	395
8	Congenital anomalies	104	Nephritis, nephrotic syndrome and nephrosis	329
9	Suicide	90	Alzheimer's disease	231
10	Homicide	60	Essential (primary) hypertension and hypertensive renal disease	221
Hispanic or Latino female				
. . .	---	---	All causes	51,432
1	---	---	Diseases of heart	13,089
2	---	---	Malignant neoplasms	10,906
3	---	---	Cerebrovascular diseases	3,448
4	---	---	Diabetes mellitus	3,133
5	---	---	Unintentional injuries	2,408
6	---	---	Chronic lower respiratory diseases	1,433
7	---	---	Influenza and pneumonia	1,426
8	---	---	Certain conditions originating in the perinatal period	1,050
9	---	---	Alzheimer's disease	1,010
10	---	---	Chronic liver disease and cirrhosis	972

. . . Category not applicable.
--- Data not available.

NOTES: For cause of death code numbers based on the *International Classification of Diseases, 9th Revision* (ICD–9) in 1980 and ICD–10 in 2002, see Appendix II, tables IV and V.

SOURCES: Centers for Disease Control and Prevention, National Center for Health Statistics, National Vital Statistics System; *Vital statistics of the United States, vol II, mortality, part A*, 1980. Washington: Public Health Service. 1985; Anderson RN, Smith BL. Deaths: Leading causes for 2002. National vital statistics reports. Vol 53 no 17. Hyattsville, Maryland: National Center for Health Statistics. 2005.

This table will be updated on the Web. Go to www.cdc.gov/nchs/hus.htm.

Table 32 (page 1 of 2). Leading causes of death and numbers of deaths, according to age: United States, 1980 and 2002

[Data are based on death certificates]

Age and rank order	1980 Cause of death	1980 Deaths	2002 Cause of death	2002 Deaths
Under 1 year				
...	All causes	45,526	All causes	28,034
1	Congenital anomalies	9,220	Congenital malformations, deformations and chromosomal abnormalities	5,623
2	Sudden infant death syndrome	5,510	Disorders related to short gestation and low birth weight, not elsewhere classified	4,637
3	Respiratory distress syndrome	4,989	Sudden infant death syndrome	2,295
4	Disorders relating to short gestation and unspecified low birthweight	3,648	Newborn affected by maternal complications of pregnancy	1,708
5	Newborn affected by maternal complications of pregnancy	1,572	Newborn affected by complications of placenta, cord and membranes	1,028
6	Intrauterine hypoxia and birth asphyxia	1,497	Unintentional injuries	946
7	Unintentional injuries	1,166	Respiratory distress of newborn	943
8	Birth trauma	1,058	Bacterial sepsis of newborn	749
9	Pneumonia and influenza	1,012	Diseases of circulatory system	667
10	Newborn affected by complications of placenta, cord, and membranes	985	Intrauterine hypoxia and birth asphyxia	583
1–4 years				
...	All causes	8,187	All causes	4,858
1	Unintentional injuries	3,313	Unintentional injuries	1,641
2	Congenital anomalies	1,026	Congenital malformations, deformations and chromosomal abnormalities	530
3	Malignant neoplasms	573	Homicide	423
4	Diseases of heart	338	Malignant neoplasms	402
5	Homicide	319	Diseases of heart	165
6	Pneumonia and influenza	267	Influenza and pneumonia	110
7	Meningitis	223	Septicemia	79
8	Meningococcal infection	110	Chronic lower respiratory diseases	65
8	...	...	Certain conditions originating in the perinatal period	65
9	Certain conditions originating in the perinatal period	84	...	...
10	Septicemia	71	In situ neoplasms, benign neoplasms and neoplasms of uncertain or unknown behavior	60
5–14 years				
...	All causes	10,689	All causes	7,150
1	Unintentional injuries	5,224	Unintentional injuries	2,718
2	Malignant neoplasms	1,497	Malignant neoplasms	1,072
3	Congenital anomalies	561	Congenital malformations, deformations and chromosomal abnormalities	417
4	Homicide	415	Homicide	356
5	Diseases of heart	330	Suicide	264
6	Pneumonia and influenza	194	Diseases of heart	255
7	Suicide	142	Chronic lower respiratory diseases	136
8	Benign neoplasms	104	Septicemia	95
9	Cerebrovascular diseases	95	Cerebrovascular diseases	91
9	...	...	Influenza and pneumonia	91
10	Chronic obstructive pulmonary diseases	85	...	...
15–24 years				
...	All causes	49,027	All causes	33,046
1	Unintentional injuries	26,206	Unintentional injuries	15,412
2	Homicide	6,537	Homicide	5,219
3	Suicide	5,239	Suicide	4,010
4	Malignant neoplasms	2,683	Malignant neoplasms	1,730
5	Diseases of heart	1,223	Diseases of heart	1,022
6	Congenital anomalies	600	Congenital malformations, deformations and chromosomal abnormalities	492
7	Cerebrovascular diseases	418	Chronic lower respiratory diseases	192
8	Pneumonia and influenza	348	Human immunodeficiency virus (HIV) disease	178
9	Chronic obstructive pulmonary diseases	141	Diabetes mellitus	171
9	...	...	Cerebrovascular diseases	171
10	Anemias	133	...	...

See footnotes at end of table.

This table will be updated on the Web. Go to www.cdc.gov/nchs/hus.htm.

Table 32 (page 2 of 2). Leading causes of death and numbers of deaths, according to age: United States, 1980 and 2002

[Data are based on death certificates]

Age and rank order	1980 Cause of death	1980 Deaths	2002 Cause of death	2002 Deaths
25–44 years				
. . .	All causes	108,658	All causes	132,495
1	Unintentional injuries	26,722	Unintentional injuries	29,279
2	Malignant neoplasms	17,551	Malignant neoplasms	19,957
3	Diseases of heart	14,513	Diseases of heart	16,853
4	Homicide	10,983	Suicide	11,897
5	Suicide	9,855	Homicide	7,728
6	Chronic liver disease and cirrhosis	4,782	Human immunodeficiency virus (HIV) disease	7,546
7	Cerebrovascular diseases	3,154	Chronic liver disease and cirrhosis	3,528
8	Diabetes mellitus	1,472	Cerebrovascular diseases	2,992
9	Pneumonia and influenza	1,467	Diabetes mellitus	2,806
10	Congenital anomalies	817	Influenza and pneumonia	1,316
45–64 years				
. . .	All causes	425,338	All causes	425,727
1	Diseases of heart	148,322	Malignant neoplasms	143,028
2	Malignant neoplasms	135,675	Diseases of heart	101,804
3	Cerebrovascular diseases	19,909	Unintentional injuries	23,020
4	Unintentional injuries	18,140	Cerebrovascular diseases	15,952
5	Chronic liver disease and cirrhosis	16,089	Diabetes mellitus	15,518
6	Chronic obstructive pulmonary diseases	11,514	Chronic lower respiratory diseases	14,755
7	Diabetes mellitus	7,977	Chronic liver disease and cirrhosis	13,313
8	Suicide	7,079	Suicide	9,926
9	Pneumonia and influenza	5,804	Human immunodeficiency virus (HIV) disease	5,821
10	Homicide	4,019	Septicemia	5,434
65 years and over				
. . .	All causes	1,341,848	All causes	1,811,720
1	Diseases of heart	595,406	Diseases of heart	576,301
2	Malignant neoplasms	258,389	Malignant neoplasms	391,001
3	Cerebrovascular diseases	146,417	Cerebrovascular diseases	143,293
4	Pneumonia and influenza	45,512	Chronic lower respiratory diseases	108,313
5	Chronic obstructive pulmonary diseases	43,587	Influenza and pneumonia	58,826
6	Atherosclerosis	28,081	Alzheimer's disease	58,289
7	Diabetes mellitus	25,216	Diabetes mellitus	54,715
8	Unintentional injuries	24,844	Nephritis, nephrotic syndrome and nephrosis	34,316
9	Nephritis, nephrotic syndrome, and nephrosis	12,968	Unintentional injuries	33,641
10	Chronic liver disease and cirrhosis	9,519	Septicemia	26,670

. . . Category not applicable.

NOTES: For cause of death code numbers based on the *International Classification of Diseases, 9th Revision* (ICD–9) in 1980 and ICD–10 in 2002, see Appendix II, tables IV and V.

SOURCES: Centers for Disease Control and Prevention, National Center for Health Statistics, National Vital Statistics System; *Vital statistics of the United States, vol II, mortality, part A*, 1980. Washington: Public Health Service. 1985; Anderson RN, Smith BL. Deaths: Leading causes for 2002. National vital statistics reports. Vol 53 no 17. Hyattsville, Maryland: National Center for Health Statistics. 2005.

This table will be updated on the Web. Go to www.cdc.gov/nchs/hus.htm.

Table 33 (page 1 of 3). Age-adjusted death rates, according to race, sex, region, and urbanization level: United States, average annual 1994–96, 1997–99, and 2000–2002

[Data are based on the National Vital Statistics System]

Sex, region, and urbanization level[1]	*All races*			*White*			*Black or African American*		
	1994–96	*1997–99*	*2000–2002*	*1994–96*	*1997–99*	*2000–2002*	*1994–96*	*1997–99*	*2000–2002*
Both sexes	Age-adjusted death rate per 100,000 standard population[2]								
All regions:									
Metropolitan counties:									
Large	902.5	860.8	833.1	870.6	836.6	813.0	1,198.6	1,115.7	1,079.3
Medium	881.9	857.7	844.6	860.9	839.7	829.1	1,188.9	1,136.7	1,114.9
Small	906.1	885.9	875.1	883.8	865.8	856.4	1,212.6	1,167.6	1,153.4
Nonmetropolitan counties:									
Micropolitan	926.2	910.4	897.7	904.9	889.9	880.7	1,233.9	1,200.1	1,158.7
Nonmicropolitan	945.8	929.7	914.3	921.7	906.0	894.2	1,215.4	1,190.7	1,149.4
Northeast:									
Metropolitan counties:									
Large	908.8	847.6	815.0	880.2	831.5	803.9	1,135.4	1,007.6	966.4
Medium	873.1	841.9	823.3	860.5	833.5	816.5	1,162.1	1,048.9	1,020.5
Small	884.8	845.5	834.3	878.8	841.6	830.9	1,195.7	1,080.7	1,068.6
Nonmetropolitan counties:									
Micropolitan	896.6	868.6	843.9	895.6	868.1	845.4	*	*	*
Nonmicropolitan	907.5	888.0	864.1	905.9	885.5	863.4	*	*	*
Midwest:									
Metropolitan counties:									
Large	934.2	902.6	878.1	885.4	859.7	838.0	1,253.3	1,189.9	1,162.5
Medium	894.6	876.2	861.6	874.1	857.4	845.1	1,199.8	1,163.0	1,131.6
Small	874.7	856.0	842.5	860.9	843.9	831.7	1,230.3	1,148.4	1,151.7
Nonmetropolitan counties:									
Micropolitan	884.5	869.9	851.8	879.9	865.2	849.6	1,231.8	1,212.6	1,108.6
Nonmicropolitan	883.7	862.5	843.7	874.0	853.3	836.5	1,351.3	1,377.7	1,068.2
South:									
Metropolitan counties:									
Large	916.6	884.1	867.6	862.7	837.9	827.2	1,223.8	1,156.8	1,119.4
Medium	905.1	883.1	877.0	861.3	843.8	841.1	1,201.6	1,156.1	1,140.4
Small	962.5	946.8	940.9	925.7	913.4	910.9	1,217.2	1,182.1	1,163.9
Nonmetropolitan counties:									
Micropolitan	983.9	971.3	967.2	940.9	931.5	935.5	1,244.2	1,210.0	1,175.3
Nonmicropolitan	1,014.1	1,004.7	995.1	983.1	975.3	971.7	1,213.3	1,187.7	1,157.2
West:									
Metropolitan counties:									
Large	848.2	809.2	771.2	854.0	819.3	783.4	1,156.4	1,088.3	1,051.3
Medium	832.5	807.6	789.9	843.1	820.2	805.2	1,080.2	1,041.3	974.7
Small	838.4	816.3	800.5	837.5	816.5	800.1	1,055.9	986.6	1,010.4
Nonmetropolitan counties:									
Micropolitan	874.3	857.2	843.2	875.6	856.8	842.4	*	*	*
Nonmicropolitan	883.6	858.6	835.5	862.3	836.6	816.9	*	*	*

See footnotes at end of table.

This table will be updated on the Web. Go to www.cdc.gov/nchs/hus.htm.

Table 33 (page 2 of 3). Age-adjusted death rates, according to race, sex, region, and urbanization level: United States, average annual 1994–96, 1997–99, and 2000–2002

[Data are based on the National Vital Statistics System]

Sex, region, and urbanization level[1]	*All races*			*White*			*Black or African American*		
	1994–96	*1997–99*	*2000–2002*	*1994–96*	*1997–99*	*2000–2002*	*1994–96*	*1997–99*	*2000–2002*
Male	Age-adjusted death rate per 100,000 standard population[2]								
All regions:									
Metropolitan counties:									
Large	1,130.6	1,050.6	999.2	1,087.6	1,018.7	973.0	1,567.5	1,415.4	1,343.6
Medium	1,103.5	1,051.3	1,013.1	1,076.5	1,028.3	993.2	1,532.4	1,435.0	1,375.7
Small	1,141.3	1,094.2	1,055.3	1,113.6	1,069.1	1,032.2	1,555.5	1,472.8	1,433.8
Nonmetropolitan counties:									
Micropolitan	1,169.3	1,130.2	1,088.1	1,142.4	1,104.1	1,067.4	1,604.3	1,532.7	1,442.7
Nonmicropolitan	1,201.5	1,160.5	1,114.7	1,171.4	1,131.0	1,090.4	1,577.7	1,522.0	1,439.2
Northeast:									
Metropolitan counties:									
Large	1,146.8	1,041.9	986.2	1,107.7	1,020.6	971.7	1,502.6	1,284.6	1,214.0
Medium	1,099.0	1,039.6	995.2	1,082.9	1,029.5	987.7	1,485.2	1,309.4	1,234.7
Small	1,113.6	1,049.8	1,002.7	1,106.5	1,046.2	999.1	1,500.0	1,329.3	1,329.6
Nonmetropolitan counties:									
Micropolitan	1,123.7	1,073.0	1,024.2	1,122.5	1,073.4	1,027.7	*	*	*
Nonmicropolitan	1,132.3	1,081.5	1,040.0	1,131.0	1,079.5	1,039.6	*	*	*
Midwest:									
Metropolitan counties:									
Large	1,174.9	1,112.6	1,058.0	1,110.3	1,057.9	1,007.4	1,633.3	1,511.0	1,447.7
Medium	1,122.8	1,082.6	1,038.9	1,097.7	1,059.9	1,020.1	1,509.7	1,444.0	1,369.0
Small	1,105.9	1,064.9	1,026.5	1,089.5	1,050.3	1,013.5	1,532.1	1,420.1	1,414.7
Nonmetropolitan counties:									
Micropolitan	1,124.6	1,086.2	1,040.1	1,119.4	1,080.7	1,038.5	1,540.2	1,501.8	1,313.1
Nonmicropolitan	1,124.6	1,081.0	1,033.3	1,113.0	1,069.7	1,025.5	1,682.3	1,735.5	1,312.0
South:									
Metropolitan counties:									
Large	1,153.1	1,081.4	1,039.2	1,080.1	1,020.5	987.4	1,607.3	1,475.1	1,394.7
Medium	1,141.2	1,085.4	1,053.7	1,082.7	1,032.9	1,007.2	1,571.5	1,481.5	1,427.3
Small	1,227.5	1,178.9	1,141.0	1,180.8	1,135.8	1,102.1	1,579.8	1,507.4	1,460.4
Nonmetropolitan counties:									
Micropolitan	1,256.0	1,218.6	1,178.2	1,199.3	1,166.2	1,137.2	1,635.4	1,563.6	1,481.6
Nonmicropolitan	1,302.5	1,266.2	1,223.6	1,263.3	1,229.0	1,194.6	1,582.8	1,524.2	1,456.4
West:									
Metropolitan counties:									
Large	1,046.5	970.1	915.7	1,053.2	980.4	928.4	1,459.9	1,331.7	1,274.1
Medium	1,020.4	972.3	934.7	1,033.6	987.1	948.9	1,311.5	1,216.5	1,154.9
Small	1,026.4	982.9	945.0	1,025.6	983.1	945.0	1,254.8	1,127.1	1,130.7
Nonmetropolitan counties:									
Micropolitan	1,063.1	1,029.5	996.7	1,065.7	1,027.2	992.9	*	*	*
Nonmicropolitan	1,079.5	1,038.7	984.7	1,054.4	1,011.8	959.7	*	*	*

See footnotes at end of table.

This table will be updated on the Web. Go to www.cdc.gov/nchs/hus.htm.

Table 33 (page 3 of 3). Age-adjusted death rates, according to race, sex, region, and urbanization level: United States, average annual 1994–96, 1997–99, and 2000–2002

[Data are based on the National Vital Statistics System]

Sex, region, and urbanization level[1]	All races			White			Black or African American		
	1994–96	1997–99	2000–2002	1994–96	1997–99	2000–2002	1994–96	1997–99	2000–2002
Female	Age-adjusted death rate per 100,000 standard population[2]								
All regions:									
Metropolitan counties:									
Large	737.4	722.6	707.9	714.0	703.4	691.3	944.5	912.7	896.9
Medium	721.4	715.6	715.2	705.5	701.2	702.6	946.6	930.0	928.7
Small	737.4	734.4	737.9	719.0	717.5	721.9	974.5	958.2	958.2
Nonmetropolitan counties:									
Micropolitan	748.7	747.7	750.5	731.6	731.0	735.8	978.2	974.0	959.7
Nonmicropolitan	753.0	752.8	754.9	733.5	733.3	737.6	957.3	956.5	943.0
Northeast:									
Metropolitan counties:									
Large	743.0	711.9	691.1	721.9	698.8	681.2	895.1	828.8	804.3
Medium	718.8	705.3	698.5	709.6	698.2	692.8	923.7	869.3	860.0
Small	725.5	704.0	709.6	720.8	699.8	706.4	977.5	924.1	908.0
Nonmetropolitan counties:									
Micropolitan	737.0	721.2	710.3	736.6	720.5	710.6	*	*	*
Nonmicropolitan	740.7	741.0	725.1	739.1	738.4	724.3	*	*	*
Midwest:									
Metropolitan counties:									
Large	768.6	756.5	747.1	733.7	723.2	715.4	987.3	966.7	960.7
Medium	738.6	733.0	732.0	722.3	717.5	717.7	976.0	960.8	953.1
Small	716.0	709.3	708.7	704.5	699.6	699.7	1,005.1	940.7	955.4
Nonmetropolitan counties:									
Micropolitan	716.4	716.0	712.3	712.1	711.7	709.9	1,012.3	1,023.1	947.8
Nonmicropolitan	703.9	696.3	694.5	696.0	689.0	688.2	1,124.4	1,140.1	918.2
South:									
Metropolitan counties:									
Large	742.8	737.8	736.0	702.4	700.8	702.3	960.5	942.7	930.7
Medium	729.9	730.6	737.3	695.9	698.9	707.1	948.6	937.1	942.9
Small	775.3	780.5	789.1	744.7	752.2	763.4	972.1	966.7	962.9
Nonmetropolitan counties:									
Micropolitan	786.3	790.3	804.2	751.7	757.5	776.9	979.3	973.8	965.7
Nonmicropolitan	801.1	809.3	817.4	775.5	784.4	796.4	952.3	951.2	945.6
West:									
Metropolitan counties:									
Large	694.8	684.7	656.9	699.6	693.7	667.7	926.5	908.9	883.1
Medium	687.4	679.1	674.4	697.8	691.1	690.1	886.6	892.8	825.1
Small	689.0	683.1	682.2	688.1	683.8	681.6	881.3	838.7	894.8
Nonmetropolitan counties:									
Micropolitan	716.5	712.2	710.3	717.8	714.1	711.6	*	*	*
Nonmicropolitan	715.8	702.8	702.2	699.5	686.2	689.5	*	*	*

* Estimates of death rates for the black population in nonmetropolitan counties in the Northeast and West may be unreliable, possibly due to anomalies in population estimates for the black population in nonmetropolitan counties in these regions.

[1]Urbanization levels are for county of residence of decedent. See Appendix II, Urbanization for definition of urbanization levels.

[2]Average annual death rates, age-adjusted using the year 2000 standard population. See Appendix II, Age adjustment. Denominators for rates are population estimates for the middle year of each 3-year period multiplied by 3. The 1995 and 1998 population estimates used to compute rates for 1994–96 and 1997–99 are intercensal population estimates based on census 2000. See Appendix I, Population Census and Population Estimates.

NOTE: The race groups, white and black, include persons of Hispanic and non-Hispanic origin.

SOURCE: Centers for Disease Control and Prevention, National Center for Health Statistics, National Vital Statistics System, Compressed Mortality File.

This table will be updated on the Web. Go to www.cdc.gov/nchs/hus.htm.

Table 34 (page 1 of 2). Age-adjusted death rates for persons 25–64 years of age for selected causes of death, according to sex and educational attainment: Selected States, 1994–2002

[Data are based on death certificates]

	Both sexes			*Male*			*Female*		
	Years of educational attainment[1]			*Years of educational attainment*[1]			*Years of educational attainment*[1]		
Cause of death[2] *and year*	*Less than 12*	*12*	*13 or more*	*Less than 12*	*12*	*13 or more*	*Less than 12*	*12*	*13 or more*
All causes	Age-adjusted death rate per 100,000 population[3]								
1994	594.6	506.4	254.8	793.6	707.1	323.5	397.3	342.9	182.1
1995	604.7	512.5	251.9	801.1	713.2	316.8	408.6	348.1	183.5
1996	579.6	492.5	241.8	763.9	669.6	300.7	396.6	344.2	180.3
1997	554.1	473.4	232.7	719.7	634.4	283.4	387.2	337.5	180.2
1998	561.6	465.8	223.9	727.6	627.1	271.9	395.6	330.9	174.3
1999	585.3	474.5	219.1	763.7	636.7	264.2	409.9	337.3	172.6
2000	591.0	484.5	216.7	780.2	641.8	260.8	409.0	347.7	171.9
2001	576.6	480.9	214.6	745.8	631.2	257.3	407.1	348.6	171.5
2002	575.1	490.9	211.3	726.1	650.2	253.5	416.6	350.7	168.8
Chronic and noncommunicable diseases									
1994	440.5	380.7	193.7	561.9	504.4	228.4	325.0	286.8	155.5
1995	445.1	384.0	192.1	563.4	507.3	224.4	332.1	290.0	156.3
1996	432.7	375.3	189.0	550.6	486.9	222.1	321.2	287.7	153.4
1997	419.0	368.8	187.4	527.0	474.1	219.0	316.0	284.6	153.8
1998	425.2	362.9	180.9	534.4	470.2	211.3	321.3	277.9	148.6
1998 comparability-modified[4]	429.5	366.5	182.7	539.7	474.9	213.4	324.5	280.7	150.1
1999[5]	447.0	369.8	177.2	563.0	477.6	205.5	337.2	283.6	147.4
2000	446.2	377.6	175.7	567.2	481.5	202.9	334.3	292.3	147.2
2001	436.5	370.7	171.1	545.1	468.2	195.7	331.7	290.3	145.5
2002	432.0	374.4	168.6	528.9	478.2	193.9	334.9	288.5	142.6
Injuries									
1994	95.8	73.4	31.9	149.4	119.2	45.7	38.9	31.7	17.9
1995	96.6	74.3	31.6	149.4	120.3	45.3	40.0	32.1	17.8
1996	92.3	73.0	32.0	139.8	116.2	45.7	40.6	32.7	18.4
1997	92.7	73.5	31.9	138.8	116.4	45.5	41.1	33.4	18.4
1998	93.9	73.8	31.2	139.4	116.6	44.4	43.8	33.7	18.3
1998 comparability-modified[4]	95.4	75.0	31.7	141.6	118.4	45.1	44.5	34.2	18.6
1999[5]	95.5	75.5	30.6	145.1	118.9	43.3	42.6	34.4	18.1
2000	100.4	76.7	30.3	155.1	119.2	43.1	43.7	35.3	17.9
2001[6]	97.9	80.7	33.2	147.0	122.7	47.6	44.8	38.6	19.3
2002	99.6	85.2	32.2	143.3	129.6	45.5	49.2	41.0	19.2
Communicable diseases									
1994	57.5	51.6	28.9	81.5	82.8	49.1	32.5	23.7	8.4
1995	62.1	53.4	27.9	87.3	84.7	46.7	35.8	25.2	8.9
1996	53.7	43.3	20.2	72.5	65.6	32.6	33.8	23.0	8.0
1997	41.6	30.1	12.9	53.1	42.9	18.4	29.3	18.7	7.6
1998	41.5	28.2	11.4	52.8	39.4	15.7	29.6	18.4	7.0
1998 comparability-modified[4]	35.6	24.2	9.8	45.3	33.8	13.5	25.4	15.8	6.0
1999[5]	42.1	28.5	10.8	54.8	39.5	15.1	29.4	18.8	6.6
2000	43.5	29.4	10.3	56.9	40.4	14.3	30.3	19.5	6.4
2001	41.4	28.7	9.9	52.9	39.4	13.6	29.7	19.0	6.3
2002	42.7	30.5	10.2	53.0	41.6	13.8	31.8	20.4	6.7
HIV disease:									
1994	36.2	36.5	21.4	54.7	63.0	39.7	16.8	12.3	2.9
1995	39.7	38.0	20.6	59.0	64.4	37.8	19.0	13.7	3.5
1996	31.9	27.7	13.1	45.4	45.4	23.8	17.2	11.2	2.4
1997	19.4	14.3	5.8	26.3	23.0	10.1	11.8	6.2	1.6
1998	17.3	11.7	4.3	23.4	18.3	7.5	10.6	5.6	1.1
1998 comparability-modified[4]	18.7	12.7	4.7	25.3	19.8	8.1	11.5	6.1	1.2
1999[5]	19.0	13.1	4.6	26.1	20.1	7.9	11.7	6.6	1.4
2000	19.8	13.2	4.1	26.9	19.8	7.1	12.6	7.1	1.2
2001	18.4	12.5	3.8	25.0	18.6	6.4	11.6	6.8	1.2
2002	18.2	12.6	3.8	23.4	18.6	6.3	12.6	6.9	1.3

See footnotes at end of table.

Table 34 (page 2 of 2). Age-adjusted death rates for persons 25–64 years of age for selected causes of death, according to sex and educational attainment: Selected States, 1994–2002

[Data are based on death certificates]

	Both sexes			Male			Female		
	Years of educational attainment[1]			Years of educational attainment[1]			Years of educational attainment[1]		
Cause of death[2] and year	Less than 12	12	13 or more	Less than 12	12	13 or more	Less than 12	12	13 or more
	Age-adjusted death rate per 100,000 population[3]								
Other communicable diseases:									
1994	21.2	15.1	7.5	26.8	19.7	9.4	15.7	11.4	5.5
1995	22.4	15.5	7.2	28.2	20.3	8.8	16.8	11.5	5.5
1996	21.8	15.7	7.2	27.2	20.2	8.8	16.7	11.9	5.6
1997	22.2	15.9	7.1	26.8	19.9	8.2	17.6	12.5	6.0
1998	24.2	16.5	7.1	29.4	21.1	8.2	19.0	12.8	5.9
1998 comparability-modified[4]	19.4	13.2	5.7	23.5	16.9	6.6	15.2	10.2	4.7
1999[5]	23.1	15.4	6.2	28.8	19.4	7.2	17.6	12.2	5.3
2000	23.7	16.2	6.2	30.0	20.6	7.2	17.7	12.4	5.1
2001	22.9	16.2	6.1	27.9	20.8	7.1	18.1	12.2	5.1
2002	24.5	17.9	6.4	29.6	23.0	7.5	19.1	13.5	5.4

[1]Educational attainment for the numerator is based on the death certificate item "highest grade completed." Educational attainment for the denominator is based on answers to the Current Population Survey question "What is the highest level of school completed or highest degree received?" (Kominski R, Adams A. Educational Attainment in the United States: March 1993 and 1992, U.S. Bureau of the Census, Current Population Reports, P20–476, Washington, DC. 1994.)
[2]Underlying cause of death was coded according to the Ninth Revision of the *International Classification of Diseases* (ICD) in 1994–98 and the Tenth Revision starting in 1999. See Appendix II, tables IV and V.
[3]Age-adjusted rates are calculated using the proportion distribution of the four age groups, 25–34, 35–44, 45–54, 55–64 from the year 2000 standard population. See Appendix II, Age adjustment and Table I.
Death records that are missing information about decedent's education are not included. Percent with not stated education averages 2–9 percent of the deaths comprising the age-adjusted death rates for causes of death in this table. Age-adjusted death rates for 1994–2000 were calculated using 1990-based postcensal population estimates in the denominator. Starting in 2001, rates were computed using 2000-based postcensal estimates. See Appendix I, Population Census and Population Estimates.
[4]Calculated by multiplying the 1998 rate by its comparability ratio to adjust for differences between ICD–9 and ICD–10. See Appendix II, Comparability ratio and table VI.
[5]Starting with 1999 data, cause of death is coded according to ICD–10. To estimate change between 1998 and 1999, compare the 1999 rate with the comparability-modified rate for 1998. See Appendix II, Comparability ratio and tables V and VI.
[6]Figures include September 11, 2001-related deaths for which death certificates were filed as of October 24, 2002. See Appendix II table V for terrorism-related ICD–10 codes.

NOTES: Based on data from 45–47 States and the District of Columbia. Death rates for age groups 65 years and over are not shown because reporting quality of educational attainment on the death certificate is poorer at older than younger ages. See Appendix II, Education, for information about reporting states and sources of bias in death rates by educational attainment. Comparability-modified 1998 rates were recomputed with final comparability ratios and 1999–2002 injury data were revised; these data may differ from previous editions of *Health, United States.*

SOURCES: Centers for Disease Control and Prevention, National Center for Health Statistics, National Vital Statistics System; numerator data from annual mortality files; denominator data from unpublished population estimates prepared by the Housing and Household Economic Statistics Division, U.S. Bureau of the Census.

Table 35 (page 1 of 4). Death rates for all causes, according to sex, race, Hispanic origin, and age: United States, selected years 1950–2002

[Data are based on death certificates]

Sex, race, Hispanic origin, and age	*1950*[1]	*1960*[1]	*1970*	*1980*	*1990*	*1995*	*1999*	*2000*	*2001*	*2002*
All persons					Deaths per 100,000 resident population					
All ages, age adjusted[2]	1,446.0	1,339.2	1,222.6	1,039.1	938.7	909.8	875.6	869.0	854.5	845.3
All ages, crude	963.8	954.7	945.3	878.3	863.8	868.3	857.0	854.0	848.5	847.3
Under 1 year	3,299.2	2,696.4	2,142.4	1,288.3	971.9	780.3	736.0	736.7	683.4	695.0
1–4 years	139.4	109.1	84.5	63.9	46.8	40.4	34.2	32.4	33.3	31.2
5–14 years	60.1	46.6	41.3	30.6	24.0	22.2	18.6	18.0	17.3	17.4
15–24 years	128.1	106.3	127.7	115.4	99.2	93.4	79.3	79.9	80.7	81.4
25–34 years	178.7	146.4	157.4	135.5	139.2	137.3	102.2	101.4	105.2	103.6
35–44 years	358.7	299.4	314.5	227.9	223.2	239.4	198.0	198.9	203.6	202.9
45–54 years	853.9	756.0	730.0	584.0	473.4	454.3	418.2	425.6	428.9	430.1
55–64 years	1,901.0	1,735.1	1,658.8	1,346.3	1,196.9	1,104.7	1,005.0	992.2	964.6	952.4
65–74 years	4,104.3	3,822.1	3,582.7	2,994.9	2,648.6	2,549.0	2,457.3	2,399.1	2,353.3	2,314.7
75–84 years	9,331.1	8,745.2	8,004.4	6,692.6	6,007.2	5,811.3	5,714.5	5,666.5	5,582.4	5,556.9
85 years and over	20,196.9	19,857.5	16,344.9	15,980.3	15,327.4	15,248.6	15,554.6	15,524.4	15,112.8	14,828.3
Male										
All ages, age adjusted[2]	1,674.2	1,609.0	1,542.1	1,348.1	1,202.8	1,143.9	1,067.0	1,053.8	1,029.1	1,013.7
All ages, crude	1,106.1	1,104.5	1,090.3	976.9	918.4	900.8	859.2	853.0	846.4	846.6
Under 1 year	3,728.0	3,059.3	2,410.0	1,428.5	1,082.8	856.3	805.0	806.5	749.8	761.5
1–4 years	151.7	119.5	93.2	72.6	52.4	44.5	37.9	35.9	37.0	35.2
5–14 years	70.9	55.7	50.5	36.7	28.5	26.4	21.5	20.9	19.8	20.0
15–24 years	167.9	152.1	188.5	172.3	147.4	137.4	113.1	114.9	117.0	117.3
25–34 years	216.5	187.9	215.3	196.1	204.3	198.0	139.7	138.6	143.7	142.2
35–44 years	428.8	372.8	402.6	299.2	310.4	331.0	254.9	255.2	259.6	257.5
45–54 years	1,067.1	992.2	958.5	767.3	610.3	589.9	533.1	542.8	545.1	547.5
55–64 years	2,395.3	2,309.5	2,282.7	1,815.1	1,553.4	1,400.7	1,252.0	1,230.7	1,192.7	1,184.0
65–74 years	4,931.4	4,914.4	4,873.8	4,105.2	3,491.5	3,263.8	3,073.7	2,979.6	2,911.5	2,855.3
75–84 years	10,426.0	10,178.4	10,010.2	8,816.7	7,888.6	7,399.6	7,083.3	6,972.6	6,833.0	6,760.5
85 years and over	21,636.0	21,186.3	17,821.5	18,801.1	18,056.6	17,861.0	17,597.2	17,501.4	16,744.8	16,254.5
Female										
All ages, age adjusted[2]	1,236.0	1,105.3	971.4	817.9	750.9	739.4	734.0	731.4	721.8	715.2
All ages, crude	823.5	809.2	807.8	785.3	812.0	837.2	854.9	855.0	850.4	848.0
Under 1 year	2,854.6	2,321.3	1,863.7	1,141.7	855.7	700.5	663.6	663.4	613.9	625.3
1–4 years	126.7	98.4	75.4	54.7	41.0	36.0	30.3	28.7	29.5	27.0
5–14 years	48.9	37.3	31.8	24.2	19.3	17.9	15.6	15.0	14.6	14.7
15–24 years	89.1	61.3	68.1	57.5	49.0	47.3	43.7	43.1	42.6	43.7
25–34 years	142.7	106.6	101.6	75.9	74.2	76.1	64.1	63.5	66.0	64.0
35–44 years	290.3	229.4	231.1	159.3	137.9	149.3	141.8	143.2	148.2	148.8
45–54 years	641.5	526.7	517.2	412.9	342.7	324.1	307.6	312.5	316.8	316.9
55–64 years	1,404.8	1,196.4	1,098.9	934.3	878.8	835.2	777.6	772.2	754.0	738.0
65–74 years	3,333.2	2,871.8	2,579.7	2,144.7	1,991.2	1,975.8	1,952.3	1,921.2	1,890.8	1,864.7
75–84 years	8,399.6	7,633.1	6,677.6	5,440.1	4,883.1	4,818.6	4,825.4	4,814.7	4,760.5	4,757.9
85 years and over	19,194.7	19,008.4	15,518.0	14,746.9	14,274.3	14,242.3	14,731.3	14,719.2	14,429.9	14,209.6
White male[3]										
All ages, age adjusted[2]	1,642.5	1,586.0	1,513.7	1,317.6	1,165.9	1,107.5	1,040.0	1,029.4	1,006.1	992.9
All ages, crude	1,089.5	1,098.5	1,086.7	983.3	930.9	921.0	892.1	887.8	881.9	884.0
Under 1 year	3,400.5	2,694.1	2,113.2	1,230.3	896.1	720.7	667.0	667.6	627.6	650.9
1–4 years	135.5	104.9	83.6	66.1	45.9	39.0	33.9	32.6	34.2	31.5
5–14 years	67.2	52.7	48.0	35.0	26.4	24.3	19.7	19.8	18.4	18.4
15–24 years	152.4	143.7	170.8	167.0	131.3	120.1	102.8	105.8	108.0	109.7
25–34 years	185.3	163.2	176.6	171.3	176.1	171.9	125.4	124.1	130.3	128.3
35–44 years	380.9	332.6	343.5	257.4	268.2	286.8	230.8	233.6	239.7	239.3
45–54 years	984.5	932.2	882.9	698.9	548.7	528.3	484.6	496.9	501.3	505.4
55–64 years	2,304.4	2,225.2	2,202.6	1,728.5	1,467.2	1,319.3	1,179.7	1,163.3	1,127.5	1,118.6
65–74 years	4,864.9	4,848.4	4,810.1	4,035.7	3,397.7	3,173.3	2,998.7	2,905.7	2,842.3	2,795.4
75–84 years	10,526.3	10,299.6	10,098.8	8,829.8	7,844.9	7,347.3	7,040.1	6,933.1	6,799.7	6,738.8
85 years and over	22,116.3	21,750.0	18,551.7	19,097.3	18,268.3	18,050.7	17,752.9	17,716.4	16,935.4	16,473.2

See footnotes at end of table.

This table will be updated on the Web. Go to www.cdc.gov/nchs/hus.htm.

Table 35 (page 2 of 4). Death rates for all causes, according to sex, race, Hispanic origin, and age: United States, selected years 1950–2002

[Data are based on death certificates]

Sex, race, Hispanic origin, and age	1950[1]	1960[1]	1970	1980	1990	1995	1999	2000	2001	2002
Black or African American male[3]				Deaths per 100,000 resident population						
All ages, age adjusted[2]	1,909.1	1,811.1	1,873.9	1,697.8	1,644.5	1,585.7	1,432.6	1,403.5	1,375.0	1,341.4
All ages, crude	1,257.7	1,181.7	1,186.6	1,034.1	1,008.0	960.2	847.4	834.1	823.9	816.7
Under 1 year	---	5,306.8	4,298.9	2,586.7	2,112.4	1,664.7	1,592.8	1,567.6	1,426.4	1,351.5
1–4 years[4]	1,412.6	208.5	150.5	110.5	85.8	73.1	59.0	54.5	53.2	54.4
5–14 years	95.1	75.1	67.1	47.4	41.2	38.5	32.0	28.2	27.7	28.9
15–24 years	289.7	212.0	320.6	209.1	252.2	246.6	184.6	181.4	180.7	172.6
25–34 years	503.5	402.5	559.5	407.3	430.8	407.4	258.6	261.0	259.2	264.5
35–44 years	878.1	762.0	956.6	689.8	699.6	716.8	469.2	453.0	445.0	434.7
45–54 years	1,905.0	1,624.8	1,777.5	1,479.9	1,261.0	1,238.9	1,030.7	1,017.7	996.1	983.0
55–64 years	3,773.2	3,316.4	3,256.9	2,873.0	2,618.4	2,382.0	2,145.6	2,080.1	2,025.3	2,039.2
65–74 years	5,310.3	5,798.7	5,803.2	5,131.1	4,946.1	4,707.8	4,352.3	4,253.5	4,166.6	4,024.5
75–84 years[5]	10,101.9	8,605.1	9,454.9	9,231.6	9,129.5	8,862.0	8,559.1	8,486.0	8,355.9	8,169.6
85 years and over	---	14,844.8	12,222.3	16,098.8	16,954.9	17,016.0	17,304.5	16,791.0	16,439.9	15,635.5
American Indian or Alaska Native male[3]										
All ages, age adjusted[2]	---	---	---	1,111.5	916.2	932.0	925.9	841.5	798.9	794.2
All ages, crude	---	---	---	597.1	476.4	459.4	431.8	415.6	424.2	439.6
Under 1 year	---	---	---	1,598.1	1,056.6	696.0	721.8	700.2	720.2	896.8
1–4 years	---	---	---	82.7	77.4	73.3	46.6	44.9	47.6	48.3
5–14 years	---	---	---	43.7	33.4	27.0	18.8	20.2	25.2	22.0
15–24 years	---	---	---	311.1	219.8	182.1	154.2	136.2	142.9	145.1
25–34 years	---	---	---	360.6	256.1	263.6	189.6	179.1	180.0	193.1
35–44 years	---	---	---	556.8	365.4	377.4	296.5	295.2	311.4	321.5
45–54 years	---	---	---	871.3	619.9	601.0	554.8	520.0	536.9	539.4
55–64 years	---	---	---	1,547.5	1,211.3	1,276.0	1,122.4	1,090.4	1,053.4	1,059.2
65–74 years	---	---	---	2,968.4	2,461.7	2,660.8	2,786.2	2,478.3	2,393.5	2,366.5
75–84 years	---	---	---	5,607.0	5,389.2	5,787.7	6,157.2	5,351.2	4,775.3	4,748.3
85 years and over	---	---	---	12,635.2	11,243.9	10,604.7	11,769.3	10,725.8	9,758.0	9,219.2
Asian or Pacific Islander male[3]										
All ages, age adjusted[2]	---	---	---	786.5	716.4	693.4	641.2	624.2	597.4	578.4
All ages, crude	---	---	---	375.3	334.3	341.4	333.2	332.9	335.0	331.4
Under 1 year	---	---	---	816.5	605.3	468.3	451.0	529.4	438.8	461.9
1–4 years	---	---	---	50.9	45.0	28.0	28.9	23.3	23.5	27.1
5–14 years	---	---	---	23.4	20.7	19.6	13.5	12.9	13.6	14.4
15–24 years	---	---	---	80.8	76.0	73.0	51.6	55.2	59.2	58.6
25–34 years	---	---	---	83.5	79.6	75.4	57.3	55.0	62.4	54.5
35–44 years	---	---	---	128.3	130.8	124.9	108.2	104.9	108.2	100.0
45–54 years	---	---	---	342.3	287.1	273.0	240.1	249.7	253.6	248.4
55–64 years	---	---	---	881.1	789.1	714.2	661.0	642.4	625.5	594.5
65–74 years	---	---	---	2,236.1	2,041.4	1,894.8	1,689.5	1,661.0	1,556.0	1,487.1
75–84 years	---	---	---	5,389.5	5,008.6	4,729.9	4,457.0	4,328.2	4,168.9	4,090.8
85 years and over	---	---	---	13,753.6	12,446.3	13,252.0	12,732.5	12,125.3	11,308.9	10,938.5
Hispanic or Latino male[3,6]										
All ages, age adjusted[2]	---	---	---	---	886.4	897.6	830.5	818.1	802.5	766.7
All ages, crude	---	---	---	---	411.6	391.6	332.6	331.3	332.9	328.7
Under 1 year	---	---	---	---	921.8	684.6	623.4	637.1	624.4	644.0
1–4 years	---	---	---	---	53.8	39.3	32.9	31.5	33.8	34.2
5–14 years	---	---	---	---	26.0	24.6	17.8	17.9	16.6	17.4
15–24 years	---	---	---	---	159.3	147.3	104.1	107.7	111.5	114.4
25–34 years	---	---	---	---	234.0	196.7	120.6	120.2	118.0	112.5
35–44 years	---	---	---	---	341.8	333.6	215.1	211.0	208.5	192.5
45–54 years	---	---	---	---	533.9	528.5	444.4	439.0	443.9	423.4
55–64 years	---	---	---	---	1,123.7	1,076.9	974.8	965.7	923.9	937.4
65–74 years	---	---	---	---	2,368.2	2,429.3	2,368.9	2,287.9	2,242.6	2,193.4
75–84 years	---	---	---	---	5,369.1	5,557.4	5,379.2	5,395.3	5,258.0	5,043.5
85 years and over	---	---	---	---	12,272.1	13,295.9	13,485.9	13,086.2	12,888.3	11,674.1

See footnotes at end of table.

This table will be updated on the Web. Go to www.cdc.gov/nchs/hus.htm.

Table 35 (page 3 of 4). Death rates for all causes, according to sex, race, Hispanic origin, and age: United States, selected years 1950–2002

[Data are based on death certificates]

Sex, race, Hispanic origin, and age	1950[1]	1960[1]	1970	1980	1990	1995	1999	2000	2001	2002
White, not Hispanic or Latino male[6]				Deaths per 100,000 resident population						
All ages, age adjusted[2]	---	---	---	---	1,170.9	1,105.6	1,045.5	1,035.4	1,012.8	1,002.2
All ages, crude	---	---	---	---	985.9	984.8	979.6	978.5	975.6	983.9
Under 1 year	---	---	---	---	865.4	703.8	658.1	658.7	611.6	643.5
1–4 years	---	---	---	---	43.8	37.8	33.4	32.4	33.7	30.3
5–14 years	---	---	---	---	25.7	23.5	19.9	20.0	18.6	18.3
15–24 years	---	---	---	---	123.4	111.5	100.8	103.5	105.1	106.7
25–34 years	---	---	---	---	165.3	163.5	124.5	123.0	131.5	130.9
35–44 years	---	---	---	---	257.1	276.5	230.0	233.9	241.6	244.9
45–54 years	---	---	---	---	544.5	520.7	483.7	497.7	502.6	509.9
55–64 years	---	---	---	---	1,479.7	1,322.7	1,187.4	1,170.9	1,136.3	1,126.5
65–74 years	---	---	---	---	3,434.5	3,188.5	3,023.2	2,930.5	2,869.4	2,824.1
75–84 years	---	---	---	---	7,920.4	7,367.4	7,088.0	6,977.8	6,851.5	6,801.7
85 years and over	---	---	---	---	18,505.4	18,132.6	17,871.2	17,853.2	17,055.3	16,641.9
White female[3]										
All ages, age adjusted[2]	1,198.0	1,074.4	944.0	796.1	728.8	718.7	716.6	715.3	706.7	701.3
All ages, crude	803.3	800.9	812.6	806.1	846.9	883.2	910.4	912.3	907.9	907.0
Under 1 year	2,566.8	2,007.7	1,614.6	962.5	690.0	574.4	542.0	550.5	511.5	519.4
1–4 years	112.2	85.2	66.1	49.3	36.1	31.3	27.5	25.5	27.1	24.5
5–14 years	45.1	34.7	29.9	22.9	17.9	16.5	14.6	14.1	13.9	13.7
15–24 years	71.5	54.9	61.6	55.5	45.9	43.7	41.5	41.1	40.8	42.4
25–34 years	112.8	85.0	84.1	65.4	61.5	62.9	56.2	55.1	58.6	56.9
35–44 years	235.8	191.1	193.3	138.2	117.4	125.5	123.2	125.7	131.0	133.2
45–54 years	546.4	458.8	462.9	372.7	309.3	291.9	277.9	281.4	286.8	286.8
55–64 years	1,293.8	1,078.9	1,014.9	876.2	822.7	783.4	731.0	730.9	712.2	698.7
65–74 years	3,242.8	2,779.3	2,470.7	2,066.6	1,923.5	1,913.2	1,893.9	1,868.3	1,840.2	1,819.7
75–84 years	8,481.5	7,696.6	6,698.7	5,401.7	4,839.1	4,775.3	4,787.8	4,785.3	4,738.5	4,742.5
85 years and over	19,679.5	19,477.7	15,980.2	14,979.6	14,400.6	14,405.8	14,900.6	14,890.7	14,597.6	14,382.8
Black or African American female[3]										
All ages, age adjusted[2]	1,545.5	1,369.7	1,228.7	1,033.3	975.1	955.9	933.6	927.6	912.5	901.8
All ages, crude	1,002.0	905.0	829.2	733.3	747.9	743.2	734.3	733.0	727.7	724.4
Under 1 year	---	4,162.2	3,368.8	2,123.7	1,735.5	1,399.9	1,317.4	1,279.8	1,176.3	1,172.0
1–4 years[4]	1,139.3	173.3	129.4	84.4	67.6	59.5	46.1	45.3	41.7	39.5
5–14 years	72.8	53.8	43.8	30.5	27.5	25.4	20.9	20.0	18.7	19.9
15–24 years	213.1	107.5	111.9	70.5	68.7	68.9	58.6	58.3	54.9	54.4
25–34 years	393.3	273.2	231.0	150.0	159.5	162.8	117.6	121.8	117.9	116.4
35–44 years	758.1	568.5	533.0	323.9	298.6	324.9	279.4	271.9	278.0	272.3
45–54 years	1,576.4	1,177.0	1,043.9	768.2	639.4	612.1	569.8	588.3	579.1	579.4
55–64 years	3,089.4	2,510.9	1,986.2	1,561.0	1,452.6	1,354.3	1,262.7	1,227.2	1,215.5	1,184.2
65–74 years	4,000.2	4,064.2	3,860.9	3,057.4	2,865.7	2,837.5	2,751.5	2,689.6	2,616.1	2,545.0
75–84 years[5]	8,347.0	6,730.0	6,691.5	6,212.1	5,688.3	5,671.9	5,742.4	5,696.5	5,591.6	5,584.4
85 years and over	---	13,052.6	10,706.6	12,367.2	13,309.5	13,073.3	13,805.9	13,941.3	13,849.9	13,734.2
American Indian or Alaska Native female[3]										
All ages, age adjusted[2]	---	---	---	662.4	561.8	643.9	668.2	604.5	594.0	581.1
All ages, crude	---	---	---	380.1	330.4	360.1	367.1	346.1	360.2	367.7
Under 1 year	---	---	---	1,352.6	688.7	780.6	682.6	492.2	577.5	744.1
1–4 years	---	---	---	87.5	37.8	54.4	34.2	39.8	48.5	42.0
5–14 years	---	---	---	33.5	25.5	20.0	17.6	17.7	18.6	21.2
15–24 years	---	---	---	90.3	69.0	60.4	59.6	58.9	59.6	61.7
25–34 years	---	---	---	178.5	102.3	106.3	106.9	84.8	81.4	87.5
35–44 years	---	---	---	286.0	156.4	171.9	168.9	171.9	172.6	176.8
45–54 years	---	---	---	491.4	380.9	349.1	298.7	284.9	334.3	324.7
55–64 years	---	---	---	837.1	805.9	876.2	852.3	772.1	749.4	747.5
65–74 years	---	---	---	1,765.5	1,679.4	1,935.6	2,015.8	1,899.8	1,801.7	1,828.9
75–84 years	---	---	---	3,612.9	3,073.2	4,067.6	4,266.5	3,850.0	3,839.7	3,667.4
85 years and over	---	---	---	8,567.4	8,201.1	9,201.8	10,639.6	9,118.2	8,492.0	7,866.4

See footnotes at end of table.

This table will be updated on the Web. Go to www.cdc.gov/nchs/hus.htm.

Table 35 (page 4 of 4). Death rates for all causes, according to sex, race, Hispanic origin, and age: United States, selected years 1950–2002

[Data are based on death certificates]

Sex, race, Hispanic origin, and age	1950[1]	1960[1]	1970	1980	1990	1995	1999	2000	2001	2002
Asian or Pacific Islander female[3]					Deaths per 100,000 resident population					
All ages, age adjusted[2]	---	---	---	425.9	469.3	446.7	427.5	416.8	412.0	395.9
All ages, crude	---	---	---	222.5	234.3	250.4	262.5	262.3	274.4	269.7
Under 1 year	---	---	---	755.8	518.2	396.6	425.3	434.3	385.0	391.4
1–4 years	---	---	---	35.4	32.0	24.9	20.9	20.0	21.1	19.6
5–14 years	---	---	---	21.5	13.0	15.4	11.9	11.7	10.8	10.4
15–24 years	---	---	---	32.3	28.8	31.1	26.1	22.4	26.6	23.8
25–34 years	---	---	---	45.4	37.5	35.6	29.5	27.6	32.9	26.6
35–44 years	---	---	---	89.7	69.9	66.2	59.0	65.6	61.9	53.9
45–54 years	---	---	---	214.1	182.7	184.1	164.4	155.5	158.5	149.5
55–64 years	---	---	---	440.8	483.4	457.7	408.7	390.9	379.9	372.0
65–74 years	---	---	---	1,027.7	1,089.2	1,037.8	1,070.8	996.4	1,059.9	1,024.7
75–84 years	---	---	---	2,833.6	3,127.9	3,089.9	2,930.8	2,882.4	2,814.4	2,713.6
85 years and over	---	---	---	7,923.3	10,254.0	9,406.1	9,126.7	9,052.2	8,706.2	8,400.6
Hispanic or Latino female[3,6]										
All ages, age adjusted[2]	---	---	---	---	537.1	546.1	555.9	546.0	544.2	518.3
All ages, crude	---	---	---	---	285.4	281.9	277.2	274.6	279.0	274.0
Under 1 year	---	---	---	---	746.6	572.0	542.3	553.6	518.9	539.1
1–4 years	---	---	---	---	42.1	33.1	28.7	27.5	27.2	25.3
5–14 years	---	---	---	---	17.3	15.0	13.3	13.4	12.7	13.5
15–24 years	---	---	---	---	40.6	37.5	32.9	31.7	33.7	34.1
25–34 years	---	---	---	---	62.9	58.6	44.9	43.4	45.2	40.0
35–44 years	---	---	---	---	109.3	118.9	97.4	100.5	97.0	94.9
45–54 years	---	---	---	---	253.3	238.8	224.9	223.8	226.7	219.8
55–64 years	---	---	---	---	607.5	602.3	555.8	548.4	543.0	524.3
65–74 years	---	---	---	---	1,453.8	1,457.2	1,448.8	1,423.2	1,408.0	1,368.7
75–84 years	---	---	---	---	3,351.3	3,506.4	3,675.7	3,624.5	3,589.8	3,526.4
85 years and over	---	---	---	---	10,098.7	10,540.5	11,547.3	11,202.8	11,300.5	10,186.0
White, non-Hispanic or Latino female[6]										
All ages, age adjusted[2]	---	---	---	---	734.6	721.1	722.3	721.5	713.5	709.9
All ages, crude	---	---	---	---	903.6	951.7	1,001.3	1,007.3	1,006.1	1,010.6
Under 1 year	---	---	---	---	655.3	553.9	524.6	530.9	496.4	504.8
1–4 years	---	---	---	---	34.0	30.3	26.7	24.4	26.3	23.8
5–14 years	---	---	---	---	17.6	16.4	14.7	13.9	13.9	13.6
15–24 years	---	---	---	---	46.0	44.0	42.9	42.6	41.9	43.8
25–34 years	---	---	---	---	60.6	62.2	57.8	56.8	60.9	60.3
35–44 years	---	---	---	---	116.8	124.1	125.6	128.1	134.9	138.3
45–54 years	---	---	---	---	312.1	293.0	281.0	285.0	291.0	292.1
55–64 years	---	---	---	---	834.5	789.8	741.6	742.1	723.5	710.5
65–74 years	---	---	---	---	1,940.2	1,925.9	1,915.1	1,891.0	1,864.1	1,846.0
75–84 years	---	---	---	---	4,887.3	4,794.9	4,817.7	4,819.3	4,777.3	4,787.9
85 years and over	---	---	---	---	14,533.1	14,450.9	14,967.5	14,971.7	14,670.6	14,504.3

- - - Data not available.

[1]Includes deaths of persons who were not residents of the 50 States and the District of Columbia.

[2]Age-adjusted rates are calculated using the year 2000 standard population. See Appendix II, Age adjustment.

[3]The race groups, white, black, Asian or Pacific Islander, and American Indian or Alaska Native, include persons of Hispanic and non-Hispanic origin. Persons of Hispanic origin may be of any race. Death rates for the American Indian or Alaska Native and Asian or Pacific Islander populations are known to be underestimated. See Appendix II, Race, for a discussion of sources of bias in death rates by race and Hispanic origin.

[4]In 1950 rate is for the age group under 5 years.

[5]In 1950 rate is for the age group 75 years and over.

[6]Prior to 1997, excludes data from States lacking an Hispanic-origin item on the death certificate. See Appendix II, Hispanic origin.

NOTES: Starting with *Health, United States, 2003*, rates for 1991–99 were revised using intercensal population estimates based on census 2000. Rates for 2000 were revised based on census 2000 counts. Rates for 2001 and 2002 were computed using 2000-based postcensal estimates. See Appendix I, Population Census and Population Estimates. Data for additional years are available. See Appendix III.

SOURCES: Centers for Disease Control and Prevention, National Center for Health Statistics, National Vital Statistics System; Grove RD, Hetzel AM. *Vital statistics rates in the United States, 1940–60.* Washington: U.S. Government Printing Office, 1968; numerator data from National Vital Statistics System, annual mortality files; denominator data from national population estimates for race groups from table 1 and unpublished Hispanic population estimates for 1985–96 prepared by the Housing and Household Economic Statistics Division, U.S. Bureau of the Census; additional mortality tables are available at www.cdc.gov/nchs/datawh/statab/unpubd/mortabs.htm; Kochanek KD, Murphy SL, Anderson RN, Scott C. Deaths: Final data for 2002. National vital statistics reports. Vol 53 no 5. Hyattsville, Maryland: National Center for Health Statistics. 2004.

This table will be updated on the Web. Go to www.cdc.gov/nchs/hus.htm.

Table 36 (page 1 of 3). Death rates for diseases of heart, according to sex, race, Hispanic origin, and age: United States, selected years 1950–2002

[Data are based on death certificates]

Sex, race, Hispanic origin, and age	*1950*[1]	*1960*[1]	*1970*	*1980*	*1990*	*2000*[2]	*2001*	*2002*
All persons				Deaths per 100,000 resident population				
All ages, age adjusted[3]	586.8	559.0	492.7	412.1	321.8	257.6	247.8	240.8
All ages, crude	355.5	369.0	362.0	336.0	289.5	252.6	245.8	241.7
Under 1 year	3.5	6.6	13.1	22.8	20.1	13.0	11.9	12.4
1–4 years	1.3	1.3	1.7	2.6	1.9	1.2	1.5	1.1
5–14 years	2.1	1.3	0.8	0.9	0.9	0.7	0.7	0.6
15–24 years	6.8	4.0	3.0	2.9	2.5	2.6	2.5	2.5
25–34 years	19.4	15.6	11.4	8.3	7.6	7.4	8.0	7.9
35–44 years	86.4	74.6	66.7	44.6	31.4	29.2	29.6	30.5
45–54 years	308.6	271.8	238.4	180.2	120.5	94.2	92.9	93.7
55–64 years	808.1	737.9	652.3	494.1	367.3	261.2	246.9	241.5
65–74 years	1,839.8	1,740.5	1,558.2	1,218.6	894.3	665.6	635.1	615.9
75–84 years	4,310.1	4,089.4	3,683.8	2,993.1	2,295.7	1,780.3	1,725.7	1,677.2
85 years and over	9,150.6	9,317.8	7,891.3	7,777.1	6,739.9	5,926.1	5,664.2	5,446.8
Male								
All ages, age adjusted[3]	697.0	687.6	634.0	538.9	412.4	320.0	305.4	297.4
All ages, crude	423.4	439.5	422.5	368.6	297.6	249.8	242.5	240.7
Under 1 year	4.0	7.8	15.1	25.5	21.9	13.3	11.8	12.9
1–4 years	1.4	1.4	1.9	2.8	1.9	1.4	1.5	1.1
5–14 years	2.0	1.4	0.9	1.0	0.9	0.8	0.7	0.7
15–24 years	6.8	4.2	3.7	3.7	3.1	3.2	3.2	3.3
25–34 years	22.9	20.1	15.2	11.4	10.3	9.6	10.3	10.5
35–44 years	118.4	112.7	103.2	68.7	48.1	41.4	41.7	43.1
45–54 years	440.5	420.4	376.4	282.6	183.0	140.2	136.6	138.4
55–64 years	1,104.5	1,066.9	987.2	746.8	537.3	371.7	349.8	343.4
65–74 years	2,292.3	2,291.3	2,170.3	1,728.0	1,250.0	898.3	851.3	827.1
75–84 years	4,825.0	4,742.4	4,534.8	3,834.3	2,968.2	2,248.1	2,177.3	2,110.1
85 years and over	9,659.8	9,788.9	8,426.2	8,752.7	7,418.4	6,430.0	6,040.5	5,823.5
Female								
All ages, age adjusted[3]	484.7	447.0	381.6	320.8	257.0	210.9	203.9	197.2
All ages, crude	288.4	300.6	304.5	305.1	281.8	255.3	249.0	242.7
Under 1 year	2.9	5.4	10.9	20.0	18.3	12.5	12.0	11.8
1–4 years	1.2	1.1	1.6	2.5	1.9	1.0	1.4	1.0
5–14 years	2.2	1.2	0.8	0.9	0.8	0.5	0.7	0.6
15–24 years	6.7	3.7	2.3	2.1	1.8	2.1	1.8	1.7
25–34 years	16.2	11.3	7.7	5.3	5.0	5.2	5.6	5.2
35–44 years	55.1	38.2	32.2	21.4	15.1	17.2	17.6	18.0
45–54 years	177.2	127.5	109.9	84.5	61.0	49.8	50.7	50.6
55–64 years	510.0	429.4	351.6	272.1	215.7	159.3	151.8	147.2
65–74 years	1,419.3	1,261.3	1,082.7	828.6	616.8	474.0	455.9	440.1
75–84 years	3,872.0	3,582.7	3,120.8	2,497.0	1,893.8	1,475.1	1,428.9	1,389.7
85 years and over	8,796.1	9,016.8	7,591.8	7,350.5	6,478.1	5,720.9	5,506.8	5,283.3
White male[4]								
All ages, age adjusted[3]	700.2	694.5	640.2	539.6	409.2	316.7	301.8	294.1
All ages, crude	433.0	454.6	438.3	384.0	312.7	265.8	257.8	256.0
45–54 years	423.6	413.2	365.7	269.8	170.6	130.7	127.0	128.6
55–64 years	1,081.7	1,056.0	979.3	730.6	516.7	351.8	330.8	324.0
65–74 years	2,308.3	2,297.9	2,177.2	1,729.7	1,230.5	877.8	829.1	807.8
75–84 years	4,907.3	4,839.9	4,617.6	3,883.2	2,983.4	2,247.0	2,175.8	2,112.0
85 years and over	9,950.5	10,135.8	8,818.0	8,958.0	7,558.7	6,560.8	6,157.2	5,939.8
Black or African American male[4]								
All ages, age adjusted[3]	639.4	615.2	607.3	561.4	485.4	392.5	384.5	371.0
All ages, crude	346.2	330.6	330.3	301.0	256.8	211.1	209.0	206.3
45–54 years	622.5	514.0	512.8	433.4	328.9	247.2	242.6	246.0
55–64 years	1,433.1	1,236.8	1,135.4	987.2	824.0	631.2	602.2	605.3
65–74 years	2,139.1	2,281.4	2,237.8	1,847.2	1,632.9	1,268.8	1,245.8	1,192.7
75–84 years[5]	4,106.1	3,533.6	3,783.4	3,578.8	3,107.1	2,597.6	2,569.3	2,449.6
85 years and over	- - -	6,037.9	5,367.6	6,819.5	6,479.6	5,633.5	5,459.9	5,125.7

See footnotes at end of table.

This table will be updated on the Web. Go to www.cdc.gov/nchs/hus.htm.

Table 36 (page 2 of 3). Death rates for diseases of heart, according to sex, race, Hispanic origin, and age: United States, selected years 1950–2002

[Data are based on death certificates]

Sex, race, Hispanic origin, and age	*1950*[1]	*1960*[1]	*1970*	*1980*	*1990*	*2000*[2]	*2001*	*2002*
	Deaths per 100,000 resident population							
American Indian or Alaska Native male[4]								
All ages, age adjusted[3]	---	---	---	320.5	264.1	222.2	200.7	201.2
All ages, crude	---	---	---	130.6	108.0	90.1	89.1	92.0
45–54 years	---	---	---	238.1	173.8	108.5	109.1	104.2
55–64 years	---	---	---	496.3	411.0	285.0	301.1	273.2
65–74 years	---	---	---	1,009.4	839.1	748.2	682.1	638.4
75–84 years	---	---	---	2,062.2	1,788.8	1,655.7	1,384.5	1,422.7
85 years and over	---	---	---	4,413.7	3,860.3	3,318.3	2,895.7	3,162.4
Asian or Pacific Islander male[4]								
All ages, age adjusted[3]	---	---	---	286.9	220.7	185.5	169.8	169.8
All ages, crude	---	---	---	119.8	88.7	90.6	87.3	89.4
45–54 years	---	---	---	112.0	70.4	61.1	60.1	60.6
55–64 years	---	---	---	306.7	226.1	182.6	162.0	154.2
65–74 years	---	---	---	852.4	623.5	482.5	439.1	422.4
75–84 years	---	---	---	2,010.9	1,642.2	1,354.7	1,273.8	1,252.4
85 years and over	---	---	---	5,923.0	4,617.8	4,154.2	3,688.1	3,841.3
Hispanic or Latino male[4,6]								
All ages, age adjusted[3]	---	---	---	---	270.0	238.2	232.6	219.8
All ages, crude	---	---	---	---	91.0	74.7	74.6	74.0
45–54 years	---	---	---	---	116.4	84.3	82.9	80.5
55–64 years	---	---	---	---	363.0	264.8	242.2	256.0
65–74 years	---	---	---	---	829.9	684.8	683.7	657.7
75–84 years	---	---	---	---	1,971.3	1,733.2	1,702.7	1,599.5
85 years and over	---	---	---	---	4,711.9	4,897.5	4,784.3	4,301.8
White, not Hispanic or Latino male[6]								
All ages, age adjusted[3]	---	---	---	---	413.6	319.9	304.8	297.7
All ages, crude	---	---	---	---	336.5	297.5	289.5	289.2
45–54 years	---	---	---	---	172.8	134.3	130.7	133.1
55–64 years	---	---	---	---	521.3	356.3	335.8	327.6
65–74 years	---	---	---	---	1,243.4	885.1	834.7	813.5
75–84 years	---	---	---	---	3,007.7	2,261.9	2,190.4	2,129.9
85 years and over	---	---	---	---	7,663.4	6,606.6	6,195.4	5,994.1
White female[4]								
All ages, age adjusted[3]	478.0	441.7	376.7	315.9	250.9	205.6	198.7	192.1
All ages, crude	289.4	306.5	313.8	319.2	298.4	274.5	267.7	261.0
45–54 years	141.9	103.4	91.4	71.2	50.2	40.9	41.5	41.7
55–64 years	460.2	383.0	317.7	248.1	192.4	141.3	134.3	130.6
65–74 years	1,400.9	1,229.8	1,044.0	796.7	583.6	445.2	429.0	414.7
75–84 years	3,925.2	3,629.7	3,143.5	2,493.6	1,874.3	1,452.4	1,407.9	1,368.2
85 years and over	9,084.7	9,280.8	7,839.9	7,501.6	6,563.4	5,801.4	5,582.5	5,350.6
Black or African American female[4]								
All ages, age adjusted[3]	536.9	488.9	435.6	378.6	327.5	277.6	269.8	263.2
All ages, crude	287.6	268.5	261.0	249.7	237.0	212.6	208.6	205.0
45–54 years	525.3	360.7	290.9	202.4	155.3	125.0	125.9	124.9
55–64 years	1,210.2	952.3	710.5	530.1	442.0	332.8	323.1	312.3
65–74 years	1,659.4	1,680.5	1,553.2	1,210.3	1,017.5	815.2	768.0	734.0
75–84 years[5]	3,499.3	2,926.9	2,964.1	2,707.2	2,250.9	1,913.1	1,849.6	1,821.9
85 years and over	---	5,650.0	5,003.8	5,796.5	5,766.1	5,298.7	5,207.3	5,111.2

See footnotes at end of table.

This table will be updated on the Web. Go to www.cdc.gov/nchs/hus.htm.

Table 36 (page 3 of 3). Death rates for diseases of heart, according to sex, race, Hispanic origin, and age: United States, selected years 1950–2002

[Data are based on death certificates]

Sex, race, Hispanic origin, and age	1950[1]	1960[1]	1970	1980	1990	2000[2]	2001	2002
American Indian or Alaska Native female[4]				Deaths per 100,000 resident population				
All ages, age adjusted[3]	---	---	---	175.4	153.1	143.6	127.0	123.6
All ages, crude	---	---	---	80.3	77.5	71.9	68.2	68.5
45–54 years	---	---	---	65.2	62.0	40.2	42.7	29.7
55–64 years	---	---	---	193.5	197.0	149.4	126.5	124.3
65–74 years	---	---	---	577.2	492.8	391.8	384.2	365.8
75–84 years	---	---	---	1,364.3	1,050.3	1,044.1	934.3	1,002.5
85 years and over	---	---	---	2,893.3	2,868.7	3,146.3	2,510.3	2,372.5
Asian or Pacific Islander female[4]								
All ages, age adjusted[3]	---	---	---	132.3	149.2	115.7	112.9	108.1
All ages, crude	---	---	---	57.0	62.0	65.0	67.9	67.4
45–54 years	---	---	---	28.6	17.5	15.9	18.4	16.4
55–64 years	---	---	---	92.9	99.0	68.8	62.8	61.8
65–74 years	---	---	---	313.3	323.9	229.6	241.7	239.9
75–84 years	---	---	---	1,053.2	1,130.9	866.2	848.7	796.9
85 years and over	---	---	---	3,211.0	4,161.2	3,367.2	3,186.3	3,067.4
Hispanic or Latino female[4,6]								
All ages, age adjusted[3]	---	---	---	---	177.2	163.7	161.0	149.7
All ages, crude	---	---	---	---	79.4	71.5	71.8	69.7
45–54 years	---	---	---	---	43.5	28.2	27.9	30.2
55–64 years	---	---	---	---	153.2	111.2	107.2	105.7
65–74 years	---	---	---	---	460.4	366.3	363.1	346.4
75–84 years	---	---	---	---	1,259.7	1,169.4	1,155.7	1,090.8
85 years and over	---	---	---	---	4,440.3	4,605.8	4,521.1	4,032.8
White, not Hispanic or Latino female[6]								
All ages, age adjusted[3]	---	---	---	---	252.6	206.8	200.0	193.7
All ages, crude	---	---	---	---	320.0	304.9	298.4	292.3
45–54 years	---	---	---	---	50.2	41.9	42.7	42.6
55–64 years	---	---	---	---	193.6	142.9	136.0	132.0
65–74 years	---	---	---	---	584.7	448.5	431.8	417.4
75–84 years	---	---	---	---	1,890.2	1,458.9	1,414.7	1,377.2
85 years and over	---	---	---	---	6,615.2	5,822.7	5,601.6	5,384.5

- - - Data not available.
[1]Includes deaths of persons who were not residents of the 50 States and the District of Columbia.
[2]Starting with 1999 data, cause of death is coded according to ICD–10. See Appendix II, Comparability ratio and tables V and VI.
[3]Age-adjusted rates are calculated using the year 2000 standard population. See Appendix II, Age adjustment.
[4]The race groups, white, black, Asian or Pacific Islander, and American Indian or Alaska Native, include persons of Hispanic and non-Hispanic origin. Persons of Hispanic origin may be of any race. Death rates for the American Indian or Alaska Native and Asian or Pacific Islander populations are known to be underestimated. See Appendix II, Race, for a discussion of sources of bias in death rates by race and Hispanic origin.
[5]In 1950 rate is for the age group 75 years and over.
[6]Prior to 1997, excludes data from States lacking an Hispanic-origin item on the death certificate. See Appendix II, Hispanic origin.

NOTES: Starting with *Health, United States, 2003*, rates for 1991–99 were revised using intercensal population estimates based on census 2000. Rates for 2000 were revised based on census 2000 counts. Rates for 2001 and 2002 were computed using 2000-based postcensal estimates. See Appendix I, Population Census and Population Estimates. Underlying cause of death code numbers are based on the applicable revision of the *International Classification of Diseases* (ICD) for data years shown. For the period 1980–98, causes were coded using ICD–9 codes that are most nearly comparable with the 113 cause list for ICD–10. See Appendix II, tables IV and V. Age groups were selected to minimize the presentation of unstable age-specific death rates based on small numbers of deaths and for consistency among comparison groups. Data for additional years are available. See Appendix III.

SOURCES: Centers for Disease Control and Prevention, National Center for Health Statistics, National Vital Statistics System; numerator data from annual mortality files; denominator data from national population estimates for race groups from table 1 and unpublished Hispanic population estimates for 1985–96 prepared by the Housing and Household Economic Statistics Division, U.S. Bureau of the Census; additional mortality tables are available at www.cdc.gov/nchs/datawh/statab/unpubd/mortabs.htm; Kochanek KD, Murphy SL, Anderson RN, Scott C. Deaths: Final data for 2002. National vital statistics reports. Vol 53 no 5. Hyattsville, Maryland: National Center for Health Statistics. 2004.

This table will be updated on the Web. Go to www.cdc.gov/nchs/hus.htm.

Table 37 (page 1 of 3). Death rates for cerebrovascular diseases, according to sex, race, Hispanic origin, and age: United States, selected years 1950–2002

[Data are based on death certificates]

Sex, race, Hispanic origin, and age	1950[1]	1960[1]	1970	1980	1990	2000[2]	2001	2002
All persons	Deaths per 100,000 resident population							
All ages, age adjusted[3]	180.7	177.9	147.7	96.2	65.3	60.9	57.9	56.2
All ages, crude	104.0	108.0	101.9	75.0	57.8	59.6	57.4	56.4
Under 1 year	5.1	4.1	5.0	4.4	3.8	3.3	2.7	2.9
1–4 years	0.9	0.8	1.0	0.5	0.3	0.3	0.4	0.3
5–14 years	0.5	0.7	0.7	0.3	0.2	0.2	0.2	0.2
15–24 years	1.6	1.8	1.6	1.0	0.6	0.5	0.5	0.4
25–34 years	4.2	4.7	4.5	2.6	2.2	1.5	1.5	1.4
35–44 years	18.7	14.7	15.6	8.5	6.4	5.8	5.5	5.4
45–54 years	70.4	49.2	41.6	25.2	18.7	16.0	15.1	15.1
55–64 years	194.2	147.3	115.8	65.1	47.9	41.0	38.0	37.2
65–74 years	554.7	469.2	384.1	219.0	144.2	128.6	123.4	120.3
75–84 years	1,499.6	1,491.3	1,254.2	786.9	498.0	461.3	443.9	431.0
85 years and over	2,990.1	3,680.5	3,014.3	2,283.7	1,628.9	1,589.2	1,500.2	1,445.9
Male								
All ages, age adjusted[3]	186.4	186.1	157.4	102.2	68.5	62.4	59.0	56.5
All ages, crude	102.5	104.5	94.5	63.4	46.7	46.9	45.2	44.2
Under 1 year	6.4	5.0	5.8	5.0	4.4	3.8	3.1	3.2
1–4 years	1.1	0.9	1.2	0.4	0.3	*	0.3	0.4
5–14 years	0.5	0.7	0.8	0.3	0.2	0.2	0.2	0.2
15–24 years	1.8	1.9	1.8	1.1	0.7	0.5	0.5	0.5
25–34 years	4.2	4.5	4.4	2.6	2.1	1.5	1.6	1.4
35–44 years	17.5	14.6	15.7	8.7	6.8	5.8	5.7	5.3
45–54 years	67.9	52.2	44.4	27.2	20.5	17.5	16.7	16.7
55–64 years	205.2	163.8	138.7	74.6	54.3	47.2	43.4	42.7
65–74 years	589.6	530.7	449.5	258.6	166.6	145.0	140.4	135.0
75–84 years	1,543.6	1,555.9	1,361.6	866.3	551.1	490.8	467.3	445.9
85 years and over	3,048.6	3,643.1	2,895.2	2,193.6	1,528.5	1,484.3	1,380.2	1,317.9
Female								
All ages, age adjusted[3]	175.8	170.7	140.0	91.7	62.6	59.1	56.4	55.2
All ages, crude	105.6	111.4	109.0	85.9	68.4	71.8	69.2	68.2
Under 1 year	3.7	3.2	4.0	3.8	3.1	2.7	2.3	2.5
1–4 years	0.7	0.7	0.7	0.5	0.3	0.4	0.4	0.3
5–14 years	0.4	0.6	0.6	0.3	0.2	0.2	0.2	0.2
15–24 years	1.5	1.6	1.4	0.8	0.6	0.5	0.5	0.3
25–34 years	4.3	4.9	4.7	2.6	2.2	1.5	1.5	1.4
35–44 years	19.9	14.8	15.6	8.4	6.1	5.7	5.4	5.5
45–54 years	72.9	46.3	39.0	23.3	17.0	14.5	13.6	13.6
55–64 years	183.1	131.8	95.3	56.8	42.2	35.3	32.9	32.1
65–74 years	522.1	415.7	333.3	188.7	126.7	115.1	109.3	108.1
75–84 years	1,462.2	1,441.1	1,183.1	740.1	466.2	442.1	428.6	421.2
85 years and over	2,949.4	3,704.4	3,081.0	2,323.1	1,667.6	1,632.0	1,550.4	1,501.5
White male[4]								
All ages, age adjusted[3]	182.1	181.6	153.7	98.7	65.5	59.8	56.5	54.2
All ages, crude	100.5	102.7	93.5	63.1	46.9	48.4	46.6	45.7
45–54 years	53.7	40.9	35.6	21.7	15.4	13.6	12.7	12.9
55–64 years	182.2	139.0	119.9	64.0	45.7	39.7	36.1	35.6
65–74 years	569.7	501.0	420.0	239.8	152.9	133.8	128.5	123.8
75–84 years	1,556.3	1,564.8	1,361.6	852.7	539.2	480.0	458.8	437.5
85 years and over	3,127.1	3,734.8	3,018.1	2,230.8	1,545.4	1,490.7	1,386.2	1,327.4
Black or African American male[4]								
All ages, age adjusted[3]	228.8	238.5	206.4	142.0	102.2	89.6	85.4	81.7
All ages, crude	122.0	122.9	108.8	73.0	53.0	46.1	44.6	43.5
45–54 years	211.9	166.1	136.1	82.1	68.4	49.5	48.8	46.5
55–64 years	522.8	439.9	343.4	189.7	141.7	115.4	111.9	110.3
65–74 years	783.6	899.2	780.1	472.3	326.9	268.5	269.2	262.9
75–84 years[5]	1,504.9	1,475.2	1,445.7	1,066.3	721.5	659.2	613.9	587.8
85 years and over	- - -	2,700.0	1,963.1	1,873.2	1,421.5	1,458.8	1,349.1	1,252.2

See footnotes at end of table.

This table will be updated on the Web. Go to www.cdc.gov/nchs/hus.htm.

Table 37 (page 2 of 3). Death rates for cerebrovascular diseases, according to sex, race, Hispanic origin, and age: United States, selected years 1950–2002

[Data are based on death certificates]

Sex, race, Hispanic origin, and age	1950[1]	1960[1]	1970	1980	1990	2000[2]	2001	2002
American Indian or Alaska Native male[4]				Deaths per 100,000 resident population				
All ages, age adjusted[3]	---	---	---	66.4	44.3	46.1	37.5	37.1
All ages, crude	---	---	---	23.1	16.0	16.8	14.2	15.4
45–54 years	---	---	---	*	*	13.3	12.6	15.4
55–64 years	---	---	---	72.0	39.8	48.6	24.1	34.5
65–74 years	---	---	---	170.5	120.3	144.7	131.5	96.6
75–84 years	---	---	---	523.9	325.9	373.3	247.8	276.4
85 years and over	---	---	---	1,384.7	949.8	834.9	833.0	768.3
Asian or Pacific Islander male[4]								
All ages, age adjusted[3]	---	---	---	71.4	59.1	58.0	55.3	50.8
All ages, crude	---	---	---	28.7	23.3	27.2	27.5	25.9
45–54 years	---	---	---	17.0	15.6	15.0	15.9	14.9
55–64 years	---	---	---	59.9	51.8	49.3	46.2	40.4
65–74 years	---	---	---	197.9	167.9	135.6	134.7	112.9
75–84 years	---	---	---	619.5	483.9	438.7	409.8	390.3
85 years and over	---	---	---	1,399.0	1,196.6	1,415.6	1,327.7	1,233.6
Hispanic or Latino male[4,6]								
All ages, age adjusted[3]	---	---	---	---	46.5	50.5	48.9	44.3
All ages, crude	---	---	---	---	15.6	15.8	15.7	15.0
45–54 years	---	---	---	---	20.0	18.1	18.7	18.6
55–64 years	---	---	---	---	49.2	48.8	43.5	45.0
65–74 years	---	---	---	---	126.4	136.1	127.2	124.6
75–84 years	---	---	---	---	356.6	392.9	386.3	338.5
85 years and over	---	---	---	---	866.3	1,029.9	1,005.6	856.7
White, not Hispanic or Latino male[6]								
All ages, age adjusted[3]	---	---	---	---	66.3	59.9	56.5	54.4
All ages, crude	---	---	---	---	50.6	53.9	52.0	51.3
45–54 years	---	---	---	---	14.9	13.0	11.9	12.1
55–64 years	---	---	---	---	45.1	38.7	35.1	34.5
65–74 years	---	---	---	---	154.5	133.1	128.0	123.2
75–84 years	---	---	---	---	547.3	482.3	460.5	441.1
85 years and over	---	---	---	---	1,578.7	1,505.9	1,399.0	1,345.9
White female[4]								
All ages, age adjusted[3]	169.7	165.0	135.5	89.0	60.3	57.3	54.5	53.4
All ages, crude	103.3	110.1	109.8	88.6	71.6	76.9	74.0	73.0
45–54 years	55.0	33.8	30.5	18.6	13.5	11.2	10.2	10.4
55–64 years	156.9	103.0	78.1	48.6	35.8	30.2	27.6	27.4
65–74 years	498.1	383.3	303.2	172.5	116.1	107.3	99.9	99.5
75–84 years	1,471.3	1,444.7	1,176.8	728.8	456.5	434.2	421.6	414.1
85 years and over	3,017.9	3,795.7	3,167.6	2,362.7	1,685.9	1,646.7	1,563.5	1,516.9
Black or African American female[4]								
All ages, age adjusted[3]	238.4	232.5	189.3	119.6	84.0	76.2	73.7	71.8
All ages, crude	128.3	127.7	112.2	77.8	60.7	58.3	56.9	55.8
45–54 years	248.9	166.2	119.4	61.8	44.1	38.1	37.3	35.7
55–64 years	567.7	452.0	272.4	138.4	96.9	76.4	74.4	70.1
65–74 years	754.4	830.5	673.5	361.7	236.7	190.9	189.5	181.2
75–84 years[5]	1,496.7	1,413.1	1,338.3	917.5	595.0	549.2	530.3	532.2
85 years and over	---	2,578.9	2,210.5	1,891.6	1,495.2	1,556.5	1,491.2	1,434.3

See footnotes at end of table.

This table will be updated on the Web. Go to www.cdc.gov/nchs/hus.htm.

Table 37 (page 3 of 3). Death rates for cerebrovascular diseases, according to sex, race, Hispanic origin, and age: United States, selected years 1950–2002

[Data are based on death certificates]

Sex, race, Hispanic origin, and age	1950[1]	1960[1]	1970	1980	1990	2000[2]	2001	2002
American Indian or Alaska Native female[4]				Deaths per 100,000 resident population				
All ages, age adjusted[3]	- - -	- - -	- - -	51.2	38.4	43.7	44.0	38.0
All ages, crude	- - -	- - -	- - -	22.0	19.3	21.5	23.3	21.5
45–54 years	- - -	- - -	- - -	*	*	14.4	15.1	13.5
55–64 years	- - -	- - -	- - -	*	40.7	37.9	30.4	33.1
65–74 years	- - -	- - -	- - -	128.3	100.5	79.5	133.3	112.4
75–84 years	- - -	- - -	- - -	404.2	282.0	391.1	359.9	304.8
85 years and over	- - -	- - -	- - -	1,095.5	776.2	931.5	830.5	689.9
Asian or Pacific Islander female[4]								
All ages, age adjusted[3]	- - -	- - -	- - -	60.8	54.9	49.1	48.2	45.4
All ages, crude	- - -	- - -	- - -	26.4	24.3	28.7	29.8	29.2
45–54 years	- - -	- - -	- - -	20.3	19.7	13.3	11.3	12.6
55–64 years	- - -	- - -	- - -	43.7	42.1	33.3	35.2	32.1
65–74 years	- - -	- - -	- - -	136.1	124.0	102.8	113.2	112.5
75–84 years	- - -	- - -	- - -	446.6	396.6	386.0	359.6	331.7
85 years and over	- - -	- - -	- - -	1,545.2	1,395.0	1,246.6	1,236.8	1,149.8
Hispanic or Latino female[4,6]								
All ages, age adjusted[3]	- - -	- - -	- - -	- - -	43.7	43.0	41.6	38.6
All ages, crude	- - -	- - -	- - -	- - -	20.1	19.4	19.1	18.4
45–54 years	- - -	- - -	- - -	- - -	15.2	12.4	13.1	12.0
55–64 years	- - -	- - -	- - -	- - -	38.5	31.9	28.2	27.6
65–74 years	- - -	- - -	- - -	- - -	102.6	95.2	89.6	85.6
75–84 years	- - -	- - -	- - -	- - -	308.5	311.3	310.7	307.2
85 years and over	- - -	- - -	- - -	- - -	1,055.3	1,108.9	1,061.2	918.5
White, not Hispanic or Latino female[6]								
All ages, age adjusted[3]	- - -	- - -	- - -	- - -	61.0	57.6	54.8	53.9
All ages, crude	- - -	- - -	- - -	- - -	77.2	85.5	82.6	82.1
45–54 years	- - -	- - -	- - -	- - -	13.2	10.9	9.8	10.1
55–64 years	- - -	- - -	- - -	- - -	35.7	29.9	27.4	27.2
65–74 years	- - -	- - -	- - -	- - -	116.9	107.6	100.3	100.2
75–84 years	- - -	- - -	- - -	- - -	461.9	438.3	425.6	418.4
85 years and over	- - -	- - -	- - -	- - -	1,714.7	1,661.6	1,577.4	1,536.7

- - - Data not available.

* Rates based on fewer than 20 deaths are considered unreliable and are not shown.

[1]Includes deaths of persons who were not residents of the 50 States and the District of Columbia.

[2]Starting with 1999 data, cause of death is coded according to ICD–10. See Appendix II, Comparability ratio and tables V and VI.

[3]Age-adjusted rates are calculated using the year 2000 standard population. See Appendix II, Age adjustment.

[4]The race groups, white, black, Asian or Pacific Islander, and American Indian or Alaska Native, include persons of Hispanic and non-Hispanic origin. Persons of Hispanic origin may be of any race. Death rates for the American Indian or Alaska Native and Asian or Pacific Islander populations are known to be underestimated. See Appendix II, Race, for a discussion of sources of bias in death rates by race and Hispanic origin.

[5]In 1950 rate is for the age group 75 years and over.

[6]Prior to 1997, excludes data from States lacking an Hispanic-origin item on the death certificate. See Appendix II, Hispanic origin.

NOTES: Starting with *Health, United States, 2003*, rates for 1991–99 were revised using intercensal population estimates based on census 2000. Rates for 2000 were revised based on census 2000 counts. Rates for 2001 and 2002 were computed using 2000-based postcensal estimates. See Appendix I, Population Census and Population Estimates. Underlying cause of death code numbers are based on the applicable revision of the *International Classification of Diseases* (ICD) for data years shown. For the period 1980–98, causes were coded using ICD–9 codes that are most nearly comparable with the 113 cause list for ICD–10. See Appendix II, tables IV and V. Age groups were selected to minimize the presentation of unstable age-specific death rates based on small numbers of deaths and for consistency among comparison groups. Data for additional years are available. See Appendix III.

SOURCES: Centers for Disease Control and Prevention, National Center for Health Statistics, National Vital Statistics System; Grove RD, Hetzel AM. Vital statistics rates in the United States, 1940–1960. Washington: U.S. Government Printing Office. 1968; numerator data from National Vital Statistics System, annual mortality files; denominator data from national population estimates for race groups from table 1 and unpublished Hispanic population estimates for 1985–96 prepared by the Housing and Household Economic Statistics Division, U.S. Bureau of the Census; additional mortality tables are available at www.cdc.gov/nchs/datawh/statab/unpubd/mortabs.htm; Kochanek KD, Murphy SL, Anderson RN, Scott C. Deaths: Final data for 2002. National vital statistics reports. Vol 53 no 5. Hyattsville, Maryland: National Center for Health Statistics. 2004.

This table will be updated on the Web. Go to www.cdc.gov/nchs/hus.htm.

Table 38 (page 1 of 4). Death rates for malignant neoplasms, according to sex, race, Hispanic origin, and age: United States, selected years 1950–2002

[Data are based on death certificates]

Sex, race, Hispanic origin, and age	1950[1]	1960[1]	1970	1980	1990	2000[2]	2001	2002
All persons	Deaths per 100,000 resident population							
All ages, age adjusted[3]	193.9	193.9	198.6	207.9	216.0	199.6	196.0	193.5
All ages, crude	139.8	149.2	162.8	183.9	203.2	196.5	194.4	193.2
Under 1 year	8.7	7.2	4.7	3.2	2.3	2.4	1.6	1.8
1–4 years	11.7	10.9	7.5	4.5	3.5	2.7	2.7	2.6
5–14 years	6.7	6.8	6.0	4.3	3.1	2.5	2.5	2.6
15–24 years	8.6	8.3	8.3	6.3	4.9	4.4	4.3	4.3
25–34 years	20.0	19.5	16.5	13.7	12.6	9.8	10.1	9.7
35–44 years	62.7	59.7	59.5	48.6	43.3	36.6	36.8	35.8
45–54 years	175.1	177.0	182.5	180.0	158.9	127.5	126.5	123.8
55–64 years	390.7	396.8	423.0	436.1	449.6	366.7	356.5	351.1
65–74 years	698.8	713.9	754.2	817.9	872.3	816.3	802.8	792.1
75–84 years	1,153.3	1,127.4	1,169.2	1,232.3	1,348.5	1,335.6	1,315.8	1,311.9
85 years and over	1,451.0	1,450.0	1,320.7	1,594.6	1,752.9	1,819.4	1,765.6	1,723.9
Male								
All ages, age adjusted[3]	208.1	225.1	247.6	271.2	280.4	248.9	243.7	238.9
All ages, crude	142.9	162.5	182.1	205.3	221.3	207.2	205.3	203.8
Under 1 year	9.7	7.7	4.4	3.7	2.4	2.6	1.5	2.0
1–4 years	12.5	12.4	8.3	5.2	3.7	3.0	2.9	2.7
5–14 years	7.4	7.6	6.7	4.9	3.5	2.7	2.5	2.9
15–24 years	9.7	10.2	10.4	7.8	5.7	5.1	5.0	4.9
25–34 years	17.7	18.8	16.3	13.4	12.6	9.2	9.3	9.2
35–44 years	45.6	48.9	53.0	44.0	38.5	32.7	32.6	31.5
45–54 years	156.2	170.8	183.5	188.7	162.5	130.9	130.3	128.0
55–64 years	413.1	459.9	511.8	520.8	532.9	415.8	405.2	399.8
65–74 years	791.5	890.5	1,006.8	1,093.2	1,122.2	1,001.9	984.6	964.8
75–84 years	1,332.6	1,389.4	1,588.3	1,790.5	1,914.4	1,760.6	1,727.1	1,711.3
85 years and over	1,668.3	1,741.2	1,720.8	2,369.5	2,739.9	2,710.7	2,613.6	2,491.1
Female								
All ages, age adjusted[3]	182.3	168.7	163.2	166.7	175.7	167.6	164.7	163.1
All ages, crude	136.8	136.4	144.4	163.6	186.0	186.2	183.9	183.0
Under 1 year	7.6	6.8	5.0	2.7	2.2	2.3	1.8	1.6
1–4 years	10.8	9.3	6.7	3.7	3.2	2.5	2.5	2.4
5–14 years	6.0	6.0	5.2	3.6	2.8	2.2	2.4	2.4
15–24 years	7.6	6.5	6.2	4.8	4.1	3.6	3.5	3.6
25–34 years	22.2	20.1	16.7	14.0	12.6	10.4	10.9	10.2
35–44 years	79.3	70.0	65.6	53.1	48.1	40.4	41.0	40.0
45–54 years	194.0	183.0	181.5	171.8	155.5	124.2	122.7	119.8
55–64 years	368.2	337.7	343.2	361.7	375.2	321.3	311.5	306.0
65–74 years	612.3	560.2	557.9	607.1	677.4	663.6	652.2	648.5
75–84 years	1,000.7	924.1	891.9	903.1	1,010.3	1,058.5	1,045.4	1,046.7
85 years and over	1,299.7	1,263.9	1,096.7	1,255.7	1,372.1	1,456.4	1,410.7	1,391.1
White male[4]								
All ages, age adjusted[3]	210.0	224.7	244.8	265.1	272.2	243.9	239.2	235.2
All ages, crude	147.2	166.1	185.1	208.7	227.7	218.1	216.4	215.5
25–34 years	17.7	18.8	16.2	13.6	12.3	9.2	9.3	9.1
35–44 years	44.5	46.3	50.1	41.1	35.8	30.9	31.3	30.5
45–54 years	150.8	164.1	172.0	175.4	149.9	123.5	123.6	121.8
55–64 years	409.4	450.9	498.1	497.4	508.2	401.9	392.1	386.0
65–74 years	798.7	887.3	997.0	1,070.7	1,090.7	984.3	969.4	954.8
75–84 years	1,367.6	1,413.7	1,592.7	1,779.7	1,883.2	1,736.0	1,704.6	1,695.3
85 years and over	1,732.7	1,791.4	1,772.2	2,375.6	2,715.1	2,693.7	2,597.6	2,486.8
Black or African American male[4]								
All ages, age adjusted[3]	178.9	227.6	291.9	353.4	397.9	340.3	330.9	319.6
All ages, crude	106.6	136.7	171.6	205.5	221.9	188.5	184.5	181.5
25–34 years	18.0	18.4	18.8	14.1	15.7	10.1	10.5	11.2
35–44 years	55.7	72.9	81.3	73.8	64.3	48.4	44.6	43.0
45–54 years	211.7	244.7	311.2	333.0	302.6	214.2	204.8	197.3
55–64 years	490.8	579.7	689.2	812.5	859.2	626.4	604.2	610.3
65–74 years	636.5	938.5	1,168.9	1,417.2	1,613.9	1,363.8	1,335.3	1,274.7
75–84 years[5]	853.5	1,053.3	1,624.8	2,029.6	2,478.3	2,351.8	2,290.0	2,223.0
85 years and over	- - -	1,155.2	1,387.0	2,393.9	3,238.3	3,264.8	3,209.9	2,976.1

See footnotes at end of table.

This table will be updated on the Web. Go to www.cdc.gov/nchs/hus.htm.

Table 38 (page 2 of 4). Death rates for malignant neoplasms, according to sex, race, Hispanic origin, and age: United States, selected years 1950–2002

[Data are based on death certificates]

Sex, race, Hispanic origin, and age	*1950*[1]	*1960*[1]	*1970*	*1980*	*1990*	*2000*[2]	*2001*	*2002*
American Indian or Alaska Native male[4]				Deaths per 100,000 resident population				
All ages, age adjusted[3]	---	---	---	140.5	145.8	155.8	155.3	141.9
All ages, crude	---	---	---	58.1	61.4	67.0	72.4	70.4
25–34 years	---	---	---	*	*	*	*	*
35–44 years	---	---	---	*	22.8	21.4	22.9	18.9
45–54 years	---	---	---	86.9	86.9	70.3	77.1	76.1
55–64 years	---	---	---	213.4	246.2	255.6	256.0	261.4
65–74 years	---	---	---	613.0	530.6	648.0	673.9	604.9
75–84 years	---	---	---	936.4	1,038.4	1,152.5	1,093.0	1,069.3
85 years and over	---	---	---	1,471.2	1,654.4	1,584.2	1,487.5	1,036.3
Asian or Pacific Islander male[4]								
All ages, age adjusted[3]	---	---	---	165.2	172.5	150.8	147.0	137.9
All ages, crude	---	---	---	81.9	82.7	85.2	87.0	84.0
25–34 years	---	---	---	6.3	9.2	7.4	7.1	7.9
35–44 years	---	---	---	29.4	27.7	26.1	24.8	22.7
45–54 years	---	---	---	108.2	92.6	78.5	83.9	82.8
55–64 years	---	---	---	298.5	274.6	229.2	234.8	224.7
65–74 years	---	---	---	581.2	687.2	559.4	515.1	481.7
75–84 years	---	---	---	1,147.6	1,229.9	1,086.1	1,095.9	1,012.7
85 years and over	---	---	---	1,798.7	1,837.0	1,823.2	1,676.4	1,544.3
Hispanic or Latino male[4,6]								
All ages, age adjusted[3]	---	---	---	---	174.7	171.7	168.2	161.4
All ages, crude	---	---	---	---	65.5	61.3	62.2	61.2
25–34 years	---	---	---	---	8.0	6.9	6.3	6.3
35–44 years	---	---	---	---	22.5	20.1	21.7	18.4
45–54 years	---	---	---	---	96.6	79.4	81.5	78.4
55–64 years	---	---	---	---	294.0	253.1	253.5	254.3
65–74 years	---	---	---	---	655.5	651.2	642.8	622.3
75–84 years	---	---	---	---	1,233.4	1,306.4	1,258.3	1,190.8
85 years and over	---	---	---	---	2,019.4	2,049.7	1,967.4	1,869.0
White, not Hispanic or Latino male[6]								
All ages, age adjusted[3]	---	---	---	---	276.7	247.7	243.1	239.6
All ages, crude	---	---	---	---	246.2	244.4	243.4	243.8
25–34 years	---	---	---	---	12.8	9.7	10.0	9.8
35–44 years	---	---	---	---	36.8	32.3	32.6	32.5
45–54 years	---	---	---	---	153.9	127.2	127.3	125.9
55–64 years	---	---	---	---	520.6	412.0	401.7	395.5
65–74 years	---	---	---	---	1,109.0	1,002.1	988.2	975.3
75–84 years	---	---	---	---	1,906.6	1,750.2	1,721.8	1,716.5
85 years and over	---	---	---	---	2,744.4	2,714.1	2,616.8	2,507.7
White female[4]								
All ages, age adjusted[3]	182.0	167.7	162.5	165.2	174.0	166.9	163.9	162.4
All ages, crude	139.9	139.8	149.4	170.3	196.1	199.4	196.7	195.8
25–34 years	20.9	18.8	16.3	13.5	11.9	10.1	10.4	9.9
35–44 years	74.5	66.6	62.4	50.9	46.2	38.2	39.3	38.5
45–54 years	185.8	175.7	177.3	166.4	150.9	120.1	118.9	115.3
55–64 years	362.5	329.0	338.6	355.5	368.5	319.7	308.6	303.1
65–74 years	616.5	562.1	554.7	605.2	675.1	665.6	652.9	650.4
75–84 years	1,026.6	939.3	903.5	905.4	1,011.8	1,063.4	1,049.8	1,053.1
85 years and over	1,348.3	1,304.9	1,126.6	1,266.8	1,372.3	1,459.1	1,416.7	1,395.1

See footnotes at end of table.

This table will be updated on the Web. Go to www.cdc.gov/nchs/hus.htm.

Table 38 (page 3 of 4). Death rates for malignant neoplasms, according to sex, race, Hispanic origin, and age: United States, selected years 1950–2002

[Data are based on death certificates]

Sex, race, Hispanic origin, and age	1950[1]	1960[1]	1970	1980	1990	2000[2]	2001	2002
Black or African American female[4]				Deaths per 100,000 resident population				
All ages, age adjusted[3]	174.1	174.3	173.4	189.5	205.9	193.8	191.3	190.3
All ages, crude	111.8	113.8	117.3	136.5	156.1	151.8	151.3	151.7
25–34 years	34.3	31.0	20.9	18.3	18.7	13.5	15.0	13.3
35–44 years	119.8	102.4	94.6	73.5	67.4	58.9	57.3	56.2
45–54 years	277.0	254.8	228.6	230.2	209.9	173.9	166.8	168.2
55–64 years	484.6	442.7	404.8	450.4	482.4	391.0	390.9	385.4
65–74 years	477.3	541.6	615.8	662.4	773.2	753.1	748.4	741.1
75–84 years[5]	605.3	696.3	763.3	923.9	1,059.9	1,124.0	1,125.0	1,123.1
85 years and over	- - -	728.9	791.5	1,159.9	1,431.3	1,527.7	1,457.5	1,468.0
American Indian or Alaska Native female[4]								
All ages, age adjusted[3]	- - -	- - -	- - -	94.0	106.9	108.3	114.1	112.9
All ages, crude	- - -	- - -	- - -	50.4	62.1	61.3	68.8	71.0
25–34 years	- - -	- - -	- - -	*	*	*	*	9.4
35–44 years	- - -	- - -	- - -	36.9	31.0	23.7	25.7	23.6
45–54 years	- - -	- - -	- - -	96.9	104.5	59.7	79.4	80.6
55–64 years	- - -	- - -	- - -	198.4	213.3	200.9	221.7	202.5
65–74 years	- - -	- - -	- - -	350.8	438.9	458.3	463.8	473.2
75–84 years	- - -	- - -	- - -	446.4	554.3	714.0	752.7	703.9
85 years and over	- - -	- - -	- - -	786.5	843.7	983.2	905.2	1,001.2
Asian or Pacific Islander female[4]								
All ages, age adjusted[3]	- - -	- - -	- - -	93.0	103.0	100.7	99.3	95.9
All ages, crude	- - -	- - -	- - -	54.1	60.5	72.1	74.0	72.6
25–34 years	- - -	- - -	- - -	9.5	7.3	8.1	8.0	6.4
35–44 years	- - -	- - -	- - -	38.7	29.8	28.9	25.6	23.6
45–54 years	- - -	- - -	- - -	99.8	93.9	78.2	82.5	78.5
55–64 years	- - -	- - -	- - -	174.7	196.2	176.5	167.7	171.2
65–74 years	- - -	- - -	- - -	301.9	346.2	357.4	373.3	358.1
75–84 years	- - -	- - -	- - -	522.1	641.4	650.1	633.1	606.4
85 years and over	- - -	- - -	- - -	800.0	971.7	988.5	929.2	910.1
Hispanic or Latino female[4,6]								
All ages, age adjusted[3]	- - -	- - -	- - -	- - -	111.9	110.8	108.6	106.1
All ages, crude	- - -	- - -	- - -	- - -	60.7	58.5	58.7	58.1
25–34 years	- - -	- - -	- - -	- - -	9.7	7.8	8.3	7.5
35–44 years	- - -	- - -	- - -	- - -	34.8	30.7	29.8	28.4
45–54 years	- - -	- - -	- - -	- - -	100.5	84.7	84.2	78.0
55–64 years	- - -	- - -	- - -	- - -	205.4	192.5	196.7	179.8
65–74 years	- - -	- - -	- - -	- - -	404.8	410.0	394.5	395.6
75–84 years	- - -	- - -	- - -	- - -	663.0	716.5	681.2	692.2
85 years and over	- - -	- - -	- - -	- - -	1,022.7	1,056.5	1,068.6	1,031.2

See footnotes at end of table.

This table will be updated on the Web. Go to www.cdc.gov/nchs/hus.htm.

Table 38 (page 4 of 4). Death rates for malignant neoplasms, according to sex, race, Hispanic origin, and age: United States, selected years 1950–2002

[Data are based on death certificates]

Sex, race, Hispanic origin, and age	1950[1]	1960[1]	1970	1980	1990	2000[2]	2001	2002
White, not Hispanic or Latino female[6]				Deaths per 100,000 resident population				
All ages, age adjusted[3]	- - -	- - -	- - -	- - -	177.5	170.0	167.2	165.9
All ages, crude	- - -	- - -	- - -	- - -	210.6	220.6	218.4	218.5
25–34 years	- - -	- - -	- - -	- - -	11.9	10.5	10.7	10.3
35–44 years	- - -	- - -	- - -	- - -	47.0	38.9	40.4	39.9
45–54 years	- - -	- - -	- - -	- - -	154.9	123.0	121.9	118.7
55–64 years	- - -	- - -	- - -	- - -	379.5	328.9	317.3	312.8
65–74 years	- - -	- - -	- - -	- - -	688.5	681.0	669.7	667.7
75–84 years	- - -	- - -	- - -	- - -	1,027.2	1,075.3	1,064.4	1,068.3
85 years and over	- - -	- - -	- - -	- - -	1,385.7	1,468.7	1,425.1	1,405.4

- - - Data not available.
* Rates based on fewer than 20 deaths are considered unreliable and are not shown.
[1]Includes deaths of persons who were not residents of the 50 States and the District of Columbia.
[2]Starting with 1999 data, cause of death is coded according to ICD–10. See Appendix II, Comparability ratio and tables V and VI.
[3]Age-adjusted rates are calculated using the year 2000 standard population. See Appendix II, Age adjustment.
[4]The race groups, white, black, Asian or Pacific Islander, and American Indian or Alaska Native, include persons of Hispanic and non-Hispanic origin. Persons of Hispanic origin may be of any race. Death rates for the American Indian or Alaska Native and Asian or Pacific Islander populations are known to be underestimated. See Appendix II, Race, for a discussion of sources of bias in death rates by race and Hispanic origin.
[5]In 1950 rate is for the age group 75 years and over.
[6]Prior to 1997, excludes data from States lacking an Hispanic-origin item on the death certificate. See Appendix II, Hispanic origin.

NOTES: Starting with *Health, United States, 2003*, rates for 1991–99 were revised using intercensal population estimates based on census 2000. Rates for 2000 were revised based on census 2000 counts. Rates for 2001 and 2002 were computed using 2000-based postcensal estimates. See Appendix I, Population Census and Population Estimates. Underlying cause of death code numbers are based on the applicable revision of the *International Classification of Diseases* (ICD) for data years shown. See Appendix II, tables IV and V. Age groups were selected to minimize the presentation of unstable age-specific death rates based on small numbers of deaths and for consistency among comparison groups. Data for additional years are available. See Appendix III.

SOURCES: Centers for Disease Control and Prevention, National Center for Health Statistics, National Vital Statistics System; Grove RD, Hetzel AM. Vital statistics rates in the United States, 1940–1960. Washington: U.S. Government Printing Office. 1968; numerator data from National Vital Statistics System, annual mortality files; denominator data from national population estimates for race groups from table 1 and unpublished Hispanic population estimates for 1985–96 prepared by the Housing and Household Economic Statistics Division, U.S. Bureau of the Census; additional mortality tables are available at www.cdc.gov/nchs/datawh/statab/unpubd/mortabs.htm; Kochanek KD, Murphy SL, Anderson RN, Scott C. Deaths: Final data for 2002. National vital statistics reports. Vol 53 no 5. Hyattsville, Maryland: National Center for Health Statistics. 2004.

This table will be updated on the Web. Go to www.cdc.gov/nchs/hus.htm.

Table 39 (page 1 of 3). Death rates for malignant neoplasms of trachea, bronchus, and lung, according to sex, race, Hispanic origin, and age: United States, selected years 1950–2002

[Data are based on death certificates]

Sex, race, Hispanic origin, and age	1950[1]	1960[1]	1970	1980	1990	2000[2]	2001	2002
All persons	Deaths per 100,000 resident population							
All ages, age adjusted[3]	15.0	24.1	37.1	49.9	59.3	56.1	55.3	54.9
All ages, crude	12.2	20.3	32.1	45.8	56.8	55.3	54.8	54.7
Under 25 years	0.1	0.0	0.1	0.0	0.0	0.0	0.0	0.0
25–34 years	0.8	1.0	0.9	0.6	0.7	0.5	0.4	0.4
35–44 years	4.5	6.8	11.0	9.2	6.8	6.1	6.2	6.0
45–54 years	20.4	29.6	43.4	54.1	46.8	31.6	30.7	30.3
55–64 years	48.7	75.3	109.1	138.2	160.6	122.4	117.7	115.3
65–74 years	59.7	108.1	164.5	233.3	288.4	284.2	279.7	275.0
75–84 years	55.8	91.5	163.2	240.5	333.3	370.8	371.4	377.6
85 years and over	42.3	65.6	101.7	176.0	242.5	302.1	302.7	297.2
Male								
All ages, age adjusted[3]	24.6	43.6	67.5	85.2	91.1	76.7	75.2	73.2
All ages, crude	19.9	35.4	53.4	68.6	75.1	65.5	64.7	63.7
Under 25 years	0.0	0.0	0.1	0.1	0.0	*	*	0.0
25–34 years	1.1	1.4	1.3	0.8	0.9	0.5	0.4	0.4
35–44 years	7.1	10.5	16.1	11.9	8.5	6.9	6.7	6.2
45–54 years	35.0	50.6	67.5	76.0	59.7	38.5	37.4	36.6
55–64 years	83.8	139.3	189.7	213.6	222.9	154.0	147.1	144.0
65–74 years	98.7	204.3	320.8	403.9	430.4	377.9	370.0	355.9
75–84 years	82.6	167.1	330.8	488.8	572.9	532.2	529.5	527.9
85 years and over	62.5	107.7	194.0	368.1	513.2	521.2	512.4	482.2
Female								
All ages, age adjusted[3]	5.8	7.5	13.1	24.4	37.1	41.3	41.0	41.6
All ages, crude	4.5	6.4	11.9	24.3	39.4	45.4	45.3	46.0
Under 25 years	0.1	0.0	0.0	*	*	*	*	*
25–34 years	0.5	0.5	0.5	0.5	0.5	0.5	0.4	0.4
35–44 years	1.9	3.2	6.1	6.5	5.2	5.3	5.7	5.8
45–54 years	5.8	9.2	21.0	33.7	34.5	25.0	24.3	24.3
55–64 years	13.6	15.4	36.8	72.0	105.0	93.3	90.5	88.8
65–74 years	23.3	24.4	43.1	102.7	177.6	206.9	204.9	207.7
75–84 years	32.9	32.8	52.4	94.1	190.1	265.6	267.5	277.8
85 years and over	28.2	38.8	50.0	91.9	138.1	212.8	215.0	217.0
White male[4]								
All ages, age adjusted[3]	25.1	43.6	67.1	83.8	89.0	75.7	74.2	72.5
All ages, crude	20.8	36.4	54.6	70.2	77.8	69.4	68.6	67.7
45–54 years	35.1	49.2	63.3	70.9	55.2	35.7	34.9	34.2
55–64 years	85.4	139.2	186.8	205.6	213.7	150.8	143.8	139.3
65–74 years	101.5	207.5	325.0	401.0	422.1	374.9	368.1	356.4
75–84 years	85.5	170.4	336.7	493.5	572.2	529.9	526.4	527.8
85 years and over	67.4	109.4	199.6	374.1	516.3	522.4	513.9	486.6
Black or African American male[4]								
All ages, age adjusted[3]	17.8	42.6	75.4	107.6	125.4	101.1	99.1	95.0
All ages, crude	12.1	28.1	47.7	66.6	73.7	58.3	57.2	56.0
45–54 years	34.4	68.4	115.4	133.8	114.9	70.7	66.2	64.6
55–64 years	68.3	146.8	234.3	321.1	358.6	223.5	215.2	223.6
65–74 years	53.8	168.3	300.5	472.3	585.4	488.8	476.4	444.6
75–84 years[5]	36.2	107.3	271.6	472.9	645.4	642.5	659.8	626.2
85 years and over	- - -	82.8	137.0	311.3	499.5	562.8	549.2	484.6
American Indian or Alaska Native male[4]								
All ages, age adjusted[3]	- - -	- - -	- - -	31.7	47.5	42.9	42.1	41.3
All ages, crude	- - -	- - -	- - -	14.2	20.0	18.1	19.6	19.8
45–54 years	- - -	- - -	- - -	*	26.6	14.5	20.0	14.9
55–64 years	- - -	- - -	- - -	72.0	97.8	86.0	78.7	92.7
65–74 years	- - -	- - -	- - -	202.8	194.3	184.8	205.4	185.2
75–84 years	- - -	- - -	- - -	*	356.2	367.9	354.6	326.2
85 years and over	- - -	- - -	- - -	*	*	*	*	*

See footnotes at end of table.

This table will be updated on the Web. Go to www.cdc.gov/nchs/hus.htm.

Table 39 (page 2 of 3). Death rates for malignant neoplasms of trachea, bronchus, and lung, according to sex, race, Hispanic origin, and age: United States, selected years 1950–2002

[Data are based on death certificates]

Sex, race, Hispanic origin, and age	1950[1]	1960[1]	1970	1980	1990	2000[2]	2001	2002
Asian or Pacific Islander male[4]				Deaths per 100,000 resident population				
All ages, age adjusted[3]	---	---	---	43.3	44.2	40.9	39.2	36.3
All ages, crude	---	---	---	22.1	20.7	22.7	22.5	21.5
45–54 years	---	---	---	33.3	18.8	17.2	16.7	15.6
55–64 years	---	---	---	94.4	74.4	61.4	62.4	64.9
65–74 years	---	---	---	174.3	215.8	183.2	161.7	137.7
75–84 years	---	---	---	301.3	307.5	323.2	311.5	301.2
85 years and over	---	---	---	*	421.3	378.0	402.3	346.5
Hispanic or Latino male[4,6]								
All ages, age adjusted[3]	---	---	---	---	44.1	39.0	36.8	36.2
All ages, crude	---	---	---	---	16.2	13.3	13.1	13.1
45–54 years	---	---	---	---	21.5	14.8	14.2	12.6
55–64 years	---	---	---	---	80.7	58.6	59.5	60.7
65–74 years	---	---	---	---	195.5	167.3	163.7	161.7
75–84 years	---	---	---	---	313.4	327.5	293.8	299.1
85 years and over	---	---	---	---	420.7	368.8	335.2	307.9
White, not Hispanic or Latino male[6]								
All ages, age adjusted[3]	---	---	---	---	91.1	77.9	76.6	75.0
All ages, crude	---	---	---	---	84.7	78.9	78.4	77.8
45–54 years	---	---	---	---	57.8	37.7	37.0	36.5
55–64 years	---	---	---	---	221.0	157.7	150.3	145.7
65–74 years	---	---	---	---	431.4	387.3	381.1	369.5
75–84 years	---	---	---	---	580.4	537.7	536.5	538.3
85 years and over	---	---	---	---	520.9	527.3	520.0	493.3
White female[4]								
All ages, age adjusted[3]	5.9	6.8	13.1	24.5	37.6	42.3	42.1	42.6
All ages, crude	4.7	5.9	12.3	25.6	42.4	49.9	49.8	50.7
45–54 years	5.7	9.0	20.9	33.0	34.6	24.8	24.3	24.2
55–64 years	13.7	15.1	37.2	71.9	105.7	96.1	93.3	91.0
65–74 years	23.7	24.8	42.9	104.6	181.3	213.2	211.9	215.1
75–84 years	34.0	32.7	52.6	95.2	194.6	272.7	274.0	285.8
85 years and over	29.3	39.1	50.6	92.4	138.3	215.9	218.1	220.2
Black or African American female[4]								
All ages, age adjusted[3]	4.5	6.8	13.7	24.8	36.8	39.8	38.7	40.1
All ages, crude	2.8	4.3	9.4	18.3	28.1	30.8	30.2	31.6
45–54 years	7.5	11.3	23.9	43.4	41.3	32.9	29.5	31.7
55–64 years	12.9	17.9	33.5	79.9	117.9	95.3	92.0	95.3
65–74 years	14.0	18.1	46.1	88.0	164.3	194.1	186.7	189.3
75–84 years[5]	*	31.3	49.1	79.4	148.1	224.3	231.3	242.6
85 years and over	---	34.2	44.8	85.8	134.9	185.9	181.0	191.0
American Indian or Alaska Native female[4]								
All ages, age adjusted[3]	---	---	---	11.7	19.3	24.8	28.1	27.1
All ages, crude	---	---	---	6.0	11.2	14.0	16.2	16.4
45–54 years	---	---	---	*	22.9	12.1	15.1	11.4
55–64 years	---	---	---	*	53.7	52.6	56.9	52.5
65–74 years	---	---	---	*	78.5	151.5	140.2	162.8
75–84 years	---	---	---	*	111.8	136.3	201.4	163.4
85 years and over	---	---	---	*	*	*	*	168.3

See footnotes at end of table.

This table will be updated on the Web. Go to www.cdc.gov/nchs/hus.htm.

Table 39 (page 3 of 3). Death rates for malignant neoplasms of trachea, bronchus, and lung, according to sex, race, Hispanic origin, and age: United States, selected years 1950–2002

[Data are based on death certificates]

Sex, race, Hispanic origin, and age	1950[1]	1960[1]	1970	1980	1990	2000[2]	2001	2002
Asian or Pacific Islander female[4]	Deaths per 100,000 resident population							
All ages, age adjusted[3]	---	---	---	15.4	18.9	18.4	20.0	17.5
All ages, crude	---	---	---	8.4	10.5	12.6	14.1	12.9
45–54 years	---	---	---	13.5	11.3	9.9	11.4	9.0
55–64 years	---	---	---	24.6	38.3	30.4	29.4	28.9
65–74 years	---	---	---	62.4	71.6	77.0	83.6	79.9
75–84 years	---	---	---	117.7	137.9	135.0	147.5	116.8
85 years and over	---	---	---	*	172.9	175.3	212.1	170.4
Hispanic or Latino female[4,6]								
All ages, age adjusted[3]	---	---	---	---	14.1	14.7	14.5	14.6
All ages, crude	---	---	---	---	7.2	7.2	7.4	7.6
45–54 years	---	---	---	---	8.7	7.1	7.3	7.3
55–64 years	---	---	---	---	25.1	22.2	24.6	23.2
65–74 years	---	---	---	---	66.8	66.0	64.6	69.5
75–84 years	---	---	---	---	94.3	112.3	107.0	104.6
85 years and over	---	---	---	---	118.2	137.5	135.0	130.1
White, not Hispanic or Latino female[6]								
All ages, age adjusted[3]	---	---	---	---	39.0	44.1	44.0	44.6
All ages, crude	---	---	---	---	46.2	56.4	56.6	57.9
45–54 years	---	---	---	---	36.6	26.4	26.0	26.0
55–64 years	---	---	---	---	111.3	102.2	99.2	96.8
65–74 years	---	---	---	---	186.4	222.9	222.3	225.9
75–84 years	---	---	---	---	199.1	279.2	281.3	294.3
85 years and over	---	---	---	---	139.0	218.0	220.6	223.4

0.0 Quantity more than zero but less than 0.05.
* Rates based on fewer than 20 deaths are considered unreliable and are not shown.
- - - Data not available.
[1]Includes deaths of persons who were not residents of the 50 States and the District of Columbia.
[2]Starting with 1999 data, cause of death is coded according to ICD–10. See Appendix II, Comparability ratio and tables V and VI.
[3]Age-adjusted rates are calculated using the year 2000 standard population. See Appendix II, Age adjustment.
[4]The race groups, white, black, Asian or Pacific Islander, and American Indian or Alaska Native, include persons of Hispanic and non-Hispanic origin. Persons of Hispanic origin may be of any race. Death rates for the American Indian or Alaska Native and Asian or Pacific Islander populations are known to be underestimated. See Appendix II, Race, for a discussion of sources of bias in death rates by race and Hispanic origin.
[5]In 1950 rate is for the age group 75 years and over.
[6]Prior to 1997, excludes data from States lacking an Hispanic-origin item on the death certificate. See Appendix II, Hispanic origin.

NOTES: Starting with *Health, United States, 2003*, rates for 1991–99 were revised using intercensal population estimates based on census 2000. Rates for 2000 were revised based on census 2000 counts. Rates for 2001 and 2002 were computed using 2000-based postcensal estimates. See Appendix I, Population Census and Population Estimates. Underlying cause of death code numbers are based on the applicable revision of the *International Classification of Diseases* (ICD) for data years shown. For the period 1980–98, causes were coded using ICD–9 codes that are most nearly comparable with the 113 cause list for ICD–10. See Appendix II, tables IV and V. Age groups were selected to minimize the presentation of unstable age-specific death rates based on small numbers of deaths and for consistency among comparison groups. Data for additional years are available. See Appendix III.

SOURCES: Centers for Disease Control and Prevention, National Center for Health Statistics, National Vital Statistics System; Grove RD, Hetzel AM. Vital statistics rates in the United States, 1940–1960. Washington: U.S. Government Printing Office. 1968; numerator data from National Vital Statistics System, annual mortality files; denominator data from national population estimates for race groups from table 1 and unpublished Hispanic population estimates for 1985–96 prepared by the Housing and Household Economic Statistics Division, U.S. Bureau of the Census; additional mortality tables are available at www.cdc.gov/nchs/datawh/statab/unpubd/mortabs.htm; Kochanek KD, Murphy SL, Anderson RN, Scott C. Deaths: Final data for 2002. National vital statistics reports. Vol 53 no 5. Hyattsville, Maryland: National Center for Health Statistics. 2004.

This table will be updated on the Web. Go to www.cdc.gov/nchs/hus.htm.

Table 40 (page 1 of 2). Death rates for malignant neoplasm of breast for females, according to race, Hispanic origin, and age: United States, selected years 1950–2002

[Data are based on death certificates]

Race, Hispanic origin, and age	*1950*[1]	*1960*[1]	*1970*	*1980*	*1990*	*2000*[2]	*2001*	*2002*
All females	Deaths per 100,000 resident population							
All ages, age adjusted[3]	31.9	31.7	32.1	31.9	33.3	26.8	26.0	25.6
All ages, crude	24.7	26.1	28.4	30.6	34.0	29.2	28.6	28.3
Under 25 years	*	*	*	*	*	*	*	*
25–34 years	3.8	3.8	3.9	3.3	2.9	2.3	2.4	2.1
35–44 years	20.8	20.2	20.4	17.9	17.8	12.4	12.4	12.0
45–54 years	46.9	51.4	52.6	48.1	45.4	33.0	32.8	31.4
55–64 years	69.9	70.8	77.6	80.5	78.6	59.3	57.5	56.2
65–74 years	95.0	90.0	93.8	101.1	111.7	88.3	85.8	84.4
75–84 years	139.8	129.9	127.4	126.4	146.3	128.9	125.8	125.9
85 years and over	195.5	191.9	157.1	169.3	196.8	205.7	188.9	191.5
White[4]								
All ages, age adjusted[3]	32.4	32.0	32.5	32.1	33.2	26.3	25.5	25.0
All ages, crude	25.7	27.2	29.9	32.3	35.9	30.7	29.8	29.5
35–44 years	20.8	19.7	20.2	17.3	17.1	11.3	11.3	10.7
45–54 years	47.1	51.2	53.0	48.1	44.3	31.2	31.0	29.4
55–64 years	70.9	71.8	79.3	81.3	78.5	57.9	56.0	55.0
65–74 years	96.3	91.6	95.9	103.7	113.3	89.3	85.6	84.6
75–84 years	143.6	132.8	129.6	128.4	148.2	130.2	126.9	126.5
85 years and over	204.2	199.7	161.9	171.7	198.0	205.5	189.9	192.6
Black or African American[4]								
All ages, age adjusted[3]	25.3	27.9	28.9	31.7	38.1	34.5	34.4	34.0
All ages, crude	16.4	18.7	19.7	22.9	29.0	27.9	28.3	28.2
35–44 years	21.0	24.8	24.4	24.1	25.8	20.9	20.8	22.0
45–54 years	46.5	54.4	52.0	52.7	60.5	51.5	50.3	49.8
55–64 years	64.3	63.2	64.7	79.9	93.1	80.9	79.8	76.6
65–74 years	67.0	72.3	77.3	84.3	112.2	98.6	106.6	101.1
75–84 years[5]	81.0	87.5	101.8	114.1	140.5	139.8	141.8	145.0
85 years and over	- - -	92.1	112.1	149.9	201.5	238.7	205.9	209.1
American Indian or Alaska Native[4]								
All ages, age adjusted[3]	- - -	- - -	- - -	10.8	13.7	13.6	11.8	13.8
All ages, crude	- - -	- - -	- - -	6.1	8.6	8.7	8.2	9.6
35–44 years	- - -	- - -	- - -	*	*	*	*	*
45–54 years	- - -	- - -	- - -	*	23.9	14.4	18.9	18.7
55–64 years	- - -	- - -	- - -	*	*	40.0	31.4	28.5
65–74 years	- - -	- - -	- - -	*	*	42.5	41.5	48.7
75–84 years	- - -	- - -	- - -	*	*	71.8	*	*
85 years and over	- - -	- - -	- - -	*	*	*	*	*
Asian or Pacific Islander[4]								
All ages, age adjusted[3]	- - -	- - -	- - -	11.9	13.7	12.3	12.9	12.8
All ages, crude	- - -	- - -	- - -	8.2	9.3	10.2	10.9	10.8
35–44 years	- - -	- - -	- - -	10.4	8.4	8.1	8.8	6.8
45–54 years	- - -	- - -	- - -	23.4	26.4	22.3	22.3	21.3
55–64 years	- - -	- - -	- - -	35.7	33.8	31.3	33.1	33.1
65–74 years	- - -	- - -	- - -	*	38.5	34.7	36.5	38.3
75–84 years	- - -	- - -	- - -	*	48.0	37.5	44.8	48.7
85 years and over	- - -	- - -	- - -	*	*	68.2	65.8	69.3
Hispanic or Latino[4,6]								
All ages, age adjusted[3]	- - -	- - -	- - -	- - -	19.5	16.9	16.3	15.5
All ages, crude	- - -	- - -	- - -	- - -	11.5	9.7	9.7	9.2
35–44 years	- - -	- - -	- - -	- - -	11.7	8.7	9.2	7.8
45–54 years	- - -	- - -	- - -	- - -	32.8	23.9	23.8	21.6
55–64 years	- - -	- - -	- - -	- - -	45.8	39.1	41.5	33.5
65–74 years	- - -	- - -	- - -	- - -	64.8	54.9	49.3	48.7
75–84 years	- - -	- - -	- - -	- - -	67.2	74.9	64.7	73.1
85 years and over	- - -	- - -	- - -	- - -	102.8	105.8	102.4	105.3

See footnotes at end of table.

This table will be updated on the Web. Go to www.cdc.gov/nchs/hus.htm.

Table 40 (page 2 of 2). Death rates for malignant neoplasm of breast for females, according to race, Hispanic origin, and age: United States, selected years 1950–2002

[Data are based on death certificates]

Race, Hispanic origin, and age	1950[1]	1960[1]	1970	1980	1990	2000[2]	2001	2002
White, not Hispanic or Latino[6]	Deaths per 100,000 resident population							
All ages, age adjusted[3]	- - -	- - -	- - -	- - -	33.9	26.8	26.0	25.6
All ages, crude	- - -	- - -	- - -	- - -	38.5	33.8	32.9	32.9
35–44 years	- - -	- - -	- - -	- - -	17.5	11.6	11.5	11.1
45–54 years	- - -	- - -	- - -	- - -	45.2	31.7	31.6	30.0
55–64 years	- - -	- - -	- - -	- - -	80.6	59.2	57.0	56.7
65–74 years	- - -	- - -	- - -	- - -	115.7	91.4	88.0	87.0
75–84 years	- - -	- - -	- - -	- - -	151.4	132.2	129.4	128.9
85 years and over	- - -	- - -	- - -	- - -	201.5	208.3	192.6	195.8

* Rates based on fewer than 20 deaths are considered unreliable and are not shown.
0.0 Quantity more than zero but less than 0.05.
- - - Data not available.
[1]Includes deaths of persons who were not residents of the 50 States and the District of Columbia.
[2]Starting with 1999 data, cause of death is coded according to ICD–10. See Appendix II, Comparability ratio and tables V and VI.
[3]Age-adjusted rates are calculated using the year 2000 standard population. See Appendix II, Age adjustment.
[4]The race groups, white, black, Asian or Pacific Islander, and American Indian or Alaska Native, include persons of Hispanic and non-Hispanic origin. Persons of Hispanic origin may be of any race. Death rates for the American Indian or Alaska Native and Asian or Pacific Islander populations are known to be underestimated. See Appendix II, Race, for a discussion of sources of bias in death rates by race and Hispanic origin.
[5]In 1950 rate is for the age group 75 years and over.
[6]Prior to 1997, excludes data from States lacking an Hispanic-origin item on the death certificate. See Appendix II, Hispanic origin.

NOTES: Starting with *Health, United States, 2003*, rates for 1991–99 were revised using intercensal population estimates based on census 2000. Rates for 2000 were revised based on census 2000 counts. Rates for 2001 and 2002 were computed using 2000-based postcensal estimates. See Appendix I, Population Census and Population Estimates. Underlying cause of death code numbers are based on the applicable revision of the *International Classification of Diseases* (ICD) for data years shown. See Appendix II, tables IV and V. Age groups were selected to minimize the presentation of unstable age-specific death rates based on small numbers of deaths and for consistency among comparison groups. Data for additional years are available. See Appendix III.

SOURCES: Centers for Disease Control and Prevention, National Center for Health Statistics, National Vital Statistics System; numerator data from annual mortality files; denominator data from national population estimates for race groups from table 1 and unpublished Hispanic population estimates for 1985–96 prepared by the Housing and Household Economic Statistics Division, U.S. Bureau of the Census; additional mortality tables are available at www.cdc.gov/nchs/datawh/statab/unpubd/mortabs.htm; Kochanek KD, Murphy SL, Anderson RN, Scott C. Deaths: Final data for 2002. National vital statistics reports. Vol 53 no 5. Hyattsville, Maryland: National Center for Health Statistics. 2004.

This table will be updated on the Web. Go to www.cdc.gov/nchs/hus.htm.

Table 41 (page 1 of 3). Death rates for chronic lower respiratory diseases, according to sex, race, Hispanic origin, and age: United States, selected years 1980–2002

[Data are based on death certificates]

Sex, race, Hispanic origin, and age	*1980*	*1990*	*1995*	*1999*[1]	*2000*	*2001*	*2002*
All persons			Deaths per 100,000 resident population				
All ages, age adjusted[2]	28.3	37.2	40.1	45.4	44.2	43.7	43.5
All ages, crude	24.7	34.9	38.6	44.5	43.4	43.2	43.3
Under 1 year	1.6	1.4	1.1	0.9	0.9	1.0	1.0
1–4 years	0.4	0.4	0.2	0.4	0.3	0.3	0.4
5–14 years	0.2	0.3	0.4	0.3	0.3	0.3	0.3
15–24 years	0.3	0.5	0.7	0.5	0.5	0.4	0.5
25–34 years	0.5	0.7	0.9	0.8	0.7	0.7	0.8
35–44 years	1.6	1.6	1.9	2.0	2.1	2.2	2.2
45–54 years	9.8	9.1	8.7	8.5	8.6	8.5	8.7
55–64 years	42.7	48.9	46.8	47.5	44.2	44.1	42.4
65–74 years	129.1	152.5	159.6	177.2	169.4	167.9	163.0
75–84 years	224.4	321.1	349.3	397.8	386.1	379.8	386.7
85 years and over	274.0	433.3	520.1	646.0	648.6	644.7	637.6
Male							
All ages, age adjusted[2]	49.9	55.5	54.8	58.7	55.8	54.0	53.5
All ages, crude	35.1	40.8	41.4	45.6	43.5	42.7	42.9
Under 1 year	1.9	1.6	1.4	*	1.2	1.1	1.1
1–4 years	0.5	0.5	0.2	0.4	0.4	0.4	0.6
5–14 years	0.2	0.4	0.5	0.4	0.4	0.3	0.4
15–24 years	0.4	0.5	0.7	0.6	0.6	0.5	0.6
25–34 years	0.6	0.7	0.9	0.8	0.8	0.7	0.8
35–44 years	1.7	1.7	1.7	1.8	1.9	2.0	2.2
45–54 years	12.1	9.4	8.8	8.6	9.0	8.8	9.1
55–64 years	59.9	58.6	52.3	52.3	47.8	46.9	45.2
65–74 years	210.0	204.0	195.6	210.7	195.2	191.3	184.8
75–84 years	437.4	500.0	483.8	513.2	488.5	475.1	480.8
85 years and over	583.4	815.1	889.8	996.7	967.9	916.9	894.8
Female							
All ages, age adjusted[2]	14.9	26.6	31.8	37.7	37.4	37.6	37.4
All ages, crude	15.0	29.2	36.0	43.4	43.2	43.7	43.7
Under 1 year	1.3	1.2	*	*	*	*	*
1–4 years	*	*	*	0.3	0.3	*	0.3
5–14 years	0.3	0.3	0.2	0.2	0.3	0.2	0.3
15–24 years	0.3	0.5	0.6	0.5	0.4	0.4	0.4
25–34 years	0.5	0.7	0.9	0.9	0.7	0.7	0.7
35–44 years	1.5	1.5	2.2	2.1	2.2	2.3	2.3
45–54 years	7.7	8.8	8.7	8.4	8.3	8.1	8.2
55–64 years	27.6	40.3	41.9	43.1	41.0	41.5	39.8
65–74 years	67.1	112.3	130.8	149.8	148.2	148.5	144.9
75–84 years	98.7	214.2	265.3	322.9	319.2	317.3	324.1
85 years and over	138.7	286.0	377.7	504.6	518.5	530.8	526.0
White male[3]							
All ages, age adjusted[2]	51.6	56.6	55.9	60.0	57.2	55.5	54.9
All ages, crude	37.9	44.3	45.5	50.6	48.3	47.6	47.8
35–44 years	1.2	1.3	1.4	1.5	1.6	1.7	1.8
45–54 years	11.4	8.6	8.1	8.1	8.4	8.6	8.8
55–64 years	60.0	58.7	52.7	53.1	48.6	48.0	46.0
65–74 years	218.4	208.1	200.0	217.3	201.4	198.3	192.3
75–84 years	459.8	513.5	497.9	525.4	503.6	489.4	495.2
85 years and over	611.2	847.0	918.3	1,029.4	997.4	943.6	923.4
Black or African American male[3]							
All ages, age adjusted[2]	34.0	47.6	47.4	51.5	47.5	46.3	46.3
All ages, crude	19.3	25.2	24.4	26.2	24.3	23.6	24.1
35–44 years	5.8	5.3	4.3	4.7	4.8	4.7	5.7
45–54 years	19.7	18.8	16.9	15.3	15.0	13.3	14.4
55–64 years	66.6	67.4	60.5	59.3	54.6	49.8	52.3
65–74 years	142.0	184.5	178.7	184.6	176.9	168.0	158.0
75–84 years	229.8	390.9	370.0	434.4	370.3	380.8	392.2
85 years and over	271.6	498.0	624.1	701.9	693.1	671.7	645.4

See footnotes at end of table.

This table will be updated on the Web. Go to www.cdc.gov/nchs/hus.htm.

Table 41 (page 2 of 3). Death rates for chronic lower respiratory diseases, according to sex, race, Hispanic origin, and age: United States, selected years 1980–2002

[Data are based on death certificates]

Sex, race, Hispanic origin, and age	1980	1990	1995	1999[1]	2000	2001	2002
			Deaths per 100,000 resident population				
American Indian or Alaska Native male[3]							
All ages, age adjusted[2]	23.0	38.3	35.6	41.8	43.7	35.0	35.9
All ages, crude	8.4	13.8	12.3	14.0	15.3	13.1	14.3
35–44 years	*	*	*	*	*	*	*
45–54 years	*	*	*	*	*	*	*
55–64 years	*	*	36.5	34.2	46.4	35.7	34.5
65–74 years	*	135.7	132.1	165.0	111.3	115.1	126.1
75–84 years	*	363.8	307.3	393.0	416.6	306.0	348.9
85 years and over	*	*	*	576.7	770.7	614.8	500.3
Asian or Pacific Islander male[3]							
All ages, age adjusted[2]	21.5	29.8	28.9	29.6	28.3	27.0	25.0
All ages, crude	8.7	11.3	11.8	13.1	12.6	12.7	12.0
35–44 years	*	*	*	*	*	*	*
45–54 years	*	*	*	*	4.8	3.6	2.6
55–64 years	*	22.1	15.7	14.3	8.8	14.4	11.5
65–74 years	70.6	91.4	87.9	81.9	71.3	65.5	58.5
75–84 years	155.7	258.6	240.6	270.6	254.3	239.3	235.9
85 years and over	472.4	615.2	650.4	652.3	670.7	640.4	582.5
Hispanic or Latino male[3,4]							
All ages, age adjusted[2]	---	28.6	31.8	33.0	28.8	27.6	27.2
All ages, crude	---	8.4	8.9	8.9	8.0	7.8	8.1
35–44 years	---	*	1.1	1.4	0.9	0.7	1.0
45–54 years	---	4.1	3.9	3.6	3.4	3.2	3.8
55–64 years	---	17.2	19.1	17.6	18.2	16.1	17.5
65–74 years	---	81.0	82.4	81.9	72.4	75.5	69.2
75–84 years	---	252.4	292.0	272.7	250.3	224.0	243.3
85 years and over	---	613.9	689.0	836.8	671.1	676.1	602.4
White, not Hispanic or Latino male[4]							
All ages, age adjusted[2]	---	57.9	56.6	61.3	58.5	56.9	56.5
All ages, crude	---	48.5	50.2	57.3	55.1	54.6	55.1
35–44 years	---	1.4	1.4	1.5	1.7	1.9	2.0
45–54 years	---	9.0	8.4	8.5	8.9	9.1	9.3
55–64 years	---	61.3	54.6	55.6	50.8	50.5	48.3
65–74 years	---	213.4	204.3	224.9	208.8	206.1	200.4
75–84 years	---	523.7	501.7	534.9	513.6	500.9	506.7
85 years and over	---	860.6	922.6	1,033.5	1,008.6	951.5	935.4
White female[3]							
All ages, age adjusted[2]	15.5	27.8	33.3	39.7	39.5	39.8	39.7
All ages, crude	16.4	32.8	40.8	49.8	49.7	50.3	50.5
35–44 years	1.3	1.2	1.7	1.8	1.8	1.9	2.0
45–54 years	7.6	8.3	8.4	8.1	7.9	8.0	8.1
55–64 years	28.7	41.9	44.0	45.6	43.2	44.1	42.4
65–74 years	71.0	118.8	139.0	160.3	159.6	160.4	157.0
75–84 years	104.0	226.3	279.5	341.5	339.1	338.3	345.4
85 years and over	144.2	298.4	395.5	529.7	544.8	557.9	554.5
Black or African American female[3]							
All ages, age adjusted[2]	9.1	16.6	20.2	23.4	22.7	22.4	22.6
All ages, crude	6.8	12.6	15.5	18.0	17.6	17.5	17.7
35–44 years	3.4	3.8	5.4	4.6	4.7	4.9	4.6
45–54 years	9.3	14.0	12.8	12.6	13.4	11.7	11.6
55–64 years	20.8	33.4	34.7	34.9	35.3	33.3	31.5
65–74 years	32.7	64.7	78.7	88.9	82.9	84.3	82.0
75–84 years	41.1	96.0	132.7	166.4	158.4	151.7	167.4
85 years and over	63.2	133.0	185.8	254.5	255.0	266.1	262.0

See footnotes at end of table.

This table will be updated on the Web. Go to www.cdc.gov/nchs/hus.htm.

Table 41 (page 3 of 3). Death rates for chronic lower respiratory diseases, according to sex, race, Hispanic origin, and age: United States, selected years 1980–2002

[Data are based on death certificates]

Sex, race, Hispanic origin, and age	1980	1990	1995	1999[1]	2000	2001	2002
	Deaths per 100,000 resident population						
American Indian or Alaska Native female[3]							
All ages, age adjusted[2]	7.7	16.8	22.8	30.4	26.2	27.3	26.4
All ages, crude	3.8	8.7	11.5	14.7	13.4	14.8	15.1
35–44 years	*	*	*	*	*	*	*
45–54 years	*	*	*	*	*	*	*
55–64 years	*	*	38.8	39.6	31.6	37.3	34.1
65–74 years	*	56.4	79.5	109.1	136.8	114.2	119.1
75–84 years	*	116.7	191.3	301.1	175.8	217.9	194.8
85 years and over	*	*	*	322.8	362.2	345.3	353.4
Asian or Pacific Islander female[3]							
All ages, age adjusted[2]	5.8	11.0	12.1	12.1	11.7	11.1	9.3
All ages, crude	2.6	5.2	6.3	7.0	6.8	6.8	6.0
35–44 years	*	*	*	*	*	*	*
45–54 years	*	*	3.6	*	*	*	*
55–64 years	*	15.2	9.6	7.7	6.2	7.0	4.9
65–74 years	*	26.5	29.2	39.9	29.2	30.2	24.6
75–84 years	*	80.6	113.2	94.1	88.9	79.4	77.0
85 years and over	*	232.5	227.8	268.0	299.5	288.5	219.1
Hispanic or Latino female[3,4]							
All ages, age adjusted[2]	- - -	13.4	16.9	17.7	16.3	16.5	16.2
All ages, crude	- - -	6.3	7.7	8.0	7.2	7.5	7.6
35–44 years	- - -	*	1.4	1.8	1.3	1.2	1.4
45–54 years	- - -	4.9	4.6	4.2	3.3	4.1	3.1
55–64 years	- - -	14.4	12.9	12.0	10.8	12.1	10.6
65–74 years	- - -	36.6	43.1	47.5	38.0	40.3	41.5
75–84 years	- - -	101.1	125.0	142.9	136.0	132.7	129.8
85 years and over	- - -	269.0	402.6	391.0	387.8	384.4	385.5
White, not Hispanic or Latino female[4]							
All ages, age adjusted[2]	- - -	28.5	34.0	40.8	40.7	41.1	41.2
All ages, crude	- - -	35.7	44.7	55.9	56.2	57.2	57.7
35–44 years	- - -	1.2	1.7	1.8	1.9	2.0	2.1
45–54 years	- - -	8.5	8.5	8.5	8.3	8.3	8.6
55–64 years	- - -	43.7	46.2	48.3	45.8	46.8	45.1
65–74 years	- - -	122.8	143.0	167.4	167.6	168.8	165.5
75–84 years	- - -	231.9	284.5	348.8	347.2	347.3	355.7
85 years and over	- - -	302.1	393.7	532.8	548.7	562.7	559.8

* Rates based on fewer than 20 deaths are considered unreliable and are not shown.

- - - Data not available.

[1]Starting with 1999 data, cause of death is coded according to ICD–10. To estimate change between 1998 and 1999, compare the 1999 rate with the comparability-modified rate for 1998. See Appendix II, Comparability ratio and tables V and VI.

[2]Age-adjusted rates are calculated using the year 2000 standard population. See Appendix II, Age adjustment.

[3]The race groups, white, black, Asian or Pacific Islander, and American Indian or Alaska Native, include persons of Hispanic and non-Hispanic origin. Persons of Hispanic origin may be of any race. Death rates for the American Indian or Alaska Native and Asian or Pacific Islander populations are known to be underestimated. See Appendix II, Race, for a discussion of sources of bias in death rates by race and Hispanic origin.

[4]Prior to 1997, excludes data from States lacking an Hispanic-origin item on the death certificate. See Appendix II, Hispanic origin.

NOTES: Starting with *Health, United States, 2003*, rates for 1991–99 were revised using intercensal population estimates based on census 2000. Rates for 2000 were revised based on census 2000 counts. Rates for 2001 and 2002 were computed using 2000-based postcensal estimates. See Appendix I, Population Census and Population Estimates. Underlying cause of death code numbers are based on the applicable revision of the *International Classification of Diseases* (ICD) for data years shown. For the period 1980–98, causes were coded using ICD–9 codes that are most nearly comparable with the 113 cause list for ICD–10. See Appendix II, tables IV and V. Age groups were selected to minimize the presentation of unstable age-specific death rates based on small numbers of deaths and for consistency among comparison groups. Data for additional years are available. See Appendix III.

SOURCES: Centers for Disease Control and Prevention, National Center for Health Statistics, National Vital Statistics System; numerator data from annual mortality files; denominator data from national population estimates for race groups from table 1 and unpublished Hispanic population estimates for 1985–96 prepared by the Housing and Household Economic Statistics Division, U.S. Bureau of the Census; additional mortality tables are available at www.cdc.gov/nchs/datawh/statab/unpubd/mortabs.htm; Kochanek KD, Murphy SL, Anderson RN, Scott C. Deaths: Final data for 2002. National vital statistics reports. Vol 53 no 5. Hyattsville, Maryland: National Center for Health Statistics. 2004.

This table will be updated on the Web. Go to www.cdc.gov/nchs/hus.htm.

Table 42 (page 1 of 2). Death rates for human immunodeficiency virus (HIV) disease, according to sex, race, Hispanic origin, and age: United States, selected years 1987–2002

[Data are based on death certificates]

Sex, race, Hispanic origin, and age	1987	1990	1995	1999[1]	2000	2001	2002
All persons				Deaths per 100,000 resident population			
All ages, age adjusted[2]	5.6	10.2	16.2	5.3	5.2	5.0	4.9
All ages, crude	5.6	10.1	16.2	5.3	5.1	5.0	4.9
Under 1 year	2.3	2.7	1.5	*	*	*	*
1–4 years	0.7	0.8	1.3	0.2	*	*	*
5–14 years	0.1	0.2	0.5	0.2	0.1	0.1	0.1
15–24 years	1.3	1.5	1.7	0.5	0.5	0.6	0.4
25–34 years	11.7	19.7	28.3	6.8	6.1	5.3	4.6
35–44 years	14.0	27.4	44.2	13.8	13.1	13.0	12.7
45–54 years	8.0	15.2	26.0	10.7	11.0	10.5	11.2
55–64 years	3.5	6.2	10.9	4.8	5.1	5.2	5.1
65–74 years	1.3	2.0	3.6	2.2	2.2	2.1	2.2
75–84 years	0.8	0.7	0.7	0.6	0.7	0.7	0.8
85 years and over	*	*	*	*	*	*	*
Male							
All ages, age adjusted[2]	10.4	18.5	27.3	8.2	7.9	7.5	7.4
All ages, crude	10.2	18.5	27.6	8.2	7.9	7.6	7.4
Under 1 year	2.2	2.4	1.7	*	*	*	*
1–4 years	0.7	0.8	1.2	*	*	*	*
5–14 years	0.2	0.3	0.5	0.2	0.1	0.1	*
15–24 years	2.2	2.2	2.0	0.5	0.5	0.5	0.4
25–34 years	20.7	34.5	45.5	9.5	8.0	7.1	5.9
35–44 years	26.3	50.2	75.5	21.0	19.8	19.5	18.8
45–54 years	15.5	29.1	46.2	17.5	17.8	16.8	17.7
55–64 years	6.8	12.0	19.7	8.3	8.7	8.6	8.5
65–74 years	2.4	3.7	6.4	3.8	3.8	3.5	3.9
75–84 years	1.2	1.1	1.3	1.0	1.3	1.5	1.4
85 years and over	*	*	*	*	*	*	*
Female							
All ages, age adjusted[2]	1.1	2.2	5.3	2.5	2.5	2.5	2.5
All ages, crude	1.1	2.2	5.3	2.5	2.5	2.5	2.5
Under 1 year	2.5	3.0	1.2	*	*	*	*
1–4 years	0.7	0.8	1.5	*	*	*	*
5–14 years	*	0.2	0.5	0.2	0.1	*	*
15–24 years	0.3	0.7	1.4	0.5	0.4	0.6	0.4
25–34 years	2.8	4.9	10.9	4.1	4.2	3.5	3.3
35–44 years	2.1	5.2	13.3	6.7	6.5	6.7	6.7
45–54 years	0.8	1.9	6.6	4.1	4.4	4.4	4.8
55–64 years	0.5	1.1	2.8	1.6	1.8	2.0	1.9
65–74 years	0.5	0.8	1.4	0.8	0.8	0.9	0.8
75–84 years	0.5	0.4	0.3	0.3	0.3	*	0.3
85 years and over	*	*	*	*	*	*	*
All ages, age adjusted[2]							
White male	8.7	15.7	20.4	4.9	4.6	4.4	4.3
Black or African American male	26.2	46.3	89.0	36.1	35.1	33.8	33.3
American Indian or Alaska Native male	*	3.3	10.5	4.2	3.5	4.2	3.4
Asian or Pacific Islander male	2.5	4.3	6.0	1.4	1.2	1.2	1.5
Hispanic or Latino male[3]	18.8	28.8	40.8	10.9	10.6	9.7	9.1
White, not Hispanic or Latino male[3]	10.7	14.1	17.9	4.0	3.8	3.6	3.5
White female	0.6	1.1	2.5	1.0	1.0	0.9	0.9
Black or African American female	4.6	10.1	24.4	13.1	13.2	13.4	13.4
American Indian or Alaska Native female	*	*	2.5	1.0	1.0	*	*
Asian or Pacific Islander female	*	*	0.6	0.2	0.2	*	*
Hispanic or Latino female[3]	2.1	3.8	8.8	3.0	2.9	2.7	2.6
White, not Hispanic or Latino female[3]	0.5	0.7	1.7	0.7	0.7	0.6	0.6

See footnotes at end of table.

This table will be updated on the Web. Go to www.cdc.gov/nchs/hus.htm.

Table 42 (page 2 of 2). Death rates for human immunodeficiency virus (HIV) disease, according to sex, race, Hispanic origin, and age: United States, selected years 1987–2002

[Data are based on death certificates]

Sex, race, Hispanic origin, and age	*1987*	*1990*	*1995*	*1999*[1]	*2000*	*2001*	*2002*
Age 25–44 years			Deaths per 100,000 resident population				
All persons	12.7	23.2	36.3	10.5	9.8	9.4	8.9
White male	19.2	35.0	46.1	9.7	8.8	8.3	7.7
Black or African American male	60.2	102.0	179.4	59.3	55.4	53.5	49.9
American Indian or Alaska Native male	*	7.7	28.5	9.1	5.5	7.3	8.3
Asian or Pacific Islander male	4.1	8.1	12.1	2.4	1.9	2.1	1.8
Hispanic or Latino male[3]	36.8	59.3	73.9	16.5	14.3	12.4	11.5
White, not Hispanic or Latino male[3]	23.3	31.6	41.2	8.2	7.4	7.2	6.6
White female	1.2	2.3	5.9	2.2	2.1	1.9	1.8
Black or African American female	11.6	23.6	53.6	26.6	26.7	26.0	25.9
American Indian or Alaska Native female	*	*	*	*	*	*	*
Asian or Pacific Islander female	*	*	1.2	*	*	*	*
Hispanic or Latino female[3]	4.9	8.9	17.2	5.3	4.6	4.3	3.8
White, not Hispanic or Latino female[3]	1.0	1.5	4.2	1.6	1.6	1.3	1.3
Age 45–64 years							
All persons	5.8	11.1	19.9	8.4	8.7	8.4	8.7
White male	9.9	18.6	26.0	7.8	8.1	7.7	7.8
Black or African American male	27.3	53.0	133.2	70.7	71.6	68.8	70.7
American Indian or Alaska Native male	*	*	*	*	*	7.8	*
Asian or Pacific Islander male	*	6.5	9.1	2.3	2.1	1.9	3.4
Hispanic or Latino male[3]	25.8	37.9	67.1	21.2	23.3	21.5	20.3
White, not Hispanic or Latino male[3]	12.6	16.9	22.4	6.4	6.5	6.1	6.4
White female	0.5	0.9	2.4	1.2	1.3	1.2	1.4
Black or African American female	2.6	7.5	27.0	18.6	19.6	20.8	21.4
American Indian or Alaska Native female	*	*	*	*	*	*	*
Asian or Pacific Islander female	*	*	*	*	*	*	*
Hispanic or Latino female[3]	*	3.1	12.6	5.1	5.8	5.4	5.7
White, not Hispanic or Latino female[3]	0.5	0.7	1.5	0.8	0.9	0.8	0.9

* Rates based on fewer than 20 deaths are considered unreliable and are not shown.
[1]Starting with 1999 data, cause of death is coded according to ICD–10. To estimate change between 1998 and 1999, compare the 1999 rate with the comparability-modified rate for 1998. See Appendix II, Comparability ratio and tables V and VI.
[2]Age-adjusted rates are calculated using the year 2000 standard population. See Appendix II, Age adjustment.
[3]Prior to 1997, excludes data from States lacking an Hispanic-origin item on the death certificate. See Appendix II, Hispanic origin.

NOTES: Starting with *Health, United States, 2003*, rates for 1991–99 were revised using intercensal population estimates based on census 2000. Rates for 2000 were revised based on census 2000 counts. Rates for 2001 and 2002 were computed using 2000-based postcensal estimates. See Appendix I, Population Census and Population Estimates. The race groups, white, black, Asian or Pacific Islander, and American Indian or Alaska Native, include persons of Hispanic and non-Hispanic origin. Persons of Hispanic origin may be of any race. Death rates for the American Indian or Alaska Native and Asian or Pacific Islander populations are known to be underestimated. See Appendix II, Race, for a discussion of sources of bias in death rates by race and Hispanic origin. Categories for the coding and classification of human immunodeficiency virus (HIV) disease were introduced in the United States in 1987. Underlying cause of death code numbers are based on the applicable revision of the *International Classification of Diseases* (ICD) for data years shown. See Appendix II, tables IV and V. Data for additional years are available. See Appendix III.

SOURCES: Centers for Disease Control and Prevention, National Center for Health Statistics, National Vital Statistics System; numerator data from annual mortality files; denominator data from national population estimates for race groups from table 1 and unpublished Hispanic population estimates for 1987–96 prepared by the Housing and Household Economic Statistics Division, U.S. Bureau of the Census; additional mortality tables are available at www.cdc.gov/nchs/datawh/statab/unpubd/mortabs.htm; Kochanek KD, Murphy SL, Anderson RN, Scott C. Deaths: Final data for 2002. National vital statistics reports. Vol 53 no 5. Hyattsville, Maryland: National Center for Health Statistics. 2004.

This table will be updated on the Web. Go to www.cdc.gov/nchs/hus.htm.

Table 43. Maternal mortality for complications of pregnancy, childbirth, and the puerperium, according to race, Hispanic origin, and age: United States, selected years 1950–2002

[Data are based on death certificates]

Race, Hispanic origin, and age	1950[1]	1960[1]	1970	1980	1990	1995	1999[2]	2000	2001	2002
					Number of deaths					
All persons	2,960	1,579	803	334	343	277	391	396	399	357
White	1,873	936	445	193	177	129	214	240	228	190
Black or African American	1,041	624	342	127	153	133	154	137	150	148
American Indian or Alaska Native	- - -	- - -	- - -	3	4	1	5	6	5	–
Asian or Pacific Islander	- - -	- - -	- - -	11	9	14	18	13	16	19
Hispanic or Latino[3]	- - -	- - -	- - -	- - -	47	43	67	81	81	62
White, not Hispanic or Latino[3]	- - -	- - -	- - -	- - -	125	84	149	160	151	128
All persons					Deaths per 100,000 live births					
All ages, age adjusted[4]	73.7	32.1	21.5	9.4	7.6	6.3	8.3	8.2	8.8	7.6
All ages, crude	83.3	37.1	21.5	9.2	8.2	7.1	9.9	9.8	9.9	8.9
Under 20 years	70.7	22.7	18.9	7.6	7.5	3.9	6.6	*	8.8	6.7
20–24 years	47.6	20.7	13.0	5.8	6.1	5.7	6.2	7.4	6.9	5.8
25–29 years	63.5	29.8	17.0	7.7	6.0	6.0	8.2	7.9	8.5	7.5
30–34 years	107.7	50.3	31.6	13.6	9.5	7.3	10.1	10.0	10.1	9.3
35 years and over[5]	222.0	104.3	81.9	36.3	20.7	15.9	23.0	22.7	18.9	18.4
White										
All ages, age adjusted[4]	53.1	22.4	14.4	6.7	5.1	3.6	5.5	6.2	6.5	4.8
All ages, crude	61.1	26.0	14.3	6.6	5.4	4.2	6.8	7.5	7.2	6.0
Under 20 years	44.9	14.8	13.8	5.8	*	*	*	*	7.4	*
20–24 years	35.7	15.3	8.4	4.2	3.9	3.5	4.0	5.6	5.3	3.4
25–29 years	45.0	20.3	11.1	5.4	4.8	4.0	5.4	5.9	5.8	4.6
30–34 years	75.9	34.3	18.7	9.3	5.0	4.0	7.0	7.1	8.1	6.7
35 years and over[5]	174.1	73.9	59.3	25.5	12.6	9.1	16.6	18.0	11.4	13.3
Black or African American										
All ages, age adjusted[4]	- - -	92.0	65.5	24.9	21.7	20.9	23.3	20.1	22.4	22.9
All ages, crude	- - -	103.6	60.9	22.4	22.4	22.1	25.4	22.0	24.7	24.9
Under 20 years	- - -	54.8	32.3	13.1	*	*	*	*	*	*
20–24 years	- - -	56.9	41.9	13.9	14.7	15.3	14.0	15.3	14.6	14.9
25–29 years	- - -	92.8	65.2	22.4	14.9	21.0	26.6	21.8	24.7	27.1
30–34 years	- - -	150.6	117.8	44.0	44.2	31.2	36.1	34.8	30.6	28.4
35 years and over[5]	- - -	299.5	207.5	100.6	79.7	61.4	69.9	62.8	71.0	62.9
Hispanic or Latino[3,6]										
All ages, age adjusted[4]	- - -	- - -	- - -	- - -	7.4	5.4	7.9	9.0	8.8	6.0
All ages, crude	- - -	- - -	- - -	- - -	7.9	6.3	8.8	9.9	9.5	7.1
White, not Hispanic or Latino[3]										
All ages, age adjusted[4]	- - -	- - -	- - -	- - -	4.4	3.3	4.9	5.5	5.8	4.4
All ages, crude	- - -	- - -	- - -	- - -	4.8	3.5	6.4	6.8	6.5	5.6

- - - Data not available.
– Quantity zero.
* Rates based on fewer than 20 deaths are considered unreliable and are not shown.
[1]Includes deaths of persons who were not residents of the 50 States and the District of Columbia.
[2]Starting with 1999 data, changes were made in the classification and coding of maternal deaths under ICD–10. The large increase in the number of maternal deaths between 1998 and 1999 is due to changes associated with ICD–10. See Appendix II, *International Classification of Diseases* (ICD); Maternal death.
[3]Prior to 1997, excludes data from States lacking an Hispanic-origin item on the death certificate. See Appendix II, Hispanic origin.
[4]Rates are age adjusted to the 1970 distribution of live births by mother's age in the United States. See Appendix II, Age adjustment.
[5]Rates computed by relating deaths of women 35 years and over to live births to women 35–49 years. See Appendix II, Rate: Death and related rates.
[6]Age-specific maternal mortality rates are not calculated because rates based on fewer than 20 deaths are considered unreliable.

NOTES: Underlying cause of death code numbers are based on the applicable revision of the *International Classification of Diseases* (ICD) for data years shown. See Appendix II, tables IV and V. The race groups, white, black, Asian or Pacific Islander, and American Indian or Alaska Native, include persons of Hispanic and non-Hispanic origin. Persons of Hispanic origin may be of any race. For 1950 and 1960, rates were based on live births by race of child; for all other years, rates are based on live births by race of mother. See Appendix II, Race. Rates are not calculated for American Indian or Alaska Native and Asian or Pacific Islander mothers because rates based on fewer than 20 deaths are considered unreliable. Data for additional years are available. See Appendix III.

SOURCES: Centers for Disease Control and Prevention, National Center for Health Statistics, National Vital Statistics System; numerator data from annual mortality files; denominator data from annual natality files; Kochanek KD, Murphy SL, Anderson RN, Scott C. Deaths: Final data for 2002. National vital statistics reports. Vol 53 no 5. Hyattsville, Maryland: National Center for Health Statistics. 2004.

This table will be updated on the Web. Go to www.cdc.gov/nchs/hus.htm.

Table 44 (page 1 of 4). Death rates for motor vehicle-related injuries, according to sex, race, Hispanic origin, and age: United States, selected years 1950–2002

[Data are based on death certificates]

Sex, race, Hispanic origin, and age	*1950*[1]	*1960*[1]	*1970*	*1980*	*1990*	*2000*[2]	*2001*	*2002*
All persons				Deaths per 100,000 resident population				
All ages, age adjusted[3]	24.6	23.1	27.6	22.3	18.5	15.4	15.3	15.7
All ages, crude	23.1	21.3	26.9	23.5	18.8	15.4	15.4	15.7
Under 1 year	8.4	8.1	9.8	7.0	4.9	4.4	3.6	3.0
1–14 years	9.8	8.6	10.5	8.2	6.0	4.3	4.1	3.9
1–4 years	11.5	10.0	11.5	9.2	6.3	4.2	4.1	3.9
5–14 years	8.8	7.9	10.2	7.9	5.9	4.3	4.1	3.9
15–24 years	34.4	38.0	47.2	44.8	34.1	26.9	26.8	28.2
15–19 years	29.6	33.9	43.6	43.0	33.1	26.0	25.7	27.6
20–24 years	38.8	42.9	51.3	46.6	35.0	28.0	28.0	28.8
25–34 years	24.6	24.3	30.9	29.1	23.6	17.3	17.5	17.8
35–44 years	20.3	19.3	24.9	20.9	16.9	15.3	15.7	15.8
45–64 years	25.2	23.0	26.5	18.0	15.7	14.3	14.0	14.5
45–54 years	22.2	21.4	25.5	18.6	15.6	14.2	14.2	14.8
55–64 years	29.0	25.1	27.9	17.4	15.9	14.4	13.7	14.1
65 years and over	43.1	34.7	36.2	22.5	23.1	21.4	21.3	21.5
65–74 years	39.1	31.4	32.8	19.2	18.6	16.5	16.3	17.0
75–84 years	52.7	41.8	43.5	28.1	29.1	25.7	26.3	25.7
85 years and over	45.1	37.9	34.2	27.6	31.2	30.4	27.8	28.0
Male								
All ages, age adjusted[3]	38.5	35.4	41.5	33.6	26.5	21.7	21.8	22.1
All ages, crude	35.4	31.8	39.7	35.3	26.7	21.3	21.5	21.9
Under 1 year	9.1	8.6	9.3	7.3	5.0	4.6	3.2	3.3
1–14 years	12.3	10.7	13.0	10.0	7.0	4.9	4.8	4.6
1–4 years	13.0	11.5	12.9	10.2	6.9	4.7	4.5	4.5
5–14 years	11.9	10.4	13.1	9.9	7.0	5.0	4.9	4.6
15–24 years	56.7	61.2	73.2	68.4	49.5	37.4	38.0	39.3
15–19 years	46.3	51.7	64.1	62.6	45.5	33.9	34.0	36.0
20–24 years	66.7	73.2	84.4	74.3	53.3	41.2	42.1	42.6
25–34 years	40.8	40.1	49.4	46.3	35.7	25.5	26.2	26.5
35–44 years	32.5	29.9	37.7	31.7	24.7	22.0	22.4	22.3
45–64 years	37.7	33.3	38.9	26.5	21.9	20.2	19.9	20.7
45–54 years	33.6	31.6	37.2	27.6	22.0	20.4	20.5	21.3
55–64 years	43.1	35.6	40.9	25.4	21.7	19.8	19.0	19.9
65 years and over	66.6	52.1	54.4	33.9	32.1	29.5	29.5	29.8
65–74 years	59.1	45.8	47.3	27.3	24.2	21.7	21.5	22.7
75–84 years	85.0	66.0	68.2	44.3	41.2	35.6	37.3	35.3
85 years and over	78.1	62.7	63.1	56.1	64.5	57.5	51.1	51.7
Female								
All ages, age adjusted[3]	11.5	11.7	14.9	11.8	11.0	9.5	9.3	9.6
All ages, crude	10.9	11.0	14.7	12.3	11.3	9.7	9.5	9.8
Under 1 year	7.6	7.5	10.4	6.7	4.9	4.2	4.0	2.8
1–14 years	7.2	6.3	7.9	6.3	4.9	3.7	3.4	3.3
1–4 years	10.0	8.4	10.0	8.1	5.6	3.8	3.6	3.3
5–14 years	5.7	5.4	7.2	5.7	4.7	3.6	3.3	3.3
15–24 years	12.6	15.1	21.6	20.8	17.9	15.9	15.1	16.6
15–19 years	12.9	16.0	22.7	22.8	20.0	17.5	16.9	18.9
20–24 years	12.2	14.0	20.4	18.9	16.0	14.2	13.4	14.3
25–34 years	9.3	9.2	13.0	12.2	11.5	8.8	8.7	8.8
35–44 years	8.5	9.1	12.9	10.4	9.2	8.8	9.1	9.3
45–64 years	12.6	13.1	15.3	10.3	10.1	8.7	8.4	8.7
45–54 years	10.9	11.6	14.5	10.2	9.6	8.2	8.1	8.6
55–64 years	14.9	15.2	16.2	10.5	10.8	9.5	8.8	8.9
65 years and over	21.9	20.3	23.1	15.0	17.2	15.8	15.5	15.7
65–74 years	20.6	19.0	21.6	13.0	14.1	12.3	12.0	12.3
75–84 years	25.2	23.0	27.2	18.5	21.9	19.2	19.2	19.3
85 years and over	22.1	22.0	18.0	15.2	18.3	19.3	18.0	17.7
White male[4]								
All ages, age adjusted[3]	37.9	34.8	40.4	33.8	26.3	21.8	22.0	22.4
All ages, crude	35.1	31.5	39.1	35.9	26.7	21.6	21.9	22.4
Under 1 year	9.1	8.8	9.1	7.0	4.8	4.2	3.1	2.9
1–14 years	12.4	10.6	12.5	9.8	6.6	4.8	4.6	4.5
15–24 years	58.3	62.7	75.2	73.8	52.5	39.6	40.0	41.9
25–34 years	39.1	38.6	47.0	46.6	35.4	25.1	26.4	26.6
35–44 years	30.9	28.4	35.2	30.7	23.7	21.8	22.4	22.3
45–64 years	36.2	31.7	36.5	25.2	20.6	19.7	19.5	20.6
65 years and over	67.1	52.1	54.2	32.7	31.4	29.4	29.9	29.8

See footnotes at end of table.

This table will be updated on the Web. Go to www.cdc.gov/nchs/hus.htm.

Table 44 (page 2 of 4). Death rates for motor vehicle-related injuries, according to sex, race, Hispanic origin, and age: United States, selected years 1950–2002

[Data are based on death certificates]

Sex, race, Hispanic origin, and age	1950[1]	1960[1]	1970	1980	1990	2000[2]	2001	2002
Black or African American male[4]				Deaths per 100,000 resident population				
All ages, age adjusted[3]	34.8	39.6	51.0	34.2	29.9	24.4	23.5	23.2
All ages, crude	37.2	33.1	44.3	31.1	28.1	22.5	22.0	21.5
Under 1 year	- - -	*	10.6	7.8	*	6.7	*	*
1–14 years[5]	10.4	11.2	16.3	11.4	8.9	5.5	6.1	5.3
15–24 years	42.5	46.4	58.1	34.9	36.1	30.2	31.4	29.6
25–34 years	54.4	51.0	70.4	44.9	39.5	32.6	29.9	31.7
35–44 years	46.7	43.6	59.5	41.2	33.5	27.2	26.1	25.3
45–64 years	54.6	47.8	61.7	39.5	33.3	27.1	26.7	24.8
65 years and over	52.6	48.2	53.4	42.4	36.3	32.1	28.1	30.4
American Indian or Alaska Native male[4]								
All ages, age adjusted[3]	- - -	- - -	- - -	78.9	48.3	35.8	34.6	39.0
All ages, crude	- - -	- - -	- - -	74.6	47.6	33.6	33.2	37.3
1–14 years	- - -	- - -	- - -	15.1	11.6	7.8	8.4	7.1
15–24 years	- - -	- - -	- - -	126.1	75.2	56.8	55.7	57.2
25–34 years	- - -	- - -	- - -	107.0	78.2	49.8	43.2	49.9
35–44 years	- - -	- - -	- - -	82.8	57.0	36.3	42.3	47.2
45–64 years	- - -	- - -	- - -	77.4	45.9	32.0	30.7	40.7
65 years and over	- - -	- - -	- - -	97.0	43.0	48.5	40.4	45.9
Asian or Pacific Islander male[4]								
All ages, age adjusted[3]	- - -	- - -	- - -	19.0	17.9	10.6	10.4	10.8
All ages, crude	- - -	- - -	- - -	17.1	15.8	9.8	9.7	10.0
1–14 years	- - -	- - -	- - -	8.2	6.3	2.5	2.2	2.5
15–24 years	- - -	- - -	- - -	27.2	25.7	17.0	19.3	20.0
25–34 years	- - -	- - -	- - -	18.8	17.0	10.4	10.0	8.9
35–44 years	- - -	- - -	- - -	13.1	12.2	6.9	7.3	7.8
45–64 years	- - -	- - -	- - -	13.7	15.1	10.1	7.9	8.7
65 years and over	- - -	- - -	- - -	37.3	33.6	21.1	21.8	23.3
Hispanic or Latino male[4,6]								
All ages, age adjusted[3]	- - -	- - -	- - -	- - -	29.5	21.3	22.2	22.2
All ages, crude	- - -	- - -	- - -	- - -	29.2	20.1	21.0	21.3
1–14 years	- - -	- - -	- - -	- - -	7.2	4.4	4.4	5.1
15–24 years	- - -	- - -	- - -	- - -	48.2	34.7	36.9	38.9
25–34 years	- - -	- - -	- - -	- - -	41.0	24.9	26.8	26.4
35–44 years	- - -	- - -	- - -	- - -	28.0	21.6	23.1	22.6
45–64 years	- - -	- - -	- - -	- - -	28.9	21.7	20.5	19.9
65 years and over	- - -	- - -	- - -	- - -	35.3	28.9	31.0	30.7
White, not Hispanic or Latino male[6]								
All ages, age adjusted[3]	- - -	- - -	- - -	- - -	25.7	21.7	21.7	22.2
All ages, crude	- - -	- - -	- - -	- - -	26.0	21.5	21.7	22.3
1–14 years	- - -	- - -	- - -	- - -	6.4	4.9	4.6	4.2
15–24 years	- - -	- - -	- - -	- - -	52.3	40.3	40.1	42.1
25–34 years	- - -	- - -	- - -	- - -	34.0	24.7	25.9	26.1
35–44 years	- - -	- - -	- - -	- - -	23.1	21.6	21.9	22.0
45–64 years	- - -	- - -	- - -	- - -	19.8	19.3	19.2	20.4
65 years and over	- - -	- - -	- - -	- - -	31.1	29.3	29.7	29.6
White female[4]								
All ages, age adjusted[3]	11.4	11.7	14.9	12.2	11.2	9.8	9.5	9.8
All ages, crude	10.9	11.2	14.8	12.8	11.6	10.0	9.8	10.1
Under 1 year	7.8	7.5	10.2	7.1	4.7	3.5	3.8	2.2
1–14 years	7.2	6.2	7.5	6.2	4.8	3.7	3.3	3.2
15–24 years	12.6	15.6	22.7	23.0	19.5	17.1	16.0	17.9
25–34 years	9.0	9.0	12.7	12.2	11.6	8.9	8.8	9.0
35–44 years	8.1	8.9	12.3	10.6	9.2	8.9	9.3	9.4
45–64 years	12.7	13.1	15.1	10.4	9.9	8.7	8.4	8.7
65 years and over	22.2	20.8	23.7	15.3	17.4	16.2	16.0	16.3

See footnotes at end of table.

This table will be updated on the Web. Go to www.cdc.gov/nchs/hus.htm.

Table 44 (page 3 of 4). Death rates for motor vehicle-related injuries, according to sex, race, Hispanic origin, and age: United States, selected years 1950–2002

[Data are based on death certificates]

Sex, race, Hispanic origin, and age	1950[1]	1960[1]	1970	1980	1990	2000[2]	2001	2002
Black or African American female[4]				Deaths per 100,000 resident population				
All ages, age adjusted[3]	9.3	10.4	14.1	8.5	9.6	8.4	8.5	8.2
All ages, crude	10.2	9.7	13.4	8.3	9.4	8.2	8.2	8.0
Under 1 year	---	8.1	11.9	*	7.0	*	*	*
1–14 years[5]	7.2	6.9	10.2	6.3	5.3	3.9	3.7	3.5
15–24 years	11.6	9.9	13.4	8.0	9.9	11.7	11.7	11.6
25–34 years	10.8	9.8	13.3	10.6	11.1	9.4	8.9	8.8
35–44 years	11.1	11.0	16.1	8.3	9.4	8.2	9.2	9.4
45–64 years	11.8	12.7	16.7	9.2	10.7	9.0	8.3	8.4
65 years and over	14.3	13.2	15.7	9.5	13.5	10.4	11.8	9.5
American Indian or Alaska Native female[4]								
All ages, age adjusted[3]	---	---	---	32.0	17.5	19.5	17.6	19.3
All ages, crude	---	---	---	32.0	17.3	18.6	16.9	19.1
1–14 years	---	---	---	15.0	8.1	6.5	7.6	6.8
15–24 years	---	---	---	42.3	31.4	30.3	30.7	29.2
25–34 years	---	---	---	52.5	18.8	22.3	15.5	21.1
35–44 years	---	---	---	38.1	18.2	22.0	13.1	24.4
45–64 years	---	---	---	32.6	17.6	17.8	18.1	20.9
65 years and over	---	---	---	*	*	24.0	25.3	*
Asian or Pacific Islander female[4]								
All ages, age adjusted[3]	---	---	---	9.3	10.4	6.7	6.1	6.2
All ages, crude	---	---	---	8.2	9.0	5.9	5.9	5.7
1–14 years	---	---	---	7.4	3.6	2.3	2.2	1.9
15–24 years	---	---	---	7.4	11.4	6.0	7.6	7.3
25–34 years	---	---	---	7.3	7.3	4.5	4.8	4.4
35–44 years	---	---	---	8.6	7.5	4.9	5.4	3.7
45–64 years	---	---	---	8.5	11.8	6.4	7.0	7.3
65 years and over	---	---	---	18.6	24.3	18.5	11.8	15.6
Hispanic or Latino female[4,6]								
All ages, age adjusted[3]	---	---	---	---	9.6	7.9	7.8	8.1
All ages, crude	---	---	---	---	8.9	7.2	7.2	7.4
1–14 years	---	---	---	---	4.8	3.9	3.3	3.2
15–24 years	---	---	---	---	11.6	10.6	11.2	12.4
25–34 years	---	---	---	---	9.4	6.5	6.5	7.2
35–44 years	---	---	---	---	8.0	7.3	6.9	7.3
45–64 years	---	---	---	---	11.4	8.3	8.4	8.4
65 years and over	---	---	---	---	14.9	13.4	12.9	13.1

See footnotes at end of table.

This table will be updated on the Web. Go to www.cdc.gov/nchs/hus.htm.

Table 44 (page 4 of 4). Death rates for motor vehicle-related injuries, according to sex, race, Hispanic origin, and age: United States, selected years 1950–2002

[Data are based on death certificates]

Sex, race, Hispanic origin, and age	1950[1]	1960[1]	1970	1980	1990	2000[2]	2001	2002
White, not Hispanic or Latino female[6]				Deaths per 100,000 resident population				
All ages, age adjusted[3]	---	---	---	---	11.3	10.0	9.7	10.1
All ages, crude	---	---	---	---	11.7	10.3	10.1	10.5
1–14 years	---	---	---	---	4.7	3.5	3.2	3.2
15–24 years	---	---	---	---	20.4	18.4	17.0	19.0
25–34 years	---	---	---	---	11.7	9.3	9.3	9.4
35–44 years	---	---	---	---	9.3	9.0	9.6	9.7
45–64 years	---	---	---	---	9.7	8.7	8.3	8.6
65 years and over	---	---	---	---	17.5	16.3	16.1	16.5

- - - Data not available.
* Rates based on fewer than 20 deaths are considered unreliable and are not shown.
[1]Includes deaths of persons who were not residents of the 50 States and the District of Columbia.
[2]Starting with 1999 data, cause of death is coded according to ICD–10. See Appendix II, Comparability ratio and tables V and VI.
[3]Age-adjusted rates are calculated using the year 2000 standard population. See Appendix II, Age adjustment.
[4]The race groups, white, black, Asian or Pacific Islander, and American Indian or Alaska Native, include persons of Hispanic and non-Hispanic origin. Persons of Hispanic origin may be of any race. Death rates for the American Indian or Alaska Native and Asian or Pacific Islander populations are known to be underestimated. See Appendix II, Race, for a discussion of sources of bias in death rates by race and Hispanic origin.
[5]In 1950 rate is for the age group under 15 years.
[6]Prior to 1997, excludes data from States lacking an Hispanic-origin item on the death certificate. See Appendix II, Hispanic origin.

NOTES: Starting with *Health, United States, 2003*, rates for 1991–99 were revised using intercensal population estimates based on census 2000. Rates for 2000 were revised based on census 2000 counts. Rates for 2001 and 2002 were computed using 2000-based postcensal estimates. See Appendix I, Population Census and Population Estimates. Underlying cause of death code numbers are based on the applicable revision of the *International Classification of Diseases* (ICD) for data years shown. See Appendix II, tables IV and V. Age groups were selected to minimize the presentation of unstable age-specific death rates based on small numbers of deaths and for consistency among comparison groups. For additional injury-related statistics, see www.cdc.gov/ncipc/wisqars, a Web-based interactive database for injury data. Data for additional years are available. See Appendix III.

SOURCES: Centers for Disease Control and Prevention, National Center for Health Statistics, National Vital Statistics System; Grove RD, Hetzel AM. Vital statistics rates in the United States, 1940–1960. Washington: U.S. Government Printing Office. 1968; numerator data from National Vital Statistics System, annual mortality files; denominator data from national population estimates for race groups from table 1 and unpublished Hispanic population estimates for 1985–96 prepared by the Housing and Household Economic Statistics Division, U.S. Bureau of the Census; additional mortality tables are available at www.cdc.gov/nchs/datawh/statab/unpubd/mortabs.htm; Kochanek KD, Murphy SL, Anderson RN, Scott C. Deaths: Final data for 2002. National vital statistics reports. Vol 53 no 5. Hyattsville, Maryland: National Center for Health Statistics. 2004.

This table will be updated on the Web. Go to www.cdc.gov/nchs/hus.htm.

Table 45 (page 1 of 3). Death rates for homicide, according to sex, race, Hispanic origin, and age: United States, selected years 1950–2002

[Data are based on death certificates]

Sex, race, Hispanic origin, and age	1950[1]	1960[1]	1970	1980	1990	2000[2]	2001	2002
All persons			Deaths per 100,000 resident population					
All ages, age adjusted[3]	5.1	5.0	8.8	10.4	9.4	5.9	7.1	6.1
All ages, crude	5.0	4.6	8.1	10.6	9.9	6.0	7.1	6.1
Under 1 year	4.4	4.8	4.3	5.9	8.4	9.2	8.2	7.5
1–14 years	0.6	0.6	1.1	1.5	1.8	1.3	1.3	1.4
1–4 years	0.6	0.7	1.9	2.5	2.5	2.3	2.7	2.7
5–14 years	0.5	0.5	0.9	1.2	1.5	0.9	0.8	0.9
15–24 years	5.8	5.6	11.3	15.4	19.7	12.6	13.3	12.9
15–19 years	3.9	3.9	7.7	10.5	16.9	9.5	9.4	9.3
20–24 years	8.5	7.7	15.6	20.2	22.2	16.0	17.3	16.5
25–44 years	8.9	8.5	14.9	17.5	14.7	8.7	11.2	9.1
25–34 years	9.3	9.2	16.2	19.3	17.4	10.4	13.1	11.2
35–44 years	8.4	7.8	13.5	14.9	11.6	7.1	9.5	7.2
45–64 years	5.0	5.3	8.7	9.0	6.3	4.0	5.4	4.1
45–54 years	5.9	6.1	10.0	11.0	7.5	4.7	6.3	4.8
55–64 years	3.9	4.1	7.1	7.0	5.0	3.0	4.0	3.2
65 years and over	3.0	2.7	4.6	5.5	4.0	2.4	2.7	2.3
65–74 years	3.2	2.8	4.9	5.7	3.8	2.4	2.9	2.3
75–84 years	2.5	2.3	4.0	5.2	4.3	2.4	2.5	2.3
85 years and over	2.3	2.4	4.2	5.3	4.6	2.4	2.4	2.1
Male								
All ages, age adjusted[3]	7.9	7.5	14.3	16.6	14.8	9.0	10.8	9.4
All ages, crude	7.7	6.8	13.1	17.1	15.9	9.3	11.1	9.6
Under 1 year	4.5	4.7	4.5	6.3	8.8	10.4	9.5	7.9
1–14 years	0.6	0.6	1.2	1.6	2.0	1.5	1.5	1.5
1–4 years	0.5	0.7	1.9	2.7	2.7	2.5	3.0	2.9
5–14 years	0.6	0.5	1.0	1.2	1.7	1.1	0.9	0.9
15–24 years	8.6	8.4	18.2	24.0	32.5	20.9	22.2	21.5
15–19 years	5.5	5.7	12.1	15.9	27.8	15.5	15.7	15.3
20–24 years	13.5	11.8	25.6	32.2	36.9	26.7	28.9	27.7
25–44 years	13.8	12.8	24.4	28.9	23.5	13.3	17.2	14.2
25–34 years	14.4	13.9	26.8	31.9	27.7	16.7	20.8	18.2
35–44 years	13.2	11.7	21.7	24.5	18.6	10.3	13.9	10.7
45–64 years	8.1	8.1	14.8	15.2	10.2	6.0	8.1	6.2
45–54 years	9.5	9.4	16.8	18.4	11.9	6.9	9.5	7.1
55–64 years	6.3	6.4	12.1	11.8	8.0	4.6	5.9	4.8
65 years and over	4.8	4.3	7.7	8.8	5.8	3.3	3.6	3.2
65–74 years	5.2	4.6	8.5	9.2	5.8	3.4	4.0	3.3
75–84 years	3.9	3.7	5.9	8.1	5.7	3.2	3.1	3.1
85 years and over	2.5	3.6	7.4	7.5	6.7	3.3	3.2	3.0
Female								
All ages, age adjusted[3]	2.4	2.6	3.7	4.4	4.0	2.8	3.3	2.8
All ages, crude	2.4	2.4	3.4	4.5	4.2	2.8	3.3	2.7
Under 1 year	4.2	4.9	4.1	5.6	8.0	7.9	6.9	7.1
1–14 years	0.6	0.5	1.0	1.4	1.6	1.1	1.1	1.3
1–4 years	0.7	0.7	1.9	2.2	2.3	2.1	2.4	2.5
5–14 years	0.5	0.4	0.7	1.1	1.2	0.7	0.7	0.8
15–24 years	3.0	2.8	4.6	6.6	6.2	3.9	3.9	3.8
15–19 years	2.4	1.9	3.2	4.9	5.4	3.1	2.7	2.9
20–24 years	3.7	3.8	6.2	8.2	7.0	4.7	5.1	4.6
25–44 years	4.2	4.3	5.8	6.4	6.0	4.0	5.2	4.0
25–34 years	4.5	4.6	6.0	6.9	7.1	4.1	5.3	4.2
35–44 years	3.8	4.0	5.7	5.7	4.8	4.0	5.1	3.8
45–64 years	1.9	2.5	3.1	3.4	2.8	2.1	2.8	2.2
45–54 years	2.3	2.9	3.7	4.1	3.2	2.5	3.2	2.6
55–64 years	1.4	2.0	2.5	2.8	2.3	1.6	2.2	1.6
65 years and over	1.4	1.3	2.3	3.3	2.8	1.8	2.0	1.6
65–74 years	1.3	1.3	2.2	3.0	2.2	1.6	2.0	1.4
75–84 years	1.4	1.3	2.7	3.5	3.4	2.0	2.1	1.8
85 years and over	2.1	1.6	2.5	4.3	3.8	2.0	2.0	1.7
White male[4]								
All ages, age adjusted[3]	3.8	3.9	7.2	10.4	8.3	5.2	7.1	5.3
All ages, crude	3.6	3.6	6.6	10.7	8.8	5.2	7.2	5.4
Under 1 year	4.3	3.8	2.9	4.3	6.4	8.2	7.3	6.2
1–14 years	0.4	0.5	0.7	1.2	1.3	1.2	1.1	1.0
15–24 years	3.2	5.0	7.6	15.1	15.2	9.9	11.2	10.6
25–44 years	5.4	5.5	11.6	17.2	13.0	7.4	11.5	7.7
25–34 years	4.9	5.7	12.5	18.5	14.7	8.4	12.3	8.9
35–44 years	6.1	5.2	10.8	15.2	11.1	6.5	10.7	6.8
45–64 years	4.8	4.6	8.3	9.8	6.9	4.1	6.4	4.2
65 years and over	3.8	3.1	5.4	6.7	4.1	2.5	3.0	2.6

See footnotes at end of table.

This table will be updated on the Web. Go to www.cdc.gov/nchs/hus.htm.

Table 45 (page 2 of 3). Death rates for homicide, according to sex, race, Hispanic origin, and age: United States, selected years 1950–2002

[Data are based on death certificates]

Sex, race, Hispanic origin, and age	1950[1]	1960[1]	1970	1980	1990	2000[2]	2001	2002
Black or African American male[4]				Deaths per 100,000 resident population				
All ages, age adjusted[3]	47.0	42.3	78.2	69.4	63.1	35.4	36.2	36.4
All ages, crude	44.7	35.0	66.0	65.7	68.5	37.2	38.3	38.4
Under 1 year	---	10.3	14.3	18.6	21.4	23.3	21.0	16.3
1–14 years[5]	1.8	1.5	4.4	4.1	5.8	3.1	3.6	3.8
15–24 years	53.8	43.2	98.3	82.6	137.1	85.3	85.7	83.1
25–44 years	92.8	80.5	140.2	130.0	105.4	55.8	58.1	60.0
25–34 years	104.3	86.4	154.5	142.9	123.7	73.9	78.8	82.2
35–44 years	80.0	74.4	124.0	109.3	81.2	38.5	38.5	38.8
45–64 years	46.0	44.6	82.3	70.6	41.4	21.9	22.7	22.9
65 years and over	16.5	17.3	33.3	30.9	25.7	12.8	11.5	11.2
American Indian or Alaska Native male[4]								
All ages, age adjusted[3]	---	---	---	23.3	16.7	10.7	9.3	11.6
All ages, crude	---	---	---	23.1	16.6	10.7	9.6	12.0
15–24 years	---	---	---	35.4	25.1	17.0	16.1	18.8
25–44 years	---	---	---	39.2	25.7	17.0	13.6	18.3
45–64 years	---	---	---	22.1	14.8	*	8.9	9.9
Asian or Pacific Islander male[4]								
All ages, age adjusted[3]	---	---	---	9.1	7.3	4.3	6.0	4.2
All ages, crude	---	---	---	8.3	7.9	4.4	6.3	4.5
15–24 years	---	---	---	9.3	14.9	7.8	9.1	9.7
25–44 years	---	---	---	11.3	9.6	4.6	8.5	4.9
45–64 years	---	---	---	10.4	7.0	6.1	7.7	4.1
Hispanic or Latino male[4,6]								
All ages, age adjusted[3]	---	---	---	---	27.4	11.8	12.9	11.6
All ages, crude	---	---	---	---	31.0	13.4	14.5	13.2
Under 1 year	---	---	---	---	8.7	6.6	7.9	6.6
1–14 years	---	---	---	---	3.1	1.7	1.5	1.6
15–24 years	---	---	---	---	55.4	28.5	30.5	29.6
25–44 years	---	---	---	---	46.4	17.2	19.2	16.5
25–34 years	---	---	---	---	50.9	19.9	21.6	19.8
35–44 years	---	---	---	---	39.3	13.5	15.9	12.1
45–64 years	---	---	---	---	20.5	9.1	9.8	8.6
65 years and over	---	---	---	---	9.4	4.4	5.5	4.4
White, not Hispanic or Latino male[6]								
All ages, age adjusted[3]	---	---	---	---	5.6	3.6	5.6	3.7
All ages, crude	---	---	---	---	5.8	3.6	5.6	3.8
Under 1 year	---	---	---	---	5.4	8.3	6.8	5.8
1–14 years	---	---	---	---	0.9	1.0	1.0	0.8
15–24 years	---	---	---	---	7.5	4.7	5.7	5.2
25–44 years	---	---	---	---	8.7	5.2	9.4	5.5
25–34 years	---	---	---	---	9.3	5.2	9.3	5.3
35–44 years	---	---	---	---	8.0	5.2	9.5	5.6
45–64 years	---	---	---	---	5.7	3.6	5.9	3.7
65 years and over	---	---	---	---	3.7	2.3	2.8	2.4
White female[4]								
All ages, age adjusted[3]	1.4	1.5	2.3	3.2	2.7	2.1	2.6	2.0
All ages, crude	1.4	1.4	2.1	3.2	2.8	2.1	2.6	2.0
Under 1 year	3.9	3.5	2.9	4.3	5.1	5.0	5.1	4.6
1–14 years	0.4	0.4	0.7	1.1	1.0	0.8	0.9	0.9
15–24 years	1.3	1.5	2.7	4.7	4.0	2.7	3.0	2.5
25–44 years	2.0	2.1	3.3	4.2	3.8	2.9	4.0	2.8
45–64 years	1.5	1.7	2.1	2.6	2.3	1.8	2.4	1.9
65 years and over	1.2	1.2	1.9	2.9	2.2	1.6	1.8	1.4
Black or African American female[4]								
All ages, age adjusted[3]	11.1	11.4	14.7	13.2	12.5	7.1	7.4	6.9
All ages, crude	11.5	10.4	13.2	13.5	13.4	7.2	7.4	7.0
Under 1 year	---	13.8	10.7	12.8	22.8	22.2	16.7	18.5
1–14 years[5]	1.8	1.2	3.1	3.3	4.7	2.7	2.1	2.6
15–24 years	16.5	11.9	17.7	18.4	18.9	10.7	8.9	10.3
25–44 years	22.5	22.7	25.3	22.6	21.0	11.0	12.5	11.1
45–64 years	6.8	10.3	13.4	10.8	6.5	4.5	5.7	4.5
65 years and over	3.6	3.0	7.4	8.0	9.4	3.5	3.7	3.1

See footnotes at end of table.

This table will be updated on the Web. Go to www.cdc.gov/nchs/hus.htm.

Table 45 (page 3 of 3). Death rates for homicide, according to sex, race, Hispanic origin, and age: United States, selected years 1950–2002

[Data are based on death certificates]

Sex, race, Hispanic origin, and age	1950[1]	1960[1]	1970	1980	1990	2000[2]	2001	2002
American Indian or Alaska Native female[4]			Deaths per 100,000 resident population					
All ages, age adjusted[3]	---	---	---	8.1	4.6	3.0	4.2	5.2
All ages, crude	---	---	---	7.7	4.8	2.9	4.2	5.3
15–24 years	---	---	---	*	*	*	*	*
25–44 years	---	---	---	13.7	6.9	5.9	5.9	6.3
45–64 years	---	---	---	*	*	*	*	*
Asian or Pacific Islander female[4]								
All ages, age adjusted[3]	---	---	---	3.1	2.8	1.7	2.5	1.8
All ages, crude	---	---	---	3.1	2.8	1.7	2.7	1.8
15–24 years	---	---	---	*	*	*	*	2.1
25–44 years	---	---	---	4.6	3.8	2.2	4.0	2.4
45–64 years	---	---	---	*	*	2.0	2.7	1.6
Hispanic or Latino female[4,6]								
All ages, age adjusted[3]	---	---	---	---	4.3	2.8	3.1	2.5
All ages, crude	---	---	---	---	4.7	2.8	3.2	2.6
Under 1 year	---	---	---	---	*	7.4	5.5	5.9
1–14 years	---	---	---	---	1.9	1.0	1.0	1.2
15–24 years	---	---	---	---	8.1	3.7	4.0	3.8
25–44 years	---	---	---	---	6.1	3.7	4.8	3.4
45–64 years	---	---	---	---	3.3	2.9	3.0	2.3
65 years and over	---	---	---	---	*	2.4	2.0	*
White, not Hispanic or Latino female[6]								
All ages, age adjusted[3]	---	---	---	---	2.5	1.9	2.5	1.9
All ages, crude	---	---	---	---	2.5	1.9	2.4	1.9
Under 1 year	---	---	---	---	4.4	4.1	4.7	4.1
1–14 years	---	---	---	---	0.8	0.8	0.9	0.9
15–24 years	---	---	---	---	3.3	2.3	2.7	2.2
25–44 years	---	---	---	---	3.5	2.7	3.7	2.6
45–64 years	---	---	---	---	2.2	1.6	2.3	1.8
65 years and over	---	---	---	---	2.2	1.6	1.8	1.4

- - - Data not available.
* Rates based on fewer than 20 deaths are considered unreliable and are not shown.
[1]Includes deaths of persons who were not residents of the 50 States and the District of Columbia.
[2]Starting with 1999 data, cause of death is coded according to ICD–10. See Appendix II, Comparability ratio and tables V and VI.
[3]Age-adjusted rates are calculated using the year 2000 standard population. See Appendix II, Age adjustment.
[4]The race groups, white, black, Asian or Pacific Islander, and American Indian or Alaska Native, include persons of Hispanic and non-Hispanic origin. Persons of Hispanic origin may be of any race. Death rates for the American Indian or Alaska Native and Asian or Pacific Islander populations are known to be underestimated. See Appendix II, Race, for a discussion of sources of bias in death rates by race and Hispanic origin.
[5]In 1950 rate is for the age group under 15 years.
[6]Prior to 1997, excludes data from States lacking an Hispanic-origin item on the death certificate. See Appendix II, Hispanic origin.

NOTES: Starting with *Health, United States, 2003*, rates for 1991–99 were revised using intercensal population estimates based on census 2000. Rates for 2000 were revised based on census 2000 counts. Rates for 2001 and 2002 were computed using 2000-based postcensal estimates. See Appendix I, Population Census and Population Estimates. Figures for 2001 include September 11-related deaths for which death certificates were filed as of October 24, 2002. Underlying cause of death code numbers are based on the applicable revision of the *International Classification of Diseases* (ICD) for data years shown. For the period 1980–98, causes were coded using ICD–9 codes that are most nearly comparable with the 113 cause list for ICD–10. See Appendix II, tables IV and V for terrorism-related ICD–10 codes. Age groups were selected to minimize the presentation of unstable age-specific death rates based on small numbers of deaths and for consistency among comparison groups. For additional injury-related statistics, see www.cdc.gov/ncipc/wisqars, a Web-based interactive database for injury data. Data for additional years are available. See Appendix III.

SOURCES: Centers for Disease Control and Prevention, National Center for Health Statistics, National Vital Statistics System; Grove RD, Hetzel AM. Vital statistics rates in the United States, 1940–1960. Washington: U.S. Government Printing Office. 1968; numerator data from National Vital Statistics System, annual mortality files; denominator data from national population estimates for race groups from table 1 and unpublished Hispanic population estimates for 1985–96 prepared by the Housing and Household Economic Statistics Division, U.S. Bureau of the Census; additional mortality tables are available at www.cdc.gov/nchs/datawh/statab/unpubd/mortabs.htm; Kochanek KD, Murphy SL, Anderson RN, Scott C. Deaths: Final data for 2002. National vital statistics reports. Vol 53 no 5. Hyattsville, Maryland: National Center for Health Statistics. 2004.

This table will be updated on the Web. Go to www.cdc.gov/nchs/hus.htm.

Table 46 (page 1 of 3). Death rates for suicide, according to sex, race, Hispanic origin, and age: United States, selected years 1950–2002

[Data are based on death certificates]

Sex, race, Hispanic origin, and age	1950[1]	1960[1]	1970	1980	1990	2000[2]	2001	2002
All persons			Deaths per 100,000 resident population					
All ages, age adjusted[3]	13.2	12.5	13.1	12.2	12.5	10.4	10.7	10.9
All ages, crude	11.4	10.6	11.6	11.9	12.4	10.4	10.8	11.0
Under 1 year	. . .	. . .	. . .	. . .	. . .	. . .	. . .	. . .
1–4 years	. . .	. . .	. . .	. . .	. . .	. . .	. . .	. . .
5–14 years	0.2	0.3	0.3	0.4	0.8	0.7	0.7	0.6
15–24 years	4.5	5.2	8.8	12.3	13.2	10.2	9.9	9.9
15–19 years	2.7	3.6	5.9	8.5	11.1	8.0	7.9	7.4
20–24 years	6.2	7.1	12.2	16.1	15.1	12.5	12.0	12.4
25–44 years	11.6	12.2	15.4	15.6	15.2	13.4	13.8	14.0
25–34 years	9.1	10.0	14.1	16.0	15.2	12.0	12.8	12.6
35–44 years	14.3	14.2	16.9	15.4	15.3	14.5	14.7	15.3
45–64 years	23.5	22.0	20.6	15.9	15.3	13.5	14.4	14.9
45–54 years	20.9	20.7	20.0	15.9	14.8	14.4	15.2	15.7
55–64 years	26.8	23.7	21.4	15.9	16.0	12.1	13.1	13.6
65 years and over	30.0	24.5	20.8	17.6	20.5	15.2	15.3	15.6
65–74 years	29.6	23.0	20.8	16.9	17.9	12.5	13.3	13.5
75–84 years	31.1	27.9	21.2	19.1	24.9	17.6	17.4	17.7
85 years and over	28.8	26.0	19.0	19.2	22.2	19.6	17.5	18.0
Male								
All ages, age adjusted[3]	21.2	20.0	19.8	19.9	21.5	17.7	18.2	18.4
All ages, crude	17.8	16.5	16.8	18.6	20.4	17.1	17.6	17.9
Under 1 year	. . .	. . .	. . .	. . .	. . .	. . .	. . .	. . .
1–4 years	. . .	. . .	. . .	. . .	. . .	. . .	. . .	. . .
5–14 years	0.3	0.4	0.5	0.6	1.1	1.2	1.0	0.9
15–24 years	6.5	8.2	13.5	20.2	22.0	17.1	16.6	16.5
15–19 years	3.5	5.6	8.8	13.8	18.1	13.0	12.9	12.2
20–24 years	9.3	11.5	19.3	26.8	25.7	21.4	20.5	20.8
25–44 years	17.2	17.9	20.9	24.0	24.4	21.3	22.1	22.2
25–34 years	13.4	14.7	19.8	25.0	24.8	19.6	21.0	20.5
35–44 years	21.3	21.0	22.1	22.5	23.9	22.8	23.1	23.7
45–64 years	37.1	34.4	30.0	23.7	24.3	21.3	22.5	23.5
45–54 years	32.0	31.6	27.9	22.9	23.2	22.4	23.4	24.4
55–64 years	43.6	38.1	32.7	24.5	25.7	19.4	21.1	22.2
65 years and over	52.8	44.0	38.4	35.0	41.6	31.1	31.5	31.8
65–74 years	50.5	39.6	36.0	30.4	32.2	22.7	24.6	24.7
75–84 years	58.3	52.5	42.8	42.3	56.1	38.6	37.8	38.1
85 years and over	58.3	57.4	42.4	50.6	65.9	57.5	51.1	50.7
Female								
All ages, age adjusted[3]	5.6	5.6	7.4	5.7	4.8	4.0	4.0	4.2
All ages, crude	5.1	4.9	6.6	5.5	4.8	4.0	4.1	4.3
Under 1 year	. . .	. . .	. . .	. . .	. . .	. . .	. . .	. . .
1–4 years	. . .	. . .	. . .	. . .	. . .	. . .	. . .	. . .
5–14 years	0.1	0.1	0.2	0.2	0.4	0.3	0.3	0.3
15–24 years	2.6	2.2	4.2	4.3	3.9	3.0	2.9	2.9
15–19 years	1.8	1.6	2.9	3.0	3.7	2.7	2.7	2.4
20–24 years	3.3	2.9	5.7	5.5	4.1	3.2	3.1	3.5
25–44 years	6.2	6.6	10.2	7.7	6.2	5.4	5.5	5.8
25–34 years	4.9	5.5	8.6	7.1	5.6	4.3	4.4	4.6
35–44 years	7.5	7.7	11.9	8.5	6.8	6.4	6.4	6.9
45–64 years	9.9	10.2	12.0	8.9	7.1	6.2	6.6	6.7
45–54 years	9.9	10.2	12.6	9.4	6.9	6.7	7.2	7.4
55–64 years	9.9	10.2	11.4	8.4	7.3	5.4	5.7	5.7
65 years and over	9.4	8.4	8.1	6.1	6.4	4.0	3.9	4.1
65–74 years	10.1	8.4	9.0	6.5	6.7	4.0	3.9	4.1
75–84 years	8.1	8.9	7.0	5.5	6.3	4.0	4.0	4.2
85 years and over	8.2	6.0	5.9	5.5	5.4	4.2	3.4	3.8
White male[4]								
All ages, age adjusted[3]	22.3	21.1	20.8	20.9	22.8	19.1	19.6	20.0
All ages, crude	19.0	17.6	18.0	19.9	22.0	18.8	19.5	19.9
15–24 years	6.6	8.6	13.9	21.4	23.2	17.9	17.6	17.7
25–44 years	17.9	18.5	21.5	24.6	25.4	22.9	24.0	24.0
45–64 years	39.3	36.5	31.9	25.0	26.0	23.2	24.7	25.9
65 years and over	55.8	46.7	41.1	37.2	44.2	33.3	33.7	34.2
65–74 years	53.2	42.0	38.7	32.5	34.2	24.3	26.3	26.8
75–84 years	61.9	55.7	45.5	45.5	60.2	41.1	40.2	40.6
85 years and over	61.9	61.3	45.8	52.8	70.3	61.6	55.0	53.9

See footnotes at end of table.

This table will be updated on the Web. Go to www.cdc.gov/nchs/hus.htm.

Table 46 (page 2 of 3). Death rates for suicide, according to sex, race, Hispanic origin, and age: United States, selected years 1950–2002

[Data are based on death certificates]

Sex, race, Hispanic origin, and age	1950[1]	1960[1]	1970	1980	1990	2000[2]	2001	2002
Black or African American male[4]				Deaths per 100,000 resident population				
All ages, age adjusted[3]	7.5	8.4	10.0	11.4	12.8	10.0	9.8	9.8
All ages, crude	6.3	6.4	8.0	10.3	12.0	9.4	9.2	9.1
15–24 years	4.9	4.1	10.5	12.3	15.1	14.2	13.0	11.3
25–44 years	9.8	12.6	16.1	19.2	19.6	14.3	14.4	15.1
45–64 years	12.7	13.0	12.4	11.8	13.1	9.9	9.7	9.6
65 years and over	9.0	9.9	8.7	11.4	14.9	11.5	11.5	11.7
65–74 years	10.0	11.3	8.7	11.1	14.7	11.1	10.7	9.7
75–84 years[5]	*	*	*	10.5	14.4	12.1	13.5	13.8
85 years and over	---	*	*	*	*	*	*	*
American Indian or Alaska Native male[4]								
All ages, age adjusted[3]	---	---	---	19.3	20.1	16.0	17.4	16.4
All ages, crude	---	---	---	20.9	20.9	15.9	17.0	16.8
15–24 years	---	---	---	45.3	49.1	26.2	24.7	27.9
25–44 years	---	---	---	31.2	27.8	24.5	27.6	26.8
45–64 years	---	---	---	*	*	15.4	17.0	14.1
65 years and over	---	---	---	*	*	*	*	*
Asian or Pacific Islander male[4]								
All ages, age adjusted[3]	---	---	---	10.7	9.6	8.6	8.4	8.0
All ages, crude	---	---	---	8.8	8.7	7.9	7.7	7.6
15–24 years	---	---	---	10.8	13.5	9.1	9.1	8.7
25–44 years	---	---	---	11.0	10.6	9.9	9.3	9.3
45–64 years	---	---	---	13.0	9.7	9.7	8.2	9.1
65 years and over	---	---	---	18.6	16.8	15.4	18.3	14.4
Hispanic or Latino male[4,6]								
All ages, age adjusted[3]	---	---	---	---	13.7	10.3	10.1	9.9
All ages, crude	---	---	---	---	11.4	8.4	8.3	8.3
15–24 years	---	---	---	---	14.7	10.9	9.5	10.6
25–44 years	---	---	---	---	16.2	11.2	11.8	10.9
45–64 years	---	---	---	---	16.1	12.0	11.4	11.9
65 years and over	---	---	---	---	23.4	19.5	18.5	17.5
White, not Hispanic or Latino male[6]								
All ages, age adjusted[3]	---	---	---	---	23.5	20.2	21.0	21.4
All ages, crude	---	---	---	---	23.1	20.4	21.4	21.9
15–24 years	---	---	---	---	24.4	19.5	19.6	19.3
25–44 years	---	---	---	---	26.4	25.1	26.4	26.9
45–64 years	---	---	---	---	26.8	24.0	25.9	27.2
65 years and over	---	---	---	---	45.4	33.9	34.4	35.1
White female[4]								
All ages, age adjusted[3]	6.0	5.9	7.9	6.1	5.2	4.3	4.5	4.7
All ages, crude	5.5	5.3	7.1	5.9	5.3	4.4	4.6	4.8
15–24 years	2.7	2.3	4.2	4.6	4.2	3.1	3.1	3.1
25–44 years	6.6	7.0	11.0	8.1	6.6	6.0	6.2	6.6
45–64 years	10.6	10.9	13.0	9.6	7.7	6.9	7.3	7.5
65 years and over	9.9	8.8	8.5	6.4	6.8	4.3	4.1	4.3
Black or African American female[4]								
All ages, age adjusted[3]	1.8	2.0	2.9	2.4	2.4	1.8	1.8	1.6
All ages, crude	1.5	1.6	2.6	2.2	2.3	1.7	1.7	1.5
15–24 years	1.8	*	3.8	2.3	2.3	2.2	1.3	1.7
25–44 years	2.3	3.0	4.8	4.3	3.8	2.6	2.6	2.4
45–64 years	2.7	3.1	2.9	2.5	2.9	2.1	2.6	2.1
65 years and over	*	*	2.6	*	1.9	1.3	1.6	1.1

See footnotes at end of table.

This table will be updated on the Web. Go to www.cdc.gov/nchs/hus.htm.

Table 46 (page 3 of 3). Death rates for suicide, according to sex, race, Hispanic origin, and age: United States, selected years 1950–2002

[Data are based on death certificates]

Sex, race, Hispanic origin, and age	*1950*[1]	*1960*[1]	*1970*	*1980*	*1990*	*2000*[2]	*2001*	*2002*
American Indian or Alaska Native female[4]				Deaths per 100,000 resident population				
All ages, age adjusted[3]	- - -	- - -	- - -	4.7	3.6	3.8	4.0	4.1
All ages, crude	- - -	- - -	- - -	4.7	3.7	4.0	4.1	4.3
15–24 years	- - -	- - -	- - -	*	*	*	*	7.4
25–44 years	- - -	- - -	- - -	10.7	*	7.2	6.1	5.6
45–64 years	- - -	- - -	- - -	*	*	*	*	*
65 years and over	- - -	- - -	- - -	*	*	*	*	*
Asian or Pacific Islander female[4]								
All ages, age adjusted[3]	- - -	- - -	- - -	5.5	4.1	2.8	2.9	3.0
All ages, crude	- - -	- - -	- - -	4.7	3.4	2.7	2.8	2.9
15–24 years	- - -	- - -	- - -	*	3.9	2.7	3.6	*
25–44 years	- - -	- - -	- - -	5.4	3.8	3.3	2.9	3.3
45–64 years	- - -	- - -	- - -	7.9	5.0	3.2	3.8	3.8
65 years and over	- - -	- - -	- - -	*	8.5	5.2	4.9	6.8
Hispanic or Latino female[4,6]								
All ages, age adjusted[3]	- - -	- - -	- - -	- - -	2.3	1.7	1.6	1.8
All ages, crude	- - -	- - -	- - -	- - -	2.2	1.5	1.5	1.6
15–24 years	- - -	- - -	- - -	- - -	3.1	2.0	2.3	2.1
25–44 years	- - -	- - -	- - -	- - -	3.1	2.1	2.0	2.0
45–64 years	- - -	- - -	- - -	- - -	2.5	2.5	2.3	2.5
65 years and over	- - -	- - -	- - -	- - -	*	*	*	1.9
White, not Hispanic or Latino female[6]								
All ages, age adjusted[3]	- - -	- - -	- - -	- - -	5.4	4.7	4.9	5.1
All ages, crude	- - -	- - -	- - -	- - -	5.6	4.9	5.0	5.3
15–24 years	- - -	- - -	- - -	- - -	4.3	3.3	3.3	3.4
25–44 years	- - -	- - -	- - -	- - -	7.0	6.7	6.9	7.5
45–64 years	- - -	- - -	- - -	- - -	8.0	7.3	7.8	8.0
65 years and over	- - -	- - -	- - -	- - -	7.0	4.4	4.3	4.5

. . . Category not applicable.
* Rates based on fewer than 20 deaths are considered unreliable and are not shown.
- - - Data not available.
[1]Includes deaths of persons who were not residents of the 50 States and the District of Columbia.
[2]Starting with 1999 data, cause of death is coded according to ICD–10. See Appendix II, Comparability ratio and tables V and VI.
[3]Age-adjusted rates are calculated using the year 2000 standard population. See Appendix II, Age adjustment.
[4]The race groups, white, black, Asian or Pacific Islander, and American Indian or Alaska Native, include persons of Hispanic and non-Hispanic origin. Persons of Hispanic origin may be of any race. Death rates for the American Indian or Alaska Native and Asian or Pacific Islander populations are known to be underestimated. See Appendix II, Race, for a discussion of sources of bias in death rates by race and Hispanic origin.
[5]In 1950 rate is for the age group 75 years and over.
[6]Prior to 1997, excludes data from States lacking an Hispanic-origin item on the death certificate. See Appendix II, Hispanic origin.

NOTES: Starting with *Health, United States, 2003*, rates for 1991–99 were revised using intercensal population estimates based on census 2000. Rates for 2000 were revised based on census 2000 counts. Rates for 2001 and 2002 were computed using 2000-based postcensal estimates. See Appendix I, Population Census and Population Estimates. Figures for 2001 include September 11-related deaths for which death certificates were filed as of October 24, 2002. Underlying cause of death code numbers are based on the applicable revision of the *International Classification of Diseases* (ICD) for data years shown. See Appendix II, tables IV and V for terrorism-related ICD–10 codes. Age groups were selected to minimize the presentation of unstable age-specific death rates based on small numbers of deaths and for consistency among comparison groups. For additional injury-related statistics, see www.cdc.gov/ncipc/wisqars, a Web-based interactive database for injury data. Data for additional years are available. See Appendix III.

SOURCES: Centers for Disease Control and Prevention, National Center for Health Statistics, National Vital Statistics System; Grove RD, Hetzel AM. Vital statistics rates in the United States, 1940–1960. Washington: U.S. Government Printing Office. 1968; numerator data from National Vital Statistics System, annual mortality files; denominator data from national population estimates for race groups from table 1 and unpublished Hispanic population estimates for 1985–96 prepared by the Housing and Household Economic Statistics Division, U.S. Bureau of the Census; additional mortality tables are available at www.cdc.gov/nchs/datawh/statab/unpubd/mortabs.htm; Kochanek KD, Murphy SL, Anderson RN, Scott C. Deaths: Final data for 2002. National vital statistics reports. Vol 53 no 5. Hyattsville, Maryland: National Center for Health Statistics. 2004.

This table will be updated on the Web. Go to www.cdc.gov/nchs/hus.htm.

Table 47 (page 1 of 3). Death rates for firearm-related injuries, according to sex, race, Hispanic origin, and age: United States, selected years 1970–2002

[Data are based on death certificates]

Sex, race, Hispanic origin, and age	1970	1980	1990	1995	2000[1]	2001	2002
All persons				Deaths per 100,000 resident population			
All ages, age adjusted[2]	14.3	14.8	14.6	13.4	10.2	10.3	10.4
All ages, crude	13.1	14.9	14.9	13.5	10.2	10.4	10.5
Under 1 year	*	*	*	*	*	*	*
1–14 years	1.6	1.4	1.5	1.6	0.7	0.7	0.7
1–4 years	1.0	0.7	0.6	0.6	0.3	0.5	0.4
5–14 years	1.7	1.6	1.9	1.9	0.9	0.8	0.8
15–24 years	15.5	20.6	25.8	26.7	16.8	16.7	16.7
15–19 years	11.4	14.7	23.3	24.1	12.9	12.4	12.1
20–24 years	20.3	26.4	28.1	29.2	20.9	21.2	21.3
25–44 years	20.9	22.5	19.3	16.9	13.1	13.5	13.7
25–34 years	22.2	24.3	21.8	19.6	14.5	15.5	15.4
35–44 years	19.6	20.0	16.3	14.3	11.9	11.7	12.1
45–64 years	17.6	15.2	13.6	11.7	10.0	10.3	10.6
45–54 years	18.1	16.4	13.9	12.0	10.5	10.5	10.8
55–64 years	17.0	13.9	13.3	11.3	9.4	10.1	10.2
65 years and over	13.8	13.5	16.0	14.1	12.2	12.4	12.4
65–74 years	14.5	13.8	14.4	12.8	10.6	10.9	10.9
75–84 years	13.4	13.4	19.4	16.3	13.9	14.3	14.4
85 years and over	10.2	11.6	14.7	14.4	14.2	12.8	12.5
Male							
All ages, age adjusted[2]	24.8	25.9	26.1	23.8	18.1	18.5	18.6
All ages, crude	22.2	25.7	26.2	23.6	17.8	18.2	18.4
Under 1 year	*	*	*	*	*	*	*
1–14 years	2.3	2.0	2.2	2.3	1.1	1.0	1.0
1–4 years	1.2	0.9	0.7	0.8	0.4	0.5	0.5
5–14 years	2.7	2.5	2.9	2.9	1.4	1.2	1.2
15–24 years	26.4	34.8	44.7	46.5	29.4	29.6	29.3
15–19 years	19.2	24.5	40.1	41.6	22.4	21.8	21.1
20–24 years	35.1	45.2	49.1	51.5	37.0	37.7	37.6
25–44 years	34.1	38.1	32.6	28.4	22.0	22.8	23.1
25–34 years	36.5	41.4	37.0	33.2	24.9	26.7	26.5
35–44 years	31.6	33.2	27.4	23.6	19.4	19.2	20.1
45–64 years	31.0	25.9	23.4	20.0	17.1	17.6	18.1
45–54 years	30.7	27.3	23.2	20.1	17.6	17.8	18.2
55–64 years	31.3	24.5	23.7	19.8	16.3	17.4	18.0
65 years and over	29.7	29.7	35.3	30.7	26.4	26.8	26.9
65–74 years	29.5	27.8	28.2	25.1	20.3	21.1	21.3
75–84 years	31.0	33.0	46.9	37.8	32.2	32.8	32.9
85 years and over	26.2	34.9	49.3	47.1	44.7	40.2	38.9
Female							
All ages, age adjusted[2]	4.8	4.7	4.2	3.8	2.8	2.8	2.8
All ages, crude	4.4	4.7	4.3	3.8	2.8	2.8	2.8
Under 1 year	*	*	*	*	*	*	*
1–14 years	0.8	0.7	0.8	0.8	0.3	0.4	0.5
1–4 years	0.9	0.5	0.5	0.5	*	0.4	0.3
5–14 years	0.8	0.7	1.0	0.9	0.4	0.4	0.5
15–24 years	4.8	6.1	6.0	5.9	3.5	3.2	3.5
15–19 years	3.5	4.6	5.7	5.6	2.9	2.6	2.7
20–24 years	6.4	7.7	6.3	6.1	4.2	3.8	4.2
25–44 years	8.3	7.4	6.1	5.5	4.2	4.2	4.1
25–34 years	8.4	7.5	6.7	5.8	4.0	4.0	4.0
35–44 years	8.2	7.2	5.4	5.2	4.4	4.3	4.2
45–64 years	5.4	5.4	4.5	3.9	3.4	3.4	3.4
45–54 years	6.4	6.2	4.9	4.2	3.6	3.5	3.6
55–64 years	4.2	4.6	4.0	3.5	3.0	3.3	3.1
65 years and over	2.4	2.5	3.1	2.8	2.2	2.2	2.0
65–74 years	2.8	3.1	3.6	3.0	2.5	2.4	2.3
75–84 years	1.7	1.7	2.9	2.8	2.0	2.2	2.1
85 years and over	*	1.3	1.3	1.8	1.7	1.3	1.1
White male[3]							
All ages, age adjusted[2]	19.7	22.1	22.0	20.1	15.9	16.3	16.2
All ages, crude	17.6	21.8	21.8	19.9	15.6	16.2	16.1
1–14 years	1.8	1.9	1.9	1.9	1.0	0.9	0.8
15–24 years	16.9	28.4	29.5	30.8	19.6	19.5	19.4
25–44 years	24.2	29.5	25.7	23.2	18.0	18.9	18.5
25–34 years	24.3	31.1	27.8	25.2	18.1	19.9	18.5
35–44 years	24.1	27.1	23.3	21.2	17.9	18.0	18.5
45–64 years	27.4	23.3	22.8	19.5	17.4	18.3	18.7
65 years and over	29.9	30.1	36.8	32.2	28.2	28.6	28.9

See footnotes at end of table.

This table will be updated on the Web. Go to www.cdc.gov/nchs/hus.htm.

Table 47 (page 2 of 3). Death rates for firearm-related injuries, according to sex, race, Hispanic origin, and age: United States, selected years 1970–2002

[Data are based on death certificates]

Sex, race, Hispanic origin, and age	*1970*	*1980*	*1990*	*1995*	*2000*[1]	*2001*	*2002*
Black or African American male[3]			Deaths per 100,000 resident population				
All ages, age adjusted[2]	70.8	60.1	56.3	49.2	34.2	34.5	36.0
All ages, crude	60.8	57.7	61.9	52.9	36.1	36.4	37.8
1–14 years	5.3	3.0	4.4	4.4	1.8	1.6	1.8
15–24 years	97.3	77.9	138.0	138.7	89.3	90.3	87.1
25–44 years	126.2	114.1	90.3	70.2	54.1	54.8	60.6
25–34 years	145.6	128.4	108.6	92.3	74.8	77.7	85.6
35–44 years	104.2	92.3	66.1	46.3	34.3	33.2	36.9
45–64 years	71.1	55.6	34.5	28.3	18.4	17.2	18.6
65 years and over	30.6	29.7	23.9	21.8	13.8	14.9	14.2
American Indian or Alaska Native male[3]							
All ages, age adjusted[2]	---	24.0	19.4	19.4	13.1	13.0	14.8
All ages, crude	---	27.5	20.5	20.9	13.2	12.9	15.3
15–24 years	---	55.3	49.1	40.9	26.9	24.3	30.0
25–44 years	---	43.9	25.4	31.2	16.6	18.8	21.7
45–64 years	---	*	*	14.2	12.2	9.6	12.4
65 years and over	---	*	*	*	*	*	*
Asian or Pacific Islander male[3]							
All ages, age adjusted[2]	---	7.8	8.8	9.2	6.0	5.2	5.5
All ages, crude	---	8.2	9.4	10.0	6.2	5.4	5.7
15–24 years	---	10.8	21.0	24.3	9.3	9.6	11.7
25–44 years	---	12.8	10.9	10.6	8.1	6.6	6.3
45–64 years	---	10.4	8.1	8.2	7.4	5.7	5.8
65 years and over	---	*	*	*	*	5.3	*
Hispanic or Latino male[3,4]							
All ages, age adjusted[2]	---	---	27.6	23.8	13.6	13.7	13.4
All ages, crude	---	---	29.9	26.2	14.2	14.6	14.2
1–14 years	---	---	2.6	2.8	1.0	0.7	0.9
15–24 years	---	---	55.5	61.7	30.8	31.4	32.1
25–44 years	---	---	42.7	31.4	17.3	19.1	17.6
25–34 years	---	---	47.3	36.4	20.3	22.7	21.2
35–44 years	---	---	35.4	24.2	13.2	14.4	12.9
45–64 years	---	---	21.4	17.2	12.0	10.0	9.9
65 years and over	---	---	19.1	16.5	12.2	12.0	12.3
White, not Hispanic or Latino male[4]							
All ages, age adjusted[2]	---	---	20.6	18.6	15.5	16.0	16.0
All ages, crude	---	---	20.4	18.5	15.7	16.3	16.3
1–14 years	---	---	1.6	1.6	1.0	1.0	0.7
15–24 years	---	---	24.1	23.5	16.2	16.0	15.6
25–44 years	---	---	23.3	21.4	17.9	18.6	18.4
25–34 years	---	---	24.7	22.5	17.2	18.9	17.4
35–44 years	---	---	21.6	20.4	18.4	18.4	19.3
45–64 years	---	---	22.7	19.5	17.8	19.0	19.4
65 years and over	---	---	37.4	32.5	29.0	29.4	29.8
White female[3]							
All ages, age adjusted[2]	4.0	4.2	3.8	3.5	2.7	2.7	2.7
All ages, crude	3.7	4.1	3.8	3.5	2.7	2.7	2.7
15–24 years	3.4	5.1	4.8	4.5	2.8	2.7	2.6
25–44 years	6.9	6.2	5.3	4.9	3.9	3.9	3.8
45–64 years	5.0	5.1	4.5	4.0	3.5	3.7	3.6
65 years and over	2.2	2.5	3.1	2.8	2.4	2.3	2.2

See footnotes at end of table.

This table will be updated on the Web. Go to www.cdc.gov/nchs/hus.htm.

Table 47 (page 3 of 3). Death rates for firearm-related injuries, according to sex, race, Hispanic origin, and age: United States, selected years 1970–2002

[Data are based on death certificates]

Sex, race, Hispanic origin, and age	*1970*	*1980*	*1990*	*1995*	*2000*[1]	*2001*	*2002*
Black or African American female[3]				Deaths per 100,000 resident population			
All ages, age adjusted[2]	11.1	8.7	7.3	6.2	3.9	3.8	4.1
All ages, crude	10.0	8.8	7.8	6.5	4.0	3.8	4.2
15–24 years	15.2	12.3	13.3	13.2	7.6	6.1	8.1
25–44 years	19.4	16.1	12.4	9.8	6.5	6.9	6.7
45–64 years	10.2	8.2	4.8	4.1	3.1	2.6	3.0
65 years and over	4.3	3.1	3.1	2.6	1.3	1.4	1.2
American Indian or Alaska Native female[3]							
All ages, age adjusted[2]	- - -	5.8	3.3	3.8	2.9	2.8	3.1
All ages, crude	- - -	5.8	3.4	4.1	2.9	2.9	3.4
15–24 years	- - -	*	*	*	*	*	*
25–44 years	- - -	10.2	*	7.0	5.5	5.0	*
45–64 years	- - -	*	*	*	*	*	*
65 years and over	- - -	*	*	*	*	*	*
Asian or Pacific Islander female[3]							
All ages, age adjusted[2]	- - -	2.0	1.9	2.0	1.1	1.0	1.1
All ages, crude	- - -	2.1	2.1	2.1	1.2	1.1	1.2
15–24 years	- - -	*	*	3.9	*	*	*
25–44 years	- - -	3.2	2.7	2.7	1.5	1.5	1.7
45–64 years	- - -	*	*	*	*	*	*
65 years and over	- - -	*	*	*	*	*	*
Hispanic or Latino female[3,4]							
All ages, age adjusted[2]	- - -	- - -	3.3	3.1	1.8	1.7	1.6
All ages, crude	- - -	- - -	3.6	3.3	1.8	1.7	1.6
15–24 years	- - -	- - -	6.9	6.1	2.9	3.3	2.8
25–44 years	- - -	- - -	5.1	4.7	2.5	2.5	2.4
45–64 years	- - -	- - -	2.4	2.4	2.2	1.6	1.6
65 years and over	- - -	- - -	*	*	*	*	*
White, not Hispanic or Latino female[4]							
All ages, age adjusted[2]	- - -	- - -	3.7	3.4	2.8	2.8	2.8
All ages, crude	- - -	- - -	3.7	3.5	2.9	2.9	2.8
15–24 years	- - -	- - -	4.3	4.1	2.7	2.5	2.5
25–44 years	- - -	- - -	5.1	4.8	4.2	4.1	4.1
45–64 years	- - -	- - -	4.6	4.1	3.6	3.8	3.8
65 years and over	- - -	- - -	3.2	2.8	2.4	2.4	2.3

* Rates based on fewer than 20 deaths are considered unreliable and are not shown.
- - - Data not available.
[1]Starting with 1999 data, cause of death is coded according to ICD–10. See Appendix II, Comparability ratio and tables V and VI.
[2]Age-adjusted rates are calculated using the year 2000 standard population. See Appendix II, Age adjustment.
[3]The race groups, white, black, Asian or Pacific Islander, and American Indian or Alaska Native, include persons of Hispanic and non-Hispanic origin. Persons of Hispanic origin may be of any race. Death rates for the American Indian or Alaska Native and Asian or Pacific Islander populations are known to be underestimated. See Appendix II, Race, for a discussion of sources of bias in death rates by race and Hispanic origin.
[4]Prior to 1997, excludes data from States lacking an Hispanic-origin item on the death certificate. See Appendix II, Hispanic origin.

NOTES: Starting with *Health, United States, 2003*, rates for 1991–99 were revised using intercensal population estimates based on census 2000. Rates for 2000 were revised based on census 2000 counts. Rates for 2001 and 2002 were computed using 2000-based postcensal estimates. See Appendix I, Population Census and Population Estimates. Underlying cause of death code numbers are based on the applicable revision of the *International Classification of Diseases* (ICD) for data years shown. See Appendix II, tables IV and V. Age groups were selected to minimize the presentation of unstable age-specific death rates based on small numbers of deaths and for consistency among comparison groups. For additional injury-related statistics, see www.cdc.gov/ncipc/wisqars, a Web-based interactive database for injury data. Data for additional years are available. See Appendix III.

SOURCES: Centers for Disease Control and Prevention, National Center for Health Statistics, National Vital Statistics System; numerator data from annual mortality files; denominator data from national population estimates for race groups from table 1 and unpublished Hispanic population estimates for 1985–96 prepared by the Housing and Household Economic Statistics Division, U.S. Bureau of the Census; additional mortality tables are available at www.cdc.gov/nchs/datawh/statab/unpubd/mortabs.htm; Kochanek KD, Murphy SL, Anderson RN, Scott C. Deaths: Final data for 2002. National vital statistics reports. Vol 53 no 5. Hyattsville, Maryland: National Center for Health Statistics. 2004.

This table will be updated on the Web. Go to www.cdc.gov/nchs/hus.htm.

Table 48. Deaths from selected occupational diseases for persons 15 years of age and over: United States, selected years 1980–2002

[Data are based on death certificates]

Cause of death[1]	1980	1985	1990	1995	1999[2]	2000	2001	2002
Underlying and nonunderlying cause of death	Number of death certificates with cause-of-death code(s) mentioned							
Angiosarcoma of liver[3]	- - -	- - -	- - -	- - -	4	16	25	23
Malignant mesothelioma[4]	699	715	874	897	2,485	2,531	2,508	2,573
Pneumoconiosis[5]	4,151	3,783	3,644	3,151	2,739	2,859	2,743	2,715
Coal workers' pneumoconiosis	2,576	2,615	1,990	1,413	1,002	949	886	858
Asbestosis	339	534	948	1,169	1,259	1,486	1,449	1,467
Silicosis	448	334	308	242	185	151	163	146
Other (including unspecified)	814	321	413	343	310	290	260	263
Underlying cause of death	Number of deaths							
Angiosarcoma of liver[3]	- - -	- - -	- - -	- - -	3	15	22	20
Malignant mesothelioma[4]	531	573	725	780	2,343	2,384	2,371	2,429
Pneumoconiosis	1,581	1,355	1,335	1,117	1,081	1,142	1,110	1,094
Coal workers' pneumoconiosis	982	958	734	533	409	389	367	354
Asbestosis	101	139	302	355	449	558	550	529
Silicosis	207	143	150	114	102	71	82	89
Other (including unspecified)	291	115	149	115	121	124	111	122

- - - Data not available.

[1]Cause-of-death titles for selected occupational diseases and corresponding code numbers according to the *International Classification of Diseases*, Ninth and Tenth Revisions. See Appendix II, table IV.

Cause of death	ICD–9 code	ICD–10 code
Angiosarcoma of liver	- - -	C22.3
Malignant mesothelioma	158.8,158.9,163	C45
Pneumoconiosis	500–505	J60-J66
Coal workers' pneumoconiosis	500	J60
Asbestosis	501	J61
Silicosis	502	J62
Other (including unspecified)	503–505	J63-J66

[2]Starting with 1999 data, ICD–10 was introduced for coding cause of death. Discontinuities exist between 1998 and 1999 due to ICD–10 coding and classification changes. Caution should be exercised in interpreting trends for the causes of death in this table, especially for those with major ICD–10 changes (e.g., malignant mesothelioma). See Appendix II, *International Classification of Diseases* (ICD).
[3]Prior to 1999 there was no discrete code for this condition.
[4]Prior to 1999 the combined ICD–9 categories of malignant neoplasm of peritoneum and malignant neoplasm of pleura served as a crude surrogate for malignant mesothelioma under ICD–10.
[5]For underlying and nonunderlying cause of death, counts for pneumoconiosis subgroups may sum to slightly more than total pneumoconiosis due to the reporting of more than one type of pneumoconiosis on some death certificates.

NOTES: See Appendix I, National Vital Statistics System, Multiple Cause of Death File for information about tabulating cause-of-death data in this table. Selection of occupational diseases is based on definitions in Mullan RJ, Murthy LI. Occupational sentinel health events: An updated list for physician recognition and public health surveillance. *Am J Ind Med* 19:775–799, 1991. For more detailed information about pneumoconiosis deaths, see *Work-Related Lung Disease Surveillance Report 2002*, DHHS (NIOSH) Publication Number 2003–111 at www.cdc.gov/niosh/docs/2003-1112003–111.html. Data for additional years are available. See Appendix III.

SOURCE: Centers for Disease Control and Prevention, National Center for Health Statistics, National Vital Statistics System; annual mortality files for underlying and multiple cause of death.

This table will be updated on the Web. Go to www.cdc.gov/nchs/hus.htm.

Table 49 (page 1 of 2). Occupational injury deaths and rates by industry, sex, age, race, and Hispanic origin: United States, selected years 1992–2003

[Data are compiled from various Federal, State, and local administrative sources]

Characteristic	*1992*[1]	*1995*	*1997*	*1998*	*1999*	*2000*	*2001*[2]	*2002*	*2003*
	Deaths per 100,000 employed workers[3]								
Total work force	5.2	4.9	4.7	4.5	4.5	4.3	4.3	4.0	4.0
Sex									
Male	---	8.3	8.1	7.7	7.7	7.4	7.4	6.9	7.0
Female	---	0.9	0.8	0.8	0.7	0.7	0.7	0.7	0.7
Age									
16–17 years	---	1.6	1.5	1.2	1.6	1.6	1.3	1.1	1.2
18–19 years	---	3.3	2.8	3.1	2.7	2.7	2.8	2.2	2.3
20–24 years	---	3.8	3.9	3.3	3.4	3.3	3.2	3.2	3.4
25–34 years	---	4.3	4.1	3.9	3.8	3.8	3.8	3.3	3.4
35–44 years	---	4.6	4.2	4.2	4.1	4.0	4.1	4.0	3.8
45–54 years	---	5.2	4.9	4.6	4.6	4.4	4.5	4.0	4.1
55–64 years	---	7.2	7.1	6.5	6.1	6.1	5.5	5.0	4.8
65 years and over	---	14.0	13.8	14.5	14.6	12.0	12.7	11.5	11.3
Race and Hispanic origin[4]									
White	---	4.7	4.6	4.5	4.4	---	---	---	---
Black or African American	---	5.1	4.8	4.0	4.1	---	---	---	---
Hispanic or Latino	---	5.5	5.1	5.2	5.2	5.6	6.0	5.0	4.5
Not Hispanic or Latino	---	4.9	4.7	4.5	4.4	4.2	4.1	3.9	4.0
White	---	---	---	---	---	4.2	4.2	3.9	4.0
Black or African American	---	---	---	---	---	3.9	3.8	3.5	3.8
Asian, Native Hawaiian or Other Pacific Islander	---	---	---	---	---	---	---	---	2.8
Industry[5]									
Private sector	...	...	...	...	...	...	...	...	4.7
Goods producing	...	...	...	...	...	...	...	...	9.1
Natural resources and mining	...	...	...	...	...	...	...	...	55.7
Construction	...	...	...	...	...	...	...	...	14.3
Manufacturing	...	...	...	...	...	...	...	...	2.5
Service providing	...	...	...	...	...	...	...	...	3.2
Trade, transportation, and utilities	...	...	...	...	...	...	...	...	5.6
Information	...	...	...	...	...	...	...	...	1.9
Financial activities	...	...	...	...	...	...	...	...	1.5
Professional and business services	...	...	...	...	...	...	...	...	3.9
Educational and health services	...	...	...	...	...	...	...	...	0.8
Leisure and hospitality	...	...	...	...	...	...	...	...	2.6
Other services, except public administration	...	...	...	...	...	...	...	...	3.4
Government[6]	...	...	...	...	...	...	...	...	2.7
	Number of deaths[7]								
Total work force	6,217	6,275	6,238	6,055	6,054	5,920	5,915	5,534	5,575
Sex									
Male	5,774	5,736	5,761	5,569	5,612	5,471	5,442	5,092	5,129
Female	443	539	477	486	442	449	473	442	446
Age									
Under 16 years	27	26	21	33	26	29	20	16	25
16–17 years	41	42	41	32	46	44	33	25	28
18–19 years	107	130	113	137	122	127	122	92	84
20–24 years	544	486	503	421	451	446	441	436	462
25–34 years	1,556	1,409	1,325	1,238	1,175	1,163	1,142	1,023	1,018
35–44 years	1,538	1,571	1,524	1,525	1,510	1,473	1,478	1,403	1,329
45–54 years	1,167	1,256	1,302	1,279	1,333	1,313	1,368	1,253	1,301
55–64 years	767	827	875	836	816	831	775	784	802
65 years and over	467	515	520	541	565	488	530	495	523
Unspecified	3	13	14	13	10	6	6	7	3

See footnotes at end of table.

Table 49 (page 2 of 2). Occupational injury deaths and rates by industry, sex, age, race, and Hispanic origin: United States, selected years 1992–2003

[Data are compiled from various Federal, State, and local administrative sources]

Characteristic	*1992*[1]	*1995*	*1997*	*1998*	*1999*	*2000*	*2001*[2]	*2002*	*2003*
Race and Hispanic origin				Number of deaths[8]					
White	5,173	5,120	5,108	5,041	4,990	- - -	- - -	- - -	- - -
Black or African American	624	697	677	594	626	- - -	- - -	- - -	- - -
Hispanic or Latino	533	619	658	707	730	815	895	841	794
Not Hispanic or Latino	5,684	5,656	5,580	5,348	5,324	5,105	5,020	4,693	4,781
White	4,712	4,599	4,576	4,478	4,410	4,244	4,175	3,926	3,988
Black or African American	618	684	661	583	616	575	565	491	543
American Indian or Alaska Native	36	27	34	28	54	33	48	40	42
Asian[8]	192	188	218	164	180	171	173	131	147
Native Hawaiian or Other Pacific Islander	- - -	- - -	- - -	- - -	- - -	14	9	9	11
Multiple races	- - -	- - -	- - -	- - -	- - -	- - -	6	4	3
Other races or not reported	126	158	91	95	64	68	44	92	47
Industry[5]									
Private sector	- - -	- - -	- - -	- - -	- - -	- - -	- - -	- - -	5,043
Goods producing	- - -	- - -	- - -	- - -	- - -	- - -	- - -	- - -	2,401
Natural resources and mining	- - -	- - -	- - -	- - -	- - -	- - -	- - -	- - -	850
Construction	- - -	- - -	- - -	- - -	- - -	- - -	- - -	- - -	1,131
Manufacturing	- - -	- - -	- - -	- - -	- - -	- - -	- - -	- - -	420
Service providing	- - -	- - -	- - -	- - -	- - -	- - -	- - -	- - -	2,642
Trade, transportation, and utilities	- - -	- - -	- - -	- - -	- - -	- - -	- - -	- - -	1,375
Information	- - -	- - -	- - -	- - -	- - -	- - -	- - -	- - -	64
Financial activities	- - -	- - -	- - -	- - -	- - -	- - -	- - -	- - -	129
Professional and business services	- - -	- - -	- - -	- - -	- - -	- - -	- - -	- - -	453
Educational and health services	- - -	- - -	- - -	- - -	- - -	- - -	- - -	- - -	143
Leisure and hospitality	- - -	- - -	- - -	- - -	- - -	- - -	- - -	- - -	275
Other services, except public administration	- - -	- - -	- - -	- - -	- - -	- - -	- - -	- - -	194
Government[6]	- - -	- - -	- - -	- - -	- - -	- - -	- - -	- - -	532

- - - Data not available.
. . . Data not applicable.
[1]1992 and 1993 employment data by demographic characteristics are not available from the Current Population Survey (CPS) for calculation of rates.
[2]2,871 fatalities due to the September 11 terrorist attacks are not included.
[3]Numerator excludes deaths to workers under the age of 16 years. 2003 employment data in denominators are average annual estimates of employed civilians 16 years of age and over from the CPS; in prior years, also included resident armed forces figures from the Bureau of the Census (1992–98) and Department of Defense (1999–2002).
[4]Employment data for American Indian or Alaska Native workers and, prior to 2003, Asian or Pacific Islander workers were not available for the calculation of rates; employment data for non-Hispanic white and non-Hispanic black workers were not available before the year 2000. In 1999 and earlier years, the race groups white and black included persons of Hispanic and non-Hispanic origin.
[5]Beginning with the 2003 data year, establishments were classified by industry according to the 2002 North American Industry Classification System (NAICS). Prior to 2003, the Standard Industrial Classification (SIC) system was used. Because of substantial differences between these systems, industry data classified by these two systems are not comparable. Industry data for 1992–2002 classified by SIC are available in *Health, United States, 2004*, table 49 at www.cdc.gov/nchs/hus.htm. See Appendix II, Industry of employment.
[6]Includes fatalities to workers employed by governmental organizations, regardless of industry.
[7]Includes fatalities to all workers, regardless of age.
[8]In 1999 and earlier years, category also included Native Hawaiian or Other Pacific Islander.

NOTES: Fatalities and rates are based on revised data and may differ from originally published data from the Census of Fatal Occupational Injuries (CFOI). See Appendix I, CFOI. CFOI began collecting fatality data in 1992. For data for prior years, see CDC. Fatal Occupational Injuries—United States, 1980–1997. MMWR 2001; 50(16):317–320, which reports trend data from the National Traumatic Occupational Fatalities (NTOF) surveillance system. NTOF was established at the National Institute of Occupational Safety and Health (NIOSH) to monitor occupational injury deaths through death certificates. Some numbers for 2002 in this table were revised and differ from the previous edition of *Health, United States*. Data for additional years are available. See Appendix III.

SOURCE: Department of Labor, Bureau of Labor Statistics, Census of Fatal Occupational Injuries. Revised annual data.

Table 50. Occupational injuries and illnesses with days away from work, job transfer, or restriction in the private sector, according to industry: United States, 2003

[Data are based on employer records from a sample of business establishments]

Industry	*Injuries and illnesses with days away from work, job transfer, or restriction*	
	Cases per 100 full-time workers[1]	*Number of cases in thousands*[2]
Total private industry[3]	2.6	2,301.9
Goods producing	3.7	796.5
Natural resources and mining[4]	2.8	40.5
Agriculture, forestry, fishing, and hunting[4]	3.3	29.3
Mining	2.0	11.2
Construction	3.6	218.0
Manufacturing	3.8	538.0
Service providing	2.3	1,505.4
Trade, transportation, and utilities	3.2	683.2
Wholesale trade	2.8	147.4
Retail trade	2.7	319.6
Transportation and warehousing	5.4	204.0
Utilities	2.2	12.2
Information	1.1	30.8
Financial activities	0.8	56.9
Finance and insurance	0.4	21.3
Real estate and rental and leasing	2.1	35.6
Professional and business services	1.4	157.7
Professional, scientific, and technical services	0.6	36.0
Management of companies and enterprises	1.6	25.1
Administrative and support and waste management and remediation services	2.4	96.7
Educational and health services	2.9	355.8
Educational services	1.2	17.9
Health care and social assistance	3.1	337.9
Leisure and hospitality	2.1	169.3
Arts, entertainment, and recreation	2.9	34.1
Accommodation and food services	2.0	135.2
Other services, except public administration	1.7	51.7

[1]Incidence rate calculated as (N/EH) x 200,000, where N = total number of injuries and illnesses, EH = total hours worked by all employees during the calendar year, and 200,000 = base for 100 full-time equivalent employees working 40 hours per week, 50 weeks per year.
[2]Because of rounding, components may not add to totals.
[3]Totals include data for industries not shown separately. Excludes self-employed, private households, and employers in Federal, state, and local government agencies.
[4]Excludes farms with fewer than 11 employees.

NOTES: Beginning with the 2003 data year, the Survey of Occupational Injuries and Illnesses began using the 2002 North American Industry Classification System (NAICS) to classify establishments by industry. Prior to 2003, the survey used the Standard Industrial Classification (SIC) system. Because of substantial differences between these systems, the data measured by these surveys are not directly comparable. Data for previous years are available in *Health, United States, 2004*, table 50 at www.cdc.gov/nchs/hus.htm. See Appendix I, Survey of Occupational Injuries and Illnesses.

SOURCE: U.S. Department of Labor, Bureau of Labor Statistics, Survey of Occupational Injuries and Illnesses: Workplace injuries and illnesses, 2003 edition. Summary News Release. 2004. Internet address: www.bls.gov/iif/home.htm.

Table 51. Selected notifiable disease rates, according to disease: United States, selected years 1950–2003

[Data are based on reporting by State health departments]

Disease	1950	1960	1970	1980	1990	2000	2001	2002	2003
					Cases per 100,000 population				
Diphtheria	3.83	0.51	0.21	0.00	0.00	0.00	0.00	0.00	0.00
Haemophilus influenzae, invasive	- - -	- - -	- - -	- - -	- - -	0.51	0.57	0.62	0.70
Hepatitis A	- - -	- - -	27.87	12.84	12.64	4.91	3.77	3.13	2.66
Hepatitis B	- - -	- - -	4.08	8.39	8.48	2.95	2.79	2.84	2.61
Lyme disease	- - -	- - -	- - -	- - -	- - -	6.53	6.05	8.44	7.39
Meningococcal disease	- - -	- - -	1.23	1.25	0.99	0.83	0.83	0.64	0.61
Mumps	- - -	- - -	55.55	3.86	2.17	0.13	0.10	0.10	0.08
Pertussis (whooping cough)	79.82	8.23	2.08	0.76	1.84	2.88	2.69	3.47	4.04
Poliomyelitis, total	22.02	1.77	0.02	0.00	0.00	–	–	–	–
Paralytic[1]	- - -	1.40	0.02	0.00	0.00	–	–	–	–
Rocky Mountain spotted fever	- - -	- - -	0.19	0.52	0.26	0.18	0.25	0.39	0.38
Rubella (German measles)	- - -	- - -	27.75	1.72	0.45	0.06	0.01	0.01	0.00
Rubeola (measles)	211.01	245.42	23.23	5.96	11.17	0.03	0.04	0.02	0.02
Salmonellosis, excluding typhoid fever	- - -	3.85	10.84	14.88	19.54	14.51	14.39	15.73	15.16
Shigellosis	15.45	6.94	6.79	8.41	10.89	8.41	7.19	8.37	8.19
Tuberculosis[2]	- - -	30.83	18.28	12.25	10.33	6.01	5.68	5.36	5.17
Sexually transmitted diseases:[3]									
Syphilis[4]	146.02	68.78	45.26	30.51	54.32	11.20	11.31	11.41	11.89
Primary and secondary	16.73	9.06	10.89	12.06	20.26	2.12	2.14	2.38	2.49
Early latent	39.71	10.11	8.08	9.00	22.19	3.35	3.05	2.92	2.90
Late and late latent[5]	70.22	45.91	24.94	9.30	10.32	5.53	5.95	6.00	6.35
Congenital[6]	8.97	2.48	0.97	0.12	1.55	0.21	0.18	0.16	0.14
Chlamydia[7]	- - -	- - -	- - -	- - -	160.19	251.38	274.52	289.41	304.29
Gonorrhea[8]	192.50	145.40	297.22	445.10	276.43	128.67	126.77	122.01	116.21
Chancroid	3.34	0.94	0.70	0.30	1.69	0.03	0.01	0.02	0.02
					Number of cases				
Diphtheria	5,796	918	435	3	4	1	2	1	1
Haemophilus influenzae, invasive	- - -	- - -	- - -	- - -	- - -	1,398	1,597	1,743	2,013
Hepatitis A	- - -	- - -	56,797	29,087	31,441	13,397	10,609	8,795	7,653
Hepatitis B	- - -	- - -	8,310	19,015	21,102	8,036	7,843	7,996	7,526
Lyme disease	- - -	- - -	- - -	- - -	- - -	17,730	17,029	23,763	21,273
Meningococcal disease	- - -	- - -	2,505	2,840	2,451	2,256	2,333	1,814	1,756
Mumps	- - -	- - -	104,953	8,576	5,292	338	266	270	231
Pertussis (whooping cough)	120,718	14,809	4,249	1,730	4,570	7,867	7,580	9,771	11,647
Poliomyelitis, total	33,300	3,190	33	9	6	–	–	–	–
Paralytic[1]	- - -	2,525	31	9	6	–	–	–	–
Rocky Mountain spotted fever	- - -	- - -	380	1,163	651	495	695	1,104	1,091
Rubella (German measles)	- - -	- - -	56,552	3,904	1,125	176	23	18	7
Rubeola (measles)	319,124	441,703	47,351	13,506	27,786	86	116	44	56
Salmonellosis, excluding typhoid fever	- - -	6,929	22,096	33,715	48,603	39,574	40,495	44,264	43,657
Shigellosis	23,367	12,487	13,845	19,041	27,077	22,922	20,221	23,541	23,581
Tuberculosis[2]	- - -	55,494	37,137	27,749	25,701	16,377	15,989	15,075	14,874
Sexually transmitted diseases:[3]									
Syphilis[4]	217,558	122,538	91,382	68,832	135,590	31,616	32,278	32,912	34,270
Primary and secondary	23,939	16,145	21,982	27,204	50,578	5,979	6,103	6,862	7,177
Early latent	59,256	18,017	16,311	20,297	55,397	9,465	8,701	8,429	8,361
Late and late latent[5]	113,569	81,798	50,348	20,979	25,750	15,594	16,976	17,168	18,319
Congenital[6]	13,377	4,416	1,953	277	3,865	578	498	453	413
Chlamydia[7]	- - -	- - -	- - -	- - -	323,663	709,452	783,242	834,555	877,478
Gonorrhea[8]	286,746	258,933	600,072	1,004,029	690,042	363,136	361,705	351,852	335,104
Chancroid	4,977	1,680	1,416	788	4,212	78	38	48	54

0.00 Rate greater than zero but less than 0.005. – Quantity zero. - - - Data not available.

[1]Data beginning in 1986 may be updated due to retrospective case evaluations or late reports.

[2]Case reporting for tuberculosis began in 1953. Data prior to 1975 are not comparable with subsequent years' data because of changes in reporting criteria effective in 1975. 2003 data were updated through the Division of Tuberculosis Elimination, NCHSTP, as of April 1, 2004.

[3]Reported civilian cases include military cases beginning in 1991. Adjustments to the number of cases from State health departments were made for hardcopy forms and for electronic data submissions through April 30, 2004. For 1950, data for Alaska and Hawaii were not included.

[4]Includes stage of syphilis not stated.

[5]Includes cases of unknown duration.

[6]Data reported for 1989 and later years reflect change in case definition introduced in 1988. Through 1994, all cases of congenitally acquired syphilis; as of 1995, congenital syphilis less than 1 year of age. See STD Surveillance Report for congenital syphilis rates per 100,000 live births. In 2003 the rate was 10.3 congenital syphilis cases per 100,000 live births.

[7]Chlamydia was nonnotifiable in 1994 and earlier years. In 1994–99, cases for New York based exclusively on those reported by New York City. Starting in 2000, includes cases for New York State.

[8]Data for 1994 do not include cases from Georgia.

NOTES: The total resident population was used to calculate all rates except sexually transmitted diseases (STDs), which used the civilian resident population prior to 1991. For STDs, rates for the period 1990–2002 have been revised and may differ from previous editions of *Health, United States*. Revised rates are due to population estimates revised to incorporate bridged single race estimates. 2002 population estimates were used to calculate 2003 STD rates. Population data from those States where diseases were not notifiable or not available were excluded from the rate calculation. See Appendix I for information on underreporting of notifiable diseases. Data for additional years are available. See Appendix III.

SOURCES: Centers for Disease Control and Prevention. Summary of notifiable diseases, United States, 2003. Morbidity and mortality weekly report; 52(54). Atlanta, Georgia: Public Health Service. 2005; National Center for HIV, STD, and TB Prevention, Division of STD Prevention. Sexually transmitted disease surveillance, 2003. Atlanta, Georgia: U.S. Department of Health and Human Services, Centers for Disease Control and Prevention, 2004.

Table 52 (page 1 of 2). Acquired immunodeficiency syndrome (AIDS) cases, according to year of diagnosis and selected characteristics of persons: United States, 1999–2003

[Data are based on reporting by State health departments]

Sex, race and Hispanic origin, region of residence	All years[1]	Year of diagnosis 1999	2000	2001	2002	2003
		Estimated number of cases[2]				
All persons[3]	929,985	41,356	41,267	40,833	41,289	43,171
Sex						
Male, 13 years and over	749,887	31,159	30,387	30,074	30,517	31,614
Female, 13 years and over	170,679	10,010	10,763	10,639	10,666	11,498
Children, under 13 years	9,419	187	117	119	105	59
Not Hispanic or Latino:						
White	376,834	12,626	12,047	11,620	11,960	12,222
Black or African American	368,169	19,960	20,312	20,291	20,476	21,304
American Indian or Alaska Native	3,026	162	186	179	196	196
Asian or Pacific Islander	7,166	369	373	409	452	497
Hispanic or Latino[4]	172,993	8,141	8,233	8,204	8,021	8,757
Age at diagnosis						
Under 13 years	9,419	187	117	119	105	59
13–14 years	891	57	56	76	68	59
15–24 years	37,599	1,541	1,642	1,625	1,810	1,991
25–34 years	311,137	11,349	10,385	9,947	9,504	9,605
35–44 years	365,432	17,165	17,295	16,890	17,008	17,633
45–54 years	148,347	8,099	8,566	8,929	9,310	10,051
55–64 years	43,451	2,218	2,422	2,468	2,724	2,888
65 years and over	13,711	739	783	779	759	886
Region of residence						
Northeast	285,040	11,885	12,516	11,350	10,551	11,461
Midwest	91,926	4,069	4,139	4,094	4,337	4,498
South	337,409	17,224	16,757	17,693	18,482	19,609
West	186,100	6,892	6,661	6,468	6,843	6,667
U.S. dependencies, possessions, and associated nations	29,511	1,286	1,194	1,228	1,075	935
		Percent distribution[5]				
All persons[3]	100.0	100.0	100.0	100.0	100.0	100.0
Sex						
Male, 13 years and over	80.6	75.3	73.6	73.7	73.9	73.2
Female, 13 years and over	18.4	24.2	26.1	26.1	25.8	26.6
Children, under 13 years	1.0	0.5	0.3	0.3	0.3	0.1
Not Hispanic or Latino:						
White	40.5	30.5	29.2	28.5	29.0	28.3
Black or African American	39.6	48.3	49.2	49.7	49.6	49.3
American Indian or Alaska Native	0.3	0.4	0.5	0.4	0.5	0.5
Asian or Pacific Islander	0.8	0.9	0.9	1.0	1.1	1.2
Hispanic or Latino[4]	18.6	19.7	20.0	20.1	19.4	20.3

See footnotes at end of table.

Table 52 (page 2 of 2). Acquired immunodeficiency syndrome (AIDS) cases, according to year of diagnosis and selected characteristics of persons: United States, 1999–2003

[Data are based on reporting by State health departments]

Sex, race and Hispanic origin, region of residence	All years[1]	Year of diagnosis 1999	2000	2001	2002	2003
Age at diagnosis		Percent distribution[5]				
Under 13 years	1.0	0.5	0.3	0.3	0.3	0.1
13–14 years	0.1	0.1	0.1	0.2	0.2	0.1
15–24 years	4.0	3.7	4.0	4.0	4.4	4.6
25–34 years	33.5	27.4	25.2	24.4	23.0	22.2
35–44 years	39.3	41.5	41.9	41.4	41.2	40.8
45–54 years	16.0	19.6	20.8	21.9	22.5	23.3
55–64 years	4.7	5.4	5.9	6.0	6.6	6.7
65 years and over	1.5	1.8	1.9	1.9	1.8	2.1
Region of residence						
Northeast	30.6	28.7	30.3	27.8	25.6	26.5
Midwest	9.9	9.8	10.0	10.0	10.5	10.4
South	36.3	41.6	40.6	43.3	44.8	45.4
West	20.0	16.7	16.1	15.8	16.6	15.4
U.S. dependencies, possessions, and associated nations	3.2	3.1	2.9	3.0	2.6	2.2

[1]Based on cases reported to the Centers for Disease Control and Prevention from the beginning of the epidemic through 2003.
[2]Numbers are point estimates that result from adjustments for reporting delays to AIDS case counts. The estimates do not include adjustments for incomplete reporting. Data are provisional. See Appendix I, AIDS Surveillance.
[3]Total for all years includes 1,796 persons of unknown race or multiple races and one person of unknown sex. All persons totals were calculated independent of values for subpopulations. Consequently sums of subpopulations may not equal total for all persons.
[4]Persons of Hispanic origin may be of any race.
[5]Percents may not sum to 100 percent due to rounding and because 0.2 percent unknown race and Hispanic origin are included in totals.

NOTES: See Appendix II, AIDS, for discussion of AIDS case reporting definitions and other issues affecting interpretation of trends. This table presents adjusted data (point estimates) by year of diagnosis and replaces surveillance data by year of report in previous editions of *Health, United States.*

SOURCES: Centers for Disease Control and Prevention, National Center for HIV, STD, and TB Prevention, Division of HIV/AIDS Prevention—Surveillance and Epidemiology, AIDS Surveillance; HIV/AIDS Surveillance Report, 2003 (vol. 15) table 3. Atlanta: US Department of Health and Human Services, Centers for Disease Control and Prevention. 2004. Also available at www.cdc.gov/hiv/stats/hasrlink.htm.

Table 53 (page 1 of 3). Age-adjusted cancer incidence rates for selected cancer sites, according to sex, race, and Hispanic origin: Selected geographic areas, 1990–2001

[Data are based on the Surveillance, Epidemiology, and End Results (SEER) Program's 12 population-based cancer registries]

Site, sex, race, and Hispanic origin	*1990*	*1995*	*1996*	*1997*	*1998*	*1999*	*2000*	*2001*	*1990–2001 APC*[1]
All sites	Number of new cases per 100,000 population[2]								
All persons	476.0	469.9	471.0	476.5	477.0	476.1	465.9	457.1	^–0.5
White	483.3	475.9	477.7	483.7	485.8	485.1	476.2	468.0	^–0.4
Black or African American	514.9	532.6	528.4	533.3	523.7	526.1	511.6	486.2	^–0.7
American Indian or Alaska Native	263.8	269.6	254.3	269.7	249.7	252.2	213.0	212.7	^–2.0
Asian or Pacific Islander	335.8	337.8	333.6	345.1	337.1	339.6	331.7	331.6	^–0.4
Hispanic or Latino	343.0	361.1	357.3	352.6	363.2	362.8	346.7	334.5	–0.2
White, not Hispanic or Latino	490.9	485.0	488.5	495.1	494.2	496.9	488.9	480.1	–0.3
Male	584.4	562.3	560.5	562.9	558.8	561.4	552.5	537.3	^–1.3
White	590.8	561.1	561.9	562.4	560.5	562.9	555.7	542.2	^–1.3
Black or African American	690.1	729.5	707.4	717.1	701.8	701.3	686.6	642.9	^–1.2
American Indian or Alaska Native	313.9	320.0	276.5	312.8	258.6	292.9	217.1	244.9	^–3.0
Asian or Pacific Islander	387.6	396.0	385.3	397.1	381.6	391.6	387.0	374.7	^–0.8
Hispanic or Latino	407.2	442.1	433.2	423.2	430.4	432.9	416.7	399.5	–0.6
White, not Hispanic or Latino	598.9	566.8	568.6	569.5	563.6	569.7	564.6	549.4	^–1.3
Female	411.7	409.6	412.8	420.1	424.1	419.8	407.3	402.0	0.0
White	421.6	422.2	424.4	433.9	439.0	434.9	423.6	418.2	0.2
Black or African American	404.4	400.9	410.5	411.7	408.1	410.6	393.7	378.4	–0.3
American Indian or Alaska Native	229.8	237.2	241.6	241.0	245.3	226.4	215.9	191.3	–1.0
Asian or Pacific Islander	295.2	295.1	296.6	308.3	307.0	304.1	293.4	302.9	0.2
Hispanic or Latino	307.7	311.5	311.7	309.6	322.3	320.5	305.4	294.3	0.0
White, not Hispanic or Latino	428.2	433.0	437.3	447.9	450.9	449.6	437.7	433.0	^0.4
Lung and bronchus									
Male	95.4	87.0	84.4	82.7	83.2	80.0	76.5	73.6	^–2.2
White	94.6	85.2	82.9	81.1	82.1	78.6	75.3	72.8	^–2.2
Black or African American	134.8	136.8	128.9	126.4	123.5	119.4	109.2	108.2	^–2.2
Asian or Pacific Islander	64.5	60.4	61.1	62.5	61.3	62.1	62.2	54.7	^–1.1
Hispanic or Latino	59.3	52.6	48.3	48.4	50.5	44.2	44.7	39.6	^–2.6
White, not Hispanic or Latino	95.2	85.6	84.4	81.8	83.1	80.1	76.6	74.0	^–2.1
Female	47.4	49.4	50.2	50.3	50.8	50.2	48.0	46.4	0.0
White	48.7	51.8	52.5	53.0	53.1	52.2	50.2	48.3	0.2
Black or African American	53.4	50.4	53.9	50.8	56.9	58.0	54.3	52.5	0.2
Asian or Pacific Islander	28.4	27.8	27.8	29.9	28.5	29.0	27.2	28.3	0.1
Hispanic or Latino	24.7	24.4	25.6	25.7	26.0	24.4	22.9	21.3	–1.0
White, not Hispanic or Latino	49.9	54.1	54.7	55.3	54.8	54.8	52.1	50.1	0.3
Colon and rectum									
Male	72.4	63.1	64.5	66.3	65.7	63.8	61.9	59.5	^–1.4
White	73.1	62.5	64.9	66.1	65.6	63.8	61.6	58.9	^–1.5
Black or African American	73.1	73.4	67.4	74.1	76.8	73.8	72.0	68.3	–0.6
Asian or Pacific Islander	61.4	58.3	56.1	59.6	57.5	54.1	56.4	54.7	^–0.8
Hispanic or Latino	46.0	46.4	51.0	50.5	52.0	50.1	48.9	47.3	0.4
White, not Hispanic or Latino	74.4	63.0	65.2	65.8	66.1	65.2	62.7	59.6	^–1.4
Female	50.2	45.8	46.0	47.1	48.5	46.8	45.5	44.1	^–0.8
White	49.8	45.5	45.6	47.0	48.2	46.1	45.1	43.3	^–0.8
Black or African American	61.1	54.7	54.1	57.5	56.3	57.5	57.2	54.0	–0.4
Asian or Pacific Islander	38.1	38.5	39.1	35.6	40.5	40.2	36.7	39.7	–0.4
Hispanic or Latino	32.6	33.1	32.1	32.1	34.1	34.4	32.9	29.7	–0.1
White, not Hispanic or Latino	50.8	46.0	46.8	48.5	49.5	47.3	46.6	44.2	^–0.7
Prostate									
Male	166.7	165.5	165.4	170.4	167.6	177.7	174.6	171.4	–1.8
White	168.1	160.1	160.8	165.6	161.9	172.2	169.5	167.8	^–2.1
Black or African American	219.2	272.4	268.8	271.0	275.3	278.1	281.2	251.3	–0.7
American Indian or Alaska Native	84.8	65.4	76.6	71.0	50.6	59.8	29.8	48.4	^–6.7
Asian or Pacific Islander	88.9	103.3	94.0	96.9	92.8	105.1	104.3	103.9	–0.9
Hispanic or Latino	115.7	139.2	135.4	138.2	140.7	144.7	140.6	136.2	0.0
White, not Hispanic or Latino	169.6	160.3	161.1	166.1	159.1	171.3	169.4	167.5	^–2.1
Breast									
Female	129.3	130.6	131.8	135.4	138.3	137.4	132.9	132.1	^0.5
White	134.3	136.1	136.9	141.1	144.6	144.1	139.8	139.0	^0.6
Black or African American	116.6	122.4	122.4	123.5	122.8	122.7	119.5	111.9	0.0
American Indian or Alaska Native	46.0	65.4	76.3	57.1	57.9	55.2	53.0	49.5	–1.1
Asian or Pacific Islander	87.0	86.7	89.9	98.6	99.0	97.5	91.7	97.8	^1.5
Hispanic or Latino	84.7	89.1	91.2	87.0	91.9	92.0	92.1	85.4	0.5
White, not Hispanic or Latino	138.6	142.1	144.1	148.6	152.2	152.9	147.5	148.3	0.9

See footnotes at end of table.

Table 53 (page 2 of 3). Age-adjusted cancer incidence rates for selected cancer sites, according to sex, race, and Hispanic origin: Selected geographic areas, 1990–2001

[Data are based on the Surveillance, Epidemiology, and End Results (SEER) Program's 12 population-based cancer registries]

Site, sex, race, and Hispanic origin	*1990*	*1995*	*1996*	*1997*	*1998*	*1999*	*2000*	*2001*	*1990–2001 APC*[1]
Cervix uteri	Number of new cases per 100,000 population[2]								
Female	11.9	9.9	10.6	9.8	9.8	9.3	8.8	8.6	^–2.5
White	11.2	9.2	9.9	9.2	9.3	9.0	8.8	8.3	^–2.2
Black or African American	16.2	14.4	13.6	13.1	12.4	12.9	10.6	10.5	^–3.3
Asian or Pacific Islander	12.1	10.9	13.0	11.1	10.9	8.3	8.0	9.8	^–3.2
Hispanic or Latino	21.2	18.1	18.5	16.2	15.7	17.3	16.8	14.9	^–2.9
White, not Hispanic or Latino	9.5	7.7	8.3	7.8	8.0	7.5	6.7	6.7	^–2.5
Corpus uteri									
Female	24.7	24.9	24.5	25.2	24.9	24.5	23.7	24.2	–0.1
White	26.4	26.4	25.9	26.9	26.5	26.2	25.4	25.6	–0.1
Black or African American	17.0	17.9	19.2	18.0	18.3	18.0	16.9	19.7	^–1.0
Asian or Pacific Islander	13.2	17.7	16.6	17.5	17.2	17.5	16.4	17.7	^1.8
Hispanic or Latino	16.3	17.2	16.2	17.3	18.0	16.6	15.3	16.9	0.2
White, not Hispanic or Latino	27.0	27.4	27.0	27.9	27.6	27.1	26.5	26.6	0.0
Ovary									
Female	15.6	14.5	14.0	14.2	14.0	14.1	13.8	13.6	^–1.2
White	16.4	15.4	15.1	14.9	14.9	15.0	14.7	14.7	^–1.0
Black or African American	11.1	10.8	9.1	10.3	10.7	10.3	10.4	8.7	–1.2
Asian or Pacific Islander	11.1	10.4	9.4	11.3	10.2	10.8	9.9	9.5	–0.8
Hispanic or Latino	12.1	11.6	12.4	11.2	12.2	11.0	10.6	11.9	–0.6
White, not Hispanic or Latino	17.0	15.7	15.4	15.3	15.2	15.6	15.3	15.0	^–1.0
Oral cavity and pharynx									
Male	19.2	16.9	17.4	16.9	16.4	15.2	15.7	14.6	^–2.2
White	18.7	16.8	17.0	16.7	16.2	15.1	15.5	14.8	^–2.1
Black or African American	26.3	22.4	23.3	19.8	21.7	19.3	19.2	17.7	^–2.9
Asian or Pacific Islander	15.1	11.8	14.2	14.7	12.9	11.1	13.0	9.7	^–2.1
Hispanic or Latino	11.0	13.1	11.5	10.5	10.1	10.2	8.7	9.0	^–2.4
White, not Hispanic or Latino	19.2	16.7	17.4	17.4	16.7	15.9	16.2	15.3	^–2.0
Female	7.3	7.0	6.9	6.9	6.6	6.3	6.1	6.4	^–1.4
White	7.4	7.1	6.9	6.9	6.7	6.1	6.1	6.4	^–1.5
Black or African American	6.3	6.7	7.3	7.1	6.4	5.9	5.4	6.3	–1.3
Asian or Pacific Islander	6.0	5.2	5.7	6.5	4.5	6.5	6.1	5.5	–0.7
Hispanic or Latino	3.7	3.8	3.7	3.9	3.5	4.5	3.6	3.9	–0.3
White, not Hispanic or Latino	7.7	7.3	7.3	7.3	7.2	6.3	6.4	6.4	^–1.7
Stomach									
Male	14.7	13.6	13.8	13.5	12.9	12.9	12.5	11.5	^–2.0
White	12.9	12.0	12.0	11.4	11.1	11.2	10.6	10.0	^–2.1
Black or African American	21.9	18.5	22.5	22.0	20.4	17.1	18.7	16.3	^–2.5
Asian or Pacific Islander	26.9	23.9	23.7	24.7	21.1	22.6	22.2	19.1	^–2.9
Hispanic or Latino	20.1	19.8	17.8	19.0	19.5	20.1	16.1	15.1	^–2.1
White, not Hispanic or Latino	11.9	10.8	11.1	10.1	9.8	9.7	9.9	8.9	^–2.4
Female	6.7	6.2	6.1	6.1	6.4	6.5	6.0	5.6	^–1.2
White	5.7	5.2	5.1	4.9	5.2	5.4	5.0	4.5	^–1.6
Black or African American	9.9	9.9	9.3	10.9	10.9	10.5	8.5	9.0	–0.6
Asian or Pacific Islander	15.5	13.1	13.7	12.2	12.8	12.2	12.8	11.9	^–2.6
Hispanic or Latino	10.9	11.2	10.1	10.1	11.0	9.4	10.4	9.3	–1.1
White, not Hispanic or Latino	5.0	4.4	4.3	4.0	4.3	4.7	4.1	3.5	^–2.4
Pancreas									
Male	13.1	12.7	12.6	12.9	12.9	12.5	12.6	12.0	^–0.4
White	12.7	12.4	12.3	12.5	12.9	12.3	12.4	12.2	–0.1
Black or African American	19.7	18.9	19.1	18.2	17.2	18.4	18.0	14.1	^–1.4
Asian or Pacific Islander	11.2	10.5	10.6	12.1	10.5	9.2	10.4	9.3	–1.7
Hispanic or Latino	11.1	12.5	11.4	12.0	9.8	9.7	11.5	9.4	–0.5
White, not Hispanic or Latino	12.4	12.1	12.1	12.5	13.0	12.7	12.4	12.1	0.1
Female	10.1	10.0	10.0	10.2	10.1	9.6	9.7	9.2	^–0.6
White	9.8	9.7	9.7	9.7	9.9	9.3	9.5	8.9	^–0.6
Black or African American	13.0	15.7	15.1	17.0	13.8	13.4	12.7	13.0	–1.4
Asian or Pacific Islander	9.9	8.1	7.9	8.4	8.4	8.5	9.1	8.8	0.5
Hispanic or Latino	9.7	8.7	9.1	10.0	9.8	10.0	9.1	8.4	–0.7
White, not Hispanic or Latino	9.6	9.6	9.7	9.3	9.8	9.0	9.4	8.5	^–0.7

See footnotes at end of table.

Table 53 (page 3 of 3). Age-adjusted cancer incidence rates for selected cancer sites, according to sex, race, and Hispanic origin: Selected geographic areas, 1990–2001

[Data are based on the Surveillance, Epidemiology, and End Results (SEER) Program's 12 population-based cancer registries]

Site, sex, race, and Hispanic origin	*1990*	*1995*	*1996*	*1997*	*1998*	*1999*	*2000*	*2001*	*1990–2001 APC*[1]
Urinary bladder	Number of new cases per 100,000 population[2]								
Male	37.2	35.3	35.6	35.8	36.7	36.2	36.4	35.5	^–0.3
White	40.7	38.7	39.2	39.5	40.5	39.8	40.3	39.4	–0.2
Black or African American	19.8	19.5	19.3	21.0	20.5	22.3	19.6	18.5	–0.3
Asian or Pacific Islander	15.6	16.7	15.6	15.3	16.0	16.8	16.5	16.6	0.8
Hispanic or Latino	21.5	18.6	18.4	18.4	18.5	18.2	19.2	18.7	–0.8
White, not Hispanic or Latino	41.8	39.8	40.7	40.9	41.7	41.3	41.4	40.9	–0.1
Female	9.5	9.3	9.0	9.3	9.0	9.3	9.0	8.8	^–0.5
White	9.9	10.1	9.8	9.9	9.8	10.0	9.7	9.7	–0.2
Black or African American	8.6	7.4	7.2	8.1	6.7	8.6	7.8	7.0	–0.7
Asian or Pacific Islander	5.3	4.5	3.9	5.1	4.7	4.1	4.1	4.5	–0.4
Hispanic or Latino	5.4	5.3	5.5	5.1	4.8	4.4	5.4	5.0	–0.7
White, not Hispanic or Latino	10.1	10.4	10.1	10.6	10.2	10.5	10.0	10.0	0.0
Non-Hodgkin's lymphoma									
Male	22.7	25.0	24.6	23.9	22.8	23.9	23.0	22.8	–0.1
White	23.8	26.2	25.7	24.7	24.0	25.0	24.3	23.8	–0.1
Black or African American	17.6	21.5	18.9	22.9	17.0	17.9	16.9	17.1	–0.5
Asian or Pacific Islander	16.5	16.3	16.8	16.2	15.3	18.9	16.0	17.0	0.3
Hispanic or Latino	17.2	21.8	21.9	17.7	19.8	18.1	19.8	17.2	–0.1
White, not Hispanic or Latino	24.6	27.0	26.1	25.2	24.8	26.0	24.6	24.6	–0.1
Female	14.6	15.1	15.2	15.9	16.1	15.8	15.5	15.4	^0.9
White	15.4	15.8	15.9	16.7	16.9	16.9	16.3	16.1	^0.8
Black or African American	10.4	10.0	11.4	11.9	12.5	10.6	11.8	11.7	^1.9
Asian or Pacific Islander	9.1	11.7	9.5	11.0	11.0	11.1	11.0	12.5	1.7
Hispanic or Latino	13.1	12.7	13.5	14.4	13.4	13.8	12.5	13.7	0.8
White, not Hispanic or Latino	15.4	16.0	16.0	16.9	17.3	17.1	16.6	16.5	^0.9
Leukemia									
Male	17.0	17.4	16.3	16.6	16.5	15.9	15.3	15.2	^–1.0
White	17.9	18.7	17.1	17.7	17.5	16.8	16.2	16.1	^–0.9
Black or African American	15.6	13.0	13.5	13.8	13.3	12.8	12.9	11.4	^–1.4
Asian or Pacific Islander	8.5	10.0	11.0	8.8	9.9	10.5	9.5	9.4	–0.1
Hispanic or Latino	11.6	15.6	12.4	12.3	11.7	11.2	12.2	9.8	–0.5
White, not Hispanic or Latino	17.7	19.0	17.1	17.9	17.7	17.0	16.2	16.4	^–0.8
Female	9.8	10.0	9.8	9.6	9.7	8.9	9.6	9.0	^–0.8
White	10.2	10.6	10.3	10.3	10.3	9.4	10.1	9.5	–0.5
Black or African American	8.3	8.1	8.1	7.9	7.4	7.5	8.7	8.2	–0.9
Asian or Pacific Islander	6.1	6.3	6.5	5.7	6.7	6.2	6.0	4.9	–1.4
Hispanic or Latino	8.3	8.2	7.2	8.4	8.3	7.7	7.5	6.2	–1.0
White, not Hispanic or Latino	10.1	10.4	10.3	10.2	10.0	9.3	9.7	9.4	^–0.7

^ Annual percent change (APC) is significantly different from 0 ($p < 0.05$).
0.0 APC is greater than –0.05 but less than 0.05.
[1]APC has been calculated by fitting a linear regression model to the natural logarithm of the yearly rates from 1990–2001.
[2]Age adjusted by 5-year age groups to the year 2000 U.S. standard population. Age-adjusted rates are based on at least 25 cases. See Appendix II, Age adjustment.

NOTES: Estimates are based on 12 SEER areas November 2003 submission and differ from published estimates based on 9 SEER areas or other submission dates. Estimates for Hispanic population exclude data from Alaska, Detroit, and Hawaii. See Appendix I, SEER. Numbers have been revised and differ from previous editions of *Health, United States*. The race groups, white, black, Asian or Pacific Islander, and American Indian or Alaska Native, include persons of Hispanic and non-Hispanic origin. Conversely, persons of Hispanic origin may be of any race. Estimates for American Indian or Alaska Native are not shown for some sites because of the small number of annual cases.

SOURCE: National Institutes of Health, National Cancer Institute, Surveillance, Epidemiology, and End Results (SEER) Program at www.seer.cancer.gov.

Table 54. Five-year relative cancer survival rates for selected cancer sites, according to race and sex: Selected geographic areas, 1974–79, 1980–82, 1983–85, 1986–88, 1989–91, and 1992–2000

[Data are based on the Surveillance, Epidemiology, and End Results (SEER) Program's 9 population-based cancer registries]

Sex and site	White						Black or African American					
	1974–79	*1980–82*	*1983–85*	*1986–88*	*1989–91*	*1992–2000*	*1974–79*	*1980–82*	*1983–85*	*1986–88*	*1989–91*	*1992–2000*
Both sexes	Percent of patients											
All sites	50.9	52.1	53.9	56.8	60.3	64.8	39.3	39.8	39.8	42.7	46.2	54.0
Oral cavity and pharynx	55.0	55.7	55.4	55.4	55.6	60.1	36.6	31.1	35.2	34.8	33.3	37.0
Esophagus	5.5	7.3	9.3	10.7	11.7	15.7	3.2	5.4	5.9	7.2	8.9	9.4
Stomach	15.2	16.5	16.3	19.2	18.4	21.4	15.6	19.1	18.9	19.3	24.8	21.8
Colon	51.9	55.6	58.5	61.6	63.2	63.5	47.3	49.4	49.5	53.1	53.9	53.2
Rectum	49.8	53.1	55.9	59.2	60.5	63.6	40.3	38.3	44.1	51.3	54.5	54.3
Pancreas	2.4	2.8	2.9	3.2	4.1	4.5	3.3	4.5	5.0	6.0	3.9	3.8
Lung and bronchus	13.1	13.5	13.8	13.5	14.4	15.3	11.3	12.1	11.4	11.9	10.8	12.6
Urinary bladder	75.0	78.9	78.3	80.7	82.2	82.6	51.6	58.5	59.8	62.8	62.0	63.4
Non-Hodgkin's lymphoma	48.3	51.9	54.5	52.8	52.1	58.2	50.3	50.5	45.1	50.4	43.7	47.9
Leukemia	36.7	39.5	42.1	44.3	46.4	48.3	30.8	32.9	33.6	38.0	34.9	38.9
Male												
All sites	43.5	46.7	48.6	51.9	57.8	64.8	32.1	34.4	34.5	37.8	43.5	55.8
Oral cavity and pharynx	54.5	54.6	54.5	52.3	52.2	59.2	31.2	26.5	29.9	29.6	28.9	31.5
Esophagus	5.2	6.4	7.7	11.3	11.8	15.4	2.1	4.6	4.7	7.0	8.0	9.5
Stomach	13.8	15.6	14.6	16.2	15.1	20.0	15.2	18.2	18.4	15.3	22.3	20.0
Colon	51.0	55.9	59.0	62.5	63.8	64.2	45.5	46.9	48.3	52.8	53.8	53.8
Rectum	48.9	51.7	55.2	58.9	60.3	62.6	36.7	36.4	43.1	46.7	56.4	52.7
Pancreas	2.6	2.5	2.6	3.0	3.9	4.3	2.6	3.2	4.4	6.1	3.1	3.4
Lung and bronchus	11.6	12.2	12.1	12.0	12.8	13.5	9.9	10.9	10.2	12.0	9.6	11.3
Prostate gland	70.3	74.5	76.2	82.7	92.0	99.0	60.7	64.8	63.9	69.3	80.8	94.3
Urinary bladder	76.0	79.9	79.6	82.3	84.4	84.6	59.1	63.0	64.8	67.6	65.7	68.4
Non-Hodgkin's lymphoma	47.3	51.0	53.5	50.1	47.8	55.3	44.7	47.8	43.6	47.0	38.3	43.2
Leukemia	35.6	39.6	41.7	45.7	46.9	49.2	30.7	30.1	32.3	36.3	30.1	38.7
Female												
All sites	57.5	57.1	58.9	61.5	62.8	64.9	46.9	46.1	45.6	47.9	49.2	51.8
Colon	52.6	55.4	58.0	60.7	62.6	63.0	48.8	51.4	50.3	53.4	54.1	52.8
Rectum	50.8	54.7	56.8	59.5	60.8	64.9	43.8	40.6	44.9	56.0	52.6	56.0
Pancreas	2.3	3.0	3.2	3.4	4.4	4.6	4.1	5.8	5.5	6.0	4.6	4.2
Lung and bronchus	16.7	16.2	17.0	15.8	16.6	17.5	15.7	15.6	14.2	11.7	13.0	14.8
Melanoma of skin	86.0	88.3	89.6	91.5	91.8	92.2	69.9	*	70.1	*	94.0	71.9
Breast	75.4	77.1	79.3	83.9	86.2	88.3	63.1	65.8	63.6	69.2	71.2	74.1
Cervix uteri	69.8	68.2	70.6	71.9	72.5	73.3	63.1	61.5	60.8	55.7	62.6	62.6
Corpus uteri	87.7	82.8	84.5	84.4	85.7	86.3	59.5	55.2	54.3	57.5	57.8	60.8
Ovary	37.2	38.7	40.3	39.4	41.2	43.4	40.5	39.3	41.5	36.6	30.7	42.0
Non-Hodgkin's lymphoma	49.3	52.9	55.5	56.2	57.4	61.7	57.5	53.7	46.9	54.8	51.2	55.4

* Data for population groups with fewer than 25 cases are not shown because estimates are considered unreliable.

NOTES: Rates are based on followup of patients through 2002. The rate is the ratio of the observed survival rate for the patient group to the expected survival rate for persons in the general population similar to the patient group with respect to age, sex, race, and calendar year of observation. It estimates the chance of surviving the effects of cancer. The race groups white and black include persons of Hispanic and non-Hispanic origin. Numbers have been revised and differ from previous editions of *Health, United States*.

SOURCE: National Institutes of Health, National Cancer Institute, Surveillance, Epidemiology, and End Results (SEER) Program at www.seer.cancer.gov.

Table 55. Diabetes among adults 20 years of age and over, according to sex, age, and race and Hispanic origin: United States, 1988–94 and 1999–2002

[Data are based on physical examinations of a sample of the civilian noninstitutionalized population]

Sex, age, and race and Hispanic origin[3]	Physician-diagnosed and undiagnosed diabetes[1,2]		Physician-diagnosed diabetes[1]		Undiagnosed diabetes[2]	
	1988–94	1999–2002	1988–94	1999–2002	1988–94	1999–2002
20 years and over, age adjusted[4]			Percent of population			
All persons[5]	8.4	9.4	5.4	6.6	3.0	2.9
Male	8.8	10.7	5.4	7.1	3.5	3.8
Female	8.0	8.3	5.4	6.2	2.6	2.2
Not Hispanic or Latino:						
White	7.5	8.0	5.0	5.3	2.6	2.8
Black or African American	12.6	14.8	8.6	11.2	4.2	*3.9
Mexican	14.1	13.6	9.7	10.5	4.7	3.5
20 years and over, crude						
All persons[5]	7.8	9.3	5.1	6.5	2.7	2.8
Male	7.9	10.2	4.8	6.7	3.0	3.5
Female	7.8	8.5	5.4	6.3	2.4	2.2
Not Hispanic or Latino:						
White	7.5	8.5	5.0	5.6	2.5	2.9
Black or African American	10.4	13.2	6.9	9.9	3.4	*3.3
Mexican	9.0	8.3	5.6	6.5	3.4	1.8
Age						
20–39 years	1.6	*	1.1	1.7	0.6	*
40–59 years	8.9	9.8	5.5	6.6	3.4	3.3
60 years and over	18.9	20.9	12.8	15.1	6.1	5.8

* Estimates are considered unreliable. Data preceded by an asterisk have a relative standard error (RSE) of 20–30 percent. Data not shown have an RSE of greater than 30 percent.

[1]Physician-diagnosed diabetes was obtained by self-report and excludes women who reported diabetes only during pregnancy.

[2]Undiagnosed diabetes is defined as a fasting blood glucose of at least 126 mg/dL and no reported physician diagnosis.

[3]Persons of Mexican origin may be of any race. Starting with data year 1999, race-specific estimates are tabulated according to 1997 Standards for Federal data on Race and Ethnicity and are not strictly comparable with estimates for earlier years. The two non-Hispanic race categories shown in the table conform to 1997 Standards. The 1999–2002 race-specific estimates are for persons who reported only one racial group. Data for 1988–94 were tabulated according to 1977 Standards. Estimates for single race categories prior to 1999 included persons who reported one race or, if they reported more than one race, identified one race as best representing their race. See Appendix II, Race.

[4]Estimates are age adjusted to the year 2000 standard population using three age groups: 20–39 years, 40–59 years, and 60 years and over. Age-adjusted estimates in this table may differ from other age-adjusted estimates based on the same data and presented elsewhere if different age groups are used in the adjustment procedure. See Appendix II, Age adjustment.

[5]Includes all other races and Hispanic origins not shown separately.

NOTE: Standard errors are available in the spreadsheet version of this table. See www.cdc.gov/nchs/hus.htm.

SOURCE: Centers for Disease Control and Prevention, National Center for Health Statistics, National Health and Nutrition Examination Survey.

Table 56 (page 1 of 2). Respiratory conditions among adults 18 years of age and over, according to selected characteristics: United States, selected years 1997–2003

[Data are based on household interviews of a sample of the civilian noninstitutionalized population]

Characteristic	Asthma attack[1]			Sinusitis[2]			Hay fever[2]		
	1997	2002	2003	1997	2002	2003	1997	2002	2003
	Percent of adults								
Total, age-adjusted[3,4]	3.7	3.7	3.3	16.3	14.1	13.9	9.2	8.8	8.6
Total, crude[4]	3.7	3.7	3.3	16.3	14.2	14.0	9.3	8.8	8.6
Age									
18–44 years	4.0	4.0	3.4	15.3	12.3	11.9	9.9	8.4	8.5
18–24 years	4.8	4.6	3.5	11.0	8.2	8.3	8.1	6.2	5.1
25–44 years	3.8	3.8	3.4	16.6	13.7	13.2	10.5	9.2	9.7
45–64 years	3.6	3.7	3.7	19.3	17.8	17.3	9.7	10.8	9.8
45–54 years	4.1	3.9	3.7	19.7	17.4	16.9	10.4	11.7	10.4
55–64 years	2.9	3.4	3.7	18.5	18.4	17.7	8.7	9.6	9.0
65 years and over	2.7	3.0	2.3	14.5	13.2	13.9	6.3	6.1	6.6
65–74 years	3.1	3.4	2.8	15.6	14.2	15.4	7.2	7.0	7.6
75 years and over	2.2	2.4	1.7	13.2	12.0	12.2	5.2	5.0	5.3
Sex[3]									
Male	2.6	2.3	2.0	11.5	10.3	10.0	8.5	7.9	7.6
Female	4.7	5.0	4.5	20.8	17.6	17.5	10.0	9.6	9.5
Sex and age									
Male:									
18–44 years	2.7	2.5	2.3	10.8	8.9	8.4	9.0	7.7	7.5
45–54 years	2.7	2.1	2.0	13.4	12.3	12.3	9.7	10.7	9.8
55–64 years	1.9	2.4	*1.8	12.9	13.3	12.5	8.2	7.7	7.7
65–74 years	2.8	*2.3	*1.6	11.8	11.3	11.1	6.5	7.1	6.7
75 years and over	*2.0	*1.7	*	9.4	9.6	10.0	4.4	4.3	4.4
Female:									
18–44 years	5.3	5.4	4.5	19.7	15.6	15.4	10.8	9.2	9.5
45–54 years	5.4	5.5	5.4	25.8	22.3	21.3	11.1	12.6	11.0
55–64 years	3.9	4.4	5.4	23.6	23.1	22.6	9.1	11.3	10.3
65–74 years	3.4	4.4	3.7	18.6	16.7	18.9	7.7	7.0	8.4
75 years and over	2.3	2.9	2.3	15.6	13.5	13.5	5.7	5.5	5.9
Race[3,5]									
White only	3.7	3.7	3.3	16.6	14.5	14.1	9.4	9.1	8.9
Black or African American only	3.9	4.3	3.7	16.8	14.6	14.3	8.7	7.0	6.7
American Indian and Alaska Native only	*6.3	*	*	18.3	*8.3	15.4	*12.0	*	*9.5
Asian only	*2.2	*2.5	*	9.9	7.1	5.5	10.8	8.4	6.5
Native Hawaiian and Other Pacific Islander only	---	*	*	---	*	*	---	*	*
2 or more races	---	9.3	*5.5	---	19.2	14.5	---	8.8	12.0
Hispanic origin and race[3,5]									
Hispanic or Latino	2.8	2.3	2.8	10.0	8.6	8.5	6.3	6.8	6.2
Mexican	1.7	1.6	1.9	9.1	7.8	7.8	5.6	6.2	5.6
Not Hispanic or Latino	3.8	3.9	3.4	17.0	14.9	14.7	9.6	9.1	9.0
White only	3.9	3.9	3.4	17.4	15.4	15.2	9.7	9.6	9.5
Black or African American only	3.9	4.2	3.6	16.9	14.4	14.4	8.8	6.9	6.8
Education[6,7]									
25 years of age and over:									
No high school diploma or GED	4.4	3.5	3.8	15.9	12.5	11.6	7.8	6.3	6.3
High school diploma or GED	3.2	3.4	3.0	16.5	14.6	13.1	7.9	8.1	6.6
Some college or more	3.4	3.7	3.2	17.9	15.8	16.5	10.9	10.5	11.3

See footnotes at end of table.

Table 56 (page 2 of 2). Respiratory conditions among adults 18 years of age and over, according to selected characteristics: United States, selected years 1997–2003

[Data are based on household interviews of a sample of the civilian noninstitutionalized population]

Characteristic	Asthma attack[1]			Sinusitis[2]			Hay fever[2]		
	1997	2002	2003	1997	2002	2003	1997	2002	2003
	Percent of adults								
Poverty status[3,8]									
Poor	5.9	5.5	5.3	16.1	14.0	12.8	8.7	7.9	6.5
Near poor	4.4	3.9	4.1	15.5	14.7	13.5	8.6	7.7	8.2
Nonpoor	3.1	3.4	2.9	16.7	14.0	14.1	9.6	9.2	9.1
Hispanic origin and race and poverty status[3,5,8]									
Hispanic or Latino:									
Poor	3.3	3.7	3.5	8.1	8.4	8.0	5.4	6.9	5.3
Near poor	3.0	*2.0	*2.7	8.6	7.9	7.9	6.4	7.4	6.8
Nonpoor	2.4	1.9	2.7	11.5	9.2	9.1	6.9	6.6	6.4
Not Hispanic or Latino:									
White only:									
Poor	7.2	6.4	6.2	18.4	16.2	14.5	9.7	9.1	7.6
Near poor	4.6	4.7	4.4	17.0	16.8	15.4	9.4	8.5	9.0
Nonpoor	3.4	3.5	3.0	17.4	15.0	15.2	9.9	9.9	9.8
Black or African American only:									
Poor	6.0	5.6	5.9	18.9	15.8	14.5	9.2	7.3	6.0
Near poor	5.4	4.2	4.9	16.1	17.4	14.3	8.8	6.2	7.9
Nonpoor	2.2	3.6	2.3	16.5	12.6	14.3	8.8	6.9	6.4
Geographic region[3]									
Northeast	3.4	4.0	3.5	15.0	13.4	13.2	9.2	9.4	9.3
Midwest	3.7	4.0	3.5	15.7	13.0	14.1	8.6	7.7	8.0
South	3.7	3.3	3.0	19.6	16.6	16.1	8.7	7.7	7.4
West	3.9	4.0	3.4	12.6	11.3	10.3	11.1	11.5	10.8
Location of residence[3]									
Within MSA[9]	3.7	3.6	3.3	15.8	13.6	13.4	9.3	8.8	8.6
Outside MSA[9]	3.5	4.1	3.3	18.4	15.9	15.7	9.0	8.5	8.6

* Estimates are considered unreliable. Data preceded by an asterisk have a relative standard error (RSE) of 20–30 percent. Data not shown have an RSE of greater than 30 percent.

- - - Data not available.

[1]Only respondents who had ever been told by a doctor or other health professional that they had asthma were asked, "During the past 12 months, have you had an episode of asthma or an asthma attack?"

[2]Respondents were asked in two separate questions, "During the past 12 months, have you been told by a doctor or other health professional that you had sinusitis? ...hay fever?"

[3]Estimates are age adjusted to the year 2000 standard population using five age groups: 18–44 years, 45–54 years, 55–64 years, 65–74 years, and 75 years and over. Age-adjusted estimates in this table may differ from other age-adjusted estimates based on the same data and presented elsewhere if different age groups are used in the adjustment procedure. See Appendix II, Age adjustment.

[4]Includes all other races not shown separately.

[5]The race groups, white, black, American Indian and Alaska Native, Asian, Native Hawaiian and Other Pacific Islander, and 2 or more races, include persons of Hispanic and non-Hispanic origin. Persons of Hispanic origin may be of any race. Starting with data year 1999 race-specific estimates are tabulated according to 1997 Standards for Federal data on Race and Ethnicity and are not strictly comparable with estimates for earlier years. The five single race categories plus multiple race categories shown in the table conform to 1997 Standards. Starting with data year 1999, race-specific estimates are for persons who reported only one racial group; the category "2 or more races" includes persons who reported more than one racial group. Prior to data year 1999, data were tabulated according to 1977 Standards with four racial groups and the category "Asian only" included Native Hawaiian and Other Pacific Islander. Estimates for single race categories prior to 1999 included persons who reported one race or, if they reported more than one race, identified one race as best representing their race. See Appendix II, Race.

[6]Estimates are for persons 25 years of age and over and are age adjusted to the year 2000 standard population using five age groups: 25–44 years, 45–54 years, 55–64 years, 65–74 years, and 75 years and over. See Appendix II, Age adjustment.

[7]GED stands for General Educational Development high school equivalency diploma. See Appendix II, Education.

[8]Poor persons are defined as below the poverty threshold. Near poor persons have incomes of 100 percent to less than 200 percent of the poverty threshold. Nonpoor persons have incomes of 200 percent or greater than the poverty threshold. Missing family income data were imputed for 27 percent of persons 18 years of age and over in 1997, 34 percent in 2002, and 36 percent in 2003. See Appendix II, Family Income; Poverty level.

[9]MSA is metropolitan statistical area.

NOTES: Data for additional years are available. See Appendix III. Standard errors are available in the spreadsheet version of this table. See www.cdc.gov/nchs/hus.htm. Starting with *Health, United States, 2005*, estimates for 2000 and later years use weights derived from the 2000 census.

SOURCE: Centers for Disease Control and Prevention, National Center for Health Statistics, National Health Interview Survey, sample adult questionnaire.

Table 57 (page 1 of 2). Severe headache or migraine, low back pain, and neck pain among adults 18 years of age and over, according to selected characteristics: United States, selected years 1997–2003

[Data are based on household interviews of a sample of the civilian noninstitutionalized population]

Characteristic	Severe headache or migraine[1]			Low back pain[1]			Neck pain[1]		
	1997	*2002*	*2003*	*1997*	*2002*	*2003*	*1997*	*2002*	*2003*
	Percent of adults with pain during past 3 months								
Total, age-adjusted[2,3]	15.8	15.0	15.1	28.2	26.4	27.4	14.7	13.8	14.7
Total, crude[3]	16.0	15.1	15.2	28.1	26.4	27.5	14.6	13.8	14.8
Age									
18–44 years	18.7	17.6	17.8	26.1	23.7	24.2	13.3	11.9	12.5
18–24 years	18.7	17.3	16.8	21.9	20.8	19.6	9.8	7.7	9.1
25–44 years	18.7	17.6	18.1	27.3	24.6	25.8	14.3	13.3	13.7
45–64 years	15.8	15.2	15.1	31.3	29.8	31.5	17.0	16.9	18.2
45–54 years	17.8	17.0	16.5	31.3	29.2	30.2	17.3	17.2	17.9
55–64 years	12.7	12.5	13.1	31.2	30.8	33.4	16.6	16.5	18.5
65 years and over	7.0	6.6	6.9	29.5	28.8	29.9	15.0	14.1	15.1
65–74 years	8.2	7.9	7.9	30.2	28.9	30.8	15.0	14.1	15.6
75 years and over	5.4	5.2	5.7	28.6	28.8	28.9	15.0	14.0	14.5
Sex[2]									
Male	9.9	9.2	9.2	26.5	24.3	25.1	12.6	11.7	12.0
Female	21.4	20.6	20.7	29.6	28.3	29.4	16.6	15.7	17.1
Sex and age									
Male:									
18–44 years	11.9	10.7	10.8	24.8	22.1	22.4	11.6	10.4	10.3
45–54 years	10.3	10.3	9.7	29.4	27.6	29.3	13.9	13.8	14.7
55–64 years	8.8	8.4	8.5	30.7	27.9	30.5	14.6	12.7	15.2
65–74 years	5.0	4.1	5.8	29.0	25.9	25.6	13.6	13.2	12.5
75 years and over	*2.4	3.6	3.2	22.5	23.8	25.1	12.6	13.0	12.6
Female:									
18–44 years	25.4	24.3	24.6	27.3	25.2	26.0	14.9	13.4	14.7
45–54 years	24.9	23.5	22.9	33.1	30.7	31.1	20.6	20.4	21.0
55–64 years	16.3	16.3	17.5	31.7	33.4	36.1	18.4	20.0	21.6
65–74 years	10.7	11.0	9.6	31.1	31.3	35.0	16.1	14.9	18.2
75 years and over	7.4	6.1	7.4	32.4	31.9	31.4	16.5	14.7	15.8
Race[2,4]									
White only	15.9	15.2	15.1	28.7	26.9	27.9	15.1	14.1	15.2
Black or African American only	16.7	14.9	15.2	26.9	24.0	25.0	13.3	11.7	12.1
American Indian and Alaska Native only	18.9	24.8	28.6	33.3	34.3	32.2	16.2	*18.2	17.4
Asian only	11.7	8.4	11.9	21.0	19.2	19.7	9.2	8.1	9.1
Native Hawaiian and Other Pacific Islander only	- - -	*	*	- - -	*	*	- - -	*	*
2 or more races	- - -	27.0	23.2	- - -	34.0	34.9	- - -	22.3	20.5
Hispanic origin and race[2,4]									
Hispanic or Latino	15.5	13.5	15.9	26.4	24.2	26.5	13.9	13.5	14.6
Mexican	14.6	12.5	15.3	25.2	23.2	24.6	12.9	12.3	12.5
Not Hispanic or Latino	15.9	15.4	15.2	28.4	26.7	27.6	14.9	13.9	14.9
White only	16.1	15.6	15.3	29.1	27.4	28.4	15.4	14.4	15.6
Black or African American only	16.8	14.9	15.2	26.9	23.9	24.9	13.3	11.6	12.0
Education[5,6]									
25 years of age and over:									
No high school diploma or GED	19.2	17.9	17.7	33.6	31.6	31.6	16.5	16.4	17.0
High school diploma or GED	16.0	15.9	15.3	30.2	28.6	29.6	15.5	15.1	14.8
Some college or more	13.8	13.2	13.8	26.9	25.6	27.3	14.6	14.0	15.3

See footnotes at end of table.

Table 57 (page 2 of 2). Severe headache or migraine, low back pain, and neck pain among adults 18 years of age and over, according to selected characteristics: United States, selected years 1997–2003

[Data are based on household interviews of a sample of the civilian noninstitutionalized population]

Characteristic	*Severe headache or migraine*[1]			*Low back pain*[1]			*Neck pain*[1]		
	1997	*2002*	*2003*	*1997*	*2002*	*2003*	*1997*	*2002*	*2003*
Poverty status[2,7]	Percent of adults with pain during the past 3 months								
Poor	23.3	21.3	21.0	35.4	31.3	33.2	18.6	17.0	17.9
Near poor	18.9	17.6	18.7	30.8	30.0	30.6	16.1	15.9	16.3
Nonpoor	13.8	13.5	13.3	26.3	24.9	25.8	13.8	12.9	13.8
Hispanic origin and race and poverty status[2,4,7]									
Hispanic or Latino:									
Poor	18.9	19.3	19.8	29.5	28.3	29.7	16.4	18.5	16.1
Near poor	15.7	13.8	16.4	26.8	24.3	26.6	12.9	14.6	16.9
Nonpoor	13.4	11.5	13.8	24.3	22.7	25.3	13.3	11.3	12.9
Not Hispanic or Latino:									
White only:									
Poor	26.2	23.3	21.7	38.9	33.7	35.9	20.5	17.3	19.7
Near poor	20.1	20.0	21.0	33.3	33.2	33.0	18.0	17.7	18.0
Nonpoor	14.1	14.1	13.6	27.1	25.7	26.8	14.4	13.6	14.7
Black or African American only:									
Poor	22.7	20.2	21.0	34.5	30.1	31.2	17.9	14.2	16.0
Near poor	17.6	17.3	15.9	27.7	26.9	27.6	14.0	13.6	12.7
Nonpoor	13.4	11.9	12.5	23.1	20.6	22.0	10.9	10.1	10.3
Geographic region[2]									
Northeast	14.5	13.9	14.1	27.1	27.4	27.3	14.0	14.0	14.3
Midwest	15.6	15.1	14.9	28.7	27.6	29.0	15.3	13.4	15.2
South	17.1	15.4	15.6	27.5	24.5	25.1	13.9	13.2	13.5
West	15.3	15.2	15.6	30.0	27.6	29.5	16.1	15.2	16.5
Location of residence[2]									
Within MSA[8]	15.2	14.2	14.6	27.0	25.7	26.5	14.2	13.2	14.5
Outside MSA[8]	18.1	18.1	17.4	32.5	29.2	30.7	16.4	15.9	15.2

* Estimates are considered unreliable. Data preceded by an asterisk have a relative standard error (RSE) of 20–30 percent. Data not shown have an RSE of greater than 30 percent.

- - - Data not available.

[1]In three separate questions, respondents were asked, "During the past 3 months, did you have a severe headache or migraine? ...low back pain? ...neck pain?" Respondents were instructed to report pain that had lasted a whole day or more and, conversely, not to report fleeting or minor aches or pains. Persons may be represented in more than one column.

[2]Estimates are age adjusted to the year 2000 standard population using five age groups: 18–44 years, 45–54 years, 55–64 years, 65–74 years, and 75 years and over. Age-adjusted estimates in this table may differ from other age-adjusted estimates based on the same data and presented elsewhere if different age groups are used in the adjustment procedure. See Appendix II, Age adjustment.

[3]Includes all other races not shown separately.

[4]The race groups, white, black, American Indian and Alaska Native, Asian, Native Hawaiian and Other Pacific Islander, and 2 or more races, include persons of Hispanic and non-Hispanic origin. Persons of Hispanic origin may be of any race. Starting with data year 1999 race-specific estimates are tabulated according to 1997 Standards for Federal data on Race and Ethnicity and are not strictly comparable with estimates for earlier years. The five single race categories plus multiple race categories shown in the table conform to 1997 Standards. Starting with data year 1999, race-specific estimates are for persons who reported only one racial group; the category "2 or more races" includes persons who reported more than one racial group. Prior to data year 1999, data were tabulated according to 1977 Standards with four racial groups and the category "Asian only" included Native Hawaiian and Other Pacific Islander. Estimates for single race categories prior to 1999 included persons who reported one race or, if they reported more than one race, identified one race as best representing their race. See Appendix II, Race.

[5]Estimates are for persons 25 years of age and over and are age adjusted to the year 2000 standard population using five age groups: 25–44 years, 45–54 years, 55–64 years, 65–74 years, and 75 years and over. See Appendix II, Age adjustment.

[6]GED stands for General Educational Development high school equivalency diploma. See Appendix II, Education.

[7]Poor persons are defined as below the poverty threshold. Near poor persons have incomes of 100 percent to less than 200 percent of the poverty threshold. Nonpoor persons have incomes of 200 percent or greater than the poverty threshold. Missing family income data were imputed for 27 percent of persons 18 years of age and over in 1997, 34 percent in 2002, and 36 percent in 2003. See Appendix II, Family Income; Poverty level.

[8]MSA is metropolitan statistical area.

NOTES: Data for additional years are available. See Appendix III. Standard errors are available in the spreadsheet version of this table. See www.cdc.gov/nchs/hus.htm. Starting with *Health, United States, 2005*, estimates for 2000 and later years use weights derived from the 2000 census.

SOURCE: Centers for Disease Control and Prevention, National Center for Health Statistics, National Health Interview Survey, sample adult questionnaire.

Table 58 (page 1 of 3). Limitation of activity caused by chronic conditions, according to selected characteristics: United States, selected years 1997–2003

[Data are based on household interviews of a sample of the civilian noninstitutionalized population]

Characteristic	1997	2001	2002	2003
All ages	Percent of persons with any activity limitation[1]			
Total[2,3]	13.3	12.1	12.3	12.1
Age				
Under 18 years	6.6	6.8	7.1	6.9
Under 5 years	3.5	3.3	3.2	3.6
5–17 years	7.8	8.0	8.5	8.1
18–44 years	7.0	6.0	6.2	6.0
18–24 years	5.1	4.6	4.3	4.1
25–44 years	7.6	6.5	6.8	6.6
45–54 years	14.2	13.1	13.8	13.0
55–64 years	22.2	20.7	21.1	21.1
65 years and over	38.7	34.6	34.5	34.6
65–74 years	30.0	26.0	25.2	26.3
75 years and over	50.2	44.7	45.2	44.0
Sex[3]				
Male	13.1	12.2	12.3	11.9
Female	13.4	11.9	12.3	12.2
Race[3,4]				
White only	13.1	11.8	12.1	11.8
Black or African American only	17.1	15.6	14.9	15.3
American Indian and Alaska Native only	23.1	18.9	19.5	21.2
Asian only	7.5	6.7	6.4	6.4
Native Hawaiian and Other Pacific Islander only	---	*	*	*
2 or more races	---	19.8	22.0	20.2
Black or African American; White	---	14.8	*8.3	*16.8
American Indian and Alaska Native; White	---	22.0	30.0	24.8
Hispanic origin and race[3,4]				
Hispanic or Latino	12.8	10.5	10.7	10.2
Mexican	12.5	10.3	10.8	9.7
Not Hispanic or Latino	13.5	12.4	12.6	12.4
White only	13.2	12.1	12.4	12.2
Black or African American only	17.0	15.5	15.0	15.4
Poverty status[3,5]				
Poor	25.4	22.3	22.9	23.1
Near poor	17.9	17.1	17.4	17.0
Nonpoor	10.1	9.5	9.5	9.2
Hispanic origin and race and poverty status[3,4,5]				
Hispanic or Latino:				
Poor	19.2	16.2	16.3	15.5
Near poor	12.7	10.9	12.2	9.9
Nonpoor	9.2	7.9	7.7	8.2
Not Hispanic or Latino:				
White only:				
Poor	27.8	24.8	25.4	26.2
Near poor	19.2	18.8	19.5	19.3
Nonpoor	10.4	9.7	9.7	9.4
Black or African American only:				
Poor	28.2	24.8	25.0	26.1
Near poor	19.5	20.1	17.9	19.0
Nonpoor	10.7	10.0	10.0	9.7
Geographic region[3]				
Northeast	13.0	11.1	11.8	11.3
Midwest	13.1	13.3	13.1	13.3
South	13.9	12.3	12.6	12.4
West	13.0	11.5	11.5	11.1
Location of residence[3]				
Within MSA[6]	12.7	11.3	11.4	11.2
Outside MSA[6]	15.5	15.3	15.9	15.7

See footnotes at end of table.

Table 58 (page 2 of 3). Limitation of activity caused by chronic conditions, according to selected characteristics: United States, selected years 1997–2003

[Data are based on household interviews of a sample of the civilian noninstitutionalized population]

Characteristic	1997	2001	2002	2003	1997	2001	2002	2003
65 years of age and over	Percent with ADL limitation[7]				Percent with IADL limitation[7]			
All adults 65 years of age and over[2,8]	6.7	6.4	6.1	6.4	13.7	12.6	12.2	12.2
Age								
65–74 years	3.4	3.4	2.7	3.1	6.9	6.7	6.0	6.5
75 years and over	10.4	9.6	9.8	9.9	21.2	18.9	19.1	18.4
Sex[8]								
Male	5.2	6.0	4.7	5.2	9.1	9.6	7.8	8.6
Female	7.7	6.5	7.0	7.2	16.9	14.6	15.2	14.6
Race[4,8]								
White only	6.3	5.7	5.6	5.9	13.1	11.8	11.5	11.5
Black or African American only	11.7	11.8	10.0	10.5	21.3	18.8	18.5	19.2
American Indian and Alaska Native only	*	*	*	*	*	*	*	*
Asian only	*	*9.2	*	*	*9.1	15.9	*11.2	*11.8
Native Hawaiian and Other Pacific Islander only	- - -	*	*	*	- - -	*	*	*
2 or more races	- - -	*	*	*	- - -	*16.0	*20.8	*20.4
Hispanic origin and race[4,8]								
Hispanic or Latino	10.8	11.2	9.2	10.3	16.3	17.0	13.1	13.8
Mexican	11.4	10.6	10.2	9.8	18.8	17.0	14.0	15.1
Not Hispanic or Latino	6.5	6.1	5.9	6.1	13.6	12.3	12.2	12.1
White only	6.1	5.5	5.5	5.7	13.0	11.6	11.5	11.4
Black or African American only	11.7	11.9	10.1	10.4	21.2	18.8	18.7	19.0
Poverty status[5,8]								
Poor	12.5	11.2	9.5	10.4	25.3	22.9	21.1	21.6
Near poor	7.4	7.5	6.9	7.0	15.8	14.9	14.7	15.0
Nonpoor	5.3	5.0	5.1	5.5	10.4	9.7	9.5	9.4
Hispanic origin and race and poverty status[4,5,8]								
Hispanic or Latino:								
Poor	16.0	13.5	12.5	*15.2	25.5	24.0	17.3	20.1
Near poor	11.1	11.3	10.0	*8.4	15.5	16.4	15.6	12.3
Nonpoor	*6.6	8.8	*6.7	*8.5	10.2	12.2	8.7	*11.1
Not Hispanic or Latino:								
White only:								
Poor	11.8	9.9	8.2	8.9	24.9	23.0	20.4	20.7
Near poor	6.6	6.5	6.3	6.4	15.2	14.1	14.2	14.8
Nonpoor	5.0	4.6	4.8	5.1	10.3	9.2	9.2	9.0
Black or African American only:								
Poor	13.5	15.9	13.8	14.0	27.8	25.8	26.6	28.3
Near poor	12.4	12.3	*9.8	10.4	22.4	18.6	19.3	18.9
Nonpoor	9.8	9.3	8.1	8.4	15.1	14.9	13.4	13.9

See footnotes at end of table.

Table 58 (page 3 of 3). Limitation of activity caused by chronic conditions, according to selected characteristics: United States, selected years 1997–2003

[Data are based on household interviews of a sample of the civilian noninstitutionalized population]

Characteristic	*1997*	*2001*	*2002*	*2003*	*1997*	*2001*	*2002*	*2003*
Geographic region[8]	Percent with ADL limitation[7]				Percent with IADL limitation[7]			
Northeast	6.1	6.5	6.3	6.6	12.2	11.3	11.0	11.4
Midwest	5.8	4.9	5.2	4.7	13.1	12.6	11.7	11.3
South	8.2	7.5	6.3	7.2	15.8	13.3	13.0	13.1
West	5.9	6.0	6.5	6.5	12.4	12.6	12.7	12.1
Location of residence[8]								
Within MSA[6]	6.6	6.1	6.2	6.3	13.5	12.2	12.1	12.0
Outside MSA[6]	7.2	7.3	5.6	6.7	14.4	13.8	12.6	12.8

* Estimates are considered unreliable. Data preceded by an asterisk have a relative standard error (RSE) of 20–30 percent. Data not shown have an RSE of greater than 30 percent.

- - - Data not available.

[1]Limitation of activity is assessed by asking respondents a series of questions about limitations in their ability to perform activities usual for their age group because of a physical, mental, or emotional problem. The category limitation of activity includes limitations in personal care (ADL), routine needs (IADL), and other limitations due to a chronic condition. See Appendix II, Limitation of activity; Activities of daily living; Condition; Instrumental activities of daily living.

[2]Includes all other races not shown separately.

[3]Estimates for all persons are age adjusted to the year 2000 standard population using six age groups: Under 18 years, 18–44 years, 45–54 years, 55–64 years, 65–74 years, and 75 years and over. Age-adjusted estimates in this table may differ from other age-adjusted estimates based on the same data and presented elsewhere if different age groups are used in the adjustment procedure. See Appendix II, Age adjustment.

[4]The race groups, white, black, American Indian and Alaska Native, Asian, Native Hawaiian and Other Pacific Islander, and 2 or more races, include persons of Hispanic and non-Hispanic origin. Persons of Hispanic origin may be of any race. Starting with data year 1999 race-specific estimates are tabulated according to 1997 Standards for Federal data on Race and Ethnicity and are not strictly comparable with estimates for earlier years. The five single race categories plus multiple race categories shown in the table conform to 1997 Standards. Starting with data year 1999 race-specific estimates are for persons who reported only one racial group; the category "2 or more races" includes persons who reported more than one racial group. Prior to data year 1999, data were tabulated according to 1977 Standards with four racial groups and the category "Asian only" included Native Hawaiian and Other Pacific Islander. Estimates for single race categories prior to 1999 included persons who reported one race or, if they reported more than one race, identified one race as best representing their race. See Appendix II, Race.

[5]Poor persons are defined as below the poverty threshold. Near poor persons have incomes of 100 percent to less than 200 percent of the poverty threshold. Nonpoor persons have incomes of 200 percent or greater than the poverty threshold. Missing family income data were imputed for 25 percent of persons in 1997 and 32–35 percent in 1999–2003. See Appendix II, Family income; Poverty level.

[6]MSA is metropolitan statistical area.

[7]These estimates are for noninstitutionalized older persons. ADL is activities of daily living and IADL is instrumental activities of daily living. Respondents were asked about needing the help of another person with personal care (ADL) and routine needs such as chores and shopping (IADL) because of a physical, mental, or emotional problem. See Appendix II, Activities of daily living; Condition; Instrumental activities of daily living.

[8]Estimates are age adjusted to the year 2000 standard population using two age groups: 65–74 years and 75 years and over. See Appendix II, Age adjustment.

NOTES: Standard errors for selected years are available in the spreadsheet version of this table. See www.cdc.gov/nchs/hus.htm. Data for additional years are available. See Appendix III. Starting with *Health, United States, 2005*, estimates for 2000 and later years use weights derived from the 2000 census. Estimates for 2000–2002 were recalculated using 2000-based weights and may differ from previous editions of *Health, United States*.

SOURCE: Centers for Disease Control and Prevention, National Center for Health Statistics, National Health Interview Survey, family core questionnaire.

Table 59 (page 1 of 2). Vision and hearing limitations among adults 18 years of age and over, according to selected characteristics: United States, selected years 1997–2003

[Data are based on household interviews of a sample of the civilian noninstitutionalized population]

Characteristic	*Any trouble seeing, even with glasses or contacts*[1]				*A lot of trouble hearing or deaf*[2]			
	1997	*2000*	*2002*	*2003*	*1997*	*2000*	*2002*	*2003*
	Percent of adults							
Total, age-adjusted[3,4]	10.0	9.0	9.3	8.8	3.2	3.2	3.2	3.1
Total, crude[4]	9.8	8.9	9.3	8.7	3.1	3.1	3.1	3.0
Age								
18–44 years	6.2	5.3	5.6	5.2	1.0	0.9	0.9	0.9
18–24 years	5.4	4.2	4.4	5.1	*0.5	*0.7	*	*
25–44 years	6.5	5.7	6.0	5.2	1.2	1.0	1.1	1.0
45–64 years	12.0	10.7	11.0	10.6	3.1	3.0	2.8	2.8
45–54 years	12.2	10.9	11.5	10.5	2.6	2.3	1.9	1.9
55–64 years	11.6	10.5	10.3	10.7	3.9	4.0	4.2	4.1
65 years and over	18.1	17.4	17.6	16.6	9.8	10.5	11.1	10.5
65–74 years	14.2	13.6	14.5	13.1	6.6	7.4	7.2	6.7
75 years and over	23.1	21.9	21.1	20.6	14.1	14.3	15.6	14.9
Sex[3]								
Male	8.8	7.9	8.1	7.3	4.2	4.3	4.2	4.0
Female	11.1	10.1	10.4	10.1	2.4	2.3	2.4	2.3
Sex and age								
Male:								
18–44 years	5.3	4.4	4.8	4.1	1.2	1.1	1.0	1.1
45–54 years	10.1	8.8	10.1	8.6	3.6	2.9	2.2	2.7
55–64 years	10.5	9.5	8.7	8.6	5.4	6.2	5.8	5.4
65–74 years	13.2	12.8	13.3	11.8	9.4	10.8	10.8	10.2
75 years and over	21.4	20.7	18.6	18.1	17.7	18.0	19.7	17.8
Female:								
18–44 years	7.1	6.2	6.5	6.2	0.9	0.8	0.7	0.7
45–54 years	14.2	12.8	12.9	12.3	1.7	1.8	1.5	1.2
55–64 years	12.6	11.5	11.9	12.5	2.6	1.9	2.7	2.8
65–74 years	15.0	14.4	15.5	14.1	4.4	4.5	4.1	3.8
75 years and over	24.2	22.7	22.6	22.3	11.7	12.1	13.0	12.9
Race[3,5]								
White only	9.7	8.8	9.0	8.5	3.4	3.4	3.3	3.3
Black or African American only	12.8	10.6	11.7	10.8	2.0	1.6	1.6	1.7
American Indian and Alaska Native only	19.2	16.6	*11.1	18.9	14.1	*	*10.1	*
Asian only	6.2	6.3	7.2	6.1	*	*2.4	*2.3	*
Native Hawaiian and Other Pacific Islander only	- - -	*	*	*	- - -	*	*	*
2 or more races	- - -	16.2	14.9	11.6	- - -	*5.7	*6.3	*
Hispanic origin and race[3,5]								
Hispanic or Latino	10.0	9.7	9.0	9.1	1.5	2.3	2.0	2.0
Mexican	10.2	8.3	8.6	9.0	1.8	3.0	3.0	2.6
Not Hispanic or Latino	10.0	9.1	9.4	8.8	3.3	3.3	3.3	3.2
White only	9.8	8.9	9.1	8.6	3.5	3.5	3.5	3.4
Black or African American only	12.8	10.6	11.8	10.7	2.0	1.6	1.6	1.8
Education[6,7]								
25 years of age and over:								
No high school diploma or GED	15.0	12.2	14.4	12.6	4.8	4.6	4.6	4.9
High school diploma or GED	10.6	9.5	10.3	9.3	3.7	3.9	3.9	3.5
Some college or more	8.9	8.9	8.7	8.1	2.9	2.8	3.3	2.8

See footnotes at end of table.

Table 59 (page 2 of 2). Vision and hearing limitations among adults 18 years of age and over, according to selected characteristics: United States, selected years 1997–2003

[Data are based on household interviews of a sample of the civilian noninstitutionalized population]

Characteristic	Any trouble seeing, even with glasses or contacts[1]				A lot of trouble hearing or deaf[2]			
	1997	2000	2002	2003	1997	2000	2002	2003
	Percent of adults							
Poverty status[3,5]								
Poor	17.0	12.9	14.5	13.7	4.5	3.7	4.4	3.9
Near poor	12.9	11.6	12.0	11.6	3.6	4.2	3.6	3.6
Nonpoor	8.2	7.8	8.0	7.3	3.0	2.8	3.0	2.8
Hispanic origin and race and poverty status[3,5,8]								
Hispanic or Latino:								
Poor	12.8	11.0	12.9	12.4	*1.9	3.3	*2.3	*3.4
Near poor	11.2	9.4	9.4	10.3	*1.5	*2.3	*1.7	*1.6
Nonpoor	7.8	9.7	7.2	6.7	*1.2	*1.7	*1.9	*1.4
Not Hispanic or Latino:								
White only:								
Poor	17.9	13.1	14.7	14.3	5.8	4.5	5.2	4.7
Near poor	13.1	12.0	12.7	11.8	4.3	5.0	4.5	4.2
Nonpoor	8.2	7.8	7.9	7.3	3.2	3.0	3.1	3.1
Black or African American only:								
Poor	17.9	13.6	16.6	14.2	3.3	*1.6	*2.3	*2.1
Near poor	16.0	12.9	14.6	13.0	*2.0	*2.0	*	*2.3
Nonpoor	8.5	8.1	9.1	8.5	*	*	*1.6	*
Geographic region[3]								
Northeast	8.6	7.4	7.8	7.5	2.2	2.4	2.7	2.9
Midwest	9.5	9.6	9.3	9.3	3.5	3.5	3.1	3.3
South	11.4	9.2	9.9	9.4	3.5	3.3	3.3	3.0
West	9.7	9.9	9.7	8.1	3.4	3.5	3.8	3.2
Location of residence[3]								
Within MSA[9]	9.5	8.5	8.7	8.2	2.9	3.0	3.0	2.7
Outside MSA[9]	12.0	11.1	11.5	10.7	4.5	3.9	3.8	4.4

* Estimates are considered unreliable. Data preceded by an asterisk have a relative standard error (RSE) of 20–30 percent. Data not shown have an RSE of greater than 30 percent.
- - - Data not available.
[1]Respondents were asked, "Do you have any trouble seeing, even when wearing glasses or contact lenses?" In 2003, 0.4 percent of adults 18 years of age and over identified themselves as blind.
[2]Respondents were asked, "Which statement best describes your hearing without a hearing aid: good, a little trouble, a lot of trouble, or deaf?" For this table, "a lot of trouble" and "deaf" are combined into one category.
In 2003, 0.3 percent of adults 18 years of age and over identified themselves as deaf.
[3]Estimates are age adjusted to the year 2000 standard population using five age groups: 18–44 years, 45–54 years, 55–64 years, 65–74 years, and 75 years and over. Age-adjusted estimates in this table may differ from other age-adjusted estimates based on the same data and presented elsewhere if different age groups are used in the adjustment procedure. See Appendix II, Age adjustment.
[4]Includes all other races not shown separately.
[5]The race groups, white, black, American Indian and Alaska Native, Asian, Native Hawaiian and Other Pacific Islander, and 2 or more races, include persons of Hispanic and non-Hispanic origin. Persons of Hispanic origin may be of any race. Starting with data year 1999 race-specific estimates are tabulated according to 1997 Standards for Federal data on Race and Ethnicity and are not strictly comparable with estimates for earlier years. The five single race categories plus multiple race categories shown in the table conform to 1997 Standards. Starting with data year 1999, race-specific estimates are for persons who reported only one racial group; the category "2 or more races" includes persons who reported more than one racial group. Prior to data year 1999, data were tabulated according to 1977 Standards with four racial groups and the category "Asian only" included Native Hawaiian and Other Pacific Islander. Estimates for single race categories prior to 1999 included persons who reported one race or, if they reported more than one race, identified one race as best representing their race. See Appendix II, Race.
[6]Estimates are for persons 25 years of age and over and are age adjusted to the year 2000 standard population using five age groups: 25–44 years, 45–54 years, 55–64 years, 65–74 years, and 75 years and over. See Appendix II, Age adjustment.
[7]GED stands for General Educational Development high school equivalency diploma. See Appendix II, Education.
[8]Poor persons are defined as below the poverty threshold. Near poor persons have incomes of 100 percent to less than 200 percent of the poverty threshold. Nonpoor persons have incomes of 200 percent or greater than the poverty threshold. Missing family income data were imputed for 27 percent of persons 18 years of age and over in 1997, 34 percent in 2000 and 2002, and 36 percent in 2003. See Appendix II, Family Income; Poverty level.
[9]MSA is metropolitan statistical area.

NOTES: Data for additional years are available. See Appendix III. Standard errors are available in the spreadsheet version of this table. See www.cdc.gov/nchs/hus.htm. Starting with *Health, United States, 2005,* estimates for 2000 and later years use weights derived from the 2000 census.

SOURCE: Centers for Disease Control and Prevention, National Center for Health Statistics, National Health Interview Survey, sample adult questionnaire.

Table 60 (page 1 of 2). Respondent-assessed health status according to selected characteristics: United States, selected years 1991–2003

[Data are based on household interviews of a sample of the civilian noninstitutionalized population]

Characteristic	1991[1]	1995[1]	1997	1999	2000	2001	2002	2003
	Percent of persons with fair or poor health[2]							
Total[3,4]	10.4	10.6	9.2	8.9	9.0	9.2	9.3	9.2
Age								
Under 18 years	2.6	2.6	2.1	1.6	1.7	1.8	1.9	1.8
Under 6 years	2.7	2.7	1.9	1.4	1.5	1.6	1.6	1.4
6–17 years	2.6	2.5	2.1	1.8	1.8	1.9	2.1	2.0
18–44 years	6.1	6.6	5.3	5.1	5.1	5.4	5.5	5.6
18–24 years	4.8	4.5	3.4	3.4	3.3	3.3	3.6	3.8
25–44 years	6.4	7.2	5.9	5.6	5.7	6.0	6.2	6.3
45–54 years	13.4	13.4	11.7	11.5	11.9	11.8	12.7	12.1
55–64 years	20.7	21.4	18.2	18.5	17.9	19.1	17.9	18.9
65 years and over	29.0	28.3	26.7	26.1	26.9	26.5	26.3	25.5
65–74 years	26.0	25.6	23.1	22.7	22.5	22.9	22.0	22.3
75 years and over	33.6	32.2	31.5	30.2	32.1	30.7	31.3	29.2
Sex[3]								
Male	10.0	10.1	8.8	8.6	8.8	9.0	8.9	8.8
Female	10.8	11.1	9.7	9.2	9.3	9.5	9.6	9.5
Race[3,5]								
White only	9.6	9.7	8.3	8.0	8.2	8.2	8.5	8.5
Black or African American only	16.8	17.2	15.8	14.6	14.6	15.4	14.1	14.7
American Indian and Alaska Native only	18.3	18.7	17.3	14.7	17.2	14.5	13.2	16.3
Asian only	7.8	9.3	7.8	8.6	7.4	8.1	6.7	7.4
Native Hawaiian and Other Pacific Islander only	---	---	---	*	*	*	*	*
2 or more races	---	---	---	12.9	16.2	13.9	12.5	14.7
Black or African American; White	---	---	---	*20.5	*14.5	*10.1	13.8	21.4
American Indian and Alaska Native; White	---	---	---	14.5	18.7	15.0	13.5	18.1
Hispanic origin and race[3,5]								
Hispanic or Latino	15.6	15.1	13.0	11.9	12.8	12.6	13.1	13.9
Mexican	17.0	16.7	13.1	12.3	12.8	12.4	13.3	13.7
Not Hispanic or Latino	#	#	8.9	8.6	8.7	8.9	8.9	8.7
White only	9.1	9.1	8.0	7.7	7.9	7.9	8.2	7.9
Black or African American only	16.8	17.3	15.8	14.6	14.6	15.5	14.0	14.6
Poverty status[3,6]								
Poor	22.8	23.7	20.8	20.6	19.6	20.2	20.3	20.4
Near poor	14.7	15.5	13.9	14.0	14.1	14.5	14.6	14.4
Nonpoor	6.8	6.7	6.1	6.0	6.3	6.4	6.4	6.1
Hispanic origin and race and poverty status[3,5,6]								
Hispanic or Latino:								
Poor	23.6	22.7	19.9	18.3	18.7	18.6	20.8	20.6
Near poor	18.0	16.9	13.5	13.8	15.3	14.7	15.4	15.5
Nonpoor	9.3	8.7	8.5	8.0	8.4	8.7	8.7	9.8
Not Hispanic or Latino:								
White only:								
Poor	21.9	22.8	19.7	19.4	18.8	19.1	19.1	19.5
Near poor	14.0	14.8	13.3	13.5	13.4	13.6	14.3	13.9
Nonpoor	6.4	6.2	5.6	5.7	5.8	5.9	6.0	5.6
Black or African American only:								
Poor	25.8	27.7	25.3	25.9	23.8	24.9	24.5	24.4
Near poor	17.0	19.3	19.2	17.5	18.2	19.6	17.4	18.6
Nonpoor	10.9	9.9	9.7	8.3	9.7	9.9	8.8	9.1

See footnotes at end of table.

Table 60 (page 2 of 2). Respondent-assessed health status according to selected characteristics: United States, selected years 1991–2003

[Data are based on household interviews of a sample of the civilian noninstitutionalized population]

Characteristic	1991[1]	1995[1]	1997	1999	2000	2001	2002	2003
Geographic region[3]	Percent of persons with fair or poor health[2]							
Northeast	8.3	9.1	8.0	7.5	7.6	7.4	8.1	8.2
Midwest	9.1	9.7	8.1	8.0	8.0	8.8	8.3	8.3
South	13.1	12.3	10.8	10.5	10.7	10.8	10.9	10.7
West	9.7	10.1	8.8	8.7	8.8	8.5	8.7	8.4
Location of residence[3]								
Within MSA[7]	9.9	10.1	8.7	8.3	8.5	8.7	8.7	8.6
Outside MSA[7]	11.9	12.6	11.1	11.1	11.1	11.0	11.7	11.5

* Estimates are considered unreliable. Data preceded by an asterisk have an relative standard error (RSE) of 20–30 percent. Data not shown have an RSE of greater than 30 percent.
- - - Data not available.
#Estimates calculated upon request.
[1]Data prior to 1997 are not strictly comparable with data for later years due to the 1997 questionnaire redesign. See Appendix I, National Health Interview Survey.
[2]See Appendix II, Health status, respondent-assessed.
[3]Estimates are age adjusted to the year 2000 standard population using six age groups: Under 18 years, 18–44 years, 45–54 years, 55–64 years, 65–74 years, and 75 years and over. See Appendix II, Age adjustment.
[4]Includes all other races not shown separately.
[5]The race groups, white, black, American Indian and Alaska Native, Asian, Native Hawaiian and Other Pacific Islander, and 2 or more races, include persons of Hispanic and non-Hispanic origin. Persons of Hispanic origin may be of any race. Starting with data year 1999 race-specific estimates are tabulated according to 1997 Standards for Federal data on Race and Ethnicity and are not strictly comparable with estimates for earlier years. The five single race categories plus multiple race categories shown in the table conform to 1997 Standards. Starting with data year 1999 race-specific estimates are for persons who reported only one racial group; the category "2 or more races" includes persons who reported more than one racial group. Prior to data year 1999, data were tabulated according to 1977 Standards with four racial groups and the category "Asian only" included Native Hawaiian and Other Pacific Islander. Estimates for single race categories prior to 1999 included persons who reported one race or, if they reported more than one race, identified one race as best representing their race. See Appendix II, Race.
[6]Poor persons are defined as below the poverty threshold. Near poor persons have incomes of 100 percent to less than 200 percent of the poverty threshold. Nonpoor persons have incomes of 200 percent or greater than the poverty threshold. Missing family income data were imputed for 16–18 percent of persons in 1991 and 1995, 25–29 percent of persons in 1997–98, and 32–35 percent in 1999–2003. See Appendix II, Family income; Poverty level.
[7]MSA is metropolitan statistical area.

NOTES: Standard errors for selected years are available in the spreadsheet version of this table. See www.cdc.gov/nchs/hus.htm. Data for additional years are available. See Appendix III. Starting with *Health, United States, 2005*, estimates for 2000 and later years use weights derived from the 2000 census. Estimates for 2000–2002 were recalculated using 2000-based weights and may differ from previous editions of *Health, United States*.

SOURCE: Centers for Disease Control and Prevention, National Center for Health Statistics, National Health Interview Survey, family core questionnaire.

Table 61 (page 1 of 2). Serious psychological distress among persons 18 years of age and over according to selected characteristics: United States, average annual 1997–98, 2000–2001, and 2002–03

[Data are based on household interviews of a sample of the civilian noninstitutionalized population]

Characteristic	1997–98	2000–2001	2002–03
	Percent of persons with serious psychological distress[1]		
Total, age adjusted[2,3]	3.2	3.2	3.1
Total, crude[3]	3.2	3.2	3.1
Age			
18–44 years	2.9	3.1	2.9
18–24 years	2.7	2.7	2.8
25–44 years	3.0	3.2	2.9
45–64 years	3.7	3.7	4.0
45–54 years	3.9	3.7	4.2
55–64 years	3.4	3.8	3.6
65 years and over	3.1	2.7	2.3
65–74 years	2.5	2.8	2.3
75 years and over	3.8	2.5	2.3
Sex[2]			
Male	2.5	2.4	2.3
Female	3.8	3.9	3.9
Race[2,4]			
White only	3.1	3.1	3.0
Black or African American only	4.0	3.5	3.4
American Indian and Alaska Native only	7.8	*9.3	*7.1
Asian only	2.0	*	*1.9
Native Hawaiian and Other Pacific Islander only	- - -	*	*
2 or more races	- - -	5.2	7.3
Hispanic origin and race[2,4]			
Hispanic or Latino	5.0	4.2	3.9
Mexican	5.2	4.0	3.7
Not Hispanic or Latino	3.0	3.1	3.1
White only	2.9	3.1	3.0
Black or African American only	3.9	3.5	3.2
Poverty status[2,5]			
Poor	9.1	8.3	8.7
Near poor	5.0	5.3	5.4
Nonpoor	1.8	2.0	1.8
Hispanic origin and race and poverty status[2,4,5]			
Hispanic or Latino:			
Poor	8.6	7.2	7.4
Near poor	5.4	4.4	3.8
Nonpoor	2.9	2.8	2.4
Not Hispanic or Latino:			
White only:			
Poor	9.6	9.4	10.1
Near poor	5.2	6.1	6.4
Nonpoor	1.8	2.0	1.7
Black or African American only:			
Poor	8.7	7.3	7.3
Near poor	4.3	4.9	*4.0
Nonpoor	1.6	*1.6	*1.3

See footnotes at end of table.

Table 61 (page 2 of 2). Serious psychological distress among persons 18 years of age and over according to selected characteristics: United States, average annual 1997–98, 2000–2001, and 2002–03

[Data are based on household interviews of a sample of the civilian noninstitutionalized population]

Characteristic	1997–98	2000–2001	2002–03
Geographic region[2]	Percent of persons with serious psychological distress[1]		
Northeast	2.7	3.1	3.0
Midwest	2.6	3.0	2.7
South	3.8	3.4	3.5
West	3.3	3.2	3.0
Location of residence[2]			
Within MSA[6]	3.0	3.1	2.9
Outside MSA[6]	3.9	3.5	3.9

* Estimates are considered unreliable. Data preceded by an asterisk have a relative standard error (RSE) of 20–30 percent. Data not shown have an RSE of greater than 30 percent.
- - - Data not available.
[1]Serious psychological distress is measured by a six-question scale that asks respondents how often they experience each of six symptoms of psychological distress. See Appendix II, Serious psychological distress.
[2]Estimates are age adjusted to the year 2000 standard population using five age groups: 18–44 years, 45–54 years, 55–64 years, 65–74 years, and 75 years and over. See Appendix II, Age adjustment.
[3]Includes all other races not shown separately.
[4]The race groups, white, black, American Indian and Alaska Native, Asian, Native Hawaiian and Other Pacific Islander, and 2 or more races, include persons of Hispanic and non-Hispanic origin. Persons of Hispanic origin may be of any race. Starting with data year 1999 race-specific estimates are tabulated according to 1997 Standards for Federal data on Race and Ethnicity and are not strictly comparable with estimates for earlier years. The five single race categories plus multiple race categories shown in the table conform to 1997 Standards. Starting with data year 1999, race-specific estimates are for persons who reported only one racial group; the category "2 or more races" includes persons who reported more than one racial group. Prior to data year 1999, data were tabulated according to 1977 Standards with four racial groups and the category "Asian only" included Native Hawaiian and Other Pacific Islander. Estimates for single race categories prior to 1999 included persons who reported one race or, if they reported more than one race, identified one race as best representing their race. See Appendix II, Race.
[5]Poor persons are defined as below the poverty threshold. Near poor persons have incomes of 100 percent to less than 200 percent of the poverty threshold. Nonpoor persons have incomes of 200 percent or greater than the poverty threshold. Missing family income data were imputed for 27 percent of persons 18 years of age and over in 1997, 31 percent in 1998, and 34–36 percent in 2000–2003. See Appendix II, Family Income; Poverty level.
[6]MSA is metropolitan statistical area.

NOTES: Standard errors for selected years are available in the spreadsheet version of this table. See www.cdc.gov/nchs/hus.htm. Starting with *Health, United States, 2005*, estimates for 2000 and later years use weights derived from the 2000 census.

SOURCE: Centers for Disease Control and Prevention, National Center for Health Statistics, National Health Interview Survey, family core questionnaire.

Table 62 (page 1 of 2). Suicidal ideation, suicide attempts, and injurious suicide attempts among students in grades 9–12, by sex, grade level, race, and Hispanic origin: United States, selected years 1991–2003

[Data are based on a national sample of high school students, grades 9–12]

Sex, grade level, race, and Hispanic origin	*1991*	*1993*	*1995*	*1997*	*1999*	*2001*	*2003*
	Percent of students who seriously considered suicide [1]						
Total	29.0	24.1	24.1	20.5	19.3	19.0	16.9
Male							
Total	20.8	18.8	18.3	15.1	13.7	14.2	12.8
9th grade	17.6	17.7	18.2	16.1	11.9	14.7	11.9
10th grade	19.5	18.0	16.7	14.5	13.7	13.8	13.2
11th grade	25.3	20.6	21.7	16.6	13.7	14.1	12.9
12th grade	20.7	18.3	16.3	13.5	15.6	13.7	13.2
Not Hispanic or Latino:							
White	21.7	19.1	19.1	14.4	12.5	14.9	12.0
Black or African American	13.3	15.4	16.7	10.6	11.7	9.2	10.3
Hispanic or Latino	18.0	17.9	15.7	17.1	13.6	12.2	12.9
Female							
Total	37.2	29.6	30.4	27.1	24.9	23.6	21.3
9th grade	40.3	30.9	34.4	28.9	24.4	26.2	22.2
10th grade	39.7	31.6	32.8	30.0	30.1	24.1	23.8
11th grade	38.4	28.9	31.1	26.2	23.0	23.6	20.0
12th grade	30.7	27.3	23.9	23.6	21.2	18.9	18.0
Not Hispanic or Latino:							
White	38.6	29.7	31.6	26.1	23.2	24.2	21.2
Black or African American	29.4	24.5	22.2	22.0	18.8	17.2	14.7
Hispanic or Latino	34.6	34.1	34.1	30.3	26.1	26.5	23.4
	Percent of students who attempted suicide [1]						
Total	7.3	8.6	8.7	7.7	8.3	8.8	8.5
Male							
Total	3.9	5.0	5.6	4.5	5.7	6.2	5.4
9th grade	4.5	5.8	6.8	6.3	6.1	8.2	5.8
10th grade	3.3	5.9	5.4	3.8	6.2	6.7	5.5
11th grade	4.1	3.4	5.8	4.4	4.8	4.9	4.6
12th grade	3.8	4.5	4.7	3.7	5.4	4.4	5.2
Not Hispanic or Latino:							
White	3.3	4.4	5.2	3.2	4.5	5.3	3.7
Black or African American	3.3	5.4	7.0	5.6	7.1	7.5	7.7
Hispanic or Latino	3.7	7.4	5.8	7.2	6.6	8.0	6.1
Female							
Total	10.7	12.5	11.9	11.6	10.9	11.2	11.5
9th grade	13.8	14.4	14.9	15.1	14.0	13.2	14.7
10th grade	12.2	13.1	15.1	14.3	14.8	12.2	12.7
11th grade	8.7	13.6	11.4	11.3	7.5	11.5	10.0
12th grade	7.8	9.1	6.6	6.2	5.8	6.5	6.9
Not Hispanic or Latino:							
White	10.4	11.3	10.4	10.3	9.0	10.3	10.3
Black or African American	9.4	11.2	10.8	9.0	7.5	9.8	9.0
Hispanic or Latino	11.6	19.7	21.0	14.9	18.9	15.9	15.0

See footnotes at end of table.

Table 62 (page 2 of 2). Suicidal ideation, suicide attempts, and injurious suicide attempts among students in grades 9–12, by sex, grade level, race, and Hispanic origin: United States, selected years 1991–2003

[Data are based on a national sample of high school students, grades 9–12]

Sex, grade level, race, and Hispanic origin	*1991*	*1993*	*1995*	*1997*	*1999*	*2001*	*2003*
			Percent of students with an injurious suicide attempt[1,2]				
Total	1.7	2.7	2.8	2.6	2.6	2.6	2.9
Male							
Total	1.0	1.6	2.2	2.0	2.1	2.1	2.4
9th grade	1.0	2.1	2.3	3.2	2.6	2.6	3.1
10th grade	0.5	1.3	2.4	1.4	1.8	2.5	2.1
11th grade	1.5	1.1	2.0	2.6	2.1	1.6	2.0
12th grade	0.9	1.5	2.2	1.0	1.7	1.5	1.8
Not Hispanic or Latino:							
White	1.0	1.4	2.1	1.5	1.6	1.7	1.1
Black or African American	0.4	2.0	2.8	1.8	3.4	3.6	5.2
Hispanic or Latino	0.5	2.0	2.9	2.1	1.4	2.5	4.2
Female							
Total	2.5	3.8	3.4	3.3	3.1	3.1	3.2
9th grade	2.8	3.5	6.3	5.0	3.8	3.8	3.9
10th grade	2.6	5.1	3.8	3.7	4.0	3.6	3.2
11th grade	2.1	3.9	2.9	2.8	2.8	2.8	2.9
12th grade	2.4	2.9	1.3	2.0	1.3	1.7	2.2
Not Hispanic or Latino:							
White	2.3	3.6	2.9	2.6	2.3	2.9	2.4
Black or African American	2.9	4.0	3.6	3.0	2.4	3.1	2.2
Hispanic or Latino	2.7	5.5	6.6	3.8	4.6	4.2	5.7

[1]Response is for the 12 months preceding the survey.
[2]A suicide attempt that required medical attention.

NOTES: Only youths attending school participated in the survey. Persons of Hispanic origin may be of any race. Standard errors for selected years are available in the spreadsheet version of this table. See www.cdc.gov/nchs/hus.htm.

SOURCE: Centers for Disease Control and Prevention, National Center for Chronic Disease Prevention and Health Promotion, National Youth Risk Behavior Survey (YRBS).

Table 63 (page 1 of 2). Current cigarette smoking for adults 18 years of age and over according to sex, race, and age: United States, selected years 1965–2003

[Data are based on household interviews of a sample of the civilian noninstitutionalized population]

Sex, race, and age	1965[1]	1974[1]	1979[1]	1985[1]	1990[1]	1995[1]	1998	1999	2000	2001	2002	2003
18 years and over, age adjusted[2]	Percent of persons who are current cigarette smokers[3]											
All persons	41.9	37.0	33.3	29.9	25.3	24.6	24.0	23.3	23.1	22.6	22.3	21.5
Male	51.2	42.8	37.0	32.2	28.0	26.5	25.9	25.2	25.2	24.6	24.6	23.7
Female	33.7	32.2	30.1	27.9	22.9	22.7	22.1	21.6	21.1	20.7	20.0	19.4
White male[4]	50.4	41.7	36.4	31.3	27.6	26.2	26.0	25.0	25.4	24.8	24.9	23.8
Black or African American male[4]	58.8	53.6	43.9	40.2	32.8	29.4	29.0	28.4	25.7	27.5	26.6	25.3
White female[4]	33.9	32.0	30.3	27.9	23.5	23.4	23.0	22.5	22.0	22.0	21.0	20.1
Black or African American female[4]	31.8	35.6	30.5	30.9	20.8	23.5	21.1	20.5	20.7	18.0	18.3	17.9
18 years and over, crude												
All persons	42.4	37.1	33.5	30.1	25.5	24.7	24.1	23.5	23.2	22.7	22.4	21.6
Male	51.9	43.1	37.5	32.6	28.4	27.0	26.4	25.7	25.6	25.1	25.1	24.1
Female	33.9	32.1	29.9	27.9	22.8	22.6	22.0	21.5	20.9	20.6	19.8	19.2
White male[4]	51.1	41.9	36.8	31.7	28.0	26.6	26.3	25.3	25.7	25.0	25.0	24.0
Black or African American male[4]	60.4	54.3	44.1	39.9	32.5	28.5	29.0	28.6	26.2	27.6	27.0	25.7
White female[4]	34.0	31.7	30.1	27.7	23.4	23.1	22.6	22.1	21.4	21.5	20.6	19.7
Black or African American female[4]	33.7	36.4	31.1	31.0	21.2	23.5	21.1	20.6	20.8	18.1	18.5	18.1
All males												
18–24 years	54.1	42.1	35.0	28.0	26.6	27.8	31.3	29.5	28.1	30.2	32.1	26.3
25–34 years	60.7	50.5	43.9	38.2	31.6	29.5	28.5	29.1	28.9	26.9	27.2	28.7
35–44 years	58.2	51.0	41.8	37.6	34.5	31.5	30.2	30.0	30.2	27.3	29.7	28.1
45–64 years	51.9	42.6	39.3	33.4	29.3	27.1	27.7	25.8	26.4	26.4	24.5	23.9
65 years and over	28.5	24.8	20.9	19.6	14.6	14.9	10.4	10.5	10.2	11.5	10.1	10.1
White male[4]												
18–24 years	53.0	40.8	34.3	28.4	27.4	28.4	34.1	30.5	30.4	32.3	34.3	27.7
25–34 years	60.1	49.5	43.6	37.3	31.6	29.9	29.2	30.8	29.7	28.7	27.7	28.8
35–44 years	57.3	50.1	41.3	36.6	33.5	31.2	29.6	29.5	30.6	27.8	29.7	28.8
45–64 years	51.3	41.2	38.3	32.1	28.7	26.3	27.0	24.5	25.8	25.1	24.4	23.3
65 years and over	27.7	24.3	20.5	18.9	13.7	14.1	10.0	10.0	9.8	10.7	9.3	9.6
Black or African American male[4]												
18–24 years	62.8	54.9	40.2	27.2	21.3	*14.6	19.7	23.6	20.9	21.6	22.7	18.6
25–34 years	68.4	58.5	47.5	45.6	33.8	25.1	25.2	22.7	23.2	23.8	28.9	31.0
35–44 years	67.3	61.5	48.6	45.0	42.0	36.3	36.1	34.8	30.7	29.9	28.3	23.6
45–64 years	57.9	57.8	50.0	46.1	36.7	33.9	37.3	35.7	32.2	34.3	29.8	30.1
65 years and over	36.4	29.7	26.2	27.7	21.5	28.5	16.3	17.3	14.2	21.1	19.4	18.0
All females												
18–24 years	38.1	34.1	33.8	30.4	22.5	21.8	24.5	26.3	24.9	23.2	24.5	21.5
25–34 years	43.7	38.8	33.7	32.0	28.2	26.4	24.6	23.5	22.3	22.7	21.3	21.3
35–44 years	43.7	39.8	37.0	31.5	24.8	27.1	26.4	26.5	26.2	25.7	23.7	24.2
45–64 years	32.0	33.4	30.7	29.9	24.8	24.0	22.5	21.0	21.7	21.4	21.1	20.2
65 years and over	9.6	12.0	13.2	13.5	11.5	11.5	11.2	10.7	9.3	9.1	8.6	8.3
White female[4]												
18–24 years	38.4	34.0	34.5	31.8	25.4	24.9	28.1	29.6	28.5	27.1	26.7	23.6
25–34 years	43.4	38.6	34.1	32.0	28.5	27.3	26.9	25.5	24.9	25.2	23.8	22.5
35–44 years	43.9	39.3	37.2	31.0	25.0	27.0	26.6	26.9	26.6	26.9	24.4	25.2
45–64 years	32.7	33.0	30.6	29.7	25.4	24.3	22.5	21.2	21.4	21.6	21.5	20.1
65 years and over	9.8	12.3	13.8	13.3	11.5	11.7	11.2	10.5	9.1	9.4	8.5	8.4
Black or African American female[4]												
18–24 years	37.1	35.6	31.8	23.7	10.0	*8.8	*8.1	14.8	14.2	10.0	17.1	10.8
25–34 years	47.8	42.2	35.2	36.2	29.1	26.7	21.5	18.2	15.5	16.8	13.9	17.0
35–44 years	42.8	46.4	37.7	40.2	25.5	31.9	30.0	28.8	30.2	24.0	24.0	23.2
45–64 years	25.7	38.9	34.2	33.4	22.6	27.5	25.4	22.3	25.6	22.6	22.2	23.3
65 years and over	7.1	*8.9	*8.5	14.5	11.1	13.3	11.5	13.5	10.2	9.3	9.4	8.0

Table 63 (page 2 of 2). Current cigarette smoking for adults 18 years of age and over according to sex, race, and age: United States, selected years 1965–2003

[Data are based on household interviews of a sample of the civilian noninstitutionalized population]

* Estimates are considered unreliable. Data preceded by an asterisk have a relative standard error of 20–30 percent.
[1]Data prior to 1997 are not strictly comparable with data for later years due to the 1997 questionnaire redesign. See Appendix I, National Health Interview Survey.
[2]Estimates are age adjusted to the year 2000 standard population using five age groups: 18–24 years, 25–34 years, 35–44 years, 45–64 years, 65 years and over. Age-adjusted estimates in this table may differ from other age-adjusted estimates based on the same data and presented elsewhere if different age groups are used in the adjustment procedure. See Appendix II, Age adjustment.
[3]Beginning in 1993 current cigarette smokers reported ever smoking 100 cigarettes in their lifetime and smoking now on every day or some days. See Appendix II, Cigarette smoking.
[4]The race groups, white and black, include persons of Hispanic and non-Hispanic origin. Starting with data year 1999 race-specific estimates are tabulated according to 1997 Standards for Federal data on Race and Ethnicity and are not strictly comparable with estimates for earlier years. The single race categories shown in the table conform to 1997 Standards. Starting with data year 1999 race-specific estimates are for persons who reported only one racial group. Prior to data year 1999, data were tabulated according to 1977 Standards. Estimates for single race categories prior to 1999 included persons who reported one race or, if they reported more than one race, identified one race as best representing their race. See Appendix II, Race. For additional data on cigarette smoking by racial groups, see table 65 of *Health, United States, 2005*.

NOTES: Data for additional years are available. See Appendix III. Standard errors for selected years are available in the spreadsheet version of this table. See www.cdc.gov/nchs/hus.htm. For more data on cigarette smoking see the Early Release reports on the National Health Interview Survey home page: www.cdc.gov/nchs/nhis.htm. Starting with *Health, United States, 2005*, estimates for 2000 and later years use weights derived from the 2000 census. Estimates for 2000–2002 were recalculated using 2000-based weights and may differ from previous editions of *Health, United States*.

SOURCES: Centers for Disease Control and Prevention, National Center for Health Statistics, National Health Interview Survey. Data are from the core questionnaire (1965) and the following questionnaire supplements: hypertension (1974), smoking (1979), alcohol and health practices (1983), health promotion and disease prevention (1985, 1990–91), cancer control and cancer epidemiology (1992), and year 2000 objectives (1993–95). Starting with 1997, data are from the family core and sample adult questionnaires.

Table 64. Age-adjusted prevalence of current cigarette smoking for adults 25 years of age and over, according to sex, race, and education: United States, selected years 1974–2003

[Data are based on household interviews of a sample of the civilian noninstitutionalized population]

Sex, race, and education	*1974*[1]	*1979*[1]	*1985*[1]	*1990*[1]	*1995*[1]	*1998*	*1999*	*2000*	*2001*	*2002*	*2003*
25 years and over, age adjusted[2]	Percent of persons who are current cigarette smokers[3]										
All persons[4]	36.9	33.1	30.0	25.4	24.5	23.4	22.7	22.6	22.0	21.4	21.1
No high school diploma or GED	43.7	40.7	40.8	36.7	35.6	34.4	32.2	31.6	30.5	30.5	29.7
High school diploma or GED	36.2	33.6	32.0	29.1	29.1	28.9	28.0	29.2	28.1	27.9	27.8
Some college, no bachelor's degree	35.9	33.2	29.5	23.4	22.6	23.5	23.3	21.7	22.2	21.5	21.1
Bachelor's degree or higher	27.2	22.6	18.5	13.9	13.6	10.9	11.1	10.9	10.8	10.0	10.2
All males[4]	42.9	37.3	32.8	28.2	26.4	25.1	24.5	24.7	23.8	23.5	23.3
No high school diploma or GED	52.3	47.6	45.7	42.0	39.7	37.5	36.2	36.0	34.2	34.0	34.4
High school diploma or GED	42.4	38.9	35.5	33.1	32.7	32.0	30.4	32.1	30.2	31.0	29.9
Some college, no bachelor's degree	41.8	36.5	32.9	25.9	23.7	25.4	24.8	23.3	24.3	23.2	22.7
Bachelor's degree or higher	28.3	22.7	19.6	14.5	13.8	11.0	11.8	11.6	11.2	11.0	11.2
White males[4,5]	41.9	36.7	31.7	27.6	25.9	24.8	24.2	24.7	23.7	23.5	23.2
No high school diploma or GED	51.5	47.6	45.0	41.8	38.7	37.4	36.3	38.2	34.8	35.6	33.6
High school diploma or GED	42.0	38.5	34.8	32.9	32.9	32.2	30.5	32.4	30.3	31.0	29.6
Some college, no bachelor's degree	41.6	36.4	32.2	25.4	23.3	25.2	24.7	23.5	24.5	23.2	23.3
Bachelor's degree or higher	27.8	22.5	19.1	14.4	13.4	10.9	11.8	11.3	11.2	11.1	11.2
Black or African American males[4,5]	53.4	44.4	42.1	34.5	31.6	30.4	29.1	26.4	28.4	27.2	26.3
No high school diploma or GED	58.1	49.7	50.5	41.6	41.9	42.9	43.8	38.2	37.9	37.2	37.4
High school diploma or GED	*50.7	48.6	41.8	37.4	36.6	32.8	32.5	29.0	33.4	31.3	33.4
Some college, no bachelor's degree	*45.3	39.2	41.8	28.1	26.4	28.4	23.4	19.9	24.1	25.6	19.5
Bachelor's degree or higher	*41.4	*36.8	*32.0	*20.8	*17.3	*15.3	11.3	14.6	11.3	*10.8	*10.3
All females[4]	32.0	29.5	27.5	22.9	22.9	21.7	20.9	20.5	20.4	19.3	19.1
No high school diploma or GED	36.6	34.8	36.5	31.8	31.7	31.3	28.2	27.1	26.9	26.9	24.9
High school diploma or GED	32.2	29.8	29.5	26.1	26.4	26.2	25.9	26.6	26.4	25.2	25.8
Some college, no bachelor's degree	30.1	30.0	26.3	21.0	21.6	21.8	21.9	20.4	20.4	20.0	19.7
Bachelor's degree or higher	25.9	22.5	17.1	13.3	13.3	10.7	10.4	10.1	10.5	9.0	9.3
White females[4,5]	31.7	29.7	27.3	23.3	23.1	22.3	21.4	21.0	21.3	20.2	19.6
No high school diploma or GED	36.8	35.8	36.7	33.4	32.4	33.0	29.5	28.4	29.2	29.0	25.0
High school diploma or GED	31.9	29.9	29.4	26.5	26.8	27.1	27.2	27.8	28.3	26.8	26.8
Some college, no bachelor's degree	30.4	30.7	26.7	21.2	22.2	22.2	22.3	21.1	21.3	20.5	20.6
Bachelor's degree or higher	25.5	21.9	16.5	13.4	13.5	11.5	10.5	10.2	10.9	9.6	9.4
Black or African American females[4,5]	35.6	30.3	32.0	22.4	25.7	23.0	21.4	21.6	19.1	18.4	18.9
No high school diploma or GED	36.1	31.6	39.4	26.3	32.3	32.8	30.1	31.1	26.3	27.1	26.9
High school diploma or GED	40.9	32.6	32.1	24.1	27.8	24.3	22.4	25.4	21.3	19.5	23.3
Some college, no bachelor's degree	32.3	*28.9	23.9	22.7	20.8	21.7	22.3	20.4	17.4	20.7	17.0
Bachelor's degree or higher	*36.3	*43.3	26.6	17.0	17.3	9.0	13.4	10.8	11.6	*7.7	11.4

* Estimates are considered unreliable. Data preceded by an asterisk have a relative standard error of 20–30 percent.

[1]Data prior to 1997 are not strictly comparable with data for later years due to the 1997 questionnaire redesign. See Appendix I, National Health Interview Survey.

[2]Estimates are age adjusted to the year 2000 standard population using four age groups: 25–34 years, 35–44 years, 45–64 years, 65 years and over. See Appendix II, Age adjustment. For age groups where percent smoking was 0 or 100, the age-adjustment procedure was modified to substitute the percent smoking from the next lower education group.

[3]Beginning in 1993 current cigarette smokers reported ever smoking 100 cigarettes in their lifetime and smoking now on every day or some days. See Appendix II, Cigarette smoking.

[4]Includes unknown education. Education categories shown are for 1997 and subsequent years. GED stands for General Educational Development high school equivalency diploma. In 1974–95 the following categories based on number of years of school completed were used: less than 12 years, 12 years, 13–15 years, 16 years or more. See Appendix II, Education.

[5]The race groups, white and black, include persons of Hispanic and non-Hispanic origin. Starting with data year 1999 race-specific estimates are tabulated according to 1997 Standards for Federal data on Race and Ethnicity and are not strictly comparable with estimates for earlier years. The single race categories shown in the table conform to 1997 Standards. Starting with data year 1999 race-specific estimates are for persons who reported only one racial group. Prior to data year 1999, data were tabulated according to 1977 Standards. Estimates for single race categories prior to 1999 included persons who reported one race or, if they reported more than one race, identified one race as best representing their race. See Appendix II, Race. For additional data on cigarette smoking by racial groups, see table 65 of *Health, United States, 2005.*

NOTES: Data for additional years are available. See Appendix III. Standard errors for selected years are available in the spreadsheet version of this table. See www.cdc.gov/nchs/hus.htm. For more data on cigarette smoking see the Early Release reports on the National Health Interview Survey home page: www.cdc.gov/nchs/nhis.htm.

Starting with *Health, United States, 2005,* estimates for 2000 and later years use weights derived from the 2000 census. Estimates for 2000–2002 were recalculated using 2000-based weights and may differ from previous editions of *Health, United States.*

SOURCES: Centers for Disease Control and Prevention, National Center for Health Statistics, National Health Interview Survey. Data are from the following questionnaire supplements: hypertension (1974), smoking (1979), alcohol and health practices (1983), health promotion and disease prevention (1985, 1990–91), cancer control and cancer epidemiology (1992), and year 2000 objectives (1993–95). Starting with 1997, data are from the family core and sample adult questionnaires.

Table 65 (page 1 of 2). Current cigarette smoking for adults according to sex, race, Hispanic origin, age, and education: United States, average annual 1990–92, 1995–98, and 2001–03

[Data are based on household interviews of a sample of the civilian noninstitutionalized population]

Characteristic	*Male*			*Female*		
	1990–92[1]	*1995–98*[1]	*2001–03*	*1990–92*[1]	*1995–98*[1]	*2001–03*
18 years of age and over, age adjusted[2]	Percent of persons who are current cigarette smokers[3]					
All persons[4]	27.9	26.5	24.3	23.7	22.1	20.0
Race[5]						
White only	27.4	26.4	24.5	24.3	22.9	21.0
Black or African American only	33.9	30.7	26.5	23.1	21.8	18.0
American Indian and Alaska Native only	34.2	40.5	32.8	36.7	28.9	31.0
Asian only	24.8	18.1	17.4	6.3	11.0	6.3
Native Hawaiian and Other Pacific Islander only	- - -	- - -	*	- - -	- - -	*
2 or more races	- - -	- - -	32.3	- - -	- - -	30.9
American Indian and Alaska Native; White	- - -	- - -	39.3	- - -	- - -	38.0
Hispanic origin and race[5]						
Hispanic or Latino	25.7	24.4	21.1	15.8	13.7	10.9
Mexican	26.2	24.5	21.3	14.8	12.0	9.6
Not Hispanic or Latino	28.1	26.9	24.9	24.4	23.1	21.4
White only	27.7	26.9	25.2	25.2	24.1	22.7
Black or African American only	33.9	30.7	26.5	23.2	21.9	18.1
18 years of age and over, crude						
All persons[4]	28.4	27.0	24.8	23.6	22.0	19.9
Race[5]						
White only	27.8	26.8	24.7	24.1	22.6	20.6
Black or African American only	33.2	30.6	26.8	23.3	21.8	18.2
American Indian and Alaska Native only	35.5	39.2	35.0	37.3	31.2	33.0
Asian only	24.9	20.0	18.4	6.3	11.2	6.5
Native Hawaiian and Other Pacific Islander only	- - -	- - -	*	- - -	- - -	*
2 or more races	- - -	- - -	33.4	- - -	- - -	31.5
American Indian and Alaska Native; White	- - -	- - -	39.9	- - -	- - -	37.9
Hispanic origin and race[5]						
Hispanic or Latino	26.5	25.5	22.2	16.6	13.8	11.0
Mexican	27.1	25.2	22.3	15.0	11.6	9.4
Not Hispanic or Latino	28.5	27.2	25.1	24.2	22.9	21.0
White only	28.0	27.0	25.0	24.8	23.5	21.8
Black or African American only	33.3	30.6	26.8	23.3	21.9	18.3
18–24 years:						
Hispanic or Latino	19.3	26.5	23.1	12.8	12.0	9.8
Not Hispanic or Latino:						
White only	28.9	35.5	33.2	28.7	31.6	28.8
Black or African American only	17.7	21.3	20.9	10.8	9.8	12.9
25–34 years:						
Hispanic or Latino	29.9	25.9	21.9	19.2	12.6	10.3
Not Hispanic or Latino:						
White only	32.7	30.5	30.1	30.9	28.5	26.9
Black or African American only	34.6	28.5	27.4	29.2	22.0	15.8
35–44 years:						
Hispanic or Latino	32.1	26.2	24.8	19.9	17.6	12.8
Not Hispanic or Latino:						
White only	32.3	31.5	29.3	27.3	28.1	27.5
Black or African American only	44.1	34.7	27.3	31.3	30.3	23.7
45–64 years:						
Hispanic or Latino	26.6	26.8	22.1	17.1	14.7	13.4
Not Hispanic or Latino:						
White only	28.4	26.8	24.4	26.1	22.3	21.8
Black or African American only	38.0	38.8	31.7	26.1	26.9	22.9
65 years and over:						
Hispanic or Latino	16.1	14.7	12.2	6.6	9.4	5.4
Not Hispanic or Latino:						
White only	14.2	10.6	9.7	12.3	11.6	8.9
Black or African American only	25.2	20.9	19.5	10.7	11.2	9.0

See footnotes at end of table.

Table 65 (page 2 of 2). Current cigarette smoking for adults according to sex, race, Hispanic origin, age, and education: United States, average annual 1990–92, 1995–98, and 2001–03

[Data are based on household interviews of a sample of the civilian noninstitutionalized population]

Characteristic	Male			Female		
	1990–92[1]	1995–98[1]	2001–03	1990–92[1]	1995–98[1]	2001–03
Education, Hispanic origin, and race[5,6]	Percent of persons who are current cigarette smokers[3]					
25 years of age and over, age adjusted[7]						
No high school diploma or GED:						
Hispanic or Latino	30.2	27.6	23.6	15.8	13.3	10.5
Not Hispanic or Latino:						
White only	46.1	43.9	43.6	40.4	40.7	41.1
Black or African American only	45.4	44.6	37.9	31.3	30.0	26.9
High school diploma or GED:						
Hispanic or Latino	29.6	26.7	21.2	18.4	16.4	12.1
Not Hispanic or Latino:						
White only	32.9	32.8	31.5	28.4	28.8	29.3
Black or African American only	38.2	35.7	32.7	25.4	26.6	21.5
Some college or more:						
Hispanic or Latino	20.4	16.6	16.0	14.3	13.5	10.7
Not Hispanic or Latino:						
White only	19.3	18.3	17.3	18.1	17.2	15.9
Black or African American only	25.6	23.3	18.7	22.8	18.9	15.4

* Estimates are considered unreliable. Data preceded by an asterisk have a relative standard error (RSE) of 20–30 percent. Data not shown have an RSE of greater than 30 percent.

- - - Data not available.

[1]Data prior to 1997 are not strictly comparable with data for later years due to the 1997 questionnaire redesign. See Appendix I, National Health Interview Survey. Cigarette smoking data were not collected in 1996.

[2]Estimates are age adjusted to the year 2000 standard population using five age groups: 18–24 years, 25–34 years, 35–44 years, 45–64 years, and 65 years and over. See Appendix II, Age adjustment. For age groups where percent smoking is 0 or 100, the age-adjustment procedure was modified to substitute the percent smoking from the previous 3-year period.

[3]Beginning in 1993 current cigarette smokers reported ever smoking 100 cigarettes in their lifetime and smoking now on every day or some days. See Appendix II, Cigarette smoking.

[4]Includes all other races not shown separately.

[5]The race groups, white, black, American Indian and Alaska Native (AI/AN), Asian, Native Hawaiian and Other Pacific Islander, and 2 or more races, include persons of Hispanic and non-Hispanic origin. Persons of Hispanic origin may be of any race. Starting with data year 1999 race-specific estimates are tabulated according to 1997 Standards for Federal data on Race and Ethnicity and are not strictly comparable with estimates for earlier years. The five single race categories plus multiple race categories shown in the table conform to 1997 Standards. The 2001–03 race-specific estimates are for persons who reported only one racial group; the category "2 or more races" includes persons who reported more than one racial group. Prior to data years 2001–03, data were tabulated according to 1977 Standards with four racial groups and the category "Asian only" included Native Hawaiian and Other Pacific Islander. Estimates for single race categories prior to 2001–03 included persons who reported one race or, if they reported more than one race, identified one race as best representing their race. See Appendix II, Race.

[6]Education categories shown are for 1997 and subsequent years. GED stands for General Educational Development high school equivalency diploma. In years prior to 1997 the following categories based on number of years of school completed were used: less than 12 years, 12 years, 13 years or more. See Appendix II, Education.

[7]Estimates are age adjusted to the year 2000 standard using four age groups: 25–34 years, 35–44 years, 45–64 years, and 65 years and over. See Appendix II, Age adjustment.

NOTES: Data for additional years are available. See Appendix III. Standard errors for selected years are available in the spreadsheet version of this table. See www.cdc.gov/nchs/hus.htm. For more data on cigarette smoking see the Early Release reports on the National Health Interview Survey home page: www.cdc.gov/nchs/nhis.htm. Starting with *Health, United States, 2005*, estimates for 2000 and later years use weights derived from the 2000 census. Estimates for 2000–2002 were recalculated using 2000-based weights and may differ from previous editions of *Health, United States*.

SOURCES: Centers for Disease Control and Prevention, National Center for Health Statistics, National Health Interview Survey. Data are from the following questionnaire supplements: health promotion and disease prevention (1990–91), cancer control and cancer epidemiology (1992), and year 2000 objectives (1993–95). Starting with 1997 data are from the family core and sample adult questionnaires.

Table 66 (page 1 of 2). Use of selected substances in the past month by persons 12 years of age and over, according to age, sex, race, and Hispanic origin: United States, 2002–2003

[Data are based on household interviews of a sample of the civilian noninstitutionalized population 12 years of age and over]

Age, sex, race, and Hispanic origin	Any illicit drug[1]		Marijuana		Nonmedical use of any psychotherapeutic drug[2]	
	2002	2003	2002	2003	2002	2003
	Percent of population					
12 years and over	8.3	8.2	6.2	6.2	2.6	2.7
Age						
12–13 years	4.2	3.8	1.4	1.0	1.7	1.8
14–15 years	11.2	10.9	7.6	7.2	4.0	4.1
16–17 years	19.8	19.2	15.7	15.6	6.2	6.1
18–25 years	20.2	20.3	17.3	17.0	5.4	6.0
26–34 years	10.5	10.7	7.7	8.4	3.6	3.4
35 years and over	4.6	4.4	3.1	3.0	1.6	1.5
Sex						
Male	10.3	10.0	8.1	8.1	2.7	2.7
Female	6.4	6.5	4.4	4.4	2.6	2.6
Age and sex						
12–17 years	11.6	11.2	8.2	7.9	4.0	4.0
Male	12.3	11.4	9.1	8.6	3.6	3.7
Female	10.9	11.1	7.2	7.2	4.3	4.2
Hispanic origin and race[3]						
Not Hispanic or Latino:						
White only	8.5	8.3	6.5	6.4	2.8	2.8
Black or African American only	9.7	8.7	7.4	6.7	2.0	1.8
American Indian and Alaska Native only	10.1	12.1	6.7	10.3	3.2	4.8
Native Hawaiian and Other Pacific Islander only	7.9	11.1	4.4	7.3	3.8	3.2
Asian only	3.5	3.8	1.8	1.9	0.7	1.7
2 or more races	11.4	12.0	9.0	9.3	3.5	2.4
Hispanic or Latino	7.2	8.0	4.3	4.9	2.9	3.0

Age, sex, race, and Hispanic origin	Alcohol use		Binge alcohol use[4]		Heavy alcohol use[5]	
	2002	2003	2002	2003	2002	2003
	Percent of population					
12 years and over	51.0	50.1	22.9	22.6	6.7	6.8
Age						
12–13 years	4.3	4.5	1.8	1.6	0.3	0.1
14–15 years	16.6	17.0	9.2	9.4	1.9	2.2
16–17 years	32.6	31.8	21.4	21.2	5.6	5.5
18–25 years	60.5	61.4	40.9	41.6	14.9	15.1
26–34 years	61.4	60.2	33.1	32.9	9.0	9.4
35 years and over	52.1	50.7	18.6	18.1	5.2	5.1
Sex						
Male	57.4	57.3	31.2	30.9	10.8	10.4
Female	44.9	43.2	15.1	14.8	3.0	3.4
Age and sex						
12–17 years	17.6	17.7	10.7	10.6	2.5	2.6
Male	17.4	17.1	11.4	11.1	3.1	2.9
Female	17.9	18.3	9.9	10.1	1.9	2.3
Hispanic origin and race[3]						
Not Hispanic or Latino:						
White only	55.0	54.4	23.4	23.6	7.5	7.7
Black or African American only	39.9	37.9	21.0	19.0	4.4	4.5
American Indian and Alaska Native only	44.7	42.0	27.9	29.6	8.7	10.0
Native Hawaiian and Other Pacific Islander only	*	43.3	25.2	29.8	8.3	10.4
Asian only	37.1	39.8	12.4	11.0	2.6	2.3
2 or more races	49.9	44.4	19.8	21.8	7.5	6.1
Hispanic or Latino	42.8	41.5	24.8	24.2	5.9	5.2

See footnotes at end of table.

Table 66 (page 2 of 2). Use of selected substances in the past month by persons 12 years of age and over, according to age, sex, race, and Hispanic origin: United States, 2002–2003

[Data are based on household interviews of a sample of the civilian noninstitutionalized population 12 years of age and over]

Age, sex, race, and Hispanic origin	*Any tobacco*[6]		*Cigarettes*		*Cigars*	
	2002	*2003*	*2002*	*2003*	*2002*	*2003*
	Percent of population					
12 years and over	30.4	29.8	26.0	25.4	5.4	5.4
Age						
12–13 years	3.8	3.2	3.2	2.5	0.7	0.8
14–15 years	13.4	13.3	11.2	11.0	3.8	3.9
16–17 years	29.0	27.0	24.9	23.2	9.3	8.8
18–25 years	45.3	44.8	40.8	40.2	11.0	11.4
26–34 years	38.2	38.8	32.7	33.4	6.6	6.9
35 years and over	27.9	27.0	23.4	22.6	4.1	3.9
Sex						
Male	37.0	35.9	28.7	28.1	9.4	9.0
Female	24.3	24.0	23.4	23.0	1.7	2.0
Age and sex						
12–17 years	15.2	14.4	13.0	12.2	4.5	4.5
Male	16.0	15.6	12.3	11.9	6.2	6.2
Female	14.4	13.3	13.6	12.5	2.7	2.7
Hispanic origin and race[3]						
Not Hispanic or Latino:						
White only	32.0	31.6	26.9	26.6	5.5	5.4
Black or African American only	28.8	30.0	25.3	25.9	6.8	7.2
American Indian and Alaska Native only	44.3	41.8	37.1	36.1	5.2	8.3
Native Hawaiian and Other Pacific Islander only	28.8	37.0	*	33.1	4.1	8.0
Asian only	18.6	13.8	17.7	12.6	1.1	1.8
2 or more races	38.1	34.4	35.0	30.7	5.5	6.2
Hispanic or Latino	25.2	23.7	23.0	21.4	5.0	4.9

* Estimates are considered unreliable; relative standard error greater than 17.5 percent of the log transformation of the proportion or minimum effective sample size less than 68 or minimum nominal sample size less than 100 or prevalence close to 0 or 100 percent. See Appendix I, National Survey on Drug Use & Health (NSDUH).

[1]Any illicit drug includes marijuana/hashish, cocaine (including crack), heroin, hallucinogens (including LSD and PCP), inhalants, or any prescription-type psychotherapeutic drug used nonmedically.

[2]Psychotherapeutic drugs include prescription-type pain relievers, tranquilizers, stimulants, or sedatives; does not include over-the-counter drugs.

[3]Persons of Hispanic origin may be of any race. Race and Hispanic origin were collected using the 1997 Standards for Federal data on Race and Ethnicity. Single race categories shown include persons who reported only one racial group. The category, 2 or more races, includes persons who reported more than one racial group. See Appendix II, Race.

[4]Binge alcohol use is defined as drinking five or more drinks on the same occasion on at least 1 day in the past 30 days. Occasion is defined as at the same time or within a couple of hours of each other.

[5]Heavy alcohol use is defined as drinking five or more drinks on the same occasion on each of 5 or more days in the past 30 days; all heavy alcohol users are also "binge" alcohol users.

[6]Any tobacco product includes cigarettes, smokeless tobacco (i.e., chewing tobacco or snuff), cigars, or pipe tobacco.

NOTES: The National Survey on Drug Use & Health (NSDUH), formerly called the National Household Survey on Drug Abuse (NHSDA), began a new baseline in 2002 and cannot be compared with previous years. Because of methodological differences among the National Survey on Drug Use & Health, Monitoring the Future Study (MTF), and Youth Risk Behavior Survey (YRBS), rates of substance use measured by these surveys are not directly comparable. See Appendix I, NSDUH, MTF, and YRBS. Some data for 2002 have been revised and differ from the previous edition of *Health, United States*.

SOURCE: Substance Abuse and Mental Health Services Administration, Office of Applied Studies, National Survey on Drug Use & Health, www.oas.samhsa.gov/nhsda.htm.

Table 67 (page 1 of 3). Use of selected substances by high school seniors, tenth-, and eighth-graders, according to sex and race: United States, selected years 1980–2004

[Data are based on a survey of high school seniors, tenth–, and eighth-graders in the coterminous United States]

Substance, sex, race, and grade in school	*1980*	*1990*	*1991*	*1995*	*2000*	*2001*	*2002*	*2003*	*2004*
Cigarettes			Percent using substance in the past month						
All seniors	30.5	29.4	28.3	33.5	31.4	29.5	26.7	24.4	25.0
Male	26.8	29.1	29.0	34.5	32.8	29.7	27.4	26.2	25.3
Female	33.4	29.2	27.5	32.0	29.7	28.7	25.5	22.1	24.1
White	31.0	32.5	31.8	37.3	36.6	34.1	30.9	28.2	28.2
Black or African American	25.2	12.0	9.4	15.0	13.6	12.9	11.3	9.0	11.3
All tenth-graders	---	---	20.8	27.9	23.9	21.3	17.7	16.7	16.0
Male	---	---	20.8	27.7	23.8	20.9	16.7	16.2	16.2
Female	---	---	20.7	27.9	23.6	21.5	18.6	17.0	15.7
White	---	---	23.9	31.2	27.3	24.0	20.8	19.3	18.1
Black or African American	---	---	6.4	12.2	11.3	10.9	9.1	8.8	9.6
All eighth-graders	---	---	14.3	19.1	14.6	12.2	10.7	10.2	9.2
Male	---	---	15.5	18.8	14.3	12.2	11.0	9.6	8.3
Female	---	---	13.1	19.0	14.7	12.0	10.4	10.6	9.9
White	---	---	15.0	21.7	16.4	12.8	11.1	10.6	9.4
Black or African American	---	---	5.3	8.2	8.4	8.0	7.3	6.4	7.5
Marijuana									
All seniors	33.7	14.0	13.8	21.2	21.6	22.4	21.5	21.2	19.9
Male	37.8	16.1	16.1	24.6	24.7	25.6	25.3	24.7	23.0
Female	29.1	11.5	11.2	17.2	18.3	19.1	17.4	17.3	16.6
White	34.2	15.6	15.0	21.5	22.0	23.9	22.8	22.8	21.5
Black or African American	26.5	5.2	6.5	17.8	17.5	16.5	16.4	16.1	14.2
All tenth-graders	---	---	8.7	17.2	19.7	19.8	17.8	17.0	15.9
Male	---	---	10.1	19.2	23.3	22.7	19.3	19.0	17.4
Female	---	---	7.3	15.0	16.2	16.8	16.4	15.0	14.2
White	---	---	9.4	17.7	20.1	20.4	19.1	17.4	15.8
Black or African American	---	---	3.8	15.1	17.0	16.5	14.4	15.6	17.2
All eighth-graders	---	---	3.2	9.1	9.1	9.2	8.3	7.5	6.4
Male	---	---	3.8	9.8	10.2	11.0	9.5	8.5	6.3
Female	---	---	2.6	8.2	7.8	7.3	7.1	6.4	6.3
White	---	---	3.0	9.0	8.3	8.6	7.9	7.0	5.5
Black or African American	---	---	2.1	7.0	8.5	7.7	7.1	7.4	8.1
Cocaine									
All seniors	5.2	1.9	1.4	1.8	2.1	2.1	2.3	2.1	2.3
Male	6.0	2.3	1.7	2.2	2.7	2.5	2.7	2.6	2.9
Female	4.3	1.3	0.9	1.3	1.6	1.6	1.8	1.4	1.7
White	5.4	1.8	1.3	1.7	2.2	2.3	2.8	2.1	2.5
Black or African American	2.0	0.5	0.8	0.4	1.0	0.6	0.2	1.0	0.9
All tenth-graders	---	---	0.7	1.7	1.8	1.3	1.6	1.3	1.7
Male	---	---	0.7	1.8	2.1	1.5	1.8	1.3	1.9
Female	---	---	0.6	1.5	1.4	1.2	1.4	1.3	1.4
White	---	---	0.6	1.7	1.7	1.2	1.7	1.4	1.7
Black or African American	---	---	0.2	0.4	0.4	0.3	0.4	0.5	0.4
All eighth-graders	---	---	0.5	1.2	1.2	1.2	1.1	0.9	0.9
Male	---	---	0.7	1.1	1.3	1.1	1.1	1.0	0.8
Female	---	---	0.4	1.2	1.1	1.2	1.1	0.8	1.0
White	---	---	0.4	1.0	1.1	1.1	1.0	0.8	0.8
Black or African American	---	---	0.4	0.4	0.5	0.4	0.5	0.5	0.8

See footnotes at end of table.

Table 67 (page 2 of 3). Use of selected substances by high school seniors, tenth-, and eighth-graders, according to sex and race: United States, selected years 1980–2004

[Data are based on a survey of high school seniors, tenth–, and eighth-graders in the coterminous United States]

Substance, sex, race, and grade in school	*1980*	*1990*	*1991*	*1995*	*2000*	*2001*	*2002*	*2003*	*2004*
Inhalants	Percent using substance in the past month								
All seniors	1.4	2.7	2.4	3.2	2.2	1.7	1.5	1.5	1.5
Male	1.8	3.5	3.3	3.9	2.9	2.3	2.2	2.0	1.7
Female	1.0	2.0	1.6	2.5	1.7	1.1	0.8	1.1	1.3
White	1.4	3.0	2.4	3.7	2.1	1.8	1.3	1.7	1.6
Black or African American	1.0	1.5	1.5	1.1	2.1	1.3	1.2	0.7	1.0
All tenth-graders	---	---	2.7	3.5	2.6	2.5	2.4	2.2	2.4
Male	---	---	2.9	3.8	3.0	2.5	2.3	2.3	2.4
Female	---	---	2.6	3.2	2.2	2.4	2.4	2.2	2.3
White	---	---	2.9	3.9	2.8	2.5	2.6	2.6	2.6
Black or African American	---	---	2.0	1.2	1.5	0.9	1.5	0.5	1.4
All eighth-graders	---	---	4.4	6.1	4.5	4.0	3.8	4.1	4.5
Male	---	---	4.1	5.6	4.1	3.6	3.5	3.4	4.0
Female	---	---	4.7	6.6	4.8	4.3	3.9	4.7	5.1
White	---	---	4.5	7.0	4.5	4.1	3.9	4.3	4.4
Black or African American	---	---	2.3	2.3	2.3	2.6	2.7	2.3	3.8
MDMA (Ecstasy)									
All seniors	---	---	---	---	3.6	2.8	2.4	1.3	1.2
Male	---	---	---	---	4.1	3.7	2.6	1.3	1.6
Female	---	---	---	---	3.1	2.0	2.1	1.2	0.9
White	---	---	---	---	3.9	2.8	2.5	1.3	1.2
Black or African American	---	---	---	---	1.9	0.9	0.5	0.6	1.1
All tenth-graders	---	---	---	---	2.6	2.6	1.8	1.1	0.8
Male	---	---	---	---	2.5	3.5	1.6	1.2	1.0
Female	---	---	---	---	2.5	1.6	1.8	1.1	0.6
White	---	---	---	---	2.5	2.6	2.3	1.2	0.9
Black or African American	---	---	---	---	1.8	1.0	0.5	0.7	0.1
All eighth-graders	---	---	---	---	1.4	1.8	1.4	0.7	0.8
Male	---	---	---	---	1.6	1.9	1.5	0.7	0.7
Female	---	---	---	---	1.2	1.8	1.3	0.7	0.9
White	---	---	---	---	1.4	2.0	1.0	0.7	0.6
Black or African American	---	---	---	---	0.8	1.1	0.6	0.4	1.2
Alcohol[1]									
All seniors	72.0	57.1	54.0	51.3	50.0	49.8	48.6	47.5	48.0
Male	77.4	61.3	58.4	55.7	54.0	54.7	52.3	51.7	51.1
Female	66.8	52.3	49.0	47.0	46.1	45.1	45.1	43.8	45.1
White	75.8	62.2	57.7	54.8	55.3	55.3	52.7	52.0	52.5
Black or African American	47.7	32.9	34.4	37.4	29.3	29.6	30.7	29.2	29.2
All tenth-graders	---	---	42.8	38.8	41.0	39.0	35.4	35.4	35.2
Male	---	---	45.5	39.7	43.3	41.1	35.3	35.3	36.3
Female	---	---	40.3	37.8	38.6	36.8	35.7	35.3	34.0
White	---	---	45.7	41.3	44.3	41.0	39.0	38.4	37.3
Black or African American	---	---	30.2	24.9	24.7	26.0	23.2	24.0	25.4
All eighth-graders	---	---	25.1	24.6	22.4	21.5	19.6	19.7	18.6
Male	---	---	26.3	25.0	22.5	22.3	19.1	19.4	17.9
Female	---	---	23.8	24.0	22.0	20.6	20.0	19.8	19.0
White	---	---	26.0	25.4	23.9	22.5	20.4	19.9	18.6
Black or African American	---	---	17.8	17.3	15.1	14.9	14.7	16.5	16.0

See footnotes at end of table.

Table 67 (page 3 of 3). Use of selected substances by high school seniors, tenth-, and eighth-graders, according to sex and race: United States, selected years 1980–2004

[Data are based on a survey of high school seniors, tenth–, and eighth-graders in the coterminous United States]

Substance, sex, race, and grade in school	*1980*	*1990*	*1991*	*1995*	*2000*	*2001*	*2002*	*2003*	*2004*
Binge drinking[2]					Percent in last 2 weeks				
All seniors	41.2	32.2	29.8	29.8	30.0	29.7	28.6	27.9	29.2
Male	52.1	39.1	37.8	36.9	36.7	36.0	34.2	34.2	34.3
Female	30.5	24.4	21.2	23.0	23.5	23.7	23.0	22.1	24.2
White	44.6	36.2	32.9	32.9	34.4	34.5	32.9	31.9	33.1
Black or African American	17.0	11.6	11.8	15.5	11.0	12.6	10.4	11.1	11.7
All tenth-graders	- - -	- - -	22.9	24.0	26.2	24.9	22.4	22.2	22.0
Male	- - -	- - -	26.4	26.4	29.8	28.6	23.8	23.2	23.8
Female	- - -	- - -	19.5	21.5	22.5	21.4	21.0	21.2	20.2
White	- - -	- - -	24.4	25.7	28.5	26.4	24.6	24.3	23.7
Black or African American	- - -	- - -	14.4	12.3	12.9	12.3	12.4	11.7	11.5
All eighth-graders	- - -	- - -	12.9	14.5	14.1	13.2	12.4	11.9	11.4
Male	- - -	- - -	14.3	15.1	14.4	13.7	12.5	12.2	10.8
Female	- - -	- - -	11.4	13.9	13.6	12.4	12.1	11.6	11.8
White	- - -	- - -	12.6	14.5	14.6	13.1	12.3	11.4	11.2
Black or African American	- - -	- - -	9.9	10.0	9.3	8.8	9.9	10.9	8.6

- - - Data not available.
0.0 Quantity more than zero but less than 0.05.
[1]In 1993 the alcohol question was changed to indicate that a "drink" meant "more than a few sips." 1993 data, available in the spreadsheet version of this table, are based on a half sample.
[2]Five or more alcoholic drinks in a row at least once in the prior 2-week period.

NOTES: Because of methodological differences among the National Survey on Drug Use & Health (NSDUH), Monitoring the Future Study (MTF), and Youth Risk Behavior Survey (YRBS), rates of substance use measured by these surveys are not directly comparable. See Appendix I, NSDUH, MTF, and YRBS. Data for additional years are available. See Appendix III.

SOURCE: National Institutes of Health, National Institute on Drug Abuse (NIDA), Monitoring the Future Study, Annual surveys.

Table 68 (page 1 of 3). Alcohol consumption by adults 18 years of age and over, according to selected characteristics: United States, selected years 1997–2003

[Data are based on household interviews of a sample of the civilian noninstitutionalized population]

Characteristic	Both sexes			Male			Female		
	1997	2002	2003	1997	2002	2003	1997	2002	2003
Drinking status[1]	Percent distribution								
18 years and over, age adjusted[2]									
All	100.0	100.0	100.0	100.0	100.0	100.0	100.0	100.0	100.0
Lifetime abstainer	21.4	22.3	24.9	14.1	14.8	17.8	27.8	28.8	31.3
Former drinker[3]	15.8	15.3	14.3	16.4	15.8	15.2	15.4	14.9	13.6
Infrequent	9.0	8.4	7.7	7.8	7.4	7.1	10.2	9.3	8.4
Regular	6.8	6.8	6.5	8.6	8.3	8.0	5.3	5.5	5.2
Current drinker[3]	62.8	62.5	60.8	69.5	69.4	67.1	56.8	56.3	55.2
Infrequent	13.9	13.3	12.9	10.2	9.8	9.8	17.4	16.6	15.9
Regular	48.5	48.7	47.4	58.7	58.9	56.7	39.2	39.3	39.0
18 years and over, crude									
All	100.0	100.0	100.0	100.0	100.0	100.0	100.0	100.0	100.0
Lifetime abstainer	21.3	22.2	24.8	14.1	14.8	17.7	27.8	28.9	31.4
Former drinker[3]	15.6	15.2	14.3	15.7	15.3	14.9	15.5	15.1	13.7
Infrequent	8.9	8.4	7.8	7.5	7.2	7.0	10.2	9.4	8.5
Regular	6.7	6.8	6.5	8.2	8.0	7.9	5.3	5.6	5.2
Current drinker[3]	63.1	62.6	60.9	70.2	69.9	67.4	56.7	56.0	54.9
Infrequent	14.0	13.3	13.0	10.2	9.8	9.8	17.4	16.6	15.9
Regular	48.8	48.8	47.5	59.4	59.4	57.1	39.1	39.1	38.7
Age	Percent current drinkers among all adults								
All persons:									
18–44 years	68.5	68.8	66.4	73.8	75.6	72.3	63.3	62.3	60.7
18–24 years	61.3	63.7	59.5	65.5	70.5	64.6	57.0	56.8	54.5
25–44 years	70.6	70.6	68.7	76.3	77.4	74.9	65.2	64.1	62.8
45–64 years	62.7	62.5	60.4	69.8	67.7	65.7	55.9	57.7	55.4
45–54 years	66.5	65.6	63.8	73.0	70.5	68.0	60.3	60.9	59.9
55–64 years	56.7	57.9	55.5	64.8	63.3	62.4	49.2	53.0	49.0
65 years and over	42.8	40.8	42.4	52.0	51.1	51.1	36.0	33.1	36.0
65–74 years	47.9	44.9	46.5	56.1	55.6	53.7	41.4	36.0	40.6
75 years and over	36.0	35.9	37.8	45.9	45.0	47.6	29.7	30.0	31.4
Race[2,4]									
White only	65.3	65.3	63.3	71.0	71.4	69.1	60.1	59.7	58.0
Black or African American only	46.7	46.9	47.4	55.5	56.4	54.7	40.0	39.6	41.8
American Indian and Alaska Native only	52.2	52.0	46.5	64.6	60.2	47.8	43.4	46.8	45.2
Asian only	45.7	47.7	39.1	59.8	58.5	49.4	31.6	35.0	30.3
Native Hawaiian and Other Pacific Islander only	- - -	*	*	- - -	*	*	- - -	*	*
2 or more races	- - -	62.4	54.5	- - -	62.8	62.4	- - -	61.9	48.4
Hispanic origin and race[2,4]									
Hispanic or Latino	52.9	50.5	49.5	63.9	64.2	61.7	41.9	37.8	37.3
Mexican	52.7	50.7	47.5	66.3	64.6	60.9	38.7	36.6	33.4
Not Hispanic or Latino	63.3	63.7	62.1	69.3	69.8	67.4	58.0	58.3	57.4
White only	66.7	67.2	65.7	71.7	72.4	70.3	62.2	62.4	61.6
Black or African American only	46.7	46.7	47.2	55.7	55.9	54.3	39.8	39.6	41.8
Geographic region[2]									
Northeast	67.9	69.3	67.8	73.4	74.7	73.7	63.3	64.8	62.9
Midwest	65.7	66.4	64.5	71.6	73.4	68.8	60.3	60.1	60.7
South	55.5	55.7	54.3	63.0	63.5	61.7	48.7	48.6	47.6
West	64.4	62.3	60.4	71.2	68.8	67.0	58.1	56.1	54.1
Location of residence[2]									
Within MSA[5]	63.9	63.7	62.3	70.1	70.4	68.2	58.5	57.6	57.0
Outside MSA[5]	56.5	56.6	53.8	64.6	64.0	61.5	48.8	50.0	47.1

See footnotes at end of table.

Table 68 (page 2 of 3). Alcohol consumption by adults 18 years of age and over, according to selected characteristics: United States, selected years 1997–2003

[Data are based on household interviews of a sample of the civilian noninstitutionalized population]

	Both sexes			Male			Female		
Characteristic	*1997*	*2002*	*2003*	*1997*	*2002*	*2003*	*1997*	*2002*	*2003*
Level of alcohol consumption in past year for current drinkers[6]	Percent distribution of current drinkers[7]								
18 years and over, age adjusted[2]									
All drinking levels	100.0	100.0	100.0	100.0	100.0	100.0	100.0	100.0	100.0
Light	69.6	68.5	68.4	59.5	58.8	58.9	81.0	79.6	78.9
Moderate	22.5	23.4	23.7	31.8	32.7	32.8	12.0	12.8	13.7
Heavier	7.9	8.1	7.9	8.7	8.5	8.3	7.0	7.6	7.4
18 years and over, crude									
All drinking levels	100.0	100.0	100.0	100.0	100.0	100.0	100.0	100.0	100.0
Light	69.8	68.7	68.6	59.6	58.9	59.1	81.4	79.9	79.2
Moderate	22.3	23.2	23.5	31.7	32.6	32.5	11.7	12.5	13.5
Heavier	7.9	8.1	7.9	8.8	8.5	8.4	6.9	7.5	7.3
Number of days in the past year with 5 or more drinks	Percent distribution of current drinkers								
18 years and over, crude									
All current drinkers	100.0	100.0	100.0	100.0	100.0	100.0	100.0	100.0	100.0
No days	65.8	67.7	68.1	54.5	57.6	58.1	78.5	79.1	79.1
At least 1 day	34.2	32.3	31.9	45.5	42.4	41.9	21.5	20.9	20.9
1–11 days	18.5	16.8	17.0	22.0	19.7	19.5	14.6	13.5	14.2
12 or more days	15.6	15.5	14.9	23.5	22.8	22.4	6.9	7.4	6.7
Hispanic origin, race, and age[4]	Percent of adults with five or more drinks on at least 1 day among current drinkers								
All persons:									
18 years and over, age adjusted[2]	32.4	31.0	30.8	43.4	40.7	40.3	20.2	20.0	20.3
18 years and over, crude	34.2	32.3	31.9	45.5	42.4	41.9	21.5	20.9	20.9
18–44 years	42.5	42.0	41.1	54.8	53.1	52.1	28.7	29.1	28.7
18–24 years	51.6	53.5	51.2	61.5	63.1	59.3	40.2	41.7	41.9
25–44 years	40.2	38.5	38.2	53.0	50.0	50.0	25.8	25.4	24.9
45–64 years	25.3	22.3	23.9	36.1	31.9	33.5	12.8	12.0	13.2
45–54 years	28.5	25.5	26.3	40.2	35.9	37.0	15.2	14.3	14.9
55–64 years	19.5	16.9	19.8	28.8	25.1	28.0	8.3	8.2	10.2
65 years and over	11.2	9.2	8.4	17.8	14.0	12.5	4.3	3.7	4.2
65–74 years	13.8	12.4	10.8	21.6	17.9	16.1	5.4	5.5	5.0
75 years and over	6.6	4.5	5.2	10.8	7.5	7.3	*2.5	*	*3.1
Race[2,4]									
White only	33.3	31.8	31.9	44.4	41.8	41.3	20.9	20.7	21.4
Black or African American only	23.9	22.7	21.6	32.0	29.2	31.0	15.0	15.3	12.2
American Indian and Alaska Native only	54.4	40.8	34.1	70.5	49.0	43.8	37.6	38.6	*23.1
Asian only	25.6	20.7	15.3	30.8	26.8	20.3	16.6	*9.6	*8.4
Native Hawaiian and Other Pacific Islander only	- - -	*	*	- - -	*	*	- - -	*	*
Hispanic origin and race[2,4]									
Hispanic or Latino	37.0	34.3	30.2	46.6	45.0	39.1	22.4	17.5	15.4
Mexican	39.1	39.4	34.2	50.2	50.7	43.0	20.3	19.6	18.2
Not Hispanic or Latino	31.9	30.3	30.6	42.8	39.7	40.1	20.0	20.0	20.6
White only	33.2	31.8	32.3	44.5	41.8	41.9	21.0	21.0	22.1
Black or African American only	23.7	22.8	21.2	32.0	29.3	30.5	14.5	15.4	11.9

See footnotes at end of table.

Table 68 (page 3 of 3). Alcohol consumption by adults 18 years of age and over, according to selected characteristics: United States, selected years 1997–2003

[Data are based on household interviews of a sample of the civilian noninstitutionalized population]

Characteristic	Both sexes			Male			Female		
	1997	2002	2003	1997	2002	2003	1997	2002	2003
	Percent of adults with five or more drinks on at least 1 day in the past year among current drinkers								
Geographic region[2]									
Northeast	31.4	29.1	29.1	43.3	39.2	37.2	19.0	18.9	21.0
Midwest	33.7	33.8	33.9	44.6	43.5	44.6	21.6	22.9	22.5
South	30.9	28.5	28.2	40.6	37.3	36.9	19.3	17.8	17.9
West	33.5	31.7	31.5	44.7	41.9	41.7	20.7	19.8	19.6
Location of residence[2]									
Within MSA[5]	31.7	30.4	29.9	42.4	39.7	39.0	19.9	19.8	19.8
Outside MSA[5]	34.9	31.7	33.2	45.7	42.0	43.7	21.2	19.9	21.2

* Estimates are considered unreliable. Data preceded by an asterisk have a relative standard error (RSE) of 20–30 percent. Data not shown have an RSE of greater than 30 percent.

- - - Data not available.

[1]Drinking status categories are based on self-reported responses to questions about alcohol consumption. Lifetime abstainers had fewer than 12 drinks in their lifetime. Former drinkers had at least 12 drinks in their lifetime and none in the past year. Former infrequent drinkers are former drinkers who had fewer than 12 drinks in any one year. Former regular drinkers are former drinkers who had at least 12 drinks in any one year. Current drinkers had 12 drinks in their lifetime and at least one drink in the past year. Current infrequent drinkers are current drinkers who had fewer than 12 drinks in the past year. Current regular drinkers are current drinkers who had at least 12 drinks in the past year. See Appendix II, Alcohol consumption.

[2]Estimates are age adjusted to the year 2000 standard population using four age groups: 18–24 years, 25–44 years, 45–64 years, and 65 years and over. Age-adjusted estimates in this table may differ from other age-adjusted estimates based on the same data and presented elsewhere if different age groups are used in the adjustment procedure. See Appendix II, Age adjustment.

[3]The totals for current and former drinkers include a small number of adults who did not provide sufficient information on frequency or amount of drinking; infrequent or regular drinking status could not be determined for these current and former drinkers.

[4]The race groups, white, black, American Indian and Alaska Native, Asian, Native Hawaiian and Other Pacific Islander, and 2 or more races, include persons of Hispanic and non-Hispanic origin. Persons of Hispanic origin may be of any race. Starting with data year 1999 race-specific estimates are tabulated according to 1997 Standards for Federal data on Race and Ethnicity and are not strictly comparable with estimates for earlier years. The five single race categories plus multiple race categories shown in the table conform to 1997 Standards. Starting with data year 1999 race-specific estimates are for persons who reported only one racial group; the category "2 or more races" includes persons who reported more than one racial group. Prior to data year 1999, data were tabulated according to 1977 Standards with four racial groups and the category "Asian only" included Native Hawaiian and Other Pacific Islander. Estimates for single race categories prior to 1999 included persons who reported one race or, if they reported more than one race, identified one race as best representing their race. See Appendix II, Race.

[5]MSA is metropolitan statistical area.

[6]Level of alcohol consumption categories are based on self-reported responses to questions about average alcohol consumption and defined as follows: light drinkers: three drinks or fewer per week; moderate drinkers: more than three drinks and up to 14 drinks per week for men and more than three drinks and up to seven drinks per week for women; heavier drinkers: more than 14 drinks per week for men and more than seven drinks per week for women. (Most drinking guidelines consider more than seven drinks per week to be a heavier level of consumption for women. U.S. Department of Agriculture: Dietary Guidelines for Americans, 2000, 5th edition.)

[7]Percent based on current drinkers with known frequency and amount of drinking.

NOTES: Data for additional years are available. See Appendix III. Standard errors are available in the spreadsheet version of this table. See www.cdc.gov/nchs/hus.htm. For more data on alcohol consumption see the Early Release reports on the National Health Interview Survey home page: www.cdc.gov/nchs/nhis.htm. Starting with *Health, United States, 2005,* estimates for 2000 and later years use weights derived from the 2000 census. Estimates for 2000–2002 were recalculated using 2000-based weights and may differ from previous editions of *Health, United States.*

SOURCE: Centers for Disease Control and Prevention, National Center for Health Statistics, National Health Interview Survey, family core and sample adult questionnaires.

Table 69 (page 1 of 2). Hypertension (elevated blood pressure) among persons 20 years of age and over, according to sex, age, race and Hispanic origin, and poverty status: United States, 1988–94 and 1999–2002

[Data are based on physical examinations of a sample of the civilian noninstitutionalized population]

Sex, age, race and Hispanic origin[1], and poverty status	Elevated blood pressure or taking antihypertensive medication[2,3]		Elevated blood pressure[2]	
	1988–94	1999–2002	1988–94	1999–2002
20–74 years, age adjusted[4]	Percent of population (standard error)			
Both sexes[5,6]	21.7	25.6	15.4	16.4
Male	23.4	25.2	18.2	16.3
Female[5]	20.0	25.7	12.6	16.1
Not Hispanic or Latino:				
White only, male	22.6	24.0	17.3	14.8
White only, female[5]	18.4	23.3	11.2	14.1
Black or African American only, male	34.3	36.9	27.9	25.6
Black or African American only, female[5]	35.0	39.5	23.5	25.7
Mexican male	23.4	22.6	19.1	18.2
Mexican female[5]	21.0	23.4	16.5	17.2
Poverty status:[7]				
Poor	27.5	29.0	19.0	19.3
Near poor	22.6	29.3	15.8	19.5
Nonpoor	20.4	24.1	14.6	14.9
20 years and over, age adjusted[4]				
Both sexes[5,6]	25.5	30.0	18.5	19.9
Male	26.4	28.8	20.6	19.1
Female[5]	24.4	30.6	16.4	20.2
Not Hispanic or Latino:				
White only, male	25.6	27.6	19.7	17.6
White only, female[5]	23.0	28.5	15.1	18.5
Black or African American only, male	37.5	40.6	30.3	28.2
Black or African American only, female[5]	38.3	43.5	26.4	28.9
Mexican male	26.9	26.8	22.2	21.5
Mexican female[5]	25.0	27.9	20.4	21.2
Poverty status:[7]				
Poor	31.7	33.9	22.5	23.3
Near poor	26.6	33.5	19.3	23.0
Nonpoor	23.9	28.2	17.5	18.2
20 years and over, crude				
Both sexes[5,6]	24.1	30.2	17.6	19.9
Male	23.8	27.6	18.7	18.2
Female[5]	24.4	32.7	16.5	21.6
Not Hispanic or Latino:				
White only, male	24.3	28.3	18.7	17.8
White only, female[5]	24.6	32.9	16.4	21.6
Black or African American only, male	31.1	35.9	25.5	25.2
Black or African American only, female[5]	32.5	42.1	22.2	27.3
Mexican male	16.4	16.5	13.9	14.1
Mexican female[5]	15.9	18.8	12.7	13.8
Poverty status:[7]				
Poor	25.7	30.3	18.7	21.1
Near poor	26.7	34.8	19.8	24.1
Nonpoor	22.2	28.2	16.2	17.8
Male				
20–34 years	7.1	*8.1	6.6	*7.3
35–44 years	17.1	17.1	15.2	12.1
45–54 years	29.2	31.0	21.9	20.4
55–64 years	40.6	45.0	28.4	24.8
65–74 years	54.4	59.6	39.9	34.9
75 years and over	60.4	69.0	49.7	50.6
Female[5]				
20–34 years	2.9	*2.7	*2.4	*1.4
35–44 years	11.2	15.1	6.4	8.5
45–54 years	23.9	31.8	13.7	19.1
55–64 years	42.6	53.9	27.0	31.9
65–74 years	56.2	72.7	38.2	53.0
75 years and over	73.6	83.1	59.9	64.4

See footnotes at end of table.

Table 69 (page 2 of 2). Hypertension (elevated blood pressure) among persons 20 years of age and over, according to sex, age, race and Hispanic origin, and poverty status: United States, 1988–94 and 1999–2002

[Data are based on physical examinations of a sample of the civilian noninstitutionalized population]

---

* Estimates are considered unreliable. Data preceded by an asterisk have a relative standard error of 20–30 percent.
[1]Persons of Mexican origin may be of any race. Starting with data year 1999 race-specific estimates are tabulated according to 1997 Standards for Federal data on Race and Ethnicity and are not strictly comparable with estimates for earlier years. The two non-Hispanic race categories shown in the table conform to 1997 Standards. The 1999–2002 race-specific estimates are for persons who reported only one racial group. Prior to data year 1999, data were tabulated according to 1977 Standards. Estimates for single race categories prior to 1999 included persons who reported one race or, if they reported more than one race, identified one race as best representing their race. See Appendix II, Race.
[2]Elevated blood pressure is defined as having systolic pressure of at least 140 mmHg or diastolic pressure of at least 90 mmHg. Those with elevated blood pressure may be taking prescribed medicine for high blood pressure.
[3]Respondents were asked, "Are you now taking prescribed medicine for your high blood pressure?"
[4]Age adjusted to the 2000 standard population using five age groups. Age-adjusted estimates may differ from other age-adjusted estimates based on the same data and presented elsewhere if different age groups are used in the adjustment procedure. See Appendix II, Age adjustment.
[5]Excludes pregnant women.
[6]Includes persons of all races and Hispanic origins, not just those shown separately.
[7]Poor persons are defined as below the poverty threshold. Near poor persons have incomes of 100 percent to less than 200 percent of the poverty threshold. Nonpoor persons have incomes of 200 percent or greater than the poverty threshold. Persons with unknown poverty status are excluded. See Appendix II, Family income; Poverty level.

NOTES: Percents are based on the average of blood pressure measurements taken. In 1999–2002, 78 percent of participants had 3 blood pressure readings. See *Health, United States, 2003* table 66 for a longer trend based on a single blood pressure measurement, which provides comparable data across five time periods (1960–62 through 1999–2000). Data have been revised and differ from the previous edition of *Health, United States*. Estimates for persons 20 years and over are used for setting and tracking *Healthy People 2010* objectives. Standard errors are available in the spreadsheet version of this table. See www.cdc.gov/nchs/hus.htm.

SOURCE: Centers for Disease Control and Prevention, National Center for Health Statistics, National Health and Nutrition Examination Survey.

Table 70 (page 1 of 3). Serum cholesterol levels among persons 20 years of age and over, according to sex, age, race and Hispanic origin, and poverty status: United States, 1960–62, 1971–74, 1976–80, 1988–94, and 1999–2002

[Data are based on physical examinations of a sample of the civilian noninstitutionalized population]

Sex, age, race and Hispanic origin[1], and poverty status	*1960–62*	*1971–74*	*1976–80*[2]	*1988–94*	*1999–2002*
20–74 years, age adjusted[3]	Percent of population with high serum cholesterol				
Both sexes[4]	33.3	28.6	27.8	19.7	17.0
Male	30.6	27.9	26.4	18.8	16.9
Female	35.6	29.1	28.8	20.5	17.0
Not Hispanic or Latino:					
White only, male	---	---	26.4	18.7	17.0
White only, female	---	---	29.6	20.7	17.4
Black or African American only, male	---	---	25.5	16.4	12.5
Black or African American only, female	---	---	26.3	19.9	16.6
Mexican male	---	---	20.3	18.7	17.6
Mexican female	---	---	20.5	17.7	12.7
Poverty status:[5]					
Poor	---	24.4	23.5	19.3	17.8
Near poor	---	28.9	26.5	19.4	18.8
Nonpoor	---	28.9	29.0	19.6	16.5
20 years and over, age adjusted[3]					
Both sexes[4]	---	---	---	20.8	17.3
Male	---	---	---	19.0	16.4
Female	---	---	---	22.0	17.8
Not Hispanic or Latino:					
White only, male	---	---	---	18.8	16.5
White only, female	---	---	---	22.2	18.1
Black or African American only, male	---	---	---	16.9	12.4
Black or African American only, female	---	---	---	21.4	17.7
Mexican male	---	---	---	18.5	17.4
Mexican female	---	---	---	18.7	13.8
Poverty status:[5]					
Poor	---	---	---	20.6	18.3
Near poor	---	---	---	20.6	19.1
Nonpoor	---	---	---	20.4	16.5
20 years and over, crude					
Both sexes[4]	---	---	---	19.6	17.3
Male	---	---	---	17.7	16.6
Female	---	---	---	21.3	18.0
Not Hispanic or Latino:					
White only, male	---	---	---	18.0	16.9
White only, female	---	---	---	22.5	19.1
Black or African American only, male	---	---	---	14.7	12.2
Black or African American only, female	---	---	---	18.2	16.1
Mexican male	---	---	---	15.4	15.0
Mexican female	---	---	---	14.3	10.7
Poverty status:[5]					
Poor	---	---	---	17.6	16.4
Near poor	---	---	---	19.8	18.2
Nonpoor	---	---	---	19.5	16.9
Male					
20–34 years	15.1	12.4	11.9	8.2	9.8
35–44 years	33.9	31.8	27.9	19.4	19.8
45–54 years	39.2	37.5	36.9	26.6	23.6
55–64 years	41.6	36.2	36.8	28.0	19.9
65–74 years	38.0	34.7	31.7	21.9	13.7
75 years and over	---	---	---	20.4	10.2
Female					
20–34 years	12.4	10.9	9.8	7.3	8.9
35–44 years	23.1	19.3	20.7	12.3	12.4
45–54 years	46.9	38.7	40.5	26.7	21.4
55–64 years	70.1	53.1	52.9	40.9	25.6
65–74 years	68.5	57.7	51.6	41.3	32.3
75 years and over	---	---	---	38.2	26.5

See footnotes at end of table.

Table 70 (page 2 of 3). Serum cholesterol levels among persons 20 years of age and over, according to sex, age, race and Hispanic origin, and poverty status: United States, 1960–62, 1971–74, 1976–80, 1988–94, and 1999–2002

[Data are based on physical examinations of a sample of the civilian noninstitutionalized population]

Sex, age, race and Hispanic origin[1], and poverty status	*1960–62*	*1971–74*	*1976–80[2]*	*1988–94*	*1999–2002*
20–74 years, age adjusted[3]	Mean serum cholesterol level, mg/dL				
Both sexes[4]	222	216	215	205	203
Male	220	216	213	204	203
Female	224	217	216	205	202
Not Hispanic or Latino:					
White only, male	---	---	213	204	202
White only, female	---	---	216	206	204
Black or African American only, male	---	---	211	201	195
Black or African American only, female	---	---	216	204	200
Mexican male	---	---	209	206	205
Mexican female	---	---	209	204	198
Poverty status:[5]					
Poor	---	211	211	203	200
Near poor	---	217	213	203	203
Nonpoor	---	217	216	206	203
20 years and over, age adjusted[3]					
Both sexes[4]	---	---	---	206	203
Male	---	---	---	204	202
Female	---	---	---	207	204
Not Hispanic or Latino:					
White only, male	---	---	---	205	202
White only, female	---	---	---	208	205
Black or African American only, male	---	---	---	202	195
Black or African American only, female	---	---	---	207	202
Mexican male	---	---	---	206	204
Mexican female	---	---	---	206	199
Poverty status:[5]					
Poor	---	---	---	205	201
Near poor	---	---	---	205	204
Nonpoor	---	---	---	207	203
20 years and over, crude					
Both sexes[4]	---	---	---	204	203
Male	---	---	---	202	202
Female	---	---	---	206	204
Not Hispanic or Latino:					
White only, male	---	---	---	203	203
White only, female	---	---	---	208	206
Black or African American only, male	---	---	---	198	194
Black or African American only, female	---	---	---	201	199
Mexican male	---	---	---	199	200
Mexican female	---	---	---	198	194
Poverty status:[5]					
Poor	---	---	---	200	198
Near poor	---	---	---	202	202
Nonpoor	---	---	---	205	204
Male					
20–34 years	198	194	192	186	188
35–44 years	227	221	217	206	207
45–54 years	231	229	227	216	215
55–64 years	233	229	229	216	212
65–74 years	230	226	221	212	202
75 years and over	---	---	---	205	195
Female					
20–34 years	194	191	189	184	185
35–44 years	214	207	207	195	198
45–54 years	237	232	232	217	211
55–64 years	262	245	249	235	221
65–74 years	266	250	246	233	224
75 years and over	---	---	---	229	217

See footnotes at end of table.

Table 70 (page 3 of 3). Serum cholesterol levels among persons 20 years of age and over, according to sex, age, race and Hispanic origin, and poverty status: United States, 1960–62, 1971–74, 1976–80, 1988–94, and 1999–2002

[Data are based on physical examinations of a sample of the civilian noninstitutionalized population]

* Estimates are considered unreliable. Data preceded by an asterisk have a relative standard error of 20–30 percent.
- - - Data not available.
[1]Persons of Mexican origin may be of any race. Starting with data year 1999 race-specific estimates are tabulated according to 1997 Standards for Federal data on Race and Ethnicity and are not strictly comparable with estimates for earlier years. The two non-Hispanic race categories shown in the table conform to 1997 Standards. The 1999–2002 race-specific estimates are for persons who reported only one racial group. Prior to data year 1999, data were tabulated according to 1977 Standards. Estimates for single race categories prior to 1999 included persons who reported one race or, if they reported more than one race, identified one race as best representing their race. See Appendix II, Race.
[2]Data for Mexicans are for 1982–84. See Appendix I, National Health and Nutrition Examination Survey (NHANES).
[3]Age adjusted to the 2000 standard population using five age groups. Age-adjusted estimates may differ from other age-adjusted estimates based on the same data and presented elsewhere if different age groups are used in the adjustment procedure. See Appendix II, Age adjustment.
[4]Includes persons of all races and Hispanic origins, not just those shown separately.
[5]Poor persons are defined as below the poverty threshold. Near poor persons have incomes of 100 percent to less than 200 percent of the poverty threshold. Nonpoor persons have incomes of 200 percent or greater than the poverty threshold. Persons with unknown poverty status are excluded. See Appendix II, Family income; Poverty level.

NOTES: High serum cholesterol is defined as greater than or equal to 240 mg/dL (6.20 mmol/L). Risk levels have been defined by the Second Report of the National Cholesterol Education Program Expert Panel on Detection, Evaluation and Treatment of High Blood Cholesterol in Adults. National Heart, Lung, and Blood Institute, National Institutes of Health. September 1993. (Summarized in *JAMA* 269(23):3015–23. June 16, 1993.) Standard errors for selected years are available in the spreadsheet version of this table. See www.cdc.gov/nchs/hus.htm.

SOURCES: Centers for Disease Control and Prevention, National Center for Health Statistics, National Health and Nutrition Examination Survey, Hispanic Health and Nutrition Examination Survey (1982–84), and National Health Examination Survey (1960–62).

Table 71. Mean energy and macronutrient intake among persons 20–74 years of age, according to sex and age: United States, 1971–74, 1976–80, 1988–94, and 1999–2000

[Data are based on dietary recall interviews of a sample of the civilian noninstitutionalized population]

Sex and age	1971–1974	1976–1980	1988–1994	1999–2000
	Energy intake in kcals			
Male, age adjusted[1]	2,450	2,439	2,666	2,618
20–39 years	2,784	2,753	2,965	2,828
40–59 years	2,303	2,315	2,568	2,590
60–74 years	1,918	1,906	2,105	2,123
Female, age adjusted[1]	1,542	1,522	1,798	1,877
20–39 years	1,652	1,643	1,958	2,028
40–59 years	1,510	1,473	1,736	1,828
60–74 years	1,325	1,322	1,522	1,596
	Percent kcals from carbohydrate			
Male, age adjusted[1]	42.4	42.6	48.2	49.0
20–39 years	42.2	43.1	48.1	50.0
40–59 years	41.6	41.5	47.8	47.5
60–74 years	44.8	44.1	49.7	49.7
Female, age adjusted[1]	45.4	46.0	50.6	51.6
20–39 years	45.8	46.0	50.6	52.6
40–59 years	44.4	45.0	50.0	50.9
60–74 years	46.8	48.6	52.5	51.1
	Percent kcals from total fat			
Male, age adjusted[1]	36.9	36.8	33.9	32.8
20–39 years	37.0	36.2	34.0	32.1
40–59 years	36.9	37.3	34.2	33.4
60–74 years	36.4	36.9	32.9	33.0
Female, age adjusted[1]	36.1	36.0	33.4	32.8
20–39 years	36.3	36.0	33.6	32.3
40–59 years	36.3	36.5	34.0	33.1
60–74 years	34.9	34.7	31.6	33.3
	Percent kcals from saturated fat			
Male, age adjusted[1]	13.5	13.2	11.3	10.9
20–39 years	13.6	13.1	11.5	10.8
40–59 years	13.5	13.5	11.3	11.1
60–74 years	13.3	13.1	10.9	10.7
Female, age adjusted[1]	13.0	12.5	11.2	11.0
20–39 years	13.0	12.6	11.4	10.9
40–59 years	13.1	12.7	11.3	11.1
60–74 years	12.4	11.8	10.4	10.9

[1]Age adjusted to the 2000 standard population using three age groups, 20–39 years, 40–59 years, and 60–74 years. See Appendix II, Age adjustment.

NOTES: Estimates of energy intake include kilocalories (kcals) from all foods and beverages, including alcoholic beverages, consumed during the preceding 24 hours. Standard errors are available in the spreadsheet version of this table. See www.cdc.gov/nchs/hus.htm.

SOURCE: Centers for Disease Control and Prevention, National Center for Health Statistics, National Health and Nutrition Examination Survey. Wright JD, Kennedy-Stephenson J, Wang CY, McDowell MA, Johnson CL. Trends in intake of energy and macronutrients - United States, 1971–2000. MMWR 53(04):80–2, 2004.

Table 72 (page 1 of 2). Leisure-time physical activity among adults 18 years of age and over, according to selected characteristics: United States, selected years 1998–2003

[Data are based on household interviews of a sample of the civilian noninstitutionalized population]

Characteristic	Inactive[1]			Some leisure-time activity[1]			Regular leisure-time activity[1]		
	1998	2002	2003	1998	2002	2003	1998	2002	2003
	Percent of adults								
Total, age-adjusted[2,3]	40.5	38.2	37.6	30.0	30.1	29.5	29.5	31.7	32.8
Total, crude[3]	40.2	38.1	37.6	30.0	30.1	29.6	29.8	31.7	32.8
Age									
18–44 years	35.2	33.1	32.9	31.4	31.0	30.3	33.5	35.9	36.8
18–24 years	32.8	32.9	29.6	30.1	28.3	28.2	37.1	38.8	42.3
25–44 years	35.9	33.2	34.0	31.8	31.9	31.0	32.4	34.9	34.9
45–64 years	41.2	38.4	38.2	30.6	31.5	30.5	28.2	30.1	31.3
45–54 years	38.9	37.5	36.5	31.4	31.2	30.8	29.8	31.3	32.8
55–64 years	44.9	39.7	40.8	29.3	32.0	30.1	25.8	28.3	29.2
65 years and over	55.4	53.6	51.4	24.7	24.8	25.3	19.9	21.6	23.3
65–74 years	49.1	46.9	45.8	26.5	27.1	25.8	24.4	26.0	28.4
75 years and over	63.3	61.3	57.5	22.4	22.2	24.8	14.3	16.6	17.7
Sex[2]									
Male	37.8	36.1	35.4	28.7	28.8	29.2	33.5	35.1	35.4
Female	42.9	40.1	39.5	31.1	31.3	29.9	26.0	28.7	30.6
Sex and age									
Male:									
18–44 years	32.0	30.6	30.9	30.7	29.7	29.5	37.2	39.7	39.6
45–54 years	37.7	37.5	36.4	29.6	29.8	30.5	32.6	32.8	33.2
55–64 years	44.5	39.1	39.5	26.9	30.9	29.7	28.6	30.0	30.8
65–74 years	45.3	44.3	43.0	23.6	26.1	24.9	31.1	29.6	32.1
75 years and over	57.4	55.6	48.1	21.6	21.0	28.9	20.9	23.5	23.0
Female:									
18–44 years	38.2	35.6	34.9	32.0	32.3	31.1	29.8	32.1	34.0
45–54 years	39.9	37.5	36.5	33.0	32.6	31.1	27.1	29.9	32.4
55–64 years	45.2	40.2	41.9	31.5	33.0	30.4	23.3	26.8	27.6
65–74 years	52.2	49.0	48.0	28.7	27.9	26.6	19.0	23.1	25.4
75 years and over	67.0	64.8	63.7	22.9	22.9	22.0	10.1	12.3	14.3
Race[2,4]									
White only	38.8	36.5	36.3	30.5	30.4	29.8	30.7	33.1	33.9
Black or African American only	52.2	48.5	48.5	25.2	27.1	26.1	22.6	24.4	25.5
American Indian and Alaska Native only	49.2	45.4	54.7	19.0	28.9	20.0	31.8	25.7	25.2
Asian only	39.4	39.0	35.9	35.2	33.1	31.1	25.4	27.9	33.1
Native Hawaiian and Other Pacific Islander only	- - -	*	*	- - -	*	*	- - -	*	*
2 or more races	- - -	30.6	33.3	- - -	32.5	34.1	- - -	36.9	32.6
Hispanic origin and race[2,4]									
Hispanic or Latino	55.5	53.9	51.9	23.4	23.5	23.6	21.1	22.7	24.4
Mexican	56.7	54.9	52.0	23.9	23.1	23.7	19.4	22.0	24.3
Not Hispanic or Latino	38.8	36.0	35.5	30.7	30.9	30.3	30.5	33.1	34.2
White only	36.7	33.9	33.4	31.3	31.5	30.9	32.0	34.6	35.8
Black or African American only	52.2	48.6	48.5	25.1	26.9	26.0	22.6	24.6	25.5
Education[5,6]									
No high school diploma or GED	64.8	63.2	61.2	19.4	19.5	20.6	15.8	17.2	18.1
High school diploma or GED	47.6	45.4	45.5	28.7	28.5	27.5	23.7	26.2	27.0
Some college or more	30.2	28.1	28.1	34.3	34.7	33.8	35.5	37.1	38.2

See footnotes at end of table.

Table 72 (page 2 of 2). Leisure-time physical activity among adults 18 years of age and over, according to selected characteristics: United States, selected years 1998–2003

[Data are based on household interviews of a sample of the civilian noninstitutionalized population]

Characteristic	*Inactive*[1]			*Some leisure-time activity*[1]			*Regular leisure-time activity*[1]		
	1998	*2002*	*2003*	*1998*	*2002*	*2003*	*1998*	*2002*	*2003*
Poverty status[2,7]					Percent of adults				
Poor	59.4	56.5	55.1	20.5	22.5	22.0	20.1	21.0	22.9
Near poor	52.2	50.5	50.5	26.2	25.8	24.8	21.6	23.7	24.7
Nonpoor	34.7	32.3	31.4	32.4	32.3	32.0	33.0	35.4	36.7
Hispanic origin and race and poverty status[2,4,7]									
Hispanic or Latino:									
Poor	68.6	65.5	64.2	18.0	19.0	19.1	13.4	15.5	16.7
Near poor	60.8	61.0	58.8	21.2	20.5	21.0	18.0	18.5	20.3
Nonpoor	45.6	45.5	41.8	27.6	26.3	27.3	26.8	28.1	30.9
Not Hispanic or Latino:									
White only:									
Poor	53.7	49.8	49.3	22.5	25.1	22.6	23.8	25.1	28.0
Near poor	49.0	46.4	45.7	27.6	27.5	27.4	23.4	26.1	27.0
Nonpoor	32.7	29.8	29.2	32.9	32.9	32.4	34.4	37.3	38.3
Black or African American only:									
Poor	64.3	64.6	61.3	17.4	18.5	20.9	18.3	16.8	17.8
Near poor	55.6	52.8	55.3	24.4	25.4	22.9	19.9	21.8	21.8
Nonpoor	46.0	40.6	40.7	28.7	30.8	29.1	25.3	28.6	30.2
Geographic region[2]									
Northeast	39.4	35.0	34.4	31.3	31.5	29.2	29.4	33.5	36.4
Midwest	37.3	35.5	34.7	31.7	32.7	32.2	31.0	31.8	33.1
South	46.9	42.5	42.6	27.1	28.2	27.7	26.0	29.2	29.7
West	33.9	36.5	34.9	31.6	29.0	29.9	34.6	34.5	35.2
Location of residence[2]									
Within MSA[8]	39.3	36.9	36.4	30.6	30.7	29.9	30.0	32.4	33.7
Outside MSA[8]	44.7	43.5	42.4	27.5	27.7	28.1	27.8	28.9	29.5

* Estimates are considered unreliable. Data not shown have a relative standard error of greater than 30 percent.
- - - Data not available.
[1]Respondents were asked about the frequency and duration of vigorous and light/moderate physical activity during leisure time. Adults classified as inactive reported no sessions of light/moderate or vigorous leisure-time activity of at least 10 minutes duration; adults classified with some leisure-time activity reported at least one session of light/moderate or vigorous physical activity of at least 10 minutes duration but did not meet the definition for regular leisure-time activity; adults classified with regular leisure-time activity reported three or more sessions per week of vigorous activity lasting at least 20 minutes or five or more sessions per week of light/moderate activity lasting at least 30 minutes in duration. See Appendix II, Physical activity, leisure-time.
[2]Estimates are age adjusted to the year 2000 standard population using five age groups: 18–44 years, 45–54 years, 55–64 years, 65–74 years, and 75 years and over. Age-adjusted estimates in this table may differ from other age-adjusted estimates based on the same data and presented elsewhere if different age groups are used in the adjustment procedure. See Appendix II, Age adjustment.
[3]Includes all other races not shown separately and unknown education.
[4]The race groups, white, black, American Indian and Alaska Native, Asian, Native Hawaiian and Other Pacific Islander, and 2 or more races, include persons of Hispanic and non-Hispanic origin. Persons of Hispanic origin may be of any race. Starting with data year 1999 race-specific estimates are tabulated according to 1997 Standards for Federal data on Race and Ethnicity and are not strictly comparable with estimates for earlier years. The five single race categories plus multiple race categories shown in the table conform to 1997 Standards. Starting with data year 1999 race-specific estimates are for persons who reported only one racial group; the category "2 or more races" includes persons who reported more than one racial group. Prior to data year 1999, data were tabulated according to 1977 Standards with four racial groups and the category "Asian only" included Native Hawaiian and Other Pacific Islander. Estimates for single race categories prior to 1999 included persons who reported one race or, if they reported more than one race, identified one race as best representing their race. See Appendix II, Race.
[5]Estimates are for persons 25 years of age and over and are age adjusted to the year 2000 standard population using five age groups: 25–44 years, 45–54 years, 55–64 years, 65–74 years, and 75 years and over. See Appendix II, Age adjustment.
[6]GED stands for General Educational Development high school equivalency diploma. See Appendix II, Education.
[7]Poor persons are defined as below the poverty threshold. Near poor persons have incomes of 100 percent to less than 200 percent of the poverty threshold. Nonpoor persons have incomes of 200 percent or greater than the poverty threshold. Missing family income data were imputed for 31–36 percent of adults 18 years of age and over in 1998–2003. See Appendix II, Family Income; Poverty level.
[8]MSA is metropolitan statistical area.

NOTES: For more data on leisure-time physical activity, see National Health Interview Survey home page: www.cdc.gov/nchs/nhis/htm. Data for additional years are available. See Appendix III. Standard errors are available in the spreadsheet version of this table. See www.cdc.gov/nchs/hus.htm.
Startingwith *Health, United States, 2005*, estimates for 2000 and later years use weights derived from the 2000 census.

SOURCE: Centers for Disease Control and Prevention, National Center for Health Statistics, National Health Interview Survey, family core and sample adult questionnaires.

Table 73 (page 1 of 4). Overweight, obesity, and healthy weight among persons 20 years of age and over, according to sex, age, race and Hispanic origin, and poverty status: United States, 1960–62, 1971–74, 1976–80, 1988–94, and 1999–2002

[Data are based on measured height and weight of a sample of the civilian noninstitutionalized population]

Sex, age, race and Hispanic origin[1], and poverty status	Overweight[2]				
	1960–62	1971–74	1976–80[3]	1988–94	1999–2002
20–74 years, age adjusted[4]	Percent of population				
Both sexes[5,6]	44.8	47.7	47.4	56.0	65.2
Male	49.5	54.7	52.9	61.0	68.8
Female[5]	40.2	41.1	42.0	51.2	61.7
Not Hispanic or Latino:					
White only, male	---	---	53.8	61.6	69.5
White only, female[5]	---	---	38.7	47.2	57.0
Black or African American only, male	---	---	51.3	58.2	62.0
Black or African American only, female[5]	---	---	62.6	68.5	77.5
Mexican male	---	---	61.6	69.4	74.1
Mexican female[5]	---	---	61.7	69.6	71.4
Poverty status:[7]					
Poor	---	49.3	50.0	59.8	65.2
Near poor	---	50.9	49.0	58.2	68.0
Nonpoor	---	46.7	46.6	54.5	64.9
20 years and over, age adjusted[4]					
Both sexes[5,6]	---	---	---	56.0	65.1
Male	---	---	---	60.9	68.8
Female[5]	---	---	---	51.4	61.6
Not Hispanic or Latino:					
White only, male	---	---	---	61.6	69.4
White only, female[5]	---	---	---	47.5	57.2
Black or African American only, male	---	---	---	57.8	62.6
Black or African American only, female[5]	---	---	---	68.2	77.1
Mexican male	---	---	---	68.9	73.2
Mexican female[5]	---	---	---	68.9	71.2
Poverty status:[7]					
Poor	---	---	---	59.6	64.6
Near poor	---	---	---	58.0	67.3
Nonpoor	---	---	---	54.8	65.1
20 years and over, crude					
Both sexes[5,6]	---	---	---	54.9	65.2
Male	---	---	---	59.4	68.6
Female[5]	---	---	---	50.7	62.0
Not Hispanic or Latino:					
White only, male	---	---	---	60.6	69.9
White only, female[5]	---	---	---	47.4	58.2
Black or African American only, male	---	---	---	56.7	61.7
Black or African American only, female[5]	---	---	---	66.0	76.8
Mexican male	---	---	---	63.9	70.1
Mexican female[5]	---	---	---	65.9	69.3
Poverty status:[7]					
Poor	---	---	---	56.8	62.5
Near poor	---	---	---	55.7	66.2
Nonpoor	---	---	---	54.2	65.8
Male					
20–34 years	42.7	42.8	41.2	47.5	57.4
35–44 years	53.5	63.2	57.2	65.5	70.5
45–54 years	53.9	59.7	60.2	66.1	75.7
55–64 years	52.2	58.5	60.2	70.5	75.4
65–74 years	47.8	54.6	54.2	68.5	76.2
75 years and over	---	---	---	56.5	67.4
Female[5]					
20–34 years	21.2	25.8	27.9	37.0	52.8
35–44 years	37.2	40.5	40.7	49.6	60.6
45–54 years	49.3	49.0	48.7	60.3	65.1
55–64 years	59.9	54.5	53.7	66.3	72.2
65–74 years	60.9	55.9	59.5	60.3	70.9
75 years and over	---	---	---	52.3	59.9

See footnotes at end of table.

Table 73 (page 2 of 4). Overweight, obesity, and healthy weight among persons 20 years of age and over, according to sex, age, race and Hispanic origin, and poverty status: United States, 1960–62, 1971–74, 1976–80, 1988–94, and 1999–2002

[Data are based on measured height and weight of a sample of the civilian noninstitutionalized population]

Sex, age, race and Hispanic origin[1], and poverty status	Obesity[8]				
	1960–62	*1971–74*	*1976–80*[3]	*1988–94*	*1999–2002*
20–74 years, age adjusted[4]	Percent of population				
Both sexes[5,6]	13.3	14.6	15.1	23.3	31.1
Male	10.7	12.2	12.8	20.6	28.1
Female[5]	15.7	16.8	17.1	26.0	34.0
Not Hispanic or Latino:					
White only, male	- - -	- - -	12.4	20.7	28.7
White only, female[5]	- - -	- - -	15.4	23.3	31.3
Black or African American only, male	- - -	- - -	16.5	21.3	27.9
Black or African American only, female[5]	- - -	- - -	31.0	39.1	49.6
Mexican male	- - -	- - -	15.7	24.4	29.0
Mexican female[5]	- - -	- - -	26.6	36.1	38.9
Poverty status:[7]					
Poor	- - -	20.7	21.9	29.2	36.0
Near poor	- - -	18.4	18.7	26.6	35.4
Nonpoor	- - -	12.4	12.9	21.4	29.2
20 years and over, age adjusted[4]					
Both sexes[5,6]	- - -	- - -	- - -	22.9	30.4
Male	- - -	- - -	- - -	20.2	27.5
Female[5]	- - -	- - -	- - -	25.5	33.2
Not Hispanic or Latino:					
White only, male	- - -	- - -	- - -	20.3	28.0
White only, female[5]	- - -	- - -	- - -	22.9	30.7
Black or African American only, male	- - -	- - -	- - -	20.9	27.8
Black or African American only, female[5]	- - -	- - -	- - -	38.3	48.8
Mexican male	- - -	- - -	- - -	23.8	27.8
Mexican female[5]	- - -	- - -	- - -	35.2	38.0
Poverty status:[7]					
Poor	- - -	- - -	- - -	28.1	34.7
Near poor	- - -	- - -	- - -	26.1	34.1
Nonpoor	- - -	- - -	- - -	21.1	28.7
20 years and over, crude					
Both sexes[5,6]	- - -	- - -	- - -	22.3	30.5
Male	- - -	- - -	- - -	19.5	27.5
Female[5]	- - -	- - -	- - -	25.0	33.4
Not Hispanic or Latino:					
White only, male	- - -	- - -	- - -	19.9	28.4
White only, female[5]	- - -	- - -	- - -	22.7	31.3
Black or African American only, male	- - -	- - -	- - -	20.7	27.5
Black or African American only, female[5]	- - -	- - -	- - -	36.7	48.8
Mexican male	- - -	- - -	- - -	20.6	26.0
Mexican female[5]	- - -	- - -	- - -	33.3	37.0
Poverty status:[7]					
Poor	- - -	- - -	- - -	25.9	33.0
Near poor	- - -	- - -	- - -	24.3	32.8
Nonpoor	- - -	- - -	- - -	20.9	29.3
Male					
20–34 years	9.2	9.7	8.9	14.1	21.7
35–44 years	12.1	13.5	13.5	21.5	28.5
45–54 years	12.5	13.7	16.7	23.2	30.6
55–64 years	9.2	14.1	14.1	27.2	35.5
65–74 years	10.4	10.9	13.2	24.1	31.9
75 years and over	- - -	- - -	- - -	13.2	18.0
Female[5]					
20–34 years	7.2	9.7	11.0	18.5	28.4
35–44 years	14.7	17.7	17.8	25.5	32.1
45–54 years	20.3	18.9	19.6	32.4	36.9
55–64 years	24.4	24.1	22.9	33.7	42.1
65–74 years	23.2	22.0	21.5	26.9	39.3
75 years and over	- - -	- - -	- - -	19.2	23.6

See footnotes at end of table.

Table 73 (page 3 of 4). Overweight, obesity, and healthy weight among persons 20 years of age and over, according to sex, age, race and Hispanic origin, and poverty status: United States, 1960–62, 1971–74, 1976–80, 1988–94, and 1999–2002

[Data are based on measured height and weight of a sample of the civilian noninstitutionalized population]

Sex, age, race and Hispanic origin[1], and poverty status	*Healthy weight*[9]				
	1960–62	*1971–74*	*1976–80*[3]	*1988–94*	*1999–2002*
20–74 years, age adjusted[4]			Percent of population		
Both sexes[5,6]	51.2	48.8	49.6	41.7	32.9
Male	48.3	43.0	45.4	37.9	30.2
Female[5]	54.1	54.3	53.7	45.3	35.6
Not Hispanic or Latino:					
White only, male	---	---	45.3	37.4	29.5
White only, female[5]	---	---	56.7	49.2	39.7
Black or African American only, male	---	---	46.6	40.0	35.5
Black or African American only, female[5]	---	---	35.0	28.9	21.3
Mexican male	---	---	37.1	29.8	25.6
Mexican female[5]	---	---	36.4	29.0	27.5
Poverty status:[7]					
Poor	---	45.8	45.1	37.3	32.4
Near poor	---	45.1	47.6	39.2	29.7
Nonpoor	---	50.2	51.0	43.4	33.5
20 years and over, age adjusted[4]					
Both sexes[5,6]	---	---	---	41.6	33.0
Male	---	---	---	37.9	30.2
Female[5]	---	---	---	45.0	35.7
Not Hispanic or Latino:					
White only, male	---	---	---	37.3	29.6
White only, female[5]	---	---	---	48.7	39.5
Black or African American only, male	---	---	---	40.1	34.7
Black or African American only, female[5]	---	---	---	29.2	21.7
Mexican male	---	---	---	30.2	26.5
Mexican female[5]	---	---	---	29.7	27.5
Poverty status:[7]					
Poor	---	---	---	37.5	32.7
Near poor	---	---	---	39.3	30.5
Nonpoor	---	---	---	43.1	33.4
20 years and over, crude					
Both sexes[5,6]	---	---	---	42.6	32.9
Male	---	---	---	39.4	30.4
Female[5]	---	---	---	45.7	35.4
Not Hispanic or Latino:					
White only, male	---	---	---	38.2	29.2
White only, female[5]	---	---	---	48.8	38.7
Black or African American only, male	---	---	---	41.5	35.9
Black or African American only, female[5]	---	---	---	31.2	21.9
Mexican male	---	---	---	35.2	29.4
Mexican female[5]	---	---	---	32.4	29.4
Poverty status:[7]					
Poor	---	---	---	39.8	34.5
Near poor	---	---	---	41.5	31.5
Nonpoor	---	---	---	43.6	32.8
Male					
20–34 years	55.3	54.7	57.1	51.1	40.3
35–44 years	45.2	35.2	41.3	33.4	29.0
45–54 years	44.8	38.5	38.7	33.6	24.0
55–64 years	44.9	38.3	38.7	28.6	23.8
65–74 years	46.2	42.1	42.3	30.1	22.8
75 years and over	---	---	---	40.9	32.0
Female[5]					
20–34 years	67.6	65.8	65.0	57.9	42.6
35–44 years	58.4	56.7	55.6	47.1	37.1
45–54 years	47.6	49.3	48.7	37.2	33.1
55–64 years	38.1	41.1	43.5	31.5	27.6
65–74 years	36.4	40.6	37.8	37.0	26.4
75 years and over	---	---	---	43.0	36.9

See footnotes at end of table.

Table 73 (page 4 of 4). Overweight, obesity, and healthy weight among persons 20 years of age and over, according to sex, age, race and Hispanic origin, and poverty status: United States, 1960–62, 1971–74, 1976–80, 1988–94, and 1999–2002

[Data are based on measured height and weight of a sample of the civilian noninstitutionalized population]

- - - Data not available.

[1]Persons of Mexican origin may be of any race. Starting with data year 1999 race-specific estimates are tabulated according to 1997 Standards for Federal data on Race and Ethnicity and are not strictly comparable with estimates for earlier years. The two non-Hispanic race categories shown in the table conform to 1997 Standards. The 1999–2002 race-specific estimates are for persons who reported only one racial group. Prior to data year 1999, data were tabulated according to 1977 Standards. Estimates for single race categories prior to 1999 included persons who reported one race or, if they reported more than one race, identified one race as best representing their race. See Appendix II, Race.

[2]Body mass index (BMI) greater than or equal to 25. See Appendix II, Body mass index.

[3]Data for Mexicans are for 1982–84. See Appendix I, National Health and Nutrition Examination Survey (NHANES).

[4]Age adjusted to the 2000 standard population using five age groups. Age-adjusted estimates in this table may differ from other age-adjusted estimates based on the same data and presented elsewhere if different age groups are used in the adjustment procedure. See Appendix II, Age adjustment.

[5]Excludes pregnant women.

[6]Includes persons of all races and Hispanic origins, not just those shown separately.

[7]Poor persons are defined as below the poverty threshold. Near poor persons have incomes of 100 percent to less than 200 percent of the poverty threshold. Nonpoor persons have incomes of 200 percent or greater than the poverty threshold. Persons with unknown poverty status are excluded. See Appendix II, Family income; Poverty level.

[8]Body mass index (BMI) greater than or equal to 30.

[9]BMI of 18.5 to less than 25 kilograms/meter^2.

NOTES: Percents do not sum to 100 because the percent of persons with BMI less than 18.5 is not shown and the percent of persons with obesity is a subset of the percent with overweight. Height was measured without shoes; two pounds were deducted from data for 1960–62 to allow for weight of clothing. Standard errors for selected years are available in the spreadsheet version of this table. See www.cdc.gov/nchs/hus.htm.

SOURCES: Centers for Disease Control and Prevention, National Center for Health Statistics, National Health and Nutrition Examination Survey, Hispanic Health and Nutrition Examination Survey (1982–84), and National Health Examination Survey (1960–62).

Table 74. Overweight among children and adolescents 6–19 years of age, according to sex, age, race and Hispanic origin, and poverty status: United States, selected years 1963–65 through 1999–2002

[Data are based on physical examinations of a sample of the civilian noninstitutionalized population]

Sex, age, race and Hispanic origin[1], and poverty status	1963–65 1966–70[2]	1971–74	1976–80[3]	1988–94	1999–2002
			Percent of population		
6–11 years of age					
Both sexes[4]	4.2	4.0	6.5	11.3	15.8
Boys	4.0	*4.3	6.6	11.6	16.9
Not Hispanic or Latino:					
White only	- - -	- - -	6.1	10.7	14.0
Black or African American only	- - -	- - -	6.8	12.3	17.0
Mexican	- - -	- - -	13.3	17.5	26.5
Girls[5]	4.5	*3.6	6.4	11.0	14.7
Not Hispanic or Latino:					
White only	- - -	- - -	5.2	*9.8	13.1
Black or African American only	- - -	- - -	11.2	17.0	22.8
Mexican	- - -	- - -	9.8	15.3	17.1
Poverty status:[6]					
Poor	- - -	- - -	- - -	11.4	19.1
Near poor	- - -	- - -	- - -	11.1	16.4
Nonpoor	- - -	- - -	- - -	11.1	14.3
12–19 years of age					
Both sexes[4]	4.6	6.1	5.0	10.5	16.1
Boys	4.5	6.1	4.8	11.3	16.7
Not Hispanic or Latino:					
White only	- - -	- - -	3.8	11.6	14.6
Black or African American only	- - -	- - -	6.1	10.7	18.7
Mexican	- - -	- - -	7.7	14.1	24.7
Girls[5]	4.7	6.2	5.3	9.7	15.4
Not Hispanic or Latino:					
White only	- - -	- - -	4.6	8.9	12.7
Black or African American only	- - -	- - -	10.7	16.3	23.6
Mexican	- - -	- - -	8.8	*13.4	19.9
Poverty status:[6]					
Poor	- - -	- - -	- - -	15.8	19.9
Near poor	- - -	- - -	- - -	11.2	15.2
Nonpoor	- - -	- - -	- - -	7.9	14.9

* Estimates are considered unreliable. Data preceded by an asterisk have a relative standard error of 20–30 percent.

- - - Data not available.

[1]Persons of Mexican origin may be of any race. Starting with data year 1999 race-specific estimates are tabulated according to 1997 Standards for Federal data on Race and Ethnicity and are not strictly comparable with estimates for earlier years. The two non-Hispanic race categories shown in the table conform to 1997 Standards. The 1999–2002 race-specific estimates are for persons who reported only one racial group. Prior to data year 1999, data were tabulated according to 1977 Standards. Estimates for single race categories prior to 1999 included persons who reported one race or, if they reported more than one race, identified one race as best representing their race. See Appendix II, Race.

[2]Data for 1963–65 are for children 6–11 years of age; data for 1966–70 are for adolescents 12–17 years of age, not 12–19 years.

[3]Data for Mexicans are for 1982–84. See Appendix I, National Health and Nutrition Examination Survey (NHANES).

[4]Includes persons of all races and Hispanic origins, not just those shown separately.

[5]Excludes pregnant women starting with 1971–74. Pregnancy status not available for 1963–65 and 1966–70.

[6]Poverty status is based on family income and family size. Poor persons are defined as below the poverty threshold. Near poor persons have incomes of 100 percent to less than 200 percent of the poverty threshold. Nonpoor persons have incomes of 200 percent or greater than the poverty threshold. Persons with unknown poverty status are excluded. See Appendix II, Family income; Poverty level.

NOTES: Overweight is defined as body mass index (BMI) at or above the sex- and age-specific 95th percentile BMI cutoff points from the 2000 CDC Growth Charts: United States. Advance data from vital and health statistics; no 314. Hyattsville, Maryland: National Center for Health Statistics. 2000. Age is at time of examination at mobile examination center. Crude rates, not age-adjusted rates, are shown. Standard errors for selected years are available in the spreadsheet version of this table. See www.cdc.gov/nchs/hus.htm.

SOURCES: Centers for Disease Control and Prevention, National Center for Health Statistics, National Health and Nutrition Examination Survey, Hispanic Health and Nutrition Examination Survey (1982–84), and National Health Examination Survey (1963–65 and 1966–70).

Table 75 (page 1 of 3). Health care visits to doctor's offices, emergency departments, and home visits within the past 12 months, according to selected characteristics: United States, selected years 1997–2003

[Data are based on household interviews of a sample of the civilian noninstitutionalized population]

Characteristic	None 1997	None 2002	None 2003	1–3 visits 1997	1–3 visits 2002	1–3 visits 2003	4–9 visits 1997	4–9 visits 2002	4–9 visits 2003	10 or more visits 1997	10 or more visits 2002	10 or more visits 2003
	Percent distribution											
All persons[2,3]	16.5	15.9	15.8	46.2	45.5	45.8	23.6	25.2	24.8	13.7	13.4	13.6
Age												
Under 18 years	11.8	10.6	11.3	54.1	55.1	54.5	25.2	27.1	26.7	8.9	7.2	7.5
Under 6 years	5.0	5.6	5.5	44.9	47.0	46.0	37.0	37.1	39.0	13.0	10.4	9.4
6–17 years	15.3	13.0	14.0	58.7	59.0	58.7	19.3	22.3	20.8	6.8	5.7	6.6
18–44 years	21.7	22.6	22.4	46.7	45.7	46.7	19.0	19.4	19.1	12.6	12.4	11.8
18–24 years	22.0	24.8	23.6	46.8	45.6	47.2	20.0	18.7	18.2	11.2	10.8	11.0
25–44 years	21.6	21.8	22.0	46.7	45.7	46.6	18.7	19.6	19.4	13.0	12.9	12.0
45–64 years	16.9	14.8	14.7	42.9	41.9	42.2	24.7	26.9	26.6	15.5	16.4	16.5
45–54 years	17.9	17.0	16.9	43.9	43.3	44.2	23.4	25.4	24.5	14.8	14.3	14.3
55–64 years	15.3	11.5	11.4	41.3	39.7	39.2	26.7	29.0	29.8	16.7	19.7	19.6
65 years and over	8.9	8.2	6.3	34.7	31.3	31.5	32.5	36.4	35.8	23.8	24.1	26.4
65–74 years	9.8	9.1	7.1	36.9	33.7	34.0	31.6	36.8	35.7	21.6	20.5	23.3
75 years and over	7.7	7.3	5.4	31.8	28.6	28.6	33.8	35.8	36.0	26.6	28.3	30.0
Sex[3]												
Male	21.3	20.6	20.6	47.1	46.5	46.8	20.6	22.2	21.9	11.0	10.7	10.7
Female	11.8	11.4	11.1	45.4	44.5	44.9	26.5	28.0	27.7	16.3	16.1	16.3
Race[3,4]												
White only	16.0	15.6	15.7	46.1	45.1	45.6	23.9	25.4	25.1	14.0	13.8	13.6
Black or African American only	16.8	15.3	14.7	46.1	45.8	45.8	23.2	26.0	25.2	13.9	13.0	14.3
American Indian and Alaska Native only	17.1	18.1	23.3	38.0	43.7	41.4	24.2	21.7	20.6	20.7	16.6	14.7
Asian only	22.8	21.2	22.6	49.1	49.7	47.8	19.7	20.3	20.7	8.3	8.8	8.9
Native Hawaiian and Other Pacific Islander only	---	*	*	---	*	*	---	*	*	---	*	*
2 or more races	---	13.5	11.1	---	43.7	44.9	---	27.3	23.0	---	15.4	21.0
Hispanic origin and race[3,4]												
Hispanic or Latino	24.9	25.7	25.3	42.3	41.5	42.9	20.3	21.1	20.3	12.5	11.7	11.5
Mexican	28.9	28.8	27.8	40.8	40.5	42.5	18.5	19.3	18.8	11.8	11.5	11.0
Not Hispanic or Latino	15.4	14.5	14.1	46.7	46.0	46.3	24.0	25.8	25.6	13.9	13.7	14.0
White only	14.7	14.0	13.5	46.6	45.8	46.2	24.4	26.1	26.1	14.3	14.2	14.2
Black or African American only	16.9	15.3	14.6	46.1	45.7	45.9	23.1	26.0	25.3	13.8	13.1	14.2
Respondent-assessed health status[3]												
Fair or poor	7.8	10.1	8.7	23.3	22.2	23.2	29.0	29.4	28.8	39.9	38.3	39.3
Good to excellent	17.2	16.6	16.4	48.4	47.7	48.1	23.3	24.9	24.5	11.1	10.8	10.9
Poverty status[3,5]												
Poor	20.6	19.9	20.9	37.8	38.3	37.8	22.7	23.9	23.7	18.9	17.9	17.6
Near poor	20.1	20.0	19.8	43.3	41.2	41.5	21.7	23.8	23.6	14.9	15.0	15.1
Nonpoor	14.5	14.2	13.7	48.7	47.6	48.4	24.2	25.7	25.4	12.6	12.4	12.6

Number of health care visits[1]

See footnotes at end of table.

Table 75 (page 2 of 3). Health care visits to doctor's offices, emergency departments, and home visits within the past 12 months, according to selected characteristics: United States, selected years 1997–2003

[Data are based on household interviews of a sample of the civilian noninstitutionalized population]

Characteristic	None 1997	None 2002	None 2003	1–3 visits 1997	1–3 visits 2002	1–3 visits 2003	4–9 visits 1997	4–9 visits 2002	4–9 visits 2003	10 or more visits 1997	10 or more visits 2002	10 or more visits 2003
	Number of health care visits[1]											
Hispanic origin and race and poverty status[3,4,5]	*Percent distribution*											
Hispanic or Latino:												
Poor	30.2	30.0	29.9	34.8	35.4	37.0	19.9	18.9	18.5	15.0	15.7	14.6
Near poor	28.7	30.2	28.6	39.7	37.8	40.2	20.4	19.9	20.6	11.2	12.2	10.5
Nonpoor	18.9	21.1	20.7	48.8	46.8	47.7	20.4	22.3	21.2	11.9	9.8	10.3
Not Hispanic or Latino:												
White only:												
Poor	17.0	16.1	17.0	38.3	38.4	37.5	23.9	25.6	25.9	20.9	19.9	19.5
Near poor	17.3	16.7	16.6	44.1	41.3	41.0	22.2	25.0	24.9	16.3	17.0	17.4
Nonpoor	13.8	13.3	12.5	48.2	47.3	48.1	24.9	26.4	26.3	13.1	13.1	13.1
Black or African American only:												
Poor	17.4	17.3	15.7	38.5	39.7	38.1	23.4	25.9	26.5	20.7	17.1	19.6
Near poor	18.8	15.6	15.4	43.7	43.4	44.2	22.9	26.9	25.9	14.5	14.1	14.5
Nonpoor	15.6	14.4	13.7	51.7	49.1	50.6	22.7	25.3	24.3	10.0	11.1	11.4
Health insurance status[6,7]												
Under 65 years of age:												
Insured	14.3	13.3	12.8	49.0	48.7	49.1	23.6	25.1	25.2	13.1	12.9	12.9
Private	14.7	13.6	13.2	50.6	50.5	51.1	23.1	24.8	24.6	11.6	11.1	11.1
Medicaid	9.8	9.9	9.9	35.5	34.9	35.2	26.5	27.4	28.1	28.2	27.7	26.8
Uninsured	33.7	36.3	38.1	42.8	42.1	42.4	15.3	14.7	13.4	8.2	6.9	6.1
65 years of age and over:												
Medicare HMO	8.9	7.7	5.4	35.8	30.9	30.6	33.1	40.9	38.9	22.3	20.5	25.2
Private	7.3	6.1	4.8	35.9	32.0	33.5	34.0	38.1	35.9	22.7	23.8	25.8
Medicaid	9.3	9.3	*4.9	19.2	15.8	21.1	27.9	34.2	29.7	43.7	40.8	44.3
Medicare fee-for-service only	15.5	14.4	11.6	34.0	33.4	28.7	28.1	30.7	35.3	22.4	21.4	24.5
Poverty status and health insurance status[5,6,7]												
Under 65 years of age:												
Poor:												
Insured	14.0	12.5	13.0	39.2	41.4	40.8	25.1	26.5	25.9	21.7	19.5	20.4
Uninsured	37.0	39.8	41.8	39.6	37.5	38.4	14.4	13.6	13.5	8.9	9.1	6.3
Near poor:												
Insured	15.8	14.9	13.8	46.2	44.1	44.4	22.3	24.5	24.8	15.8	16.6	16.8
Uninsured	34.8	38.1	37.9	42.0	39.8	40.0	15.1	16.3	15.4	8.1	5.8	6.7
Nonpoor:												
Insured	13.8	13.1	12.5	51.0	50.3	51.0	23.6	25.1	25.2	11.7	11.5	11.4
Uninsured	29.7	32.8	35.5	46.0	46.3	47.3	16.3	14.2	11.6	8.0	6.7	5.6
Geographic region[3]												
Northeast	13.2	11.0	10.4	45.9	45.5	47.6	26.0	27.7	27.0	14.9	15.7	15.0
Midwest	15.9	14.4	14.2	47.7	47.7	47.2	22.8	25.0	25.4	13.6	13.0	13.2
South	17.2	17.4	16.5	46.1	44.7	45.1	23.3	25.2	24.8	13.5	12.8	13.6
West	19.1	19.9	21.0	44.8	44.2	44.2	22.8	23.0	22.2	13.3	12.9	12.6

See footnotes at end of table.

Table 75 (page 3 of 3). Health care visits to doctor's offices, emergency departments, and home visits within the past 12 months, according to selected characteristics: United States, selected years 1997–2003

[Data are based on household interviews of a sample of the civilian noninstitutionalized population]

	Number of health care visits[1]											
	None			*1–3 visits*			*4–9 visits*			*10 or more visits*		
Characteristic	*1997*	*2002*	*2003*	*1997*	*2002*	*2003*	*1997*	*2002*	*2003*	*1997*	*2002*	*2003*
Location of residence[3]	Percent distribution											
Within MSA[8]	16.2	15.8	16.0	46.4	45.8	45.9	23.7	25.1	24.8	13.7	13.3	13.3
Outside MSA[8]	17.3	16.3	15.0	45.4	44.1	45.6	23.3	25.6	24.9	13.9	14.0	14.5

* Estimates are considered unreliable. Data not shown have a relative standard error (RSE) of greater than 30 percent. Data preceded by an asterisk have an RSE of 20–30 percent.
- - - Data not available.
[1]This table presents a summary measure of health care visits to doctor's offices, emergency departments, and home visits during a 12-month period. See Appendix II, Health care contact; Emergency department visit; Home visit.
[2]Includes all other races not shown separately and unknown health insurance status.
[3]Estimates are age adjusted to the year 2000 standard population using six age groups: Under 18 years, 18–44 years, 45–54 years, 55–64 years, 65–74 years, and 75 years and over. See Appendix II, Age adjustment.
[4]The race groups, white, black, American Indian and Alaska Native, Asian, Native Hawaiian and Other Pacific Islander, and 2 or more races, include persons of Hispanic and non-Hispanic origin. Persons of Hispanic origin may be of any race. Starting with data year 1999 race-specific estimates are tabulated according to 1997 Standards for Federal data on Race and Ethnicity and are not strictly comparable with estimates for earlier years. The five single race categories plus multiple race categories shown in the table conform to 1997 Standards. Starting with data year 1999, race-specific estimates are for persons who reported only one racial group; the category "2 or more races" includes persons who reported more than one racial group. Prior to data year 1999, data were tabulated according to 1977 Standards with four racial groups and the category "Asian only" included Native Hawaiian and Other Pacific Islander. Estimates for single race categories prior to 1999 included persons who reported one race or, if they reported more than one race, identified one race as best representing their race. See Appendix II, Race.
[5]Poor persons are defined as below the poverty threshold. Near poor persons have incomes of 100 percent to less than 200 percent of poverty threshold. Nonpoor persons have incomes of 200 percent or greater than the poverty threshold. Missing family income data were imputed for 25–29 percent of persons in 1997–98 and 32–35 percent in 1999–2003. See Appendix II, Family income; Poverty level.
[6]Estimates for persons under 65 years of age are age adjusted to the year 2000 standard using four age groups: Under 18 years, 18–44 years, 45–54 years, and 55–64 years of age. Estimates for persons 65 years of age and over are age adjusted to the year 2000 standard using two age groups: 65–74 years and 75 years and over. See Appendix II, Age adjustment.
[7]Health insurance categories are mutually exclusive. Persons who reported both Medicaid and private coverage are classified as having private coverage. Starting in 1997 Medicaid includes State-sponsored health plans and State Children's Health Insurance Program (SCHIP). In addition to private and Medicaid the category "insured" also includes military plans, other government-sponsored health plans, and Medicare, not shown separately. Persons 65 years of age and over who reported Medicare HMO (health maintenance organization) and some other type of health insurance coverage are classified as having Medicare HMO. For persons 65 years of age and over the category "private" includes private and Medicare coverage. See Appendix II, Health insurance coverage.
[8]MSA is metropolitan statistical area.

NOTES: In 1997 the National Health Interview Survey questionnaire was redesigned. See Appendix I, National Health Interview Survey. Data for additional years are available. See Appendix III. Standard errors are available in the spreadsheet version of this table. See www.cdc.gov/nchs/hus.htm. Starting with *Health, United States, 2005*, estimates for 2000 and later years use weights derived from the 2000 census.

SOURCE: Centers for Disease Control and Prevention, National Center for Health Statistics, National Health Interview Survey, family core and sample adult questionnaires.

Table 76 (page 1 of 2). Influenza and pneumococcal vaccination among persons 18 years of age and over, according to selected characteristics: United States, selected years 1989–2003

[Data are based on household interviews of a sample of the civilian noninstitutionalized population]

Characteristic	1989	1995	2002	2003	1989	1995	2002	2003
	Percent receiving influenza vaccination during past 12 months[1]				Percent ever receiving pneumococcal vaccination[2]			
Total, age-adjusted[3,4]	9.5	23.5	28.2	29.1	4.6	11.7	16.4	16.3
Total, crude[4]	9.1	24.4	28.0	29.0	4.4	12.5	16.0	16.0
Age								
18–44 years	3.3	12.3	14.8	15.4	2.1	6.3	5.3	5.1
18–24 years	3.2	11.2	13.3	14.9	2.9	10.3	5.7	6.4
25–44 years	3.3	12.5	15.3	15.5	1.8	5.4	5.2	4.7
45–64 years	8.8	24.5	30.7	32.9	3.7	9.1	13.4	14.0
45–54 years	5.6	21.0	25.9	27.7	2.3	6.9	8.7	9.8
55–64 years	12.6	29.2	37.9	40.4	5.2	12.1	20.4	20.0
65 years and over	30.4	57.0	65.7	65.5	14.1	32.9	56.0	55.6
65–74 years	28.0	54.0	60.9	60.5	13.1	30.3	50.2	49.8
75 years and over	34.2	61.2	71.3	71.0	15.7	36.7	62.8	62.1
50 years and over	19.9	43.0	47.7	48.9	9.0	22.4	33.3	33.1
Sex[3]								
Male	9.5	22.9	27.1	27.9	4.7	13.2	16.5	15.9
Female	9.6	24.2	29.4	30.3	4.5	10.7	16.3	16.6
Sex and age								
Male:								
18–44 years	3.2	12.1	13.6	14.3	2.4	8.9	5.6	5.7
45–54 years	4.6	18.3	22.9	25.3	2.2	7.4	8.8	8.6
55–64 years	11.8	25.7	35.8	37.4	4.9	11.2	19.0	18.2
65–74 years	28.3	54.1	62.1	60.4	12.6	28.9	49.3	47.9
75 years and over	37.5	65.3	74.1	73.2	16.3	39.7	65.2	61.2
50 years and over	19.2	40.9	45.1	46.8	8.4	21.2	31.5	30.2
Female:								
18–44 years	3.3	12.3	16.0	16.4	1.8	4.4	5.0	4.5
45–54 years	6.5	23.3	28.8	30.1	2.5	6.4	8.7	11.0
55–64 years	13.2	32.1	39.9	43.1	5.4	12.8	21.7	21.6
65–74 years	27.8	53.9	59.9	60.7	13.5	31.3	51.0	51.4
75 years and over	32.3	59.3	69.6	69.6	15.3	35.3	61.4	62.7
50 years and over	20.6	44.4	49.8	50.7	9.4	23.2	34.9	35.4
Race[3,5]								
White only	9.8	24.0	28.7	29.5	4.7	11.5	16.8	16.5
Black or African American only	7.3	20.5	23.9	24.4	3.7	12.0	13.1	14.1
American Indian and Alaska Native only	12.8	22.6	29.2	24.3	9.4	20.1	*16.2	16.1
Asian only	5.7	23.8	28.4	28.9	*	8.7	11.0	11.3
Native Hawaiian and Other Pacific Islander only	- - -	- - -	*	*	- - -	- - -	*	*
2 or more races	- - -	- - -	30.8	34.2	- - -	- - -	21.9	18.7
Hispanic origin and race[3,5]								
Hispanic or Latino	8.0	21.1	21.4	21.2	3.6	9.6	9.2	10.0
Mexican	7.3	22.4	21.0	20.8	4.0	8.9	9.3	10.1
Not Hispanic or Latino	9.5	23.9	28.9	30.0	4.6	11.8	16.9	16.8
White only	9.8	24.3	29.3	30.6	4.7	11.7	17.3	17.1
Black or African American only	7.2	20.5	24.0	24.5	3.6	11.8	13.2	14.1
Education[6,7]								
25 years of age and over:								
No high school diploma or GED	9.5	22.6	24.8	24.6	4.6	12.2	16.1	15.7
High school diploma or GED	10.5	25.0	29.2	29.4	5.0	13.1	18.6	17.9
Some college or more	11.9	26.9	33.3	34.4	5.8	13.3	19.1	18.9

See footnotes at end of table.

Table 76 (page 2 of 2). Influenza and pneumococcal vaccination among persons 18 years of age and over, according to selected characteristics: United States, selected years 1989–2003

[Data are based on household interviews of a sample of the civilian noninstitutionalized population]

Characteristic	1989	1995	2002	2003	1989	1995	2002	2003
	Percent receiving influenza vaccination during past 12 months[1]				Percent ever receiving pneumococcal vaccination[2]			
Poverty status[3,8]								
Poor	9.4	21.1	24.0	23.9	5.2	12.4	14.7	15.9
Near poor	9.6	22.2	24.5	25.6	5.0	12.9	15.8	17.9
Nonpoor	10.3	25.1	29.8	30.8	4.7	11.7	16.9	16.1
Hispanic or Latino:								
Poor	7.3	19.3	20.2	18.4	*3.3	9.2	8.4	8.9
Near poor	10.3	22.5	19.7	18.1	4.3	11.0	8.5	8.1
Nonpoor	9.2	23.3	23.3	24.5	3.8	8.9	10.4	12.1
Not Hispanic or Latino:								
White only:								
Poor	10.2	22.7	23.4	26.1	6.2	14.4	16.4	18.8
Near poor	9.8	22.2	25.6	26.9	5.0	13.3	17.3	19.8
Nonpoor	10.4	25.4	30.8	31.9	4.8	11.6	17.5	16.5
Black or African American only:								
Poor	7.9	20.2	26.8	23.2	4.3	9.7	12.9	14.3
Near poor	6.7	19.0	22.5	25.2	4.2	11.9	13.8	16.3
Nonpoor	8.3	22.8	23.7	24.4	3.2	13.7	13.1	13.3
Geographic region[3]								
Northeast	8.4	21.8	28.0	29.8	3.3	9.8	15.4	14.9
Midwest	9.3	23.6	29.2	29.6	4.4	11.0	16.9	16.4
South	9.8	24.6	27.8	29.7	5.0	12.4	16.1	17.2
West	10.4	23.6	28.1	26.9	5.6	13.4	17.2	15.9
Location of residence[3]								
Within MSA[9]	9.5	23.5	28.1	29.0	4.6	11.7	16.2	16.1
Outside MSA[9]	9.3	26.3	28.8	29.6	4.2	12.6	17.1	17.3

* Estimates are considered unreliable. Data preceded by an asterisk have a relative standard error (RSE) of 20–30 percent. Data not shown have an RSE of greater than 30 percent.

- - - Data not available.

[1]Respondents were asked, "During the past 12 months, have you had a flu shot? A flu shot is usually given in the fall and protects against influenza for the flu season."

[2]Respondents were asked, "Have you ever had a pneumonia shot? This shot is usually given only once or twice in a person's lifetime and is different from the flu shot. It is also called the pneumococcal vaccine."

[3]Estimates are age adjusted to the year 2000 standard population using five age groups: 18–44 years, 45–54 years, 55–64 years, 65–74 years, and 75 years and over. See Appendix II, Age adjustment.

[4]Includes all other races not shown separately and, prior to 1990, unknown poverty status.

[5]The race groups, white, black, American Indian and Alaska Native, Asian, Native Hawaiian and Other Pacific Islander, and 2 or more races, include persons of Hispanic and non-Hispanic origin. Persons of Hispanic origin may be of any race. Starting with data year 1999, race-specific estimates are tabulated according to 1997 Standards for Federal data on Race and Ethnicity and are not strictly comparable with estimates for earlier years. The five single race categories plus multiple race categories shown in the table conform to 1997 Standards. Starting with data year 1999, race-specific estimates are for persons who reported only one racial group; the category "2 or more races" includes persons who reported more than one racial group. Prior to data year 1999, data were tabulated according to 1977 Standards with four racial groups and the category "Asian only" included Native Hawaiian and Other Pacific Islander. Estimates for single race categories prior to 1999 included persons who reported one race or, if they reported more than one race, identified one race as best representing their race. See Appendix II, Race.

[6]Estimates are for persons 25 years of age and over and are age-adjusted to the year 2000 standard population using five age groups: 25–44 years, 45–54 years, 55–64 years, 65–74 years, and 75 years and over. See Appendix II, Age adjustment.

[7]Education categories shown are for 1998 and subsequent years. GED stands for General Educational Development high school equivalency diploma. In years prior to 1998 the following categories based on number of years of school completed were used: less than 12 years, 12 years, 13 years or more. See Appendix II, Education.

[8]Poor persons are defined as below the poverty threshold. Near poor persons have incomes of 100 percent to less than 200 percent of the poverty threshold. Nonpoor persons have incomes of 200 percent or greater than the poverty threshold. Poverty status was unknown for 11 percent of persons 18 years of age and over in 1989. Missing family income data were imputed for 16 percent of persons 18 years of age and over in 1995, 34 percent in 2002, and 36 percent in 2003. See Appendix II, Family Income; Poverty level.

[9]MSA is metropolitan statistical area.

NOTES: In 2000, the Advisory Committee on Immunization Practices (ACIP) of the Centers for Disease Control and Prevention (CDC) recommended universal influenza vaccination for persons 50 years of age and over (CDC. Prevention and Control of Influenza, United States, 2000. Morbidity and mortality weekly report; 49(RR03). Atlanta, Georgia: Public Health Service. 2000). Data for additional years are available. See Appendix III. Standard errors for selected years are available in the spreadsheet version of this table. See www.cdc.gov/nchs/hus.htm. Starting with *Health, United States, 2005*, estimates for 2000 and later years use weights derived from the 2000 census.

SOURCE: Centers for Disease Control and Prevention, National Center for Health Statistics, National Health Interview Survey, sample adult questionnaire.

Table 77 (page 1 of 2). Vaccinations of children 19–35 months of age for selected diseases, according to race, Hispanic origin, poverty status, and residence in metropolitan statistical area (MSA): United States, 1995–2003

[Data are based on telephone interviews of a sample of the civilian noninstitutionalized population supplemented by a survey of immunization providers for interview participants]

Vaccination and year	Race and Hispanic origin[1]								Poverty status		Location of residence		
		Not Hispanic or Latino									Inside MSA[2]		
	All	White	Black or African American	American Indian or Alaska Native	Asian[3]	Native Hawaiian or Other Pacific Islander[3]	2 or more races	Hispanic or Latino	Below poverty	At or above poverty	Central city	Remaining areas	Outside MSA[2]
	Percent of children 19–35 months of age												
Combined series (4:3:1:3):[4]													
1995	74	76	70	69	76	---	---	68	67	77	72	75	75
1998	79	82	73	78	79	---	---	75	74	82	77	81	81
1999	78	81	74	75	77	---	---	75	73	81	77	79	80
2000	76	79	71	69	75	---	---	73	71	78	73	78	79
2001	77	79	71	76	77	---	---	77	72	79	75	78	79
2002	78	80	71	*	83	*	74	76	72	79	75	80	77
2003	81	84	75	77	81	*	81	79	76	83	80	82	81
DTP/DT/DTaP (4 doses or more):[5]													
1995	78	80	74	71	84	---	---	75	71	81	77	79	78
1998	84	87	77	83	89	---	---	81	80	86	82	85	85
1999	83	86	79	80	87	---	---	80	79	85	82	84	83
2000	82	84	76	75	85	---	---	79	76	84	80	83	83
2001	82	84	76	77	84	---	---	83	77	84	81	83	82
2002	82	84	76	*	88	*	78	79	75	84	79	84	80
2003	85	88	80	80	89	*	84	82	80	87	84	86	83
Polio (3 doses or more):													
1995	88	89	84	86	90	---	---	87	85	89	87	88	89
1998	91	92	88	85	93	---	---	89	90	92	89	91	93
1999	90	90	87	88	90	---	---	89	87	91	89	90	90
2000	90	91	87	90	93	---	---	88	87	90	88	90	91
2001	89	90	85	88	90	---	---	91	87	90	88	90	91
2002	90	91	87	*	92	95	87	90	88	91	89	91	90
2003	92	93	89	91	91	90	91	90	89	93	91	92	92
Measles, Mumps, Rubella:													
1995	90	91	87	88	95	---	---	88	86	91	90	90	89
1998	92	93	89	91	92	---	---	91	90	93	92	92	93
1999	92	92	90	92	93	---	---	90	90	92	91	92	90
2000	91	92	88	87	90	---	---	90	89	91	90	91	91
2001	91	92	89	94	90	---	---	92	89	92	91	92	91
2002	92	93	90	84	95	94	89	91	90	92	90	93	90
2003	93	93	92	92	96	*	94	93	92	93	93	93	92
Hib (3 doses or more):[6]													
1995	91	93	88	93	90	---	---	89	88	93	91	92	92
1998	93	95	90	90	92	---	---	92	91	95	92	94	94
1999	94	95	92	91	90	---	---	92	91	95	92	95	93
2000	93	95	93	90	92	---	---	91	90	95	92	94	95
2001	93	94	90	91	92	---	---	93	90	94	91	94	93
2002	93	94	92	*	95	93	90	92	90	94	92	94	93
2003	94	95	92	89	91	*	93	93	91	95	94	94	94
Hepatitis B (3 doses or more):													
1995	68	68	66	52	80	---	---	70	65	69	69	71	59
1998	87	88	84	82	89	---	---	86	85	88	85	88	87
1999	88	89	87	*	88	---	---	87	87	89	87	89	88
2000	90	91	89	91	91	---	---	88	87	91	89	90	92
2001	89	90	85	86	90	---	---	90	87	90	88	90	89
2002	90	91	88	*	94	94	84	90	88	90	89	91	90
2003	92	93	92	90	94	*	93	91	91	93	92	93	93
Varicella:[7]													
1998	43	42	42	28	53	---	---	47	41	44	45	45	34
1999	58	56	58	*	64	---	---	61	55	58	59	61	47
2000	68	66	67	62	77	---	---	70	64	69	69	70	60
2001	76	75	75	69	82	---	---	80	74	77	78	78	68
2002	81	79	83	71	87	*	79	82	79	81	81	83	75
2003	85	84	85	81	91	*	86	86	84	85	86	86	80
PCV (3 doses or more):[8]													
2002	41	44	34	33	55	*	38	37	33	43	41	45	32
2003	68	71	62	60	71	*	66	66	62	71	68	71	61

See footnotes at end of table.

This table will be updated on the Web. Go to www.cdc.gov/nchs/hus.htm.

Table 77 (page 2 of 2). Vaccinations of children 19–35 months of age for selected diseases, according to race, Hispanic origin, poverty status, and residence in metropolitan statistical area (MSA): United States, 1995–2003

[Data are based on telephone interviews of a sample of the civilian noninstitutionalized population supplemented by a survey of immunization providers for interview participants]

	Not Hispanic or Latino					
	White		Black or African American		Hispanic or Latino	
Vaccination and year	Below poverty	At or above poverty	Below poverty	At or above poverty	Below poverty	At or above poverty
	Percent of children 19–35 months of age					
Combined series (4:3:1:3):[4]						
1995	69	78	70	73	63	72
1998	77	83	72	74	73	79
1999	76	82	72	77	73	78
2000	73	80	69	72	70	74
2001	71	80	69	74	73	79
2002	72	81	68	72	75	76
2003	79	85	70	79	78	81

- - - Data not available.

* Estimates are considered unreliable. Percents not shown if the unweighted sample size for the numerator was less than 30 or relative standard error greater than 50 percent or confidence interval half width greater than 10 percentage points.

[1]Persons of Hispanic origin may be of any race. Starting with data for 2002, estimates were tabulated using the 1997 Standards for Federal data on Race and Ethnicity. Estimates for earlier years were tabulated using the 1977 Standards on Race and Ethnicity. See Appendix II, Race.

[2]Metropolitan statistical area.

[3]Prior to data year 2002 the category "Asian" included "Native Hawaiian and Other Pacific Islander."

[4]The 4:3:1:3 combined series consists of 4 or more doses of diphtheria and tetanus toxoids and pertussis vaccine (DTP), diphtheria and tetanus toxoids (DT), or diphtheria and tetanus toxoids and acellular pertussis vaccine (DTaP), 3 or more doses of any poliovirus vaccine, 1 or more doses of a measles-containing vaccine (MCV), and 3 or more doses of *Haemophilus influenzae* type b vaccine (Hib).

[5]Diphtheria and tetanus toxoids and pertussis vaccine, diphtheria and tetanus toxoids, and diphtheria and tetanus toxoids and acellular pertussis vaccine.

[6]*Haemophilus influenzae* type b vaccine (Hib).

[7]Recommended in 1996. Data collection for varicella began in July 1996.

[8]Pneumococcal conjugate vaccine. Recommended in 2000. Data collection for PCV began in July 2001.

NOTES: Final estimates from the National Immunization Survey include an adjustment for children with missing immunization provider data. Poverty status is based on family income and family size using U.S. Bureau of the Census poverty thresholds. Children missing information about poverty status were omitted from analysis by poverty level. In 2003, 13.0 percent of all children, 20.0 percent of Hispanic, 10.2 percent of non-Hispanic white, and 11.3 percent of non-Hispanic black children were missing information about poverty status and were omitted. See Appendix I, National Immunization Survey. Data for additional years are available . See Appendix III.

SOURCE: Centers for Disease Control and Prevention, National Center for Health Statistics and National Immunization Program, National Immunization Survey. Data are available on the CDC Web site at www.cdc.gov/nip/coverage/ and www.cdc.gov/nis/.

This table will be updated on the Web. Go to www.cdc.gov/nchs/hus.htm.

Table 78 (page 1 of 2). Vaccination coverage among children 19–35 months of age according to geographic division, State, and selected urban areas: United States, 1995–2003

[Data are based on telephone interviews of a sample of the civilian noninstitutionalized population supplemented by a survey of immunization providers for interview participants]

Geographic division and State	1995	1996	1997	1998	1999	2000	2001	2002	2003
	Percent of children 19–35 months of age with 4:3:1:3 series[1]								
United States	74	76	76	79	78	76	77	78	81
New England:									
Connecticut	86	88	86	90	86	85	84	86	95
Maine	88	86	87	86	83	83	82	83	82
Massachusetts	81	87	88	87	85	85	81	89	92
New Hampshire	89	83	85	82	85	83	84	87	88
Rhode Island	83	84	82	86	87	82	84	86	87
Vermont	87	87	87	86	91	83	88	87	90
Middle Atlantic:									
New Jersey	70	75	76	82	81	76	76	80	76
New York	74	80	75	85	81	75	81	81	82
Pennsylvania	77	79	79	83	86	78	82	77	87
East North Central:									
Illinois	78	75	74	78	77	75	76	80	85
Indiana	74	70	72	78	74	76	74	78	82
Michigan	68	75	75	78	74	75	74	84	83
Ohio	71	78	72	78	78	72	75	77	84
Wisconsin	74	77	81	78	85	80	83	82	83
West North Central:									
Iowa	83	81	77	82	83	83	79	80	83
Kansas	70	72	84	82	79	76	76	73	78
Minnesota	75	84	78	82	85	86	79	79	84
Missouri	75	75	79	85	75	78	78	77	84
Nebraska	71	78	74	76	82	79	80	79	82
North Dakota	79	80	80	79	80	81	83	79	83
South Dakota	79	81	77	74	82	78	79	81	83
South Atlantic:									
Delaware	68	81	80	79	78	75	79	81	80
District of Columbia	69	76	71	71	78	71	74	72	77
Florida	74	79	74	79	80	74	77	77	83
Georgia	77	81	78	80	82	81	80	82	77
Maryland	77	79	81	77	79	78	78	81	84
North Carolina	80	78	80	83	82	87	85	87	89
South Carolina	78	85	81	88	81	80	81	80	85
Virginia	69	76	72	80	80	74	78	77	85
West Virginia	71	71	81	82	81	76	81	79	77
East South Central:									
Alabama	73	74	87	82	78	81	83	80	82
Kentucky	81	76	78	82	88	81	79	74	81
Mississippi	79	81	80	84	82	81	84	78	84
Tennessee	74	79	79	82	78	81	84	80	81
West South Central:									
Arkansas	73	70	80	73	77	72	74	74	80
Louisiana	77	79	77	78	77	75	69	69	72
Oklahoma	74	72	70	75	73	71	76	67	72
Texas	71	71	74	74	72	69	74	71	77
Mountain:									
Arizona	69	70	71	76	72	72	73	70	79
Colorado	75	80	74	76	76	74	75	64	69
Idaho	66	65	71	76	69	74	74	73	82
Montana	71	75	75	82	83	77	82	71	85
Nevada	67	67	70	76	73	74	72	78	78
New Mexico	74	78	73	71	73	68	71	67	77
Utah	65	65	69	76	80	77	74	79	80
Wyoming	71	77	75	80	83	79	81	77	77
Pacific:									
Alaska	74	72	75	81	80	77	74	78	81
California	70	74	74	76	75	75	75	76	80
Hawaii	75	80	77	79	82	75	73	81	83
Oregon	71	70	72	76	72	79	73	75	79
Washington	76	78	79	81	75	77	76	73	80

See footnotes at end of table.

This table will be updated on the Web. Go to www.cdc.gov/nchs/hus.htm.

Table 78 (page 2 of 2). Vaccination coverage among children 19–35 months of age according to geographic division, State, and selected urban areas: United States, 1995–2003

[Data are based on telephone interviews of a sample of the civilian noninstitutionalized population supplemented by a survey of immunization providers for interview participants]

Geographic division and urban areas	1995	1996	1997	1998	1999	2000	2001	2002	2003
	Percent of children 19–35 months of age with 4:3:1:3 series[1]								
New England:									
Boston, Massachusetts	85	85	86	89	84	79	85	80	90
Middle Atlantic:									
New York City, New York	72	78	72	81	78	68	76	81	77
Newark, New Jersey	67	64	68	64	67	63	64	60	74
Philadelphia, Pennsylvania	67	74	81	80	81	74	74	74	80
East North Central:									
Chicago, Illinois	70	72	66	64	71	65	69	72	77
Cuyahoga County (Cleveland), Ohio	72	79	70	75	74	73	73	74	75
Detroit, Michigan	54	60	60	70	66	59	63	66	71
Franklin County (Columbus), Ohio	75	80	73	78	78	77	78	84	83
Marion County (Indianapolis), Indiana	77	72	80	78	79	69	72	75	79
Milwaukee County (Milwaukee), Wisconsin	69	70	72	73	74	69	70	70	81
South Atlantic:									
Baltimore, Maryland	*	80	84	81	72	70	72	75	81
Dade County (Miami), Florida	78	79	75	75	84	78	78	73	83
District of Columbia	67	76	71	71	78	71	74	72	77
Duval County (Jacksonville), Florida	69	76	69	79	78	79	76	77	81
Fulton/DeKalb Counties (Atlanta), Georgia	*	76	74	71	83	80	75	79	75
East South Central:									
Davidson County (Nashville), Tennessee	72	80	76	80	73	73	82	80	83
Shelby County (Memphis), Tennessee	69	70	70	71	75	77	74	73	77
Jefferson County (Birmingham), Alabama	86	76	83	85	85	79	87	82	83
West South Central:									
Bexar County (San Antonio), Texas	76	74	79	79	70	68	73	76	79
Dallas County (Dallas), Texas	70	68	75	71	72	67	67	76	75
El Paso County (El Paso), Texas	72	61	63	78	73	70	69	77	81
Houston, Texas	64	62	62	61	63	65	69	64	75
Orleans Parish (New Orleans), Louisiana	78	72	69	79	72	70	68	63	74
Mountain:									
Maricopa County (Phoenix), Arizona	67	72	70	77	71	71	72	73	80
Pacific:									
King County (Seattle), Washington	84	82	81	86	77	75	72	77	83
Los Angeles County (Los Angeles), California	68	75	72	76	76	77	73	77	84
San Diego County (San Diego), California	72	74	76	77	75	76	80	78	81
Santa Clara County (Santa Clara), California	76	80	69	84	82	76	77	84	85

* Estimates are considered unreliable. Percents not shown if the unweighted sample size for the numerator was less than 30 or relative standard error greater than 50 percent or confidence interval half width greater than 10 percentage points.

[1]The 4:3:1:3 combined series consists of 4 or more doses of diphtheria and tetanus toxoids and pertussis vaccine (DTP), diphtheria and tetanus toxoids (DT), or diphtheria and tetanus toxoids and acellular pertussis vaccine (DTaP), 3 or more doses of any poliovirus vaccine, 1 or more doses of a measles-containing vaccine (MCV), and 3 or more doses of *Haemophilus influenzae* type b vaccine (Hib).

NOTES: Urban areas were originally selected because they were at risk for undervaccination. Final estimates from the National Immunization Survey include an adjustment for children with missing immunization provider data.

SOURCE: Centers for Disease Control and Prevention, National Center for Health Statistics and National Immunization Program, National Immunization Survey. Data are available on the CDC Web site at www.cdc.gov/nip/coverage/ and www.cdc.gov/nis/.

This table will be updated on the Web. Go to www.cdc.gov/nchs/hus.htm.

Table 79 (page 1 of 2). No health care visits to an office or clinic within the past 12 months among children under 18 years of age, according to selected characteristics: United States, average annual 1997–98, 2000–01, and 2002–03

[Data are based on household interviews of a sample of the civilian noninstitutionalized population]

Characteristic	Under 18 years of age			Under 6 years of age			6–17 years of age		
	1997–98	2000–01	2002–03	1997–98	2000–01	2002–03	1997–98	2000–01	2002–03
	Percent of children without a health care visit[1]								
All children[2]	12.8	12.9	11.8	5.7	6.6	6.2	16.3	15.9	14.5
Race[3]									
White only	12.2	12.1	11.7	5.5	6.6	6.3	15.5	14.7	14.3
Black or African American only	14.3	15.0	11.4	6.5	6.3	6.1	18.1	19.0	13.9
American Indian and Alaska Native only	13.8	22.4	*15.6	*	*	*	*17.6	*25.0	*18.6
Asian only	16.3	15.2	17.1	*5.6	*8.8	*7.8	22.1	18.9	21.9
Native Hawaiian and Other Pacific Islander only	- - -	*	*	- - -	*	*	- - -	*	*
2 or more races	- - -	8.5	8.5	- - -	*	*	- - -	13.5	12.4
Hispanic origin and race[3]									
Hispanic or Latino	19.3	19.8	18.6	9.7	10.0	10.1	25.3	25.5	23.5
Not Hispanic or Latino	11.6	11.4	10.3	4.8	5.8	5.3	14.9	14.0	12.6
White only	10.7	10.4	9.7	4.3	5.5	5.0	13.7	12.6	11.8
Black or African American only	14.5	14.7	11.4	6.5	6.5	6.0	18.3	18.4	13.9
Poverty status[4]									
Poor	17.6	18.2	15.3	8.1	9.9	8.0	23.6	22.8	19.5
Near poor	16.2	17.0	14.7	7.2	9.2	8.5	20.8	21.1	18.0
Nonpoor	9.9	9.9	9.7	4.1	4.5	4.7	12.6	12.3	11.9
Hispanic origin and race and poverty status[3,4]									
Hispanic or Latino:									
Poor	23.2	23.6	20.6	11.7	11.6	10.5	31.1	30.8	26.9
Near poor	20.9	22.6	21.2	9.7	13.4	11.4	28.1	28.0	26.8
Nonpoor	13.4	14.1	14.6	7.2	5.1	8.3	16.8	18.8	17.8
Not Hispanic or Latino:									
White only:									
Poor	14.0	15.1	12.4	*5.6	*9.6	*6.6	19.7	18.2	15.7
Near poor	14.1	14.1	12.2	6.0	7.5	7.8	18.0	17.4	14.6
Nonpoor	9.2	8.9	8.7	3.6	4.3	3.9	11.7	10.8	10.7
Black or African American only:									
Poor	15.8	16.1	12.6	7.6	*8.2	*6.9	20.5	20.1	15.4
Near poor	16.4	16.7	11.5	*7.7	*7.1	*6.1	20.4	21.2	13.8
Nonpoor	11.8	12.3	10.5	*4.1	*4.4	*5.3	14.8	15.5	12.9
Health insurance status[5]									
Insured	10.4	10.6	9.5	4.5	5.2	5.1	13.4	13.2	11.7
Private	10.4	10.4	9.5	4.3	4.7	4.9	13.1	12.9	11.5
Medicaid	10.1	11.1	9.3	5.0	6.3	5.3	14.4	14.2	12.1
Uninsured	28.8	30.8	31.8	14.6	18.8	18.5	34.9	35.9	37.0
Poverty status and health insurance status[4]									
Poor:									
Insured	13.0	13.2	11.2	6.0	7.5	6.1	17.8	16.6	14.3
Uninsured	34.3	37.0	36.8	18.2	20.8	21.6	41.3	44.3	42.7
Near poor:									
Insured	12.6	13.4	11.0	4.9	6.5	6.4	16.7	17.2	13.6
Uninsured	28.2	31.8	33.7	16.0	21.9	21.0	33.7	36.3	39.2
Nonpoor:									
Insured	9.0	9.1	8.6	3.8	4.1	4.3	11.4	11.3	10.6
Uninsured	22.7	23.0	26.0	*7.8	11.8	*12.8	28.7	27.1	30.5

See footnotes at end of table.

Table 79 (page 2 of 2). No health care visits to an office or clinic within the past 12 months among children under 18 years of age, according to selected characteristics: United States, average annual 1997–98, 2000–01, and 2002–03

[Data are based on household interviews of a sample of the civilian noninstitutionalized population]

Characteristic	*Under 18 years of age*			*Under 6 years of age*			*6–17 years of age*		
	1997–98	*2000–01*	*2002–03*	*1997–98*	*2000–01*	*2002–03*	*1997–98*	*2000–01*	*2002–03*
Geographic region	Percent of children without a health care visit[1]								
Northeast	7.0	6.5	5.1	3.1	4.6	3.1	8.9	7.4	6.1
Midwest	12.2	10.5	10.5	5.9	5.3	4.8	15.3	12.9	13.3
South	14.3	15.2	13.1	5.6	7.4	7.1	18.5	19.0	16.1
West	16.3	17.0	16.5	7.9	8.2	8.9	20.7	21.5	20.3
Location of residence									
Within MSA[6]	12.3	12.4	11.4	5.4	6.6	6.0	15.9	15.3	14.1
Outside MSA[6]	14.6	14.8	13.3	6.9	6.8	7.4	17.9	18.2	16.0

* Estimates are considered unreliable. Data preceded by an asterisk have a relative standard error (RSE) of 20–30 percent. Data not shown have an RSE of greater than 30 percent.

- - - Data not available.

[1]Respondents were asked how many times a doctor or other health care professional was seen in the past 12 months at a doctor's office, clinic, or some other place. Excluded are visits to emergency rooms, hospitalizations, home visits, and telephone calls. Beginning in 2000 dental visits were also excluded. See Appendix II, Health care contact.

[2]Includes all other races not shown separately and unknown health insurance status.

[3]The race groups, white, black, American Indian and Alaska Native, Asian, Native Hawaiian and Other Pacific Islander, and 2 or more races, include persons of Hispanic and non-Hispanic origin. Persons of Hispanic origin may be of any race. Starting with data year 1999 race-specific estimates are tabulated according to 1997 Standards for Federal data on Race and Ethnicity and are not strictly comparable with estimates for earlier years. The five single race categories plus multiple race categories shown in the table conform to 1997 Standards. Starting with data year 1999 race-specific estimates are for persons who reported only one racial group; the category "2 or more races" includes persons who reported more than one racial group. Prior to data year 1999, data were tabulated according to 1977 Standards with four racial groups and the category "Asian only" included Native Hawaiian and Other Pacific Islander. Estimates for single race categories prior to 1999 included persons who reported one race or, if they reported more than one race, identified one race as best representing their race. See Appendix II, Race.

[4]Poor persons are defined as below the poverty threshold. Near poor persons have incomes of 100 percent to less than 200 percent of the poverty threshold. Nonpoor persons have incomes of 200 percent or greater than the poverty threshold. Missing family income data were imputed for 21–25 percent of children under 18 years of age in 1997–98 and 28–31 percent in 1999–2003. See Appendix II, Family income; Poverty level.

[5]Health insurance categories are mutually exclusive. Persons who reported both Medicaid and private coverage are classified as having private coverage. Starting in 1997 Medicaid includes state-sponsored health plans and State Children's Health Insurance Program (SCHIP). The category "insured" also includes military, other government, and Medicare coverage. See Appendix II, Health insurance coverage.

[6]MSA is metropolitan statistical area.

NOTES: In 1997 the National Health Interview Survey questionnaire was redesigned. See Appendix I, National Health Interview Survey. Standard errors for selected years are available in the spreadsheet version of this table. See www.cdc.gov/nchs/hus.htm. Starting with *Health, United States, 2005*, estimates for 2000 and later years use weights derived from the 2000 census. Estimates for 2000–2002 were recalculated using 2000-based weights and may differ from previous editions of *Health, United States*.

SOURCE: Centers for Disease Control and Prevention, National Center for Health Statistics, National Health Interview Survey, family core and sample child questionnaires.

Table 80 (page 1 of 2). No usual source of health care among children under 18 years of age, according to selected characteristics: United States, average annual selected years 1993–94 through 2002–03

[Data are based on household interviews of a sample of the civilian noninstitutionalized population]

Characteristic	Under 18 years of age			Under 6 years of age			6–17 years of age		
	1993–94[1]	2000–01	2002–03	1993–94[1]	2000–01	2002–03	1993–94[1]	2000–01	2002–03
	Percent of children without a usual source of health care[2]								
All children[3]	7.7	6.5	5.7	5.2	4.4	4.1	9.0	7.4	6.5
Race[4]									
White only	7.0	5.7	5.2	4.7	4.2	3.9	8.3	6.4	5.8
Black or African American only	10.3	7.4	6.7	7.6	4.0	3.3	11.9	8.9	8.2
American Indian and Alaska Native only	*9.3	*6.8	*	*	*	*	*8.7	*	*
Asian only	9.7	9.9	10.3	*3.4	*7.4	*	13.5	11.3	13.3
Native Hawaiian and Other Pacific Islander only	- - -	*	*	- - -	*	*	- - -	*	*
2 or more races	- - -	6.0	6.3	- - -	*	*6.7	- - -	*7.9	*6.0
Hispanic origin and race[4]									
Hispanic or Latino	14.3	14.2	12.1	9.3	9.3	8.3	17.7	17.0	14.3
Not Hispanic or Latino	6.7	4.8	4.3	4.4	3.2	3.0	7.8	5.6	5.0
White only	5.7	3.9	3.4	3.7	2.8	2.7	6.7	4.4	3.7
Black or African American only	10.2	7.4	6.7	7.7	4.0	3.3	11.6	8.9	8.2
Poverty status[5]									
Poor	13.9	12.5	10.6	9.4	7.6	7.1	16.8	15.2	12.6
Near poor	9.8	9.9	8.4	6.7	7.3	6.6	11.6	11.3	9.5
Nonpoor	3.7	3.5	3.3	1.8	2.2	1.9	4.6	4.1	3.9
Hispanic origin and race and poverty status[4,5]									
Hispanic or Latino:									
Poor	19.6	20.0	15.0	12.7	12.3	10.1	24.8	24.7	18.1
Near poor	15.3	16.4	15.0	9.9	11.6	10.6	18.9	19.2	17.6
Nonpoor	5.0	7.1	7.0	*2.7	4.2	*4.4	6.5	8.6	8.3
Not Hispanic or Latino:									
White only:									
Poor	10.2	9.2	7.2	6.5	*	*6.2	12.7	11.0	7.7
Near poor	8.7	6.5	5.2	6.3	5.1	*4.8	10.1	7.2	5.5
Nonpoor	3.4	2.6	2.4	1.6	1.7	1.4	4.2	3.0	2.8
Black or African American only:									
Poor	13.7	9.1	9.6	10.9	*4.7	*	15.5	11.3	12.7
Near poor	9.1	9.3	6.7	*6.0	*5.8	*	10.8	11.0	7.6
Nonpoor	4.6	4.7	4.3	*	*	*2.7	5.8	5.7	5.1
Health insurance status[6]									
Insured	5.0	3.5	3.1	3.3	2.5	2.0	5.9	4.0	3.6
Private	3.8	2.9	2.4	1.9	1.9	1.3	4.6	3.4	2.8
Medicaid	8.9	5.1	5.0	6.4	3.9	3.3	11.3	5.9	6.1
Uninsured	23.5	29.3	29.2	18.0	20.9	25.5	26.0	32.9	30.6
Poverty status and health insurance status[5]									
Poor:									
Insured	9.1	5.7	5.1	6.0	3.4	3.2	11.5	7.1	6.2
Uninsured	29.4	37.6	39.0	25.0	26.2	34.4	31.5	42.9	40.8
Near poor:									
Insured	6.0	5.2	4.2	4.0	4.2	3.1	7.2	5.8	4.8
Uninsured	22.9	29.0	30.3	18.0	21.2	27.6	25.3	32.6	31.5
Nonpoor:									
Insured	2.9	2.4	2.2	1.5	1.6	1.2	3.6	2.8	2.7
Uninsured	14.5	20.6	19.9	6.4	13.8	15.0	18.1	23.0	21.5

See footnotes at end of table.

Table 80 (page 2 of 2). No usual source of health care among children under 18 years of age, according to selected characteristics: United States, average annual selected years 1993–94 through 2002–03

[Data are based on household interviews of a sample of the civilian noninstitutionalized population]

Characteristic	*Under 18 years of age*			*Under 6 years of age*			*6–17 years of age*		
	1993–94[1]	*2000–01*	*2002–03*	*1993–94*[1]	*2000–01*	*2002–03*	*1993–94*[1]	*2000–01*	*2002–03*
Geographic region	Percent of children without a usual source of health care[2]								
Northeast	4.1	2.4	2.6	2.9	2.1	*2.2	4.8	2.5	2.7
Midwest	5.2	4.8	3.6	4.1	3.6	3.5	5.9	5.4	3.7
South	10.9	7.7	7.2	7.3	4.9	4.4	12.7	9.1	8.6
West	8.6	9.6	8.1	5.3	6.3	5.5	10.6	11.3	9.4
Location of residence									
Within MSA[7]	7.7	6.5	5.6	5.0	4.6	4.0	9.2	7.4	6.4
Outside MSA[7]	7.8	6.4	6.1	6.0	3.5	4.2	8.7	7.6	6.9

* Estimates are considered unreliable. Data preceded by an asterisk have a relative standard error (RSE) of 20–30 percent. Data not shown have an RSE of greater than 30 percent.
- - - Data not available.
[1]Data prior to 1997 are not strictly comparable with data for later years due to the 1997 questionnaire redesign. See Appendix I, National Health Interview Survey.
[2]Persons who report the emergency department as the place of their usual source of care are defined as having no usual source of care. See Appendix II, Usual source of care.
[3]Includes all other races not shown separately and unknown health insurance status.
[4]The race groups, white, black, American Indian and Alaska Native, Asian, Native Hawaiian and Other Pacific Islander, and 2 or more races, include persons of Hispanic and non-Hispanic origin. Persons of Hispanic origin may be of any race. Starting with data year 1999 race-specific estimates are tabulated according to 1997 Standards for Federal data on Race and Ethnicity and are not strictly comparable with estimates for earlier years. The five single race categories plus multiple race categories shown in the table conform to 1997 Standards. Starting with data year 1999 race-specific estimates are for persons who reported only one racial group; the category "2 or more races" includes persons who reported more than one racial group. Prior to data year 1999, data were tabulated according to 1977 Standards with four racial groups and the category "Asian only" included Native Hawaiian and Other Pacific Islander. Estimates for single race categories prior to 1999 included persons who reported one race or, if they reported more than one race, identified one race as best representing their race. See Appendix II, Race.
[5]Poor persons are defined as below the poverty threshold. Near poor persons have incomes of 100 percent to less than 200 percent of the poverty threshold. Nonpoor persons have incomes of 200 percent or greater than the poverty threshold. Missing family income data were imputed for 14 percent of children in 1993–96, 21–25 percent in 1997–98, and 28–31 percent in 1999–2003. See Appendix II, Family income; Poverty level.
[6]Health insurance categories are mutually exclusive. Persons who reported both Medicaid and private coverage are classified as having private coverage. Medicaid includes other public assistance through 1996. Starting in 1997 Medicaid includes state-sponsored health plans and State Children's Health Insurance Program (SCHIP). The category "insured" also includes military, other government, and Medicare coverage. Health insurance status was unknown for 8–9 percent of children in the sample in 1993–96 and 1 percent in 1997–2003. See Appendix II, Health insurance coverage.
[7]MSA is metropolitan statistical area.

NOTES: Data for additional years are available. See Appendix III. For more data on usual source of care, see National Health Interview Survey home page: www.cdc.gov/nchs/nhis/htm. Standard errors for selected years are available in the spreadsheet version of this table. See www.cdc.gov/nchs/hus.htm.
Starting with *Health, United States, 2005*, estimates for 2000 and later years use weights derived from the 2000 census. Estimates for 2000–2002 were recalculated using 2000-based weights and may differ from previous editions of *Health, United States.*

SOURCES: Centers for Disease Control and Prevention, National Center for Health Statistics, National Health Interview Survey, access to care and health insurance supplements (1993–96). Starting in 1997 data are from the family core and sample child questionnaires.

Table 81 (page 1 of 3). Emergency department visits within the past 12 months among children under 18 years of age, according to selected characteristics: United States, selected years 1997–2003

[Data are based on household interviews of a sample of the civilian noninstitutionalized population]

Characteristic	Under 18 years of age			Under 6 years of age			6–17 years of age		
	1997	2002	2003	1997	2002	2003	1997	2002	2003
	Percent of children with 1 or more emergency department visits[1]								
All children[2]	19.9	22.4	20.9	24.3	28.0	26.5	17.7	19.7	18.2
Race[3]									
White only	19.4	21.3	20.3	22.6	26.1	25.2	17.8	19.1	17.9
Black or African American only	24.0	27.9	23.9	33.1	36.6	32.0	19.4	23.8	20.2
American Indian and Alaska Native only	*24.1	*	*22.7	*24.3	*	*	*24.0	*	*21.0
Asian only	12.6	14.4	14.2	20.8	*19.5	*20.7	8.6	*11.5	*11.0
Native Hawaiian and Other Pacific Islander only	- - -	*	*	- - -	*	*	- - -	*	*
2 or more races	- - -	28.4	26.1	- - -	37.5	34.0	- - -	20.3	20.3
Hispanic origin and race[3]									
Hispanic or Latino	21.1	20.6	20.3	25.7	26.8	27.9	18.1	17.1	16.0
Not Hispanic or Latino	19.7	22.8	21.0	24.0	28.3	26.1	17.6	20.3	18.7
White only	19.2	21.7	20.4	22.2	26.3	24.6	17.7	19.7	18.5
Black or African American only	23.6	27.8	23.8	32.7	36.3	31.9	19.2	23.9	20.1
Poverty status[4]									
Poor	25.1	26.7	27.0	29.5	34.3	34.7	22.2	22.3	22.7
Near poor	22.0	26.6	22.8	28.0	32.8	28.8	19.0	23.4	19.4
Nonpoor	17.3	19.6	18.3	20.5	23.9	22.5	15.8	17.7	16.5
Hispanic origin and race and poverty status[3,4]									
Hispanic or Latino:									
Poor	21.9	22.3	23.7	25.0	30.3	31.5	19.6	17.2	18.9
Near poor	20.8	21.5	19.8	28.8	25.4	27.8	15.6	19.5	14.8
Nonpoor	20.4	18.4	17.6	23.4	24.8	24.2	18.7	15.0	14.3
Not Hispanic or Latino:									
White only:									
Poor	25.5	27.1	28.1	27.2	36.2	34.1	24.4	22.1	24.8
Near poor	22.3	27.9	23.4	25.8	33.8	27.0	20.7	25.0	21.3
Nonpoor	17.2	19.4	18.6	20.1	22.6	22.2	15.9	18.1	17.0
Black or African American only:									
Poor	29.3	30.3	27.2	39.5	38.6	33.7	23.0	26.2	24.0
Near poor	22.5	32.2	27.5	31.7	40.8	44.4	18.5	27.8	21.1
Nonpoor	17.7	23.0	18.8	22.6	30.9	23.5	15.9	19.6	16.6
Health insurance status[5]									
Insured	19.8	22.9	21.4	24.4	28.7	26.7	17.5	20.1	18.7
Private	17.5	20.0	18.1	20.9	24.5	21.6	15.9	18.1	16.6
Medicaid	28.2	30.7	28.9	33.0	37.6	35.1	24.1	26.2	24.5
Uninsured	20.2	18.2	17.1	23.0	22.0	23.9	18.9	16.6	14.7
Poverty status and health insurance status[4]									
Poor:									
Insured	26.6	28.3	29.2	31.3	36.5	36.6	23.1	23.5	24.7
Uninsured	19.9	17.7	16.7	19.8	*21.5	22.6	20.0	15.9	14.7
Near poor:									
Insured	22.2	28.0	23.8	28.5	34.7	29.5	18.9	24.5	20.4
Uninsured	21.3	19.3	17.5	26.2	23.2	23.9	19.2	17.4	15.2
Nonpoor:									
Insured	17.1	19.8	18.5	20.2	24.0	22.4	15.7	17.9	16.7
Uninsured	18.9	17.6	16.9	22.6	*20.9	25.0	17.3	16.3	14.3
Geographic region									
Northeast	18.5	23.3	21.8	20.7	27.4	26.3	17.4	21.4	19.7
Midwest	19.5	22.7	21.4	26.0	28.4	27.2	16.4	20.0	18.7
South	21.8	24.4	21.7	25.6	31.4	27.8	19.9	21.0	18.6
West	18.5	17.9	18.3	23.5	22.4	23.6	15.9	15.6	15.8
Location of residence									
Within MSA[6]	19.7	21.7	20.2	23.9	27.1	25.2	17.4	19.0	17.8
Outside MSA[6]	20.8	25.4	23.6	26.2	32.3	31.8	18.6	22.4	19.7

See footnotes at end of table.

Table 81 (page 2 of 3). Emergency department visits within the past 12 months among children under 18 years of age, according to selected characteristics: United States, selected years 1997–2003

[Data are based on household interviews of a sample of the civilian noninstitutionalized population]

Characteristic	*Under 18 years of age*			*Under 6 years of age*			*6–17 years of age*		
	1997	*2002*	*2003*	*1997*	*2002*	*2003*	*1997*	*2002*	*2003*
	Percent of children with 2 or more emergency department visits[1]								
All children[2]	7.1	7.5	7.0	9.6	10.2	8.7	5.8	6.2	6.2
Race[3]									
White only	6.6	6.6	6.3	8.4	8.8	7.6	5.7	5.6	5.7
Black or African American only	9.6	11.1	10.4	14.9	17.4	13.9	6.9	8.1	8.8
American Indian and Alaska Native only	*	*	*	*	*	*	*	*	*
Asian only	*5.7	*	*6.7	*12.9	*	*	*	*	*
Native Hawaiian and Other Pacific Islander only	- - -	*	*	- - -	*	*	- - -	*	*
2 or more races	- - -	12.5	8.7	- - -	17.2	*10.1	- - -	*8.2	*7.6
Hispanic origin and race[3]									
Hispanic or Latino	8.9	8.0	7.4	11.8	11.7	10.8	7.0	5.9	5.5
Not Hispanic or Latino	6.8	7.4	6.9	9.2	9.8	8.2	5.7	6.2	6.4
White only	6.2	6.3	6.0	7.8	7.8	6.6	5.5	5.7	5.8
Black or African American only	9.3	11.2	10.6	14.6	17.5	14.4	6.8	8.2	8.9
Poverty status[4]									
Poor	11.1	12.3	11.6	14.5	17.2	12.9	8.9	9.5	10.8
Near poor	8.3	8.8	8.6	12.2	11.2	10.7	6.3	7.6	7.4
Nonpoor	5.3	5.5	5.1	6.5	7.3	6.3	4.7	4.8	4.5
Hispanic origin and race and poverty status[3,4]									
Hispanic or Latino:									
Poor	10.4	8.8	9.9	13.9	14.2	13.5	8.0	*5.4	7.7
Near poor	8.2	9.2	7.2	12.0	12.9	11.7	5.7	*7.3	4.5
Nonpoor	7.6	6.2	5.3	8.4	8.5	7.0	7.1	*5.0	4.5
Not Hispanic or Latino:									
White only:									
Poor	10.7	12.0	10.1	12.2	15.8	*9.7	9.8	*9.9	*10.3
Near poor	8.0	8.1	8.8	11.2	8.8	8.0	6.4	7.7	9.2
Nonpoor	5.0	5.1	4.8	5.8	6.2	5.7	4.6	4.6	4.4
Black or African American only:									
Poor	12.7	15.4	14.5	19.1	23.0	14.7	8.8	11.6	14.4
Near poor	9.2	10.4	11.8	*13.5	*14.6	21.9	*7.2	*8.3	*7.9
Nonpoor	5.5	8.1	6.8	*8.2	14.6	*9.8	*4.5	*5.3	*5.4
Health insurance status[5]									
Insured	7.0	7.5	7.1	9.6	10.2	8.7	5.7	6.2	6.3
Private	5.2	5.6	5.1	6.8	7.2	5.4	4.5	4.9	4.9
Medicaid	13.1	12.7	11.7	16.2	16.5	14.0	10.4	10.3	10.1
Uninsured	7.7	7.0	6.6	9.8	9.1	*8.8	6.8	6.2	5.9
Poverty status and health insurance status[4]									
Poor:									
Insured	12.1	13.1	12.3	15.7	18.3	13.4	9.5	10.1	11.7
Uninsured	7.6	*8.0	*8.1	*8.3	*	*	*7.3	*	*7.3
Near poor:									
Insured	8.4	9.1	9.1	12.3	11.4	10.8	6.3	7.9	8.0
Uninsured	7.9	*7.0	*6.1	*11.1	*10.9	*	6.5	*	*5.0
Nonpoor:									
Insured	5.1	5.5	5.0	6.2	7.3	6.3	4.6	4.7	4.5
Uninsured	7.7	*6.3	*5.8	*10.1	*	*	*6.7	*6.5	*5.5

See footnotes at end of table.

Table 81 (page 3 of 3). Emergency department visits within the past 12 months among children under 18 years of age, according to selected characteristics: United States, selected years 1997–2002

[Data are based on household interviews of a sample of the civilian noninstitutionalized population]

Characteristic	Under 18 years of age			Under 6 years of age			6–17 years of age		
	1997	2002	2003	1997	2002	2003	1997	2002	2003
Geographic region	Percent of children with 2 or more emergency department visits[1]								
Northeast	6.2	7.2	7.8	7.6	9.3	8.0	5.4	6.3	7.6
Midwest	6.6	6.9	6.3	10.4	8.3	8.5	4.8	6.3	5.3
South	8.0	8.7	8.0	10.1	12.3	9.5	6.9	7.0	7.3
West	7.1	6.1	5.5	10.0	9.5	8.1	5.6	4.4	4.2
Location of residence									
Within MSA[6]	7.2	7.1	6.7	9.6	9.9	8.3	5.9	5.8	6.0
Outside MSA[6]	6.8	8.8	8.2	9.7	11.4	10.3	5.6	7.6	7.2

* Estimates are considered unreliable. Data preceded by an asterisk have a relative standard error (RSE) of 20–30 percent. Data not shown have an RSE of greater than 30 percent.

- - - Data not available.

[1]See Appendix II, Emergency department visit.

[2]Includes all other races not shown separately and unknown health insurance status.

[3]The race groups, white, black, American Indian and Alaska Native, Asian, Native Hawaiian and Other Pacific Islander, and 2 or more races, include persons of Hispanic and non-Hispanic origin. Persons of Hispanic origin may be of any race. Starting with data year 1999 race-specific estimates are tabulated according to 1997 Standards for Federal data on Race and Ethnicity and are not strictly comparable with estimates for earlier years. The five single race categories plus multiple race categories shown in the table conform to 1997 Standards. Starting with data year 1999 race-specific estimates are for persons who reported only one racial group; the category "2 or more races" includes persons who reported more than one racial group. Prior to data year 1999, data were tabulated according to 1977 Standards with four racial groups and the category "Asian only" included Native Hawaiian and Other Pacific Islander. Estimates for single race categories prior to 1999 included persons who reported one race or, if they reported more than one race, identified one race as best representing their race. See Appendix II, Race.

[4]Poor persons are defined as below the poverty threshold. Near poor persons have incomes of 100 percent to less than 200 percent of the poverty threshold. Nonpoor persons have incomes of 200 percent or greater than the poverty threshold. Missing family income data were imputed for 21–25 percent of children in 1997–98 and 28–31 percent in 1999–2003. See Appendix II, Family income; Poverty level.

[5]Health insurance categories are mutually exclusive. Persons who reported both Medicaid and private coverage are classified as having private coverage. Starting in 1997 Medicaid includes state-sponsored health plans and State Children's Health Insurance Program (SCHIP). The category "insured" also includes military, other government, and Medicare coverage. See Appendix II, Health insurance coverage.

[6]MSA is metropolitan statistical area.

NOTES: Data for additional years are available. See Appendix III. Standard errors for selected years are available in the spreadsheet version of this table. See www.cdc.gov/nchs/hus.htm. Starting with *Health, United States, 2005*, estimates for 2000 and later years use weights derived from the 2000 census. Estimates for 2000–2002 were recalculated using 2000-based weights and may differ from previous editions of *Health, United States*.

SOURCE: Centers for Disease Control and Prevention, National Center for Health Statistics, National Health Interview Survey, family core and sample child questionnaires.

Table 82 (page 1 of 2). No usual source of health care among adults 18–64 years of age, according to selected characteristics: United States, average annual 1993–94 through 2002–03

[Data are based on household interviews of a sample of the civilian noninstitutionalized population]

Characteristic	*1993–94*[1]	*1995–96*[1]	*1997–98*	*2000–01*	*2002–03*
	Percent of adults without a usual source of health care[2]				
All adults 18–64 years of age[3,4]	18.5	16.6	17.5	16.5	16.6
Age					
18–44 years	21.7	19.6	21.1	20.3	20.7
18–24 years	26.6	22.6	27.0	26.1	27.0
25–44 years	20.3	18.8	19.3	18.4	18.6
45–64 years	12.8	11.3	11.2	9.9	9.5
45–54 years	14.1	12.2	12.6	10.9	10.8
55–64 years	11.1	9.8	9.0	8.3	7.6
Sex[4]					
Male	23.3	21.0	23.2	21.8	21.8
Female	13.9	12.5	11.9	11.4	11.6
Race[4,5]					
White only	18.2	16.3	16.9	15.8	16.1
Black or African American only	19.2	17.6	18.7	16.8	17.6
American Indian and Alaska Native only	19.1	15.9	20.7	15.9	19.1
Asian only	24.0	20.7	21.1	18.5	20.9
Native Hawaiian and Other Pacific Islander only	- - -	- - -	- - -	*	*
2 or more races	- - -	- - -	- - -	21.1	17.3
American Indian and Alaska Native; White	- - -	- - -	- - -	24.0	17.1
Hispanic origin and race[4,5]					
Hispanic or Latino	28.8	26.2	28.6	30.8	29.4
Mexican	30.5	28.1	33.4	34.6	31.6
Not Hispanic or Latino	17.5	15.5	16.1	14.6	14.5
White only	17.0	15.0	15.4	13.9	13.6
Black or African American only	18.9	17.4	18.6	16.7	17.4
Poverty status[4,6]					
Poor	28.2	24.9	28.2	27.8	22.7
Near poor	24.6	22.3	24.7	25.1	21.7
Nonpoor	14.8	13.5	13.9	12.7	14.0
Hispanic origin and race and poverty status[4,5,6]					
Hispanic or Latino:					
Poor	38.0	32.6	40.8	43.9	35.2
Near poor	35.7	31.6	33.3	37.3	32.6
Nonpoor	18.3	18.2	19.0	20.8	24.5
Not Hispanic or Latino:					
White only:					
Poor	27.1	22.8	24.5	22.3	17.1
Near poor	22.7	20.3	21.8	21.8	17.9
Nonpoor	14.4	13.0	13.3	11.7	12.1
Black or African American only:					
Poor	23.8	21.1	23.1	21.9	21.7
Near poor	21.6	21.2	24.7	20.9	21.1
Nonpoor	14.6	13.6	14.4	13.2	14.6
Health insurance status[4,7]					
Insured	13.3	11.4	11.4	9.7	9.3
Private	13.1	11.3	11.5	9.7	9.4
Medicaid	15.2	12.5	10.0	9.6	8.9
Uninsured	41.5	40.9	45.3	46.3	46.7
Poverty status and health insurance status[4,6]					
Poor:					
Insured	16.8	13.6	13.8	12.0	9.8
Uninsured	45.7	42.1	50.4	51.7	49.9
Near poor:					
Insured	15.3	13.1	13.9	12.3	10.4
Uninsured	42.9	41.5	46.2	48.4	46.3
Nonpoor:					
Insured	12.3	10.8	10.7	9.1	8.8
Uninsured	37.0	39.4	41.2	41.7	44.0

See footnotes at end of table.

Table 82 (page 2 of 2). No usual source of health care among adults 18–64 years of age, according to selected characteristics: United States, average annual 1993–94 through 2002–03

[Data are based on household interviews of a sample of the civilian noninstitutionalized population]

Characteristic	*1993–94*[1]	*1995–96*[1]	*1997–98*	*2000–01*	*2002–03*
Geographic region[4]	Percent of adults without a usual source of health care[2]				
Northeast	14.5	13.3	13.2	12.1	12.2
Midwest	15.8	14.5	14.9	15.2	14.3
South	21.6	18.4	20.5	17.8	18.9
West	20.5	19.5	19.8	20.0	19.5
Location of residence[4]					
Within MSA[8]	18.8	16.9	17.6	16.7	16.8
Outside MSA[8]	17.4	15.4	17.1	15.8	16.1

* Estimates are considered unreliable. Data not shown have a relative standard error of greater than 30 percent.
- - - Data not available.
[1]Data prior to 1997 are not strictly comparable with data for later years due to the 1997 questionnaire redesign. See Appendix I, National Health Interview Survey.
[2]Persons who report the emergency department as the place of their usual source of care are defined as having no usual source of care. See Appendix II, Usual source of care.
[3]Includes all other races not shown separately, and unknown health insurance status.
[4]Estimates are for persons 18–64 years of age and are age adjusted to the year 2000 standard population using three age groups: 18–44 years, 45–54 years, and 55–64 years of age. See Appendix II, Age adjustment.
[5]The race groups, white, black, American Indian and Alaska Native, Asian, Native Hawaiian and Other Pacific Islander, and 2 or more races, include persons of Hispanic and non-Hispanic origin. Persons of Hispanic origin may be of any race. Starting with data year 1999 race-specific estimates are tabulated according to 1997 Standards for Federal data on Race and Ethnicity and are not strictly comparable with estimates for earlier years. The five single race categories plus multiple race categories shown in the table conform to 1997 Standards. Starting with data year 1999 race-specific estimates are for persons who reported only one racial group; the category "2 or more races" includes persons who reported more than one racial group. Prior to data year 1999, data were tabulated according to 1977 Standards with four racial groups and the category "Asian only" included Native Hawaiian and Other Pacific Islander. Estimates for single race categories prior to 1999 included persons who reported one race or, if they reported more than one race, identified one race as best representing their race. See Appendix II, Race.
[6]Poor persons are defined as below the poverty threshold. Near poor persons have incomes of 100 percent to less than 200 percent of the poverty threshold. Nonpoor persons have incomes of 200 percent or greater than the poverty threshold. Missing family income data were imputed for 15–17 percent of persons 18–64 years of age in 1993–96, 25–29 percent in 1997–98, and 31–34 percent in 1999–2003. See Appendix II, Family income; Poverty level.
[7]Health insurance categories are mutually exclusive. Persons who reported both Medicaid and private coverage are classified as having private coverage. Medicaid includes other public assistance through 1996. Starting in 1997 Medicaid includes state-sponsored health plans and State Children's Health Insurance Program (SCHIP). The category "insured" also includes military, other government, and Medicare coverage. In 1993–96 health insurance status was unknown for 8–9 percent of adults in the sample. In 1997–2003 health insurance status was unknown for 1 percent of adults in the sample. See Appendix II, Health insurance coverage.
[8]MSA is metropolitan statistical area.

NOTES: For more data on usual source of care see the National Health Interview Survey home page: www.cdc.gov/nchs/nhis.htm. Standard errors are available in the spreadsheet version of this table. See www.cdc.gov/nchs/hus.htm. Starting with *Health, United States, 2005*, estimates for 2000 and later years use weights derived from the 2000 census. Estimates for 2000–2002 were recalculated using 2000-based weights and may differ from previous editions of *Health, United States.*

SOURCE: Centers for Disease Control and Prevention, National Center for Health Statistics, National Health Interview Survey, access to care and health insurance supplements (1993–96). Starting in 1997 data are from the family core and sample adult questionnaires.

Table 83 (page 1 of 2). Emergency department visits within the past 12 months among adults 18 years of age and over, according to selected characteristics: United States, selected years 1997–2003

[Data are based on household interviews of a sample of the civilian noninstitutionalized population]

Characteristic	1 or more emergency department visits				2 or more emergency department visits			
	1997	2000	2002	2003	1997	2000	2002	2003
	Percent of adults with emergency department visit[1]							
All adults 18 years of age and over[2,3]	19.6	20.2	20.5	20.0	6.7	6.9	7.1	7.0
Age								
18–44 years	20.7	20.5	20.7	20.0	6.8	7.0	7.1	6.8
18–24 years	26.3	25.7	24.7	23.9	9.1	8.8	8.5	8.2
25–44 years	19.0	18.8	19.4	18.6	6.2	6.4	6.6	6.4
45–64 years	16.2	17.6	18.2	18.5	5.6	5.6	6.3	6.4
45–54 years	15.7	17.9	18.1	17.8	5.5	5.8	6.7	5.9
55–64 years	16.9	17.0	18.4	19.3	5.7	5.3	5.7	7.0
65 years and over	22.0	23.7	24.0	22.9	8.1	8.6	8.3	8.7
65–74 years	20.3	21.6	21.2	19.7	7.1	7.4	7.7	7.1
75 years and over	24.3	26.2	27.1	26.6	9.3	10.0	9.0	10.4
Sex[3]								
Male	19.1	18.7	19.6	18.2	5.9	5.7	6.2	5.6
Female	20.2	21.6	21.5	21.8	7.5	7.9	7.9	8.4
Race[3,4]								
White only	19.0	19.4	19.6	19.2	6.2	6.4	6.5	6.4
Black or African American only	25.9	26.5	27.8	27.8	11.1	10.8	11.7	12.4
American Indian and Alaska Native only	24.8	30.3	25.3	22.5	13.1	*12.6	*10.0	*9.1
Asian only	11.6	13.6	13.6	12.9	*2.9	*3.8	*2.6	*3.5
Native Hawaiian and Other Pacific Islander only	- - -	*	*	*	- - -	*	*	*
2 or more races	- - -	32.5	30.8	25.2	- - -	11.3	13.3	11.1
American Indian and Alaska Native; White	- - -	33.9	37.7	29.7	- - -	*9.4	15.9	*15.1
Hispanic origin and race[3,4]								
Hispanic or Latino	19.2	18.3	18.4	18.5	7.4	7.0	6.8	7.3
Mexican	17.8	17.4	18.1	17.0	6.4	7.1	6.3	6.4
Not Hispanic or Latino	19.7	20.6	20.9	20.3	6.7	6.9	7.2	7.0
White only	19.1	19.8	20.0	19.5	6.2	6.4	6.6	6.3
Black or African American only	25.9	26.5	27.9	27.7	11.0	10.8	11.6	12.3
Poverty status[3,5]								
Poor	28.1	29.0	28.6	26.3	12.8	13.3	12.6	12.6
Near poor	23.8	23.9	24.7	23.2	9.3	9.6	9.7	9.9
Nonpoor	17.0	18.0	18.2	18.2	4.9	5.2	5.6	5.4
Hispanic origin and race and poverty status[3,4,5]								
Hispanic or Latino:								
Poor	22.1	22.4	22.3	21.2	9.8	9.7	9.0	9.6
Near poor	19.2	18.1	19.5	17.6	8.1	6.7	8.6	7.3
Nonpoor	17.6	16.8	16.7	17.9	5.4	6.1	5.0	6.4
Not Hispanic or Latino:								
White only:								
Poor	29.5	30.1	30.2	27.0	13.0	13.9	13.4	12.7
Near poor	24.3	25.5	25.9	24.0	9.1	10.4	9.6	10.0
Nonpoor	16.8	17.7	17.7	17.8	4.8	5.0	5.3	5.0
Black or African American only:								
Poor	34.6	35.4	35.3	33.4	17.5	17.4	16.7	18.1
Near poor	29.2	28.5	29.7	31.2	12.8	12.2	13.8	15.7
Nonpoor	19.7	22.6	24.3	24.0	7.2	8.0	9.1	8.7
Health insurance status[6,7]								
18–64 years of age:								
Insured	18.8	19.5	19.6	19.7	6.1	6.4	6.7	6.7
Private	16.9	17.6	17.4	17.4	4.7	5.1	5.0	5.0
Medicaid	37.6	42.2	40.4	39.7	19.7	21.0	21.9	21.6
Uninsured	20.0	19.3	20.4	18.1	7.5	6.9	7.4	6.7
65 years of age and over:								
Medicare HMO	20.2	24.4	20.3	25.6	6.7	8.5	7.4	10.8
Private	21.3	23.3	24.0	21.2	6.9	7.8	7.9	7.1
Medicaid	35.2	36.0	33.1	34.9	20.2	18.3	12.8	17.8
Medicare fee-for-service only	22.0	20.1	22.4	22.2	9.4	7.2	8.6	9.4

See footnotes at end of table.

Table 83 (page 2 of 2). Emergency department visits within the past 12 months among adults 18 years of age and over, according to selected characteristics: United States, selected years 1997–2003

[Data are based on household interviews of a sample of the civilian noninstitutionalized population]

Characteristic	1 or more emergency department visits				2 or more emergency department visits			
	1997	2000	2002	2003	1997	2000	2002	2003
Poverty status and health insurance status[5,6,7]	Percent of adults with emergency department visit[1]							
18–64 years of age:								
Poor:								
Insured	31.0	33.0	32.7	30.1	15.2	16.2	15.0	15.2
Uninsured	22.8	24.2	23.4	19.9	9.1	9.9	10.3	8.7
Near poor:								
Insured	25.3	25.9	26.1	25.5	9.6	10.6	10.5	11.2
Uninsured	20.2	18.7	21.1	18.8	8.6	6.9	8.1	7.5
Nonpoor:								
Insured	16.2	17.2	17.0	17.5	4.4	4.8	5.1	4.9
Uninsured	18.0	17.4	18.5	16.7	5.5	5.5	5.7	5.0
Geographic region[3]								
Northeast	19.5	20.0	20.5	20.3	6.9	6.2	6.2	6.9
Midwest	19.3	20.1	20.9	20.0	6.2	6.9	6.7	6.4
South	20.9	21.2	21.4	20.9	7.3	7.6	8.2	8.1
West	17.7	18.6	18.4	18.2	6.0	6.3	6.2	5.9
Location of residence[3]								
Within MSA[8]	19.1	19.6	19.8	19.5	6.4	6.6	6.6	6.6
Outside MSA[8]	21.5	22.5	23.4	22.3	7.8	7.8	8.9	8.6

* Estimates are considered unreliable. Data preceded by an asterisk have a relative standard error (RSE) of 20–30 percent. Data not shown have an RSE of greater than 30 percent.

- - - Data not available.

[1]See Appendix II, Emergency department visit.

[2]Includes all other races not shown separately and unknown health insurance status.

[3]Estimates are for persons 18 years of age and over and are age adjusted to the year 2000 standard using five age groups: 18–44 years, 45–54 years, 55–64 years, 65–74 years, and 75 years and over. See Appendix II, Age adjustment.

[4]The race groups, white, black, American Indian and Alaska Native, Asian, Native Hawaiian and Other Pacific Islander, and 2 or more races, include persons of Hispanic and non-Hispanic origin. Persons of Hispanic origin may be of any race. Starting with data year 1999 race-specific estimates are tabulated according to 1997 Standards for Federal data on Race and Ethnicity and are not strictly comparable with estimates for earlier years. The five single race categories plus multiple race categories shown in the table conform to 1997 Standards. Starting with data year 1999 race-specific estimates are for persons who reported only one racial group; the category "2 or more races" includes persons who reported more than one racial group. Prior to data year 1999, data were tabulated according to 1977 Standards with four racial groups and the category "Asian only" included Native Hawaiian and Other Pacific Islander. Estimates for single race categories prior to 1999 included persons who reported one race or, if they reported more than one race, identified one race as best representing their race. See Appendix II, Race.

[5]Poor persons are defined as below the poverty threshold. Near poor persons have incomes of 100 percent to less than 200 percent of the poverty threshold. Nonpoor persons have incomes of 200 percent or greater than the poverty threshold. Missing family income data were imputed for 27–31 percent of persons 18 years of age and over in 1997–98 and 33–36 percent in 1999–2003. See Appendix II, Family income; Poverty level.

[6]Estimates for persons 18–64 years of age are age adjusted to the year 2000 Standard using three age groups: 18–44 years, 45–54 years, and 55–64 years of age. Estimates for persons 65 years of age and over are age adjusted to the year 2000 Standard using two age groups: 65–74 years and 75 years and over. See Appendix II, Age adjustment.

[7]Health insurance categories are mutually exclusive. Persons who reported both Medicaid and private coverage are classified as having private coverage. Starting in 1997 Medicaid includes State-sponsored health plans and State Children's Health Insurance Program (SCHIP). In addition to private and Medicaid, the category "insured" also includes military plans, other government-sponsored health plans, and Medicare, not shown separately. Persons 65 years of age and over who reported Medicare HMO (health maintenance organization) and some other type of health insurance coverage are classified as having Medicare HMO. For persons 65 years of age and over the category "private" includes private and Medicare coverage. See Appendix II, Health insurance coverage.

[8]MSA is metropolitan statistical area.

NOTES: Data for additional years are available. See Appendix III. Standard errors are available in the spreadsheet version of this table. See www.cdc.gov/nchs/hus.htm. Starting with *Health, United States, 2005,* estimates for 2000 and later years use weights derived from the 2000 census. Estimates for 2000–2002 were recalculated using 2000-based weights and may differ from previous editions of *Health, United States*.

SOURCE: Centers for Disease Control and Prevention, National Center for Health Statistics, National Health Interview Survey, family core and sample adult questionnaires.

Table 84 (page 1 of 2). Dental visits in the past year according to selected characteristics: United States, selected years 1997–2003

[Data are based on household interviews of a sample of the civilian noninstitutionalized population]

Characteristic	2 years of age and over[1]			2–17 years of age			18–64 years of age			65 years of age and over[2]		
	1997	2002	2003	1997	2002	2003	1997	2002	2003	1997	2002	2003
	Percent of persons with a dental visit in the past year[3]											
Total[4]	64.9	64.4	66.3	72.7	74.2	75.0	64.1	62.6	64.8	54.8	55.5	58.0
Sex												
Male	62.6	61.5	63.6	72.3	73.7	74.1	60.4	58.4	60.9	55.4	55.4	58.4
Female	67.2	67.1	68.9	73.0	74.8	75.9	67.7	66.7	68.6	54.4	55.5	57.7
Race[5]												
White only	66.5	66.3	67.5	74.0	76.3	76.0	65.7	64.5	65.9	56.8	58.0	59.8
Black or African American only	56.5	54.5	58.4	68.8	68.8	70.5	57.0	53.5	58.1	35.4	33.9	38.7
American Indian and Alaska Native only	51.5	51.2	59.9	66.8	66.6	69.9	49.9	50.3	58.0	*	*	*49.2
Asian only	61.8	61.3	65.1	69.9	66.8	72.9	60.3	62.7	63.6	53.9	45.4	57.4
Native Hawaiian and Other Pacific Islander only	---	*	*	---	*	*	---	*	*	---	*	*
2 or more races	---	59.5	61.6	---	71.4	74.5	---	57.9	59.6	---	44.7	51.0
Black or African American; White	---	70.1	63.6	---	67.2	71.3	---	65.4	60.3	---	*	*80.7
American Indian and Alaska Native; White	---	51.9	50.0	---	64.3	52.8	---	50.2	53.7	---	*42.7	*
Hispanic origin and race[5]												
Hispanic or Latino	52.9	52.7	52.4	61.0	62.5	64.5	50.8	49.2	48.3	47.8	47.9	46.0
Not Hispanic or Latino	66.4	66.3	68.6	74.7	76.7	77.3	65.7	64.6	67.4	55.2	55.9	58.7
White only	68.2	68.6	70.5	76.4	79.4	79.4	67.5	66.7	69.3	57.2	58.4	60.9
Black or African American only	56.5	54.3	58.5	68.8	68.6	70.6	56.9	53.4	58.3	35.3	33.7	38.3
Poverty status[6]												
Poor	47.7	47.5	48.2	62.0	64.4	65.8	46.9	44.3	44.5	31.5	35.0	37.1
Near poor	50.6	51.4	52.3	62.5	66.9	66.6	48.3	47.5	49.1	40.8	43.0	43.6
Nonpoor	72.5	70.7	73.4	80.1	79.6	80.8	71.2	68.9	72.0	65.9	64.7	67.8
Hispanic origin and race and poverty status[5,6]												
Hispanic or Latino:												
Poor	42.1	43.8	42.0	55.9	60.0	62.1	39.2	38.6	35.5	33.6	38.1	33.2
Near poor	46.4	45.1	45.5	53.8	57.8	59.1	43.5	40.1	40.8	47.9	40.6	39.4
Nonpoor	64.9	61.1	62.7	73.7	68.4	71.6	62.3	58.0	59.4	58.8	61.3	60.7
Not Hispanic or Latino:												
White only:												
Poor	50.6	51.9	52.8	64.4	69.5	69.1	50.6	48.6	50.4	32.0	38.2	39.9
Near poor	52.9	55.3	55.8	66.1	71.3	69.6	50.4	51.4	52.8	42.2	45.2	45.9
Nonpoor	73.9	73.1	75.6	81.3	82.7	83.2	72.7	71.1	74.2	67.0	66.5	69.1
Black or African American only:												
Poor	47.7	42.9	45.1	66.1	63.5	66.7	46.2	39.8	40.8	27.7	23.8	27.6
Near poor	46.9	47.7	52.0	61.2	68.9	69.1	46.3	45.0	50.6	26.9	26.0	29.3
Nonpoor	66.0	61.8	66.7	77.1	72.5	74.5	66.1	61.4	67.2	49.8	45.6	51.9

See footnotes at end of table.

Table 84 (page 2 of 2). Dental visits in the past year according to selected characteristics: United States, selected years 1997–2003

[Data are based on household interviews of a sample of the civilian noninstitutionalized population]

Characteristic	2 years of age and over[1]			2–17 years of age			18–64 years of age			65 years of age and over[2]		
	1997	2002	2003	1997	2002	2003	1997	2002	2003	1997	2002	2003
Geographic region	Percent of persons with a dental visit in the past year[3]											
Northeast	69.6	70.1	72.4	77.5	80.5	81.5	69.6	69.2	71.4	55.5	55.8	61.1
Midwest	68.3	68.0	68.8	76.4	77.9	77.6	67.4	66.6	67.6	57.6	56.9	58.8
South	60.0	58.8	61.4	68.0	69.1	70.7	59.4	56.7	59.6	49.0	50.7	53.3
West	64.9	65.0	66.7	71.5	73.5	74.1	62.9	62.3	64.7	61.9	63.2	62.8
Location of residence												
Within MSA[7]	66.5	66.0	67.9	73.6	74.8	75.5	65.7	64.4	66.5	57.6	58.5	61.3
Outside MSA[7]	59.1	58.1	60.0	69.3	71.9	72.9	58.0	55.4	57.9	46.1	45.9	46.7

* Estimates are considered unreliable. Data preceded by an asterisk have a relative standard error (RSE) of 20–30 percent. Data not shown have an RSE greater than 30 percent.

- - - Data not available.

[1]Estimates are age adjusted to the year 2000 standard using six age groups: 2–17 years, 18–44 years, 45–54 years, 55–64 years, 65–74 years, and 75 years and over. See Appendix II, Age adjustment.

[2]Based on 1997–2003 National Health Interview Surveys, it was estimated that 25–30 percent of persons 65 years of age and over were edentulous (having lost all their natural teeth). In 1997–2003 about 70 percent of older dentate persons compared with 16–20 percent of older edentate persons had a dental visit in the past year.

[3]Respondents were asked "About how long has it been since you last saw or talked to a dentist?" See Appendix II, Dental visit.

[4]Includes all other races not shown separately.

[5]The race groups, white, black, American Indian and Alaska Native, Asian, Native Hawaiian and Other Pacific Islander, and 2 or more races, include persons of Hispanic and non-Hispanic origin. Persons of Hispanic origin may be of any race. Starting with data year 1999 race-specific estimates are tabulated according to 1997 Standards for Federal data on Race and Ethnicity and are not strictly comparable with estimates for earlier years. The five single race categories plus multiple race categories shown in the table conform to 1997 Standards. Starting with data year 1999 race-specific estimates are for persons who reported only one racial group; the category "2 or more races" includes persons who reported more than one racial group. Prior to data year 1999, data were tabulated according to 1977 Standards with four racial groups and the category "Asian only" included Native Hawaiian and Other Pacific Islander. Estimates for single race categories prior to 1999 included persons who reported one race or, if they reported more than one race, identified one race as best representing their race. See Appendix II, Race.

[6]Poor persons are defined as below the poverty threshold. Near poor persons have incomes of 100 percent to less than 200 percent of the poverty threshold. Nonpoor persons have incomes of 200 percent or greater than the poverty threshold. Missing family income data were imputed for 25–29 percent of persons in 1997–98 and 32–35 percent in 1999–2003. See Appendix II, Family income; Poverty level.

[7]MSA is metropolitan statistical area.

NOTES: In 1997 the National Health Interview Survey questionnaire was redesigned. See Appendix I, National Health Interview Survey. Data for additional years are available. See Appendix III. Standard errors for selected years are available in the spreadsheet version of this table. See www.cdc.gov/nchs/hus.htm. Starting with *Health, United States, 2005*, estimates for 2000 and later years use weights derived from the 2000 census. Estimates for 2000–2002 were recalculated using 2000-based weights and may differ from previous editions of *Health, United States.*

SOURCE: Centers for Disease Control and Prevention, National Center for Health Statistics, National Health Interview Survey, sample child and sample adult questionnaires.

Table 85 (page 1 of 2). Untreated dental caries, according to age, sex, race and Hispanic origin, and poverty status: United States, 1971–74, 1988–94, and 1999–2002

[Data are based on dental examinations of a sample of the civilian noninstitutionalized population]

Sex, race and Hispanic origin, and poverty status	2–5 years			6–17 years		
	1971–74	1988–94	1999–2002	1971–74	1988–94	1999–2002
	Percent of persons with untreated dental caries					
Total[1]	25.1	19.6	19.4	55.3	23.9	21.9
Sex						
Male	26.6	20.0	20.4	55.2	23.0	23.0
Female	23.6	19.3	18.4	55.4	24.8	20.8
Race and Hispanic origin[2]						
Not Hispanic or Latino:						
White	23.7	14.4	16.9	52.3	19.2	18.0
Black or African American	29.0	25.1	24.3	70.5	33.1	28.3
Mexican	34.1	35.0	31.4	60.2	37.1	32.5
Poverty status[3]						
Poor	32.0	30.6	31.9	68.9	38.4	32.6
Near poor	29.9	25.1	20.1	60.9	28.9	29.2
Nonpoor	17.9	9.7	11.0	46.2	15.1	13.2
Race, Hispanic origin, and poverty status[2,3]						
Not Hispanic or Latino:						
White:						
Poor	32.1	26.5	34.2	68.5	34.8	29.7
Near poor and nonpoor	22.1	12.2	12.8	50.4	17.0	15.8
Black or African American:						
Poor	29.1	27.7	29.3	72.7	35.7	35.8
Near poor and nonpoor	27.9	22.7	20.1	67.5	31.3	24.4
Mexican:						
Poor	*	38.9	39.1	57.1	46.4	39.2
Near poor and nonpoor	27.4	30.5	25.7	61.2	26.9	25.1

Sex, race and Hispanic origin, and poverty status	18–64 years			65–74 years		
	1971–74	1988–94	1999–2002	1971–74	1988–94	1999–2002
	Percent of persons with untreated dental caries					
Total[1]	48.4	28.2	23.8	29.7	25.4	17.0
Sex						
Male	50.9	31.2	25.9	32.6	29.8	20.1
Female	46.0	25.3	21.7	27.4	21.5	14.4
Race and Hispanic origin[2]						
Not Hispanic or Latino:						
White	45.6	23.6	18.7	28.3	22.7	14.3
Black or African American	68.2	48.0	41.7	41.5	46.7	35.0
Mexican	62.0	40.0	35.5	*	43.8	33.9
Poverty status[3]						
Poor	63.6	47.4	40.1	34.3	46.6	27.9
Near poor	56.3	42.6	36.1	35.6	40.1	28.1
Nonpoor	43.1	19.5	16.1	26.2	19.2	12.2
Race, Hispanic origin, and poverty status[2,3]						
Not Hispanic or Latino:						
White:						
Poor	59.5	42.4	33.9	33.3	*39.0	*
Near poor and nonpoor	44.5	21.6	16.8	28.3	22.7	14.0
Black or African American:						
Poor	73.1	59.3	53.5	39.8	49.7	*31.0
Near poor and nonpoor	65.8	43.4	37.2	41.1	43.8	39.0
Mexican:						
Poor	65.4	52.4	43.1	*	55.5	*45.0
Near poor and nonpoor	59.1	31.6	32.2	*	35.6	31.1

See footnotes at end of table.

Table 85 (page 2 of 2). Untreated dental caries, according to age, sex, race and Hispanic origin, and poverty status: United States, 1971–74, 1988–94, and 1999–2002

[Data are based on dental examinations of a sample of the civilian noninstitutionalized population]

Sex, race and Hispanic origin, and poverty status	75 years and over		
	1971–74	*1988–94*	*1999–2002*
	Percent of persons with untreated dental caries		
Total[1]	- - -	30.3	20.3
Sex			
Male	- - -	34.4	24.4
Female	- - -	28.1	17.4
Race and Hispanic origin[2]			
Not Hispanic or Latino:			
White	- - -	27.8	18.3
Black or African American	- - -	62.6	46.8
Mexican	- - -	55.6	48.2
Poverty status[3]			
Poor	- - -	47.1	33.0
Near poor	- - -	34.5	23.0
Nonpoor	- - -	23.2	15.8
Race, Hispanic origin, and poverty status[2,3]			
Not Hispanic or Latino:			
White:			
Poor	- - -	38.0	*32.2
Near poor and nonpoor	- - -	26.1	17.2
Black or African American:			
Poor	- - -	68.6	*
Near poor and nonpoor	- - -	60.2	43.8
Mexican:			
Poor	- - -	79.4	*
Near poor and nonpoor	- - -	*	49.7

* Estimates are considered unreliable. Data preceded by an asterisk have a relative standard error (RSE) of 20–30 percent. Data not shown have an RSE of greater than 30 percent or fewer than 30 cases.

- - - Data not available.

[1]Includes persons of all races and Hispanic origins, not just those shown separately and unknown poverty status.

[2]Persons of Mexican origin may be of any race. Starting with data year 1999 race-specific estimates are tabulated according to 1997 Standards for Federal data on Race and Ethnicity and are not strictly comparable with estimates for earlier years. The two non-Hispanic race categories shown in the table conform to 1997 Standards. The 1999–2002 race-specific estimates are for persons who reported only one racial group. Prior to data year 1999, data were tabulated according to 1977 Standards. Estimates for single race categories prior to 1999 included persons who reported one race or, if they reported more than one race, identified one race as best representing their race. See Appendix II, Race.

[3]Poor persons are defined as below the poverty threshold. Near poor persons have incomes of 100 percent to less than 200 percent of the poverty threshold. Nonpoor persons have incomes of 200 percent or greater than the poverty threshold. Persons with unknown poverty status are excluded (4 percent in 1971–74, 6 percent in 1988–94, and 8 percent in 1999–2002). See Appendix II, Family income; Poverty level.

NOTES: Excludes edentulous persons (persons without teeth) of all ages. The majority of edentulous persons are 65 years of age and over. Estimates of edentulism among persons 65 years of age and over are 46 percent in 1971–74, 33 percent in 1988–94, and 27 percent in 1999–2002. See Appendix II, Dental caries. Standard errors are available in the spreadsheet version of this table. See www.cdc.gov/nchs/hus.htm.

SOURCES: Centers for Disease Control and Prevention, National Center for Health Statistics, National Health and Nutrition Examination Survey.

Table 86 (page 1 of 2). Use of mammography for women 40 years of age and over, according to selected characteristics: United States, selected years 1987–2003

[Data are based on household interviews of a sample of the civilian noninstitutionalized population]

Characteristic	1987	1990	1991	1994	1998	1999	2000	2003
	Percent of women having a mammogram within the past 2 years[1]							
40 years and over, age adjusted[2,3]	29.0	51.7	54.7	61.0	67.0	70.3	70.4	69.5
40 years and over, crude[2]	28.7	51.4	54.6	60.9	66.9	70.3	70.4	69.7
Age								
40–49 years	31.9	55.1	55.6	61.3	63.4	67.2	64.3	64.4
50–64 years	31.7	56.0	60.3	66.5	73.7	76.5	78.7	76.2
65 years and over	22.8	43.4	48.1	55.0	63.8	66.8	67.9	67.7
65–74 years	26.6	48.7	55.7	63.0	69.4	73.9	74.0	74.6
75 years and over	17.3	35.8	37.8	44.6	57.2	58.9	61.3	60.6
Race[4]								
40 years and over, crude:								
White only	29.6	52.2	55.6	60.6	67.4	70.6	71.4	70.1
Black or African American only	24.0	46.4	48.0	64.3	66.0	71.0	67.8	70.4
American Indian and Alaska Native only	*	43.2	54.5	65.8	45.2	63.0	47.4	63.1
Asian only	*	46.0	45.9	55.8	60.2	58.3	53.5	57.6
Native Hawaiian and Other Pacific Islander only	- - -	- - -	- - -	- - -	- - -	*	*	*
2 or more races	- - -	- - -	- - -	- - -	- - -	70.2	69.2	65.3
Hispanic origin and race[4]								
40 years and over, crude:								
Hispanic or Latino	18.3	45.2	49.2	51.9	60.2	65.7	61.2	65.0
Not Hispanic or Latino	29.4	51.8	54.9	61.5	67.5	70.7	71.1	70.1
White only	30.3	52.7	56.0	61.3	68.0	71.1	72.2	70.5
Black or African American only	23.8	46.0	47.7	64.4	66.0	71.0	67.9	70.5
Age, Hispanic origin, and race[4]								
40–49 years:								
Hispanic or Latino	*15.3	45.1	44.0	47.5	55.2	61.6	54.1	59.4
Not Hispanic or Latino:								
White only	34.3	57.0	58.1	62.0	64.4	68.3	67.2	65.2
Black or African American only	27.8	48.4	48.0	67.2	65.0	69.2	60.9	68.2
50–64 years:								
Hispanic or Latino	23.0	47.5	61.7	60.1	67.2	69.7	66.5	69.4
Not Hispanic or Latino:								
White only	33.6	58.1	61.5	67.5	75.3	77.9	80.6	77.2
Black or African American only	26.4	48.4	52.4	63.6	71.2	75.0	77.7	76.2
65 years and over:								
Hispanic or Latino	*	41.1	40.9	48.0	59.0	67.2	68.3	69.5
Not Hispanic or Latino:								
White only	24.0	43.8	49.1	54.9	64.3	66.8	68.3	68.1
Black or African American only	14.1	39.7	41.6	61.0	60.6	68.1	65.5	65.4
Age and poverty status[5]								
40 years and over, crude:								
Poor	14.6	30.8	35.2	44.2	50.1	57.4	54.8	55.4
Near poor	20.9	39.1	44.4	48.6	56.1	59.5	58.1	60.8
Nonpoor	35.2	59.2	62.2	68.5	72.6	75.0	75.9	74.3
40–49 years:								
Poor	18.6	32.2	33.0	43.0	44.8	51.3	47.4	50.6
Near poor	18.4	39.0	43.8	47.6	46.9	52.8	43.6	54.0
Nonpoor	36.8	60.1	61.2	66.5	68.4	71.6	69.9	68.3
50–64 years:								
Poor	14.6	29.9	37.3	46.2	52.7	63.3	61.7	58.3
Near poor	24.2	39.8	50.2	49.0	61.8	64.9	68.3	64.0
Nonpoor	37.0	63.3	66.0	73.7	78.7	80.2	82.6	80.9
65 years and over:								
Poor	13.1	30.8	35.2	43.9	51.9	57.6	54.8	57.0
Near poor	19.9	38.6	41.8	48.8	57.8	60.2	60.3	62.8
Nonpoor	29.7	51.5	57.8	64.0	70.1	72.5	75.0	72.6

See footnotes at end of table.

Table 86 (page 2 of 2). Use of mammography for women 40 years of age and over, according to selected characteristics: United States, selected years 1987–2003

[Data are based on household interviews of a sample of the civilian noninstitutionalized population]

Characteristic	1987	1990	1991	1994	1998	1999	2000	2003
Health insurance status[6]	Percent of women having a mammogram within the past 2 years[1]							
40–64 years of age:								
Insured	- - -	- - -	- - -	68.3	72.3	75.5	76.0	75.1
Private	- - -	- - -	- - -	69.4	73.4	76.3	77.1	76.3
Medicaid	- - -	- - -	- - -	54.5	59.7	62.5	61.7	63.5
Uninsured	- - -	- - -	- - -	34.0	40.1	44.8	40.7	41.5
65 years of age and over:								
Medicare HMO	- - -	- - -	- - -	- - -	70.4	76.3	73.2	70.2
Private	- - -	- - -	- - -	59.0	67.3	70.2	71.2	72.4
Medicaid	- - -	- - -	- - -	46.2	51.1	53.8	57.6	61.2
Medicare fee-for-service only	- - -	- - -	- - -	36.8	48.1	51.3	55.8	53.4
Age and education[7]								
40 years and over, crude:								
No high school diploma or GED	17.8	36.4	40.0	48.2	54.5	56.7	57.7	58.1
High school diploma or GED	31.3	52.7	55.8	61.0	66.7	69.2	69.7	67.8
Some college or more	37.7	62.8	65.2	69.7	72.8	77.3	76.2	75.1
40–49 years of age:								
No high school diploma or GED	15.1	38.5	40.8	50.4	47.3	48.8	46.8	53.3
High school diploma or GED	32.6	53.1	52.0	55.8	59.1	60.8	59.0	60.8
Some college or more	39.2	62.3	63.7	68.7	68.3	74.4	70.6	68.1
50–64 years of age:								
No high school diploma or GED	21.2	41.0	43.6	51.6	58.8	62.3	66.5	63.4
High school diploma or GED	33.8	56.5	60.8	67.8	73.3	77.2	76.6	71.8
Some college or more	40.5	68.0	72.7	74.7	79.8	81.2	84.2	82.7
65 years of age and over:								
No high school diploma or GED	16.5	33.0	37.7	45.6	54.7	56.6	57.4	56.9
High school diploma or GED	25.9	47.5	54.0	59.1	66.8	68.4	71.8	69.7
Some college or more	32.3	56.7	57.9	64.3	71.3	77.1	74.1	75.1

* Estimates are considered unreliable. Data preceded by an asterisk have a relative standard error (RSE) of 20–30 percent. Data not shown have an RSE greater than 30 percent.

- - - Data not available.

[1]Questions concerning use of mammography differed slightly on the National Health Interview Survey across the years for which data are shown. See Appendix II, Mammography.

[2]Includes all other races not shown separately, unknown poverty status in 1987, unknown health insurance status, and unknown education.

[3]Estimates are age adjusted to the year 2000 standard population using four age groups: 40–49 years, 50–64 years, 65–74 years, and 75 years and over. See Appendix II, Age adjustment.

[4]The race groups, white, black, American Indian and Alaska Native, Asian, Native Hawaiian and Other Pacific Islander, and 2 or more races, include persons of Hispanic and non-Hispanic origin. Persons of Hispanic origin may be of any race. Starting with data year 1999 race-specific estimates are tabulated according to 1997 Standards for Federal data on Race and Ethnicity and are not strictly comparable with estimates for earlier years. The five single race categories plus multiple race categories shown in the table conform to 1997 Standards. Starting with data year 1999, race-specific estimates are for persons who reported only one racial group; the category "2 or more races" includes persons who reported more than one racial group. Prior to data year 1999, data were tabulated according to 1977 Standards with four racial groups and the category "Asian only" included Native Hawaiian and Other Pacific Islander. Estimates for single race categories prior to 1999 included persons who reported one race or, if they reported more than one race, identified one race as best representing their race. See Appendix II, Race.

[5]Poor persons are defined as below the poverty threshold. Near poor persons have incomes of 100 percent to less than 200 percent of the poverty threshold. Nonpoor persons have incomes of 200 percent or greater than the poverty threshold. Poverty status was unknown for 11 percent of women 40 years of age and over in 1987. Missing family income data were imputed for 19–23 percent of women 40 years of age and over in 1990–94 and 35–39 percent in 1998–2003. See Appendix II, Family income; Poverty level.

[6]Health insurance categories are mutually exclusive. Persons who reported both Medicaid and private coverage are classified as having private coverage. Starting in 1997 Medicaid includes State-sponsored health plans and State Children's Health Insurance Program (SCHIP). In addition to private and Medicaid, the category "insured" also includes military plans, other government-sponsored health plans, and Medicare, not shown separately. Persons 65 years of age and over who reported Medicare HMO (health maintenance organization) and some other type of health insurance coverage are classified as having Medicare HMO. For persons 65 years of age and over the category "private" includes private and Medicare coverage. See Appendix II, Health insurance coverage.

[7]Education categories shown are for 1998 and subsequent years. GED stands for General Educational Development high school equivalency diploma. In years prior to 1998 the following categories based on number of years of school completed were used: less than 12 years, 12 years, 13 years or more. See Appendix II, Education.

NOTES: Standard errors are available in the spreadsheet version of this table. See www.cdc.gov/nchs/hus.htm. Data starting in 1997 are not strictly comparable with data for earlier years due to the 1997 questionnaire redesign. See Appendix I, National Health Interview Survey. Starting with *Health, United States, 2005*, estimates for 2000 and later years use weights derived from the 2000 census. Estimates for 2000–2002 were recalculated using 2000-based weights and may differ from previous editions of *Health, United States*. Data for additional years are available. See Appendix III.

SOURCE: Centers for Disease Control and Prevention, National Center for Health Statistics, National Health Interview Survey. Data are from the following supplements: cancer control (1987), health promotion and disease prevention (1990–91), and year 2000 objectives (1993–94). Starting in 1998, data are from the family core and sample adult questionnaires.

Table 87 (page 1 of 2). Use of Pap smears for women 18 years of age and over, according to selected characteristics: United States, selected years 1987–2003

[Data are based on household interviews of a sample of the civilian noninstitutionalized population]

Characteristic	1987	1993	1994	1998	1999	2000	2003
	Percent of women having a Pap smear within the past 3 years[1]						
18 years and over, age adjusted[2,3]	74.1	77.7	76.8	79.3	80.8	81.3	79.2
18 years and over, crude[2]	74.4	77.7	76.8	79.1	80.8	81.2	79.0
Age							
18–44 years	83.3	84.6	82.8	84.4	86.8	84.9	83.9
18–24 years	74.8	78.8	76.6	73.6	76.8	73.5	75.1
25–44 years	86.3	86.3	84.6	87.6	89.9	88.5	86.8
45–64 years	70.5	77.2	77.4	81.4	81.7	84.6	81.3
45–54 years	75.7	82.1	81.9	83.7	83.8	86.3	83.6
55–64 years	65.2	70.6	71.0	78.0	78.4	82.0	77.8
65 years and over	50.8	57.6	57.3	59.8	61.0	64.5	60.8
65–74 years	57.9	64.7	64.9	67.0	70.0	71.6	70.1
75 years and over	40.4	48.0	47.3	51.2	50.8	56.7	51.1
Race[4]							
18 years and over, crude:							
White only	74.1	77.3	76.2	78.9	80.6	81.3	78.7
Black or African American only	80.7	82.7	83.5	84.2	85.7	85.1	84.0
American Indian and Alaska Native only	85.4	78.1	73.5	74.6	92.2	76.8	84.8
Asian only	51.9	68.8	66.4	68.5	64.4	66.4	68.3
Native Hawaiian and Other Pacific Islander only	- - -	- - -	- - -	- - -	*	*	*
2 or more races	- - -	- - -	- - -	- - -	86.9	80.0	81.6
Hispanic origin and race[4]							
18 years and over, crude:							
Hispanic or Latino	67.6	77.2	74.4	75.2	76.3	77.0	75.4
Not Hispanic or Latino	74.9	77.8	77.0	79.6	81.3	81.7	79.5
White only	74.7	77.3	76.5	79.3	81.0	81.8	79.3
Black or African American only	80.9	82.7	83.8	84.2	86.0	85.1	83.8
Age, Hispanic origin, and race[4]							
18–44 years:							
Hispanic or Latino	73.9	80.9	80.6	76.4	77.0	78.1	75.9
Not Hispanic or Latino:							
White only	84.5	85.3	82.9	85.7	88.7	86.6	85.8
Black or African American only	89.1	88.0	89.1	88.9	90.8	88.5	88.6
45–64 years:							
Hispanic or Latino	57.7	75.8	70.1	78.3	79.5	77.8	77.9
Not Hispanic or Latino:							
White only	71.2	77.2	77.5	81.7	81.9	85.9	81.4
Black or African American only	76.2	80.3	82.2	84.1	84.6	85.7	84.7
65 years and over:							
Hispanic or Latino	41.7	57.1	43.8	59.8	63.7	66.8	64.6
Not Hispanic or Latino:							
White only	51.8	57.1	58.2	59.7	60.5	64.2	60.7
Black or African American only	44.8	61.2	59.5	61.7	64.5	67.2	59.6
Age and poverty status[5]							
18 years and over, crude:							
Below poverty	64.3	70.3	68.8	69.8	73.6	72.0	70.5
Near poor	68.2	71.2	68.8	70.6	72.5	73.4	71.4
Nonpoor	80.0	82.1	81.9	83.5	84.3	85.0	83.0
18–44 years:							
Below poverty	77.1	77.0	78.9	77.1	79.7	77.1	77.1
Near poor	80.4	81.9	78.2	79.2	84.0	79.4	79.5
Nonpoor	86.4	87.9	85.7	87.6	89.0	88.0	86.9
45–64 years:							
Below poverty	53.6	66.5	62.0	67.6	73.1	73.6	66.0
Near poor	60.4	64.8	66.2	69.9	70.4	76.1	71.4
Nonpoor	74.9	81.4	82.0	85.1	84.6	87.4	85.1
65 years and over:							
Below poverty	33.2	47.4	44.0	48.2	51.9	53.7	52.6
Near poor	50.4	55.7	51.5	55.1	54.7	61.0	55.4
Nonpoor	60.0	62.0	66.8	65.3	66.4	68.8	65.4

See footnotes at end of table.

Table 87 (page 2 of 2). Use of Pap smears for women 18 years of age and over, according to selected characteristics: United States, selected years 1987–2003

[Data are based on household interviews of a sample of the civilian noninstitutionalized population]

Characteristic	*1987*	*1993*	*1994*	*1998*	*1999*	*2000*	*2003*
Health insurance status[6]	Percent of women having a Pap smear within the past 3 years[1]						
18–64 years of age:							
Insured	- - -	84.7	83.8	86.0	87.2	87.8	86.4
Private	- - -	84.8	83.6	86.5	87.5	88.0	87.0
Medicaid	- - -	82.7	86.2	83.0	84.2	85.8	82.8
Uninsured	- - -	69.4	68.6	69.6	73.3	70.4	66.6
65 years of age and over:							
Medicare HMO	- - -	- - -	- - -	66.1	69.6	67.6	61.4
Private	- - -	60.6	61.2	61.3	62.9	67.2	63.0
Medicaid	- - -	47.8	44.9	49.9	54.8	57.8	53.9
Medicare fee-for-service only	- - -	43.6	42.4	49.8	48.4	55.1	53.8
Age and education[7]							
25 years and over, crude:							
No high school diploma or GED	57.1	61.9	60.9	65.0	66.1	69.9	64.9
High school diploma or GED	76.4	78.2	76.0	77.4	79.3	79.8	75.9
Some college or more	84.0	84.4	85.2	86.9	87.8	88.0	86.2
25–44 years of age:							
No high school diploma or GED	75.1	73.6	73.6	76.8	79.0	79.6	71.7
High school diploma or GED	85.6	85.4	82.4	83.9	87.6	86.2	84.3
Some college or more	90.1	89.8	89.1	91.5	93.0	91.4	90.8
45–64 years of age:							
No high school diploma or GED	58.0	65.6	66.1	69.2	71.6	75.7	71.4
High school diploma or GED	72.3	77.6	75.9	81.0	79.8	81.8	77.6
Some college or more	80.1	83.0	84.7	85.5	85.7	89.1	86.2
65 years of age and over:							
No high school diploma or GED	44.0	50.7	47.7	52.4	51.8	56.6	52.5
High school diploma or GED	55.4	61.6	61.2	60.7	63.7	66.9	61.2
Some college or more	59.4	62.3	66.5	67.9	68.8	69.8	67.8

* Estimates are considered unreliable. Data not shown have a relative standard error greater than 30 percent.
- - - Data not available.
[1]Questions concerning use of Pap smears differed slightly on the National Health Interview Survey across the years for which data are shown. See Appendix II, Pap smear.
[2]Includes all other races not shown separately, unknown poverty status in 1987, unknown health insurance status, and unknown education.
[3]Estimates are age adjusted to the year 2000 standard population using five age groups: 18–44 years, 45–54 years, 55–64 years, 65–74 years, and 75 years and over. Age-adjusted estimates in this table may differ from other age-adjusted estimates based on the same data and presented elsewhere if different age groups are used in the adjustment procedure. See Appendix II, Age adjustment.
[4]The race groups, white, black, American Indian and Alaska Native, Asian, Native Hawaiian and Other Pacific Islander, and 2 or more races, include persons of Hispanic and non-Hispanic origin. Persons of Hispanic origin may be of any race. Starting with data year 1999 race-specific estimates are tabulated according to 1997 Standards for Federal data on Race and Ethnicity and are not strictly comparable with estimates for earlier years. The five single race categories plus multiple race categories shown in the table conform to 1997 Standards. Starting with data year 1999, race-specific estimates are for persons who reported only one racial group; the category "2 or more races" includes persons who reported more than one racial group. Prior to data year 1999, data were tabulated according to 1977 Standards with four racial groups and the category "Asian only" included Native Hawaiian and Other Pacific Islander. Estimates for single race categories prior to 1999 included persons who reported one race or, if they reported more than one race, identified one race as best representing their race. See Appendix II, Race.
[5]Poor persons are defined as below the poverty threshold. Near poor persons have incomes of 100 percent to less than 200 percent of the poverty threshold. Nonpoor persons have incomes of 200 percent or greater than the poverty threshold. Poverty status was unknown for 9 percent of women 18 years of age and over in 1987. Missing family income data were imputed for 17–20 percent of women 18 years of age and over in 1990–94 and 35–39 percent in 1998–2003. See Appendix II, Family income; Poverty level.
[6]Health insurance categories are mutually exclusive. Persons who reported both Medicaid and private coverage are classified as having private coverage. Starting in 1997 Medicaid includes State-sponsored health plans and State Children's Health Insurance Program (SCHIP). In addition to private and Medicaid, the category "insured" also includes military plans, other government-sponsored health plans, and Medicare, not shown separately. Persons 65 years of age and over who reported Medicare HMO (health maintenance organization) and some other type of health insurance coverage are classified as having Medicare HMO. For persons 65 years of age and over the category "private" includes private and Medicare coverage. See Appendix II, Health insurance coverage.
[7]Education categories shown are for 1998 and subsequent years. GED stands for General Educational Development high school equivalency diploma. In years prior to 1998 the following categories based on number of years of school completed were used: less than 12 years, 12 years, 13 years or more. See Appendix II, Education.

NOTES: Standard errors are available in the spreadsheet version of this table. See www.cdc.gov/nchs/hus.htm. Data starting in 1997 are not strictly comparable with data for earlier years due to the 1997 questionnaire redesign. See Appendix I, National Health Interview Survey. Starting with *Health, United States, 2005*, estimates for 2000 and later years use weights derived from the 2000 census. Estimates for 2000–2002 were recalculated using 2000-based weights and may differ from previous editions of *Health, United States*. Some data for 1993 and 1994 have been revised and differ from previous editions of *Health, United States*.

SOURCES: Centers for Disease Control and Prevention, National Center for Health Statistics, National Health Interview Survey. Data are from the following supplements: cancer control (1987), year 2000 objectives (1993–94). Starting in 1998, data are from the family core and sample adult questionnaires.

Table 88 (page 1 of 3). Visits to physician offices and hospital outpatient and emergency departments by selected characteristics: United States, selected years 1995–2003

[Data are based on reporting by a sample of office-based physicians and hospital outpatient and emergency departments]

Age, sex, and race	All places[1] 1995	All places[1] 2001	All places[1] 2002	All places[1] 2003	Physician offices 1995	Physician offices 2001	Physician offices 2002	Physician offices 2003
	Number of visits in thousands							
Total	860,859	1,142,420	1,157,798	1,114,504	697,082	951,214	964,304	906,023
Under 18 years	194,644	220,921	238,571	223,964	150,351	173,383	188,933	169,392
18–44 years	285,184	341,383	337,681	330,687	219,065	267,844	263,672	251,853
45–64 years	188,320	300,567	308,627	301,477	159,531	259,718	267,249	257,258
45–54 years	104,891	165,321	169,871	164,383	88,266	141,598	145,767	138,634
55–64 years	83,429	135,247	138,756	137,094	71,264	118,120	121,482	118,624
65 years and over	192,712	279,548	272,919	258,375	168,135	250,269	244,451	227,520
65–74 years	102,605	136,819	132,116	120,817	90,544	122,970	118,971	106,424
75 years and over	90,106	142,729	140,802	137,558	77,591	127,299	125,479	121,096
	Number of visits per 100 persons							
Total, age adjusted[2]	334	410	410	391	271	342	342	317
Total, crude	329	408	409	390	266	340	341	317
Under 18 years	275	305	328	307	213	239	260	232
18–44 years	264	311	306	300	203	244	239	229
45–64 years	364	469	466	442	309	406	404	377
45–54 years	339	425	427	406	286	364	367	343
55–64 years	401	538	525	494	343	470	459	428
65 years and over	612	829	804	754	534	742	720	664
65–74 years	560	757	733	668	494	680	660	588
75 years and over	683	913	884	850	588	814	788	748
Sex and age								
Male, age adjusted[2]	290	356	353	338	232	294	293	273
Male, crude	277	343	343	329	220	281	283	264
Under 18 years	273	306	329	317	209	238	262	241
18–44 years	190	217	214	202	139	163	161	147
45–54 years	275	349	351	335	229	294	298	280
55–64 years	351	457	448	422	300	399	393	365
65–74 years	508	726	703	633	445	654	631	558
75 years and over	711	934	850	881	616	840	762	777
Female, age adjusted[2]	377	463	465	442	309	388	388	360
Female, crude	378	470	472	449	310	395	396	368
Under 18 years	277	304	327	297	217	240	258	223
18–44 years	336	402	397	396	265	323	316	309
45–54 years	400	498	500	474	339	431	433	403
55–64 years	446	612	596	561	382	535	521	486
65–74 years	603	782	757	697	534	702	684	613
75 years and over	666	900	905	830	571	798	804	730
Race and age[3]								
White, age adjusted[2]	339	428	421	399	282	364	359	332
White, crude	338	433	426	405	281	369	364	337
Under 18 years	295	330	346	330	237	268	282	260
18–44 years	267	327	317	308	211	264	256	242
45–54 years	334	434	439	409	286	378	385	352
55–64 years	397	552	534	500	345	490	476	439
65–74 years	557	778	734	654	496	708	669	582
75 years and over	689	938	880	844	598	845	790	747
Black or African American, age adjusted	309	357	427	391	204	242	301	261
Black or African American, crude	281	329	392	363	178	217	269	236
Under 18 years	193	210	307	247	100	110	198	131
18–44 years	260	291	316	326	158	178	191	199
45–54 years	387	454	422	442	281	342	306	315
55–64 years	414	519	563	486	294	383	421	349
65–74 years	553	633	842	761	429	492	*687	602
75 years and over	534	676	*1,019	774	395	517	*842	608

See footnotes at end of table.

Table 88 (page 2 of 3). Visits to physician offices and hospital outpatient and emergency departments by selected characteristics: United States, selected years 1995–2003

[Data are based on reporting by a sample of office-based physicians and hospital outpatient and emergency departments]

Age, sex, and race	*Hospital outpatient departments* 1995	2001	2002	2003	*Hospital emergency departments* 1995	2001	2002	2003
	Number of visits in thousands							
Total	67,232	83,715	83,339	94,578	96,545	107,490	110,155	113,903
Under 18 years	17,636	21,299	21,707	25,652	26,657	26,239	27,932	28,920
18–44 years	24,299	27,430	28,216	32,386	41,820	46,109	45,792	46,449
45–64 years	14,811	21,590	21,436	23,227	13,978	19,260	19,943	20,992
45–54 years	8,029	12,016	12,054	12,889	8,595	11,707	12,050	12,861
55–64 years	6,782	9,574	9,382	10,338	5,383	7,552	7,892	8,132
65 years and over	10,486	13,396	11,980	13,313	14,090	15,883	16,488	17,542
65–74 years	6,004	7,299	6,386	7,240	6,057	6,551	6,759	7,153
75 years and over	4,482	6,097	5,595	6,073	8,033	9,332	9,728	10,389
	Number of visits per 100 persons							
Total, age adjusted[2]	26	30	29	33	37	39	39	40
Total, crude	26	30	29	33	37	38	39	40
Under 18 years	25	29	30	35	38	36	38	40
18–44 years	22	25	26	29	39	42	42	42
45–64 years	29	34	32	34	27	30	30	31
45–54 years	26	31	30	32	28	30	30	32
55–64 years	33	38	36	37	26	30	30	29
65 years and over	33	40	35	39	45	47	49	51
65–74 years	33	40	35	40	33	36	38	40
75 years and over	34	39	35	38	61	60	61	64
Sex and age								
Male, age adjusted[2]	21	25	24	27	37	37	37	39
Male, crude	21	24	23	26	36	37	37	38
Under 18 years	25	29	28	35	40	38	39	41
18–44 years	14	16	16	18	37	39	37	37
45–54 years	20	26	25	25	26	29	29	30
55–64 years	26	30	28	29	25	28	28	29
65–74 years	29	35	34	35	34	38	38	41
75 years and over	34	37	31	38	61	57	58	67
Female, age adjusted[2]	31	35	35	40	37	40	41	42
Female, crude	31	35	35	40	37	40	41	42
Under 18 years	25	29	31	36	35	34	38	38
18–44 years	31	34	35	41	40	45	46	47
45–54 years	32	36	36	38	29	31	32	33
55–64 years	38	45	43	45	26	32	32	30
65–74 years	36	45	36	45	32	35	37	39
75 years and over	34	40	38	37	61	61	63	63

See footnotes at end of table.

Table 88 (page 3 of 3). Visits to physician offices and hospital outpatient and emergency departments by selected characteristics: United States, selected years 1995–2003

[Data are based on reporting by a sample of office-based physicians and hospital outpatient and emergency departments]

Age, sex, and race	Hospital outpatient departments				Hospital emergency departments			
	1995	2001	2002	2003	1995	2001	2002	2003
Race and age[3]	Number of visits per 100 persons							
White, age adjusted[2]	23	28	27	30	34	36	36	38
White, crude	23	28	27	30	34	36	36	37
Under 18 years	23	28	28	33	35	34	36	38
18–44 years	20	23	23	27	36	40	38	39
45–54 years	23	28	27	28	25	28	27	29
55–64 years	28	34	31	33	24	28	27	28
65–74 years	29	37	30	36	32	33	35	36
75 years and over	31	36	31	35	60	58	59	62
Black or African American, age adjusted	48	51	55	59	58	65	71	71
Black or African American, crude	45	49	53	58	58	64	70	69
Under 18 years	39	44	46	55	53	55	63	61
18–44 years	38	41	46	51	64	71	79	77
45–54 years	55	56	57	62	51	56	59	65
55–64 years	73	79	78	84	47	56	65	53
65–74 years	*77	70	87	82	47	71	68	77
75 years and over	66	67	85	64	73	91	92	103

* Estimates are considered unreliable. Data preceded by an asterisk have a relative standard error of 20–30 percent.
[1]All places includes visits to physician offices and hospital outpatient and emergency departments.
[2]Estimates are age adjusted to the year 2000 standard population using six age groups: under 18 years, 18–44 years, 45–54 years, 55–64 years, 65–74 years, and 75 years and over. See Appendix II, Age adjustment.
[3]In 1999 the instruction for the race item on the Patient Record Form was changed so that more than one race could be recorded. In previous years only one race could be checked. Estimates for race in this table are for visits where only one race was recorded. Estimates for visits where multiple races were checked are unreliable and are not presented.

NOTES: Rates for 1995–2000 were computed using 1990-based postcensal estimates of the civilian noninstitutionalized population as of July 1 adjusted for net underenumeration using the 1990 National Population Adjustment Matrix from the Bureau of the Census. Rates for 2001 and later years were computed using 2000-based postcensal estimates of the civilian noninstitutionalized population as of July 1. The difference between rates for 2000 computed using 1990-based postcensal estimates and 2000 census counts is minimal. See www.cdc.gov/nchs/about/major/ahcd/census2000.htm. Starting with *Health, United States, 2005*, data for 2001 and later years for physicians offices use a revised weighting scheme. Therefore, 2001–02 data for all places and physician offices differ from the previous edition of *Health, United States*. See Appendix I, National Ambulatory Medical Care Survey. Rates will be overestimated to the extent that visits by institutionalized persons are counted in the numerator (for example, hospital emergency department visits by nursing home residents) and institutionalized persons are omitted from the denominator. Data for additional years are available. See Appendix III.

SOURCES: Centers for Disease Control and Prevention, National Center for Health Statistics, National Ambulatory Medical Care Survey and National Hospital Ambulatory Medical Care Survey.

Table 89 (page 1 of 2). Injury-related visits to hospital emergency departments by sex, age, and intent and mechanism of injury: United States, average annual 1995–96, 1998–99, and 2002–2003

[Data are based on reporting by a sample of hospital emergency departments]

Sex, age, and intent and mechanism of injury[1]	*1995–96*	*1998–99*	*2002–03*	*1995–96*	*1998–99*	*2002–03*
Both sexes	Injury-related visits in thousands			Injury-related visits per 10,000 persons		
All ages[2,3]	36,081	37,361	39,676	1,360.9	1,378.3	1,401.4
Male						
All ages[2,3]	20,030	20,445	21,467	1,530.7	1,535.2	1,548.1
Under 18 years[2]	6,238	6,054	5,974	1,720.2	1,644.3	1,604.5
Unintentional injuries[4]	5,478	5,190	4,781	1,510.5	1,409.7	1,284.2
Falls	1,402	1,247	1,228	386.5	338.7	329.9
Struck by or against objects or persons	1,011	1,398	1,315	278.9	379.7	353.2
Motor vehicle traffic	453	388	369	125.0	105.5	99.2
Cut or pierce	493	505	348	136.0	137.1	93.5
Intentional injuries	290	222	202	80.0	60.3	54.4
18–24 years[2]	2,980	2,948	2,956	2,396.9	2,295.1	2,134.3
Unintentional injuries[4]	2,423	2,319	2,019	1,948.7	1,805.3	1,457.7
Falls	299	333	289	240.8	259.5	208.3
Struck by or against objects or persons	387	389	433	311.0	303.1	312.8
Motor vehicle traffic	347	412	376	279.4	320.9	271.9
Cut or pierce	304	344	286	244.8	268.2	206.4
Intentional injuries	335	291	287	269.2	226.5	207.0
25–44 years[2]	7,245	7,112	7,157	1,767.4	1,751.7	1,758.7
Unintentional injuries[4]	5,757	5,391	4,701	1,404.3	1,327.8	1,155.2
Falls	817	847	840	199.4	208.6	206.5
Struck by or against objects or persons	619	819	698	151.0	201.6	171.5
Motor vehicle traffic	912	839	766	222.6	206.6	188.3
Cut or pierce	860	786	615	209.8	193.7	151.1
Intentional injuries	701	473	479	171.0	116.5	117.7
45–64 years[2]	2,240	2,822	3,528	883.4	1,011.9	1,082.8
Unintentional injuries[4]	1,845	2,213	2,207	727.6	793.4	677.5
Falls	445	569	518	175.6	204.0	159.0
Struck by or against objects or persons	186	197	247	73.3	70.6	75.8
Motor vehicle traffic	244	322	343	96.3	115.5	105.3
Cut or pierce	203	290	276	79.9	104.1	84.6
Intentional injuries	86	73	123	33.8	26.2	37.9
65 years and over[2]	1,327	1,509	1,854	1,000.7	1,100.3	1,285.9
Unintentional injuries[4]	1,009	1,151	1,232	760.6	839.3	854.4
Falls	505	584	649	380.9	426.0	450.4
Struck by or against objects or persons	*39	101	77	*29.4	73.3	53.4
Motor vehicle traffic	99	113	128	74.7	82.7	88.5
Cut or pierce	*81	85	91	*61.1	*61.7	62.8
Intentional injuries	*	16	22	*	*	*

See footnotes at end of table.

Table 89 (page 2 of 2). Injury-related visits to hospital emergency departments by sex, age, and intent and mechanism of injury: United States, average annual 1995–96, 1998–99, and 2002–2003

[Data are based on reporting by a sample of hospital emergency departments]

Sex, age, and intent and mechanism of injury[1]	*1995–96*	*1998–99*	*2002–03*	*1995–96*	*1998–99*	*2002–03*
Female	Injury-related visits in thousands			Injury-related visits per 10,000 persons		
All ages[2,3]	16,051	16,917	18,208	1,186.4	1,217.6	1,253.1
Under 18 years[2]	4,372	4,290	4,321	1,263.9	1,220.4	1,214.5
Unintentional injuries[4]	3,760	3,598	3,204	1,087.0	1,023.4	900.4
Falls	1,040	964	908	300.7	274.2	255.3
Struck by or against objects or persons	477	689	627	137.9	196.1	176.1
Motor vehicle traffic	447	394	368	129.3	112.1	103.5
Cut or pierce	253	258	198	73.0	73.4	55.7
Intentional injuries	220	147	216	63.6	41.7	60.7
18–24 years[2]	1,900	2,049	2,307	1,523.4	1,589.6	1,672.9
Unintentional injuries[4]	1,430	1,464	1,492	1,146.7	1,135.8	1,081.5
Falls	268	208	260	214.5	161.7	188.2
Struck by or against objects or persons	134	169	201	107.4	130.8	145.9
Motor vehicle traffic	373	442	456	298.8	342.7	330.9
Cut or pierce	131	122	129	105.3	94.8	93.2
Intentional injuries	239	230	202	191.7	178.6	146.2
25–44 years[2]	5,098	5,257	5,527	1,205.8	1,246.7	1,320.9
Unintentional injuries[4]	3,877	3,820	3,470	916.8	906.1	829.4
Falls	817	908	802	193.3	215.5	191.8
Struck by or against objects or persons	380	405	381	89.8	95.9	91.0
Motor vehicle traffic	872	794	819	206.2	188.4	195.8
Cut or pierce	338	472	337	79.8	111.9	80.4
Intentional injuries	422	422	401	99.8	100.2	95.8
45–64 years[2]	2,369	2,802	3,335	873.7	940.4	963.4
Unintentional injuries[4]	1,857	2,109	2,272	685.2	707.9	656.4
Falls	600	706	791	221.5	237.0	228.4
Struck by or against objects or persons	160	193	213	58.8	64.8	61.5
Motor vehicle traffic	343	317	388	126.5	106.4	111.9
Cut or pierce	127	214	205	46.9	71.8	59.1
Intentional injuries	*64	111	119	*23.5	37.4	34.3
65 years and over[2]	2,313	2,518	2,718	1,256.1	1,346.8	1,379.3
Unintentional injuries[4]	1,931	2,016	1,957	1,049.0	1,078.1	993.2
Falls	1,230	1,258	1,225	667.9	672.7	621.9
Struck by or against objects or persons	82	119	170	44.8	63.6	86.1
Motor vehicle traffic	169	148	175	91.6	79.3	88.6
Cut or pierce	*42	73	48	*22.7	*39.0	24.4
Intentional injuries	*	34	12	*	*	*

* Estimates are considered unreliable. Data preceded by an asterisk have a relative standard error (RSE) of 20–30 percent. Data not shown have an RSE of greater than 30 percent.

[1]Intent and mechanism of injury are based on the first-listed external cause of injury code (E code). Intentional injuries include suicide attempts and assaults. See Appendix II, External cause of injury and Appendix II, table VII for listing of E codes.

[2]Includes all injury-related visits not shown separately in table including those with undetermined intent (0.5 percent in 2002–03), insufficient or no information to code cause of injury (21.4 percent in 2002–03), and resulting from adverse effects of medical treatment (3.9 percent in 2002–03).

[3]Rates are age adjusted to the year 2000 standard population using six age groups: under 18 years, 18–24 years, 25–44 years, 45–64 years, 65–74 years, and 75 years and over. See Appendix II, Age adjustment.

[4]Includes unintentional injury-related visits with mechanism of injury not shown in table.

NOTES: An emergency department visit was considered injury related if the checkbox for injury was indicated, the physician's diagnosis was injury related (ICD–9-CM 800–999), an external cause of injury code was present (ICD–9-CM E800-E999), or the patient's reason for the visit was injury related. Rates for 1995–2000 were computed using 1990-based postcensal estimates of the civilian noninstitutionalized population as of July 1 adjusted for net underenumeration using the 1990 National Population Adjustment Matrix from the Bureau of the Census. Starting with 2001, rates were computed using 2000-based postcensal estimates of the civilian noninstitutionalized population as of July 1. The difference between rates for 2000 computed using 1990-based postcensal estimates and rates computed using estimates based on 2000 census counts is minimal. See www.cdc.gov/nchs/about/major/ahcd/census2000.htm. Rates will be overestimated to the extent that visits by institutionalized persons are counted in the numerator (for example, hospital emergency department visits by nursing home residents) and institutionalized persons are omitted from the denominator. Data for additional years are available. See Appendix III.

SOURCE: Centers for Disease Control and Prevention, National Center for Health Statistics, National Hospital Ambulatory Medical Care Survey.

Table 90 (page 1 of 2). Visits to primary care generalist and specialist physicians, according to selected characteristics and type of physician: United States, 1980, 1990, 2000, and 2003

[Data are based on reporting by a sample of office-based physicians]

	Type of primary care generalist physician[1]											
	All primary care generalists				*General and family practice*				*Internal medicine*			
Age, sex, and race	*1980*	*1990*	*2000*	*2003*	*1980*	*1990*	*2000*	*2003*	*1980*	*1990*	*2000*	*2003*
	Percent of all physician office visits											
Total	66.2	63.6	58.9	58.5	33.5	29.9	24.1	24.5	12.1	13.8	15.3	15.6
Under 18 years	77.8	79.5	79.7	78.3	26.1	26.5	19.9	19.3	2.0	2.9	*	*
18–44 years	65.3	65.2	62.1	63.7	34.3	31.9	28.2	28.5	8.6	11.8	12.7	13.0
45–64 years	60.2	55.5	51.2	52.2	36.3	32.1	26.4	27.3	19.5	18.6	20.1	19.0
45–54 years	60.2	55.6	52.3	55.1	37.4	32.0	27.8	29.7	17.1	17.1	18.7	18.3
55–64 years	60.2	55.5	49.9	48.9	35.4	32.1	24.7	24.5	21.8	20.0	21.7	19.9
65 years and over	61.6	52.6	46.5	45.2	37.5	28.1	20.2	20.6	22.7	23.3	24.5	22.4
65–74 years	61.2	52.7	46.6	46.6	37.4	28.1	19.7	20.8	22.1	23.0	24.5	22.9
75 years and over	62.3	52.4	46.4	44.0	37.6	28.0	20.8	20.5	23.5	23.7	24.5	22.0
Sex and age												
Male:												
Under 18 years	77.3	78.1	77.7	76.5	25.6	24.1	18.3	17.3	2.0	3.0	*	*
18–44 years	50.8	51.8	51.5	54.2	38.0	35.9	34.2	35.6	11.5	15.0	14.4	17.3
45–64 years	55.6	50.6	49.4	50.1	34.4	31.0	28.7	30.3	20.5	19.2	19.8	19.2
65 years and over	58.2	51.2	43.1	40.4	35.6	27.7	19.3	20.0	22.3	23.3	23.8	20.1
Female:												
Under 18 years	78.5	81.1	82.0	80.4	26.6	29.1	21.7	21.5	2.0	2.8	*	*
18–44 years	72.1	71.3	67.2	68.2	32.5	30.0	25.3	25.2	7.3	10.3	11.9	10.9
45–64 years	63.4	58.8	52.5	53.7	37.7	32.8	24.9	25.3	18.9	18.2	20.2	18.9
65 years and over	63.9	53.5	48.9	48.6	38.7	28.3	20.9	21.0	22.9	23.3	25.0	24.1
Race and age[2]												
White:												
Under 18 years	77.6	79.2	78.5	78.1	26.4	27.1	21.2	19.8	2.0	2.3	*	*
18–44 years	64.8	64.4	61.4	63.3	34.5	31.9	29.2	29.1	8.6	10.6	11.0	12.1
45–64 years	59.6	54.2	49.3	51.9	36.0	31.5	27.3	27.5	19.2	17.6	17.1	18.4
65 years and over	61.4	51.9	45.1	43.1	36.6	27.5	20.3	20.3	23.3	23.1	23.0	20.8
Black or African American:												
Under 18 years	79.9	85.5	87.3	77.3	23.7	20.2	*	*18.8	*2.2	9.8	*	*
18–44 years	68.5	68.3	65.0	66.5	31.7	31.9	22.0	25.0	9.0	18.1	20.9	*
45–64 years	66.1	61.6	61.7	56.7	38.6	31.2	23.3	26.2	22.6	26.9	35.9	23.8
65 years and over	64.6	58.6	52.8	56.0	49.0	28.9	*18.5	*20.9	14.2	28.7	33.4	31.4

See footnotes at end of table.

Table 90 (page 2 of 2). Visits to primary care generalist and specialist physicians, according to selected characteristics and type of physician: United States, 1980, 1990, 2000, and 2003

[Data are based on reporting by a sample of office-based physicians]

Age, sex, and race	Type of primary care generalist physician[1]								Specialty care physicians			
					Pediatrics							
	1980	1990	2000	2003	1980	1990	2000	2003	1980	1990	2000	2003
	Percent of all physician office visits											
Total	9.6	8.7	7.8	8.4	10.9	11.2	11.7	10.1	33.8	36.4	41.1	41.5
Under 18 years	1.3	1.2	*1.1	*1.5	48.5	48.9	57.3	52.4	22.2	20.5	20.3	21.7
18–44 years	21.7	20.8	20.4	21.5	0.7	0.7	*0.9	*0.7	34.7	34.8	37.9	36.3
45–64 years	4.2	4.6	4.5	5.6	*	*	*	*	39.8	44.5	48.8	47.8
45–54 years	5.6	6.3	5.6	6.7	*	*	*	*	39.8	44.4	47.7	44.9
55–64 years	2.9	3.1	3.3	*4.4	*	*	*	*	39.8	44.5	50.1	51.1
65 years and over	1.4	1.1	1.5	*2.0	*	*	*	*	38.4	47.4	53.5	54.8
65–74 years	1.7	1.6	2.0	*2.7	*	*	*	*	38.8	47.3	53.4	53.4
75 years and over	1.0	*0.6	*1.0	*1.4	*	*	*	*	37.7	47.6	53.6	56.0
Sex and age												
Male:												
Under 18 years	. . .	. . .	. . .	. . .	49.4	50.7	58.0	53.2	22.7	21.9	22.3	23.5
18–44 years	. . .	. . .	. . .	. . .	1.0	0.7	*1.7	*1.2	49.2	48.2	48.5	45.8
45–64 years	. . .	. . .	. . .	. . .	*	*	*	*	44.4	49.4	50.6	49.9
65 years and over	. . .	. . .	. . .	. . .	*	*	*	*	41.8	48.8	56.9	59.6
Female:												
Under 18 years	2.5	2.3	2.1	*3.2	47.4	46.9	56.5	51.4	21.5	18.9	18.0	19.6
18–44 years	31.7	30.4	29.6	31.6	0.6	0.7	*	*	27.9	28.7	32.8	31.8
45–64 years	6.7	7.7	7.3	9.2	*	*	*	*	36.6	41.2	47.5	46.3
65 years and over	2.1	1.8	2.6	*3.4	*	*	*	*	36.1	46.5	51.1	51.4
Race and age[2]												
White:												
Under 18 years	1.1	1.0	*1.2	*1.5	48.2	48.8	54.7	52.4	22.4	20.8	21.5	21.9
18–44 years	21.0	21.1	20.4	21.3	0.7	0.7	*0.8	*0.8	35.2	35.6	38.6	36.7
45–64 years	4.1	4.8	4.7	5.7	*	*	*	*	40.4	45.8	50.7	48.1
65 years and over	1.4	1.2	1.5	*1.9	*	*	*	*	38.6	48.1	54.9	56.9
Black or African American:												
Under 18 years	2.8	*3.4	*	*	51.2	52.1	75.0	51.3	20.1	14.5	*12.7	22.7
18–44 years	27.1	17.9	20.7	*25.8	*	*	*	*	31.5	31.7	35.0	33.5
45–64 years	4.8	3.5	*2.4	*	*	*	*	*	33.9	38.4	38.3	43.3
65 years and over	*	*	*	*	*	*	*	*	35.4	41.4	47.2	44.0

* Estimates are considered unreliable. Data preceded by an asterisk have a relative standard error (RSE) of 20–30 percent. Data not shown have a RSE of greater than 30 percent.

. . . Category not applicable.

[1]Type of physician is based on physician's self-designated primary area of practice. Primary care generalist physicians are defined as practitioners in the fields of general and family practice, general internal medicine, general obstetrics and gynecology, and general pediatrics and exclude primary care specialists. Primary care generalists in general and family practice exclude primary care specialities, such as sports medicine and geriatrics. Primary care internal medicine physicians exclude internal medicine specialists, such as allergists, cardiologists, endocrinologists, etc. Primary care obstetrics and gynecology physicians exclude obstetrics and gynecology specialities, such as gynecological oncology, maternal and fetal medicine, general obstetrics and gynecology critical care medicine, and reproductive endocrinology. Primary care pediatricians exclude pediatric specialists, such as adolescent medicine specialists, neonatologists, pediatric allergists, pediatric cardiologists, etc. See Appendix II, Physician specialty.

[2]Beginning in 1999, the instruction for the race item on the Patient Record Form was changed so that more than one race could be recorded. In previous years only one racial category could be checked. Estimates for racial groups presented in this table are for visits where only one race was recorded. Estimates for visits where multiple races were checked are unreliable and are not presented.

NOTES: This table presents data on visits to physician offices and excludes visits to other sites, such as hospital outpatient and emergency departments. In 1980 the survey excluded Alaska and Hawaii. Data for all other years include all 50 States. Visits with type of physician unknown are excluded. Starting with *Health, United States, 2005*, data from 2001 and onward use a revised weighting scheme. Therefore, data for survey years 2001–02 differ from the previous editions of *Health, United States*. See Appendix I, National Ambulatory Medical Care Survey. Data for additional years are available. See Appendix III.

SOURCE: Centers for Disease Control and Prevention, National Center for Health Statistics, National Ambulatory Medical Care Survey.

Table 91 (page 1 of 2). Prescription drug use in the past month by sex, age, race, and Hispanic origin: United States, 1988–94 and 1999–2002

[Data are based on a sample of the civilian noninstitutionalized population]

Sex and age	All persons[1]		Not Hispanic or Latino: White[2]		Not Hispanic or Latino: Black or African American[2]		Mexican[3]	
	1988–94	1999–2002	1988–94	1999–2002	1988–94	1999–2002	1988–94	1999–2002
	Percent of population with at least one prescription drug in past month							
Both sexes, age adjusted[4]	39.1	45.3	41.1	48.9	36.9	40.1	31.7	31.7
Male	32.7	39.9	34.2	43.1	31.1	35.4	27.5	25.8
Female	45.0	50.4	47.6	54.5	41.4	43.8	36.0	37.8
Both sexes, crude	37.8	45.1	41.4	50.9	31.2	36.0	24.0	23.7
Male	30.6	38.7	33.5	43.9	25.5	30.8	20.1	18.8
Female	44.6	51.2	48.9	57.6	36.2	40.6	28.1	28.9
Under 18 years	20.5	24.2	22.9	27.6	14.8	18.6	16.1	15.9
18–44 years	31.3	35.9	34.3	41.3	27.8	28.5	21.1	19.2
45–64 years	54.8	64.1	55.5	66.1	57.5	62.3	48.1	49.3
65 years and over	73.6	84.7	74.0	85.4	74.5	81.1	67.7	72.0
Male:								
Under 18 years	20.4	26.2	22.3	30.6	15.5	19.8	16.3	16.2
18–44 years	21.5	27.1	23.5	31.2	21.1	21.5	14.9	13.0
45–64 years	47.2	55.6	48.1	57.4	48.2	54.0	43.8	36.4
65 years and over	67.2	80.1	67.4	81.0	64.4	78.1	61.3	66.8
Female:								
Under 18 years	20.6	22.0	23.6	24.4	14.2	17.3	16.0	15.6
18–44 years	40.7	44.6	44.7	51.7	33.4	34.2	28.1	26.2
45–64 years	62.0	72.0	62.6	74.7	64.4	69.0	52.2	62.4
65 years and over	78.3	88.1	78.8	88.8	81.3	83.1	73.0	76.3
	Percent of population with three or more prescription drugs in past month							
Both sexes, age adjusted[4]	11.8	17.7	12.4	18.9	12.6	16.5	9.0	11.2
Male	9.4	14.8	9.9	15.9	10.2	14.4	7.0	9.5
Female	13.9	20.4	14.6	21.7	14.3	18.0	11.0	12.9
Both sexes, crude	11.0	17.6	12.5	20.5	9.2	13.4	4.8	6.1
Male	8.3	13.9	9.5	16.4	7.0	10.9	3.4	4.8
Female	13.6	21.1	15.4	24.5	11.1	15.6	6.4	7.5
Under 18 years	2.4	4.1	3.2	4.9	1.5	2.5	*1.2	2.1
18–44 years	5.7	8.4	6.3	10.1	5.4	6.5	3.0	2.7
45–64 years	20.0	30.8	20.9	31.6	21.9	31.1	16.0	20.7
65 years and over	35.3	51.6	35.0	52.5	41.2	50.1	31.3	39.5
Male:								
Under 18 years	2.6	4.3	3.3	5.2	1.7	3.0	*	1.9
18–44 years	3.6	6.7	4.1	8.4	4.2	4.4	*1.8	*1.7
45–64 years	15.1	23.5	15.8	24.0	18.7	26.3	11.6	18.2
65 years and over	31.3	46.0	30.9	47.0	31.7	48.2	27.6	34.2
Female:								
Under 18 years	2.3	3.9	3.0	4.7	*1.2	*2.0	*1.5	2.2
18–44 years	7.6	10.2	8.5	11.9	6.4	8.3	4.3	4.0
45–64 years	24.7	37.4	25.8	39.1	24.3	35.0	20.3	23.3
65 years and over	38.2	55.7	38.0	56.6	47.7	51.3	34.5	44.0

See footnotes at end of table.

Table 91 (page 2 of 2). Prescription drug use in the past month by sex, age, race, and Hispanic origin: United States, 1988–94 and 1999–2002

[Data are based on a sample of the civilian noninstitutionalized population]

* Estimates are considered unreliable. Data preceded by an asterisk have a relative standard error (RSE) of 20–30 percent. Data not shown have an RSE of greater than 30 percent.
[1]Includes persons of all races and Hispanic origins, not just those shown separately.
[2]Starting with data year 1999 race-specific estimates are tabulated according to 1997 Standards for Federal data on Race and Ethnicity and are not strictly comparable with estimates for earlier years. The two non-Hispanic race categories shown in the table conform to 1997 Standards. The 1999–2002 race-specific estimates are for persons who reported only one racial group. Prior to data year 1999, data were tabulated according to 1977 Standards. Estimates for single race categories prior to 1999 included persons who reported one race or, if they reported more than one race, identified one race as best representing their race. See Appendix II, Race.
[3]Persons of Mexican origin may be of any race.
[4]Age adjusted to the 2000 standard population using four age groups: Under 18 years, 18–44 years , 45–64 years, and 65 years and over. See Appendix II, Age adjustment.

NOTES: Standard errors are available in the spreadsheet version of this table. See www.cdc.gov/nchs/hus.htm.

SOURCE: Centers for Disease Control and Prevention, National Center for Health Statistics, National Health and Nutrition Examination Survey.

Table 92 (page 1 of 3). Selected prescription and nonprescription drugs recorded during physician office visits and hospital outpatient department visits, by age and sex: United States, 1995–96 and 2002–03

[Data are based on a sample of visit records from physician offices and hospital outpatient departments]

Age group and National Drug Code (NDC) therapeutic class[1] (common reasons for use)	*Total* 1995–96	*Total* 2002–03	*Male* 1995–96	*Male* 2002–03	*Female* 1995–96	*Female* 2002–03
All ages	Visits with at least one drug per 100 population[2]					
Drug visits[3]	189.8	234.9	156.5	193.7	221.5	274.1
	Number of drugs per 100 population[4]					
Total number of drugs[5]	400.3	585.7	321.1	477.6	475.6	688.8
NSAID[6] (pain relief)	19.9	30.0	16.0	24.1	23.7	35.6
Antidepressants (depression and related disorders)	13.8	27.8	9.1	19.2	18.2	36.0
Antihistamines (allergies)	13.7	23.8	10.8	18.7	16.4	28.6
Antiasthmatics/bronchodilators (asthma, breathing)	13.0	22.9	11.7	19.9	14.3	25.7
Nonnarcotic analgesics (pain relief)	14.4	21.8	13.0	20.4	15.7	23.2
Hyperlipidemia (high cholesterol)	5.4	20.8	5.4	21.5	5.4	20.2
Hypertension control drugs, not otherwise specified (high blood pressure)	6.0	20.7	4.1	17.6	7.8	23.6
Acid/peptic disorders (gastrointestinal reflux, ulcers)	12.0	19.2	9.8	15.6	14.1	22.6
Blood glucose/sugar regulators (diabetes)	9.5	18.5	8.6	17.5	10.4	19.4
ACE inhibitors (high blood pressure, heart disease)	9.6	16.6	9.0	16.3	10.2	16.9
Diuretics (high blood pressure, heart disease)	10.2	15.9	7.8	12.8	12.6	18.8
Penicillins (bacterial infections)	16.6	15.2	15.5	14.3	17.7	15.9
Narcotic analgesics (pain relief)	11.2	15.3	10.3	12.3	12.2	18.2
Vitamins/minerals (dietary supplements)	9.2	14.5	3.4	8.3	14.8	20.5
Estrogens/progestins (menopause, hot flashes)	. . .	. . .	. . .	. . .	19.8	19.2
Under 18 years	Visits with at least one drug per 100 population[2]					
Drug visits[3]	153.9	177.9	152.3	181.6	155.6	174.1
	Number of drugs per 100 population[4]					
Total number of drugs[5]	261.3	334.8	255.6	340.1	267.3	329.3
Penicillins (bacterial infections)	37.2	34.3	36.4	34.0	38.0	34.6
Antiasthmatics/bronchodilators (asthma, breathing)	13.4	26.0	14.8	27.7	11.9	24.3
Antihistamines (allergies)	17.5	25.9	16.7	26.0	18.4	25.8
Erythromycins/lincosamides (infections)	10.2	13.6	11.0	13.3	9.4	13.9
NSAID[6] (pain relief)	7.4	13.1	6.9	12.4	7.9	13.8
Cephalosporins (bacterial infections)	18.1	12.7	18.8	13.7	17.3	11.6
Nonnarcotic analgesics (pain relief)	12.1	12.0	10.4	12.5	13.9	11.4
Antitussives/expectorants (cough and cold, congestion)	11.8	10.3	11.0	10.3	12.7	10.3
Nasal corticosteroid inhalants (asthma, breathing, allergies)	3.5	9.3	3.5	9.3	3.5	9.3
Anorexiants/CNS stimulants (attention deficit disorder, hyperactivity)	3.9	8.8	5.6	12.5	2.1	4.9
Nasal decongestants (congestion)	14.0	8.3	12.4	8.0	15.7	8.5
Antidepressants (depression and related disorders)	1.9	6.8	1.9	7.7	1.9	5.9
18–44 years	Visits with at least one drug per 100 population[2]					
Drug visits[3]	136.2	161.4	90.9	108.4	180.4	213.3
	Number of drugs per 100 population[4]					
Total number of drugs[5]	251.0	330.5	168.8	227.5	331.2	431.5
Antidepressants (depression and related disorders)	14.0	26.6	9.3	17.9	18.5	35.0
NSAID[6] (pain relief)	16.7	22.2	14.5	16.7	18.8	27.6
Antihistamines (allergies)	10.8	19.0	7.5	12.8	14.1	25.0
Narcotic analgesics (pain relief)	11.7	14.0	10.8	10.6	12.7	17.4
Antiasthmatics/bronchodilator (asthma, breathing)	6.8	11.5	3.3	7.4	10.2	15.6
Vitamins/minerals (dietary supplements)	11.8	11.3	1.1	2.1	22.2	20.2
Acid/peptic disorders (gastrointestinal reflux, ulcers)	6.6	9.4	5.3	8.5	7.9	10.2
Penicillins (bacterial infections)	9.5	8.8	7.0	6.2	11.9	11.3
Nasal corticosteroid inhalants (asthma, breathing, allergies)	4.7	8.7	3.3	6.7	6.1	10.6
Erythromycins/lincosamides (infections)	7.5	8.4	5.4	5.9	9.5	10.9
Antitussives/expectorants (cough and cold, congestion)	7.7	8.1	5.8	5.4	9.5	10.7
Nonnarcotic analgesics (pain relief)	6.0	7.7	4.5	5.4	7.4	9.9
Contraceptive agents (prevent pregnancy)	. . .	. . .	. . .	. . .	13.4	22.8

See footnotes at end of table.

Table 92 (page 2 of 3). Selected prescription and nonprescription drugs recorded during physician office visits and hospital outpatient department visits, by age and sex: United States, 1995–96 and 2002–03

[Data are based on a sample of visit records from physician offices and hospital outpatient departments]

Age group and National Drug Code (NDC) therapeutic class[1] (common reasons for use)	Total		Male		Female	
	1995–96	2002–03	1995–96	2002–03	1995–96	2002–03
45–64 years	Visits with at least one drug per 100 population[2]					
Drug visits[3]	222.4	284.1	185.0	231.7	257.4	333.3
	Number of drugs per 100 population[4]					
Total number of drugs[5]	505.1	757.7	403.2	612.5	600.4	894.3
Antidepressants (depression and related disorders)	23.5	44.5	14.9	29.6	31.5	58.4
NSAID[6] (pain relief)	30.3	42.6	23.9	37.0	36.4	47.8
Hyperlipidemia (high cholesterol)	10.4	36.9	12.0	40.2	8.8	33.7
Hypertension control drugs, not otherwise specified (high blood pressure)	9.4	33.7	6.9	31.6	11.7	35.7
Blood glucose/sugar regulators (diabetes)	17.7	33.0	16.7	32.3	18.7	33.6
Acid/peptic disorders (gastrointestinal reflux, ulcers)	19.8	29.8	18.3	24.8	21.3	34.5
ACE inhibitors (high blood pressure, heart disease)	16.8	26.2	17.7	28.1	16.0	24.3
Antiasthmatics/bronchodilators (asthma, breathing)	14.4	26.2	11.4	20.1	17.1	32.0
Antihistamines (allergies)	13.5	25.5	9.1	17.3	17.7	33.2
Narcotic analgesics (pain relief)	17.5	25.5	17.0	22.8	18.0	28.1
Nonnarcotic analgesics (pain relief)	16.3	25.2	15.6	26.4	17.0	24.1
Diuretics (high blood pressure, heart disease)	13.5	22.6	11.2	18.7	15.7	26.3
Beta blockers (high blood pressure, heart disease)	10.6	20.8	10.0	18.6	11.2	22.8
Calcium channel blockers (high blood pressure, heart disease)	19.3	19.4	19.9	19.5	18.8	19.3
Estrogens/progestins (menopause, hot flashes)	. . .	. . .	. . .	. . .	55.7	43.8
65 years and over						
	Visits with at least one drug per 100 population[2]					
Drug visits[3]	399.4	496.7	378.1	462.0	414.7	522.2
	Number of drugs per 100 population[4]					
Total number of drugs[5]	1,047.4	1,606.2	956.9	1,473.8	1,112.5	1,703.1
Hypertension control drugs, not otherwise specified (high blood pressure)	29.1	91.8	22.7	81.3	33.8	99.5
Hyperlipidemia (high cholesterol)	24.7	90.4	25.1	101.5	24.5	82.3
Nonnarcotic analgesics (pain relief)	44.9	81.8	49.0	83.6	42.0	80.4
Diuretics (high blood pressure, heart disease)	55.2	77.7	48.5	74.5	60.0	80.1
ACE inhibitors (high blood pressure, heart disease)	42.6	74.1	41.2	79.8	43.6	70.0
Blood glucose/sugar regulators (diabetes)	37.5	69.0	38.0	76.9	37.1	63.1
Beta blockers (high blood pressure, heart disease)	25.5	66.9	23.6	65.7	26.8	67.7
NSAID[6] (pain relief)	41.8	66.2	31.9	52.7	49.0	76.0
Acid/peptic disorders (gastrointestinal reflux, ulcers)	42.2	64.5	36.0	54.8	46.6	71.7
Calcium channel blockers (high blood pressure, heart disease)	57.3	60.4	52.2	51.6	60.9	66.9
Antiasthmatics/bronchodilators (asthma, breathing)	31.3	46.2	37.1	46.7	27.0	45.8
Vitamins/minerals (dietary supplements)	17.1	44.1	13.1	35.8	20.0	50.2
Antidepressants (depression and related disorders)	23.5	43.7	16.7	30.4	28.5	53.5
Anticoagulants/thrombolytics (blood thinning, reduce or prevent blood clots)	20.7	42.0	24.0	48.0	18.3	37.6
Estrogens/progestins (menopause, hot flashes)	. . .	. . .	. . .	. . .	37.1	38.5
65–74 years	Visits with at least one drug per 100 population[2]					
Drug visits[3]	362.8	444.3	323.0	408.4	394.9	474.3
	Number of drugs per 100 population[4]					
Total number of drugs[5]	930.5	1,394.7	804.7	1,278.8	1,032.1	1,491.4
Hyperlipidemia (high cholesterol)	27.3	93.3	27.1	102.2	27.4	85.9
Hypertension control drugs, not otherwise specified (high blood pressure)	24.8	83.1	19.2	68.4	29.3	95.4
Blood glucose/sugar regulators (diabetes)	35.7	72.6	32.4	82.4	38.4	64.5
Nonnarcotic analgesics (pain relief)	38.0	70.0	40.5	73.6	35.9	67.0
ACE inhibitors (high blood pressure, heart disease)	37.1	67.5	35.6	73.0	38.3	62.8
NSAID[6] (pain relief)	42.0	61.2	31.2	54.0	50.8	67.1
Beta blockers (high blood pressure, heart disease)	23.7	59.1	20.7	58.2	26.1	59.8
Acid/peptic disorders (gastrointestinal reflux, ulcers)	38.7	57.1	30.6	50.8	45.2	62.3
Diuretics (high blood pressure, heart disease)	40.0	55.8	32.3	52.2	46.3	58.8
Calcium channel blockers (high blood pressure, heart disease)	48.9	52.6	46.2	44.5	51.2	59.3
Antiasthmatics/bronchodilators (asthma, breathing)	31.1	44.2	33.0	38.5	29.5	48.9
Antidepressants (depression and related disorders)	22.7	39.0	14.2	29.4	29.6	47.1
Vitamins/minerals (dietary supplements)	14.1	35.9	10.1	31.1	17.4	39.8
Antihistamines (allergies)	14.7	34.1	12.3	27.8	16.6	39.3
Estrogens/progestins (menopause, hot flashes)	. . .	. . .	. . .	. . .	47.5	45.2

See footnotes at end of table.

Table 92 (page 3 of 3). Selected prescription and nonprescription drugs recorded during physician office visits and hospital outpatient department visits, by age and sex: United States, 1995–96 and 2002–03

[Data are based on a sample of visit records from physician offices and hospital outpatient departments]

Age group and National Drug Code (NDC) therapeutic class[1] (common reasons for use)	Total		Male		Female	
	1995–96	2002–03	1995–96	2002–03	1995–96	2002–03
75 years and over	Visits with at least one drug per 100 population[2]					
Drug visits[3]	449.2	555.6	466.3	532.8	438.7	570.0
	Number of drugs per 100 population[4]					
Total number of drugs[5]	1,206.8	1,844.1	1,200.9	1,732.0	1,210.4	1,914.7
Diuretics (high blood pressure, heart disease)	75.8	102.4	74.5	104.1	76.6	101.3
Hypertension control drugs, not otherwise specified (high blood pressure)	35.1	101.6	28.4	98.5	39.2	103.5
Nonnarcotic analgesics (pain relief)	54.4	95.0	62.6	96.8	49.4	93.9
Hyperlipidemia (high cholesterol)	21.3	87.2	21.8	100.7	21.0	78.7
ACE inhibitors (high blood pressure, heart disease)	50.2	81.6	50.2	88.7	50.1	77.1
Beta blockers (high blood pressure, heart disease)	27.9	75.7	28.3	75.7	27.6	75.7
Acid/peptic disorders (gastrointestinal reflux, ulcers)	47.0	72.9	44.7	60.1	48.3	81.0
NSAID[6] (pain relief)	41.5	71.8	33.1	51.0	46.7	84.9
Calcium channel blockers (high blood pressure, heart disease)	68.6	69.3	61.8	61.0	72.7	74.5
Blood glucose/sugar regulators (diabetes)	39.8	64.8	46.9	69.7	35.5	61.8
Anticoagulants/thrombolytics (blood thinning, reduce or prevent blood clots)	28.6	57.5	34.9	68.8	24.7	50.3
Vitamins/minerals (dietary supplements)	21.2	53.4	18.0	42.0	23.2	60.6
Antidepressants (depression and related disorders)	24.6	49.0	20.7	31.7	27.0	59.9
Antiasthmatics/bronchodilators (asthma, breathing)	31.5	48.4	43.7	57.5	24.0	42.7
Thyroid/antithyroid (hyper- and hypothyroidism)	27.1	45.1	15.1	25.0	34.4	57.8

. . . Category not applicable.

[1]The National Drug Code (NDC) therapeutic class is a general therapeutic or pharmacological classification scheme for drug products reported to the Food and Drug Administration (FDA) under the provisions of the Drug Listing Act. See Appendix II, National Drug Code (NDC) Directory therapeutic class and table XI.

[2]Estimated number of drug visits during the 2-year period divided by the sum of population estimates for both years times 100.

[3]Drug visits are physician office and hospital outpatient department visits in which at least one prescription or nonprescription drug was recorded on the patient record form.

[4]Estimated number of drugs recorded during visits during the 2-year period divided by the sum of population estimates for both years times 100.

[5]Until 2002, up to six prescription and nonprescription medications were recorded on the patient record form. Beginning in 2003, up to eight prescription and nonprescription medications are recorded on the patient record form. If 2003 data were restricted to six instead of eight drugs, the 2002–03 total drug rate for all ages would be 2.7 percent lower. See Appendix II, Drugs.

[6]NSAID is nonsteroidal anti-inflammatory drug. Aspirin was not included as an NSAID in this analysis. See Appendix II, National Drug Classification (NDC) system.

NOTE: Drugs recorded on the patient record form are those prescribed, continued, administered, or provided during a physician office visit or hospital outpatient department visit.

SOURCE: Centers for Disease Control and Prevention, National Center for Health Statistics, National Ambulatory Medical Care Survey and National Hospital Ambulatory Medical Care Survey.

Table 93. Additions to mental health organizations according to type of service and organization: United States, selected years 1986–2002

[Data are based on inventories of mental health organizations]

Service and organization	1986	1990	1994[1]	2000	2002[2]	1986	1990	1994[1]	2000	2002[2]
24-hour hospital and residential treatment[3]	Additions[4] in thousands					Additions per 100,000 civilian population[5]				
All organizations	1,819	2,035	2,267	2,029	2,193	759.9	833.7	874.6	719.3	760.4
State and county mental hospitals	333	276	238	236	239	139.1	113.2	92.0	83.6	82.7
Private psychiatric hospitals	235	407	485	451	477	98.0	166.5	187.1	159.8	165.6
Non-Federal general hospital psychiatric services	849	960	1,067	994	1,095	354.8	393.2	411.5	352.3	379.6
Department of Veterans Affairs medical centers[6]	180	198	173	171	182	75.1	81.2	66.9	60.5	63.1
Residential treatment centers for emotionally disturbed children	25	42	47	46	60	10.2	17.0	18.0	16.2	20.7
All other organizations[7]	198	153	257	132	141	82.7	62.6	99.0	46.8	48.7
Less than 24-hour care[8]										
All organizations	2,955	3,298	3,516	4,057	3,575	1,233.4	1,352.4	1,356.8	1,438.1	1,239.7
State and county mental hospitals	68	48	42	49	53	28.4	19.8	16.1	17.2	18.3
Private psychiatric hospitals	132	163	214	265	426	55.2	66.9	82.4	94.1	147.6
Non-Federal general hospital psychiatric services	533	659	498	1,103	546	222.4	270.0	192.0	391.0	189.4
Department of Veterans Affairs medical centers[6]	133	184	132	139	80	55.3	75.3	51.1	49.1	27.7
Residential treatment centers for emotionally disturbed children	67	100	167	199	208	28.1	40.8	64.6	70.6	72.0
All other organizations[7]	2,022	2,145	2,464	2,302	2,263	844.0	879.6	950.7	816.0	784.7

[1]Beginning in 1994 data for supportive residential clients (moderately staffed housing arrangements such as supervised apartments, group homes, and halfway houses) are included in the totals and "All other organizations." This change affects the comparability of trend data prior to 1994 with data for 1994 and later years.
[2]Preliminary data.
[3]These data exclude mental health care provided in nonpsychiatric units of hospitals such as general medical units.
[4]See Appendix II, Addition.
[5]Civilian population estimates for 2000 and beyond are based on 2000 Census as of July 1; population estimates for 1992–98 are 1990 postcensal estimates.
[6]Includes Department of Veterans Affairs (VA) neuropsychiatric hospitals, VA general hospital psychiatric services, and VA psychiatric outpatient clinics.
[7]Includes freestanding psychiatric outpatient clinics, partial care organizations, and multiservice mental health organizations. See Appendix I, Survey of Mental Health Organizations.
[8]Formerly reported as partial care and outpatient treatment, the survey format was changed in 1994 and the reporting of these services was combined due to similarities in the care provided. These data exclude office-based mental health care (psychiatrists, psychologists, licensed clinical social workers, and psychiatric nurses).

NOTES: Data for 2000 are revised and differ from the previous edition of *Health, United States*. Data for additional years are available. See Appendix III.

SOURCES: Substance Abuse and Mental Health Services Administration, Center for Mental Health Services (CMHS). Manderscheid RW and Henderson MJ. *Mental Health, United States, 2002*. Washington, DC. U.S. Government Printing Office, 2004; and Survey of Mental Health Organizations, unpublished data.

Table 94. Home health care patients, according to age, sex, and diagnosis: United States, selected years 1992–2000

[Data are based on a survey of current home health care patients]

Age, sex, and diagnosis	*1992*	*1994*	*1996*	*1998*	*2000*
	Number of current patients				
Total home health care patients	1,232,200	1,889,327	2,427,483	1,881,768	1,355,290
	Current patients per 10,000 population				
Total	47.8	71.8	90.6	69.6	48.7
Age at time of survey:					
Under 65 years, crude	12.6	21.0	27.8	25.0	16.4
65 years and over, crude	295.4	424.9	526.3	375.7	277.0
65 years and over, age adjusted[1]	315.8	449.6	546.6	381.0	276.5
65–74 years	151.7	209.1	240.1	202.0	130.2
75–84 years	398.3	542.2	753.6	470.3	347.6
85 years and over	775.9	1,206.1	1,253.4	885.4	694.1
Sex:					
Male, total	32.6	47.8	60.9	47.9	35.1
Under 65 years, crude	10.9	17.8	22.1	22.9	15.6
65 years and over, crude	219.2	303.1	386.4	255.2	199.6
65 years and over, age adjusted[1]	255.8	350.0	438.3	277.6	216.4
65–74 years	121.8	169.9	187.0	159.7	100.7
75–84 years	322.0	427.5	598.7	321.4	270.0
85 years and over	635.2	893.1	1,044.3	653.0	553.9
Female, total	62.4	94.7	118.9	90.4	61.8
Under 65 years, crude	14.3	24.2	33.6	27.0	17.2
65 years and over, crude	347.4	508.9	623.9	460.4	332.6
65 years and over, age adjusted[1]	351.5	506.6	615.0	445.8	315.5
65–74 years	175.3	240.6	283.2	236.3	154.6
75–84 years	445.3	614.5	854.0	568.8	400.4
85 years and over	830.7	1,327.6	1,337.0	981.7	754.9
	Percent distribution				
Age at time of survey:[2]					
Under 65 years	23.1	25.7	27.0	31.3	29.5
65 years and over	76.9	74.3	73.0	68.7	70.5
65–74 years	22.6	20.6	18.4	19.7	17.3
75–84 years	33.9	31.2	35.3	29.9	31.3
85 years and over	20.4	22.4	19.4	19.1	21.9
Sex:					
Male	33.2	32.5	32.9	33.6	35.2
Female	66.8	67.5	67.1	66.4	64.8
Primary admission diagnosis:[3]					
Malignant neoplasms	5.7	5.7	4.8	3.8	4.9
Diabetes	7.7	8.1	8.5	6.1	7.8
Diseases of the nervous system and sense organs	6.3	8.0	5.8	7.6	6.1
Diseases of the circulatory system	25.9	27.2	25.6	23.6	23.6
Diseases of heart	12.6	14.3	10.9	12.3	10.9
Cerebrovascular diseases	5.8	6.1	7.8	5.1	7.3
Diseases of the respiratory system	6.6	6.1	7.7	7.9	6.8
Decubitus ulcers	1.9	1.1	1.0	1.2	1.9
Diseases of the musculoskeletal system and connective tissue	9.4	8.3	8.8	8.3	9.8
Osteoarthritis	2.5	2.8	3.2	2.7	3.5
Fractures, all sites	3.8	3.7	3.3	4.0	4.1
Fracture of neck of femur (hip)	1.4	1.7	1.3	1.1	1.5
Other	32.7	31.8	34.6	37.5	34.9

[1]Age adjusted by the direct method to the year 2000 standard population using the following three age groups: 65–74 years, 75–84 years, and 85 years and over. See Appendix II, Age adjustment.

[2]Denominator excludes persons with unknown age.

[3]Denominator excludes persons with unknown diagnosis.

NOTES: Current home health care patients are those who were on the rolls of the agency as of midnight on the day immediately before the date of the survey. Rates are based on the civilian population as of July 1. Population figures are adjusted for net underenumeration using the 1990 National Population Adjustment Matrix from the U.S. Bureau of the Census. Diagnostic categories are based on the *International Classification of Diseases, 9th Revision, Clinical Modification.* For a listing of the code numbers, see Appendix II, table IX.

SOURCE: Centers for Disease Control and Prevention, National Center for Health Statistics, National Home and Hospice Care Survey.

Table 95. Hospice patients, according to age, sex, and diagnosis: United States, selected years 1992–2000

[Data are based on a survey of current hospice patients]

Age, sex, and diagnosis	1992	1994	1996	1998	2000
	Number of current patients				
Total hospice patients	52,100	60,783	59,363	79,837	105,496
	Current patients per 10,000 population				
Total	2.0	2.3	2.2	3.0	3.8
Age at time of survey:					
Under 65 years, crude	0.5	0.8	0.5	0.7	0.8
65 years and over, crude	13.1	12.9	13.9	18.2	24.9
65 years and over, age adjusted[1]	13.7	13.6	14.4	18.4	24.9
65–74 years	7.8	7.3	7.8	9.9	10.1
75–84 years	19.2	16.9	16.9	22.0	31.9
85 years and over	23.4	30.6	34.7	44.7	67.3
Sex:					
Male, total	1.9	2.1	2.0	2.6	3.3
Under 65 years, crude	0.5	0.9	0.5	0.7	0.8
65 years and over, crude	13.9	12.5	14.8	18.5	24.8
65 years and over, age adjusted[1]	16.0	14.4	16.1	20.3	26.9
65–74 years	6.3	7.0	10.4	10.2	13.0
75–84 years	25.8	18.2	18.5	25.2	32.6
85 years and over	28.8	34.8	33.9	49.2	69.9
Female, total	2.1	2.5	2.4	3.3	4.3
Under 65 years, crude	0.4	0.7	0.6	0.8	0.9
65 years and over, crude	12.6	13.2	13.2	18.0	25.0
65 years and over, age adjusted[1]	12.6	13.2	12.9	17.3	23.3
65–74 years	8.9	7.5	5.8	9.6	7.6
75–84 years	15.1	16.1	15.9	19.9	31.5
85 years and over	21.4	29.0	35.0	42.9	66.2
	Percent distribution				
Age at time of survey:[2]					
Under 65 years	19.5	30.1	21.3	21.6	18.6
65 years and over	80.5	69.9	78.7	78.4	81.4
65–74 years	27.3	22.2	24.5	22.7	17.2
75–84 years	38.6	30.1	32.4	32.9	37.0
85 years and over	14.6	17.6	21.9	22.7	27.3
Sex:					
Male	46.1	44.7	44.9	42.7	42.6
Female	53.9	55.3	55.1	57.3	57.4
Primary admission diagnosis:[3]					
Malignant neoplasms	65.7	57.2	58.3	55.5	51.9
Large intestine and rectum	9.0	8.0	4.0	6.4	4.9
Trachea, bronchus, and lung	21.1	12.5	15.8	13.0	12.3
Breast	3.9	4.8	6.2	4.9	4.8
Prostate	6.0	5.9	6.6	6.1	7.7
Diseases of heart	10.2	9.3	8.3	9.7	12.8
Diseases of the respiratory system	4.3	6.6	7.3	10.6	6.5
Other	19.8	27.0	26.1	24.3	28.8

[1]Age adjusted by the direct method to the year 2000 standard population using the following three age groups: 65–74 years, 75–84 years, and 85 years and over. See Appendix II, Age adjustment.
[2]Denominator excludes persons with unknown age.
[3]Denominator excludes persons with unknown diagnosis.

NOTES: Current hospice patients are those who were on the rolls of the agency as of midnight on the day immediately before the date of the survey. Rates are based on the civilian population as of July 1. Population figures are adjusted for net underenumeration using the 1990 National Population Adjustment Matrix from the U.S. Bureau of the Census. Diagnostic categories are based on the *International Classification of Diseases, 9th Revision, Clinical Modification.* For a listing of the code numbers, see Appendix II, table IX.

SOURCE: Centers for Disease Control and Prevention, National Center for Health Statistics, National Home and Hospice Care Survey.

Table 96 (page 1 of 3). Discharges, days of care, and average length of stay in short-stay hospitals, according to selected characteristics: United States, selected years 1997–2003

[Data are based on household interviews of a sample of the civilian noninstitutionalized population]

Characteristic	Discharges[1]			Days of care[1]			Average length of stay[1]		
	1997	2002	2003	1997	2002	2003	1997	2002	2003
	Number per 1,000 population						Number of days		
Total[2,3]	124.3	122.9	119.9	601.2	541.3	558.9	4.8	4.4	4.7
Age									
Under 18 years	90.8	81.0	72.0	319.0	269.3	258.7	3.5	3.3	3.6
Under 6 years	203.5	188.9	169.8	632.6	601.0	610.9	3.1	3.2	3.6
6–17 years	34.0	29.2	24.3	163.1	110.3	86.9	4.8	3.8	3.6
18–44 years	96.8	94.7	93.2	358.8	311.2	352.7	3.7	3.3	3.8
45–64 years	124.9	124.3	129.5	631.1	574.5	676.5	5.1	4.6	5.2
45–54 years	99.2	106.8	107.5	527.5	495.8	543.4	5.3	4.6	5.1
55–64 years	164.8	150.7	161.6	792.4	693.0	871.1	4.8	4.6	5.4
65 years and over	274.4	293.2	283.9	1,852.5	1,745.3	1,607.8	6.8	6.0	5.7
65–74 years	249.1	250.5	242.9	1,595.2	1,269.6	1,261.7	6.4	5.1	5.2
75 years and over	307.3	342.0	330.3	2,188.4	2,290.1	2,000.4	7.1	6.7	6.1
Under 65 years of age									
All persons under 65 years of age[2,4]	102.2	98.1	96.0	416.4	365.5	406.2	4.1	3.7	4.2
Sex[4]									
Male	79.1	72.8	74.1	374.9	312.9	363.1	4.7	4.3	4.9
Female	124.7	122.9	117.5	456.6	416.7	448.7	3.7	3.4	3.8
Race[4,5]									
White only	100.8	96.4	93.2	385.8	342.5	378.3	3.8	3.6	4.1
Black or African American only	126.3	121.3	124.8	688.6	536.4	623.7	5.5	4.4	5.0
American Indian and Alaska Native only	*	*	*	*	*	*	*	*	*
Asian only	61.7	45.0	53.2	*	*	*	*	*	*
Native Hawaiian and Other Pacific Islander only	---	*	*	---	*	*	---	*	*
2 or more races	---	*	*135.9	---	*	*	---	*	*
Hispanic origin and race[4,5]									
Hispanic or Latino	109.9	94.9	95.6	416.7	377.4	393.5	3.8	4.0	4.1
Not Hispanic or Latino	101.2	98.8	96.3	415.4	365.2	407.1	4.1	3.7	4.2
White only	99.6	97.2	93.7	382.7	345.0	376.7	3.8	3.5	4.0
Black or African American only	125.7	121.2	124.2	692.6	517.9	629.3	5.5	4.3	5.1
Poverty status[4,6]									
Poor	186.0	157.9	150.3	922.0	747.1	694.9	5.0	4.7	4.6
Near poor	119.3	124.0	117.2	530.5	491.7	571.1	4.4	4.0	4.9
Nonpoor	82.7	83.1	82.4	308.9	283.3	323.5	3.7	3.4	3.9
Hispanic origin and race and poverty status[4,5,6]									
Hispanic or Latino:									
Poor	152.3	132.8	132.3	592.3	*	*557.3	3.9	*	*4.2
Near poor	92.7	103.6	99.3	*415.0	*377.7	*378.9	*4.5	*3.6	*3.8
Nonpoor	92.1	72.8	78.6	294.5	*289.1	*335.0	3.2	*4.0	*4.3
Not Hispanic or Latino:									
White only:									
Poor	205.2	159.6	144.2	955.5	695.9	*721.7	4.7	4.4	*5.0
Near poor	124.3	129.1	125.9	503.4	488.1	*557.4	4.0	3.8	*4.4
Nonpoor	83.1	85.3	82.9	303.0	287.1	311.9	3.6	3.4	3.8
Black or African American only:									
Poor	199.0	199.4	*207.2	*	*	*	*	*	*
Near poor	139.1	*129.8	*121.4	*819.0	*	*	*5.9	*	*
Nonpoor	85.2	93.3	93.1	*402.1	292.6	*418.8	*4.7	3.1	*4.5
Health insurance status[4,7]									
Insured	108.1	104.2	101.5	442.5	390.4	441.5	4.1	3.7	4.3
Private	85.6	84.3	80.1	310.2	275.1	323.0	3.6	3.3	4.0
Medicaid	311.6	277.4	268.8	1,575.3	1,301.2	1,397.1	5.1	4.7	5.2
Uninsured	75.3	68.7	69.3	296.3	247.2	251.2	3.9	3.6	3.6

See footnotes at end of table.

Table 96 (page 2 of 3). Discharges, days of care, and average length of stay in short-stay hospitals, according to selected characteristics: United States, selected years 1997–2003

[Data are based on household interviews of a sample of the civilian noninstitutionalized population]

Characteristic	Discharges[1] 1997	Discharges[1] 2002	Discharges[1] 2003	Days of care[1] 1997	Days of care[1] 2002	Days of care[1] 2003	Average length of stay[1] 1997	Average length of stay[1] 2002	Average length of stay[1] 2003
Poverty status and health insurance status[4,6]	Number per 1,000 population						Number of days		
Poor:									
Insured	234.6	193.0	184.5	1,243.1	958.1	912.3	5.3	5.0	4.9
Uninsured	102.8	90.2	*86.7	*407.7	*355.3	*306.8	*4.0	*3.9	*3.5
Near poor:									
Insured	141.2	146.1	139.5	640.0	603.7	*714.7	4.5	4.1	*5.1
Uninsured	72.0	75.2	69.4	*285.3	*252.9	*	*4.0	*3.4	*
Nonpoor:									
Insured	85.5	86.8	85.6	315.6	294.4	340.4	3.7	3.4	4.0
Uninsured	*58.5	54.5	59.3	*	*193.4	*201.6	*	*3.6	*3.4
Geographic region[4]									
Northeast	96.0	92.8	82.3	455.4	348.0	384.4	4.7	3.8	4.7
Midwest	108.7	104.9	95.7	384.4	382.6	368.1	3.5	3.6	3.8
South	111.8	106.6	112.5	466.1	400.6	467.4	4.2	3.8	4.2
West	82.9	80.9	79.0	327.2	300.8	359.8	3.9	3.7	4.6
Location of residence[4]									
Within MSA[8]	99.3	94.6	91.7	411.8	355.4	406.6	4.1	3.8	4.4
Outside MSA[8]	113.2	112.4	113.8	435.9	407.5	405.8	3.8	3.6	3.6
65 years of age and over									
All persons 65 years of age and over[2,9]	276.9	294.2	284.6	1,878.4	1,756.9	1,614.4	6.8	6.0	5.7
Sex[9]									
Male	291.6	312.5	273.0	2,077.4	1,804.6	1,614.1	7.1	5.8	5.9
Female	265.2	280.6	293.7	1,727.4	1,708.5	1,609.3	6.5	6.1	5.5
Hispanic origin and race[5,9]									
Hispanic or Latino	312.7	290.8	311.2	*2,512.1	1,489.4	*1,725.2	*8.0	5.1	*5.5
Not Hispanic or Latino	274.6	294.6	283.0	1,846.3	1,771.4	1,603.4	6.7	6.0	5.7
White only	274.8	293.0	280.6	1,808.2	1,683.5	1,547.2	6.6	5.7	5.5
Black or African American only	290.8	*373.3	349.4	2,423.5	*	*2,327.8	8.3	*	*6.7
Poverty status[6,9]									
Poor	342.3	361.2	359.5	2,566.3	*	2,110.0	7.5	*	5.9
Near poor	311.5	314.8	329.1	2,269.4	1,836.0	1,724.6	7.3	5.8	5.2
Nonpoor	251.5	273.8	256.5	1,606.7	1,575.4	1,501.8	6.4	5.8	5.9
Health insurance status[7,9]									
Medicare HMO	217.8	239.7	290.5	1,355.3	1,072.2	1,508.4	6.2	4.5	5.2
Private	271.9	295.7	265.6	1,756.1	1,782.6	1,537.6	6.5	6.0	5.8
Medicaid	539.7	487.1	463.2	3,810.6	2,505.1	3,008.3	7.1	5.1	6.5
Medicare fee-for-service only	252.9	258.2	*294.1	1,906.6	*	1,442.7	7.5	*	*4.9
Geographic region[9]									
Northeast	265.0	281.8	*300.4	1,828.5	1,659.3	1,604.1	6.9	5.9	*5.3
Midwest	285.2	306.3	275.2	1,971.1	1,765.3	1,588.6	6.9	5.8	5.8
South	298.1	319.7	298.5	2,140.2	2,075.3	1,834.8	7.2	6.5	6.1
West	237.2	243.6	249.4	1,299.2	1,234.8	1,200.3	5.5	5.1	4.8

See footnotes at end of table.

Table 96 (page 3 of 3). Discharges, days of care, and average length of stay in short-stay hospitals, according to selected characteristics: United States, selected years 1997–2003

[Data are based on household interviews of a sample of the civilian noninstitutionalized population]

Characteristic	Discharges[1]			Days of care[1]			Average length of stay[1]		
	1997	2002	2003	1997	2002	2003	1997	2002	2003
Location of residence[9]	Number per 1,000 population						Number of days		
Within MSA[8]	271.3	283.5	286.9	1,875.9	1,661.8	1,593.8	6.9	5.9	5.6
Outside MSA[8]	295.1	329.5	276.7	1,893.6	*2,070.2	1,683.6	6.4	*6.3	6.1

* Estimates are considered unreliable. Data preceded by an asterisk have a relative standard error of 20–30 percent. Data not shown have a relative standard error of greater than 30 percent.
- - - Data not available.
[1]See Appendix II, Discharge; Days of care; Average length of stay.
[2]Includes all other races not shown separately and unknown health insurance status.
[3]Estimates for all persons are age adjusted to the year 2000 standard population using six age groups: Under 18 years, 18–44 years, 45–54 years, 55–64 years, 65–74 years, and 75 years of age and over. See Appendix II, Age adjustment.
[4]Estimates are for persons under 65 years of age and are age adjusted to the year 2000 standard population using four age groups: Under 18 years, 18–44 years, 45–54 years, and 55–64 years of age. See Appendix II, Age adjustment.
[5]The race groups, white, black, American Indian and Alaska Native, Asian, Native Hawaiian and Other Pacific Islander, and 2 or more races, include persons of Hispanic and non-Hispanic origin. Persons of Hispanic origin may be of any race. Starting with data year 1999 race-specific estimates are tabulated according to 1997 Standards for Federal data on Race and Ethnicity and are not strictly comparable with estimates for earlier years. The five single race categories plus multiple race categories shown in the table conform to 1997 Standards. Starting with data year 1999 race-specific estimates are for persons who reported only one racial group; the category "2 or more races" includes persons who reported more than one racial group. Prior to data year 1999, data were tabulated according to 1977 Standards with four racial groups and the category "Asian only" included Native Hawaiian and Other Pacific Islander. Estimates for single race categories prior to 1999 included persons who reported one race or, if they reported more than one race, identified one race as best representing their race. See Appendix II, Race.
[6]Poor persons are defined as below the poverty threshold. Near poor persons have incomes of 100 percent to less than 200 percent of the poverty threshold. Nonpoor persons have incomes of 200 percent or greater than the poverty threshold. Missing family income data were imputed for 24–28 percent of persons under 65 years of age in 1997–98 and 30–33 percent in 1999–2003; and 36–41 percent of persons 65 years of age and over in 1997–98 and 44–47 percent in 1999–2003. See Appendix II, Poverty level; Family income.
[7]Health insurance categories are mutually exclusive. Persons who reported both Medicaid and private coverage are classified as having private coverage. Starting in 1997 Medicaid includes state-sponsored health plans and State Children's Health Insurance Program (SCHIP). In addition to private and Medicaid, the category "insured" also includes military plans, other government-sponsored health plans, and Medicare, not shown separately. Persons 65 years of age and over who reported Medicare HMO (health maintenance organization) and some other type of health insurance coverage are classified as having Medicare HMO. For persons 65 years of age and over the category "private" includes private and Medicare coverage. See Appendix II, Health insurance coverage.
[8]MSA is metropolitan statistical area.
[9]Estimates are for persons 65 years of age and over and are age adjusted to the year 2000 standard population using two age groups: 65–74 years and 75 years and over. See Appendix II, Age adjustment.

NOTES: Estimates of hospital utilization presented in *Health, United States* utilize two data sources: the National Health Interview Survey (NHIS) and the National Hospital Discharge Survey (NHDS). Differences in estimates from the two surveys are particularly evident for children and persons 65 years of age and over. See Appendix II, Hospital utilization. Data for additional years are available. See Appendix III. Standard errors are available in the spreadsheet version of this table. See www.cdc.gov/nchs/hus.htm. Starting with *Health, United States, 2005*, estimates for 2000 and later years use weights derived from the 2000 census. Estimates for 2000–2002 were recalculated using 2000-based weights and may differ from previous editions of *Health, United States.*

SOURCE: Centers for Disease Control and Prevention, National Center for Health Statistics, National Health Interview Survey, family core questionnaire.

Table 97 (page 1 of 2). Discharges, days of care, and average length of stay in non-Federal short-stay hospitals, according to selected characteristics: United States, selected years 1980–2003

[Data are based on a sample of hospital records]

Characteristic	1980[1]	1985[1]	1990	1995	1998	2000	2001	2002	2003
	Discharges per 1,000 population								
Total[2]	173.4	151.4	125.2	118.0	117.9	113.3	115.1	117.3	119.5
Age									
Under 18 years	75.6	61.4	46.4	42.4	40.4	40.3	43.4	43.4	43.6
18–44 years	155.3	128.0	102.7	91.4	88.8	84.9	87.3	90.3	91.3
45–54 years	174.8	146.8	112.4	98.5	92.7	92.1	94.4	95.6	99.5
55–64 years	215.4	194.8	163.3	148.3	155.1	141.5	139.3	146.5	145.7
65 years and over	383.7	369.8	334.1	347.7	365.3	353.4	354.3	357.5	367.9
65–74 years	315.8	297.2	261.6	260.0	267.6	254.6	256.1	254.0	265.1
75 years and over	489.3	475.6	434.0	459.1	477.4	462.0	460.0	466.6	475.2
Sex[2]									
Male	153.2	137.3	113.0	104.8	102.8	99.1	100.0	102.4	104.4
Female	195.0	167.3	139.0	131.7	133.3	127.7	130.6	132.9	135.1
Geographic region[2]									
Northeast	162.0	142.6	133.2	133.5	127.3	127.5	125.2	123.5	127.6
Midwest	192.1	158.1	128.8	113.3	116.4	110.9	113.5	113.6	117.1
South	179.7	155.5	132.5	125.2	126.4	120.9	126.3	126.7	125.8
West	150.5	145.7	100.7	96.7	97.1	89.4	88.8	99.7	103.9
	Days of care per 1,000 population								
Total[3]	1,297.0	997.5	818.9	638.6	598.6	557.7	562.2	570.9	574.6
Age									
Under 18 years	341.4	281.2	226.3	184.7	182.4	179.0	192.5	195.2	195.5
18–44 years	818.6	619.2	467.7	351.7	328.3	309.4	322.7	333.9	339.7
45–54 years	1,314.9	967.8	699.7	516.2	452.9	437.4	455.4	456.7	477.2
55–64 years	1,889.4	1,436.9	1,172.3	867.2	836.1	729.1	732.2	752.2	735.9
65 years and over	4,098.3	3,228.0	2,895.6	2,373.7	2,264.2	2,111.9	2,064.2	2,085.1	2,088.3
65–74 years	3,147.0	2,437.3	2,087.8	1,684.7	1,596.1	1,439.0	1,449.5	1,411.9	1,428.9
75 years and over	5,578.8	4,381.3	4,009.1	3,247.8	3,030.8	2,851.9	2,725.5	2,795.0	2,776.1
Sex[2]									
Male	1,239.7	973.3	805.8	623.9	576.7	535.9	534.5	549.5	546.7
Female	1,365.2	1,033.1	840.5	654.9	622.9	581.0	591.9	596.0	605.2
Geographic region[2]									
Northeast	1,400.6	1,113.0	1,026.7	839.0	731.0	718.6	697.7	690.0	694.4
Midwest	1,484.8	1,078.6	830.6	590.9	552.5	500.5	491.6	502.1	507.9
South	1,262.3	957.7	820.4	666.0	643.9	592.5	623.6	618.6	609.8
West	956.9	824.7	575.5	451.1	450.4	408.2	408.3	454.7	476.4
	Average length of stay in days								
Total[2]	7.5	6.6	6.5	5.4	5.1	4.9	4.9	4.9	4.8
Age									
Under 18 years	4.5	4.6	4.9	4.4	4.5	4.4	4.4	4.5	4.5
18–44 years	5.3	4.8	4.6	3.8	3.7	3.6	3.7	3.7	3.7
45–54 years	7.5	6.6	6.2	5.2	4.9	4.8	4.8	4.8	4.8
55–64 years	8.8	7.4	7.2	5.8	5.4	5.2	5.3	5.1	5.1
65 years and over	10.7	8.7	8.7	6.8	6.2	6.0	5.8	5.8	5.7
65–74 years	10.0	8.2	8.0	6.5	6.0	5.7	5.7	5.6	5.4
75 years and over	11.4	9.2	9.2	7.1	6.3	6.2	5.9	6.0	5.8
Sex[2]									
Male	8.1	7.1	7.1	6.0	5.6	5.4	5.3	5.4	5.2
Female	7.0	6.2	6.0	5.0	4.7	4.6	4.5	4.5	4.5

See footnotes at end of table.

Table 97 (page 2 of 2). Discharges, days of care, and average length of stay in non-Federal short-stay hospitals, according to selected characteristics: United States, selected years 1980–2003

[Data are based on a sample of hospital records]

Characteristic	*1980*[1]	*1985*[1]	*1990*	*1995*	*1998*	*2000*	*2001*	*2002*	*2003*
Geographic region[2]	Average length of stay in days								
Northeast	8.6	7.8	7.7	6.3	5.7	5.6	5.6	5.6	5.4
Midwest	7.7	6.8	6.5	5.2	4.7	4.5	4.3	4.4	4.3
South	7.0	6.2	6.2	5.3	5.1	4.9	4.9	4.9	4.8
West	6.4	5.7	5.7	4.7	4.6	4.6	4.6	4.6	4.6

[1]Comparisons of data from 1980–85 with data from later years should be made with caution as estimates of change may reflect improvements in the design rather than true changes in hospital use. See Appendix I, National Hospital Discharge Survey.
[2]Estimates are age adjusted to the year 2000 standard population using six age groups: under 18 years, 18–44 years, 45–54 years, 55–64 years, 65–74 years, and 75 years and over. See Appendix II, Age adjustment.

NOTES: Rates are based on the civilian population as of July 1. Starting with *Health, United States, 2003*, rates for 2000 and beyond are based on the 2000 census. Rates for 1990–99 use population estimates based on the 1990 census adjusted for net underenumeration using the 1990 National Population Adjustment Matrix from the U.S. Bureau of the Census. Rates for 1990–99 are not strictly comparable with rates for 2000 and beyond because population estimates for 1990–99 have not been revised to reflect Census 2000. See Appendix I, National Hospital Discharge Survey; Population Census and Population Estimates. Estimates of hospital utilization from the National Health Interview Survey (NHIS) and the National Hospital Discharge Survey (NHDS) may differ because NHIS data are based on household interviews of the civilian noninstitutionalized population, whereas NHDS data are based on hospital discharge records of all persons. See Appendix II, Hospital utilization. Data for additional years are available. See Appendix III.

SOURCE: Centers for Disease Control and Prevention, National Center for Health Statistics, National Hospital Discharge Survey.

Table 98 (page 1 of 3). Rates of discharges and days of care in non-Federal short-stay hospitals, according to sex, age, and selected first-listed diagnoses: United States, selected years 1990–2003

[Data are based on a sample of hospital records]

Sex, age, and first-listed diagnosis	Discharges			Days of care		
	1990	2000	2003	1990	2000	2003
Both sexes	Number per 1,000 population					
Total[1,2]	125.2	113.3	119.5	818.9	557.7	574.6
Male						
All ages[1,2]	113.0	99.1	104.4	805.8	535.9	546.7
Under 18 years[2]	46.3	40.9	44.9	233.6	195.6	200.0
Pneumonia	5.3	5.4	5.9	22.6	17.3	19.1
Asthma	3.3	3.5	2.0	9.3	7.4	4.7
Injuries and poisoning	6.8	5.0	5.5	30.1	21.4	21.6
Fracture, all sites	2.2	1.8	2.0	9.3	7.2	6.1
18–44 years[2]	57.9	45.0	47.7	351.7	217.5	236.0
HIV infection	*0.3	0.6	0.5	*3.0	*5.4	4.3
Alcohol and drug[3]	3.7	4.0	3.6	33.1	19.1	14.9
Serious mental illness[4]	3.4	*5.3	5.8	47.1	*43.6	46.2
Diseases of heart	3.0	2.7	3.0	16.3	9.4	*13.5
Intervertebral disc disorders	2.6	1.5	1.2	10.7	3.2	2.9
Injuries and poisoning	13.1	7.3	8.4	65.7	33.2	40.8
Fracture, all sites	4.0	2.5	3.0	22.7	12.8	15.5
45–64 years[2]	140.3	112.7	120.1	943.4	570.4	605.0
HIV infection	*0.1	*0.5	*0.7	*	*	*
Malignant neoplasms	10.6	6.2	6.6	99.1	42.1	44.7
Trachea, bronchus, lung	2.7	0.9	0.9	19.1	5.2	6.1
Diabetes	2.9	3.7	3.1	21.2	22.5	14.8
Alcohol and drug[3]	3.5	3.5	4.2	29.7	15.8	18.7
Serious mental illness[4]	2.5	*4.0	4.4	34.8	*34.6	39.9
Diseases of heart	31.7	26.4	24.7	185.0	101.5	99.0
Ischemic heart disease	22.6	17.7	14.8	128.2	63.8	56.1
Acute myocardial infarction	7.4	5.9	4.8	55.8	27.8	25.0
Congestive heart failure	3.0	3.3	3.9	19.7	17.2	18.5
Cerebrovascular diseases	4.1	3.8	3.8	40.7	19.8	16.6
Pneumonia	3.5	3.4	4.1	27.4	20.5	24.9
Injuries and poisoning	11.6	8.8	11.0	82.6	49.8	60.9
Fracture, all sites	3.3	2.5	3.1	24.2	16.2	18.0
65–74 years[2]	287.8	264.9	276.5	2,251.5	1,489.7	1,465.3
Malignant neoplasms	27.9	17.6	19.3	277.6	121.2	124.7
Large intestine and rectum	3.0	3.0	2.1	34.2	27.3	17.0
Trachea, bronchus, lung	6.4	2.8	3.6	55.7	19.2	21.0
Prostate	5.1	3.7	3.9	33.1	14.0	12.7
Diabetes	4.4	4.7	5.1	39.8	29.0	27.9
Serious mental illness[4]	2.5	*3.4	2.8	43.8	39.9	28.6
Diseases of heart	69.4	70.6	66.3	487.2	331.9	290.0
Ischemic heart disease	42.0	39.7	35.2	285.2	171.2	147.4
Acute myocardial infarction	14.0	12.5	12.5	122.4	66.5	66.9
Congestive heart failure	11.4	13.4	13.5	90.2	76.8	65.6
Cerebrovascular diseases	13.8	13.2	13.4	114.8	59.0	57.8
Pneumonia	11.4	12.8	12.9	107.8	82.0	77.2
Hyperplasia of prostate	14.4	5.4	3.8	65.0	15.0	10.5
Osteoarthritis	5.0	9.6	8.7	44.9	46.7	34.7
Injuries and poisoning	17.6	17.9	19.2	139.0	105.7	105.6
Fracture, all sites	4.5	4.7	4.6	45.9	29.9	27.5
Fracture of neck of femur (hip)	1.5	*2.0	*1.5	*18.1	*15.9	*10.4

See footnotes at end of table.

Table 98 (page 2 of 3). Rates of discharges and days of care in non-Federal short-stay hospitals, according to sex, age, and selected first-listed diagnoses: United States, selected years 1990–2003

[Data are based on a sample of hospital records]

Sex, age, and first-listed diagnosis	Discharges			Days of care		
	1990	2000	2003	1990	2000	2003
Male—Con.	Number per 1,000 population					
75 years and over[2]	478.5	467.4	483.1	4,231.6	2,888.0	2,844.9
Malignant neoplasms	41.0	21.9	24.1	408.3	165.2	166.8
Large intestine and rectum	5.4	4.2	4.0	80.7	44.1	36.9
Trachea, bronchus, lung	5.4	3.0	4.1	53.4	18.3	29.3
Prostate	9.7	3.2	2.3	65.6	*19.4	*10.4
Diabetes	4.6	6.5	6.6	51.2	43.2	*36.5
Serious mental illness[4]	*2.6	2.9	2.5	*40.5	*32.6	*25.2
Diseases of heart	106.2	113.3	110.3	855.7	600.9	560.2
Ischemic heart disease	49.1	53.0	47.2	398.1	276.1	238.8
Acute myocardial infarction	23.1	23.0	21.6	227.5	136.5	142.6
Congestive heart failure	31.0	30.5	31.1	242.3	175.4	170.6
Cerebrovascular diseases	30.2	30.2	29.1	298.3	171.2	142.2
Pneumonia	38.6	37.2	39.7	393.6	233.3	245.2
Hyperplasia of prostate	17.9	6.8	5.4	109.2	21.6	17.0
Osteoarthritis	5.8	6.2	9.7	60.7	28.7	42.3
Injuries and poisoning	31.2	33.6	34.6	341.3	257.7	226.1
Fracture, all sites	13.7	14.4	15.3	145.1	*119.2	108.0
Fracture of neck of femur (hip)	8.5	8.4	9.7	97.8	63.3	67.2
Female						
All ages[1,2]	139.0	127.7	135.1	840.5	581.0	605.2
Under 18 years[2]	46.4	39.6	42.2	218.7	161.5	190.9
Pneumonia	4.0	4.8	4.5	17.4	17.2	13.9
Asthma	2.2	2.4	1.3	6.8	5.5	*3.1
Injuries and poisoning	4.3	3.1	3.6	16.7	*12.0	*15.4
Fracture, all sites	1.3	0.9	1.1	6.4	2.3	3.6
18–44 years[2]	146.8	124.8	135.2	582.0	401.1	444.2
HIV infection	*	0.3	0.3	*	*2.1	2.5
Delivery	69.9	64.5	69.5	195.0	160.2	179.6
Alcohol and drug[3]	1.6	*2.1	1.9	14.1	*10.8	*9.5
Serious mental illness[4]	3.7	*5.4	6.0	54.3	*41.1	48.2
Diseases of heart	1.3	1.7	1.8	7.2	6.3	7.5
Intervertebral disc disorders	1.5	1.0	1.1	7.3	2.4	2.6
Injuries and poisoning	6.7	4.3	4.8	36.6	18.1	18.9
Fracture, all sites	1.6	1.0	1.0	10.7	4.5	4.8
45–64 years[2]	131.0	110.2	116.5	886.5	533.6	560.9
HIV infection	*	*	*	*	*	*
Malignant neoplasms	12.7	6.1	6.4	107.4	34.7	37.9
Trachea, bronchus, lung	1.7	0.5	0.8	14.8	3.4	5.3
Breast	2.8	1.3	1.0	12.1	2.6	2.5
Diabetes	2.9	2.9	2.8	25.8	15.0	15.3
Alcohol and drug[3]	1.0	1.5	1.6	8.0	*7.1	*8.2
Serious mental illness[4]	4.0	4.6	5.4	60.5	42.7	48.1
Diseases of heart	16.6	14.6	14.1	101.1	59.5	59.7
Ischemic heart disease	9.9	7.8	6.9	57.4	29.5	25.0
Acute myocardial infarction	2.8	2.0	1.9	21.6	10.0	8.2
Congestive heart failure	2.1	2.9	3.1	15.8	13.6	14.5
Cerebrovascular diseases	3.0	3.5	3.0	32.1	19.5	15.3
Pneumonia	3.4	3.6	3.9	26.5	20.8	21.3
Injuries and poisoning	9.4	7.7	8.8	63.3	41.2	48.8
Fracture, all sites	3.1	2.7	2.0	25.0	13.3	9.5

See footnotes at end of table.

Table 98 (page 3 of 3). Rates of discharges and days of care in non-Federal short-stay hospitals, according to sex, age, and selected first-listed diagnoses: United States, selected years 1990–2003

[Data are based on a sample of hospital records]

Sex, age, and first-listed diagnosis	Discharges			Days of care		
	1990	2000	2003	1990	2000	2003
Female—Con.	Number per 1,000 population					
65–74 years[2]	241.1	246.1	255.5	1,959.3	1,397.1	1,398.4
Malignant neoplasms	20.9	14.1	14.5	189.8	101.0	98.5
Large intestine and rectum	2.4	1.7	2.0	34.9	15.2	17.1
Trachea, bronchus, lung	2.6	2.4	2.5	26.9	*17.5	16.8
Breast	3.9	2.8	2.2	17.6	*	*4.3
Diabetes	5.8	4.6	5.1	46.8	26.1	26.8
Serious mental illness[4]	3.9	4.0	4.4	62.8	46.3	44.1
Diseases of heart	45.1	52.1	48.0	316.9	256.0	229.6
Ischemic heart disease	24.4	23.3	20.5	153.8	113.9	86.8
Acute myocardial infarction	7.5	8.0	7.6	58.1	52.8	40.6
Congestive heart failure	9.2	12.7	11.6	81.8	68.4	61.8
Cerebrovascular diseases	11.3	12.3	11.1	96.0	59.4	58.4
Pneumonia	8.7	11.7	11.8	81.8	73.5	65.6
Osteoarthritis	6.9	9.3	13.2	68.9	43.6	54.7
Injuries and poisoning	17.8	18.3	18.5	166.2	109.9	103.2
Fracture, all sites	8.4	7.7	7.3	97.3	43.8	39.8
Fracture of neck of femur (hip)	3.6	3.2	2.8	*59.6	21.1	16.8
75 years and over[2]	409.6	458.8	470.5	3,887.1	2,830.8	2,734.8
Malignant neoplasms	22.1	17.6	15.9	257.3	125.7	124.5
Large intestine and rectum	4.6	3.4	2.8	69.8	28.4	26.8
Trachea, bronchus, lung	2.1	1.9	2.0	20.6	14.0	*16.2
Breast	3.9	2.5	1.4	22.0	*8.9	*4.4
Diabetes	4.6	6.3	6.2	55.3	34.0	28.6
Serious mental illness[4]	4.2	4.7	3.3	78.4	49.2	37.2
Diseases of heart	84.6	99.1	97.2	672.8	523.4	480.1
Ischemic heart disease	33.7	35.5	32.1	253.2	185.5	150.8
Acute myocardial infarction	13.1	16.5	15.8	125.9	110.7	95.1
Congestive heart failure	28.0	32.2	29.6	236.6	181.7	159.4
Cerebrovascular diseases	29.6	27.6	24.5	302.0	156.8	138.3
Pneumonia	23.9	30.5	29.7	260.1	209.7	189.9
Osteoarthritis	5.3	8.7	10.6	54.1	40.4	45.8
Injuries and poisoning	46.3	44.7	46.2	489.2	275.4	271.0
Fracture, all sites	31.5	30.0	29.4	352.7	190.0	173.5
Fracture of neck of femur (hip)	18.8	17.9	15.5	236.3	125.3	98.6

* Estimates are considered unreliable. Data preceded by an asterisk have a relative standard error (RSE) of 20–30 percent. Data not shown have an RSE of greater than 30 percent.

[1]Estimates are age adjusted to the year 2000 standard population using six age groups: under 18 years, 18–44 years, 45–54 years, 55–64 years, 65–74 years, and 75 years and over. See Appendix II, Age adjustment.

[2]Includes discharges with first-listed diagnoses not shown in table.

[3]Includes abuse, dependence, and withdrawal. These estimates are for non-Federal short-stay hospitals and do not include alcohol and drug discharges from other types of facilities or programs such as the Department of Veterans Affairs or day treatment programs.

[4]These estimates are for non-Federal short-stay hospitals and do not include serious mental illness discharges from other types of facilities or programs such as the Department of Veterans Affairs or long-term hospitals.

NOTES: Excludes newborn infants. Diagnostic categories are based on the *International Classification of Diseases, Ninth Revision, Clinical Modification* (ICD–9-CM). See Appendix II, Diagnosis; Human immunodeficiency virus (HIV) infection; Table IX for ICD–9-CM codes. Rates are based on the civilian population as of July 1. Starting with *Health, United States, 2003*, rates for 2000 and beyond are based on the 2000 census. Rates for 1990–99 use population estimates based on the 1990 census adjusted for net underenumeration using the 1990 National Population Adjustment Matrix from the U.S. Bureau of the Census. Rates for 1990–99 are not strictly comparable with rates for 2000 and beyond because population estimates for 1990–99 have not been revised to reflect Census 2000. See Appendix I, National Hospital Discharge Survey; Population Census and Population Estimates. Data for additional years are available. See Appendix III.

SOURCE: Centers for Disease Control and Prevention, National Center for Health Statistics, National Hospital Discharge Survey.

Table 99 (page 1 of 3). Discharges and average length of stay in non-Federal short-stay hospitals, according to sex, age, and selected first-listed diagnoses: United States, selected years 1990–2003

[Data are based on a sample of hospital records]

Sex, age, and first-listed diagnosis	Discharges			Average length of stay		
	1990	2000	2003	1990	2000	2003
Both sexes	Number in thousands			Number of days		
Total[1,2]	30,788	31,706	34,738	6.5	4.9	4.8
Male						
All ages[1,2]	12,280	12,514	13,874	7.1	5.4	5.2
Under 18 years[2]	1,572	1,515	1,679	5.0	4.8	4.5
Pneumonia	178	199	221	4.3	3.2	3.2
Asthma	111	129	74	2.8	2.1	2.4
Injuries and poisoning	232	185	207	4.4	4.3	3.9
Fracture, all sites	76	68	77	4.2	3.9	3.0
18–44 years[2]	3,120	2,498	2,683	6.1	4.8	4.9
HIV infection	*15	32	28	*10.6	*9.4	8.6
Alcohol and drug[3]	201	224	203	8.9	4.7	4.1
Serious mental illness[4]	184	*296	323	13.8	*8.2	8.0
Diseases of heart	163	148	169	5.4	3.5	*4.5
Intervertebral disc disorders	138	81	69	4.2	2.2	2.3
Injuries and poisoning	704	408	470	5.0	4.5	4.9
Fracture, all sites	217	141	171	5.6	5.0	5.1
45–64 years[2]	3,115	3,424	4,016	6.7	5.1	5.0
HIV infection	*3	*15	*22	*7.1	*	*
Malignant neoplasms	235	188	221	9.4	6.8	6.7
Trachea, bronchus, lung	60	26	30	7.1	6.0	6.9
Diabetes	65	114	105	7.3	6.0	4.7
Alcohol and drug[3]	77	106	140	8.5	4.5	4.5
Serious mental illness[4]	56	*120	147	13.7	*8.8	9.1
Diseases of heart	704	802	827	5.8	3.8	4.0
Ischemic heart disease	502	539	494	5.7	3.6	3.8
Acute myocardial infarction	165	178	161	7.5	4.7	5.2
Congestive heart failure	66	101	129	6.7	5.2	4.8
Cerebrovascular diseases	91	116	126	10.0	5.2	4.4
Pneumonia	77	104	137	7.9	6.0	6.1
Injuries and poisoning	257	266	369	7.2	5.7	5.5
Fracture, all sites	74	77	102	7.2	6.4	5.9
65–74 years[2]	2,268	2,199	2,309	7.8	5.6	5.3
Malignant neoplasms	220	146	161	9.9	6.9	6.5
Large intestine and rectum	24	24	18	11.4	9.2	8.0
Trachea, bronchus, lung	50	23	30	8.7	6.8	5.8
Prostate	40	31	33	6.5	3.8	3.2
Diabetes	34	39	42	9.1	6.2	5.5
Serious mental illness[4]	20	*28	24	17.4	*11.7	10.1
Diseases of heart	547	586	553	7.0	4.7	4.4
Ischemic heart disease	331	329	294	6.8	4.3	4.2
Acute myocardial infarction	110	104	105	8.8	5.3	5.3
Congestive heart failure	90	112	113	7.9	5.7	4.9
Cerebrovascular diseases	108	109	112	8.3	4.5	4.3
Pneumonia	90	106	108	9.5	6.4	6.0
Hyperplasia of prostate	113	45	32	4.5	2.8	2.8
Osteoarthritis	39	80	72	9.0	4.9	4.0
Injuries and poisoning	139	149	160	7.9	5.9	5.5
Fracture, all sites	36	39	38	10.2	6.4	6.0
Fracture of neck of femur (hip)	12	*17	*12	*11.8	*7.9	*7.1

See footnotes at end of table.

Table 99 (page 2 of 3). Discharges and average length of stay in non-Federal short-stay hospitals, according to sex, age, and selected first-listed diagnoses: United States, selected years 1990–2003

[Data are based on a sample of hospital records]

Sex, age, and first-listed diagnosis	Discharges			Average length of stay		
	1990	2000	2003	1990	2000	2003
Male—Con.	Number in thousands			Number of days		
75 years and over[2]	2,203	2,878	3,188	8.8	6.2	5.9
Malignant neoplasms	189	135	159	10.0	7.6	6.9
Large intestine and rectum	25	26	26	15.0	10.6	9.2
Trachea, bronchus, lung	25	18	27	10.0	6.1	7.2
Prostate	45	20	16	6.8	*6.1	*4.4
Diabetes	21	40	44	11.0	6.6	*5.5
Serious mental illness[4]	*12	18	17	*15.5	*11.2	*10.0
Diseases of heart	489	697	728	8.1	5.3	5.1
Ischemic heart disease	226	326	311	8.1	5.2	5.1
Acute myocardial infarction	106	141	142	9.9	5.9	6.6
Congestive heart failure	143	188	205	7.8	5.7	5.5
Cerebrovascular diseases	139	186	192	9.9	5.7	4.9
Pneumonia	178	229	262	10.2	6.3	6.2
Hyperplasia of prostate	82	42	36	6.1	3.2	3.1
Osteoarthritis	27	38	64	10.5	4.6	4.4
Injuries and poisoning	144	207	228	10.9	7.7	6.5
Fracture, all sites	63	89	101	10.6	*8.3	7.1
Fracture of neck of femur (hip)	39	52	64	11.5	7.5	6.9
Female						
All ages[1,2]	18,508	19,192	20,864	6.0	4.5	4.5
Under 18 years[2]	1,500	1,397	1,504	4.7	4.1	4.5
Pneumonia	129	168	159	4.4	3.6	3.1
Asthma	71	85	46	3.1	2.3	*2.4
Injuries and poisoning	138	111	128	3.9	*3.8	*4.3
Fracture, all sites	42	32	38	5.0	2.5	3.4
18–44 years[2]	8,018	6,941	7,537	4.0	3.2	3.3
HIV infection	*	15	19	*	*7.5	7.4
Delivery	3,815	3,588	3,874	2.8	2.5	2.6
Alcohol and drug[3]	85	*116	106	9.1	*5.2	*5.0
Serious mental illness[4]	200	*300	333	14.8	*7.6	8.1
Diseases of heart	73	95	102	5.4	3.7	4.1
Intervertebral disc disorders	84	58	60	4.7	2.3	2.4
Injuries and poisoning	366	237	268	5.5	4.2	3.9
Fracture, all sites	85	57	57	6.9	4.4	4.7
45–64 years[2]	3,129	3,534	4,104	6.8	4.8	4.8
HIV infection	*	*	*	*	*	*
Malignant neoplasms	303	195	226	8.5	5.7	5.9
Trachea, bronchus, lung	41	17	27	8.6	6.4	6.8
Breast	67	40	37	4.3	2.1	2.4
Diabetes	70	93	99	8.9	5.2	5.4
Alcohol and drug[3]	23	47	55	8.2	*4.8	*5.2
Serious mental illness[4]	95	146	191	15.2	9.4	8.8
Diseases of heart	397	470	498	6.1	4.1	4.2
Ischemic heart disease	237	251	242	5.8	3.8	3.6
Acute myocardial infarction	68	64	66	7.6	5.0	4.4
Congestive heart failure	51	94	110	7.4	4.6	4.6
Cerebrovascular diseases	72	113	104	10.7	5.5	5.2
Pneumonia	80	117	136	7.9	5.7	5.5
Injuries and poisoning	225	248	310	6.7	5.3	5.5
Fracture, all sites	75	87	71	7.9	4.9	4.7

See footnotes at end of table.

Table 99 (page 3 of 3). Discharges and average length of stay in non-Federal short-stay hospitals, according to sex, age, and selected first-listed diagnoses: United States, selected years 1990–2003

[Data are based on a sample of hospital records]

Sex, age, and first-listed diagnosis	Discharges			Average length of stay		
	1990	2000	2003	1990	2000	2003
Female—Con.	Number in thousands			Number of days		
65–74 years[2]	2,421	2,479	2,552	8.1	5.7	5.5
Malignant neoplasms	210	142	144	9.1	7.2	6.8
Large intestine and rectum	24	17	20	14.5	9.0	8.4
Trachea, bronchus, lung	26	25	25	10.2	*7.1	6.8
Breast	40	29	22	4.5	*	*2.0
Diabetes	59	47	51	8.0	5.6	5.2
Serious mental illness[4]	39	40	43	16.3	11.7	10.1
Diseases of heart	453	525	480	7.0	4.9	4.8
Ischemic heart disease	245	235	205	6.3	4.9	4.2
Acute myocardial infarction	75	81	76	7.8	6.6	5.4
Congestive heart failure	92	128	116	8.9	5.4	5.3
Cerebrovascular diseases	114	124	111	8.5	4.8	5.3
Pneumonia	87	117	117	9.4	6.3	5.6
Osteoarthritis	69	94	132	10.0	4.7	4.1
Injuries and poisoning	179	185	184	9.3	6.0	5.6
Fracture, all sites	85	77	73	11.5	5.7	5.4
Fracture of neck of femur (hip)	36	32	28	*16.7	6.7	5.9
75 years and over[2]	3,440	4,840	5,168	9.5	6.2	5.8
Malignant neoplasms	185	186	175	11.7	7.1	7.8
Large intestine and rectum	39	36	31	15.1	8.4	9.6
Trachea, bronchus, lung	18	20	22	9.9	7.3	*8.1
Breast	33	27	15	5.7	*3.5	*3.2
Diabetes	39	67	68	11.9	5.4	4.6
Serious mental illness[4]	35	49	37	18.7	10.5	11.2
Diseases of heart	711	1,045	1,067	8.0	5.3	4.9
Ischemic heart disease	283	375	352	7.5	5.2	4.7
Acute myocardial infarction	110	174	174	9.6	6.7	6.0
Congestive heart failure	235	339	325	8.5	5.6	5.4
Cerebrovascular diseases	249	292	269	10.2	5.7	5.6
Pneumonia	201	322	327	10.9	6.9	6.4
Osteoarthritis	45	91	117	10.2	4.7	4.3
Injuries and poisoning	389	472	507	10.6	6.2	5.9
Fracture, all sites	265	316	323	11.2	6.3	5.9
Fracture of neck of femur (hip)	158	189	171	12.5	7.0	6.3

* Estimates are considered unreliable. Data preceded by an asterisk have a relative standard error (RSE) of 20–30 percent. Data not shown have an RSE of greater than 30 percent.

[1]Average length of stay estimates are age adjusted to the year 2000 standard population using six age groups: under 18 years, 18–44 years, 45–54 years, 55–64 years, 65–74 years, and 75 years and over. See Appendix II, Age adjustment.

[2]Includes discharges with first-listed diagnoses not shown in table.

[3]Includes abuse, dependence, and withdrawal. These estimates are for non-Federal short-stay hospitals and do not include alcohol and drug discharges from other types of facilities or programs such as the Department of Veterans Affairs or day treatment programs.

[4]These estimates are for non-Federal short-stay hospitals and do not include serious mental illness discharges from other types of facilities or programs such as the Department of Veterans Affairs or long-term hospitals.

NOTES: Excludes newborn infants. Diagnostic categories are based on the *International Classification of Diseases, Ninth Revision, Clinical Modification* (ICD-9-CM). See Appendix II, Diagnosis; Human immunodeficiency virus (HIV) infection; Table IX for ICD–9–CM codes. Data for additional years are available. See Appendix III.

SOURCE: Centers for Disease Control and Prevention, National Center for Health Statistics, National Hospital Discharge Survey.

Table 100 (page 1 of 3). Hospital stays with at least one procedure, according to sex, age, and selected procedures: United States, average annual 1992–93 and 2002–03

[Data are based on a sample of hospital records]

Age and procedure category	Both sexes 1992–93	Both sexes 2002–03	Male 1992–93	Male 2002–03	Female 1992–93	Female 2002–03
18 years of age and over	Number in thousands[1]					
Hospital stays with at least one procedure[2]	18,700	19,283	6,953	7,084	11,748	12,199
18 years of age and over, age adjusted[3]	Number per 10,000 population[4]					
Hospital stays with at least one procedure[2]	992.3	897.3	845.8	729.0	1,152.6	1,076.2
Cardiac catheterization	54.6	58.8	74.4	78.8	37.9	42.2
Insertion, replacement, removal, and revision of pacemaker leads or device	8.8	10.4	10.9	12.2	7.4	9.1
Incision, excision, and occlusion of vessels	40.3	64.1	46.9	68.2	35.5	61.1
Angiocardiography using contrast material	45.6	47.5	61.3	61.5	32.3	35.8
Operations on vessels of heart	37.0	43.1	56.4	64.4	20.8	25.4
Removal of coronary artery obstruction and insertion of stent(s)	21.0	30.2	30.7	43.5	12.7	18.9
Insertion of coronary artery stent(s)[5]	. . .	25.0	. . .	36.8	. . .	15.1
Coronary artery bypass graft	16.9	13.2	27.1	21.3	8.6	6.6
Diagnostic procedures on small intestine	44.8	47.1	47.1	46.7	43.1	47.8
Diagnostic procedures on large intestine	28.7	26.7	27.7	24.8	29.6	28.3
Diagnostic radiology	78.0	35.1	80.4	34.9	76.6	35.6
Computerized axial tomography	54.9	28.4	59.2	28.5	51.2	28.1
Diagnostic ultrasound	66.1	32.7	61.5	33.8	71.1	32.2
Joint replacement of lower extremity	22.6	35.6	18.2	30.9	25.7	39.3
Total hip replacement	6.8	9.5	6.2	9.2	7.1	9.6
Partial hip replacement	4.9	5.0	2.9	3.5	6.1	6.0
Total knee replacement	8.9	17.7	6.9	15.1	10.5	20.0
Reduction of fracture and dislocation	27.5	24.2	24.7	23.3	28.3	23.6
Excision or destruction of intervertebral disc	17.3	14.4	19.6	16.2	15.2	12.9
Cholecystectomy	27.2	19.7	18.9	14.9	35.4	24.4
Laparoscopic cholecystectomy	18.1	14.5	10.9	9.6	25.0	19.3
Lysis of peritoneal adhesions	18.0	15.2	7.3	5.9	28.1	24.1
18–44 years of age	Number in thousands[1]					
Hospital stays with at least one procedure[2]	7,855	7,238	1,874	1,481	5,981	5,757
	Number per 10,000 population[4]					
Hospital stays with at least one procedure[2]	719.2	646.5	344.9	263.8	1,089.5	1,031.3
Repair of hernia	4.7	4.2	5.0	2.6	4.3	5.9
Cesarean section and removal of fetus[6]	. . .	. . .	. . .	. . .	163.1	191.0
Forceps, vacuum, and breech delivery[6]	. . .	. . .	. . .	. . .	77.1	55.6
Other procedures inducing or assisting delivery[6,7]	. . .	. . .	. . .	. . .	399.6	399.5
Dilation and curettage of uterus[6]	. . .	. . .	. . .	. . .	20.9	7.1
Total abdominal hysterectomy[6]	. . .	. . .	. . .	. . .	38.5	36.5
Vaginal hysterectomy[6]	. . .	. . .	. . .	. . .	20.3	18.8
Cardiac catheterization	8.3	9.1	12.3	12.3	4.4	5.9
Incision, excision, and occlusion of vessels	11.9	20.2	12.3	20.2	11.4	20.3
Angiocardiography using contrast material	7.4	8.2	11.0	10.6	3.8	5.7
Operations on vessels of heart	3.6	4.5	6.2	7.0	1.0	2.0
Removal of coronary artery obstruction and insertion of stent(s)	2.6	3.6	4.5	5.5	*0.7	1.7
Insertion of coronary artery stent(s)[5]	. . .	3.0	. . .	4.7	. . .	1.2
Coronary artery bypass graft	1.0	0.9	1.8	1.5	*	*
Diagnostic procedures on small intestine	12.9	13.4	13.8	11.4	12.1	15.5
Diagnostic procedures on large intestine	6.7	6.3	6.6	5.7	6.9	6.9
Diagnostic radiology	33.2	14.7	32.4	12.7	33.9	16.6
Computerized axial tomography	21.2	11.4	24.7	11.4	17.6	11.3
Diagnostic ultrasound	29.0	10.6	15.8	7.7	42.0	13.6
Reduction of fracture and dislocation	15.9	13.4	21.3	18.9	10.5	7.9
Excision or destruction of intervertebral disc	15.0	10.6	18.7	11.6	11.5	9.7
Cholecystectomy	16.1	12.0	6.3	5.0	25.8	19.0
Laparoscopic cholecystectomy	11.9	10.2	4.1	3.7	19.5	16.8
Lysis of peritoneal adhesions	15.2	12.4	2.1	1.6	28.2	23.2

See footnotes at end of table.

Table 100 (page 2 of 3). Hospital stays with at least one procedure, according to sex, age, and selected procedures: United States, average annual 1992–93 and 2002–03

[Data are based on a sample of hospital records]

Age and procedure category	Both sexes 1992–93	Both sexes 2002–03	Male 1992–93	Male 2002–03	Female 1992–93	Female 2002–03
45–64 years of age			Number in thousands[1]			
Hospital stays with at least one procedure[2]	4,227	4,924	2,105	2,457	2,122	2,467
			Number per 10,000 population[4]			
Hospital stays with at least one procedure[2]	866.5	727.8	892.3	746.2	842.2	710.4
Transurethral prostatectomy[8]	. . .	. . .	21.2	6.5	. . .	. . .
Repair of hernia	15.7	13.5	18.6	12.2	12.9	14.6
Total abdominal hysterectomy[6]	. . .	. . .	. . .	. . .	49.6	47.2
Vaginal hysterectomy[6]	. . .	. . .	. . .	. . .	19.4	21.1
Cardiac catheterization	86.5	79.8	120.3	106.7	54.9	54.3
Insertion, replacement, removal, and revision of pacemaker leads or device	6.1	4.3	7.6	5.5	4.8	3.1
Incision, excision, and occlusion of vessels	43.2	65.0	48.1	68.5	38.6	61.6
Angiocardiography using contrast material	72.9	64.4	99.1	83.2	48.3	46.5
Operations on vessels of heart	59.5	58.6	91.8	88.4	29.3	30.3
Removal of coronary artery obstruction and insertion of stent(s)	35.3	41.4	52.2	61.2	19.5	22.6
Insertion of coronary artery stent(s)[5]	. . .	34.4	. . .	52.0	. . .	17.6
Coronary artery bypass graft	25.8	17.6	42.1	27.7	10.7	8.0
Diagnostic procedures on small intestine	42.2	41.5	44.2	41.7	40.3	41.3
Diagnostic procedures on large intestine	27.2	20.9	26.3	18.0	28.1	23.7
Diagnostic radiology	76.8	31.5	77.7	31.4	75.9	31.5
Computerized axial tomography	48.8	24.0	51.1	25.5	46.6	22.7
Diagnostic ultrasound	60.6	30.4	63.3	34.2	58.2	26.9
Joint replacement of lower extremity	18.0	34.8	15.2	31.0	20.7	38.4
Total hip replacement	6.5	10.4	7.1	11.6	5.9	9.4
Partial hip replacement	1.6	1.2	*	*1.0	2.2	1.3
Total knee replacement	7.8	20.2	5.2	16.1	10.2	24.1
Reduction of fracture and dislocation	21.1	16.4	18.4	17.8	23.6	15.0
Excision or destruction of intervertebral disc	23.7	21.0	25.1	23.2	22.4	18.9
Cholecystectomy	31.9	20.5	21.1	17.3	41.9	23.4
Laparoscopic cholecystectomy	23.0	14.6	14.2	11.1	31.4	17.8
Lysis of peritoneal adhesions	16.6	14.9	7.6	5.7	25.0	23.6
65–74 years of age			Number in thousands[1]			
Hospital stays with at least one procedure[2]	3,216	2,889	1,605	1,421	1,611	1,468
			Number per 10,000 population[4]			
Hospital stays with at least one procedure[2]	1,749.6	1,578.4	1,974.0	1,707.4	1,571.7	1,470.7
Transurethral prostatectomy[8]	. . .	. . .	128.6	50.5	. . .	. . .
Repair of hernia	36.2	27.1	51.1	29.5	24.4	25.0
Total abdominal hysterectomy[6]	. . .	. . .	. . .	. . .	23.8	18.0
Vaginal hysterectomy[6]	. . .	. . .	. . .	. . .	14.2	13.9
Cardiac catheterization	175.7	178.1	227.5	230.0	134.7	134.8
Insertion, replacement, removal, and revision of pacemaker leads or device	24.3	27.8	28.9	28.6	20.6	27.0
Incision, excision, and occlusion of vessels	109.5	154.9	131.5	167.1	92.0	144.7
Angiocardiography using contrast material	144.0	139.4	185.2	174.3	111.3	110.2
Operations on vessels of heart	127.5	144.8	184.6	208.5	82.1	91.7
Removal of coronary artery obstruction and insertion of stent(s)	67.0	97.3	91.8	134.5	47.4	66.3
Insertion of coronary artery stent(s)[5]	. . .	81.8	. . .	113.9	. . .	55.0
Coronary artery bypass graft	64.0	48.6	97.8	75.9	37.1	25.9
Diagnostic procedures on small intestine	104.6	110.7	104.2	114.9	105.0	107.2
Diagnostic procedures on large intestine	64.4	67.9	57.9	64.4	69.6	70.8
Diagnostic radiology	159.7	75.8	169.5	77.9	151.9	74.1
Computerized axial tomography	120.6	59.1	129.4	56.5	113.7	61.3
Diagnostic ultrasound	142.7	75.5	152.2	78.5	135.2	73.0
Joint replacement of lower extremity	79.0	120.3	61.2	95.2	93.1	141.2
Total hip replacement	24.4	30.5	20.5	26.5	27.6	33.8
Partial hip replacement	8.0	8.3	*3.7	5.9	11.5	10.3
Total knee replacement	40.4	70.1	30.7	52.9	48.1	84.4
Reduction of fracture and dislocation	38.4	36.8	28.4	26.7	46.4	45.2
Excision or destruction of intervertebral disc	17.6	16.8	15.6	19.1	19.3	15.0
Cholecystectomy	54.5	40.1	48.7	38.8	59.1	41.1
Laparoscopic cholecystectomy	31.6	27.5	24.2	24.9	37.5	29.6
Lysis of peritoneal adhesions	24.5	20.9	21.3	16.8	27.0	24.3

See footnotes at end of table.

Table 100 (page 3 of 3). Hospital stays with at least one procedure, according to sex, age, and selected procedures: United States, average annual 1992–93 and 2002–03

[Data are based on a sample of hospital records]

Age and procedure category	Both sexes 1992–93	Both sexes 2002–03	Male 1992–93	Male 2002–03	Female 1992–93	Female 2002–03
75 years of age and over			Number in thousands[1]			
Hospital stays with at least one procedure[2]	3,402	4,232	1,369	1,725	2,033	2,507
			Number per 10,000 population[4]			
Hospital stays with at least one procedure[2]	2,455.5	2,424.5	2,756.6	2,638.9	2,287.3	2,296.1
Transurethral prostatectomy[8]	. . .	. . .	225.9	81.2	. . .	. . .
Repair of hernia	41.5	27.2	58.4	32.1	32.0	24.3
Total abdominal hysterectomy[6]	. . .	. . .	. . .	. . .	13.8	13.0
Vaginal hysterectomy[6]	. . .	. . .	. . .	. . .	9.1	6.8
Cardiac catheterization	114.2	176.7	150.0	246.0	94.2	135.2
Insertion, replacement, removal, and revision of pacemaker leads or device	57.6	78.7	72.6	94.5	49.3	69.2
Incision, excision, and occlusion of vessels	143.6	249.1	180.2	272.4	123.1	235.1
Angiocardiography using contrast material	93.2	142.8	120.2	191.7	78.1	113.4
Operations on vessels of heart	78.9	128.3	120.6	194.3	55.6	88.8
Removal of coronary artery obstruction and insertion of stent(s)	41.0	90.0	59.2	127.5	30.8	67.5
Insertion of coronary artery stent(s)[5]	. . .	73.3	. . .	106.7	. . .	53.3
Coronary artery bypass graft	39.0	39.1	63.5	67.7	25.4	22.0
Diagnostic procedures on small intestine	200.0	219.1	214.9	220.8	191.6	218.2
Diagnostic procedures on large intestine	141.0	136.2	138.8	131.2	142.1	139.2
Diagnostic radiology	289.9	137.9	309.1	146.2	279.2	132.8
Computerized axial tomography	228.9	121.8	240.8	121.2	222.2	122.2
Diagnostic ultrasound	248.8	139.2	258.0	155.0	243.6	129.8
Joint replacement of lower extremity	118.1	162.9	91.7	145.6	132.8	173.3
Total hip replacement	27.7	37.1	22.4	33.2	30.7	39.4
Partial hip replacement	44.7	48.0	27.7	32.0	54.2	57.6
Total knee replacement	36.1	63.3	30.8	64.7	39.1	62.5
Reduction of fracture and dislocation	115.7	109.9	65.9	68.9	143.6	134.4
Excision or destruction of intervertebral disc	8.1	12.1	9.4	16.7	7.4	9.3
Cholecystectomy	54.4	44.9	61.8	44.0	50.2	45.4
Laparoscopic cholecystectomy	26.6	28.1	28.7	25.9	25.4	29.4
Lysis of peritoneal adhesions	34.0	28.1	25.8	23.3	38.7	31.0

* Estimates are considered unreliable. Rates for inpatient procedures preceded by an asterisk are based on 5,000–8,999 estimated procedures; those based on fewer than 5,000 are not shown. Estimates that are not shown generally have a relative standard error of greater than 30 percent.
. . . Category not applicable.
[1]Average number of procedures per year.
[2]Includes stays for procedures not shown separately.
[3]Estimates are age adjusted to the year 2000 standard population using five age groups: 18–44 years, 45–54 years, 55–64 years, 65–74 years, and 75 years and over. See Appendix II, Age adjustment.
[4]Average annual rate.
[5]The procedure code for insertion of coronary artery stents (36.06) first appears in the 1996 data. A second procedure code for the insertion of drug-eluting stents (36.07) first appears in the 2003 data.
[6]Rate for female population only.
[7]Includes artificial rupture of membranes, surgical and medical induction of labor, and episiotomy.
[8]Rate for male population only.

NOTES: Up to four procedures were coded for each hospital stay. If more than one procedure with the same code (e.g., a coronary artery bypass graft) was performed during the hospital stay, it is counted only once. Procedure categories are based on the *International Classification of Diseases, Ninth Revision, Clinical Modification (ICD–9-CM)*. See Appendix II, Procedure; and table X for ICD–9-CM codes. Rates are based on the civilian population as of July 1. Rates for 1990–99 use population estimates based on the 1990 census adjusted for net underenumeration using the 1990 National Population Adjustment Matrix from the U.S. Bureau of the Census. Rates prior to 2000 are not strictly comparable with rates after 2000 because population estimates for data years before 2000 have not been revised to reflect Census 2000. See Appendix I, National Hospital Discharge Survey.

SOURCE: Centers for Disease Control and Prevention, National Center for Health Statistics, National Hospital Discharge Survey.

Table 101. Hospital admissions, average length of stay, and outpatient visits, according to type of ownership and size of hospital, and percent outpatient surgery: United States, selected years 1975–2003

[Data are based on reporting by a census of hospitals]

Type of ownership and size of hospital	1975	1980	1990	1995	2000	2001	2002	2003
Admissions				Number in thousands				
All hospitals	36,157	38,892	33,774	33,282	34,891	35,644	36,326	36,611
Federal	1,913	2,044	1,759	1,559	1,034	1,001	1,027	973
Non-Federal[1]	34,243	36,848	32,015	31,723	33,946	34,644	35,299	35,637
Community[2]	33,435	36,143	31,181	30,945	33,089	33,814	34,478	34,783
Nonprofit	23,722	25,566	22,878	22,557	24,453	27,983	25,425	25,668
For profit	2,646	3,165	3,066	3,428	4,141	4,197	4,365	4,481
State-local government	7,067	7,413	5,236	4,961	4,496	4,634	4,688	4,634
6–24 beds	174	159	95	124	141	140	162	162
25–49 beds	1,431	1,254	870	944	995	1,030	1,062	1,098
50–99 beds	3,675	3,700	2,474	2,299	2,355	2,422	2,471	2,464
100–199 beds	7,017	7,162	5,833	6,288	6,735	6,778	6,826	6,817
200–299 beds	6,174	6,596	6,333	6,495	6,702	6,630	6,800	6,887
300–399 beds	4,739	5,358	5,091	4,693	5,135	5,328	5,607	5,590
400–499 beds	3,689	4,401	3,644	3,413	3,617	3,779	3,593	3,591
500 beds or more	6,537	7,513	6,840	6,690	7,410	7,706	7,958	8,174
Average length of stay				Number of days				
All hospitals	11.4	9.9	9.1	7.8	6.8	6.7	6.6	6.6
Federal	20.3	16.8	14.9	13.1	12.8	13.2	11.7	11.5
Non-Federal[1]	10.9	9.6	8.8	7.5	6.6	6.6	6.5	6.4
Community[2]	7.7	7.6	7.2	6.5	5.8	5.7	5.7	5.7
Nonprofit	7.8	7.7	7.3	6.4	5.7	5.6	5.6	5.5
For profit	6.6	6.5	6.4	5.8	5.4	5.4	5.3	5.3
State-local government	7.6	7.3	7.7	7.4	6.7	6.7	6.6	6.6
6–24 beds	5.6	5.3	5.4	5.5	4.2	4.0	4.1	4.0
25–49 beds	6.0	5.8	6.1	5.7	5.1	5.0	5.0	5.0
50–99 beds	6.8	6.7	7.2	7.0	6.4	6.4	6.4	6.3
100–199 beds	7.1	7.0	7.1	6.4	5.7	5.7	5.7	5.6
200–299 beds	7.5	7.4	6.9	6.2	5.7	5.6	5.5	5.4
300–399 beds	7.8	7.6	7.0	6.1	5.5	5.4	5.5	5.4
400–499 beds	8.1	7.9	7.3	6.3	5.6	5.6	5.5	5.5
500 beds or more	9.1	8.7	8.1	7.1	6.2	6.1	6.1	6.1
Outpatient visits[3]				Number in thousands				
All hospitals	254,844	262,951	368,184	483,195	592,673	612,276	640,515	648,560
Federal	51,957	50,566	58,527	59,934	63,402	64,035	75,781	74,240
Non-Federal[1]	202,887	212,385	309,657	423,261	531,972	548,242	564,734	574,320
Community[2]	190,672	202,310	301,329	414,345	521,405	538,480	556,404	563,186
Nonprofit	131,435	142,156	221,073	303,851	393,168	404,901	416,910	424,215
For profit	7,713	9,696	20,110	31,940	43,378	44,706	45,215	44,246
State-local government	51,525	50,459	60,146	78,554	84,858	88,873	94,280	94,725
6–24 beds	915	1,155	1,471	3,644	4,555	4,556	5,930	6,512
25–49 beds	5,855	6,227	10,812	19,465	27,007	27,941	29,726	31,261
50–99 beds	16,303	17,976	27,582	38,597	49,385	51,331	53,342	52,959
100–199 beds	35,156	36,453	58,940	91,312	114,183	114,921	117,573	119,856
200–299 beds	32,772	36,073	60,561	84,080	99,248	99,596	102,424	100,095
300–399 beds	29,169	30,495	43,699	54,277	73,444	75,242	79,092	80,938
400–499 beds	22,127	25,501	33,394	44,284	52,205	59,580	57,841	57,203
500 beds or more	48,375	48,430	64,870	78,685	101,378	105,314	110,475	114,362
Outpatient surgery				Percent of total surgeries[4]				
Community hospitals[2]	- - -	16.3	50.5	58.1	62.7	63.0	63.4	63.3

- - - Data not available.

[1]The category of non-Federal hospitals comprises psychiatric, tuberculosis and other respiratory diseases hospitals, and long-term and short-term general and other special hospitals. See Appendix II, Hospital.

[2]Community hospitals are non-Federal short-term general and special hospitals whose facilities and services are available to the public. See Appendix II, Hospital.

[3]Outpatient visits include visits to the emergency department, outpatient department, referred visits (pharmacy, EKG, radiology), and outpatient surgery. See Appendix II, Outpatient visit.

[4]Total surgeries is a measure of patients with at least one surgical procedure. Persons with multiple surgical procedures are counted only once.

NOTE: Data for additional years are available. See Appendix III.

SOURCES: American Hospital Association Annual Survey of Hospitals. Hospital Statistics, 1976, 1981, 1991–2005 Editions. Chicago. (Copyrights 1976, 1981, 1991–2005: Used with the permission of Health Forum LLC, an affiliate of the American Hospital Association.)

Table 102. Nursing home residents 65 years of age and over, according to age, sex, and race: United States, 1973–74, 1985, 1995, and 1999

[Data are based on a sample of nursing home residents]

Age, sex, and race	Residents				Residents per 1,000 population			
	1973–74	1985	1995	1999	1973–74	1985	1995	1999
Age								
65 years and over, age adjusted [1]	. . .	. . .	. . .	. . .	58.5	54.0	45.9	43.3
65 years and over, crude	961,500	1,318,300	1,422,600	1,469,500	44.7	46.2	42.4	42.9
65–74 years	163,100	212,100	190,200	194,800	12.3	12.5	10.1	10.8
75–84 years	384,900	509,000	511,900	517,600	57.7	57.7	45.9	43.0
85 years and over	413,600	597,300	720,400	757,100	257.3	220.3	198.6	182.5
Male								
65 years and over, age adjusted [1]	. . .	. . .	. . .	. . .	42.5	38.8	32.8	30.6
65 years and over, crude	265,700	334,400	356,800	377,800	30.0	29.0	26.1	26.5
65–74 years	65,100	80,600	79,300	84,100	11.3	10.8	9.5	10.3
75–84 years	102,300	141,300	144,300	149,500	39.9	43.0	33.3	30.8
85 years and over	98,300	112,600	133,100	144,200	182.7	145.7	130.8	116.5
Female								
65 years and over, age adjusted [1]	. . .	. . .	. . .	. . .	67.5	61.5	52.3	49.8
65 years and over, crude	695,800	983,900	1,065,800	1,091,700	54.9	57.9	53.7	54.6
65–74 years	98,000	131,500	110,900	110,700	13.1	13.8	10.6	11.2
75–84 years	282,600	367,700	367,600	368,100	68.9	66.4	53.9	51.2
85 years and over	315,300	484,700	587,300	612,900	294.9	250.1	224.9	210.5
White [2]								
65 years and over, age adjusted [1]	. . .	. . .	. . .	. . .	61.2	55.5	45.4	41.9
65 years and over, crude	920,600	1,227,400	1,271,200	1,279,600	46.9	47.7	42.3	42.1
65–74 years	150,100	187,800	154,400	157,200	12.5	12.3	9.3	10.0
75–84 years	369,700	473,600	453,800	440,600	60.3	59.1	44.9	40.5
85 years and over	400,800	566,000	663,000	681,700	270.8	228.7	200.7	181.8
Black or African American [2]								
65 years and over, age adjusted [1]	. . .	. . .	. . .	. . .	28.2	41.5	50.4	55.6
65 years and over, crude	37,700	82,000	122,900	145,900	22.0	35.0	45.2	51.1
65–74 years	12,200	22,500	29,700	30,300	11.1	15.4	18.4	18.2
75–84 years	13,400	30,600	47,300	58,700	26.7	45.3	57.2	66.5
85 years and over	12,100	29,000	45,800	56,900	105.7	141.5	167.1	183.1

. . . Category not applicable.
[1]Age adjusted by the direct method to the year 2000 population standard using the following three age groups: 65–74 years, 75–84 years, and 85 years and over.
[2]Beginning in 1999 the instruction for the race item on the Current Resident Questionnaire was changed so that more than one race could be recorded. In previous years only one racial category could be checked. Estimates for racial groups presented in this table are for residents for whom only one race was recorded. Estimates for residents where multiple races were checked are unreliable due to small sample sizes and are not shown.

NOTES: Excludes residents in personal care or domiciliary care homes. Age refers to age at time of interview. Civilian population estimates used to compute rates for the 1990s are 1990-based postcensal estimates, as of July 1. Starting in 1997, population figures are adjusted for net underenumeration using the 1990 National Population Adjustment Matrix from the U.S. Bureau of the Census. Data for additional years are available. See Appendix III.

SOURCES: Hing E, Sekscenski E, Strahan G. The National Nursing Home Survey: 1985 summary for the United States. National Center for Health Statistics. Vital Health Stat 13(97). 1989; and Centers for Disease Control and Prevention, National Center for Health Statistics, National Nursing Home Survey for other data years.

Table 103. Nursing home residents 65 years of age and over, according to selected functional status and age, sex, and race: United States, 1985, 1995, and 1999

[Data are based on a sample of nursing home residents]

	Functional status[1]											
	Dependent mobility			*Incontinent*			*Dependent eating*			*Dependent mobility, eating, and incontinent*		
Age, sex, and race	*1985*	*1995*	*1999*	*1985*	*1995*	*1999*	*1985*	*1995*	*1999*	*1985*	*1995*	*1999*
All persons	Percent											
65 years and over, age adjusted[2]	75.7	79.0	80.3	55.0	63.8	65.7	40.9	44.9	47.3	32.5	36.5	36.9
65 years and over, crude	74.8	79.0	80.4	54.5	63.8	65.7	40.5	44.9	47.4	32.1	36.5	37.0
65–74 years	61.2	73.0	73.9	42.9	61.9	58.5	33.5	43.8	43.1	25.7	35.8	31.7
75–84 years	70.5	76.5	77.8	55.1	62.5	64.2	39.4	45.2	46.6	30.6	35.3	35.4
85 years and over	83.3	82.4	83.8	58.1	65.3	68.6	43.9	45.0	49.0	35.6	37.5	39.4
Male												
65 years and over, age adjusted[2]	71.2	76.6	76.6	54.2	63.8	66.6	36.0	42.1	45.2	28.0	34.3	35.0
65 years and over, crude	67.8	75.8	75.9	51.9	63.9	66.0	34.9	42.7	45.1	26.9	34.8	35.0
65–74 years	55.8	70.6	70.5	38.8	63.4	59.6	32.8	44.2	45.0	24.1	36.9	34.8
75–84 years	65.7	76.6	76.9	54.4	64.6	68.9	32.6	44.1	44.7	25.5	35.5	35.2
85 years and over	79.2	78.2	78.1	58.1	63.4	66.8	39.2	40.2	45.7	30.9	32.7	34.9
Female												
65 years and over, age adjusted[2]	77.3	79.7	81.5	55.4	63.6	65.0	42.4	45.6	47.8	33.9	36.9	37.2
65 years and over, crude	77.1	80.1	81.9	55.4	63.8	65.6	42.4	45.6	48.1	33.8	37.0	37.7
65–74 years	64.5	74.8	76.4	45.4	60.9	57.7	34.0	43.6	41.6	26.7	35.0	29.3
75–84 years	72.3	76.5	78.2	55.3	61.7	62.2	42.0	45.7	47.4	32.6	35.2	35.6
85 years and over	84.3	83.3	85.2	58.1	65.7	69.0	45.0	46.0	49.7	36.7	38.6	40.4
White[3]												
65 years and over, age adjusted[2]	75.2	78.5	79.9	54.6	63.2	64.9	40.4	44.2	46.1	32.1	35.7	35.7
65 years and over, crude	74.3	78.7	80.2	54.2	63.3	65.1	40.1	44.2	46.2	31.7	35.7	35.8
65–74 years	60.2	71.4	72.6	42.2	60.2	57.1	32.6	41.9	40.7	24.9	33.8	28.8
75–84 years	69.6	76.4	77.5	54.2	61.8	63.8	38.9	44.9	45.8	30.1	34.7	34.8
85 years and over	83.1	81.9	83.6	58.2	65.0	67.8	43.5	44.3	47.7	35.5	36.9	38.1
Black or African American[3]												
65 years and over, age adjusted[2]	83.4	83.2	82.1	61.0	69.3	71.9	49.2	52.2	55.9	38.2	44.0	46.8
65 years and over, crude	81.1	82.1	81.5	59.9	69.1	70.6	47.9	51.7	54.9	37.7	43.7	45.7
65–74 years	70.9	79.6	78.7	48.6	68.3	64.6	43.1	51.2	53.3	33.8	43.1	42.6
75–84 years	82.5	77.8	80.1	70.1	68.9	67.5	47.9	49.5	49.7	40.6	42.3	41.0
85 years and over	87.4	88.0	84.5	57.9	69.8	77.0	51.7	54.3	61.0	37.6	45.5	52.1

[1]Nursing home residents who are dependent in mobility and eating require the assistance of a person or special equipment. Nursing home residents who are incontinent have difficulty in controlling bowels and/or bladder or have an ostomy or indwelling catheter.
[2]Age adjusted by the direct method to the 1995 National Nursing Home Survey population using the following three age groups: 65–74 years, 75–84 years, and 85 years and over.
[3]Beginning in 1999 the instruction for the race item on the Current Resident Questionnaire was changed so that more than one race could be recorded. In previous years only one racial category could be checked. Estimates for racial groups presented in this table are for residents for whom only one race was recorded. Estimates for residents where multiple races were checked are unreliable due to small sample sizes and are not shown.

NOTES: Age refers to age at time of interview. Excludes residents in personal care or domiciliary care homes. Data for additional years are available. See Appendix III.

SOURCES: Hing E, Sekscenski E, Strahan G. The National Nursing Home Survey: 1985 summary for the United States. National Center for Health Statistics. Vital Health Stat 13(97). 1989; and Centers for Disease Control and Prevention, National Center for Health Statistics, National Nursing Home Survey for other data years.

Table 104. Persons employed in health service sites, according to sex: United States, selected years 2000–04

[Data are based on household interviews of a sample of the civilian noninstitutionalized population]

Site	2000	2001	2002	2003	2004
Both sexes	Number of persons in thousands				
All employed civilians[1]	136,891	136,933	136,485	137,736	139,252
All health service sites[2]	12,211	12,558	13,069	13,615	13,817
Offices and clinics of physicians	1,387	1,499	1,533	1,673	1,727
Offices and clinics of dentists	672	701	734	771	780
Offices and clinics of chiropractors	120	111	132	142	156
Offices and clinics of optometrists	95	102	113	92	93
Offices and clinics of other health practitioners[3]	143	140	149	250	274
Outpatient care centers	772	830	850	873	885
Home health care services	548	582	636	741	750
Other health care services[4]	1,027	1,101	1,188	943	976
Hospitals	5,202	5,256	5,330	5,652	5,700
Nursing care facilities	1,593	1,568	1,715	1,877	1,858
Residential care facilities, without nursing	652	668	689	601	618
Men					
All health service sites[2]	2,756	2,778	2,838	2,986	3,067
Offices and clinics of physicians	354	379	370	414	424
Offices and clinics of dentists	158	150	151	163	158
Offices and clinics of chiropractors	32	39	47	53	63
Offices and clinics of optometrists	26	27	29	29	24
Offices and clinics of other health practitioners[3]	38	41	42	63	69
Outpatient care centers	186	185	172	200	203
Home health care services	45	51	54	56	65
Other health care services[4]	304	345	362	297	314
Hospitals	1,241	1,187	1,195	1,263	1,333
Nursing care facilities	195	189	223	267	251
Residential care facilities, without nursing	177	185	193	181	164
Women					
All health service sites[2]	9,457	9,782	10,232	10,631	10,750
Offices and clinics of physicians	1,034	1,120	1,164	1,259	1,302
Offices and clinics of dentists	514	551	584	607	623
Offices and clinics of chiropractors	88	72	85	90	93
Offices and clinics of optometrists	69	75	84	64	69
Offices and clinics of other health practitioners[3]	106	99	106	186	204
Outpatient care centers	586	646	678	673	683
Home health care services	503	531	582	685	685
Other health care services[4]	723	756	826	646	662
Hospitals	3,961	4,069	4,135	4,390	4,366
Nursing care facilities	1,398	1,380	1,492	1,611	1,607
Residential care facilities, without nursing	475	483	496	420	454
Both sexes	Percent of employed civilians				
All health service sites	8.9	9.2	9.6	9.9	9.9
	Percent distribution				
All health service sites	100.0	100.0	100.0	100.0	100.0
Offices and clinics of physicians	11.4	11.9	11.7	12.3	12.5
Offices and clinics of dentists	5.5	5.6	5.6	5.7	5.6
Offices and clinics of chiropractors	1.0	0.9	1.0	1.0	1.1
Offices and clinics of optometrists	0.8	0.8	0.9	0.7	0.7
Offices and clinics of other health practitioners[3]	1.2	1.1	1.1	1.8	2.0
Outpatient care centers	6.3	6.6	6.5	6.4	6.4
Home health care services	4.5	4.6	4.9	5.4	5.4
Other health care services[4]	8.4	8.8	9.1	6.9	7.1
Hospitals	42.6	41.9	40.8	41.5	41.3
Nursing care facilities	13.0	12.5	13.1	13.8	13.4
Residential care facilities, without nursing	5.3	5.3	5.3	4.4	4.5

[1]Excludes workers under the age of 16 years.
[2]Data for health service sites for men and women may not sum to total for all health service sites for both sexes due to rounding.
[3]Includes health service sites such as acupuncture, nutritionists' offices, speech defect clinics, and other offices and clinics. For a complete list of clinics under this category, see www.census.gov/hhes/www/ioindex/cens_797_847.html, Census Industry Code 808.
[4]Includes health service sites such as ambulance services, blood banks, CT-SCAN (computer tomography) centers, and other offices and clinics. For a complete list of clinics under this category, see www.census.gov/hhes/www/ioindex/cens_797_847.html, Census Industry Code 818.

NOTES: Annual data are based on data collected each month and averaged over the year. Health service sites are based on the 2002 North American Industry Classification System. See Appendix II, Industry of employment.

SOURCES: U.S. Department of Labor, Bureau of Labor Statistics, Current Population Survey: Employment and Earnings, January 2005 at www.bls.gov/cps/home.htm#annual (table 18) and unpublished data.

Table 105 (page 1 of 2). Active physicians and doctors of medicine in patient care, according to geographic division and State: United States, 1975, 1985, 1995, and 2003

[Data are based on reporting by physicians]

Geographic division and State	Total physicians[1] 1975	1985	1995[3]	2003[4,5]	Doctors of medicine in patient care[2] 1975	1985	1995	2003[5]
	Number per 10,000 civilian population							
United States	15.3	20.7	24.2	26.6	13.5	18.0	21.3	23.5
New England	19.1	26.7	32.5	36.3	16.9	22.9	28.8	32.3
Connecticut	19.8	27.6	32.8	34.9	17.7	24.3	29.5	31.2
Maine	12.8	18.7	22.3	29.9	10.7	15.6	18.2	24.1
Massachusetts	20.8	30.2	37.5	40.8	18.3	25.4	33.2	36.5
New Hampshire	14.3	18.1	21.5	26.3	13.1	16.7	19.8	24.0
Rhode Island	17.8	23.3	30.4	34.3	16.1	20.2	26.7	30.7
Vermont	18.2	23.8	26.9	35.0	15.5	20.3	24.2	32.1
Middle Atlantic	19.5	26.1	32.4	34.3	17.0	22.2	28.0	29.6
New Jersey	16.2	23.4	29.3	32.1	14.0	19.8	24.9	27.3
New York	22.7	29.0	35.3	37.1	20.2	25.2	31.6	33.1
Pennsylvania	16.6	23.6	30.1	31.5	13.9	19.2	24.6	25.7
East North Central	13.9	19.3	23.3	25.9	12.0	16.4	19.8	22.2
Illinois	14.5	20.5	24.8	27.1	13.1	18.2	22.1	23.9
Indiana	10.6	14.7	18.4	21.8	9.6	13.2	16.6	19.7
Michigan	15.4	20.8	24.8	26.7	12.0	16.0	19.0	20.9
Ohio	14.1	19.9	23.8	26.5	12.2	16.8	20.0	22.6
Wisconsin	12.5	17.7	21.5	24.8	11.4	15.9	19.6	22.8
West North Central	13.3	18.3	21.8	24.6	11.4	15.6	18.9	21.3
Iowa	11.4	15.6	19.2	21.6	9.4	12.4	15.1	16.6
Kansas	12.8	17.3	20.8	23.0	11.2	15.1	18.0	19.8
Minnesota	14.9	20.5	23.4	27.0	13.7	18.5	21.5	24.8
Missouri	15.0	20.5	23.9	25.7	11.6	16.3	19.7	21.3
Nebraska	12.1	15.7	19.8	23.6	10.9	14.4	18.3	21.9
North Dakota	9.7	15.8	20.5	23.5	9.2	14.9	18.9	21.8
South Dakota	8.2	13.4	16.7	21.3	7.7	12.3	15.7	19.9
South Atlantic	14.0	19.7	23.4	26.4	12.6	17.6	21.0	23.6
Delaware	14.3	19.7	23.4	26.6	12.7	17.1	19.7	22.6
District of Columbia	39.6	55.3	63.6	70.7	34.6	45.6	53.6	60.2
Florida	15.2	20.2	22.9	25.4	13.4	17.8	20.3	22.4
Georgia	11.5	16.2	19.7	21.8	10.6	14.7	18.0	19.8
Maryland	18.6	30.4	34.1	39.1	16.5	24.9	29.9	33.6
North Carolina	11.7	16.9	21.1	24.5	10.6	15.0	19.4	22.6
South Carolina	10.0	14.7	18.9	22.5	9.3	13.6	17.6	20.9
Virginia	12.9	19.5	22.5	26.4	11.9	17.8	20.8	24.4
West Virginia	11.0	16.3	21.0	24.2	10.0	14.6	17.9	20.5
East South Central	10.5	15.0	19.2	22.3	9.7	14.0	17.8	20.5
Alabama	9.2	14.2	18.4	21.1	8.6	13.1	17.0	19.3
Kentucky	10.9	15.1	19.2	22.4	10.1	13.9	18.0	20.6
Mississippi	8.4	11.8	13.9	18.3	8.0	11.1	13.0	16.7
Tennessee	12.4	17.7	22.5	25.1	11.3	16.2	20.8	23.3
West South Central	11.9	16.4	19.5	21.4	10.5	14.5	17.3	19.1
Arkansas	9.1	13.8	17.3	20.2	8.5	12.8	16.0	18.6
Louisiana	11.4	17.3	21.7	25.1	10.5	16.1	20.3	23.7
Oklahoma	11.6	16.1	18.8	19.9	9.4	12.9	14.7	15.5
Texas	12.5	16.8	19.4	21.0	11.0	14.7	17.3	18.9
Mountain	14.3	17.8	20.2	22.5	12.6	15.7	17.8	19.8
Arizona	16.7	20.2	21.4	22.7	14.1	17.1	18.2	18.9
Colorado	17.3	20.7	23.7	26.2	15.0	17.7	20.6	22.8
Idaho	9.5	12.1	13.9	17.7	8.9	11.4	13.1	16.1
Montana	10.6	14.0	18.4	23.0	10.1	13.2	17.1	21.4
Nevada	11.9	16.0	16.7	19.0	10.9	14.5	14.6	17.2
New Mexico	12.2	17.0	20.2	23.5	10.1	14.7	18.0	21.1
Utah	14.1	17.2	19.2	20.8	13.0	15.5	17.6	19.1
Wyoming	9.5	12.9	15.3	19.4	8.9	12.0	13.9	18.1

See footnotes at end of table.

Table 105 (page 2 of 2). Active physicians and doctors of medicine in patient care, according to geographic division and State: United States, 1975, 1985, 1995, and 2003

[Data are based on reporting by physicians]

Geographic division and State	Total physicians[1]				Doctors of medicine in patient care[2]			
	1975	1985	1995[3]	2003[4,5]	1975	1985	1995	2003[5]
	Number per 10,000 civilian population							
Pacific	17.9	22.5	23.3	25.5	16.3	20.5	21.2	23.1
Alaska	8.4	13.0	15.7	23.2	7.8	12.1	14.2	20.4
California	18.8	23.7	23.7	25.2	17.3	21.5	21.7	22.8
Hawaii	16.2	21.5	24.8	30.9	14.7	19.8	22.8	28.1
Oregon	15.6	19.7	21.6	25.9	13.8	17.6	19.5	23.5
Washington	15.3	20.2	22.5	26.1	13.6	17.9	20.2	23.7

[1]Includes active doctors of medicine and active doctors of osteopathy. See Appendix II, Physician.
[2]Excludes doctors of osteopathy (DOs); States with more than 2,500 active DOs are Pennsylvania, Michigan, Florida, Ohio, California, New York, and New Jersey. States with fewer than 100 active DOs are Wyoming, Vermont, North Dakota, District of Columbia, South Dakota, Montana, and Nebraska. Excludes doctors of medicine in medical teaching, administration, research, and other nonpatient care activities.
[3]Data for doctors of osteopathy are as of July 1996.
[4]Data for doctors of osteopathy are as of June 2003.
[5]Data for the year 2003 include Federal and non-Federal physicians. Prior to the year 2003, the data include non-Federal physicians only.

NOTES: Data for doctors of medicine are as of December 31. Data for additional years are available. See Appendix III.

SOURCES: American Medical Association (AMA). Physician distribution and medical licensure in the U.S., 1975; Physician characteristics and distribution in the U.S., 1986 edition; 1996–97 edition; 2005 edition; Department of Physician Practice and Communication Information, Division of Survey and Data Resources, AMA. (Copyrights 1976, 1986, 1997, 2005: Used with the permission of the AMA); American Osteopathic Association: 1975–76 Yearbook and Directory of Osteopathic Physicians, 1985–86 Yearbook and Directory of Osteopathic Physicians; American Association of Colleges of Osteopathic Medicine: 2003 Annual Report on Osteopathic Medical Education, 2004.

Table 106. Doctors of medicine, according to activity and place of medical education: United States and outlying U.S. areas, selected years 1975–2003

[Data are based on reporting by physicians]

Activity and place of medical education	1975	1985	1995	1999	2000	2001	2002	2003[1]
	Number of doctors of medicine							
Doctors of medicine	393,742	552,716	720,325	797,634	813,770	836,156	853,187	871,535
Professionally active[2]	340,280	497,140	625,443	669,949	692,368	713,375	719,431	736,211
Place of medical education:								
U.S. medical graduates	- - -	392,007	481,137	510,738	525,691	537,529	544,779	558,167
International medical graduates[3]	- - -	105,133	144,306	158,211	164,437	171,639	172,770	178,044
Activity:								
Non-Federal	312,089	475,573	604,364	650,899	672,987	693,358	699,249	- - -
Patient care[4]	287,837	431,527	564,074	610,656	631,431	652,328	658,123	691,873
Office-based practice	213,334	329,041	427,275	473,241	490,398	514,016	516,246	529,836
General and family practice	46,347	53,862	59,932	66,246	67,534	70,030	71,696	73,508
Cardiovascular diseases	5,046	9,054	13,739	15,586	16,300	16,991	16,989	17,301
Dermatology	3,442	5,325	6,959	7,788	7,969	8,199	8,282	8,477
Gastroenterology	1,696	4,135	7,300	8,185	8,515	8,905	9,044	9,326
Internal medicine	28,188	52,712	72,612	84,633	88,699	94,674	96,496	99,670
Pediatrics	12,687	22,392	33,890	40,502	42,215	44,824	46,097	47,996
Pulmonary diseases	1,166	3,035	4,964	5,745	6,095	6,596	6,672	6,919
General surgery	19,710	24,708	24,086	26,822	24,475	25,632	24,902	25,284
Obstetrics and gynecology	15,613	23,525	29,111	31,103	31,726	32,582	32,738	33,636
Ophthalmology	8,795	12,212	14,596	15,238	15,598	15,994	16,052	16,240
Orthopedic surgery	8,148	13,033	17,136	16,974	17,367	17,829	18,118	18,423
Otolaryngology	4,297	5,751	7,139	7,282	7,581	7,866	8,001	8,103
Plastic surgery	1,706	3,299	4,612	5,127	5,308	5,545	5,593	5,725
Urological surgery	5,025	7,081	7,991	8,229	8,460	8,636	8,615	8,804
Anesthesiology	8,970	15,285	23,770	26,635	27,624	28,868	28,661	29,254
Diagnostic radiology	1,978	7,735	12,751	14,259	14,622	15,596	15,896	16,403
Emergency medicine	- - -	- - -	11,700	13,932	14,541	15,823	16,907	17,727
Neurology	1,862	4,691	7,623	8,065	8,559	9,156	9,034	9,304
Pathology, anatomical/clinical	4,195	6,877	9,031	10,074	10,267	10,554	10,103	10,209
Psychiatry	12,173	18,521	23,334	24,393	24,955	25,653	25,350	25,656
Radiology	6,970	7,355	5,994	6,523	6,674	6,830	6,916	7,010
Other specialty	15,320	28,453	29,005	29,900	35,314	37,233	34,084	34,861
Hospital-based practice	74,503	102,486	136,799	137,225	141,033	138,312	141,877	162,037
Residents and interns[5]	53,527	72,159	93,650	92,461	95,125	92,935	96,547	100,033
Full-time hospital staff	20,976	30,327	43,149	44,764	45,908	45,377	45,330	62,004
Other professional activity[6]	24,252	44,046	40,290	41,243	41,556	41,118	41,126	44,338
Federal[7]	28,191	21,567	21,079	18,050	19,381	20,017	20,182	- - -
Patient care	24,100	17,293	18,057	14,678	15,999	16,611	16,701	- - -
Office-based practice	2,095	1,156	. . .	. . .	. . .	. . .	. . .	- - -
Hospital-based practice	22,005	16,137	18,057	14,678	15,999	16,611	16,701	- - -
Residents and interns	4,275	3,252	2,702	375	600	739	390	- - -
Full-time hospital staff	17,730	12,885	15,355	14,303	15,399	15,872	16,311	- - -
Other professional activity[6]	4,091	4,274	3,022	3,372	3,382	3,406	3,481	- - -
Inactive	21,449	38,646	72,326	75,893	75,168	81,520	84,166	84,360
Not classified	26,145	13,950	20,579	50,906	45,136	38,314	49,067	50,447
Unknown address	5,868	2,980	1,977	886	1,098	2,947	523	517

- - - Data not available.
. . . Category not applicable.
[1]Activity data for the year 2003 include Federal and non-Federal physicians.
[2]Excludes inactive, not classified, and address unknown. See Appendix II, Physician.
[3]International medical graduates received their medical education in schools outside the United States and Canada.
[4]Specialty information based on the physician's self-designated primary area of practice. Categories include generalists and specialists. See Appendix II, Physician specialty.
[5]Beginning in 1990 clinical fellows are included in this category. In prior years clinical fellows were included in Other professional activity.
[6]Includes medical teaching, administration, research, and other. Prior to 1990 this category also included clinical fellows.
[7]Beginning in 1993 data collection for Federal physicians was revised.

NOTES: Data for doctors of medicine are as of December 31, except for 1990–94 data, which are as of January 1. Outlying areas include Puerto Rico, Virgin Islands, and the Pacific islands of Canton, Caroline, Guam, Mariana, Marshall, American Samoa, and Wake. Data for additional years are available. See Appendix III.

SOURCES: American Medical Association (AMA). Distribution of physicians in the United States, 1970; Physician distribution and medical licensure in the U.S., 1975; Physician characteristics and distribution in the U.S., 1981, 1986, 1989, 1990, 1992, 1993, 1994, 1995–96, 1996–97, 1997–98, 1999, 2000–2001, 2001–2002, 2002–2003, 2003–2004, 2004, 2005 editions, Department of Physician Practice and Communications Information, Division of Survey and Data Resources, AMA. (Copyrights 1971, 1976, 1982, 1986, 1989, 1990, 1992, 1993, 1994, 1996, 1997, 1997, 1999, 2000, 2001, 2002, 2003, 2005: Used with the permission of the AMA.)

Table 107. Doctors of medicine in primary care, according to specialty: United States and outlying U.S. areas, selected years 1949–2003

[Data are based on reporting by physicians]

Specialty	1949[1]	1960[1]	1970	1980	1990	1995	2000	2001	2002	2003
					Number					
Total doctors of medicine[2]	201,277	260,484	334,028	467,679	615,421	720,325	813,770	836,156	853,187	871,535
Active doctors of medicine[3]	191,577	247,257	310,929	435,545	559,988	646,022	737,504	751,689	768,498	786,658
General primary care specialists	113,222	125,359	134,354	170,705	213,514	241,329	274,653	283,583	286,294	293,701
General practice/family medicine	95,980	88,023	57,948	60,049	70,480	75,976	86,312	88,597	89,357	91,545
Internal medicine	12,453	26,209	39,924	58,462	76,295	88,240	101,353	105,229	106,499	109,317
Obstetrics/Gynecology	---	---	18,532	24,612	30,220	33,519	35,922	36,869	36,810	37,725
Pediatrics	4,789	11,127	17,950	27,582	36,519	43,594	51,066	52,888	53,628	55,114
Primary care subspecialists	---	---	3,161	16,642	30,911	39,659	52,294	55,871	57,929	60,589
Family medicine	---	---	---	---	---	236	483	564	627	691
Internal medicine	---	---	1,948	13,069	22,054	26,928	34,831	37,558	38,821	40,598
Obstetrics/Gynecology	---	---	344	1,693	3,477	4,133	4,319	4,173	4,228	4,191
Pediatrics	---	---	869	1,880	5,380	8,362	12,661	13,576	14,253	15,109
					Percent of active doctors of medicine					
General primary care specialists	59.1	50.7	43.2	39.2	38.1	37.4	37.2	37.7	37.3	37.3
General practice/family medicine	50.1	35.6	18.6	13.8	12.6	11.8	11.7	11.8	11.6	11.6
Internal medicine	6.5	10.6	12.8	13.4	13.6	13.7	13.7	14.0	13.9	13.9
Obstetrics/Gynecology	---	---	6.0	5.7	5.4	5.2	4.9	4.9	4.8	4.8
Pediatrics	2.5	4.5	5.8	6.3	6.5	6.7	6.9	7.0	7.0	7.0
Primary care subspecialists	---	---	1.0	3.8	5.5	6.1	7.1	7.4	7.5	7.7
Family medicine	---	---	---	---	---	0.0	0.1	0.1	0.1	0.1
Internal medicine	---	---	0.6	3.0	3.9	4.2	4.7	5.0	5.1	5.2
Obstetrics/Gynecology	---	---	0.1	0.4	0.6	0.6	0.6	0.6	0.6	0.5
Pediatrics	---	---	0.3	0.4	1.0	1.3	1.7	1.8	1.9	1.9

0.0 Percent greater than zero but less than 0.05.
--- Data not available.
[1]Estimated by the Bureau of Health Professions, Health Resources Administration. Active doctors of medicine (M.D.'s) include those with address unknown and primary specialty not classified.
[2]Includes M.D.'s engaged in Federal and non-Federal patient care (office-based or hospital-based) and other professional activities.
[3]Beginning in 1970, M.D.'s who are inactive, have unknown address, or primary specialty not classified are excluded. See Appendix II, Physician.

NOTES: See Appendix II, Physician specialty. Data are as of December 31 except for 1990–94 data, which are as of January 1, and 1949 data, which are as of midyear. Outlying areas include Puerto Rico, Virgin Islands, and the Pacific islands of Canton, Caroline, Guam, Mariana, Marshall, American Samoa, and Wake. Data for additional years are available. See Appendix III.

SOURCES: Health Manpower Source Book: Medical Specialists, USDHEW, 1962; American Medical Association (AMA). Distribution of physicians in the United States, 1970; Physician characteristics and distribution in the U.S., 1981, 1992, 1996–97, 1997–98, 1999, 2000–2001, 2001–2002, 2002–2003, 2003–2004, 2004, 2005 editions, Department of Data Survey and Planning, Division of Survey and Data Resources, AMA. (Copyrights 1971, 1982, 1992, 1996, 1997, 1997, 1999, 2000, 2001, 2002, 2003, 2004, 2005: Used with the permission of the AMA.)

Table 108. Active health personnel according to occupation: United States, selected years 1980–2001

[Data are compiled by the Bureau of Health Professions]

Occupation	1980	1985[1]	1990	1995	1999	2000[2]	2001
			Number of active health personnel				
Chiropractors	25,600	35,000	42,400	52,100	61,500	64,100	66,800
Dentists[3]	121,900	133,500	147,500	158,600	164,700	168,000	- - -
Nurses, registered[4]	1,272,900	1,538,100	1,789,600	2,115,800	2,201,800	- - -	- - -
Associate and diploma	908,300	1,024,500	1,107,300	1,235,100	1,237,400	- - -	- - -
Baccalaureate	297,300	419,900	549,000	673,200	731,200	- - -	- - -
Masters and doctorate	67,300	93,700	133,300	207,500	229,200	- - -	- - -
Nutritionists/Dieticians	32,000	- - -	57,000	- - -	- - -	90,000	- - -
Occupational therapists	25,000	- - -	42,000	- - -	- - -	72,000	- - -
Optometrists	21,900	24,000	26,000	28,900	31,500	32,200	- - -
Pharmacists	142,400	153,500	168,000	181,000	193,400	196,000	- - -
Physical therapists	50,000	- - -	92,000	- - -	- - -	130,000	- - -
Physicians	427,122	542,653	567,610	672,859	753,176	772,296	793,263
Federal	17,642	23,305	20,784	21,153	17,338	19,228	20,017
Doctors of medicine[5]	16,585	21,938	19,166	19,830	17,224	19,110	20,017
Doctors of osteopathy[6]	1,057	1,367	1,618	1,323	114	118	- - -
Non-Federal	409,480	519,348	546,826	651,706	735,838	753,068	773,246
Doctors of medicine[5]	393,407	497,473	520,450	617,362	693,345	708,463	731,672
Doctors of osteopathy[6]	16,073	21,875	26,376	34,344	42,493	44,605	41,574
Podiatrists[7]	7,780	9,620	10,353	10,304	11,853	12,242	- - -
Speech therapists	50,000	- - -	65,000	- - -	- - -	121,000	- - -
			Number per 100,000 population				
Chiropractors	11.3	14.6	17.0	19.6	22.0	22.8	23.5
Dentists[3]	54.0	56.5	59.1	59.6	59.0	59.5	- - -
Nurses, registered[4]	560.0	641.4	716.9	794.6	789.1	- - -	- - -
Associate and diploma	399.9	425.8	443.6	463.8	443.4	- - -	- - -
Baccalaureate	130.9	175.6	219.9	252.8	262.0	- - -	- - -
Masters and doctorate	29.6	39.9	53.4	77.9	82.1	- - -	- - -
Nutritionists/Dieticians	14.0	- - -	22.8	- - -	- - -	31.9	- - -
Occupational therapists	10.9	- - -	16.8	- - -	- - -	25.5	- - -
Optometrists	9.6	10.1	10.4	10.9	11.3	11.4	- - -
Pharmacists	62.5	66.3	67.3	68.0	69.3	69.5	- - -
Physical therapists	21.8	- - -	36.9	- - -	- - -	46.1	- - -
Physicians	189.8	221.3	223.9	248.9	265.9	269.7	274.3
Federal	7.8	9.5	8.2	7.8	6.1	6.7	6.9
Doctors of medicine[5]	7.4	8.9	7.6	7.3	6.1	6.7	6.9
Doctors of osteopathy[6]	0.5	0.6	0.6	0.5	0.0	0.0	- - -
Non-Federal	182.0	211.8	215.7	241.1	259.8	263.0	267.3
Doctors of medicine[5]	174.9	202.9	205.3	228.4	244.8	247.4	253.0
Doctors of osteopathy[6]	7.1	8.9	10.4	12.7	15.0	15.6	14.4
Podiatrists[7]	3.4	4.0	4.1	3.9	4.3	4.4	- - -
Speech therapists	21.8	- - -	26.0	- - -	- - -	42.9	- - -

- - - Data not available.
[1]Osteopath, podiatric, and chiropractic data are for 1986.
[2]Data for speech therapists are for 1996.
[3]Excludes dentists in military service, U.S. Public Health Service, and Department of Veterans Affairs.
[4]See Appendix II, Nurse Supply Estimates. In 1999 the total number of registered nurses includes an estimated 4,000 nurses whose highest nursing-related educational preparation was not known.
[5]Excludes physicians with unknown addresses and those who do not practice or practice fewer than 20 hours per week. 1990 data for doctors of medicine are as of January 1; in other years these data are as of December 31. See Appendix II, Physician.
[6]Beginning in 2001, doctors of osteopathy include Federal and non-Federal doctors of osteopathy.
[7]Podiatrists in patient care.

NOTE: Ratios for all health occupations are based on resident population.

SOURCES: National Center for Health Workforce Analysis, Bureau of Health Professions: United States Health Personnel FACTBOOK. Health Resources and Services Administration. Rockville, Md., June 2003 and unpublished data; American Medical Association. Physician characteristics and distribution in the U.S., 1981, 1986, 1992, 1996–97, 2001–2002, 2002–2003, and 2003–2004 editions. Chicago, 1982, 1986, 1992, 1997, 2001, 2002, and 2003; American Osteopathic Association. 1980–81 Yearbook and Directory of Osteopathic Physicians. Chicago, 1980. American Association of Colleges of Osteopathic Medicine. Annual statistical report, 1990, 1997, 1999, 2000, and 2001 editions. Rockville, MD, 1990, 1997, 2000, 2001, and 2002; Bureau of Labor Statistics: unpublished data.

Table 109. First-year enrollment and graduates of health professions schools and number of schools, according to profession: United States, selected years 1980–2003

[Data are based on reporting by health professions schools]

Profession	1980	1985	1990	1995	2000	2002	2003
First-year enrollment				Number			
Dentistry	6,132	5,047	3,979	4,121	4,314	4,407	4,448
Medicine (Allopathic)	16,930	16,997	16,756	17,085	16,856	16,875	16,953
Medicine (Osteopathic)	1,426	1,750	1,844	2,217	2,848	3,043	3,079
Nursing:							
Licensed practical	56,316	47,034	52,969	57,906	- - -	- - -	- - -
Registered, total	105,952	118,224	108,580	127,184	- - -	- - -	- - -
Baccalaureate	35,414	39,573	29,858	43,451	- - -	- - -	- - -
Associate degree	53,633	63,776	68,634	76,016	- - -	- - -	- - -
Diploma	16,905	14,875	10,088	7,717	- - -	- - -	- - -
Optometry	1,202	1,187	1,258	1,390	1,410	- - -	1,416
Pharmacy	8,035	6,986	8,267	8,740	8,382	9,128	9,909
Podiatry	695	811	561	630	475	419	441
Public Health[1]	- - -	- - -	4,392	5,332	5,840	6,329	6,786
Graduates							
Dentistry	5,256	5,353	4,233	3,908	4,171	4,349	4,443
Medicine (Allopathic)	15,113	16,318	15,398	15,883	15,718	15,648	15,499
Medicine (Osteopathic)	1,059	1,474	1,529	1,843	2,279	2,536	2,607
Nursing:[2]							
Licensed practical	41,892	36,955	35,417	44,234	- - -	- - -	- - -
Registered, total	75,523	82,075	66,088	97,052	- - -	72,882	- - -
Baccalaureate	24,994	24,975	18,571	31,254	- - -	30,522	- - -
Associate degree	36,034	45,208	42,318	58,749	- - -	40,073	- - -
Diploma	14,495	11,892	5,199	7,049	- - -	2,287	- - -
Occupational therapy	- - -	- - -	2,424	3,473	- - -	- - -	- - -
Optometry	1,073	1,114	1,115	1,219	1,315	1,309	1,305
Pharmacy	7,432	5,735	6,956	7,837	7,260	7,573	7,488
Podiatry	597	582	679	558	583	478	436
Public Health	3,326	3,047	3,549	4,636	5,879	5,664	5,906
Schools							
Dentistry	60	60	58	54	55	56	56
Medicine (Allopathic)	126	127	127	125	125	125	126
Medicine (Osteopathic)	14	15	15	16	19	19	19
Nursing:[3]							
Licensed practical	1,299	1,165	1,154	1,210	- - -	- - -	- - -
Registered, total	1,385	1,473	1,470	1,516	- - -	1,459	- - -
Baccalaureate	377	441	489	521	- - -	526	- - -
Associate degree	697	776	829	876	- - -	857	- - -
Diploma	311	256	152	119	- - -	76	- - -
Occupational therapy	50	61	69	98	142	- - -	- - -
Optometry	16	17	17	17	17	17	17
Pharmacy	72	72	74	75	81	83	89
Podiatry	5	7	7	7	7	7	7
Public Health	21	23	25	27	28	32	33

- - - Data not available.
[1]Number of students entering Schools of Public Health for the first time.
[2]Data for 2000–2002 exclude American Samoa, Guam, Puerto Rico, and the Virgin Islands.
[3]Some nursing schools offer more than one type of program. Numbers shown for nursing are number of nursing programs.

NOTES: Some numbers in this table have been revised and differ from previous editions of *Health, United States*. Data on the number of schools are reported as of the beginning of the academic year while data on first-year enrollment and number of graduates are reported as of the end of the academic year.

SOURCES: Association of American Medical Colleges: AAMC Data Book, Statistical Information Related to Medical Schools and Teaching Hospitals, 2004. Washington, DC. 2004 and unpublished data (Copyright 2005: Used with the permission of the AMA); Bureau of Health Professions: United States Health Personnel FACTBOOK. Health Resources and Services Administration. Rockville, MD. 2003; National League for Nursing: unpublished data; American Dental Association: 2002–03 Survey of Predoctoral Dental Education, vol.1, Academic Programs, Enrollments, and Graduates, Chicago. 2004; American Dental Education Association: www.adea.org/ADEA.html; American Association of Colleges of Osteopathic Medicine. 2003 Annual Report on Osteopathic Medical Education, Chevy Chase, MD. 2004; Association of Schools of Public Health: 2003 Annual Data Report. Washington, DC. 2004; Association of Schools and Colleges of Optometry: Annual Student Data Report Academic Year 2003–2004 and unpublished data; American Association of Colleges of Pharmacy: Academic Pharmacy's Vital Statistics, 2004 and unpublished data; American Association of Colleges of Podiatric Medicine: unpublished data; American Medical Association: Health Professions Career and Education Directory, 29th edition. Chicago. 2001.

Table 110 (page 1 of 2). Total enrollment of minorities in schools for selected health occupations, according to detailed race and Hispanic origin: United States, academic years 1980–81, 1990–91, 2001–02, and 2002–03

[Data are based on reporting by health professions associations]

Occupation, detailed race, and Hispanic origin	*1980–81*	*1990–91*	*2001–02*	*2002–03*	*1980–81*	*1990–91*	*2001–02*	*2002–03*[1]
Dentistry	Number of students				Percent distribution of students			
All races	22,842	15,951	17,487	17,657	100.0	100.0	100.0	100.0
Not Hispanic or Latino:								
White[2]	19,947	11,185	11,411	11,243	87.3	70.1	65.3	63.7
Black or African American	1,022	940	854	904	4.5	5.9	4.9	5.1
Hispanic or Latino[3]	780	1,254	1,030	1,066	3.4	7.9	5.9	6.0
American Indian or Alaska Native	53	53	74	80	0.2	0.3	0.4	0.5
Asian or Pacific Islander	1,040	2,519	4,118	4,041	4.6	15.8	23.5	22.9
Medicine (Allopathic)								
All races[2,4]	65,189	65,163	66,989	66,334	100.0	100.0	100.0	100.0
Not Hispanic or Latino:								
White	55,434	47,893	41,737	42,435	85.0	73.5	62.3	64.0
Black or African American	3,708	4,241	4,746	4,905	5.7	6.5	7.1	7.4
Hispanic or Latino	2,761	3,538	4,167	4,264	4.2	5.4	6.2	6.4
Mexican	951	1,109	1,630	1,614	1.5	1.7	2.4	2.4
Mainland Puerto Rican	329	457	447	321	0.5	0.7	0.7	0.5
Other Hispanic or Latino[5]	1,481	1,972	2,090	2,329	2.3	3.0	3.1	3.5
American Indian or Alaska Native[6]	221	277	527	567	0.3	0.4	0.8	0.9
Asian or Pacific Islander	1,924	8,436	13,139	13,589	3.0	12.9	19.6	20.5
Medicine (Osteopathic)								
All races[2]	4,940	6,792	11,101	11,432	100.0	100.0	100.0	100.0
Not Hispanic or Latino:								
White	4,688	5,680	8,062	8,410	94.9	83.6	72.6	73.6
Black or African American	94	217	407	404	1.9	3.2	3.7	3.5
Hispanic or Latino	52	277	386	420	1.1	4.1	3.5	3.7
American Indian or Alaska Native	19	36	68	82	0.4	0.5	0.6	0.7
Asian or Pacific Islander	87	582	1,817	1,782	1.8	8.6	16.4	15.6
Nursing, registered[7]								
All races	230,966	221,170	221,334	- - -	- - -	100.0	100.0	- - -
Not Hispanic or Latino:								
White[2]	- - -	183,102	173,585	- - -	- - -	82.8	78.4	- - -
Black or African American	- - -	23,094	26,026	- - -	- - -	10.4	11.8	- - -
Hispanic or Latino	- - -	6,580	10,886	- - -	- - -	3.0	4.9	- - -
American Indian or Alaska Native	- - -	1,803	2,516	- - -	- - -	0.8	1.1	- - -
Asian or Pacific Islander	- - -	6,591	8,321	- - -	- - -	3.0	3.8	- - -
Optometry								
All races[2]	4,641	4,760	- - -	5,354	100.0	100.0	- - -	100.0
Not Hispanic or Latino:								
White	4,221	3,706	- - -	3,230	91.0	77.9	- - -	60.3
Black or African American	57	134	- - -	171	1.2	2.8	- - -	3.2
Hispanic or Latino	108	296	- - -	302	2.3	6.2	- - -	5.6
American Indian or Alaska Native	12	21	- - -	35	0.3	0.4	- - -	0.7
Asian or Pacific Islander	243	603	- - -	1,254	5.2	12.7	- - -	23.4
Pharmacy[8]								
All races[2]	21,628	29,797	35,885	38,902	100.0	100.0	100.0	100.0
Not Hispanic or Latino:								
White	19,153	21,717	21,088	22,764	88.6	80.5	58.8	58.5
Black or African American	945	2,103	3,407	3,826	4.4	5.7	9.5	9.8
Hispanic or Latino	459	1,118	1,322	1,466	2.1	4.2	3.7	3.8
American Indian or Alaska Native	36	85	179	168	0.2	0.3	0.5	0.4
Asian or Pacific Islander	1,035	3,346	7,506	8,263	4.8	9.4	20.9	21.2

See footnotes at end of table.

Table 110 (page 2 of 2). Total enrollment of minorities in schools for selected health occupations, according to detailed race and Hispanic origin: United States, academic years 1980–81, 1990–91,2001–02, and 2002–03

[Data are based on reporting by health professions associations]

Occupation, detailed race, and Hispanic origin	*1980–81*	*1990–91*	*2001–02*	*2002–03*	*1980–81*	*1990–91*	*2001–02*	*2002–03*[1]
Podiatry	Number of students				Percent distribution of students			
All races[2]	2,577	2,221	1,783	1,637	100.0	100.0	100.0	100.0
Not Hispanic or Latino:								
White	2,353	1,671	1,108	993	91.3	75.2	62.1	60.7
Black or African American	110	235	190	192	4.3	10.6	10.7	11.7
Hispanic or Latino	39	149	116	119	1.5	6.7	6.5	7.3
American Indian or Alaska Native	6	7	14	11	0.2	0.3	0.8	0.7
Asian or Pacific Islander	69	159	234	208	2.7	7.2	13.1	12.7

- - - Data not available.
[1]Data for optometry are for 2003–04.
[2]Includes other and unknown races; foreign students were included in total for osteopathic medicine and optometry; starting in 1992–93, foreign students were excluded from total for allopathic medicine.
[3]Includes students from University of Puerto Rico.
[4]Starting in 2002–03, counts by race and ethnicity are in combination or alone and do not sum to the unduplicated total.
[5]Includes The Commonwealth of Puerto Rico students.
[6]Starting in 1997–98, includes American Indian, Alaska Native, and Native Hawaiian; prior to 1997, included only American Indian and Alaska Native.
[7]In 1990 the National League for Nursing developed a new system for analyzing minority data. In evaluating the former system, much underreporting was noted. Therefore, race-specific data before 1990 would not be comparable and are not shown. Additional changes in the minority data question were introduced for academic years 2000–01 and 2001–02, resulting in a discontinuity in the trend.
[8]Prior to 1992–93, pharmacy total enrollment data were for students in the final 3 years of pharmacy education. Beginning in 1992–93, pharmacy data are for all students.

NOTES: Total enrollment data are collected at the beginning of the academic year. Data for chiropractic students, occupational and physical therapy students, and public health students were not available for this table. Some numbers have been revised and differ from the previous edition of *Health, United States*.

SOURCES: Association of American Medical Colleges: AAMC Data Book: Statistical Information Related to Medical Education. Washington, DC. 2004 (Copyright 2005: Used with the permission of the AAMC.). AAMC Data Warehouse, unpublished data; American Association of Colleges of Osteopathic Medicine: 2003 Annual Report on Osteopathic Medical Education. Chevy Chase, Maryland. 2004; Bureau of Health Professions: Minorities and Women in the Health Fields, 1990 Edition; American Dental Association: 2002–03 Survey of Predoctoral Dental Education, vol.1, Academic Programs, Enrollments, and Graduates, Chicago. 2004; American Dental Education Association: www.adea.org/ADEA.html and unpublished data; Association of Schools and Colleges of Optometry: Annual Student Data Report Academic Year 2003–2004 and unpublished data; American Association of Colleges of Pharmacy: Profile of Pharmacy Students, Fall 2002; American Association of Colleges of Podiatric Medicine: unpublished data; National League for Nursing: unpublished data.

Table 111. First-year and total enrollment of women in schools for selected health occupations, according to detailed race and Hispanic origin: United States, academic years 1980–81, 1990–91, and 2002–03

[Data are based on reporting by health professions associations]

Enrollment, occupation, detailed race, and Hispanic origin	Both sexes			Women		
	1980–81	1990–91	2002–03[1]	1980–81	1990–91[2]	2002–03[1]
First-year enrollment	Number of students			Percent of students		
Dentistry	6,030	4,001	4,448	19.8	37.9	44.0
Medicine (Allopathic)[3]	17,186	16,876	16,953	28.9	38.8	49.0
Not Hispanic or Latino:						
White	14,262	11,830	11,404	27.4	37.7	- - -
Black or African American	1,128	1,263	1,394	45.5	55.3	- - -
Hispanic or Latino	818	933	1,227	31.5	42.0	- - -
Mexican	258	285	428	30.6	39.3	- - -
Mainland Puerto Rican	95	120	112	43.2	43.3	- - -
Other Hispanic or Latino[4]	465	528	687	29.7	43.3	- - -
American Indian or Alaska Native[5]	67	76	194	35.8	40.8	- - -
Asian or Pacific Islander	572	2,527	3,657	31.5	40.3	- - -
Medicine (Osteopathic)	1,496	1,950	3,079	22.0	34.2	47.5
Nurses, registered[6]	110,201	113,526	- - -	92.7	89.3	- - -
Optometry	1,258	1,239	1,416	25.3	50.6	62.7
Pharmacy[7]	7,377	8,267	9,128	48.4	- - -	67.7
Podiatry	695	561	419	- - -	28.0	45.0
Public Health	3,348	4,289	6,329	- - -	62.1	68.3
Total enrollment						
Dentistry	22,842	15,951	17,657	17.0	34.4	- - -
Medicine (Allopathic)[3]	65,189	65,163	66,334	26.5	37.3	46.8
Not Hispanic or Latino:						
White	55,434	47,893	42,435	25.0	35.4	- - -
Black or African American	3,708	4,241	4,905	44.3	55.8	- - -
Hispanic or Latino	2,761	3,538	4,264	30.1	39.0	- - -
Mexican	951	1,109	1,614	26.4	38.5	- - -
Mainland Puerto Rican	329	457	321	35.9	43.1	- - -
Other Hispanic[4]	1,481	1,972	2,329	31.1	38.4	- - -
American Indian or Alaska Native[5]	221	277	567	28.5	42.6	- - -
Asian or Pacific Islander	1,924	8,436	13,589	30.4	37.7	- - -
Medicine (Osteopathic)	4,940	6,792	11,432	19.7	32.7	44.6
Nurses, registered[6]	230,966	221,170	- - -	94.3	- - -	- - -
Optometry	4,641	4,760	5,354	- - -	47.3	60.4
Pharmacy	26,617	29,797	38,902	47.4	62.4	67.1
Podiatry	2,577	2,154	1,637	11.9	28.9	41.7
Public Health	8,486	11,386	17,878	55.2	62.5	66.4

- - - Data not available.

[1]Data for optometry are for 2003–04.

[2]Percent of women podiatry students is for 1991–92.

[3]Includes race and ethnicity unspecified; for first year enrollment, starting in 2000–2001, also includes foreign students; for total enrollment, starting in 1992–93, excludes foreign students.

[4]Includes Commonwealth Puerto Rican students.

[5]Starting in 1997–98, includes American Indian, Alaska Native, and Native Hawaiian; prior to 1997, included only American Indian and Alaska Native.

[6]Excludes American Samoa, Guam, Puerto Rico, and Virgin Islands.

[7]Pharmacy first-year enrollment is for students in the first year of the final 3 years of pharmacy education.

NOTES: Total enrollment data are collected at the beginning of the academic year while first-year enrollment data are collected during the academic year. Data for chiropractic students and occupational, physical, and speech therapy students were not available for this table. Some numbers in this table have been revised and differ from the previous edition of *Health, United States.*

SOURCES: Association of American Medical Colleges: AAMC Data Book: Statistical Information Related to Medical Education. Washington, DC. 2004 (Copyright 2005: Used with the permission of the AAMC); American Association of Colleges of Osteopathic Medicine: 2003 Annual Report on Osteopathic Medical Education. Chevy Chase, Maryland. 2004; Bureau of Health Professions: Minorities and Women in the Health Fields, 1990 edition; American Dental Association: 2002–03 Survey of Predoctoral Dental Education, vol.1, Academic Programs, Enrollments, and Graduates, Chicago. 2004 and unpublished data; Association of Schools and Colleges of Optometry: Annual Student Data Report Academic Year 2003–04 and unpublished data; American Association of Colleges of Pharmacy: Profile of Pharmacy Students, Fall 2002 and unpublished data; American Association of Colleges of Podiatric Medicine: unpublished data; National League for Nursing: Nursing Data Review. New York. 1997; Nursing data book. New York. 1982 and unpublished data; State-Approved Schools of Nursing-RN. New York. 1973; Association of Schools of Public Health: 2003 Annual Data Report. Washington, DC. 2004.

Table 112. Hospitals, beds, and occupancy rates, according to type of ownership and size of hospital: United States, selected years 1975–2003

[Data are based on reporting by a census of hospitals]

Type of ownership and size of hospital	*1975*	*1980*	*1990*	*1995*	*2000*	*2001*	*2002*	*2003*
Hospitals				Number				
All hospitals	7,156	6,965	6,649	6,291	5,810	5,801	5,794	5,764
Federal	382	359	337	299	245	243	240	239
Non-Federal[1]	6,774	6,606	6,312	5,992	5,565	5,558	5,554	5,525
Community[2]	5,875	5,830	5,384	5,194	4,915	4,908	4,927	4,895
Nonprofit	3,339	3,322	3,191	3,092	3,003	2,998	3,025	2,984
For profit	775	730	749	752	749	754	766	790
State-local government	1,761	1,778	1,444	1,350	1,163	1,156	1,136	1,121
6–24 beds	299	259	226	278	288	281	321	327
25–49 beds	1,155	1,029	935	922	910	916	931	965
50–99 beds	1,481	1,462	1,263	1,139	1,055	1,070	1,072	1,031
100–199 beds	1,363	1,370	1,306	1,324	1,236	1,218	1,190	1,168
200–299 beds	678	715	739	718	656	635	625	624
300–399 beds	378	412	408	354	341	348	358	349
400–499 beds	230	266	222	195	182	191	174	172
500 beds or more	291	317	285	264	247	249	256	256
Beds								
All hospitals	1,465,828	1,364,516	1,213,327	1,080,601	983,628	987,440	975,962	965,256
Federal	131,946	117,328	98,255	77,079	53,067	51,900	49,838	47,456
Non-Federal[1]	1,333,882	1,247,188	1,115,072	1,003,522	930,561	935,540	926,124	917,800
Community[2]	941,844	988,387	927,360	872,736	823,560	825,966	820,653	813,307
Nonprofit	658,195	692,459	656,755	609,729	582,988	585,070	582,179	574,587
For profit	73,495	87,033	101,377	105,737	109,883	108,718	108,422	109,671
State-local government	210,154	208,895	169,228	157,270	130,689	132,178	130,052	129,049
6–24 beds	5,615	4,932	4,427	5,085	5,156	4,964	5,629	5,635
25–49 beds	41,783	37,478	35,420	34,352	33,333	33,263	33,200	33,613
50–99 beds	106,776	105,278	90,394	82,024	75,865	76,924	76,882	74,025
100–199 beds	192,438	192,892	183,867	187,381	175,778	174,024	171,625	167,451
200–299 beds	164,405	172,390	179,670	175,240	159,807	154,420	152,682	152,487
300–399 beds	127,728	139,434	138,938	121,136	117,220	119,753	123,399	119,903
400–499 beds	101,278	117,724	98,833	86,459	80,763	84,745	77,145	76,333
500 beds or more	201,821	218,259	195,811	181,059	175,638	177,873	180,091	183,860
Occupancy rate[3]				Percent				
All hospitals	76.7	77.7	69.5	65.7	66.1	66.7	67.8	68.1
Federal	80.7	80.1	72.9	72.6	68.2	69.8	66.0	64.8
Non-Federal[1]	76.3	77.4	69.2	65.1	65.9	66.5	67.9	68.3
Community[2]	75.0	75.6	66.8	62.8	63.9	64.5	65.8	66.2
Nonprofit	77.5	78.2	69.3	64.5	65.5	65.8	67.2	67.7
For profit	65.9	65.2	52.8	51.8	55.9	57.8	59.0	59.6
State-local government	70.4	71.1	65.3	63.7	63.2	64.1	64.9	65.3
6–24 beds	48.0	46.8	32.3	36.9	31.7	31.3	32.4	31.9
25–49 beds	56.7	52.8	41.3	42.6	41.3	42.5	44.0	44.6
50–99 beds	64.7	64.2	53.8	54.1	54.8	55.5	56.7	57.2
100–199 beds	71.2	71.4	61.5	58.8	60.0	60.7	61.7	62.6
200–299 beds	77.1	77.4	67.1	63.1	65.0	65.5	66.7	67.0
300–399 beds	79.7	79.7	70.0	64.8	65.7	66.4	68.2	68.5
400–499 beds	81.1	81.2	73.5	68.1	69.1	68.9	70.5	70.7
500 beds or more	80.9	82.1	77.3	71.4	72.2	72.8	74.0	74.2

[1]The category of non-Federal hospitals comprises psychiatric, tuberculosis and other respiratory diseases hospitals, and long-term and short-term general and other special hospitals. See Appendix II, Hospital.
[2]Community hospitals are non-Federal short-term general and special hospitals whose facilities and services are available to the public. See Appendix II, Hospital.
[3]Estimated percent of staffed beds that are occupied. See Appendix II, Occupancy rate.

NOTE: Data for additional years are available. See Appendix III.

SOURCES: American Hospital Association Annual Survey of Hospitals. Hospital Statistics, 1976, 1981, 1991–2005 Editions. Chicago. (Copyrights 1976, 1981, 1991–2005: Used with the permission of Health Forum LLC, an affiliate of the American Hospital Association.)

Table 113. Mental health organizations and beds for 24-hour hospital and residential treatment according to type of organization: United States, selected years 1986–2002

[Data are based on inventories of mental health organizations]

Type of organization	1986	1990	1994[1]	1998	2000	2002[2]
	Number of mental health organizations					
All organizations	4,747	5,284	5,392	5,722	4,541	4,301
State and county mental hospitals	285	273	256	229	223	222
Private psychiatric hospitals	314	462	430	348	269	253
Non-Federal general hospital psychiatric services	1,351	1,674	1,612	1,707	1,373	1,285
Department of Veterans Affairs medical centers[3]	139	141	161	145	142	140
Residential treatment centers for emotionally disturbed children	437	501	459	461	475	508
All other organizations[4]	2,221	2,233	2,474	2,832	2,059	1,893
	Number of beds					
All organizations	267,613	272,253	290,604	267,796	212,621	211,199
State and county mental hospitals	119,033	98,789	81,911	68,872	60,675	57,263
Private psychiatric hospitals	30,201	44,871	42,399	33,408	26,484	25,095
Non-Federal general hospital psychiatric services	45,808	53,479	52,984	54,434	39,690	40,202
Department of Veterans Affairs medical centers[3]	26,874	21,712	21,146	16,973	9,363	9,672
Residential treatment centers for emotionally disturbed children	24,547	29,756	32,110	31,965	33,375	39,049
All other organizations[4]	21,150	23,646	60,054	62,144	43,034	39,918
	Beds per 100,000 civilian population[5]					
All organizations	111.7	111.6	112.1	99.5	75.4	73.2
State and county mental hospitals	49.7	40.5	31.6	25.6	21.5	19.9
Private psychiatric hospitals	12.6	18.4	16.4	12.4	9.4	8.7
Non-Federal general hospital psychiatric services	19.1	21.9	20.4	20.2	14.1	13.9
Department of Veterans Affairs medical centers[3]	11.2	8.9	8.2	6.3	3.3	3.4
Residential treatment centers for emotionally disturbed children	10.3	12.2	12.4	11.9	11.8	13.5
All other organizations[4]	8.8	9.7	23.2	23.1	15.3	13.8

[1]Beginning in 1994 data for supportive residential clients (moderately staffed housing arrangements such as supervised apartments, group homes, and halfway houses) are included in the totals and "All other organizations." This change affects the comparability of trend data prior to 1994 with data for 1994 and later years.
[2]Preliminary data.
[3]Includes Department of Veterans Affairs (VA) neuropsychiatric hospitals, VA general hospital psychiatric services, and VA psychiatric outpatient clinics.
[4]Includes freestanding psychiatric outpatient clinics, partial care organizations, and multiservice mental health organizations. See Appendix I, Survey of Mental Health Organizations.
[5]Civilian population estimates for 2000 and beyond are based on 2000 Census as of July 1; population estimates for 1992–98 are 1990 postcensal estimates.

NOTES: Data for 2000 are revised and differ from the previous edition of *Health, United States.* These data exclude mental health care provided in nonpsychiatric units of hospitals such as general medical units. Data for additional years are available. See Appendix III.

SOURCES: Substance Abuse and Mental Health Services Administration, Center for Mental Health Services (CMHS). Manderscheid RW and Henderson MJ. *Mental Health, United States, 2002.* Washington, DC. U.S. Government Printing Office, 2004; and Survey of Mental Health Organizations, unpublished data.

Table 114. Community hospital beds and average annual percent change, according to geographic division and State: United States, selected years 1960–2003

[Data are based on reporting by a census of hospitals]

Geographic division and State	1960[1,2]	1970[1]	1980[1]	1990[3]	2000[3]	2003[3]	1960–70[1,2]	1970–80[1]	1980–90[4]	1990–2000[3]	2000–03[3]
	Beds per 1,000 resident population[5]						Average annual percent change				
United States	3.6	4.3	4.5	3.7	2.9	2.8	1.8	0.5	–1.9	–2.4	–1.2
New England	3.9	4.1	4.1	3.4	2.5	2.4	0.5	0.0	–1.9	–3.0	–1.4
Connecticut	3.4	3.4	3.5	2.9	2.3	2.1	0.0	0.3	–1.9	–2.3	–3.0
Maine	3.4	4.7	4.7	3.7	2.9	2.8	3.3	0.0	–2.4	–2.4	–1.2
Massachusetts	4.2	4.4	4.4	3.6	2.6	2.5	0.5	0.0	–2.0	–3.2	–1.3
New Hampshire	4.4	4.0	3.9	3.1	2.3	2.2	–0.9	–0.3	–2.3	–2.9	–1.5
Rhode Island	3.7	4.0	3.8	3.2	2.3	2.2	0.8	–0.5	–1.7	–3.2	–1.5
Vermont	4.5	4.5	4.4	3.0	2.7	2.4	0.0	–0.2	–3.8	–1.0	–3.9
Middle Atlantic	4.0	4.4	4.6	4.1	3.4	3.2	1.0	0.4	–1.1	–1.9	–2.0
New Jersey	3.1	3.6	4.2	3.7	3.0	2.6	1.5	1.6	–1.3	–2.1	–4.7
New York	4.3	4.6	4.5	4.1	3.5	3.4	0.7	–0.2	–0.9	–1.6	–1.0
Pennsylvania	4.1	4.7	4.8	4.4	3.4	3.3	1.4	0.2	–0.9	–2.5	–1.0
East North Central	3.6	4.4	4.7	3.9	2.9	2.8	2.0	0.7	–1.8	–2.9	–1.2
Illinois	4.0	4.7	5.1	4.0	3.0	2.8	1.6	0.8	–2.4	–2.8	–2.3
Indiana	3.1	4.0	4.5	3.9	3.2	3.1	2.6	1.2	–1.4	–2.0	–1.1
Michigan	3.3	4.3	4.4	3.7	2.6	2.6	2.7	0.2	–1.7	–3.5	0.0
Ohio	3.4	4.2	4.7	4.0	3.0	2.9	2.1	1.1	–1.6	–2.8	–1.1
Wisconsin	4.3	5.2	4.9	3.8	2.9	2.7	1.9	–0.6	–2.5	–2.7	–2.4
West North Central	4.3	5.7	5.8	4.9	3.9	3.7	2.9	0.2	–1.7	–2.3	–1.7
Iowa	3.9	5.6	5.7	5.1	4.0	3.7	3.7	0.2	–1.1	–2.4	–2.6
Kansas	4.2	5.4	5.8	4.8	4.0	3.9	2.5	0.7	–1.9	–1.8	–0.8
Minnesota	4.8	6.1	5.7	4.4	3.4	3.2	2.4	–0.7	–2.6	–2.5	–2.0
Missouri	3.9	5.1	5.7	4.8	3.6	3.4	2.7	1.1	–1.7	–2.8	–1.9
Nebraska	4.4	6.2	6.0	5.5	4.8	4.3	3.5	–0.3	–0.9	–1.4	–3.6
North Dakota	5.2	6.8	7.4	7.0	6.0	5.7	2.7	0.8	–0.6	–1.5	–1.7
South Dakota	4.5	5.6	5.5	6.1	5.7	5.8	2.2	–0.2	1.0	–0.7	0.6
South Atlantic	3.3	4.0	4.5	3.7	2.9	2.8	1.9	1.2	–1.9	–2.4	–1.2
Delaware	3.7	3.7	3.6	3.0	2.3	2.5	0.0	–0.3	–1.8	–2.6	2.8
District of Columbia	5.9	7.4	7.3	7.6	5.8	6.0	2.3	–0.1	0.4	–2.7	1.1
Florida	3.1	4.4	5.1	3.9	3.2	3.0	3.6	1.5	–2.6	–2.0	–2.1
Georgia	2.8	3.8	4.6	4.0	2.9	2.8	3.1	1.9	–1.4	–3.2	–1.2
Maryland	3.3	3.1	3.6	2.8	2.1	2.1	–0.6	1.5	–2.5	–2.8	0.0
North Carolina	3.4	3.8	4.2	3.3	2.9	2.8	1.1	1.0	–2.4	–1.3	–1.2
South Carolina	2.9	3.7	3.9	3.3	2.9	2.7	2.5	0.5	–1.7	–1.3	–2.4
Virginia	3.0	3.7	4.1	3.3	2.4	2.3	2.1	1.0	–2.1	–3.1	–1.4
West Virginia	4.1	5.4	5.5	4.7	4.4	4.3	2.8	0.2	–1.6	–0.7	–0.8
East South Central	3.0	4.4	5.1	4.7	3.8	3.7	3.9	1.5	–0.8	–2.1	–0.9
Alabama	2.8	4.3	5.1	4.6	3.7	3.5	4.4	1.7	–1.0	–2.2	–1.8
Kentucky	3.0	4.0	4.5	4.3	3.7	3.6	2.9	1.2	–0.5	–1.5	–0.9
Mississippi	2.9	4.4	5.3	5.0	4.8	4.5	4.3	1.9	–0.6	–0.4	–2.1
Tennessee	3.4	4.7	5.5	4.8	3.6	3.5	3.3	1.6	–1.4	–2.8	–0.9
West South Central	3.3	4.3	4.7	3.8	3.0	2.9	2.7	0.9	–2.1	–2.3	–1.1
Arkansas	2.9	4.2	5.0	4.6	3.7	3.6	3.8	1.8	–0.8	–2.2	–0.9
Louisiana	3.9	4.2	4.8	4.6	3.9	4.0	0.7	1.3	–0.4	–1.6	0.8
Oklahoma	3.2	4.5	4.6	4.0	3.2	3.1	3.5	0.2	–1.4	–2.2	–1.1
Texas	3.3	4.3	4.7	3.5	2.7	2.6	2.7	0.9	–2.9	–2.6	–1.3
Mountain	3.5	4.3	3.8	3.1	2.3	2.2	2.1	–1.2	–2.0	–2.9	–1.5
Arizona	3.0	4.1	3.6	2.7	2.1	1.9	3.2	–1.3	–2.8	–2.5	–3.3
Colorado	3.8	4.6	4.2	3.2	2.2	2.1	1.9	–0.9	–2.7	–3.7	–1.5
Idaho	3.2	4.0	3.7	3.2	2.7	2.5	2.3	–0.8	–1.4	–1.7	–2.5
Montana	5.1	5.8	5.9	5.8	4.7	4.7	1.3	0.2	–0.2	–2.1	0.0
Nevada	3.9	4.2	4.2	2.8	1.9	1.9	0.7	0.0	–4.0	–3.8	0.0
New Mexico	2.9	3.5	3.1	2.8	1.9	2.0	1.9	–1.2	–1.0	–3.8	1.7
Utah	2.8	3.6	3.1	2.6	1.9	1.9	2.5	–1.5	–1.7	–3.1	0.0
Wyoming	4.6	5.5	3.6	4.8	3.9	3.5	1.8	–4.1	2.9	–2.1	–3.5
Pacific	3.1	3.7	3.5	2.7	2.1	2.1	1.8	–0.6	–2.6	–2.5	0.0
Alaska	2.4	2.3	2.7	2.3	2.3	2.2	–0.4	1.6	–1.6	0.0	–1.5
California	3.0	3.8	3.6	2.7	2.1	2.1	2.4	–0.5	–2.8	–2.5	0.0
Hawaii	3.7	3.4	3.1	2.7	2.5	2.5	–0.8	–0.9	–1.4	–0.8	0.0
Oregon	3.5	4.0	3.5	2.8	1.9	1.9	1.3	–1.3	–2.2	–3.8	0.0
Washington	3.3	3.5	3.1	2.5	1.9	1.8	0.6	–1.2	–2.1	–2.7	–1.8

[1]Data exclude facilities for the mentally retarded. See Appendix II, Hospital.
[2]1960 data include hospital units of institutions such as prisons and college infirmaries.
[3]Starting with 1990, data exclude hospital units of institutions, facilities for the mentally retarded, and alcoholism and chemical dependency hospitals. See Appendix II, Hospital.
[4]1990 data used in this calculation (not shown in table) exclude only facilities for the mentally retarded, consistent with exclusions from 1980 data.
[5]Civilian population for 1997 and earlier years.

NOTE: Data for additional years are available. See Appendix III.

SOURCES: American Hospital Association (AHA): Hospitals. *JAHA* 35(15):383–430, 1961 (Copyright 1961: Used with permission of AHA); National Center for Health Statistics, Division of Health Care Statistics and AHA Annual Survey of Hospitals for 1970, 1980; Hospital Statistics 1991–92, 2001–2005 Editions. Chicago (Copyrights 1971, 1981, 1991, 2001, 2002, 2003, 2005: Used with permission of Health Forum LLC, an affiliate of the American Hospital Association).

Table 115. Occupancy rates in community hospitals and average annual percent change, according to geographic division and State: United States, selected years 1960–2003

[Data are based on reporting by a census of hospitals]

Geographic division and State	*1960*[1,2]	*1970*[1]	*1980*[1]	*1990*[3]	*2000*[3]	*2003*[3]	*1960–70*[1,2]	*1970–80*[1]	*1980–90*[4]	*1990–2000*[3]	*2000–03*[3]
	Occupancy rate[5]						Average annual percent change				
United States	75	77	75	67	64	66	0.3	–0.3	–1.1	–0.5	1.0
New England	75	80	80	74	70	72	0.6	0.0	–0.8	–0.6	0.9
Connecticut	78	83	80	77	75	77	0.6	–0.4	–0.4	–0.3	0.9
Maine	73	73	75	72	64	60	0.0	0.3	–0.4	–1.2	–2.1
Massachusetts	76	80	82	74	71	75	0.5	0.2	–1.0	–0.4	1.8
New Hampshire	67	73	73	67	59	62	0.9	0.0	–0.9	–1.3	1.7
Rhode Island	76	83	86	79	72	75	0.9	0.4	–0.8	–0.9	1.4
Vermont	69	76	74	67	67	62	1.0	–0.3	–1.0	0.0	–2.6
Middle Atlantic	78	82	83	81	74	74	0.5	0.1	–0.2	–0.9	0.0
New Jersey	78	83	83	80	69	74	0.6	0.0	–0.4	–1.5	2.4
New York	79	83	86	86	79	78	0.5	0.4	0.0	–0.8	–0.4
Pennsylvania	76	82	80	73	68	69	0.8	–0.2	–0.9	–0.7	0.5
East North Central	78	80	77	65	61	63	0.3	–0.4	–1.7	–0.6	1.1
Illinois	76	79	75	66	60	64	0.4	–0.5	–1.3	–0.9	2.2
Indiana	80	80	78	61	56	58	0.0	–0.3	–2.4	–0.9	1.2
Michigan	81	81	78	66	65	66	0.0	–0.4	–1.7	–0.2	0.5
Ohio	81	82	79	65	61	62	0.1	–0.4	–1.9	–0.6	0.5
Wisconsin	74	73	74	65	60	62	–0.1	0.1	–1.3	–0.8	1.1
West North Central	72	74	71	62	60	61	0.3	–0.4	–1.3	–0.3	0.6
Iowa	73	72	69	62	58	59	–0.1	–0.4	–1.1	–0.7	0.6
Kansas	69	71	69	56	53	56	0.3	–0.3	–2.1	–0.5	1.9
Minnesota	72	74	74	67	67	69	0.3	0.0	–1.0	0.0	1.0
Missouri	76	79	75	62	58	62	0.4	–0.5	–1.9	–0.7	2.2
Nebraska	66	70	67	58	59	58	0.6	–0.4	–1.4	0.2	–0.6
North Dakota	71	67	69	64	60	59	–0.6	0.3	–0.7	–0.6	–0.6
South Dakota	66	66	61	62	65	62	0.0	–0.8	0.2	0.5	–1.6
South Atlantic	75	78	76	67	65	68	0.4	–0.3	–1.3	–0.3	1.5
Delaware	70	79	82	77	75	81	1.2	0.4	–0.6	–0.3	2.6
District of Columbia	81	78	83	75	74	73	–0.4	0.6	–1.0	–0.1	–0.5
Florida	74	76	72	62	61	65	0.3	–0.5	–1.5	–0.2	2.1
Georgia	72	77	70	66	63	67	0.7	–0.9	–0.6	–0.5	2.1
Maryland	74	79	84	79	73	75	0.7	0.6	–0.6	–0.8	0.9
North Carolina	74	79	78	73	70	71	0.7	–0.1	–0.7	–0.4	0.5
South Carolina	77	76	77	71	69	73	–0.1	0.1	–0.8	–0.3	1.9
Virginia	78	81	78	67	68	69	0.4	–0.4	–1.5	0.1	0.5
West Virginia	75	79	76	63	61	62	0.5	–0.4	–1.9	–0.3	0.5
East South Central	72	78	75	63	59	61	0.8	–0.4	–1.7	–0.7	1.1
Alabama	71	80	73	63	60	62	1.2	–0.9	–1.5	–0.5	1.1
Kentucky	73	80	77	62	62	62	0.9	–0.4	–2.1	0.0	0.0
Mississippi	63	74	71	59	59	57	1.6	–0.4	–1.8	0.0	–1.1
Tennessee	76	78	76	64	56	61	0.3	–0.3	–1.7	–1.3	2.9
West South Central	69	73	70	58	58	62	0.6	–0.4	–1.9	0.0	2.2
Arkansas	70	74	70	62	59	58	0.6	–0.6	–1.2	–0.5	–0.6
Louisiana	68	74	70	57	56	60	0.8	–0.6	–2.0	–0.2	2.3
Oklahoma	71	73	68	58	56	59	0.3	–0.7	–1.6	–0.4	1.8
Texas	68	73	70	57	59	63	0.7	–0.4	–2.0	0.3	2.2
Mountain	70	71	70	61	61	64	0.1	–0.1	–1.4	0.0	1.6
Arizona	74	73	74	62	63	68	–0.1	0.1	–1.8	0.2	2.6
Colorado	81	74	72	64	58	65	–0.9	–0.3	–1.2	–1.0	3.9
Idaho	56	66	65	56	53	56	1.7	–0.2	–1.5	–0.5	1.9
Montana	60	66	66	61	67	66	1.0	0.0	–0.8	0.9	–0.5
Nevada	71	73	69	60	71	71	0.3	–0.6	–1.4	1.7	0.0
New Mexico	65	70	66	58	58	58	0.7	–0.6	–1.3	0.0	0.0
Utah	70	74	70	59	56	57	0.6	–0.6	–1.7	–0.5	0.6
Wyoming	61	63	57	54	56	53	0.3	–1.0	–0.5	0.4	–1.8
Pacific	71	71	69	64	65	67	0.0	–0.3	–0.7	0.2	1.0
Alaska	54	59	58	50	57	54	0.9	–0.2	–1.5	1.3	–1.8
California	74	71	69	64	66	69	–0.4	–0.3	–0.7	0.3	1.5
Hawaii	62	76	75	85	76	72	2.1	–0.1	1.3	–1.1	–1.8
Oregon	66	69	69	57	59	59	0.4	0.0	–1.9	0.3	0.0
Washington	63	70	72	63	60	61	1.1	0.3	–1.3	–0.5	0.6

[1]Data exclude facilities for the mentally retarded. See Appendix II, Hospital.
[2]1960 data include hospital units of institutions such as prisons and college infirmaries.
[3]Starting with 1990, data exclude hospital units of institutions, facilities for the mentally retarded, and alcoholism and chemical dependency hospitals. See Appendix II, Hospital.
[4]1990 data used in this calculation (not shown in table) exclude only facilities for the mentally retarded, consistent with exclusions from 1980 data.
[5]Estimated percent of staffed beds that are occupied. See Appendix II, Occupancy rate.

NOTE: Data for additional years are available. See Appendix III.

SOURCES: American Hospital Association (AHA): Hospitals. *JAHA* 35(15):383–430, 1961. (Copyright 1961: Used with permission of AHA); AHA Annual Survey of Hospitals, 1970 and 1980 unpublished; Hospital Statistics 1991–92, 2001–2005 Editions. Chicago (Copyrights 1971, 1981, 1991, 2001, 2002, 2003, 2004, 2005: Used with permission of Health Forum LLC, an affiliate of the American Hospital Association).

Table 116 (page 1 of 2). Nursing homes, beds, occupancy, and residents, according to geographic division and State: United States, 1995–2003

[Data are based on a census of certified nursing facilities]

Geographic division and State	Nursing homes			Beds		
	1995	2000	2003	1995	2000	2003
United States	16,389	16,886	16,323	1,751,302	1,795,388	1,756,699
New England	1,140	1,137	1,067	115,488	118,562	111,892
Connecticut	267	259	252	32,827	32,433	31,248
Maine	132	126	119	9,243	8,248	7,552
Massachusetts	550	526	478	54,532	56,030	52,323
New Hampshire	74	83	81	7,412	7,837	7,811
Rhode Island	94	99	94	9,612	10,271	9,376
Vermont	23	44	43	1,862	3,743	3,582
Middle Atlantic	1,650	1,796	1,767	244,342	267,772	264,041
New Jersey	300	361	356	43,967	52,195	50,551
New York	624	665	671	107,750	120,514	122,633
Pennsylvania	726	770	740	92,625	95,063	90,857
East North Central	3,171	3,301	3,182	367,879	369,657	360,504
Illinois	827	869	827	103,230	110,766	106,734
Indiana	556	564	527	59,538	56,762	55,475
Michigan	432	439	431	49,473	50,696	49,225
Ohio	943	1,009	989	106,884	105,038	106,426
Wisconsin	413	420	408	48,754	46,395	42,644
West North Central	2,258	2,281	2,212	200,109	193,754	186,548
Iowa	419	467	454	39,959	37,034	35,428
Kansas	429	392	374	30,016	27,067	27,045
Minnesota	432	433	425	43,865	42,149	39,336
Missouri	546	551	534	52,679	54,829	54,415
Nebraska	231	236	228	18,169	17,877	16,378
North Dakota	87	88	84	7,125	6,954	6,582
South Dakota	114	114	113	8,296	7,844	7,364
South Atlantic	2,215	2,418	2,374	243,069	264,147	263,651
Delaware	42	43	42	4,739	4,906	4,679
District of Columbia	19	20	21	3,206	3,078	3,114
Florida	627	732	693	72,656	83,365	82,546
Georgia	352	363	360	38,097	39,817	39,998
Maryland	218	255	243	28,394	31,495	29,362
North Carolina	391	410	423	38,322	41,376	43,022
South Carolina	166	178	178	16,682	18,102	18,306
Virginia	271	278	278	30,070	30,595	31,472
West Virginia	129	139	136	10,903	11,413	11,152
East South Central	1,014	1,071	1,065	99,707	106,250	108,105
Alabama	221	225	228	23,353	25,248	26,369
Kentucky	288	307	296	23,221	25,341	25,629
Mississippi	183	190	204	16,059	17,068	18,149
Tennessee	322	349	337	37,074	38,593	37,958
West South Central	2,264	2,199	2,069	224,695	224,100	217,469
Arkansas	256	255	242	29,952	25,715	24,791
Louisiana	337	337	314	37,769	39,430	38,397
Oklahoma	405	392	370	33,918	33,903	32,733
Texas	1,266	1,215	1,143	123,056	125,052	121,548
Mountain	800	827	785	70,134	75,152	73,464
Arizona	152	150	135	16,162	17,458	16,451
Colorado	219	225	215	19,912	20,240	20,127
Idaho	76	84	80	5,747	6,181	6,258
Montana	100	104	101	7,210	7,667	7,489
Nevada	42	51	44	3,998	5,547	5,197
New Mexico	83	80	81	6,969	7,289	7,443
Utah	91	93	90	7,101	7,651	7,438
Wyoming	37	40	39	3,035	3,119	3,061
Pacific	1,877	1,856	1,802	185,879	175,994	171,025
Alaska	15	15	14	814	821	806
California	1,382	1,369	1,342	140,203	131,762	129,658
Hawaii	34	45	45	2,513	4,006	4,059
Oregon	161	150	141	13,885	13,500	12,789
Washington	285	277	260	28,464	25,905	23,713

See footnotes at end of table.

Table 116 (page 2 of 2). Nursing homes, beds, occupancy, and residents, according to geographic division and State: United States, 1995–2003

[Data are based on a census of certified nursing facilities]

Geographic division and State	Residents			Occupancy rate[1]			Resident rate[2]		
	1995	2000	2003	1995	2000	2003	1995	2000	2003
United States	1,479,550	1,480,076	1,451,672	84.5	82.4	82.6	404.5	349.1	308.0
New England	105,792	106,308	101,561	91.6	89.7	90.8	474.2	419.5	359.2
Connecticut	29,948	29,657	28,622	91.2	91.4	91.6	541.7	461.4	386.8
Maine	8,587	7,298	6,954	92.9	88.5	92.1	417.9	313.0	274.9
Massachusetts	49,765	49,805	46,993	91.3	88.9	89.8	477.3	426.8	366.8
New Hampshire	6,877	7,158	7,145	92.8	91.3	91.5	434.1	392.6	346.7
Rhode Island	8,823	9,041	8,528	91.8	88.0	91.0	476.9	432.6	363.1
Vermont	1,792	3,349	3,319	96.2	89.5	92.7	207.0	335.0	296.7
Middle Atlantic	228,649	242,674	239,286	93.6	90.6	90.6	384.0	354.2	313.8
New Jersey	40,397	45,837	44,356	91.9	87.8	87.7	351.6	337.0	290.3
New York	103,409	112,957	113,456	96.0	93.7	92.5	371.8	362.6	330.5
Pennsylvania	84,843	83,880	81,474	91.6	88.2	89.7	419.2	353.1	305.9
East North Central	294,319	289,404	278,339	80.0	78.3	77.2	476.1	414.3	358.1
Illinois	83,696	83,604	79,833	81.1	75.5	74.8	495.3	435.4	377.4
Indiana	44,328	42,328	40,623	74.5	74.6	73.2	548.9	462.3	401.9
Michigan	43,271	42,615	41,547	87.5	84.1	84.4	345.0	299.1	256.5
Ohio	79,026	81,946	79,839	73.9	78.0	75.0	499.5	463.5	406.5
Wisconsin	43,998	38,911	36,497	90.2	83.9	85.6	518.9	406.9	343.2
West North Central	164,660	157,224	149,004	82.3	81.1	79.9	489.6	429.8	378.5
Iowa	27,506	29,204	27,805	68.8	78.9	78.5	458.0	448.5	394.8
Kansas	25,140	22,230	21,085	83.8	82.1	78.0	528.9	429.4	384.5
Minnesota	41,163	38,813	36,231	93.8	92.1	92.1	537.4	453.4	380.0
Missouri	39,891	38,586	37,345	75.7	70.4	68.6	432.8	391.5	361.1
Nebraska	16,166	14,989	13,598	89.0	83.8	83.0	501.4	441.5	376.0
North Dakota	6,868	6,343	6,137	96.4	91.2	93.2	522.0	430.7	380.8
South Dakota	7,926	7,059	6,803	95.5	90.0	92.4	543.3	438.8	391.4
South Atlantic	217,303	227,818	232,185	89.4	86.2	88.1	335.4	291.9	264.6
Delaware	3,819	3,900	3,962	80.6	79.5	84.7	448.7	369.7	318.6
District of Columbia	2,576	2,858	2,861	80.3	92.9	91.9	297.6	318.4	306.0
Florida	61,845	69,050	71,987	85.1	82.8	87.2	228.2	208.4	193.7
Georgia	35,933	36,559	36,372	94.3	91.8	90.9	496.0	416.1	375.4
Maryland	24,716	25,629	25,270	87.0	81.4	86.1	432.7	383.1	326.1
North Carolina	35,511	36,658	37,936	92.7	88.6	88.2	401.1	347.6	320.1
South Carolina	14,568	15,739	16,220	87.3	86.9	88.6	366.0	313.1	278.1
Virginia	28,119	27,091	27,614	93.5	88.5	87.7	385.2	310.4	277.9
West Virginia	10,216	10,334	9,963	93.7	90.5	89.3	355.2	325.2	298.4
East South Central	91,563	96,348	95,938	91.8	90.7	88.7	416.6	385.5	363.2
Alabama	21,691	23,089	23,564	92.9	91.4	89.4	370.1	343.1	329.6
Kentucky	20,696	22,730	22,814	89.1	89.7	89.0	391.9	390.1	370.5
Mississippi	15,247	15,815	16,057	94.9	92.7	88.5	405.3	368.7	366.8
Tennessee	33,929	34,714	33,503	91.5	89.9	88.3	479.6	426.1	383.6
West South Central	169,047	159,160	156,297	75.2	71.0	71.9	486.1	397.6	368.7
Arkansas	20,823	19,317	17,997	69.5	75.1	72.6	508.3	415.5	365.9
Louisiana	32,493	30,735	29,151	86.0	77.9	75.9	639.3	523.8	470.0
Oklahoma	26,377	23,833	21,679	77.8	70.3	66.2	499.1	416.8	372.6
Texas	89,354	85,275	87,470	72.6	68.2	72.0	439.9	358.4	343.7
Mountain	58,738	59,379	58,451	83.8	79.0	79.6	335.9	271.2	229.4
Arizona	12,382	13,253	13,245	76.6	75.9	80.5	233.3	193.4	163.7
Colorado	17,055	17,045	16,344	85.7	84.2	81.2	420.6	353.5	300.7
Idaho	4,697	4,640	4,754	81.7	75.1	76.0	321.7	257.0	224.2
Montana	6,415	5,973	5,739	89.0	77.9	76.6	491.4	389.5	328.1
Nevada	3,645	3,657	4,308	91.2	65.9	82.9	312.0	215.3	195.3
New Mexico	6,051	6,503	6,280	86.8	89.2	84.4	332.0	279.0	236.9
Utah	5,832	5,703	5,306	82.1	74.5	71.3	323.5	262.2	213.3
Wyoming	2,661	2,605	2,475	87.7	83.5	80.9	468.2	386.8	334.2
Pacific	149,479	141,761	140,611	80.4	80.5	82.2	302.4	241.3	207.7
Alaska	634	595	619	77.9	72.5	76.8	348.0	225.9	185.2
California	109,805	106,460	107,578	78.3	80.8	83.0	302.9	250.1	220.2
Hawaii	2,413	3,558	3,806	96.0	88.8	93.8	178.5	202.6	172.4
Oregon	11,673	9,990	8,640	84.1	74.0	67.6	244.9	173.9	131.0
Washington	24,954	21,158	19,968	87.7	81.7	84.2	362.5	251.6	205.9

[1]Percent of beds occupied (number of nursing home residents per 100 nursing home beds).

[2]Number of nursing home residents (all ages) per 1,000 resident population 85 years of age and over. Resident rates for 1995–99 are based on population estimates projected from the 1990 census. Starting with 2000, resident rates are based on the 2000 census.

NOTES: Annual numbers of nursing homes, beds, and residents are based on a 15-month OSCAR reporting cycle. See Appendix I, Online Survey Certification and Reporting Database (OSCAR). Data for additional years are available. See Appendix III.

SOURCES: Cowles CM, 1995 Nursing Home Statistical Yearbook. Anacortes, WA: Cowles Research Group, 1995; Cowles CM, 2000 Nursing Home Statistical Yearbook. Washington, DC: American Association of Homes and Services for the Aging, 2001; and Cowles Research Group, unpublished data. Based on data from the Centers for Medicare & Medicaid Services' Online Survey Certification and Reporting (OSCAR) database.

Table 117. Medicare-certified providers and suppliers: United States, selected years 1980–2003

[Data are compiled from various Centers for Medicare & Medicaid Services data systems]

Providers or suppliers	*1980*	*1985*	*1990*	*1996*	*1997*	*2000*	*2001*	*2002*	*2003*
				Number of providers or suppliers					
Home health agencies	2,924	5,679	5,730	8,437	10,807	7,857	7,099	6,813	6,928
Clinical Lab Improvement Act Facilities	---	---	---	159,907	164,054	171,018	168,333	173,807	176,947
End stage renal disease facilities	999	1,393	1,937	2,876	3,367	3,787	3,991	4,113	4,309
Outpatient physical therapy	419	854	1,195	2,302	2,758	2,867	2,874	2,836	2,961
Portable X-ray	216	308	443	555	656	666	675	644	641
Rural health clinics	391	428	551	2,775	3,673	3,453	3,334	3,283	3,306
Comprehensive outpatient rehabilitation facilities	---	72	186	307	531	522	518	524	587
Ambulatory surgical centers	---	336	1,197	2,112	2,480	2,894	3,147	3,371	3,597
Hospices	---	164	825	1,927	2,344	2,326	2,267	2,275	2,323

--- Data not available.

NOTES: Provider and supplier data for 1980–90 are as of July 1. Provider and supplier data for 1996–98 are as of December. Provider and supplier data for 2000, 2001, 2002, and 2003 are as of December 1999, December 2000, December 2001, and December 2002, respectively. Providers and suppliers certified for Medicare are deemed to meet Medicaid standards.

SOURCE: Centers for Medicare & Medicaid Services, Office of Research, Development, and Information.

Table 118. Total health expenditures as a percent of gross domestic product and per capita health expenditures in dollars: Selected countries and years 1960–2002

[Data compiled by the Organization for Economic Cooperation and Development]

Country	1960	1970	1980	1990	1995	1998	1999	2000	2001[1]	2002
				Health expenditures as a percent of gross domestic product						
Australia	4.1	---	7.0	7.8	8.2	8.6	8.8	9.0	9.1	---
Austria	4.3	5.3	7.6	7.1	8.2	7.7	7.8	7.7	7.6	7.7
Belgium	---	4.0	6.4	7.4	8.7	8.6	8.7	8.8	9.0	9.1
Canada	5.4	7.0	7.1	9.0	9.2	9.2	9.0	8.9	9.4	9.6
Czech Republic	---	---	---	5.0	7.3	7.1	7.1	7.1	7.3	7.4
Denmark	---	---	9.1	8.5	8.2	8.4	8.5	8.4	8.6	8.8
Finland	3.8	5.6	6.4	7.8	7.5	6.9	6.9	6.7	7.0	7.3
France	3.8	5.4	7.1	8.6	9.5	9.3	9.3	9.3	9.4	9.7
Germany	---	6.2	8.7	8.5	10.6	10.6	10.6	10.6	10.8	10.9
Greece	---	6.1	6.6	7.4	9.6	9.4	9.6	9.7	9.4	9.5
Hungary	---	---	---	---	7.5	7.3	7.4	7.1	7.4	7.8
Iceland	3.0	4.7	6.2	8.0	8.4	8.6	9.4	9.2	9.2	9.9
Ireland	3.7	5.1	8.4	6.1	6.8	6.2	6.3	6.4	6.9	7.3
Italy	---	---	---	8.0	7.4	7.7	7.8	8.1	8.3	8.5
Japan	3.0	4.5	6.5	5.9	6.8	7.2	7.4	7.6	7.8	---
Korea	---	---	---	4.2	4.1	4.4	4.7	4.6	5.3	5.1
Luxembourg	---	3.6	5.9	6.1	6.4	5.8	6.2	5.5	5.9	6.2
Mexico	---	---	---	4.8	5.6	5.4	5.6	5.6	6.0	6.1
Netherlands	---	---	7.5	8.0	8.4	8.1	8.2	8.2	8.5	9.1
New Zealand	---	5.1	5.9	6.9	7.2	7.9	7.8	7.9	8.0	8.5
Norway	2.9	4.4	7.0	7.7	7.9	8.5	8.5	7.7	8.9	9.6
Poland	---	---	---	4.9	5.6	6.0	5.9	5.7	6.0	6.1
Portugal	---	2.6	5.6	6.2	8.2	8.4	8.7	9.2	9.3	9.3
Slovak Republic	---	---	---	---	---	5.7	5.8	5.5	5.6	5.7
Spain	1.5	3.6	5.4	6.7	7.6	7.5	7.5	7.5	7.5	7.6
Sweden	---	6.9	9.1	8.4	8.1	8.3	8.4	8.4	8.8	9.2
Switzerland	4.9	5.4	7.3	8.3	9.7	10.3	10.5	10.4	10.9	11.2
Turkey	---	2.4	3.3	3.6	3.4	4.8	6.4	6.6	---	---
United Kingdom	3.9	4.5	5.6	6.0	7.0	6.9	7.2	7.3	7.5	7.7
United States	5.1	7.0	8.8	12.0	13.4	13.2	13.2	13.3	14.1	14.9
				Per capita health expenditures[1]						
Australia	$ 93	---	$ 684	$1,300	$1,737	$2,077	$2,231	$2,379	$2,504	---
Austria	77	190	762	1,344	1,865	1,953	2,069	2,147	2,174	2,220
Belgium	---	147	627	1,340	1,882	2,041	2,139	2,288	2,441	2,515
Canada	121	289	770	1,714	2,044	2,291	2,400	2,541	2,743	2,931
Czech Republic	---	---	---	553	876	918	932	977	1,083	1,118
Denmark	---	---	943	1,554	1,843	2,141	2,297	2,353	2,520	2,583
Finland	62	190	584	1,414	1,428	1,607	1,641	1,698	1,841	1,943
France	69	206	699	1,555	2,025	2,231	2,306	2,416	2,588	2,736
Germany	---	266	955	1,729	2,263	2,470	2,563	2,640	2,735	2,817
Greece	---	171	464	838	1,269	1,428	1,517	1,617	1,670	1,814
Hungary	---	---	---	---	674	775	820	847	961	1,079
Iceland	57	163	698	1,598	1,853	2,252	2,540	2,559	2,680	2,807
Ireland	42	117	511	791	1,208	1,487	1,623	1,774	2,059	2,367
Italy	---	---	---	1,397	1,524	1,800	1,853	2,001	2,107	2,166
Japan	29	144	559	1,105	1,530	1,742	1,829	1,958	2,077	---
Korea	---	---	---	329	491	589	714	777	943	996
Luxembourg	---	161	637	1,533	2,053	2,291	2,734	2,682	2,900	3,065
Mexico	---	---	---	290	380	427	463	494	536	553
Netherlands	---	---	750	1,419	1,827	2,016	2,098	2,196	2,455	2,643
New Zealand	---	205	488	987	1,238	1,441	1,527	1,611	1,710	1,857
Norway	49	140	659	1,385	1,892	2,314	2,561	2,747	3,258	3,409
Poland	---	---	---	298	423	563	571	578	629	654
Portugal	---	54	283	661	1,080	1,290	1,424	1,570	1,662	1,702
Slovak Republic	---	---	---	---	---	559	578	591	633	698
Spain	16	97	363	865	1,195	1,371	1,467	1,493	1,567	1,646
Sweden	---	305	924	1,566	1,733	1,961	2,119	2,243	2,370	2,517
Switzerland	166	350	1,031	2,040	2,555	2,967	2,985	3,111	3,288	3,446
Turkey	---	24	76	165	184	312	392	446	---	---
United Kingdom	84	160	472	977	1,393	1,607	1,725	1,839	2,012	2,160
United States	143	348	1,067	2,738	3,698	4,098	4,302	4,560	4,914	5,317

--- Data not available.

[1]Per capita health expenditures for each country have been adjusted to U.S. dollars using gross domestic product purchasing power parities (PPP) for each year.

NOTE: These data include revisions in health expenditures and may differ from previous editions of *Health, United States*.

SOURCES: All countries except United States from the Organization for Economic Cooperation and Development Health Data File 2004, 3rd edition following the annual update, www.oecd.org/els/health; United States data from the Centers for Medicare & Medicaid Services, Office of the Actuary, National Health Statistics Group, National health expenditures, 2003. Internet address: cms.hhs.gov/statistics/nhe.

Table 119. Gross domestic product, Federal and State and local government expenditures, national health expenditures, and average annual percent change: United States, selected years 1960–2003

[Data are compiled from various sources by the Centers for Medicare & Medicaid Services]

Gross domestic product, government expenditures, and national health expenditures	1960	1970	1980	1990	1995	2000	2001	2002	2003
					Amount in billions				
Gross domestic product (GDP)	$ 527	$1,040	$2,796	$ 5,803	$ 7,401	$ 9,817	$ 10,128	$ 10,487	$ 11,004
Federal government expenditures	85.8	198.6	576.6	1,228.7	1,575.7	1,864.4	1,969.5	2,101.8	2,241.6
State and local government expenditures	38.1	107.5	307.8	660.8	902.5	1,269.5	1,368.2	1,436.9	1,498.1
National health expenditures	26.7	73.1	245.8	696.0	990.2	1,309.9	1,426.4	1,559.0	1,678.9
Private	20.1	45.4	140.9	413.5	533.6	717.5	771.8	841.0	913.2
Public	6.6	27.6	104.8	282.5	456.6	592.4	654.6	718.0	765.7
Federal government	2.8	17.6	71.3	192.7	322.4	416.0	463.8	508.6	541.7
State and local government	3.8	10.0	33.5	89.8	134.2	176.4	190.8	209.4	224.0
					Amount per capita				
National health expenditures	$ 143	$ 348	$1,067	$ 2,738	$ 3,698	$ 4,560	$ 4,914	$ 5,317	$ 5,671
Private	108	216	612	1,627	1,993	2,498	2,659	2,869	3,084
Public	35	131	455	1,111	1,705	2,062	2,255	2,449	2,586
					Percent				
National health expenditures as percent of GDP	5.1	7.0	8.8	12.0	13.4	13.3	14.1	14.9	15.3
Health expenditures as a percent of total government expenditures									
Federal	3.3	8.9	12.4	15.7	20.5	22.3	23.5	24.2	24.2
State and local	9.9	9.3	10.9	13.6	14.9	13.9	13.9	14.6	15.0
					Percent distribution				
National health expenditures	100.0	100.0	100.0	100.0	100.0	100.0	100.0	100.0	100.0
Private	75.2	62.2	57.3	59.4	53.9	54.8	54.1	53.9	54.4
Public	24.8	37.8	42.7	40.6	46.1	45.2	45.9	46.1	45.6
					Average annual percent change from previous year shown				
Gross domestic product	. . .	7.0	10.4	7.6	5.0	5.8	3.2	3.5	4.9
Federal government expenditures	. . .	8.8	11.2	7.9	5.1	3.1	5.6	6.7	6.7
State and local government expenditures	. . .	10.9	11.1	7.9	6.4	5.4	7.8	5.0	4.3
National health expenditures	. . .	10.6	12.9	11.0	7.3	5.8	8.9	9.3	7.7
Private	. . .	8.5	12.0	11.4	5.2	6.1	7.6	9.0	8.6
Public	. . .	15.4	14.3	10.4	10.1	5.3	10.5	9.7	6.6
Federal government	. . .	20.1	15.0	10.5	10.8	5.2	11.5	9.7	6.5
State and local government	. . .	10.2	12.8	10.4	8.4	5.6	8.2	9.7	7.0
National health expenditures, per capita	. . .	9.3	11.9	9.9	6.2	4.5	7.8	8.2	6.6
Private	. . .	7.2	11.0	10.3	4.1	4.9	6.5	7.9	7.5
Public	. . .	14.0	13.2	9.3	8.9	4.1	9.4	8.6	5.6

. . . Category not applicable.

NOTES: These data include revisions in health expenditures and may differ from previous editions of *Health, United States.* They reflect U.S. Bureau of the Census resident population estimates as of July 2004. Federal and State and local government total expenditures reflect September 2004 revisions from the Bureau of Economic Analysis. Percents are calculated using unrounded data.

SOURCE: Centers for Medicare & Medicaid Services, Office of the Actuary, National Health Statistics Group, National health accounts, National health expenditures, 2003. Internet address: www.cms.hhs.gov/statistics/nhe/.

Table 120. Consumer Price Index and average annual percent change for all items, selected items, and medical care components: United States, selected years 1960–2004

[Data are based on reporting by samples of providers and other retail outlets]

Items and medical care components	*1960*	*1970*	*1980*	*1990*	*1995*	*2000*	*2001*	*2002*	*2003*	*2004*
	Consumer Price Index (CPI)									
All items	29.6	38.8	82.4	130.7	152.4	172.2	177.1	179.9	184.0	188.9
All items excluding medical care	30.2	39.2	82.8	128.8	148.6	167.3	171.9	174.3	178.1	182.7
All services	24.1	35.0	77.9	139.2	168.7	195.3	203.4	209.8	216.5	222.8
Food	30.0	39.2	86.8	132.4	148.4	167.8	173.1	176.2	180.0	186.2
Apparel	45.7	59.2	90.9	124.1	132.0	129.6	127.3	124.0	120.9	120.4
Housing	- - -	36.4	81.1	128.5	148.5	169.6	176.4	180.3	184.8	189.5
Energy	22.4	25.5	86.0	102.1	105.2	124.6	129.3	121.7	136.5	151.4
Medical care	22.3	34.0	74.9	162.8	220.5	260.8	272.8	285.6	297.1	310.1
Components of medical care										
Medical care services	19.5	32.3	74.8	162.7	224.2	266.0	278.8	292.9	306.0	321.3
Professional services	- - -	37.0	77.9	156.1	201.0	237.7	246.5	253.9	261.2	271.5
Physicians' services	21.9	34.5	76.5	160.8	208.8	244.7	253.6	260.6	267.7	278.3
Dental services	27.0	39.2	78.9	155.8	206.8	258.5	269.0	281.0	292.5	306.9
Eye glasses and eye care[1]	- - -	- - -	- - -	117.3	137.0	149.7	154.5	155.5	155.9	159.3
Services by other medical professionals[1]	- - -	- - -	- - -	120.2	143.9	161.9	167.3	171.8	177.1	181.9
Hospital and related services	- - -	- - -	69.2	178.0	257.8	317.3	338.3	367.8	394.8	417.9
Hospital services[2]	- - -	- - -	- - -	- - -	- - -	115.9	123.6	134.7	144.7	153.4
Inpatient hospital services[2,3]	- - -	- - -	- - -	- - -	- - -	113.8	121.0	131.2	140.1	148.1
Outpatient hospital services[1,3]	- - -	- - -	- - -	138.7	204.6	263.8	281.1	309.8	337.9	356.3
Hospital rooms	9.3	23.6	68.0	175.4	251.2	- - -	- - -	- - -	- - -	- - -
Other inpatient services[1]	- - -	- - -	- - -	142.7	206.8	- - -	- - -	- - -	- - -	- - -
Nursing homes and adult day care[2]	- - -	- - -	- - -	- - -	- - -	117.0	121.8	127.9	135.2	140.4
Medical care commodities	46.9	46.5	75.4	163.4	204.5	238.1	247.6	256.4	262.8	269.3
Prescription drugs and medical supplies	54.0	47.4	72.5	181.7	235.0	285.4	300.9	316.5	326.3	337.1
Nonprescription drugs and medical supplies[1]	- - -	- - -	- - -	120.6	140.5	149.5	150.6	150.4	152.0	152.3
Internal and respiratory over-the-counter drugs	- - -	42.3	74.9	145.9	167.0	176.9	178.9	178.8	181.2	180.9
Nonprescription medical equipment and supplies	- - -	- - -	79.2	138.0	166.3	178.1	178.2	177.5	178.1	179.7
	Average annual percent change from previous year shown									
All items	. . .	2.7	7.8	4.7	3.1	2.5	2.8	1.6	2.3	2.7
All items excluding medical care	. . .	2.6	7.8	4.5	2.9	2.4	2.7	1.4	2.2	2.6
All services	. . .	3.8	8.3	6.0	3.9	3.0	4.1	3.1	3.2	2.9
Food	. . .	2.7	8.3	4.3	2.3	2.5	3.2	1.8	2.2	3.4
Apparel	. . .	2.6	4.4	3.2	1.2	–0.4	–1.8	–2.6	–2.5	–0.4
Housing	. . .	- - -	8.3	4.7	2.9	2.7	4.0	2.2	2.5	2.5
Energy	. . .	1.3	12.9	1.7	0.6	3.4	3.8	–5.9	12.2	10.9
Medical care	. . .	4.3	8.2	8.1	6.3	3.4	4.6	4.7	4.0	4.4
Components of medical care										
Medical care services	. . .	5.2	8.8	8.1	6.6	3.5	4.8	5.1	4.5	5.0
Professional services	. . .	- - -	7.7	7.2	5.2	3.4	3.7	3.0	2.9	3.9
Physicians' services	. . .	4.6	8.3	7.7	5.4	3.2	3.6	2.8	2.7	4.0
Dental services	. . .	3.8	7.2	7.0	5.8	4.6	4.1	4.5	4.1	4.9
Eye glasses and eye care[1]	. . .	- - -	- - -	- - -	3.2	1.8	3.2	0.6	0.3	2.2
Services by other medical professionals[1]	. . .	- - -	- - -	- - -	3.7	2.4	3.3	2.7	3.1	2.7
Hospital and related services	. . .	- - -	- - -	9.9	7.7	4.2	6.6	8.7	7.3	5.9
Hospital services[2]	. . .	- - -	- - -	- - -	- - -	- - -	6.6	9.0	7.4	6.0
Inpatient hospital services[2,3]	. . .	- - -	- - -	- - -	- - -	- - -	6.3	8.4	6.8	5.7
Outpatient hospital services[1,3]	. . .	- - -	- - -	- - -	8.1	5.2	6.6	10.2	9.1	5.4
Hospital rooms	. . .	9.8	11.2	9.9	7.4	- - -	- - -	- - -	- - -	- - -
Other inpatient services[1]	. . .	- - -	- - -	- - -	7.7	- - -	- - -	- - -	- - -	- - -
Nursing homes and adult day care[2]	. . .	- - -	- - -	- - -	- - -	- - -	4.1	5.0	5.7	3.8
Medical care commodities	. . .	–0.1	5.0	8.0	4.6	3.1	4.0	3.6	2.5	2.5
Prescription drugs and medical supplies	. . .	–1.3	4.3	9.6	5.3	4.0	5.4	5.2	3.1	3.3
Nonprescription drugs and medical supplies[1]	. . .	- - -	- - -	- - -	3.1	1.2	0.7	–0.1	1.1	0.2
Internal and respiratory over-the-counter drugs	. . .	- - -	5.9	6.9	2.7	1.2	1.1	–0.1	1.3	–0.2
Nonprescription medical equipment and supplies	. . .	- - -	- - -	5.7	3.8	1.4	0.1	–0.4	0.3	0.9

- - - Data not available.
. . . Category not applicable.
[1]December 1986 = 100.
[2]December 1996 = 100.
[3]Special index based on a substantially smaller sample.

NOTES: Consumer Price Index for all urban consumers (CPI-U) U.S. city average, detailed expenditure categories. 1982–84 = 100, except where noted. Data are not seasonally adjusted.

SOURCE: U.S. Department of Labor, Bureau of Labor Statistics, Consumer Price Index. Various releases. 2004 data available from the Bureau of Labor Statistics Web site at www.bls.gov/cpi/cpid04av.pdf.

Table 121. Growth in personal health care expenditures and percent distribution of factors affecting growth: United States, 1960–2003

[Data are compiled from various sources by the Centers for Medicare & Medicaid Services]

Period	Average annual percent increase	Factors affecting growth				
			Inflation[1]			
		All factors	Economy-wide	Medical	Population	Intensity[2]
		Percent distribution[3]				
1960–2003	10.1	100	39	17	11	32
1960–65	8.2	100	17	10	18	55
1965–70	12.7	100	33	12	8	46
1970–75	12.3	100	55	1	8	36
1975–80	13.7	100	55	12	7	26
1980–85	11.7	100	46	32	9	13
1980–81	16.1	100	60	17	7	16
1981–82	12.4	100	51	36	9	5
1982–83	10.1	100	40	35	10	14
1983–84	9.7	100	40	39	10	11
1984–85	10.1	100	31	41	10	18
1985–90	10.4	100	32	26	10	31
1985–86	8.7	100	26	31	11	31
1986–87	9.6	100	29	23	10	38
1987–88	11.3	100	31	25	9	35
1988–89	10.6	100	37	29	10	24
1989–90	11.7	100	34	24	11	31
1990–95	7.3	100	35	30	18	17
1990–91	10.3	100	35	21	14	30
1991–92	8.5	100	28	35	17	20
1992–93	6.4	100	37	37	21	5
1993–94	5.2	100	41	31	24	4
1994–95	6.0	100	35	27	21	18
1995–2000	5.6	100	30	19	21	30
1995–96	5.2	100	37	21	22	21
1996–97	5.3	100	32	9	23	36
1997–98	5.3	100	21	21	23	35
1998–99	5.5	100	27	24	21	28
1999–2000	6.6	100	34	18	17	31
2000–2003	8.2	100	25	22	13	40
2000–2001	8.7	100	28	17	12	43
2001–2002	8.7	100	20	27	12	42
2002–2003	7.3	100	26	24	14	36

[1]Total inflation is economy-wide and medical inflation is the medical inflation above economy-wide inflation.
[2]The residual percent of growth which cannot be attributed to price increases or population growth represents changes in use or kinds of services and supplies.
[3]Percents may not sum to 100 due to rounding.

NOTES: These data include revisions in health expenditures for 1995 forward and revisions in population for 1990 forward. Additionally, the implicit price deflator for Gross Domestic Product (GDP) is now used to measure economy-wide inflation for all years 1960–2003. Previous estimates of the factors accounting for growth used GDP chain-type price index. All indexes used to calculate the factors affecting growth were rebased in 2003 with base year 2000.

SOURCE: Centers for Medicare & Medicaid Services, Office of the Actuary, National Health Statistics Group, National health accounts, National health expenditures, 2003. Internet address: www.cms.hhs.gov/statistics/nhe/.

Table 122 (page 1 of 2). National health expenditures, average annual percent change, and percent distribution, according to type of expenditure: United States, selected years 1960–2003

[Data are compiled from various sources by the Centers for Medicare & Medicaid Services]

Type of national health expenditure	*1960*	*1970*	*1980*	*1990*	*1995*	*2000*	*2001*	*2002*	*2003*
					Amount in billions				
National health expenditures	$26.7	$73.1	$245.8	$696.0	$990.2	$1,309.9	$1,426.4	$1,559.0	$1,678.9
Health services and supplies	25.0	67.3	233.5	669.6	957.6	1,260.9	1,373.8	1,499.8	1,614.2
Personal health care	23.4	63.2	214.6	609.4	865.7	1,136.1	1,235.5	1,342.9	1,440.8
Hospital care	9.2	27.6	101.5	253.9	343.6	413.1	446.4	484.2	515.9
Professional services	8.3	20.7	67.3	216.9	316.5	426.4	464.4	503.0	542.0
Physician and clinical services	5.4	14.0	47.1	157.5	220.5	290.2	315.1	340.8	369.7
Other professional services	0.4	0.7	3.6	18.2	28.6	38.8	42.6	46.1	48.5
Dental services	2.0	4.7	13.3	31.5	44.5	60.7	65.6	70.9	74.3
Other personal health care	0.6	1.3	3.3	9.6	22.9	36.7	41.1	45.3	49.5
Nursing home and home health	0.9	4.4	20.1	65.3	105.1	126.9	134.9	143.1	150.8
Home health care[1]	0.1	0.2	2.4	12.6	30.5	31.6	33.7	36.5	40.0
Nursing home care[1]	0.8	4.2	17.7	52.7	74.6	95.3	101.2	106.6	110.8
Retail outlet sales of medical products	5.0	10.5	25.7	73.3	100.5	169.7	189.7	212.6	232.1
Prescription drugs	2.7	5.5	12.0	40.3	60.8	121.5	140.8	161.8	179.2
Other medical products	2.3	5.0	13.7	33.1	39.7	48.1	48.9	50.7	52.9
Government administration and net cost of private health insurance	1.2	2.8	12.1	40.0	60.5	81.0	90.9	105.7	119.7
Government public health activities[2]	0.4	1.4	6.7	20.2	31.4	43.9	47.4	51.2	53.8
Investment	1.7	5.7	12.3	26.4	32.6	49.0	52.6	59.2	64.6
Research[3]	0.7	2.0	5.5	12.7	17.1	29.1	32.9	36.5	40.2
Construction	1.0	3.8	6.8	13.7	15.5	19.8	19.7	22.7	24.5
					Average annual percent change from previous year shown				
National health expenditures	. . .	10.6	12.9	11.0	7.3	5.8	8.9	9.3	7.7
Health services and supplies	. . .	10.4	13.2	11.1	7.4	5.7	9.0	9.2	7.6
Personal health care	. . .	10.5	13.0	11.0	7.3	5.6	8.7	8.7	7.3
Hospital care	. . .	11.7	13.9	9.6	6.2	3.8	8.1	8.5	6.5
Professional services	. . .	9.5	12.5	12.4	7.9	6.1	8.9	8.3	7.8
Physician and clinical services	. . .	10.1	12.9	12.8	7.0	5.6	8.6	8.2	8.5
Other professional services	. . .	6.6	17.1	17.5	9.5	6.3	9.9	8.0	5.3
Dental services	. . .	9.1	11.1	9.0	7.1	6.4	8.0	8.0	4.8
Other personal health care	. . .	7.2	10.0	11.4	18.9	9.9	12.1	10.1	9.2
Nursing home and home health	. . .	17.2	16.3	12.5	10.0	3.8	6.3	6.1	5.4
Home health care[1]	. . .	14.5	26.9	18.1	19.4	0.7	6.5	8.5	9.5
Nursing home care[1]	. . .	17.4	15.4	11.5	7.2	5.0	6.2	5.3	4.0
Retail outlet sales of medical products	. . .	7.8	9.4	11.1	6.5	11.0	11.8	12.0	9.2
Prescription drugs	. . .	7.5	8.2	12.8	8.6	14.9	15.9	14.9	10.7
Other medical products	. . .	8.1	10.6	9.2	3.8	3.9	1.7	3.6	4.2
Government administration and net cost of private health insurance	. . .	8.6	15.9	12.7	8.6	6.0	12.3	16.3	13.2
Government public health activities	. . .	13.2	17.4	11.6	9.2	6.9	8.1	7.9	5.1
Investment	. . .	12.9	7.9	8.0	4.3	8.5	7.4	12.7	9.1
Research[3]	. . .	10.9	10.8	8.8	6.2	11.3	12.9	11.0	10.0
Construction	. . .	14.1	6.1	7.3	2.4	5.1	–0.7	15.5	7.7

See footnotes at end of table.

Table 122 (page 2 of 2). National health expenditures, average annual percent change, and percent distribution, according to type of expenditure: United States, selected years 1960–2003

[Data are compiled from various sources by the Centers for Medicare & Medicaid Services]

Type of national health expenditure	*1960*	*1970*	*1980*	*1990*	*1995*	*2000*	*2001*	*2002*	*2003*
	Percent distribution								
National health expenditures	100.0	100.0	100.0	100.0	100.0	100.0	100.0	100.0	100.0
Health services and supplies	93.6	92.2	95.0	96.2	96.7	96.3	96.3	96.2	96.1
Personal health care	87.6	86.5	87.3	87.6	87.4	86.7	86.6	86.1	85.8
Hospital care	34.4	37.8	41.3	36.5	34.7	31.5	31.3	31.1	30.7
Professional services	31.3	28.3	27.4	31.2	32.0	32.6	32.6	32.3	32.3
Physician and clinical services	20.1	19.1	19.2	22.6	22.3	22.2	22.1	21.9	22.0
Other professional services	1.5	1.0	1.5	2.6	2.9	3.0	3.0	3.0	2.9
Dental services	7.4	6.4	5.4	4.5	4.5	4.6	4.6	4.5	4.4
Other personal health care	2.4	1.7	1.3	1.4	2.3	2.8	2.9	2.9	2.9
Nursing home and home health	3.4	6.1	8.2	9.4	10.6	9.7	9.5	9.2	9.0
Home health care[1]	0.2	0.3	1.0	1.8	3.1	2.4	2.4	2.3	2.4
Nursing home care[1]	3.2	5.8	7.2	7.6	7.5	7.3	7.1	6.8	6.6
Retail outlet sales of medical products	18.6	14.3	10.5	10.5	10.2	13.0	13.3	13.6	13.8
Prescription drugs	10.0	7.5	4.9	5.8	6.1	9.3	9.9	10.4	10.7
Other medical products	8.5	6.8	5.6	4.7	4.0	3.7	3.4	3.3	3.1
Government administration and net cost of private health insurance	4.5	3.8	4.9	5.7	6.1	6.2	6.4	6.8	7.1
Government public health activities	1.5	1.9	2.7	2.9	3.2	3.3	3.3	3.3	3.2
Investment	6.4	7.8	5.0	3.8	3.3	3.7	3.7	3.8	3.9
Research[3]	2.6	2.7	2.2	1.8	1.7	2.2	2.3	2.3	2.4
Construction	3.8	5.2	2.8	2.0	1.6	1.5	1.4	1.5	1.5

. . . Category not applicable.

[1]Freestanding facilities only. Additional services of this type are provided in hospital-based facilities and counted as hospital care.

[2]Includes personal care services delivered by government public health agencies.

[3]Research and development expenditures of drug companies and other manufacturers and providers of medical equipment and supplies are excluded from "research expenditures," but are included in the expenditure class in which the product falls in that they are covered by the payment received for that product.

NOTES: These data include revisions in health expenditures and differ from previous editions of *Health, United States*. Percents are calculated using unrounded data.

SOURCE: Centers for Medicare & Medicaid Services, Office of the Actuary, National Health Statistics Group, National health accounts, National health expenditures, 2003. Internet address: www.cms.hhs.gov/statistics/nhe/.

Table 123 (page 1 of 2). Personal health care expenditures, according to type of expenditure and source of funds: United States, selected years 1960–2003

[Data are compiled from various sources by the Centers for Medicare & Medicaid Services]

Type of personal health care expenditures and source of funds	*1960*	*1970*	*1980*	*1990*	*1995*	*2000*	*2001*	*2002*	*2003*
					Amount				
Per capita	$ 126	$ 301	$ 931	$2,398	$3,233	$ 3,955	$ 4,257	$ 4,580	$ 4,866
					Amount in billions				
All personal health care expenditures[1]	$ 23.4	$ 63.2	$214.6	$609.4	$865.7	$1,136.1	$1,235.5	$1,342.9	$1,440.8
					Percent distribution				
All sources of funds	100.0	100.0	100.0	100.0	100.0	100.0	100.0	100.0	100.0
Out-of-pocket payments	55.2	39.7	27.1	22.5	16.9	17.0	16.3	16.0	16.0
Private health insurance	21.4	22.3	28.3	33.4	33.4	35.1	35.4	35.7	36.0
Other private funds	2.0	2.8	4.3	5.0	5.1	4.8	4.4	4.2	4.2
Government	21.4	35.2	40.3	39.0	44.6	43.1	43.8	44.2	43.8
Federal	8.7	22.9	29.3	28.6	34.1	32.7	33.5	33.7	33.3
State and local	12.6	12.3	11.1	10.5	10.5	10.4	10.3	10.5	10.5
					Amount in billions				
Hospital care expenditures[2]	$ 9.2	$ 27.6	$101.5	$253.9	$343.6	$ 413.1	$ 446.4	$ 484.2	$ 515.9
					Percent distribution				
All sources of funds	100.0	100.0	100.0	100.0	100.0	100.0	100.0	100.0	100.0
Out-of-pocket payments	20.8	9.1	5.2	4.4	3.1	3.1	3.0	3.1	3.2
Private health insurance	35.8	32.6	35.6	38.3	32.5	33.4	33.6	33.8	34.4
Other private funds	1.2	3.3	4.9	4.1	4.3	4.9	4.4	4.1	4.1
Government[3]	42.2	55.1	54.3	53.2	60.1	58.6	59.1	59.0	58.3
Medicaid[4]	. . .	9.6	10.4	10.9	15.9	16.9	16.6	17.1	16.9
Medicare	. . .	19.4	26.0	26.7	31.2	30.6	31.1	30.7	30.3
					Amount in billions				
Physician services expenditures	$ 5.4	$ 14.0	$ 47.1	$157.5	$220.5	$ 290.2	$ 315.1	$ 340.8	$ 369.7
					Percent distribution				
All sources of funds	100.0	100.0	100.0	100.0	100.0	100.0	100.0	100.0	100.0
Out-of-pocket payments	61.6	46.1	30.2	19.3	11.9	11.1	10.5	10.2	10.2
Private health insurance	29.8	30.1	35.3	43.0	48.5	48.5	48.6	49.1	49.7
Other private funds	1.4	1.6	3.9	7.2	8.0	7.3	7.1	6.9	6.9
Government[3]	7.2	22.2	30.5	30.6	31.6	33.1	33.8	33.8	33.3
Medicaid[4]	. . .	4.6	5.2	4.5	6.7	6.6	6.9	7.2	7.1
Medicare	. . .	11.8	17.4	19.1	19.0	20.4	20.7	20.2	19.9
					Amount in billions				
Nursing home expenditures[5]	$ 0.8	$ 4.2	$ 17.7	$ 52.7	$ 74.6	$ 95.3	$ 101.2	$ 106.6	$ 110.8
					Percent distribution				
All sources of funds	100.0	100.0	100.0	100.0	100.0	100.0	100.0	100.0	100.0
Out-of-pocket payments	77.9	53.6	40.0	37.5	26.9	28.7	27.9	26.6	27.9
Private health insurance	0.0	0.2	1.2	5.8	7.5	7.9	7.8	7.6	7.6
Other private funds	6.3	4.9	4.5	7.5	6.4	4.5	3.8	3.6	3.8
Government[3]	15.7	41.2	54.2	49.2	59.1	58.9	60.4	62.3	60.7
Medicaid[4]	. . .	22.3	50.2	43.9	47.5	46.7	46.1	47.4	46.1
Medicare	. . .	3.4	1.7	3.2	9.3	10.0	12.0	12.7	12.4

See footnotes at end of table.

Table 123 (page 2 of 2). Personal health care expenditures, according to type of expenditure and source of funds: United States, selected years 1960–2003

[Data are compiled from various sources by the Centers for Medicare & Medicaid Services]

Type of personal health care expenditures and source of funds	*1960*	*1970*	*1980*	*1990*	*1995*	*2000*	*2001*	*2002*	*2003*
	Amount in billions								
Prescription drug expenditures	$ 2.7	$ 5.5	$ 12.0	$ 40.3	$ 60.8	$121.5	$140.8	$161.8	$179.2
	Percent distribution								
All sources of funds	100.0	100.0	100.0	100.0	100.0	100.0	100.0	100.0	100.0
Out-of-pocket payments	96.0	82.4	69.4	59.1	42.7	31.5	30.2	29.5	29.7
Private health insurance	1.3	8.8	16.7	24.4	37.1	46.5	47.5	47.7	46.3
Other private funds	0.0	0.0	0.0	0.0	0.0	0.0	0.0	0.0	0.0
Government[3]	2.7	8.8	13.9	16.6	20.1	21.9	22.3	22.9	24.1
Medicaid[4]	. . .	7.6	11.7	12.6	16.0	17.1	17.4	17.7	18.8
Medicare	. . .	0.0	0.0	0.5	1.3	1.9	1.8	1.6	1.6
	Amount in billions								
All other personal health care expenditures[6]	$ 5.3	$ 11.9	$ 36.3	$104.9	$166.2	$216.0	$232.0	$249.5	$265.1
	Percent distribution								
All sources of funds	100.0	100.0	100.0	100.0	100.0	100.0	100.0	100.0	100.0
Out-of-pocket payments	84.2	78.6	64.3	49.6	38.3	38.3	36.5	35.5	34.9
Private health insurance	1.6	3.3	15.5	24.7	25.2	26.2	25.8	25.3	25.0
Other private funds	4.2	3.6	4.3	4.7	4.3	4.0	3.7	3.5	3.4
Government[3]	10.1	14.5	16.0	20.9	32.2	31.6	34.0	35.7	36.7
Medicaid[4]	. . .	3.3	3.9	6.5	12.5	15.7	17.2	18.3	19.1
Medicare	. . .	1.1	3.8	7.1	13.1	9.0	9.8	10.4	10.6

. . . Category not applicable.
[1]Includes all expenditures for specified health services and supplies other than expenses for program administration, net cost of private health insurance, and government public health activities.
[2]Includes expenditures for hospital-based nursing home care and home health agency care.
[3]Includes other government expenditures for these health care services, for example, Medicaid State Children's Health Insurance Program (SCHIP) expansion and SCHIP, care funded by the Department of Veterans Affairs, and State and locally financed subsidies to hospitals.
[4]Excludes Medicaid SCHIP expansion and SCHIP.
[5]Includes expenditures for care in freestanding nursing homes. Expenditures for care in facility-based nursing homes are included with hospital care.
[6]Includes expenditures for dental services, other professional services, home health care, nonprescription drugs and other medical nondurables, vision products and other medical durables, and other personal health care, not shown separately.

NOTES: These data include revisions in health expenditures and differ from previous editions of *Health, United States*. Percents are calculated using unrounded data.

SOURCE: Centers for Medicare & Medicaid Services, Office of the Actuary, National Health Statistics Group, National health accounts, National health expenditures, 2003. Internet address: www.cms.hhs.gov/statistics/nhe/.

Table 124 (page 1 of 2). Expenses for health care and prescribed medicine according to selected population characteristics: United States, selected years 1987–2002

[Data are based on household interviews of a sample of the noninstitutionalized population and a sample of medical providers]

Characteristic	Population in millions[2]			Total expenses[1]							
				Percent of persons with expense				Mean annual expense per person with expense[3]			
	1997	2000	2002	1987	1997	2000	2002	1987	1997	2000	2002
All ages	271.3	278.4	288.2	84.5	84.1	83.5	85.2	$2,474	$2,717	$2,821	$3,302
Under 65 years:											
Total	237.1	243.6	251.9	83.2	82.5	81.8	83.6	$1,926	$2,060	$2,222	$2,557
Under 6 years	23.8	24.1	23.3	88.9	88.0	86.7	88.8	1,636	962	1,174	1,364
6–17 years	48.1	48.4	49.5	80.2	81.7	80.0	83.6	1,078	1,079	1,167	1,228
18–44 years	108.9	109.0	111.2	81.5	78.3	77.7	78.5	1,693	1,867	1,990	2,233
45–64 years	56.3	62.1	68.0	87.0	89.2	88.5	90.0	3,278	3,616	3,721	4,321
Sex											
Male	118.0	120.9	125.4	78.8	77.6	76.6	78.2	1,816	1,862	2,127	2,350
Female	119.1	122.7	126.6	87.5	87.4	87.0	89.0	2,019	2,235	2,305	2,737
Hispanic origin and race[4]											
Hispanic or Latino	29.4	32.0	37.5	71.0	69.5	69.0	69.6	1,536	1,715	1,514	1,793
Not Hispanic or Latino:											
White	166.2	169.2	165.8	86.9	87.2	86.6	88.7	1,932	2,210	2,324	2,761
Black or African American	31.3	32.1	31.8	72.2	72.1	71.3	76.1	2,330	1,652	2,360	2,557
Other	10.2	10.2	16.8	72.8	75.8	76.0	78.6	1,278	1,370	1,894	1,790
Insurance status[5]											
Any private insurance	174.0	181.6	181.5	86.5	86.5	85.9	88.2	1,847	2,099	2,117	2,485
Public insurance only	29.8	29.7	36.7	82.4	83.3	83.6	84.7	3,098	2,504	3,373	3,590
Uninsured all year	33.3	32.3	33.7	61.8	61.1	57.3	57.4	1,204	1,231	1,567	1,491
65 years and over	34.2	34.8	36.3	93.7	95.2	95.5	96.3	$6,110	$6,666	$6,415	$7,797
Sex											
Male	14.6	15.0	15.4	92.0	94.5	93.4	95.8	6,252	7,491	6,878	8,186
Female	19.6	19.8	20.8	94.9	95.7	97.1	96.7	6,010	6,058	6,077	7,511
Hispanic origin and race[4]											
Hispanic or Latino	1.7	1.9	2.2	82.5	94.2	92.5	90.2	5,818	6,975	5,756	7,925
Not Hispanic or Latino:											
White	28.8	28.9	29.6	94.9	95.9	95.9	97.2	6,015	6,699	6,512	7,824
Black or African American	2.8	2.9	3.0	88.5	92.2	94.0	93.8	7,364	6,565	6,169	7,938
Other	*	*	1.4	*	*	*	92.5	*	*	*	6,678
Insurance status[6]											
Medicare only	8.8	12.0	11.1	85.9	92.1	94.8	95.1	4,813	6,141	5,508	7,180
Medicare and private insurance	21.7	19.2	20.4	95.4	97.0	96.0	97.6	6,045	6,501	6,578	7,814
Medicare and other public coverage	3.2	3.2	4.3	94.4	93.2	96.3	95.3	9,388	9,395	8,802	9,606

See footnotes at end of table.

Table 124 (page 2 of 2). Expenses for health care and prescribed medicine according to selected population characteristics: United States, selected years 1987–2002

[Data are based on household interviews of a sample of the noninstitutionalized population and a sample of medical providers]

	Prescribed medicine expenses							
	Percent of persons with expense				*Mean annual out-of-pocket expense per person with out-of-pocket expense*[3,7]			
Characteristic	*1987*	*1997*	*2000*	*2002*	*1987*	*1997*	*2000*	*2002*
All ages	57.3	62.1	62.3	64.4	$146	$226	$286	$344
Under 65 years:								
Total	54.0	58.7	58.5	60.6	$108	$160	$208	242
Under 6 years	61.8	61.3	56.9	58.4	38	39	39	43
6–17 years	44.3	48.2	46.2	50.0	71	61	73	86
18–44 years	51.3	55.9	56.0	56.8	84	137	158	191
45–64 years	65.3	71.8	73.3	75.3	204	298	392	434
Sex								
Male	46.5	51.5	51.3	53.2	100	142	183	212
Female	61.4	65.8	65.6	67.9	114	174	228	265
Hispanic origin and race[4]								
Hispanic or Latino	41.6	47.7	45.0	45.5	78	106	153	177
Not Hispanic or Latino:								
White	57.7	63.1	63.8	66.7	112	174	224	259
Black or African American	44.1	50.0	47.6	51.2	95	129	171	227
Other	41.1	44.8	47.8	51.6	79	139	146	181
Insurance status[5]								
Any private insurance	56.5	61.6	61.6	64.9	111	152	179	217
Public insurance only	56.5	62.0	62.4	60.1	74	158	298	267
Uninsured all year	35.1	40.2	37.6	38.1	119	231	345	426
65 years and over	81.6	86.0	88.3	90.5	$336	$541	651	817
Sex								
Male	78.0	82.8	83.9	89.1	312	488	488	674
Female	84.0	88.3	91.5	91.4	350	578	764	920
Hispanic origin and race[4]								
Hispanic or Latino	74.7	87.5	83.9	83.4	443	442	548	678
Not Hispanic or Latino:								
White	82.3	86.7	89.0	91.6	342	559	675	840
Black or African American	79.5	85.3	85.3	87.8	263	449	556	742
Other	*	*	*	83.2	*	*	*	667
Insurance status[6]								
Medicare only	70.6	82.1	87.7	89.6	371	625	777	1,067
Medicare and private insurance	83.4	88.1	89.0	91.7	348	549	602	753
Medicare and other public coverage	88.2	85.0	88.5	89.4	127	303	515	507

* Estimates are considered unreliable. Data not shown are based on fewer than 100 sample cases. Data preceded by an asterisk have a relative standard error equal to or greater than 30 percent.

[1]Includes expenses for inpatient hospital and physician services, ambulatory physician and nonphysician services, prescribed medicines, home health services, dental services, and other medical equipment, supplies, and services that were purchased or rented during the year. Excludes expenses for over-the-counter medications, alternative care services, phone contacts with health providers, and premiums for health insurance.

[2]Includes persons in the civilian noninstitutionalized population for all or part of the year. Expenditures for persons only in this population for part of the year are restricted to those incurred during periods of eligibility (e.g., expenses incurred during periods of institutionalization and military service are not included in estimates).

[3]Estimates of expenses have been updated to 2002 dollars using the Consumer Price Index (all items) and differ from the previous edition of *Health, United States.* See Appendix II, Consumer Price Index (CPI).

[4]Persons of Hispanic origin may be of any race. Beginning in 2002, MEPS respondents were allowed to report multiple races and these persons are included in the "Other" category. As a result, there is a slight increase in percent of persons classified in the "Other" category in 2002 compared with prior years.

[5]Any private insurance includes individuals with insurance that provided coverage for hospital and physician care at any time during the year, other than Medicare, Medicaid, or other public coverage for hospital or physician services. Public insurance only includes individuals who were not covered by private insurance at any time during the year but were covered by Medicare, Medicaid, other public coverage for hospital or physician services, and/or CHAMPUS/CHAMPVA (TRICARE) at any point during the year. Uninsured includes persons not covered by either private or public insurance throughout the entire year or period of eligibility for the survey.

[6]Populations do not add to total because uninsured persons and persons with unknown insurance status were excluded.

[7]Includes expenses for all prescribed medications that were purchased or refilled during the survey year.

NOTES: 1987 estimates are based on National Medical Expenditure Survey (NMES) while estimates for other years are based on Medical Expenditure Panel Survey (MEPS). Because expenditures in NMES were based primarily on charges while those for MEPS were based on payments, NMES data were adjusted to be more comparable to MEPS using estimated charge to payment ratios for 1987. Overall, this resulted in about an 11-percent reduction from the unadjusted 1987 NMES expenditure estimates. See Zuvekas S and Cohen S. A guide to comparing health care estimates in the 1996 Medical Expenditure Panel Survey to the 1987 National Medical Expenditure Survey. Inquiry. vol. 39. Spring 2002. Data for additional years are available. See Appendix III.

SOURCE: Agency for Healthcare Research and Quality, Center for Cost and Financing Studies. 1987 National Medical Expenditure Survey and 1996–2002 Medical Expenditure Panel Surveys.

Table 125 (page 1 of 2). Sources of payment for health care according to selected population characteristics: United States, selected years 1987–2002

[Data are based on household interviews of a sample of the noninstitutionalized population and a sample of medical providers]

Characteristic	All sources	Out of pocket 1987	Out of pocket 1997	Out of pocket 2000	Out of pocket 2002	Private insurance[1] 1987	Private insurance[1] 1997	Private insurance[1] 2000	Private insurance[1] 2002
		Percent distribution							
All ages	100.0	24.8	19.4	19.4	19.1	36.6	40.3	40.3	38.8
Under 65 years:									
Total	100.0	26.2	21.1	20.3	20.3	46.6	53.1	52.5	51.1
Under 6 years	100.0	18.5	14.2	10.3	9.1	39.5	49.3	51.2	36.1
6–17 years	100.0	35.7	29.0	27.7	25.6	47.3	53.2	48.8	43.7
18–44 years	100.0	27.4	21.1	19.9	20.7	46.8	52.9	51.2	51.8
45–64 years	100.0	24.0	20.1	20.2	20.2	47.8	53.6	54.5	53.7
Sex									
Male	100.0	24.5	21.3	18.1	18.5	44.6	50.3	52.2	49.3
Female	100.0	27.5	21.0	22.1	21.6	48.1	55.1	52.7	52.5
Hispanic origin and race[2]									
Hispanic or Latino	100.0	22.0	18.8	20.5	18.2	36.1	42.3	45.8	35.2
Not Hispanic or Latino:									
White	100.0	28.2	21.8	21.7	21.5	50.1	55.8	55.1	54.5
Black or African American	100.0	15.5	17.1	11.8	13.3	30.0	42.3	40.5	41.6
Other	100.0	27.2	21.2	17.0	21.4	46.7	45.2	51.2	49.0
Insurance status									
Any private insurance[3]	100.0	29.0	21.6	21.2	21.4	60.0	67.6	70.2	69.0
Public insurance only[4]	100.0	8.9	10.6	9.8	8.7	. . .	. . .	. . .	. . .
Uninsured all year[5]	100.0	40.6	41.3	40.4	49.3	. . .	. . .	. . .	. . .
65 years and over	100.0	22.0	16.3	17.5	16.9	15.8	16.5	14.9	14.3
Sex									
Male	100.0	21.7	14.2	14.2	14.2	17.6	20.1	16.8	15.6
Female	100.0	22.2	18.1	20.2	19.0	14.4	13.2	13.3	13.3
Hispanic origin and race[2]									
Hispanic or Latino	100.0	*13.5	13.6	13.9	10.6	*4.7	5.9	8.4	4.2
Not Hispanic or Latino:									
White	100.0	23.7	17.0	18.3	17.9	16.7	17.9	15.2	15.5
Black or African American	100.0	11.2	11.4	13.6	12.3	*11.9	8.8	9.3	10.5
Other	100.0	*	*	*	14.1	*	*	*	10.6
Insurance status									
Medicare only	100.0	29.8	19.8	22.2	21.4	. . .	. . .	. . .	. . .
Medicare and private insurance	100.0	23.4	17.3	17.0	16.9	18.9	25.7	25.3	24.3
Medicare and other public coverage	100.0	*6.2	5.2	9.1	7.9	. . .	. . .	. . .	. . .

See footnotes at end of table.

Table 125 (page 2 of 2). Sources of payment for health care according to selected population characteristics: United States, selected years 1987–2002

[Data are based on household interviews of a sample of the noninstitutionalized population and a sample of medical providers]

	Sources of payment for health care							
	Public coverage[6]				Other[7]			
Characteristic	1987	1997	2000	2002	1987	1997	2000	2002
	Percent distribution							
All ages	34.1	34.4	35.4	37.1	4.5	5.9	5.0	5.0
Under 65 years:								
Total	21.3	18.1	21.3	22.5	6.0	7.7	6.0	6.1
Under 6 years	35.8	25.4	33.6	49.3	6.2	11.2	4.9	*5.4
6–17 years	11.8	14.1	20.1	25.4	5.2	3.7	3.4	5.2
18–44 years	19.4	15.7	21.1	20.9	6.4	10.3	7.8	6.7
45–64 years	22.4	20.3	20.2	20.3	5.8	6.0	5.2	5.9
Sex								
Male	23.9	19.5	23.5	26.5	7.1	8.9	6.3	5.7
Female	19.2	17.0	19.5	19.5	5.2	6.8	5.7	6.4
Hispanic origin and race[2]								
Hispanic or Latino	35.8	28.9	27.5	35.1	6.0	10.0	6.2	11.5
Not Hispanic or Latino:								
White	15.9	15.3	18.0	18.5	5.8	7.1	5.2	5.4
Black or African American	47.2	30.7	38.8	38.9	7.3	9.9	8.8	6.2
Other	21.0	23.7	19.0	23.4	5.1	9.9	*12.8	6.2
Insurance status								
Any private insurance[3]	6.2	6.6	5.3	6.3	4.8	4.2	3.3	3.3
Public insurance only[4]	87.2	80.7	84.4	83.9	3.9	8.7	5.8	7.4
Uninsured all year[5]	28.6	7.5	*21.2	9.4	30.9	51.1	38.4	41.4
65 years and over	60.8	64.8	64.7	66.0	1.5	2.5	2.9	2.8
Sex								
Male	58.8	63.4	66.9	67.4	*1.9	2.3	2.2	2.8
Female	62.3	65.9	63.0	64.9	1.1	2.7	3.5	2.8
Hispanic origin and race[2]								
Hispanic or Latino	80.2	77.8	75.6	77.2	*1.6	*2.7	*2.2	*8.0
Not Hispanic or Latino:								
White	58.0	62.6	64.1	64.0	1.6	2.5	2.4	2.6
Black or African American	76.3	77.6	68.3	75.5	0.6	2.2	*8.9	1.8
Other	*	*	*	73.7	*	*	*	*1.6
Insurance status								
Medicare only	68.8	72.4	72.2	71.4	1.4	7.7	5.7	7.2
Medicare and private insurance	56.1	56.3	57.1	57.8	1.6	0.6	*0.6	*1.0
Medicare and other public coverage	92.9	92.7	87.3	89.8	1.0	*2.1	*3.6	1.4

. . . Category not applicable. *Estimates are considered unreliable. Data not shown are based on fewer than 100 sample cases. Data preceded by an asterisk have a relative standard error greater than or equal to 30 percent.

[1]Private insurance—Includes any type of private insurance payments reported for people with private health insurance coverage during the year.

[2]Persons of Hispanic origin may be of any race. Beginning in 2002, MEPS respondents were allowed to report multiple races and these persons are included in the "Other" category. As a result, there is a slight increase in percent of persons classified in the "Other" category in 2002 compared with prior years.

[3]Includes individuals with insurance that provided coverage for hospital and physician care at any time during the year, other than Medicare, Medicaid, or other public coverage for hospital or physician services.

[4]Includes individuals who were not covered by private insurance at any time during the year but were covered by Medicare, Medicaid, other public coverage for hospital or physician services, and/or CHAMPUS/CHAMPVA (TRICARE) at any point during the year.

[5]Includes individuals not covered by either private or public insurance throughout the entire year or period of eligibility for the survey. However, a portion of expenses for the uninsured were paid by sources that were not defined as health insurance coverage, such as the Department of Veterans Affairs, community and neighborhood clinics, the Indian Health Service, State and local health departments, State programs other than Medicaid, Workers' Compensation, and other unclassified sources (e.g., automobile, homeowner's, liability insurance).

[6]Public coverage—Includes payments made by Medicare, Medicaid, the Department of Veterans Affairs, other Federal sources (e.g., Indian Health Service, military treatment facilities, and other care provided by the Federal Government), and various State and local sources (e.g., community and neighborhood clinics, State and local health departments, and State programs other than Medicaid).

[7]Other sources—Includes Workers' Compensation, unclassified sources (automobile, homeowner's, or liability insurance, and other miscellaneous or unknown sources), Medicaid payments reported for people who were not enrolled in the program at any time during the year, and any type of private insurance payments reported for people without private health insurance coverage during the year as defined in the survey.

NOTES: 1987 estimates are based on the National Medical Expenditure Survey (NMES) while estimates for other years are based on the Medical Expenditure Panel Survey (MEPS). Because expenditures in NMES were based primarily on charges while those for MEPS were based on payments, data for NMES were adjusted to be more comparable to MEPS using estimated charge to payment ratios for 1987. Overall, this resulted in an approximate 11-percent reduction from the unadjusted 1987 NMES expenditure estimates. For a detailed explanation of this adjustment, see Zuvekas S and Cohen S. A guide to comparing health care estimates in the 1996 Medical Expenditure Panel Survey to the 1987 National Medical Expenditure Survey. Inquiry. vol. 39. Spring 2002. Data for additional years are available. See Appendix III.

SOURCE: Agency for Healthcare Research and Quality, Center for Cost and Financing Studies. 1987 National Medical Expenditure Survey and 1996–2002 Medical Expenditure Panel Surveys.

Table 126. Out-of-pocket health care expenses for persons with medical expenses by age: United States, selected years 1987–2002

[Data are based on household interviews for a sample of the noninstitutionalized population and a sample of medical providers]

Age and year	Percent of persons with expense	Amount paid out of pocket for persons with expense[1]						
		Total	$0	$1–124	$125–249	$250–499	$500–999	$1,000+
		Percent distribution						
All ages								
1987	84.5	100.0	10.4	29.2	16.6	17.4	13.3	13.1
1998	83.8	100.0	7.7	36.5	15.8	16.1	12.2	11.8
1999	84.3	100.0	7.4	35.9	15.5	15.6	12.8	12.7
2000	83.5	100.0	6.9	34.8	15.0	16.2	13.0	14.1
2001	85.4	100.0	7.1	31.7	14.7	16.6	13.8	16.2
2002	85.2	100.0	7.8	29.8	14.3	15.7	14.8	17.6
Under 6 years								
1987	88.9	100.0	19.2	38.7	18.9	14.7	5.3	3.2
1998	87.6	100.0	17.4	60.1	12.4	6.8	2.3	0.9
1999	87.9	100.0	17.7	60.5	12.2	5.9	2.6	1.1
2000	86.7	100.0	16.7	61.0	11.1	7.5	2.4	1.3
2001	88.8	100.0	18.5	57.8	12.9	7.6	2.1	1.1
2002	88.8	100.0	21.5	51.7	14.0	7.7	3.9	1.3
6–17 years								
1987	80.2	100.0	15.5	37.9	18.2	12.4	8.5	7.6
1998	80.6	100.0	16.3	47.0	15.0	11.1	5.6	5.1
1999	81.5	100.0	15.0	46.6	15.4	11.2	6.0	5.8
2000	80.0	100.0	14.7	46.5	14.5	11.2	6.5	6.6
2001	83.2	100.0	15.0	45.2	15.0	11.1	6.0	7.7
2002	83.6	100.0	16.6	43.2	14.7	12.0	6.8	6.7
18–44 years								
1987	81.5	100.0	10.1	32.3	17.7	18.2	11.9	9.8
1998	78.0	100.0	6.4	40.2	17.9	17.0	10.7	7.7
1999	78.9	100.0	6.4	40.2	17.6	16.6	11.1	8.1
2000	77.7	100.0	5.8	39.1	17.8	17.1	11.7	8.5
2001	79.3	100.0	6.0	34.8	17.5	18.8	13.3	9.7
2002	78.5	100.0	6.7	34.2	17.4	17.1	13.9	10.8
45–64 years								
1987	87.0	100.0	5.7	20.4	15.6	20.7	18.8	18.8
1998	89.2	100.0	2.9	25.6	16.2	20.1	17.7	17.5
1999	88.9	100.0	2.7	24.0	16.4	19.7	19.0	18.2
2000	88.5	100.0	2.6	22.3	15.6	19.9	18.8	20.9
2001	89.9	100.0	2.4	19.6	13.9	20.4	19.8	23.8
2002	90.0	100.0	2.3	18.8	12.8	19.1	21.3	25.8
65–74 years								
1987	92.8	100.0	5.3	15.4	11.6	18.5	22.1	27.1
1998	94.3	100.0	2.0	17.8	13.3	20.7	20.6	25.6
1999	95.3	100.0	1.4	16.1	11.3	17.9	23.7	29.6
2000	94.7	100.0	1.5	14.4	10.6	20.2	20.1	33.2
2001	95.6	100.0	1.5	14.4	9.9	18.3	21.7	34.2
2002	96.1	100.0	1.8	10.1	9.9	16.4	22.5	39.3
75 years or more								
1987	95.1	100.0	5.6	12.9	10.0	17.1	21.2	33.2
1998	96.3	100.0	3.0	14.3	11.6	17.7	22.2	31.3
1999	95.3	100.0	2.6	14.5	10.2	18.6	20.2	33.8
2000	96.5	100.0	2.6	14.2	8.4	18.2	22.0	34.6
2001	97.0	100.0	1.7	10.1	9.2	14.4	21.1	43.6
2002	96.5	100.0	2.2	9.0	7.7	14.4	20.4	46.2

[1] 1987 dollars were converted to 1998 dollars using the national Consumer Price Index (CPI). Starting in 1998, percent distributions are based on actual dollars (non-adjusted).

NOTES: Out-of-pocket expenses include expenditures for inpatient hospital and physician services, ambulatory physician and nonphysician services, prescribed medicines, home health services, dental services, and various other medical equipment, supplies, and services that were purchased or rented during the year. Out-of-pocket expenses for over-the-counter medications, alternative care services, phone contacts with health providers, and premiums for health insurance policies are not included in these estimates. 1987 estimates are based on the National Medical Expenditure Survey (NMES) while estimates for other years are based on the Medical Expenditure Panel Survey (MEPS). Because expenditures in NMES were based primarily on charges while those for MEPS were based on payments, data for the NMES were adjusted to be more comparable to MEPS using estimated charge to payment ratios for 1987. Overall this resulted in an approximate 11-percent reduction from the unadjusted 1987 NMES expenditure estimates. For a detailed explanation of this adjustment, see Zuvekas S and Cohen S. A guide to comparing health care estimates in the 1996 Medical Expenditure Panel Survey to the 1987 National Medical Expenditure Survey. Inquiry. vol 39. Spring 2002.

SOURCES: Agency for Healthcare Research and Quality, Center for Cost and Financing Studies. 1987 National Medical Expenditure Survey and 1998–2002 Medical Expenditure Panel Surveys.

Table 127 (page 1 of 2). Expenditures for health services and supplies and percent distribution, by type of payer: United States, selected calendar years 1987–2003

[Data are compiled from various sources by the Centers for Medicare & Medicaid Services]

Type of payer	*1987*	*1993*	*1997*	*1998*	*1999*	*2000*	*2001*	*2002*	*2003*
					Amount in billions				
Total[1]	$477.8	$856.3	$1,055.8	$1,112.6	$1,180.2	$1,260.9	$1,373.8	$1,499.8	$1,614.2
Private	331.2	546.8	664.7	714.0	760.2	812.2	862.9	923.4	992.2
Private business	122.4	221.2	268.0	287.7	313.4	342.6	369.3	395.2	423.0
Employer contribution to private health insurance premiums	84.4	161.5	194.9	209.9	229.6	251.3	274.5	297.4	320.6
Private employer contribution to Medicare hospital insurance trust fund[2]	24.6	35.8	49.5	53.8	57.6	62.3	63.4	62.9	64.3
Workers compensation and temporary disability insurance	11.7	21.1	20.0	20.2	22.3	24.7	27.1	30.3	33.2
Industrial inplant health services	1.7	2.8	3.6	3.8	4.0	4.2	4.4	4.7	4.9
Household	186.4	289.4	348.2	374.8	393.5	418.3	442.4	475.3	512.6
Employee contribution to private health insurance premiums and individual policy premiums	41.9	86.9	107.8	114.6	117.5	126.3	139.5	157.3	174.1
Employee and self-employment contributions and voluntary premiums paid to Medicare hospital insurance trust fund[2]	29.4	43.7	63.0	69.2	75.0	82.5	82.9	84.1	86.0
Premiums paid by individuals to Medicare supplementary medical insurance trust fund	6.2	11.9	15.4	15.5	16.3	16.3	18.0	19.6	22.0
Out-of-pocket health spending	108.9	146.9	162.0	175.6	184.7	193.1	202.0	214.2	230.5
Other private revenues	22.4	36.2	48.5	51.5	53.3	51.3	51.1	52.9	56.6
Public	146.6	309.5	391.1	398.7	420.0	448.8	510.9	576.4	622.0
Federal Government	75.1	175.6	220.1	215.0	222.5	236.9	278.1	318.3	344.0
Employer contributions to private health insurance premiums	4.9	11.5	11.4	11.4	13.2	14.3	15.8	17.7	19.7
Medicaid[3]	28.1	78.1	97.1	101.8	110.4	120.1	133.7	150.5	160.9
Other[4]	45.9	83.6	109.2	99.4	96.4	99.9	126.0	147.2	160.2
State and local government	71.5	133.9	171.0	183.6	197.5	211.9	232.8	258.1	278.1
Employer contributions to private health insurance premiums	16.7	38.2	46.7	48.8	53.5	58.6	66.9	77.1	86.2
Medicaid[3]	22.8	45.8	66.3	73.5	80.0	86.5	93.5	104.2	111.8
Other[5]	28.8	45.0	51.8	54.8	57.0	59.4	64.5	68.4	71.5
					Percent distribution				
Total	100.0	100.0	100.0	100.0	100.0	100.0	100.0	100.0	100.0
Private	69.3	63.9	63.0	64.2	64.4	64.4	62.8	61.6	61.5
Private business	25.6	25.8	25.4	25.9	26.6	27.2	26.9	26.4	26.2
Employer contribution to private health insurance premiums	17.7	18.9	18.5	18.9	19.5	19.9	20.0	19.8	19.9
Private employer contribution to Medicare hospital insurance trust fund[2]	5.2	4.2	4.7	4.8	4.9	4.9	4.6	4.2	4.0
Workers compensation and temporary disability insurance	2.4	2.5	1.9	1.8	1.9	2.0	2.0	2.0	2.1
Industrial inplant health services	0.4	0.3	0.3	0.3	0.3	0.3	0.3	0.3	0.3
Household	39.0	33.8	33.0	33.7	33.3	33.2	32.2	31.7	31.8
Employee contribution to private health insurance premiums and individual policy premiums	8.8	10.1	10.2	10.3	10.0	10.0	10.2	10.5	10.8
Employee and self-employment contributions and voluntary premiums paid to Medicare hospital insurance trust fund[2]	6.2	5.1	6.0	6.2	6.4	6.5	6.0	5.6	5.3
Premiums paid by individuals to Medicare supplementary medical insurance trust fund	1.3	1.4	1.5	1.4	1.4	1.3	1.3	1.3	1.4
Out-of-pocket health spending	22.8	17.2	15.3	15.8	15.7	15.3	14.7	14.3	14.3
Other private revenues	4.7	4.2	4.6	4.6	4.5	4.1	3.7	3.5	3.5

See footnotes at end of table.

Table 127 (page 2 of 2). Expenditures for health services and supplies and percent distribution, by type of payer: United States, selected calendar years 1987–2003

[Data are compiled from various sources by the Centers for Medicare & Medicaid Services]

Type of payer	1987	1993	1997	1998	1999	2000	2001	2002	2003
	Percent distribution								
Public	30.7	36.1	37.0	35.8	35.6	35.6	37.2	38.4	38.5
Federal Government	15.7	20.5	20.8	19.3	18.9	18.8	20.2	21.2	21.3
Employer contributions to private health insurance premiums	1.0	1.3	1.1	1.0	1.1	1.1	1.1	1.2	1.2
Medicaid[3]	5.9	9.1	9.2	9.2	9.4	9.5	9.7	10.0	10.0
Other[4]	9.6	9.8	10.3	8.9	8.2	7.9	9.2	9.8	9.9
State and local government	15.0	15.6	16.2	16.5	16.7	16.8	16.9	17.2	17.2
Employer contributions to private health insurance premiums	3.5	4.5	4.4	4.4	4.5	4.6	4.9	5.1	5.3
Medicaid[3]	4.8	5.3	6.3	6.6	6.8	6.9	6.8	6.9	6.9
Other[5]	6.0	5.2	4.9	4.9	4.8	4.7	4.7	4.6	4.4

[1]Excludes research and construction.
[2]Includes one-half of self-employment contribution to Medicare hospital insurance trust fund.
[3]Includes Medicaid buy-in premiums for Medicare.
[4]Includes expenditures for Medicare with adjustments for contributions by employers and individuals and premiums paid to the Medicare insurance trust fund and maternal and child health, vocational rehabilitation, Substance Abuse and Mental Health Services Administration, Indian Health Service, Federal workers' compensation, and other miscellaneous general hospital and medical programs, public health activities, Department of Defense, and Department of Veterans Affairs.
[5]Includes other public and general assistance, maternal and child health, vocational rehabilitation, public health activities, hospital subsidies, and employer contributions to Medicare hospital insurance trust fund.

NOTES: This table disaggregates health expenditures according to four classes of payers: businesses, households (individuals), Federal Government, and State and local governments with a small amount of revenue coming from nonpatient revenue sources such as philanthropy. Where businesses or households pay dedicated funds into government health programs (for example, Medicare) or employers and employees share in the cost of health premiums, these costs are assigned to businesses or households accordingly. This results in a lower share of expenditures being assigned to the Federal Government than for tabulations of expenditures by source of funds. Estimates of national health expenditure by source of funds aim to track government-sponsored health programs over time and do not delineate the role of business employers in paying for health care. Figures may not sum to totals due to rounding. These data were revised and differ from previous editions of *Health, United States*.

SOURCE: Centers for Medicare & Medicaid Services, Office of the Actuary, National Health Statistics Group. Financing Health Care: Businesses, Households and Governments, 1987–2003. Health Care Financing Review Web Exclusive vol. 1, no. 2. Washington. July 2005.

Table 128 (page 1 of 2). Employers' costs per employee-hour worked for total compensation, wages and salaries, and health insurance, according to selected characteristics: United States, selected years 1991–2005

[Data are based on surveys of employers]

Characteristic	1991	1994	1996	1998	2000	2001	2002	2003	2004	2005
	Amount per employee-hour worked									
State and local government	$22.31	$25.27	$25.73	$27.28	$29.05	$30.06	$31.29	$32.62	$34.21	$35.50
Total private industry	15.40	17.08	17.49	18.50	19.85	20.81	21.71	22.37	23.29	24.17
Industry:										
Goods producing	18.48	20.85	21.27	22.26	23.55	24.40	25.44	26.25	27.19	28.48
Service providing	14.31	15.82	16.28	17.31	18.72	19.74	20.66	21.30	22.33	23.11
Occupational group:[1]										
White collar	18.15	20.26	21.10	22.38	24.19	25.34	26.43	28.85	- - -	- - -
Blue collar	15.15	16.92	17.04	17.56	18.73	19.35	20.15	21.21	- - -	- - -
Service	7.82	8.38	8.61	9.37	9.72	10.32	10.95	13.68	- - -	- - -
Management, professional and related	- - -	- - -	- - -	- - -	- - -	- - -	- - -	- - -	40.23	42.09
Sales and office	- - -	- - -	- - -	- - -	- - -	- - -	- - -	- - -	18.42	19.30
Service	- - -	- - -	- - -	- - -	- - -	- - -	- - -	- - -	11.66	12.07
Natural resources, construction and maintenance	- - -	- - -	- - -	- - -	- - -	- - -	- - -	- - -	26.55	27.26
Production, transportation and material moving	- - -	- - -	- - -	- - -	- - -	- - -	- - -	- - -	20.21	20.82
Census region:										
Northeast	17.56	20.03	20.57	20.38	22.67	23.91	25.00	25.70	26.29	27.09
Midwest	15.05	16.26	16.30	18.15	19.22	20.47	21.25	22.40	23.26	24.23
South	13.68	15.05	15.62	16.45	17.81	18.59	19.49	19.95	20.80	21.36
West	15.97	18.08	18.78	19.94	20.88	21.86	22.68	23.07	24.54	25.98
Union status:										
Union	19.76	23.26	23.31	23.59	25.88	27.80	29.42	30.68	31.94	33.17
Nonunion	14.54	16.04	16.61	17.80	19.07	19.98	20.79	21.36	22.28	23.09
Establishment employment size:										
1–99 employees	13.38	14.58	14.85	15.92	17.16	17.86	18.51	18.93	19.47	20.22
100 or more	17.34	19.45	20.09	21.20	22.81	24.19	25.48	26.42	27.81	28.94
100–499	14.31	15.88	16.61	17.52	19.30	20.97	21.99	22.62	23.91	24.44
500 or more	20.60	23.35	24.03	25.56	26.93	28.17	29.79	30.94	32.54	34.59
	Wages and salaries as a percent of total compensation									
State and local government	69.6	69.5	69.8	70.3	70.8	71.0	70.8	70.0	69.2	68.3
Total private industry	72.3	71.1	71.9	72.8	73.0	72.9	72.8	72.2	71.5	71.0
Industry:										
Goods producing	68.7	66.5	67.6	69.0	69.0	69.1	68.7	67.7	66.7	65.5
Service providing	73.9	73.1	73.8	74.4	74.5	74.4	74.2	73.7	72.9	72.6
Occupational group:[1]										
White collar	73.8	72.7	73.2	73.9	74.0	73.8	73.7	72.9	- - -	- - -
Blue collar	68.4	66.8	68.1	69.2	69.4	69.7	69.5	68.5	- - -	- - -
Service	76.2	75.5	75.8	77.4	77.9	77.5	76.9	72.4	- - -	- - -
Management, professional and related	- - -	- - -	- - -	- - -	- - -	- - -	- - -	- - -	72.1	71.5
Sales and office	- - -	- - -	- - -	- - -	- - -	- - -	- - -	- - -	73.0	72.6
Service	- - -	- - -	- - -	- - -	- - -	- - -	- - -	- - -	75.8	75.7
Natural resources, construction and maintenance	- - -	- - -	- - -	- - -	- - -	- - -	- - -	- - -	69.1	68.0
Production, transportation and material moving	- - -	- - -	- - -	- - -	- - -	- - -	- - -	- - -	66.9	66.2
Census region:										
Northeast	72.0	70.5	70.9	72.1	72.2	72.0	71.9	71.2	70.4	70.4
Midwest	71.1	69.7	71.1	71.6	72.4	71.8	72.0	71.6	71.1	70.1
South	73.3	72.1	72.7	73.9	73.5	73.7	73.6	73.2	72.5	72.1
West	72.8	72.0	73.1	74.0	74.0	74.1	73.5	72.6	71.6	70.9
Union status:										
Union	65.9	63.5	64.0	65.2	65.2	66.0	65.7	65.0	63.6	62.6
Nonunion	74.1	72.9	73.6	74.2	74.4	74.1	74.0	73.5	72.8	72.4
Establishment employment size:										
1–99 employees	74.7	73.5	74.7	75.4	75.5	75.1	75.0	74.6	74.3	73.9
100 or more	70.5	69.3	69.9	70.8	71.0	71.1	70.9	70.2	69.1	68.5
100–499	72.1	71.6	71.6	72.3	72.8	72.5	72.2	71.4	70.7	70.2
500 or more	69.3	67.6	68.6	69.6	69.4	69.8	69.8	69.1	67.7	67.0

See footnotes at end of table.

Table 128 (page 2 of 2). Employers' costs per employee-hour worked for total compensation, wages and salaries, and health insurance, according to selected characteristics: United States, selected years 1991–2005

[Data are based on surveys of employers]

Characteristic	*1991*	*1994*	*1996*	*1998*	*2000*	*2001*	*2002*	*2003*	*2004*	*2005*
	Health insurance as a percent of total compensation									
State and local government	6.9	8.2	7.7	7.5	7.8	8.5	8.6	9.2	9.8	10.2
Total private industry	6.0	6.7	5.9	5.4	5.5	6.2	5.9	6.3	6.6	6.8
Industry:										
Goods producing	6.9	8.1	7.2	6.6	6.9	7.6	7.2	7.5	7.8	8.0
Service providing	5.5	6.0	5.4	4.9	4.9	5.6	5.5	5.9	6.2	6.4
Occupational group:[1]										
White collar	5.6	6.2	5.5	5.0	5.0	5.6	5.4	6.4	---	---
Blue collar	7.0	8.0	7.2	6.7	6.8	7.5	7.3	8.0	---	---
Service	4.6	5.4	4.8	4.3	4.3	5.0	5.1	7.0	---	---
Management, professional and related	---	---	---	---	---	---	---	---	5.4	5.5
Sales and office	---	---	---	---	---	---	---	---	7.3	7.5
Service	---	---	---	---	---	---	---	---	6.0	6.1
Natural resources, construction and maintenance	---	---	---	---	---	---	---	---	6.9	7.5
Production, transportation and material moving	---	---	---	---	---	---	---	---	8.5	8.9
Census region:										
Northeast	6.2	6.9	6.2	5.6	5.6	6.3	5.9	6.3	6.5	6.8
Midwest	6.3	7.3	6.3	5.7	5.8	6.6	6.4	6.6	7.0	7.3
South	5.5	6.3	5.9	5.3	5.4	6.2	5.8	6.2	6.5	6.6
West	5.8	6.1	5.2	4.9	5.0	5.4	5.6	6.0	6.3	6.3
Union status:										
Union	8.2	9.8	8.8	8.4	8.4	8.9	8.7	9.1	9.6	10.3
Nonunion	5.4	5.9	5.3	4.8	5.0	5.7	5.4	5.8	6.1	6.2
Establishment employment size:										
1–99 employees	5.1	5.7	5.0	4.6	4.8	5.3	5.2	5.5	5.8	5.9
100 or more	6.6	7.3	6.6	6.0	6.0	6.9	6.6	7.0	7.2	7.5
100–499	6.3	6.5	6.3	5.8	5.6	6.6	6.4	6.9	7.1	7.5
500 or more	6.8	7.9	6.9	6.2	6.4	7.1	6.7	7.0	7.3	7.6

- - - Data not available.

[1]Starting in 2004, sample establishments were classified by industry categories based on the 2000 North American Industry Classification (NAICS) system, as defined by the U.S. Office of Management and Budget. Within a sample establishment, specific job categories were selected and classified into about 800 occupational classifications according to the 2000 Standard Occupational Classification (SOC) system. Individual occupations were combined to represent one of five higher-level aggregations such as management, professional, and related occupations. For more detailed information on NAICS and SOC, including background and definitions, see the Bureau of Labor Statistics Web sites: www.bls.gov/bls/naics.htm and www.bls.gov/soc/home.htm. NAICS and SOC replace the 1987 Standard Industrial Classification System (SIC) and the Occupational Classification System (OCS).

NOTES: Costs are calculated from March survey data each year. Total compensation includes wages and salaries, and benefits. See Appendix II, Employer costs for employee compensation. Data for additional years are available. See Appendix III.

SOURCES: U.S. Department of Labor, Bureau of Labor Statistics, National Compensation Survey, Employer Costs for Employee Compensation, March release; News pub no 05–1056, June 16, 2005. Washington, DC. Data are available on the Bureau of Labor Statistics Web site at www.bls.gov/ncs/ect/home.htm.

Table 129. Hospital expenses, according to type of ownership and size of hospital: United States, selected years 1980–2003

[Data are based on reporting by a census of hospitals]

Type of ownership and size of hospital	*1980*	*1990*	*1995*	*2000*	*2002*	*2003*	*1980–90*	*1990–95*	*1995–2000*	*2000–03*
Total expenses	Amount in billions						Average annual percent change			
All hospitals	$ 91.9	$234.9	$320.3	$395.4	$ 462.2	$ 498.1	9.8	6.4	4.3	8.0
Federal	7.9	15.2	20.2	23.9	29.7	30.9	6.8	5.9	3.4	8.9
Non-Federal[1]	84.0	219.6	300.0	371.5	432.5	467.2	10.1	6.4	4.4	7.9
Community[2]	76.9	203.7	285.6	356.6	416.6	450.1	10.2	7.0	4.5	8.1
Nonprofit	55.8	150.7	209.6	267.1	312.7	337.7	10.4	6.8	5.0	8.1
For profit	5.8	18.8	26.7	35.0	40.1	44.0	12.5	7.3	5.6	7.9
State-local government	15.2	34.2	49.3	54.5	63.8	68.5	8.4	7.6	2.0	7.9
6–24 beds	0.2	0.5	1.1	1.5	2.2	2.5	9.6	17.1	6.4	18.6
25–49 beds	1.7	4.0	7.2	10.4	12.6	14.0	8.9	12.5	7.6	10.4
50–99 beds	5.4	12.6	17.8	22.3	26.1	28.2	8.8	7.2	4.6	8.1
100–199 beds	12.5	33.3	50.7	63.4	71.4	75.6	10.3	8.8	4.6	6.0
200–299 beds	13.4	38.7	55.8	67.1	75.6	81.0	11.2	7.6	3.8	6.5
300–399 beds	11.5	33.1	43.3	54.3	66.1	70.4	11.2	5.5	4.6	9.0
400–499 beds	10.5	25.3	33.7	41.3	47.4	51.6	9.2	5.9	4.2	7.7
500 beds or more	21.6	56.2	76.1	96.3	115.1	126.9	10.0	6.3	4.8	9.6
Expenses per inpatient day	Amount									
Community[2]	$ 245	$ 687	$ 968	$1,149	$ 1,290	$ 1,379	10.9	7.1	3.5	6.3
Nonprofit	246	692	994	1,182	1,329	1,430	10.9	7.5	3.5	6.6
For profit	257	752	947	1,057	1,181	1,265	11.3	4.7	2.2	6.2
State-local government	239	634	878	1,064	1,188	1,238	10.2	6.7	3.9	5.2
6–24 beds	203	526	678	896	1,028	1,111	10.0	5.2	5.7	7.4
25–49 beds	197	489	696	891	987	1,032	9.5	7.3	5.1	5.0
50–99 beds	191	493	647	745	816	893	9.9	5.6	2.9	6.2
100–199 beds	215	585	796	925	1,038	1,082	10.5	6.4	3.0	5.4
200–299 beds	239	665	943	1,122	1,263	1,343	10.8	7.2	3.5	6.2
300–399 beds	248	731	1,070	1,277	1,398	1,522	11.4	7.9	3.6	6.0
400–499 beds	215	756	1,135	1,353	1,583	1,714	13.4	8.5	3.6	8.2
500 beds or more	239	825	1,212	1,468	1,641	1,750	13.2	8.0	3.9	6.0
Expenses per inpatient stay										
Community[2]	$1,851	$4,947	$6,216	$6,649	$ 7,355	$ 7,796	10.3	4.7	1.4	5.4
Nonprofit	1,902	5,001	6,279	6,717	7,458	7,905	10.2	4.7	1.4	5.6
For profit	1,676	4,727	5,425	5,642	6,161	6,590	10.9	2.8	0.8	5.3
State-local government	1,750	4,838	6,445	7,106	7,773	8,205	10.7	5.9	2.0	4.9
6–24 beds	1,072	2,701	3,578	3,652	4,135	4,372	9.7	5.8	0.4	6.2
25–49 beds	1,138	2,967	3,797	4,381	4,848	5,005	10.1	5.1	2.9	4.5
50–99 beds	1,271	3,461	4,427	4,760	5,197	5,553	10.5	5.0	1.5	5.3
100–199 beds	1,512	4,109	5,103	5,305	5,935	6,191	10.5	4.4	0.8	5.3
200–299 beds	1,767	4,618	5,851	6,392	6,951	7,317	10.1	4.8	1.8	4.6
300–399 beds	1,881	5,096	6,512	6,988	7,635	8,184	10.5	5.0	1.4	5.4
400–499 beds	2,090	5,500	7,164	7,629	8,762	9,396	10.2	5.4	1.3	7.2
500 beds or more	2,517	6,667	8,531	9,149	10,007	10,640	10.2	5.1	1.4	5.2

[1]The category of non-Federal hospitals comprises psychiatric, tuberculosis and other respiratory diseases hospitals, and long-term and short-term general and other special hospitals. See Appendix II, Hospital.

[2]Community hospitals are non-Federal short-term general and special hospitals whose facilities and services are available to the public. See Appendix II, Hospital.

NOTES: In 2003 employee payroll and benefit expenses comprised 52 percent of expenses in community hospitals and 64 percent in Federal hospitals. Data for additional years are available. See Appendix III.

SOURCES: American Hospital Association Annual Survey of Hospitals. Hospital Statistics, 1981, 1991–2005 Editions. Chicago, 1981, 1991–2005 (Copyrights 1981, 1991–2005: Used with the permission of the Health Forum LLC, an affiliate of the American Hospital Association); and unpublished data.

Table 130. Nursing home average monthly charges per resident and percent of residents, according to primary source of payments and selected facility characteristics: United States, 1985, 1995, and 1999

[Data are based on reporting by a sample of nursing homes]

Facility characteristic	Primary source of payment									
	All sources	Own income or family support[1]			Medicare			Medicaid		
	1999	1985	1995	1999	1985	1995	1999	1985	1995	1999
	Average monthly charge[2]									
All facilities	$3,891	$1,450	$3,081	$3,947	$2,141	$5,546	$5,764	$1,504	$2,769	$3,505
Ownership										
Proprietary	3,698	1,444	3,190	3,984	2,058	5,668	5,275	1,363	2,560	3,312
Nonprofit and government	4,225	1,462	2,967	3,903	*	5,304	6,548	1,851	3,201	3,918
Certification										
Both Medicare and Medicaid	4,060	- - -	3,365	4,211	- - -	5,472	5,887	- - -	2,910	3,626
Medicare only	4,437	- - -	3,344	3,873	- - -	*	*	. . .	. . .	. . .
Medicaid only	2,508	- - -	2,352	2,533	. . .	. . .	. . .	- - -	2,069	2,501
Neither	2,360	- - -	2,390	2,685	. . .	. . .	. . .	. . .	. . .	. . .
Bed size										
Less than 50 beds	3,808	886	3,377	3,358	*	*	*	1,335	2,990	3,533
50–99 beds	3,627	1,388	2,849	3,698	1,760	4,929	*	1,323	2,335	3,121
100–199 beds	3,867	1,567	3,138	4,160	2,192	4,918	5,318	1,413	2,659	3,487
200 beds or more	4,281	1,701	3,316	4,029	2,767	4,523	5,912	1,919	3,520	4,011
Geographic region										
Northeast	4,852	1,645	4,117	5,300	2,109	4,883	6,368	2,035	3,671	4,397
Midwest	3,474	1,398	2,650	3,413	2,745	5,439	4,726	1,382	2,478	3,239
South	3,263	1,359	2,945	3,467	2,033	4,889	4,859	1,200	2,333	2,943
West	4,725	1,498	3,666	4,868	1,838	8,825	*	1,501	2,848	3,865
	Percent of residents									
All facilities	100.0	41.6	27.8	23.7	1.4	9.9	14.7	50.4	60.2	58.7
Ownership										
Proprietary	100.0	40.1	24.1	20.2	1.6	10.4	14.2	52.1	63.8	62.9
Nonprofit and government	100.0	44.9	34.3	30.2	*	9.2	15.5	46.6	54.0	51.1
Certification										
Both Medicare and Medicaid	100.0	- - -	23.1	21.5	- - -	11.6	15.5	- - -	63.9	60.4
Medicare only	100.0	- - -	71.2	71.4	- - -	16.2	*21.0	. . .	. . .	. . .
Medicaid only	100.0	- - -	32.1	21.9	. . .	. . .	. . .	- - -	63.0	69.5
Neither	100.0	- - -	91.0	73.6	. . .	. . .	. . .	. . .	. . .	. . .
Bed size										
Less than 50 beds	100.0	53.1	35.3	40.3	*	13.1	*15.9	33.8	49.9	42.5
50–99 beds	100.0	49.5	34.5	28.3	*	6.2	12.4	42.9	57.6	56.9
100–199 beds	100.0	39.6	26.2	21.8	1.5	10.6	15.0	55.2	61.5	61.0
200 beds or more	100.0	30.1	22.0	20.1	*	12.1	16.3	57.7	62.4	58.1
Geographic region										
Northeast	100.0	34.8	18.2	18.0	1.7	14.0	16.4	52.9	64.9	62.3
Midwest	100.0	49.1	36.3	32.9	*	6.7	13.3	45.9	55.8	51.1
South	100.0	39.4	26.1	19.2	*	10.1	14.9	53.8	62.2	63.5
West	100.0	40.4	27.9	23.9	*	10.5	13.9	49.2	57.9	57.8

* Estimates are considered unreliable. Data not shown have a relative standard error greater than 30 percent. After 1995 data preceded by an asterisk have a relative standard error of 20–30 percent.
- - - Data not available.
. . . Category not applicable.
[1]Includes private health insurance.
[2]Includes life-care residents and no-charge residents.

NOTE: Data for additional years are available. See Appendix III.

SOURCES: Hing E, Sekscenski E, Strahan G. The National Nursing Home Survey: 1985 summary for the United States. National Center for Health Statistics. Vital Health Stat 13(97). 1989; and Centers for Disease Control and Prevention, National Center for Health Statistics, National Nursing Home Survey for other data years.

Table 131. Mental health expenditures, percent distribution, and per capita expenditures, according to type of mental health organization: United States, selected years 1975–2002

[Data are based on an inventory of Mental Health Organizations (SMHO)]

Type of organization	1975	1979	1983	1986	1990	1994[1]	1998	2000	2002[2]
	Amount in millions								
All organizations	$6,564	$8,764	$14,432	$18,458	$28,410	$33,136	$38,512	$34,528	$34,302
State and county psychiatric hospitals	3,185	3,757	5,491	6,326	7,774	7,825	7,117	7,485	7,616
Private psychiatric hospitals	467	743	1,712	2,629	6,101	6,468	4,106	3,885	3,929
Non-Federal general hospital psychiatric services	621	723	2,176	2,878	4,662	5,344	5,589	5,853	5,179
Department of Veterans Affairs medical centers[3]	699	848	1,316	1,338	1,480	1,386	1,690	976	1,018
Residential treatment centers for emotionally disturbed children	279	436	573	978	1,969	2,360	3,557	3,781	4,496
All other organizations[4]	1,313	2,256	3,164	4,310	6,424	9,753	16,454	12,549	12,063
	Percent distribution								
All organizations	100.0	100.0	100.0	100.0	100.0	100.0	100.0	100.0	100.0
State and county psychiatric hospitals	48.5	42.9	38.0	34.3	27.4	23.6	18.5	21.7	22.2
Private psychiatric hospitals	7.1	8.5	11.9	14.2	21.5	19.5	10.7	11.3	11.5
Non-Federal general hospital psychiatric services	9.5	8.2	15.1	15.6	16.4	16.1	14.5	17.0	15.1
Department of Veterans Affairs medical centers[3]	10.6	9.7	9.1	7.2	5.2	4.2	4.4	2.8	3.0
Residential treatment centers for emotionally disturbed children	4.2	5.0	4.0	5.3	6.9	7.1	9.2	11.0	13.1
All other organizations[4]	20.0	25.7	21.9	23.3	22.6	29.4	42.7	36.4	35.2
	Amount per capita[5]								
All organizations	$ 31	$ 40	$ 62	$ 77	$ 116	$ 128	$ 143	$ 122	$ 119
State and county psychiatric hospitals	15	17	24	26	32	30	26	27	26
Private psychiatric hospitals	2	3	7	11	25	25	15	14	14
Non-Federal general hospital psychiatric services	3	3	9	12	19	21	21	21	18
Department of Veterans Affairs medical centers[3]	3	4	6	6	6	5	6	3	4
Residential treatment centers for emotionally disturbed children	1	2	2	4	8	9	13	13	16
All other organizations[4]	6	10	14	18	26	38	61	44	42

[1]Beginning in 1994 data for supportive residential clients (moderately staffed housing arrangements such as supervised apartments, group homes, and halfway houses) are included in the totals and all other organizations. This change affects the comparability of trend data prior to 1994 with data for 1994 and later years.
[2]Preliminary data.
[3]Includes Department of Veterans Affairs neuropsychiatric hospitals, general hospital psychiatric services, and psychiatric outpatient clinics.
[4]Includes freestanding psychiatric outpatient clinics, partial care organizations, multiservice mental health organizations, residential treatment centers for adults, substance abuse organizations, and in 1975 and 1979 Federally funded community mental health centers.
[5]Civilian population as of January 1 each year through 1998. The rates for 2000 and later years are based on the decennial census sample civilian population.

NOTES: Changes in reporting procedures and definitions may affect the comparability of data prior to 1980 with those of later years. Mental health expenditures include salaries, other operating expenditures, and capital expenditures. These data exclude mental health care provided in nonpsychiatric units of hospitals such as general medical units. These data include revisions for 1998 data and differ from the previous editions of *Health, United States.*

SOURCES: Substance Abuse and Mental Health Services Administration, Center for Mental Health Services. Manderscheid RW, Henderson MJ. *Mental health, United States, 2002.* Washington, DC. U.S. Government Printing Office, 2004.

Table 132 (page 1 of 3). Private health insurance coverage among persons under 65 years of age, according to selected characteristics: United States, selected years 1984–2003

[Data are based on household interviews of a sample of the civilian noninstitutionalized population]

Characteristic	*1984*	*1989*	*1995*	*1997*[1]	*1998*	*1999*	*2000*	*2001*	*2002*	*2003*
					Number in millions					
Total[2]	157.5	162.7	164.2	165.8	170.8	174.3	174.0	175.3	172.4	173.6
					Percent of population					
Total[2]	76.8	75.9	71.3	70.7	72.1	72.8	71.5	71.2	69.4	68.9
Age										
Under 18 years	72.6	71.8	65.2	66.1	68.4	68.8	66.6	66.3	63.5	63.0
Under 6 years	68.1	67.9	59.5	61.3	64.7	64.7	62.7	62.9	60.2	58.2
6–17 years	74.9	74.0	68.3	68.5	70.2	70.9	68.5	67.9	65.1	65.3
18–44 years	76.5	75.5	70.9	69.4	71.1	72.0	70.5	70.1	68.7	67.7
18–24 years	67.4	64.5	60.8	59.3	61.5	63.2	60.3	60.3	60.2	58.8
25–34 years	77.4	75.9	70.1	68.1	70.6	71.2	70.1	70.0	68.0	65.6
35–44 years	83.9	82.7	77.7	76.4	76.9	77.9	77.0	76.2	74.6	75.1
45–64 years	83.3	82.5	80.1	79.0	79.0	79.3	78.7	78.6	77.3	77.3
45–54 years	83.3	83.4	80.9	80.4	80.0	80.4	80.0	79.4	77.5	77.9
55–64 years	83.3	81.6	79.0	76.9	77.3	77.7	76.7	77.4	76.9	76.5
Sex										
Male	77.3	76.1	71.6	70.9	72.2	72.9	71.6	71.2	69.0	69.0
Female	76.2	75.7	70.9	70.5	72.0	72.8	71.3	71.2	69.8	68.9
Race[3]										
White only	79.9	79.1	74.5	74.2	75.9	76.9	75.7	75.1	73.4	71.5
Black or African American only	58.1	57.7	53.0	54.7	54.7	57.2	55.9	56.5	55.1	54.9
American Indian and Alaska Native only	49.1	45.5	45.3	39.4	43.4	39.5	43.7	49.0	37.9	45.0
Asian only	69.9	71.9	68.4	68.0	72.2	73.3	72.1	72.3	70.9	71.4
Native Hawaiian and Other Pacific Islander only	- - -	- - -	- - -	- - -	- - -	*	*	*	*	*
2 or more races	- - -	- - -	- - -	- - -	- - -	62.7	61.4	61.5	57.1	56.3
Hispanic origin and race[3]										
Hispanic or Latino	55.7	51.5	46.4	46.4	48.7	48.9	47.8	46.1	44.4	41.9
Mexican	53.3	46.8	42.6	42.3	44.3	46.0	45.4	43.1	42.1	39.3
Puerto Rican	48.4	45.6	47.6	47.0	51.7	50.4	51.1	50.5	50.0	48.6
Cuban	72.5	70.3	63.6	71.0	71.7	71.3	63.9	66.1	62.0	55.9
Other Hispanic or Latino	61.6	61.0	51.4	49.9	51.9	52.8	50.7	49.9	46.2	45.3
Not Hispanic or Latino	78.7	78.4	74.4	74.0	75.5	76.3	75.2	75.3	73.7	73.7
White only	82.3	82.4	78.6	78.1	79.7	80.4	79.5	79.4	77.9	77.8
Black or African American only	58.3	57.8	53.4	54.9	54.9	57.3	56.0	56.7	55.2	55.5
Age and percent of poverty level[4]										
All ages:[3]										
Below 100 percent	32.2	27.0	22.6	23.3	24.0	25.5	25.2	25.3	25.2	23.9
100–149 percent	62.2	55.1	47.8	43.6	45.3	42.9	41.7	41.7	38.4	37.5
150–199 percent	77.2	71.0	65.1	62.9	62.2	59.4	58.5	56.7	56.2	52.2
200 percent or more	91.5	90.8	88.3	86.4	86.8	87.1	85.7	85.5	83.9	84.6
Under 18 years:										
Below 100 percent	28.5	22.3	16.9	18.3	19.2	20.4	19.5	18.2	16.9	15.9
100–149 percent	66.2	59.6	48.5	43.5	46.9	42.8	39.8	40.7	35.2	33.9
150–199 percent	80.9	75.9	67.4	65.7	66.1	61.0	59.7	56.3	55.3	50.9
200 percent or more	92.3	92.5	89.5	87.8	88.6	89.0	86.7	86.8	84.5	85.1
Geographic region										
Northeast	80.5	82.0	75.4	74.2	76.5	77.1	76.3	76.4	73.9	74.7
Midwest	80.6	81.5	77.3	77.1	79.0	80.1	78.8	78.1	76.4	75.9
South	74.3	71.4	66.9	67.3	67.7	68.0	66.8	66.0	64.6	64.0
West	71.9	71.2	67.5	65.4	67.4	68.6	66.5	67.9	66.1	64.7
Location of residence										
Within MSA[5]	77.5	76.5	72.1	71.2	73.0	74.1	72.3	72.2	70.7	70.2
Outside MSA[5]	75.2	73.8	67.9	68.4	68.9	67.8	67.8	67.0	64.2	63.7

See footnotes at end of table.

Table 132 (page 2 of 3). Private health insurance coverage among persons under 65 years of age, according to selected characteristics: United States, selected years 1984–2003

[Data are based on household interviews of a sample of the civilian noninstitutionalized population]

Characteristic	1984	1989	1995	1997[1]	1998	1999	2000	2001	2002	2003
	Private insurance obtained through workplace[6]									
	Number in millions									
Total[2]	141.8	146.3	150.7	155.6	159.3	162.6	162.5	164.2	161.3	159.3
	Percent of population									
Total[2]	69.1	68.3	65.4	66.3	67.3	68.0	66.7	66.7	65.0	63.3
Age										
Under 18 years	66.5	65.8	60.4	62.7	64.1	64.6	62.7	62.8	60.1	58.6
Under 6 years	62.1	62.3	55.1	58.2	60.9	60.8	58.8	59.1	57.0	53.9
6–17 years	68.7	67.7	63.3	64.9	65.7	66.5	64.6	64.5	61.7	60.9
18–44 years	69.6	68.4	65.3	65.5	66.5	67.7	66.1	65.9	64.3	62.2
18–24 years	58.7	55.3	53.5	54.7	55.7	57.8	54.9	55.3	54.3	52.3
25–34 years	71.2	69.5	65.0	64.5	66.7	67.2	66.1	66.0	63.9	60.3
35–44 years	77.4	76.2	72.7	72.6	72.5	73.8	72.8	72.1	70.8	70.0
45–64 years	71.8	71.6	72.2	72.6	72.7	72.7	72.5	72.5	71.4	70.0
45–54 years	74.6	74.4	74.7	75.4	75.1	75.1	75.3	74.5	72.9	71.5
55–64 years	69.0	68.3	68.4	68.3	69.1	69.2	68.1	69.5	69.1	68.0
Sex										
Male	69.8	68.7	65.9	66.6	67.4	68.0	67.0	66.7	64.7	63.3
Female	68.4	67.9	64.9	66.0	67.1	68.0	66.5	66.6	65.2	63.3
Race[3]										
White only	72.0	71.2	68.4	69.6	70.7	71.6	70.6	70.2	68.7	65.6
Black or African American only	52.4	52.8	49.3	52.5	52.0	54.6	53.1	54.2	52.4	51.5
American Indian and Alaska Native only	45.8	40.9	40.2	37.1	41.2	36.5	41.6	47.0	35.8	40.5
Asian only	59.0	61.1	59.6	61.4	63.8	65.4	65.1	65.9	62.5	62.1
Native Hawaiian and Other Pacific Islander only	- - -	- - -	- - -	- - -	- - -	*	*	*	*	*
2 or more races	- - -	- - -	- - -	- - -	- - -	59.3	59.7	57.9	54.5	53.1
Hispanic origin and race[3]										
Hispanic or Latino	52.0	47.3	43.4	43.9	45.8	46.1	45.0	43.8	41.9	38.9
Mexican	50.5	44.2	40.9	40.7	42.2	43.7	43.2	41.2	40.1	36.7
Puerto Rican	45.9	42.3	44.5	45.1	49.3	47.4	49.3	47.5	48.0	45.0
Cuban	57.4	56.5	54.0	58.1	60.2	63.5	53.4	56.6	52.1	51.1
Other Hispanic or Latino	57.4	54.7	46.7	46.9	48.5	49.6	47.0	47.6	43.1	41.6
Not Hispanic or Latino	70.6	70.4	68.2	69.4	70.3	71.2	70.2	70.5	68.8	67.6
White only	74.0	74.0	72.1	73.1	74.2	74.8	74.1	74.1	72.8	71.3
Black or African American only	52.6	53.0	49.8	52.8	52.2	54.6	53.3	54.4	52.6	52.0
Age and percent of poverty level[4]										
All ages:										
Below 100 percent	24.1	19.9	17.5	19.9	20.1	21.8	20.9	21.8	21.4	19.9
100–149 percent	52.4	46.4	42.1	38.8	40.4	38.4	37.1	37.0	34.3	31.8
150–199 percent	69.5	63.1	58.8	58.3	56.6	53.9	53.4	51.9	50.9	46.8
200 percent or more	85.0	83.7	82.3	81.9	81.9	82.1	81.0	80.9	79.3	78.6
Under 18 years:										
Below 100 percent	23.0	17.5	13.6	16.2	16.8	17.5	16.5	16.2	14.8	14.0
100–149 percent	58.3	52.5	43.6	39.6	42.6	39.2	36.3	37.0	32.5	30.1
150–199 percent	75.8	70.1	61.8	62.5	61.6	56.3	55.6	52.9	50.8	47.0
200 percent or more	86.9	86.6	84.4	83.9	83.9	84.4	82.5	82.9	80.8	79.9

See footnotes at end of table.

Table 132 (page 3 of 3). Private health insurance coverage among persons under 65 years of age, according to selected characteristics: United States, selected years 1984–2003

[Data are based on household interviews of a sample of the civilian noninstitutionalized population]

Characteristic	Private insurance obtained through workplace[6]									
	1984	*1989*	*1995*	*1997*[1]	*1998*	*1999*	*2000*	*2001*	*2002*	*2003*
Geographic region	Percent of population									
Northeast	74.0	75.0	69.8	70.9	73.0	73.5	72.1	72.9	70.5	69.4
Midwest	72.0	73.3	71.2	72.4	73.6	75.3	74.5	73.7	72.2	70.4
South	66.2	63.6	61.8	62.8	63.2	63.6	62.2	61.6	60.3	58.8
West	64.7	63.9	60.4	60.6	61.3	61.7	60.6	62.1	59.9	57.5
Location of residence										
Within MSA[5]	70.9	69.6	66.6	67.2	68.4	69.5	67.8	67.9	66.3	64.6
Outside MSA[5]	65.3	63.5	60.7	62.7	63.0	61.9	62.4	61.7	59.2	58.0

* Estimates are considered unreliable. Data not shown have a relative standard error of greater than 30 percent.
- - - Data not available.
[1]In 1997 the National Health Interview Survey (NHIS) was redesigned, including changes to the questions on health insurance coverage. See Appendix I, National Health Interview Survey and Appendix II, Health insurance coverage.
[2]Includes all other races not shown separately and, in 1984 and 1989, unknown poverty level.
[3]The race groups, white, black, American Indian and Alaska Native, Asian, Native Hawaiian and Other Pacific Islander, and 2 or more races, include persons of Hispanic and non-Hispanic origin. Persons of Hispanic origin may be of any race. Starting with data year 1999 race-specific estimates are tabulated according to 1997 Standards for Federal data on Race and Ethnicity and are not strictly comparable with estimates for earlier years. The five single race categories plus multiple race categories shown in the table conform to 1997 Standards. Starting with data year 1999, race-specific estimates are for persons who reported only one racial group; the category "2 or more races" includes persons who reported more than one racial group. Prior to data year 1999, data were tabulated according to 1977 Standards with four racial groups and the category "Asian only" included Native Hawaiian and Other Pacific Islander. Estimates for single race categories prior to 1999 included persons who reported one race or, if they reported more than one race, identified one race as best representing their race. Starting in 2003, race responses of "other race" and "unspecified multiple race" were treated as missing, and then race was imputed if these were the only race responses. Almost all persons with a race response of "other race" were of Hispanic origin. See Appendix II, Race.
[4]Poverty status was unknown for 10–11 percent of persons under 65 years of age in 1984 and 1989. Missing family income data were imputed for 15–16 percent of persons under 65 years of age in 1994–96, 24 percent in 1997, and 28–31 percent in 1998–2003. See Appendix II, Family income; Poverty level.
[5]MSA is metropolitan statistical area.
[6]Private insurance originally obtained through a present or former employer or union. Starting in 1997 also includes private insurance obtained through workplace, self-employment, or professional association.

NOTES: Standard errors are available in the spreadsheet version of this table. See www.cdc.gov/nchs/hus.htm. Starting with *Health, United States, 2005*, estimates for 2000 and later years use weights derived from the 2000 census. Estimates for 2000–2002 were recalculated using 2000-based weights and may differ from previous editions of *Health, United States.* Data for additional years are available. See Appendix III.

SOURCES: Centers for Disease Control and Prevention, National Center for Health Statistics, National Health Interview Survey, health insurance supplements (1984, 1989, 1994–1996). Starting with data year 1997 data are from the family core questionnaires.

Table 133 (page 1 of 2). Medicaid coverage among persons under 65 years of age, according to selected characteristics: United States, selected years 1984–2003

[Data are based on household interviews of a sample of the civilian noninstitutionalized population]

Characteristic	*1984*	*1989*	*1995*	*1997*[1]	*1998*	*1999*	*2000*	*2001*	*2002*	*2003*
					Number in millions					
Total[2]	14.0	15.4	26.6	22.9	21.1	21.9	23.2	25.5	29.4	30.9
					Percent of population					
Total[2]	6.8	7.2	11.5	9.7	8.9	9.1	9.5	10.4	11.8	12.3
Age										
Under 18 years	11.9	12.6	21.5	18.4	17.1	18.1	19.6	21.5	24.8	26.0
Under 6 years	15.5	15.7	29.3	24.7	22.4	23.5	24.7	26.2	30.0	32.3
6–17 years	10.1	10.9	17.4	15.2	14.5	15.5	17.2	19.2	22.3	23.0
18–44 years	5.1	5.2	7.8	6.6	5.8	5.7	5.6	6.3	7.1	7.4
18–24 years	6.4	6.8	10.4	8.8	8.0	8.1	8.1	8.4	9.9	9.6
25–34 years	5.3	5.2	8.2	6.8	5.7	5.7	5.5	6.2	6.6	7.8
35–44 years	3.5	4.0	5.9	5.2	4.6	4.3	4.3	5.1	5.9	5.6
45–64 years	3.4	4.3	5.6	4.6	4.5	4.4	4.5	4.7	5.3	5.3
45–54 years	3.2	3.8	5.1	4.0	4.1	3.9	4.2	4.4	5.1	5.0
55–64 years	3.6	4.9	6.4	5.6	5.0	5.3	4.9	5.2	5.8	5.8
Sex										
Male	5.4	5.7	9.6	8.4	7.7	7.9	8.2	9.1	10.6	10.9
Female	8.1	8.6	13.4	11.1	10.1	10.3	10.8	11.6	13.0	13.6
Race[3]										
White only	4.6	5.1	8.9	7.4	6.7	6.9	7.1	8.0	9.3	10.4
Black or African American only	20.5	19.0	28.5	22.4	21.2	20.1	21.2	22.1	23.2	23.7
American Indian and Alaska Native only	*28.2	29.7	19.0	19.6	15.2	21.4	15.1	16.2	21.1	18.5
Asian only	*8.7	*8.8	10.5	9.6	6.7	7.9	7.5	8.4	9.8	8.0
Native Hawaiian and Other Pacific Islander only	- - -	- - -	- - -	- - -	- - -	*	*	*	*	*
2 or more races	- - -	- - -	- - -	- - -	- - -	19.7	19.1	17.5	21.6	23.5
Hispanic origin and race[3]										
Hispanic or Latino	13.3	13.5	21.9	17.6	15.5	15.7	15.5	17.5	20.8	21.8
Mexican	12.2	12.4	21.6	17.2	14.3	14.5	14.0	16.6	20.2	21.7
Puerto Rican	31.5	27.3	33.4	31.0	26.1	28.6	29.4	30.3	29.0	31.0
Cuban	*4.8	*7.7	13.4	7.3	*8.9	7.6	9.2	11.1	14.9	13.8
Other Hispanic or Latino	7.9	11.1	18.2	15.3	15.0	14.7	14.5	15.6	19.6	19.3
Not Hispanic or Latino	6.2	6.6	10.2	8.7	8.0	8.2	8.5	9.2	10.3	10.6
White only	3.7	4.2	7.1	6.1	5.6	5.8	6.1	6.7	7.7	8.0
Black or African American only	20.7	19.0	28.1	22.1	21.0	20.1	21.0	22.0	23.2	23.4
Age and percent of poverty level[4]										
All ages:[3]										
Below 100 percent	33.0	37.6	48.4	40.5	38.9	38.8	38.4	40.0	42.8	43.2
100–149 percent	7.7	10.9	19.1	17.9	16.2	18.8	20.7	23.3	27.6	26.9
150–199 percent	3.2	5.1	8.3	8.3	7.9	10.8	11.5	14.1	16.1	17.1
200 percent or more	0.6	1.1	1.7	1.8	1.9	2.1	2.3	2.6	3.1	3.3
Under 18 years:										
Below 100 percent	43.2	47.9	66.0	58.0	57.0	57.7	58.5	61.5	66.4	67.5
100–149 percent	9.0	12.3	27.2	28.7	25.1	31.4	35.0	38.9	47.1	49.1
150–199 percent	4.4	6.1	13.1	13.0	13.1	17.9	21.3	25.9	29.1	33.6
200 percent or more	0.8	1.8	3.3	3.1	3.4	4.2	5.1	5.7	7.2	7.6

See footnotes at end of table.

Table 133 (page 2 of 2). Medicaid coverage among persons under 65 years of age, according to selected characteristics: United States, selected years 1984–2003

[Data are based on household interviews of a sample of the civilian noninstitutionalized population]

Characteristic	*1984*	*1989*	*1995*	*1997*[1]	*1998*	*1999*	*2000*	*2001*	*2002*	*2003*
Geographic region					Percent of population					
Northeast	8.6	6.6	11.7	11.3	9.8	10.0	10.6	10.8	12.5	12.9
Midwest	7.4	7.6	10.5	8.4	7.7	7.4	8.0	8.9	10.3	10.8
South	5.1	6.5	11.3	8.7	8.6	9.0	9.4	10.7	12.0	12.6
West	7.0	8.5	12.9	11.7	10.1	10.7	10.4	11.0	12.7	12.8
Location of residence										
Within MSA[5]	7.1	7.0	11.3	9.7	8.6	8.5	8.9	9.9	11.0	11.5
Outside MSA[5]	6.1	7.9	12.3	10.1	10.0	11.7	11.9	12.4	15.2	15.3

* Estimates are considered unreliable. Data preceded by an asterisk have a relative standard error (RSE) of 20–30 percent. Data not shown have an RSE of greater than 30 percent.
- - - Data not available.
[1]In 1997 the National Health Interview Survey (NHIS) was redesigned, including changes to the questions on health insurance coverage. See Appendix I, National Health Interview Survey and Appendix II, Health insurance coverage.
[2]Includes all other races not shown separately and, in 1984 and 1989, unknown poverty level.
[3]The race groups, white, black, American Indian and Alaska Native, Asian, Native Hawaiian and Other Pacific Islander, and 2 or more races, include persons of Hispanic and non-Hispanic origin. Persons of Hispanic origin may be of any race. Starting with data year 1999 race-specific estimates are tabulated according to 1997 Standards for Federal data on Race and Ethnicity and are not strictly comparable with estimates for earlier years. The five single race categories plus multiple race categories shown in the table conform to 1997 Standards. Starting with data year 1999, race-specific estimates are for persons who reported only one racial group; the category "2 or more races" includes persons who reported more than one racial group. Prior to data year 1999, data were tabulated according to 1977 Standards with four racial groups and the category "Asian only" included Native Hawaiian and Other Pacific Islander. Estimates for single race categories prior to 1999 included persons who reported one race or, if they reported more than one race, identified one race as best representing their race. See Appendix II, Race.
[4]Poverty status was unknown for 10–11 percent of persons under 65 years of age in 1984 and 1989. Missing family income data were imputed for 15–16 percent of persons under 65 years of age in 1994–96, 24 percent in 1997, and 28–31 percent in 1998–2003. See Appendix II, Family income; Poverty level.
[5]MSA is metropolitan statistical area.

NOTES: Medicaid includes other public assistance through 1996. Starting in 1997 includes state-sponsored health plans. Starting in 1999 includes State Children's Health Insurance Program (SCHIP). In 2003, 9.4 percent of persons under 65 years of age were covered by Medicaid, 1.2 percent by state-sponsored health plans, and 1.7 percent by SCHIP. Standard errors are available in the spreadsheet version of this table. See www.cdc.gov/nchs/hus.htm. Starting with *Health, United States, 2005*, estimates for 2000 and later years use weights derived from the 2000 census. Estimates for 2000–2002 were recalculated using 2000-based weights and may differ from previous editions of *Health, United States*. Data for additional years are available. See Appendix III.

SOURCES: Centers for Disease Control and Prevention, National Center for Health Statistics, National Health Interview Survey, health insurance supplements (1984, 1989, 1994–1996). Starting with data year 1997 data are from the family core questionnaires.

Table 134 (page 1 of 2). No health insurance coverage among persons under 65 years of age, according to selected characteristics: United States, selected years 1984–2003

[Data are based on household interviews of a sample of the civilian noninstitutionalized population]

Characteristic	1984	1989	1995	1997[1]	1998	1999	2000	2001	2002	2003
	Number in millions									
Total[2]	29.8	33.4	37.1	41.0	39.2	38.5	41.4	40.3	41.7	41.6
	Percent of population									
Total[2]	14.5	15.6	16.1	17.5	16.6	16.1	17.0	16.4	16.8	16.5
Age										
Under 18 years	13.9	14.7	13.4	14.0	12.7	11.9	12.6	11.2	10.9	9.8
Under 6 years	14.9	15.1	11.8	12.5	11.5	11.0	11.8	9.9	9.2	8.2
6–17 years	13.4	14.5	14.3	14.7	13.3	12.3	13.0	11.8	11.7	10.6
18–44 years	17.1	18.4	20.4	22.4	21.4	21.0	22.4	22.2	23.0	23.5
18–24 years	25.0	27.1	28.0	30.1	29.0	27.4	30.4	29.9	28.8	30.1
25–34 years	16.2	18.3	21.1	23.8	22.2	22.1	23.3	23.1	24.6	25.4
35–44 years	11.2	12.3	15.1	16.7	16.4	16.3	16.9	16.8	18.0	17.5
45–64 years	9.6	10.5	10.9	12.4	12.2	12.2	12.6	12.2	13.1	12.5
45–54 years	10.5	11.0	11.6	12.8	12.6	12.8	12.8	13.0	14.1	13.6
55–64 years	8.7	10.0	9.9	11.8	11.4	11.4	12.4	11.0	11.5	10.9
Sex										
Male	15.3	16.8	17.4	18.7	17.6	17.2	18.1	17.5	18.4	17.7
Female	13.8	14.4	14.8	16.3	15.6	15.0	15.9	15.3	15.2	15.3
Race[3]										
White only	13.6	14.5	15.5	16.4	15.2	14.6	15.4	14.9	15.5	16.0
Black or African American only	19.9	21.6	18.0	20.1	20.4	19.3	19.5	18.8	18.8	18.4
American Indian and Alaska Native only	22.5	28.4	34.3	38.1	38.7	38.2	38.4	33.1	39.1	35.0
Asian only	18.5	16.9	18.6	19.5	18.3	16.8	17.6	17.3	17.4	18.2
Native Hawaiian and Other Pacific Islander only	---	---	---	---	---	*	*	*	*	*
2 or more races	---	---	---	---	---	14.5	16.8	16.6	17.6	15.9
Hispanic origin and race[3]										
Hispanic or Latino	29.5	33.7	31.4	34.5	34.1	34.0	35.6	35.0	33.9	34.7
Mexican	33.8	39.9	35.6	39.4	40.1	38.2	39.9	39.4	37.1	37.8
Puerto Rican	18.3	24.7	17.6	19.0	18.9	19.4	16.4	15.5	19.2	17.7
Cuban	21.6	20.6	22.3	21.1	18.5	20.4	25.4	20.4	20.8	29.1
Other Hispanic or Latino	27.4	25.8	30.2	33.0	31.2	30.7	33.4	33.2	33.2	33.4
Not Hispanic or Latino	13.2	13.7	14.2	15.2	14.1	13.5	14.0	13.3	13.9	13.3
White only	12.0	12.2	13.0	13.8	12.5	12.1	12.5	11.8	12.5	11.9
Black or African American only	19.6	21.4	17.9	20.0	20.4	19.2	19.5	18.7	18.7	18.1
Age and percent of poverty level[4]										
All ages:										
Below 100 percent	33.9	35.0	29.6	33.7	34.1	33.8	34.2	33.1	30.3	31.1
100–149 percent	27.2	31.1	31.6	35.1	35.4	34.1	34.9	31.7	32.2	31.9
150–199 percent	17.3	21.7	24.0	26.3	25.9	26.9	27.0	26.4	25.2	27.6
200 percent or more	6.0	7.1	8.7	10.1	9.3	9.2	10.1	10.0	11.1	10.0
Under 18 years:										
Below 100 percent	29.0	31.4	20.0	23.2	22.7	22.3	22.0	20.7	17.0	16.8
100–149 percent	22.8	26.1	24.8	26.5	27.4	24.2	25.4	19.6	19.4	16.2
150–199 percent	12.7	15.8	18.0	19.9	17.5	19.1	17.7	17.4	14.3	14.9
200 percent or more	4.2	4.5	6.4	7.1	6.0	5.4	6.5	5.8	6.7	5.5

See footnotes at end of table.

Table 134 (page 2 of 2). No health insurance coverage among persons under 65 years of age, according to selected characteristics: United States, selected years 1984–2003

[Data are based on household interviews of a sample of the civilian noninstitutionalized population]

Characteristic	1984	1989	1995	1997[1]	1998	1999	2000	2001	2002	2003
Geographic region	Percent of population									
Northeast	10.2	10.9	13.3	13.5	12.3	12.2	12.2	11.7	12.8	11.3
Midwest	11.3	10.7	12.2	13.2	11.9	11.5	12.3	11.7	12.5	12.4
South	17.7	19.7	19.4	20.9	20.1	19.9	20.5	20.2	20.3	19.8
West	18.2	18.8	17.9	20.6	20.0	18.5	20.7	19.0	19.1	19.9
Location of residence										
Within MSA[5]	13.6	15.2	15.5	16.9	15.9	15.4	16.6	15.9	16.3	16.0
Outside MSA[5]	16.6	17.0	18.6	19.8	19.1	18.8	18.6	18.2	18.7	18.7

* Estimates are considered unreliable. Data not shown have a relative standard error of greater than 30 percent.
- - - Data not available.
[1]In 1997 the National Health Interview Survey (NHIS) was redesigned, including changes to the questions on health insurance coverage. See Appendix I, National Health Interview Survey and Appendix II, Health insurance coverage.
[2]Includes all other races not shown separately and, in 1984 and 1989, unknown poverty level.
[3]The race groups, white, black, American Indian and Alaska Native, Asian, Native Hawaiian and Other Pacific Islander, and 2 or more races, include persons of Hispanic and non-Hispanic origin. Persons of Hispanic origin may be of any race. Starting with data year 1999 race-specific estimates are tabulated according to 1997 Standards for Federal data on Race and Ethnicity and are not strictly comparable with estimates for earlier years. The five single race categories plus multiple race categories shown in the table conform to 1997 Standards. Starting with data year 1999, race-specific estimates are for persons who reported only one racial group; the category "2 or more races" includes persons who reported more than one racial group. Prior to data year 1999, data were tabulated according to 1977 Standards with four racial groups and the category "Asian only" included Native Hawaiian and Other Pacific Islander. Estimates for single race categories prior to 1999 included persons who reported one race or, if they reported more than one race, identified one race as best representing their race. See Appendix II, Race.
[4]Poverty status was unknown for 10–11 percent of persons under 65 years of age in 1984 and 1989. Missing family income data were imputed for 15–16 percent of persons under 65 years of age in 1994–96, 24 percent in 1997, and 28–31 percent in 1998–2003. See Appendix II, Family income; Poverty level.
[5]MSA is metropolitan statistical area.

NOTES: Persons not covered by private insurance, Medicaid, State Children's Health Insurance Program (SCHIP), public assistance (through 1996), state-sponsored or other government-sponsored health plans (starting in 1997), Medicare, or military plans are considered to have no health insurance coverage and are included in this table. See Appendix II, Health insurance coverage. Standard errors are available in the spreadsheet version of this table. See www.cdc.gov/nchs/hus.htm. Starting with *Health, United States, 2005*, estimates for 2000 and later years use weights derived from the 2000 census. Estimates for 2000–2002 were recalculated using 2000-based weights and may differ from previous editions of *Health, United States*. Data for additional years are available. See Appendix III.

SOURCES: Centers for Disease Control and Prevention, National Center for Health Statistics, National Health Interview Survey, health insurance supplements (1984, 1989, 1994–1996). Starting with data year 1997 data are from the family core questionnaires.

Table 135 (page 1 of 3). Health insurance coverage for persons 65 years of age and over, according to type of coverage and selected characteristics: United States, selected years 1989–2003

[Data are based on household interviews of a sample of the civilian noninstitutionalized population]

	Private insurance[1]						*Private insurance obtained through workplace*[1,2]					
Characteristic	*1989*	*1995*	*2000*	*2001*	*2002*	*2003*	*1989*	*1995*	*2000*	*2001*	*2002*	*2003*
	Number in millions											
Total[3]	22.4	23.5	21.2	21.3	20.6	21.5	11.2	12.4	12.0	12.2	11.8	11.9
	Percent of population											
Total[3]	76.5	74.6	63.4	63.1	60.9	62.7	38.4	39.5	35.9	36.2	34.9	34.8
Age												
65–74 years	78.2	75.1	63.1	63.4	60.9	62.3	43.7	43.3	39.6	39.8	38.0	38.2
75 years and over	73.9	73.9	63.9	62.7	60.8	63.1	30.2	34.1	31.4	32.0	31.4	31.0
75–84 years	75.9	75.7	64.9	64.2	61.7	64.0	32.0	36.0	33.2	33.4	33.1	32.5
85 years and over	65.5	67.3	59.8	57.4	57.7	59.8	22.8	27.3	24.8	26.8	25.4	26.2
Sex												
Male	77.5	76.4	64.7	64.2	62.2	64.1	43.5	44.2	40.4	40.6	39.2	38.6
Female	75.8	73.3	62.5	62.3	59.9	61.6	34.8	36.2	32.6	33.0	31.8	32.0
Race[4]												
White only	80.1	78.3	67.2	66.7	64.3	65.7	39.9	41.0	37.4	37.6	36.0	35.7
Black or African American only	43.0	41.8	36.1	38.3	36.5	37.6	24.8	26.5	25.7	28.5	27.2	28.3
American Indian and Alaska Native only	46.8	*39.9	*	*32.6	*	*37.3	*21.3	*29.4	*	*	*	*
Asian only	48.4	45.8	42.9	41.3	40.7	40.2	*30.2	27.0	25.0	23.8	28.0	25.9
Native Hawaiian and Other Pacific Islander only	---	---	*	*	*	*	---	---	*	*	*	*
2 or more races	---	---	65.5	48.5	55.1	53.0	---	---	49.7	31.2	35.2	31.7
Hispanic origin and race[4]												
Hispanic or Latino	44.8	40.9	24.6	25.3	23.8	24.0	24.5	20.3	16.4	17.6	17.3	17.6
Mexican	36.4	33.3	21.7	25.8	22.3	25.7	22.2	17.8	13.8	18.0	16.8	19.5
Not Hispanic or Latino	77.6	76.3	65.5	65.2	63.1	65.1	38.9	40.5	36.9	37.3	35.9	35.9
White only	81.4	80.4	69.1	68.8	66.4	68.6	40.4	42.2	38.3	38.6	37.0	37.0
Black or African American only	43.0	41.5	36.1	38.3	36.6	37.6	24.8	26.1	25.7	28.6	27.2	28.1
Percent of poverty level[5]												
Below 100 percent	46.3	40.3	34.1	32.8	30.7	33.2	11.5	13.9	12.7	15.2	12.7	12.9
100–149 percent	67.5	67.6	47.0	48.3	46.9	47.2	22.3	26.7	18.9	22.6	19.8	16.8
150–199 percent	81.1	75.9	61.8	61.8	58.7	61.8	39.5	38.8	29.2	28.8	28.6	26.9
200 percent or more	86.6	85.7	72.8	71.4	69.7	71.1	52.3	50.6	45.5	44.1	43.4	44.0
Geographic region												
Northeast	76.5	76.1	66.9	66.4	65.8	70.6	43.6	44.9	38.9	38.9	39.8	39.5
Midwest	82.2	82.3	76.0	72.5	71.8	74.5	41.0	45.3	41.3	40.7	37.2	39.1
South	73.4	71.1	58.8	60.6	57.6	56.0	33.2	34.6	32.4	34.5	33.6	31.4
West	75.1	68.9	51.9	52.1	48.3	51.4	38.2	34.2	31.9	30.7	29.4	30.7
Location of residence												
Within MSA[6]	77.1	74.8	61.7	61.5	60.1	62.1	41.3	41.5	37.2	36.8	35.9	36.7
Outside MSA[6]	75.0	74.1	68.8	68.3	63.5	64.6	30.8	32.6	32.0	34.2	31.6	28.5

See footnotes at end of table.

Table 135 (page 2 of 3). Health insurance coverage for persons 65 years of age and over, according to type of coverage and selected characteristics: United States, selected years 1989–2003

[Data are based on household interviews of a sample of the civilian noninstitutionalized population]

Characteristic	*Medicare health maintenance organization*[1,7]						*Medicaid*[1,8]					
	1989	*1995*	*2000*	*2001*	*2002*	*2003*	*1989*	*1995*	*2000*	*2001*	*2002*	*2003*
	Number in millions											
Total[3]	---	---	5.1	4.3	4.0	3.4	2.0	3.0	2.5	2.7	2.7	2.7
	Percent of population											
Total[3]	---	---	15.2	12.9	11.8	10.0	7.0	9.4	7.5	8.0	7.8	8.0
Age	Percent of population											
65–74 years	---	---	15.7	12.7	11.7	9.5	6.3	8.4	7.6	7.6	7.9	8.0
75 years and over	---	---	14.5	13.1	11.9	10.6	8.2	10.9	7.4	8.4	7.7	7.9
75–84 years	---	---	15.4	13.4	12.6	10.9	7.9	9.9	7.1	7.9	7.8	7.6
85 years and over	---	---	11.0	11.9	9.2	9.7	9.7	14.3	8.4	10.1	7.3	9.1
Sex												
Male	---	---	15.5	12.4	12.3	9.9	4.9	5.7	5.4	5.9	5.6	5.7
Female	---	---	14.9	13.2	11.4	10.2	8.5	12.1	9.0	9.5	9.5	9.6
Race[4]												
White only	---	---	15.1	12.9	11.6	10.0	5.5	7.2	5.5	6.1	6.1	6.2
Black or African American only	---	---	14.6	11.4	10.6	9.4	20.5	27.5	19.4	19.9	19.5	19.2
American Indian and Alaska Native only	---	---	*	*	*	*	*30.9	*	*35.4	*	*	*32.7
Asian only	---	---	16.7	13.4	18.6	15.2	*21.3	33.6	21.0	22.9	20.0	28.5
Native Hawaiian and Other Pacific Islander only	---	---	*	*	*	*	---	---	*	*	*	*
2 or more races	---	---	*30.4	*16.5	*15.2	*	---	---	*	*19.1	*	*15.5
Hispanic origin and race[4]												
Hispanic or Latino	---	---	24.7	19.9	21.8	18.9	25.6	31.1	28.4	29.0	27.9	27.3
Mexican	---	---	23.7	18.2	19.0	14.5	27.4	31.6	26.6	25.7	23.6	25.7
Not Hispanic or Latino	---	---	14.6	12.5	11.2	9.5	6.4	8.3	6.3	6.8	6.6	6.8
White only	---	---	14.5	12.5	11.1	9.3	4.8	5.9	4.6	4.9	5.0	4.8
Black or African American only	---	---	14.5	11.4	10.5	9.5	20.4	27.6	19.4	19.8	19.4	18.8
Percent of poverty level[5]												
Below 100 percent	---	---	15.1	9.1	9.1	9.4	28.1	36.2	28.1	31.0	29.5	31.8
100–149 percent	---	---	16.4	12.8	11.8	10.7	9.0	12.8	13.7	15.0	12.8	13.3
150–199 percent	---	---	15.7	14.1	12.8	11.7	4.7	5.8	5.4	6.8	6.6	6.4
200 percent or more	---	---	14.8	13.3	12.0	9.7	2.2	2.2	2.8	3.0	3.1	3.1
Geographic region												
Northeast	---	---	12.6	13.5	10.3	10.3	5.4	8.9	7.2	7.7	7.5	6.5
Midwest	---	---	8.4	7.5	5.9	4.0	3.6	5.8	4.5	5.1	5.1	4.9
South	---	---	13.1	10.1	8.8	8.0	9.2	11.4	9.3	9.2	9.2	9.1
West	---	---	30.6	23.8	26.4	21.9	9.3	11.3	8.4	9.7	9.0	11.3
Location of residence												
Within MSA[6]	---	---	18.6	15.7	14.5	12.5	6.4	8.8	7.0	7.9	7.4	7.7
Outside MSA[6]	---	---	4.4	3.1	3.0	*1.7	8.6	11.5	8.8	8.3	9.3	8.8

See footnotes at end of table.

Table 135 (page 3 of 3). Health insurance coverage for persons 65 years of age and over, according to type of coverage and selected characteristics: United States, selected years 1989–2003

[Data are based on household interviews of a sample of the civilian noninstitutionalized population]

* Estimates are considered unreliable. Data preceded by an asterisk have a relative standard error (RSE) of 20–30 percent. Data not shown have an RSE of greater than 30 percent.
- - - Data not available.
[1]Almost all persons 65 years of age and over are also covered by Medicare.
[2]Private insurance originally obtained through a present or former employer or union. Starting in 1997, also includes private insurance obtained through workplace, self-employed, or professional association.
[3]Includes all other races not shown separately and, in 1984 and 1989, unknown poverty level.
[4]The race groups, white, black, American Indian and Alaska Native, Asian, Native Hawaiian and Other Pacific Islander, and 2 or more races, include persons of Hispanic and non-Hispanic origin. Persons of Hispanic origin may be of any race. Starting with data year 1999, race-specific estimates are tabulated according to 1997 Standards for Federal data on Race and Ethnicity and are not strictly comparable with estimates for earlier years. The five single race categories plus multiple race categories shown in the table conform to 1997 Standards. Starting with data year 1999, race-specific estimates are for persons who reported only one racial group; the category "2 or more races" includes persons who reported more than one racial group. Prior to data year 1999, data were tabulated according to 1977 Standards with four racial groups and the category "Asian only" included Native Hawaiian and Other Pacific Islander. Estimates for single race categories prior to 1999 included persons who reported one race or, if they reported more than one race, identified one race as best representing their race. See Appendix II, Race.
[5]Poverty status was unknown for 15–18 percent of persons 65 years of age and over in 1984 and 1989. Missing family income data were imputed for 22–25 percent of persons 65 years of age and over in 1994–96, 36 percent in 1997, 41 percent in 1998, and 44–47 percent in 1999–2003. See Appendix II, Family income; Poverty level.
[6]MSA is metropolitan statistical area.
[7]Persons reporting Medicare coverage are considered to have health maintenance organization (HMO) coverage if they responded yes when asked if they were under a Medicare managed care arrangement such as an HMO.
[8]Includes public assistance through 1996. Starting with data year 1997 includes State-sponsored health plans. In 2003 the percent of the population 65 years of age and over covered by Medicaid was 7.3 percent, and 0.6 percent were covered by State-sponsored health plans.

NOTES: In 1997 the National Health Interview Survey (NHIS) was redesigned, including changes to the questions on health insurance coverage. See Appendix I, National Health Interview Survey and Appendix II, Health insurance coverage. Percents do not add to 100 because (1) elderly persons with more than one type of insurance in addition to Medicare appear in more than one column, (2) elderly persons with Medicare fee-for-service only are not shown, and (3) the percent of elderly persons without health insurance (1.1 percent in 2003) is not shown. Standard errors are available in the spreadsheet version of this table. See www.cdc.gov/nchs/hus.htm. Starting with *Health, United States, 2005*, estimates for 2000 and later years use weights derived from the 2000 census. Estimates for 2000–2002 were recalculated using 2000-based weights and may differ from previous editions of *Health, United States*. Data for additional years are available. See Appendix III.

SOURCES: Centers for Disease Control and Prevention, National Center for Health Statistics, National Health Interview Survey, health insurance supplements (1984, 1989, 1994–1996). Starting with data year 1997, data are from the family core questionnaires.

Table 136 (page 1 of 2). Health maintenance organization (HMO) coverage among persons under 65 years of age by private insurance and Medicaid, according to selected characteristics: United States, 1998–2003

[Data are based on household interviews of a sample of the civilian noninstitutionalized population]

Characteristic	Total[1]				Private[2]				Medicaid[3]			
	1998	2000	2002	2003	1998	2000	2002	2003	1998	2000	2002	2003
	Number of persons in millions											
Total under age 65 years[4]	83.2	82.9	77.0	71.2	72.3	71.8	64.0	57.8	10.7	10.9	13.0	13.3
	Percent of population											
Total under age 65 years[4]	35.2	34.0	31.0	28.3	30.5	29.5	25.8	22.9	4.5	4.5	5.2	5.3
Age												
Under 18 years	39.4	37.6	35.4	33.1	30.1	28.3	24.6	21.9	9.4	9.4	11.0	11.3
Under 6 years	41.7	39.8	37.4	35.1	29.2	27.6	23.4	20.7	12.7	12.4	14.2	14.5
6–17 years	38.3	36.6	34.5	32.1	30.5	28.6	25.1	22.5	7.7	8.0	9.5	9.8
18–44 years	33.4	32.5	29.2	25.9	30.6	29.8	25.9	22.6	2.8	2.7	3.3	3.2
18–24 years	28.8	28.3	25.6	21.8	25.0	24.3	21.3	17.9	3.9	4.0	4.4	3.9
25–34 years	34.8	33.8	30.4	25.8	31.8	31.3	27.1	22.3	2.9	2.6	3.3	3.5
35–44 years	34.9	33.7	30.4	28.5	32.7	31.8	27.8	25.9	2.0	1.9	2.5	2.5
45–64 years	33.0	32.6	29.3	27.0	31.0	30.4	26.8	24.6	1.6	1.8	2.1	2.1
45–54 years	34.3	33.4	30.3	27.9	32.5	31.4	28.1	25.7	1.6	1.9	2.1	2.1
55–64 years	31.1	31.4	27.7	25.7	28.7	28.8	24.9	23.0	1.7	1.8	2.2	2.2
Sex												
Male	34.2	33.1	30.2	27.3	30.4	29.2	25.6	22.7	3.7	3.8	4.6	4.6
Female	36.1	35.0	31.8	29.2	30.7	29.7	25.9	23.2	5.3	5.1	5.8	6.0
Race[5]												
White only	33.9	32.9	29.4	26.8	30.6	29.7	25.5	22.6	3.2	3.2	3.8	4.2
Black or African American only	40.9	40.1	37.9	36.3	29.1	29.3	26.5	24.0	11.6	10.8	11.5	12.3
American Indian and Alaska Native only	30.3	22.2	18.7	19.7	21.9	14.6	*10.8	13.4	*8.2	*6.9	*	*6.0
Asian only	41.6	39.6	36.2	31.5	37.5	36.3	32.0	28.8	4.0	*3.1	4.3	*2.6
Native Hawaiian and Other Pacific Islander only	---	*	*	*	---	*	*	*	---	*	*	*
2 or more races	---	39.9	34.2	33.5	---	29.6	24.2	21.9	---	10.4	10.3	11.6
Hispanic origin and race[5]												
Hispanic or Latino	34.6	33.7	32.9	29.5	26.8	26.2	23.5	20.0	7.7	7.6	9.4	9.5
Mexican	31.6	31.2	31.4	27.6	24.9	24.0	21.6	18.6	6.6	7.3	9.7	9.1
Puerto Rican	44.8	43.9	39.7	39.9	27.9	29.3	27.3	22.7	16.2	14.6	12.5	17.4
Cuban	42.0	40.3	41.7	30.3	36.5	35.4	36.1	26.3	*	*4.2	*5.3	*3.4
Other Hispanic or Latino	35.3	35.4	32.9	30.7	28.4	29.7	25.3	22.5	6.9	5.8	7.6	8.1
Not Hispanic or Latino	35.2	34.1	30.7	28.1	31.1	30.0	26.2	23.5	4.1	4.0	4.5	4.6
White only	34.0	32.7	29.1	26.4	31.2	30.0	25.9	23.2	2.7	2.7	3.1	3.1
Black or African American only	40.6	40.0	37.9	36.3	29.1	29.3	26.5	24.2	11.3	10.7	11.5	12.2
Percent of poverty level[6]												
Below 100 percent	30.9	29.2	29.3	28.0	9.3	9.8	8.2	7.3	21.3	19.4	21.2	20.6
100–149 percent	26.6	26.3	26.9	23.3	18.7	16.8	14.7	11.9	7.8	9.2	12.1	11.2
150–199 percent	30.3	30.0	27.6	24.8	26.9	24.6	21.3	17.6	3.2	5.3	6.3	7.2
200 percent or more	37.8	36.5	32.3	29.5	36.9	35.5	31.3	28.3	0.8	0.9	1.0	1.1
Geographic region												
Northeast	44.4	44.6	39.4	37.8	39.7	40.7	35.1	32.3	4.8	3.9	4.4	5.4
Midwest	29.9	26.6	25.3	23.4	25.8	23.5	21.0	18.9	4.0	3.0	4.3	4.6
South	30.7	30.4	27.4	24.2	26.2	25.2	21.2	18.4	4.3	5.1	6.1	5.8
West	40.7	39.3	36.4	32.9	35.4	33.7	30.7	27.6	5.1	5.5	5.6	5.2

See footnotes at end of table.

Table 136 (page 2 of 2). Health maintenance organization (HMO) coverage among persons under 65 years of age by private insurance and Medicaid, according to selected characteristics: United States, 1998–2003

[Data are based on household interviews of a sample of the civilian noninstitutionalized population]

	Total[1]				*Private*[2]				*Medicaid*[3]			
Characteristic	*1998*	*2000*	*2002*	*2003*	*1998*	*2000*	*2002*	*2003*	*1998*	*2000*	*2002*	*2003*
	Percent of population											
Location of residence												
Within MSA[7]	38.4	36.8	33.5	30.6	33.7	32.4	28.5	25.4	4.5	4.3	5.0	5.1
Outside MSA[7]	22.9	22.4	20.6	18.6	18.4	17.3	14.4	12.7	4.5	5.0	6.3	5.9

- - - Data not available.
* Estimates are considered unreliable. Data preceded by an asterisk have a relative standard error (RSE) of 20–30 percent. Data not shown have an RSE of greater than 30 percent.
[1]Includes persons with private, Medicaid, or Medicare health maintenance organization (HMO) coverage.
[2]Persons reporting private health insurance coverage are considered to have HMO coverage if they responded HMO or Individual Practice Association (IPA) when asked their plan type.
[3]Persons reporting Medicaid coverage are considered to have HMO coverage if they must choose from a book or list of doctors or the doctor is assigned or if they are required to sign up with a certain primary care doctor, group of doctors, or certain clinic for all routine care.
[4]Includes all other races not shown separately.
[5]The race groups, white, black, American Indian and Alaska Native, Asian, Native Hawaiian and Other Pacific Islander, and 2 or more races, include persons of Hispanic and non-Hispanic origin. Persons of Hispanic origin may be of any race. Starting with data year 1999 race-specific estimates are tabulated according to 1997 Standards for Federal data on Race and Ethnicity and are not strictly comparable with estimates for earlier years. The five single race categories plus multiple race categories shown in the table conform to 1997 Standards. Starting with data year 1999, race-specific estimates are for persons who reported only one racial group; the category "2 or more races" includes persons who reported more than one racial group. Prior to data year 1999, data were tabulated according to 1977 Standards with four racial groups and the category "Asian only" included Native Hawaiian and Other Pacific Islander. Estimates for single race categories prior to 1999 included persons who reported one race or, if they reported more than one race, identified one race as best representing their race. See Appendix II, Race.
[6]Missing family income data were imputed for 24 percent of persons under 65 years of age in 1997 and 28–31 percent in 1998–2003. See Appendix II, Family income; Poverty level.
[7]MSA is metropolitan statistical area.

NOTES: Standard errors for selected years are available in the spreadsheet version of this table. See www.cdc.gov/nchs/hus.htm. Starting with *Health, United States, 2005*, estimates for 2000 and later years use weights derived from the 2000 census. Estimates for 2000–2002 were recalculated using 2000-based weights and may differ from previous editions of *Health, United States.* Data for additional years are available. See Appendix III.

SOURCE: Centers for Disease Control and Prevention, National Center for Health Statistics, National Health Interview Survey. Data are from the family core questionnaires.

Table 137. Health maintenance organizations (HMOs) and enrollment, according to model type, geographic region, and Federal program: United States, selected years 1976–2004

[Data are based on a census of health maintenance organizations]

Plans and enrollment	1976	1980	1985	1990	1995	1998	2000	2003	2004
Plans					Number				
All plans	174	235	478	572	562	651	568	435	412
Model type:[1]									
Individual practice association[2]	41	97	244	360	332	317	278	188	176
Group[3]	122	138	234	212	108	116	101	102	96
Mixed	---	---	---	---	122	212	188	145	140
Geographic region:									
Northeast	29	55	81	115	100	107	98	81	77
Midwest	52	72	157	160	157	185	161	130	126
South	23	45	141	176	196	237	203	138	126
West	70	63	99	121	109	122	106	86	83
Enrollment[1]					Number of persons in millions				
Total	6.0	9.1	21.0	33.0	50.9	76.6	80.9	71.8	68.8
Model type:[1]									
Individual practice association[2]	0.4	1.7	6.4	13.7	20.1	32.6	33.4	27.9	24.6
Group[3]	5.6	7.4	14.6	19.3	13.3	13.8	15.2	16.1	15.3
Mixed	---	---	---	---	17.6	30.1	32.3	27.8	28.9
Federal program:[4]									
Medicaid[5]	---	0.3	0.6	1.2	3.5	7.8	10.8	14.5	14.3
Medicare	---	0.4	1.1	1.8	2.9	5.7	6.6	4.9	4.9
					Percent of HMO enrollees				
Model type:[1]									
Individual practice association[2]	6.6	18.7	30.4	41.6	39.4	42.6	41.3	38.9	35.8
Group[3]	93.4	81.3	69.6	58.4	26.0	18.0	18.9	22.4	22.2
Mixed	---	---	---	---	34.5	39.2	39.9	38.7	42.0
Federal program:[4]									
Medicaid[5]	---	2.9	2.7	3.5	6.9	10.2	13.3	20.2	20.8
Medicare	---	4.3	5.1	5.4	5.7	7.4	8.1	6.9	7.1
					Percent of population enrolled in HMOs				
Total	2.8	4.0	8.9	13.4	19.4	28.6	30.0	24.6	23.4
Geographic region:									
Northeast	2.0	3.1	7.9	14.6	24.4	37.8	36.5	31.8	30.1
Midwest	1.5	2.8	9.7	12.6	16.4	22.7	23.2	19.7	18.7
South	0.4	0.8	3.8	7.1	12.4	21.0	22.6	17.1	16.0
West	9.7	12.2	17.3	23.2	28.6	39.1	41.7	35.8	34.4

- - - Data not available.

[1]Enrollment or number of plans may not equal total because some plans did not report these characteristics.

[2]An HMO operating under an individual practice association model contracts with an association of physicians from various settings (a mixture of solo and group practices) to provide health services.

[3]Group includes staff, group, and network model types. See Appendix II, Health maintenance organization.

[4]Federal program enrollment in HMOs refers to enrollment by Medicaid or Medicare beneficiaries, where the Medicaid or Medicare program contracts directly with the HMO to pay the appropriate annual premium.

[5]Data for 1990 and later include enrollment in managed care health insuring organizations.

NOTES: Data as of June 30 in 1976–80, and January 1 from 1990 onward. Open-ended enrollment in HMO plans, amounting to 6.9 million on January 1, 2004, is included from 1994 onward. See Appendix II, Health maintenance organization. HMOs in Guam are included starting in 1994; HMOs in Puerto Rico, starting in 1998. In 2004 HMO enrollment in Guam was 28,000 and in Puerto Rico, 1,618,000. Some data for 2003 have been revised and differ from the previous edition of *Health, United States*. Data for additional years are available. See Appendix III.

SOURCES: InterStudy National Health Maintenance Organization Census. Annual Report on the Growth of HMOs in the U.S., 1984–1985 editions; The InterStudy Edge, 1990, vol. 2; The InterStudy Competitive Edge, Part II Managed Care Industry Report, 1991–2004. St. Paul, Minnesota (Copyrights 1985, 1990, 1991–2004: Used with the permission of InterStudy); Office of Health Maintenance Organizations: Summary of the National HMO census of prepaid plans—June 1976 and National HMO Census 1980. Public Health Service. Washington. U.S. Government Printing Office. DHHS Pub. No. (PHS) 80–50159; Population estimates used for calculations of regional percents from the U.S. Bureau of the Census at www.census.gov/popest/states/tables/NST-EST2004–08.xls.

Table 138 (page 1 of 2). Medical care benefits for employees of private establishments by size of establishment and occupation: United States, selected years 1990–97

[Data are based on a survey of employers]

Size of establishment and type of benefit	All			Professional, technical, and related			Clerical and sales			Blue collar and service		
	1990	1994	1996	1990	1994	1996	1990	1994	1996	1990	1994	1996
Small private establishments[1]	Percent of all employees											
Participation in medical care benefit:												
Full-time employees	69	66	64	82	80	76	75	70	69	60	57	56
Part-time employees	6	7	6	6	11	14	7	9	9	6	5	3
Type of medical care benefit among participating full-time employees	Percent of participating full-time employees											
Fee arrangement	100	100	100	100	100	100	100	100	100	100	100	100
Traditional fee-for-service	74	55	36	69	53	31	77	55	34	73	57	41
Preferred provider organization (PPO)	13	24	35	16	27	41	13	24	36	11	23	32
Health maintenance organization (HMO)	14	19	27	15	20	27	10	19	28	15	20	25
Other	0	1	2	0	0	1	0	2	2	0	0	2
Individual coverage:												
Employee contributions not required	58	47	48	56	49	49	53	44	46	62	48	48
Employee contributions required	42	53	52	44	51	51	47	56	54	38	52	51
Family coverage:												
Employee contributions not required	32	19	24	28	17	21	29	15	20	37	23	29
Employee contributions required	68	81	75	72	83	78	71	85	80	63	77	70
	Average monthly contribution											
Individual coverage:												
Average monthly employee contribution:												
Total	$ 25	$ 41	$ 43	$ 24	$ 47	$ 41	$ 24	$ 41	$ 42	$ 27	$ 38	$ 44
Non-HMO	25	39	43	24	46	40	24	38	43	28	36	45
HMO	25	49	41	24	48	42	27	50	42	25	47	41
Family coverage:												
Average monthly employee contribution:												
Total	109	160	182	112	181	190	106	160	181	111	149	177
Non-HMO	104	151	181	110	173	192	102	155	181	101	137	175
HMO	135	190	182	118	204	183	134	178	183	145	191	182

See footnotes at end of table.

Table 138 (page 2 of 2). Medical care benefits for employees of private establishments by size of establishment and occupation: United States, selected years 1990–97

[Data are based on a survey of employers]

Size of establishment and type of benefit	All 1991	All 1995	All 1997	Professional, technical, and related 1991	Professional, technical, and related 1995	Professional, technical, and related 1997	Clerical and sales 1991	Clerical and sales 1995	Clerical and sales 1997	Blue collar and service 1991	Blue collar and service 1995	Blue collar and service 1997
Medium and large private establishments[2]	Percent of all employees											
Participation in medical care benefit:												
Full-time employees	83	77	76	85	80	79	81	76	78	84	75	74
Part-time employees	28	19	21	42	31	29	26	20	20	26	15	19
Type of medical care benefit among participating full-time employees	Percent of participating full-time employees											
Fee arrangement	100	100	100	100	100	100	100	100	100	100	100	100
Traditional fee-for-service	67	37	27	62	29	20	59	30	22	73	45	33
Preferred provider organization (PPO)	16	34	40	19	36	40	21	36	42	12	33	39
Health maintenance organization (HMO)	17	27	33	18	33	40	19	32	36	14	21	28
Other	0	1	1	1	1	0	0	2	0	0	1	0
Individual coverage:												
Employee contributions not required	49	33	31	45	21	20	43	24	24	55	44	40
Employee contributions required	51	67	69	55	79	80	57	76	76	45	56	60
Family coverage:												
Employee contributions not required	31	22	20	25	11	10	27	15	14	37	33	29
Employee contributions required	69	78	80	75	89	90	73	85	86	63	67	71
	Average monthly contribution											
Individual coverage:												
Average monthly employee contribution:												
Total	$ 27	$ 34	$ 39	$ 26	$ 35	$ 37	$ 28	$ 36	$ 39	$ 26	$ 32	$ 40
Non-HMO	26	33	42	26	33	40	27	34	41	25	32	43
HMO	29	36	34	29	38	33	32	39	36	28	32	34
Family coverage:												
Average monthly employee contribution:												
Total	97	118	130	96	120	125	108	127	135	91	112	131
Non-HMO	92	112	132	93	116	128	104	120	134	84	106	134
HMO	118	133	126	110	128	120	121	141	138	122	130	124

[1]Less than 100 employees in all private nonfarm industries.
[2]100 or more employees in all private nonfarm industries.

NOTE: In 1992–93, 88 percent of full-time employees in private establishments were offered health care plans by their employers (96 percent in medium and large private establishments and 80 percent in small private establishments). In 1999 the National Compensation Survey was redesigned. Starting in 1999, only participation rates in medical care benefits for full-time and part-time employees are available for this table, but not details on type of coverage or employee contributions. In 2000 in medium and large private establishments, the participation rate in health benefits was 67 percent for full-time employees and 28 percent for part-time employees; in small private establishments, 56 percent of full-time and 6 percent of part-time employees received health benefits through their employers.

SOURCES: U.S. Department of Labor, Bureau of Labor Statistics, National Compensation Survey; Employee benefits in small private establishments, 1990 Bulletin 2388, September 1991, 1994 Bulletin 2475, April 1996, and 1996 Bulletin 2507, April 1999. Employee benefits in medium and large private establishments, 1991 Bulletin 2422, May 1993, 1997 Bulletin 2517, Sept. 1999, and news release USDL 97–246. July 25, 1997. Blostin AP and Pfuntner JN. Employee medical care contributions on the rise. Compensation and Working Conditions, Spring 1998.

Table 139 (page 1 of 2). Medicare enrollees and expenditures and percent distribution, according to type of service: United States and other areas, selected years 1970–2004

[Data are compiled from various sources by the Centers for Medicare & Medicaid Services]

Type of service	*1970*	*1980*	*1990*	*1995*	*2000*	*2001*	*2002*	*2003*	*2004*[1]
Enrollees					Number in millions				
Total[2]	20.4	28.4	34.3	37.6	39.7	40.1	40.5	41.1	41.7
Hospital insurance	20.1	28.0	33.7	37.2	39.3	39.7	40.1	40.6	41.2
Supplementary medical insurance	19.5	27.3	32.6	35.6	37.3	37.7	38.0	38.4	38.8
Expenditures					Amount in billions				
Total	$ 7.5	$ 36.8	$110.8	$184.0	$221.8	$244.8	$265.7	$280.8	$308.9
Total hospital insurance (HI)	5.3	25.6	66.8	117.4	131.1	143.4	152.5	154.6	170.6
HI payments to managed care organizations[3]	- - -	0.0	2.7	6.7	21.4	20.8	19.2	19.5	20.8
HI payments for fee-for-service utilization	5.3	25.5	64.2	110.7	109.7	122.6	133.3	135.1	149.8
Inpatient hospital	4.8	24.1	56.9	82.3	87.1	95.6	104.1	108.6	116.2
Skilled nursing facility	0.2	0.4	2.5	9.1	11.1	13.4	15.3	14.8	16.9
Home health agency	0.1	0.5	3.7	16.2	3.8	4.2	5.0	4.8	5.8
Home health agency transfer[4]	- - -	- - -	- - -	- - -	1.7	3.1	1.2	–2.2	–
Hospice	- - -	- - -	0.3	1.9	3.0	3.7	4.9	6.2	7.6
Administrative expenses[5]	0.2	0.5	0.8	1.2	2.9	2.5	2.8	2.8	3.3
Total supplementary medical insurance (SMI)	2.2	11.2	44.0	66.6	90.7	101.4	113.2	126.1	138.3
SMI payments to managed care organizations[3]	0.0	0.2	2.8	6.6	18.4	17.6	17.5	17.3	18.7
SMI payments for fee-for-service utilization[6]	2.2	11.0	41.2	60.0	72.3	83.8	95.7	108.9	119.6
Physician/supplies[7]	1.8	8.2	29.6	- - -	- - -	- - -	- - -	- - -	- - -
Outpatient hospital[8]	0.1	1.9	8.5	- - -	- - -	- - -	- - -	- - -	- - -
Independent laboratory[9]	0.0	0.1	1.5	- - -	- - -	- - -	- - -	- - -	- - -
Physician fee schedule	- - -	- - -	- - -	31.7	37.0	42.0	44.8	48.2	53.8
Durable medical equipment	- - -	- - -	- - -	3.7	4.7	5.4	6.6	7.7	8.0
Laboratory[10]	- - -	- - -	- - -	4.3	4.0	4.4	5.0	5.5	6.0
Other[11]	- - -	- - -	- - -	9.9	13.7	16.0	19.6	22.6	25.0
Hospital[12]	- - -	- - -	- - -	8.7	8.5	12.8	13.5	15.3	17.4
Home health agency	–	0.2	0.1	0.2	4.4	4.4	5.1	5.1	5.9
Home health agency transfer[4]	- - -	- - -	- - -	- - -	–1.7	–3.1	–1.2	2.2	–
Administrative expenses[5]	0.2	0.6	1.5	1.6	1.8	1.8	2.3	2.4	3.4
					Percent distribution of expenditures				
Total hospital insurance (HI)	100.0	100.0	100.0	100.0	100.0	100.0	100.0	100.0	100.0
HI payments to managed care organizations[3]	- - -	0.0	4.0	5.7	16.3	14.5	12.6	12.6	12.2
HI payments for fee-for-service utilization	100.0	99.6	96.1	94.3	83.7	85.5	87.4	87.4	87.8
Inpatient hospital	90.6	94.5	85.1	70.1	66.5	66.7	68.2	70.3	68.1
Skilled nursing facility	3.8	1.6	3.7	7.8	8.5	9.4	10.1	9.6	9.9
Home health agency	1.9	2.0	5.5	13.8	2.9	2.9	3.3	3.1	3.4
Home health agency transfer[4]	- - -	- - -	- - -	- - -	1.3	2.2	0.8	–1.4	–
Hospice	- - -	- - -	0.4	1.6	2.3	2.6	3.2	4.0	4.4
Administrative expenses[5]	3.8	2.0	1.2	1.0	2.2	1.7	1.9	1.8	2.0

See footnotes at end of table.

Table 139 (page 2 of 2). Medicare enrollees and expenditures and percent distribution, according to type of service: United States and other areas, selected years 1970–2004

[Data are compiled from various sources by the Centers for Medicare & Medicaid Services]

Type of service	1970	1980	1990	1995	2000	2001	2002	2003	2004[1]
				Percent distribution of expenditures					
Total supplementary medical insurance (SMI)	100.0	100.0	100.0	100.0	100.0	100.0	100.0	100.0	100.0
SMI payments to managed care organizations[3]	0.0	1.8	6.4	9.9	20.3	17.3	15.5	13.7	13.5
SMI payments for fee-for-service utilization[6]	100.0	98.2	93.6	90.1	79.8	82.7	84.5	86.3	86.5
Physician/supplies[7]	85.7	73.2	67.3	- - -	- - -	- - -	- - -	- - -	- - -
Outpatient hospital[8]	4.8	17.0	19.3	- - -	- - -	- - -	- - -	- - -	- - -
Independent laboratory[9]	0.0	0.9	3.4	- - -	- - -	- - -	- - -	- - -	- - -
Physician fee schedule	- - -	- - -	- - -	47.5	40.8	41.5	39.6	38.2	38.9
Durable medical equipment	- - -	- - -	- - -	5.5	5.2	5.4	5.8	6.1	5.8
Laboratory[10]	- - -	- - -	- - -	6.4	4.4	4.3	4.4	4.3	4.3
Other[11]	- - -	- - -	- - -	14.8	15.1	15.8	17.3	17.9	18.1
Hospital[12]	- - -	- - -	- - -	13.0	9.4	12.6	12.0	12.2	12.6
Home health agency	0.0	1.8	0.2	0.3	4.8	4.4	4.5	4.0	4.2
Home health agency transfer[4]	- - -	- - -	- - -	0.0	–1.9	–3.1	–1.1	1.7	–
Administrative expenses[5]	9.5	5.4	3.4	2.4	2.0	1.8	2.0	1.9	2.5

- - - Data not available.
0.0 Quantity greater than 0 but less than 0.05.
– Quantity zero.
[1]Preliminary figures.
[2]Average number enrolled in the hospital insurance (HI) and/or supplementary medical insurance (SMI) programs for the calendar year. See Appendix II, Medicare.
[3]Medicare-approved managed care organizations.
[4]Reflects home health transfer amounts between HI and SMI.
[5]Includes research, costs of experiments and demonstration projects, and peer review activity.
[6]Type of service reporting categories for fee-for-service reimbursement differ before and after 1991.
[7]Includes payment for physicians, practitioners, durable medical equipment, and all suppliers other than Independent laboratory, which is shown separately through 1990. Beginning in 1991, those physician services subject to the Physician fee schedule are so broken out. Payments for laboratory services paid under the Laboratory fee schedule and performed in a physician office are included under "Laboratory" beginning in 1991. Payments for durable medical equipment are broken out and so labeled beginning in 1991. The remaining services from the "Physician" category are included in "Other."
[8]Includes payments for hospital outpatient department services, for skilled nursing facility outpatient services, for Part B services received as an inpatient in a hospital or skilled nursing facility setting, and for other types of outpatient facilities. Beginning in 1991, payments for hospital outpatient department services, except for laboratory services, are listed under "Hospital." Hospital outpatient laboratory services are included in the "Laboratory" line.
[9]Beginning in 1991, those independent laboratory services that were paid under the laboratory fee schedule (most of Independent lab) are included in the "Laboratory" line; the remaining services are included in "Physician fee schedule" and "Other" lines.
[10]Payments for laboratory services paid under the laboratory fee schedule performed in a physician office, independent lab, or in a hospital outpatient department.
[11]Includes payments for physician-administered drugs; free-standing ambulatory surgical center facility services; ambulance services; supplies; free-standing end-stage renal disease (ESRD) dialysis facility services; rural health clinics; outpatient rehabilitation facilities; psychiatric hospitals; and federally qualified health centers.
[12]Includes the hospital facility costs for Medicare Part B services that are predominantly in the outpatient department, with the exception of hospital outpatient laboratory services, which are included on the "Laboratory" line. Physician reimbursement is included on the "Physician fee schedule" line.

NOTES: Percents are calculated using unrounded data. Table includes service disbursements as of February 2005 for Medicare enrollees residing in Puerto Rico, Virgin Islands, Guam, other outlying areas, foreign countries, and unknown residence. Totals do not necessarily equal the sum of rounded components. Some numbers in this table have been revised and differ from previous editions of *Health, United States*. Data for additional years are available. See Appendix III.

SOURCE: Centers for Medicare & Medicaid Services, Office of the Actuary, Medicare and Medicaid Cost Estimates Group, Medicare Administrative Data.

Table 140. Medicare enrollees and program payments among fee-for-service Medicare beneficiaries, according to sex and age: United States and other areas, 1994–2002

[Data are compiled from administrative data by the Centers for Medicare & Medicaid Services]

Sex and age	*1994*	*1995*	*1996*	*1997*	*1998*	*1999*	*2000*	*2001*	*2002*
	Fee-for-service enrollees in thousands								
Total	34,076	34,062	33,704	33,009	32,349	32,179	32,740	33,860	34,977
Sex									
Male	14,533	14,563	14,440	14,149	13,902	13,872	14,195	14,746	15,314
Female	19,543	19,499	19,264	18,860	18,477	18,307	18,545	19,113	19,664
Age									
Under 65 years	4,031	4,239	4,413	4,498	4,617	4,742	4,907	5,172	5,448
65–74 years	16,713	16,373	15,810	15,099	14,433	14,072	14,230	14,689	15,107
75–84 years	9,845	9,911	9,915	9,847	9,722	9,748	9,919	10,211	10,533
85 years and over	3,486	3,540	3,566	3,565	3,577	3,618	3,684	3,787	3,889
	Fee-for-service program payments in millions								
Total	$146,549	$158,980	$167,063	$175,423	$168,164	$166,687	$174,261	$197,505	$215,411
Sex									
Male	63,907	68,758	71,011	75,357	72,883	73,171	76,230	86,314	94,292
Female	82,642	90,222	95,052	100,066	95,281	93,516	98,031	111,190	121,118
Age									
Under 65 years	18,835	21,029	24,160	25,798	23,746	24,262	25,773	29,720	33,248
65–74 years	55,147	58,093	58,737	59,687	57,342	56,031	57,494	64,634	70,018
75–84 years	50,719	55,256	58,058	61,708	59,745	59,518	62,685	70,850	77,073
85 years and over	21,847	24,602	26,108	28,231	27,331	26,875	28,309	32,300	35,072
	Percent distribution of fee-for-service program payments								
Total	100.0	100.0	100.0	100.0	100.0	100.0	100.0	100.0	100.0
Sex									
Male	43.6	43.2	42.5	43.0	43.3	43.9	43.7	43.7	43.8
Female	56.4	56.8	56.9	57.0	56.7	56.1	56.3	56.3	56.2
Age									
Under 65 years	12.9	13.2	14.5	14.7	14.1	14.6	14.8	15.0	15.4
65–74 years	37.6	36.5	35.2	34.0	34.1	33.6	33.0	32.7	32.5
75–84 years	34.6	34.8	34.8	35.2	35.5	35.7	36.0	35.9	35.8
85 years and over	14.9	15.5	15.6	16.1	16.3	16.1	16.2	16.4	16.3
	Average fee-for-service payment per enrollee								
Total	$ 4,301	$ 4,667	$ 4,957	$ 5,314	$ 5,198	$ 5,180	$ 5,323	$ 5,833	$ 6,159
Sex									
Male	4,397	4,721	4,918	5,326	5,243	5,275	5,370	5,853	6,157
Female	4,229	4,627	4,934	5,306	5,165	5,108	5,286	5,818	6,159
Age									
Under 65 years	4,673	4,960	5,475	5,735	5,143	5,117	5,252	5,746	6,102
65–74 years	3,300	3,548	3,715	3,953	3,973	3,982	4,040	4,400	4,635
75–84 years	5,152	5,576	5,856	6,267	6,145	6,106	6,320	6,939	7,317
85 years and over	6,267	6,950	7,321	7,919	7,641	7,428	7,684	8,529	9,019

NOTES: Table includes data for Medicare enrollees residing in Puerto Rico, Virgin Islands, Guam, other outlying areas, foreign countries, and unknown residence. Number of fee-for-service enrollees is based on 5-percent annual Denominator File using the Centers for Medicare & Medicaid Services' (CMS) Enrollment Database and Group Health Plan data. Fee-for-service program payments are based on a 5-percent annual Denominator File and fee-for-service billing reimbursement for a 5-percent sample of Medicare beneficiaries as recorded in CMS' National Claims History using CMS' Enrollment Database, Group Health Plan, and National Claims History data.

SOURCE: Centers for Medicare & Medicaid Services, Office of Research, Development, and Information. Health Care Financing Review: Medicare and Medicaid Statistical Supplements for years 1996 to 2004. Website: www.cms.hhs.gov/review/supp/.

Table 141 (page 1 of 2). Medicare beneficiaries by race and ethnicity, according to selected characteristics: United States, 1992 and 2001

[Data are based on household interviews of a sample of current Medicare beneficiaries and Medicare administrative records]

			Not Hispanic or Latino					
	All		White		Black or African American		Hispanic or Latino	
Characteristic	1992	2001	1992	2001	1992	2001	1992	2001
	Number of beneficiaries in millions							
All Medicare beneficiaries	36.8	41.2	30.9	32.7	3.3	3.8	1.9	3.0
	Percent distribution of beneficiaries							
All Medicare beneficiaries	100.0	100.00	84.2	79.8	8.9	9.3	5.2	7.2
Medical care use	Percent of beneficiaries with at least one service							
All Medicare beneficiaries:								
Long-term care facility stay	7.7	9.1	8.0	9.8	6.2	8.1	4.2	4.8
Community-only residents:								
Inpatient hospital	17.9	19.8	18.1	20.1	18.4	20.2	16.6	16.2
Outpatient hospital	57.9	70.3	57.8	71.4	61.1	69.1	53.1	61.6
Physician/supplier [1]	92.4	95.3	93.0	96.3	89.1	92.1	87.9	91.8
Dental	40.4	44.0	43.1	48.3	23.5	21.8	29.1	30.9
Prescription medicine	85.2	91.6	85.5	92.1	83.1	90.3	84.6	90.2
Expenditures	Expenditures per beneficiary							
All Medicare beneficiaries:								
Total health care [2]	$6,716	$11,403	$6,816	$11,478	$7,043	$13,279	$5,784	$8,903
Long-term care facility [3]	1,581	2,503	1,674	2,636	1,255	2,753	*758	1,486
Community-only residents:								
Total personal health care	5,054	8,626	4,988	8,636	5,530	9,483	4,938	7,121
Inpatient hospital	2,098	2,771	2,058	2,739	2,493	3,411	1,999	2,835
Outpatient hospital	504	957	478	896	668	1,483	511	812
Physician/supplier [1]	1,524	2,760	1,525	2,801	1,398	2,581	1,587	2,609
Dental	142	271	153	300	70	107	97	206
Prescription medicine	468	1,338	481	1,369	417	1,271	389	1,069
Long-term care facility residents only:								
Long-term care facility [4]	23,054	$35,384	23,177	33,939	21,272	33,903	*25,026	31,788
Sex	Percent distribution of beneficiaries							
Both sexes	100.0	100.0	100.0	100.0	100.0	100.0	100.0	100.0
Male	42.9	43.8	42.7	43.6	42.0	42.2	46.7	46.7
Female	57.1	56.2	57.3	56.4	58.0	57.9	53.3	54.3
Eligibility criteria and age								
All Medicare beneficiaries [5]	100.0	100.0	100.0	100.0	100.0	100.0	100.0	100
Disabled	10.2	13.9	8.6	11.9	19.1	25.6	16.5	19.2
Under 45 years	3.5	3.8	2.9	3.2	7.6	7.9	6.9	4.6
45–64 years	6.5	10.1	5.8	8.7	11.5	17.8	9.6	14.6
Aged	89.8	86.1	91.4	88.1	81.0	74.4	83.5	80.8
65–74 years	51.5	45.3	52.0	45.5	48.0	40.0	49.4	48.2
75–84 years	28.8	30.2	29.5	31.3	24.0	25.7	27.1	24.0
85 years and over	9.7	10.7	9.9	11.3	9.0	8.7	6.9	8.7
Living arrangement								
All living arrangements	100.0	100.0	100.0	100.0	100.0	100.0	100.0	100.0
Alone	27.0	28.9	27.5	29.3	27.7	30.7	20.2	24.9
With spouse	51.2	49.5	53.3	51.6	33.3	30.7	50.4	49.3
With children	9.1	9.3	7.7	7.3	16.8	21.0	16.6	13.5
With others	7.6	7.4	6.2	6.5	18.1	13.3	10.8	9.3
Long-term care facility	5.1	5.0	5.3	5.3	4.0	4.4	*2.0	2.9

See footnotes at end of table.

Table 141 (page 2 of 2). Medicare beneficiaries by race and ethnicity, according to selected characteristics: United States, 1992 and 2001

[Data are based on household interviews of a sample of current Medicare beneficiaries and Medicare administrative records]

			Not Hispanic or Latino					
	All		White		Black or African American		Hispanic or Latino	
Characteristic	1992	2001	1992	2001	1992	2001	1992	2001
Age and limitation of activity[6]			Percent distribution of beneficiaries					
Disabled	100.0	100.0	100.0	100.0	100.0	100.0	100.0	100.0
None	22.7	28.3	21.8	27.0	26.2	32.9	21.2	27.4
IADL only	39.0	35.3	38.9	34.5	35.8	36.0	46.1	36.6
1 or 2 ADL	21.2	20.2	21.5	21.6	21.2	20.0	*20.9	14.4
3–5 ADL	17.2	16.2	17.9	16.9	*16.8	11.2	*11.9	21.6
65–74 years	100.0	100.0	100.0	100.0	100.0	100.0	100.0	100.0
None	67.0	70.9	68.7	27.0	55.1	64.2	59.2	69.7
IADL only	17.8	16.1	17.0	34.5	22.9	20.3	*20.9	16.4
1 or 2 ADL	10.4	8.4	9.6	21.6	14.4	8.5	*15.7	8.4
3–5 ADL	4.8	4.6	4.6	4.2	*7.6	7.0	*4.2	5.5
75–84 years	100.0	100.0	100.0	100.0	100.0	100.0	100.0	100.0
None	46.6	52.6	47.5	53.5	42.0	45.9	44.3	49.9
IADL only	23.9	23.2	23.6	23.0	26.7	25.0	*27.8	23.7
1 or 2 ADL	16.5	13.0	16.8	12.8	15.3	14.0	*14.9	15.6
3–5 ADL	13.0	11.2	12.2	10.8	*15.9	15.1	*13.0	*10.78
85 years and over	100.0	100.0	100.0	100.0	100.0	100.0	100.0	100.0
None	19.9	25.1	20.2	25.8	*19.6	23.0	*19.7	*19.1
IADL only	20.9	24.8	20.2	24.6	*22.1	24.5	*24.7	25.0
1 or 2 ADL	23.5	20.9	23.5	20.7	*24.3	21.7	*23.7	*22.24
3–5 ADL	35.8	29.3	36.1	28.9	*34.0	30.8	*31.8	33.7

* Estimates are considered unreliable. Cell is based on 50 persons or fewer or the estimate has a relative standard error of 30 percent or higher.

[1]Physician/supplier services include medical and osteopathic doctor and health practitioner visits; diagnostic laboratory and radiology services; medical and surgical services; and durable medical equipment and nondurable medical supplies.

[2]Total health care expenditures by Medicare beneficiaries, including expenses paid by Medicare and all other sources of payment for the following services: inpatient hospital, outpatient hospital, physician/supplier, dental, prescription medicine, home health, and hospice and long-term care facility care. Does not include health insurance premiums.

[3]Expenditures for long-term care in facilities include facility room and board expenses for beneficiaries who resided in a facility for the full year, for beneficiaries who resided in a facility for part of the year and in the community for part of the year, and expenditures for short-term facility stays for full-year or part-year community residents. See Appendix II, Long-term care facility.

[4]Expenditures for long-term care in facilities include facility room and board expenses for beneficiaries who resided in a facility for the full year and for beneficiaries who resided in a facility for part of the year and in the community for part of the year. It does not include expenditures for short-term facility stays for full-year community residents. See Appendix II, Long-term care facility.

[5]Medicare beneficiaries with end-stage renal disease (ESRD) are included within the subgroups "Aged" and "Disabled."

[6]See Appendix II for definitions of Activities of Daily Living (ADL) and Instrumental Activities of Daily Living (IADL). Includes data for both community and long-term care facility residents.

NOTES: Percents and percent distributions are calculated using unrounded numbers. Data for additional years are available. See Appendix III.

SOURCE: Centers for Medicare & Medicaid Services, Medicare Current Beneficiary Survey, Health and Health Care of the Medicare Population; www.cms.hhs.gov/mcbs/Publdt.asp.

Table 142. Medicaid recipients and medical vendor payments, according to basis of eligibility, and race and ethnicity: United States, selected fiscal years 1972–2001

[Data are compiled by the Centers for Medicare & Medicaid Services from the Medicaid Data System]

Basis of eligibility and race and ethnicity	1972	1980	1990	1995	1997	1998[1]	1999[2]	2000	2001
Recipients					Number in millions				
All recipients	17.6	21.6	25.3	36.3	34.9	40.6	40.1	42.8	46.0
					Percent of recipients				
Basis of eligibility:[3]									
Aged (65 years and over)	18.8	15.9	12.7	11.4	11.3	9.8	9.4	8.7	8.3
Blind and disabled	9.8	13.5	14.7	16.1	17.6	16.3	16.7	16.1	15.4
Adults in families with dependent children[4]	17.8	22.6	23.8	21.0	19.5	19.5	18.7	20.5	21.1
Children under age 21[5]	44.5	43.2	44.4	47.3	45.3	46.7	46.9	46.1	45.7
Other Title XIX[6]	9.0	6.9	3.9	1.7	6.3	7.8	8.4	8.6	9.5
Race and ethnicity:[7]									
White	---	---	42.8	45.5	44.4	41.3	---	---	40.2
Black or African American	---	---	25.1	24.7	23.5	24.2	---	---	23.1
American Indian or Alaska Native	---	---	1.0	0.8	1.0	0.8	---	---	1.3
Asian or Pacific Islander	---	---	2.0	2.2	1.9	2.5	---	---	3.0
Hispanic or Latino	---	---	15.2	17.2	14.3	15.6	---	---	17.9
Unknown	---	---	14.0	9.6	14.9	15.5	---	---	14.6
Vendor payments[8]					Amount in billions				
All payments	$ 6.3	$ 23.3	$ 64.9	$120.1	$124.4	$ 142.3	$ 153.5	$ 168.3	$ 186.3
					Percent distribution				
Total	100.0	100.0	100.0	100.0	100.0	100.0	100.0	100.0	100.0
Basis of eligibility:									
Aged (65 years and over)	30.6	37.5	33.2	30.4	30.3	28.5	27.7	26.4	25.9
Blind and disabled	22.2	32.7	37.6	41.1	43.5	42.4	42.9	43.2	43.1
Adults in families with dependent children[4]	15.3	13.9	13.2	11.2	9.9	10.4	10.3	10.6	10.7
Children under age 21[5]	18.1	13.4	14.0	15.0	14.1	16.0	15.7	15.9	16.3
Other Title XIX[6]	13.9	2.6	1.6	1.2	2.2	2.6	3.4	3.9	3.9
Race and ethnicity:[7]									
White	---	---	53.4	54.3	55.0	54.3	---	---	54.4
Black or African American	---	---	18.3	19.2	18.5	19.6	---	---	19.8
American Indian or Alaska Native	---	---	0.6	0.5	0.6	0.8	---	---	1.1
Asian or Pacific Islander	---	---	1.0	1.2	0.9	1.4	---	---	2.5
Hispanic or Latino	---	---	5.3	7.3	6.8	8.2	---	---	9.4
Unknown	---	---	21.3	17.6	18.2	15.7	---	---	12.9
Vendor payments per recipient[8]					Amount				
All recipients	$ 358	$1,079	$2,568	$3,311	$3,568	$ 3,501	$ 3,819	$ 3,936	$ 4,053
Basis of eligibility:									
Aged (65 years and over)	580	2,540	6,717	8,868	9,538	10,242	11,268	11,929	12,725
Blind and disabled	807	2,618	6,564	8,435	8,832	9,095	9,832	10,559	11,318
Adults in families with dependent children[4]	307	662	1,429	1,777	1,809	1,876	2,104	2,030	2,059
Children under age 21[5]	145	335	811	1,047	1,111	1,203	1,282	1,358	1,448
Other Title XIX[6]	555	398	1,062	2,380	1,242	1,166	1,532	1,778	1,680
Race and ethnicity:[7]									
White	---	---	3,207	3,953	4,421	4,609	---	---	5,489
Black or African American	---	---	1,878	2,568	2,798	2,836	---	---	3,480
American Indian or Alaska Native	---	---	1,706	2,142	2,500	3,297	---	---	3,452
Asian or Pacific Islander	---	---	1,257	1,713	1,610	1,924	---	---	3,283
Hispanic or Latino	---	---	903	1,400	1,699	1,842	---	---	2,126
Unknown	---	---	3,909	6,099	4,356	3,531	---	---	3,576

- - - Data not available.

[1]Prior to 1999 recipient counts exclude those individuals who only received coverage under prepaid health care and for whom no direct vendor payments were made during the year; and vendor payments exclude payments to health maintenance organizations and other prepaid health plans ($19.3 billion in 1998 and $18 billion in 1997). The total number of persons who were Medicaid eligible and enrolled was 41.4 million in 1998, 41.6 million in 1997, and 41.2 million in 1996 (HCFA Medicaid Statistics, Program and Financial Statistics FY1996, FY1997, and FY1998, unpublished).

[2]Starting in 1999, the Medicaid data system was changed. See Appendix I, Medicaid Data System.

[3]In 1980 and 1985 recipients are included in more than one category. In 1990–96, 0.2–2.5 percent of recipients have unknown basis of eligibility. From 1997 onwards, unknowns are included in Other Title XIX.

[4]Includes adults in the Aid to Families with Dependent Children (AFDC) program. From 1997 onwards includes adults in the Temporary Assistance for Needy Families (TANF) program. From 2001 onwards includes women in the Breast and Cervical Cancer Prevention and Treatment Program.

[5]Includes children in the AFDC program. From 1997 onwards includes children and foster care children in the TANF program.

[6]Includes some participants in the Supplemental Security Income program and other people deemed medically needy in participating States. From 1997 onwards excludes foster care children and includes unknown eligibility.

[7]Race and ethnicity as determined on initial Medicaid application. Categories are mutually exclusive. Starting in 2001, Hispanic category included Hispanic persons regardless of race. Persons indicating more than one race were included in the unknown category.

[8]Vendor payments exclude disproportionate share hospital payments ($15.5 billion in FY2001).

NOTES: 1972 data are for fiscal year ending June 30. All other years are for fiscal year ending September 30. Data for additional years are available. See Appendix III.

SOURCE: Centers for Medicare & Medicaid Services, Office of Information Services, Enterprise Databases Group, Division of Information Distribution, Medicaid Data System. Before 1999 Medicaid Statistical Report HCFA–2082. From 1999 onwards Medicaid Statistical Information System, MSIS. www.cms.hhs.gov/medicaid/msis/mstats.asp.

Table 143 (page 1 of 2). Medicaid recipients and medical vendor payments, according to type of service: United States, selected fiscal years 1972–2001

[Data are compiled by the Centers for Medicare & Medicaid Services from the Medicaid Data System]

Type of service	*1972*	*1980*	*1990*	*1995*	*1997*	*1998*[1]	*1999*[2]	*2000*	*2001*
Recipients					Number in millions				
All recipients	17.6	21.6	25.3	36.3	34.9	40.6	40.2	42.8	46.0
					Percent of recipients				
Inpatient hospital	16.1	17.0	18.2	15.3	13.6	10.5	11.2	11.5	10.6
Mental health facility	0.2	0.3	0.4	0.2	0.3	0.3	0.2	0.2	0.2
Mentally retarded intermediate care facility	---	0.6	0.6	0.4	0.4	0.3	0.3	0.3	0.3
Nursing facility	---	---	---	4.6	4.6	4.0	4.0	4.0	3.7
Skilled	3.1	2.8	2.4	---	---	---	---	---	---
Intermediate care	---	3.7	3.4	---	---	---	---	---	---
Physician	69.8	63.7	67.6	65.6	60.7	45.6	45.7	44.7	43.5
Dental	13.6	21.5	18.0	17.6	17.0	12.2	14.0	13.8	15.3
Other practitioner	9.1	15.0	15.3	15.2	14.7	10.7	9.9	11.1	11.1
Outpatient hospital	29.6	44.9	49.0	46.1	39.1	29.9	30.9	30.9	29.8
Clinic	2.8	7.1	11.1	14.7	13.5	13.0	16.8	17.9	18.4
Laboratory and radiological	20.0	14.9	35.5	36.0	31.8	23.1	25.4	26.6	26.8
Home health	0.6	1.8	2.8	4.5	5.3	3.0	2.0	2.3	2.2
Prescribed drugs	63.3	63.4	68.5	65.4	60.1	47.6	49.4	48.0	47.6
Family planning	. . .	5.2	6.9	6.9	6.0	4.9	---	---	---
Early and periodic screening	. . .	. . .	11.7	18.2	18.5	15.2	---	---	---
Rural health clinic	. . .	. . .	0.9	3.4	4.1	---	---	---	---
Capitated payment services	---	---	---	---	---	49.7	51.5	49.7	50.5
Primary care case management	---	---	---	---	---	---	9.7	13.0	13.9
Personal support	---	---	---	---	---	---	10.1	10.6	10.8
Other care	14.4	11.9	20.3	31.5	35.5	36.0	21.6	21.4	21.5
Vendor payments[3]					Amount in billions				
All payments	$ 6.3	$ 23.3	$ 64.9	$120.1	$124.4	$142.3	$153.5	$168.3	$186.3
					Percent distribution				
Total	100.0	100.0	100.0	100.0	100.0	100.0	100.0	100.0	100.0
Inpatient hospital	40.6	27.5	25.7	21.9	18.6	15.1	14.5	14.4	13.9
Mental health facility	1.8	3.3	2.6	2.1	1.6	2.0	1.1	1.1	1.1
Mentally retarded intermediate care facility	---	8.5	11.3	8.6	7.9	6.7	6.1	5.6	5.2
Nursing facility	---	---	---	24.2	24.5	22.4	21.7	20.5	20.0
Skilled	23.3	15.8	12.4	---	---	---	---	---	---
Intermediate care	---	18.0	14.9	---	---	---	---	---	---
Physician	12.6	8.0	6.2	6.1	5.7	4.3	4.3	4.0	4.0
Dental	2.7	2.0	0.9	0.8	0.8	0.6	0.8	0.8	1.0
Other practitioner	0.9	0.8	0.6	0.8	0.8	0.4	0.3	0.4	0.4
Outpatient hospital	5.8	4.7	5.1	5.5	5.0	4.0	4.0	4.2	4.0
Clinic	0.7	1.4	2.6	3.6	3.4	2.8	3.8	3.7	3.0
Laboratory and radiological	1.3	0.5	1.1	1.0	0.8	0.7	0.8	0.8	0.9
Home health	0.4	1.4	5.2	7.8	9.8	1.9	1.9	1.9	1.9
Prescribed drugs	8.1	5.7	6.8	8.1	9.6	9.5	10.8	11.9	12.7
Family planning	. . .	0.3	0.4	0.4	0.3	0.3	---	---	---
Early and periodic screening	. . .	. . .	0.3	1.0	1.3	0.9	---	---	---
Rural health clinic	. . .	. . .	0.1	0.2	0.2	---	---	---	---
Capitated payment services	---	---	---	---	---	13.6	14.0	14.5	15.7
Primary care case management	---	---	---	---	---	---	0.3	0.1	0.1
Personal support	---	---	---	---	---	---	6.9	6.9	7.0
Other care	1.8	1.9	3.7	7.7	8.9	13.6	8.6	8.8	9.2

See footnotes at end of table.

Table 143 (page 2 of 2). Medicaid recipients and medical vendor payments, according to type of service: United States, selected fiscal years 1972–2001

[Data are compiled by the Centers for Medicare & Medicaid Services from the Medicaid Data System]

Type of service	1972	1980	1990	1995	1997	1998[1]	1999[2]	2000	2001
Vendor payments per recipient[3]					Amount				
Total payment per recipient	$ 358	$ 1,079	$ 2,568	$ 3,311	$ 3,568	$ 3,501	$ 3,819	$ 3,936	$ 4,053
Inpatient hospital	903	1,742	3,630	4,735	4,877	5,031	4,943	4,919	5,313
Mental health facility	2,825	11,742	18,548	29,847	22,990	20,701	18,094	17,800	21,482
Mentally retarded intermediate care facility	- - -	16,438	50,048	68,613	72,033	74,960	76,443	79,330	83,227
Nursing facility	- - -	- - -	- - -	17,424	19,029	19,379	20,568	20,220	21,894
Skilled	2,665	6,081	13,356	- - -	- - -	- - -	- - -	- - -	- - -
Intermediate care	- - -	5,326	11,236	- - -	- - -	- - -	- - -	- - -	- - -
Physician	65	136	235	309	333	327	357	356	371
Dental	71	99	130	160	175	182	214	238	270
Other practitioner	37	61	96	178	190	135	118	139	149
Outpatient hospital	70	113	269	397	453	474	491	533	546
Clinic	82	209	602	804	902	742	860	805	662
Laboratory and radiological	23	38	80	90	93	100	114	113	131
Home health	229	847	4,733	5,740	6,575	2,206	3,571	3,135	3,478
Prescribed drugs	46	96	256	413	571	699	837	975	1,083
Family planning	. . .	72	151	206	200	223	- - -	- - -	- - -
Early and periodic screening	. . .	. . .	67	177	251	216	- - -	- - -	- - -
Rural health clinic	. . .	. . .	154	174	213	- - -	- - -	- - -	- - -
Capitated payment services	- - -	- - -	- - -	- - -	- - -	955	1,040	1,148	1,257
Primary care case management	- - -	- - -	- - -	- - -	- - -	- - -	119	30	29
Personal support	- - -	- - -	- - -	- - -	- - -	- - -	2,583	2,543	2,639
Other care	44	172	465	807	891	1,331	1,508	1,600	1,734

- - - Data not available.
. . . Category not applicable.
[1]Prior to 1999 recipient counts exclude those individuals who only received coverage under prepaid health care and for whom no direct vendor payments were made during the year; and vendor payments exclude payments to health maintenance organizations and other prepaid health plans ($19.3 billion in 1998 and $18 billion in 1997). The total number of persons who were Medicaid eligible and enrolled was 41.4 million in 1998, 41.6 million in 1997, and 41.2 million in 1996 (HCFA Medicaid Statistics, Program and Financial Statistics FY1996, FY1997, and FY1998, unpublished).
[2]Starting in 1999, the Medicaid data system was changed. See Appendix I, Medicaid Data System.
[3]Payments exclude disproportionate share hospital payments ($15.5 billion in FY2001).

NOTES: 1972 data are for fiscal year ending June 30. All other years are for fiscal year ending September 30. Unknown services are included with Other care (0.1 percent of recipients and 0.2 percent of payments in 2001). Data for additional years are available. See Appendix III.

SOURCE: Centers for Medicare & Medicaid Services, Office of Information Services, Enterprise Databases Group, Division of Information Distribution, Medicaid Data System. Before 1999 Medicaid Statistical Report HCFA–2082. From 1999 onwards Medicaid Statistical Information System, MSIS. www.cms.hhs.gov/medicaid/msis/mstats.asp.

Table 144. Department of Veterans Affairs health care expenditures and use, and persons treated according to selected characteristics: United States, selected fiscal years 1970–2003

[Data are compiled from patient records, enrollment information, and budgetary data by the Department of Veterans Affairs]

	1970	*1980*	*1990*	*1995*	*1999*	*2000*	*2001*	*2002*	*2003*
Health care expenditures					Amount in millions				
All expenditures [1]	$1,689	$ 5,981	$11,500	$16,126	$17,876	$19,327	$21,316	$23,003	$25,647
					Percent distribution				
All services	100.0	100.0	100.0	100.0	100.0	100.0	100.0	100.0	100.0
Inpatient hospital	71.3	64.3	57.5	49.0	38.8	37.3	34.7	33.6	32.2
Outpatient care	14.0	19.1	25.3	30.2	44.0	45.7	48.0	48.8	49.5
Nursing home care	5.5	7.1	9.5	10.0	8.5	8.2	8.1	8.0	8.1
All other [2]	9.1	9.6	7.7	10.8	8.7	8.8	9.2	9.6	10.2
Health care use					Number in thousands				
Inpatient hospital stays [3]	787	1,248	1,029	879	611	579	584	590	588
Outpatient visits	7,312	17,971	22,602	27,527	36,928	38,370	42,901	46,058	49,760
Nursing home stays [4]	47	57	75	79	92	91	93	87	93
Inpatients [5]									
Total	---	---	598	527	447	417	426	436	443
					Percent distribution				
Total	---	---	100.0	100.0	100.0	100.0	100.0	100.0	100.0
Veterans with service-connected disability	---	---	38.9	39.3	33.8	34.4	34.6	35.2	36.2
Veterans without service-connected disability	---	---	60.3	59.9	65.3	64.7	64.5	63.9	62.9
Low income	---	---	54.8	56.2	44.8	41.7	41.4	40.9	40.8
Veterans receiving aid and attendance or housebound benefits or who are catastrophically disabled [6]	---	---	---	---	12.8	16.0	15.7	13.6	13.5
Veterans receiving medical care subject to copayments [7]	---	---	2.8	2.8	4.7	5.2	6.0	7.7	8.0
Other and unknown [8]	---	---	2.7	0.9	3.0	1.8	1.4	1.7	0.6
Nonveterans	---	---	0.8	0.8	0.9	0.9	0.9	0.9	0.8
Outpatients [5]					Number in thousands				
Total	---	---	2,564	2,790	3,400	3,657	4,072	4,456	4,715
					Percent distribution				
Total	---	---	100.0	100.0	100.0	100.0	100.0	100.0	100.0
Veterans with service-connected disability	---	---	38.3	37.5	30.5	30.7	30.0	29.5	30.3
Veterans without service-connected disability	---	---	49.8	50.5	60.6	60.8	62.5	63.9	63.4
Low income	---	---	41.1	42.2	38.8	37.6	36.6	34.1	32.7
Veterans receiving aid and attendance or housebound benefits or who are catastrophically disabled [6]	---	---	---	---	3.2	3.8	3.7	3.3	3.4
Veterans receiving medical care subject to copayments [7]	---	---	3.6	4.2	11.7	15.4	19.9	23.6	26.1
Other and unknown [8]	---	---	5.1	4.1	6.9	4.0	2.3	2.9	1.1
Nonveterans	---	---	11.8	12.0	8.9	8.5	7.5	6.6	6.3

- - - Data not available.

[1] Health care expenditures exclude construction, medical administration, and miscellaneous operating expenses at Department of Veterans Affairs headquarters.

[2] Includes miscellaneous benefits and services, contract hospitals, education and training, subsidies to State veterans hospitals, nursing homes and residential rehabilitation treatment programs (formerly domiciliaries), and the Civilian Health and Medical Program of the Department of Veterans Affairs.

[3] One-day dialysis patients were included in 1980. Interfacility transfers were included beginning in 1990.

[4] Includes Department of Veterans Affairs nursing home and residential rehabilitation treatment program (formerly domiciliary) stays, and community nursing home care stays.

[5] Individuals. The inpatient and outpatient totals are not additive since almost all inpatients are also treated as outpatients.

[6] Veterans who are receiving aid and attendance or housebound benefits; veterans who have been determined by the Department of Veterans Affairs to be catastrophically disabled.

[7] Financial means-tested veterans who receive medical care subject to copayments according to income level.

[8] Prisoner of war, exposed to Agent Orange, and so forth. Prior to fiscal year 1994, veterans who reported exposure to Agent Orange were classified as exempt. Beginning in fiscal year 1994 those veterans reporting Agent Orange exposure but not treated for it were means tested and placed in the low income or other group depending on income.

NOTES: Figures may not add to totals due to rounding. In 1970, the fiscal year ended June 30; 1980 and later the fiscal year ended September 30. The veteran population was estimated at 25.2 million at the end of FY 2003, with 38 percent age 65 or over, compared with 11 percent in 1980. Seventeen percent had served during World War II, 14 percent during the Korean conflict, 33 percent during the Vietnam era, 15 percent during the Persian Gulf War, and 25 percent during peacetime. These percentages add to more than 100 due to veterans serving during more than one war. Beginning in fiscal year 1995 categories for health care expenditures and health care use were revised. In fiscal year 1999 a new priority system for reporting data was introduced and starting in 1999, data reflect the new categories. Data for additional years are available. See Appendix III.

SOURCES: Department of Veterans Affairs (VA), Office of the Assistant Deputy Under Secretary for Health, National Patient Care Database, National Enrollment Database, budgetary data, and unpublished data. Veteran population estimates were provided by the VA's Office of the Actuary.

Table 145 (page 1 of 2). Personal health care per capita expenditures, by geographic region and State: United States, selected years 1991–98

[Data are compiled from various sources by the Centers for Medicare & Medicaid Services]

Geographic region and State[1]	1991	1994	1995	1996	1997	1998	1991–98	1998
	Per capita expenditures						Average annual percent change	Ratio to U.S. per capita expenditures
United States	$2,685	$3,193	$3,334	$3,472	$3,606	$3,759	4.9	1.00
New England	3,115	3,745	3,945	4,092	4,303	4,540	5.5	1.21
Connecticut	3,338	3,900	4,138	4,250	4,442	4,656	4.9	1.24
Maine	2,464	3,018	3,256	3,512	3,755	4,025	7.3	1.07
Massachusetts	3,334	4,056	4,200	4,347	4,556	4,810	5.4	1.28
New Hampshire	2,511	3,029	3,264	3,441	3,650	3,840	6.3	1.02
Rhode Island	2,943	3,569	3,867	3,978	4,235	4,497	6.2	1.20
Vermont	2,393	2,890	3,133	3,273	3,455	3,654	6.2	0.97
Mideast[2]	3,108	3,748	3,905	4,063	4,209	4,386	5.0	1.17
Delaware	2,878	3,565	3,737	3,847	4,083	4,258	5.8	1.13
Maryland	2,796	3,291	3,401	3,573	3,696	3,848	4.7	1.02
New Jersey	2,966	3,622	3,830	4,009	4,080	4,197	5.1	1.12
New York	3,288	3,997	4,162	4,346	4,486	4,706	5.3	1.25
Pennsylvania	2,988	3,547	3,683	3,791	4,003	4,168	4.9	1.11
Great Lakes	2,666	3,172	3,318	3,467	3,606	3,733	4.9	0.99
Illinois	2,743	3,259	3,394	3,535	3,653	3,801	4.8	1.01
Indiana	2,508	3,052	3,156	3,196	3,416	3,566	5.2	0.95
Michigan	2,643	3,114	3,289	3,457	3,602	3,676	4.8	0.98
Ohio	2,709	3,209	3,353	3,542	3,635	3,747	4.7	1.00
Wisconsin	2,610	3,138	3,306	3,476	3,654	3,845	5.7	1.02
Plains	2,544	3,115	3,271	3,436	3,592	3,797	5.9	1.01
Iowa	2,524	3,014	3,165	3,368	3,519	3,765	5.9	1.00
Kansas	2,574	3,067	3,249	3,412	3,573	3,707	5.3	0.99
Minnesota	2,606	3,246	3,439	3,614	3,791	3,986	6.3	1.06
Missouri	2,555	3,159	3,262	3,390	3,531	3,754	5.6	1.00
Nebraska	2,383	2,947	3,083	3,287	3,407	3,627	6.2	0.96
North Dakota	2,555	3,155	3,420	3,540	3,680	3,881	6.2	1.03
South Dakota	2,394	2,880	3,068	3,253	3,453	3,650	6.2	0.97
Southeast	2,557	3,081	3,241	3,400	3,557	3,686	5.4	0.98
Alabama	2,561	3,059	3,234	3,422	3,626	3,630	5.1	0.97
Arkansas	2,408	2,840	3,012	3,177	3,355	3,540	5.7	0.94
Florida	2,976	3,523	3,632	3,774	3,875	4,046	4.5	1.08
Georgia	2,527	3,007	3,170	3,291	3,412	3,505	4.8	0.93
Kentucky	2,424	2,898	3,098	3,300	3,519	3,711	6.3	0.99
Louisiana	2,619	3,243	3,376	3,496	3,639	3,742	5.2	1.00
Mississippi	2,190	2,686	2,933	3,145	3,286	3,474	6.8	0.92
North Carolina	2,271	2,854	3,040	3,232	3,420	3,535	6.5	0.94
South Carolina	2,276	2,839	2,985	3,131	3,399	3,529	6.5	0.94
Tennessee	2,594	3,186	3,415	3,569	3,728	3,808	5.6	1.01
Virginia	2,378	2,743	2,858	3,009	3,155	3,284	4.7	0.87
West Virginia	2,568	3,233	3,442	3,649	3,858	4,044	6.7	1.08
Southwest	2,373	2,794	2,934	3,075	3,194	3,339	5.0	0.89
Arizona	2,407	2,729	2,769	2,862	2,935	3,100	3.7	0.82
New Mexico	2,211	2,609	2,744	2,943	3,058	3,209	5.5	0.85
Oklahoma	2,336	2,819	3,014	3,188	3,268	3,397	5.5	0.90
Texas	2,387	2,821	2,975	3,117	3,255	3,397	5.2	0.90
Rocky Mountains	2,267	2,608	2,751	2,874	3,010	3,145	4.8	0.84
Colorado	2,481	2,835	2,977	3,071	3,202	3,331	4.3	0.89
Idaho	2,082	2,436	2,580	2,765	2,883	3,035	5.5	0.81
Montana	2,304	2,655	2,876	2,917	3,114	3,314	5.3	0.88
Utah	1,960	2,250	2,349	2,506	2,638	2,731	4.8	0.73
Wyoming	2,234	2,658	2,850	3,046	3,185	3,381	6.1	0.90

See footnotes at end of table.

Table 145 (page 2 of 2). Personal health care per capita expenditures, by geographic region and State: United States, selected years 1991–98

[Data are compiled from various sources by the Centers for Medicare & Medicaid Services]

Geographic region and State[1]	*1991*	*1994*	*1995*	*1996*	*1997*	*1998*	*1991–98*	*1998*
	Per capita expenditures						Average annual percent change	Ratio to U.S. per capita expenditures
Far West	$2,634	$3,028	$3,109	$3,183	$3,255	$3,414	3.8	0.91
Alaska	2,459	2,811	3,050	3,227	3,340	3,442	4.9	0.92
California	2,690	3,071	3,132	3,200	3,265	3,429	3.5	0.91
Hawaii	2,638	3,248	3,462	3,656	3,664	3,770	5.2	1.00
Nevada	2,393	2,829	2,881	2,949	3,028	3,147	4.0	0.84
Oregon	2,337	2,780	2,924	3,019	3,160	3,334	5.2	0.89
Washington	2,545	2,946	3,075	3,142	3,225	3,382	4.1	0.90

[1]Data are shown for Bureau of Economic Analysis (BEA) regions that are constructed to show economically interdependent states. These BEA geographic regions differ from Bureau of the Census geographic divisions shown in some *Health, United States* tables. See Appendix II, Geographic region and division.
[2]The Mideast region includes spending in the District of Columbia (DC), although it is not listed separately. Per capita spending in DC is substantially higher than per capita spending in most states. Most of this higher spending comes from spending on hospital care. One contributing factor to higher spending is the concentration of several higher-cost academic medical centers in a very small geographic area populated with a small number of people. Another factor could be the inability of current data sources and methods to accurately portray spending flows between providers located in DC and beneficiary resident locations. As a result, per capita spending in DC is not shown.

NOTES: Personal health care includes the following types of services: hospital care, physician and other professional services, nursing home care and home health care, drugs and nondurable products, dental services, durable products, and other personal health care not otherwise specified. Per capita expenditures for each category except the last three are shown in tables 141–144. Services not shown separately accounted for 6 percent of personal health care expenditures in 1991 and 10 percent in 1998. Data for additional years are available. See Appendix III.

SOURCE: Centers for Medicare & Medicaid Services, Office of the Actuary, National Health Statistics Group, National Health Accounts, State Health Expenditures. www.cms.hhs.gov/statistics/nhe/state-estimates-residence/.

Table 146 (page 1 of 2). Hospital care per capita expenditures, by geographic region and State: United States, selected years 1991–98

[Data are compiled from various sources by the Centers for Medicare & Medicaid Services]

Geographic region and State[1]	*1991*	*1994*	*1995*	*1996*	*1997*	*1998*	*1991–98*	*1998*
	Per capita expenditures						Average annual percent change	Ratio to U.S. per capita expenditures
United States	$1,109	$1,279	$1,310	$1,344	$1,372	$1,405	3.4	1.00
New England	1,253	1,438	1,463	1,503	1,562	1,613	3.7	1.15
Connecticut	1,206	1,345	1,343	1,387	1,423	1,478	2.9	1.05
Maine	1,015	1,204	1,296	1,385	1,441	1,501	5.7	1.07
Massachusetts	1,416	1,636	1,635	1,675	1,738	1,807	3.5	1.29
New Hampshire	987	1,123	1,180	1,187	1,235	1,234	3.2	0.88
Rhode Island	1,191	1,368	1,473	1,498	1,632	1,626	4.5	1.16
Vermont	948	1,135	1,244	1,259	1,304	1,328	4.9	0.95
Mideast[2]	1,320	1,553	1,575	1,616	1,645	1,656	3.3	1.18
Delaware	1,187	1,457	1,513	1,467	1,565	1,581	4.2	1.13
Maryland	1,158	1,312	1,360	1,424	1,457	1,486	3.6	1.06
New Jersey	1,187	1,430	1,424	1,509	1,467	1,481	3.2	1.05
New York	1,380	1,646	1,672	1,726	1,754	1,769	3.6	1.26
Pennsylvania	1,332	1,520	1,548	1,538	1,610	1,599	2.6	1.14
Great Lakes	1,134	1,317	1,361	1,405	1,455	1,471	3.8	1.05
Illinois	1,238	1,416	1,455	1,491	1,531	1,558	3.3	1.11
Indiana	1,048	1,239	1,273	1,228	1,365	1,413	4.4	1.01
Michigan	1,129	1,318	1,393	1,444	1,474	1,489	4.0	1.06
Ohio	1,132	1,325	1,366	1,434	1,459	1,437	3.5	1.02
Wisconsin	998	1,151	1,173	1,266	1,336	1,377	4.7	0.98
Plains	1,069	1,269	1,317	1,365	1,415	1,460	4.6	1.04
Iowa	1,095	1,269	1,325	1,406	1,455	1,520	4.8	1.08
Kansas	1,083	1,278	1,333	1,369	1,412	1,428	4.0	1.02
Minnesota	933	1,060	1,104	1,156	1,249	1,254	4.3	0.89
Missouri	1,170	1,437	1,464	1,476	1,494	1,566	4.3	1.11
Nebraska	1,043	1,258	1,316	1,419	1,433	1,507	5.4	1.07
North Dakota	1,062	1,357	1,466	1,532	1,647	1,741	7.3	1.24
South Dakota	1,106	1,269	1,370	1,436	1,499	1,534	4.8	1.09
Southeast	1,085	1,253	1,297	1,343	1,378	1,409	3.8	1.00
Alabama	1,109	1,284	1,376	1,445	1,473	1,432	3.7	1.02
Arkansas	1,028	1,167	1,228	1,320	1,354	1,430	4.8	1.02
Florida	1,130	1,267	1,290	1,317	1,322	1,371	2.8	0.98
Georgia	1,089	1,249	1,270	1,299	1,309	1,329	2.9	0.95
Kentucky	1,067	1,220	1,266	1,340	1,411	1,479	4.8	1.05
Louisiana	1,207	1,453	1,502	1,520	1,563	1,601	4.1	1.14
Mississippi	1,025	1,231	1,365	1,456	1,443	1,551	6.1	1.10
North Carolina	972	1,169	1,246	1,306	1,366	1,373	5.1	0.98
South Carolina	1,073	1,303	1,326	1,345	1,467	1,480	4.7	1.05
Tennessee	1,122	1,311	1,296	1,346	1,379	1,375	3.0	0.98
Virginia	1,016	1,113	1,167	1,212	1,258	1,286	3.4	0.92
West Virginia	1,186	1,381	1,452	1,562	1,635	1,693	5.2	1.20
Southwest	992	1,137	1,157	1,191	1,205	1,255	3.4	0.89
Arizona	920	1,000	998	1,012	1,022	1,085	2.4	0.77
New Mexico	1,051	1,213	1,218	1,267	1,313	1,389	4.1	0.99
Oklahoma	1,000	1,152	1,210	1,275	1,282	1,307	3.9	0.93
Texas	1,001	1,159	1,179	1,211	1,225	1,274	3.5	0.91
Rocky Mountains	921	1,013	1,067	1,097	1,131	1,164	3.4	0.83
Colorado	986	1,067	1,114	1,111	1,139	1,147	2.2	0.82
Idaho	848	933	978	1,073	1,094	1,163	4.6	0.83
Montana	983	1,111	1,232	1,206	1,333	1,440	5.6	1.02
Utah	781	882	917	978	995	1,016	3.8	0.72
Wyoming	1,038	1,142	1,238	1,341	1,380	1,439	4.8	1.02

See footnotes at end of table.

Table 146 (page 2 of 2). Hospital care per capita expenditures, by geographic region and State: United States, selected years 1991–98

[Data are compiled from various sources by the Centers for Medicare & Medicaid Services]

Geographic region and State[1]	*1991*	*1994*	*1995*	*1996*	*1997*	*1998*	*1991–98*	*1998*
	Per capita expenditures						Average annual percent change	Ratio to U.S. per capita expenditures
Far West	$ 974	$1,093	$1,099	$1,098	$1,088	$1,146	2.3	0.82
Alaska	1,118	1,306	1,447	1,496	1,502	1,496	4.3	1.06
California	998	1,106	1,103	1,092	1,076	1,145	2.0	0.81
Hawaii	1,074	1,318	1,371	1,462	1,413	1,391	3.8	0.99
Nevada	879	1,013	1,001	1,021	1,027	1,033	2.3	0.74
Oregon	822	964	1,001	1,021	1,049	1,112	4.4	0.79
Washington	904	1,038	1,061	1,078	1,085	1,116	3.1	0.79

[1]Data are shown for Bureau of Economic Analysis (BEA) regions that are constructed to show economically interdependent states. These BEA geographic regions differ from Bureau of the Census geographic divisions shown in some *Health, United States* tables. See Appendix II, Geographic region and division.
[2]The Mideast region includes spending in the District of Columbia (DC), although it is not listed separately. Per capita spending in DC is substantially higher than per capita spending in most states. Most of this higher spending comes from spending on hospital care. One contributing factor to higher spending is the concentration of several higher-cost academic medical centers in a very small geographic area populated with a small number of people. Another factor could be the inability of current data sources and methods to accurately portray spending flows between providers located in DC and beneficiary resident locations. As a result, per capita spending in DC is not shown.

NOTE: Data for additional years are available. See Appendix III.

SOURCE: Centers for Medicare & Medicaid Services, Office of the Actuary, National Health Statistics Group, National Health Accounts, State Health Expenditures. www.cms.hhs.gov/statistics/nhe/state-estimates-residence/.

Table 147. Physician and other professional services per capita expenditures, by geographic region and State: United States, selected years 1991–98

[Data are compiled from various sources by the Centers for Medicare & Medicaid Services]

Geographic region and State[1]	*1991*	*1994*	*1995*	*1996*	*1997*	*1998*	*1991–98*	*1998*
	Per capita expenditures						Average annual percent change	Ratio to U.S. per capita expenditures
United States	$ 795	$ 932	$ 972	$1,003	$1,043	$1,095	4.7	1.00
New England	823	980	1,045	1,080	1,163	1,246	6.1	1.14
Connecticut	945	1,072	1,182	1,188	1,249	1,304	4.7	1.19
Maine	621	736	796	847	929	1,020	7.4	0.93
Massachusetts	845	1,035	1,073	1,117	1,224	1,316	6.5	1.20
New Hampshire	726	881	964	1,039	1,101	1,189	7.3	1.09
Rhode Island	751	890	974	974	1,022	1,128	6.0	1.03
Vermont	634	752	796	838	911	988	6.5	0.90
Mideast[2]	812	982	1,027	1,044	1,079	1,136	4.9	1.04
Delaware	843	1,002	1,011	1,024	1,084	1,123	4.2	1.03
Maryland	871	1,056	1,060	1,080	1,099	1,140	3.9	1.04
New Jersey	879	1,052	1,153	1,155	1,193	1,225	4.9	1.12
New York	758	936	982	1,006	1,044	1,112	5.6	1.01
Pennsylvania	806	954	980	998	1,034	1,103	4.6	1.01
Great Lakes	747	882	914	944	963	1,015	4.5	0.93
Illinois	751	901	929	970	991	1,046	4.9	0.95
Indiana	681	820	828	860	883	944	4.8	0.86
Michigan	744	855	889	918	937	973	3.9	0.89
Ohio	776	882	911	943	941	992	3.6	0.91
Wisconsin	751	955	1,030	1,033	1,083	1,151	6.3	1.05
Plains	690	852	892	937	983	1,051	6.2	0.96
Iowa	662	798	823	856	888	956	5.4	0.87
Kansas	757	879	940	969	993	1,039	4.6	0.95
Minnesota	775	1,020	1,107	1,189	1,260	1,347	8.2	1.23
Missouri	649	781	787	822	869	938	5.4	0.86
Nebraska	580	723	724	750	790	839	5.4	0.77
North Dakota	671	826	915	911	880	914	4.5	0.83
South Dakota	590	733	764	815	908	998	7.8	0.91
Southeast	765	899	936	969	1,018	1,059	4.8	0.97
Alabama	777	902	913	941	1,020	1,075	4.7	0.98
Arkansas	707	808	842	836	903	941	4.2	0.86
Florida	1,033	1,182	1,178	1,201	1,235	1,273	3.0	1.16
Georgia	767	883	966	1,007	1,066	1,091	5.2	1.00
Kentucky	656	783	862	898	935	976	5.8	0.89
Louisiana	702	829	844	867	917	968	4.7	0.88
Mississippi	564	661	719	757	838	879	6.5	0.80
North Carolina	627	782	811	854	891	941	6.0	0.86
South Carolina	571	705	747	784	846	896	6.7	0.82
Tennessee	720	877	999	1,052	1,112	1,149	6.9	1.05
Virginia	716	822	827	865	894	928	3.8	0.85
West Virginia	682	862	896	923	983	1,040	6.2	0.95
Southwest	718	809	856	887	935	989	4.7	0.90
Arizona	856	920	918	949	982	1,037	2.8	0.95
New Mexico	591	689	735	810	843	878	5.8	0.80
Oklahoma	656	765	804	841	886	948	5.4	0.87
Texas	711	803	861	887	941	995	4.9	0.91
Rocky Mountains	678	764	796	830	877	925	4.5	0.84
Colorado	788	897	929	964	1,007	1,058	4.3	0.97
Idaho	618	693	739	767	813	852	4.7	0.78
Montana	609	639	696	730	777	825	4.4	0.75
Utah	557	629	637	675	726	763	4.6	0.70
Wyoming	594	693	746	760	811	896	6.0	0.82
Far West	977	1,108	1,148	1,181	1,212	1,261	3.7	1.15
Alaska	701	740	792	866	902	953	4.5	0.87
California	1,039	1,184	1,221	1,259	1,290	1,340	3.7	1.22
Hawaii	799	1,012	1,118	1,214	1,235	1,311	7.3	1.20
Nevada	898	960	993	1,000	1,035	1,085	2.7	0.99
Oregon	737	854	899	911	963	1,001	4.5	0.91
Washington	831	914	957	969	988	1,037	3.2	0.95

[1]Data are shown for Bureau of Economic Analysis (BEA) regions that are constructed to show economically interdependent states. These BEA geographic regions differ from Bureau of the Census geographic divisions shown in some *Health, United States* tables. See Appendix II, Geographic region and division.
[2]The Mideast region includes spending in the District of Columbia (DC), although it is not listed separately.

NOTE: Data for additional years are available. See Appendix III.

SOURCE: Centers for Medicare & Medicaid Services, Office of the Actuary, National Health Statistics Group, National Health Accounts, State Health Expenditures. www.cms.hhs.gov/statistics/nhe/state-estimates-residence/.

Table 148. Nursing home care and home health care per capita expenditures, by geographic region and State: United States, selected years 1991–98

[Data are compiled from various sources by the Centers for Medicare & Medicaid Services]

Geographic region and State[1]	*1991*	*1994*	*1995*	*1996*	*1997*	*1998*	*1991–98*	*1998*
	Per capita expenditures						Average annual percent change	Ratio to U.S. per capita expenditures
United States	$290	$374	$398	$420	$430	$433	5.9	1.00
New England	492	618	656	688	693	702	5.2	1.62
Connecticut	578	734	780	827	847	860	5.8	1.99
Maine	384	492	516	525	532	538	4.9	1.24
Massachusetts	534	664	702	735	733	739	4.7	1.71
New Hampshire	268	375	419	450	465	470	8.3	1.08
Rhode Island	443	541	571	587	574	606	4.6	1.40
Vermont	316	357	378	403	412	411	3.9	0.95
Mideast[2]	447	548	578	609	623	648	5.5	1.50
Delaware	328	417	455	492	495	520	6.8	1.20
Maryland	247	323	344	354	369	395	7.0	0.91
New Jersey	309	425	474	499	513	514	7.5	1.19
New York	628	730	749	784	789	827	4.0	1.91
Pennsylvania	353	452	489	530	559	582	7.4	1.34
Great Lakes	306	381	405	425	442	445	5.5	1.03
Illinois	286	359	379	391	403	409	5.2	0.94
Indiana	331	426	443	459	470	464	4.9	1.07
Michigan	246	295	316	339	374	342	4.8	0.79
Ohio	341	438	468	500	511	549	7.1	1.27
Wisconsin	360	424	454	466	480	478	4.2	1.10
Plains	327	404	425	453	465	474	5.5	1.09
Iowa	326	400	424	461	476	502	6.4	1.16
Kansas	289	357	374	404	420	421	5.5	0.97
Minnesota	412	490	502	505	496	503	2.9	1.16
Missouri	285	371	401	443	473	476	7.6	1.10
Nebraska	289	378	397	431	441	459	6.8	1.06
North Dakota	378	405	423	442	455	470	3.2	1.09
South Dakota	274	345	359	387	391	401	5.6	0.93
Southeast	240	340	368	396	406	404	7.7	0.93
Alabama	213	303	333	357	369	360	7.8	0.83
Arkansas	251	332	359	376	410	415	7.4	0.96
Florida	282	404	439	464	465	471	7.6	1.09
Georgia	201	288	303	311	308	308	6.3	0.71
Kentucky	253	345	377	411	446	458	8.8	1.06
Louisiana	265	389	424	471	470	431	7.2	1.00
Mississippi	210	307	327	367	382	366	8.3	0.84
North Carolina	242	355	381	413	433	430	8.5	0.99
South Carolina	197	274	304	337	340	349	8.5	0.81
Tennessee	286	410	448	478	491	474	7.5	1.09
Virginia	177	236	247	271	289	296	7.6	0.68
West Virginia	237	329	375	411	414	414	8.3	0.96
Southwest	205	287	318	346	358	340	7.5	0.79
Arizona	162	247	248	257	251	242	5.9	0.56
New Mexico	149	190	221	239	242	238	6.9	0.55
Oklahoma	257	363	412	440	426	402	6.6	0.93
Texas	209	291	327	361	381	362	8.2	0.84
Rocky Mountains	193	248	260	274	283	277	5.3	0.64
Colorado	203	254	266	289	307	307	6.1	0.71
Idaho	176	254	266	279	281	272	6.4	0.63
Montana	249	336	346	331	322	317	3.5	0.73
Utah	166	189	203	213	218	202	2.9	0.47
Wyoming	173	266	281	301	308	296	8.0	0.68
Far West	173	226	236	240	242	245	5.1	0.57
Alaska	95	121	127	99	97	90	–0.8	0.21
California	155	208	218	224	228	232	5.9	0.54
Hawaii	160	189	195	206	215	223	4.8	0.51
Nevada	143	249	229	218	207	203	5.1	0.47
Oregon	246	267	275	288	299	300	2.8	0.69
Washington	256	321	344	329	323	326	3.5	0.75

[1]Data are shown for Bureau of Economic Analysis (BEA) regions that are constructed to show economically interdependent states. These BEA geographic regions differ from Bureau of the Census geographic divisions shown in some *Health, United States* tables. See Appendix II, Geographic region and division.
[2]The Mideast region includes spending in the District of Columbia (DC), although it is not listed separately.

NOTE: Data for additional years are available. See Appendix III.

SOURCE: Centers for Medicare & Medicaid Services, Office of the Actuary, National Health Statistics Group, National Health Accounts, State Health Expenditures. www.cms.hhs.gov/statistics/nhe/state-estimates-residence/.

Table 149. Drugs and other nondurables per capita expenditures, by geographic region and State: United States, selected years 1991–98

[Data are compiled from various sources by the Centers for Medicare & Medicaid Services]

Geographic region and State[1]	1991	1994	1995	1996	1997	1998	1991–98	1998
	Per capita expenditures						Average annual percent change	Ratio to U.S. per capita expenditures
United States	$260	$313	$337	$370	$406	$451	8.2	1.00
New England	265	323	348	380	418	479	8.8	1.06
Connecticut	280	344	375	410	448	521	9.3	1.15
Maine	225	277	301	342	398	449	10.4	1.00
Massachusetts	267	323	347	375	410	469	8.4	1.04
New Hampshire	261	314	336	366	402	455	8.2	1.01
Rhode Island	281	343	373	413	451	511	8.9	1.13
Vermont	230	277	298	321	351	401	8.2	0.89
Mideast[2]	274	337	365	405	449	506	9.1	1.12
Delaware	267	324	349	395	456	524	10.1	1.16
Maryland	274	306	319	356	406	449	7.3	0.99
New Jersey	304	381	416	455	498	562	9.2	1.25
New York	262	326	356	399	437	492	9.4	1.09
Pennsylvania	274	337	366	404	452	513	9.4	1.14
Great Lakes	261	319	345	381	413	453	8.2	1.00
Illinois	255	310	335	368	393	430	7.7	0.95
Indiana	264	331	361	389	422	449	7.9	1.00
Michigan	279	341	371	418	458	498	8.6	1.10
Ohio	260	313	338	371	407	448	8.1	0.99
Wisconsin	245	298	320	352	379	434	8.5	0.96
Plains	246	298	320	348	379	429	8.3	0.95
Iowa	240	292	316	348	375	426	8.6	0.94
Kansas	245	292	312	344	379	413	7.7	0.92
Minnesota	233	286	309	340	372	424	8.9	0.94
Missouri	263	316	336	355	387	442	7.7	0.98
Nebraska	257	319	345	380	414	476	9.2	1.06
North Dakota	237	286	307	332	358	392	7.4	0.87
South Dakota	220	264	280	302	323	363	7.4	0.81
Southeast	268	328	356	392	434	482	8.8	1.07
Alabama	271	327	351	385	432	471	8.2	1.04
Arkansas	266	322	346	388	418	464	8.3	1.03
Florida	285	359	395	444	488	552	9.9	1.22
Georgia	255	308	333	364	403	441	8.1	0.98
Kentucky	275	335	363	399	444	499	8.9	1.11
Louisiana	272	330	357	381	415	456	7.6	1.01
Mississippi	253	304	325	355	396	444	8.4	0.98
North Carolina	251	305	331	366	411	452	8.8	1.00
South Carolina	240	298	325	364	412	449	9.4	0.99
Tennessee	286	348	376	408	453	507	8.5	1.12
Virginia	254	307	333	360	393	434	7.9	0.96
West Virginia	287	357	392	422	477	524	9.0	1.16
Southwest	258	309	332	362	392	433	7.7	0.96
Arizona	254	313	342	371	400	443	8.3	0.98
New Mexico	228	268	284	312	332	363	6.9	0.80
Oklahoma	246	304	333	362	384	424	8.1	0.94
Texas	264	313	333	364	397	439	7.5	0.97
Rocky Mountains	231	280	301	328	353	390	7.7	0.86
Colorado	231	281	304	325	347	389	7.8	0.86
Idaho	226	275	297	325	352	386	7.9	0.86
Montana	236	289	311	338	358	397	7.7	0.88
Utah	236	282	302	336	369	394	7.6	0.87
Wyoming	222	259	275	304	332	370	7.5	0.82
Far West	243	274	288	308	339	374	6.4	0.83
Alaska	228	257	275	301	323	360	6.7	0.80
California	239	264	275	292	323	355	5.8	0.79
Hawaii	314	353	372	388	407	431	4.7	0.96
Nevada	256	329	362	391	429	472	9.1	1.05
Oregon	238	294	316	349	378	422	8.5	0.94
Washington	252	290	308	335	369	416	7.4	0.92

[1]Data are shown for Bureau of Economic Analysis (BEA) regions that are constructed to show economically interdependent states. These BEA geographic regions differ from Bureau of the Census geographic divisions shown in some *Health, United States* tables. See Appendix II, Geographic region and division.
[2]The Mideast region includes spending in the District of Columbia (DC), although it is not listed separately.

NOTE: Data for additional years are available. See Appendix III.

SOURCE: Centers for Medicare & Medicaid Services, Office of the Actuary, National Health Statistics Group, National Health Accounts, State Health Expenditures. www.cms.hhs.gov/statistics/nhe/state-estimates-residence/.

Table 150. Medicare expenditures as a percent of total personal health care expenditures by geographic region and State: United States, 1991–98

[Data are compiled from various sources by the Centers for Medicare & Medicaid Services]

Geographic region and State[1]	*1991*	*1992*	*1993*	*1994*	*1995*	*1996*	*1997*	*1998*
				Percent				
United States	17.3	17.9	18.3	19.5	20.5	21.0	21.2	20.6
New England	16.5	17.4	18.1	19.1	20.3	21.2	21.0	20.2
Connecticut	15.5	16.5	17.4	18.5	19.7	20.6	20.5	20.5
Maine	16.4	16.6	16.8	18.2	19.1	19.5	19.6	19.0
Massachusetts	17.4	18.4	19.2	20.1	21.7	22.6	22.1	20.7
New Hampshire	13.9	14.5	14.5	15.8	16.4	16.9	16.7	16.6
Rhode Island	17.9	18.5	18.8	20.1	20.5	22.4	22.8	22.0
Vermont	15.0	15.4	15.6	16.5	17.2	17.6	17.3	16.6
Mideast	17.5	18.2	18.6	19.3	20.1	20.6	21.1	21.1
Delaware	15.1	15.9	16.0	16.3	16.5	17.4	16.9	17.4
District of Columbia	13.1	12.3	12.6	13.2	14.0	15.2	16.1	16.9
Maryland	16.3	17.2	17.4	17.9	18.1	18.3	18.8	19.2
New Jersey	16.8	18.5	18.8	19.1	19.7	19.8	21.1	21.4
New York	16.1	16.6	17.0	17.8	18.9	19.3	19.8	19.6
Pennsylvania	21.2	21.6	22.3	23.0	24.1	24.9	24.9	24.8
Great Lakes	17.0	17.6	17.7	18.8	19.8	20.0	20.1	20.0
Illinois	16.9	17.3	17.5	18.7	19.4	19.5	19.5	19.2
Indiana	16.8	17.5	17.6	18.6	19.9	20.5	20.4	19.8
Michigan	17.7	18.6	18.9	20.2	21.4	21.7	21.8	22.0
Ohio	17.5	18.1	18.1	19.1	20.2	20.3	20.9	21.1
Wisconsin	15.2	15.6	15.3	16.0	16.6	16.8	16.8	16.2
Plains	17.0	17.4	17.4	17.9	18.7	18.8	18.9	18.1
Iowa	17.5	18.0	17.7	18.1	18.7	18.6	18.8	17.8
Kansas	17.4	17.9	18.0	18.8	19.8	19.8	20.4	19.6
Minnesota	14.4	14.6	14.3	14.4	15.0	15.2	15.1	14.7
Missouri	19.1	20.0	20.3	21.2	22.4	22.4	22.4	21.1
Nebraska	15.9	15.7	15.7	16.4	17.2	17.4	18.0	17.2
North Dakota	16.4	16.4	16.7	17.1	17.3	17.0	17.2	16.7
South Dakota	16.5	17.0	16.7	17.2	17.8	17.8	17.7	17.3
Southeast	19.3	20.0	20.3	21.8	22.9	23.3	23.3	22.5
Alabama	19.6	20.8	21.3	22.6	23.6	23.7	23.4	22.6
Arkansas	21.8	21.7	21.3	22.7	23.7	23.9	23.8	23.1
Florida	23.3	24.2	25.1	27.2	28.6	28.8	29.0	28.1
Georgia	15.9	17.0	16.6	17.5	18.3	18.5	18.4	17.3
Kentucky	18.8	19.2	19.5	20.8	21.2	21.4	21.2	20.2
Louisiana	19.4	20.1	20.5	22.9	24.9	26.5	26.9	26.3
Mississippi	21.0	22.5	22.4	24.1	25.4	26.7	27.0	25.1
North Carolina	17.5	17.4	17.3	18.1	19.4	19.6	19.4	19.3
South Carolina	15.1	15.9	16.3	18.6	19.4	20.2	19.8	19.7
Tennessee	18.7	19.4	19.9	21.1	21.7	22.1	21.6	20.6
Virginia	14.9	15.8	15.9	17.1	17.9	18.3	18.5	18.0
West Virginia	20.5	21.3	20.5	21.7	22.5	23.7	23.9	23.1
Southwest	16.4	16.8	17.3	19.4	21.1	21.9	22.3	21.0
Arizona	19.7	19.6	19.3	20.4	21.7	22.2	22.6	21.1
New Mexico	14.7	14.6	14.6	16.1	17.2	17.4	17.5	16.9
Oklahoma	19.1	19.7	20.0	22.4	24.3	25.0	25.5	24.0
Texas	15.4	15.9	16.6	19.0	20.8	21.6	22.0	20.9
Rocky Mountains	13.9	14.6	15.1	16.2	17.2	17.4	17.2	16.4
Colorado	13.4	14.0	14.6	15.8	16.9	17.4	17.1	16.5
Idaho	15.1	15.9	15.9	17.3	18.3	18.3	18.6	17.7
Montana	17.1	17.9	18.4	19.1	18.9	19.1	19.1	18.4
Utah	12.4	13.2	13.8	14.7	16.1	16.1	15.8	14.7
Wyoming	14.3	15.2	16.2	17.2	18.1	17.3	17.1	16.1
Far West	16.1	16.2	17.0	18.2	19.2	19.7	20.1	19.3
Alaska	6.5	6.9	7.1	7.8	8.7	9.0	9.3	9.1
California	16.5	16.5	17.5	18.9	20.1	20.7	21.1	20.1
Hawaii	12.1	12.6	12.8	13.0	13.6	13.4	14.3	14.1
Nevada	16.3	16.7	18.1	19.1	20.2	20.9	21.7	20.7
Oregon	17.2	17.5	17.4	18.3	19.0	19.4	19.5	19.1
Washington	15.0	15.3	15.2	15.8	16.3	16.5	17.0	16.7

[1]Data are shown for Bureau of Economic Analysis (BEA) regions that are constructed to show economically interdependent states. These BEA geographic regions differ from Bureau of the Census geographic divisions shown in some *Health, United States* tables. See Appendix II, Geographic region and division.

SOURCE: Centers for Medicare & Medicaid Services, Office of the Actuary, National Health Statistics Group, National Health Accounts, State Health Expenditures. www.cms.hhs.gov/statistics/nhe/state-estimates-residence/.

Table 151. Medicaid expenditures as a percent of total personal health care expenditures by geographic region and State: United States, 1991–98

[Data are compiled from various sources by the Centers for Medicare & Medicaid Services]

Geographic region and State[1]	*1991*	*1992*	*1993*	*1994*	*1995*	*1996*	*1997*	*1998*
				Percent				
United States	13.2	13.7	14.7	15.2	15.6	15.9	15.7	15.7
New England	17.0	16.7	16.6	18.0	18.8	17.8	18.6	18.8
Connecticut	15.7	14.8	15.9	17.0	18.0	17.7	18.5	17.5
Maine	18.3	19.0	21.3	22.1	21.1	21.1	21.9	21.1
Massachusetts	18.1	17.3	16.2	18.0	19.2	17.3	18.3	19.3
New Hampshire	11.7	12.4	13.2	14.5	15.6	15.1	15.7	15.6
Rhode Island	18.6	21.5	20.9	21.2	20.7	20.6	21.4	21.6
Vermont	15.6	15.2	15.6	16.7	17.0	17.6	17.3	18.0
Mideast	18.1	18.5	19.3	20.1	21.0	21.7	21.5	22.2
Delaware	10.2	10.4	11.0	11.4	12.7	14.3	12.6	12.5
District of Columbia	19.2	18.5	20.5	21.7	20.9	20.9	22.5	20.5
Maryland	11.7	12.2	12.5	13.2	13.5	13.5	13.8	12.7
New Jersey	13.1	12.3	13.6	13.9	14.0	13.9	14.6	14.0
New York	26.4	26.5	27.5	28.4	29.8	30.7	29.7	31.5
Pennsylvania	10.4	12.3	12.0	13.3	14.0	15.4	16.1	16.3
Great Lakes	12.2	13.3	14.4	14.3	14.4	14.8	14.6	14.5
Illinois	9.1	11.8	13.2	13.5	14.2	15.1	15.1	14.8
Indiana	14.0	14.9	16.4	14.0	12.0	13.2	12.1	12.0
Michigan	12.2	12.6	14.2	14.6	15.0	15.1	15.3	14.9
Ohio	14.0	14.5	15.0	15.2	15.6	15.4	15.4	15.6
Wisconsin	14.1	14.0	14.0	14.0	13.7	13.6	13.5	13.4
Plains	12.1	13.0	13.4	13.8	13.9	13.9	13.8	14.3
Iowa	11.9	12.0	12.5	12.8	12.8	13.0	12.8	15.4
Kansas	9.7	10.3	11.3	11.4	10.7	10.7	10.8	10.8
Minnesota	15.5	15.2	16.0	16.7	16.9	16.5	15.4	15.4
Missouri	10.3	13.0	12.7	13.2	13.6	13.5	14.3	14.4
Nebraska	11.4	11.8	12.9	12.8	12.6	13.2	13.4	14.4
North Dakota	14.9	14.1	14.5	14.0	13.6	14.3	14.2	13.8
South Dakota	12.7	13.0	13.7	13.8	13.7	13.8	13.1	13.4
Southeast	11.7	12.2	13.4	14.0	14.4	14.2	14.1	14.0
Alabama	8.8	10.1	10.8	11.5	12.2	12.7	13.1	13.0
Arkansas	13.6	14.9	15.4	15.3	15.5	15.6	15.3	15.5
Florida	8.5	9.1	9.9	10.2	10.6	10.4	10.7	10.4
Georgia	12.1	11.8	12.8	14.0	13.8	13.5	12.8	12.2
Kentucky	13.8	15.4	16.2	16.6	16.1	16.6	17.7	16.9
Louisiana	17.8	17.7	22.1	24.3	23.1	20.0	18.9	19.1
Mississippi	14.8	14.7	15.4	16.4	16.8	16.8	16.8	15.8
North Carolina	12.9	13.3	14.3	14.8	16.7	17.3	17.2	16.9
South Carolina	14.8	15.3	15.9	16.5	16.7	16.6	16.0	16.6
Tennessee	12.6	13.9	14.1	15.6	17.1	16.3	16.4	17.4
Virginia	8.9	9.0	9.8	9.8	10.1	10.1	10.2	9.9
West Virginia	15.3	17.5	19.7	19.5	18.6	17.7	17.0	17.3
Southwest	11.1	12.1	13.0	13.7	13.5	13.6	13.2	12.6
Arizona	8.6	11.0	11.3	12.0	11.8	12.2	12.2	12.0
New Mexico	12.1	13.1	14.3	15.5	16.5	18.3	17.9	17.7
Oklahoma	12.3	12.5	12.2	11.2	11.0	10.9	10.9	11.8
Texas	11.4	12.2	13.4	14.3	14.1	14.0	13.5	12.5
Rocky Mountains	10.2	10.9	11.4	11.8	11.8	12.2	11.9	11.9
Colorado	9.1	10.1	10.5	11.1	11.3	11.6	11.5	11.4
Idaho	10.7	11.1	11.3	11.3	11.3	12.1	12.2	12.1
Montana	13.5	13.7	15.2	15.2	14.4	15.4	14.3	13.8
Utah	10.8	11.3	11.7	11.8	11.8	12.0	11.4	11.8
Wyoming	10.1	11.3	11.8	12.7	12.6	12.9	12.7	12.3
Far West	10.9	10.9	12.4	12.8	13.3	14.3	14.0	13.3
Alaska	13.8	14.7	17.3	16.3	15.9	17.1	17.5	16.9
California	10.8	10.7	12.3	12.6	12.9	14.1	13.7	12.7
Hawaii	9.1	8.7	10.0	12.5	16.0	13.9	13.4	14.2
Nevada	7.7	8.7	9.2	8.7	9.2	9.0	9.0	9.1
Oregon	10.4	10.8	11.8	13.2	14.8	15.2	14.5	15.3
Washington	12.9	13.1	14.3	14.8	15.3	16.3	16.3	16.2

[1]Data are shown for Bureau of Economic Analysis (BEA) regions that are constructed to show economically interdependent states. These BEA geographic regions differ from Bureau of the Census geographic divisions shown in some *Health, United States* tables. See Appendix II, Geographic region and division.

SOURCE: Centers for Medicare & Medicaid Services, Office of the Actuary, National Health Statistics Group, National Health Accounts, State Health Expenditures. www.cms.hhs.gov/statistics/nhe/state-estimates-residence/.

Table 152 (page 1 of 2). State mental health agency per capita expenditures for mental health services and average annual percent change by geographic region and State: United States, selected fiscal years 1981–2002

[Data are based on reporting by State mental health agencies]

Geographic region and State[1]	*1981*	*1983*	*1985*	*1987*	*1990*	*1993*	*1997*	*2001*	*2002*	*1981–90*	*1990–2002*
	Amount per capita									Average annual percent change	
United States	$ 27	$31	$35	$ 38	$ 48	$ 54	$ 64	$ 81	$ 88	6.6	5.2
New England:											
Connecticut	32	39	44	56	73	82	99	129	138	9.6	5.4
Maine	25	32	36	42	67	70	88	107	118	11.6	4.8
Massachusetts	32	36	46	62	84	83	90	107	107	11.3	2.0
New Hampshire	35	39	42	36	63	78	99	112	116	6.7	5.2
Rhode Island	36	32	35	41	50	61	63	88	88	3.7	4.8
Vermont	32	40	44	44	54	74	92	130	145	6.0	8.6
Mideast:											
Delaware	44	51	46	41	55	56	73	93	86	2.5	3.8
District of Columbia[2]	- - -	23	28	130	268	315	337	398	409	- - -	3.6
Maryland	33	37	40	49	61	64	76	127	136	7.1	6.9
New Jersey	26	31	36	43	57	68	69	90	120	9.1	6.4
New York	67	74	90	99	118	131	113	176	184	6.5	3.8
Pennsylvania	41	47	52	50	57	68	68	152	166	3.7	9.3
Great Lakes:											
Illinois	18	21	24	25	34	36	51	64	69	7.3	6.1
Indiana	19	23	27	31	47	39	40	65	69	10.6	3.3
Michigan	33	39	49	61	74	75	87	90	91	9.4	1.7
Ohio	25	29	30	34	41	47	52	61	61	5.7	3.4
Wisconsin	22	27	28	31	37	35	44	72	91	5.9	7.8
Plains:											
Iowa	8	10	11	12	17	13	29	73	53	8.7	9.9
Kansas	18	22	27	28	35	48	59	60	70	7.7	5.9
Minnesota[3]	17	30	32	42	54	69	87	105	115	8.8	6.5
Missouri	24	25	28	32	35	41	56	60	69	4.3	5.8
Nebraska	17	19	21	21	29	34	39	51	56	6.1	5.6
North Dakota	39	42	36	42	40	43	48	79	82	0.3	6.2
South Dakota	17	21	22	27	25	47	54	61	65	4.4	8.3
Southeast:											
Alabama	20	24	28	29	38	43	47	57	60	7.4	3.9
Arkansas	17	20	24	24	26	30	30	28	28	4.8	0.6
Florida	20	23	26	25	37	31	44	35	44	7.1	1.5
Georgia	25	26	23	32	51	49	47	46	47	8.2	–0.7
Kentucky	15	17	19	23	23	25	35	49	51	4.9	6.9
Louisiana	19	23	26	25	28	39	43	45	48	4.4	4.6
Mississippi	14	16	24	22	34	41	56	87	89	10.4	8.3
North Carolina	24	29	38	41	46	50	62	76	50	7.5	0.7
South Carolina	31	33	33	45	51	56	64	74	70	5.7	2.7
Tennessee	18	20	23	24	29	37	23	69	84	5.4	9.3
Virginia	23	29	32	35	45	40	49	65	67	7.7	3.4
West Virginia	20	20	22	23	24	22	23	26	47	2.0	5.8
Southwest:											
Arizona	10	10	12	16	27	60	68	89	102	11.7	11.7
New Mexico	24	25	25	24	23	24	31	33	29	–0.5	2.0
Oklahoma	22	33	31	30	36	38	41	39	41	5.6	1.1
Texas	13	16	17	19	23	31	39	38	38	6.5	4.3
Rocky Mountains:											
Colorado	24	25	28	30	34	41	57	64	67	3.9	5.8
Idaho	13	15	15	17	20	26	29	46	40	4.9	5.9
Montana	25	28	29	28	28	34	93	124	132	1.3	13.8
Utah	13	16	17	19	21	25	28	33	69	5.5	10.4
Wyoming	23	28	31	30	35	42	43	61	78	4.8	6.9

See footnotes at end of table.

Table 152 (page 2 of 2). State mental health agency per capita expenditures for mental health services and average annual percent change by geographic region and State: United States, selected fiscal years 1981–2002

[Data are based on reporting by State mental health agencies]

Geographic region and State[1]	1981	1983	1985	1987	1990	1993	1997	2001	2002	1981–90	1990–2002
	Amount per capita									Average annual percent change	
Far West:											
Alaska	$38	$41	$45	$50	$72	$86	$79	$ 81	$ 88	7.4	1.7
California	28	29	34	30	42	50	58	92	105	4.6	7.9
Hawaii	19	22	23	26	38	71	85	175	162	8.0	12.8
Nevada	22	25	26	28	33	32	45	57	59	4.6	5.0
Oregon	21	21	25	28	41	60	68	97	60	7.7	3.2
Washington	18	24	30	37	43	66	79	88	92	10.2	6.5

- - - Data not available.
[1]Data are shown for Bureau of Economic Analysis (BEA) regions that are constructed to show economically interdependent states. These BEA geographic divisions differ from Bureau of the Census geographic divisions shown in some *Health, United States* tables. See Appendix II, Geographic region and division.
[2]Transfer of St. Elizabeths Hospital from the National Institute of Mental Health to the District of Columbia Office of Mental Health took place over the years 1985–93.
[3]Data for 1981 not comparable with later years' data for Minnesota. Average annual percent change is for 1983–90.

NOTES: Expenditures are for mental illness, excluding mental retardation and substance abuse. Starting in 1990 data for Puerto Rico, and starting in 1993 data for Guam are included in the U.S. total. States may vary in type of funds included in mental health expenditures. Medicaid revenues for community programs and children's mental health expenditures are not included by some states. Funds for mental health services in jails or prisons are included by some states. State data omissions and inclusions are likely to be consistent across years.

SOURCES: National Association of State Mental Health Program Directors and the National Association of State Mental Health Program Directors Research Institute, Inc. Lutterman T, Hollen V, Shaw R. Funding sources and expenditures of state mental health agencies: fiscal year 2002. Final report. Oct. 2004; Website: www.nri-inc.org.

Table 153 (page 1 of 2). Medicare enrollees, enrollees in managed care, payments per enrollee, and short-stay hospital utilization by geographic region and State: United States, 1994 and 2002

[Data are compiled by the Centers for Medicare & Medicaid Services]

Geographic division and State[1]	Enrollment in thousands[2]	Percent of enrollees in managed care[3]		Payment per fee-for-service enrollee		Short-stay hospital utilization: Discharges per 1,000 enrollees[4]		Short-stay hospital utilization: Average length of stay in days[4]	
	2002	1994	2002	1994	2002	1994	2002	1994	2002
United States[5]	39,597	7.9	13.9	$4,375	$6,271	345	370	7.5	5.9
New England:									
Connecticut	520	2.6	6.2	4,426	6,772	287	317	8.1	6.1
Maine	223	0.1	0.1	3,464	5,037	322	308	7.6	5.6
Massachusetts	958	6.1	21.8	5,147	7,065	350	363	7.6	5.7
New Hampshire	175	0.2	1.1	3,414	5,030	281	268	7.6	5.6
Rhode Island	170	7.0	33.1	4,148	5,907	312	346	8.1	6.2
Vermont	92	0.1	0.0	3,182	5,070	283	265	7.6	5.8
Mideast:									
Delaware	120	0.2	1.1	4,712	6,356	326	332	8.1	6.4
District of Columbia	75	3.9	6.6	5,655	7,731	376	389	10.1	7.5
Maryland	665	1.4	3.1	4,997	7,284	362	393	7.5	5.4
New Jersey	1,219	2.6	8.9	4,531	7,834	354	378	10.2	7.2
New York	2,722	6.2	17.1	4,855	7,180	334	369	11.2	7.7
Pennsylvania	2,098	3.3	24.0	5,212	6,781	379	406	8.0	6.0
Great Lakes:									
Illinois	1,641	5.5	6.2	4,324	6,193	374	420	7.3	5.7
Indiana	858	2.6	2.7	3,945	5,534	345	354	6.9	5.6
Michigan	1,420	0.7	2.4	4,307	6,582	328	376	7.6	5.9
Ohio	1,719	2.4	14.3	3,982	6,037	350	390	7.1	5.5
Wisconsin	788	2.0	3.2	3,246	5,114	310	326	6.8	5.3
Plains:									
Iowa	477	3.1	3.6	3,080	4,931	322	350	6.6	5.3
Kansas	387	3.3	6.1	3,847	5,500	348	372	6.5	5.4
Minnesota	667	19.6	12.8	3,394	5,213	334	354	5.7	4.9
Missouri	875	3.4	14.2	4,191	5,826	349	406	7.3	5.6
Nebraska	258	2.2	3.8	2,926	5,189	281	287	6.3	5.3
North Dakota	103	0.6	0.6	3,218	4,703	327	295	6.3	5.3
South Dakota	119	0.1	1.3	2,952	4,498	356	324	6.1	5.0
Southeast:									
Alabama	709	0.8	6.8	4,454	5,973	413	456	7.0	5.5
Arkansas	438	0.2	0.5	3,719	5,466	366	404	7.0	5.8
Florida	2,900	13.8	19.9	5,027	7,055	326	376	7.1	5.8
Georgia	963	0.4	4.2	4,402	5,839	378	369	6.9	5.8
Kentucky	637	2.3	3.2	3,862	5,783	396	421	7.2	5.6
Louisiana	612	0.4	12.2	5,468	7,417	399	466	7.2	6.1
Mississippi	428	0.1	0.7	4,189	6,265	423	450	7.4	6.4
North Carolina	1,180	0.5	4.4	3,465	5,557	314	370	8.0	5.8
South Carolina	592	0.1	0.3	3,777	5,900	319	382	8.3	6.2
Tennessee	861	0.3	6.0	4,441	6,152	375	398	7.1	5.9
Virginia	929	1.5	2.0	3,748	5,296	348	349	7.3	5.8
West Virginia	342	8.3	7.1	3,798	5,585	420	432	7.1	5.7
Southwest:									
Arizona	707	24.8	29.9	4,442	5,499	292	313	5.9	5.1
New Mexico	243	13.6	15.2	3,110	4,735	301	279	6.0	5.4
Oklahoma	517	2.5	8.3	4,098	6,112	355	416	7.0	5.7
Texas	2,342	4.1	8.1	4,703	6,736	333	387	7.2	5.9
Rocky Mountains:									
Colorado	487	17.2	28.5	3,935	5,448	302	306	6.0	4.9
Idaho	174	2.5	9.3	3,045	4,867	274	290	5.2	4.7
Montana	140	0.4	0.5	3,114	4,653	306	299	5.9	4.9
Utah	216	9.4	3.2	3,443	4,752	238	257	5.4	4.7
Wyoming	68	3.3	1.7	3,537	4,896	315	318	5.6	4.9

See footnotes at end of table.

Table 153 (page 2 of 2). Medicare enrollees, enrollees in managed care, payments per enrollee, and short-stay hospital utilization by geographic region and State: United States, 1994 and 2002

[Data are compiled by the Centers for Medicare & Medicaid Services]

Geographic division and State[1]	Enrollment in thousands[2]	Percent of enrollees in managed care[3]		Payment per fee-for-service enrollee		Short-stay hospital utilization: Discharges per 1,000 enrollees[4]		Short-stay hospital utilization: Average length of stay in days[4]	
	2002	1994	2002	1994	2002	1994	2002	1994	2002
Far West:									
Alaska	45	0.6	0.6	3,687	5,642	269	294	6.3	5.9
California	4,004	30.0	35.1	5,219	6,942	366	328	6.1	6.1
Hawaii	174	29.8	33.9	3,069	4,454	301	225	9.1	7.5
Nevada	269	19.0	30.9	4,306	6,070	291	302	7.0	6.2
Oregon	512	27.7	34.3	3,285	4,933	305	315	5.2	4.6
Washington	762	12.5	17.8	3,401	5,280	269	271	5.3	4.9

0.0 less than 0.05.
[1]Data are shown for Bureau of Economic Analysis (BEA) regions that are constructed to show economically interdependent States. These BEA geographic regions differ from Bureau of the Census geographic divisions shown in some *Health, United States* tables. See Appendix II, Geographic region and division.
[2]Total persons enrolled in hospital insurance, supplementary medical insurance, or both, as of July 1. Includes fee-for-service and managed care enrollees.
[3]Includes enrollees in Medicare-approved managed care organizations.
[4]Data are for fee-for-service enrollees only.
[5]Includes residents of any of the 50 States and the District of Columbia. Excludes Puerto Rico, Guam, Virgin Islands, residence unknown, foreign countries, and other outlying areas not shown separately.

NOTES: Enrollment and percent of enrollees in managed care are based on a 5-percent annual Denominator File using the Centers for Medicare & Medicaid Services' (CMS) Enrollment Database and Group Health Plan data. Payments per fee-for-service enrollee are based on fee-for-service billing reimbursement for a 5-percent sample of Medicare beneficiaries as recorded in CMS' National Claims History. Short-stay hospital utilization is based on the Medicare Provider Analysis and Review (MEDPAR) stay records for a 20-percent sample of Medicare beneficiaries.
Figures may not sum to totals due to rounding. Data for additional years are available. See Appendix III.

SOURCE: Centers for Medicare & Medicaid Services, Office of Research, Development, and Information. Health Care Financing Review: Medicare and Medicaid Statistical Supplements for the years 1996 to 2004. Website: www.cms.hhs.gov/review/supp/.

Table 154 (page 1 of 2). Medicaid recipients, recipients in managed care, payments per recipient, and recipients per 100 persons below the poverty level by geographic region and State: United States, selected fiscal years 1989–2001

[Data are compiled from Medicaid administrative records by the Centers for Medicare & Medicaid Services]

Geographic region and State[1]	Recipients in thousands		Percent of recipients in managed care		Payments per recipient			Recipients per 100 persons below the poverty level	
	1996[2]	2001	1996[2]	2001	1990	1996[2]	2001	1989–90	2000–2001
United States	36,118	45,972	40	57	$2,568	$3,369	$4,053	75	139
New England:									
Connecticut	329	685	61	72	4,829	6,179	4,324	167	236
Maine	167	252	1	43	3,248	4,321	5,808	88	187
Massachusetts	715	1,055	70	65	4,622	5,285	5,486	103	177
New Hampshire	100	97	16	8	5,423	5,496	7,121	53	134
Rhode Island	130	188	63	68	3,778	5,280	5,823	163	198
Vermont	102	150	–	61	2,530	2,954	3,616	108	222
Mideast:									
Delaware	82	123	78	82	3,004	3,773	4,891	68	190
District of Columbia	143	141	55	64	2,629	4,955	5,900	86	159
Maryland	399	656	64	68	3,300	5,138	5,041	74	171
New Jersey	714	881	43	60	4,054	5,217	5,693	83	126
New York	3,281	3,591	23	26	5,099	6,811	7,725	95	137
Pennsylvania	1,168	1,558	53	76	2,449	3,993	4,901	88	137
Great Lakes:									
Illinois	1,454	1,658	13	9	2,271	3,689	4,916	69	120
Indiana	594	777	31	70	3,859	4,130	4,319	45	146
Michigan	1,172	1,353	73	90	2,094	2,867	3,930	85	141
Ohio	1,478	1,498	32	21	2,566	3,729	5,365	98	120
Wisconsin	434	637	32	52	3,179	4,384	5,027	95	129
Plains:									
Iowa	308	320	41	89	2,589	3,534	5,197	80	152
Kansas	251	273	32	58	2,524	3,425	5,026	71	103
Minnesota	455	601	33	64	3,709	5,342	6,271	70	180
Missouri	636	979	35	45	2,002	3,171	3,709	63	191
Nebraska	191	243	27	75	2,595	3,548	4,487	61	154
North Dakota	61	64	55	58	3,955	4,889	5,933	58	85
South Dakota	77	110	65	97	3,368	4,114	3,896	51	164
Southeast:									
Alabama	546	882	11	54	1,731	2,675	3,338	43	112
Arkansas	363	532	39	58	2,267	3,375	3,250	55	109
Florida	1,638	2,472	64	62	2,273	2,851	3,474	55	131
Georgia	1,185	1,514	32	84	3,190	2,604	2,677	64	145
Kentucky	641	807	53	81	2,089	3,014	4,031	81	162
Louisiana	778	805	6	7	2,247	3,154	3,582	58	109
Mississippi	510	708	7	51	1,354	2,633	3,081	67	146
North Carolina	1,130	1,310	37	70	2,531	3,255	4,201	66	131
South Carolina	503	761	1	6	2,343	3,026	4,071	52	144
Tennessee	1,409	1,602	100	100	1,896	2,049	2,534	67	195
Virginia	623	620	68	61	2,596	2,849	4,383	53	114
West Virginia	395	349	30	46	1,443	2,855	4,487	80	127
Southwest:									
Arizona	528	763	86	96	- - -	- - -	3,214	- - -	106
New Mexico	318	385	45	64	2,120	2,757	3,851	39	122
Oklahoma	358	589	19	68	2,516	2,852	3,422	56	108
Texas	2,572	2,660	4	41	1,928	2,672	3,626	47	86
Rocky Mountains:									
Colorado	271	393	80	92	2,705	3,815	4,969	45	107
Idaho	119	157	37	28	2,973	3,402	4,541	36	92
Montana	101	108	59	64	2,793	3,478	4,390	47	83
Utah	152	233	82	93	2,279	2,775	4,571	72	102
Wyoming	51	51	1	–	2,036	3,571	4,755	59	101

See footnotes at end of table.

Table 154 (page 2 of 2). Medicaid recipients, recipients in managed care, payments per recipient, and recipients per 100 persons below the poverty level by geographic region and State: United States, selected fiscal years 1989–2001

[Data are compiled from Medicaid administrative records by the Centers for Medicare & Medicaid Services]

Geographic region and State[1]	Recipients in thousands		Percent of recipients in managed care		Payments per recipient			Recipients per 100 persons below the poverty level	
	1996[2]	2001	1996[2]	2001	1990	1996[2]	2001	1989–90	2000–2001
Far West:									
Alaska	69	105	–	–	3,562	4,027	5,314	70	188
California	5,107	8,583	23	52	1,795	2,178	2,315	88	188
Hawaii	41	- - -	80	78	2,252	6,574	- - -	73	- - -
Nevada	109	154	41	38	3,161	3,361	3,886	37	91
Oregon	450	582	91	87	2,283	2,915	3,245	74	142
Washington	621	958	100	100	2,128	2,242	2,833	98	151

– Quantity zero.
- - - Data not available.
[1]Data are shown for Bureau of Economic Analysis (BEA) regions that are constructed to show economically interdependent States. These BEA geographic regions differ from Bureau of the Census geographic divisions shown in some *Health, United States* tables. See Appendix II, Geographic region and division.
[2]Prior to 1999 recipient counts exclude those individuals who only received coverage under prepaid health care and for whom no direct vendor payments were made during the year; and vendor payments exclude payments to health maintenance organizations and other prepaid health plans ($15 billion in 1996). The total number of persons who were Medicaid eligible and enrolled was 41.2 million in 1996 (CMS Medicaid Statistics, Program and Financial Statistics FY1996, unpublished).

NOTES: Payments exclude disproportionate share hospital payments ($15.5 billion in FY2001). Data for additional years are available. See Appendix III.

SOURCES: Centers for Medicare & Medicaid Services, Office of Information Services, Enterprise Databases Group, Division of Information Distribution, Medicaid Data System; Department of Commerce, Bureau of the Census, Housing and Household Economic Statistics Division.

Table 155. Persons enrolled in health maintenance organizations (HMOs) by geographic region and State: United States, selected years 1980–2004

[Data are based on a census of health maintenance organizations]

Geographic region and State[1]	2004	1980	1985	1990	1995	1998	2000	2003	2004
	Number in thousands	Percent of population							
United States[2]	68,808	4.0	7.9	13.4	19.4	28.6	30.0	24.6	23.4
New England:									
Connecticut	1,362	2.4	7.1	19.9	21.2	42.9	44.6	37.8	39.1
Maine	259	0.4	0.3	2.6	7.0	19.1	22.3	21.1	19.8
Massachusetts	2,405	2.9	13.7	26.5	39.0	54.2	53.0	38.7	37.4
New Hampshire	284	1.2	5.6	9.6	18.5	33.8	33.7	25.9	22.1
Rhode Island	340	3.7	9.1	20.6	19.6	29.8	38.1	31.7	31.6
Vermont	59	–	–	6.4	12.5	–	4.6	9.9	9.6
Mideast:									
Delaware	120	–	3.9	17.5	18.4	48.1	22.0	15.3	14.7
District of Columbia[3]	162	- - -	- - -	- - -	- - -	33.0	35.2	27.8	28.8
Maryland[4]	1,698	2.0	4.8	14.2	29.5	43.6	43.9	30.6	30.8
New Jersey	2,136	2.0	5.6	12.3	14.7	31.3	30.9	27.0	24.7
New York	5,743	5.5	8.0	15.1	26.6	37.8	35.8	32.4	29.9
Pennsylvania	3,856	1.2	5.0	12.5	21.5	37.1	33.9	31.7	31.2
Great Lakes:									
Illinois	1,625	1.9	7.1	12.6	17.2	20.8	21.0	14.7	12.8
Indiana	702	0.5	3.6	6.1	8.3	14.0	12.4	11.9	11.3
Michigan	2,744	2.4	9.9	15.2	20.5	25.3	27.1	26.0	27.2
Ohio	2,059	2.2	6.7	13.3	16.3	23.4	25.1	18.6	18.0
Wisconsin	1,556	8.5	17.8	21.7	24.0	30.8	30.2	29.1	28.4
Plains:									
Iowa	295	0.2	4.8	10.1	4.5	4.9	7.4	9.5	10.0
Kansas	175	–	3.3	7.9	4.7	14.4	17.9	7.8	6.4
Minnesota	1,335	9.9	22.2	16.4	26.5	32.4	29.9	27.6	26.4
Missouri	1,564	2.3	6.0	8.2	18.5	33.7	35.2	32.3	27.4
Nebraska	130	1.1	1.8	5.1	8.6	16.9	11.2	8.8	7.5
North Dakota	2	0.4	2.5	1.7	1.2	2.2	2.5	0.4	0.3
South Dakota	82	–	–	3.3	2.8	5.1	6.7	10.6	10.7
Southeast:									
Alabama	128	0.3	0.9	5.3	7.3	10.8	7.2	3.8	2.8
Arkansas	145	–	0.1	2.2	3.8	10.7	10.4	7.1	5.3
Florida	4,225	1.5	5.6	10.6	18.8	31.5	31.4	26.0	24.8
Georgia	1,193	0.1	2.9	4.8	7.6	15.5	17.4	13.4	13.7
Kentucky	1,164	0.9	1.6	5.7	16.1	35.1	31.5	31.2	28.3
Louisiana	524	0.6	0.9	5.4	7.2	16.6	17.0	12.2	11.7
Mississippi	12	–	–	–	0.7	3.6	1.1	0.8	0.4
North Carolina	836	0.6	1.6	4.8	8.3	17.1	17.8	11.6	9.9
South Carolina	253	0.2	1.0	1.9	5.5	9.9	9.9	6.5	6.1
Tennessee	749	–	1.8	3.7	12.2	24.1	33.0	18.0	12.8
Virginia[4]	1,343	–	1.1	6.1	7.7	16.9	18.5	16.5	18.2
West Virginia[4]	179	0.7	1.7	3.9	5.8	10.7	10.3	10.1	9.9
Southwest:									
Arizona	1,112	6.0	10.3	16.2	25.8	30.3	30.9	21.3	19.9
New Mexico	577	1.4	2.0	12.7	15.1	32.3	37.7	30.3	30.8
Oklahoma	277	–	2.1	5.5	7.6	13.8	14.7	13.9	7.9
Texas	2,354	0.6	3.4	6.9	12.0	17.8	18.5	12.8	10.6
Rocky Mountains:									
Colorado	1,244	6.9	10.8	20.0	23.3	36.4	39.5	30.3	27.3
Idaho	39	1.2	–	1.8	1.4	5.7	7.9	2.8	2.9
Montana	86	–	–	1.0	2.4	3.9	7.0	5.2	9.3
Utah	598	0.6	8.8	13.9	25.1	35.6	35.3	25.9	25.4
Wyoming	11	–	–	–	–	0.7	1.4	2.4	2.2
Far West:									
Alaska	–	–	–	–	–	–	–	–	–
California	17,022	16.8	22.5	30.7	36.0	47.1	53.5	48.5	48.0
Hawaii	373	15.3	18.1	21.6	21.0	32.8	30.0	30.0	29.7
Nevada	538	–	5.8	8.5	15.9	26.8	23.5	21.1	24.0
Oregon	778	12.0	14.0	24.7	40.0	45.3	41.1	24.2	21.8
Washington	786	9.4	8.7	14.6	18.7	26.3	15.2	15.1	12.8

– Quantity zero. - - - Data not available.

[1]Data are shown for Bureau of Economic Analysis (BEA) regions that are constructed to show economically interdependent states. These BEA geographic regions differ from Bureau of the Census geographic regions and divisions shown in some *Health, United States* tables. See Appendix II, Geographic region and division.

[2]HMOs in Guam are included starting in 1994; HMOs in Puerto Rico, starting in 1998. In 2004 HMO enrollment in Guam was 28,000 and in Puerto Rico, 1,618,000.

[3]Data for District of Columbia (DC) not included for 1980–96 because data not adjusted for high proportion of enrollees of DC-based HMOs living in Maryland and Virginia. [4]Includes partial enrollment for five plans serving the District of Columbia.

NOTES: 1980–90 are for pure HMO enrollment at midyear. Starting in 1994 data are for pure and open-ended enrollment as of January 1. In 1990 open-ended enrollment accounted for 3 percent of HMO enrollment compared with 10 percent in 2004. See Appendix II, Health maintenance organization. Data for additional years are available. See Appendix III.

SOURCE: InterStudy National Health Maintenance Organization Census. The InterStudy Edge, Managed care: A decade in review 1980–1990. The InterStudy Competitive Edge, Part II Managed Care Industry Report, 1995–2004. St. Paul, Minnesota (Copyrights 1991, 1995–2004: Used with the permission of InterStudy).

Table 156. Persons without health insurance coverage by State: United States, average annual 1995–97, 1998–2000, and 2001–03

[Data are based on household interviews of a sample of the civilian noninstitutionalized population]

Geographic region and State[1]	*1995–97*	*1998–2000*	*2001–03*
		Percent of population	
United States	15.7	14.4	15.1
New England:			
Connecticut	10.6	9.5	10.4
Maine	13.5	11.5	10.7
Massachusetts	12.0	9.2	9.6
New Hampshire	10.4	8.6	9.9
Rhode Island	11.0	6.9	9.3
Vermont	11.3	10.3	9.9
Mideast:			
Delaware	14.1	11.2	10.1
District of Columbia	16.1	14.5	13.3
Maryland	13.4	11.9	13.2
New Jersey	15.8	12.9	13.7
New York	16.6	15.3	15.5
Pennsylvania	9.8	8.3	10.7
Great Lakes:			
Illinois	11.6	13.3	14.0
Indiana	11.5	11.3	12.9
Michigan	10.1	10.6	11.0
Ohio	11.6	10.2	11.7
Wisconsin	7.9	9.3	9.5
Plains:			
Iowa	11.6	8.2	9.5
Kansas	11.8	11.0	10.9
Minnesota	9.1	8.2	8.2
Missouri	13.5	9.0	10.9
Nebraska	10.4	9.5	10.3
North Dakota	11.1	12.1	10.5
South Dakota	10.2	12.0	11.0
Southeast:			
Alabama	14.0	14.2	13.3
Arkansas	21.3	15.3	16.6
Florida	18.9	17.2	17.6
Georgia	17.8	15.2	16.4
Kentucky	15.0	13.1	13.3
Louisiana	18.8	19.5	19.4
Mississippi	19.4	15.7	17.0
North Carolina	15.3	13.7	16.1
South Carolina	16.2	13.8	13.1
Tennessee	14.5	10.8	11.8
Virginia	12.9	12.9	12.5
West Virginia	15.8	15.2	14.8
Southwest:			
Arizona	23.0	19.5	17.3
New Mexico	23.5	22.6	21.3
Oklahoma	18.0	17.7	18.7
Texas	24.4	22.2	24.6
Rocky Mountains:			
Colorado	15.5	14.1	16.3
Idaho	16.1	16.5	17.5
Montana	15.3	18.3	16.1
Utah	12.4	13.2	13.6
Wyoming	15.0	15.1	16.5
Far West:			
Alaska	14.7	18.1	17.8
California	20.7	19.2	18.7
Hawaii	8.3	9.8	9.9
Nevada	17.3	17.5	18.3
Oregon	13.7	13.7	14.8
Washington	12.4	12.8	14.3

[1]Data are shown for Bureau of Economic Analysis (BEA) regions that are constructed to show economically interdependent States. These BEA geographic regions differ from Bureau of the Census geographic divisions shown in some *Health, United States* tables. See Appendix II, Geographic region and division.

NOTES: Methodology and sample size changed in 1999 and 2000. Beginning with data for 1997, people with no coverage other than access to the Indian Health Service are no longer considered covered by health insurance. The effect of this change on the number uninsured is negligible. Starting in 1999 estimates reflect the results of follow-up verification questions and implementation of Census 2000-based population controls. In 1999 the use of verification questions decreased the percent uninsured by 1.2 percentage points. See Appendix I, Current Population Survey.

SOURCES: U.S. Bureau of the Census, Current Population Survey, Bennefield RL. Health Insurance Coverage: 1997; Mills RJ. Health Insurance Coverage: 2000; DeNavas-Walt C, Proctor BD, and Mills RJ. Income, Poverty, and Health Insurance Coverage in the United States: 2003. Current population reports, series P–60 nos 202; 215; 226. Washington, DC: U.S. Government Printing Office, 2004. Available at www.census.gov/hhes/www/hlthins/reports.html.

Appendixes

Appendix Contents

Appendix II Tables

Appendix II Figures

Appendix I

Data Sources

This report consolidates the most current data on the health of the population of the United States, the availability and use of health resources, and health care expenditures. Information was obtained from data files and published reports of many Federal Government and private and global agencies and organizations. In each case, the sponsoring agency or organization collected data using its own methods and procedures. Therefore, data in this report vary considerably with respect to source, method of collection, definitions, and reference period.

Although a detailed description and comprehensive evaluation of each data source are beyond the scope of this Appendix, users should be aware of the general strengths and weaknesses of the different data collection systems. For example, population-based surveys obtain socioeconomic data, data on family characteristics, and information on the impact of an illness, such as days lost from work or limitation of activity. These data are limited by the amount of information a respondent remembers or is willing to report. A respondent may not know detailed medical information, such as precise diagnoses or the types of operations performed, and therefore cannot report it. In contrast, record-based surveys, which collect data from physician and hospital records, usually have good diagnostic information but little or no information about the socioeconomic characteristics of individuals or the impact of illnesses on individuals.

The populations covered by different data collection systems may not be the same, and understanding the differences is critical to interpreting the data. Data on vital statistics and national expenditures cover the entire population. Most data on morbidity and utilization of health resources cover only the civilian noninstitutionalized population. Such statistics may not include data for military personnel, who are usually young; for institutionalized people, who may be any age; or for nursing home residents, who are usually old.

All data collection systems are subject to error, and records may be incomplete or contain inaccurate information. Respondents may not remember essential information, a question may not mean the same thing to different respondents, and some institutions or individuals may not respond at all. It is not always possible to measure the magnitude of these errors or their effect on the data. Where possible, table notes describe the universe and method of data collection to assist users in evaluating data quality.

Some information is collected in more than one survey, and estimates of the same statistic may vary among surveys because of different survey methodologies, sampling frames, questionnaires, definitions, and tabulation categories. For example, cigarette use is measured by the National Health Interview Survey, the National Survey on Drug Use & Health, the Monitoring the Future Survey, and the Youth Risk Behavior Survey, all of which use slightly different questions of persons of differing ages and interview in different settings (at school compared with at home), so estimates will differ.

Overall estimates generally have relatively small sampling errors, but estimates for certain population subgroups may be based on small numbers and have relatively large sampling errors. Numbers of births and deaths from the vital statistics system represent complete counts (except for births in those States where data are based on a 50-percent sample for certain years). Therefore, they are not subject to sampling error. However, when the figures are used for analytical purposes, such as the comparison of rates over a period, the number of events that actually occurred may be considered as one of a large series of possible results that could have arisen under the same circumstances. When the number of events is small and the probability of such an event is rare, estimates may be unstable and considerable caution must be observed in interpreting the statistics. Estimates that are unreliable because of large sampling errors or small numbers of events are noted with asterisks in selected tables. The criteria used to designate unreliable estimates are indicated in notes to the applicable tables.

Government data sources are listed alphabetically by data set name; private and global sources are listed separately. To the extent possible, government data systems are described using a standard format. "Overview" is a brief, general statement about the purpose or objectives of the data system. "Selected Content" lists major data elements that are collected or estimated using interpolation or modeling. "Data Years" gives the years that the survey or data system has existed or been fielded. "Coverage" describes the population that the data system represents; for example, residents of the United States, the noninstitutionalized population, persons in specific population groups, or other entities that comprise the survey. The "Methodology" section presents a short description of methods used to collect data. "Sample Size and Response Rates" are given for surveys. "Issues Affecting Interpretation" describes major changes in the data collection methodology or other factors that must be considered when analyzing trends—for example, a major survey redesign that may introduce a discontinuity in the trend. For more information about the methodology, data files, and history of a data source, consult the "References" and Web sites at the end of each summary. For more information about private and global organizations' data sources, refer to the organization's Web sites.

Government Sources

Abortion Surveillance

Centers for Disease Control and Prevention National Center for Chronic Disease Prevention and Health Promotion

Overview: The abortion surveillance program documents the number and characteristics of women obtaining legal induced abortions, monitors unintended pregnancy, and assists efforts to identify and reduce preventable causes of morbidity and mortality associated with abortions.

Selected Content: Content includes age, race/ethnicity, marital status, previous live births, period of gestation, and previous induced abortions of women obtaining legal induced abortions.

Data Years: Between 1973 and 1997, the number of abortions is based on reporting from 52 reporting areas: 50 States, the District of Columbia, and New York City. In 1998 and 1999, the Centers for Disease Control and Prevention (CDC) compiled abortion data from 48 reporting areas: Alaska, California, New Hampshire, and Oklahoma did not report, and data for these areas were not estimated. In 2000 and 2001, Oklahoma again reported these data, increasing the number of reporting areas to 49.

Coverage: The system includes women of all ages, including adolescents, who obtain legal induced abortions.

Methodology: Beginning with data year 2000, data concerning the number and characteristics of women who obtain legal induced abortions are provided for 49 reporting areas by central health agencies, such as State health departments and the health departments of New York City and the District of Columbia and by hospitals and other medical facilities. In general, the procedures are reported by the State in which the procedure is performed (i.e., State of occurrence). In 2000, three States (Delaware, Maryland, and Wisconsin) reported characteristics only for women who were residents and who obtained abortions in the State. One State (Iowa) provided numbers and characteristics only for State residents. While the total number of legal induced abortions is available for those 49 reporting areas, not all areas collect information on the characteristics of women who obtain abortions. The number of areas reporting each characteristic and the number of areas with complete data for each characteristic vary from year to year. For example, in 2000, the number of areas reporting different characteristics ranged from 26 areas reporting Hispanic ethnicity and 37 areas reporting race and marital status to 47 areas reporting age. Data from reporting areas with more than 15 percent unknown for a given characteristic are excluded from the analysis of that characteristic.

Issues Affecting Interpretation: Between 1989 and 1997, the total number of abortions reported to CDC was about 10 percent less than the total estimated independently by the Alan Guttmacher Institute (AGI), a not-for-profit organization for reproductive health research, policy analysis, and public education. In 1998–99, the total number of abortions reported to CDC was about 33 percent less than the total estimated by AGI. The four reporting areas (the largest of which was California) that did not report abortions to CDC in 1998 accounted for 18 percent of all abortions tallied by AGI's 1995–96 survey. See Appendix I, *Alan Guttmacher Institute Abortion Provider Survey*.

Reference:

Centers for Disease Control and Prevention, CDC Surveillance Summaries, November 26, 2004. MMWR 2004; 53(SS09);1–32, Abortion Surveillance—United States, 2001.

For More Information: See the NCCDPHP surveillance and research Web site at http://www.cdc.gov/reproductivehealth/Data_Stats/index.htm.

AIDS Surveillance

Centers for Disease Control and Prevention National Center for HIV, STD, and TB Prevention

Overview: Acquired immunodeficiency syndrome (AIDS) surveillance data are used to detect and monitor cases of human immunodeficiency virus (HIV) disease and AIDS in the United States, identify epidemiologic trends, identify unusual cases requiring follow-up, and inform public health efforts to prevent and control the disease.

Selected Content: Data collected on cases diagnosed with AIDS include age, sex, race/ethnicity, mode of exposure, and geographic region.

Data Years: Reports on AIDS cases are available from the beginning of the epidemic in 1981.

Coverage: All 50 States, the District of Columbia, U.S. dependencies and possessions, and independent nations in free association with the United States report AIDS cases to CDC using a uniform surveillance case definition and case report form.

Methodology: AIDS surveillance is conducted by health departments in each State or territory and the District of Columbia. Although surveillance activities range from passive to active, most areas employ multifaceted active surveillance programs, which include four major reporting sources of AIDS information: hospitals and hospital-based physicians, physicians in nonhospital practice, public and private clinics, and medical record systems (death certificates, tumor registries, hospital discharge abstracts, and communicable disease reports). Using a standard confidential case report form, the health departments collect information that is then transmitted electronically without personal identifiers to CDC.

Adjustments of the estimated data on HIV infection (not AIDS) and on AIDS to account for reporting delays are calculated by a maximum likelihood statistical procedure that takes into account the differences in reporting delays among exposure, geographic, racial/ethnic, age, sex, and vital status categories and is based on the assumption that reporting delays in these categories have not changed over time. AIDS surveillance data are provisional and are updated annually.

Issues Affecting Interpretation: Although completeness of reporting of AIDS cases to State and local health departments differs by geographic region and patient population, studies conducted by State and local health departments indicate that the reporting of AIDS cases in most areas of the United States is more than 85 percent complete. To assess trends in AIDS cases, deaths, and prevalence, it is preferable to use case data adjusted for reporting delays and presented by year of diagnosis instead of straight counts of cases presented by year of report.

The original definition of AIDS was modified in 1985 and 1987. The case definition for adults and adolescents was modified again in 1993. The revisions incorporated a broader range of AIDS-indicator diseases and conditions and used HIV diagnostic tests to improve the sensitivity and specificity of the definition. Laboratory and diagnostic criteria for the 1987 pediatric case definition were updated in 1994. Effective January 2000, the surveillance case definition for HIV infection was revised to reflect advances in laboratory HIV virologic tests. The definition incorporates the reporting criteria for HIV infection and AIDS into a single case definition for adults and children.

Decreases in AIDS incidence and in the number of AIDS deaths, first noted in 1996, have been ascribed to the effect of new treatments, which prevent or delay the onset of AIDS and premature death among HIV-infected persons and result in an increase in the number of persons living with HIV and AIDS. A growing number of States require confidential reporting of persons with HIV infection and participate in CDC's integrated HIV/AIDS surveillance system that compiles information on the population of persons newly diagnosed and living with HIV infection.

Reference:

Centers for Disease Control and Prevention, HIV/AIDS Surveillance Report, published annually at www.cdc.gov/hiv/stats/hasrlink.htm.

For More Information: See the NCHSTP Web site at www.cdc.gov/nchstp/od/nchstp.html.

Census of Fatal Occupational Injuries (CFOI)

Bureau of Labor Statistics

Overview: The Census of Fatal Occupational Injuries (CFOI) compiles comprehensive and timely information on fatal work injuries occurring in the 50 States and the District of

Columbia to monitor workplace safety and to inform private and public health efforts to improve workplace safety.

Selected Content: Information is collected about each workplace fatality, including occupation and other worker characteristics, equipment involved, and circumstances of the event.

Data Years: Data have been collected annually since 1992.

Coverage: The data cover all 50 States and the District of Columbia.

Methodology: CFOI is administered by the Bureau of Labor Statistics (BLS) in conjunction with participating State agencies to compile counts that are as complete as possible to identify, verify, and profile fatal work injuries. Key information about each workplace fatality (occupation and other worker characteristics, equipment or machinery involved, and circumstances of the event) is obtained by cross-referencing source records. For a fatality to be included in the census, the decedent must have been employed (that is, working for pay, compensation, or profit) at the time of the event, engaged in a legal work activity, or present at the site of the incident as a requirement of his or her job. These criteria are generally broader than those used by Federal and State agencies administering specific laws and regulations. Fatalities that occur during a person's commute to or from work are excluded from the census counts.

Data for the CFOI are compiled from various Federal, State, and local administrative sources—including death certificates, workers' compensation reports and claims, reports to various regulatory agencies, medical examiner reports, and police reports—as well as news reports. Diverse sources are used because studies have shown that no single source captures all job-related fatalities. Source documents are matched so that each fatality is counted only once. To ensure that a fatality occurred while the decedent was at work, information is verified from two or more independent source documents or from a source document and a follow-up questionnaire.

Issues Affecting Interpretation: The number of occupational fatalities and fatality rates are periodically revised. States have up to 1 year to update their initial published State counts. States may identify additional fatal work injuries after data collection closeout for a reference year. In addition, other fatalities excluded from the published count because of insufficient information to determine work relationship may subsequently be verified as work related. Increases in the published counts based on additional information have averaged less than 100 fatalities per year, or less than 1.5 percent of the total.

Beginning with the 2003 data year, CFOI began using the 2002 North American Industry Classification System (NAICS) to classify industries. Prior to 2003, the program used the Standard Industrial Classification (SIC) system and the Census Bureau occupational classification system. Although some titles in SIC and NAICS are similar, there is limited compatibility between the two systems because the industry groupings are defined differently. See Appendix II, *Industry of employment.*

Reference:

Bureau of Labor Statistics. National Census of Fatal Occupational Injuries in 2003. Washington, DC: U.S. Department of Labor, September 2004.

For More Information: See the CFOI Web site at www.bls.gov/iif/oshcfoi1.htm.

Consumer Price Index (CPI)

Bureau of Labor Statistics

Overview: The Consumer Price Index (CPI) is designed to produce a monthly measure of the average change in the prices paid by urban consumers for a fixed market basket of goods and services.

Selected Content: Price indexes are available for the United States, the four census regions, size of city, cross-classifications of regions and size-classes, and 26 local areas. Indexes are available for major groups of consumer expenditures (food and beverages, housing, apparel, transportation, medical care, recreation, education and communications, and other goods and services), for items within each group, and for special categories, such as services. Monthly indexes are available for the United States, the four census regions, and some local areas. More detailed item indexes are available for the United States than for regions and local areas. Indexes are available for two population groups: a CPI for All Urban Consumers (CPI-U), which covers approximately 87 percent of the total population, and a CPI for Urban Wage Earners and Clerical Workers (CPI-W), which covers 32 percent of the population.

Data Years: The index has been constructed annually since 1978.

Coverage: The all-urban index (CPI-U) introduced in 1978 covers residents of metropolitan areas as well as residents of urban parts of nonmetropolitan areas (about 87 percent of the U.S. population in 2000).

Methodology: In calculating the index, price changes for the various items in each location were averaged together with weights that represent their importance in the spending of all urban consumers. Local data were then combined to obtain a U.S. city average.

The index measures price changes from a designated reference date, 1982–84, which equals 100. An increase of 22 percent, for example, is shown as 122. Change can also be expressed in dollars as follows: the price of a base period "market basket" of goods and services bought by all urban consumers has risen from $100 in 1982–84 to $184 in 2003.

The current revision of the CPI, completed in 2000, reflects spending patterns based on the Survey of Consumer Expenditures from 1993 to 1995, the 1990 Census of Population, and the ongoing Point-of-Purchase Survey. Using an improved sample design, prices for the goods and services required to calculate the index are collected in urban areas throughout the country and from retail and service establishments. Data on rents are collected from tenants of rented housing and residents of owner-occupied housing units. Food, fuels, and other goods and services are priced monthly in urban locations. Price information is obtained through visits or calls by trained BLS field representatives using computer-assisted telephone interviews.

Issues Affecting Interpretation: A 1987 revision changed the treatment of health insurance in the cost-weight definitions for medical care items. This change has no effect on the overall index result but provides a clearer picture of the role of health insurance in the CPI. As part of the revision, three new indexes have been created by separating previously combined items, for example, eye care is separated from other professional services, and inpatient and outpatient treatment is separated from other hospital and medical care services.

Effective January 1997, the hospital index was restructured by combining the three categories—room, inpatient services, and outpatient services—into one category: hospital services. In addition, new procedures for hospital data collection identify a payor, diagnosis, and the payor's reimbursement arrangement from selected hospital bills.

References:

Bureau of Labor Statistics. Handbook of Methods. BLS Bulletin 2490. Washington, DC: U.S. Department of Labor. April 1997; Revising the Consumer Price Index, Monthly Labor Review, Dec 1996.

Ford IK, Ginsburg DH. "Medical Care in the Consumer Price Index," in Medical Care Output and Productivity Studies in Income and Wealth, vol 62, Cutler DM, Berndt ER, eds., Chicago: University of Chicago Press, pp. 203–19, 2001.

For More Information: See the BLS/CPI Web site at www.bls.gov/cpi/home.htm.

Current Population Survey (CPS)

Census Bureau Bureau of Labor Statistics

Overview: The Current Population Survey (CPS) provides current estimates and trends in employment, unemployment, and other characteristics of the general labor force, the population as a whole, and various population subgroups.

Selected Content: Estimates of poverty and health insurance coverage presented in *Health, United States* from the CPS are derived from the Annual Social and Economic Supplement (ASEC), formerly called the Annual Demographic Supplement (ADS), or simply the "March Supplement." The ASEC includes a series of questions asked each March in addition to core CPS questions. Information is gathered on more than 50 different sources of income, including noncash income sources such as food stamps, school lunch program, employer-provided group health insurance plan, employer-provided pension plan, personal health insurance, Medicaid, Medicare, CHAMPUS or military health care, and energy assistance. Comprehensive work experience information is given on the employment status, occupation, and industry of persons interviewed.

Data Years: The basic CPS has been conducted since 1945, although some data were collected prior to that time. Collection of income data began in 1948.

Coverage: The CPS sample is located in 754 sample areas, with coverage in every State and the District of Columbia.

The adult universe (i.e., population of marriageable age) is composed of persons 15 years of age and over in the civilian noninstitutionalized population for CPS labor force data. The sample for the March CPS supplement is expanded to include members of the Armed Forces who are living in civilian housing or with their family on a military base, as well as additional Hispanic households that are not included in the monthly labor force estimates.

Methodology: The basic CPS sample is selected from multiple frames using multiple stages of selection. Each unit is selected with a known probability to represent similar units in the universe. The sample design is a State-based design, with the sample in each State being independent of the others.

The additional Hispanic sample is from the previous November's basic CPS sample. If a person is identified as being of Hispanic origin from the November interview and is still residing at the same address in March, that housing unit is eligible for the March survey. This amounts to a near doubling of the Hispanic sample since there is no overlap of housing units between the basic CPS samples in November and March.

For all CPS data files a single weight is prepared and used to compute the monthly labor force status estimates. An additional weight was prepared for the earnings universe that roughly corresponds to wage and salary workers in the two outgoing rotations. The difference in content of the March CPS supplement requires the presentation of additional weights: a household weight, a family weight, and a March supplement weight. The final weight is the product of (1) the basic weight, (2) adjustments for special weighting, (3) noninterview adjustment, (4) first stage ratio adjustment factor, and (5) second-stage ratio adjustment factor. This final weight should be used when producing estimates from the basic CPS data. Differences in the questionnaire, sample, and data uses for the March CPS supplement result in the need for additional adjustment procedures to produce what is called the March supplement weight.

Sample Size and Response Rate: Beginning with 2001, the State Children's Health Insurance Program (SCHIP) sample expansion was introduced. This included an increase in the basic CPS sample to 60,000 households per month. Prior to 2001 estimates were based on 50,000 households per month. The expansion also included an additional 12,000 households that were allocated differentially across States, based on prior information of the number of uninsured children in each State, to produce statistically reliable current State data on the number of low-income children who do not have health insurance coverage. In an average month, the nonresponse rate for the basic CPS is about 6–7 percent.

Issues Affecting Interpretation: Over the years, the number of income questions has expanded, questions on work experience and other characteristics have been added, and the month of interview was moved to March.

In 1994, major changes were introduced, which included a complete redesign of the questionnaire including new health insurance questions and the introduction of computer-assisted interviewing for the entire survey. In addition, there were revisions to some of the labor force concepts and definitions. Prior to the redesign, CPS data were primarily collected using a paper-and-pencil form. Beginning in 1994, population controls were based on the 1990 census and adjusted for the estimated population undercount. Starting with *Health, United States, 2003*, poverty estimates for data years 2000 and beyond were recalculated based on the expanded SCHIP sample, and census 2000-based population controls were implemented. Beginning with 2002 data, 1997 race standards were implemented in which people could report more than one race.

Reference:

U.S. Census Bureau. Technical Paper 63RV. Current Population Survey: Design and Methodology. TP63RV, March 2002 found at www.census.gov/prod/2002pubs/tp63rv.pdf.

For More Information: See the CPS Web site at www.bls.census.gov/cps/cpsmain.htm.

Department of Veterans Affairs National Patient Care Database and National Enrollment Database

Department of Veterans Affairs

Overview: The Department of Veterans Affairs (VA) compiles and analyzes multiple data sets on the health and health care of its clients and other veterans to monitor access and quality of care and to conduct program and policy evaluations.

Selected Content: VA maintains the National Patient Care Database (NPCD) and the National Enrollment Database (NED).

The NPCD is a nationwide system that contains a statistical record for each episode of care provided under VA auspices in VA and non-VA hospitals, nursing homes, VA residential rehabilitation treatment programs (formerly called domiciliaries), and VA outpatient clinics. Three major extracts from the NPCD are the patient treatment file (PTF), the patient census file (PCF), and the outpatient clinic file (OPC).

The PTF collects data at the time of the patient's discharge on each episode of inpatient care provided to patients at VA hospitals, VA nursing homes, VA residential rehabilitation treatment programs, community nursing homes, and other non-VA facilities. The PTF record contains the scrambled social security number (SSN), dates of inpatient treatment, date of birth, State and county of residence, type of disposition, place of disposition after discharge, and ICD–9–CM diagnostic and procedure or operative codes for each episode of care.

The PCF collects data on each patient remaining in a VA medical facility at midnight at the end of each quarter of the fiscal year. The census record includes information similar to that reported in the PTF record.

The outpatient clinic file (OPC) collects data on each instance of medical treatment provided to a veteran in an outpatient setting. The OPC record includes the age, scrambled social security number, State and county of residence, VA eligibility code, clinic(s) visited, purpose of visit, and date of visit for each episode of care.

The VA also maintains the National Enrollment Database (NED) as the official repository of enrollment information for each veteran enrolled in the VA health care system.

Coverage: U.S. veterans who receive services within the VA medical system are included. Data are available for some nonveterans who receive care at VA facilities.

Methodology: NPCD is the source data for the Veterans Health Administration (VHA) Medical SAS Datasets. NPCD is the VHA's centralized relational database (a data warehouse) that receives encounter data from VHA clinical information systems. It is updated daily. Data are collected locally at each VA medical center and are transmitted electronically to the VA Austin Automation Center for use in providing nationwide statistics, reports, and comparisons.

In all of the medical data sets, each patient has a unique identifier, which is a formula-based encryption of the individual's SSN. The identifier is consistent for a given patient across data sets and fiscal years. An extract containing selected information from the NPCD, the NED, and the cost distribution system is produced by the Austin Automation Center.

Issues Affecting Interpretation: The databases include users of the VA health care system. VA eligibility is a hierarchy based on service-connected disabilities, income, age, and availability of services. Therefore, different VA programs may serve populations with different sociodemographic characteristics than other health care systems.

For More Information: See the VHA Information Systems Web site at www.virec.research.med.va.gov/Support/Training-newUsersToolkit/IntroToVAData.htm.

Employee Benefits Survey—See National Compensation Survey

Medicaid Data System

Centers for Medicare & Medicaid Services

Overview: The Centers for Medicare & Medicaid Services (CMS) works with its State partners to collect data on persons served by the Medicaid program to monitor and evaluate access and quality of care, trends in program eligibility, characteristics of enrollees, changes in payment policy, and other program-related issues.

Selected Content: Data collected include medical vendor payments for Medicaid recipients by type of service and information on the characteristics of Medicaid recipients, including race/ethnicity, age, and basis of eligibility.

Data Years: Selected State data are available from 1992 on. Data for the 50 States and the District of Columbia are available from 1999 on.

Coverage: The data include individuals enrolled in the Medicaid program or receiving Medicaid benefits.

Methodology: The primary data sources for Medicaid statistical data are the Medicaid Statistical Information System (MSIS) and the CMS-64 reports.

MSIS is the basic source of State-reported eligibility and claims data on the Medicaid population, and their characteristics, utilization, and payments. Beginning in FY 1999, as a result of legislation enacted from the Balanced Budget Act of 1997, States are required to submit individual eligibility and claims data tapes to CMS quarterly through MSIS. Prior to FY 1999, States were required to submit an annual HCFA-2082 report, designed to collect aggregated statistical data on eligibles, recipients, services, and expenditures during a Federal fiscal year (October 1 through September 30). The data reported for each year represented people on the Medicaid rolls, recipients of Medicaid services, and payments for claims adjudicated during the year. The data reflected bills adjudicated or processed during the year, rather than services used during the year. States summarized and reported the data processed through their own Medicaid claims processing and payment operations, unless they opted to participate in MSIS, in which case the HCFA-2082 report was produced by the Health Care Financing Administration (the predecessor to CMS).

The CMS-64 is a product of the financial budget and grant system. The CMS-64 is a statement of expenditures for the Medicaid program that States submit to CMS 30 days after each quarter. The report is an accounting statement of actual expenditures made by the States for which they are entitled to receive Federal reimbursement under title XIX for that quarter. The amount claimed on the CMS-64 is a summary of expenditures derived from source documents, such as invoices, cost reports, and eligibility records.

The CMS-64 shows the disposition of Medicaid grant funds for the quarter being reported and previous years, the recoupments made or refunds received, and income earned on grant funds. The data on the CMS-64 are used to reconcile the monetary advance made on the basis of States' funding estimates filed prior to the beginning of the quarter on the CMS-37. As such, the CMS-64 is the primary source for making adjustments for any identified overpayments and underpayments to the States. Also incorporated into this process are disallowance actions forwarded from other Federal financial adjustments. Finally, the CMS-64 provides information that forms the basis for a series of Medicaid financial reports and budget analyses. Also included are third party liability (TPL) collections tables. TPL refers to the legal obligation of certain health care sources to pay the medical claims of Medicaid recipients before Medicaid pays these claims. Medicaid pays only after the TPL sources have met their legal obligation to pay.

Issues Affecting Interpretation: Health, United States Medicaid tables are based on MSIS data. Users of Medicaid data may note apparent inconsistencies in Medicaid data that are primarily due to the difference in information captured in MSIS versus CMS-64 reports. The most substantive difference is due to payments made to "disproportionate share hospitals." Payments to disproportionate share hospitals do not appear in MSIS because States directly reimburse these hospitals and there is no fee-for-service billing. Other less significant differences between MSIS and CMS-64 occur because adjudicated claims data are used in MSIS versus actual payments reflected in the CMS-64. Differences also may occur because of internal State practices for capturing and reporting these data through two separate systems. Finally, national totals for the CMS-64 are different because they include other jurisdictions, such as the Northern Mariana Islands and American Samoa.

For More Information: See the CMS Web site at http://www.cms.hhs.gov/medicaid/ or the Research Data Assistance Center (ResDAC) Web site at www.resdac.umn.edu/medicaid/data_available.asp. Also see Appendix II, *Medicaid.*

Medical Expenditure Panel Survey (MEPS)

Agency for Healthcare Research and Quality

Overview: The Medical Expenditure Panel Survey (MEPS) produces nationally representative estimates of health care use, expenditures, sources of payment, insurance coverage, and quality of care for the U.S. civilian noninstitutionalized population.

Selected Content: MEPS data in *Health, United States* include total health care expenses and prescribed medicine expenses, presented by sociodemographic characteristics, type of health insurance, and sources of payment.

Data Years: The 1977 National Medical Care Expenditure Survey and the 1987 National Medical Expenditure Survey (NMES) are earlier versions of this survey. Since 1996, MEPS has been conducted on an annual basis.

Coverage: U.S. civilian noninstitutionalized population is the primary population represented. The 1987 and 1996 surveys also had an institutionalized population component.

Methodology: MEPS is a national probability survey conducted on an annual basis since 1996. The panel design of the survey features several rounds of interviewing covering 2 full calendar years. The MEPS consists of three components: the Household Component (HC), the Medical Provider Component (MPC), and the Insurance Component (IC).

The HC is a nationally representative survey of the civilian noninstitutionalized population drawn from a subsample of households that participated in the prior year's National Health Interview Survey conducted by the National Center for Health Statistics. Missing expenditure data are imputed using data collected in the MPC whenever possible.

Data are collected in MPC to improve the accuracy of expenditure estimates derived solely from the HC. The MPC is particularly useful in obtaining expenditure information for persons enrolled in managed care plans and Medicaid recipients. The MPC collects data from hospitals, physicians, and home health providers that were reported in the HC as providing care to MEPS sample persons. Sample sizes for the MPC vary from year to year depending on the HC sample size and the MPC sampling rates for providers.

The IC consists of two subcomponent samples: a household sample and list sample. The household sample collects detailed information from employers on the health insurance held by and offered to respondents to the MEPS-HC. The list sample collects data on the types and costs of workplace health insurance from a total of about 40,000 business establishments and governments each year.

The MEPS updates the 1987 NMES. The NMES consists of two components: the Household Survey (HS) and the Medical Provider Survey (MPS). The NMES-HS Component was designed to provide nationally representative estimates of health insurance status, health insurance coverage, and health care use for the U.S. civilian noninstitutionalized population for the calendar year 1987. Data from the NMES-MPS component were used in conjunction with HS data to produce estimates of health care expenditures. The NMES-HS consisted of four rounds of household interviews. Income was collected in a special supplement administered early in 1988. Events under the scope of the NMES-MPS included medical services provided by or under the direction of a physician, all hospital events, and home health care. The sample of events included in the NMES-MPS was all events for persons covered by Medicaid and for a 25 percent sample of NMES-HS respondents. Missing expenditure data were imputed.

Sample Size and Response Rate: For MEPS first core household interview, 17,500 households were selected. The sample sizes for the MEPS-HC are approximately 10,000 families in 1996 and 1998–2000, 13,500 families in 1997 and 2001, and 15,000 families annually beginning in 2002. The full-year household core response rate has generally been about 66 percent. The 12-month joint core questionnaire/ health questionnaire/access supplement response rate for the household component of the NMES was 80 percent.

Issues Affecting Interpretation: The 1987 estimates are based on the NMES, and 1996 and later years estimates are based on the MEPS. Because expenditures in NMES were based primarily on charges while those for MEPS were based on payments, data for NMES were adjusted to be more comparable to MEPS using estimated charge-to-payment ratios for 1987. For a detailed explanation of this adjustment, see Zuvekas and Cohen, 2002.

References:

Hahn B, Lefkowitz D. Annual expenses and sources of payment for health care services (AHRQ pub no 93–0007). National Medical Expenditure Survey Research Findings 14, Agency for Healthcare Research and Quality pub no 93–0007. Rockville, MD: Public Health Service, November 1992.

Cohen SB. Sample design of the 1997 Medical Expenditure Panel Survey Household Component. MEPS Methodology Report No. 11. AHRQ pub no. 01–0001. Rockville MD: Agency for Healthcare Research and Quality. 2000.

Zuvekas S, Cohen S. A guide to comparing health care estimates in the 1996 Medical Expenditure Panel Survey to the 1987 National Medical Expenditure Survey. Inquiry; 39(1):76–86. 2002.

For More Information: See the MEPS Web site at www.meps.ahrq.gov.

Medicare Administrative Data

Centers for Medicare & Medicaid Services

Overview: The Centers for Medicare & Medicaid Services (CMS) collects and synthesizes Medicare enrollment, spending, and claims data to monitor and evaluate access to and quality of care, trends in utilization, changes in payment policy, and other program-related issues.

Selected Content: Data include claims information for services furnished to Medicare beneficiaries and Medicare enrollment data. Claims data include type of service, procedures, diagnoses, dates of service, and claim amount. Enrollment data include date of birth, sex, race/ethnicity, and reason for entitlement.

Data Years: Some data files are available as far back as 1987, but CMS no longer provides technical support for files with data prior to 1996.

Coverage: Enrollment data are for all persons enrolled in the Medicare program. Claims data include data for Medicare beneficiaries who filed claims.

Methodology: The claims and utilization data files contain extensive utilization information at various levels of summarization for a variety of providers and services. There are many types and levels of these files, including the National Claims History (NCH) files, the Standard Analytic Files (SAF), Medicare Provider and Analysis Review (MedPAR) files, Medicare enrollment files, and various other files.

The National Claims History (NCH) 100 Percent Nearline File contains all institutional and noninstitutional claims and provides records of every Medicare claim submitted, including adjustment claims. The Standard Analytical Files (SAFs) contain final action claims data in which all adjustments have been resolved. These files contain information collected by Medicare to pay for health care services provided to a Medicare beneficiary. SAFs are available for each institutional (inpatient, outpatient, skilled nursing facility, hospice, or home health agency) and noninstitutional (physician and durable medical equipment providers) claim type. The record unit of SAFs is the claim (some episodes of care may have more than one claim). SAF files include the Inpatient SAF, the Skilled Nursing Facility SAF, the Outpatient SAF, the Home Health Agency SAF, the Hospice SAF, the Clinical Laboratory SAF, and the Durable Medical Equipment SAF.

Medicare Provider and Analysis Review (MedPAR) files contain inpatient hospital and skilled nursing facility (SNF) final action stay records. Each MedPAR record represents a stay in an inpatient hospital or SNF. An inpatient "stay" record summarizes all services rendered to a beneficiary from the time of admission to a facility through discharge. Each MedPAR record may represent one claim or multiple claims, depending on the length of a beneficiary's stay and the amount of inpatient services used throughout the stay.

The Denominator File contains demographic and enrollment information about each beneficiary enrolled in Medicare during a calendar year. The information in the Denominator File is "frozen" in March of the following calendar year. Some of the information contained in this file includes the beneficiary unique identifier, State and county codes, ZIP code, date of birth, date of death, sex, race, age, monthly entitlement indicators (for Medicare Part A, Medicare Part B, or Part A and Part B), reasons for entitlement, State buy-in indicators, and monthly managed care indicators (yes/no). The Denominator File is used to determine beneficiary demographic characteristics, entitlement, and beneficiary participation in Medicare Managed Care Organizations.

The Vital Status File contains demographic information about each beneficiary ever entitled to Medicare. Some of the information contained in this file includes the beneficiary unique identifier, State and county codes, ZIP code, date of birth, date of death, sex, race, and age. Often the Vital Status File is used to obtain recent death information for a cohort of Medicare beneficiaries.

The Group Health Plan (GHP) Master File contains data on beneficiaries who are currently enrolled or have ever been enrolled in a Managed Care Organization (MCO) under contract with CMS. Each record represents one beneficiary, and each beneficiary has one record. Some of the information contained in this file includes the Beneficiary Unique Identifier number, date of birth, date of death, State and county, and managed care enrollment information such as dates of membership and MCO contract number. The GHP Master File is used to identify the exact MCO in which beneficiaries were enrolled.

Issues Affecting Interpretation: Because Medicare managed care programs may not file claims, files based only on claims data will exclude care for persons enrolled in Medicare managed care programs. In addition, to maintain a manageable file size, some files are based on a sample of enrollees, rather than on all Medicare enrollees. Coding changes and interpretation of Medicare coverage rules have also changed over the life of the Medicare program.

For More Information: See the CMS Research Data Assistance Center (ResDAC) Web site at http://www.resdac.umn.edu/medicare/index.asp or the CMS Web site at http://www.cms.hhs.gov/medicare/. Also see Appendix II, *Medicare*.

Medicare Current Beneficiary Survey (MCBS)

Centers for Medicare & Medicaid Services

Overview: The Medicare Current Beneficiary Survey (MCBS) produces nationally representative estimates of health status, health care use and expenditures, health insurance coverage, and socioeconomic and demographic characteristics of Medicare beneficiaries. It is used to estimate expenditures and sources of payment for all services used by Medicare beneficiaries, including co-payments, deductibles, and noncovered services; to ascertain all types of health insurance coverage and relate coverage to sources of payment; and to trace processes over time, such as changes in health status, spending down to Medicaid eligibility, and the effects of program changes.

Selected Content: The survey collects data on utilization of health services, health and functional status, health care expenditures, and health insurance and beneficiary information (such as income, assets, living arrangement, family assistance, and quality of life).

Data Years: The first round of interviewing was conducted from September through December 1991, and the survey has been continuously in the field since then. The data are designed to support both cross-sectional and longitudinal analyses.

Coverage: The MCBS is a continuous survey of a nationally representative sample of aged, institutionalized, and disabled Medicare beneficiaries.

Methodology: The longitudinal design of the survey allows each sample person to be interviewed three times a year for 4 years, whether he or she resides in the community or a facility or moves between the two settings, using the version of the questionnaire appropriate to the setting. Sample persons in the community are interviewed using computer-assisted personal interviewing (CAPI) survey instruments. Because long-term care facility residents often are in poor health, information about institutionalized patients is collected from proxy respondents, such as nurses and other primary caregivers affiliated with the facility. The sample is selected from the Medicare enrollment files, with oversampling among disabled persons under age 65 years and among persons 80 years of age and over.

Medicare claims are linked to survey-reported events to produce the Cost and Use file that provides complete expenditure and source of payment data on all health care services, including those not covered by Medicare. The Access to Care file contains information on beneficiaries' access to health care, satisfaction with care, and usual source of care. The sample for this file represents the "always enrolled" population—those who participated in the Medicare program for the entire year. In contrast, the Cost and Use file represents the "ever enrolled" population, including those who enter Medicare during the year and those who died.

Sample Size and Response Rate: Each fall, about one-third of the sample is retired and roughly 6,000 new sample persons are included in the survey—the exact number chosen is based on projections of target samples of 12,000 persons with 3 years of cost and use information distributed appropriately across the sample cells. In the community, response rates for initial interviews range in the mid- to high 80s; once respondents have completed the first interview, their participation in subsequent rounds is 95 percent or more. In recent rounds, data have been collected from approximately 15,000 to 19,000 beneficiaries, with the peaks occurring in fall rounds because of the annual and HMO samples. Roughly 90 percent of the sample is made up of persons who live in the community, with the remaining persons living in long-term care facilities. Response rates for facility interviews approach 100 percent.

Issues Affecting Interpretation: Because only Medicare enrollees are included in the survey, the survey excludes a small proportion of persons age 65 and over who are not enrolled in Medicare, which should be noted when using the MCBS to make estimates of the entire population age 65 and over in the United States.

References:

Adler GS. A profile of the Medicare Current Beneficiary Survey. Health Care Financ Rev; 15(4):153–163. 1994.

Lo A, Chu A, Apodaca R. Redesign of the Medicare Current Beneficiary Survey Sample, Rockville, MD: Westat, Inc., 2003, found at www.cms.hhs.gov/MCBS/PublBIB/Mbibl8.pdf.

For More Information: See the MCBS Web site at www.cms.hhs.gov/mcbs/default.asp.

Monitoring the Future Study (MTF)

National Institute on Drug Abuse

Overview: Monitoring the Future (MTF) is an ongoing study of the behaviors, attitudes, and values of American secondary school students, college students, and young adults.

Selected Content: Data collected include lifetime, annual, and 30-day prevalence of use of specific illegal drugs and substances, inhalants, tobacco, and alcohol. Data are also collected on usage levels, frequency of use, perceived risks associated with use, opinions about whether use is approved or disapproved by others, and opinions about availability of the substances.

Data Years: MTF has been conducted annually since 1975, initially with high school seniors; ongoing panel studies of representative samples from each graduating class have been conducted by mail since 1976; annual surveys of 8th and 10th graders were initiated in 1991.

Coverage: MTF surveys a sample of high school seniors, 10th graders, and 8th graders selected to be representative of all seniors, 10th graders, and 8th graders in public and private high schools in the continental United States.

Methodology: The survey design is a multistage random sample with stage one being selection of particular geographic areas, stage two selection of one or more schools in each area, and stage three selection of students within each school. Data are collected using self-administered questionnaires conducted in the classroom by representatives of the Institute for Social Research. Dropouts and students who are absent on the day of the survey are excluded. Recognizing that the dropout population is at higher risk for drug use, this survey was expanded to include similar nationally representative samples of 8th and 10th graders in 1991, who have lower dropout rates than seniors and include future high-risk 12th grade dropouts. Statistics that are published in the *Dropout Rates in the United States: 2001* (published by the National Center for Educational Statistics, Pub. No. NCES 2005–046) stated that, among persons 15–16 years of age, 3.9 percent have dropped out of school, 2.8 percent for persons 17 years of age, 6.6 percent for persons 18 years of age, and 8.4 percent for persons 19 years of age but dropout rates are higher for certain race and ethnic groups, notably Hispanics.

Sample Size and Response Rates: In 2004 approximately 49,500 8th, 10th, and 12th graders in 406 schools were surveyed. The annual senior samples comprised roughly 15,200 seniors in 128 public and private high schools nationwide. The 10th-grade samples involved about 16,800 students in 131 schools, and the 8th-grade samples had approximately 17,400 students in 147 schools. Response rates were 82 percent, 88 percent, and 89 percent for 12th, 10th and 8th graders and have been relatively constant across time. Absentees constitute virtually all of the nonresponding students.

Issues Affecting Interpretation: Estimates of substance use for youth based on the National Survey on Drug Use & Health (NSDUH) are not directly comparable with estimates based on the MTF and the Youth Risk Behavior Surveillance System (YRBSS). In addition to the fact that the MTF excludes dropouts and absentees, rates are not directly comparable across these surveys because of differences in populations covered, sample design, questionnaires, interview setting, and statistical approaches to make the survey estimates generalizable to the entire population. The NSDUH survey collects data in homes, whereas the MTF and YRBSS collect data in school classrooms. The NSDUH estimates are tabulated by age, while the MTF and YRBSS estimates are tabulated by grade, representing different ages as well as different populations.

References:

Johnston LD, O'Malley PM, Bachman JG, Schulenberg, JE. Monitoring the Future national results on adolescent drug use: Overview of key findings, 2004. NIH pub no 05–5726. Bethesda, MD: National Institute on Drug Abuse, 2005.

Johnston LD, O'Malley PM, Bachman JG. Monitoring the Future national survey results on drug use, 1975–2002. Vol I: Secondary school students. NIH pub no 03–5375.

Bethesda, MD: National Institute on Drug Abuse. 2003, found at http://monitoringthefuture.org/pubs/monographs/vol1_2002.pdf.

Cowan CD. Coverage, sample design, and weighting in three Federal surveys. Journal of Drug Issues; 31(3):595–614. 2001.

For More Information: See the NIDA Web site at http://www.nida.nih.gov/Infofax/HSYouthtrends.html or the Monitoring the Future Web site at www.monitoringthefuture.org/.

National Ambulatory Medical Care Survey (NAMCS)

Centers for Disease Control and Prevention National Center for Health Statistics

Overview: The National Ambulatory Medical Care Survey (NAMCS) is a national survey designed to provide information about the provision and use of medical care services in office-based physician practices in the United States.

Selected Content: Data are collected from medical records on type of providers seen; reason for visit; diagnoses; drugs ordered, provided, or continued; and selected procedures and tests ordered or performed during the visit. Patient data include age, sex, race, and expected source of payment. Data are also collected on selected characteristics of physician practices.

Data Years: The NAMCS, which began in 1973, was conducted annually until 1981, once in 1985, and resumed an annual schedule in 1989.

Coverage: The scope of the survey covers patient encounters in the offices of nonfederally employed physicians classified by the American Medical Association or American Osteopathic Association as "office-based, patient care" physicians. Patient encounters with physicians engaged in prepaid practices—health maintenance organizations (HMOs), independent practice organizations (IPAs), and other prepaid practices—are included in NAMCS. Excluded are visits to hospital-based physicians, visits to specialists in anesthesiology, pathology, and radiology, and visits to physicians who are principally engaged in teaching, research, or administration. Telephone contacts and nonoffice visits are also excluded.

Methodology: A multistage probability design is employed. The first-stage sample consisted of 84 primary sampling units (PSUs) in 1985, and beginning in 1989, 112 PSUs, which were selected from about 1,900 such units into which the United States had been divided. In each sample PSU, a sample of practicing non-Federal office-based physicians is selected from master files maintained by the American Medical Association and the American Osteopathic Association. The final stage involves systematic random samples of office visits during randomly assigned 7-day reporting periods. In 1985 the survey excluded Alaska and Hawaii. Starting in 1989, the survey included all 50 States and the District of Columbia.

The U.S. Census Bureau acts as the data collection agent for the NAMCS. Screening interviews are conducted by Census field representatives to obtain information about physicians' office-based practices and to ensure that the practice is within the scope of the survey. Field representatives visit eligible physicians prior to their participation in the survey to provide them with survey materials and instruct them on how to sample patient visits and complete "Patient Record" forms. Participants are asked to complete forms for a systematic random sample of approximately 30 office visits occurring during a randomly assigned 1-week period, but increasingly Patient Record forms are abstracted by field representatives.

Sample data are weighted to produce national estimates. The estimation procedure used in the NAMCS has three basic components: inflation by the reciprocal of the probability of selection, adjustment for nonresponse, and ratio adjustment to fixed totals.

Sample Size and Response Rate: In the 2002 survey, a sample of 3,150 physicians was selected: 2,095 were in scope and 1,492 participated for a response rate of 71 percent. Data were provided on 28,738 visits. In 2003 a sample of 3,000 physicians was selected; 2,007 were in scope and 1,407 participated for a response rate of 67 percent. Data were provided for 25,288 visits.

Issues Affecting Interpretation: The NAMCS Patient Record form is modified approximately every 2 years to reflect changes in physician practice characteristics, patterns of care, and technological innovations. Examples of recent changes include the number of drugs recorded on the Patient Record form, and checkboxes for specific tests or procedures performed. Some physician practices are out of scope (e.g., single-specialty radiology practices) which affects the generalizability of results. Sample sizes vary by survey year. For some years, it is suggested that analysts combine 2 or more years of data if they wish to examine relatively rare populations or events. In *Health, United States, 2005,* data for survey years 2001–02 were revised to be consistent with the weighting scheme introduced in the 2003 NAMCS data. For more information on the new weighting scheme, see "National Ambulatory Medical Care Survey: 2003 summary," Advance Data From Vital and Health Statistics (forthcoming).

Reference:

Woodwell DA , Cherry DK. National Ambulatory Medical Care Survey: 2002 summary. Advance data from vital and health statistics; no 346. Hyattsville, MD: National Center for Health Statistics. 2004.

For More Information: See the Ambulatory Health Care Data Web site at www.cdc.gov/nchs/about/major/ahcd/ahcd1.htm.

National Compensation Survey

Bureau of Labor Statistics

Overview: The National Compensation Survey (NCS) provides comprehensive measures of occupational earnings, compensation cost trends, benefit incidence, and detailed plan provisions.

Selected Content: Detailed occupational earnings are collected for metropolitan and nonmetropolitan areas and broad geographic regions, and on a national basis. The Employment Cost Index (ECI) and Employer Costs for Employee Compensation (ECEC) are compensation measures derived from the NCS. ECI measures changes in labor costs. Average hourly employer cost for employee compensation is presented in the ECEC. National benefits data are presented for three broad occupational groupings: professional, technical, and related; clerical and sales; and blue-collar and service employees. Data are also available by goods- and service-producing occupations, union affiliation, and full- and part-time status.

Data Years: The NCS replaces three existing BLS surveys: Employment Cost Index (ECI), Occupational Compensation Survey Program (OCSP), and Employee Benefits Survey (EBS). The ECI and EBS were fully integrated into the NCS in 1999. Prior to 1999, the EBS were collected for small private establishments (those employing fewer than 100 workers) and from State and local governments (regardless of employment size). In odd-numbered years, data were collected for medium and large private establishments (those employing 100 workers or more). The ECI was created in the mid-1970s. The EBS was added to an existing data collection effort, the National Pay Survey, in the late 1970s. The Employer Cost for Employee Compensation product was developed in 1987.

Coverage: The NCS provides information for the Nation, for 81 metropolitan areas and 73 nonmetropolitan counties representing the United States, and for the 9 census divisions (although not all areas have information for all occupations). It includes both full-time and part-time workers who are paid a wage or salary. It excludes agriculture, fishing and forestry industries, private household workers, and the Federal Government. The NCS only includes establishments with at least 50 workers.

Methodology: Conducted quarterly by The Bureau of Labor Statistics' Office of Compensation and Working Conditions, the sample for the NCS is selected using a three-stage design. The first stage involves the selection of areas. The NCS sample consists of 154 metropolitan and nonmetropolitan areas that represent the Nation's 326 metropolitan statistical areas and the remaining portions of the 50 States. In the second stage, establishments are systematically selected with probability of selection proportionate to their relative employment size within the industry. Use of this technique means that the larger an establishment's employment, the greater its chance of selection.

The third stage of sampling is a probability sample of occupations within a sampled establishment. This step is performed by the BLS field economist during an interview with the respondent establishment in which selection of an occupation is based on probability of selection proportionate to employment in the establishment. Each occupation is classified under its corresponding major occupational group using the Occupational Classification System Manual (OCSM) and the Census Occupation Index, which are based on the 1990 U.S. Census.

Data collection is conducted by BLS field economists. Data are gathered from each establishment on the primary business activity of the establishment, types of occupations, number of employees, wages and salaries and benefits, hours of work, and duties and responsibilities. Wage data obtained by occupation and work level allows NCS to publish occupational wage statistics for localities, census divisions, and the Nation.

Sample Size and Response Rates: The NCS sample consists of 154 metropolitan and nonmetropolitan areas that represent the Nation's 326 metropolitan statistical areas and the remaining portions of the 50 States. The 2003 NCS benefits incidence survey obtained data from 2,924 private industry establishments, representing nearly 103 million workers; of this number, nearly 79 million were full-time workers, and the remainder were part-time workers.

Issues Affecting Interpretation: Because the NCS merges separate surveys, trend analyses prior to 2000 should be interpreted with care. The industrial coverage, establishment size coverage, and geographic coverage for the EBS survey changed since 1990. All surveys conducted from 1979 to 1989 excluded part-time employees and establishments in Alaska and Hawaii. The surveys conducted from 1979 to 1986 covered only medium and large private establishments and excluded most of the service industries. Establishments that employed at least 50, 100, or 250 workers, depending on the industry, were included. The survey conducted in 1987 consisted of State and local governments with 50 or more employees. The surveys carried out in 1988 and 1989 included all private-sector establishments that employed 100 or more employees.

The Employer Costs for Employee Compensation (ECEC) switched to new industry and occupation classification systems with the release of the March 2004 data. The 2002 North American Industry Classification System (NAICS) is now used to classify industries and the 2000 Standard Occupational Classification (SOC) system is used to classify occupations. ECEC data by the present classification systems—the 1987 Standard Industrial Classification System (SIC) and the 1990 Occupational Classification System (OCS)—will no longer be produced. The ECEC was the first National Compensation Survey product to make this transition. For more information about this transition see http://www.bls.gov/ncs/ect/sp/ecsm0001.htm.

References:

U.S. Department of Labor, Bureau of Labor Statistics, Employer Costs for Employee Compensation Summary—March, 2004, found at www.bls.gov/news.release/ecec.nr0.htm.

The National Compensation Survey: Compensation Statistics for the 21st Century, found at www.bls.gov/opub/cwc/archive/winter2000art1.pdf.

For More Information: See the National Compensation Survey Web site at www.bls.gov/ncs.

National Health Accounts

Centers for Medicare & Medicaid Services

Overview: National Health Accounts provide estimates of how much money is spent on different types of health care-related services and programs in the United States.

Selected Content: National Health Expenditures measure spending for health care in the United States by type of service delivered (such as hospital care, physician services, nursing home care) and source of funding for those services (such as private health insurance, Medicare, Medicaid, and out-of-pocket spending).

Data Years: Expenditure estimates are available starting from 1960 in data files or in published articles.

Methodology: The American Hospital Association (AHA) data on hospital finances are the primary source for estimates relating to hospital care. The salaries of physicians and dentists on the staffs of hospitals, hospital outpatient clinics, hospital-based home health agencies, and nursing home care provided in the hospital setting are considered to be components of hospital care. Expenditures for home health care and for services of health professionals (for example, doctors, chiropractors, private duty nurses, therapists, and podiatrists) are estimated primarily using a combination of data from the U.S. Census Bureau Services Annual Survey and the quinquennial Census of Service Industries.

The estimates of retail spending for prescription drugs are based on household and industry data on prescription drug transactions. Expenditures for other medical nondurables and for vision products and other medical durables purchased in retail outlets are based on estimates of personal consumption expenditures prepared by the U.S. Department of Commerce's Bureau of Economic Analysis, U.S. Bureau of Labor Statistics/Consumer Expenditure Survey; the 1987 National Medical Expenditure Survey and the 1996 Medical Expenditure Panel Survey conducted by the Agency for Healthcare Research and Quality; and spending by Medicare and Medicaid. Those durable and nondurable products provided to inpatients in hospitals or nursing homes, and those provided by licensed professionals or through home health agencies are excluded here, but they are included with the expenditure estimates of the provider service category.

Nursing home expenditures cover care rendered in establishments providing inpatient nursing and health-related personal care through active treatment programs for medical and health-related conditions. These establishments cover skilled nursing and intermediate care facilities, including those for the mentally retarded. Spending estimates are primarily based on data from the U.S. Census Bureau's Services Annual Survey and the quinquennial Census of Service Industries.

Expenditures for construction include those spent on the erection or renovation of hospitals, nursing homes, medical clinics, and medical research facilities, but not for private office buildings providing office space for private practitioners. Expenditures for noncommercial research (the cost of commercial research by drug companies is assumed to be imbedded in the price charged for the product; to include this item again would result in double counting) are developed from information gathered by the National Institutes of Health and the National Science Foundation.

Source of funding estimates likewise come from a multiplicity of sources. Data on the Federal health programs are taken from administrative records maintained by the servicing agencies. Among the sources used to estimate State and local government spending for health are the U.S Census Bureau's Government Finances and the National Academy of Social Insurance reports on State-operated workers' compensation programs. Federal and State and local expenditures for education and training of medical personnel are excluded from these measures where they are separable. For the private financing of health care, data on the financial experience of health insurance organizations come from special Centers for Medicare & Medicaid Services analyses of private health insurers and from the Bureau of Labor Statistics' survey on the cost of employer-sponsored health insurance and on consumer expenditures. Information on out-of-pocket spending from the U.S. Census Bureau Services Annual Survey; U.S. Bureau of Labor Statistics Consumer Expenditure Survey; the 1987 National Medical Expenditure Survey and the Medical Expenditure Panel Surveys conducted by the Agency for Healthcare Research and Quality; and from private surveys conducted by the American Hospital Association, American Medical Association, American Dental Association, and IMS Health, an organization that collects data from the pharmaceutical industry, is used to develop estimates of direct spending by customers.

References:

Growth Slows In 2003. Health Affairs; 4(1):185–194. 2005.

Levit K, Smith C, Cowan C, Sensenig A, Catlin A, and the Health Accounts Team. Health Spending Rebound Continues in 2002. Health Affairs; 23(1):147–159. 2004.

For More Information: See the Centers for Medicare & Medicaid Services National Health Accounts Web site at http://cms.hhs.gov/statistics/nhe.

State Health Expenditures

Overview: Estimates of personal health care spending by State are created using the same definitions of health care sectors used in producing the National Health Expenditures (NHE). These estimates are useful in measuring the role of health spending in States' economies.

Selected Content: Health Accounts by State provide estimates of health care spending by type of establishment delivering care (such as hospitals, physicians and clinics, and nursing homes) and for medical products (such as prescription drugs, over-the-counter medicines and sundries, and durable medical products such as eyeglasses and hearing aids) purchased in retail outlets. Source of funding estimates by State are also provided for Medicare and Medicaid.

Data Years: Annual State health expenditures are available for 1980–98.

Methodology: The same data sources used in creating NHE are also used to create State estimates whenever possible. Additional sources are employed when surveys used to create valid national estimates lack sufficient sample size to create valid State-level estimates. State-level data are used to estimate State-by-State distribution of health spending, and NHE national totals for the specific type of service or source of funds are used to control the level of State-by-State distributions. This procedure implicitly assumes that national spending estimates can be created more accurately than State-specific expenditures.

The NHE data that were used as national totals for these State estimates were published in *Health, United States, 2001*, and differ from the sum of State estimates because national totals included expenditures for persons living in U.S. territories and for military and Federal civilian employees and their families stationed overseas. The sum of the State-level expenditures exclude health spending for those groups. Starting with *Health, United States, 2002*, NHE reflect new data and benchmark revisions incorporated after completion of the State estimates and incorporate a conceptual revision to exclude spending for persons living in U.S. territories and military and Federal civilian employees and their families living overseas.

Starting in *Health, United States, 2002,* State estimates are based on the location of the beneficiary's residence. This differs from previous estimates published in *Health, United States*, which presented spending based on the health care provider's location. State estimates were first constructed based on the provider's location because data available to estimate spending by State primarily comes from providers and represents the State-of-provider location. However, the most useful unit for analyzing spending trends and differences are per capita units, which are based on spending estimates for the State in which people reside. Therefore, State-of-provider-based expenditures are adjusted to a State-of-residence basis using interstate border-crossing flow patterns that represent travel patterns across State borders for health care.

Data for the interstate border-crossing flow patterns are based on Medicare claims. Medicare is the only comprehensive source on which to base interstate flows of spending between State-of-provider and State-of-beneficiary residence. Data for non-Medicare payers (excluding Medicaid) are also based on Medicare flow patterns but are further adjusted for age-specific service mix variation in hospital and physician services. Medicaid services are not adjusted because it is assumed that care provided to eligible State residents is most often provided by in-State providers and further assumed that spending by Medicaid is identical on a residence and provider basis.

In addition to differences noted earlier, national totals for residence-based State health expenditures may differ slightly from national totals for provider-based expenditures because of inflows and outflows of health care spending to the U.S. territories. Because flow patterns are based on Medicare data, we are able to adjust for services that Medicare beneficiaries receive outside of the United States and for services received by Medicare beneficiaries in the United States who either live in the U.S. territories or in other countries. Similar adjustments for the non-Medicare, non-Medicaid population are not possible.

For More Information: See the Centers for Medicare & Medicaid Services National Health Expenditures Web site at http://cms.hhs.gov/statistics/nhe/#state.

National Health Care Survey (NHCS)

Centers for Disease Control and Prevention

National Center for Health Statistics

Overview: The National Health Care Survey (NHCS) is a family of surveys that collect data from medical records of health care providers and establishments about the utilization of health services and characteristics of providers and their patients.

Selected Content: The components of the NHCS represent the major sectors of the U.S. health care system providing data on ambulatory, inpatient, and long-term care settings. This family of surveys includes the following components:

- National Ambulatory Medical Care Survey (NAMCS)
- National Hospital Ambulatory Medical Care Survey (NHAMCS)
- National Hospital Discharge Survey (NHDS)
- National Survey of Ambulatory Surgery (NSAS)
- National Home and Hospice Care Survey (NHHCS)
- National Nursing Home Survey (NHHS)

Methodology: Each survey in the family is based on a multistage sampling design that includes the health care facilities or providers and their records. Data are collected through abstraction of medical records, completion of encounter forms, compilation of data from State and professional associations, purchase of data from commercial abstraction services, and surveys of providers. Data from all survey components are collected from the establishment, and in no case is information received directly from the person receiving care.

For More Information: See the NHCS Web site at www.cdc.gov/nchs/nhcs.htm.

National Health and Nutrition Examination Survey (NHANES)

Centers for Disease Control and Prevention

National Center for Health Statistics

Overview: The National Health and Nutrition Examination Survey (NHANES) program includes a series of cross-sectional nationally representative health examination surveys conducted in mobile examination units or clinics (MECs). In the first series of surveys, the National Health Examination Survey (NHES), data were collected on the prevalence of certain chronic diseases, the distributions of various physical and psychological measures, and measures of growth and development. In 1971 a nutrition surveillance component was added and the survey name changed to the National Health and Nutrition Examination Survey.

Selected Content: The NHANES surveys have collected data on chronic disease prevalence and conditions (including undiagnosed conditions) and risk factors such as obesity and smoking, serum cholesterol levels, hypertension, diet and nutritional status, immunization status, infectious disease prevalence, health insurance, and measures of environmental exposures. Other topics addressed include hearing, vision, mental health, anemia, diabetes, cardiovascular disease, osteoporosis, oral health, mental health, pharmaceuticals used, and physical fitness.

NHES I data were collected on the prevalence of certain chronic diseases as well as the distributions of various physical and psychological measures, including blood pressure and serum cholesterol levels. NHES II and NHES III focused on factors related to growth and development in children and youth.

In NHANES I, data were collected on indicators of the nutritional and health status of the American people through dietary intake data, biochemical tests, physical measurements, and clinical assessments for evidence of nutritional deficiency. Detailed examinations were given by dentists, ophthalmologists, and dermatologists, with an assessment of need for treatment. In addition, data were obtained for a subsample of adults on overall health care needs and behavior, and more detailed examination data were collected on cardiovascular, respiratory, arthritic, and hearing conditions. For NHANES II the nutrition component was expanded. In the medical area primary emphasis was placed on diabetes, kidney and liver functions, allergy, and speech pathology. The third National Health and Nutrition Examination Survey (NHANES III) also included data on antibodies, spirometry, and bone health.

Beginning in 1999 with continuous NHANES, new topics include cardiorespiratory fitness, physical functioning, lower extremity disease, full body scan (DXA) for body fat as well as bone density, and tuberculosis infection.

Data Years: Data have been collected from surveys conducted during 1960–62 (NHES I), 1963–65 (NHES II), 1966–70 (NHES III), 1971–74 (NHANES I), 1976–80 (NHANES II), 1982–84 (HHANES), and 1988–94 (NHANES III). Beginning in 1999, the survey has been conducted continuously.

Coverage: With the exception of the Hispanic Health and Nutrition Examination Survey (see *Methodology*, below), the NHES and NHANES provide estimates of the health status of the civilian noninstitutionalized population of the United States. NHES II and NHES III examined probability samples of the Nation's noninstitutionalized children ages 6–11 years and 12–17 years, respectively.

The NHANES I target population was the civilian noninstitutionalized population 1–74 years of age residing in the coterminous United States, except for people residing on any of the reservation lands set aside for the use of American Indians.

The NHANES II target population was the civilian noninstitutionalized population 6 months–74 years of age residing in the United States, including Alaska and Hawaii.

In Hispanic Health and Nutrition Examination Survey (HHANES) three geographically and ethnically distinct populations were studied: Mexican Americans living in Texas, New Mexico, Arizona, Colorado, and California; Cuban Americans living in Dade County, Florida; and Puerto Ricans living in parts of New York, New Jersey, and Connecticut.

The NHANES III target population was the civilian noninstitutionalized population 2 months of age and over. The sample design provided for oversampling among children 2–35 months of age, persons 70 years of age and over, black Americans, and Mexican Americans.

Beginning in 1999 NHANES oversampled low-income persons, adolescents 12–19 years of age, persons 60 years of age and over, African Americans, and Mexican Americans.

The sample is not designed to give a nationally representative sample for the total population of Hispanics residing in the United States.

Methodology: The NHANES includes clinical examinations, selected medical and laboratory tests, and self-reported data. The NHANES and previous surveys interviewed persons in their homes and conducted medical examinations, including laboratory analysis of blood, urine, and other tissue samples. Medical examinations and laboratory tests follow very specific protocols and are as standard as possible to ensure comparability across sites and providers. In addition to the MEC examinations, a small number of survey participants receive an abbreviated health examination in their homes if they are unable to come to the MEC.

For the first program or cycle of the NHES I, a highly stratified multistage probability sample was selected to represent the 111 million civilian noninstitutionalized adults 18–79 years of age in the United States at that time. The sample areas consisted of 42 primary sampling units (PSUs) from the 1,900 geographic units. NHES II and NHES III were also multistage stratified probability samples of clusters of households in land-based segments. NHES II and III used the same 40 PSUs.

For NHANES I the sample areas consisted of 65 PSUs. A subsample of persons 25–74 years of age was selected to receive the more detailed health examination. Groups at high risk of malnutrition were oversampled.

NHANES II used a multistage probability design that involved selection of PSUs, segments (clusters of households) within PSUs, households, eligible persons, and finally, sample persons. The sample design provided for oversampling among persons 6 months–5 years of age, 60–74 years of age, and those living in poverty areas.

HHANES was similar in content and design to NHANES I and II. The major difference between HHANES and the previous national surveys is that HHANES used a probability sample of three special subgroups of the population living in selected areas of the United States rather than a national probability sample. The three HHANES universes included approximately 84, 57, and 59 percent of the respective 1980 Mexican-, Cuban-, and Puerto Rican-origin populations in the continental United States.

The survey for the NHANES III was conducted from 1988 to 1994 and consisted of two phases of equal length and sample size. Phase 1 and Phase 2 comprised random samples of the civilian U.S. population living in households. About 40,000 persons 2 months of age and over were selected and asked to complete an extensive interview and an examination. Participants were selected from households in 81 counties across the United States. Children age 2 months to 5 years and persons 60 years of age and over were oversampled to provide precise descriptive information on the health status of selected population groups of the United States

Beginning in 1999, NHANES became a continuous, annual survey, which also allows increased flexibility in survey content. Since April 1999, NHANES collects data every year from a representative sample of the civilian U.S. population, newborns and older, by in-home personal interviews and physical examinations in the MEC. The sample design is a complex, multistage, clustered design using unequal probabilities of selection. The first-stage sample frame for continuous NHANES during 1999–2001 was the list of PSUs selected for the design of the National Health Interview Survey (NHIS). Typically, an NHANES PSU is a county. For 2002, an independent sample of PSUs (based on current census data) was selected. This independent design will be used for the period 2002–06. For 1999, because of delay in the start of data collection, 12 distinct PSUs were in the annual sample. For each year 2000–02, 15 PSUs were selected. The within-PSU design involves forming secondary sampling units that are nested within census tracts, selecting dwelling units within secondary units, and then selecting sample persons within dwelling units. The final sample person selection involves differential probabilities of selection according to demographic variables sex (male or female), race/ethnicity (Mexican American, black, all others), and age. Because of the differential probabilities of selection, dwelling units are screened for potential sample persons. Sample weights are available and should be used in estimation of descriptive statistics. The complex design features should be used in estimating standard errors for the descriptive estimates.

The estimation procedure used to produce national statistics for all NHANES involved inflation by the reciprocal of the probability of selection, adjustment for nonresponse, and poststratified ratio adjustment to population totals. Sampling errors also were estimated to measure the reliability of the statistics.

Sample Size and Response Rates: NHES I sampled 7,710 adults. The examination response rate was 86.5 percent. NHES II sampled 7,417 children and reported a response rate of 96 percent for the questionnaire sample and 73 percent for the examination sample. NHES III sampled 7,514 youths and reported a response rate of 90 percent.

A sample of 28,043 persons was selected for NHANES I. Household interviews were completed for more than 96 percent of the persons selected, and about 75 percent (20,749) were examined. A sample of 27,801 persons was selected for NHANES II; 73.1 percent (20,322 persons) were examined.

In the HHANES, 9,894 persons in the Southwest were selected (75 percent or 7,462 were examined); in Dade County, 2,244 persons were selected (60 percent or 1,357 were examined); and, in the Northeast, 3,786 persons were selected (75 percent or 2,834 were examined). Over the 6-year survey period of NHANES III, 39,695 persons were selected, the household interview response rate was 86 percent, and the medical examination response rate was 78 percent.

In the sample selection for NHANES 1999–2000, there were 22,839 dwelling units screened. Of these, 6,005 households had at least one eligible sample person identified for interviewing. A total of 12,160 eligible sample persons were identified. The overall response rate in NHANES 1999–2000 for those interviewed was 81.9 percent (9,965 of 12,160), and the response rate for those examined was 76.3 percent (9,282 of 12,160). For NHANES 2001–02 there were 13,156 persons selected in the sample, of which 83.9 percent (11,039) were interviewed and 79.7 percent (10,480) of the 13,156 selected completed the health examination component of the survey.

Issues Affecting Interpretation: Data elements, lab tests performed, and the technological sophistication of medical examination and laboratory equipment have changed over time. Therefore, trend analyses should carefully examine how specific data elements were collected across the different NHANES and NHES surveys.

References:

Gordon T, Miller HW. Cycle I of the Health Examination Survey: Sample and response, United States, 1960–62. National Center for Health Statistics. Vital Health Stat Series no 11(1). 1974.

Plan, operation, and response results of a program of children's examinations. National Center for Health Statistics. Vital Health Stat Series no 1(5). 1967.

Schaible WL. Quality control in a National Health Examination Survey. National Center for Health Statistics. Vital Health Stat Series no 2 (44). 1972.

Miller HW. Plan and operation of the Health and Nutrition Examination Survey, United States, 1971–73. National Center for Health Statistics. Vital Health Stat Series no 1(10a) and 1(10b). 1977 and 1978.

Engel A, Murphy RS, Maurer K, Collins E. Plan and operation of the NHANES I Augmentation Survey of Adults 25–74 years, United States, 1974–75. National Center for Health Statistics. Vital Health Stat Series no 1(14). 1978.

McDowell A, Engel A, Massey JT, Maurer K. Plan and operation of the second National Health and Nutrition Examination Survey, 1976–80. National Center for Health Statistics. Vital Health Stat Series no 1(15), 1981.

Maurer K. Plan and operation of the Hispanic Health and Nutrition Examination Survey, 1982–84. National Center for Health Statistics. Vital Health Stat Series no 1(19). 1985.

Ezzati TM, Massey JT, Waksberg J, et al. Sample design: Third National Health and Nutrition Examination Survey. National Center for Health Statistics. Vital Health Stat Series no 2(113). 1992.

Plan and operation of the Third National Health and Nutrition Examination Survey, 1988–94. National Center for Health Statistics. Vital Health Stat Series no 1(32). 1994.

For More Information: See the NHANES Web site at www.cdc.gov/nchs/about/major/nhanes/nhanes.htm.

National Health Interview Survey (NHIS)

Centers for Disease Control and Prevention

National Center for Health Statistics

Overview: The National Health Interview Survey (NHIS) monitors the health of the U.S. population through the collection and analysis of data on a broad range of health topics. A major strength of this survey lies in the ability to analyze health measures by many demographic and socioeconomic characteristics.

Selected Content: The NHIS obtains information during household interviews on illnesses, injuries, activity limitation, chronic conditions, health insurance coverage, utilization of health care, and other health topics. Demographic data include gender, age, education, race/ethnicity (reported by respondent or proxy), place of birth, income, and place of residence. Other data collected include risk factors, such as lack of exercise, smoking, alcohol consumption, and use of prevention services such as vaccinations, mammography, and pap smears. Special modules and supplements focus on different issues each year and have included topics, such as HIV/AIDS, aging, cancer screening, prevention, alternative and complementary medicine, and many other topics.

Data Years: The NHIS has been conducted annually since 1957, with a major redesign every 10–15 years.

Coverage: The NHIS covers the civilian noninstitutionalized population of the United States. Excluded are patients in long-term care facilities, persons on active duty with the Armed Forces (although their dependents are included), and U.S. nationals living in foreign countries.

Methodology: The NHIS is a cross-sectional household interview survey. Sampling and interviewing are continuous throughout each year. The sampling plan follows a multistage area probability design that permits the representative sampling of households. The sampling plan was last redesigned in 1995. Information for only the current sampling plan covering the design years of 1995–2004 is presented. The first stage consists of a sample of 358 primary sampling units (PSUs) drawn from approximately 1,900 geographically defined PSUs that cover the 50 States and the District of Columbia. A PSU consists of a county, a small group of contiguous counties, or a metropolitan statistical area.

Within a PSU, two types of second-stage units are used: area segments and permit area segments. Area segments are defined geographically and contain an expected 8 or 12 addresses. Permit area segments cover geographical areas containing housing units built after the 1990 census. The permit area segments are defined using updated lists of building permits issued in the PSU since 1990 and contain an expected four addresses. Within each segment all occupied households at the sample addresses are targeted for interview.

The total NHIS sample of PSUs is subdivided into four separate panels, or subdesigns, such that each panel is a representative sample of the U.S. population. This design feature has a number of advantages, including flexibility for the total sample size. The households selected for interview each week in the NHIS are a probability sample representative of the target population.

The NHIS that was fielded from 1982–96 consisted of two parts: (1) a set of basic health and demographic items (known as the Core questionnaire), and (2) one or more sets of questions on current health topics (known as Supplements). The Core questionnaire remained the same over that time period whereas the current health topics changed depending on data needs.

The NHIS questionnaire revision first implemented in 1997 has three parts or modules: a Basic module, a Periodic module, and a Topical module. The Basic module corresponds to the core questionnaire before revision. It remains largely unchanged from year to year and allows for trend analysis and for data from more than 1 year to be pooled to increase sample size for analytic purposes. The Basic module contains three components: the Family Core, the Sample Adult Core, and the Sample Child Core. The Family Core component collects information on everyone in the family and allows the NHIS to serve as a sampling frame for additional integrated surveys as needed. Information collected on the Family Core for all family members includes household composition and sociodemographic characteristics, tracking information, information for matches to administrative data bases, health insurance coverage, and basic indicators of health status and utilization of health care services.

From each family in the NHIS, one sample adult and, for families with children under 18 years of age, one sample child are randomly selected to participate in the Sample Adult Core and the Sample Child Core questionnaires. Because some health issues are different for children and adults, these two questionnaires differ in some items but both collect basic information on health status, use of health care services, health conditions, and health behaviors.

Sample Size and Response Rates: Since 1997, the sample numbered about 100,000 persons with about 30,000 persons participating in the sample adult and about 15,000 persons in the sample child questionnaire. In recent years, the total household response rate was about 90 percent. Response rates for special health topics (supplements) have generally been lower. For example, the response rate was 80 percent for the 1994 Year 2000 Supplement, which included questions about cigarette smoking and use of such preventive services as mammography. Since 1997, the final response rate for the sample adult supplement was 70–80 percent and 78–84 percent for the sample child supplement.

Issues Affecting Interpretation: In 1997, the questionnaire was redesigned and some basic concepts were changed and other concepts were measured in different ways. For some questions, there was a change in the reference period. Also in 1997, the collection methodology changed from paper and pencil questionnaires to computer-assisted personal interviewing (CAPI). Because of the major redesigns of the questionnaire in 1997, most trend tables in *Health, United States* begin with 1997 data. Starting with *Health, United States, 2005*, estimates for 2000 and later years use weights derived from the 2000 census.

References:

Massey JT, Moore TF, Parsons VL, Tadros W. Design and estimation for the National Health Interview Survey, 1985–94. National Center for Health Statistics. Vital Health Stat Series no 2(110). 1989.

National Center for Health Statistics. National Health Interview Survey: Research for the 1995–2004 redesign. National Center for Health Statistics. Vital Health Stat Series no 2(126). 1999.

Botman SL, Moore TF, Moriarity CL, Parsons VL. Design and estimation for the National Health Interview Survey, 1995–2004. National Center for Health Statistics. Vital Health Stat Series no 2(130). 2000.

For More Information: See the NHIS Web site at http://www.cdc.gov/nchs/nhis.htm.

National Health Provider Inventory (NHPI)

Centers for Disease Control and Prevention

National Center for Health Statistics

Overview: The National Health Provider Inventory (NHPI) is an inventory of nursing homes, home health agencies, and hospices. The NHPI and its predecessor inventories served as sampling frames for the NCHS National Nursing Home Survey and National Home and Hospice Care Survey.

Selected Content: Information collected included facility ownership, size, services provided, geographic location, and some resident or client characteristics.

Data Years: The NHPI was conducted in 1991 and has not been repeated.

Coverage: The NHPI included nursing homes, board and care homes, home health agencies, and hospices.

Methodology: The National Master Facility Inventories (NMFIs), forerunners of the National Health Provider Inventory (NHPI), were a series of inventories of inpatient health facilities in the United States conducted by NCHS. The inventories included hospitals, nursing and related-care homes, and other custodial care facilities. The last NMFI was conducted in 1982. In 1986 the inventory was changed to the Inventory of Long-Term Care Places (ILTCP) and included nursing and related-care homes and facilities for the mentally retarded. In 1991 the inventory was changed to NHPI.

National Home and Hospice Care Survey (NHHCS)

Centers for Disease Control and Prevention

National Center for Health Statistics

Overview: The National Home and Hospice Care Survey (NHHCS) collects data on the characteristics and care provided by home health care agencies and hospices as well as characteristics of patients receiving these services.

Selected Content: The NHHCS provides information on home health and hospice care from two perspectives—that of the provider of services and that of the recipient. Data collected at the home health care and hospice agency level include number of clients served, ownership and affiliations, certification status, and services provided. At the patient level, data are collected on demographic characteristics, diagnoses, living arrangements, caregiver status, enrollment date, discharge disposition (for discharge sample), selected therapies and treatments provided, aids and special devices used, activities of daily living (ADL) assistance received from the agency, vision and hearing impairments, continence, payment source, and care charges.

Data Years: Initiated in 1992, the NHHCS was also conducted in 1993, 1994, 1996, 1998, and 2000. The survey is currently undergoing a major redesign.

Coverage: The survey covers agencies and the current patients and discharges from agencies that provide home health and hospice care services in the United States. Agencies may be freestanding health facilities or units of larger organizations, such as hospitals or nursing homes. Agencies providing only durable medical equipment are excluded. Only agencies providing home health or hospice care services to patients at the time of the survey are eligible to participate.

Methodology: The sample design for the 1992–94 NHHCS was a stratified three-stage probability design. Primary sampling units were selected at the first stage, agencies were selected at the second stage, and up to six current patients and six discharges were selected at the third stage. The sample design for the 1996, 1998, and 2000 NHHCS was a two-stage probability design in which agencies were selected at the first stage and current patients and discharges were selected at the second stage. Current patients were those on the rolls of the agency as of midnight the day before the survey. Discharges were selected to estimate the number of discharges from the agency during the 12 months before the survey. Agency characteristics were obtained through interviews with the agency administrators and staff. Sample patients and discharges were selected, and questionnaires were completed by interviewing the staff member most familiar with the care provided to the patient. Respondents were requested to refer to the medical records for the patient.

Estimates based on the NHHCS are derived by a multistage estimation procedure that has three principle components: inflation by the reciprocals of the probabilities of sample selection; adjustment for nonresponse; and ratio adjustment to fixed totals. The data from the surveys are adjusted for three types of nonresponse: an in-scope sample agency did not respond; an agency did not complete the sampling lists used to select the patient or discharge samples; and the agency did not complete the questionnaire for the sample patient or discharge.

Sample Size and Response Rates: The original sampling frame consisted of all home health care agencies and hospices identified in the 1991 National Health Provider Inventory (NHPI). The 1992 sample contained 1,500 agencies. These agencies were revisited during the 1993 survey (excluding agencies that had been found to be out of scope for the survey). In 1994 in-scope agencies identified in the 1993 survey were revisited, along with 100 newly identified agencies added to the sample. In 1996, the universe was again updated and a new sample of 1,200 agencies was drawn. In 1998, a sample of 1,350 agencies was selected from a universe of home health agencies and hospices obtained from various national organizations and other sources. In 2000, 1,800 agencies were sampled from the universe that was obtained from SMG Home Healthcare Market Database and the membership list of the National Hospice and Palliative Care Organization. The response rates during the 1992–2000 survey years have been greater than 92 percent at the agency level, mid-90 to mid-80 percent for current patients, and low 90 to low 80 percent for discharges.

Issues Affecting Interpretation: Characteristics of agencies and current patients reflect the situation on a given day when the survey was being conducted. Because frequent short-term users are less likely to be enrolled with the agency on any given day than long-term users, the current patient component tends to underestimate those patients with a very short length of service. The discharge component is designed to estimate the number of discharges that occur over a 12-month period. Estimates of discharges may underestimate those patients who tend to receive care for longer periods of time. Caution should be made in comparing estimates from the resident and discharge samples. Finally, various survey items have been added or modified over the survey years, which may preclude comparisons from previous years or trend analyses.

References:

Haupt BJ. Development of the National Home and Hospice Care Survey. National Center for Health Statistics. Vital Health Stat Series 1(33). 1994.

Haupt BJ. The National Home and Hospice Care Survey: 1992 Summary. National Center for Health Statistics. Vital Health Stat Series 13(117). 1994.

Jones A, Strahan G. The National Home and Hospice Care Survey: 1994 Summary. National Center for Health Statistics. Vital Health Stat Series 13(126). 1997.

Haupt BJ, Jones A. National Home and Hospice Care Survey: Annual Summary, 1996. National Center for Health Statistics. Vital Health Stat Series 13(141). 1999.

Haupt BJ. Characteristics of hospice care discharges and their length of service: United States, 2000. National Center for Health Statistics. Vital Health Stat Series 13 (154). 2003.

For More Information: See the National Health Care Survey (NHCS) Web site at www.cdc.gov/nchs/nhcs.htm or the National Home and Hospice Care Survey Web site at www.cdc.gov/nchs/about/major/nhhcsd/nhhcsd.htm.

National Hospital Ambulatory Medical Care Survey (NHAMCS)

Centers for Disease Control and Prevention

National Center for Health Statistics

Overview: The National Hospital Ambulatory Medical Care Survey (NHAMCS) collects data on the utilization and provision of medical care services provided in hospital emergency and outpatient departments.

Selected Content: Data are collected from medical records on type of providers seen; reason for visit; diagnoses; drugs ordered, provided, or continued; and selected procedures and tests performed during the visit. Patient data include age, sex, race, and expected source of payment. Data are also collected on selected characteristics of hospitals included in the survey.

Data Years: Annual data collection began in 1992.

Coverage: The survey is a representative sample of visits to emergency departments (EDs) and outpatient departments (OPDs) of non-Federal, short-stay, or general hospitals. Telephone contacts are excluded.

Methodology: A four-stage probability sample design is used in NHAMCS, involving samples of primary sampling units (PSUs), hospitals within PSUs, clinics within OPDs, and patient visits within clinics. The first stage sample of the NHAMCS consists of 112 PSUs selected from 1,900 such units comprising the United States. Within PSUs, 600 general and short-stay hospitals were sampled and assigned to 1 of 16 panels. In any given year, 13 panels are included. Each panel is assigned to a 4-week reporting period during the calendar year.

In the NHAMCS outpatient department survey, a clinic is defined as an administrative unit of the OPD in which ambulatory medical care is provided under the supervision of a physician. Clinics where only ancillary services, such as radiology, laboratory services, physical rehabilitation, renal dialysis, and pharmacy, are provided, or other settings in which physician services are not typically provided, are considered out of scope. If a hospital OPD has five or fewer in-scope clinics, all are included in the sample. For hospital OPDs with more than five clinics, a systematic sample of clinics proportional to size is included in the survey.

The U.S. Census Bureau acts as the data collection agent for the NHAMCS. Census field representatives contact sample hospitals to determine whether they have a 24-hour ED or an OPD that offers physician services. Visits to eligible EDs and OPDs are systematically sampled over the 4-week reporting period such that about 100 ED encounters and about 200 OPD encounters are selected. Hospital staff are asked to complete "Patient Record" forms for each sampled visit, but Census field representatives typically abstract data for more than half of these visits.

Sample data are weighted to produce national estimates. The estimation procedure used in the NHAMCS has three basic components: inflation by the reciprocal of the probability of selection, adjustment for nonresponse, and ratio adjustment to fixed totals.

Sample Size and Response Rates: In any given year, the hospital sample consists of approximately 500 hospitals, of which 80 percent have EDs and about half have eligible OPDs. Typically, about 1,000 clinics are selected from participating hospital OPDs. In 2002 the number of patient record forms (PRFs) completed for EDs was 37,337 and for OPDs 35,586. In 2003 the number of PRFs completed for EDs was 40, 253 and for OPDs 34,492. In 2002 the hospital response rate for NHAMCS was 95 percent for EDs and 87 percent for OPDs. In 2003 the hospital response rate was 85 percent for EDs and 83 percent for OPDs.

Issues Affecting Interpretation: The NHAMCS PRF is modified approximately every 2 years to reflect change in physician practice characteristics, patterns of care, and technological innovations. Examples of recent changes are the number of drugs recorded on the PRF form, and checkboxes of specific tests or procedures performed. For analyses that present visit rates per population, the civilian noninstitutionalized population is used as the denominator. However, visits to hospital EDs or OPDs can also include persons who reside in institutional settings.

Reference:

McCaig LF, McLemore T. Plan and operation of the National Hospital Ambulatory Medical Care Survey.

National Center for Health Statistics. Vital Health Stat Series no 1(34). 1994.

For More Information: See the National Health Care Survey (NHCS) Web site at www.cdc.gov/nchs/nhcs.htm or the Ambulatory Health Care Web site at www.cdc.gov/nchs/about/major/ahcd/ahcd1.htm.

National Hospital Discharge Survey (NHDS)

Centers for Disease Control and Prevention

National Center for Health Statistics

Overview: The National Hospital Discharge Survey (NHDS) collects and produces national estimates on characteristics of inpatient stays in non-Federal short-stay hospitals in the United States.

Selected Content: Patient information collected includes demographics, length of stay, diagnoses, and procedures. Hospital characteristics collected include region, ownership, and bedsize.

Data Years: The NHDS has been conducted annually since 1965.

Coverage: The survey design covers the 50 States and the District of Columbia. Included in the survey are hospitals with an average length of stay of less than 30 days for all inpatients, general hospitals, and children's general hospitals. Excluded are Federal, military, and Department of Veterans Affairs hospitals, as well as hospital units of institutions (such as prison hospitals), and hospitals with fewer than six beds staffed for patient use. All discharged patients from in-scope hospitals are included in the survey; however, newborns are not included in *Health, United States.*

Methodology: The design implemented in 1965 continued through 1987, and a redesign with a new sample of hospitals fielded in 1988 is currently in place. The sample for the 1965 NHDS was selected in 1964 from a frame of short-stay hospitals listed in the National Master Facility Inventory. A two-stage stratified sample design was used, with hospitals stratified according to bedsize and geographic region. Sample hospitals were selected with probabilities ranging from certainty for the largest hospitals to 1 in 40 for the smallest hospitals. Within each participating hospital, a systematic random sample was selected from a daily listing sheet of discharges. Within-hospital sampling rates for discharges varied inversely with the probability of hospital selection, so the overall probability of selecting a discharge was approximately the same across the sample.

Data collection was conducted by means of manual abstraction of patient information from sampled medical records. Sample selection and transcription of information from inpatient medical records to NHDS survey forms were performed by hospital staff, representatives of NCHS, or both. In 1985, a second data collection procedure was introduced. The procedure involved the purchase of computer data tapes from commercial abstracting services that contained automated discharge data for some hospitals participating in the NHDS. This procedure was used in approximately 17 percent of the sample hospitals for 1985–87. Discharges on these computer files were subjected to the NHDS sampling specifications as well as the computer edits and estimation procedures. Two data collection methods, manual and automated, continue to be used in the NHDS.

A redesign of the NHDS was implemented for the 1988 survey. Under the redesign, hospitals were selected using a modified three-stage stratified design. Units selected at the first stage consisted of either hospitals or geographic areas. The geographic areas were Primary Sample Units (PSUs) used for the 1985–94 National Health Interview Survey, which are geographic areas such as counties or townships. Hospitals within PSUs were then selected at the second stage. Strata at this stage were defined by geographic region, PSU size, abstracting service status, and hospital specialty-size groups. Within these strata, hospitals were selected with probabilities proportional to their annual number of discharges. At the third stage, a sample of discharges was selected by a systematic random sampling technique. The sampling rate was determined by the hospital's sampling stratum and the type of data collection system (manual or automated) used. Discharge records from hospitals submitting data via commercial abstracting services and selected State data systems (approximately 41 percent of sample hospitals) were arrayed by primary diagnoses, patient sex and age group, and date of discharge, before sampling.

The NHDS hospital sample is updated every 3 years by continuing the sampling process among hospitals that become eligible for the survey during the intervening years and by deleting hospitals that were no longer eligible. This process was conducted in 1991, 1994, 1997, 2000, and 2003.

The basic unit of estimation for NHDS is a sampled discharge. The basic estimation procedure involves inflation by the reciprocal of the probability of selection. There are adjustments for nonresponding hospitals and discharges; a postratio adjustment to fixed totals is employed.

Sample Size and Response Rate: In 2003, 501 hospitals were selected: 479 were within scope, 426 participated (89 percent), and approximately 320,000 medical records were abstracted.

Issues Affecting Interpretation: In 1988, the NHDS was redesigned. Caution is required in comparing trend data from before and after the redesign There are also annual modifications to the ICD–9–CM affecting diagnoses and procedure categories. See related Appendix II, *ICD–9–CM*; tables IX and X.

Hospital utilization rates per 1,000 population were computed using estimates of the civilian population of the United States as of July 1 of each year. Rates for 1990 through 1999 use postcensal estimates of the civilian population based on the 1990 census adjusted for net underenumeration using the 1990 National Population Adjustment Matrix from the U.S. Census Bureau. The estimates for 2000 and beyond that appear in *Health, United States, 2003* and later editions were calculated using estimates of the civilian population based on census 2000, and therefore are not strictly comparable with postcensal rates calculated for the 1990s. See related *Population Census and Population Estimates* in Appendix I.

References:

DeFrances CJ, Hall MJ, Podgornik MN. 2003 National Hospital Discharge Survey. Advance data from vital and health statistics; no 359. Hyattsville, MD: National Center for Health Statistics. 2005.

Dennison C, Pokras R. Design and operation of the National Hospital Discharge Survey: 1988 redesign. National Center for Health Statistics. Vital Health Stat Series no 1(39). 2000.

Haupt BJ, Kozak LJ. Estimates from two survey designs: National Hospital Discharge Survey. National Center for Health Statistics. Vital Health Stat Series no 13(111). 1992.

For More Information: See the National Health Care Survey Web site at www.cdc.gov/nchs.nhcs.htm or the National Hospital Discharge Survey Web site at www.cdc.gov/nchs/about/major/hdasd/nhds.htm.

National Immunization Survey (NIS)

Centers for Disease Control and Prevention

National Center for Health Statistics and National Immunization Program

Overview: The National Immunization Survey (NIS) is a continuing nationwide telephone sample survey to monitor vaccination coverage rates among children 19–35 months of age.

Selected Content: Data collected include vaccination status and timing for diphtheria, tetanus toxoids, and pertussis vaccine (DTP/DT/DTaP); Polio vaccine; Measles, mumps, and rubella vaccine (MMR); Haemophilius influenzae type b vaccine (Hib); Hepatitis B vaccine (Hep B); Varicella vaccine; Pneumococcal conjugate vaccine (PCV); and Combined series (4:3:1:3) by race/ethnicity, poverty status, location of residence, geographic division, State, and selected urban areas.

Data Years: Annual data collection was initiated beginning with the data year 1994. Data collection for Varicella began in July 1996; data collection for PCV began in July 2001.

Coverage: Children 19–35 months of age in the civilian noninstitutionalized population are represented in this survey. Estimates of vaccine-specific coverage are available for the Nation, States, and 28 urban areas. In 2003, about 81.3 percent of the age-eligible children were up-to-date for the 4:3:1:3 series.

Methodology: The NIS is a nationwide telephone sample survey of households with age-eligible children. The NIS uses a two-phase sample design. First, a random-digit dialing (RDD) sample of telephone numbers is drawn. When households with age-eligible children are contacted, the interviewer collects information on the vaccinations received by all age-eligible children and obtains permission to contact the children's immunization providers. In the second phase, immunization providers are sent vaccination history questionnaires by mail. Providers' responses are compared with information obtained from households to provide a more accurate estimate of vaccination coverage levels. Final estimates are adjusted for households without telephones and nonresponse.

Sample Size and Response Rates: In 2003, vaccination data were collected for 30,930 children aged 19–35 months. In 2003 the household interview rate was 69.8 percent. Vaccination information from providers was obtained for 69 percent of all children who were eligible for provider follow-up in 2003.

Issues Affecting Interpretation: For the 1998 data year, a new estimation procedure was implemented to obtain vaccination coverage rates from the provider data. Published estimates of vaccination coverage based on NIS data for years prior to 1998 (e.g., estimates published in MMWR articles) may differ slightly from estimates published in *Health, United States* and on the NIS Web site for the same NIS data. All public-use data files include the sampling weight for the new estimation procedure.

References:

National, State, and urban area vaccination levels among children aged 19–35 months—United States, 2003. MMWR; 53(29);658–661. 2004, found at http://www.cdc.gov/mmwr/preview/mmwrhtml/mm5329a3.htm.

Smith PJ, Hoaglin DC, Battaglia M, Michael P, Khare, M, Barker LE. Statistical methodology of the National Immunization Survey, 1994–2002. National Center for Health Statistics. Vital Health Stat 2(138). 2005.

For More Information: See the NIS Web site at http://www.cdc.gov/nis.

National Medical Expenditure Survey (NMES)—See Medical Expenditure Panel Survey

National Notifiable Disease Surveillance System (NNDSS)

Centers for Disease Control and Prevention

Overview: This system provides weekly provisional information on the occurrence of diseases defined as notifiable by the Council of State and Territorial Epidemiologists.

Selected Content: Data include incidence of reportable diseases using uniform case definitions.

Data Years: The first annual summary of The Notifiable Diseases in 1912 included reports of 10 diseases from 19 States, the District of Columbia, and Hawaii. By 1928, all States, the District of Columbia, Hawaii, and Puerto Rico were participating in national reporting of 29 specified diseases. At their annual meeting in 1950, the State and Territorial Health Officers authorized a conference of State and territorial epidemiologists whose purpose was to determine which diseases should be reported to the Public Health Service. In 1961, CDC assumed responsibility for the collection and publication of data concerning nationally notifiable diseases.

Coverage: Notifiable disease reports are received from health departments in the 50 States, five territories, New York City, and the District of Columbia. Policies for reporting notifiable disease cases can vary by disease or reporting jurisdiction, depending on case status classification (i.e., confirmed, probable, or suspect).

Methodology: CDC, in partnership with the Council of State and Territorial Epidemiologists (CSTE), operates the National Notifiable Diseases Surveillance System (NNDSS). Notifiable disease surveillance is conducted by public health practitioners at local, State, and national levels to support disease prevention and control activities. The system also provides annual summaries of the data. CSTE and CDC annually review the status of national infectious disease surveillance and recommend additions or deletions to the list of nationally notifiable diseases based on the need to respond to emerging priorities. For example, Q fever and tularemia became nationally notifiable in 2000. However, reporting nationally notifiable diseases to CDC is voluntary. Reporting is currently mandated by law or regulation only at the local and State level. Therefore, the list of diseases that are considered notifiable varies slightly by State. For example, reporting of cyclosporiasis to CDC is not done by some States in which this disease is not notifiable to local or State authorities.

State epidemiologists report cases of notifiable diseases to CDC, which tabulates and publishes these data in the *Morbidity and Mortality Weekly Report (MMWR)* and the *Summary of Notifiable Diseases, United States* (entitled *Annual Summary* before 1985).

Issues Affecting Interpretation: These data must be interpreted in light of reporting practices. Some diseases that cause severe clinical illness (for example, plague and rabies) are most likely reported accurately if diagnosed by a clinician. However, persons who have diseases that are clinically mild and infrequently associated with serious consequences (for example, salmonellosis) might not seek medical care from a health care provider. Even if these less severe diseases are diagnosed, they are less likely to be reported.

The degree of completeness of data reporting also is influenced by the diagnostic facilities available, the control measures in effect, public awareness of a specific disease, and the interests, resources, and priorities of State and local officials responsible for disease control and public health surveillance. Finally, factors such as changes in case definitions for public health surveillance, introduction of new diagnostic tests, or discovery of new disease entities can cause changes in disease reporting that are independent of the true incidence of disease.

Reference:

Centers for Disease Control and Prevention. Summary of notifiable diseases—United States, 2003. MMWR 52 no 54. April 22, 2005. found at http://www.cdc.gov/mmwr/summary.html.

For More Information: See the NNDSS Web site at www.cdc.gov/epo/dphsi/nndsshis.htm.

National Nursing Home Survey (NNHS)

Centers for Disease Control and Prevention

National Center for Health Statistics

Overview: The National Nursing Home Survey (NNHS) provides information on characteristics of nursing homes and their residents and staff.

Selected Content: The NNHS provides information on nursing homes from two perspectives—that of the provider of services and that of the recipient. Data about the facilities include characteristics, such as bed size, ownership, affiliation, Medicare/Medicaid certification, specialty units, services offered, number and characteristics of staff, expenses, and charges. Data about the current residents and discharges include demographic characteristics, health status, level of assistance needed with activities of daily living, vision and hearing impairment, continence, services received, sources of payment, and discharge disposition (for discharges).

Data Years: NCHS conducted six NNHS: the first survey August 1973–April 1974; the second May–December 1977; the third August 1985–January 1986; the fourth July–December 1995; the fifth July–December 1997; and the sixth July–December 1999. The next NNHS, which has undergone a major redesign, was conducted in 2004 and data will be released some time in 2006.

Coverage: The initial NNHS, conducted in 1973–74, included the universe of nursing homes that provided some level of nursing care and excluded homes providing only personal or domiciliary care. The 1977 NNHS encompassed all types of nursing homes, including personal care and domiciliary care homes. The 1985 NNHS was designed to be similar to the 1973–74 survey in that it excluded personal or domiciliary care homes. However in 1985, an unknown number of residential care facilities were present in the sampling frame. These facilities were identified in the 1986 inventory survey and can be removed from the estimate of facilities and beds for 1985. The 1995, 1997, and 1999 NNHS also included only nursing homes that provided some level of nursing care and excluded homes providing only personal or domiciliary care, similar to the 1985 and 1973–74 surveys.

Data were collected from nursing homes in all 50 States and the District of Columbia (DC) in the 1995–1999 surveys, but in 1973–74, 1977, and 1985, data were only collected in the 48 contiguous States and DC. Data on current residents were collected in all surveys; data on discharges were collected in 1977, 1985, 1997, and 1999. Expense data were collected in 1977, 1985, and 1995. Data on characteristics of staff were collected in 1973–74, 1977, and 1985.

Methodology: The survey uses a stratified two-stage probability design. The first stage is the selection of facilities, and the second stage is the selection of residents and discharges. Up to six current residents and six discharges are selected. Information on the facility is collected through a personal interview with the administrator or staff designated by the administrator. Resident data were provided by staff familiar with the care provided to the resident. Staff relied on the medical record and personal knowledge of the resident. In addition to employee data that were collected during the interview with the administrator, in several years staffing data were collected via a self-administered questionnaire. Discharge data were based on information recorded in the medical record.

Current residents are those on the facility's roster as of the night before the survey. Included are all residents for whom beds are maintained even though they may be away on an overnight leave or in the hospital. Discharges are those who are formally discharged from care by the facility during a designated month randomly selected for each facility before data collection. Both live and deceased discharges are included. Residents were counted more than once if they were discharged more than once during the reference period.

Statistics for the NNHS are derived by a multistage estimation procedure that has three major components: (a) inflation by the reciprocals of the probabilities of sample selection; (b) adjustment for nonresponse; and (c) ratio adjustment to fixed totals. The surveys are adjusted for four types of nonresponse: (1) when an eligible nursing facility did not respond; (2) when the facility failed to complete the sampling lists; (3) when the facility did not complete the facility questionnaire but did complete the questionnaire for residents in the facility; and (4) when the facility did not provide information to complete the questionnaire for the sample resident or discharge.

Sample Size and Response Rates: In 1973–74 the sample of 2,118 homes was selected from the 1971 National Master Facility Inventory (NMFI) and from those that opened for business in 1972. For the 1977 NNHS the sample of 1,698 facilities was selected from nursing homes in the sampling frame, which consisted of all homes listed in the 1973 NMFI and those opening for business between 1973 and December 1976. The sample for the 1985 survey consisted of the 1,220 facilities selected from the 1982 NMFI, data for homes identified in the 1982 Complement Survey of the NMFI, data on hospital-based nursing homes obtained from the Health Care Financing Administration (now known as the Centers for Medicare & Medicaid Services), and data on nursing homes open for business between 1982 and June 1, 1984. The 1995 sample of 1,500 homes was selected from a sampling frame consisting of nursing homes from the 1991 National Health Provider Inventory (NHPI) and updated lists from the Agency Reporting System (ARS). ARS was an ongoing system designed to periodically update the NHPI and consisted primarily of lists or directories of facilities from State agencies, Federal agencies, and national voluntary organizations. For the 1997 survey, data were obtained from about 1,488 nursing homes from a sampling frame consisting of nursing homes listed on the 1991 NHPI that was updated with a current listing of nursing facilities supplied by the Health Care Finance Administration and other national organizations. The facility frame for the 1999 NNHS consisted of all nursing homes identified in the 1997 NNHS and updated with current nursing facilities listed by the Centers for Medicare & Medicaid Services and other national organizations. The 1999 sample consisted of 1,496 nursing homes. In 1995, 1997, and 1999, facility-level response rates were over 93 percent.

Issues Affecting Interpretation: Samples of discharges and residents contain different populations with different characteristics. The resident sample is more likely to contain long-term nursing home residents and, conversely, to underestimate short nursing home stays. Because short-term residents are less likely to be on the nursing home rolls on a given night, they are less likely to be sampled. Estimates of discharges underestimate long nursing home stays. In addition, analysts should ensure that the underlying populations are similar across survey years—for example, whether the survey includes personal or domiciliary care homes.

References:

Meiners MR. Selected operating and financial characteristics of nursing homes, United States, 1973–74 National Nursing Home Survey. National Center for Health Statistics. Vital Health Stat Series no 13(22). 1975.

Van Nostrand JF, Zappolo A, Hing E, et al. The National Nursing Home Survey, 1977 summary for the United States. National Center for Health Statistics. Vital Health Stat Series no 13(43). 1979.

Hing E, Sekscenski E, Strahan G. The National Nursing Home Survey: 1985 summary for the United States. National Center for Health Statistics. Vital Health Stat Series no 13(97). 1989.

Strahan G. An overview of nursing homes and their current residents: Data from the 1995 National Nursing Home Survey. Advance data from vital and health statistics; no 280. Hyattsville, MD: National Center for Health Statistics. 1997.

The National Nursing Home Survey: 1997 summary. National Center for Health Statistics. Vital Health Stat Series no 13(147). 2000.

The National Nursing Home Survey: 1999 summary. National Center for Health Statistics. Vital Health Stat Series no 13(152). 2002.

For More Information: See the National Health Care Survey Web site at www.cdc.gov/nchs/nhcs.htm and the NNHS Web site at www.cdc.gov/nchs/about/major/nnhsd/nnhsd.htm.

National Survey on Drug Use and Health (NSDUH)

Substance Abuse and Mental Health Services Administration

Overview: The National Survey on Drug Use & Health (NSDUH), formerly called the National Household Survey on Drug Abuse (NHSDA), collects data on substance abuse and dependence, mental health problems, and receipt of substance abuse and mental health treatment.

Selected Content: NSDUH reports on the prevalence, patterns, and consequences of drug and alcohol use and abuse in the general U.S. civilian noninstitutionalized population age 12 and over. Data are collected on the use of illicit drugs, the nonmedical use of licit drugs, and use of alcohol and tobacco products. The survey is conducted annually and is designed to produce drug and alcohol use incidence and prevalence estimates. Data are also collected periodically on special topics of interest such as criminal behavior, treatment, mental health, and attitudes about drugs.

Data Years: The NHSDA survey has been conducted since 1971. In 1999, the NHSDA underwent a major redesign affecting the method of data collection, sample design, sample size, and oversampling. In 2002, the survey underwent a name change to NSDUH as well as additional improvements and modifications to the survey.

Coverage: The survey is representative of persons 12 years of age and over in the civilian noninstitutionalized population in the United States. This includes civilians living on military bases and persons living in noninstitutionalized group quarters, such as college dormitories, rooming houses, and shelters. Persons excluded from the survey include homeless people who do not use shelters, active military personnel, and residents of institutional group quarters, such as jails and hospitals.

Methodology: The data collection method is in-person interviews conducted with a sample of individuals at their place of residence. Prior to 1999, the NSDUH used a paper-and-pencil interviewing (PAPI) methodology. Since 1999, the interview has been carried out with computer assisted interviewing (CAI) methodology. The survey uses a combination of computer-assisted personal-interviewing (CAPI), conducted by the interviewer for some basic demographic information, and audio computer-assisted self-interviewing (ACASI) for most of the questions. ACASI provides a highly private and confidential means of responding to questions to increase the level of honest reporting of illicit drug use and other sensitive behavior. The 2003 NSDUH employed a 50-State sample design with an independent, multistage area probability sample for each of the 50 States and the District of Columbia to support the development of both national and State-level estimates. Each State was stratified into regions (48 regions in each of 8 large States, 12 regions in each of 42 small States and the District of Columbia). At the first stage of sampling, 8 area segments were selected in each region, for a total of 7,200 sample units nationally. The design also oversampled youths and young adults, so that each State's sample was approximately equally distributed among three major age groups: 12–17 years, 18–25 years, and 26 years or over.

Sample Size and Response Rate: Nationally, 130,605 addresses were screened for the 2003 survey, and 67,784 completed interviews were obtained. The survey was conducted from January to December 2003. Weighted response rates for household screening and for interviewing were 90.7 and 77.4 percent, respectively.

Issues Affecting Interpretation: Several improvements to the survey were implemented in 2002. In addition to the name change, respondents were offered a $30 incentive payment for participation in the survey starting in 2002, and quality control procedures for data collection were enhanced in 2001 and 2002. Because of these improvements and modifications, estimates from the NSDUH completed in 2002 and later should not be compared with estimates from the 2001 or earlier versions of the survey. The data collected in 2002 represent a new baseline for tracking trends in substance use and other measures. Estimates of substance use for youth based on the NSDUH are not directly comparable with estimates based on Monitoring the Future (MTF) and Youth Risk Behavior Surveillance System (YRBSS). In addition to the fact that the MTF excludes dropouts and absentees, rates are not directly comparable across these surveys because of differences in populations covered, sample design, questionnaires, interview setting, and statistical approaches to make the survey estimates generalizable to the entire population. The NSDUH survey collects data in homes, whereas the MTF and YRBSS collect data in school classrooms. The NSDUH estimates are tabulated by age, while the MTF and YRBSS estimates are tabulated by grade, representing different ages as well as different populations.

References:

Substance Abuse and Mental Health Services Administration. Results from the 2003 National Survey on Drug Use and Health: National Findings. Office of Applied Studies, NSDUH Series H–25, DHHS Publication No. SMA 04–3964. Rockville, MD. 2004.

Wright D, Sathe N. State estimates of substance use from the 2002–2003 national surveys on drug use and health (DHHS Publication No. SMA 05–3989, NSDUH Series H-26). Substance Abuse and Mental Health Services Administration. Rockville, MD: Office of Applied Studies. 2004.

Cowan CD. Coverage, sample design, and weighting in three Federal surveys. Journal of Drug Issues; 31(3):595–614. 2001.

For More Information: See the NSDUH Web site at https://nsduhweb.rti.org/ or the SAMHSA Office of Applied Studies Web site at http://oas.samhsa.gov/.

National Survey of Family Growth (NSFG)

Centers for Disease Control and Prevention National Center for Health Statistics

Overview: The National Survey of Family Growth (NSFG) provides national data on factors affecting birth and pregnancy rates, adoption, and maternal and infant health.

Selected Content: Data elements include sexual activity, marriage, divorce and remarriage, unmarried cohabitation, contraception and sterilization, infertility, breastfeeding, pregnancy loss, low birthweight, and use of medical care for family planning and infertility.

Data Years: Six cycles of the survey have been completed: 1973, 1976, 1982, 1988, 1995, and 2002.

Coverage: The 1973–95 cycles of the National Survey of Family Growth (NSFG) were based on samples of women ages 15–44 years in the civilian noninstitutionalized population of the United States. The first and second cycles (1973 and 1976) excluded most women who had never been married. The third, fourth, and fifth cycles (1982, 1988, and 1995) included all women ages 15–44 years in the civilian noninstitutional population of the United States. The sixth cycle (2002) included men and women 15–44 years of age in the household population of the United States.

Methodology: Interviews are conducted in person by professional female interviewers using a standardized questionnaire. In all cycles, black women were sampled at higher rates than white women so that detailed statistics for black women could be produced. In cycles 5 and 6 (1995 and 2002), Hispanics were also oversampled.

To make national estimates from the sample for the millions of women ages 15–44 years in the United States, data for the interviewed sample women were (a) inflated by the reciprocal of the probability of selection at each stage of sampling (for example, if there was a 1 in 5,000 chance that a woman would be selected for the sample, her sampling weight was 5,000); (b) adjusted for nonresponse; and (c) poststratified, or forced to agree with benchmark population values based on data from the U.S. Census Bureau.

Sample Size and Response Rates: For Cycle 1, from 101 PSUs, 10,879 women 15–44 years of age were selected, 9,797 of these were interviewed. In Cycle 2, from 79 PSUs, 10,202 eligible women were identified; of these, 8,611 were interviewed. In Cycle 3, household screener interviews were completed in 29,511 households (95.1 percent). Of the 9,964 eligible women identified, 7,969 were interviewed. In Cycle 4, 10,566 eligible women ages 15–44 years were sampled. Interviews were completed with 8,450 women. The response rate for the 1990 telephone reinterview was 68 percent of those responding to the 1988 survey and still eligible for the 1990 survey. In Cycle 5, of the 13,795 eligible women in the sample, 10,847 were interviewed. In Cycle 6, from 120 PSUs, 7,643 (about 80 percent) of interviews were completed with eligible women and 4,928 (78 percent) interviews were completed with men.

References:

French DK. National Survey of Family Growth, Cycle I: Sample design, estimation procedures, and variance estimation. National Center for Health Statistics. Vital Health Stat Series no 2(76). 1978.

Grady WR. National Survey of Family Growth, Cycle II: Sample design, estimation procedures, and variance estimation. National Center for Health Statistics. Vital Health Stat Series no 2(87). 198l.

Bachrach CA, Horn MC, Mosher WD, Shimizu I. National Survey of Family Growth, Cycle III: Sample design, weighting, and variance estimation. National Center for Health Statistics. Vital Health Stat Series no 2(98). 1985.

Judkins DR, Mosher WD, Botman SL. National Survey of Family Growth: Design, estimation, and inference. National Center for Health Statistics. Vital Health Stat Series no 2(109). 1991.

Goksel H, Judkins DR, Mosher WD. Nonresponse adjustments for a telephone follow-up to a National In-Person Survey. Journal of Official Statistics; 8(4):417–32. 1992.

Kelly JE, Mosher WD, Duffer AP, Kinsey SH. Plan and operation of the 1995 National Survey of Family Growth. Vital Health Stat 1(36). 1997.

Potter FJ, Iannacchione VG, Mosher WD, Mason RE, Kavee JD. Sampling weights, imputation, and variance estimation in the 1995 National Survey of Family Growth. Vital Health Stat Series no 2(124). 1998.

Groves R, Mosher W, Benson G, et al. Plan and operation of the 2002 National Survey of Family Growth. National Center for Health Statistics. Vital Health Stat Series no 1(42). Forthcoming.

For More Information: See the NCHS Web site at www.cdc.gov/nchs/nsfg.htm.

National Vital Statistics System (NVSS)

Centers for Disease Control and Prevention

National Center for Health Statistics

Overview: The National Vital Statistics System (NVSS) collects and publishes official national statistics on births, deaths, fetal deaths, and prior to 1996, marriages and divorces occurring in the United States based on U.S. Standard Certificates. Fetal deaths are classified and tabulated separately from other deaths. Detailed descriptions of the five Vital Statistics files (birth file, mortality file, multiple cause of death file, linked birth/infant death data set, and compressed mortality file) are presented separately below.

Data Years: The death-registration area for 1900 consisted of 10 States, the District of Columbia, and a number of cities located in nonregistration States; it covered 40 percent of the continental U.S. population. The birth registration area was established in 1915 with 10 States and the District of Columbia. The birth and death registration areas continued to expand until 1933, when they included all 48 States and the District of Columbia. Alaska and Hawaii were added to both registration areas in 1959 and 1960, the years in which they gained statehood.

Coverage: The NVSS collects and presents U.S. resident data for the aggregate of 50 States, New York City, and the District of Columbia, as well as for each individual State and the District of Columbia. Vital events occurring in the United States to non-U.S. residents and vital events occurring abroad to U.S. residents are excluded.

Methodology: NCHS's Division of Vital Statistics obtains information on births and deaths from the registration offices of each of the 50 States, New York City, the District of Columbia, Puerto Rico, the U.S. Virgin Islands, Guam, American Samoa, and Northern Mariana Islands. Until 1972 microfilm copies of all death certificates and a 50-percent sample of birth certificates were received from all registration areas and processed by NCHS. In 1972, some States began sending their data to NCHS through the Cooperative Health Statistics System (CHSS). States that participated in the CHSS program processed 100 percent of their death and birth records and sent the entire data file to NCHS on computer tapes. Currently, data are sent to NCHS through the Vital Statistics Cooperative Program (VSCP), following the same procedures as CHSS. The number of participating States grew from 6 in 1972 to 46 in 1984. Starting in 1985 all 50 States and the District of Columbia participated in VSCP.

U.S. Standard Certificates—U.S. Standard Live Birth and Death Certificates and Fetal Death Reports are revised periodically, allowing evaluation and addition, modification, and deletion of items. Beginning with 1989 revised standard certificates replaced the 1978 versions. The 1989 revision of the birth certificate included items to identify the Hispanic parentage of newborns and to expand information about maternal and infant health characteristics. The 1989 revision of the death certificate included items on educational attainment and Hispanic origin of decedents, as well as changes to improve the medical certification of cause of death. Standard certificates recommended by NCHS are modified in each registration area to serve the area's needs.

However, most certificates conform closely in content and arrangement to the standard certificate, and all certificates contain a minimum data set specified by NCHS. Following 1989, the next revisions of vital records went into effect in some States beginning in 2003, but full implementation in all States will be phased in over several years.

Birth File

Overview: Vital statistics natality data are a fundamental source of demographic, geographic, and medical and health information on all births occurring in the United States. This is one of the few sources of comparable health-related data for small geographic areas over an extended time period. The data are used to present the characteristics of babies and their mothers, track trends such as birth rates for teenagers, and compare natality trends with other countries.

Selected Content: The natality file includes characteristics about the baby such as sex, birthweight, weeks of gestation; demographic information about the parents such as age, race, Hispanic origin, parity, educational attainment, marital status, and State of residence; medical and health information such as prenatal care based on hospital records; and behavioral risk factors for the birth such as mother's tobacco use during pregnancy.

Data Years: The birth registration area began in 1915 with 10 States and the District of Columbia.

Methodology: In the United States, State laws require birth certificates to be completed for all births. The registration of births is the responsibility of the professional attendant at birth, generally a physician or midwife. The birth certificate must be filed with the local registrar of the district in which the birth occurs. Each birth must be reported promptly—the reporting requirements vary from State to State, ranging from 24 hours after the birth to as much as 10 days.

Federal law mandates national collection and publication of birth and other vital statistics data. The National Vital Statistics System is the result of cooperation between NCHS and the States to provide access to statistical information from birth certificates. Standard forms for the collection of the data and model procedures for the uniform registration of the events are developed and recommended for State use through cooperative activities of the States and NCHS. NCHS shares the costs incurred by the States in providing vital statistics data for national use.

Issues Affecting Interpretation: In 2003, two States, Pennsylvania and Washington, implemented the 2003 revision of the U.S. Standard Certificate of Live Birth (revised). Data on mother's educational attainment, tobacco use during pregnancy, and prenatal care based on the 2003 revision are not comparable with data based on the 1989 revision of the U.S. Standard Certificate of Live Birth (revised), and are excluded from *Health, United States* statistics. Prior to 2003, the number of States reporting information on maternal education, Hispanic origin, marital status, and tobacco use during pregnancy increased over the years. Interpretation of trend data should take into consideration expansion of reporting areas and immigration. See Appendix II for methodological and reporting area changes for the following birth certificate items: *Age* (maternal age); *Education* (maternal education); *Hispanic origin; Marital status; Prenatal care; Race;* and *Tobacco use.*

Reference:

National Center for Health Statistics, Vital Statistics of the United States 2000, Vol. I Natality, Technical Appendix, found at http://www.cdc.gov/nchs/data/techap00.pdf.

For More Information: See the Birth Data Web site at www.cdc.gov/nchs/births.htm.

Mortality File

Overview: Vital statistics mortality data are a fundamental source of demographic, geographic, and cause-of-death information. This is one of the few sources of comparable health-related data for small geographic areas over an extended time period. The data are used to present the characteristics of those dying in the United States, to determine life expectancy, and to compare mortality trends with other countries.

Selected Content: The mortality file includes demographic information on age, sex, race, Hispanic origin, State of residence, and educational attainment, and medical information on cause of death.

Data Years: The death registration area began in 1900 with 10 States and the District of Columbia.

Methodology: By law, the registration of deaths is the responsibility of the funeral director. The funeral director obtains demographic data for the death certificate from an informant. The physician in attendance at the death is required to certify the cause of death. Where death is from other than natural causes, a coroner or medical examiner may be required to examine the body and certify the cause of death. Data for the entire United States refer to events occurring within the United States; data for geographic areas are by place of residence. See Appendix II for methodological and reporting area changes for the following death certificate items: *Education; Hispanic origin;* and *Race.*

Issues Affecting Interpretation: International Classification of Diseases (ICD), by which cause of death is coded and classified, is revised approximately every 10 to 15 years. Revisions of the ICD may cause discontinuities in trend data by cause of death. Comparing death rates by cause of death across ICD revisions should be conducted with caution and with reference to the comparability ratio. (See Appendix II, *Comparability ratio.*) The death certificate has been revised periodically. A revised U.S. Standard Certificate of Death was recommended for State use beginning on January 1, 1989. Among the changes were the addition of a new item on educational attainment and Hispanic origin of decedent and changes to improve the medical certification of cause of death.

References:

Grove RD, Hetzel AM. Vital statistics rates in the United States, 1940–60. Washington: Government Printing Office. 1968.

National Center for Health Statistics, Vital Statistics of the United States, Vol II Mortality part A, Technical Appendix, available at www.cdc.gov/nchs/datawh/statab/pubd/ta.htm.

For More Information: See the Mortality Data Web site at www.cdc.gov/nchs/about/major/dvs/mortdata.htm.

Multiple Cause-of-Death File

Overview: Multiple cause-of-death data reflect all medical information reported on death certificates and complement traditional underlying cause-of-death data. Multiple cause data give information on diseases that are a factor in death whether or not they are the underlying cause of death, on associations among diseases, and on injuries leading to death.

Selected Content: In addition to the same demographic variables listed for the mortality file, the multiple cause-of-death file includes record axis and entity axis cause-of-death data (see *Methodology* section).

Data Years: Multiple cause-of-death data files are available for every data year since 1968.

Methodology: NCHS is responsible for compiling and publishing annual national statistics on causes of death. In carrying out this responsibility, NCHS adheres to the World Health Organization Nomenclature Regulations. These Regulations require that (1) cause of death be coded in accordance with the applicable revision of the *International Classification of Diseases* (ICD) (see Appendix II, table IV and *ICD*); and (2) underlying cause of death be selected in accordance with international rules. Traditionally, national mortality statistics have been based on a count of deaths, with one underlying cause assigned for each death.

Starting with data year 1968, electronic files exist with multiple cause-of-death information. These files contain codes for all diagnostic terms and related codable information recorded on the death certificate. These codes make up the entity axis and are the input for a software program called TRANSAX. The TRANSAX program eliminates redundant entity axis codes and combines other entity axis codes to create the best set of ICD codes for a record. The output of the TRANSAX program is the record axis. Record axis data are generally used for research and analysis of multiple or nonunderlying cause of death. Because the function of the TRANSAX program is not to select a single underlying cause of death, record axis data may or may not include the underlying cause. Tabulations of underlying and nonunderlying cause of death in table 48 (selected occupational diseases) are compiled by searching both underlying cause of death and record axis data.

Reference: Multiple Causes of Death in the United States. Monthly vital statistics report; vol 32 no 10, supp 2. Hyattsville, MD: National Center for Health Statistics. February 17, 1984.

For More Information: See the mortality multiple cause-of-death data file page at www.cdc.gov/nchs/products/elec_prods/subject/mortmcd.htm.

Linked Birth/Infant Death Data Set

Overview: National linked files of live births and infant deaths are used for research on infant mortality.

Selected Content: The linked birth/infant death data set includes all variables on the natality file, including racial and ethnic information, as well as variables on the mortality file, including cause of death and age at death.

Data Years: National linked files of live births and infant deaths were first produced for the 1983 birth cohort. Birth cohort linked file data are available for 1983–91 and period linked file data starting with 1995. National linked files do not exist for 1992–94.

Methodology: To create the linked data files, death certificates are linked with corresponding birth certificates for infants who die in the United States before their first birthday. About 97–99 percent of files can be linked. The linkage makes available extensive information about the pregnancy, maternal risk factors, infant characteristics, and health items at birth that can be used in analyses of infant mortality.

Starting with data year 1995, more timely linked file data are produced in a period data format preceding the release of the corresponding birth cohort format. Other changes to the data set starting with 1995 data include addition of record weights to correct for the 1.0–1.4 percent in 2000–2002 (2.1–2.5 percent in 1995–99) of records that could not be linked and for the addition of an imputation for not stated birthweight. The 1995–2001 weighted mortality rates are from less than 1 percent to 4.1 percent higher than unweighted rates for the same period. The 1995–2001 weighted mortality rates with imputed birthweight are less than 1 percent to 6.3 percent higher than unweighted rates with imputed birthweight for the same period.

Issues Affecting Interpretation: Period linked file data starting with 1995 are not strictly comparable with birth cohort data for 1983–91. While birth cohort linked files have methodological advantages, their production incurs substantial delays in data availability, since it is necessary to wait until the close of a second data year to include all infant deaths to the birth cohort.

Reference:

Mathews TJ, Menacker F, MacDorman MF. Infant mortality statistics from the 2002 period linked birth/infant death data set. National vital statistics report; vol 53 no 10. Hyattsville, Maryland: National Center for Health Statistics. 2004.

For More Information: See the NCHS Linked Birth and Infant Death Data Web site at www.cdc.gov/nchs/linked.htm.

Compressed Mortality File

Overview: The Compressed Mortality File (CMF) is a county-level national mortality and population database.

Selected Content: The compressed mortality database contains mortality data derived from the detailed mortality files of the National Vital Statistics System and from the U.S. Census Bureau estimates of U.S. national, State, and county resident populations. Number of deaths, crude death rates, and age-adjusted death rates can be obtained by place of residence (total U.S., State, and county), age group, race (white, black, and other), sex, year of death, and underlying cause of death.

Data Years: The CMF spans the years 1968–2002. On CDC WONDER, data are available starting with 1979.

Methodology: In *Health, United States*, the CMF is used to compute death rates by urbanization level of decedent's county of residence. Counties are categorized according to level of urbanization based on an NCHS-modified version of the 1993 rural-urban continuum codes for metropolitan and nonmetropolitan counties developed by the Economic Research Service, U.S. Department of Agriculture. See Appendix II, *Urbanization*.

For More Information: See the Compressed Mortality File Web site at: http://www.cdc.gov/nchs/products/elec_prods/subject/mcompres.htm; or see the CDC Wonder Web site at http://wonder.cdc.gov/mortSQL.html.

Online Survey Certification and Reporting Database (OSCAR)

Centers for Medicare & Medicaid Services

Overview: The Online Survey Certification and Reporting (OSCAR) is an administrative database containing detailed information on all Medicare and Medicaid certified institutional health care providers, including all currently and previously certified Medicare and Medicaid nursing homes in the United States and Territories. (Data for the Territories are not shown in *(Health, United States)*. The purpose of the nursing home survey certification process is to ensure that nursing facilities meet the current Centers for Medicare & Medicaid Services

(CMS) care requirements and thus can be reimbursed for services furnished to Medicare and Medicaid beneficiaries.

Selected Content: OSCAR contains information on facility and patient characteristics and health deficiencies issued by the government during State surveys.

Data Years: OSCAR has been maintained by CMS, formerly the Health Care Financing Administration (HCFA), since 1992. OSCAR is an updated version of the Medicare and Medicaid Automated Certification System that had been in existence since 1972.

Coverage: All nursing homes in the United States that receive Medicare or Medicaid payments are included. Nursing homes that are intermediate care facilities for the mentally retarded and Department of Veterans Affairs nursing homes are excluded.

Methodology: Information on the number of beds and other facility characteristics comes from HCFA form 671, and information on residents and resident characteristics is collected on HCFA form 672. A nursing home representative fills out the forms, and they are submitted to CMS. The information provided on HCFA forms 671 and 672 can be audited at any time.

All certified nursing homes are inspected by representatives of the State survey agency (generally the department of health) at least once every 15 months. Therefore, a complete census must be based on a 15-month reporting cycle rather than a 12-month cycle. Some nursing homes are inspected twice or more often during any given reporting cycle. To avoid overcounting, the data must be edited and duplicates removed. Data editing and compilation were performed by Cowles Research Group and published in the group's *Nursing Home Statistical Yearbook* series.

References:

Cowles CM. 1995; 1996; 1997 Nursing home statistical yearbook. Anacortes, WA: Cowles Research Group (CRG). 1995; 1997; 1998.

Cowles CM, 1998; 1999; 2000; 2001 Nursing home statistical yearbook. Washington: American Association of Homes and Services for the Aging (AAHSA). 1999; 2000; 2001; 2002.

For More Information: See the CRG Web site at www.longtermcareinfo.com/crg or the AAHSA Web site at www.aahsa.org.

Population Census and Population Estimates

Bureau of the Census

Decennial Census

The census of population (decennial census) has been held in the United States every 10 years since 1790. The decennial census has enumerated the resident population as of April 1 of the census year ever since 1930. Data on sex, race, age, and marital status are collected from 100 percent of the enumerated population. More detailed information, such as income, education, housing, occupation, and industry, are collected from a representative sample of the population.

Race Data on the 1990 Census

The question on race on the 1990 census was based on the Office of Management and Budget's (OMB) "1977 Statistical Policy Directive 15, Race and Ethnicity Standards for Federal Statistics and Administrative Reporting." This document specified rules for the collection, tabulation, and reporting of race and ethnicity data within the Federal statistical system. The 1977 standards required Federal agencies to report race-specific tabulations using four single-race categories: American Indian or Alaska Native, Asian or Pacific Islander, black, and white. Under the 1977 standards, race and ethnicity were considered to be two separate and distinct concepts. Thus, persons of Hispanic origin may be of any race.

Race Data on the 2000 Census

The question on race on the 2000 census was based on OMB's 1997 "Revisions of the Standards for the Classification of Federal Data on Race and Ethnicity" (see Appendix II, *Race*). The 1997 Standards incorporated two major changes in the collection, tabulation, and presentation of race data. First, the 1997 standards increased from four to five the minimum set of categories to be used by Federal agencies for identification of race: American Indian or Alaska Native, Asian, Black or African American, Native Hawaiian or Other Pacific Islander, and white. Second, the 1997 standards included the requirement that Federal data collection programs allow respondents to select one or more race categories when responding to a query on their racial identity.

This provision means that there are potentially 31 race groups, depending on whether an individual selects one, two, three, four, or all five of the race categories. The 1997 standards continue to call for use, when possible, of a separate question on Hispanic or Latino ethnicity and specify that the ethnicity question should appear before the question on race. Thus, under the 1997 standards, as under the 1977 standards, Hispanics may be of any race.

Modified Decennial Census Files

For several decades, the Census Bureau has produced modified decennial census files. These modified files incorporate adjustments to the 100 percent April 1 count data for 1) errors in the census data discovered subsequent to publication, 2) misreported age data, and 3) nonspecified race.

For the 1990 census, the Census Bureau modified the age, race, and sex data on the census and produced the Modified Age Race Sex (MARS) file. The differences between the population counts on the original census file and the MARS file are primarily due to modification of the race data. Of the 248.7 million persons enumerated in 1990, 9.8 million persons did not specify their race (over 95 percent were of Hispanic origin). For the 1990 MARS file, these persons were assigned the race reported by a nearby person with an identical response to the Hispanic origin question.

For the 2000 census, the Census Bureau modified the race data on the census and produced the Modified Race Data Summary File. For this file, persons who reported "Some other race" as part of their race response were assigned to one of the 31 race groups, which are the single- and multiple-race combinations of the five race categories specified in the 1997 race and ethnicity standards. Persons who did not specify their race were assigned to one of the 31 race groups using imputation. Of the 18.5 million persons who reported "Some other race" as part of their race response, or who did not specify their race, 16.8 million (90.4 percent) were of Hispanic origin.

Bridged-Race Population Estimates for Census 2000

Race data on the 2000 census are not comparable with race data on other data systems that are continuing to collect data using the 1977 standards on race and ethnicity during the transition to full implementation of the 1997 standards. For example, most of the States in the Vital Statistics Cooperative Program will revise their birth and death certificates to conform to the 1997 standards after 2000. Thus, population estimates for 2000 and beyond with race categories comparable to the 1977 categories are needed so that race-specific birth and death rates can be calculated. To meet this need, NCHS, in collaboration with the U.S. Census Bureau, developed methodology to bridge the 31 race groups in census 2000 to the four single-race categories specified under the 1977 standards.

The bridging methodology was developed using information from the 1997–2000 National Health Interview Survey (NHIS) The NHIS provides a unique opportunity to investigate multiple-race groups because, since 1982, the NHIS has allowed respondents to choose more than one race but has also asked respondents reporting multiple races to choose a "primary" race. The bridging methodology developed by NCHS involved the application of regression models relating person-level and county-level covariates to the selection of a particular primary race by the multiple-race respondents. Bridging proportions derived from these models were applied by the U.S. Census Bureau to the Census 2000 Modified Race Data Summary File. This application resulted in bridged counts of the April 1, 2000, resident single-race populations for four racial groups, American Indian or Alaska Native, Asian or Pacific Islander, black, and white.

For More Information about bridged-race population estimates, see Ingram DD, Parker JD, Schenker N, et al. United States Census 2000 population with bridged race categories. National Center for Health Statistics. Vital Health Stat 2(135). 2003; and the NCHS Web site for U.S. Census Populations with Bridged Race Categories www.cdc.gov/nchs/about/major/dvs/popbridge/popbridge.htm.

Postcensal Population Estimates

Postcensal population estimates are estimates made for the years following a census, before the next census has been taken. National postcensal population estimates are derived by updating the resident population enumerated in the decennial census using a components of population change approach. The following formula is used to update the decennial census counts:

(1) decennial census enumerated resident population
(2) + births to U.S. resident women,
(3) – deaths to U.S. residents,
(4) + net international migration,

(5) + net movement of U.S. Armed Forces and U.S. civilian citizens

State postcensal estimates are based on similar data and on a variety of other data series, including school statistics from State departments of education and parochial school systems. The postcensal estimates are consistent with official decennial census figures and do not reflect estimated decennial census underenumeration.

The Census Bureau has produced a postcensal series of estimates of the July 1 resident population of the United States based on census 2000 by applying the components of change methodology to the Modified Race Data Summary File. These postcensal estimates have race data for 31 race groups, in accordance with the 1997 race and ethnicity standards. So that the race data for the 2000-based postcensal estimates would be comparable with race data on vital records, the Census Bureau applied the NHIS bridging methodology to the 31-race group postcensal population estimates to obtain postcensal estimates for the four single-race categories (American Indian or Alaska Native, Asian or Pacific Islander, black, and white). Bridged-race postcensal population estimates are available at www.cdc.gov/nchs/about/major/dvs/popbridge/popbridge.htm.

Note that before the bridged-race April 1, 2000, population counts and the bridged-race 2000-based postcensal estimates were available, the Census Bureau extended their postcensal series of estimates based on the 1990 census (with the four single-race categories needed to compute vital rates) to July 1, 2001. NCHS initially calculated vital rates for 2000 using 1990-based July 1, 2000, postcensal population estimates and vital rates for 2001 using 1990-based July 1, 2001, postcensal estimates. Vital rates for 2000 have been revised using the bridged-race April 1, 2000, population counts, and vital rates for 2001 have been revised using the 2000-based bridged-race July 1, 2001, postcensal population estimates.

Intercensal Population Estimates

The further from the census year on which the postcensal estimates are based, the less accurate are the postcensal estimates. With the completion of the decennial census at the end of the decade, intercensal estimates for the preceding decade were prepared to replace the less accurate postcensal estimates. Intercensal population estimates take into account the census of population at the beginning and end of the decade. Thus intercensal estimates are more accurate than postcensal estimates because they correct for the "error of closure" or difference between the estimated population at the end of the decade and the census count for that date. The "error of closure" at the national level was quite small for the 1960s (379,000). However, for the 1970s, it amounted to almost 5 million; for the 1980s, 1.5 million; for the 1990s, about 6 million. The error of closure differentially affects age, race, sex, and Hispanic origin subgroup populations as well as the rates based on these populations. Vital rates that were calculated using postcensal population estimates are routinely revised when intercensal estimates become available because the intercensal estimates correct for the error of closure.

Intercensal estimates for the 1990s with race data comparable to the 1977 standards have been derived so that vital rates for the 1990s could be revised to reflect census 2000. Calculation of the intercensal population estimates for the 1990s was complicated by the incomparability of the race data on the 1990 and 2000 censuses. The Census Bureau, in collaboration with National Cancer Institute and NCHS, derived race-specific intercensal population estimates for the 1990s using the 1990 MARS file as the beginning population base and the bridged-race population estimates for April 1, 2000, as the ending population base. Bridged-race intercensal population estimates are available at www.cdc.gov/nchs/about/major/dvs/popbridge/popbridge.htm.

Special Population Estimates

Special population estimates are prepared for the education reporting area for mortality statistics because educational attainment of decedent is not reported by all 50 States. The Housing and Household Economics Statistics Division of the U.S. Bureau of the Census currently produces unpublished estimates of populations by age, race, sex, and educational attainment for NCHS. These population estimates are based on the Current Population Survey, adjusted to resident population controls. The control totals used for July 1, 1994–96 are 1990-based population estimates for 45 reporting States and the District of Columbia (DC); for July 1, 1997–2000, 1990-based postcensal population estimates for 46 reporting States and DC; and for July 1, 2001–02, 2000-based postcensal population estimates for 47 reporting States and DC. See Appendix II, *Education*.

For More Information: See the U.S. Census Bureau Web site at www.census.gov/.

Sexually Transmitted Disease (STD) Surveillance

Centers for Disease Control and Prevention

National Center of HIV, STD, and TB Prevention

Overview: Surveillance information on incidence and prevalence of sexually transmitted diseases (STDs) is used to inform public and private health efforts to control these diseases.

Selected Content: Case reporting data are available for nationally notifiable chanchroid, chlamydia, gonorrhea, and syphilis; surveillance of other STDs, such as genital herpes simplex virus (HSV), genital warts or other human papillomavirus infections, and trichomoniasis, are based on estimates of office visits in physicians' office practices provided by the National Disease and Therapeutic Index (NDTI).

Data Years: STD national surveillance data have been collected since 1941.

Coverage: Case reports of STDs are reported to CDC by STD surveillance systems operated by State and local STD control programs and health departments in 50 States, the District of Columbia, selected cities, 3,139 U.S. counties, and outlying areas comprised of U.S. dependencies, possessions, and independent nations in free association with the United States. Data from outlying areas are not included in *Health, United States.*

Methodology: Information is obtained from the following sources of data: (1) case reports from STD project areas; (2) prevalence data from the Regional Infertility Prevention Program, the National Job Training Program (formerly the Job Corps), the Jail STD Prevalence Monitoring Projects, the adolescent Women Reproductive Health Monitoring Project, the Men Who Have Sex With Men (MSM) Prevalence Monitoring Project, and the Indian Health Service; (3) sentinel surveillance of gonococcal antimicrobial resistance from the Gonococcal Isolate Surveillance Project (GISP); and (4) national sample surveys implemented by Federal and private organizations. STD data are submitted to CDC on a variety of hard-copy summary reporting forms (monthly, quarterly, and annually) and in electronic summary or individual case-specific (line-listed) formats via the National Electronic Telecommunications System for Surveillance (NETSS).

Issues Affecting Interpretation: Because of incomplete diagnosis and reporting, the number of STD cases reported to CDC undercounts the actual number of cases occurring among the U.S. population. Reference: Centers for Disease Control and Prevention. Sexually Transmitted Disease Surveillance, 2002. Atlanta, GA: Department of Health and Human Services. 2003.

For More Information: See the STD Surveillance Report Web site at http://www.cdc.gov/std/stats/ or the STD Prevention Web site at: http://www.cdc.gov/std/default.htm.

Surveillance, Epidemiology, and End Results (SEER) Program

National Cancer Institute

Overview: The Surveillance, Epidemiology, and End Results (SEER) program tracks incidence of persons diagnosed with cancer during the year as well as follow-up information on all previously diagnosed patients until death.

Selected Content: SEER registries routinely collect data on patient demographics, primary tumor site, morphology, stage at diagnosis, first course of treatment, and follow-up for vital status.

Data Years: Case ascertainment for SEER began on January 1, 1973, and has continued for more than 30 years.

Coverage: SEER cancer registries were initiated in 1973 in Connecticut, Iowa, New Mexico, Utah, Hawaii, Detroit, and San Francisco-Oakland. Registries were added as follows: in 1974–75, Atlanta and Seattle-Puget Sound; in 1978, 10 predominantly black rural counties in Georgia; in 1980, American Indians in Arizona; New Orleans, Louisiana (1974–77, rejoined 2001); New Jersey (1979–89, rejoined 2001); and Puerto Rico (1973–89); in 1992, Alaska Native populations in Alaska and Hispanics in Los Angeles County and San Jose-Monterey; in 2001, Kentucky, Greater California, New Jersey, and Louisiana. The SEER Program currently collects and publishes cancer incidence and survival data from 14 population-based cancer registries and three supplemental registries covering approximately 26 percent of the U.S. population.

The following combination of SEER registries are commonly used for statistical analyses and are used for analysis of cancer survival rates in *Health, United States*: the SEER 9 registries of Atlanta, Connecticut, Detroit, Hawaii, Iowa, New Mexico, San Francisco-Oakland, Seattle-Puget Sound, and Utah. Analysis of cancer incidence covers residents in the following SEER 12 registries: the SEER 9 registries plus Los Angeles, San Jose-Monterey, and the Alaska Native Tumor Registry.

Methodology: A cancer registry (or tumor registry) collects and stores data on cancers diagnosed in a specific hospital or medical facility (hospital-based registry) or in a defined geographic area (population-based registry). A population-based registry is generally composed of a number of hospital-based registries. In SEER registry areas, trained coders abstract medical records using the *International Classification of Diseases for Oncology, Third Edition* (ICD–O–3), which provides a coding system for onset and stage of specific cancers. The third edition, implemented in 2001, is the first complete review and revision of the text and guidelines since its original publication in 1988.

Population estimates used to calculate incidence rates are obtained from the U.S. Census Bureau. NCI uses estimation procedures as needed to obtain estimates for years and races not included in data provided by the U.S. Census Bureau. Life tables used to determine normal life expectancy when calculating relative survival rates were obtained from NCHS and in-house calculations. Separate life tables are used for each race-sex-specific group included in the SEER Program.

Issues Affecting Interpretation: Because of the addition of registries over time, analysis of long-term incidence and survival trends is limited to those registries that have been in SEER for similar lengths of time. Analysis of Hispanic, American Indian and Alaska Native data is limited to shorter trends. Rates presented in this report may differ somewhat from previous reports due to revised population estimates and the addition and deletion of small numbers of incidence cases.

Reference:

Ries LAG, Eisner MP, Kosary CL, et al. (eds). SEER Cancer Statistics Review 1975–2001. Bethesda, MD: National Cancer Institute. 2004, available at http://seer.cancer.gov/csr/1975_2001.

For More Information: See the SEER Web site at www.seer.cancer.gov.

Survey of Mental Health Organizations (SMHO)

Substance Abuse and Mental Health Services Administration (SAMHSA)

Overview: The Survey of Mental Health Organizations and General Hospital Mental Health Services (SMHO/GHMHS) collects data on number and characteristics of specialty mental health organizations in the United States.

Selected Content: The inventory collects basic information, such as types of mental health organizations, ownership, number of additions and residents, and number of beds. The sample survey is a more detailed questionnaire that covers types of services provided, revenues and expenditures, staffing, and many items addressed to managed behavioral health care.

Data Years: The Inventory of Mental Health Organizations (IMHO/GHMHS) was conducted biannually from 1986 until 1994. The SMHO replaced the IMHO/GHMHS in 1998. The SMHO and the inventory used as its sampling frame have been conducted biannually starting in 1998.

Coverage: Organizations included are State and county mental hospitals, private psychiatric hospitals, non-Federal general hospitals with separate psychiatric services, Department of Veterans Affairs medical centers, residential treatment centers for emotionally disturbed children, freestanding outpatient psychiatric clinics, partial care organizations, freestanding day-night organizations, and multiservice mental health organizations not elsewhere classified.

Methodology: The IMHO was an inventory of all mental health organizations. Its core questionnaire included versions designed for specialty mental health organizations and another for non-Federal general hospitals with separate psychiatric services. The data system was based on questionnaires mailed every other year to mental health organizations in the United States. In 1998, the IMHO was replaced by the SMHO. The SMHO is made up of two parts. A complete inventory is done by postcard gathering a limited amount of information. The inventory is used as a sampling frame for the SMHO, which contains most of the information from the IMHO core questionnaire as well as new items about managed behavioral health care.

Sample Size and Response Rate: Phase I, all organizations were inventoried by postcard (about 10,000). A complete enumeration was needed to define the sampling frame for the sample survey. In Phase II, general hospitals without separate mental health units, community residential organizations, and managed behavioral health care organizations are dropped from the sampling frame. From this number, approximately between 1,600 and 2,200 organizations are drawn for the sample survey and sent a questionnaire with a response rate of approximately 90 percent.

Issues Affecting Interpretation: Revisions to definitions of providers include phasing out Community Mental Health Centers as a category after 1981–82; increasing the number of multiservice mental health organizations from 1981 to 1986; increasing the number of psychiatric outpatient clinics in 1981–82, but decreasing the number in 1983–84, 1986, 1990, and 1992; and increasing the number of partial care services in 1983–84. These changes should be noted when interyear comparisons for the affected organizations and service types are made. The increase in the number of general hospitals with separate psychiatric services was partially due to a more concerted effort to identify these organizations. Forms had been sent only to those hospitals previously identified as having a separate psychiatric service. Beginning in 1980–81, a screener form was sent to general hospitals not previously identified as providing a separate psychiatric service to determine whether they had such a service.

Reference:

Center for Mental Health Services. Mental Health, United States, 2002. Manderscheid R, Henderson MJ, eds. DHHS pub no (SMA) SMA04–3938. Washington: Department of Health and Human Services. 2004, available at http:/ www.mentalhealth.samhsa.gov/ publications/allpubs/SMA04–3938.

For More Information: See the Center for Mental Health Services Web site at www.samhsa.gov/centers/cmhs/ cmhs.html.

Survey of Occupational Injuries and Illnesses (SOII)

Bureau of Labor Statistics

Overview: The Survey of Occupational Injuries and Illnesses (SOII) is a Federal/State program that collects statistics used to identify problems with workplace safety and develop programs to improve workplace safety.

Selected Content: Data include the number of injuries and illnesses by industry. The case and demographic data provide additional details on workers injured, the nature of the disabling condition, and the event and source producing that condition for those cases that involve one or more days away from work.

Data Years: The Bureau of Labor Statistics (BLS) has conducted an annual survey since 1971.

Coverage: The data represent persons employed in private industry establishments in the United States. The survey excludes the self-employed, farms with fewer than 11 employees, private households, Federal Government agencies, and State and local government agencies.

Methodology: Survey estimates of occupational injuries and illnesses are based on a scientifically selected probability sample of establishments rather than a census of all establishments. An independent sample is selected for each State and the District of Columbia that represents industries in that jurisdiction. BLS includes all the State samples in the national sample.

Establishments included in the survey are instructed in a mailed questionnaire to provide summary totals of all entries for the previous calendar year to its Log and Summary of Occupational Injuries and Illnesses (OSHA No. 200 form). In addition, from the selected establishments, approximately 550,000 injuries and illnesses with days away from work are sampled to obtain demographic and detailed case characteristic information. An occupational injury is any injury such as a cut, fracture, sprain, or amputation that results from a work-related event or from a single instantaneous exposure in the work environment. An occupational illness is any abnormal condition or disorder other than one resulting from an occupational injury, caused by exposure to factors associated with employment. It includes acute and chronic illnesses or diseases that may be caused by inhalation, absorption, ingestion, or direct contact. Prior to 2002, injury and illness cases involved days away from work, days of restricted work activity, or both (lost workday cases). Starting in 2002, injury and illness cases may involve days away from work, job transfer, or restricted work activity. Restriction may involve shortened hours, a temporary job change, or temporary restrictions on certain duties (for example, no heavy lifting) of a worker's regular job.

Sample Size and Response Rates: Employer reports were collected from about 183,700 private industry establishments in 2003. Survey response rates have typically exceeded 90 percent.

Issues Affecting Interpretation: The number of injuries and illnesses reported in any given year can be influenced by the level of economic activity, working conditions and work practices, worker experience and training, and number of hours worked. Long-term latent illnesses caused by exposure to carcinogens are believed to be understated in the survey's illness measures. In contrast, new illnesses, such as contact dermatitis and carpal tunnel syndrome, are easier to relate directly to workplace activity.

Effective January 1, 2002, the Occupational Safety and Health Administration (OSHA) revised its requirement for recording occupational injuries and illnesses. Because of the revised recordkeeping rule, the estimates from the 2002 survey are not comparable with those from previous years. See www.osha-slc.gov/recordkeeping/index.html for details about the revised recordkeeping requirements.

Data for the mining industry and for railroad activities are provided by Department of Labor's Mine Safety and Health Administration and Department of Transportation's Federal Railroad Administration. Neither of these agencies adopted the revised OSHA recordkeeping requirements for 2002. Therefore, estimates for these industries for 2002 are not comparable with estimates for other industries but are comparable with estimates for prior years. Excluded from the survey are self-employed individuals, farmers with fewer than 11 employees, private households, Federal Government agencies, and employees in State and local government agencies.

Beginning with the 2003 data year, SOII began using the 2002 North American Industry Classification System (NAICS) to classify industries. Prior to 2003, the program used the Standard Industrial Classification (SIC) system and the Bureau of the Census occupational classification system. Although some titles in SIC and NAICS are similar, there is limited compatibility because industry groupings are defined differently between the two systems. See Appendix II, *Industry of employment.*

Reference:

Bureau of Labor Statistics. Workplace Injuries and Illnesses in 2003. Washington: Department of Labor. December 2004.

For More Information: See the BLS occupational safety and health Web site at www.bls.gov/iif/home.htm.

Youth Risk Behavior Survey (YRBS)

Centers for Disease Control and Prevention

National Center for Chronic Disease Prevention and Health Promotion

Overview: The national Youth Risk Behavior Survey (YRBS) monitors health risk behaviors among students in grades 5–12 that contribute to morbidity and mortality in both adolescence and adulthood.

Selected Content: Data are collected on tobacco use, dietary behaviors, physical activity, alcohol and other drug use, sexual behaviors that contribute to unintended pregnancy and sexually transmitted diseases including HIV infection, and behaviors that contribute to unintentional injuries and violence.

Data Years: The national YRBS of high school students was conducted in 1990, 1991, 1993, 1995, 1997, 1999, 2001, and 2003.

Coverage: Data are representative of high school students in public and private schools in the United States.

Methodology: The national YRBS school-based surveys employ a three-stage cluster sample design to produce a nationally representative sample of students in grades 5–12 attending public and private high schools. The first-stage sampling frame contains primary sampling units (PSUs) consisting of large counties or groups of smaller, adjacent counties. The PSUs are then stratified based on degree of urbanization and relative percentage of black and Hispanic students in the PSU. The PSUs are selected from these strata with probability proportional to school enrollment size. At the second sampling stage, schools are selected with probability proportional to school enrollment size. To enable separate analysis of data for black and Hispanic students, schools with substantial numbers of black and Hispanic students are sampled at higher rates than all other schools. The third stage of sampling consists of randomly selecting one or two intact classes of a required subject from grades 5–12 at each chosen school. All students in the selected classes are eligible to participate in the survey. A weighting factor is applied to each student record to adjust for nonresponse and for the varying probabilities of selection, including those resulting from the oversampling of black and Hispanic students.

Sample Size and Response Rate: The sample size for the 2003 YRBS was 15,240 students in 158 schools. The school response rate was 81 percent and the student response rate was 83 percent, for an overall response rate of 67 percent.

Issues Affecting Interpretation: National YRBS data are subject to at least two limitations. First, these data apply only to adolescents who attend regular high school. These students may not be representative of all persons in this age group because those who have dropped out of high school or attend an alternative high school are not surveyed. Second, the extent of underreporting or overreporting cannot be determined, although the survey questions demonstrate good test-retest reliability.

Estimates of substance use for youths based on the YRBS differ from the National Survey on Drug Use & Health (NSDUH) and Monitoring the Future (MTF). Rates are not directly comparable across these surveys because of differences in populations covered, sample design, questionnaires, interview setting, and statistical approaches to make the survey estimates generalizable to the entire population. The NSDUH survey collects data in homes, whereas the MTF and YRBS collect data in school classrooms. The NSDUH estimates are tabulated by age, while the MTF and YRBS estimates are tabulated by grade, representing different ages as well as different populations.

References:

Grunbaum JA, Kann L, Kinchen S, et al. Youth risk behavior surveillance—United States, 2003. In: Surveillance Summaries May 21, 2004. Morbidity & Mortality Weekly Report 53(SS-2):1–29. 2004.

Cowan CD. Coverage, sample design, and weighting in three Federal surveys. Journal of Drug Issues; 1(3):595–614. 2004.

For More Information: See the Division of Adolescent and School Health Web site at www.cdc.gov/nccdphp/dash/.

Private and Global Sources

Alan Guttmacher Institute (AGI) Abortion Provider Survey

The Alan Guttmacher Institute (AGI), a not-for-profit organization focused on reproductive health research, policy analysis, and public education, conducts periodic surveys of abortion providers to provide nationally representative statistics on abortion incidence.

Number of induced abortions; number, types, and locations of providers; and types of procedures performed, are presented by State and region. *Health, United States* presents the total for each data year. Thirteen provider surveys have been conducted for selected data years 1973 to midyear 2001. Data were collected from clinics, physicians, and hospitals identified as potential providers of abortion services. Mailed questionnaires were sent to all potential providers, with two additional mailings and telephone follow-up for nonresponse. No surveys were conducted in 1983, 1986, 1989, 1990, 1993, 1994, 1997, or 1998. For 1999–2000, a version of the survey questionnaire was created for each of the three major categories of providers, modeled on the survey questionnaire used for AGI's data collection in 1997. All surveys asked the number of induced abortions performed at the provider's location. State health statistics agencies were contacted, requesting all available data reported by providers to each State health agency on the number of abortions performed in the survey year. For States that provided data to AGI, the health agency figures were used for providers who did not respond to the survey. Estimates of the number of abortions performed by some providers were ascertained from knowledgeable sources in the community.

Of the 2,442 potential providers surveyed for 1999–2000, 1,931 performed abortions between January 1999 and June 2001. Of abortions reported for data year 2000, 77 percent were reported by providers, 10 percent came from health department data, 11 percent were estimated by knowledgeable sources, and 2 percent were projections or other estimates.

To estimate the number of abortions performed in 2001 and 2002, AGI first estimated the change in the number of abortions between 2000 and 2001, beginning with the number of abortions occurring in each State, as reported by the CDC, in each of those 2 years. The three States without reporting systems were excluded. AGI also eliminated the States with very incomplete or inconsistent reporting (Arizona, Maryland, and Nevada, as well as the District of Columbia). AGI summed the number of abortions that took place in the 44 remaining States for each year. The percentage change between 2000 and 2001 was then applied to AGI's more complete nationwide count of 1,312,990 abortions in 2000 to arrive at the national estimate for 2001. The same procedure was used to estimate the change in the number of abortions between 2001 and 2002, except that the data for both years were collected directly from State health departments because the CDC abortion surveillance report for 2002 was not yet available. For 2002, no data were available for Wyoming (in addition to the States with no reporting systems), and AGI eliminated Arizona, Colorado, the District of Columbia, and Maryland because of inconsistent reporting. AGI used the remaining 43 States for the calculations.

The number of abortions estimated by AGI through the mid- to late-1980s was about 20 percent higher than the number reported to the CDC. Between 1989 and 1997, the AGI estimates were about 12 percent higher than those reported by CDC. Beginning in 1998, health departments of four States did not report abortion data to CDC. The four reporting areas (the largest of which is California) that did not report abortions to CDC in 1998 accounted for 18 percent of all abortions tallied by AGI's 1995–96 survey. FDA approval of Mifepristone (medical abortion) in September of 2000 accounted for a small proportion (approx 6 percent) of abortions performed in nonhospital facilities during the first half of 2001.

References:

Finer LB, Henshaw SK. Abortion incidence and services in the United States in 2000. Perspect Sex Reprod Health; 35(1):6–15. 2003.

Finer LB, Henshaw SK. Estimates of U.S. Abortion Incidence in 2001 and 2002. The Alan Guttmacher Institute. May 2005. found at http://www.guttmacher.org/pubs/2005/05/18/ab_incidence.pdf.

For More Information: See the AGI Web site at http://www.guttmacher.org or write to The Alan Guttmacher Institute, 120 Wall Street, New York, NY 10005.

American Association of Colleges of Pharmacy

The American Association of Colleges of Pharmacy (AACP) compiles data on the Colleges of Pharmacy, including information on student enrollment and types of degrees conferred. Data are collected through an annual survey; the response rate is 100 percent.

For More Information: See *Profile of Pharmacy Students.* The American Association of Colleges of Pharmacy, 1426 Prince Street, Alexandria, VA; or the AACP Web site at www.aacp.org.

American Association of Colleges of Podiatric Medicine

The American Association of Colleges of Podiatric Medicine (AACPM) compiles data on the Colleges of Podiatric Medicine, including information on the schools and enrollment. Data are collected annually through written questionnaires. The response rate is 100 percent.

For More Information: Write to The American Association of Colleges of Podiatric Medicine, 15850 Crabbs Branch Way, Suite 320, Rockville, MD 20855; or see the AACPM Web site at www.aacpm.org.

American Dental Association

The Division of Educational Measurement of the American Dental Association (ADA) conducts annual surveys of predoctoral dental educational institutions. The questionnaire, mailed to all dental schools, collects information on student characteristics, financial management, and curricula.

For More Information: See the American Dental Association, *2002–03 Survey of Predoctoral Dental Education, vol.1, Academic Programs, Enrollments, and Graduates, Chicago. 2004* or the ADA Web site at www.ada.org.

American Hospital Association Annual Survey of Hospitals

Data from the American Hospital Association (AHA) annual survey are based on questionnaires sent to all AHA-registered and nonregistered hospitals in the United States and its associated areas. U.S. Government hospitals located outside the United States are excluded. Overall, the average response rate over the past 5 years has been approximately 83 percent. For nonreporting hospitals and for the survey questionnaires of reporting hospitals on which some information was missing, estimates are made for all data, except those on beds, bassinets, and facilities. Data for beds and bassinets of nonreporting hospitals are based on the most recent information available from those hospitals. Data for facilities and services are based only on reporting hospitals.

Estimates of other types of missing data are based on data reported the previous year, if available. When unavailable, estimates are based on data furnished by reporting hospitals similar in size, control, major service provided, length of stay, and geographic and demographic characteristics.

For More Information: Write to the AHA Annual Survey of Hospitals, Health Forum, LLC, an American Hospital Association Company, One North Franklin Street, Chicago, IL 60606; or see the AHA Web site at www.aha.org.

American Medical Association Physician Masterfile

A masterfile of physicians has been maintained by the American Medical Association (AMA) since 1906. The Physician Masterfile contains data on all physicians in the United States, both members and nonmembers of the AMA, and on those graduates of American medical schools temporarily practicing overseas. The file also includes international medical graduates (IMGs) who are graduates of foreign medical schools residing in the United States and who meet education standards for primary recognition as physicians.

A file is initiated on each individual upon entry into medical school or, in the case of IMGs, upon entry into the United States. Between 1965 and 1985, a mail questionnaire survey was conducted every 4 years to update the file information on professional activities, self-designated area of specialization, and present employment status. Since 1985, approximately one-third of all physicians are surveyed each year.

For More Information: See Division of Survey and Data Resources, American Medical Association, *Physician Characteristics and Distribution in the U.S., 2005* ed. Chicago, IL. 2004; or the AMA Web site at http://www.ama-assn.org/.

Association of American Medical Colleges

The Association of American Medical Colleges (AAMC) collects information on student enrollment in medical schools through the annual Liaison Committee on Medical Education questionnaire, the fall enrollment questionnaire, and the American Medical College Application Service (AMCAS) data system. Other data sources are the institutional profile system, the premedical students questionnaire, the minority student opportunities in medicine questionnaire, the faculty roster system, data from the Medical College Admission Test, and one-time surveys developed for special projects.

For More Information: See the Association of American Medical Colleges, *Statistical Information Related to Medical Schools and Teaching Hospitals*, Washington, DC. 2004; or the AAMC Web site at www.aamc.org.

Association of Schools and Colleges of Optometry

The Association of Schools and Colleges of Optometry (ASCO) compiles data on various aspects of optometric education including data on schools and enrollment. Questionnaires are sent annually to all schools and colleges of optometry. The response rate is 100 percent.

For More Information: Write to the Annual Survey of Optometric Educational Institutions, Association of Schools and Colleges of Optometry, 6110 Executive Blvd., Suite 510, Rockville, MD 20852; or see the ASCO Web site at www.opted.org.

Association of Schools of Public Health

The Association of Schools of Public Health (ASPH) compiles data on schools of public health in the United States and Puerto Rico. Questionnaires are sent annually to all member schools. The response rate is 100 percent.

Unlike health professional schools that emphasize specific clinical occupations, schools of public health offer study in specialty areas such as biostatistics, epidemiology, environmental health, occupational health, health administration, health planning, nutrition, maternal and child health, social and behavioral sciences, and other population-based sciences.

For More Information: Write to the Association of Schools of Public Health, 1101 15th Street, NW, Suite 910, Washington, DC 20005; or see the ASPH Web site at www.asph.org.

European Health for All Database

World Health Organization Regional Office for Europe

The WHO Regional Office for Europe (WHO/Europe) provides country-specific and topic-specific health information via the Internet for people who influence health policy in the WHO European Region and the media.

WHO/Europe collects statistics on health and makes them widely available through

- The European health for all database (HFA-DB), which contains data on about 600 health indicators collected from national counterparts in 51 European countries, and data from other WHO technical programs and some international organizations.
- Highlights on health in countries in the WHO European Region that give an overview of the health situation in each country in comparison with other countries. Highlights complement the public health reports produced by a number of member States in the region.
- Health status overview for countries of central and eastern Europe that are candidates for accession to the European Union (Bulgaria, the Czech Republic, Estonia, Hungary, Latvia, Lithuania, Poland, Romania, Slovakia, and Slovenia).

WHO/Europe helps countries strengthen their national health information systems, particularly by supporting

- the development of national health indicator databases
- the exchange of experience on national public health reports between countries; a database of public health reports is maintained and available for consultation and networking
- implementation of international classifications and definitions in countries
- regional networks of health information professionals

For More Information: See the European health for all database at http://hfadb.who.dk/hfa/.

InterStudy National Health Maintenance Organization Census

From 1976 to 1980, the Office of Health Maintenance Organizations conducted a census of health maintenance organizations (HMOs). Since 1981, InterStudy has conducted the census. A questionnaire is sent to all HMOs in the United States asking for updated enrollment, profit status, and Federal qualification status. New HMOs, are also asked to provide information on model type. When necessary, information is obtained, supplemented, or clarified by telephone. For nonresponding HMOs State-supplied information or the most current available data are used.

In 1985, a large increase in the number of HMOs and enrollment was partly attributable to a change in the categories of HMOs included in the census: Medicaid-only and Medicare-only HMOs have been added. Component HMOs, which have their own discrete management, can be listed separately, whereas previously, the oldest HMO reported for all of its component or expansion sites, even when the components had different operational dates or were different model types.

For More Information: See *Rebecca L. Waller RL, Lauer TM, Greenberger MA, et al. The InterStudy Competitive Edge, Fall 2004 Part II: Managed Care Industry Report. St. Paul, MN: Decision Resources, Inc., 2004* or the InterStudy Web site at www.hmodata.com.

National League for Nursing

The division of research of the National League for Nursing (NLN) conducts The Annual Survey of Schools of Nursing in October of each year. Questionnaires are sent to all graduate nursing programs (master's and doctoral), baccalaureate programs designed exclusively for registered nurses, basic registered nursing programs (baccalaureate, associate degree, and diploma), and licensed practical nursing programs. Data on enrollments, first-time admissions, and graduates are completed for all nursing education programs. Response rates of approximately 80 percent are achieved for other areas of inquiry.

For More Information: See the NLN Web site at www.nln.org.

Organization for Economic Cooperation and Development Health Data

The Organization for Economic Cooperation and Development (OECD) provides annual data on statistical indicators on health and economic policies collected from 30 member countries since the 1960s. The international comparability of health expenditure estimates depends on the quality of national health accounts in OECD member countries. In recent years, the OECD health accounts have become an informal standard for reporting on health care systems. Additional limitations in international comparisons include differing boundaries between health care and other social care, particularly for the disabled and elderly, and underestimation of private expenditures on health.

The OECD was established in 1961 with a mandate to promote policies to achieve the highest sustainable economic growth and a rising standard of living among member countries. The Organization now comprises 30 member countries: Australia, Austria, Belgium, Canada, Czech Republic, Denmark, Finland, France, Germany, Greece, Hungary, Iceland, Ireland, Italy, Japan, Korea, Luxembourg, Mexico, The Netherlands, New Zealand, Norway, Poland, Portugal, Slovak Republic, Spain, Sweden, Switzerland, Turkey, the United Kingdom, and the United States.

As part of its mission, the OECD has developed a number of activities in relation to health and health care systems. The main aim of OECD work on health policy is to conduct cross-national studies of the performance of OECD health systems and to facilitate exchanges between member countries of their experiences of financing, delivering, and managing health services. To support this work, each year the OECD compiles cross-country data in OECD Health Data, one of the most comprehensive sources of comparable health-related statistics. OECD Health Data is an essential tool to carry out comparative analyses and to draw lessons from international comparisons of diverse health care systems. This international database now incorporates the first results arising from the implementation of the OECD manual, A System of Health Accounts (2000), which provide a standard framework for producing a set of comprehensive, consistent, and internationally comparable data on health spending. The OECD collaborates with other international organizations such as the WHO.

For More Information: See the OECD Web site at www.oecd.org/health.

United Nations Demographic Yearbook

The Statistical Office of the United Nations prepares the *Demographic Yearbook*, a comprehensive collection of international demographic statistics.

Questionnaires are sent annually and monthly to more than 220 national statistical services and other appropriate government offices. Data forwarded on these questionnaires are supplemented, to the extent possible, by data taken from official national publications and by correspondence with the national statistical services. To ensure comparability, rates, ratios, and percents have been calculated in the statistical office of the United Nations.

Lack of international comparability among estimates arises from differences in concepts, definitions, and time of data collection. The comparability of population data is affected by several factors, including (a) definitions of the total population, (b) definitions used to classify the population into its urban and rural components, (c) difficulties relating to age reporting, (d) extent of over- or under-enumeration, and (e) quality of population estimates. The completeness and accuracy of vital statistics data also vary from one country to another. Differences in statistical definitions of vital events may also influence comparability.

International demographic trend data are available on a CD-ROM entitled United Nations, 2000. Demographic Yearbook—Historical Supplement 1948–97. CD-ROM Special Issue. United Nations publication sales number E/F.99.XIII.12.

For More Information: See the United Nations, Statistics Division Web site at http://unstats.un.org/unsd/demographic/products/dyb/dyb2.htm.

World Health Statistics Annual

World Health Organization

The World Health Organization (WHO) prepares the *World Health Statistics Annual*, an annual volume of information on vital statistics and causes of death designed for use by the medical and public health professions. Each volume is the result of a joint effort by the national health and statistical administrations of many countries, the United Nations, and

WHO. United Nations estimates of vital rates and population size and composition, where available, are reprinted directly in the *Statistics Annual.* For those countries for which the United Nations does not prepare demographic estimates, primarily smaller populations, the latest available data reported to the United Nations and based on reasonably complete coverage of events are used.

Information published on infant mortality is based entirely on official national data either reported directly or made available to WHO.

Selected life table functions are calculated from the application of a uniform methodology to national mortality data provided to WHO, to enhance their value for international comparisons. The life table procedure used by WHO may often lead to discrepancies with national figures published by countries, because of differences in methodology or degree of age detail maintained in calculations.

The international comparability of estimates published in the *World Health Statistics Annual* is affected by the same problems as is the United Nations *Demographic Yearbook.* Cross-national differences in statistical definitions of vital events, in the completeness and accuracy of vital statistics data, and in the comparability of population data are the primary factors affecting comparability.

For More Information: See the World Health Organization, *World Health Statistics Annual 2005* at http://www3.who.int/statistics/ or the WHO Web site at www.who.int.

Appendix II

Definitions and Methods

Appendix II is an alphabetical listing of terms used in *Health, United States*. It includes cross-references to related terms and synonyms. It also describes the methods used for calculating age-adjusted rates, average annual rates of change, relative standard errors, birth rates, death rates, and years of potential life lost. Appendix II includes standard populations used for age adjustment (tables I, II, and III); *International Classification of Diseases* (ICD) codes for cause of death from the Sixth through Tenth Revisions and the years when the Revisions were in effect (tables IV and V); comparability ratios between ICD–9 and ICD–10 for selected causes (table VI); ICD–9–CM codes for external cause of injury, diagnostic, and procedure categories (tables VII, IX, and X); classification of generic analgesic drugs (table XI); and industry codes from the North American Industry Classification System (NAICS) that has replaced the Standard Industrial Classification (SIC) system (table VIII). Standards for presenting Federal data on race and ethnicity are described under *Race*, and sample tabulations of National Health Interview Survey (NHIS) data comparing the 1977 and 1997 Standards for Federal data on race and Hispanic origin are presented in tables XII and XIII.

Acquired immunodeficiency syndrome (AIDS)—Human immunodeficiency virus (HIV) disease is the pathogen that causes AIDS and encompasses all the condition's stages, from infection to the deterioration of the immune system and the onset of opportunistic diseases. However, AIDS is still the name that most people use to refer to the immune deficiency caused by HIV. An AIDS diagnosis (indicating that the person has reached the late stages of the disease) is given to people with HIV who have counts below 200 CD4+ cells/mm^3 (also known as T cells or T4 cells, which are the main target of HIV) or when they become diagnosed with at least one of a set of opportunistic diseases. All 50 States and the District of Columbia report AIDS cases to CDC using a uniform surveillance case definition and case report form. The case reporting definitions were expanded in 1985 *(MMWR* 1985; 34:373–5); 1987 *(MMWR* 1987; 36(No. SS-1):1S–15S); 1993 for adults and adolescents *(MMWR* 1992; 41(no. RR-17): 1–19); and 1994 for pediatric cases *(MMWR* 1994; 43(no. RR-12):1–19). The revisions incorporated a broader range of AIDS-indicator diseases and conditions and used HIV diagnostic tests to improve the sensitivity and specificity of the definition. The 1993 expansion of the case definition caused a temporary distortion of AIDS incidence trends. In 1995, new treatments (protease inhibitors) for HIV and AIDS were approved. These therapies have prevented or delayed the onset of AIDS and premature death among many HIV-infected persons, which should be considered when interpreting trend data. AIDS surveillance data are published annually by CDC in the HIV/AIDS Surveillance Report at www.cdc.gov/hiv/stats/hasrlink.htm. See related *Human immunodeficiency virus (HIV) disease.*

Active physician—See *Physician.*

Activities of daily living (ADL)—Activities of daily living are activities related to personal care and include bathing or showering, dressing, getting in or out of bed or a chair, using the toilet, and eating. In the National Health Interview Survey, respondents were asked whether they or family members 3 years of age and over need the help of another person with personal care because of a physical, mental, or emotional problem. Persons are considered to have an ADL limitation if any condition(s) causing the respondent to need help with the specific activities was chronic.

In the Medicare Current Beneficiary Survey (table 141), if a sample person had any difficulty performing an activity by him or herself and without special equipment or did not perform the activity at all because of health problems, the person was categorized as having a limitation in that activity. The limitation may have been temporary or chronic at the time of the interview. Sample persons who were administered a community interview answered health status and functioning questions themselves, if able to do so. A proxy such as a nurse answered questions about the sample person's health status and functioning for those in a long-term care facility. Beginning in 1997, interview questions for persons in long-term care facilities were changed slightly from those administered to persons in the community to differentiate residents who were independent from those who received supervision or assistance with transferring, locomotion on unit, dressing, eating, toilet use, and bathing. See related *Condition; Instrumental activities of daily living (IADL); Limitation of activity.*

Addition—An addition to a mental health organization is defined by the Substance Abuse and Mental Health Services

Administration's Center for Mental Health Services as a new admission, a readmission, a return from long-term leave, or a transfer from another service of the same organization or another organization. See related *Mental health organization; Mental health service type*.

Admission—The American Hospital Association defines admissions as persons, excluding newborns, accepted for inpatient services during the survey reporting period. See related *Days of care; Discharge; Inpatient*.

Age—Age is reported as age at last birthday, that is, age in completed years, often calculated by subtracting date of birth from the reference date, with the reference date being the date of the examination, interview, or other contact with an individual.

Mother's (maternal) age is reported on the birth certificate by all States. Birth statistics are presented for mothers age 10–49 years through 1996 and 10–54 years starting in 1997, based on mother's date of birth or age as reported on the birth certificate. The age of mother is edited for upper and lower limits. When the age of the mother is computed to be under 10 years or 55 years or over (50 years or over in 1964–96), it is considered not stated and imputed according to the age of the mother from the previous birth record of the same race and total birth order (total of fetal deaths and live births). Before 1963 not stated ages were distributed in proportion to the known ages for each racial group. Beginning in 1997 the birth rate for the maternal age group 45–49 years includes data for mothers age 50–54 years in the numerator and is based on the population of women 45–49 years in the denominator.

Age adjustment—Age adjustment is used to compare risks of two or more populations at one point in time or one population at two or more points in time. Age-adjusted rates are computed by the direct method by applying age-specific rates in a population of interest to a standardized age distribution, to eliminate differences in observed rates that result from age differences in population composition. Age-adjusted rates should be viewed as relative indexes rather than actual measures of risk.

Age-adjusted rates are calculated by the direct method as follows:

$$\sum_{i=1}^{n} r_i \times (p_i / P)$$

Table I. United States standard population and proportion distribution by age for age adjusting death rates

Age	Population	Proportion distribution (weights)	Standard million
Total	274,634,000	1.000000	1,000,000
Under 1 year	3,795,000	0.013818	13,818
1–4 years	15,192,000	0.055317	55,317
5–14 years	39,977,000	0.145565	145,565
15–24 years	38,077,000	0.138646	138,646
25–34 years	37,233,000	0.135573	135,573
35–44 years	44,659,000	0.162613	162,613
45–54 years	37,030,000	0.134834	134,834
55–64 years	23,961,000	0.087247	87,247
65–74 years	18,136,000	0.066037	66,037
75–84 years	12,315,000	*0.044842	44,842
85 years and over	4,259,000	0.015508	15,508

*Figure is rounded up instead of down to force total to 1.0.

SOURCE: Anderson RN, Rosenberg HM. Age Standardization of Death Rates: Implementation of the Year 2000 Standard. National vital statistics reports; vol 47 no 3. Hyattsville, Maryland: National Center for Health Statistics. 1998.

Table II. Numbers of live births and mother's age groups used to adjust maternal mortality rates to live births in the United States in 1970

Mother's age	Number
All ages	3,731,386
Under 20 years	656,460
20–24 years	1,418,874
25–29 years	994,904
30–34 years	427,806
35 years and over	233,342

SOURCE: U.S. Bureau of the Census: Population estimates and projections. *Current Population Reports.* Series P-25, No. 499. Washington, D.C.: U.S. Government Printing Office, May 1973.

where r_i = rate in age group i in the population of interest

p_i = standard population in age group i

$$P = \sum_{i=1}^{n} p_i$$

n = total number of age groups over the age range of the age-adjusted rate

Age adjustment by the direct method requires use of a standard age distribution. The standard for age adjusting death rates and estimates from surveys in *Health, United States* is the projected year 2000 U.S. resident population. Starting with *Health, United States, 2001*, the year 2000 U.S. standard population replaces the 1940 U.S. population for age adjusting mortality statistics. The U.S. standard population also replaces the 1970 civilian noninstitutionalized population and 1980 U.S. resident population, which previously had been used as standard age distributions for age adjusting estimates from NCHS surveys.

Changing the standard population has implications for racial and ethnic differentials in mortality. For example, the mortality ratio for the black to white populations is reduced from 1.6 using the 1940 standard to 1.4 using the 2000 standard, reflecting the greater weight that the 2000 standard gives to the older population where race differentials in mortality are smaller.

Age-adjusted estimates from any data source presented in *Health, United States* may differ from age-adjusted estimates based on the same data presented in other reports if different age groups are used in the adjustment procedure.

For more information on implementing the 2000 population standard for age adjusting death rates, see Anderson RN, Rosenberg HM. Age Standardization of Death Rates: Implementation of the Year 2000 Standard. National vital statistics reports; vol 47 no 3. Hyattsville, MD: National Center for Health Statistics. 1998. For more information on the derivation of age-adjustment weights for use with NCHS survey data, see Klein RJ, Schoenborn CA. Age Adjustment Using the 2000 Projected U.S. Population. Healthy People Statistical Notes no. 20. Hyattsville, MD: National Center for Health Statistics. 2001. Both reports are available through the NCHS home page at www.cdc.gov/nchs. The U.S. standard population is available through the Census Bureau's home page at www.census.gov/prod/1/pop/p25–1130/.

Mortality data—Death rates are age adjusted to the year 2000 U.S. standard population (table I). Age-adjusted rates are calculated using age-specific death rates per 100,000 population rounded to one decimal place. Adjustment is based on 11 age groups with two exceptions. First, age-adjusted death rates for black males and black females in 1950 are based on nine age groups, with under 1 year and 1–4 years of age combined as one group and 75–84 years and 85 years of age combined as one group. Second, age-adjusted death rates by educational attainment for the age group 25–64 years are based on four 10-year age groups (25–34 years, 35–44 years, 45–54 years, and 55–64 years).

Age-adjusted rates for years of potential life lost before age 75 years also use the year 2000 standard population and are based on eight age groups (under 1 year, 1–14 years, 15–24 years, and 10-year age groups through 65–74 years).

Maternal mortality rates for pregnancy, childbirth, and the puerperium are calculated as the number of deaths per 100,000 live births. These rates are age adjusted to the 1970 distribution of live births by mother's age in the United States as shown in table II. See related *Rate: Death and related rates; Years of potential life lost.*

National Health and Nutrition Examination Survey (NHANES)—Estimates based on the National Health Examination Survey (NHES) and NHANES are age adjusted to the year 2000 U.S. standard population generally using five age groups: 20–34 years, 35–44 years, 45–54 years, 55–64 years, and 65–74 years or 65 years and over (see table III). Prior to *Health, United States, 2000*, these estimates were age adjusted to the 1980 U.S. resident population.

National Health Care Surveys—Estimates based on the National Hospital Discharge Survey, the National Ambulatory Medical Care Survey, the National Hospital Ambulatory Medical Care Survey, the National Nursing Home Survey, and the National Home and Hospice Care Survey are age adjusted to the year 2000 U.S. standard population (table III). Information on the age groups used in the age-adjustment procedure is contained in the footnotes to the relevant tables.

National Health Interview Survey (NHIS)—Estimates based on the NHIS are age adjusted to the year 2000 U.S. standard population (table III). Prior to the 2000 edition of *Health, United States,* National Health Interview Survey estimates were age adjusted to the 1970 civilian noninstitutionalized population. Information on the age groups used in the age-adjustment procedure is contained in the footnotes to the relevant tables.

AIDS—See *Acquired immunodeficiency syndrome.*

Alcohol consumption—Alcohol consumption is measured differently in various data systems.

Monitoring the Future Study—This school-based survey of secondary school students collects information on alcohol use using self-completed questionnaires.

Information on consumption of alcoholic beverages, defined as beer, wine, wine coolers, and liquor, is based on the following question: "On how many occasions (if any) have you had alcohol to drink—more than just a few sips—in the last 30 days?" Students responding affirmatively are then asked "How many times have you had five or more drinks in a row in the last 2 weeks?" For this question, a "drink" means a 12-ounce can or bottle of beer, a 4-ounce glass of wine, a 12-ounce bottle or can of wine cooler, or a mixed drink or shot of liquor.

National Health Interview Survey (NHIS)—Starting with the 1997 NHIS, information on alcohol consumption is collected in the sample adult questionnaire. Adult respondents are asked two screening questions about their lifetime alcohol consumption: "In any one year, have you had at least 12 drinks of any type of alcoholic beverage? In your entire life, have you had at least 12 drinks of any type of alcoholic beverage?" Persons who report at least 12 drinks in a lifetime are then asked a series of questions about alcohol consumption during the past year: "In the past year, how often did you drink any type of alcoholic beverage? In the past year, on those days that you drank alcoholic beverages, on the average, how many drinks did you have? In the past year, on how many days did you have 5 or more drinks of any alcoholic beverage?"

National Survey on Drug Use and Health (NSDUH)—Starting in 1999, NSDUH information about the frequency of the consumption of alcoholic beverages during the past 30 days has been obtained for all persons surveyed who are 12 years of age and over. An extensive list of examples of the kinds of beverages covered was given to respondents prior to the question administration. A "drink" is defined as a can or bottle of beer, a glass of wine or a wine cooler, a shot of liquor, or a mixed drink with liquor in it. Those times when the respondent had only a sip or two from a drink are not considered consumption. Alcohol use is based on the following questions: "During the past 30 days, on how many days did you drink one or more drinks of an alcoholic beverage?" "On the days that you drank during the past 30 days, how many drinks did you usually have?" And "During the past 30 days, on how many days did you have 5 or more drinks on the same occasion?"

Table III. United States standard population and age groups used to age adjust survey data

Survey and age	*Number in thousands*
NHIS, NAMCS, NHAMCS, NHHCS, NNHS, and NHDS	
All ages	274,634
18 years and over	203,851
25 years and over	117,593
40 years and over	118,180
65 years and over	34,710
Under 18 years	70,783
2–17 years	63,229
18–44 years	108,150
18–24 years	26,258
25–34 years	37,233
35–44 years	44,659
45–64 years	60,991
45–54 years	37,030
55–64 years	23,961
65–74 years	18,136
75 years and over	16,574
18–49 years	127,956
40–64 years:	
40–49 years	42,285
50–64 years	41,185
NHES and NHANES	
20 years and over	195,850
20–74 years	179,276
20–34 years	55,490
35–44 years	44,659
45–54 years	37,030
55–64 years	23,961
65–74 years	18,136
or	
65 years and over	34,710
NHANES (Tables 55 and 71 only)	
20–39 years	77,670
40–59 years	72,816
60–74 years	28,790
or	
60 years and over	45,364
NHANES (Table 91 only)	
Under 18 years	70,783
18–44 years	108,150
45–64 years	60,991
65 years and over	34,710

SOURCE: U.S. Census Bureau: Current Population Reports. P25–1130. Population Projections of the United States by Age, Sex, Race, and Hispanic Origin, table 2. U.S. Government Printing Office, Washington: 1996.

Any-listed diagnosis—See *Diagnosis.*

Average annual rate of change (percent change)—In *Health, United States* average annual rates of change or growth rates are calculated as follows:

$$[(P_n / P_o)^{1/N} - 1] \times 100$$

where P_n = later time period

P_o = earlier time period

N = number of years in interval.

This geometric rate of change assumes that a variable increases or decreases at the same rate during each year between the two time periods.

Average length of stay—In the National Health Interview Survey, average length of stay per discharged inpatient is computed by dividing the total number of hospital days for a specified group by the total number of discharges for that group. Similarly, in the National Hospital Discharge Survey, average length of stay is computed by dividing the total number of days of care, counting the date of admission but not the date of discharge, by the number of patients discharged. The American Hospital Association computes average length of stay by dividing the number of inpatient days by the number of admissions. See related *Days of care; Discharge; Inpatient.*

Bed—The American Hospital Association defines the bed count as the number of beds, cribs, and pediatric bassinets that are set up and staffed for use by inpatients on the last day of the reporting period. In the Center for Medicare & Medicaid Service's Online Survey Certification and Reporting (OSCAR) database, all beds in certified facilities are counted on the day of certification inspection. The World Health Organization defines a hospital bed as one regularly maintained and staffed for the accommodation and full-time care of a succession of inpatients and situated in a part of the hospital where continuous medical care for inpatients is provided. The Center for Mental Health Services counts the number of beds set up and staffed for use in inpatient and residential treatment services on the last day of the survey reporting period. See related *Hospital; Mental health organization; Mental health service type; Occupancy rate.*

Birth cohort—A birth cohort consists of all persons born within a given period of time, such as a calendar year.

Birth rate—See *Rate: Birth and related rates.*

Birthweight—Birthweight is the first weight of the newborn obtained after birth. Low birthweight is defined as less than 2,500 grams or 5 pounds 8 ounces. Very low birthweight is defined as less than 1,500 grams or 3 pounds 4 ounces. Before 1979, low birthweight was defined as 2,500 grams or less and very low birthweight as 1,500 grams or less.

Body mass index (BMI)—BMI is a measure that adjusts bodyweight for height. It is calculated as weight in kilograms divided by height in meters squared. Overweight for children and adolescents is defined as BMI at or above the sex- and age-specific 95th percentile BMI cut points from the 2000 CDC Growth Charts (www.cdc.gov/growthcharts/). Healthy weight for adults is defined as a BMI of 18.5 to less than 25; overweight, as greater than or equal to a BMI of 25; and obesity, as greater than or equal to a BMI of 30. BMI cut points are defined in the Report of the Dietary Guidelines Advisory Committee on the Dietary Guidelines for Americans, 2000. U.S. Department of Agriculture, Agricultural Research Service, Dietary Guidelines Advisory Committee, p. 23, or on the Internet at www.health.gov/dietaryguidelines/dgac/; NHLBI Obesity Education Initiative Expert Panel on the Identification, Evaluation, and Treatment of Overweight and Obesity in Adults. Clinical Guidelines on the Identification, Evaluation, and Treatment of Overweight and Obesity in Adults—The Evidence Report. *Obes Res* 1998. 6:51S-209S or on the Internet at www.nhlbi.nih.gov/guidelines/obesity/ob_gdlns.htm; and in U.S. Department of Health and Human Services. *Tracking Healthy People 2010.* Washington, DC: U.S. Government Printing Office, November 2000. Objectives 19.1, 19.2, and 19.3, or on the Internet at www.health.gov/healthypeople/document/html/volume2/19nutrition.htm.

Cause of death—For the purpose of national mortality statistics, every death is attributed to one underlying condition, based on information reported on the death certificate and using the international rules for selecting the underlying cause of death from the conditions stated on the death certificate. The underlying cause is defined by the World Health Organization (WHO) as the disease or injury that initiated the train of events leading directly to death, or the circumstances of the accident or violence that produced the fatal injury. Generally more medical information is reported on death certificates than is directly reflected in the underlying cause of death. The conditions that are not selected as

Table IV. Revision of the *International Classification of Diseases (ICD)* according to year of conference by which adopted and years in use in the United States

Revision of the International Classification of Diseases	Year of conference by which adopted	Years in use in United States
First	1900	1900–1909
Second	1909	1910–1920
Third	1920	1921–1929
Fourth	1929	1930–1938
Fifth	1938	1939–1948
Sixth	1948	1949–1957
Seventh	1955	1958–1967
Eighth	1965	1968–1978
Ninth	1975	1979–1998
Tenth	1992	1999–

underlying cause of death constitute the nonunderlying causes of death, also known as multiple cause of death.

Cause of death is coded according to the appropriate revision of the *International Classification of Diseases* (ICD) (see table IV). Effective with deaths occurring in 1999, the United States began using the Tenth Revision of the ICD (ICD–10); during the period 1979–98, causes of death were coded and classified according to the Ninth Revision (ICD–9). Table V lists ICD codes for the Sixth through Tenth Revisions for causes of death shown in *Health, United States.*

Each of these revisions has produced discontinuities in cause-of-death trends. These discontinuities are measured using comparability ratios. These measures of discontinuity are essential to the interpretation of mortality trends. For further discussion, see the Mortality Technical Appendix available on the NCHS Web site at www.cdc.gov/nchs/about/major/dvs/mortdata.htm. See related *Comparability ratio; International Classification of Diseases (ICD); Appendix I, National Vital Statistics System, Multiple Cause-of-Death File.*

Cause-of-death ranking—Selected causes of death of public health and medical importance comprise tabulation lists and are ranked according to the number of deaths assigned to these causes. The top-ranking causes determine the leading causes of death. Certain causes on the tabulation lists are not ranked if, for example, the category title represents a group title (such as Major cardiovascular diseases and Symptoms, signs, and abnormal clinical and laboratory findings, not elsewhere classified); or the category title begins with the words "Other" and "All other." In addition when one of the titles that represents a subtotal (such as Malignant neoplasms) is ranked, its component parts are not ranked. The tabulation lists used for ranking in the *Tenth Revision of the International Classification of Diseases* (ICD) include the List of 113 Selected Causes of Death, which replaces the ICD–9 List of 72 Selected Causes, HIV infection and Alzheimer's disease; and the ICD–10 List of 130 Selected Causes of Infant Death, which replaces the ICD–9 List of 60 Selected Causes of Infant Death and HIV infection. Causes that are tied receive the same rank; the next cause is assigned the rank it would have received had the lower-ranked causes not been tied, that is, skip a rank. See related *International Classification of Diseases (ICD).*

Chronic condition—See *Condition.*

Cigarette smoking—Cigarette smoking and related tobacco use are measured in several different data systems.

Birth File—Information on cigarette smoking by the mother during pregnancy is based on Yes/No responses to the birth certificate item "Other risk factors for this pregnancy: Tobacco use during pregnancy" and the average number of cigarettes per day with no specificity on timing during pregnancy. This information became available for the first time in 1989 with revision of the U.S. Standard Certificate of Live Birth. In 1989, 43 States and the District of Columbia collected data on tobacco use. The following States did not require the reporting of tobacco use in the standard format on the birth certificate: California, Indiana, Louisiana, Nebraska, New York, Oklahoma, and South Dakota. In 1990, information on tobacco use became available from Louisiana and Nebraska, increasing the number of reporting States to 45 and the District of Columbia. In 1991–93, with the addition of Oklahoma to the reporting area, information on tobacco use was available for 46 States and the District of Columbia; in 1994–98, 46 States, the District of Columbia, and New York City reported tobacco use; in 1999 information on tobacco use became available from Indiana and New York, increasing the number of reporting States to 48 and the District of Columbia; starting in 2000, with the addition of South Dakota, the reporting area includes 49 States and the District of Columbia. During 1989–2002, California did not require the reporting of tobacco use. The areas reporting tobacco use comprised 87 percent of U.S. births in 1999–2002. In 2003, data on smoking during pregnancy was included for all States except California,

Table V. Cause-of-death codes, according to applicable revision of *International Classification of Diseases (ICD)*

Cause of death (Tenth Revision titles)	*Sixth and Seventh Revisions*	*Eighth Revision*	*Ninth Revision*	*Tenth Revision*
Communicable diseases	. . .	. . .	001–139, 460–466, 480–487, 771.3	A00–B99, J00–J22
Chronic and noncommunicable diseases	. . .	. . .	140–459, 470–478, 490–799	C00–I99, J30–R99
Injuries[1]	. . .	. . .	E800–E869, E880–E929, E950–E999	*U01–*U03, V01–Y36, Y85–Y87, Y89
Meningococcal Infection	. . .	. . .	036	A39
Septicemia	. . .	. . .	038	A40–A41
Human immunodeficiency virus (HIV) disease[2]	. . .	. . .	*042–*044	B20–B24
Malignant neoplasms	140–205	140–209	140–208	C00–C97
Colon, rectum, and anus	153–154	153–154	153, 154	C18–C21
Trachea, bronchus, and lung	162–163	162	162	C33–C34
Breast	170	174	174–175	C50
Prostate	177	185	185	C61
In situ neoplasms and benign neoplasms	. . .	. . .	210–239	D00–D48
Diabetes mellitus	260	250	250	E10–E14
Anemias	. . .	. . .	280–285	D50–D64
Meningitis	. . .	. . .	320–322	G00, G03
Alzheimer's disease	. . .	. . .	331.0	G30
Diseases of heart	6th: 410–443 7th: 400–402, 410–443	390–398, 402, 404, 410–429	390–398, 402, 404, 410–429	I00–I09, I11, I13, I20–I51
Ischemic heart disease	. . .	. . .	410–414, 429.2	I20–I25
Cerebrovascular diseases	330–334	430–438	430–434, 436–438	I60–I69
Atherosclerosis	. . .	. . .	440	I70
Influenza and pneumonia	480–483, 490–493	470–474, 480–486	480–487	J10–J18
Chronic lower respiratory diseases	241, 501, 502, 527.1	490–493, 519.3	490–494, 496	J40–J47
Chronic liver disease and cirrhosis	581	571	571	K70, K73–K74
Nephritis, nephrotic syndrome, and nephrosis	. . .	. . .	580–589	N00–N07, N17–N19, N25–N27
Pregnancy, childbirth, and the puerperium	640–689	630–678	630–676	A34, O00–O95, O98–O99
Congenital malformations, deformations, and chromosomal abnormalities	. . .	. . .	740–759	Q00–Q99
Certain conditions originating in the perinatal period	. . .	. . .	760–779	P00–P96
Newborn affected by maternal complications of pregnancy	. . .	. . .	761	P01
Newborn affected by complications of placenta, cord, and membranes	. . .	. . .	762	P02
Disorders related to short gestation and low birthweight, not elsewhere classified	. . .	. . .	765	P07
Birth trauma	. . .	. . .	767	P10–P15
Intrauterine hypoxia and birth asphyxia	. . .	. . .	768	P20–P21
Respiratory distress of newborn	. . .	. . .	769	P22
Sudden infant death syndrome	. . .	. . .	798.0	R95
Unintentional injuries[3]	E800–E936, E960–E965	E800–E929, E940–E946	E800–E869, E880–E929	V01–X59, Y85–Y86
Motor vehicle-related injuries[3]	E810–E835	E810–E823	E810–E825	V02–V04, V09.0, V09.2, V12–V14, V19.0–V19.2, V19.4–V19.6, V20–V79, V80.3–V80.5, V81.0–V81.1, V82.0–V82.1, V83–V86, V87.0–V87.8, V88.0–V88.8, V89.0, V89.2
Suicide[1]	E963, E970–E979	E950–E959	E950–E959	*U03, X60–X84, Y87.0
Homicide[1]	E964, E980–E983	E960–E969	E960–E969	*U01–*U02, X85–Y09, Y87.1
Injury by firearms	. . .	E922, E955, E965, E970, E985	E922, E955.0–E955.4, E965.0–E965.4, E970, E985.0–E985.4	*U01.4, W32–W34, X72–X74, X93–X95, Y22–Y24, Y35.0

. . . Cause-of-death code numbers are not provided for causes not shown in *Health, United States*.
[1]Beginning with 2001 data, NCHS introduced categories *U01–*U03 for classifying and coding deaths due to acts of terrorism. The * indicates codes are not part of the Tenth Revision.
[2]Categories for coding human immunodeficiency virus infection were introduced in 1987. The * indicates codes are not part of the Ninth Revision.
[3]In the public health community, the term "unintentional injuries" is preferred to "accidents" and "motor vehicle-related injuries" to "motor vehicle accidents."

Pennsylvania, and Washington, and comprised 81 percent of births. California did not report this information. Pennsylvania and Washington implemented the 2003 revision of the U.S. Standard Certificate of Live Birth, which asked for the number of cigarettes smoked at different intervals before and during pregnancy. Data from the 2003 revision of the birth certificate are not comparable with data from the 1989 revision used by other reporting areas.

Monitoring the Future Survey—Information on current cigarette smoking is obtained for high school seniors (starting in 1975) and 8th and 10th graders (starting in 1991) based on the following question: "How frequently have you smoked cigarettes during the past 30 days?"

National Health Interview Survey (NHIS)—Information about cigarette smoking is obtained for adults 18 years of age and over. Starting in 1993, current smokers are identified by asking the following two questions: "Have you smoked at least 100 cigarettes in your entire life?" and "Do you now smoke cigarettes every day, some days, or not at all?" Persons who smoked 100 cigarettes and who now smoke every day or some days are defined as current smokers. Before 1992, current smokers were identified based on positive responses to the following two questions: "Have you smoked 100 cigarettes in your entire life?" and "Do you smoke now?" (traditional definition). In 1992, the definition of current smoker in the NHIS was modified to specifically include persons who smoked on "some days" (revised definition). In 1992 cigarette smoking data were collected for a half sample with half the respondents (one-quarter sample) using the traditional smoking questions and the other half of the respondents (one-quarter sample) using the revised smoking question ("Do you smoke every day, some days, or not at all?"). An unpublished analysis of the 1992 traditional smoking measure revealed that the crude percentage of current smokers 18 years of age and over remained the same as for 1991. The statistics for 1992 combine data collected using the traditional and the revised questions.

In 1993–95 estimates of cigarette smoking prevalence were based on a half sample. Smoking data were not collected in 1996. Starting in 1997 smoking data were collected in the sample adult questionnaire. For further information on survey methodology and sample sizes pertaining to the NHIS cigarette smoking data for data years 1965–92 and other sources of cigarette smoking data available from the National Center for Health Statistics, see National Center for Health Statistics. *Bibliographies and Data Sources, Smoking Data Guide,* no 1, DHHS pub no (PHS) 91–1308-1, Public Health Service. Washington: U.S. Government Printing Office. 1991.

National Survey on Drug Use & Health (NSDUH)—Information on current cigarette smoking is obtained for all persons surveyed who are 12 years of age and over based on the following question: "During the past 30 days, have you smoked part or all of a cigarette?"

Youth Risk Behavior Survey—Information on current cigarette smoking is obtained from high school students (starting in 1991) based on the following question: "During the past 30 days, on how many days did you smoke cigarettes?"

Civilian noninstitutionalized population; Civilian population—See *Population.*

Cohort fertility—Cohort fertility refers to the fertility of the same women at successive ages. Women born during a 12-month period constitute a birth cohort. Cohort fertility for birth cohorts of women is measured by central birth rates, which represent the number of births occurring to women of an exact age divided by the number of women of that exact age. Cumulative birth rates by a given exact age represent the total childbearing experience of women in a cohort up to that age. Cumulative birth rates are sums of central birth rates for specified cohorts and show the number of children ever born up to the indicated age. For example, the cumulative birth rate for women exactly 30 years of age as of January 1, 1960, is the sum of the central birth rates for the 1930 birth cohort for the years 1944 (when its members were age 14) through 1959 (when they were age 29). Cumulative birth rates are also calculated for specific birth orders at each exact age of woman. The percentage of women who have not had at least one live birth by a certain age is found by subtracting the cumulative first birth rate for women of that age from 1,000 and dividing by 10. For method of calculation, see Heuser RL. *Fertility tables for birth cohorts by color: United States, 1917–73.* Rockville, MD: NCHS. 1976. See related *Rate: Birth and related rates.*

Community hospitals—See *Hospital.*

Comparability ratio—About every 10–20 years, the *International Classification of Diseases* (ICD) is revised to stay abreast of advances in medical science and changes in medical terminology. Each of these revisions produces breaks in the continuity of cause-of-death statistics. Discontinuities across revisions are due to changes in classification and rules for selecting underlying cause of death. Classification and rule changes affect cause-of-death trend data by shifting deaths away from some cause-of-death categories and into others. Comparability ratios measure the effect of changes in classification and coding rules. For causes shown in table VI, comparability ratios range between 0.6974 and 1.1404. Influenza and pneumonia had the lowest comparability ratio (0.6974), indicating that influenza and pneumonia is about 30 percent less likely to be selected as the underlying cause of death in ICD–10 than in ICD–9. Pregnancy, childbirth, and the puerperium had the highest comparability ratio (1.1404), indicating that pregnancy is more than 14 percent more likely to be selected as the underlying cause using ICD–10 coding.

For selected causes of death, the ICD–9 codes used to calculate death rates for 1980–1998 differ from the ICD–9 codes most nearly comparable with the corresponding ICD–10 cause-of-death category, which also affects the ability to compare death rates across ICD revisions. Examples of these causes are ischemic heart disease; cerebrovascular diseases; trachea, bronchus, and lung cancer; unintentional injuries; and homicide. To address this source of discontinuity, mortality trends for 1980–98 were recalculated, using ICD–9 codes that are more comparable with codes for corresponding ICD–10 categories. Table V shows the ICD–9 codes used for these causes. Although this modification may lessen the discontinuity between the Ninth and Tenth Revisions, the effect on the discontinuity between the Eighth and Ninth Revisions is not measured.

Comparability ratios shown in table VI are based on a comparability study in which the same deaths were coded by both the Ninth and Tenth Revisions. The comparability ratio was calculated by dividing the number of deaths classified by ICD–10 by the number of deaths classified by ICD–9. The resulting ratios represent the net effect of the Tenth Revision on cause-of-death statistics and can be used to adjust mortality statistics for causes of death classified by the Ninth Revision to be comparable with cause-specific mortality statistics classified by the Tenth Revision.

The application of comparability ratios to mortality statistics helps make the analysis of change between 1998 and 1999 more accurate and complete. The 1998 comparability-modified death rate is calculated by multiplying the comparability ratio by the 1998 death rate. Comparability-modified rates should be used to estimate mortality change between 1998 and 1999.

Table VI. Comparability of selected causes of death between the Ninth and Tenth Revisions of the *International Classification of Diseases (ICD)*

Cause of death[1]	*Final comparability ratio*[2]
Human immunodeficiency virus (HIV) disease	1.0821
Malignant neoplasms	1.0093
Colon, rectum, and anus	0.9988
Trachea, bronchus, and lung	0.9844
Breast	1.0073
Prostate	1.0144
Diabetes mellitus	1.0193
Diseases of heart	0.9852
Ischemic heart diseases	1.0006
Cerebrovascular diseases	1.0502
Influenza and pneumonia	0.6974
Chronic lower respiratory diseases	1.0411
Chronic liver disease and cirrhosis	1.0321
Pregnancy, childbirth, and the puerperium	1.1404
Unintentional injuries	1.0251
Motor vehicle-related injuries	0.9527
Suicide	1.0022
Homicide	1.0020
Injury by firearms	1.0012
Chronic and noncommunicable diseases	1.0100
Injuries	1.0159
Communicable diseases	0.8582
HIV disease	1.0821
Other communicable diseases	0.7997

[1]See table V for ICD–9 and ICD–10 cause-of-death codes.
[2]Ratio of number of deaths classified by ICD–10 to number of deaths classified by ICD–9.

SOURCE: Final and preliminary comparability ratios for 113 selected causes of death at ftp://ftp.cdc.gov/pub/Health_Statistics/NCHS/Datasets/Comparability/icd9_icd/10.

Caution should be taken when applying the comparability ratios presented in table VI to age-, race-, and sex-specific mortality data. Demographic subgroups may sometimes differ with regard to their cause-of-death distribution, and this would result in demographic variation in cause-specific comparability ratios.

For more information, see Anderson RN, Minino AM, Hoyert DL, Rosenberg HM. Comparability of cause of death between ICD–9 and ICD–10: Preliminary estimates; Kochanek KD, Smith BL, Anderson RN. Deaths: Preliminary data for 1999. National vital statistics reports. Vol. 49 no. 2 and vol. 49 no. 3. Hyattsville, MD: National Center for Health Statistics. 2001; and Final and preliminary comparability ratios for 113 selected causes of death at ftp://ftp.cdc.gov/pub/Health_Statistics/NCHS/Datasets/Comparability/icd9_icd10/. See related *Cause of death; International Classification of Diseases (ICD); tables IV, V, and VI.*

Compensation—See *Employer costs for employee compensation.*

Condition—A health condition is a departure from a state of physical or mental well-being. In the National Health Interview Survey, each condition reported as a cause of an individual's activity limitation has been classified as "chronic," "not chronic," or "unknown if chronic," based on the nature and duration of the condition. Conditions that are not cured once acquired (such as heart disease, diabetes, and birth defects in the original response categories, and amputee and old age in the ad hoc categories) are considered chronic, whereas conditions related to pregnancy are always considered not chronic. In addition, other conditions must have been present 3 months or longer to be considered chronic. An exception is made for children less than 1 year of age who have had a condition "since birth," as these conditions are always considered chronic. The National Nursing Home Survey uses a specific list of chronic conditions, disregarding time of onset.

Consumer Price Index (CPI)—The CPI is prepared by the U.S. Bureau of Labor Statistics. It is a monthly measure of the average change in the prices paid by urban consumers for a fixed market basket of goods and services. The medical care component of CPI shows trends in medical care prices based on specific indicators of hospital, medical, dental, and drug prices. A revision of the definition of CPI has been in use since January 1988. See related *Gross domestic product (GDP); Health expenditures, national; Appendix I, Consumer Price Index.*

Contraception —The National Survey of Family Growth collects information on contraceptive use as reported by women 15–44 years of age, during heterosexual vaginal intercourse. For current contraceptive use, women were asked about contraceptive use during the month of interview. Women were classified by whether they reported using each of 19 methods of contraception at any time in the month of interview. Data show up to four methods used in the month of interview. Contraceptive methods listed as other methods include the following: for 2002, the female condom, foam, cervical cap, Today Sponge®, suppository or insert, jelly or cream, or other method; for 1995, the female condom or vaginal pouch, foam, cervical cap, Today Sponge®, suppository or insert, jelly or cream, or other method; for 1988, foam, douche, Today Sponge®, suppository or insert, jelly or cream, or other method; and for 1982, foam, douche, suppository or insert, or other method.

Crude birth rate; Crude death rate—See *Rate: Birth and related rates; Rate: Death and related rates.*

Days of care—Days of care is defined similarly in different data systems. See related *Admission; Average length of stay; Discharge; Hospital; Hospital utilization; Inpatient.*

American Hospital Association—Days, hospital days, or inpatient days are the number of adult and pediatric days of care rendered during the entire reporting period. Days of care for newborns are excluded.

National Health Interview Survey (NHIS)—Hospital days during the year refer to the total number of hospital days occurring in the 12-month period before the interview week. A hospital day is a night spent in the hospital for persons admitted as inpatients. Starting in 1997 hospitalization data from NHIS are for all inpatient stays, whereas estimates for prior years published in *Health, United States* excluded hospitalizations for deliveries and newborns.

National Hospital Discharge Survey—Days of care refers to the total number of patient days accumulated by inpatients at the time of discharge from non-Federal short-stay hospitals during a reporting period. All days from and including the date of admission but not including the date of discharge are counted.

Death rate—See *Rate: Death and related rates.*

Dental caries—Dental caries is evidence of dental decay on any surface of a tooth. Dental caries was determined by an oral examination conducted by a trained dentist as part of the National Health and Nutrition Examination Survey. Study participants 2 years of age and over were eligible for the examination, as long as they did not meet other exclusion criteria. Both permanent and primary (or baby) teeth were evaluated.

Dental visit—Starting in 1997, National Health Interview Survey respondents were asked "About how long has it been since you last saw or talked to a dentist? Include all types of dentists, such as orthodontists, oral surgeons, and all other dental specialists as well as hygienists." Starting in 2001, the question was modified slightly to ask respondents how long it had been since they last saw a dentist. Questions about dental visits were not asked for children under 2 years of age for years 1997–99 and under 1 year of age for 2000 and beyond. Starting with data year 1997 estimates are presented for persons with a dental visit in the past year. Prior to 1997, dental visit estimates were based on a 2-week recall period.

Diagnosis—Diagnosis is the act or process of identifying or determining the nature and cause of a disease or injury through evaluation of patient history, examination, and review of laboratory data. Diagnoses in the National Hospital Discharge Survey, the National Ambulatory Medical Care Survey, the National Hospital Ambulatory Medical Care Survey, the National Nursing Home Survey, and the National Home and Hospice Care Survey are abstracted from medical records and coded to the *International Classification of Diseases, Ninth Revision, Clinical Modification (ICD–9–CM)*. For a given medical care encounter, the first-listed diagnosis can be used to categorize the visit, or if more than one diagnosis is recorded on the survey abstraction form, the visit can be categorized based on all diagnoses recorded. Analyzing first-listed diagnoses avoids double-counting events such as visits or hospitalizations; the first-listed diagnosis is often, but not always, considered the most important or dominant condition among all comorbid conditions. For example, a hospital discharge would be considered a first-listed stroke discharge if the ICD–9–CM diagnosis code for stroke was recorded in the first diagnosis field on the survey form. An any listed stroke discharge would classify all diagnoses of stroke recorded on the survey abstraction form regardless of order. Any-listed diagnoses double count events such as visits or hospitalizations with more than one recorded diagnosis but provide information on the burden a specific diagnosis presents to the health care system. See related *External cause of injury; Injury; Injury-related visit.*

Diagnostic and other nonsurgical procedures—See *Procedure.*

Discharge—The National Health Interview Survey defines a hospital discharge as the completion of any continuous period of stay of 1 night or more in a hospital as an inpatient. According to the National Hospital Discharge Survey, a discharge is a completed inpatient hospitalization. A hospitalization may be completed by death or by releasing the patient to the customary place of residence, a nursing home, another hospital, or other locations. See related *Admission; Average length of stay; Days of care; Inpatient.*

Domiciliary care homes—See *Long-term care facility; Nursing home.*

Drug abuse—See *Illicit drug use.*

Drug class, major—Major drug class is a general therapeutic or pharmacological classification scheme for drug products reported to the Food and Drug Administration under the provisions of the Drug Listing Act. The classification scheme used was based on the AMA DRUG EVALUATIONS SUBSCRIPTION and generally follows the organization of material in that publication. The drug class for each product was determined by the labeled indication(s). See related *National Drug Code (NDC) Directory therapeutic class.*

Drugs—Drugs are pharmaceutical agents—by any route of administration—for prevention, diagnosis, or treatment of medical conditions or diseases. Data on specific drug use are collected in three NCHS surveys.

National Ambulatory Medical Care Survey (NAMCS) and *National Hospital Ambulatory Medical Care Survey (NHAMCS)*—Data collection in the NAMCS and NHAMCS outpatient department component is from the medical record of an inperson physician office or hospital outpatient department visit, rather than from the patient. Generic or brand name drugs are abstracted from the medical record, including prescription and over-the-counter drugs, immunizations, allergy shots, and anesthetics that were prescribed, ordered, supplied, administered, or continued during the visit. Prior to 1995, up to five drugs per visit could be reported on the Patient Record Form; in data years 1995 and beyond, up to six drugs could be reported. Beginning with data year 2003, eight drugs could be reported, as well as a count of the total number of drugs prescribed, ordered, supplied, administered, or continued during the visit. For more information on drugs collected by the NAMCS and NHAMCS, see the NAMCS drug database at www.cdc.gov/nchs/about/major/ahcd/ambulatory.htm, or ftp://ftp.cdc.gov/pub/Health_Statistics/NCHS/Dataset_Documentation/NAMCS/doc01.pdf. For more information on how drugs are classified into therapeutic use categories, see *National Drug Code (NDC) Directory therapeutic class.* See related *Appendix*

I, National Ambulatory Medical Care Survey and *National Hospital Ambulatory Medical Care Survey.*

National Health and Nutrition Examination Survey (NHANES)—Drug information from NHANES III and 1999–2002 NHANES was collected during an inperson interview conducted in the participant's home. Participants were asked whether they had taken a medication in the past month for which they needed a prescription. Those who answered "Yes" were asked to produce the prescription medication containers for the interviewer. For each medication reported, the interviewer entered the product's complete name from the container. If no container was available, the interviewer asked the participant to verbally report the name of the medication. In addition, participants were asked how long they had been taking the medication and the main reason for use.

All reported medication names were converted to their standard generic ingredient name. For multi-ingredient products, the ingredients were listed in alphabetical order and counted as one drug (e.g., Tylenol #3 was listed as Acetaminophen; Codeine). No trade or proprietary names are provided on the data file.

Drug data from NHANES provide a snapshot of all prescribed drugs reported by a sample of the civilian noninstitutionalized population for a 1-month period. Drugs taken on an irregular basis, such as every other day, once per week, or for a 10-day period, etc., were captured in the 1-month recall period. Data shown in *Health, United States* for the percent of the population reporting three or more prescription drugs during the past month include a range of drug utilization patterns—for example, persons who took three or more drugs on a daily basis during the past month or persons who took a different drug three separate times—as long as at least three different drugs were taken during the past month.

For more information on prescription drug data collection and coding in the NHANES 1999–2000, see www.cdc.gov/nchs/data/nhanes/frequency/rxq_rxdoc.pdf. For more information on NHANES III prescription drug data collection and coding, see www.cdc.gov/nchs/data/nhanes/nhanes3/PUPREMED-acc.pdf. See related *Appendix I, National Health and Nutrition Examination Survey.*

Education—Several approaches to defining educational categories are used in this report. In survey data, educational categories are based on information about educational credentials, such as diplomas and degrees. In vital statistics, educational attainment is based on years of school completed.

Birth File—Information on educational attainment of mother is based on number of years of school completed, as reported by the mother on the birth certificate. Between 1970 and 1992, the reporting area for maternal education expanded.

Mother's education was reported on the birth certificate by 38 States in 1970. Data were not available from Alabama, Arkansas, California, Connecticut, Delaware, District of Columbia, Georgia, Idaho, Maryland, New Mexico, Pennsylvania, Texas, and Washington. In 1975, these data became available from Connecticut, Delaware, Georgia, Maryland, and the District of Columbia, increasing the number of States reporting mother's education to 42 and the District of Columbia. Between 1980 and 1988, only three States, California, Texas, and Washington, did not report mother's education. In 1988, mother's education was also missing from New York State outside New York City. In 1989–91, mother's education was missing only from Washington and New York State outside New York City. During 1992–2002, mother's education was reported by all 50 States and the District of Columbia. In 2003, data on mother's education is included for all States except Pennsylvania and Washington, both of which implemented the 2003 revision of the U.S. Standard Certificate of Live Birth. The education item on the 2003 revision asks for the highest degree or level of school completed whereas the education item on the 1989 revision asks for highest grade completed. Data from the 1989 and 2003 certificate items on educational attainment are too dissimilar to be reliably combined.

Mortality File—Information on educational attainment of decedent became available for the first time in 1989 because of a revision of the U.S. Standard Certificate of Death. Decedent's educational attainment is reported on the death certificate by the funeral director based on information provided by an informant such as next of kin. Mortality data by educational attainment for 1989 were based on data from 20 States and by 1994–96, increased to 45 States and the District of Columbia (DC). In 1994–96, either the following States did not report educational attainment on the death certificate or the information was more than 20 percent incomplete: Georgia, Kentucky, Oklahoma, Rhode Island, and South Dakota. In 1997–2000, information on decedent's education was available from Oklahoma, increasing the reporting area to 46 States and the DC. With the addition of Kentucky, the reporting area increased to 47 States and DC in 2001 and 2002.

Calculation of unbiased death rates by educational attainment based on the National Vital Statistics System requires that the reporting of education on the death certificate be complete and consistent with the reporting of education on the Current Population Survey (CPS), the source of population estimates for denominators for death rates. Death records that are missing information about decedent's education are not included in the calculation of rates. Therefore the levels of death rates by educational attainment shown in this report are underestimated by approximately the percentage with not stated education, which ranges from 3 to 9 percent.

The validity of information about the decedent's education was evaluated by comparing self-reported education obtained in the CPS with education on the death certificate for decedents in the National Longitudinal Mortality Survey (NLMS). (Sorlie PD, Johnson NJ. Validity of education information on the death certificate. *Epidemiology* 7(4):437–9), 1996. Another analysis compared self-reported education collected in the first National Health and Nutrition Examination Survey (NHANES I) with education on the death certificate for decedents in the NHANES I Epidemiologic Followup Study. (Makuc DM, Feldman JJ, Mussolino ME. Validity of education and age as reported on death certificates. American Statistical Association. *1996 Proceedings of the Social Statistics Section 102–6).* Results of both studies indicated that there is a tendency for some people who did not graduate from high school to be reported as high school graduates on the death certificate. This tendency results in overstating the death rate for high school graduates and understating the death rate for the group with less than 12 years of education. The bias was greater among older than younger decedents and somewhat greater among black than white decedents.

In addition, educational gradients in death rates based on the National Vital Statistics System were compared with those based on the NLMS, a prospective study of persons in the CPS. Results of these comparisons indicate that educational gradients in death rates based on the National Vital Statistics System were reasonably similar to those based on NLMS for white persons 25–64 years of age and black persons 25–44 years of age. The number of deaths for persons of Hispanic origin in NLMS was too small to permit comparison for this ethnic group. For further information on measurement of education, see Kominski R and Siegel PM. Measuring education in the Current Population Survey. *Monthly Labor Review*, 34–8. September 1993.

National Health Interview Survey (NHIS)—Beginning in 1997, the NHIS questionnaire was changed to ask "What is the highest level of school ___ has completed or the highest degree received?" Responses were used to categorize adults according to educational credentials (e.g., no high school diploma or general educational development (GED) high school equivalency diploma; high school diploma or GED; some college, no bachelor's degree; bachelor's degree or higher).

Prior to 1997, the education variable in NHIS was measured by asking, "What is the highest grade or year of regular school ___ has ever attended?" and "Did ___ finish the grade/year?" Responses were used to categorize adults according to years of education completed (e.g., less than 12 years, 12 years, 13–15 years, and 16 or more years).

Data from the 1996 and 1997 NHIS were used to compare distributions of educational attainment for adults 25 years of age and over using categories based on educational credentials (1997) with categories based on years of education completed (1996). A larger percentage of persons reported "some college" than "13–15 years" of education and a correspondingly smaller percentage reported "high school diploma or GED" than "12 years of education." In 1997, 19 percent of adults reported no high school diploma, 31 percent a high school diploma or GED, 26 percent some college, and 24 percent a bachelor's degree or higher. In 1996, 18 percent of adults reported less than 12 years of education, 37 percent 12 years of education, 20 percent 13–15 years, and 25 percent 16 or more years of education.

Figure I. **Census Bureau**: Four Geographic Regions and 9 Divisions of the United States

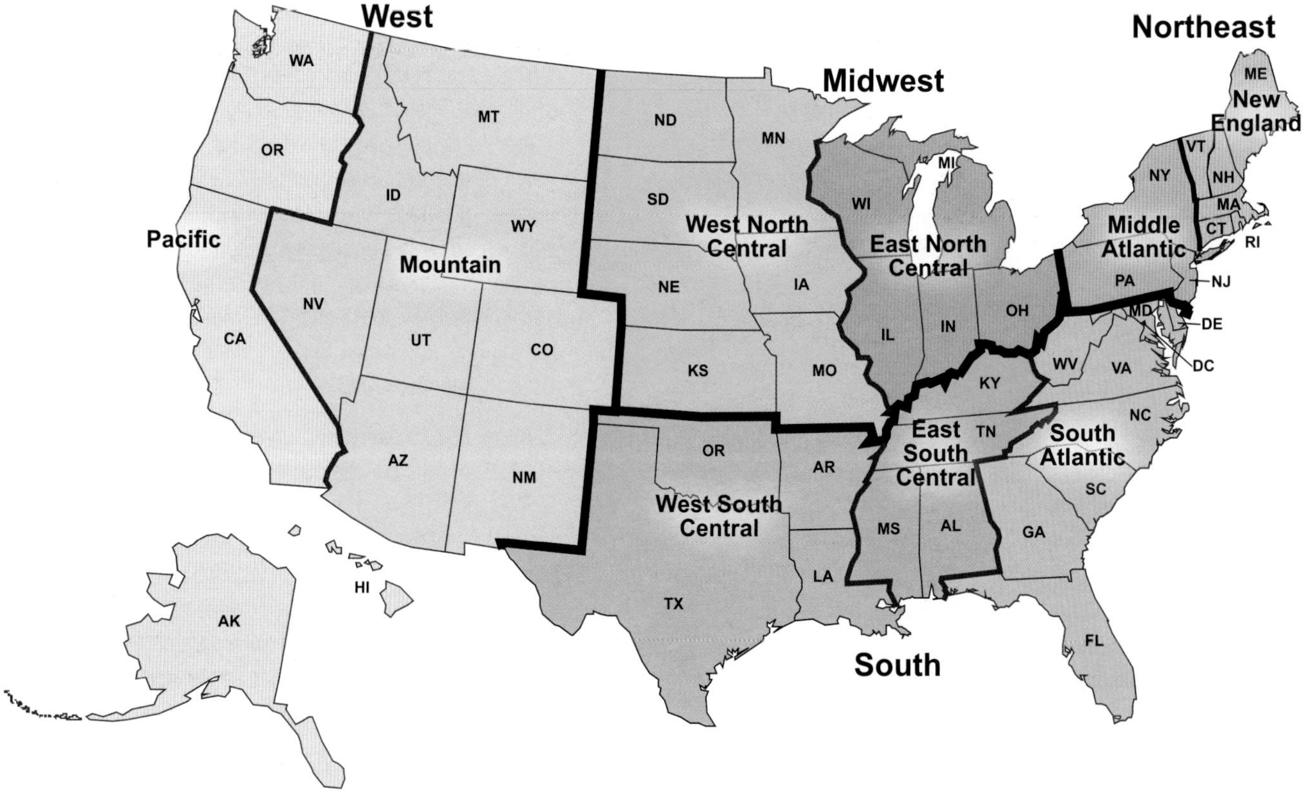

Emergency department—According to the National Hospital Ambulatory Medical Care Survey, an emergency department is a hospital facility that provides unscheduled outpatient services to patients whose conditions require immediate care and is staffed 24 hours a day. Off-site emergency departments open less than 24 hours are included if staffed by the hospital's emergency department. See related *Emergency department or emergency room visit; Outpatient department.*

Table VII. Codes for first-listed external causes of injury from the *International Classification of Diseases, Ninth Revision, Clinical Modification*

External cause of injury category	*E-Code numbers*
Unintentional	E800–E869, E880–E929
Motor vehicle traffic	E810–E819
Falls	E880–E886, E888
Struck by or against objects or persons	E916–E917
Caused by cutting and piercing instruments or objects	E920
Intentional (suicide and homicide)	E950–E969

Emergency department or emergency room visit—Starting with the 1997 National Health Interview Survey, respondents to the sample adult and sample child questionnaires (generally the parent) were asked about the number of visits to hospital emergency rooms during the past 12 months, including visits that resulted in hospitalization. In the National Hospital Ambulatory Medical Care Survey, an emergency department visit is a direct personal exchange between a patient and a physician or other health care providers working under the physician's supervision for the purpose of seeking care and receiving personal health services. See related *Emergency department; Injury-related visit.*

Employer costs for employee compensation—This is a measure of the average cost per employee hour worked to employers for wages and salaries and benefits. Wages and salaries are defined as the hourly straight-time wage rate or, for workers not paid on an hourly basis, straight-time earnings divided by the corresponding hours. Straight-time wage and salary rates are total earnings before payroll deductions, excluding premium pay for overtime and for work on

Figure II. **Bureau of Economic Analysis:** Eight Geographic Regions of the United States

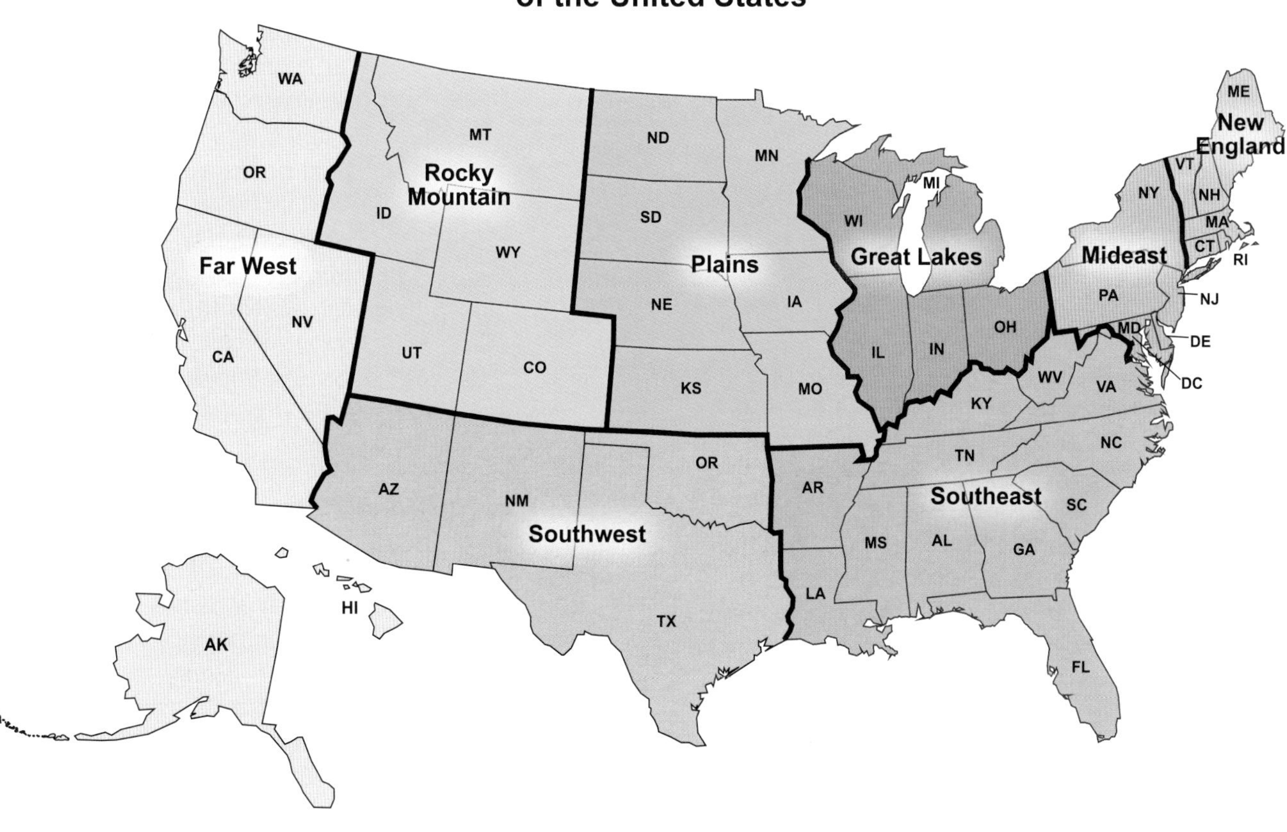

weekends and holidays, shift differentials, nonproduction bonuses, and lump-sum payments provided in lieu of wage increases. Production bonuses, incentive earnings, commission payments, and cost-of-living adjustments are included in straight-time wage and salary rates. Benefits covered are paid leave—paid vacations, holidays, sick leave, and other leave; supplemental pay—premium pay for overtime and work on weekends and holidays, shift differentials, nonproduction bonuses, and lump-sum payments provided in lieu of wage increases; insurance benefits—life, health, and sickness and accident insurance; retirement and savings benefits—pension and other retirement plans and savings and thrift plans; legally required benefits—Social Security, railroad retirement and supplemental retirement, railroad unemployment insurance, Federal and State unemployment insurance, workers' compensation, and other benefits required by law, such as State temporary disability insurance; and other benefits—severance pay and supplemental unemployment plans. See related *Appendix I, National Compensation Survey.*

Ethnicity—See *Hispanic origin.*

Exercise—See *Physical activity, leisure-time.*

Expenditures—See *Health expenditures, national; Appendix I, National Health Accounts.*

External cause of injury—The ICD–9 External Cause Matrix is a two-dimensional array describing both the mechanism or external cause of the injury (e.g., fall, motor vehicle traffic) and the manner or intent of the injury (e.g., self-inflicted or assault). Although this matrix was originally developed for mortality, it has been adapted for use with the ICD–9–CM. For more information, see *http://www.cdc.gov/nchs/about/otheract/injury/tools.htm.*

Family income—For purposes of the National Health Interview Survey and National Health and Nutrition Examination Survey, all people within a household related to each other by blood, marriage, or adoption constitute a family. Each member of a family is classified according to the total income of the family. Unrelated individuals are classified according to their own income.

National Health Interview Survey (NHIS)—In the NHIS (prior to 1997), family income was the total income received by members of a family (or by an unrelated individual) during the 12 months before the interview. Starting in 1997, the NHIS collected family income data for the calendar year prior to the interview (e.g., 2003 family income data were based on calendar year 2002 information). Family income includes wages, salaries, rents from property, interest, dividends, profits and fees from their own businesses, pensions, and help from relatives. Family income data are used in the computation of poverty level. Starting with *Health, United States, 2004*, a new methodology for imputing family income data for NHIS data was implemented for data years 1997 and beyond. Multiple imputations were performed for survey years 1997 and beyond with five sets of imputed values created to allow for the assessment of variability caused by imputation. Family income was missing for 24–29 percent of persons in 1997–98 and 31–33 percent in 1999–2003. A detailed description of the multiple imputation procedure, as well as data files for 1997 and beyond, are available from NCHS on the NHIS Web site (www.cdc.gov/nchs/nhis.htm), via the Imputed Income Files link under that year. For data years 1990–96, about 16–18 percent of persons had missing data on poverty level. In those years, missing values were imputed for family income using a sequential hot deck within matrix cells imputation approach. A detailed description of the imputation procedure, as well as data files with imputed annual family income for 1990–96, is available from NCHS on CD-ROM, NHIS Imputed Annual Family Income 1990–96, series 10, no 9A.

National Health and Nutrition Examination Survey (NHANES)—In the NHANES 1999 and onward, family income is asked in a series of questions about possible sources of income, including wages, salaries, interest and dividends, Federal programs, child support, rents, royalties, and other possible sources of income. After the information about sources of income was obtained in the Family Interview Income section of the questionnaire, the respondent was asked to report total combined family income for themselves and the other members of their family, in dollars. If the respondent did not provide an answer or did not know the total combined family income, they were asked if the total family income was less than $20,000 or more than $20,000. If the respondent answered, a followup question asked the respondent to select an income range from a list on a printed hand card. The midpoint of the income range was then used as the total family income value. Family income values were used to calculate the Poverty Income ratio. NHANES III did not ask the detailed components of income questions but asked respondents to identify their income based on a set of ranges provided on a flashcard, whereas NHANES II did include questions on components of income. Family income was not imputed for individuals or families with no reported income information in any of the NHANES survey years. See related *Poverty level.*

Federal hospitals—See *Hospital.*

Fee-for-service health insurance—This is private (commercial) health insurance that reimburses health care providers on the basis of a fee for each health service provided to the insured person. It is also known as indemnity health insurance. Medicare Parts A and B are sometimes referred to as "Medicare fee-for-service." See related *Health insurance coverage; Medicare.*

Fertility rate—See *Rate: Birth and related rates.*

General hospitals—See *Hospital.*

General hospitals providing separate psychiatric services—See *Mental health organization.*

Geographic region and division—The U.S. Census Bureau groups the 50 States and the District of Columbia for statistical purposes into four geographic regions—Northeast, Midwest, South, and West—and nine divisions, based on geographic proximity. See figure I.

The Department of Commerce's Bureau of Economic Analysis (BEA) groups States into eight regions based on their homogeneity with respect to income characteristics, industrial composition of the employed labor force, and such noneconomic factors as demographic, social, and cultural characteristics. See figure II.

Three Census Bureau divisions—West North Central, East North Central, and New England—and three BEA regions—Plains, Great Lakes, and New England—are composed of the same States. The States composing the remaining Census Bureau divisions differ from those composing the corresponding BEA regions.

Gestation—For the National Vital Statistics System and the Centers for Disease Control and Prevention's Abortion Surveillance, the period of gestation is defined as beginning with the first day of the last normal menstrual period and ending with the day of birth or day of termination of pregnancy.

Gross domestic product (GDP)—GDP is the market value of the goods and services produced by labor and property located in the United States. As long as the labor and property are located in the United States, the suppliers (i.e., the workers and, for property, the owners) may be U.S. residents or residents of other countries. See related *Consumer Price Index (CPI); Health expenditures, national.*

Health care contact—Starting in 1997, the National Health Interview Survey has been collecting information on health care contacts with doctors and other health care professionals using the following questions: "During the past 12 months, how many times have you gone to a hospital emergency room about your own health?" "During the past 12 months, did you receive care at home from a nurse or other health care professional? What was the total number of home visits received?" "During the past 12 months, how many times have you seen a doctor or other health care professional about your own health at a doctor's office, a clinic, or some other place? Do not include times you were hospitalized overnight, visits to hospital emergency rooms, home visits, or telephone calls." Beginning in 2000 this question was amended to exclude dental visits also. For each question respondents were shown a flashcard with response categories of 0, 1, 2–3, 4–9, 10–12, or 13 or more visits in 1997–99. Starting in 2000, response categories were expanded to 0, 1, 2–3, 4–5, 6–7, 8–9, 10–12, 13–15, or 16 or more. Analyses of the percentage of persons with health care visits were tabulated as follows: For tabulation of the 1997–99 data, responses of 2–3 were recoded to 2, and responses of 4–9 were recoded to 6. Starting in 2000, tabulation of responses of 2–3 were recoded to 2, and other responses were recoded to the midpoint of the range. A summary measure of health care visits was constructed by adding recoded responses for these questions and categorizing the sum as none, 1–3, 4–9, or 10 or more health care visits during the past 12 months.

Analyses of the percent of children without a health care visit are based on the following question: "During the past 12 months, how many times has ___ seen a doctor or other health care professional about (his/her) health at a doctor's office, a clinic, or some other place? Do not include times ____ was hospitalized overnight, visits to hospital emergency rooms, home visits, or telephone calls." See related *Emergency department or emergency room visit; Home visit.*

Health expenditures, national—National Health Expenditures are estimated by the Centers for Medicare & Medicaid Services (CMS) and measure spending for health care in the United States by type of service delivered (e.g., hospital care, physician services, nursing home care) and source of funding for those services (e.g., private health insurance, Medicare, Medicaid, out-of-pocket spending). CMS produces both historical and projected estimates of health expenditures by category. See related *Consumer price index (CPI); Gross domestic product (GDP).*

Health services and supplies expenditures—These are outlays for goods and services relating directly to patient care plus expenses for administering health insurance programs and government public health activities. This category is equivalent to total national health expenditures minus expenditures for research and construction.

National health expenditures—This measure estimates the amount spent for all health services and supplies and health-related research and construction activities consumed in the United States during the calendar year. Detailed estimates are available by source of expenditures (e.g., out-of-pocket payments, private health insurance, and government programs) and by type of expenditures (e.g., hospital care, physician services, and drugs) and are in current dollars for the year of report. Data are compiled from a variety of sources.

Nursing home expenditures—These cover care rendered in establishments primarily engaged in providing inpatient nursing and rehabilitative services and continuous personal care services to persons requiring nursing care (skilled nursing and intermediate care facilities, including those for the mentally retarded) and continuing care retirement communities with on-site nursing care facilities. The costs of long-term care provided by hospitals are excluded.

Personal health care expenditures—These are outlays for goods and services relating directly to patient care. The expenditures in this category are total national health expenditures minus expenditures for research and construction, health insurance program administration, and government public health activities.

Private expenditures—These are outlays for services provided or paid for by nongovernmental sources—consumers, insurance companies, private industry, and philanthropic and other nonpatient care sources.

Public expenditures—These are outlays for services provided or paid for by Federal, State, and local government agencies or expenditures required by governmental mandate (such as worker's compensation insurance payments).

Health insurance coverage—Health insurance is broadly defined to include both public and private payors who cover medical expenditures incurred by a defined population in a variety of settings.

National Health Interview Survey (NHIS)—NHIS respondents were asked about their health insurance coverage in the previous month in 1993–96 and at the time of the interview in other years. Questions on health insurance coverage were expanded starting in 1993 compared with previous years. In 1997, the entire questionnaire was redesigned and data were collected using a computer-assisted personal interview (CAPI).

Respondents are covered by private health insurance if they indicate private health insurance or if they are covered by a single-service hospital plan, except in 1997 and 1998, when no information on single-service plans was obtained. Private health insurance includes managed care such as health maintenance organizations (HMOs).

Until 1996, persons were defined as having Medicaid or other public assistance coverage if they indicated that they had either Medicaid or other public assistance or if they reported receiving Aid to Families with Dependent Children (AFDC) or Supplemental Security Income (SSI). After welfare reform in late 1996, Medicaid was delinked from AFDC and SSI. Starting in 1997, persons are considered to be covered by Medicaid if they report Medicaid or a State-sponsored health program. Starting in 1998, persons are considered to be covered by Medicaid if they report being covered by the State Children's Health Insurance Program (SCHIP). Medicare or military health plan coverage is also determined in the interview, and starting in 1997 other government-sponsored program coverage is determined as well.

If respondents do not report coverage under one of the above types of plans and they have unknown coverage under either private health insurance or Medicaid, they are considered to have unknown coverage.

The remaining respondents are considered uninsured. The uninsured are persons who do not have coverage under private health insurance, Medicare, Medicaid, public assistance, a State-sponsored health plan, other government-sponsored programs, or a military health plan. Persons with only Indian Health Service coverage are considered uninsured. Estimates of the percentage of persons who are uninsured based on the NHIS may differ slightly from those based on the March Current Population Survey (CPS) because of differences in survey questions, recall period, and other aspects of survey methodology.

In the NHIS, less than 2 percent of persons age 65 years and over reported no current health insurance coverage, but the small sample size precludes the presentation of separate estimates for this population. Therefore, the term "uninsured" refers only to the population under age 65.

In the NHIS, the category "Medicare HMO" is defined as persons age 65 years or over who responded "Yes" when asked whether they were under a Medicare managed care arrangement such as an HMO. This is a subset of Medicare Part C. Respondents who stated they had Medicare coverage but did not answer "Yes" to the "managed care arrangement such as an HMO" are included in the Medicare fee-for-service category. Medicare fee-for-service is defined as Medicare Part A or Part B. The majority of these people had coverage from another source, primarily employer-sponsored retiree health insurance. Some tables in *Health, United States* further classify persons 65 years of age and over with "Medicare fee-for service" into "Medicare fee-for-service only" and Private (including Medicare fee-for-service) coverage.

See related *Fee-for-service health insurance; Health maintenance organization (HMO); Managed care; Medicaid;*

Medicare; State Children's Health Insurance Program (SCHIP); Uninsured.

Health maintenance organization (HMO)—An HMO is a health care system that assumes or shares both the financial risks and the delivery risks associated with providing comprehensive medical services to a voluntarily enrolled population in a particular geographic area, usually in return for a fixed, prepaid fee. Pure HMO enrollees use only the prepaid capitated health services of the HMO panel of medical care providers. Open-ended HMO enrollees use the prepaid HMO health services but, in addition, may receive medical care from providers who are not part of the HMO panel. There is usually a substantial deductible, copayment, or coinsurance associated with use of nonpanel providers.

HMO model types are these:

Group model HMO—A group model HMO is an HMO that contracts with a single multispecialty medical group to provide care to the HMO's membership. The group practice may work exclusively with the HMO, or it may provide services to non-HMO patients as well. The HMO pays the medical group a negotiated per capita rate, which the group distributes among its physicians, usually on a salaried basis.

Staff model HMO—A staff model HMO is a closed-panel HMO (where patients can receive services only through a limited number of providers) in which physicians are HMO employees. The providers see members in the HMO's own facilities.

Network model HMO—A network model HMO is an HMO that contracts with multiple physician groups to provide services to HMO members and may include single or multispecialty groups.

Individual practice association (IPA)— An individual practice association is a healthcare provider organization composed of a group of independent practicing physicians who maintain their own offices and band together for the purpose of contracting their services to HMOs, preferred provider organizations (PPOs), and insurance companies. An IPA may contract with and provide services to both HMO and non-HMO plan participants.

Mixed model HMO—A mixed model HMO combines features of more than one HMO model.

See related *Managed care; Point-of-service (POS) plan; Preferred provider organization (PPO).*

Health services and supplies expenditures—See *Health expenditures, national.*

Health status, respondent-assessed—Health status was measured in the National Health Interview Survey by asking the family respondent about his or her health or the health of a family member: "Would you say _____'s health is excellent, very good, good, fair, or poor?"

Hispanic origin—Hispanic or Latino origin includes persons of Mexican, Puerto Rican, Cuban, Central and South American, and other or unknown Latin American or Spanish origins. Persons of Hispanic origin may be of any race.

National Health Interview Survey (NHIS) and *National Health and Nutrition Examination Survey (NHANES)*—Questions on Hispanic origin are self-reported in the NHANES III and subsequent years and all years of the NHIS and precede questions on race. The NHANES sample was designed to provide estimates specifically for persons of Mexican origin and not for all Hispanic-origin persons in the United States. Persons of Hispanic origin other than Mexicans were entered into the sample with different selection probabilities that are not nationally representative of the total U.S. Hispanic population.

Birth File—The reporting area for an Hispanic-origin item on the birth certificate expanded between 1980 and 1993. Trend data on births of Hispanic and non-Hispanic parentage in this report are affected by expansion of the reporting area and by immigration. These two factors affect numbers of events, composition of the Hispanic population, and maternal and infant health characteristics.

In 1980 and 1981, information on births of Hispanic parentage was reported on the birth certificate by the following 22 States: Arizona, Arkansas, California, Colorado, Florida, Georgia, Hawaii, Illinois, Indiana, Kansas, Maine, Mississippi, Nebraska, Nevada, New Jersey, New Mexico, New York, North Dakota, Ohio, Texas, Utah, and Wyoming. In 1982, Tennessee, and in 1983, the District of Columbia, began reporting this information. Between 1983 and 1987, information on births of Hispanic parentage was available for 23 States and the District of Columbia. In 1988, this information became available for Alabama, Connecticut, Kentucky, Massachusetts, Montana, North Carolina, and Washington, increasing the number of States reporting information on births of Hispanic parentage to 30 States and the District of Columbia. In 1989 this information became available from an additional 17 States, increasing the number of Hispanic-reporting States to 47 and the District of Columbia. In 1989, only Louisiana, New Hampshire, and Oklahoma did not report Hispanic parentage on the birth certificate. With the inclusion of Oklahoma in 1989 and Louisiana in 1990 as Hispanic-reporting States, 99 percent of birth records included information on mother's origin. Hispanic origin of the mother was reported on the birth certificates of 49 States and the District of Columbia in 1991 and 1992; only New Hampshire did not provide this information. Starting in 1993 Hispanic origin of mother was reported by all 50 States and the District of Columbia.

Mortality File—The reporting area for an Hispanic-origin item on the death certificate expanded between 1985 and 1997. In 1985 mortality data by Hispanic origin of decedent were based on deaths to residents of the following 17 States and the District of Columbia whose data on the death certificate were at least 90 percent complete on a place-of-occurrence basis and of comparable format: Arizona, Arkansas, California, Colorado, Georgia, Hawaii, Illinois, Indiana, Kansas, Mississippi, Nebraska, New York, North Dakota, Ohio, Texas, Utah, and Wyoming. In 1986 New Jersey began reporting Hispanic origin of decedent, increasing the number of reporting States to 18 and the District of Columbia in 1986 and 1987. In 1988 Alabama, Kentucky, Maine, Montana, North Carolina, Oregon, Rhode Island, and Washington were added to the reporting area, increasing the number of States to 26 and the District of Columbia. In 1989 an additional 18 States were added, increasing the Hispanic reporting area to 44 States and the District of Columbia; only Connecticut, Louisiana, Maryland, New Hampshire, Oklahoma, and Virginia were not included in the reporting area. Starting with 1990 data in this book, the criterion was changed to include States whose data were at least 80 percent complete. In 1990 Maryland, Virginia, and Connecticut, in 1991 Louisiana, and in 1993 New Hampshire were added, increasing the reporting area for Hispanic origin of decedent to 47 States and the District of Columbia in 1990, 48 States and the District of Columbia in 1991 and 1992, and 49 States and the District of Columbia in 1993–96. Only Oklahoma did not provide this information in 1993–96. Starting in 1997 Hispanic origin of decedent was reported by all 50 States and the District of Columbia. Based on data from the U.S. Census Bureau, the 1990 reporting area encompassed 99.6 percent of the U.S. Hispanic population. In 1990 more than 96 percent of death records included information on Hispanic origin of decedent.

See related *Race*.

HIV—See *Human immunodeficiency virus (HIV) disease.*

Home health care—Home health care as defined by the National Home and Hospice Care Survey is care provided by a home health care agency to individuals and families in their place of residence for promoting, maintaining, or restoring health or for minimizing the effects of disability and illness including terminal illness.

Home visit—Starting in 1997, the National Health Interview Survey has been collecting information on home visits received during the past 12 months. Respondents are asked "During the past 12 months, did you receive care at home from a nurse or other health care professional? What was the total number of home visits received?" These data are combined with data on visits to doctors' offices, clinics, and emergency departments to provide a summary measure of health care visits. See related *Emergency department or emergency room visit; Health care contact.*

Hospice care—Hospice care as defined by the National Home and Hospice Care Survey is a program of palliative and supportive care services providing physical, psychological, social, and spiritual care for dying persons, their families, and other loved ones by a hospice program or agency. Hospice services are available in home and inpatient settings.

Hospital—According to the American Hospital Association, hospitals are licensed institutions with at least six beds whose primary function is to provide diagnostic and therapeutic patient services for medical conditions by an organized physician staff and that have continuous nursing services under the supervision of registered nurses. The World Health Organization considers an establishment to be a hospital if it is permanently staffed by at least one physician, can offer inpatient accommodation, and can provide active medical and nursing care. Hospitals may be classified by type of service, ownership, size in terms of number of beds, and length of stay. In the National Hospital Ambulatory Medical Care Survey, hospitals include all those with an average length of stay for all patients of less than 30 days (short-stay) or hospitals whose specialty is general (medical or surgical) or children's general. Federal hospitals and hospital units of institutions and hospitals with fewer than six beds staffed for patient use are excluded. See related *Average length of stay; Bed; Days of care; Emergency department; Inpatient; Outpatient department.*

Community hospitals—Community hospitals based on the American Hospital Association definition include all non-Federal short-term general and special hospitals whose facilities and services are available to the public. Special hospitals include obstetrics and gynecology; eye, ear, nose, and throat; rehabilitation; orthopedic; and other specialty services. Short-term general and special childrens hospitals are also considered to be community hospitals. A hospital may include a nursing-home-type unit and still be classified as short-term, provided that the majority of its patients are admitted to units where the average length of stay is less than 30 days. Hospital units of institutions such as prisons and college infirmaries that are not open to the public and are contained within a nonhospital facility are not included in the category of community hospitals. Traditionally the definition included all non-Federal short-stay hospitals except facilities for the mentally retarded. In a revised definition the following additional sites were excluded: hospital units of institutions, and alcoholism and chemical dependency facilities.

Federal hospitals—Federal hospitals are operated by the Federal Government.

For-profit hospitals—For-profit hospitals are operated for profit by individuals, partnerships, or corporations.

General hospitals—General hospitals provide diagnostic, treatment, and surgical services for patients with a variety of medical conditions. According to the World Health Organization, these hospitals provide medical and nursing care for more than one category of medical discipline (e.g., general medicine, specialized medicine, general surgery, specialized surgery, and obstetrics). Excluded are hospitals, usually in rural areas, that provide a more limited range of care.

Nonprofit hospitals—Nonprofit hospitals are controlled by nonprofit organizations, including religious organizations, fraternal societies, and others.

Psychiatric hospitals—Psychiatric hospitals are ones whose major type of service is psychiatric care. See related *Mental health organization.*

Registered hospitals—Registered hospitals are registered with the American Hospital Association. About 98 percent of hospitals are registered.

Short-stay hospitals—Short-stay hospitals in the National Hospital Discharge Survey, are those in which the average length of stay is less than 30 days. The National Health Interview Survey defines a short-stay hospitals as any hospital or hospital department in which the type of service provided is general; maternity; eye, ear, nose, and throat; children's; or osteopathic.

Specialty hospitals—Specialty hospitals such as psychiatric, tuberculosis, chronic disease, rehabilitation, maternity, and alcoholic or narcotic, provide a particular type of service to the majority of their patients.

Hospital-based physician—See *Physician.*

Hospital days—See *Days of care.*

Hospital utilization—Estimates of hospital utilization (such as hospital discharge rate, days of care rate, and average length of stay) presented in *Health, United States* are based on data from three different sources—the National Health Interview Survey (NHIS), the National Hospital Discharge Survey (NHDS), and the American Hospital Association. Estimates of hospital utilization from the NHIS and NHDS may differ because NHIS data are based on household interviews of the civilian noninstitutionalized population whereas NHDS data are based on hospital discharge records of all persons. Starting in 1997, hospital utilization data from the NHIS are for all hospital discharges whereas estimates for prior years excluded hospitalizations for delivery and newborns. NHDS includes hospital discharge records for all persons discharged alive or

Table VIII. Codes for industries, according to the 2002 North American Industry Classification System (NAICS)

Industry	Code numbers
Goods producing	
Natural resources and mining:	
Agriculture, forestry, fishing, and hunting	11
Mining	21
Construction	23
Manufacturing	31–33
Service providing	
Trade, transportation, and utilities:	
Wholesale trade	42
Retail trade	44–45
Transportation and warehousing	48–49
Utilities	22
Information	51
Financial activities:	
Finance and insurance	52
Real estate and rental and leasing	53
Professional and business services:	
Professional, scientific, and technical services	54
Management of companies and enterprises	55
Administrative and support and waste management and remediation services	56
Education and health services:	
Educational services	61
Health care and social assistance	62
Leisure and hospitality:	
Arts, entertainment, and recreation	71
Accommodation and food services	72
Other services, except public administration	81
Public administration	92

deceased and institutionalized persons and excludes data for newborn infants. Differences in hospital utilization estimated by these two surveys are particularly evident for children and the elderly. For children, NHIS estimates are higher than NHDS estimates because NHIS includes data for newborns. For the elderly NHDS estimates are higher than NHIS estimates because NHIS includes data for institutionalized persons and persons who died while hospitalized. Estimates for average length of stay between the three sources presented in *Health, United States* differ because of different methods for counting days of care. See related *Average length of stay; Days of care; Discharge; Appendix I, National Health Interview Survey, National Hospital Discharge Survey.*

Human immunodeficiency virus (HIV) disease—HIV disease is a serious disease caused by a cytopathic retrovirus that is the cause of Acquired Immunity Syndrome (AIDS). It is also called AIDS-related virus, human T-cell leukemia virus type III, human T-cell lymphotrophic virus type III, and lymphadenopathy-associated virus. Mortality and morbidity coding for HIV disease are similar and have evolved over time.

Mortality coding—Starting with data year 1999 and the introduction of the Tenth Revision of the *International Classification of Diseases* (ICD–10), the title for this cause of death was changed to "HIV disease" from "HIV infection" and the ICD codes changed to B20–B24. Beginning with data for 1987, NCHS introduced category numbers *042–*044 for classifying and coding HIV infection as a cause of death in ICD–9. The asterisk before the category numbers indicates that these codes were not part of the original ICD–9. HIV infection was formerly referred to as human T-cell lymphotropic virus-III/lymphadenopathy-associated virus (HTLV-III/LAV) infection. Before 1987 deaths involving HIV infection were classified to Deficiency of cell-mediated immunity (ICD–9 279.1) contained in the title "All other diseases"; to Pneumocystosis (ICD–9 136.3) contained in the title "All other infectious and parasitic diseases"; to "Malignant neoplasms, including neoplasms of lymphatic and hematopoietic tissues"; and to a number of other causes. Therefore, before 1987, death statistics for HIV infection are not strictly comparable with data for 1987 and later years and are not shown in this report.

Morbidity coding—The National Hospital Discharge Survey codes diagnosis data using the *International Classification of Diseases, Ninth Revision, Clinical Modification* (ICD–9–CM). Discharges with diagnosis of HIV as shown in *Health, United States* have at least one HIV diagnosis listed on the face sheet of the medical record and are not limited to the first-listed diagnosis. During 1984 and 1985 only data for AIDS (ICD–9–CM 279.19) were included. In 1986–94 discharges with the following diagnoses were included: Acquired immunodeficiency syndrome (AIDS), Human immunodeficiency virus (HIV) infection and associated conditions, and Positive serological or viral culture findings for HIV (ICD–9–CM 042–044, 279.19, and 795.8). Beginning in 1995 discharges with the following diagnoses were included: Human immunodeficiency virus (HIV) disease and Asymptomatic human immunodeficiency virus (HIV) infection status (ICD–9–CM 042 and V08).

See related *Acquired immunodeficiency syndrome (AIDS); Cause of death; International Classification of*

Diseases (ICD); International Classification of Diseases, Ninth Revision, Clinical Modification (ICD–9–CM).

ICD; ICD codes—See *Cause of death; International Classification of Diseases (ICD).*

Illicit drug use—Illicit drug use refers to use and misuse of illegal and controlled drugs.

Monitoring the Future Study—In this school-based survey of secondary school students, information on marijuana use is collected using self-completed questionnaires. The information is based on the following questions: "On how many occasions (if any) have you used marijuana in the last 30 days?" and "On how many occasions (if any) have you used hashish in the last 30 days?" Questions on cocaine use include the following: "On how many occasions (if any) have you take 'crack' (cocaine in chunk or rock form) during the last 30 days?" and "On how many occasions (if any) have you taken cocaine in any other form during the last 30 days?"

National Survey on Drug Use & Health (NSDUH)—Information on illicit drug use is collected for all persons 12 years of age and over. Information on any illicit drug use, including marijuana or hashish, cocaine, heroin, hallucinogens, and nonmedical use of prescription drugs is based on the following question: "During the past 30 days, on how many days did you use (specific illicit drug)?" See related *Substance use.*

Incidence—Incidence is the number of cases of disease having their onset during a prescribed period of time. It is often expressed as a rate (e.g., the incidence of measles per 1,000 children 5–15 years of age during a specified year). Incidence is a measure of morbidity or other events that occur within a specified period of time. See related *Prevalence.*

Income—See *Family income.*

Individual practice association (IPA)—See *Health maintenance organization (HMO).*

Industry of employment—Industries are classified according to the 2002 North American Industry Classification System (NAICS) for the presentation of health data in Health, United States, starting with data year 2003. The NAICS classification system groups establishments into industries based on their production or supply function—establishments using similar raw material inputs, capital equipment, and labor are classified in the same industry. This approach creates homogeneous categories well suited for economic analysis. NAICS uses a six-digit hierarchical coding system to classify all economic activity into 20 industry sectors. The first two digits of the six-digit code designate the highest level of aggregation, with 20 such two-digit industry sectors (table VIII). Five sectors are primarily goods-producing sectors, and 15 are entirely services-providing sectors. NAICS allows for the classification of 1,170 industries.

NAICS replaces the Standard Industrial Classification (SIC) system, originally designed in the 1930s and revised and updated periodically to reflect changes in the U.S. economy. The last SIC revision was in 1987. The SIC system focused on the manufacturing sector of the economy and provided significantly less detail for the now dominant service sector, including newly developed industries in information services, health care delivery, and high-tech manufacturing. Although some titles in SIC and NAICS are similar, there is little comparability between the two systems because industry groupings are defined differently.

Starting with *Health United States, 2005*, health data by industry from the Bureau of Labor Statistics' Census of Fatal Occupational Injuries (CFOI) and Survey of Occupational Injuries and Illnesses (SOII) data systems are classified using the NAICS system and replace trends in occupational health data based on the SIC system in previous editions of *Health, United States*. With 2003 data in which industries are classified by NAICS system, CFOI and SOII start a new trend, and the estimates of deaths, injuries, and illnesses by industry should not be compared with earlier estimates that used the SIC.

Infant death—An infant death is the death of a live-born child before his or her first birthday. Age at death may be further classified according to neonatal and postneonatal. Neonatal deaths are those that occur before the 28th day of life; postneonatal deaths are those that occur between 28 and 365 days of age. See related *Rate: Death and related rates.*

Injury—The International Classification of External Causes of Injuries (ICECI) Coordination and Maintenance Group defines injury as a (suspected) bodily lesion resulting from acute overexposure to energy (this can be mechanical, thermal, electrical, chemical, or radiant) interacting with the body in amounts or rates that exceed the threshold of physiological

Table IX. Codes for diagnostic categories from the *International Classification of Diseases, Ninth Revision, Clinical Modification*

Diagnostic category	*Code numbers*
Females with delivery	V27
Human immunodeficiency virus (HIV) (1984–85)	279.19
(1986–94)	042–044, 279.19, 795.8
(Beginning in 1995)	042, V08
Malignant neoplasms	140–208
Large intestine and rectum	153–154, 197.5
Trachea, bronchus, and lung	162, 197.0, 197.3
Breast	174–175, 198.81
Prostate	185
Diabetes	250
Alcohol and drug	291–292, 303–305
Serious mental illness	295–298
Diseases of the nervous system and sense organs	320–389
Diseases of the circulatory system	390–459
Diseases of heart	391–392.0, 393–398, 402, 404, 410–416, 420–429
Ischemic heart disease	410–414
Acute myocardial infarction	410
Congestive heart failure	428.0
Cerebrovascular diseases	430–438
Diseases of the respiratory system	460–519
Pneumonia	466.1, 480–487.0
Asthma	493
Hyperplasia of prostate	600
Decubitus ulcers	707.0
Diseases of the musculoskeletal system and connective tissue	710–739
Osteoarthritis	715
Intervertebral disc disorders	722
Injuries and poisoning	800–999
Fracture, all sites	800–829
Fracture of neck of femur (hip)	820

tolerance. In some cases an injury results from an insufficiency of any of the vital elements. Acute poisonings and toxic effects, including overdoses of substances and wrong substances given or taken in error are included, as are adverse effects and complications of therapeutic, surgical, and medical care. Psychological harm is excluded. Injuries can be intentional or unintentional (i.e., accidental). External causes of nonfatal injuries in NCHS data systems are coded to the *International Classification of Diseases, Ninth Revision, Clinical Modification* Supplementary Classification of External Causes of Injury and Poisoning, often referred to as "E-Codes." See table VII for a list of injury categories and codes. See related *Diagnosis; Injury-related visit.* See ICECI Coordination and Maintenance Group (2004). *International Classification of External Causes of Injuries* (ICECI), version 1.2. Consumer Safety Institute, Amsterdam and AIHW National Injury Surveillance Unit, Adelaide, found at www.iceci.org.

Injury-related visit—In the National Hospital Ambulatory Medical Care Survey an emergency department visit was considered injury related if, on the Patient Record Form (PRF), the checkbox for injury was indicated. In addition, injury visits were identified if the physician's diagnosis was injury related (ICD–9–CM code of 800–999), an external cause-of-injury code was present (ICD–9–CM E800–E999), or the patient's reason for visit code was injury-related. See related *Emergency department or emergency room visit; External cause of injury; Injury.*

Inpatient—An inpatient is a person who is formally admitted to the inpatient service of a hospital for observation, care, diagnosis, or treatment. See related *Admission; Average length of stay; Days of care; Discharge; Hospital.*

Inpatient care—See *Hospital utilization; Mental health service type.*

Inpatient days—See *Days of care.*

Instrumental activities of daily living (IADL)—Instrumental activities of daily living are activities related to independent living and include preparing meals, managing money, shopping for groceries or personal items, performing light or

Table X. Codes for procedure categories from the *International Classification of Diseases, Ninth Revision, Clinical Modification*

Procedure category	Code numbers
Operations on vessels of heart	36
Removal of coronary artery obstruction and insertion of stent(s)	36.0
Insertion of coronary artery stent(s)[1]	36.06, 36.07
Coronary artery bypass graft	36.1
Cardiac catheterization	37.21–37.23
Insertion, replacement, removal, and revision of pacemaker leads or device	37.7–37.8
Incision, excision, and occlusion of vessels	38
Diagnostic procedures on small intestine	45.1
Diagnostic procedures on large intestine	45.2
Cholecystectomy	51.2
Laparoscopic cholecystectomy	51.23
Repair of hernia	53
Lysis of peritoneal adhesions	54.5
Transurethral prostatectomy	60.2
Total abdominal hysterectomy	68.4
Vaginal hysterectomy	68.5
Dilation and curettage of uterus	69.0
Forceps, vacuum, and breech delivery	72
Other procedures inducing or assisting delivery	73
Cesarean section and removal of fetus	74
Reduction of fracture and dislocation	79
Excision or destruction of intervertebral disc	80.5
Joint replacement of lower extremity	81.5
Total hip replacement	81.51
Partial hip replacement	81.52
Total knee replacement	81.54
Diagnostic Radiology	87
Computerized axial tomography	87.03, 87.41, 87.71, 88.01, 88.38
Angiocardiography using contrast material	88.5
Diagnostic ultrasound	88.7

[1]The procedure code for insertion of coronary artery stents (36.06) first appears in the 1996 data. A second procedure code for the insertion of drug-eluting stents (36.07) first appears in the 2003 data.

heavy housework, and using a telephone. In the National Health Interview Survey (NHIS) respondents are asked whether they or family members 18 years of age and over need the help of another person for handling routine IADL needs because of a physical, mental, or emotional problem. Persons are considered to have an IADL limitation in the NHIS if any causal condition is chronic.

In the Medicare Current Beneficiary Survey, if a sample person had any difficulty performing an activity by him or herself and without special equipment, or did not perform the activity at all because of health problems, the person was categorized as having a limitation in that activity. The limitation may have been temporary or chronic at the time of the interview. Sample persons in the community answered health status and functioning questions themselves, if able to do so. For sample persons in a long-term care facility, a proxy such as a nurse answered questions about the sample person's health status and functioning. See related *Activities of daily living (ADL); Limitation of activity.*

Insured—See *Health insurance coverage.*

Intermediate care facilities—See *Nursing home.*

International Classification of Diseases (ICD)—The ICD provides the ground rules for coding and classifying cause-of-death data. The ICD is developed collaboratively by the World Health Organization (WHO) and 10 international centers, one of which is housed at NCHS. The purpose of the ICD is to promote international comparability in the collection, classification, processing, and presentation of health statistics. Since 1900, the ICD has been modified about once every 10 years, except for the 20-year interval between ICD–9 and ICD–10 (see table IV). The purpose of the revisions is to stay abreast with advances in medical science. New revisions usually introduce major disruptions in time series of mortality statistics (see tables V and VI). For more information, see www.cdc.gov/nchs/about/major/dvs/icd10des.htm. See related *Cause of death; Comparability ratio; International Classification of Diseases, Ninth Revision, Clinical Modification (ICD–9–CM).*

International Classification of Diseases, Ninth Revision, Clinical Modification (ICD–9–CM)—The ICD–9–CM is based on and is compatible with the World Health Organization's *International Classification of Diseases, Ninth Revision* (ICD–9). The United States currently uses ICD–9–CM to code morbidity diagnoses and inpatient procedures. ICD–9–CM consists of three volumes. Volumes 1 and 2 contain the diagnosis tabular list and index. Volume 3 contains the procedure classification (tabular and index combined).

ICD–9–CM is divided into 17 chapters and 2 supplemental classifications. The chapters are arranged primarily by body system. In addition, there are chapters for Infectious and parasitic diseases; Neoplasms; Endocrine, nutritional, and metabolic diseases; Mental disorders; Complications of pregnancy, childbirth and puerperium; Certain conditions originating in the perinatal period; Congenital anomalies; and Symptoms, signs and ill-defined conditions. The two supplemental classifications are for factors influencing health status and contact with health services ("V Codes"), and external causes of injury and poisoning ("E Codes").

In *Health, United States* morbidity data are classified using ICD–9–CM. Diagnostic categories and codes for ICD–9–CM are shown in table IX; ICD–9–CM procedure categories and codes are shown in table X. For additional information about ICD–9–CM, see www.cdc.gov/nchs/icd9.htm. See related *International Classification of Diseases (ICD).*

Late fetal death rate—See *Rate: Death and related rates.*

Leading causes of death—See *Cause-of-death ranking.*

Length of stay—See *Average length of stay.*

Life expectancy—Life expectancy is the average number of years of life remaining to a person at a particular age and is based on a given set of age-specific death rates, generally the mortality conditions existing in the period mentioned. Life expectancy may be determined by race, sex, or other characteristics using age-specific death rates for the population with that characteristic. See related *Rate: Death and related rates.*

Limitation of activity—Limitation of activity may be defined different ways, depending on the conceptual framework. In the National Health Interview Survey limitation of activity refers to a long-term reduction in a person's capacity to perform the usual kind or amount of activities associated with his or her age group as a result of a chronic condition. Limitation of activity is assessed by asking persons a series of questions about limitations in their or household members' ability to perform activities usual for their age group because of a physical, mental, or emotional problem. Persons are asked about limitations in activities of daily living, instrumental activities of daily living, play, school, work, difficulty walking or remembering, and any other activity limitations. For reported limitations, the causal health conditions are determined, and persons are considered limited if one or more of these conditions is chronic. Children under 18 years of age who receive special education or early intervention services are considered to have a limitation of activity. See related *Activities of daily living; Condition; Instrumental activities of daily living.*

Live-birth order—In the National Vital Statistics System, this item from the birth certificate refers to the total number of live births the mother has had, including the present birth as recorded on the birth certificate. Fetal deaths are excluded.

Long-term care facility—A long-term care facility is a residence that provides a specific level of personal or medical care or supervision to residents. In the Medicare Current Beneficiary Survey, a residence is considered a long-term care facility if it has three or more long-term care beds and provides personal care services to residents, continuous supervision of residents, or long-term care services throughout the facility or in a separately identifiable unit. Types of long-term care facilities include licensed nursing homes, skilled nursing homes, intermediate care facilities, retirement homes (that provide services), domiciliary or personal care facilities, distinct long-term care units in a hospital complex, mental health facilities and centers, assisted and foster care homes, and institutions for the mentally retarded and developmentally disabled. See related *Nursing home.*

Low birthweight—See *Birthweight.*

Mammography—Mammography is an x-ray image of the breast used to detect irregularities in breast tissue. In the National Health Interview Survey, questions concerning use of mammography were asked on an intermittent schedule, and question content differed slightly across years. In 1987 and 1990, women were asked to report when they had their last mammogram. In 1991, women were asked whether they had a mammogram in the past 2 years. In 1993 and 1994, women were asked whether they had a mammogram within the past year, between 1 and 2 years ago, or over 2 years ago. In 1998, women were asked whether they had a mammogram a year ago or less, more than 1 year but not more than 2 years, or more than 2 years ago. In 1999, women were asked when they had their most recent mammogram in days, weeks, months, or years. In 1999, 10 percent of women in the sample responded "2 years ago," and in this analysis these women were coded as "within the past 2 years" although a response of "2 years ago" may include women whose last mammogram was more than 2 but less than 3 years ago. Thus, estimates for 1999 are overestimated to some degree in comparison with estimates in previous years. In 2000 and 2003, women were asked when they had their most recent mammogram (give month and year). Women who did not respond were given a followup question that used the 1999 wording, and women who did not answer the followup question were asked a second followup question that used the 1998 wording. In 2000 and 2003, 2 percent of women in the sample answered "2 years ago" using the 1999 wording, and they were coded as "within the past 2 years." Thus, estimates for 2000 and 2003 may be slightly overestimated in comparison with estimates for years prior to 1999.

Managed care—Managed care is a term originally used to refer to the prepaid health care sector (health maintenance organizations or HMOs) where care is provided under a fixed budget and costs are therein capable of being managed. Increasingly, the term is being used to include preferred provider organizations (PPOs) and even forms of indemnity insurance coverage (or fee-for-service insurance) that incorporate preadmission certification and other utilization controls. See related *Health maintenance organization (HMO); Preferred provider organization (PPO).*

Marital status—Marital status is classified through self-reporting into the categories married and unmarried. The term "married" encompasses all married people including those separated from their spouses. Unmarried includes those who are single (never married), divorced, or widowed. The abortion surveillance program classified separated people as unmarried before 1978.

Birth File—In 1970, 39 States and the District of Columbia (DC) and in 1975, 38 States and DC included a direct question about mother's marital status on the birth certificate. Since 1980, national estimates of births to unmarried women have been based on two methods for determining marital status, a direct question in the birth registration process and inferential procedures. In 1980–96 marital status was reported on the birth certificates of 41–45 States and DC; with the addition of California in 1997, 46 States and DC; and in 1998–2001, 48 States and DC. In 1997, all but four States (Connecticut, Michigan, Nevada, and New York), and in 1998, all but two States (Michigan and New York) included a direct question about mother's marital status on their birth certificates. In 1998–2001, marital status was imputed as married on those 0.03–0.05 percent of birth records with missing information in the 48 States and DC where this information was obtained by a direct question.

For States lacking a direct question, marital status was inferred. Before 1980 the incidence of births to unmarried women in States with no direct question on marital status was assumed to be the same as the incidence in reporting States in the same geographic division. Starting in 1980 for States without a direct question, marital status was inferred by comparing the parents' and child's surnames. Inferential procedures in current use depend on the presence of a paternity acknowledgment or missing information on the father. Changes in reporting procedures by some States in 1995 and 1997 had little effect on national totals, but they did affect trends for age groups and some State trends. Details of the changes in reporting procedures are described in Ventura SJ, Bachrach CA. Nonmarital Childbearing in the United States, 1940–99. National vital statistics reports; vol 48 no 16. Hyattsville, MD: National Center for Health Statistics. 2000, available at www.cdc.gov/nchs/births.htm.

Maternal age—See *Age.*

Maternal death—Maternal death is defined by the World Health Organization as the death of a woman while pregnant or within 42 days of termination of pregnancy, irrespective of the duration and site of the pregnancy, from any cause related to or aggravated by the pregnancy or its management, but not from accidental or incidental causes. A maternal death is one for which the certifying physician has designated a maternal condition as the underlying cause of death. Maternal conditions are those assigned to pregnancy, childbirth, and the puerperium, ICD–10 codes A34, O00–O95, O98–O99 (see table V). Changes have been made in the classification and coding of maternal deaths between ICD–9 and ICD–10, effective with mortality data for 1999. ICD–10 changes pertain to indirect maternal causes and timing of death relative to pregnancy. If only indirect maternal causes of death (i.e., a previously existing disease or a disease that developed during pregnancy that was not due to direct obstetric causes but was aggravated by physiologic effects of pregnancy) are reported in Part I of the death certificate and pregnancy is reported in either Part I or Part II, ICD–10 classifies this as a maternal death. ICD–9 only classified the death as maternal if pregnancy was reported in Part I. Some State death certificates include a separate question regarding pregnancy status. A positive response to the question is interpreted as "pregnant" being reported in Part II of the cause-of-death section of the death certificate. If the medical certifier did not specify when death occurred relative to the pregnancy, it is assumed that the pregnancy terminated 42 days or less prior to death. Under ICD–10, a new category has been added for deaths from maternal causes that occurred more than 42 days after delivery or termination of pregnancy (O96–O97). In 1999, there were 15 such deaths, and, in 2000, there were eight. See related *Rate: Death and related rates.*

Maternal education—See *Education.*

Maternal mortality rate—See *Rate: Death and related rates.*

Medicaid—Medicaid was authorized by Title XIX of the Social Security Act in 1965 as a jointly funded cooperative venture between the Federal and State Governments to assist States in the provision of adequate medical care to eligible needy persons. Within broad Federal guidelines, each of the States establishes its own eligibility standards; determines the type, amount, duration, and scope of services; sets the rate of payment for services; and administers its own program.

Medicaid is the largest program providing medical and health-related services to America's poorest people. However, Medicaid does not provide medical assistance to all poor persons. Under the broadest provisions of the Federal statute, Medicaid does *no* provide health care services even for very poor childless adults under age 65 years unless they are disabled. Except as noted, all States must provide Medicaid coverage to the following:

- Individuals who meet the requirements for the Aid to Families with Dependent Children (AFDC) program that were in effect in their State on July 16, 1996, or, at State option, more liberal criteria (with some exceptions).
- Children under age 6 whose family income is at or below 133 percent of the Federal poverty level.
- Pregnant women whose family income is below 133 percent of the Federal poverty level (services to these women are limited to those related to pregnancy, complications of pregnancy, delivery, and postpartum care).
- Supplemental Security Income (SSI) recipients in most States (some States use more restrictive Medicaid eligibility requirements that predate SSI).
- Recipients of adoption or foster care assistance under Title IV of the Social Security Act.
- Special protected groups (typically individuals who lose their cash assistance because of earnings from work or from increased Social Security benefits but who may keep Medicaid for a period of time).
- All children under age 19 in families with incomes at or below the Federal poverty level.
- Certain Medicare beneficiaries (low income is only one test for Medicaid eligibility for those within these groups; their resources also are tested against threshold levels, as determined by each State within Federal guidelines).

States also have the option of providing Medicaid coverage for other groups.

Medicaid operates as a vendor payment program. States may pay health care providers directly on a fee-for-service basis, or States may pay for Medicaid services through various prepayment arrangements, such as health maintenance organizations (HMOs) or other forms of managed care. Within Federally imposed upper limits and specific restrictions, each State for the most part has broad discretion in determining the payment methodology and payment rate for services. Thus, the Medicaid program varies considerably from State to

State, as well as within each State over time. See related *Health expenditures, national; Health insurance coverage; Health maintenance organization (HMO); Managed care; Appendix I, Medicaid Data System.*

Medical specialties—See *Physician specialty.*

Medical vendor payments—Under the Medicaid program, medical vendor payments are payments (expenditures) to medical vendors from the State through a fiscal agent or to a health insurance plan. Adjustments are made for Indian Health Service payments to Medicaid, cost settlements, third party recoupments, refunds, voided checks, and other financial settlements that cannot be related to specific provided claims. Excluded are payments made for medical care under the emergency assistance provisions, payments made from State medical assistance funds that are not federally matchable, disproportionate share hospital payments, cost sharing or enrollment fees collected from recipients or a third party, and administration and training costs.

Medicare—This is a nationwide health insurance program providing health insurance protection to people 65 years of age and over, people entitled to Social Security disability payments for 2 years or more, and people with end-stage renal disease, regardless of income. The program was enacted July 30, 1965, as Title XVIII, *Health Insurance for the Aged of the Social Security Act*, and became effective on July 1, 1966. From its inception, it has included two separate but coordinated programs: hospital insurance (Part A) and supplementary medical insurance (Part B). In 1999, additional choices were allowed for delivering Medicare Part A and Part B benefits. "Medicare+Choice" (Part C) is an expanded set of options for the delivery of health care under Medicare, created in the Balanced Budget Act passed by Congress in 1997. The term "Medicare+Choice" refers to options other than original Medicare. While all Medicare beneficiaries can receive their benefits through the original fee-for-service (FFS) program, most beneficiaries enrolled in both Part A and Part B can choose to participate in a Medicare+Choice plan instead. Organizations that seek to contract as Medicare+Choice plans must meet specific organizational, financial, and other requirements. Most Medicare+Choice plans are coordinated care plans, which include health maintenance organizations (HMOs), provider-sponsored organizations (PSOs), preferred provider organizations (PPOs), and other certified coordinated care plans and entities that meet the standards set forth in the law. The Medicare+Choice program also includes Medical savings account (MSA) plans, which provide benefits after a single high deductible is met, and private, unrestricted FFS plans, which allow beneficiaries to select certain private providers. These programs are available in only a limited number of States. For those providers who agree to accept the plan's payment terms and conditions, this option does not place the providers at risk, nor does it vary payment rates based on utilization. Only the coordinated care plans are considered managed care plans. Except for MSA plans, all Medicare+Choice plans are required to provide at least the current Medicare benefit package, excluding hospice services. Plans may offer additional covered services and are required to do so (or return excess payments) if plan costs are lower than the Medicare payments received by the plan.

In the National Health Interview Survey (NHIS), the category "Medicare HMO" is defined as persons who are age 65 years or over and who responded "Yes" when asked whether they were under a Medicare managed care arrangement such as an HMO. This is a subset of Medicare Part C. Respondents who stated they had Medicare coverage but did not answer yes to the "managed care arrangement such as an HMO" are included in the Medicare fee-for-service category. "Medicare fee-for-service" is defined as Medicare Part A or Part B. The majority of these people had coverage from another source, primarily employer-sponsored retiree health insurance. Some tables in *Health, United States* further classify persons 65 years of age and over with Medicare fee-for service into Medicare fee-for-service only and Private (including Medicare fee-for-service) coverage.

See related *Fee-for-service health insurance; Health insurance coverage; Health maintenance organization (HMO); Managed care; Appendix I, Medicare Administrative Data.*

Mental health organization—The Center for Mental Health Services of the Substance Abuse and Mental Health Services Administration defines a mental health organization as an administratively distinct public or private agency or institution whose primary concern is provision of direct mental health services to the mentally ill or emotionally disturbed. Excluded are private office-based practices of psychiatrists, psychologists, and other mental health providers; psychiatric services of all types of hospitals or outpatient clinics operated by Federal agencies other than the Department of Veterans Affairs (e.g., Public Health Service, Indian Health Service, Department of Defense, and Bureau of Prisons); general

Table XI. National Drug Code (NDC) therapeutic class analgesic drug recodes

Narcotic analgesics	*Nonnarcotic analgesics*	*Nonsteroidal anti-inflammatory drugs (NSAIDs)*
Alfentanil Hydrochloride	Acetaminophen	Bromfenac Sodium
Alphaprodine	Acetylsalicylic Acid	Celecoxib
Bupernorphine	Aminobenzoic Acid	Diclofenac Potassium
Butorphanol	Aspirin	Diclofenac Sodium
Codeine	Auranofin	Difunisal
Dihydrocodeine	Aurothioglucose	Etodolac
Fentanyl	Butalbital	Fenoprofen
Hydrocodone Bitartrate	Capsaicin	Flurbiprofen Sodium
Hydromorphone	Carbaspirin Calcium	Ibuprofen
Levorphanol	Choline Salicylate	Indomethacin
Meperidine	Etanercept	Ketoprofen
Meperidine HCI	Fluprednisolone	Ketorolac Tromethamine
Methadone	Gold Sodium Thiomalate	Meclofenamate
Morphine	Gold Sodium Thiosulfate	Meclofenamic Acid
Morphine Sulfate	Hyaluronic Acid	Mefenamic Acid
Nalbuphine	Leflunomide	Meloxicam
Opium	Magnesium Salicylate	Nabumetone
Oxycodone	Menthol	Naproxen
Oxycodone HCI	Methotrexate	Oxaprozin
Pentazocine	Methylprednisolone	Piroxicam
Propoxyphene	Methylsulfonylmethane	Rofecoxib
Remifentanyl	Oxyphenbutazone	Sulindac
	Phenyl Salicylate	Suprofen
	Phenylbutazone	Tolmetin
	Prednisolone	Valdecoxib
	Salicylamide	
	Salsalate	
	Sodium Hyaluronate	
	Sodium Salicylate	
	Sodium Thiosalicylate	
	Tramadol	
	Triamcinilone	
	Zomepirac	

NOTE: Drugs originally classified as National Drug Code (NDC) therapeutic category 1720 (general analgesics); 1721 (narcotic analgesics); 1722 (non-narcotic analgesics); 1724 (antiarthritics); 1727 (NSAIDs); 1728 (antipyretics); and 1729 (menstrual products) were recoded into the three mutually exclusive categories shown above. NDC codes for the analgesic categories 1723 (antimigraine) and 1725 (antigout) were not recoded.

hospitals that have no separate psychiatric services but admit psychiatric patients to nonpsychiatric units; and psychiatric services of schools, colleges, halfway houses, community residential organizations, local and county jails, State prisons, and other human services providers. The major types of mental health organizations are described below.

Freestanding psychiatric outpatient clinics—These clinics provide only outpatient mental health services on either a regular or emergency basis. A psychiatrist generally assumes the medical responsibility for services.

Psychiatric hospitals—These hospitals (public or private) primarily provide 24-hour inpatient care and treatment in a hospital setting to persons with mental illnesses. Psychiatric hospitals may be under State, county, private for profit, or private nonprofit auspices.

General hospital psychiatric services—These are organizations that provide psychiatric services with assigned staff for 24-hour inpatient or residential care and/or less than 24-hour outpatient care in a separate ward, unit, floor, or wing of the hospital.

Department of Veterans Affairs medical centers—These are hospitals are hospitals operated by the Department of Veterans Affairs (formerly Veterans Administration) and include Department of Veterans Affairs general hospital psychiatric services (including large neuropsychiatric units) and Department of Veterans Affairs psychiatric outpatient clinics.

Residential treatment centers for emotionally disturbed children—These centers must meet all of the following criteria: (a) provide 24-hour residential services; (b) are not licensed as a psychiatric hospital and have the primary purpose of providing individually planned mental health treatment services in conjunction with residential care; (c) include a clinical program directed by a psychiatrist, psychologist, social worker, or psychiatric nurse with a graduate degree; (d) serve children and youth primarily under the age of 18; and (e) have the primary diagnosis as mental illness, classified as other than mental retardation, developmental disability, or substance-related disorders, according to DSM-II/ICDA-8 or DSM-IIIR/ICD–9–CM codes, for the majority of admissions.

Multiservice mental health organizations—These organizations provide services in both 24-hour and less than 24-hour settings and are not classifiable as a psychiatric hospital, general hospital, or residential treatment center for emotionally disturbed children. (The classification of a psychiatric or general hospital or residential treatment center for emotionally disturbed children takes precedence over a multiservice classification, even if two or more services are offered.)

Partial care organizations—These organizations provide a program of ambulatory mental health services or rehabilitation, habitation, or education programs.

See related *Addition; Mental health service type.*

Mental health service type—This term refers to the following types of mental health services:

24-hour mental health care, formerly called inpatient care, provides care in a mental health hospital setting.

Less than 24-hour care, formerly called outpatient or partial care treatment, provides mental health services on an ambulatory basis.

Residential treatment care provides overnight mental health care in conjunction with an intensive treatment program in a setting other than a hospital. Facilities may offer care to emotionally disturbed children or mentally ill adults.

See related *Addition; Mental health organization.*

Metropolitan statistical area (MSA)—The Office of Management and Budget (OMB) defines metropolitan areas according to published standards that are applied to Census Bureau data. An MSA is a county or group of contiguous counties that contains at least one urbanized area of 50,000 or more population. In addition to the county or counties that contain all or part of the urbanized area, an MSA may contain other counties that are metropolitan in character and that are economically and socially integrated with the main city. In New England, cities and towns, rather than counties, are used to define MSAs. Counties that are not within an MSA are considered to be nonmetropolitan.

For National Health Interview Survey (NHIS) data before 1995, metropolitan population is based on MSAs as defined by OMB in 1983 using the 1980 census. Starting with the 1995 NHIS, metropolitan population is based on MSAs as defined by OMB in 1993 using the 1990 census. For additional information about metropolitan statistical areas see www.census.gov/population/www/estimates/metrodef.html. See related *Urbanization.*

Micropolitan statistical area—The Office of Management and Budget (OMB) defines micropolitan areas based on published standards that are applied to Census Bureau data. A micropolitan statistical area is a nonmetropolitan county or group of contiguous nonmetropolitan counties that contains an urban cluster of 10,000 to 49,999 persons. A micropolitan statistical area may include surrounding counties if there are strong economic ties between the counties, based on commuting patterns. In New England, cities and towns, rather than counties, are used to define micropolitan statistical areas. Nonmetropolitan counties that are not classified as part of a micropolitan statistical area are considered nonmicropolitan. For additional information about micropolitan statistical areas see www.census.gov/population/www/estimates/metrodef.html. See related *Urbanization.*

Multiservice mental health organizations—See *Mental health organization.*

National Drug Code (NDC) Directory therapeutic class—The NDC system was originally established as an essential part of an out-of-hospital drug reimbursement program under Medicare. The NDC serves as a universal product identifier for human drugs. The current edition of the NDC is limited to prescription drugs and a few selected over-the-counter (OTC) products. The directory consists of prescription and selected OTC insulin, domestic, and foreign drug products that are in commercial distribution in the United States. The products have been listed in accordance with the Drug Listing Act and applicable Code of Federal Regulations for submitting drug product information to the Food and Drug Administation (FDA). NDC therapeutic class codes are used to identify each of 20 major drug classes to which the drug entry may belong, adapted from Standard Drug Classifications in the NDC Directory, 1995. The two-digit categories are general and represent all subcategories (e.g., Antimicrobial agents), and the specific four-digit categories represent the breakouts of the general category (e.g., Penicillin). The general two-digit codes include medications that do not fit into any of the subcategories (four-digit codes). Starting in 1995, the NDC four-digit classes were changed to include more classes than the previous classification in 1985. Therefore some drugs switched from a general two-digit class into a more specific four-digit class. In addition, drugs may be approved for several different therapeutic classes. Some drugs receive approval for additional therapeutic uses after their initial approval, so the same drug can change classes because of new uses.

Numerous drug products have many uses or indications. In an effort to categorize the vast number of the broad analgesic or pain-relief individual products in the marketplace into manageable and nonoverlapping categories, all four-digit categories within the analgesic two-digit therapeutic class were recoded by staff of the FDA's Center for Drug Center for Drug Evaluation and Research. Thus, the codes presented in *Health, United States* do not match the published NDC codes for analgesic therapeutic categories. The NDC contains the following four-digit analgesic therapeutic categories: 1720—general analgesic, 1721—narcotic analgesic, 1722—nonnarcotic analgesic, 1724—antiarthritics, 1723—antimigraine/headache, 1726—central pain syndrome, 1727—nonsteroidal anti-inflammatory drugs (NSAID), 1728—antipyretic, and 1729—menstrual products. These categories were collapsed into broader and mutually exclusive categories of narcotic analgesics, nonnarcotic analgesics, and NSAIDs. Under the NDC system, aspirin is coded as an NSAID because of its anti-inflammatory properties, but also as an analgesic, an antiarthritic, and an antipyretic. In this report aspirin has been recoded into the nonnarcotic analgesic category. Aspirin was not included as an NSAID because of its common use for cardiac therapy and its many other indications.

Table XI shows how generic analgesic drugs were reclassified for *Health, United States*. Analgesic drugs were reclassified based on the product's main ingredients or indication of use. For example, Robitussin AC contains several ingredients, one of which is codeine, a narcotic. However, its main use is not for pain but for cough suppression, and it is therefore categorized as a cough and cold product as opposed to a narcotic analgesic product. Another example is methotrexate, which is used for treating certain neoplastic diseases and severe psoriasis in some formulations, but it is also used to treat rheumatoid arthritis and therefore appears in the list of nonnarcotic analgesic drugs, which include previously defined antiarthritic drugs in table XI.

Neonatal mortality rate—See *Rate: Death and related rates.*

Nonpatient revenues—Nonpatient revenues are those revenues received for which no direct patient care services are rendered. The most widely recognized source of nonpatient revenues is philanthropy. Philanthropic support may be direct from individuals or may be obtained through philanthropic fundraising organizations, foundations, or corporations. Philanthropic revenues may be designated for direct patient care use or may be contained in an endowment fund where only the current income may be tapped.

Nonprofit hospitals—See *Hospital.*

North American Industry Classification System (NAICS)—See *Industry of employment.*

Notifiable disease—A notifiable disease is one that, when diagnosed, health providers are required, usually by law, to report to State or local public health officials. Notifiable diseases are those of public interest by reason of their contagiousness, severity, or frequency.

Nurse supply estimates—Nurse supply estimates are based on a model developed by Health Resources and Services Administration's (HRSA's) Bureau of Health Professions to meet the requirements of Section 951, P.L. 94–63. The model estimates the following for each State: (a) population of nurses currently licensed to practice; (b) supply of full-time and part-time practicing nurses (or available to practice); and (c) full-time equivalent supply of nurses practicing full-time plus one-half of those practicing part-time (or available on that basis). The three estimates are divided into three levels of highest educational preparation—associate degree or diploma, baccalaureate, and master's and doctorate. Among the factors considered are new graduates, changes in educational status, nursing employment rates, age, migration patterns, death rates, and licensure phenomena. The base data for the model are derived from the National Sample Surveys of Registered Nurses, conducted by the Division of Nursing, Bureau of Health Professions, HRSA. Other data sources include National League for Nursing for data on nursing education and National Council of State Boards of Nursing for data on licensure. For further information, see HRSA's Division of Nursing Web site at www.bhpr.hrsa.gov/nursing.

Nursing care—The following definition of nursing care applies to data collected in National Nursing Home Surveys through 1977. Nursing care is provision of any of the following services: application of dressings or bandages; bowel and bladder retraining; catheterization; enema; full bed bath; hypodermic, intramuscular, or intravenous injection; irrigation; nasal feeding; oxygen therapy; and temperature-pulse-respiration or blood pressure measurement. See related *Nursing home.*

Nursing care homes—See *Nursing home.*

Nursing home—In the Online Survey Certification and Reporting database, a nursing home is a facility that is certified and meets the Center for Medicare & Medicaid Services' long-term care requirements for Medicare and Medicaid eligibility.

In the National Master Facility Inventory (NMFI), which provided the sampling frame for 1973–74, 1977, and 1985 National Nursing Home Surveys, a nursing home was an establishment with three or more beds that provided nursing or personal care services to the aged, infirm, or chronically ill. The 1977 National Nursing Home Survey included personal care homes and domiciliary care homes, whereas the National Nursing Home Surveys of 1973–74, 1985, 1995, 1997, and 1999 excluded them. The following definitions of nursing home types applied to facilities listed in the NFMI:

Nursing care homes—These homes employ one or more full-time registered or licensed practical nurses and provide nursing care to at least one-half the residents.

Personal care homes with nursing—These homes have fewer than one-half the residents receiving nursing care. In addition, such homes employ one or more registered or licensed practical nurses or provided administration of medications and treatments in accordance with physicians' orders, supervision of self-administered medications, or three or more personal services.

Personal care homes without nursing—These homes have no residents who receive nursing care. These homes provide administration of medications and treatments in accordance with physicians' orders, supervise self-administered medications, or provide three or more personal services.

Domiciliary care homes—These homes primarily provide supervisory care and one or two personal services.

The following definitions of certification levels apply to data collected in National Nursing Home Surveys of 1973–74, 1977, and 1985:

Skilled nursing facilities—These facilities provide the most intensive nursing care available outside a hospital. Facilities certified by Medicare provide posthospital care to eligible Medicare enrollees. Facilities certified by Medicaid as skilled nursing facilities provide skilled nursing services on a daily basis to individuals eligible for Medicaid benefits.

Intermediate care facilities—These facilities are certified by the Medicaid program to provide health-related services on a regular basis to Medicaid eligibles who do not require hospital or skilled nursing facility care but do require institutional care above the level of room and board.

Not certified facilities—These facilities are not certified as providers of care by Medicare or Medicaid.

Beginning with the 1995 National Nursing Home Surveys, nursing homes have been defined as facilities that routinely provide nursing care services and have three or more beds set up for residents. Facilities may be certified by Medicare or Medicaid or not certified but licensed by the State as a nursing home. The facilities may be freestanding or a distinct unit of a larger facility.

After October 1, 1990, long-term care facilities that met the Omnibus Budget Reconciliation Act of 1987 (OBRA 87) nursing home reform requirements that were formerly certified under the Medicaid program as skilled nursing, nursing home, or intermediate care facilities were reclassified as nursing facilities. The Medicare program continues to certify skilled nursing facilities, but not intermediate care facilities. State Medicaid programs can certify intermediate care facilities for the mentally retarded or developmentally disabled. Nursing facilities must also be certified to participate in the Medicare program to be certified for participation in Medicaid except those facilities that have obtained waivers. Thus most nursing home care is now provided in skilled care facilities.

See related *Long-term care facility; Nursing care; Resident.*

Nursing home expenditures—See *Health expenditures, national.*

Obesity—See *Body mass index (BMI).*

Occupancy rate—In American Hospital Association statistics, hospital occupancy rate is calculated as the average daily census divided by the number of hospital beds, cribs, and pediatric bassinets set up and staffed on the last day of the reporting period, expressed as a percent. Average daily census is calculated by dividing the total annual number of inpatients, excluding newborns, by 365 days to derive the number of inpatients receiving care on an average day during the annual reporting period. The occupancy rate for facilities other than hospitals is calculated as the number of residents at the facility reported on the day of the interview divided by the number of reported beds. In the Online Survey Certification and Reporting database, occupancy is determined as of the day of certification inspection as the total number of residents on that day divided by the total number of beds on that day.

Office—In the National Ambulatory Medical Care Survey, a physician's ambulatory practice (office) can be in any location other than in a hospital, nursing home, other extended care facility, patient's home, industrial clinic, college clinic, or family planning clinic. Offices in health maintenance organizations and private offices in hospitals are included. See related *Office visit; Outpatient visit; Physician.*

Office-based physician—See *Physician.*

Office visit—In the National Ambulatory Medical Care Survey, an office visit is any direct personal exchange between an ambulatory patient and a physician or members of his or her staff for the purposes of seeking care and rendering health services. See related *Outpatient visit.*

Operations—See *Procedure.*

Outpatient department—According to the National Hospital Ambulatory Medical Care Survey (NHAMCS), an outpatient department (OPD) is a hospital facility where nonurgent ambulatory medical care is provided. The following types of OPDs are excluded from the NHAMCS: ambulatory surgical centers, chemotherapy, employee health services, renal dialysis, methadone maintenance, and radiology. See related *Emergency department; Outpatient visit.*

Outpatient surgery—According to the American Hospital Association, outpatient surgery is a surgical operation, whether major or minor, performed on patients who do not remain in the hospital overnight. Outpatient surgery may be performed in inpatient operating suites, outpatient surgery suites, or procedure rooms within an outpatient care facility. A surgical operation involving more than one surgical procedure is considered one surgical operation. See related *Procedure.*

Outpatient visit—The American Hospital Association defines outpatient visits as visits for receipt of medical, dental, or other services at a hospital by patients who are not lodged in the hospital. Each appearance by an outpatient to each unit of the hospital is counted individually as an outpatient visit, including all clinic visits, referred visits, observation services, outpatient surgeries, and emergency department visits. In the National Hospital Ambulatory Medical Care Survey an outpatient department visit is a direct personal exchange between a patient and a physician or other health care provider working under the physician's supervision for the purpose of seeking care and receiving personal health services. See related *Emergency department or emergency room visit; Outpatient department.*

Overweight—See *Body mass index (BMI).*

Pap smear—A Pap smear (also known as a Papanicolaou smear or Pap test) is a microscopic examination of cells scraped from the cervix that is used to detect cancerous or precancerous conditions of the cervix or other medical conditions. In the National Health Interview Survey questions concerning use of Pap smear were asked on an intermittent schedule, and the question content differed slightly across years. In 1987, women were asked to report when they had their most recent Pap smear in days, weeks, months, or years. Women who did not respond were asked a followup question, "Was it 3 years ago or less, between 3 and 5 years, or 5 years or more ago?" Pap smear data in the past 3 years were not available in 1990 and 1991. In 1993 and 1994, women were asked whether they had a Pap smear within the past year, between 1 and 3 years ago, or more than 3 years ago. In 1998 women were asked whether they had a Pap smear 1 year ago or less, more than 1 year but not more than 2 years, more than 2 years but not more than 3 years, more than 3 years but not more than 5 years, or more than 5 years ago. In 1999, women were asked when they had their most recent Pap smear in days, weeks, months, or years. In 1999, 4 percent of women in the sample responded "3 years ago." In this analysis, these women were coded as "within the past 3 years," although a response of "3 years ago" may include women whose last Pap smear was more than 3 but less than 4 years ago. Thus, estimates for 1999 are overestimated to some degree in comparison with estimates for previous years. In 2000 and 2003, women were asked when they had their most recent Pap smear (give month and year). Women who did not respond were given a followup question that used the 1999 wording and women who did not answer the followup question were asked a second followup question that used the 1998 wording. In 2000 and 2003 less than 1 percent of women in the sample answered "3 years ago" using the 1999 wording, and they were coded as "within the past 3 years." Thus, estimates for 2000 and 2003 may be slightly overestimated in comparison with estimates for years prior to 1999.

Partial care organization—See *Mental health organization.*

Partial care treatment—See *Mental health service type.*

Patient—See *Home health care; Hospice care; Inpatient; Office visit; Outpatient visit.*

Percent change—See *Average annual rate of change.*

Perinatal mortality rate; ratio—See *Rate: Death and related rates.*

Personal care homes with or without nursing—See *Nursing home.*

Personal health care expenditures—See *Health expenditures, national.*

Physical activity, leisure-time—Beginning in 1998 leisure-time physical activity is assessed in the National Health Interview Survey by asking adults a series of questions about how often they do vigorous or light/moderate physical activity of at least 10 minutes duration and for about how long these sessions generally last. Vigorous physical activity is described as causing heavy sweating or a large increase in breathing or heart rate and light/ moderate as causing light sweating or a slight to moderate increase in breathing or heart rate. Adults classified as inactive did not report any sessions of moderate or vigorous leisure-time physical activity of at least 10 minutes duration or reported they were unable to perform leisure-time physical activity. Adults classified with some leisure-time activity reported at least one session of light/moderate or vigorous activity but did not meet the requirement for regular leisure-time activity. Adults classified with regular leisure-time activity reported at least three sessions per week of vigorous leisure-time physical activity lasting at least 20 minutes in duration or at least five sessions per week of light or moderate physical activity lasting at least 30 minutes in duration.

Physician—Data on physician characteristics are obtained through physician self-report for the American Medical Association's (AMA) Physician Masterfile. The AMA tabulates data only for doctors of medicine (MDs), but some tables in *Health, United States* include data for both MDs and doctors of osteopathy (DOs).

Active (or professionally active) physicians—These physicians are currently engaged in patient care or other professional activity for a minimum of 20 hours per week. Other professional activity includes administration, medical teaching, research, and other activities, such as employment with insurance carriers, pharmaceutical companies, corporations, voluntary organizations, medical societies, and the like. Physicians who are retired, semiretired, working part-time, or not practicing are classified as inactive and are excluded. Also excluded are physicians with address unknown and physicians who did not provide information on type of practice or present employment (not classified).

Hospital-based physicians—These physicians are employed under contract with hospitals to provide direct patient care and include physicians in residency training (including clinical fellows) and full-time members of the hospital staff.

Office-based physicians—These physicians are engaged in seeing patients in solo practice, group practice, two-physician practice, other patient care employment, or inpatient services such as those provided by pathologists and radiologists.

Data for physicians are presented by type of education (doctors of medicine and doctors of osteopathy); place of education (U.S. medical graduates and international medical graduates); activity status (professionally active and inactive); area of specialty; and geographic area. See related *Office; Physician specialty*.

Physician specialty—A physician specialty is any specific branch of medicine in which a physician may concentrate. Data are based on physician self-reports of their primary area of specialty. Physician data are broadly categorized into two areas of practice: those who provide primary care, and those who provide specialty care.

Primary care generalists—These physicians are physicians who practice in the general fields of family medicine, general practice, internal medicine, obstetrics and gynecology, and pediatrics. They specifically exclude primary care specialists associated with these generalist fields.

Primary care specialists—These specialists practice in the primary care subspecialties of family medicine, internal medicine, obstetrics and gynecology, and pediatrics. Family medicine subspecialties include geriatric medicine and sports medicine. Internal medicine subspecialties include adolescent medicine, critical care medicine, diabetes, endocrinology, diabetes and metabolism, hematology, hepatology, hematology/oncology, cardiac electrophysiology, infectious diseases, clinical and laboratory immunology, geriatric medicine, sports medicine, nephrology, nutrition, medical oncology, pulmonary critical care medicine, and rheumatology. Obstetrics and gynecology subspecialties include gynecological oncology, gynecology, maternal and fetal medicine, obstetrics, critical care medicine, and reproductive endocrinology. Pediatric subspecialties include adolescent medicine, pediatric critical care medicine, pediatrics/internal medicine, neonatal-perinatal medicine, pediatric allergy, pediatric cardiology, pediatric endocrinology, pediatric infectious disease, pediatric pulmonology, medical toxicology (pediatrics), pediatric emergency medicine, pediatric gastroenterology, pediatric hematology/oncology, clinical and laboratory immunology (pediatrics), pediatric nephrology, pediatric rheumatology, and sports medicine (pediatrics).

Specialty care physicians—These physicians are sometimes called specialists, and include primary care subspecialists listed above in addition to all other physicians not included in the generalist definition. Specialty fields include allergy and immunology, aerospace medicine, anesthesiology, cardiovascular diseases, child and adolescent psychiatry, colon and rectal surgery, dermatology, diagnostic radiology, forensic pathology, gastroenterology, general surgery, medical genetics, neurology, nuclear medicine, neurological surgery, occupational medicine, ophthalmology, orthopedic surgery, otolaryngology, psychiatry, public health and general preventive medicine, physical medicine and rehabilitation, plastic surgery, anatomic and clinical pathology, pulmonary diseases, radiation oncology, thoracic surgery, urology, addiction medicine, critical care medicine, legal medicine, and clinical pharmacology.

See related *Physician*.

Point-of-service (POS) plan—This is a health plan that allows members to choose to receive services from a participating or non-participating network provider, usually with a financial disincentive for going outside the network. More of a product than an organization, POS plans can be offered by HMOs, PPOs, or self-insured employers. See related *Health maintenance organization (HMO); Managed care; Preferred provider organization (PPO)*.

Population—The U.S. Census Bureau collects and publishes data on populations in the United States according to several different definitions. Various statistical systems then use the appropriate population for calculating rates. See also *Appendix I, Population Census and Population Estimates*.

Table XII. Current cigarette smoking by persons 18 years of age and over, according to race and Hispanic origin under the 1977 and 1997 Standards for Federal data on race and ethnicity: United States, average annual 1993–95

1997 Standards	*Sample size*	*Percent*	*Standard error*	*1977 Standards*	*Sample size*	*Percent*	*Standard error*
			Race				
White only	46,228	25.2	0.26	White	46,664	25.3	0.26
Black or African American only	7,208	26.6	0.64	Black	7,334	26.5	0.63
American Indian or Alaska Native only	416	32.9	2.53	American Indian or Alaska Native	480	33.9	2.38
Asian only	1,370	15.0	1.19	Asian or Pacific Islander	1,411	15.5	1.22
2 or more races total	786	34.5	2.00				
Black or African American; White	83	*21.7	6.05				
American Indian or Alaska Native; White	461	40.0	2.58				
			Race, any mention				
White, any mention	46,882	25.3	0.26				
Black or African American, any mention	7,382	26.6	0.63				
American Indian or Alaska Native, any mention	965	36.3	1.71				
Asian, any mention	1,458	15.7	1.20				
Native Hawaiian and Other Pacific Islander, any mention	53	*17.5	5.10				
			Hispanic origin and race				
Not Hispanic or Latino:				Non-Hispanic:			
White only	42,421	25.8	0.27	White	42,976	25.9	0.27
Black or African American only	7,053	26.7	0.65	Black	7,203	26.7	0.64
American Indian or Alaska Native only	358	33.5	2.69	American Indian or Alaska Native	407	35.4	2.53
Asian only	1,320	14.8	1.21	Asian or Pacific Islander	1,397	15.3	1.24
2 or more races total	687	35.6	2.15				
Hispanic or Latino	5,175	17.8	0.65	Hispanic	5,175	17.8	0.65

*Relative standard error 20–30 percent.

NOTES: The 1997 Standards for Federal data on race and ethnicity set five single-race groups (White, Black, American Indian or Alaska Native, Asian, and Native Hawaiian or Other Pacific Islander) and allow respondents to report one or more race groups. Estimates for single-race and multiple-race groups not shown above do not meet standards for statistical reliability or confidentiality (relative standard error greater than 30 percent). Race groups under the 1997 Standards were based on the question, "What is the group or groups which represents _____ race?" For persons who selected multiple groups, race groups under the 1977 Standards were based on the additional question, "Which of those groups would you say best represents ____ race?" Race-specific estimates in this table were calculated after excluding respondents of other and unknown race. Other published race-specific estimates are based on files in which such responses have been edited. Percents are age adjusted to the year 2000 standard using three age groups: Under 18 years, 18–44 years, and 45–64 years of age. See Appendix II, Age adjustment.

SOURCE: Centers for Disease Control and Prevention, National Center for Health Statistics. National Health Interview Survey.

Total population—This is the population of the United States, including all members of the Armed Forces living in foreign countries, Puerto Rico, Guam, and the U.S. Virgin Islands. Other Americans abroad (e.g., civilian Federal employees and dependents of members of the Armed Forces or other Federal employees) are not included.

Resident population—This population includes persons whose usual place of residence (i.e., the place where one usually lives and sleeps) is in one of the 50 States or the District of Columbia. It includes members of the Armed Forces stationed in the United States and their families. It excludes international military, naval, and diplomatic personnel and their families located in this country and residing in embassies or similar quarters. Also excluded are international workers and international students in this country and Americans living abroad. The resident population is the denominator for calculating birth and death rates and incidence of disease.

Civilian population—The civilian populatin is the resident population excluding members of the Armed Forces. However, families of members of the Armed Forces are included. This population is the denominator in rates calculated for the National Hospital Discharge Survey, the National Home and Hospice Care Survey, and the National Nursing Home Survey.

Civilian noninstitutionalized population—This is the civilian population not residing in institutions such as correctional institutions, detention homes, and training

Table XIII. Private health care coverage for persons under 65 years of age, according to race and Hispanic origin under the 1977 and 1997 Standards for Federal data on race and ethnicity: United States, average annual 1993–95

1997 Standards	*Sample size*	*Percent*	*Standard error*	*1977 Standards*	*Sample size*	*Percent*	*Standard error*
			Race				
White only	168,256	76.1	0.28	White	170,472	75.9	0.28
Black or African American only	30,048	53.5	0.63	Black	30,690	53.6	0.63
American Indian or Alaska Native only	2,003	44.2	1.97	American Indian or Alaska Native	2,316	43.5	1.85
Asian only	6,896	68.0	1.39	Asian or Pacific Islander	7,146	68.2	1.34
Native Hawaiian and Other Pacific Islander only	173	75.0	7.43				
2 or more races total	4,203	60.9	1.17				
Black or African American; White	686	59.5	3.21				
American Indian or Alaska Native; White	2,022	60.0	1.71				
Asian; White	590	71.9	3.39				
Native Hawaiian and Other Pacific Islander; White	56	59.2	10.65				
			Race, any mention				
White, any mention	171,817	75.8	0.28				
Black or African American, any mention	31,147	53.6	0.62				
American Indian or Alaska Native, any mention	4,365	52.4	1.40				
Asian, any mention	7,639	68.4	1.27				
Native Hawaiian and Other Pacific Islander, any mention	283	68.7	6.23				
			Hispanic origin and race				
Not Hispanic or Latino:				Non-Hispanic:			
White only	146,109	78.9	0.27	White	149,057	78.6	0.27
Black or African American only	29,250	53.9	0.64	Black	29,877	54.0	0.63
American Indian or Alaska Native only	1,620	45.2	2.15	American Indian or Alaska Native	1,859	44.6	2.05
Asian only	6,623	68.2	1.43	Asian or Pacific Islander	6,999	68.4	1.40
Native Hawaiian and Other Pacific Islander only	145	76.4	7.79				
2 or more races total	3,365	62.6	1.18				
Hispanic or Latino	31,040	48.8	0.74	Hispanic	31,040	48.8	0.74

NOTES: The 1997 Standards for Federal data on race and ethnicity set five single-race groups (White, Black, American Indian or Alaska Native, Asian, and Native Hawaiian or Other Pacific Islander) and allow respondents to report one or more race groups. Estimates for single-race and multiple-race groups not shown above do not meet standards for statistical reliability or confidentiality (relative standard error greater than 30 percent). Race groups under the 1997 Standards were based on the question, "What is the group or groups which represents _____ race?" For persons who selected multiple groups, race groups under the 1977 Standards were based on the additional question, "Which of those groups would you say best represents ____ race?" Race-specific estimates in this table were calculated after excluding respondents of other and unknown race. Other published race-specific estimates are based on files in which such responses have been edited. Percents are age adjusted to the year 2000 standard using three age groups: Under 18 years, 18–44 years, and 45–64 years of age. See Appendix II, Age adjustment.

SOURCE: Centers for Disease Control and Prevention, National Center for Health Statistics. National Health Interview Survey.

schools for juvenile delinquents; homes for aged and dependent persons (e.g., nursing homes and convalescent homes); homes for dependent and neglected children; homes and schools for mentally or physically handicapped persons; homes for unwed mothers; psychiatric, tuberculosis, and chronic disease hospitals; and residential treatment centers. Census Bureau estimates of the civilian noninstitutionalized population are used to calculate sample weights for the National Health Interview Survey, National Health and Nutrition Examination Survey, and National Survey of Family Growth, and as denominators in rates calculated for the National Ambulatory Medical Care Survey and the National Hospital Ambulatory Medical Care Survey.

Introduction of census 2000 population estimates—Health United States, 2003 marked the transition to the use of year 2000 resident population estimates based on the 2000 census for calculation of rates. Previously, 1991–2000 rates were based on post-1990 population estimates. Birth rates and death rates for 1991–99 were revised using intercensal population estimates based on the 2000 census. Rates for 2000 were revised using Census 2000 counts. Data systems and surveys that use civilian and civilian noninstitutionalized population estimates as denominators for computation of rates for the period 1991–99 have not been updated with intercensal estimates based on the 2000 civilian and civilian noninstitutionalized populations. See *Appendix I, Population Census and Population Estimates.*

Postneonatal mortality rate—See *Rate: Death and related rates.*

Poverty level—Poverty statistics are based on definitions originally developed by the Social Security Administration. These include a set of money income thresholds that vary by family size and composition. Families or individuals with income below their appropriate thresholds are classified as below the poverty level. These thresholds are updated annually by the U.S. Census Bureau to reflect changes in the Consumer Price Index for all urban consumers (CPI-U). For example, the average poverty threshold for a family of four was $17,603 in 2000 and $13,359 in 1990. For more information, see *Consumer Income and Poverty 2003.* Series P-60. Washington, DC. U.S. Government Printing Office. 2003. Also see www.census.gov/hhes/www/poverty.html.

National Health Interview Survey (NHIS) and *National Health and Nutrition Examination Survey (NHANES)*—Poverty level, for years prior to 1997, was based on family income and family size using Census Bureau poverty thresholds. In the NHIS, beginning in 1997 poverty status is based on family income, family size, number of children in the family, and for families with two or fewer adults, the age of the adults in the family. Poverty status in the NHANES is also based on family income and family size and composition. See related *Consumer Price Index (CPI); Family income; Appendix I, Current Population Survey; National Health Interview Survey; National Health and Nutrition Examination Survey.*

Preferred provider organization (PPO)—A PPO is a type of medical plan where coverage is provided to participants through a network of selected health care providers (such as hospitals and physicians). The enrollees may go outside the network, but they would pay a greater percentage of the cost of coverage than within the network. See related *Health maintenance organization (HMO); Managed care; Point-of-service (POS) plan.*

Prenatal care—Prenatal care is medical care provided to a pregnant woman to prevent complications and decrease the incidence of maternal and prenatal mortality. Information on when pregnancy care began is recorded on the birth certificate. Between 1970 and 1980, the reporting area for prenatal care expanded. In 1970, 39 States and the District of Columbia reported prenatal care on the birth certificate. Data were not available from Alabama, Alaska, Arkansas, Connecticut, Delaware, Georgia, Idaho, Massachusetts, New Mexico, Pennsylvania, and Virginia. In 1975 these data were available from three additional States—Connecticut, Delaware, and Georgia increasing the number of States reporting prenatal care to 42 and the District of Columbia. During 1980–2002 prenatal care information was available for the entire United States. In 2003, data on prenatal care was included for all States except Pennsylvania, and Washington both of which implemented the 2003 revision of the U.S. Standard Certificate of Live Birth. The prenatal care item on the 2003 certificate, "Date of first prenatal visit," is not comparable with the prenatal care item on the 1989 revision, "Month prenatal care began." In addition the 2003 revision recommends that information on prenatal care be gathered from prenatal care or medical records whereas the 1989 revision did not recommend a source for these data.

Prevalence—Prevalence is the number of cases of a disease, infected persons, or persons with some other attribute present during a particular interval of time. It is often expressed as a rate (e.g., the prevalence of diabetes per 1,000 persons during a year). See related *Incidence.*

Primary admission diagnosis—In the National Home and Hospice Care Survey the primary admission diagnosis is the first-listed diagnosis at admission on the patient's medical record as provided by the agency staff member most familiar with the care provided to the patient.

Primary care specialties—See *Physician specialty.*

Private expenditures—See *Health expenditures, national.*

Procedure—The National Hospital Discharge Survey (NHDS) used to classify a procedure as a surgical or nonsurgical operation, diagnostic procedure, or therapeutic procedure (such as respiratory therapy); however the distinction between types of procedures has become less meaningful because of the development of minimally invasive and noninvasive surgery. Thus the practice of classifying the type of procedure has been discontinued. Procedures are coded according to the *International Classification of Diseases, Ninth Revision, Clinical Modification* (see table X). Up to four different procedures are coded in the NHDS. Procedures per hospital stay can be classified as any-listed—that is, if more than one procedure with the same code is performed it is counted only once— or all-listed where multiple occurrences of the same procedure would be counted the number of times it appears on the medical record up to the maximum of four available codes. For example, a triple coronary artery bypass graft would be counted once as "any-listed" but three times as "all-listed". All-listed procedures double-count the number of procedures of a given type that are performed, thus all listed procedure counts are greater than the number of hospital stays that occurred. Any-listed procedure counts approximate the number of hospital stays where a procedure was performed at any time during the stay. See related *Outpatient surgery*.

Proprietary hospitals—See *Hospital*.

Psychiatric hospitals—See *Hospital; Mental health organization*.

Public expenditures—See *Health expenditures, national*.

Public health activities—Public health activities may include any of the following essential services of public health—surveillance, investigations, education, community mobilization, workforce training, research, and personal care services delivered or funded by governmental agencies.

Race—In 1977, the Office of Management and Budget (OMB) issued Race and Ethnicity Standards for Federal Statistics and Administrative Reporting to promote comparability of data among Federal data systems. The 1977 Standards called for the Federal Government's data systems to classify individuals into the following four racial groups: American Indian or Alaska Native, Asian or Pacific Islander, black, and white. Depending on the data source, the classification by race was based on self-classification or on observation by an interviewer or other person filling out the questionnaire.

In 1997, new standards were announced for classification of individuals by race within the Federal Government's data systems (*Federal Register*, 62FR58781–58790). The 1997 Standards have five racial groups: American Indian or Alaska Native, Asian, Black or African American, Native Hawaiian or Other Pacific Islander, and White. These five categories are the minimum set for data on race in Federal statistics. The 1997 Standards also offer an opportunity for respondents to select more than one of the five groups, leading to many possible multiple-race categories. As with the single-race groups, data for the multiple-race groups are to be reported when estimates meet agency requirements for reliability and confidentiality. The 1997 Standards allow for observer or proxy identification of race but clearly state a preference for self-classification. The Federal Government considers race and Hispanic origin to be two separate and distinct concepts. Thus Hispanics may be of any race. Federal data systems were required to comply with the 1997 Standards by 2003.

National Health Interview Survey (NHIS)—Starting with *Health, United States, 2002*, race-specific estimates based on the NHIS were tabulated using the 1997 Standards for data year 1999 and beyond and are not strictly comparable with estimates for earlier years. The 1997 Standards specify five single-race categories plus multiple-race categories. Estimates for specific race groups are shown when they meet requirements for statistical reliability and confidentiality. The race categories "White only," "Black or African American only," "American Indian and Alaska Native only," "Asian only," and "Native Hawaiian and Other Pacific Islander only" include persons who reported only one racial group; the category "2 or more races" includes persons who reported more than one of the five racial groups in the 1997 Standards or one of the five racial groups and "Some other race." Prior to data year 1999, data were tabulated according to the 1977 Standards with four racial groups, and the category "Asian only" included Native Hawaiian and Other Pacific Islander. Estimates for single-race categories prior to 1999 included persons who reported one race or, if they reported more than one race, identified one race as best representing their race. Differences between estimates tabulated using the two Standards for data year 1999 are discussed in the footnotes for each NHIS table in the *Health, United States*, 2002, 2003, and 2004 editions.

Tables XII and XIII illustrate NHIS data tabulated by race and Hispanic origin according to the 1997 and 1977 Standards for two health statistics (cigarette smoking and private health insurance coverage). In these illustrations, three separate tabulations using the 1997 Standards are shown: 1) Race: mutually exclusive race groups, including several multiple-race combinations; 2) Race, any mention: race groups that are not mutually exclusive because each race category includes all persons who mention that race; and 3) Hispanic origin and race: detailed race and Hispanic origin with a multiple-race total category. Where applicable, comparison tabulations by race and Hispanic origin are shown based on the 1977 Standards. Because there are more race groups with the 1997 Standards, the sample size of each race group under the 1997 Standards is slightly smaller than the sample size under the 1977 Standards. Only those few multiple-race groups with sufficient numbers of observations to meet standards of statistical reliability are shown. Tables XII and XIII also illustrate changes in labels and group categories in the 1997 Standards. The race designation of Black was changed to Black or African American, and the ethnicity designation of Hispanic was changed to Hispanic or Latino.

Data systems included in *Health, United States,* other than the NHIS, the National Survey of Drug Use & Health (NSDUH), and the National Health and Nutrition Examination Survey (NHANES), generally do not permit tabulation of estimates for the detailed race and ethnicity categories shown in tables XII and XIII, either because race data based on the 1997 standard categories are not yet available or because there are insufficient numbers of observations to meet statistical reliability or confidentiality requirements.

National Health and Nutrition Examination Survey (NHANES)—Starting with *Health, United States, 2003* race-specific estimates based on NHANES were tabulated using the 1997 Standards for data years 1999 and beyond. Prior to data year 1999, the 1977 Standards were used. Because of the differences between the two Standards, the race-specific estimates shown in trend tables based on the NHANES for 1999–2002 are not strictly comparable with estimates for earlier years. Each trend table based on the NHANES includes a footnote that discusses differences between estimates tabulated using the two Standards for survey years 1999–2002. Race in NHANES I and II was determined primarily by interviewer observation; starting with NHANES III, race was self-reported by survey participants.

The NHANES sample was designed to provide estimates specifically for persons of Mexican origin and not for all Hispanic-origin persons in the United States. Persons of Hispanic origin other than Mexicans were entered into the sample with different selection probabilities that are not nationally representative of the total U.S. Hispanic population. Estimates are shown for non-Hispanic white, non-Hispanic black, and Mexican. Although data were collected according to the 1997 Standards, there are insufficient numbers of observations to meet statistical reliability or confidentiality requirements for reporting estimates for additional race categories.

National Survey on Drug Use & Health (NSDUH)—Race-specific estimates based on NSDUH are tabulated using the 1997 Standards. Estimates in the NSDUH trend table begin with the data year 1999. Estimates for specific race groups are shown when they meet requirements for statistical reliability and confidentiality. The race categories "White only," "Black or African American only," "American Indian and Alaska Native only," "Asian only," and "Native Hawaiian and Other Pacific Islander only" include persons who reported only one racial group; and the category "2 or more races" includes persons who reported more than one of the five racial groups in the 1997 Standards or one of the five racial groups and "Some other race."

National Vital Statistics System—Most of the States in the Vital Statistics Cooperative Program are still revising their birth and death records to conform to the 1997 standards on race and ethnicity. During the transition to full implementation of the 1997 standards, vital statistics data will continue to be presented for the four major race groups—white, black or African American, American Indian or Alaska Native, and Asian or Pacific Islander—in accordance with 1977 standards.

Birth File—Information about the race and Hispanic ethnicity of the mother and father are provided by the mother at the time of birth and recorded on the birth certificate and fetal death record. Since 1980, birth rates, birth characteristics, and fetal death rates for live-born infants and fetal deaths are presented in this report according to race of mother. Before 1980 data were tabulated by race of newborn and fetus, taking into account the race of both parents. If the parents were of different races and one parent was white, the child was classified according to the race of the other parent. When neither parent was white, the child was classified according to father's race, with one exception: if either parent was Hawaiian, the child was classified Hawaiian.

Before 1964, if race was unknown, the birth was classified as white. Beginning in 1964 unknown race was classified according to information on the birth record. Beginning with the 2000 data year, the race and ethnicity data used for denominators (population) to calculate birth rates are collected in accordance with 1997 revised OMB standards for race and ethnicity. However, the numerators (births) will not be compatible with the denominators until all the States revise their birth certificates to reflect the new standards. In order to compute rates, it is necessary to bridge population data for multiple-race persons to single-race categories. See *Appendix I, Population Census and Population Estimates, Bridged-Race Population Estimates for Census 2000.*

Beginning with the 2003 data year, multiple-race data were reported by both Pennsylvania and Washington, which used the 2003 revision of the U.S. Standard Certificate of Live Birth, as well as California, Hawaii, Ohio (for births occurring in December only), and Utah, which used the 1989 revision of the U.S. Standard Certificate of Live Birth. These six States, which accounted for 20.7 percent of births in the United States in 2003, reported 2.6 percent of mothers as multiracial, with levels varying from 0.7 percent (Ohio) to 37.5 percent (Hawaii). Data from the vital records of the remaining 44 States and the District of Columbia followed the 1977 OMB standards in which a single race is reported. In order to provide uniformity and comparability of the data during the transition period, before multiple-race data are available for all reporting areas, it is necessary to "bridge" the responses of those who reported more than one race to a single race. See Martin JA, Hamilton BE, et al. Births: Final Data for 2003. National vital statistics reports; forthcoming. Hyattsville, MD: National Center for Health Statistics. 2005.

Although the bridging procedure imputes multiple-race of mothers to one of the four minimum races stipulated in the 1977 race and ethnicity standards, mothers of a specified Asian or Pacific Islander (API) subgroup (Chinese, Japanese, Hawaiian, or Filipino) in combination with another race (American Indian or Alaska Native, Black, or White) or another API subgroup cannot be imputed to a single Asian or Pacific Islander subgroup. In 2003, API mothers were disproportionately represented in the six States reporting multiple-race (44 percent). Data are not shown for the API subgroups or reported alone or in combination with other races or other API subgroups because the bridging technique cannot be applied in this detail. These data are available in the 2003 Natality public-use data file, which can be found at http://www.cdc.gov/nchs/births.htm.

Mortality File—Information about the race and Hispanic ethnicity of the decedent is reported by the funeral director as provided by an informant, often the surviving next of kin, or, in the absence of an informant, on the basis of observation. Death rates by race and Hispanic origin are based on information from death certificates (numerators of the rates) and on population estimates from the Census Bureau (denominators). Race and ethnicity information from the census is by self-report. To the extent that race and Hispanic origin are inconsistent between these two data sources, death rates will be biased. Studies have shown that persons self-reported as American Indian, Asian, or Hispanic on census and survey records may sometimes be reported as white or non-Hispanic on the death certificate, resulting in an underestimation of deaths and death rates for the American Indian, Asian, and Hispanic groups. Bias also results from undercounts of some population groups in the census, particularly young black males, young white males, and elderly persons, resulting in an overestimation of death rates. The net effects of misclassification and undercoverage result in overstated death rates for the white population and black population are estimated to be 1 percent and 5 percent, respectively; understated death rates for other population groups are estimated as follows: American Indians, 21 percent; Asian or Pacific Islanders, 11 percent; and Hispanics, 2 percent. For more information, see Rosenberg HM, Maurer JD, Sorlie PD, et al. Quality of death rates by race and Hispanic origin: A summary of current research, 1999. National Center for Health Statistics. *Vital Health Stat* 2(128). 1999.

Denominators for infant and maternal mortality rates are based on number of live births rather than population estimates. Race information for the denominator is supplied from the birth certificate. Before 1980, race of child for the denominator took into account the races of both parents. Starting in 1980 race information for the denominator was based solely on race of mother. Race information for the numerator is supplied from the death certificate. For the infant mortality rate, race information for the numerator is race of the deceased child; for the maternal mortality rate, it is race of the mother.

Vital event rates for the American Indian or Alaska Native population shown in this book are based on the total U.S. resident population of American Indians and Alaska Natives, as enumerated by the U.S. Census Bureau. In contrast the Indian Health Service calculates vital event rates for this population based on U.S. Census Bureau county data for American Indians and Alaska Natives who reside on or near reservations. Interpretation of trends for the American Indian and Alaska Native population should take into account that population estimates for these groups increased by 45 percent between 1980 and 1990, partly because of better enumeration techniques in the 1990 decennial census and the increased tendency for people to identify themselves as American Indian in 1990.

Interpretation of trends for the Asian population in the United States should take into account that this population more than doubled between 1980 and 1990, primarily because of immigration. Between 1990 and 2000, the increase in the Asian population was 48 percent for persons reporting that they were Asian alone, and 72 percent for persons who reported they were either Asian alone or in combination with another race.

For more information on coding race using vital statistics, see National Center for Health Statistics, Technical Appendix. *Vital Statistics of the United States*, Vol. I, Natality, and Vol. II, Mortality, Part A available on the NCHS home page at www.cdc.gov/nchs/nvss.htm. See related *Hispanic origin; Appendix I, Population Census and Population Estimates.*

Rate—A rate is a measure of some event, disease, or condition in relation to a unit of population, along with some specification of time. See related *Age adjustment; Population.*

Birth and related rates

Birth rate is calculated by dividing the number of live births in a population in a year by the midyear resident population. For census years, rates are based on unrounded census counts of the resident population, as of April 1. For the noncensus years 1981–89, rates were based on national estimates of the resident population, as of July 1, rounded to 1,000s. Rounded population estimates for 5-year age groups were calculated by summing unrounded population estimates before rounding to 1,000s. Starting in 1991 rates were based on unrounded national population estimates. Beginning in 1997, the birth rate for the maternal age group 45–49 years includes data for mothers age 50–54 years in the numerator and is based on the population of women age 45–49 years in the denominator. Birth rates are expressed as the number of live births per 1,000 population. The rate may be restricted to births to women of specific age, race, marital status, or geographic location (specific rate), or it may be related to the entire population (crude rate). See related *Cohort fertility.*

Fertility rate is the total number of live births, regardless of age of mother, per 1,000 women of reproductive age, 15–44 years.

Death and related rates

Death rate is calculated by dividing the number of deaths in a population in a year by the midyear resident population. For census years, rates are based on unrounded census counts of the resident population, as of April 1. For the noncensus years 1981–89, rates were based on national estimates of the resident population, as of July 1, rounded to 1,000s. Rounded population estimates for 10-year age groups were calculated by summing unrounded population estimates before rounding to 1,000s. Starting in 1991, rates were based on unrounded national population estimates. Rates for the Hispanic and non-Hispanic white populations in each year are based on unrounded State population estimates for States in the Hispanic reporting area. Death rates are expressed as the number of deaths per 100,000 population. The rate may be restricted to deaths in specific age, race, sex, or geographic groups or from specific causes of death (specific rate), or it may be related to the entire population (crude rate).

Fetal death rate is the number of fetal deaths with stated or presumed gestation of 20 weeks or more divided by the sum of live births plus fetal deaths, per 1,000 live births plus fetal deaths. *Late fetal death rate* is the number of fetal deaths with stated or presumed gestation of 28 weeks or more divided by the sum of live births plus late fetal deaths, per 1,000 live births plus late fetal deaths. See related *Gestation.*

Infant mortality rate based on period files is calculated by dividing the number of infant deaths during a calendar year by the number of live births reported in the same year. It is expressed as the number of infant deaths per 1,000 live births. *Neonatal mortality rate* is the number of deaths of children under 28 days of age, per 1,000 live births. *Postneonatal mortality rate* is the number of deaths of children that occur between 28 days and 365 days after birth, per 1,000 live births. See related *Infant death.*

Birth cohort infant mortality rates are based on linked birth and infant death files. In contrast to period rates in which the births and infant deaths occur in the same period or calendar year, infant deaths constituting the numerator of a birth cohort rate may have occurred in the same year as, or in the year following, the year of birth. The birth cohort infant mortality rate is expressed as the number of infant deaths per 1,000 live births. See related *Birth cohort.*

Perinatal relates to the period surrounding the birth event. Rates and ratios are based on events reported in a calendar year. *Perinatal mortality rate* is the sum of late fetal deaths plus infant deaths within 7 days of birth divided by the sum of live births plus late fetal deaths, per 1,000 live births plus late fetal deaths.

Perinatal mortality ratio is the sum of late fetal deaths plus infant deaths within 7 days of birth divided by the number of live births, per 1,000 live births.

Maternal mortality rate is defined as the number of maternal deaths per 100,000 live births. The maternal mortality rate is a measure of the likelihood that a pregnant woman will die from maternal causes. The number of live births used in the denominator is a proxy for the population of pregnant women who are at risk of a maternal death. See related *Maternal death.*

Visit rate is a basic measure of service utilization for event-based data. Examples of events include physician office visits with drugs provided or hospital discharges. In the visit rate calculation, the numerator is the number of estimated events, and the denominator is the corresponding U.S. population estimate for those who possibly could have had events during a given period of time. The interpretation is that for every person in the population there were, on average, *x* events. It does not mean that *x* percent of the population had events, because some persons in the population had no events while others had multiple events. The only exception is when an event can occur just once for a person (e.g., if an appendectomy were performed during a hospital stay). The visit rate is best used to compare utilization across various subgroups of interest such as age or race groups or geographic regions (e.g., the rate of hospital discharges in 2002 was 43.4 per 1,000 population for children under 18 years of age and 466.6 per 1, 000 population for adults 75 years and over).

Region—See *Geographic region and division.*

Registered hospitals—See *Hospital.*

Registered nursing education—Registered nursing data are shown by level of educational preparation. Baccalaureate education requires at least 4 years of college or university; associate degree programs are based in community colleges and are usually 2 years in length; and diploma programs are based in hospitals and are usually 3 years in length.

Registration area—The United States has separate registration areas for birth, death, marriage, and divorce statistics. In general, registration areas correspond to States and include two separate registration areas for the District of Columbia and New York City. All States have adopted laws that require registration of births and deaths and reporting of fetal deaths. It is believed that more than 99 percent of births and deaths occurring in this country are registered.

The *death registration area* was established in 1900 with 10 States and the District of Columbia, and the *birth registration area* was established in 1915, also with 10 States and the District of Columbia. Beginning with 1933, all States were included in the birth and death registration areas. The specific States added year by year are shown in "History and Organization of the Vital Statistics System." Reprinted from *Vital Statistics of the United States Vol. I, 1950*, chapter 1. National Center for Health Statistics. 1978. Currently, Puerto Rico, U.S. Virgin Islands, and Guam each constitutes a separate registration area, although their data are not included in statistical tabulations of U.S. resident data. See related *Reporting area.*

Relative standard error—The relative standard error (RSE) is a measure of an estimate's reliability. The RSE of an estimate is obtained by dividing the standard error of the estimate (SE(r)) by the estimate itself (r). This quantity is expressed as a percentage of the estimate and is calculated as follows: RSE = 100 x (SE(r)/r). Estimates with large RSEs are considered unreliable. In *Health, United States* most statistics with large RSEs are preceded by an asterisk or are not presented.

Relative survival rate—The relative survival rate is the ratio of the observed survival rate for the patient group to the expected survival rate for persons in the general population similar to the patient group with respect to age, sex, race, and calendar year of observation. The 5-year relative survival rate is used to estimate the proportion of cancer patients potentially curable. Because over one-half of all cancers occur in persons 65 years of age and over, many of these individuals die of other causes with no evidence of recurrence of their cancer. Thus, because it is obtained by adjusting observed survival for the normal life expectancy of the general population of the same age, the relative survival rate is an estimate of the chance of surviving the effects of cancer.

Reporting area—In the National Vital Statistics System, the reporting area for such basic items on the birth and death certificates as age, race, and sex is based on data from residents of all 50 States in the United States and the District of Columbia (DC). The reporting area for selected items such as Hispanic origin, educational attainment, and marital status is based on data from those States that require the item to be reported, whose data meet a minimum level of completeness (such as 80 or 90 percent), and are considered to be sufficiently comparable to be used for analysis. In 1993–96 the reporting area for Hispanic origin of decedent on the death certificate included 49 States and DC. Starting in 1997 the Hispanic reporting area includes all 50 States and DC. See related *Registration area; Appendix I, National Vital Statistics System.*

Resident—In the Online Survey Certification and Reporting database, all residents in certified facilities are counted on the day of certification inspection. In the National Nursing Home Survey, a resident is a person on the roster of the nursing home as of the night before the survey. Included are all residents for whom beds are maintained even though they may be on overnight leave or in a hospital. See related *Nursing home.*

Resident population—See *Population.*

Residential treatment care—See *Mental health service type.*

Residential treatment centers for emotionally disturbed children—See *Mental health organization.*

Rural—See *Urbanization.*

Self-assessment of health—See *Health status, respondent-assessed.*

Serious psychological distress—The serious psychological distress scale (K6) is a six-item scale developed to measure serious mental illness. The K6 was asked of adults 18 years of age and older. The answers were self-reported and no proxies were allowed. The K6 is designed to identify persons with serious psychological distress using as few questions as possible. The six items included in the K6 are as follows: During the past 30 days, how often did you feel . . .

> so sad that nothing could cheer you up?
> nervous?
> restless or fidgety?
> hopeless?
> that everything was an effort?
> worthless?

Possible answers are all of the time (4 points), most of the time (3 points), some of the time (2 points), a little of the time (1 point), and none of the time (0 points).

To score the K6, the points are added together yielding a possible total of 0 to 24 points. A threshold of 13 or more is used to define serious mental illness. Persons answering "some of the time" to all six questions would not reach the threshold for serious mental illness, because to achieve a score of 13 they would need to answer "most of the time" to at least one item.

For more information, see Kessler RC, Barker PR, Colpe LJ, et al. Screening for serious mental illness in the general population. *Arch Gen Psychiatry* 60:184–189, 2003.

Short-stay hospital—See *Hospital.*

Skilled nursing facility—See *Nursing home.*

Smoker—See *Cigarette smoking.*

Specialty hospital—See *Hospital.*

State health agency—A State health agency is the agency or department within State government headed by the State or territorial health official. Generally, the State health agency is responsible for setting statewide public health priorities, carrying out national and State mandates, responding to public health hazards, and assuring access to health care for underserved State residents.

State Children's Health Insurance Program (SCHIP)—Title XXI of the Social Security Act, known as the State Children's Health Insurance Program (SCHIP), is a program initiated by the Balanced Budget Act of 1997 (BBA). SCHIP provides more Federal funds for States to provide health care coverage to low-income, uninsured children. SCHIP gives States broad flexibility in program design while protecting beneficiaries through Federal standards. Funds from SCHIP may be used to expand Medicaid or to provide medical assistance to children during a presumptive eligibility period for Medicaid. This is one of several options from which States may select to provide health care coverage for more children, as prescribed within the BBA's Title XXI program. See related *Health insurance coverage; Medicaid.*

Substance use—This term refers to the use of selected substances including alcohol, tobacco products, drugs, inhalants, and other substances that can be consumed, inhaled, injected, or otherwise absorbed into the body with possible detrimental effects.

The Monitoring the Future Study (MTF)—The MTF collects information on use of selected substances using self-completed questionnaires to a school-based survey of secondary school students. MTF has tracked 12th-graders' illicit drug use and attitudes towards drugs since 1975. In 1991, 8th and 10th graders were added to the study. The survey includes questions on abuse of substances including (but not limited to) marijuana, inhalants, illegal drugs, alcohol, cigarettes, and other tobacco products. A standard set of three questions is used to assess use of the substances in the past month. "Past month" refers to an individual's use of a substance at least once during the month preceding their response to the survey. See related *Appendix I, Monitoring the Future Study.*

National Survey on Drug Use & Health (NSDUH)—The NSDUH conducts in-person interviews of a sample of individuals 12 years of age and older at their place of residence. For illicit drug use, alcohol use, and tobacco use, information is collected about use in past month. For information on illicit drug use, respondents in the NSDUH are asked about use of marijuana/hashish, cocaine (including crack), inhalants, hallucinogens, heroin, and prescription-type drugs used nonmedically (pain relievers, tranquilizers, stimulants, and sedatives). A series of questions is asked about each substance: "Have you ever, even once, used [e.g., Ecstasy, also know as MDMA/substance]?" "Think specifically about the past 30 days, from [date] up to and including today. During the past 30 days, on how many days did you use [substance]?" Numerous probes and checks are included in the computer-assisted interview system. Nonprescription medications and legitimate uses under a doctor's supervision are not included in the survey. Summary measures such as "any illicit drug use" are produced. See related *Alcohol consumption; Cigarette smoking; Illicit drug use; Appendix I, National Survey on Drug Use & Health.*

Suicidal ideation—Suicidal ideation is having thoughts of suicide or of taking action to end one's own life. Suicidal ideation includes all thoughts of suicide, both when the thoughts include a plan to commit suicide and when they do not include a plan. Suicidal ideation is measured in the Youth Risk Behavior Survey by the question "During the past 12 months, did you ever seriously consider attempting suicide?"

Surgical operation—See *Procedure.*

Surgical specialty—See *Physician specialty.*

Tobacco use—See *Cigarette smoking.*

Uninsured—In the Current Population Survey (CPS), persons are considered uninsured if they do not have coverage through private health insurance, Medicare, Medicaid, State Children's Health Insurance Program, military or Veterans coverage, another government program, a plan of someone outside the household, or other insurance. In addition, if the respondent has missing Medicaid information but has income from certain low-income public programs, then Medicaid coverage is imputed. The questions on health insurance are administered in March and refer to the previous calendar year.

In the National Health Interview Survey (NHIS), the uninsured are persons who do not have coverage under private health insurance, Medicare, Medicaid, public assistance, a State-sponsored health plan, other government-sponsored programs, or a military health plan. Persons with only Indian Health Service coverage are considered uninsured. Estimates of the percentage of persons who are uninsured based on the NHIS (table 134) may differ slightly from those based on the March CPS (table 156) because of differences in survey questions, recall period, and other aspects of survey methodology. In 2003 in the NHIS, 1.1 percent of adults age 65 years and over had no health insurance, but the small sample size precludes the presentation of separate estimates for this population. Therefore the term "uninsured" refers only to the population under age 65. See related *Health insurance coverage; Appendix I, Current Population Survey.*

Urbanization—Urbanization is the degree of urban (city-like) character or nature of a particular geographic area. In this report death rates are presented according to the urbanization level of the decedent's county of residence. Counties and county equivalents were assigned to one of five urbanization levels using Office of Management and Budget's (OMB) standards for metropolitan statistical areas (MSAs) and micropolitan statistical areas and the Rural-Urban Continuum code system to differentiate among metropolitan areas based on population.

There are three major categories of counties. OMB classifies counties as metropolitan or micropolitan. Counties not categorized by OMB are neither metropolitan nor micropolitan.

OMB's classification of metropolitan counties are further differentiated in *Health, United States* by population size using the Rural-Urban Continuum code system (August 2003 Revision) developed by the Economic Research Service, U.S. Department of Agriculture. Metropolitan counties are classified by the population size of their metropolitan area to one of three metropolitan urbanization levels:

(a) *Large*—counties in MSAs with 1 million or more population.
(b) *Medium*— counties MSAs with 250,000 to 1 million population.
(c) *Small*—counties in MSAs with less than 250,000 population.

See *Metropolitan statistical area (MSA)* for definitions of metropolitan and nonmetropolitan counties.

Nonmetropolitan counties are categorized using the OMB's classification of nonmetropolitan micropolitan statistical areas (February 2004 Revision). Nonmetropolitan counties are classified into two categories:

(a) *Micropolitan*—counties defined by OMB as micropolitan based on population criteria.
(b) *Nonmicropolitan*—nonmetropolitan counties that do not meet the population criteria for micropolitan.

See *Micropolitan statistical area* for definitions of micropolitan and nonmicropolitan counties.

Usual source of care—Usual source of care was measured in the National Health Interview Survey (NHIS) in 1993 and 1994 by asking the respondent "Is there a particular person or place that ____ usually goes to when ____ is sick or needs advice about ___ health?" In the 1995 and 1996 NHIS, the respondent was asked "Is there one doctor, person, or place that ____ usually goes to when ____ is sick or needs advice about health?" Starting in 1997 the respondent was asked "Is there a place that ____ usually goes when he/she is sick or you need advice about (his/her) health?" Persons who report the emergency department as their usual source of care are defined as having no usual source of care in this report.

Wages and salaries—See *Employer costs for employee compensation.*

Years of potential life lost (YPLL)—YPLL is a measure of premature mortality. Starting with *Health, United States, 1996–97*, YPLL is presented for persons under 75 years of age because the average life expectancy in the United States is over 75 years. YPLL-75 is calculated using the following eight age groups: under 1 year, 1–14 years, 15–24 years, 25–34 years, 35–44 years, 45–54 years, 55–64 years, and 65–74 years. The number of deaths for each age group is multiplied by years of life lost, calculated as the difference between age 75 years and the midpoint of the age group. For the eight age groups, the midpoints are 0.5, 7.5, 19.5, 29.5, 39.5, 49.5, 59.5, and 69.5. For example, the death of a person 15–24 years of age counts as 55.5 years of life lost. Years of potential life lost is derived by summing years of life lost over all age groups. In *Health, United States, 1995* and earlier editions, YPLL was presented for persons under 65 years of age. For more information, see Centers for Disease Control. *MMWR* 35(2S):suppl. 1986. Available at: www.cdc.gov/mmwr/preview/mmwrhtml/00001773.htm.

Appendix III

Additional Data Years Available

For trend tables spanning long periods, only selected data years are shown to highlight major trends. Additional years of data are available for some of the tables in electronic spreadsheets available through the Internet and on CD-ROM.

To access spreadsheet files on the Internet, go to the *Health, United States* Web site at www.cdc.gov/nchs/hus.htm, scroll down to "Spreadsheet Files," and click on 2005 Edition.

Downloadable spreadsheet files for trend tables, many of which include more data years than are shown in the printed report, are available in Excel. Standard errors are included in spreadsheet files for trend tables based on the National Health Interview Survey (NHIS), National Health and Nutrition Examination Survey (NHANES), and National Survey of Family Growth (NSFG).

Spreadsheet files in Excel are also available on a CD-ROM. A limited supply of CD-ROMs are available from the National Center for Health Statistics upon request, while supplies last, or CD-ROMs may be purchased from the Government Printing Office.

Table number	Table topic	Additional data years available
2	Poverty	1986–89, 1991–94, 1996–99
3	Fertility rates and birth rates	1981–84, 1986–89, 1991–94, 1996
4	Live births	1972–74, 1976–79, 1981–84, 1986–89, 1991–94, 1996–99, 2001
5	Twin births	1972–74, 1976–79, 1981–84, 1986–89, 1991–94, 1996, 1998
7	Prenatal care	1981–84, 1986–89, 1991–94, 1996, 1998
9	Teenage childbearing	1981–84, 1986–89, 1991–94, 1996–97
10	Nonmarital childbearing	1981–84, 1986–89, 1991–94, 1996–97
11	Maternal education	1981–84, 1986–89, 1991–94, 1996–97
12	Maternal smoking	1991–94, 1996–97
13	Low birthweight	1981–84, 1986–89, 1991–94, 1996–97
14	Low birthweight	1991–94, 1996–97
15	Low birthweight	1972–74
16	Abortions	1981–84, 1986–89, 1991–94, 1996
19	Infant mortality rates	1996–97
20	Infant mortality rates	1984–89, 1991, 1996–2000
21	Infant mortality rates	1984, 1986–89, 1991, 1996–97, 1996–98, 1999–2001
22	Infant mortality rates	1981–84, 1986–89, 1991–94
27	Life expectancy	1975, 1981–84, 1986–89
29	Age-adjusted death rates for selected causes	1981–89, 1991–94, 1996–99
30	Years of potential life lost	1991–94, 1996–99; Crude 1999–2001
35	Death rates for all causes	1981–89, 1991–94, 1996–97
36	Diseases of heart	1981–89, 1991–99
37	Cerebrovascular diseases	1981–89, 1991–99
38	Malignant neoplasms	1981–89, 1991–99
39	Malignant neoplasms of trachea, bronchus, and lung	1981–89, 1991–99
40	Malignant neoplasm of breast	1981–89, 1991–99
41	Chronic lower respiratory diseases	1981–89, 1991–94, 1996–98
42	Human immunodeficiency virus (HIV) disease	1988–89, 1991–94, 1996–98
43	Maternal mortality	1981–89, 1991–94, 1996–98
44	Motor vehicle–related injuries	1981–89, 1991–99
45	Homicide	1981–89, 1991–99
46	Suicide	1981–89, 1991–99
47	Firearm-related injuries	1981–89, 1991–94, 1996–99
48	Occupational diseases	1981–84, 1986–89, 1991–94, 1996–98
49	Occupational injury deaths	1993–94, 1996

51	Notifiable diseases	1985, 1988–89, 1991–99
53	Cancer incidence rates	1991–94
56	Respiratory conditions	1998–2001
57	Severe headache or migraine, low back pain, and neck pain	1998–2001
58	Limitation of activity	1999–2000
59	Vision and hearing limitations	1998–99, 2001
60	Respondent-assessed health status	1998
63	Cigarette smoking	1983, 1987–88, 1991–94, 1997
64	Cigarette smoking	1983, 1987–88, 1991–94, 1997
65	Cigarette smoking	1993–95, 1994–97
67	Use of selected substances	1981–89, 1992–94, 1996–99
68	Alcohol consumption	1998–2001
72	Leisure-time physical activity	1991–2001
75	Health care visits	1998–2001
76	Influenza and pneumococcal vaccination	1991, 1993–94, 1997–2001
77	Vaccinations	1996–97
80	No usual source of health care	1995–96, 1997–98
81	Emergency department visits for children	1998–2001
83	Emergency department visits for adults	1998–99, 2001
84	Dental visits	1998–2001
85	Untreated dental caries	1999–2000
86	Mammography	1993
88	Ambulatory care visits	1997–2000
89	Injury-related visits	1997–98, 1999–2000, 2000–01, 2001–02
90	Ambulatory care visits	1980, 1997–99, 2001–02
91	Prescription drug use	1999–2000
93	Additions to mental health organizations	1992, 1998
96	Discharges	1998–2001
97	Discharges	1991–94, 1996–97, 1999
98	Rates of discharges	1995–99, 2001–02
99	Discharges	1995–99, 2001–02
100	Inpatient procedures	1991–92, 2001–02
101	Hospital admissions	1985, 1991–94, 1996–99
102	Nursing home residents	1997
103	Nursing home residents	1997
106	Physicians	1970, 1980, 1987, 1989–90, 1992–94, 1996–98
107	Primary care doctors of medicine	1994, 1996–99
109	Health professions schools	1996, 1998–99, 2001
110	Total enrollment of minorities in schools	2000–01
111	Enrollment of women in schools	2000–01, 2001–02
112	Hospitals	1985, 1991–94, 1996–99
113	Mental health organizations	1992
114	Community hospital beds	1985, 1988–89, 1995–2001
115	Occupancy rates	1985, 1988–89, 1995–99, 2001–02
116	Nursing homes	1996–99, 2001–02
117	Medicare–certified providers and suppliers	1970, 1998
124	Expenditures for health care	1996, 1998–99, 2001
125	Sources of payment for health care	1996, 1998–99, 2001
128	Employers' costs and health insurance	1992–93, 1995, 1997, 1999
129	Hospital expenses	1975, 1985, 1991–94, 1996–98, 2001
130	Nursing home average monthly charges	All: 1995, 1997; 1977, 1997
131	Mental health expenditures	1992
132	Private health insurance	1994, 1996
133	Medicaid coverage	1994, 1996

134	No health insurance coverage	1994, 1996
135	Health care coverage	1984, 1994, 1996–98
136	Health maintenance organization	1997, 1999, 2001
137	Health maintenance organizations	1984, 1986–87, 1989, 1991–94, 1996–97, 2001–02
139	Medicare	1999
141	Medicare	1993–2000
142	Medicaid	1975, 1985–89, 1991–94, 1996
143	Medicaid	1975, 1985–89, 1991–94, 1996
144	Department of Veterans Affairs	1985, 1988–89, 1991–94, 1996–98
145	Personal health care per capita expenditures	1992–93
146	Hospital care per capita expenditures	1992–93
147	Physician services per capita expenditures	1992–93
148	Nursing home care per capita expenditures	1992–93
149	Drugs per capita expenditures	1992–93
153	Medicare	1995–2001
154	Medicaid	1998, 2000
155	Health maintenance organizations	1994, 1996–97, 1999, 2001–02

Index to Trend Tables and Chartbook Figures

(Numbers refer to table numbers)

A

A—Con.

A—Con.

B

B—Con.

B—Con.

C

C—Con.

C—Con.

D

D—Con.

E

E—Con.

E—Con.

F

G

H

H—Con.

H—Con.

I

J

L

M

Table and Figure

M—Con.

Table and Figure

M—Con.

N

O

P

P—Con.

R

S

S—Con.

T

U

V

W

W—Con.

Y

ISBN 0-16-072854-1

9 780160 728549
90000